America's
Top-Rated Cities:
A Statistical Handbook

Volume 4

2021
Twenty-Eighth Edition

America's
Top-Rated Cities:
A Statistical Handbook

Volume 4: Eastern Region

A UNIVERSAL REFERENCE BOOK

Grey House
Publishing

Cover image: Charlotte, North Carolina

PRESIDENT: Richard Gottlieb
PUBLISHER: Leslie Mackenzie
EDITORIAL DIRECTOR: Laura Mars
SENIOR EDITOR: David Garoogian

RESEARCHER & WRITER: Jael Bridgemahon
PRODUCTION MANAGER: Kristen Hayes
MARKETING DIRECTOR: Jessica Moody

A Universal Reference Book
Grey House Publishing, Inc.
4919 Route 22
Amenia, NY 12501
518.789.8700 • Fax 845.373.6390
www.greyhouse.com
books@greyhouse.com

While every effort has been made to ensure the reliability of the information presented in this publication, Grey House Publishing neither guarantees the accuracy of the data contained herein nor assumes any responsibility for errors, omissions or discrepancies. Grey House accepts no payment for listing; inclusion in the publication of any organization, agency, institution, publication, service or individual does not imply endorsement of the editors or publisher.

Errors brought to the attention of the publisher and verified to the satisfaction of the publisher will be corrected in future editions.

Twenty-eighth Edition
Printed in the USA

Publisher's Cataloging-in-Publication Data
(Prepared by The Donohue Group, Inc.)

America's top-rated cities. Vol. 4, Eastern region : a statistical handbook. — 1992-

v. : ill. ; cm.
Annual, 1995-
Irregular, 1992-1993
ISSN: 1082-7102

1. Cities and towns--Ratings--Eastern States--Statistics--Periodicals. 2. Cities and towns--Eastern States--Statistics--Periodicals. 3. Social indicators--Eastern States--Periodicals. 4. Quality of life--Eastern States--Statistics--Periodicals. 5. Eastern States--Social conditions--Statistics--Periodicals. I. Title: America's top rated cities. II. Title: Eastern region

HT123.5.S6 A44
307.76/0973/05   95644648

4-Volume Set	ISBN: 978-1-64265-821-7
Volume 1	ISBN: 978-1-64265-823-1
Volume 2	ISBN: 978-1-64265-824-8
Volume 3	ISBN: 978-1-64265-825-5
Volume 4	**ISBN: 978-1-64265-826-2**

Allentown, Pennsylvania

Boston, Massachusetts

Charlotte, North Carolina

Cincinnati, Ohio

Cleveland, Ohio

Columbus, Ohio

Durham, North Carolina

Edison, New Jersey

Fayetteville, North Carolina

Greensboro, North Carolina

Lexington, Kentucky

Louisville, Kentucky

Pittsburgh, Pennsylvania

Providence, Rhode Island

Raleigh, North Carolina

Richmond, Virginia

Virginia Beach, Virginia

Winston-Salem, North Carolina

Washington, D.C.

Appendixes

Introduction

This twenty-eighth edition of *America's Top-Rated Cities* is a concise, statistical, 4-volume work identifying America's top-rated cities with estimated populations of approximately 100,000 or more. It profiles 100 cities that have received high marks for business and living from prominent sources such as *Forbes, Fortune, U.S. News & World Report, The Brookings Institution, U.S. Conference of Mayors, The Wall Street Journal,* and *CNNMoney.*

Each volume covers a different region of the country—Southern, Western, Central, Eastern—and includes a detailed Table of Contents, City Chapters, Appendices, and Maps. Each city chapter incorporates information from hundreds of resources to create the following major sections:

- **Background**—lively narrative of significant, up-to-date news for both businesses and residents. These combine historical facts with current developments, "known-for" annual events, and climate data.
- **Rankings**—fun-to-read, bulleted survey results from over 230 books, magazines, and online articles, ranging from general (Great Places to Live), to specific (Friendliest Cities), and everything in between.
- **Statistical Tables**—87 tables and detailed topics that offer an unparalleled view of each city's Business and Living Environments. They are carefully organized with data that is easy to read and understand.
- **Appendices**—five in all, appearing at the end of each volume. These range from listings of Metropolitan Statistical Areas to Comparative Statistics for all 100 cities.

This new edition of *America's Top-Rated Cities* includes cities that not only surveyed well, but ranked highest using our unique weighting system. We looked at violent crime, property crime, population growth, median household income, housing affordability, poverty, educational attainment, and unemployment. You'll find that we have included several American cities despite less-than-stellar numbers. New York, Los Angeles, and Miami remain world-class cities despite challenges faced by many large urban centers. Part of the criteria, in most cases, is that it be the "primary" city in a given metropolitan area. For example, if the metro area is Raleigh-Cary, NC, we would consider Raleigh, not Cary. This allows for a more equitable core city comparison. In general, the core city of a metro area is defined as having substantial influence on neighboring cities. A final consideration is location—we strive to include as many states in the country as possible.

New to this edition are:
Volume 1 - Memphis, TN
Volume 2 - Riverside, CA
Volume 4 - Cincnnati, OH

Praise for previous editions:

> "...[ATRC] has...proven its worth to a wide audience...from businesspeople and corporations planning to launch, relocate, or expand their operations to market researchers, real estate professionals, urban planners, job-seekers, students...interested in...reliable, attractively presented statistical information about larger U.S. cities."
> —ARBA

> "...For individuals or businesses looking to relocate, this resource conveniently reports rankings from more than 300 sources for the top 100 US cities. Recommended..."
> —Choice

> "...While patrons are becoming increasingly comfortable locating statistical data online, there is still something to be said for the ease associated with such a compendium of otherwise scattered data. A well-organized and appropriate update...
> —Library Journal

BACKGROUND
Each city begins with an informative Background that combines history with current events. These narratives often reflect changes that have occurred during the past year, and touch on the city's environment, politics, employment, cultural offerings, and climate, and include interesting trivia. For example: Peregrine Falcons were rehabilitated and released into the wild from Boise City's World Center for Birds of Prey; Grand Rapids was the first city to introduce fluoride into its drinking water in 1945; and Thomas Alva Edison discovered the phonograph and the light bulb in the city whose name was changed in 1954 from Raritan Township to Edison in his honor. This year, many backgrounds incluce an interesting fact about how the city is reacting to the COVID-19 pandemic.

RANKINGS

This section has rankings from a possible 233 books, articles, and reports. For easy reference, these Rankings are categorized into 16 topics including Business/Finance, Dating/Romance, and Health/Fitness.

The Rankings are presented in an easy-to-read, bulleted format and include results from both annual surveys and one-shot studies. **Fastest-Growing Economies . . . Best Drivers . . . Most Well-Read . . . Most Wired . . . Healthiest for Women . . . Best for Minority Entrepreneurs . . . Safest . . . Best to Retire . . . Most Polite . . . Best for Moviemakers . . . Most Frugal . . . Best for Bikes . . . Most Cultured . . . Least Stressful . . . Best for Families . . . Most Romantic . . . Most Charitable . . . Best for Telecommuters . . . Best for Singles . . . Nerdiest . . . Fittest . . . Best for Dogs . . . Most Tattooed . . . Best for Wheelchair Users**, and more. A number of these relate specifically to COVID-19.

Sources for these Rankings include both well-known magazines and other media, including *Forbes, Fortune, USA Today, Condé Nast Traveler, Gallup, Kiplinger's Personal Finance, Men's Journal,* and *Travel + Leisure,* as well as *Asthma & Allergy Foundation of America, American Lung Association, League of American Bicyclists, The Advocate, National Civic League, National Alliance to End Homelessness, MovieMaker Magazine, National Insurance Crime Bureau, Center for Digital Government, National Association of Home Builders,* and the *Milken Institute.*

Rankings cover a variety of geographic areas; see Appendix B for full geographic definitions.

STATISTICAL TABLES

Each city chapter includes a possible 87 tables and detailed topics—44 in Business and 43 in Living. Over 90% of statistical data has been updated.

Business Environment includes hard facts and figures on 8 major categories, including Demographics, Income, Economy, Employment, and Taxes. *Living Environment* includes 11 major categories, such as Cost of Living, Housing, Health, Education, Safety, and Climate.

To compile the Statistical Tables, editors have again turned to a wide range of sources, some well known, such as the *U.S. Census Bureau, U.S. Environmental Protection Agency, Bureau of Labor Statistics, Centers for Disease Control and Prevention,* and the *Federal Bureau of Investigation*, plus others like *The Council for Community and Economic Research, Texas A&M Transportation Institute,* and *Federation of Tax Administrators.*

APPENDICES: Data for all cities appear in all volumes.
- **Appendix A**—*Comparative Statistics*
- **Appendix B**—*Metropolitan Area Definitions*
- **Appendix C**—*Government Type and County*
- **Appendix D**—*Chambers of Commerce and Economic Development Organizations*
- **Appendix E**—*State Departments of Labor and Employment*

Material provided by public and private agencies and organizations was supplemented by original research, numerous library sources and Internet sites. *America's Top-Rated Cities, 2021*, is designed for a wide range of readers: private individuals considering relocating a residence or business; professionals considering expanding their businesses or changing careers; corporations considering relocating, opening up additional offices or creating new divisions; government agencies; general and market researchers; real estate consultants; human resource personnel; urban planners; investors; and urban government students.

Customers who purchase the four-volume set receive free online access to *America's Top-Rated Cities* allowing them to download city reports and sort and rank by 50-plus data points.

AMERICA'S TOP-RATED CITIES

CBSA: Core Based Statistical Area

STATE

○ Top Rated City

East Region

Central Region

West Region

South Region

©Larry Mandelin 2021

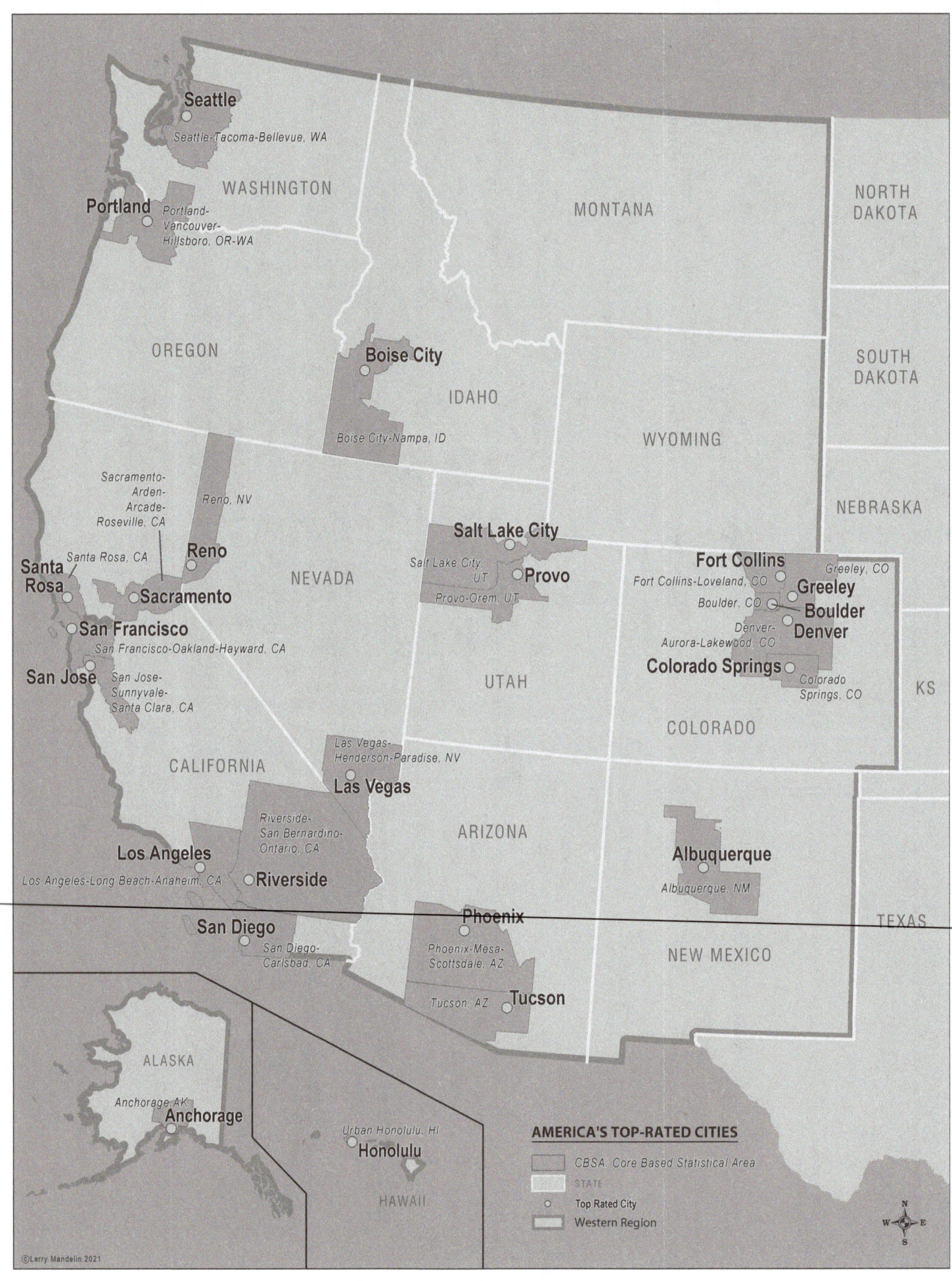

Seattle
Seattle-Tacoma-Bellevue, WA

WASHINGTON

Portland
Portland-Vancouver-Hillsboro, OR-WA

MONTANA

NORTH DAKOTA

OREGON

Boise City
Boise City-Nampa, ID

IDAHO

SOUTH DAKOTA

WYOMING

Sacramento-Arden-Arcade-Roseville, CA

Reno, NV

NEBRASKA

Santa Rosa, CA

Santa Rosa

Reno

NEVADA

Salt Lake City
Salt Lake City, UT

Provo
Provo-Orem, UT

Fort Collins
Fort Collins-Loveland, CO

Greeley, CO

Greeley

Sacramento

San Francisco
San Francisco-Oakland-Hayward, CA

Boulder, CO

Boulder

San Jose
San Jose-Sunnyvale-Santa Clara, CA

Denver

UTAH

Denver-Aurora-Lakewood, CO

Colorado Springs

KS

Colorado Springs, CO

Las Vegas-Henderson-Paradise, NV

COLORADO

CALIFORNIA

Las Vegas

ARIZONA

Riverside-San Bernardino-Ontario, CA

Los Angeles
Los Angeles-Long Beach-Anaheim, CA

Albuquerque

Riverside

Albuquerque, NM

San Diego

Phoenix

TEXAS

San Diego-Carlsbad, CA

Phoenix-Mesa-Scottsdale, AZ

NEW MEXICO

Tucson, AZ

Tucson

ALASKA

Anchorage, AK

Anchorage

Urban Honolulu, HI

Honolulu

HAWAII

AMERICA'S TOP-RATED CITIES

CBSA: Core Based Statistical Area

STATE

○ Top Rated City

Western Region

©Larry Mandelin 2021

N W E S

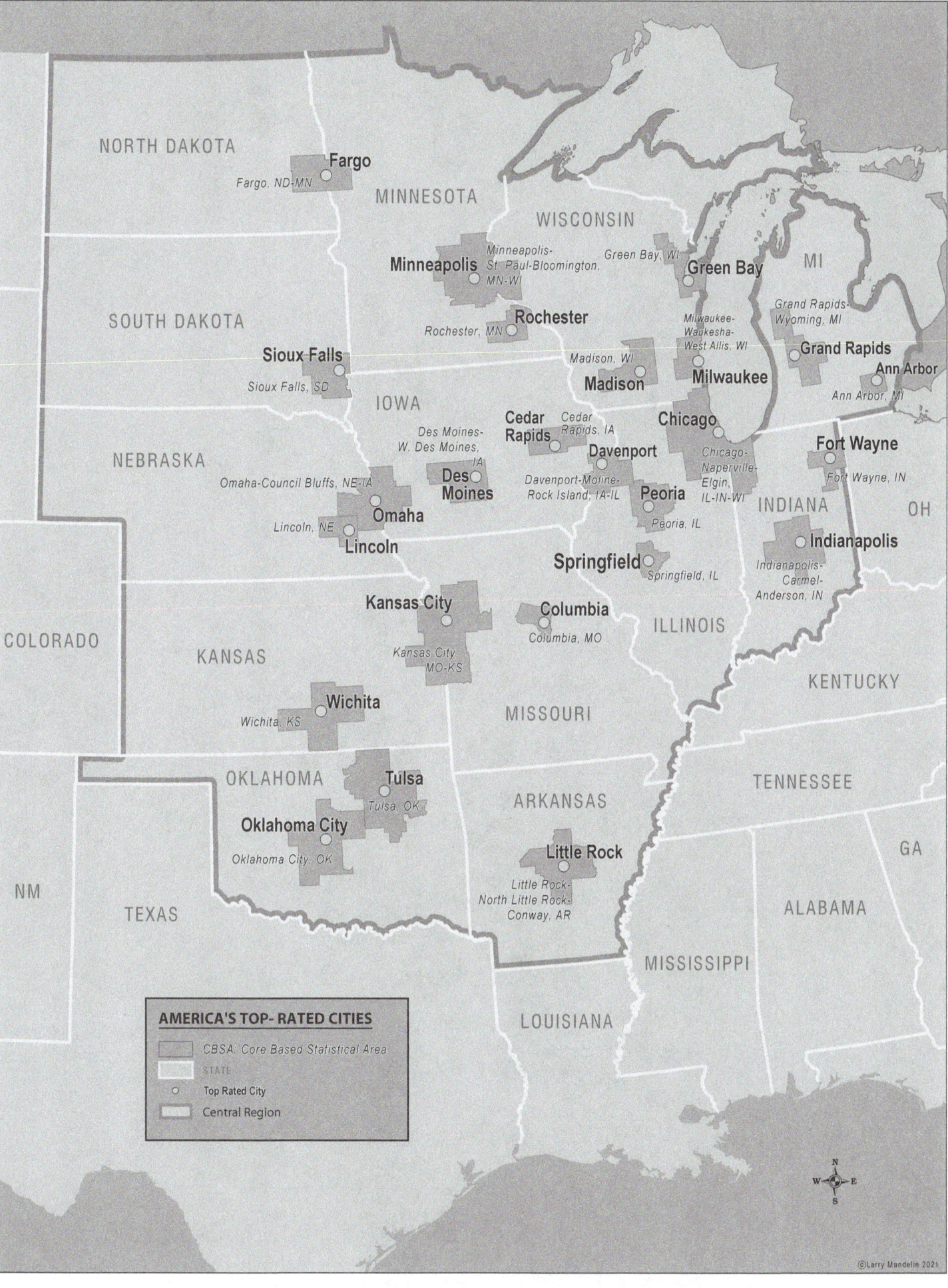

AMERICA'S TOP-RATED CITIES

- CBSA: Core Based Statistical Area
- STATE
- ○ Top Rated City
- Central Region

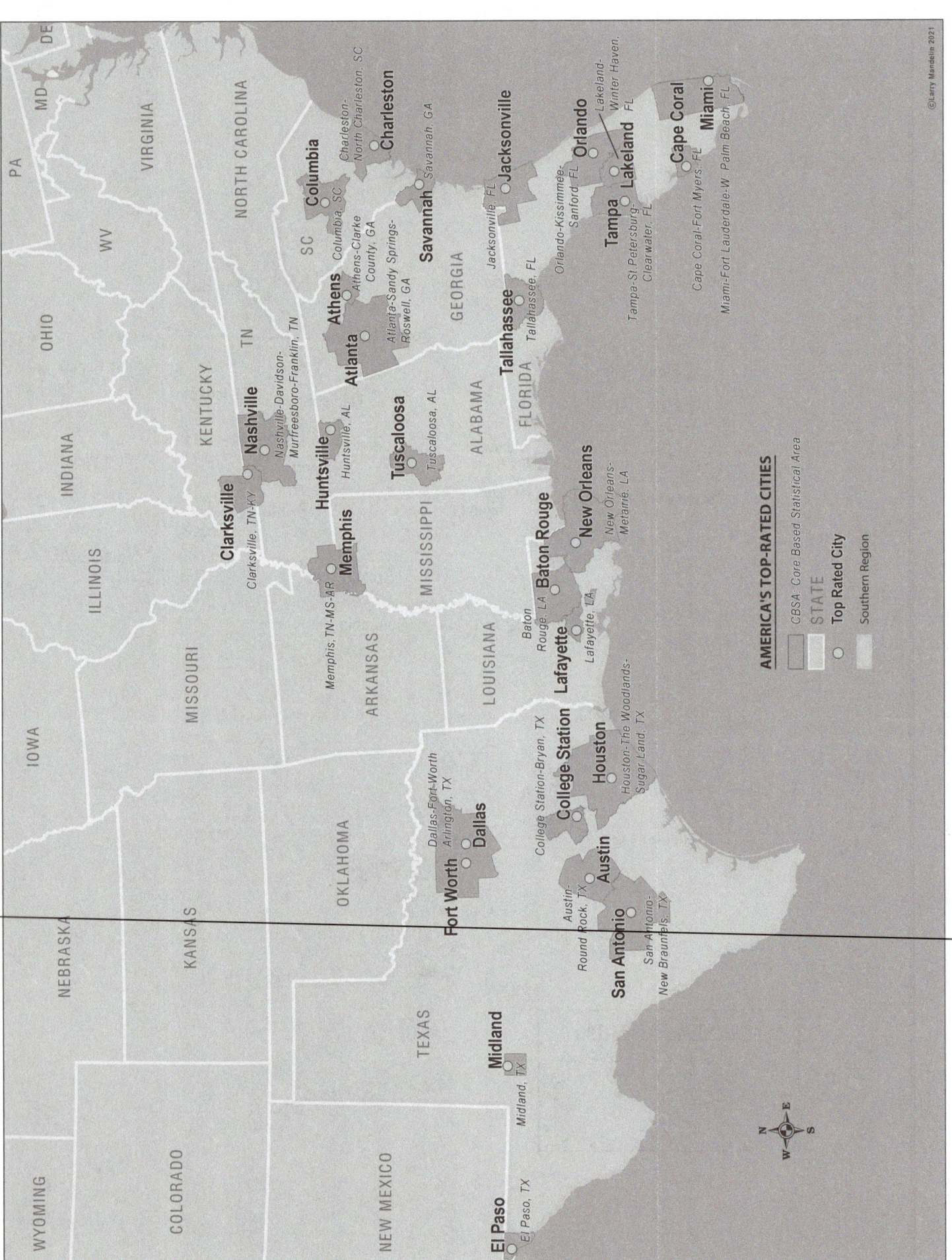

AMERICA'S TOP-RATED CITIES

CBSA: Core Based Statistical Area

STATE

○ Top Rated City

Southern Region

©Larry Mardelm 2021

AMERICA'S TOP-RATED CITIES

CBSA: Core Based Statistical Area
STATE
Top Rated City
Eastern Region

MAINE

VT
NH

NEW YORK
Manchester
Manchester-Nashua, NH
Boston-Cambridge-Newton, MA-NH
Boston
MA
Providence
CT
Providence-Warwick, RI-MA
RI
New Haven
New Haven-Milford, CT
Allentown-Bethlehem-Easton, PA-NJ
Allentown
New York
Edison
New York-Newark-Jersey City, NY-NJ-PA

MICHIGAN

Cleveland
Cleveland-Elyria, OH
PENNSYLVANIA
Pittsburgh
Pittsburgh, PA
Philadelphia
Philadelphia-Camden-Wilmington, PA-NJ-DE-MD
NJ

OHIO
Columbus
Columbus, OH
Washington
DE
MD
Washington-Arlington-Alexandria, DC-VA-MD-WV

INDIANA
Cincinnati, OH-KY-IN
WV
Richmond
Virginia Beach-Norfolk-Newport News, VA-NC
IL
Cincinnati
VA
Louisville/Jefferson County, KY-IN
Lexington
Richmond, VA
Louisville
Lexington-Fayette, KY
Virginia Beach
Durham-Chapel Hill, NC
KENTUCKY
Greensboro
Durham
Winston-Salem
Raleigh
Winston-Salem, NC
Raleigh, NC
Greensboro-High Point, NC
Fayetteville
TENNESSEE
NC
Charlotte
Fayetteville, NC
Charlotte-Concord-Gastonia, NC-SC

S.CAROLINA

N
W   E
S

MS
ALABAMA
GEORGIA

©Larry Mandelin 2021

Allentown, Pennsylvania

Background

Allentown, the third-largest city in Pennsylvania, is located in Lehigh County along the Lehigh River in the eastern part of the state. The city has gone through periods of both economic prosperity and hard times at the hands of industry, but always has managed to reinvent itself into a prosperous place for both businesses and residents. In recent years it was named a "national success story," only one of six communities in the country.

The area was first settled in 1762 by wealthy shipping merchant William Allen, who was also the Chief Justice of the Province of Pennsylvania and the former Mayor of Philadelphia. He purchased 5,000 acres in the hopes of founding a commercial trading center, given the riverside location and proximity to Philadelphia. However, the river's low water level made trade impractical. Allen gave the property to his son in the 1770s. The settlement, originally called Northamptontown, hobbled along as a small agricultural community. In 1838, its name was officially changed to Allentown (affectionately called "Allen's town") and in 1867, the settlement was incorporated as a city.

In the mid-to-late nineteenth century, the construction of the Lehigh Canal and the Lehigh Valley Railroad enabled the transport of both raw materials and finished goods. The iron industry flourished. The Panic of 1873, followed by depression ended the railroad boom and iron furnaces closed.

By the beginning of the twentieth century, Allentown rebounded as silk manufacturing became central to the city. The city's economy also now included furniture, beer and cigars. By 1928, over 140 silk and textile mills operated in the Lehigh Valley. Déjà vu set in however, when the popularity of synthetic materials sent the silk industry into a decline by the middle of the twentieth century. Though not as sudden as the iron industry's collapse, this downturn had a strong negative impact on Allenstown's economy.

In recent years, Allentown has been riding a wave of renovation and rehabilitation to its historic downtown. Downtown's centerpiece is the PPL Center, a 8,500-seat entertainment venue and minor hockey league stadium home to the Lehigh Valley Phantoms. A hotel, restaurants, and 200,000-square foot office building accompany the center complex. The city also saw the opening of a progressive new competency-based, experiential learning public school, Building 21.

Allentown is home to several national companies and major regional employers including the Lehigh Valley Hospital and Health Network, St. Luke's Hospital and Health Network, Parkland School District, Victaulic Co., B. Braun Medical Inc., Phebe Ministries senior living, and the Pleasant Valley School District.

Major attractions in Allentown include Dorney Park & Wildwater Kingdom and Coca-Cola Park, the 8,278-seat minor league baseball home of the Lehigh Valley IronPigs. Cultural and historical venues include Miller Symphony Hall, Allentown Art Museum—known for American painting and sculpture—and Old Court House County Museum, exhibiting the history of Lehigh County. The city's two institutions of higher learning are Cedar Crest College and Muhlenberg College.

Allentown has a humid season that resembles a midwestern climate more than a northeastern one. Summers are hot and muggy. Winters are cold; spring and fall are generally mild. Rainfall is distributed evenly across the twelve months of the year. Allentown's climate is affected by the Blue Mountain, a 1,600-foot-high ridge located 12 miles north of the city that separates it somewhat from regional weather systems.

Rankings

Business/Finance Rankings

- The Brookings Institution ranked the nation's largest cities based on income inequality. Allentown was ranked #92 (#1 = greatest inequality). Criteria: the "95/20 ratio," a figure representing the income at which a household earns more than 95 percent of all other households, divided by the income at which a household earns more than only 20 percent of all other households. *Brookings Institution, "Household Income Inequality, Largest Cities of 97 Large U.S. Metro Areas, 2014-2016," February 5, 2018*

- The Brookings Institution ranked the 100 largest metro areas in the U.S. based on income inequality. Allentown was ranked #87 (#1 = greatest inequality). Criteria: the "95/20 ratio," a figure representing the income at which a household earns more than 95 percent of all other households, divided by the income at which a household earns more than only 20 percent of all other households. *Brookings Institution, "Household Income Inequality, 100 Largest U.S. Metro Areas, 2014-2016," February 5, 2018*

- Allentown was cited as one of America's top metros for new and expanded facility projects in 2020. The area ranked #7 in the mid-sized metro area category (population 200,000 to 1 million). *Site Selection, "Top Metros of 2020," March 2021*

- The Allentown metro area appeared on the Milken Institute "2021 Best Performing Cities" list. Rank: #90 out of 200 large metro areas (population over 250,000). Criteria: job growth; wage and salary growth; high-tech output growth; housing affordability; household broadband access. *Milken Institute, "Best-Performing Cities 2021," February 16, 2021*

- *Forbes* ranked the 200 most populous metro areas to determine the nation's "Best Places for Business and Careers." The Allentown metro area was ranked #129. Criteria: costs (business and living); job growth (past and projected); income growth; quality of life; educational attainment (college and high school); projected economic growth; cultural and leisure opportunities; workplace tolerance laws; net migration patterns. *Forbes, "The Best Places for Business and Careers 2019: Seattle Still On Top," October 30, 2019*

Education Rankings

- Personal finance website *WalletHub* analyzed the 150 largest U.S. metropolitan statistical areas to determine where the most educated Americans are putting their degrees to work. Criteria: education levels; percentage of workers with degrees; education quality and attainment gap; public school quality rankings; quality and enrollment of each metro area's universities. Allentown was ranked #104 (#1 = most educated city). *www.WalletHub.com, "Most and Least Educated Cities in America," July 20, 2020*

Health/Fitness Rankings

- Allentown was identified as a "2021 Spring Allergy Capital." The area ranked #24 out of 100. Three groups of factors were used to identify the most challenging cities for people with allergies during the spring season: annual spring pollen levels; over the counter medicine use; number of board-certified allergy specialists. *Asthma and Allergy Foundation of America, "Spring Allergy Capitals 2021," February 23, 2021*

- Allentown was identified as a "2021 Fall Allergy Capital." The area ranked #26 out of 100. Three groups of factors were used to identify the most challenging cities for people with allergies during the fall season: annual fall pollen levels; over the counter medicine use; number of board-certified allergy specialists. *Asthma and Allergy Foundation of America, "Fall Allergy Capitals 2021," February 23, 2021*

- Allentown was identified as a "2019 Asthma Capital." The area ranked #6 out of the nation's 100 largest metropolitan areas. Criteria: estimated asthma prevalence; crude death rate from asthma; and ER visits due to asthma. Risk factors analyzed but not factored in the rankings: annual pollen score; annual air quality; public smoking laws; number of board-certified asthma specialists; rescue medication use; controller medication use; uninsured rate; poverty rate. *Asthma and Allergy Foundation of America, "Asthma Capitals 2019: The Most Challenging Places to Live With Asthma," May 7, 2019*

Real Estate Rankings

- Allentown was ranked #132 out of 268 metro areas in terms of housing affordability in 2020 by the National Association of Home Builders (#1 = most affordable). Criteria: the share of homes sold in that area affordable to a family earning the local median income, based on standard mortgage underwriting criteria. *National Association of Home Builders®, NAHB-Wells Fargo Housing Opportunity Index, 4th Quarter 2020*

Safety Rankings

- The National Insurance Crime Bureau ranked 384 metro areas in the U.S. in terms of per capita rates of vehicle theft. The Allentown metro area ranked #329 (#1 = highest rate). Criteria: number of vehicle theft offenses per 100,000 inhabitants in 2019. *National Insurance Crime Bureau, "Hot Spots 2019," July 21, 2020*

Seniors/Retirement Rankings

- From its Best Cities for Successful Aging indexes, the Milken Institute generated rankings for metropolitan areas, weighing data in nine categories—health care, wellness, living arrangements, transportation and convenience, financial characteristics, education, employment, community engagement, and overall livability. The Allentown metro area was ranked #73 overall in the large metro area category. *Milken Institute, "Best Cities for Successful Aging, 2017" March 14, 2017*

Business Environment

DEMOGRAPHICS

Population Growth

Area	1990 Census	2000 Census	2010 Census	2019* Estimate	Population Growth (%)	
					1990-2019	2010-2019
City	105,066	106,632	118,032	120,915	15.1	2.4
MSA[1]	686,666	740,395	821,173	837,610	22.0	2.0
U.S.	248,709,873	281,421,906	308,745,538	324,697,795	30.6	5.2

Note: (1) Figures cover the Allentown-Bethlehem-Easton, PA-NJ Metropolitan Statistical Area; (*) 2015-2019 5-year estimated population
Source: U.S. Census Bureau, 1990 Census, Census 2000, Census 2010, 2015-2019 American Community Survey 5-Year Estimates

Household Size

Area	Persons in Household (%)							Average Household Size
	One	Two	Three	Four	Five	Six	Seven or More	
City	27.7	28.9	15.5	13.8	8.1	3.7	2.4	2.70
MSA[1]	26.1	35.4	15.7	13.5	6.0	2.2	1.1	2.50
U.S.	27.9	33.9	15.6	12.9	6.0	2.3	1.4	2.60

Note: (1) Figures cover the Allentown-Bethlehem-Easton, PA-NJ Metropolitan Statistical Area
Source: U.S. Census Bureau, 2015-2019 American Community Survey 5-Year Estimates

Race

Area	White Alone[2] (%)	Black Alone[2] (%)	Asian Alone[2] (%)	AIAN[3] Alone[2] (%)	NHOPI[4] Alone[2] (%)	Other Race Alone[2] (%)	Two or More Races (%)
City	62.3	14.7	2.9	0.7	0.1	14.7	4.6
MSA[1]	84.0	6.0	2.9	0.2	0.0	3.7	3.1
U.S.	72.5	12.7	5.5	0.8	0.2	4.9	3.3

Note: (1) Figures cover the Allentown-Bethlehem-Easton, PA-NJ Metropolitan Statistical Area; (2) Alone is defined as not being in combination with one or more other races; (3) American Indian and Alaska Native; (4) Native Hawaiian and Other Pacific Islander
Source: U.S. Census Bureau, 2015-2019 American Community Survey 5-Year Estimates

Hispanic or Latino Origin

Area	Total (%)	Mexican (%)	Puerto Rican (%)	Cuban (%)	Other (%)
City	52.5	1.9	28.8	0.9	20.9
MSA[1]	17.0	1.2	9.2	0.3	6.2
U.S.	18.0	11.2	1.7	0.7	4.3

Note: Persons of Hispanic or Latino origin can be of any race; (1) Figures cover the Allentown-Bethlehem-Easton, PA-NJ Metropolitan Statistical Area
Source: U.S. Census Bureau, 2015-2019 American Community Survey 5-Year Estimates

Ancestry

Area	German	Irish	English	American	Italian	Polish	French[2]	Scottish	Dutch
City	10.3	4.9	1.7	2.1	4.4	1.7	0.9	0.5	1.1
MSA[1]	24.3	13.5	5.8	4.5	12.8	5.2	1.6	1.1	2.3
U.S.	13.3	9.7	7.2	6.2	5.1	2.8	2.3	1.7	1.2

Note: Figures are the percentage of the total population reporting a particular ancestry. The nine most commonly reported ancestries in the U.S. are shown. Figures include multiple ancestries (e.g. if a person reported being Irish and Italian, they were included in both columns); (1) Figures cover the Allentown-Bethlehem-Easton, PA-NJ Metropolitan Statistical Area; (2) Excludes Basque
Source: U.S. Census Bureau, 2015-2019 American Community Survey 5-Year Estimates

Foreign-born Population

Area	Percent of Population Born in								
	Any Foreign Country	Asia	Mexico	Europe	Caribbean	Central America[2]	South America	Africa	Canada
City	19.2	3.6	1.0	0.8	9.0	1.3	2.5	0.8	0.1
MSA[1]	9.3	2.8	0.4	1.6	2.2	0.6	1.2	0.5	0.1
U.S.	13.6	4.2	3.5	1.5	1.3	1.1	1.0	0.7	0.2

Note: (1) Figures cover the Allentown-Bethlehem-Easton, PA-NJ Metropolitan Statistical Area; (2) Excludes Mexico.
Source: U.S. Census Bureau, 2015-2019 American Community Survey 5-Year Estimates

Marital Status

Area	Never Married	Now Married[2]	Separated	Widowed	Divorced
City	47.4	33.2	3.6	5.4	10.4
MSA[1]	32.3	49.3	2.1	6.4	9.9
U.S.	33.4	48.1	1.9	5.8	10.9

Note: Figures are percentages and cover the population 15 years of age and older; (1) Figures cover the Allentown-Bethlehem-Easton, PA-NJ Metropolitan Statistical Area; (2) Excludes separated
Source: U.S. Census Bureau, 2015-2019 American Community Survey 5-Year Estimates

Disability by Age

Area	All Ages	Under 18 Years Old	18 to 64 Years Old	65 Years and Over
City	17.1	9.2	16.9	37.5
MSA[1]	13.3	5.7	10.8	31.8
U.S.	12.6	4.2	10.3	34.5

Note: Figures show percent of the civilian noninstitutionalized population that reported having a disability. Disability status is determined from six types of difficulty: vision, hearing, cognitive, ambulatory, self-care, and independent living. For children under 5 years old, hearing and vision difficulty are used to determine disability status. For children between the ages of 5 and 14, disability status is determined from hearing, vision, cognitive, ambulatory, and self-care difficulties. For people aged 15 years and older, they are considered to have a disability if they have difficulty with any one of the six difficulty types; Note: (1) Figures cover the Allentown-Bethlehem-Easton, PA-NJ Metropolitan Statistical Area
Source: U.S. Census Bureau, 2015-2019 American Community Survey 5-Year Estimates

Age

Area	Percent of Population									Median Age
	Under Age 5	Age 5–19	Age 20–34	Age 35–44	Age 45–54	Age 55–64	Age 65–74	Age 75–84	Age 85+	
City	7.6	22.8	24.6	11.9	11.3	10.0	6.5	3.3	2.0	31.6
MSA[1]	5.3	18.7	18.6	11.9	13.8	14.1	9.9	5.2	2.6	41.4
U.S.	6.1	19.1	20.7	12.6	13.0	12.9	9.1	4.6	1.9	38.1

Note: (1) Figures cover the Allentown-Bethlehem-Easton, PA-NJ Metropolitan Statistical Area
Source: U.S. Census Bureau, 2015-2019 American Community Survey 5-Year Estimates

Gender

Area	Males	Females	Males per 100 Females
City	59,101	61,814	95.6
MSA[1]	411,125	426,485	96.4
U.S.	159,886,919	164,810,876	97.0

Note: (1) Figures cover the Allentown-Bethlehem-Easton, PA-NJ Metropolitan Statistical Area
Source: U.S. Census Bureau, 2015-2019 American Community Survey 5-Year Estimates

Religious Groups by Family

Area	Catholic	Baptist	Non-Den.	Methodist[2]	Lutheran	LDS[3]	Pente-costal	Presby-terian[4]	Muslim[5]	Judaism
MSA[1]	23.2	0.5	1.9	3.9	8.0	0.3	0.5	6.2	0.6	0.6
U.S.	19.1	9.3	4.0	4.0	2.3	2.0	1.9	1.6	0.8	0.7

Note: Figures are the number of adherents as a percentage of the total population; (1) Figures cover the Allentown-Bethlehem-Easton, PA-NJ Metropolitan Statistical Area; (2) Methodist/Pietist; (3) Latter Day Saints; (4) Reformed; (5) Figures are estimates
Source: Association of Statisticians of American Religious Bodies, 2010 U.S. Religion Census: Religious Congregations & Membership Study

Religious Groups by Tradition

Area	Catholic	Evangelical Protestant	Mainline Protestant	Other Tradition	Black Protestant	Orthodox
MSA[1]	23.2	5.4	17.8	3.0	0.1	0.6
U.S.	19.1	16.2	7.3	4.3	1.6	0.3

Note: Figures are the number of adherents as a percentage of the total population; (1) Figures cover the Allentown-Bethlehem-Easton, PA-NJ Metropolitan Statistical Area
Source: Association of Statisticians of American Religious Bodies, 2010 U.S. Religion Census: Religious Congregations & Membership Study

ECONOMY

Gross Metropolitan Product

Area	2017	2018	2019	2020	Rank[2]
MSA[1]	43.9	46.2	48.1	49.9	64

Note: Figures are in billions of dollars; (1) Figures cover the Allentown-Bethlehem-Easton, PA-NJ Metropolitan Statistical Area; (2) Rank is based on 2018 data and ranges from 1 to 381
Source: U.S. Conference of Mayors, U.S. Metro Economies: GMP & Employment 2018-2020, September 2019

Economic Growth

Area	2015-17 (%)	2018 (%)	2019 (%)	2020 (%)	Rank[2]
MSA[1]	1.2	2.6	2.3	1.6	210
U.S.	1.9	2.9	2.3	2.1	—

Note: Figures are real gross metropolitan product (GMP) growth rates and represent average annual percent change; (1) Figures cover the Allentown-Bethlehem-Easton, PA-NJ Metropolitan Statistical Area; (2) Rank is based on 2017 2-year average annual percent change and ranges from 1 to 381
Source: U.S. Conference of Mayors, U.S. Metro Economies: GMP & Employment 2018-2020, September 2019

Metropolitan Area Exports

Area	2014	2015	2016	2017	2018	2019	Rank[2]
MSA[1]	3,152.5	3,439.9	3,657.2	3,639.4	3,423.2	3,796.3	66

Note: Figures are in millions of dollars; (1) Figures cover the Allentown-Bethlehem-Easton, PA-NJ Metropolitan Statistical Area; (2) Rank is based on 2019 data and ranges from 1 to 386
Source: U.S. Department of Commerce, International Trade Administration, Office of Trade and Economic Analysis, Industry and Analysis, Exports by Metropolitan Area, data extracted March 24, 2021

Building Permits

Area	Single-Family			Multi-Family			Total		
	2018	2019	Pct. Chg.	2018	2019	Pct. Chg.	2018	2019	Pct. Chg.
City	0	0	0.0	0	0	0.0	0	0	0.0
MSA[1]	1,082	1,078	-0.4	164	267	62.8	1,246	1,345	7.9
U.S.	855,300	862,100	0.7	473,500	523,900	10.6	1,328,800	1,386,000	4.3

Note: (1) Figures cover the Allentown-Bethlehem-Easton, PA-NJ Metropolitan Statistical Area; Figures represent new, privately-owned housing units authorized (unadjusted data); All permit data are based on estimates with imputation
Source: U.S. Census Bureau, Manufacturing, Mining, and Construction Statistics, Building Permits, 2018, 2019

Bankruptcy Filings

Area	Business Filings			Nonbusiness Filings		
	2019	2020	% Chg.	2019	2020	% Chg.
Lehigh County	16	10	-37.5	599	433	-27.7
U.S.	22,780	21,655	-4.9	752,160	522,808	-30.5

Note: Business filings include Chapter 7, Chapter 9, Chapter 11, Chapter 12, Chapter 13, Chapter 15, and Section 304; Nonbusiness filings include Chapter 7, Chapter 11, and Chapter 13
Source: Administrative Office of the U.S. Courts, Business and Nonbusiness Bankruptcy, County Cases Commenced by Chapter of the Bankruptcy Code, During the 12-Month Period Ending December 31, 2019 and Business and Nonbusiness Bankruptcy, County Cases Commenced by Chapter of the Bankruptcy Code, During the 12-Month Period Ending December 31, 2020

Housing Vacancy Rates

Area	Gross Vacancy Rate[2] (%)			Year-Round Vacancy Rate[3] (%)			Rental Vacancy Rate[4] (%)			Homeowner Vacancy Rate[5] (%)		
	2018	2019	2020	2018	2019	2020	2018	2019	2020	2018	2019	2020
MSA[1]	9.3	7.7	4.9	7.1	5.8	4.8	5.7	4.0	3.9	0.9	1.4	0.7
U.S.	12.3	12.0	10.6	9.7	9.5	8.2	6.9	6.7	6.3	1.5	1.4	1.0

Note: (1) Figures cover the Allentown-Bethlehem-Easton, PA-NJ Metropolitan Statistical Area; (2) The percentage of the total housing inventory that is vacant; (3) The percentage of the housing inventory (excluding seasonal units) that is year-round vacant; (4) The percentage of rental inventory that is vacant for rent; (5) The percentage of homeowner inventory that is vacant for sale
Source: U.S. Census Bureau, Housing Vacancies and Homeownership Annual Statistics: 2018, 2019, 2020

INCOME

Income

Area	Per Capita ($)	Median Household ($)	Average Household ($)
City	20,792	41,167	56,842
MSA[1]	34,637	67,652	88,415
U.S.	34,103	62,843	88,607

Note: (1) Figures cover the Allentown-Bethlehem-Easton, PA-NJ Metropolitan Statistical Area
Source: U.S. Census Bureau, 2015-2019 American Community Survey 5-Year Estimates

Household Income Distribution

Area	Percent of Households Earning							
	Under $15,000	$15,000 -$24,999	$25,000 -$34,999	$35,000 -$49,999	$50,000 -$74,999	$75,000 -$99,999	$100,000 -$149,999	$150,000 and up
City	15.9	13.8	13.0	15.2	19.3	10.2	8.0	4.5
MSA[1]	7.9	8.4	8.7	12.2	17.9	13.9	16.9	14.2
U.S.	10.3	8.9	8.9	12.3	17.2	12.7	15.1	14.5

Note: (1) Figures cover the Allentown-Bethlehem-Easton, PA-NJ Metropolitan Statistical Area
Source: U.S. Census Bureau, 2015-2019 American Community Survey 5-Year Estimates

Poverty Rate

Area	All Ages	Under 18 Years Old	18 to 64 Years Old	65 Years and Over
City	25.7	37.4	22.4	15.8
MSA[1]	10.4	16.3	9.3	6.8
U.S.	13.4	18.5	12.6	9.3

Note: Figures are percentage of people whose income during the past 12 months was below the poverty level;
(1) Figures cover the Allentown-Bethlehem-Easton, PA-NJ Metropolitan Statistical Area
Source: U.S. Census Bureau, 2015-2019 American Community Survey 5-Year Estimates

CITY FINANCES

City Government Finances

Component	2017 ($000)	2017 ($ per capita)
Total Revenues	174,554	1,452
Total Expenditures	203,779	1,695
Debt Outstanding	97,403	810
Cash and Securities[1]	294,551	2,450

Note: (1) Cash and security holdings of a government at the close of its fiscal year,
including those of its dependent agencies, utilities, and liquor stores.
Source: U.S. Census Bureau, State & Local Government Finances 2017

City Government Revenue by Source

Source	2017 ($000)	2017 ($ per capita)	2017 (%)
General Revenue			
From Federal Government	13,117	109	7.5
From State Government	16,182	135	9.3
From Local Governments	2,488	21	1.4
Taxes			
Property	30,800	256	17.6
Sales and Gross Receipts	0	0	0.0
Personal Income	23,841	198	13.7
Corporate Income	0	0	0.0
Motor Vehicle License	0	0	0.0
Other Taxes	15,991	133	9.2
Current Charges	45,883	382	26.3
Liquor Store	0	0	0.0
Utility	398	3	0.2
Employee Retirement	24,210	201	13.9

Source: U.S. Census Bureau, State & Local Government Finances 2017

City Government Expenditures by Function

Function	2017 ($000)	2017 ($ per capita)	2017 (%)
General Direct Expenditures			
Air Transportation	0	0	0.0
Corrections	0	0	0.0
Education	0	0	0.0
Employment Security Administration	0	0	0.0
Financial Administration	2,955	24	1.5
Fire Protection	17,324	144	8.5
General Public Buildings	5,296	44	2.6
Governmental Administration, Other	3,489	29	1.7
Health	7,233	60	3.5
Highways	31,404	261	15.4
Hospitals	0	0	0.0
Housing and Community Development	7,600	63	3.7
Interest on General Debt	3,272	27	1.6
Judicial and Legal	621	5	0.3
Libraries	0	0	0.0
Parking	0	0	0.0
Parks and Recreation	9,792	81	4.8
Police Protection	33,232	276	16.3
Public Welfare	0	0	0.0
Sewerage	0	0	0.0
Solid Waste Management	29,182	242	14.3
Veterans' Services	0	0	0.0
Liquor Store	0	0	0.0
Utility	0	0	0.0
Employee Retirement	21,479	178	10.5

Source: U.S. Census Bureau, State & Local Government Finances 2017

EMPLOYMENT

Labor Force and Employment

Area	Civilian Labor Force			Workers Employed		
	Dec. 2019	Dec. 2020	% Chg.	Dec. 2019	Dec. 2020	% Chg.
City	56,275	55,559	-1.3	52,716	50,085	-5.0
MSA[1]	448,501	434,989	-3.0	428,188	408,208	-4.7
U.S.	164,007,000	160,017,000	-2.4	158,504,000	149,613,000	-5.6

Note: Data is not seasonally adjusted and covers workers 16 years of age and older; (1) Figures cover the Allentown-Bethlehem-Easton, PA-NJ Metropolitan Statistical Area
Source: Bureau of Labor Statistics, Local Area Unemployment Statistics

Unemployment Rate

Area	2020											
	Jan.	Feb.	Mar.	Apr.	May	Jun.	Jul.	Aug.	Sep.	Oct.	Nov.	Dec.
City	6.6	6.6	8.2	20.1	18.3	19.8	19.0	16.9	12.9	12.1	10.7	9.9
MSA[1]	5.0	5.0	5.7	16.2	13.8	14.1	12.8	10.6	7.5	6.9	6.5	6.2
U.S.	4.0	3.8	4.5	14.4	13.0	11.2	10.5	8.5	7.7	6.6	6.4	6.5

Note: Data is not seasonally adjusted and covers workers 16 years of age and older; (1) Figures cover the Allentown-Bethlehem-Easton, PA-NJ Metropolitan Statistical Area
Source: Bureau of Labor Statistics, Local Area Unemployment Statistics

Average Wages

Occupation	$/Hr.	Occupation	$/Hr.
Accountants and Auditors	36.60	Maintenance and Repair Workers	22.80
Automotive Mechanics	21.50	Marketing Managers	63.70
Bookkeepers	20.20	Network and Computer Systems Admin.	37.90
Carpenters	23.10	Nurses, Licensed Practical	24.50
Cashiers	11.50	Nurses, Registered	34.20
Computer Programmers	40.10	Nursing Assistants	16.30
Computer Systems Analysts	42.50	Office Clerks, General	18.20
Computer User Support Specialists	27.10	Physical Therapists	42.50
Construction Laborers	21.90	Physicians	n/a
Cooks, Restaurant	13.70	Plumbers, Pipefitters and Steamfitters	33.00
Customer Service Representatives	17.60	Police and Sheriff's Patrol Officers	34.50
Dentists	66.60	Postal Service Mail Carriers	25.50
Electricians	27.40	Real Estate Sales Agents	20.90
Engineers, Electrical	50.30	Retail Salespersons	13.50
Fast Food and Counter Workers	11.10	Sales Representatives, Technical/Scientific	35.70
Financial Managers	75.30	Secretaries, Exc. Legal/Medical/Executive	19.00
First-Line Supervisors of Office Workers	28.90	Security Guards	14.10
General and Operations Managers	57.30	Surgeons	n/a
Hairdressers/Cosmetologists	15.20	Teacher Assistants, Exc. Postsecondary*	14.40
Home Health and Personal Care Aides	12.90	Teachers, Secondary School, Exc. Sp. Ed.*	34.30
Janitors and Cleaners	15.90	Telemarketers	13.80
Landscaping/Groundskeeping Workers	16.40	Truck Drivers, Heavy/Tractor-Trailer	23.60
Lawyers	68.70	Truck Drivers, Light/Delivery Services	17.70
Maids and Housekeeping Cleaners	13.00	Waiters and Waitresses	13.50

Note: Wage data covers the Allentown-Bethlehem-Easton, PA-NJ Metropolitan Statistical Area; (*) Hourly wages were calculated from annual wage data based on a 40 hour work week; n/a not available.
Source: Bureau of Labor Statistics, Metro Area Occupational Employment & Wage Estimates, May 2020

Employment by Industry

Sector	MSA[1]		U.S.
	Number of Employees	Percent of Total	Percent of Total
Construction, Mining, and Logging	12,900	3.5	5.5
Education and Health Services	76,000	20.8	16.3
Financial Activities	13,200	3.6	6.1
Government	38,500	10.6	15.2
Information	4,700	1.3	1.9
Leisure and Hospitality	28,200	7.7	9.0
Manufacturing	38,300	10.5	8.5
Other Services	12,600	3.5	3.8
Professional and Business Services	46,800	12.8	14.4
Retail Trade	39,600	10.9	10.9
Transportation, Warehousing, and Utilities	40,100	11.0	4.6
Wholesale Trade	14,000	3.8	3.9

Note: Figures are non-farm employment as of December 2020. Figures are not seasonally adjusted and include workers 16 years of age and older; (1) Figures cover the Allentown-Bethlehem-Easton, PA-NJ Metropolitan Statistical Area
Source: Bureau of Labor Statistics, Current Employment Statistics, Employment, Hours, and Earnings

Employment by Occupation

Occupation Classification	City (%)	MSA[1] (%)	U.S. (%)
Management, Business, Science, and Arts	21.1	35.9	38.5
Natural Resources, Construction, and Maintenance	6.9	8.1	8.9
Production, Transportation, and Material Moving	29.1	16.9	13.2
Sales and Office	20.5	22.0	21.6
Service	22.4	17.1	17.8

Note: Figures cover employed civilians 16 years of age and older; (1) Figures cover the Allentown-Bethlehem-Easton, PA-NJ Metropolitan Statistical Area
Source: U.S. Census Bureau, 2015-2019 American Community Survey 5-Year Estimates

Occupations with Greatest Projected Employment Growth: 2020 – 2022

Occupation[1]	2020 Employment	2022 Projected Employment	Numeric Employment Change	Percent Employment Change
Fast Food and Counter Workers	99,390	133,800	34,410	34.6
Retail Salespersons	114,460	140,170	25,710	22.5
Waiters and Waitresses	50,420	71,990	21,570	42.8
Home Health and Personal Care Aides	167,300	188,640	21,340	12.8
Laborers and Freight, Stock, and Material Movers, Hand	136,300	150,840	14,540	10.7
Cooks, Restaurant	30,330	44,850	14,520	47.9
Janitors and Cleaners, Except Maids and Housekeeping Cleaners	84,010	95,320	11,310	13.5
Office Clerks, General	142,930	154,180	11,250	7.9
Cashiers	119,300	129,290	9,990	8.4
First-Line Supervisors of Food Preparation and Serving Workers	24,060	32,140	8,080	33.6

Note: Projections cover Pennsylvania; (1) Sorted by numeric employment change
Source: www.projectionscentral.com, State Occupational Projections, 2020–2022 Short-Term Projections

Fastest-Growing Occupations: 2020 – 2022

Occupation[1]	2020 Employment	2022 Projected Employment	Numeric Employment Change	Percent Employment Change
Motion Picture Projectionists	160	310	150	93.8
Gaming Dealers	1,960	3,610	1,650	84.2
Gaming Change Persons and Booth Cashiers	210	380	170	81.0
Amusement and Recreation Attendants	5,330	9,600	4,270	80.1
Ushers, Lobby Attendants, and Ticket Takers	2,460	4,340	1,880	76.4
Athletes and Sports Competitors	580	1,010	430	74.1
Hotel, Motel, and Resort Desk Clerks	4,010	6,860	2,850	71.1
Funeral Attendants	1,150	1,820	670	58.3
Pressers, Textile, Garment, and Related Materials	780	1,190	410	52.6
Locker Room, Coatroom, and Dressing Room Attendants	570	860	290	50.9

Note: Projections cover Pennsylvania; (1) Sorted by percent employment change and excludes occupations with numeric employment change less than 50
Source: www.projectionscentral.com, State Occupational Projections, 2020–2022 Short-Term Projections

TAXES

State Corporate Income Tax Rates

State	Tax Rate (%)	Income Brackets ($)	Num. of Brackets	Financial Institution Tax Rate (%)[a]	Federal Income Tax Ded.
Pennsylvania	9.99	Flat rate	1	(a)	No

Note: Tax rates as of January 1, 2021; (a) Rates listed are the corporate income tax rate applied to financial institutions or excise taxes based on income. Some states have other taxes based upon the value of deposits or shares.
Source: Federation of Tax Administrators, State Corporate Income Tax Rates, January 1, 2021

State Individual Income Tax Rates

State	Tax Rate (%)	Income Brackets ($)	Personal Exemptions ($) Single	Married	Depend.	Standard Ded. ($) Single	Married
Pennsylvania	3.07	Flat rate	None	None	None	–	–

Note: Tax rates as of January 1, 2021; Local- and county-level taxes are not included; Federal income tax is not deductible on state income tax returns
Source: Federation of Tax Administrators, State Individual Income Tax Rates, January 1, 2021

Various State Sales and Excise Tax Rates

State	State Sales Tax (%)	Gasoline[1] (¢/gal.)	Cigarette[2] ($/pack)	Spirits[3] ($/gal.)	Wine[4] ($/gal.)	Beer[5] ($/gal.)	Recreational Marijuana (%)
Pennsylvania	6	58.7	2.6	7.41	0.00	0.08	Not legal

Note: All tax rates as of January 1, 2021; (1) The American Petroleum Institute has developed a methodology for determining the average tax rate on a gallon of fuel. Rates may include any of the following: excise taxes, environmental fees, storage tank fees, other fees or taxes, general sales tax, and local taxes; (2) The federal excise tax of $1.0066 per pack and local taxes are not included; (3) Rates are those applicable to off-premise sales of 40% alcohol by volume (a.b.v.) distilled spirits in 750ml containers. Local excise taxes are excluded; (4) Rates are those applicable to off-premise sales of 11% a.b.v. non-carbonated wine in 750ml containers; (5) Rates are those applicable to off-premise sales of 4.7% a.b.v. beer in 12 ounce containers.
Source: Tax Foundation, 2021 Facts & Figures: How Does Your State Compare?

State Business Tax Climate Index Rankings

State	Overall Rank	Corporate Tax Rank	Individual Income Tax Rank	Sales Tax Rank	Property Tax Rank	Unemployment Insurance Tax Rank
Pennsylvania	27	43	19	17	15	40

Note: The index is a measure of how each state's tax laws affect economic performance. The lower the rank, the more favorable a state's tax system is for business. States without a given tax are given a ranking of 1. The scores/rankings for the District of Columbia do not affect other states. The 2021 index represents the tax climate as of July 1, 2020.
Source: Tax Foundation, State Business Tax Climate Index 2021

TRANSPORTATION

Means of Transportation to Work

Area	Car/Truck/Van		Public Transportation			Bicycle	Walked	Other Means	Worked at Home
	Drove Alone	Car-pooled	Bus	Subway	Railroad				
City	67.4	17.2	4.9	0.0	0.0	0.1	5.4	1.2	3.9
MSA[1]	81.7	8.4	1.5	0.1	0.1	0.2	2.4	1.1	4.6
U.S.	76.3	9.0	2.4	1.9	0.6	0.5	2.7	1.4	5.2

Note: Figures are percentages and cover workers 16 years of age and older; (1) Figures cover the Allentown-Bethlehem-Easton, PA-NJ Metropolitan Statistical Area
Source: U.S. Census Bureau, 2015-2019 American Community Survey 5-Year Estimates

Travel Time to Work

Area	Less Than 10 Minutes	10 to 19 Minutes	20 to 29 Minutes	30 to 44 Minutes	45 to 59 Minutes	60 to 89 Minutes	90 Minutes or More
City	11.5	34.8	28.6	14.6	4.2	4.1	2.2
MSA[1]	12.4	27.6	23.1	18.1	7.4	7.3	4.1
U.S.	12.2	28.4	20.8	20.8	8.3	6.4	2.9

Note: Note: Figures are percentages and include workers 16 years old and over; (1) Figures cover the Allentown-Bethlehem-Easton, PA-NJ Metropolitan Statistical Area
Source: U.S. Census Bureau, 2015-2019 American Community Survey 5-Year Estimates

Key Congestion Measures

Measure	1982	1992	2002	2012	2017
Annual Hours of Delay, Total (000)	3,147	6,933	14,695	15,728	18,068
Annual Hours of Delay, Per Auto Commuter	11	20	33	32	38
Annual Congestion Cost, Total (million $)	24	74	199	285	337
Annual Congestion Cost, Per Auto Commuter ($)	255	386	637	535	596

Note: Covers the Allentown PA-NJ urban area
Source: Texas A&M Transportation Institute, 2019 Urban Mobility Report

Freeway Travel Time Index

Measure	1982	1987	1992	1997	2002	2007	2012	2017
Urban Area Index[1]	1.07	1.07	1.11	1.16	1.17	1.17	1.18	1.20
Urban Area Rank[1,2]	35	55	49	36	41	56	40	39

Note: Freeway Travel Time Index—the ratio of travel time in the peak period to the travel time at free-flow conditions. For example, a value of 1.30 indicates a 20-minute free-flow trip takes 26 minutes in the peak (20 minutes x 1.30 = 26 minutes); (1) Covers the Allentown PA-NJ urban area; (2) Rank is based on 101 larger urban areas (#1 = highest travel time index)
Source: Texas A&M Transportation Institute, 2019 Urban Mobility Report

Public Transportation

Agency Name / Mode of Transportation	Vehicles Operated in Maximum Service[1]	Annual Unlinked Passenger Trips[2] (in thous.)	Annual Passenger Miles[3] (in thous.)
Lehigh and Northampton Transportation Authority (LANTA)			
Bus (directly operated)	76	4,368.6	23,765.0
Bus (purchased transportation)	1	4.5	26.6
Demand Response (purchased transportation)	94	359.5	3,917.2

Note: (1) Number of revenue vehicles operated by the given mode and type of service to meet the annual maximum service requirement. This is the revenue vehicle count during the peak season of the year; on the week and day that maximum service is provided. Vehicles operated in maximum service (VOMS) exclude atypical days and one-time special events; (2) Number of passengers who boarded public transportation vehicles. Passengers are counted each time they board a vehicle no matter how many vehicles they use to travel from their origin to their destination. (3) Sum of the distances ridden by all passengers during the entire fiscal year.
Source: Federal Transit Administration, National Transit Database, 2019

Air Transportation

Airport Name and Code / Type of Service	Passenger Airlines[1]	Passenger Enplanements	Freight Carriers[2]	Freight (lbs)
Lehigh Valley International (ABE)				
Domestic service (U.S. carriers - 2020)	11	191,424	8	101,771,260
International service (U.S. carriers - 2019)	1	165	0	0

Note: (1) Includes all U.S.-based major, minor and commuter airlines that carried at least one passenger during the year; (2) Includes all U.S.-based airlines and freight carriers that transported at least one pound of freight during the year.
Source: Bureau of Transportation Statistics, The Intermodal Transportation Database, Air Carriers: T-100 Domestic Market (U.S. Carriers), 2020; Bureau of Transportation Statistics, The Intermodal Transportation Database, Air Carriers: T-100 International Market (U.S. Carriers), 2019

BUSINESSES

Major Business Headquarters

Company Name	Industry	Rankings	
		Fortune[1]	Forbes[2]
Air Products & Chemicals	Chemicals	355	-
PPL	Utilities, Gas and Electric	408	-

Note: (1) Companies that produce a 10-K are ranked 1 to 500 based on 2019 revenue; (2) All private companies with at least $2 billion in annual revenue through the end of their most current fiscal year are ranked 1 to 219; companies listed are headquartered in the city; dashes indicate no ranking
Source: Fortune, "Fortune 500," June/July 2020; Forbes, "America's Largest Private Companies," 2020

Fastest-Growing Businesses

According to *Inc.*, Allentown is home to one of America's 500 fastest-growing private companies: **Netizen Corporation** (#184). Criteria: must be an independent, privately-held, for-profit, U.S. corporation, proprietorship or partnership as of December 31, 2019; revenues must be at least $100,000 in 2016 and $2 million in 2019; must have four-year operating/sales history. *Inc., "America's 500 Fastest-Growing Private Companies," 2020*

Living Environment

COST OF LIVING

Cost of Living Index

Composite Index	Groceries	Housing	Utilities	Trans-portation	Health Care	Misc. Goods/ Services
105.9	99.7	113.5	108.0	108.3	95.2	102.7

Note: The Cost of Living Index measures regional differences in the cost of consumer goods and services, excluding taxes and non-consumer expenditures, for professional and managerial households in the top income quintile. It is based on more than 50,000 prices covering almost 60 different items for which prices are collected three times a year by chambers of commerce, economic development organizations or university applied economic centers in each participating urban area. The numbers shown should be read as a percentage above or below the national average of 100. For example, a value of 115.4 in the groceries column indicates that grocery prices are 15.4% higher than the national average. Small differences in the index numbers should not be interpreted as significant; Figures cover the Allentown PA urban area.
Source: The Council for Community and Economic Research, Cost of Living Index, 2020

Grocery Prices

Area[1]	T-Bone Steak ($/pound)	Frying Chicken ($/pound)	Whole Milk ($/half gal.)	Eggs ($/dozen)	Orange Juice ($/64 oz.)	Coffee ($/11.5 oz.)
City[2]	13.52	1.36	2.09	1.36	3.47	3.73
Avg.	11.78	1.39	2.05	1.47	3.57	4.34
Min.	8.03	0.94	1.03	0.74	2.94	3.02
Max.	15.86	2.65	4.31	3.77	5.44	8.69

Note: (1) Values for the local area are compared with the average, minimum and maximum values for all 284 areas in the Cost of Living Index; (2) Figures cover the Allentown PA urban area; *T-Bone Steak* (price per pound); *Frying Chicken* (price per pound, whole fryer); *Whole Milk* (half gallon carton); *Eggs* (price per dozen, Grade A, large); *Orange Juice* (64 oz. Tropicana or Florida Natural); *Coffee* (11.5 oz. can, vacuum-packed, Maxwell House, Hills Bros, or Folgers).
Source: The Council for Community and Economic Research, Cost of Living Index, 2020

Housing and Utility Costs

Area[1]	New Home Price ($)	Apartment Rent ($/month)	All Electric ($/month)	Part Electric ($/month)	Other Energy ($/month)	Telephone ($/month)
City[2]	397,306	1,488	-	100.14	86.52	189.10
Avg.	368,594	1,168	170.86	100.47	65.28	184.30
Min.	190,567	502	91.58	31.42	26.08	169.60
Max.	2,227,806	4,738	470.38	280.31	280.06	206.50

Note: (1) Values for the local area are compared with the average, minimum and maximum values for all 284 areas in the Cost of Living Index; (2) Figures cover the Allentown PA urban area; *New Home Price* (2,400 sf living area, 8,000 sf lot, in urban area with full utilities); *Apartment Rent* (950 sf 2 bedroom/1.5 or 2 bath, unfurnished, excluding all utilities except water); *All Electric* (average monthly cost for an all-electric home); *Part Electric* (average monthly cost for a part-electric home); *Other Energy* (average monthly cost for natural gas, fuel oil, coal, wood, and any other forms of energy except electricity); *Telephone* (price includes the base monthly rate plus taxes and fees for three lines of mobile phone service).
Source: The Council for Community and Economic Research, Cost of Living Index, 2020

Health Care, Transportation, and Other Costs

Area[1]	Doctor ($/visit)	Dentist ($/visit)	Optometrist ($/visit)	Gasoline ($/gallon)	Beauty Salon ($/visit)	Men's Shirt ($)
City[2]	75.54	110.86	106.13	2.54	43.55	25.80
Avg.	115.44	99.32	108.10	2.21	39.27	31.37
Min.	36.68	59.00	51.36	1.71	19.00	11.00
Max.	219.00	153.10	250.97	3.46	82.05	58.33

Note: (1) Values for the local area are compared with the average, minimum and maximum values for all 284 areas in the Cost of Living Index; (2) Figures cover the Allentown PA urban area; *Doctor* (general practitioners routine exam of an established patient); *Dentist* (adult teeth cleaning and periodic oral examination); *Optometrist* (full vision eye exam for established adult patient); *Gasoline* (one gallon regular unleaded, national brand, including all taxes, cash price at self-service pump if available); *Beauty Salon* (woman's shampoo, trim, and blow-dry); *Men's Shirt* (cotton/polyester dress shirt, pinpoint weave, long sleeves).
Source: The Council for Community and Economic Research, Cost of Living Index, 2020

HOUSING

Homeownership Rate

Area	2012 (%)	2013 (%)	2014 (%)	2015 (%)	2016 (%)	2017 (%)	2018 (%)	2019 (%)	2020 (%)
MSA[1]	75.5	71.5	68.2	69.2	68.9	73.1	72.1	67.8	68.8
U.S.	65.4	65.1	64.5	63.7	63.4	63.9	64.4	64.6	66.6

Note: (1) Figures cover the Allentown-Bethlehem-Easton, PA-NJ Metropolitan Statistical Area
Source: U.S. Census Bureau, Housing Vacancies and Homeownership Annual Statistics: 2012-2020

House Price Index (HPI)

Area	National Ranking[2]	Quarterly Change (%)	One-Year Change (%)	Five-Year Change (%)	Since 1991Q1 (%)
MSA[1]	59	2.10	7.47	23.78	102.86
U.S.[3]	–	3.81	10.77	38.99	205.12

Note: The HPI is a weighted repeat sales index. It measures average price changes in repeat sales or refinancings on the same properties. This information is obtained by reviewing repeat mortgage transactions on single-family properties whose mortgages have been purchased or securitized by Fannie Mae or Freddie Mac since January 1975; (1) Figures cover the Allentown-Bethlehem-Easton, PA-NJ Metropolitan Statistical Area; (2) Rankings are based on annual percentage change for all metro areas containing at least 15,000 transactions over the last 10 years and ranges from 1 to 253; (3) figures based on a weighted average of Census Division estimates using a seasonally adjusted, purchase-only index; all figures are for the period ending December 31, 2020
Source: Federal Housing Finance Agency, Change in Metropolitan Area House Price Indexes, April 7, 2021

Median Single-Family Home Prices

Area	2018	2019	2020[p]	Percent Change 2019 to 2020
MSA[1]	199.3	207.2	234.9	13.4
U.S. Average	261.6	274.6	299.9	9.2

Note: Figures are median sales prices of existing single-family homes in thousands of dollars; (p) preliminary; (1) Figures cover the Allentown-Bethlehem-Easton, PA-NJ Metropolitan Statistical Area
Source: National Association of Realtors, Median Sales Price of Existing Single-Family Homes for Metropolitan Areas, 4th Quarter 2020

Qualifying Income Based on Median Sales Price of Existing Single-Family Homes

Area	With 5% Down ($)	With 10% Down ($)	With 20% Down ($)
MSA[1]	46,661	44,205	39,294
U.S. Average	59,266	56,147	49,908

Note: Figures are preliminary; Qualifying income is based on a mortgage rate of 2.81%. Monthly principal and interest payment is limited to 25% of income; (1) Figures cover the Allentown-Bethlehem-Easton, PA-NJ Metropolitan Statistical Area
Source: National Association of Realtors, Qualifying Income Based on Median Sales Price of Existing Single-Family Homes for Metropolitan Areas, 4th Quarter 2020

Home Value Distribution

Area	Under $50,000	$50,000 -$99,999	$100,000 -$149,999	$150,000 -$199,999	$200,000 -$299,999	$300,000 -$499,999	$500,000 -$999,999	$1,000,000 or more
City	4.5	22.0	35.2	24.0	8.7	4.1	1.1	0.4
MSA[1]	3.8	7.3	14.4	20.0	28.2	21.4	4.3	0.6
U.S.	6.9	12.0	13.3	14.0	19.6	19.3	11.4	3.4

Note: Figures are percentages and cover owner-occupied housing units; (1) Figures cover the Allentown-Bethlehem-Easton, PA-NJ Metropolitan Statistical Area
Source: U.S. Census Bureau, 2015-2019 American Community Survey 5-Year Estimates

Year Housing Structure Built

Area	2010 or Later	2000 -2009	1990 -1999	1980 -1989	1970 -1979	1960 -1969	1950 -1959	1940 -1949	Before 1940	Median Year
City	2.1	5.0	3.8	5.5	10.6	12.1	16.1	7.2	37.6	1953
MSA[1]	3.0	11.5	10.6	11.1	12.0	9.7	11.2	5.3	25.5	1968
U.S.	5.2	14.0	13.9	13.4	15.2	10.6	10.3	4.9	12.6	1978

Note: Figures are percentages except for Median Year; Note: (1) Figures cover the Allentown-Bethlehem-Easton, PA-NJ Metropolitan Statistical Area
Source: U.S. Census Bureau, 2015-2019 American Community Survey 5-Year Estimates

Gross Monthly Rent

Area	Under $500	$500 -$999	$1,000 -$1,499	$1,500 -$1,999	$2,000 -$2,499	$2,500 -$2,999	$3,000 and up	Median ($)
City	10.0	39.6	38.7	10.0	1.4	0.3	0.0	1,004
MSA[1]	9.5	34.3	38.5	13.6	2.6	0.7	0.8	1,066
U.S.	9.4	36.2	30.0	14.0	5.6	2.4	2.4	1,062

Note: Figures are percentages except for Median; Gross rent is the contract rent plus the estimated average monthly cost of utilities (electricity, gas, and water and sewer) and fuels (oil, coal, kerosene, wood, etc.) if these are paid by the renter (or paid for the renter by someone else); (1) Figures cover the Allentown-Bethlehem-Easton, PA-NJ Metropolitan Statistical Area
Source: U.S. Census Bureau, 2015-2019 American Community Survey 5-Year Estimates

HEALTH

Health Risk Factors

Category	MSA[1] (%)	U.S. (%)
Adults aged 18–64 who have any kind of health care coverage	91.9	87.3
Adults who reported being in good or better health	82.9	82.4
Adults who have been told they have high blood cholesterol	31.1	33.0
Adults who have been told they have high blood pressure	32.7	32.3
Adults who are current smokers	18.6	17.1
Adults who currently use E-cigarettes	4.8	4.6
Adults who currently use chewing tobacco, snuff, or snus	2.1	4.0
Adults who are heavy drinkers[2]	6.2	6.3
Adults who are binge drinkers[3]	16.2	17.4
Adults who are overweight (BMI 25.0 - 29.9)	31.9	35.3
Adults who are obese (BMI 30.0 - 99.8)	31.7	31.3
Adults who participated in any physical activities in the past month	79.0	74.4
Adults who always or nearly always wears a seat belt	93.0	94.3

Note: (1) Figures cover the Allentown-Bethlehem-Easton, PA-NJ Metropolitan Statistical Area; (2) Heavy drinkers are classified as adult men having more than 14 drinks per week and adult women having more than 7 drinks per week; (3) Binge drinkers are classified as males having five or more drinks on one occasion or females having four or more drinks on one occasion
Source: Centers for Disease Control and Prevention, Behaviorial Risk Factor Surveillance System, SMART: Selected Metropolitan Area Risk Trends, 2017

Acute and Chronic Health Conditions

Category	MSA[1] (%)	U.S. (%)
Adults who have ever been told they had a heart attack	5.0	4.2
Adults who have ever been told they have angina or coronary heart disease	4.1	3.9
Adults who have ever been told they had a stroke	3.5	3.0
Adults who have ever been told they have asthma	14.9	14.2
Adults who have ever been told they have arthritis	27.4	24.9
Adults who have ever been told they have diabetes[2]	11.4	10.5
Adults who have ever been told they had skin cancer	6.7	6.2
Adults who have ever been told they had any other types of cancer	8.7	7.1
Adults who have ever been told they have COPD	6.5	6.5
Adults who have ever been told they have kidney disease	2.5	3.0
Adults who have ever been told they have a form of depression	19.2	20.5

Note: (1) Figures cover the Allentown-Bethlehem-Easton, PA-NJ Metropolitan Statistical Area; (2) Figures do not include pregnancy-related, borderline, or pre-diabetes
Source: Centers for Disease Control and Prevention, Behaviorial Risk Factor Surveillance System, SMART: Selected Metropolitan Area Risk Trends, 2017

Health Screening and Vaccination Rates

Category	MSA[1] (%)	U.S. (%)
Adults aged 65+ who have had flu shot within the past year	73.0	60.7
Adults aged 65+ who have ever had a pneumonia vaccination	77.1	75.4
Adults who have ever been tested for HIV	35.4	36.1
Adults who have ever had the shingles or zoster vaccine?	30.5	28.9
Adults who have had their blood cholesterol checked within the last five years	90.6	85.9

Note: n/a not available; (1) Figures cover the Allentown-Bethlehem-Easton, PA-NJ Metropolitan Statistical Area.
Source: Centers for Disease Control and Prevention, Behaviorial Risk Factor Surveillance System, SMART: Selected Metropolitan Area Risk Trends, 2017

Disability Status

Category	MSA[1] (%)	U.S. (%)
Adults who reported being deaf	9.1	6.7
Are you blind or have serious difficulty seeing, even when wearing glasses?	2.5	4.5
Are you limited in any way in any of your usual activities due of arthritis?	14.8	12.9
Do you have difficulty doing errands alone?	6.2	6.8
Do you have difficulty dressing or bathing?	5.1	3.6
Do you have serious difficulty concentrating/remembering/making decisions?	11.6	10.7
Do you have serious difficulty walking or climbing stairs?	16.0	13.6

Note: (1) Figures cover the Allentown-Bethlehem-Easton, PA-NJ Metropolitan Statistical Area.
Source: Centers for Disease Control and Prevention, Behaviorial Risk Factor Surveillance System, SMART: Selected Metropolitan Area Risk Trends, 2017

Mortality Rates for the Top 10 Causes of Death in the U.S.

ICD-10[a] Sub-Chapter	ICD-10[a] Code	Age-Adjusted Mortality Rate[1] per 100,000 population	
		County[2]	U.S.
Malignant neoplasms	C00-C97	149.2	149.2
Ischaemic heart diseases	I20-I25	68.6	90.5
Other forms of heart disease	I30-I51	64.6	52.2
Chronic lower respiratory diseases	J40-J47	26.1	39.6
Other degenerative diseases of the nervous system	G30-G31	29.3	37.6
Cerebrovascular diseases	I60-I69	30.9	37.2
Other external causes of accidental injury	W00-X59	52.2	36.1
Organic, including symptomatic, mental disorders	F01-F09	55.1	29.4
Hypertensive diseases	I10-I15	14.0	24.1
Diabetes mellitus	E10-E14	18.0	21.5

Note: (a) ICD-10 = International Classification of Diseases 10th Revision; (1) Mortality rates are a three-year average covering 2017-2019; (2) Figures cover Lehigh County.
Source: Centers for Disease Control and Prevention, National Center for Health Statistics. Underlying Cause of Death 1999-2019 on CDC WONDER Online Database

Mortality Rates for Selected Causes of Death

ICD-10[a] Sub-Chapter	ICD-10[a] Code	Age-Adjusted Mortality Rate[1] per 100,000 population	
		County[2]	U.S.
Assault	X85-Y09	3.8	6.0
Diseases of the liver	K70-K76	11.8	14.4
Human immunodeficiency virus (HIV) disease	B20-B24	Unreliable	1.5
Influenza and pneumonia	J09-J18	10.9	13.8
Intentional self-harm	X60-X84	13.5	14.1
Malnutrition	E40-E46	2.7	2.3
Obesity and other hyperalimentation	E65-E68	2.0	2.1
Renal failure	N17-N19	12.1	12.6
Transport accidents	V01-V99	5.9	12.3
Viral hepatitis	B15-B19	Unreliable	1.2

Note: (a) ICD-10 = International Classification of Diseases 10th Revision; (1) Mortality rates are a three-year average covering 2017-2019; (2) Figures cover Lehigh County; Data are suppressed when the data meet the criteria for confidentiality constraints; Mortality rates are flagged as unreliable when the rate would be calculated with a numerator of 20 or less.
Source: Centers for Disease Control and Prevention, National Center for Health Statistics. Underlying Cause of Death 1999-2019 on CDC WONDER Online Database

Health Insurance Coverage

Area	With Health Insurance	With Private Health Insurance	With Public Health Insurance	Without Health Insurance	Population Under Age 19 Without Health Insurance
City	88.8	47.3	49.7	11.2	5.0
MSA[1]	94.5	73.3	35.4	5.5	3.0
U.S.	91.2	67.9	35.1	8.8	5.1

Note: Figures are percentages that cover the civilian noninstitutionalized population; (1) Figures cover the Allentown-Bethlehem-Easton, PA-NJ Metropolitan Statistical Area
Source: U.S. Census Bureau, 2015-2019 American Community Survey 5-Year Estimates

Number of Medical Professionals

Area	MDs[3]	DOs[3,4]	Dentists	Podiatrists	Chiropractors	Optometrists
County[1] (number)	1,281	307	326	45	109	74
County[1] (rate[2])	347.8	83.3	88.3	12.2	29.5	20.0
U.S. (rate[2])	282.9	22.7	71.2	6.2	28.1	16.9
42077						

Note: Data as of 2019 unless noted; (1) Data covers Lehigh County; (2) Rate per 100,000 population; (3) Data as of 2018 and includes all active, non-federal physicians; (4) Doctor of Osteopathic Medicine
Source: U.S. Department of Health and Human Services, Health Resources and Services Administration, Bureau of Health Professions, Area Resource File (ARF) 2019-2020

EDUCATION

Public School District Statistics

District Name	Schls	Pupils	Pupil/ Teacher Ratio	Minority Pupils[1] (%)	Free Lunch Eligible[2] (%)	IEP[3] (%)
Allentown City SD	22	16,946	16.8	91.1	88.7	21.1
Parkland SD	11	9,514	15.2	35.6	21.4	17.3

Note: Table includes school districts with 2,000 or more students; (1) Percentage of students that are not non-Hispanic white; (2) Percentage of students that are eligible for the free lunch program; (3) Percentage of students that have an Individualized Education Program.
Source: U.S. Department of Education, National Center for Education Statistics, Common Core of Data, Local Education Agency (School District) Universe Survey: School Year 2018-2019; U.S. Department of Education, National Center for Education Statistics, Common Core of Data, Public Elementary/Secondary School Universe Survey: School Year 2018-2019

Highest Level of Education

Area	Less than H.S.	H.S. Diploma	Some College, No Deg.	Associate Degree	Bachelor's Degree	Master's Degree	Prof. School Degree	Doctorate Degree
City	21.0	38.0	18.3	7.4	9.6	3.9	1.0	0.8
MSA[1]	10.0	34.2	17.1	9.3	18.3	8.4	1.6	1.2
U.S.	12.0	27.0	20.4	8.5	19.8	8.8	2.1	1.4

Note: Figures cover persons age 25 and over; (1) Figures cover the Allentown-Bethlehem-Easton, PA-NJ Metropolitan Statistical Area
Source: U.S. Census Bureau, 2015-2019 American Community Survey 5-Year Estimates

Educational Attainment by Race

Area	High School Graduate or Higher (%)					Bachelor's Degree or Higher (%)				
	Total	White	Black	Asian	Hisp.[2]	Total	White	Black	Asian	Hisp.[2]
City	79.0	81.5	83.0	81.3	68.2	15.3	17.9	7.3	37.1	6.0
MSA[1]	90.0	91.1	88.0	87.5	74.9	29.5	30.1	19.5	54.6	13.2
U.S.	88.0	89.9	86.0	87.1	68.7	32.1	33.5	21.6	54.3	16.4

Note: Figures shown cover persons 25 years old and over; (1) Figures cover the Allentown-Bethlehem-Easton, PA-NJ Metropolitan Statistical Area; (2) People of Hispanic origin can be of any race
Source: U.S. Census Bureau, 2015-2019 American Community Survey 5-Year Estimates

School Enrollment by Grade and Control

Area	Preschool (%)		Kindergarten (%)		Grades 1 - 4 (%)		Grades 5 - 8 (%)		Grades 9 - 12 (%)	
	Public	Private	Public	Private	Public	Private	Public	Private	Public	Private
City	73.8	26.2	82.8	17.2	87.8	12.2	88.3	11.7	89.0	11.0
MSA[1]	49.0	51.0	85.5	14.5	89.4	10.6	90.5	9.5	91.0	9.0
U.S.	59.1	40.9	87.6	12.4	89.5	10.5	89.4	10.6	90.1	9.9

Note: Figures shown cover persons 3 years old and over; (1) Figures cover the Allentown-Bethlehem-Easton, PA-NJ Metropolitan Statistical Area
Source: U.S. Census Bureau, 2015-2019 American Community Survey 5-Year Estimates

Higher Education

Four-Year Colleges			Two-Year Colleges			Medical Schools[1]	Law Schools[2]	Voc/ Tech[3]
Public	Private Non-profit	Private For-profit	Public	Private Non-profit	Private For-profit			
0	2	0	0	0	2	0	0	3

Note: Figures cover institutions located within the city limits and include main campuses only; (1) includes schools accredited by the Liaison Committee on Medical Education and the American Osteopathic Association's Commission on Osteopathic College Accreditation; (2) includes ABA-accredited schools, schools with provisional ABA accreditation, and state accredited schools; (3) includes all schools with programs that are less than 2 years.
Source: National Center for Education Statistics, Integrated Postsecondary Education System (IPEDS), 2019-20; Wikipedia, List of Medical Schools in the United States, accessed April 2, 2021; Wikipedia, List of Law Schools in the United States, accessed April 2, 2021

According to *U.S. News & World Report*, the Allentown-Bethlehem-Easton, PA-NJ metro area is home to one of the top 200 national universities in the U.S.: **Lehigh University** (#49 tie). The indicators used to capture academic quality fall into a number of categories: assessment by administrators at peer institutions; retention of students; faculty resources; student selectivity; financial resources; alumni giving; high school counselor ratings of colleges; and graduation rate. *U.S. News & World Report, "America's Best Colleges 2021"*

According to *U.S. News & World Report*, the Allentown-Bethlehem-Easton, PA-NJ metro area is home to two of the top 100 liberal arts colleges in the U.S.: **Lafayette College** (#40 tie); **Muhlenberg College** (#72 tie). The indicators used to capture academic quality fall into a number of categories: assessment by administrators at peer institutions; retention of students; faculty resources; student selectivity; financial resources; alumni giving; high school counselor ratings of colleges; and graduation rate. *U.S. News & World Report, "America's Best Colleges 2021"*

EMPLOYERS

Major Employers

Company Name	Industry
Air Products	Manufacturer
Amazon.com	Internet retailer
B. Braun Medical	Healthcare
Crayola	Electronics
Easton Hospital	Healthcare
Giant Food Stores	Grocery stores
Good Shepard Rehabilitation Network	Healthcare
Guardian Life Insurance Co.	Life insurance
HCR Manorcare	Healthcare
KidsPeace	Healthcare
Lehigh Carbon Community College	Education
Lehigh University	Education
Lehigh Valley Hospital and Health Network	Healthcare
Lutron Electronics Co.	Electronics
Mack Trucks	Trucking
Northampton Community College	Education
PPL	Utilities
Sacred Heart Healthcare System	Healthcare
Sands Casino Resort Bethlehem	Casino resort
Sodexo	Conglomerate
St. Luke's Hospital and Health Network	Healthcare
Wal-Mart Stores	Retail stores
Wegmans Food Market	Grocery stores
Weis Markets	Grocery stores
Wells Fargo	Banking and financial services

Note: Companies shown are located within the Allentown-Bethlehem-Easton, PA-NJ Metropolitan Statistical Area.
Source: Hoovers.com; Wikipedia

PUBLIC SAFETY

Crime Rate

Area	All Crimes	Violent Crimes				Property Crimes		
		Murder	Rape[3]	Robbery	Aggrav. Assault	Burglary	Larceny -Theft	Motor Vehicle Theft
City	2,669.6	5.7	52.5	139.5	188.7	427.6	1,656.1	199.4
Suburbs[1]	n/a	n/a	n/a	n/a	n/a	n/a	n/a	n/a
Metro[2]	n/a	n/a	n/a	n/a	n/a	n/a	n/a	n/a
U.S.	2,489.3	5.0	42.6	81.6	250.2	340.5	1,549.5	219.9

Note: Figures are crimes per 100,000 population; (1) All areas within the metro area that are located outside the city limits; (2) Figures cover the Allentown-Bethlehem-Easton, PA-NJ Metropolitan Statistical Area; n/a not available; (3) All figures shown were reported using the revised Uniform Crime Reporting (UCR) definition of rape.
Source: FBI Uniform Crime Reports, 2019

Hate Crimes

Area	Number of Quarters Reported	Number of Incidents per Bias Motivation					
		Race/Ethnicity/ Ancestry	Religion	Sexual Orientation	Disability	Gender	Gender Identity
City	3	0	0	0	0	0	0
U.S.	4	3,963	1,521	1,195	157	69	198

Source: Federal Bureau of Investigation, Hate Crime Statistics 2019

Identity Theft Consumer Reports

Area	Reports	Reports per 100,000 Population	Rank[2]
MSA[1]	2,089	247	163
U.S.	1,387,615	423	-

Note: (1) Figures cover the Allentown-Bethlehem-Easton, PA-NJ Metropolitan Statistical Area; (2) Rank ranges from 1 to 391 where 1 indicates greatest number of identity theft reports per 100,000 population
Source: Federal Trade Commission, Consumer Sentinel Network Data Book 2020

Fraud and Other Consumer Reports

Area	Reports	Reports per 100,000 Population	Rank[2]
MSA[1]	7,059	836	83
U.S.	3,385,133	1,031	-

Note: (1) Figures cover the Allentown-Bethlehem-Easton, PA-NJ Metropolitan Statistical Area; (2) Rank ranges from 1 to 391 where 1 indicates greatest number of fraud and other consumer reports per 100,000 population
Source: Federal Trade Commission, Consumer Sentinel Network Data Book 2020

POLITICS

2020 Presidential Election Results

Area	Biden	Trump	Jorgensen	Hawkins	Other
Lehigh County	53.1	45.5	1.2	0.1	0.2
U.S.	51.3	46.8	1.2	0.3	0.5

Note: Results are percentages and may not add to 100% due to rounding
Source: Dave Leip's Atlas of U.S. Presidential Elections

SPORTS

Professional Sports Teams

Team Name	League	Year Established
No teams are located in the metro area		

Source: Wikipedia, Major Professional Sports Teams of the United States and Canada, April 6, 2021

CLIMATE

Average and Extreme Temperatures

Temperature	Jan	Feb	Mar	Apr	May	Jun	Jul	Aug	Sep	Oct	Nov	Dec	Yr.
Extreme High (°F)	72	76	84	93	97	100	105	100	99	90	81	72	105
Average High (°F)	35	38	48	61	71	80	85	82	75	64	52	39	61
Average Temp. (°F)	28	30	39	50	60	70	74	72	65	54	43	32	52
Average Low (°F)	20	22	29	39	49	58	63	62	54	43	34	24	42
Extreme Low (°F)	-12	-7	-1	16	30	39	48	41	31	21	11	-8	-12

Note: Figures cover the years 1948-1990
Source: National Climatic Data Center, International Station Meteorological Climate Summary, 9/96

Average Precipitation/Snowfall/Humidity

Precip./Humidity	Jan	Feb	Mar	Apr	May	Jun	Jul	Aug	Sep	Oct	Nov	Dec	Yr.
Avg. Precip. (in.)	3.2	3.0	3.5	3.8	4.2	3.6	4.3	4.4	3.9	2.9	3.8	3.6	44.2
Avg. Snowfall (in.)	9	9	6	1	Tr	0	0	0	0	Tr	1	6	32
Avg. Rel. Hum. 7am (%)	77	76	75	75	78	79	82	86	88	86	82	79	80
Avg. Rel. Hum. 4pm (%)	62	57	51	48	52	52	52	55	57	56	60	64	55

Note: Figures cover the years 1948-1990; Tr = Trace amounts (<0.05 in. of rain; <0.5 in. of snow)
Source: National Climatic Data Center, International Station Meteorological Climate Summary, 9/96

Weather Conditions

Temperature			Daytime Sky			Precipitation		
5°F & below	32°F & below	90°F & above	Clear	Partly cloudy	Cloudy	0.01 inch or more precip.	0.1 inch or more snow/ice	Thunder-storms
6	123	15	77	148	140	123	20	31

Note: Figures are average number of days per year and cover the years 1948-1990
Source: National Climatic Data Center, International Station Meteorological Climate Summary, 9/96

HAZARDOUS WASTE

Superfund Sites

The Allentown-Bethlehem-Easton, PA-NJ metro area is home to eight sites on the EPA's Superfund National Priorities List: **Heleva Landfill** (final); **Hellertown Manufacturing Co.** (final); **Industrial Lane** (final); **Novak Sanitary Landfill** (final); **Palmerton Zinc Pile** (final); **Pohatcong Valley Ground Water Contamination** (final); **Rodale Manufacturing Co., Inc.** (final); **Tonolli Corp.** (final). There are a total of 1,375 Superfund sites with a status of proposed or final on the list in the U.S.
U.S. Environmental Protection Agency, National Priorities List, April 7, 2021

AIR QUALITY

Air Quality Trends: Ozone

	1990	1995	2000	2005	2010	2015	2016	2017	2018	2019
MSA[1]	0.093	0.091	0.091	0.086	0.080	0.070	0.073	0.067	0.067	0.064
U.S.	0.088	0.089	0.082	0.080	0.073	0.068	0.069	0.068	0.069	0.065

Note: (1) Data covers the Allentown-Bethlehem-Easton, PA-NJ Metropolitan Statistical Area. The values shown are the composite ozone concentration averages among trend sites based on the highest fourth daily maximum 8-hour concentration in parts per million. These trends are based on sites having an adequate record of monitoring data during the trend period. Data from exceptional events are included.
Source: U.S. Environmental Protection Agency, Air Quality Monitoring Information, "Air Quality Trends by City, 1990-2019"

Air Quality Index

Area	Percent of Days when Air Quality was...[2]					AQI Statistics[2]	
	Good	Moderate	Unhealthy for Sensitive Groups	Unhealthy	Very Unhealthy	Maximum	Median
MSA[1]	75.3	23.6	1.1	0.0	0.0	119	42

Note: (1) Data covers the Allentown-Bethlehem-Easton, PA-NJ Metropolitan Statistical Area; (2) Based on 365 days with AQI data in 2019. Air Quality Index (AQI) is an index for reporting daily air quality. EPA calculates the AQI for five major air pollutants regulated by the Clean Air Act: ground-level ozone, particle pollution (aka particulate matter), carbon monoxide, sulfur dioxide, and nitrogen dioxide. The AQI runs from 0 to 500. The higher the AQI value, the greater the level of air pollution and the greater the health concern. There are six AQI categories: "Good" AQI is between 0 and 50. Air quality is considered satisfactory; "Moderate" AQI is between 51 and 100. Air quality is acceptable; "Unhealthy for Sensitive Groups" When AQI values are between 101 and 150, members of sensitive groups may experience health effects; "Unhealthy" When AQI values are between 151 and 200 everyone may begin to experience health effects; "Very Unhealthy" AQI values between 201 and 300 trigger a health alert; "Hazardous" AQI values over 300 trigger warnings of emergency conditions (not shown).
Source: U.S. Environmental Protection Agency, Air Quality Index Report, 2019

Air Quality Index Pollutants

Area	Percent of Days when AQI Pollutant was...[2]					
	Carbon Monoxide	Nitrogen Dioxide	Ozone	Sulfur Dioxide	Particulate Matter 2.5	Particulate Matter 10
MSA[1]	0.0	3.6	61.4	0.0	35.1	0.0

Note: (1) Data covers the Allentown-Bethlehem-Easton, PA-NJ Metropolitan Statistical Area; (2) Based on 365 days with AQI data in 2019. The Air Quality Index (AQI) is an index for reporting daily air quality. EPA calculates the AQI for five major air pollutants regulated by the Clean Air Act: ground-level ozone, particle pollution (also known as particulate matter), carbon monoxide, sulfur dioxide, and nitrogen dioxide. The AQI runs from 0 to 500. The higher the AQI value, the greater the level of air pollution and the greater the health concern.
Source: U.S. Environmental Protection Agency, Air Quality Index Report, 2019

Maximum Air Pollutant Concentrations: Particulate Matter, Ozone, CO and Lead

	Particulate Matter 10 (ug/m^3)	Particulate Matter 2.5 Wtd AM (ug/m^3)	Particulate Matter 2.5 24-Hr (ug/m^3)	Ozone (ppm)	Carbon Monoxide (ppm)	Lead (ug/m^3)
MSA[1] Level	31	8.5	26	0.065	n/a	0.04
NAAQS[2]	150	15	35	0.075	9	0.15
Met NAAQS[2]	Yes	Yes	Yes	Yes	n/a	Yes

Note: (1) Data covers the Allentown-Bethlehem-Easton, PA-NJ Metropolitan Statistical Area; Data from exceptional events are included; (2) National Ambient Air Quality Standards; ppm = parts per million; ug/m^3 = micrograms per cubic meter; n/a not available.
Concentrations: Particulate Matter 10 (coarse particulate)—highest second maximum 24-hour concentration; Particulate Matter 2.5 Wtd AM (fine particulate)—highest weighted annual mean concentration; Particulate Matter 2.5 24-Hour (fine particulate)—highest 98th percentile 24-hour concentration; Ozone—highest fourth daily maximum 8-hour concentration; Carbon Monoxide—highest second maximum non-overlapping 8-hour concentration; Lead—maximum running 3-month average
Source: U.S. Environmental Protection Agency, Air Quality Monitoring Information, "Air Quality Statistics by City, 2019"

Maximum Air Pollutant Concentrations: Nitrogen Dioxide and Sulfur Dioxide

	Nitrogen Dioxide AM (ppb)	Nitrogen Dioxide 1-Hr (ppb)	Sulfur Dioxide AM (ppb)	Sulfur Dioxide 1-Hr (ppb)	Sulfur Dioxide 24-Hr (ppb)
MSA[1] Level	11	43	n/a	6	n/a
NAAQS[2]	53	100	30	75	140
Met NAAQS[2]	Yes	Yes	n/a	Yes	n/a

Note: (1) Data covers the Allentown-Bethlehem-Easton, PA-NJ Metropolitan Statistical Area; Data from exceptional events are included; (2) National Ambient Air Quality Standards; ppm = parts per million; ug/m^3 = micrograms per cubic meter; n/a not available.
Concentrations: Nitrogen Dioxide AM—highest arithmetic mean concentration; Nitrogen Dioxide 1-Hr—highest 98th percentile 1-hour daily maximum concentration; Sulfur Dioxide AM—highest annual mean concentration; Sulfur Dioxide 1-Hr—highest 99th percentile 1-hour daily maximum concentration; Sulfur Dioxide 24-Hr—highest second maximum 24-hour concentration
Source: U.S. Environmental Protection Agency, Air Quality Monitoring Information, "Air Quality Statistics by City, 2019"

Boston, Massachusetts

Background

Who would think that Boston, a city founded upon the Puritan principles of hard work, plain living, sobriety, and unyielding religious conviction, would be known for such a radical act of throwing tea overboard from a ship? The answer lies in the wealth upon which Boston grew: ship trading. Boston sea captains reaped more profits from West Indies molasses, mahogany from Honduras, and slaves from Guinea than did the English, who decided to impose additional taxes upon her colonial subjects. In defiance, Samuel Adams led the Sons of Liberty to throw a precious cargo of tea, so dear to the English, overboard. Events escalated, and the American Revolution began.

After the Revolution, Boston continued to grow into the Yankee capital that it is today. Metropolitan Boston is the site of nearly 80 institutions of higher learning. Boston's largest universities are Boston University, Northeastern University, University of Massachusetts/Boston, and Boston College. Cambridge, across the Charles River, is home to both the Massachusetts Institute of Technology (MIT) and Harvard University, which recently expanded into nearby Allston.

Boston's moniker is "The Hub." The largest city in the six-state New England region, it has been recognized not only as a city of historic importance in the American Revolution, but as a leading educational and medical center and as a site for historic architecture and world class cultural institutions.

Historic Faneuil Hall and the nearby Quincy Market have been renovated into a historical attraction and a festival marketplace of food and shopping. The Back Bay and fashionable Newbury Street offers art galleries, fashion boutiques, and open-air cafes draw tourists and local residents. The Fenway neighborhood is home to the Boston Symphony Orchestra, Boston Pops, Berklee College of Music, Gardner Museum, and New England Conservatory. Along the city's downtown waterfront are the Museum of Science, New England Aquarium, and the Children's Museum.

Boston's historic buildings include Trinity Church, with its brilliant stained glass windows, built in 1877. The African meeting house on Beacon Hill is the oldest surviving black church in North America. Christ Church (Old North Church) is the oldest church in Boston (1723), and was part of Paul Revere's ride. Modern architecture is represented by the John Hancock Tower by I.M. Pei and luxury hotels, including the Ritz Carlton Boston Common and the Four Seasons.

The TD Garden is home to the Boston Bruins and the Boston Celtics and a venue for concerts, shows and conventions. Gillette Stadium, a 68,000 seat outdoor coliseum for football, soccer and other events opened in 2002 in nearby Foxboro. Fenway Park, the oldest major league ballpark still in use, is home to the Boston Red Sox, 2018 World Series winners. Deep pride in their sports teams is a known characteristic of Bostonians. In addition to the Red Sox victory, the Celtics won the 2008 NBA championship, and the New England Patriots won the NFL Super Bowl in 2019.

> The city's famous St. Patrick's Day Parade was canceled, but some events streamed online, and many restaurants offered takeout kits for customers to bring the pub home with them.

The Boston Marathon is the world's oldest annual marathon and best-known road racing event. During the 2013 race, two explosions occurred close to the end of the course, halting the race and preventing many from finishing. Three spectators were killed and more than 200 people were injured. Two brothers, allegedly motivated by extremist Islamist beliefs, planted the two bombs. One brother was killed by police and the other was sentenced to death.

Boston's colleges and universities have a major impact on the city's economy, attracting high-tech industries including computer hardware and software and biotech companies. Boston receives the largest amount of annual funding from the National Institutes of Health of all cities in the United States.

Boston's weather is influenced by both tropical and polar air masses, proximity to several low-pressure storm tracks, and by its moderating East Coast location. Summer heat is relieved by sea breezes. Cold winters are often alleviated by the relatively warm ocean.

Rankings

General Rankings

- *US News & World Report* conducted a survey of more than 3,000 people and analyzed the 150 largest metropolitan areas to determine what matters most when selecting the next place to live. Boston ranked #18 out of the top 25 as having the best combination of desirable factors. Criteria: cost of living; quality of life; net migration; job market; desirability; and other factors. *realestate.usnews.com, "The 25 Best Places to Live in the U.S. in 2020-21," October 13, 2020*

- Boston was selected as one of the best places to live in America by *Outside Magazine*. Criteria included population, park acreage, neighborhood and resident diversity, new and upcoming things of interest, and opportunities for outdoor adventure. *Outside Magazine, "The 12 Best Places to Live in 2019," July 11, 2019*

- The human resources consulting firm Mercer ranked 231 major cities worldwide in terms of overall quality of life. Boston ranked #36. Criteria: political, social, economic, and socio-cultural factors; medical and health considerations; schools and education; public services and transportation; recreation; consumer goods; housing; and natural environment. *Mercer, "Mercer 2019 Quality of Living Survey," March 13, 2019*

- For its 33rd annual "Readers' Choice Awards" survey, *Condé Nast Traveler* ranked its readers' favorite cities in the U.S. These places brought feelings of comfort in a time of limited travel. The list was broken into large cities and cities under 250,000. Boston ranked #3 in the big city category. *Condé Nast Traveler, Readers' Choice Awards 2020, "Best Big Cities in the U.S." October 6, 2020*

Business/Finance Rankings

- According to *Business Insider*, the Boston metro area is a prime place to run a startup or move an existing business to. The area ranked #4. Nearly 190 metro areas were analyzed on overall economic health and investments. Data was based on the 2019 U.S. Census Bureau American Community Survey, the marketing company PitchBook, Bureau of Labor Statistics employment report, and Zillow. Criteria: percentage of change in typical home values and employment rates; quarterly venture capital investment activity; and median household income. *www.businessinsider.com, "The 25 Best Cities to Start a Business-Or Move Your Current One," January 12, 2021*

- 24/7 Wall Street used metro data from the Bureau of Labor Statistics' Occupational Employment database to identify the cities with the highest percentage of those employed in jobs requiring knowledge in the science, technology, engineering, and math (STEM) fields as well as average wages for STEM jobs. The Boston metro area was #10. *247wallst.com, "15 Cities with the Most High-Tech Jobs," January 11, 2020*

- Based on metro area social media reviews, the employment opinion group Glassdoor surveyed 50 of the most populous U.S. metro areas and equally weighed cost of living, hiring opportunity, and job satisfaction to compose a list of "25 Best Cities for Jobs." Median pay and home value, and number of active job openings were also factored in. The Boston metro area was ranked #20 in overall job satisfaction. *www.glassdoor.com, "Best Cities for Jobs," February 25, 2020*

- The Brookings Institution ranked the nation's largest cities based on income inequality. Boston was ranked #7 (#1 = greatest inequality). Criteria: the "95/20 ratio," a figure representing the income at which a household earns more than 95 percent of all other households, divided by the income at which a household earns more than only 20 percent of all other households. *Brookings Institution, "Household Income Inequality, Largest Cities of 97 Large U.S. Metro Areas, 2014-2016," February 5, 2018*

- The Brookings Institution ranked the 100 largest metro areas in the U.S. based on income inequality. Boston was ranked #10 (#1 = greatest inequality). Criteria: the "95/20 ratio," a figure representing the income at which a household earns more than 95 percent of all other households, divided by the income at which a household earns more than only 20 percent of all other households. *Brookings Institution, "Household Income Inequality, 100 Largest U.S. Metro Areas, 2014-2016," February 5, 2018*

- *Forbes* ranked the 100 largest metro areas in the U.S. in terms of the "Best Cities for Young Professionals." The Boston metro area ranked #8 out of 25. Criteria: median rent of a two-bedroom apartment; job growth and unemployment rate; median salary of college graduates with 5 or less years of work experience; networking opportunities; social outlook; percentage of population 25 years of age and older with college degrees. *Forbes.com, "America's 25 Best Cities for Young Professionals in 2017," May 22, 2017*

- Payscale.com ranked the 32 largest metro areas in terms of wage growth. The Boston metro area ranked #30. Criteria: private-sector and education professional wage growth between the 4th quarter of 2019 and the 4th quarter of 2020. *PayScale, "Wage Trends by Metro Area-4th Quarter," January 11, 2021*

- The Boston metro area was identified as one of the most debt-ridden places in America by the finance site Credit.com. The metro area was ranked #16. Criteria: residents' average credit card debt as well as median income. *Credit.com, "25 Cities With the Most Credit Card Debt," February 28, 2018*

- For its annual survey of the "Most Expensive U.S. Cities to Live In," Kiplinger applied Cost of Living Index statistics developed by the Council for Community and Economic Research to U.S. Census Bureau population and median household income data for 256 urban areas. Boston was among the 20 most expensive in the country. *Kiplinger.com, "The 20 Most Expensive Cities in the U.S.," July 29, 2020*

- Boston was identified as one of America's most frugal metro areas by *Coupons.com*. The city ranked #11 out of 25. Criteria: digital coupon usage. *Coupons.com, "America's Most Frugal Cities of 2017," March 22, 2018*

- Boston was identified as one of the happiest cities to work in by CareerBliss.com, an online community for career advancement. The city ranked #6 out of 10. Criteria: an employee's relationship with his or her boss and co-workers; daily tasks; general work environment; compensation; opportunities for advancement; company culture and job reputation; and resources. *Businesswire.com, "CareerBliss Happiest Cities to Work 2019," February 12, 2019*

- The Boston metro area appeared on the Milken Institute "2021 Best Performing Cities" list. Rank: #105 out of 200 large metro areas (population over 250,000). Criteria: job growth; wage and salary growth; high-tech output growth; housing affordability; household broadband access. *Milken Institute, "Best-Performing Cities 2021," February 16, 2021*

- *Forbes* ranked the 200 most populous metro areas to determine the nation's "Best Places for Business and Careers." The Boston metro area was ranked #41. Criteria: costs (business and living); job growth (past and projected); income growth; quality of life; educational attainment (college and high school); projected economic growth; cultural and leisure opportunities; workplace tolerance laws; net migration patterns. *Forbes, "The Best Places for Business and Careers 2019: Seattle Still On Top," October 30, 2019*

- Mercer Human Resources Consulting ranked 209 cities worldwide in terms of cost-of-living. Boston ranked #41 (the lower the ranking, the higher the cost-of-living). The survey measured the comparative cost of over 200 items (such as housing, food, clothing, household goods, transportation, and entertainment) in each location. *Mercer, "2020 Cost of Living Survey," June 9, 2020*

Children/Family Rankings

- Boston was selected as one of the most playful cities in the U.S. by KaBOOM! The organization's Playful City USA initiative honors cities and towns across the nation that have made their communities more playable. Criteria: pledging to integrate play as a solution to challenges in their communities; making it easy for children to get active and balanced play; creating more family-friendly and innovative communities as a result. *KaBOOM! National Campaign for Play, "2017 Playful City USA Communities"*

Culture/Performing Arts Rankings

- Boston was selected as one of the 25 best cities for moviemakers in North America. COVID-19 has spurred a quest for great film cities that offer more creative space, lower costs, and more great outdoors. NYC & LA were intentionally excluded. Criteria: longstanding reputations as film-friendly communities; efforts to deal with pandemic-specific challenges; and establish appropriate COVID-19 guidelines. The city was ranked #9. *MovieMaker Magazine, "Best Places to Live and Work as a Moviemaker, 2021," January 26, 2021*

Dating/Romance Rankings

- Boston was selected as one of the best cities for post grads by *Rent.com*. The city ranked among the top 10. Criteria: jobs per capita; unemployment rate; mean annual income; cost of living; rental inventory. *Rent.com, "Best Cities for College Grads," December 11, 2018*

Education Rankings

- Personal finance website *WalletHub* analyzed the 150 largest U.S. metropolitan statistical areas to determine where the most educated Americans are putting their degrees to work. Criteria: education levels; percentage of workers with degrees; education quality and attainment gap; public school quality rankings; quality and enrollment of each metro area's universities. Boston was ranked #7 (#1 = most educated city). *www.WalletHub.com, "Most and Least Educated Cities in America," July 20, 2020*

- Boston was selected as one of America's most literate cities. The city ranked #13 out of the 84 largest U.S. cities. Criteria: number of booksellers; library resources; Internet resources; educational attainment; periodical publishing resources; newspaper circulation. *Central Connecticut State University, "America's Most Literate Cities, 2018," February 2019*

Environmental Rankings

- The U.S. Environmental Protection Agency (EPA) released a list of U.S. metropolitan areas with the most ENERGY STAR certified buildings in 2019. The Boston metro area was ranked #9 out of 25. *U.S. Environmental Protection Agency, "2020 Energy Star Top Cities," March 2020*

- Boston was highlighted as one of the top 98 cleanest metro areas for short-term particle pollution (24-hour PM 2.5) in the U.S. during 2016 through 2018. Monitors in these cities reported no days with unhealthful PM 2.5 levels. *American Lung Association, "State of the Air 2020," April 21, 2020*

Food/Drink Rankings

- The U.S. Chamber of Commerce Foundation conducted an in-depth study on local food truck regulations, surveyed 288 food truck owners, and ranked 20 major American cities based on how friendly they are for operating a food truck. The compiled index assessed the following: procedures for obtaining permits and licenses; complying with restrictions; and financial obligations associated with operating a food truck. Boston ranked #20 overall (1 being the best). *www.foodtrucknation.us, "Food Truck Nation," March 20, 2018*

- Boston was identified as one of the cities in America ordering the most vegan food options by GrubHub.com. The city ranked #5 out of 5. Criteria: percentage of vegan, vegetarian and plant-based food orders compared to the overall number of orders. *GrubHub.com, "State of the Plate Report 2020: Top Vegan-Friendly Cities," July 9, 2020*

Health/Fitness Rankings

- The Sharecare Community Well-Being Index evaluates 10 individual and social health factors in order to measure what matters to Americans in the communities in which they live. The Boston metro area was one of the five communities where social determinants of health were the highest. Criteria: access to food, healthcare, and community resources; housing and transportation; economic security. The area ranked #0. *www.sharecare.com, "Community Well-Being Index: 2019 Metro Area & County Rankings Report," August 31, 2020*

- For each of the 100 largest cities in the United States, the American Fitness Index®, published by the American College of Sports Medicine and the Anthem Foundation, evaluated community infrastructure and 33 health behaviors including preventive health, levels of chronic disease conditions, pedestrian safety, air quality, and community resources that support physical activity. Boston ranked #10 for "community fitness." *americanfitnessindex.org, "2020 ACSM American Fitness Index Summary Report," July 14, 2020*

- Trulia analyzed the 100 largest U.S. metro areas to identify the nation's best cities for weight loss, based on the percentage of adults who bike or walk to work, sporting goods stores, grocery stores, access to outdoor activities, weight-loss centers, gyms, and average space reserved for parks. Boston ranked #8. *Trulia.com, "Where to Live to Get in Shape in the New Year," January 4, 2018*

- Boston was identified as one of the 10 most walkable cities in the U.S. by Walk Score. The city ranked #3. Walk Score measures walkability by analyzing hundreds of walking routes to nearby amenities, and also measures pedestrian friendliness by analyzing population density and road metrics such as block length and intersection density. *WalkScore.com, April 13, 2021*

- Boston was identified as a "2021 Spring Allergy Capital." The area ranked #72 out of 100. Three groups of factors were used to identify the most challenging cities for people with allergies during the spring season: annual spring pollen levels; over the counter medicine use; number of board-certified allergy specialists. *Asthma and Allergy Foundation of America, "Spring Allergy Capitals 2021," February 23, 2021*

- Boston was identified as a "2021 Fall Allergy Capital." The area ranked #74 out of 100. Three groups of factors were used to identify the most challenging cities for people with allergies during the fall season: annual fall pollen levels; over the counter medicine use; number of board-certified allergy specialists. *Asthma and Allergy Foundation of America, "Fall Allergy Capitals 2021," February 23, 2021*

- Boston was identified as a "2019 Asthma Capital." The area ranked #8 out of the nation's 100 largest metropolitan areas. Criteria: estimated asthma prevalence; crude death rate from asthma; and ER visits due to asthma. Risk factors analyzed but not factored in the rankings: annual pollen score; annual air quality; public smoking laws; number of board-certified asthma specialists; rescue medication use; controller medication use; uninsured rate; poverty rate. *Asthma and Allergy Foundation of America, "Asthma Capitals 2019: The Most Challenging Places to Live With Asthma," May 7, 2019*

- The Sharecare Community Well-Being Index evaluates 10 individual and social health factors in order to measure what matters to Americans in the communities in which they live. The Boston metro area ranked #5 in the top 10 across all 10 domains. Criteria: access to healthcare, food, and community resources; housng and transportation; economic security; feeling of purpose; physical, financial, social, and community well-being. *www.sharecare.com, "Community Well-Being Index: 2019 Metro Area & County Rankings Report," August 31, 2020*

Real Estate Rankings

- FitSmallBusiness looked at 50 of the largest metropolitan areas in the U.S. to determine which metro was the best to start a real estate business. Data was compiled from such sources as: Zillow, Trulia, U.S. Census Bureau, and the Bureau of Labor Statistics. Criteria: location; inventory; annual wages; median sales price of homes; days on the market; median price cut percentage; and other factors that would influence real estate professional growth. The Boston metro area ranked #2. *fitsmallbusiness.com, "The Best Cities to Become a Real Estate Agent in 2018," January 30, 2018*

- *WalletHub* compared the most populated U.S. cities to determine which had the best markets for real estate agents. Boston ranked #8 where demand was high and pay was the best. Criteria: sales per agent; annual median wage for real-estate agents; monthly average starting salary for real estate agents; real estate job density and competition; unemployment rate; home turnover rate; housing-market health index; and other relevant metrics. *www.WalletHub.com, "2019's Best Places to Be a Real Estate Agent," April 24, 2019*

- The Boston metro area was identified as one of the 10 worst condo markets in the U.S. in 2020. The area ranked #58 out of 63 markets. Criteria: year-over-year change of median sales price of existing apartment condo-coop homes between the 4th quarter of 2019 and the 4th quarter of 2020. *National Association of Realtors®, Median Sales Price of Existing Apartment Condo-Coops Homes for Metropolitan Areas, 4th Quarter 2020*

- The Boston metro area was identified as one of the 20 least affordable housing markets in the U.S. in 2020. The area ranked #174 out of 183 markets. Criteria: qualification for a mortgage loan with a 10 percent down payment on a typical home. *National Association of Realtors®, Qualifying Income Based on Sales Price of Existing Single-Family Homes for Metropolitan Areas, 2020*

- Boston was ranked #225 out of 268 metro areas in terms of housing affordability in 2020 by the National Association of Home Builders (#1 = most affordable). Criteria: the share of homes sold in that area affordable to a family earning the local median income, based on standard mortgage underwriting criteria. *National Association of Home Builders®, NAHB-Wells Fargo Housing Opportunity Index, 4th Quarter 2020*

Safety Rankings

- Allstate ranked the 200 largest cities in America in terms of driver safety. Boston ranked #198. Criteria: internal property damage claims over a two-year period from January 2016 to December 2017. The report helps increase the importance of safety and awareness behind the wheel. *Allstate, "Allstate America's Best Drivers Report, 2019" June 24, 2019*

- The National Insurance Crime Bureau ranked 384 metro areas in the U.S. in terms of per capita rates of vehicle theft. The Boston metro area ranked #323 (#1 = highest rate). Criteria: number of vehicle theft offenses per 100,000 inhabitants in 2019. *National Insurance Crime Bureau, "Hot Spots 2019," July 21, 2020*

Seniors/Retirement Rankings

- From its Best Cities for Successful Aging indexes, the Milken Institute generated rankings for metropolitan areas, weighing data in nine categories—health care, wellness, living arrangements, transportation and convenience, financial characteristics, education, employment, community engagement, and overall livability. The Boston metro area was ranked #9 overall in the large metro area category. *Milken Institute, "Best Cities for Successful Aging, 2017" March 14, 2017*

Sports/Recreation Rankings

- Boston was chosen as one of America's best cities for bicycling. The city ranked #20 out of 50. Criteria: cycling infrastructure that is safe and friendly for all ages; energy and bike culture. The editors evaluated cities with populations of 100,000 or more. *Bicycling, "The 50 Best Bike Cities in America," October 10, 2018*

Transportation Rankings

- Business Insider presented an AllTransit Performance Score ranking of public transportation in major U.S. cities and towns, with populations over 250,000, in which Boston earned the #3-ranked "Transit Score," awarded for frequency of service, access to jobs, quality and number of stops, and affordability. *www.businessinsider.com, "The 17 Major U.S. Cities with the Best Public Transportation," April 17, 2018*

- The business website 24/7 Wall Street reviewed U.S. Census data to identify the 25 cities where the largest share of households do not own a vehicle. Boston held the #4 position. *247wallst.com, "Cities Where No One Wants to Drive," February 15, 2017*

- Boston was identified as one of the most congested metro areas in the U.S. The area ranked #6 out of 10. Criteria: yearly delay per auto commuter in hours. *Texas A&M Transportation Institute, "2019 Urban Mobility Report," December 2019*

- According to the INRIX "2019 Global Traffic Scorecard," Boston was identified as one of the most congested metro areas in the U.S. The area ranked #1 out of 10. Criteria: average annual time spent in traffic and average cost of congestion per motorist. *Inrix.com, "Congestion Costs Each American Nearly 100 hours, $1,400 A Year," March 9, 2020*

Women/Minorities Rankings

- The *Houston Chronicle* listed the Boston metro area as #1 in top places for young Latinos to live in the U.S. Research was largely based on housing and occupational data from the largest metropolitan areas performed by *Forbes* and NBC Universo. Criteria: percentage of 18-34 year-olds; Latino college grad rates; and diversity. *blog.chron.com, "The 15 Best Big Cities for Latino Millenials," January 26, 2016*

- *24/7 Wall St.* compared median annual earnings for men and women who worked full-time, year-round, female employment in management roles, bachelor's degree attainment among women, female life expectancy, uninsured rates, and preschool enrollment to identify the best cities for women. The U.S. metropolitan area, Boston was ranked #9 in pay disparity and other gender gaps. *24/7 Wall St., "The Easiest (and Toughest) Cities to Be a Woman," January 11, 2020*

- Personal finance website *WalletHub* compared more than 180 U.S. cities across two key dimensions, "Hispanic Business-Friendliness" and "Hispanic Purchasing Power," to arrive at the most favorable conditions for Hispanic entrepreneurs. Boston was ranked #161 out of 182. Criteria includes: share of Hispanic-Owned Businesses; Hispanic entrepreneurship rate to median annual income of Hispanics; Small Business-Friendliness score; cost of living; and number of Hispanics with at least a bachelor's degree. *WalletHub.com, "2019's Best Cities for Hispanic Entrepreneurs," May 1, 2019*

Miscellaneous Rankings

- In its roundup of St. Patrick's Day parades "Gayot" listed the best festivals and parades of all things Irish. The festivities in Boston as among the best. *www.gayot.com, "Best St. Patrick's Day Parades," March 2020*

- The watchdog site, Charity Navigator, conducted a study of charities in major markets both to analyze statistical differences in their financial, accountability, and transparency practices and to track year-to-year variations in individual philanthropic communities. The Boston metro area was ranked #23 among the 30 metro markets in the rating category of Overall Score. *www.charitynavigator.org, "2017 Metro Market Study," May 1, 2017*

- *WalletHub* compared the 150 most populated U.S. cities to determine their operating efficiency. A "Quality of City Services" score was constructed for each city and then divided by the total budget per capita to reveal which were managed the best. Boston ranked #65. Criteria: financial stability; economy; education; safety; health; infrastructure and pollution. *www.WalletHub.com, "2020's Best- & Worst-Run Cities in America," June 29, 2020*

- The National Alliance to End Homelessness listed the 25 most populous metro areas with the highest rate of homelessness. The Boston metro area had a high rate of homelessness. Criteria: number of homeless people per 10,000 population in 2016. *National Alliance to End Homelessness, "Homelessness in the 25 Most Populous U.S. Metro Areas," September 1, 2017*

Business Environment

DEMOGRAPHICS

Population Growth

Area	1990 Census	2000 Census	2010 Census	2019* Estimate	Population Growth (%) 1990-2019	Population Growth (%) 2010-2019
City	574,283	589,141	617,594	684,379	19.2	10.8
MSA[1]	4,133,895	4,391,344	4,552,402	4,832,346	16.9	6.1
U.S.	248,709,873	281,421,906	308,745,538	324,697,795	30.6	5.2

Note: (1) Figures cover the Boston-Cambridge-Newton, MA-NH Metropolitan Statistical Area; (*) 2015-2019 5-year estimated population
Source: U.S. Census Bureau, 1990 Census, Census 2000, Census 2010, 2015-2019 American Community Survey 5-Year Estimates

Household Size

Area	Persons in Household (%) One	Two	Three	Four	Five	Six	Seven or More	Average Household Size
City	36.2	32.5	15.5	9.4	3.9	1.6	0.9	2.40
MSA[1]	27.7	33.1	16.7	14.4	5.5	1.8	0.9	2.60
U.S.	27.9	33.9	15.6	12.9	6.0	2.3	1.4	2.60

Note: (1) Figures cover the Boston-Cambridge-Newton, MA-NH Metropolitan Statistical Area
Source: U.S. Census Bureau, 2015-2019 American Community Survey 5-Year Estimates

Race

Area	White Alone[2] (%)	Black Alone[2] (%)	Asian Alone[2] (%)	AIAN[3] Alone[2] (%)	NHOPI[4] Alone[2] (%)	Other Race Alone[2] (%)	Two or More Races (%)
City	52.8	25.2	9.7	0.3	0.1	6.7	5.3
MSA[1]	76.0	8.3	7.9	0.2	0.0	4.2	3.3
U.S.	72.5	12.7	5.5	0.8	0.2	4.9	3.3

Note: (1) Figures cover the Boston-Cambridge-Newton, MA-NH Metropolitan Statistical Area; (2) Alone is defined as not being in combination with one or more other races; (3) American Indian and Alaska Native; (4) Native Hawaiian and Other Pacific Islander
Source: U.S. Census Bureau, 2015-2019 American Community Survey 5-Year Estimates

Hispanic or Latino Origin

Area	Total (%)	Mexican (%)	Puerto Rican (%)	Cuban (%)	Other (%)
City	19.8	1.2	5.3	0.5	12.9
MSA[1]	11.1	0.7	2.9	0.2	7.3
U.S.	18.0	11.2	1.7	0.7	4.3

Note: Persons of Hispanic or Latino origin can be of any race; (1) Figures cover the Boston-Cambridge-Newton, MA-NH Metropolitan Statistical Area
Source: U.S. Census Bureau, 2015-2019 American Community Survey 5-Year Estimates

Ancestry

Area	German	Irish	English	American	Italian	Polish	French[2]	Scottish	Dutch
City	4.6	13.4	4.3	2.5	7.7	2.2	1.9	1.2	0.5
MSA[1]	5.9	20.8	9.4	3.5	13.1	3.4	4.5	2.3	0.6
U.S.	13.3	9.7	7.2	6.2	5.1	2.8	2.3	1.7	1.2

Note: Figures are the percentage of the total population reporting a particular ancestry. The nine most commonly reported ancestries in the U.S. are shown. Figures include multiple ancestries (e.g. if a person reported being Irish and Italian, they were included in both columns); (1) Figures cover the Boston-Cambridge-Newton, MA-NH Metropolitan Statistical Area; (2) Excludes Basque
Source: U.S. Census Bureau, 2015-2019 American Community Survey 5-Year Estimates

Foreign-born Population

Area	Any Foreign Country	Asia	Mexico	Europe	Caribbean	Central America[2]	South America	Africa	Canada
City	28.3	7.6	0.4	3.4	8.2	2.6	2.4	3.1	0.4
MSA[1]	18.9	6.1	0.2	3.3	3.4	1.6	2.1	1.6	0.5
U.S.	13.6	4.2	3.5	1.5	1.3	1.1	1.0	0.7	0.2

Note: (1) Figures cover the Boston-Cambridge-Newton, MA-NH Metropolitan Statistical Area; (2) Excludes Mexico.
Source: U.S. Census Bureau, 2015-2019 American Community Survey 5-Year Estimates

Marital Status

Area	Never Married	Now Married[2]	Separated	Widowed	Divorced
City	56.0	30.3	2.6	3.9	7.2
MSA[1]	37.1	47.5	1.5	5.1	8.7
U.S.	33.4	48.1	1.9	5.8	10.9

Note: Figures are percentages and cover the population 15 years of age and older; (1) Figures cover the Boston-Cambridge-Newton, MA-NH Metropolitan Statistical Area; (2) Excludes separated
Source: U.S. Census Bureau, 2015-2019 American Community Survey 5-Year Estimates

Disability by Age

Area	All Ages	Under 18 Years Old	18 to 64 Years Old	65 Years and Over
City	11.9	5.3	8.9	41.0
MSA[1]	10.6	4.0	7.8	31.3
U.S.	12.6	4.2	10.3	34.5

Note: Figures show percent of the civilian noninstitutionalized population that reported having a disability. Disability status is determined from six types of difficulty: vision, hearing, cognitive, ambulatory, self-care, and independent living. For children under 5 years old, hearing and vision difficulty are used to determine disability status. For children between the ages of 5 and 14, disability status is determined from hearing, vision, cognitive, ambulatory, and self-care difficulties. For people aged 15 years and older, they are considered to have a disability if they have difficulty with any one of the six difficulty types; Note: (1) Figures cover the Boston-Cambridge-Newton, MA-NH Metropolitan Statistical Area
Source: U.S. Census Bureau, 2015-2019 American Community Survey 5-Year Estimates

Age

Area	Percent of Population									Median Age
	Under Age 5	Age 5–19	Age 20–34	Age 35–44	Age 45–54	Age 55–64	Age 65–74	Age 75–84	Age 85+	
City	5.0	15.4	34.8	12.4	10.9	10.1	6.6	3.3	1.6	32.2
MSA[1]	5.3	17.7	22.2	12.5	13.7	13.2	8.8	4.4	2.1	38.7
U.S.	6.1	19.1	20.7	12.6	13.0	12.9	9.1	4.6	1.9	38.1

Note: (1) Figures cover the Boston-Cambridge-Newton, MA-NH Metropolitan Statistical Area
Source: U.S. Census Bureau, 2015-2019 American Community Survey 5-Year Estimates

Gender

Area	Males	Females	Males per 100 Females
City	328,503	355,876	92.3
MSA[1]	2,347,899	2,484,447	94.5
U.S.	159,886,919	164,810,876	97.0

Note: (1) Figures cover the Boston-Cambridge-Newton, MA-NH Metropolitan Statistical Area
Source: U.S. Census Bureau, 2015-2019 American Community Survey 5-Year Estimates

Religious Groups by Family

Area	Catholic	Baptist	Non-Den.	Methodist[2]	Lutheran	LDS[3]	Pente-costal	Presby-terian[4]	Muslim[5]	Judaism
MSA[1]	44.4	1.2	1.0	1.0	0.4	0.4	0.6	1.6	0.4	1.4
U.S.	19.1	9.3	4.0	4.0	2.3	2.0	1.9	1.6	0.8	0.7

Note: Figures are the number of adherents as a percentage of the total population; (1) Figures cover the Boston-Cambridge-Newton, MA-NH Metropolitan Statistical Area; (2) Methodist/Pietist; (3) Latter Day Saints; (4) Reformed; (5) Figures are estimates
Source: Association of Statisticians of American Religious Bodies, 2010 U.S. Religion Census: Religious Congregations & Membership Study

Religious Groups by Tradition

Area	Catholic	Evangelical Protestant	Mainline Protestant	Other Tradition	Black Protestant	Orthodox
MSA[1]	44.4	3.2	4.5	3.4	0.2	1.1
U.S.	19.1	16.2	7.3	4.3	1.6	0.3

Note: Figures are the number of adherents as a percentage of the total population; (1) Figures cover the Boston-Cambridge-Newton, MA-NH Metropolitan Statistical Area
Source: Association of Statisticians of American Religious Bodies, 2010 U.S. Religion Census: Religious Congregations & Membership Study

ECONOMY

Gross Metropolitan Product

Area	2017	2018	2019	2020	Rank[2]
MSA[1]	449.5	472.7	493.6	515.0	8

Note: Figures are in billions of dollars; (1) Figures cover the Boston-Cambridge-Newton, MA-NH Metropolitan Statistical Area; (2) Rank is based on 2018 data and ranges from 1 to 381
Source: U.S. Conference of Mayors, U.S. Metro Economies: GMP & Employment 2018-2020, September 2019

Economic Growth

Area	2015-17 (%)	2018 (%)	2019 (%)	2020 (%)	Rank[2]
MSA[1]	2.0	3.0	2.8	2.1	134
U.S.	1.9	2.9	2.3	2.1	—

Note: Figures are real gross metropolitan product (GMP) growth rates and represent average annual percent change; (1) Figures cover the Boston-Cambridge-Newton, MA-NH Metropolitan Statistical Area; (2) Rank is based on 2017 2-year average annual percent change and ranges from 1 to 381
Source: U.S. Conference of Mayors, U.S. Metro Economies: GMP & Employment 2018-2020, September 2019

Metropolitan Area Exports

Area	2014	2015	2016	2017	2018	2019	Rank[2]
MSA[1]	23,378.5	21,329.5	21,168.0	23,116.2	24,450.1	23,505.8	17

Note: Figures are in millions of dollars; (1) Figures cover the Boston-Cambridge-Newton, MA-NH Metropolitan Statistical Area; (2) Rank is based on 2019 data and ranges from 1 to 386
Source: U.S. Department of Commerce, International Trade Administration, Office of Trade and Economic Analysis, Industry and Analysis, Exports by Metropolitan Area, data extracted March 24, 2021

Building Permits

Area	Single-Family			Multi-Family			Total		
	2018	2019	Pct. Chg.	2018	2019	Pct. Chg.	2018	2019	Pct. Chg.
City	49	37	-24.5	3,553	2,956	-16.8	3,602	2,993	-16.9
MSA[1]	4,930	4,299	-12.8	9,253	10,789	16.6	14,183	15,088	6.4
U.S.	855,300	862,100	0.7	473,500	523,900	10.6	1,328,800	1,386,000	4.3

Note: (1) Figures cover the Boston-Cambridge-Newton, MA-NH Metropolitan Statistical Area; Figures represent new, privately-owned housing units authorized (unadjusted data); All permit data are based on estimates with imputation
Source: U.S. Census Bureau, Manufacturing, Mining, and Construction Statistics, Building Permits, 2018, 2019

Bankruptcy Filings

Area	Business Filings			Nonbusiness Filings		
	2019	2020	% Chg.	2019	2020	% Chg.
Suffolk County	47	37	-21.3	530	279	-47.4
U.S.	22,780	21,655	-4.9	752,160	522,808	-30.5

Note: Business filings include Chapter 7, Chapter 9, Chapter 11, Chapter 12, Chapter 13, Chapter 15, and Section 304; Nonbusiness filings include Chapter 7, Chapter 11, and Chapter 13
Source: Administrative Office of the U.S. Courts, Business and Nonbusiness Bankruptcy, County Cases Commenced by Chapter of the Bankruptcy Code, During the 12-Month Period Ending December 31, 2019 and Business and Nonbusiness Bankruptcy, County Cases Commenced by Chapter of the Bankruptcy Code, During the 12-Month Period Ending December 31, 2020

Housing Vacancy Rates

Area	Gross Vacancy Rate[2] (%)			Year-Round Vacancy Rate[3] (%)			Rental Vacancy Rate[4] (%)			Homeowner Vacancy Rate[5] (%)		
	2018	2019	2020	2018	2019	2020	2018	2019	2020	2018	2019	2020
MSA[1]	7.5	7.1	6.8	6.5	6.2	5.6	3.8	3.6	4.7	1.0	0.8	0.4
U.S.	12.3	12.0	10.6	9.7	9.5	8.2	6.9	6.7	6.3	1.5	1.4	1.0

Note: (1) Figures cover the Boston-Cambridge-Newton, MA-NH Metropolitan Statistical Area; (2) The percentage of the total housing inventory that is vacant; (3) The percentage of the housing inventory (excluding seasonal units) that is year-round vacant; (4) The percentage of rental inventory that is vacant for rent; (5) The percentage of homeowner inventory that is vacant for sale
Source: U.S. Census Bureau, Housing Vacancies and Homeownership Annual Statistics: 2018, 2019, 2020

INCOME

Income

Area	Per Capita ($)	Median Household ($)	Average Household ($)
City	44,690	71,115	107,608
MSA[1]	47,604	90,333	122,399
U.S.	34,103	62,843	88,607

Note: (1) Figures cover the Boston-Cambridge-Newton, MA-NH Metropolitan Statistical Area
Source: U.S. Census Bureau, 2015-2019 American Community Survey 5-Year Estimates

Household Income Distribution

Area	Percent of Households Earning							
	Under $15,000	$15,000 -$24,999	$25,000 -$34,999	$35,000 -$49,999	$50,000 -$74,999	$75,000 -$99,999	$100,000 -$149,999	$150,000 and up
City	16.1	8.1	6.3	8.4	13.0	10.3	15.7	22.2
MSA[1]	8.8	6.2	5.8	8.3	13.5	11.8	18.5	27.1
U.S.	10.3	8.9	8.9	12.3	17.2	12.7	15.1	14.5

Note: (1) Figures cover the Boston-Cambridge-Newton, MA-NH Metropolitan Statistical Area
Source: U.S. Census Bureau, 2015-2019 American Community Survey 5-Year Estimates

Poverty Rate

Area	All Ages	Under 18 Years Old	18 to 64 Years Old	65 Years and Over
City	18.9	27.7	16.5	20.9
MSA[1]	9.3	11.3	8.8	9.1
U.S.	13.4	18.5	12.6	9.3

Note: Figures are percentage of people whose income during the past 12 months was below the poverty level;
(1) Figures cover the Boston-Cambridge-Newton, MA-NH Metropolitan Statistical Area
Source: U.S. Census Bureau, 2015-2019 American Community Survey 5-Year Estimates

CITY FINANCES

City Government Finances

Component	2017 ($000)	2017 ($ per capita)
Total Revenues	4,698,449	7,043
Total Expenditures	4,389,645	6,580
Debt Outstanding	1,929,751	2,893
Cash and Securities[1]	8,112,442	12,160

Note: (1) Cash and security holdings of a government at the close of its fiscal year,
including those of its dependent agencies, utilities, and liquor stores.
Source: U.S. Census Bureau, State & Local Government Finances 2017

City Government Revenue by Source

Source	2017 ($000)	2017 ($ per capita)	2017 (%)
General Revenue			
From Federal Government	83,307	125	1.8
From State Government	860,576	1,290	18.3
From Local Governments	1,151	2	0.0
Taxes			
Property	2,116,268	3,172	45.0
Sales and Gross Receipts	138,488	208	2.9
Personal Income	0	0	0.0
Corporate Income	0	0	0.0
Motor Vehicle License	0	0	0.0
Other Taxes	110,286	165	2.3
Current Charges	283,225	425	6.0
Liquor Store	0	0	0.0
Utility	150,392	225	3.2
Employee Retirement	747,211	1,120	15.9

Source: U.S. Census Bureau, State & Local Government Finances 2017

City Government Expenditures by Function

Function	2017 ($000)	2017 ($ per capita)	2017 (%)
General Direct Expenditures			
Air Transportation	0	0	0.0
Corrections	0	0	0.0
Education	1,391,891	2,086	31.7
Employment Security Administration	0	0	0.0
Financial Administration	53,114	79	1.2
Fire Protection	219,945	329	5.0
General Public Buildings	38,248	57	0.9
Governmental Administration, Other	15,923	23	0.4
Health	17,716	26	0.4
Highways	117,824	176	2.7
Hospitals	266,459	399	6.1
Housing and Community Development	99,996	149	2.3
Interest on General Debt	69,206	103	1.6
Judicial and Legal	5,253	7	0.1
Libraries	48,084	72	1.1
Parking	2,265	3	0.1
Parks and Recreation	93,838	140	2.1
Police Protection	375,505	562	8.6
Public Welfare	3,312	5	0.1
Sewerage	65,073	97	1.5
Solid Waste Management	59,751	89	1.4
Veterans' Services	0	0	0.0
Liquor Store	0	0	0.0
Utility	79,930	119	1.8
Employee Retirement	580,861	870	13.2

Source: U.S. Census Bureau, State & Local Government Finances 2017

EMPLOYMENT

Labor Force and Employment

Area	Civilian Labor Force			Workers Employed		
	Dec. 2019	Dec. 2020	% Chg.	Dec. 2019	Dec. 2020	% Chg.
City	399,841	382,754	-4.3	391,993	354,899	-9.5
NECTAD[1]	1,694,809	1,609,639	-5.0	1,662,542	1,505,214	-9.5
U.S.	164,007,000	160,017,000	-2.4	158,504,000	149,613,000	-5.6

Note: Data is not seasonally adjusted and covers workers 16 years of age and older; (1) Figures cover the Boston-Cambridge-Newton, MA New England City and Town Area Division
Source: Bureau of Labor Statistics, Local Area Unemployment Statistics

Unemployment Rate

Area	2020											
	Jan.	Feb.	Mar.	Apr.	May	Jun.	Jul.	Aug.	Sep.	Oct.	Nov.	Dec.
City	2.7	2.6	2.4	14.6	16.6	19.3	18.2	12.9	11.1	7.7	6.6	7.3
NECTAD[1]	2.7	2.6	2.4	14.2	15.3	16.9	15.5	10.7	9.3	6.7	5.9	6.5
U.S.	4.0	3.8	4.5	14.4	13.0	11.2	10.5	8.5	7.7	6.6	6.4	6.5

Note: Data is not seasonally adjusted and covers workers 16 years of age and older; (1) Figures cover the Boston-Cambridge-Newton, MA New England City and Town Area Division
Source: Bureau of Labor Statistics, Local Area Unemployment Statistics

Average Wages

Occupation	$/Hr.	Occupation	$/Hr.
Accountants and Auditors	43.60	Maintenance and Repair Workers	25.60
Automotive Mechanics	24.10	Marketing Managers	74.50
Bookkeepers	25.10	Network and Computer Systems Admin.	48.80
Carpenters	31.30	Nurses, Licensed Practical	29.40
Cashiers	14.20	Nurses, Registered	47.80
Computer Programmers	49.30	Nursing Assistants	18.30
Computer Systems Analysts	50.80	Office Clerks, General	21.20
Computer User Support Specialists	33.20	Physical Therapists	41.60
Construction Laborers	28.40	Physicians	86.50
Cooks, Restaurant	17.00	Plumbers, Pipefitters and Steamfitters	40.50
Customer Service Representatives	22.70	Police and Sheriff's Patrol Officers	37.80
Dentists	100.80	Postal Service Mail Carriers	26.40
Electricians	34.10	Real Estate Sales Agents	43.80
Engineers, Electrical	55.70	Retail Salespersons	16.10
Fast Food and Counter Workers	14.10	Sales Representatives, Technical/Scientific	51.60
Financial Managers	79.10	Secretaries, Exc. Legal/Medical/Executive	24.00
First-Line Supervisors of Office Workers	34.30	Security Guards	18.40
General and Operations Managers	73.20	Surgeons	130.20
Hairdressers/Cosmetologists	21.90	Teacher Assistants, Exc. Postsecondary*	18.20
Home Health and Personal Care Aides	16.30	Teachers, Secondary School, Exc. Sp. Ed.*	39.90
Janitors and Cleaners	18.90	Telemarketers	18.30
Landscaping/Groundskeeping Workers	20.10	Truck Drivers, Heavy/Tractor-Trailer	25.00
Lawyers	84.40	Truck Drivers, Light/Delivery Services	22.30
Maids and Housekeeping Cleaners	16.40	Waiters and Waitresses	16.00

Note: Wage data covers the Boston-Cambridge-Nashua, MA-NH New England City and Town Area; (*) Hourly wages were calculated from annual wage data based on a 40 hour work week; n/a not available.
Source: Bureau of Labor Statistics, Metro Area Occupational Employment & Wage Estimates, May 2020

Employment by Industry

Sector	NECTAD[1]		U.S.
	Number of Employees	Percent of Total	Percent of Total
Construction, Mining, and Logging	72,500	4.2	5.5
Education and Health Services	396,000	22.9	16.3
Financial Activities	150,000	8.7	6.1
Government	191,000	11.0	15.2
Information	59,100	3.4	1.9
Leisure and Hospitality	110,700	6.4	9.0
Manufacturing	72,700	4.2	8.5
Other Services	55,300	3.2	3.8
Professional and Business Services	386,300	22.3	14.4
Retail Trade	139,400	8.0	10.9
Transportation, Warehousing, and Utilities	43,200	2.5	4.6
Wholesale Trade	55,700	3.2	3.9

Note: Figures are non-farm employment as of December 2020. Figures are not seasonally adjusted and include workers 16 years of age and older; (1) Figures cover the Boston-Cambridge-Newton, MA New England City and Town Area Division
Source: Bureau of Labor Statistics, Current Employment Statistics, Employment, Hours, and Earnings

Employment by Occupation

Occupation Classification	City (%)	MSA[1] (%)	U.S. (%)
Management, Business, Science, and Arts	50.6	49.7	38.5
Natural Resources, Construction, and Maintenance	3.9	6.1	8.9
Production, Transportation, and Material Moving	6.7	8.4	13.2
Sales and Office	19.1	19.5	21.6
Service	19.8	16.3	17.8

Note: Figures cover employed civilians 16 years of age and older; (1) Figures cover the Boston-Cambridge-Newton, MA-NH Metropolitan Statistical Area
Source: U.S. Census Bureau, 2015-2019 American Community Survey 5-Year Estimates

Occupations with Greatest Projected Employment Growth: 2020 – 2022

Occupation[1]	2020 Employment	2022 Projected Employment	Numeric Employment Change	Percent Employment Change
Fast Food and Counter Workers	56,360	87,340	30,980	55.0
Waiters and Waitresses	41,030	66,470	25,440	62.0
Home Health and Personal Care Aides	93,700	109,980	16,280	17.4
Retail Salespersons	72,560	86,490	13,930	19.2
Cooks, Restaurant	18,250	30,960	12,710	69.6
Passenger Vehicle Drivers, Except Bus Drivers, Transit and Intercity	13,820	23,120	9,300	67.3
Cashiers	66,900	76,110	9,210	13.8
Bartenders	13,350	21,270	7,920	59.3
Janitors and Cleaners, Except Maids and Housekeeping Cleaners	47,460	54,650	7,190	15.1
General and Operations Managers	74,410	81,550	7,140	9.6

Note: Projections cover Massachusetts; (1) Sorted by numeric employment change
Source: www.projectionscentral.com, State Occupational Projections, 2020–2022 Short-Term Projections

Fastest-Growing Occupations: 2020 – 2022

Occupation[1]	2020 Employment	2022 Projected Employment	Numeric Employment Change	Percent Employment Change
Athletes and Sports Competitors	210	470	260	123.8
Amusement and Recreation Attendants	2,900	5,740	2,840	97.9
Hotel, Motel, and Resort Desk Clerks	1,960	3,710	1,750	89.3
Ushers, Lobby Attendants, and Ticket Takers	1,210	2,240	1,030	85.1
Riggers	290	520	230	79.3
Actors	290	510	220	75.9
Fitness Trainers and Aerobics Instructors	8,800	15,260	6,460	73.4
Cooks, Restaurant	18,250	30,960	12,710	69.6
Passenger Vehicle Drivers, Except Bus Drivers, Transit and Intercity	13,820	23,120	9,300	67.3
Dancers	290	480	190	65.5

Note: Projections cover Massachusetts; (1) Sorted by percent employment change and excludes occupations with numeric employment change less than 50
Source: www.projectionscentral.com, State Occupational Projections, 2020–2022 Short-Term Projections

TAXES

State Corporate Income Tax Rates

State	Tax Rate (%)	Income Brackets ($)	Num. of Brackets	Financial Institution Tax Rate (%)[a]	Federal Income Tax Ded.
Massachusetts	8.0 (m)	Flat rate	1	9.0 (m)	No

Note: Tax rates as of January 1, 2021; (a) Rates listed are the corporate income tax rate applied to financial institutions or excise taxes based on income. Some states have other taxes based upon the value of deposits or shares; (m) Business and manufacturing corporations pay an additional tax of $2.60 per $1,000 on either taxable Massachusetts tangible property or taxable net worth allocable to the state (for intangible property corporations). The minimum tax for both corporations and financial institutions is $456.
Source: Federation of Tax Administrators, State Corporate Income Tax Rates, January 1, 2021

State Individual Income Tax Rates

State	Tax Rate (%)	Income Brackets ($)	Personal Exemptions ($)			Standard Ded. ($)	
			Single	Married	Depend.	Single	Married
Massachusetts	5.0	Flat rate	4,400	8,800	1,000	–	–

Note: Tax rates as of January 1, 2021; Local- and county-level taxes are not included; Federal income tax is not deductible on state income tax returns
Source: Federation of Tax Administrators, State Individual Income Tax Rates, January 1, 2021

Various State Sales and Excise Tax Rates

State	State Sales Tax (%)	Gasoline[1] (¢/gal.)	Cigarette[2] ($/pack)	Spirits[3] ($/gal.)	Wine[4] ($/gal.)	Beer[5] ($/gal.)	Recreational Marijuana (%)
Massachusetts	6.25	26.54	3.51	4.05	0.55	0.11	(g)

Note: All tax rates as of January 1, 2021; (1) The American Petroleum Institute has developed a methodology for determining the average tax rate on a gallon of fuel. Rates may include any of the following: excise taxes, environmental fees, storage tank fees, other fees or taxes, general sales tax, and local taxes; (2) The federal excise tax of $1.0066 per pack and local taxes are not included; (3) Rates are those applicable to off-premise sales of 40% alcohol by volume (a.b.v.) distilled spirits in 750ml containers. Local excise taxes are excluded; (4) Rates are those applicable to off-premise sales of 11% a.b.v. non-carbonated wine in 750ml containers; (5) Rates are those applicable to off-premise sales of 4.7% a.b.v. beer in 12 ounce containers; (g) 10.75% excise tax (retail price)
Source: Tax Foundation, 2021 Facts & Figures: How Does Your State Compare?

State Business Tax Climate Index Rankings

State	Overall Rank	Corporate Tax Rank	Individual Income Tax Rank	Sales Tax Rank	Property Tax Rank	Unemployment Insurance Tax Rank
Massachusetts	34	38	11	12	44	50

Note: The index is a measure of how each state's tax laws affect economic performance. The lower the rank, the more favorable a state's tax system is for business. States without a given tax are given a ranking of 1. The scores/rankings for the District of Columbia do not affect other states. The 2021 index represents the tax climate as of July 1, 2020.
Source: Tax Foundation, State Business Tax Climate Index 2021

TRANSPORTATION

Means of Transportation to Work

Area	Car/Truck/Van — Drove Alone	Car/Truck/Van — Car-pooled	Public Transportation — Bus	Public Transportation — Subway	Public Transportation — Railroad	Bicycle	Walked	Other Means	Worked at Home
City	38.3	5.9	13.5	17.8	1.1	2.3	15.1	2.6	3.4
MSA[1]	66.4	7.2	4.1	6.7	2.2	1.1	5.4	1.7	5.3
U.S.	76.3	9.0	2.4	1.9	0.6	0.5	2.7	1.4	5.2

Note: Figures are percentages and cover workers 16 years of age and older; (1) Figures cover the Boston-Cambridge-Newton, MA-NH Metropolitan Statistical Area
Source: U.S. Census Bureau, 2015-2019 American Community Survey 5-Year Estimates

Travel Time to Work

Area	Less Than 10 Minutes	10 to 19 Minutes	20 to 29 Minutes	30 to 44 Minutes	45 to 59 Minutes	60 to 89 Minutes	90 Minutes or More
City	7.1	19.1	19.6	30.3	12.1	9.6	2.2
MSA[1]	9.0	22.0	17.9	24.4	12.1	11.0	3.7
U.S.	12.2	28.4	20.8	20.8	8.3	6.4	2.9

Note: Note: Figures are percentages and include workers 16 years old and over; (1) Figures cover the Boston-Cambridge-Newton, MA-NH Metropolitan Statistical Area
Source: U.S. Census Bureau, 2015-2019 American Community Survey 5-Year Estimates

Key Congestion Measures

Measure	1982	1992	2002	2012	2017
Annual Hours of Delay, Total (000)	52,591	84,574	133,838	164,282	189,426
Annual Hours of Delay, Per Auto Commuter	31	44	63	69	80
Annual Congestion Cost, Total (million $)	396	894	1,810	2,951	3,497
Annual Congestion Cost, Per Auto Commuter ($)	983	1,087	1,342	1,291	1,443

Note: Covers the Boston MA-NH-RI urban area
Source: Texas A&M Transportation Institute, 2019 Urban Mobility Report

Freeway Travel Time Index

Measure	1982	1987	1992	1997	2002	2007	2012	2017
Urban Area Index[1]	1.14	1.18	1.20	1.25	1.29	1.29	1.29	1.30
Urban Area Rank[1,2]	12	11	15	9	10	15	17	19

Note: Freeway Travel Time Index—the ratio of travel time in the peak period to the travel time at free-flow conditions. For example, a value of 1.30 indicates a 20-minute free-flow trip takes 26 minutes in the peak (20 minutes x 1.30 = 26 minutes); (1) Covers the Boston MA-NH-RI urban area; (2) Rank is based on 101 larger urban areas (#1 = highest travel time index)
Source: Texas A&M Transportation Institute, 2019 Urban Mobility Report

Public Transportation

Agency Name / Mode of Transportation	Vehicles Operated in Maximum Service[1]	Annual Unlinked Passenger Trips[2] (in thous.)	Annual Passenger Miles[3] (in thous.)
Massachusetts Bay Transportation Authority (MBTA)			
Bus (directly operated)	779	99,301.3	255,494.5
Bus (purchased transportation)	70	951.7	2,162.1
Bus Rapid Transit (directly operated)	42	11,490.8	23,235.1
Commuter Rail (purchased transportation)	436	31,177.7	653,571.0
Demand Response (purchased transportation)	617	1,862.3	14,589.9
Ferryboat (purchased transportation)	9	1,584.4	13,942.3
Heavy Rail (directly operated)	338	160,351.8	572,046.3
Light Rail (directly operated)	151	56,975.6	137,719.1
Trolleybus (directly operated)	22	3,021.2	7,133.6

Note: (1) Number of revenue vehicles operated by the given mode and type of service to meet the annual maximum service requirement. This is the revenue vehicle count during the peak season of the year; on the week and day that maximum service is provided. Vehicles operated in maximum service (VOMS) exclude atypical days and one-time special events; (2) Number of passengers who boarded public transportation vehicles. Passengers are counted each time they board a vehicle no matter how many vehicles they use to travel from their origin to their destination. (3) Sum of the distances ridden by all passengers during the entire fiscal year.
Source: Federal Transit Administration, National Transit Database, 2019

Air Transportation

Airport Name and Code / Type of Service	Passenger Airlines[1]	Passenger Enplanements	Freight Carriers[2]	Freight (lbs)
Logan International (BOS)				
Domestic service (U.S. carriers - 2020)	26	5,258,977	15	198,746,451
International service (U.S. carriers - 2019)	11	891,908	3	13,103,096

Note: (1) Includes all U.S.-based major, minor and commuter airlines that carried at least one passenger during the year; (2) Includes all U.S.-based airlines and freight carriers that transported at least one pound of freight during the year.
Source: Bureau of Transportation Statistics, The Intermodal Transportation Database, Air Carriers: T-100 Domestic Market (U.S. Carriers), 2020; Bureau of Transportation Statistics, The Intermodal Transportation Database, Air Carriers: T-100 International Market (U.S. Carriers), 2019

BUSINESSES

Major Business Headquarters

Company Name	Industry	Rankings	
		Fortune[1]	Forbes[2]
American Tower	Telecommunications	414	-
Bain & Company	Business Services & Supplies	-	102
Boston Consulting Group	Business Services & Supplies	-	47
Fidelity Investments	Diversified Financials	-	15
Liberty Mutual Insurance Group	Insurance, Property and Casualty (Stock)	77	-
New Balance	Retailing	-	113
State Street	Superregional Banks	244	-
Suffolk	Construction	-	127
Wayfair	Internet Services and Retailing	348	-

Note: (1) Companies that produce a 10-K are ranked 1 to 500 based on 2019 revenue; (2) All private companies with at least $2 billion in annual revenue through the end of their most current fiscal year are ranked 1 to 219; companies listed are headquartered in the city; dashes indicate no ranking
Source: Fortune, "Fortune 500," June/July 2020; Forbes, "America's Largest Private Companies," 2020

Fastest-Growing Businesses

According to *Inc.*, Boston is home to four of America's 500 fastest-growing private companies: **Embark Veterinary** (#173); **Caldwell Intellectual Property Law** (#215); **Stynt** (#357); **Privy** (#451). Criteria: must be an independent, privately-held, for-profit, U.S. corporation, proprietorship or partnership as of December 31, 2019; revenues must be at least $100,000 in 2016 and $2 million in 2019; must have four-year operating/sales history. *Inc., "America's 500 Fastest-Growing Private Companies," 2020*

According to *Fortune*, Boston is home to one of the 100 fastest-growing companies in the world: **Vertex Pharmaceuticals** (#6). Companies were ranked by their revenue growth rate; their EPS growth rate; and their three-year annualized total return to investors for the period ending June 30, 2020. Criteria for inclusion: a company, foreign or domestic, must trade on a major U.S. stock exchange; must file quarterly reports with the SEC; must have a minimum market capitalization of $250 million; must have a stock price of at least $5 on June 30, 2020; must have been trading continuously since June 30, 2017; must have revenue and net income for the four quarters ended on or before April 30, 2020, of at least $50 million and $10 million, respectively; and must have posted a compound annual growth in revenue and earnings per share of at least 15% annually over the three years ending on or before April 30, 2020. Real estate investment trusts, limited-liability companies, limited parterships, business development companies, closed-end investment firms, companies about to be acquired, and companies that lost money in the quarter ending April 30, 2020 were excluded. *Fortune, "100 Fastest-Growing Companies," 2020*

According to *Initiative for a Competitive Inner City (ICIC)*, Boston is home to three of America's 100 fastest-growing "inner city" companies: **Onyx Spectrum Technology** (#18); **The Urban Grape** (#23); **Guardian Healthcare** (#60). Criteria for inclusion: company must be headquartered in or have 51 percent or more of its physical operations in an economically distressed urban area; must be an independent, for-profit corporation, partnership or proprietorship; must have 10 or more employees and have a five-year sales history that includes sales of at least $200,000 in the base year and at least $1 million in the current year with no decrease in sales over the two most recent years. Companies were ranked overall by revenue growth over the five-year period between 2015 and 2019. *Initiative for a Competitive Inner City (ICIC), "Inner City 100 Companies," 2020*

According to Deloitte, Boston is home to 10 of North America's 500 fastest-growing high-technology companies: **Transmit Security** (#5); **Drift** (#6); **Wellframe** (#120); **Motus** (#255); **Forward Financing** (#317); **LogMeIn** (#359); **LogicManager** (#375); **Onapsis** (#379); **Nasuni** (#421); **meQuilibrium** (#424). Companies are ranked by percentage growth in revenue over a four-year period. Criteria for inclusion: company must be headquartered within North America; must own proprietary intellectual property or technology that is sold to customers in products that contributes to a significant portion of the company's operating revenue; must have been in business for a minumum of four years with 2016 operating revenues of at least $50,000 USD/CD and 2019 operating revenues of at least $5 million USD/CD. *Deloitte, 2020 Technology Fast 500*™

Minority Business Opportunity

Boston is home to one company which is on the *Black Enterprise* Bank list (15 largest banks based on total assets, capital, deposits and loans, including mortgage-backed securities for the calendar year): **OneUnited Bank** (#1). Only commercial banks or savings and loans that are classified by the Federal Reserve as black institutions and have been fully operational for the previous calendar year were considered. *Black Enterprise, B.E. 100s, 2019*

Living Environment

COST OF LIVING

Cost of Living Index

Composite Index	Groceries	Housing	Utilities	Trans-portation	Health Care	Misc. Goods/ Services
150.2	113.2	225.4	122.1	108.6	120.8	127.4

Note: The Cost of Living Index measures regional differences in the cost of consumer goods and services, excluding taxes and non-consumer expenditures, for professional and managerial households in the top income quintile. It is based on more than 50,000 prices covering almost 60 different items for which prices are collected three times a year by chambers of commerce, economic development organizations or university applied economic centers in each participating urban area. The numbers shown should be read as a percentage above or below the national average of 100. For example, a value of 115.4 in the groceries column indicates that grocery prices are 15.4% higher than the national average. Small differences in the index numbers should not be interpreted as significant; Figures cover the Boston MA urban area.
Source: The Council for Community and Economic Research, Cost of Living Index, 2020

Grocery Prices

Area[1]	T-Bone Steak ($/pound)	Frying Chicken ($/pound)	Whole Milk ($/half gal.)	Eggs ($/dozen)	Orange Juice ($/64 oz.)	Coffee ($/11.5 oz.)
City[2]	13.53	1.64	2.27	2.00	3.73	4.41
Avg.	11.78	1.39	2.05	1.47	3.57	4.34
Min.	8.03	0.94	1.03	0.74	2.94	3.02
Max.	15.86	2.65	4.31	3.77	5.44	8.69

Note: (1) Values for the local area are compared with the average, minimum and maximum values for all 284 areas in the Cost of Living Index; (2) Figures cover the Boston MA urban area; **T-Bone Steak** (price per pound); **Frying Chicken** (price per pound, whole fryer); **Whole Milk** (half gallon carton); **Eggs** (price per dozen, Grade A, large); **Orange Juice** (64 oz. Tropicana or Florida Natural); **Coffee** (11.5 oz. can, vacuum-packed, Maxwell House, Hills Bros, or Folgers).
Source: The Council for Community and Economic Research, Cost of Living Index, 2020

Housing and Utility Costs

Area[1]	New Home Price ($)	Apartment Rent ($/month)	All Electric ($/month)	Part Electric ($/month)	Other Energy ($/month)	Telephone ($/month)
City[2]	744,522	3,157	-	72.47	161.39	181.10
Avg.	368,594	1,168	170.86	100.47	65.28	184.30
Min.	190,567	502	91.58	31.42	26.08	169.60
Max.	2,227,806	4,738	470.38	280.31	280.06	206.50

Note: (1) Values for the local area are compared with the average, minimum and maximum values for all 284 areas in the Cost of Living Index; (2) Figures cover the Boston MA urban area; **New Home Price** (2,400 sf living area, 8,000 sf lot, in urban area with full utilities); **Apartment Rent** (950 sf 2 bedroom/1.5 or 2 bath, unfurnished, excluding all utilities except water); **All Electric** (average monthly cost for an all-electric home); **Part Electric** (average monthly cost for a part-electric home); **Other Energy** (average monthly cost for natural gas, fuel oil, coal, wood, and any other forms of energy except electricity); **Telephone** (price includes the base monthly rate plus taxes and fees for three lines of mobile phone service).
Source: The Council for Community and Economic Research, Cost of Living Index, 2020

Health Care, Transportation, and Other Costs

Area[1]	Doctor ($/visit)	Dentist ($/visit)	Optometrist ($/visit)	Gasoline ($/gallon)	Beauty Salon ($/visit)	Men's Shirt ($)
City[2]	194.00	108.27	102.75	2.19	64.17	44.46
Avg.	115.44	99.32	108.10	2.21	39.27	31.37
Min.	36.68	59.00	51.36	1.71	19.00	11.00
Max.	219.00	153.10	250.97	3.46	82.05	58.33

Note: (1) Values for the local area are compared with the average, minimum and maximum values for all 284 areas in the Cost of Living Index; (2) Figures cover the Boston MA urban area; **Doctor** (general practitioners routine exam of an established patient); **Dentist** (adult teeth cleaning and periodic oral examination); **Optometrist** (full vision eye exam for established adult patient); **Gasoline** (one gallon regular unleaded, national brand, including all taxes, cash price at self-service pump if available); **Beauty Salon** (woman's shampoo, trim, and blow-dry); **Men's Shirt** (cotton/polyester dress shirt, pinpoint weave, long sleeves).
Source: The Council for Community and Economic Research, Cost of Living Index, 2020

HOUSING

Homeownership Rate

Area	2012 (%)	2013 (%)	2014 (%)	2015 (%)	2016 (%)	2017 (%)	2018 (%)	2019 (%)	2020 (%)
MSA[1]	66.0	66.3	62.8	59.3	58.9	58.8	61.0	60.9	61.2
U.S.	65.4	65.1	64.5	63.7	63.4	63.9	64.4	64.6	66.6

Note: (1) Figures cover the Boston-Cambridge-Newton, MA-NH Metropolitan Statistical Area
Source: U.S. Census Bureau, Housing Vacancies and Homeownership Annual Statistics: 2012-2020

House Price Index (HPI)

Area	National Ranking[2]	Quarterly Change (%)	One-Year Change (%)	Five-Year Change (%)	Since 1991Q1 (%)
MD[1]	167	1.93	5.51	29.37	228.40
U.S.[3]	–	3.81	10.77	38.99	205.12

Note: The HPI is a weighted repeat sales index. It measures average price changes in repeat sales or refinancings on the same properties. This information is obtained by reviewing repeat mortgage transactions on single-family properties whose mortgages have been purchased or securitized by Fannie Mae or Freddie Mac since January 1975; (1) Figures cover the Boston, MA Metropolitan Division; (2) Rankings are based on annual percentage change for all metro areas containing at least 15,000 transactions over the last 10 years and ranges from 1 to 253; (3) figures based on a weighted average of Census Division estimates using a seasonally adjusted, purchase-only index; all figures are for the period ending December 31, 2020
Source: Federal Housing Finance Agency, Change in Metropolitan Area House Price Indexes, April 7, 2021

Median Single-Family Home Prices

Area	2018	2019	2020p	Percent Change 2019 to 2020
MSA[1]	477.4	491.9	563.7	14.6
U.S. Average	261.6	274.6	299.9	9.2

Note: Figures are median sales prices of existing single-family homes in thousands of dollars; (p) preliminary; (1) Figures cover the Boston-Cambridge-Newton, MA-NH Metropolitan Statistical Area
Source: National Association of Realtors, Median Sales Price of Existing Single-Family Homes for Metropolitan Areas, 4th Quarter 2020

Qualifying Income Based on Median Sales Price of Existing Single-Family Homes

Area	With 5% Down ($)	With 10% Down ($)	With 20% Down ($)
MSA[1]	109,532	103,767	92,238
U.S. Average	59,266	56,147	49,908

Note: Figures are preliminary; Qualifying income is based on a mortgage rate of 2.81%. Monthly principal and interest payment is limited to 25% of income; (1) Figures cover the Boston-Cambridge-Newton, MA-NH Metropolitan Statistical Area
Source: National Association of Realtors, Qualifying Income Based on Median Sales Price of Existing Single-Family Homes for Metropolitan Areas, 4th Quarter 2020

Home Value Distribution

Area	Under $50,000	$50,000 -$99,999	$100,000 -$149,999	$150,000 -$199,999	$200,000 -$299,999	$300,000 -$499,999	$500,000 -$999,999	$1,000,000 or more
City	1.6	0.3	0.4	1.4	8.2	34.1	40.4	13.5
MSA[1]	1.6	1.0	1.6	3.6	14.5	38.5	31.8	7.4
U.S.	6.9	12.0	13.3	14.0	19.6	19.3	11.4	3.4

Note: Figures are percentages and cover owner-occupied housing units; (1) Figures cover the Boston-Cambridge-Newton, MA-NH Metropolitan Statistical Area
Source: U.S. Census Bureau, 2015-2019 American Community Survey 5-Year Estimates

Year Housing Structure Built

Area	2010 or Later	2000 -2009	1990 -1999	1980 -1989	1970 -1979	1960 -1969	1950 -1959	1940 -1949	Before 1940	Median Year
City	5.0	6.5	4.2	5.9	7.9	7.8	7.3	5.8	49.6	1941
MSA[1]	4.0	7.6	7.4	10.4	11.2	10.2	10.8	5.3	33.2	1961
U.S.	5.2	14.0	13.9	13.4	15.2	10.6	10.3	4.9	12.6	1978

Note: Figures are percentages except for Median Year; Note: (1) Figures cover the Boston-Cambridge-Newton, MA-NH Metropolitan Statistical Area
Source: U.S. Census Bureau, 2015-2019 American Community Survey 5-Year Estimates

Gross Monthly Rent

Area	Under $500	$500 -$999	$1,000 -$1,499	$1,500 -$1,999	$2,000 -$2,499	$2,500 -$2,999	$3,000 and up	Median ($)
City	16.5	11.4	16.6	22.7	15.3	8.2	9.3	1,620
MSA[1]	12.4	13.4	25.6	23.5	13.2	6.1	5.8	1,475
U.S.	9.4	36.2	30.0	14.0	5.6	2.4	2.4	1,062

Note: Figures are percentages except for Median; Gross rent is the contract rent plus the estimated average monthly cost of utilities (electricity, gas, and water and sewer) and fuels (oil, coal, kerosene, wood, etc.) if these are paid by the renter (or paid for the renter by someone else); (1) Figures cover the Boston-Cambridge-Newton, MA-NH Metropolitan Statistical Area
Source: U.S. Census Bureau, 2015-2019 American Community Survey 5-Year Estimates

HEALTH

Health Risk Factors

Category	MD[1] (%)	U.S. (%)
Adults aged 18–64 who have any kind of health care coverage	92.0	87.3
Adults who reported being in good or better health	85.1	82.4
Adults who have been told they have high blood cholesterol	31.3	33.0
Adults who have been told they have high blood pressure	26.2	32.3
Adults who are current smokers	15.5	17.1
Adults who currently use E-cigarettes	3.8	4.6
Adults who currently use chewing tobacco, snuff, or snus	3.3	4.0
Adults who are heavy drinkers[2]	7.5	6.3
Adults who are binge drinkers[3]	19.2	17.4
Adults who are overweight (BMI 25.0 - 29.9)	35.2	35.3
Adults who are obese (BMI 30.0 - 99.8)	25.6	31.3
Adults who participated in any physical activities in the past month	75.1	74.4
Adults who always or nearly always wears a seat belt	88.4	94.3

Note: (1) Figures cover the Boston, MA Metropolitan Division; (2) Heavy drinkers are classified as adult men having more than 14 drinks per week and adult women having more than 7 drinks per week; (3) Binge drinkers are classified as males having five or more drinks on one occasion or females having four or more drinks on one occasion
Source: Centers for Disease Control and Prevention, Behaviorial Risk Factor Surveillance System, SMART: Selected Metropolitan Area Risk Trends, 2017

Acute and Chronic Health Conditions

Category	MD[1] (%)	U.S. (%)
Adults who have ever been told they had a heart attack	3.1	4.2
Adults who have ever been told they have angina or coronary heart disease	3.0	3.9
Adults who have ever been told they had a stroke	3.6	3.0
Adults who have ever been told they have asthma	17.1	14.2
Adults who have ever been told they have arthritis	22.4	24.9
Adults who have ever been told they have diabetes[2]	8.7	10.5
Adults who have ever been told they had skin cancer	6.6	6.2
Adults who have ever been told they had any other types of cancer	7.4	7.1
Adults who have ever been told they have COPD	4.8	6.5
Adults who have ever been told they have kidney disease	3.8	3.0
Adults who have ever been told they have a form of depression	15.7	20.5

Note: (1) Figures cover the Boston, MA Metropolitan Division; (2) Figures do not include pregnancy-related, borderline, or pre-diabetes
Source: Centers for Disease Control and Prevention, Behaviorial Risk Factor Surveillance System, SMART: Selected Metropolitan Area Risk Trends, 2017

Health Screening and Vaccination Rates

Category	MD[1] (%)	U.S. (%)
Adults aged 65+ who have had flu shot within the past year	51.6	60.7
Adults aged 65+ who have ever had a pneumonia vaccination	74.7	75.4
Adults who have ever been tested for HIV	41.7	36.1
Adults who have ever had the shingles or zoster vaccine?	32.6	28.9
Adults who have had their blood cholesterol checked within the last five years	88.3	85.9

Note: n/a not available; (1) Figures cover the Boston, MA Metropolitan Division.
Source: Centers for Disease Control and Prevention, Behaviorial Risk Factor Surveillance System, SMART: Selected Metropolitan Area Risk Trends, 2017

Disability Status

Category	MD[1] (%)	U.S. (%)
Adults who reported being deaf	4.1	6.7
Are you blind or have serious difficulty seeing, even when wearing glasses?	2.8	4.5
Are you limited in any way in any of your usual activities due of arthritis?	10.6	12.9
Do you have difficulty doing errands alone?	5.8	6.8
Do you have difficulty dressing or bathing?	3.9	3.6
Do you have serious difficulty concentrating/remembering/making decisions?	9.2	10.7
Do you have serious difficulty walking or climbing stairs?	12.0	13.6

Note: (1) Figures cover the Boston, MA Metropolitan Division.
Source: Centers for Disease Control and Prevention, Behaviorial Risk Factor Surveillance System, SMART: Selected Metropolitan Area Risk Trends, 2017

Mortality Rates for the Top 10 Causes of Death in the U.S.

ICD-10[a] Sub-Chapter	ICD-10[a] Code	Age-Adjusted Mortality Rate[1] per 100,000 population	
		County[2]	U.S.
Malignant neoplasms	C00-C97	135.6	149.2
Ischaemic heart diseases	I20-I25	55.8	90.5
Other forms of heart disease	I30-I51	44.6	52.2
Chronic lower respiratory diseases	J40-J47	24.4	39.6
Other degenerative diseases of the nervous system	G30-G31	18.8	37.6
Cerebrovascular diseases	I60-I69	25.2	37.2
Other external causes of accidental injury	W00-X59	42.0	36.1
Organic, including symptomatic, mental disorders	F01-F09	47.7	29.4
Hypertensive diseases	I10-I15	19.3	24.1
Diabetes mellitus	E10-E14	20.3	21.5

Note: (a) ICD-10 = International Classification of Diseases 10th Revision; (1) Mortality rates are a three-year average covering 2017-2019; (2) Figures cover Suffolk County.
Source: Centers for Disease Control and Prevention, National Center for Health Statistics. Underlying Cause of Death 1999-2019 on CDC WONDER Online Database

Mortality Rates for Selected Causes of Death

ICD-10[a] Sub-Chapter	ICD-10[a] Code	Age-Adjusted Mortality Rate[1] per 100,000 population	
		County[2]	U.S.
Assault	X85-Y09	5.4	6.0
Diseases of the liver	K70-K76	11.5	14.4
Human immunodeficiency virus (HIV) disease	B20-B24	1.7	1.5
Influenza and pneumonia	J09-J18	12.1	13.8
Intentional self-harm	X60-X84	5.9	14.1
Malnutrition	E40-E46	Unreliable	2.3
Obesity and other hyperalimentation	E65-E68	1.8	2.1
Renal failure	N17-N19	15.0	12.6
Transport accidents	V01-V99	3.8	12.3
Viral hepatitis	B15-B19	1.2	1.2

Note: (a) ICD-10 = International Classification of Diseases 10th Revision; (1) Mortality rates are a three-year average covering 2017-2019; (2) Figures cover Suffolk County; Data are suppressed when the data meet the criteria for confidentiality constraints; Mortality rates are flagged as unreliable when the rate would be calculated with a numerator of 20 or less.
Source: Centers for Disease Control and Prevention, National Center for Health Statistics. Underlying Cause of Death 1999-2019 on CDC WONDER Online Database

Health Insurance Coverage

Area	With Health Insurance	With Private Health Insurance	With Public Health Insurance	Without Health Insurance	Population Under Age 19 Without Health Insurance
City	96.5	67.2	36.7	3.5	1.3
MSA[1]	97.1	76.7	32.7	2.9	1.3
U.S.	91.2	67.9	35.1	8.8	5.1

Note: Figures are percentages that cover the civilian noninstitutionalized population; (1) Figures cover the Boston-Cambridge-Newton, MA-NH Metropolitan Statistical Area
Source: U.S. Census Bureau, 2015-2019 American Community Survey 5-Year Estimates

Number of Medical Professionals

Area	MDs[3]	DOs[3,4]	Dentists	Podiatrists	Chiropractors	Optometrists
County[1] (number)	11,885	122	1,787	80	113	274
County[1] (rate[2])	1,479.8	15.2	222.3	10.0	14.1	34.1
U.S. (rate[2])	282.9	22.7	71.2	6.2	28.1	16.9

25025
Note: Data as of 2019 unless noted; (1) Data covers Suffolk County; (2) Rate per 100,000 population; (3) Data as of 2018 and includes all active, non-federal physicians; (4) Doctor of Osteopathic Medicine
Source: U.S. Department of Health and Human Services, Health Resources and Services Administration, Bureau of Health Professions, Area Resource File (ARF) 2019-2020

Best Hospitals

According to *U.S. News,* the Boston, MA metro area is home to seven of the best hospitals in the U.S.: **Beth Israel Deaconess Medical Center** (2 adult specialties); **Brigham and Women's Hospital** (Honor Roll/13 adult specialties); **Dana-Farber/Brigham and Women's Cancer Center** (1 adult specialty and 1 pediatric specialty); **Massachusetts Eye and Ear Infirmary, Massachusetts General Hospital** (2 adult specialties); **Massachusetts General Hospital** (Honor Roll/16 adult specialties and 5 pediatric specialties); **New England Baptist Hospital** (1 adult specialty); **Spaulding Rehabilitation Hospital, Massachusetts General Hospital** (1 adult specialty). The hospitals listed were nationally ranked in at least one of 16 adult or 10 pediatric specialties. Only 134 hospitals nationwide were nationally ranked in one or more adult or pediatric specialty; this number increases to

178 counting specialized centers within hospitals. Twenty hospitals in the U.S. made the Honor Roll. The Best Hospitals Honor Roll takes both the national rankings and the procedure and condition ratings into account. Hospitals received points if they were nationally ranked in one of the 16 adult specialties—the higher they ranked, the more points they got—and how many ratings of "high performing" they earned in the 10 procedures and conditions. *U.S. News Online, "America's Best Hospitals 2020-21"*

According to *U.S. News,* the Boston, MA metro area is home to three of the best children's hospitals in the U.S.: **Boston Children's Hospital** (Honor Roll/10 pediatric specialties); **Dana-Farber/Boston Children's Cancer and Blood Disorders Center** (1 adult specialty and 1 pediat); **MassGeneral Hospital for Children** (5 pediatric specialties). The hospitals listed were highly ranked in at least one of 10 pediatric specialties. Eighty-eight children's hospitals in the U.S. were nationally ranked in at least one specialty. Hospitals received points for being ranked in a specialty, and the 10 hospitals with the most points across the 10 specialties make up the Honor Roll. *U.S. News Online, "America's Best Children's Hospitals 2020-21"*

EDUCATION

Public School District Statistics

District Name	Schls	Pupils	Pupil/Teacher Ratio	Minority Pupils[1] (%)	Free Lunch Eligible[2] (%)	IEP[3] (%)
Boston	117	51,433	12.2	85.4	n/a	21.0

Note: Table includes school districts with 2,000 or more students; (1) Percentage of students that are not non-Hispanic white; (2) Percentage of students that are eligible for the free lunch program; (3) Percentage of students that have an Individualized Education Program.
Source: U.S. Department of Education, National Center for Education Statistics, Common Core of Data, Local Education Agency (School District) Universe Survey: School Year 2018-2019; U.S. Department of Education, National Center for Education Statistics, Common Core of Data, Public Elementary/Secondary School Universe Survey: School Year 2018-2019

Best High Schools

According to *U.S. News,* Boston is home to one of the top 500 high schools in the U.S.: **Boston Latin School** (#37). Nearly 18,000 public, magnet and charter schools were ranked based on their performance on state assessments and how well they prepare students for college. *U.S. News & World Report, "Best High Schools 2020"*

Highest Level of Education

Area	Less than H.S.	H.S. Diploma	Some College, No Deg.	Associate Degree	Bachelor's Degree	Master's Degree	Prof. School Degree	Doctorate Degree
City	12.8	19.7	13.1	4.6	27.0	14.5	4.8	3.4
MSA[1]	8.3	22.1	14.5	7.0	26.0	15.2	3.5	3.3
U.S.	12.0	27.0	20.4	8.5	19.8	8.8	2.1	1.4

Note: Figures cover persons age 25 and over; (1) Figures cover the Boston-Cambridge-Newton, MA-NH Metropolitan Statistical Area
Source: U.S. Census Bureau, 2015-2019 American Community Survey 5-Year Estimates

Educational Attainment by Race

Area	High School Graduate or Higher (%)					Bachelor's Degree or Higher (%)				
	Total	White	Black	Asian	Hisp.[2]	Total	White	Black	Asian	Hisp.[2]
City	87.2	93.0	83.8	78.9	70.0	49.7	65.7	21.8	53.2	23.7
MSA[1]	91.7	94.3	85.2	86.0	72.0	48.1	50.6	26.3	62.3	22.8
U.S.	88.0	89.9	86.0	87.1	68.7	32.1	33.5	21.6	54.3	16.4

Note: Figures shown cover persons 25 years old and over; (1) Figures cover the Boston-Cambridge-Newton, MA-NH Metropolitan Statistical Area; (2) People of Hispanic origin can be of any race
Source: U.S. Census Bureau, 2015-2019 American Community Survey 5-Year Estimates

School Enrollment by Grade and Control

Area	Preschool (%)		Kindergarten (%)		Grades 1 - 4 (%)		Grades 5 - 8 (%)		Grades 9 - 12 (%)	
	Public	Private	Public	Private	Public	Private	Public	Private	Public	Private
City	50.7	49.3	84.9	15.1	85.7	14.3	86.8	13.2	87.8	12.2
MSA[1]	45.7	54.3	87.7	12.3	91.2	8.8	89.8	10.2	86.9	13.1
U.S.	59.1	40.9	87.6	12.4	89.5	10.5	89.4	10.6	90.1	9.9

Note: Figures shown cover persons 3 years old and over; (1) Figures cover the Boston-Cambridge-Newton, MA-NH Metropolitan Statistical Area
Source: U.S. Census Bureau, 2015-2019 American Community Survey 5-Year Estimates

Higher Education

Four-Year Colleges			Two-Year Colleges			Medical Schools[1]	Law Schools[2]	Voc/ Tech[3]
Public	Private Non-profit	Private For-profit	Public	Private Non-profit	Private For-profit			
2	19	2	1	2	0	3	4	2

Note: Figures cover institutions located within the city limits and include main campuses only; (1) includes schools accredited by the Liaison Committee on Medical Education and the American Osteopathic Association's Commission on Osteopathic College Accreditation; (2) includes ABA-accredited schools, schools with provisional ABA accreditation, and state accredited schools; (3) includes all schools with programs that are less than 2 years.
Source: National Center for Education Statistics, Integrated Postsecondary Education System (IPEDS), 2019-20; Wikipedia, List of Medical Schools in the United States, accessed April 2, 2021; Wikipedia, List of Law Schools in the United States, accessed April 2, 2021

According to *U.S. News & World Report,* the Boston, MA metro division is home to three of the top 200 national universities in the U.S.: **Boston University** (#42 tie); **Northeastern University** (#49 tie); **Simmons University** (#133 tie). The indicators used to capture academic quality fall into a number of categories: assessment by administrators at peer institutions; retention of students; faculty resources; student selectivity; financial resources; alumni giving; high school counselor ratings of colleges; and graduation rate. *U.S. News & World Report, "America's Best Colleges 2021"*

According to *U.S. News & World Report,* the Boston, MA metro division is home to one of the top 100 liberal arts colleges in the U.S.: **Wellesley College** (#4 tie). The indicators used to capture academic quality fall into a number of categories: assessment by administrators at peer institutions; retention of students; faculty resources; student selectivity; financial resources; alumni giving; high school counselor ratings of colleges; and graduation rate. *U.S. News & World Report, "America's Best Colleges 2021"*

According to *U.S. News & World Report,* the Boston, MA metro division is home to two of the top 100 law schools in the U.S.: **Boston University** (#20); **Northeastern University** (#67 tie). The rankings are based on a weighted average of 12 measures of quality: peer assessment score; assessment score by lawyers/judges; median LSAT scores; median undergrad GPA; acceptance rate; employment rates for graduates; placement success; bar passage rate; faculty resources; expenditures per student; student/faculty ratio; and library resources. *U.S. News & World Report, "America's Best Graduate Schools, Law, 2022"*

According to *U.S. News & World Report,* the Boston, MA metro division is home to three of the top 75 medical schools for research in the U.S.: **Harvard University** (#1); **Boston University** (#33 tie); **Tufts University** (#55 tie). The rankings are based on a weighted average of 11 measures of quality: quality assessment; peer assessment score; assessment score by residency directors; research activity; total research activity; average research activity per faculty member; student selectivity; median MCAT total score; median undergraduate GPA; acceptance rate; and faculty resources. *U.S. News & World Report, "America's Best Graduate Schools, Medical, 2022"*

According to *U.S. News & World Report,* the Boston, MA metro division is home to three of the top 75 business schools in the U.S.: **Harvard University** (#5 tie); **Boston University (Questrom)** (#50 tie); **Northeastern University (School of Business)** (#55 tie). The rankings are based on a weighted average of the following nine measures: quality assessment; peer assessment; recruiter assessment; placement success; mean starting salary and bonus; student selectivity; mean GMAT and GRE scores; mean undergraduate GPA; and acceptance rate. *U.S. News & World Report, "America's Best Graduate Schools, Business, 2022"*

EMPLOYERS

Major Employers

Company Name	Industry
Beth Israel Deaconess Medical Center	General medical & surgical hospitals
BlueCross BlueShield of Massachusetts	Health insurance
Boston University	Colleges & universities
Children's Hospital Corporation	Specialty hospitals, except psychiatric
City of Lowell	Municipal government
EMC Corp.	Data management
Federal Deposit Insurance Corporation	Federal deposit insurance corporation (FDIC)
General Electric Company	Aircraft engines & engine parts
Harvard University	Colleges & universities
Internal Revenue Service	Taxation department, government
John Hancock Corp Tax Credit Fund I	Personal service agents, brokers, & bureaus
Lahey Clinic	General medical & surgical hospitals
Massachusetts General Hospital	Health care
Massachusetts Institute of Technology	Colleges & universities
MassMutual Financial Group	Life insurance, annuities, & retirement investment
Roche Bros. Supermarkets	Food/grocery
State Street Bank and Trust Company	State trust companies accepting deposits, commercial
Sun Healthcare Group	Accident & health insurance
The Admins of the Tulane Educational Fund	Hospital, medical school affiliation
Tufts Medical Center	Hospital management

Note: Companies shown are located within the Boston-Cambridge-Newton, MA-NH Metropolitan Statistical Area.
Source: Hoovers.com; Wikipedia

Best Companies to Work For

Bain & Co, headquartered in Boston, is among "The 100 Best Companies to Work For." To pick the best companies, *Fortune* partnered with the Great Place to Work Institute. Two-thirds of a company's score is based on the results of the Institute's Trust Index survey, which is sent to a random sample of employees from each company. The questions related to attitudes about management's credibility, job satisfaction, and camaraderie. The other third of the scoring is based on the company's responses to the Institute's Culture Audit, which includes detailed questions about pay and benefit programs, and a series of open-ended questions about hiring practices, internal communication, training, recognition programs, and diversity efforts. Any company that is at least five years old with more than 1,000 U.S. employees is eligible. *Fortune, "The 100 Best Companies to Work For," 2020*

Boston Consulting Group; Digitas; LEK Consulting; Publicis Sapient; State Street, headquartered in Boston, are among the "100 Best Companies for Working Mothers." Criteria: paid time off and leaves; workforce profile; benefits; women's issues and advancement; flexible work; company culture and work life programs. *Working Mother, "100 Best Companies for Working Mothers," 2020*

Liberty Mutual Insurance, headquartered in Boston, is among the "100 Best Places to Work in IT." To qualify, companies had to be U.S.-based organizations or be non-U.S.-based employers that met the following criteria: have a minimum of 300 total employees at a U.S. headquarters and a minimum of 30 IT employees in the U.S., with at least 50% of their IT employees based in the U.S. The best places to work were selected based on compensation, benefits, work/life balance, employee morale, and satisfaction with training and development programs. In addition, *InsiderPro* and *Computerworld* looked at retention efforts, programs for recognizing and rewarding outstanding performances, and benefits such as flextime, elder care and child care, and reimbursement for college tuition and the cost of pursuing technology certifications. *InsiderPro and Computerworld, "100 Best Places to Work in IT," 2020*

Boston Consulting Group; Digitas, headquartered in Boston, are among the "Top Companies for Executive Women." This list is determined by organizations filling out an in-depth survey that measures female demographics at every level, but with an emphasis on women in senior corporate roles, with profit & loss (P&L) responsibility, and those earning in the top 20 percent of the organization. *Working Mother* defines P&L as having responsibility that involves monitoring the net income after expenses for a department or entire organization, with direct influence on how company resources are allocated. *Working Mother, "Top Companies for Executive Women," 2020+*

Blue Cross Blue Shield of Massachusetts; Boston Consulting Group; LEK Consulting; Publicis Sapient; State Street, headquartered in Boston, are among the "Best Companies for Dads." *Working Mother's* newest list recognizes the growing importance companies place on giving dads time off and support for their families. Rankings are determined by measuring gender-neutral or paternity leave offered, as well as actual time taken, phase-back policies, child- and dependent-care benefits, and corporate support groups for men and dads. *Working Mother, "Best Companies for Dads," 2020*

PUBLIC SAFETY

Crime Rate

Area	All Crimes	Violent Crimes				Property Crimes		
		Murder	Rape[3]	Robbery	Aggrav. Assault	Burglary	Larceny -Theft	Motor Vehicle Theft
City	n/a	6.0	33.1	148.7	419.5	243.7	1,515.1	n/a
Suburbs[1]	n/a	1.4	30.1	41.9	212.4	126.0	804.5	n/a
Metro[2]	n/a	3.0	31.1	78.6	283.6	166.5	1,048.9	n/a
U.S.	2,489.3	5.0	42.6	81.6	250.2	340.5	1,549.5	219.9

Note: Figures are crimes per 100,000 population; (1) All areas within the metro area that are located outside the city limits; (2) Figures cover the Boston, MA Metropolitan Division; (3) All figures shown were reported using the revised Uniform Crime Reporting (UCR) definition of rape.
Source: FBI Uniform Crime Reports, 2019

Hate Crimes

Area	Number of Quarters Reported	Number of Incidents per Bias Motivation					
		Race/Ethnicity/ Ancestry	Religion	Sexual Orientation	Disability	Gender	Gender Identity
City[1]	4	113	26	47	0	1	1
U.S.	4	3,963	1,521	1,195	157	69	198

Note: (1) Figures include one incident reported with more than one bias motivation.
Source: Federal Bureau of Investigation, Hate Crime Statistics 2019

Identity Theft Consumer Reports

Area	Reports	Reports per 100,000 Population	Rank[2]
MSA[1]	33,030	678	29
U.S.	1,387,615	423	-

Note: (1) Figures cover the Boston-Cambridge-Newton, MA-NH Metropolitan Statistical Area; (2) Rank ranges from 1 to 391 where 1 indicates greatest number of identity theft reports per 100,000 population
Source: Federal Trade Commission, Consumer Sentinel Network Data Book 2020

Fraud and Other Consumer Reports

Area	Reports	Reports per 100,000 Population	Rank[2]
MSA[1]	37,609	772	119
U.S.	3,385,133	1,031	-

Note: (1) Figures cover the Boston-Cambridge-Newton, MA-NH Metropolitan Statistical Area; (2) Rank ranges from 1 to 391 where 1 indicates greatest number of fraud and other consumer reports per 100,000 population
Source: Federal Trade Commission, Consumer Sentinel Network Data Book 2020

POLITICS

2020 Presidential Election Results

Area	Biden	Trump	Jorgensen	Hawkins	Other
Suffolk County	80.6	17.5	0.9	0.5	0.5
U.S.	51.3	46.8	1.2	0.3	0.5

Note: Results are percentages and may not add to 100% due to rounding
Source: Dave Leip's Atlas of U.S. Presidential Elections

SPORTS

Professional Sports Teams

Team Name	League	Year Established
Boston Bruins	National Hockey League (NHL)	1924
Boston Celtics	National Basketball Association (NBA)	1946
Boston Red Sox	Major League Baseball (MLB)	1901
New England Patriots	National Football League (NFL)	1960
New England Revolution	Major League Soccer (MLS)	1996

Note: Includes teams located in the Boston-Cambridge-Newton, MA-NH Metropolitan Statistical Area.
Source: Wikipedia, Major Professional Sports Teams of the United States and Canada, April 6, 2021

CLIMATE

Average and Extreme Temperatures

Temperature	Jan	Feb	Mar	Apr	May	Jun	Jul	Aug	Sep	Oct	Nov	Dec	Yr.
Extreme High (°F)	72	70	85	94	95	100	102	102	100	90	83	73	102
Average High (°F)	36	38	46	56	67	76	82	80	73	63	52	41	59
Average Temp. (°F)	30	31	39	48	58	68	74	72	65	55	45	34	52
Average Low (°F)	22	23	31	40	50	59	65	64	57	47	38	27	44
Extreme Low (°F)	-12	-4	1	16	34	45	50	47	37	28	15	-7	-12

Note: Figures cover the years 1945-1990
Source: National Climatic Data Center, International Station Meteorological Climate Summary, 9/96

Average Precipitation/Snowfall/Humidity

Precip./Humidity	Jan	Feb	Mar	Apr	May	Jun	Jul	Aug	Sep	Oct	Nov	Dec	Yr.
Avg. Precip. (in.)	3.8	3.6	3.8	3.7	3.5	3.1	2.9	3.6	3.1	3.3	4.4	4.1	42.9
Avg. Snowfall (in.)	12	12	8	1	Tr	0	0	0	0	Tr	1	8	41
Avg. Rel. Hum. 7am (%)	68	68	69	68	71	72	73	76	79	77	74	70	72
Avg. Rel. Hum. 4pm (%)	58	57	56	56	58	58	58	61	61	59	61	60	59

Note: Figures cover the years 1945-1990; Tr = Trace amounts (<0.05 in. of rain; <0.5 in. of snow)
Source: National Climatic Data Center, International Station Meteorological Climate Summary, 9/96

Weather Conditions

Temperature			Daytime Sky			Precipitation		
5°F & below	32°F & below	90°F & above	Clear	Partly cloudy	Cloudy	0.01 inch or more precip.	0.1 inch or more snow/ice	Thunder-storms
4	97	12	88	127	150	253	48	18

Note: Figures are average number of days per year and cover the years 1945-1990
Source: National Climatic Data Center, International Station Meteorological Climate Summary, 9/96

HAZARDOUS WASTE

Superfund Sites

The Boston, MA metro division is home to four sites on the EPA's Superfund National Priorities List: **Baird & McGuire** (final); **BJAT** (final); **Blackburn & Union Privileges** (final); **South Weymouth Naval Air Station** (final). There are a total of 1,375 Superfund sites with a status of proposed or final on the list in the U.S. *U.S. Environmental Protection Agency, National Priorities List, April 7, 2021*

AIR QUALITY

Air Quality Trends: Ozone

	1990	1995	2000	2005	2010	2015	2016	2017	2018	2019
MSA[1]	n/a	n/a	n/a	n/a	n/a	n/a	n/a	n/a	n/a	n/a
U.S.	0.088	0.089	0.082	0.080	0.073	0.068	0.069	0.068	0.069	0.065

Note: (1) Data covers the Boston-Cambridge-Newton, MA-NH Metropolitan Statistical Area; n/a not available. The values shown are the composite ozone concentration averages among trend sites based on the highest fourth daily maximum 8-hour concentration in parts per million. These trends are based on sites having an adequate record of monitoring data during the trend period. Data from exceptional events are included.
Source: U.S. Environmental Protection Agency, Air Quality Monitoring Information, "Air Quality Trends by City, 1990-2019"

Air Quality Index

Area	Percent of Days when Air Quality was...[2]					AQI Statistics[2]	
	Good	Moderate	Unhealthy for Sensitive Groups	Unhealthy	Very Unhealthy	Maximum	Median
MSA[1]	79.7	20.0	0.3	0.0	0.0	122	43

Note: (1) Data covers the Boston-Cambridge-Newton, MA-NH Metropolitan Statistical Area; (2) Based on 365 days with AQI data in 2019. Air Quality Index (AQI) is an index for reporting daily air quality. EPA calculates the AQI for five major air pollutants regulated by the Clean Air Act: ground-level ozone, particle pollution (aka particulate matter), carbon monoxide, sulfur dioxide, and nitrogen dioxide. The AQI runs from 0 to 500. The higher the AQI value, the greater the level of air pollution and the greater the health concern. There are six AQI categories: "Good" AQI is between 0 and 50. Air quality is considered satisfactory; "Moderate" AQI is between 51 and 100. Air quality is acceptable; "Unhealthy for Sensitive Groups" When AQI values are between 101 and 150, members of sensitive groups may experience health effects; "Unhealthy" When AQI values are between 151 and 200 everyone may begin to experience health effects; "Very Unhealthy" AQI values between 201 and 300 trigger a health alert; "Hazardous" AQI values over 300 trigger warnings of emergency conditions (not shown).
Source: U.S. Environmental Protection Agency, Air Quality Index Report, 2019

Air Quality Index Pollutants

Area	Percent of Days when AQI Pollutant was...[2]					
	Carbon Monoxide	Nitrogen Dioxide	Ozone	Sulfur Dioxide	Particulate Matter 2.5	Particulate Matter 10
MSA[1]	0.0	4.1	57.5	0.0	38.4	0.0

Note: (1) Data covers the Boston-Cambridge-Newton, MA-NH Metropolitan Statistical Area; (2) Based on 365 days with AQI data in 2019. The Air Quality Index (AQI) is an index for reporting daily air quality. EPA calculates the AQI for five major air pollutants regulated by the Clean Air Act: ground-level ozone, particle pollution (also known as particulate matter), carbon monoxide, sulfur dioxide, and nitrogen dioxide. The AQI runs from 0 to 500. The higher the AQI value, the greater the level of air pollution and the greater the health concern.
Source: U.S. Environmental Protection Agency, Air Quality Index Report, 2019

Maximum Air Pollutant Concentrations: Particulate Matter, Ozone, CO and Lead

	Particulate Matter 10 (ug/m³)	Particulate Matter 2.5 Wtd AM (ug/m³)	Particulate Matter 2.5 24-Hr (ug/m³)	Ozone (ppm)	Carbon Monoxide (ppm)	Lead (ug/m³)
MSA[1] Level	34	7.5	17	0.065	1	n/a
NAAQS[2]	150	15	35	0.075	9	0.15
Met NAAQS[2]	Yes	Yes	Yes	Yes	Yes	n/a

Note: (1) Data covers the Boston-Cambridge-Newton, MA-NH Metropolitan Statistical Area; Data from exceptional events are included; (2) National Ambient Air Quality Standards; ppm = parts per million; ug/m³ = micrograms per cubic meter; n/a not available.
Concentrations: Particulate Matter 10 (coarse particulate)—highest second maximum 24-hour concentration; Particulate Matter 2.5 Wtd AM (fine particulate)—highest weighted annual mean concentration; Particulate Matter 2.5 24-Hour (fine particulate)—highest 98th percentile 24-hour concentration; Ozone—highest fourth daily maximum 8-hour concentration; Carbon Monoxide—highest second maximum non-overlapping 8-hour concentration; Lead—maximum running 3-month average
Source: U.S. Environmental Protection Agency, Air Quality Monitoring Information, "Air Quality Statistics by City, 2019"

Maximum Air Pollutant Concentrations: Nitrogen Dioxide and Sulfur Dioxide

	Nitrogen Dioxide AM (ppb)	Nitrogen Dioxide 1-Hr (ppb)	Sulfur Dioxide AM (ppb)	Sulfur Dioxide 1-Hr (ppb)	Sulfur Dioxide 24-Hr (ppb)
MSA[1] Level	14	49	n/a	10	n/a
NAAQS[2]	53	100	30	75	140
Met NAAQS[2]	Yes	Yes	n/a	Yes	n/a

Note: (1) Data covers the Boston-Cambridge-Newton, MA-NH Metropolitan Statistical Area; Data from exceptional events are included; (2) National Ambient Air Quality Standards; ppm = parts per million; ug/m³ = micrograms per cubic meter; n/a not available.
Concentrations: Nitrogen Dioxide AM—highest arithmetic mean concentration; Nitrogen Dioxide 1-Hr—highest 98th percentile 1-hour daily maximum concentration; Sulfur Dioxide AM—highest annual mean concentration; Sulfur Dioxide 1-Hr—highest 99th percentile 1-hour daily maximum concentration; Sulfur Dioxide 24-Hr—highest second maximum 24-hour concentration
Source: U.S. Environmental Protection Agency, Air Quality Monitoring Information, "Air Quality Statistics by City, 2019"

Charlotte, North Carolina

Background

Charlotte's relationship with England began amiably enough. Settled by Scotch-Irish and German migrants from Pennsylvania, New Jersey, and Virginia in 1750, the area was named for Charlotte Sophia of Mecklenburg-Strelitz, queen to England's King George III. The county in which Charlotte lies was named for Queen Charlotte Sophia's duchy of Mecklenburg.

Trouble started in 1775, however, when the citizens of Charlotte signed the Mecklenburg Resolves, a document invalidating the power of the king and the English Parliament over their lives. The British General Lord Cornwallis found subduing these "treasoners" so difficult, he called Charlotte a "hornet's nest of rebellion."

Today, a better-behaved Charlotte is a sophisticated metropolitan area, its thriving economy based in banking and finance, manufacturing, retail, education, government, health care, transportation, and telecommunications. Known as a center for the banking industry, Charlotte is the nucleus of the Carolinas crescent, an industrial arc extending from Raleigh, North Carolina, to Greenville, South Carolina. Many Fortune 500 companies have a presence in the Charlotte area.

The Charlotte region has a major base of energy-oriented organizations and is known as "Charlotte USA—The New Energy Capital." The region includes nearly 300 energy related companies, employing more than 30,000. The University of North Carolina at Charlotte has a reputation in energy education and research; its Energy Production and Infrastructure Center (EPIC) trains energy engineers and conducts research in the energy sector. Charlotte is also listed as a "gamma" global city by the Globalization and World Cities Research Network.

Charlotte offers exciting cultural and nightlife scenes, and many of the scenes from the film "Talladega Nights" were filmed in and around Charlotte. Sports in the city include the NFL's Carolina Panthers and the NBA's Charlotte Hornets. Charlotte is also a center of NASCAR racing and the NASCAR Hall of Fame opened in Charlotte in 2010. In 2019, MLS awarded Charlotte its expansion team which is scheduled to begin play in 2022.

Charlotte was host to the Republican National Convention in 2020, the same year that CNN established a Charlotte bureau.

> Bubba Wallace, the only Black driver in NASCAR, received his COVID-19 vaccine at his race team's shop in North Carolina, encouraging others to get their shot "and help get us all safely back to normal."

Attractions include the Blumenthal Performing Arts Center, which offers Broadway theater, ballet and music productions; the U.S. National Whitewater Center, the world's largest artificial whitewater river; ImaginOn: The Joe & Joan Martin Educational Center; and the Mint Museum of Art and Discovery Place, one of America's top hands-on science museums with a planetarium and IMAX® Dome theater. The Levine Museum of the New South offers the nation's most comprehensive exhibits on post-Civil War southern society.

Significant institutions of higher education in the region include Queens University, the University of North Carolina at Charlotte, Davidson College and nearby Winthrop University.

Charlotte is located in the Piedmont of the Carolinas, a transitional area of rolling country between the mountains to the west and the Coastal Plain to the east. The city enjoys a moderate climate, characterized by cool winters and warm summers. Winter weather is changeable, with occasional cold periods, but extreme cold is rare. Snow is infrequent. Summer afternoons can be hot. Rainfall is generally evenly distributed throughout the year. The city took a direct hit from Hurricane Hugo in 1989, which caused massive damage. In 2002, Charlotte, and much of central North Carolina experienced an ice storm that resulted in 1.3 million people without power for weeks.

Rankings

General Rankings

- *US News & World Report* conducted a survey of more than 3,000 people and analyzed the 150 largest metropolitan areas to determine what matters most when selecting the next place to live. Charlotte ranked #6 out of the top 25 as having the best combination of desirable factors. Criteria: cost of living; quality of life; net migration; job market; desirability; and other factors. *realestate.usnews.com, "The 25 Best Places to Live in the U.S. in 2020-21," October 13, 2020*

- The Charlotte metro area was identified as one of America's fastest-growing areas in terms of population and business growth by *MagnifyMoney*. The area ranked #13 out of 35. The 100 most populous metro areas in the U.S. were evaluated on their change from 2011-2016 in the following categories: people and housing; workforce and employment opportunities; growing industry. *www.businessinsider.com, "The 35 Cities in the US with the Biggest Influx of People, the Most Work Opportunities, and the Hottest Business Growth," August 12, 2018*

- The Charlotte metro area was identified as one of America's fastest-growing areas in terms of population and economy by *Forbes*. The area ranked #19 out of 25. The 100 most populous metro areas in the U.S. were evaluated on the following criteria: estimated population growth; employment; economic output; wages; home values. *Forbes, "America's Fastest-Growing Cities 2018," February 28, 2018*

- In their seventh annual survey, Livability.com looked at data for more than 1,000 small to mid-sized U.S. cities to determine the rankings for Livability's "Top 100 Best Places to Live" in 2020. Charlotte ranked #13. Criteria: housing and affordable living; vibrant economy; social and civic engagement; education; demographics; health care options; transportation & infrastructure; and abundant lifestyle amenities. *Livability.com, "Top 100 Best Places to Live 2020" October 2020*

Business/Finance Rankings

- According to *Business Insider*, the Charlotte metro area is a prime place to run a startup or move an existing business to. The area ranked #25. Nearly 190 metro areas were analyzed on overall economic health and investments. Data was based on the 2019 U.S. Census Bureau American Community Survey, the marketing company PitchBook, Bureau of Labor Statistics employment report, and Zillow. Criteria: percentage of change in typical home values and employment rates; quarterly venture capital investment activity; and median household income. *www.businessinsider.com, "The 25 Best Cities to Start a Business-Or Move Your Current One," January 12, 2021*

- The Brookings Institution ranked the nation's largest cities based on income inequality. Charlotte was ranked #66 (#1 = greatest inequality). Criteria: the "95/20 ratio," a figure representing the income at which a household earns more than 95 percent of all other households, divided by the income at which a household earns more than only 20 percent of all other households. *Brookings Institution, "Household Income Inequality, Largest Cities of 97 Large U.S. Metro Areas, 2014-2016," February 5, 2018*

- The Brookings Institution ranked the 100 largest metro areas in the U.S. based on income inequality. Charlotte was ranked #53 (#1 = greatest inequality). Criteria: the "95/20 ratio," a figure representing the income at which a household earns more than 95 percent of all other households, divided by the income at which a household earns more than only 20 percent of all other households. *Brookings Institution, "Household Income Inequality, 100 Largest U.S. Metro Areas, 2014-2016," February 5, 2018*

- Payscale.com ranked the 32 largest metro areas in terms of wage growth. The Charlotte metro area ranked #15. Criteria: private-sector and education professional wage growth between the 4th quarter of 2019 and the 4th quarter of 2020. *PayScale, "Wage Trends by Metro Area-4th Quarter," January 11, 2021*

- The Charlotte metro area was identified as one of the most debt-ridden places in America by the finance site Credit.com. The metro area was ranked #18. Criteria: residents' average credit card debt as well as median income. *Credit.com, "25 Cities With the Most Credit Card Debt," February 28, 2018*

- Charlotte was identified as one of America's most frugal metro areas by *Coupons.com*. The city ranked #4 out of 25. Criteria: digital coupon usage. *Coupons.com, "America's Most Frugal Cities of 2017," March 22, 2018*

- Charlotte was identified as one of the happiest cities to work in by CareerBliss.com, an online community for career advancement. The city ranked #9 out of 10. Criteria: an employee's relationship with his or her boss and co-workers; daily tasks; general work environment; compensation; opportunities for advancement; company culture and job reputation; and resources. *Businesswire.com, "CareerBliss Happiest Cities to Work 2019," February 12, 2019*

- The Charlotte metro area appeared on the Milken Institute "2021 Best Performing Cities" list. Rank: #26 out of 200 large metro areas (population over 250,000). Criteria: job growth; wage and salary growth; high-tech output growth; housing affordability; household broadband access. *Milken Institute, "Best-Performing Cities 2021," February 16, 2021*

- *Forbes* ranked the 200 most populous metro areas to determine the nation's "Best Places for Business and Careers." The Charlotte metro area was ranked #7. Criteria: costs (business and living); job growth (past and projected); income growth; quality of life; educational attainment (college and high school); projected economic growth; cultural and leisure opportunities; workplace tolerance laws; net migration patterns. *Forbes, "The Best Places for Business and Careers 2019: Seattle Still On Top," October 30, 2019*

Children/Family Rankings

- Charlotte was selected as one of the most playful cities in the U.S. by KaBOOM! The organization's Playful City USA initiative honors cities and towns across the nation that have made their communities more playable. Criteria: pledging to integrate play as a solution to challenges in their communities; making it easy for children to get active and balanced play; creating more family-friendly and innovative communities as a result. *KaBOOM! National Campaign for Play, "2017 Playful City USA Communities"*

Education Rankings

- Personal finance website *WalletHub* analyzed the 150 largest U.S. metropolitan statistical areas to determine where the most educated Americans are putting their degrees to work. Criteria: education levels; percentage of workers with degrees; education quality and attainment gap; public school quality rankings; quality and enrollment of each metro area's universities. Charlotte was ranked #54 (#1 = most educated city). *www.WalletHub.com, "Most and Least Educated Cities in America," July 20, 2020*

- Charlotte was selected as one of America's most literate cities. The city ranked #57 out of the 84 largest U.S. cities. Criteria: number of booksellers; library resources; Internet resources; educational attainment; periodical publishing resources; newspaper circulation. *Central Connecticut State University, "America's Most Literate Cities, 2018," February 2019*

Environmental Rankings

- The U.S. Environmental Protection Agency (EPA) released a list of U.S. metropolitan areas with the most ENERGY STAR certified buildings in 2019. The Charlotte metro area was ranked #19 out of 25. *U.S. Environmental Protection Agency, "2020 Energy Star Top Cities," March 2020*

- Charlotte was highlighted as one of the top 98 cleanest metro areas for short-term particle pollution (24-hour PM 2.5) in the U.S. during 2016 through 2018. Monitors in these cities reported no days with unhealthful PM 2.5 levels. *American Lung Association, "State of the Air 2020," April 21, 2020*

Health/Fitness Rankings

- For each of the 100 largest cities in the United States, the American Fitness Index®, published by the American College of Sports Medicine and the Anthem Foundation, evaluated community infrastructure and 33 health behaviors including preventive health, levels of chronic disease conditions, pedestrian safety, air quality, and community resources that support physical activity. Charlotte ranked #67 for "community fitness." *americanfitnessindex.org, "2020 ACSM American Fitness Index Summary Report," July 14, 2020*

- The Charlotte metro area was identified as one of the worst cities for bed bugs in America by pest control company Orkin. The area ranked #11 out of 50 based on the number of bed bug treatments Orkin performed from December 2019 to November 2020. *Orkin, "New Year, New Top City on Orkin's 2021 Bed Bug Cities List: Chicago," February 1, 2021*

- Charlotte was identified as a "2021 Spring Allergy Capital." The area ranked #41 out of 100. Three groups of factors were used to identify the most challenging cities for people with allergies during the spring season: annual spring pollen levels; over the counter medicine use; number of board-certified allergy specialists. *Asthma and Allergy Foundation of America, "Spring Allergy Capitals 2021," February 23, 2021*

- Charlotte was identified as a "2021 Fall Allergy Capital." The area ranked #63 out of 100. Three groups of factors were used to identify the most challenging cities for people with allergies during the fall season: annual fall pollen levels; over the counter medicine use; number of board-certified allergy specialists. *Asthma and Allergy Foundation of America, "Fall Allergy Capitals 2021," February 23, 2021*

- Charlotte was identified as a "2019 Asthma Capital." The area ranked #74 out of the nation's 100 largest metropolitan areas. Criteria: estimated asthma prevalence; crude death rate from asthma; and ER visits due to asthma. Risk factors analyzed but not factored in the rankings: annual pollen score; annual air quality; public smoking laws; number of board-certified asthma specialists; rescue medication use; controller medication use; uninsured rate; poverty rate. *Asthma and Allergy Foundation of America, "Asthma Capitals 2019: The Most Challenging Places to Live With Asthma," May 7, 2019*

Real Estate Rankings

- FitSmallBusiness looked at 50 of the largest metropolitan areas in the U.S. to determine which metro was the best to start a real estate business. Data was compiled from such sources as: Zillow, Trulia, U.S. Census Bureau, and the Bureau of Labor Statistics. Criteria: location; inventory; annual wages; median sales price of homes; days on the market; median price cut percentage; and other factors that would influence real estate professional growth. The Charlotte metro area ranked #20. *fitsmallbusiness.com, "The Best Cities to Become a Real Estate Agent in 2018," January 30, 2018*

- *WalletHub* compared the most populated U.S. cities to determine which had the best markets for real estate agents. Charlotte ranked #34 where demand was high and pay was the best. Criteria: sales per agent; annual median wage for real-estate agents; monthly average starting salary for real estate agents; real estate job density and competition; unemployment rate; home turnover rate; housing-market health index; and other relevant metrics. *www.WalletHub.com, "2019's Best Places to Be a Real Estate Agent," April 24, 2019*

- The Charlotte metro area appeared on Realtor.com's list of hot housing markets to watch in 2021. The area ranked #3. Criteria: healthy existing homes inventory; relative home affordability; local economy/population trends. *Realtor.com®, "Top 10 Housing Markets Positioned for Growth in 2021," December 7, 2020*

- Charlotte was ranked #15 in the top 20 out of the 100 largest metro areas in terms of house price appreciation in 2020 (#1 = highest rate). *Federal Housing Finance Agency, House Price Index, 4th Quarter 2020*

- The Charlotte metro area was identified as one of the 20 best housing markets in the U.S. in 2020. The area ranked #18 out of 180 markets. Criteria: year-over-year change of median sales price of existing single-family homes between the 4th quarter of 2019 and the 4th quarter of 2020. *National Association of Realtors®, Median Sales Price of Existing Single-Family Homes for Metropolitan Areas, 4th Quarter 2020*

- Charlotte was ranked #129 out of 268 metro areas in terms of housing affordability in 2020 by the National Association of Home Builders (#1 = most affordable). Criteria: the share of homes sold in that area affordable to a family earning the local median income, based on standard mortgage underwriting criteria. *National Association of Home Builders®, NAHB-Wells Fargo Housing Opportunity Index, 4th Quarter 2020*

Safety Rankings

- Allstate ranked the 200 largest cities in America in terms of driver safety. Charlotte ranked #153. Criteria: internal property damage claims over a two-year period from January 2016 to December 2017. The report helps increase the importance of safety and awareness behind the wheel. *Allstate, "Allstate America's Best Drivers Report, 2019" June 24, 2019*

- The National Insurance Crime Bureau ranked 384 metro areas in the U.S. in terms of per capita rates of vehicle theft. The Charlotte metro area ranked #103 (#1 = highest rate). Criteria: number of vehicle theft offenses per 100,000 inhabitants in 2019. *National Insurance Crime Bureau, "Hot Spots 2019," July 21, 2020*

Seniors/Retirement Rankings

- From its Best Cities for Successful Aging indexes, the Milken Institute generated rankings for metropolitan areas, weighing data in nine categories—health care, wellness, living arrangements, transportation and convenience, financial characteristics, education, employment, community engagement, and overall livability. The Charlotte metro area was ranked #72 overall in the large metro area category. *Milken Institute, "Best Cities for Successful Aging, 2017" March 14, 2017*

Sports/Recreation Rankings

- Charlotte was chosen as a bicycle friendly community by the League of American Bicyclists. A "Bicycle Friendly Community" welcomes cyclists by providing safe and supportive accommodation for cycling and encouraging people to bike for transportation and recreation. There are five award levels: Diamond; Platinum; Gold; Silver; and Bronze. The community achieved an award level of Bronze. *League of American Bicyclists, "Fall 2020 Awards-New & Renewing Bicycle Friendly Communities List," December 16, 2020*

Women/Minorities Rankings

- Personal finance website *WalletHub* compared more than 180 U.S. cities across two key dimensions, "Hispanic Business-Friendliness" and "Hispanic Purchasing Power," to arrive at the most favorable conditions for Hispanic entrepreneurs. Charlotte was ranked #91 out of 182. Criteria includes: share of Hispanic-Owned Businesses; Hispanic entrepreneurship rate to median annual income of Hispanics; Small Business-Friendliness score; cost of living; and number of Hispanics with at least a bachelor's degree. *WalletHub.com, "2019's Best Cities for Hispanic Entrepreneurs," May 1, 2019*

Miscellaneous Rankings

- Charlotte was selected as a 2020 Digital Cities Survey winner. The city ranked #6 in the large city (500,000 or more population) category. The survey examined and assessed how city governments are utilizing technology to improve transparency, enhance cybersecurity, and respond to the pandemic. Survey questions focused on ten initiatives: cybersecurity, citizen experience, disaster recovery, business intelligence, IT personnel, data governance, collaboration, infrastructure modernization, cloud computing, and mobile applications. *Center for Digital Government, "2020 Digital Cities Survey," November 10, 2020*

- *WalletHub* compared the 150 most populated U.S. cities to determine their operating efficiency. A "Quality of City Services" score was constructed for each city and then divided by the total budget per capita to reveal which were managed the best. Charlotte ranked #113. Criteria: financial stability; economy; education; safety; health; infrastructure and pollution. *www.WalletHub.com, "2020's Best-& Worst-Run Cities in America," June 29, 2020*

- The National Alliance to End Homelessness listed the 25 most populous metro areas with the highest rate of homelessness. The Charlotte metro area had a high rate of homelessness. Criteria: number of homeless people per 10,000 population in 2016. *National Alliance to End Homelessness, "Homelessness in the 25 Most Populous U.S. Metro Areas," September 1, 2017*

Business Environment

DEMOGRAPHICS

Population Growth

Area	1990 Census	2000 Census	2010 Census	2019* Estimate	Population Growth (%) 1990-2019	Population Growth (%) 2010-2019
City	428,283	540,828	731,424	857,425	100.2	17.2
MSA[1]	1,024,331	1,330,448	1,758,038	2,545,560	148.5	44.8
U.S.	248,709,873	281,421,906	308,745,538	324,697,795	30.6	5.2

Note: (1) Figures cover the Charlotte-Concord-Gastonia, NC-SC Metropolitan Statistical Area; (*) 2015-2019 5-year estimated population
Source: U.S. Census Bureau, 1990 Census, Census 2000, Census 2010, 2015-2019 American Community Survey 5-Year Estimates

Household Size

Area	One	Two	Three	Four	Five	Six	Seven or More	Average Household Size
City	32.9	32.2	15.5	12.0	4.9	1.6	0.9	2.60
MSA[1]	27.1	34.0	16.4	14.0	5.6	1.9	1.0	2.60
U.S.	27.9	33.9	15.6	12.9	6.0	2.3	1.4	2.60

Note: (1) Figures cover the Charlotte-Concord-Gastonia, NC-SC Metropolitan Statistical Area
Source: U.S. Census Bureau, 2015-2019 American Community Survey 5-Year Estimates

Race

Area	White Alone[2] (%)	Black Alone[2] (%)	Asian Alone[2] (%)	AIAN[3] Alone[2] (%)	NHOPI[4] Alone[2] (%)	Other Race Alone[2] (%)	Two or More Races (%)
City	48.8	35.2	6.5	0.4	0.1	6.1	2.8
MSA[1]	66.9	22.8	3.7	0.4	0.1	3.6	2.5
U.S.	72.5	12.7	5.5	0.8	0.2	4.9	3.3

Note: (1) Figures cover the Charlotte-Concord-Gastonia, NC-SC Metropolitan Statistical Area; (2) Alone is defined as not being in combination with one or more other races; (3) American Indian and Alaska Native; (4) Native Hawaiian and Other Pacific Islander
Source: U.S. Census Bureau, 2015-2019 American Community Survey 5-Year Estimates

Hispanic or Latino Origin

Area	Total (%)	Mexican (%)	Puerto Rican (%)	Cuban (%)	Other (%)
City	14.3	5.3	1.2	0.5	7.3
MSA[1]	10.1	4.7	1.0	0.4	4.1
U.S.	18.0	11.2	1.7	0.7	4.3

Note: Persons of Hispanic or Latino origin can be of any race; (1) Figures cover the Charlotte-Concord-Gastonia, NC-SC Metropolitan Statistical Area
Source: U.S. Census Bureau, 2015-2019 American Community Survey 5-Year Estimates

Ancestry

Area	German	Irish	English	American	Italian	Polish	French[2]	Scottish	Dutch
City	8.7	7.0	6.6	4.7	3.4	1.6	1.4	1.9	0.7
MSA[1]	11.0	8.4	7.8	9.1	3.9	1.7	1.6	2.3	0.9
U.S.	13.3	9.7	7.2	6.2	5.1	2.8	2.3	1.7	1.2

Note: Figures are the percentage of the total population reporting a particular ancestry. The nine most commonly reported ancestries in the U.S. are shown. Figures include multiple ancestries (e.g. if a person reported being Irish and Italian, they were included in both columns); (1) Figures cover the Charlotte-Concord-Gastonia, NC-SC Metropolitan Statistical Area; (2) Excludes Basque
Source: U.S. Census Bureau, 2015-2019 American Community Survey 5-Year Estimates

Foreign-born Population

Area	Any Foreign Country	Asia	Mexico	Europe	Caribbean	Central America[2]	South America	Africa	Canada
City	16.7	5.4	2.6	1.2	1.1	2.8	1.4	1.9	0.2
MSA[1]	10.1	3.0	2.1	1.1	0.6	1.4	0.9	0.9	0.2
U.S.	13.6	4.2	3.5	1.5	1.3	1.1	1.0	0.7	0.2

Note: (1) Figures cover the Charlotte-Concord-Gastonia, NC-SC Metropolitan Statistical Area; (2) Excludes Mexico.
Source: U.S. Census Bureau, 2015-2019 American Community Survey 5-Year Estimates

Marital Status

Area	Never Married	Now Married[2]	Separated	Widowed	Divorced
City	40.7	42.5	2.6	4.0	10.2
MSA[1]	32.6	49.4	2.4	5.2	10.3
U.S.	33.4	48.1	1.9	5.8	10.9

Note: Figures are percentages and cover the population 15 years of age and older; (1) Figures cover the Charlotte-Concord-Gastonia, NC-SC Metropolitan Statistical Area; (2) Excludes separated
Source: U.S. Census Bureau, 2015-2019 American Community Survey 5-Year Estimates

Disability by Age

Area	All Ages	Under 18 Years Old	18 to 64 Years Old	65 Years and Over
City	7.9	2.5	6.5	29.7
MSA[1]	10.5	3.4	8.7	32.4
U.S.	12.6	4.2	10.3	34.5

Note: Figures show percent of the civilian noninstitutionalized population that reported having a disability. Disability status is determined from six types of difficulty: vision, hearing, cognitive, ambulatory, self-care, and independent living. For children under 5 years old, hearing and vision difficulty are used to determine disability status. For children between the ages of 5 and 14, disability status is determined from hearing, vision, cognitive, ambulatory, and self-care difficulties. For people aged 15 years and older, they are considered to have a disability if they have difficulty with any one of the six difficulty types; Note: (1) Figures cover the Charlotte-Concord-Gastonia, NC-SC Metropolitan Statistical Area
Source: U.S. Census Bureau, 2015-2019 American Community Survey 5-Year Estimates

Age

Area	Percent of Population									Median Age
	Under Age 5	Age 5–19	Age 20–34	Age 35–44	Age 45–54	Age 55–64	Age 65–74	Age 75–84	Age 85+	
City	6.8	19.4	25.1	14.8	13.1	10.7	6.4	2.8	1.1	34.2
MSA[1]	6.2	20.2	20.1	13.9	14.2	12.1	8.2	3.8	1.4	37.5
U.S.	6.1	19.1	20.7	12.6	13.0	12.9	9.1	4.6	1.9	38.1

Note: (1) Figures cover the Charlotte-Concord-Gastonia, NC-SC Metropolitan Statistical Area
Source: U.S. Census Bureau, 2015-2019 American Community Survey 5-Year Estimates

Gender

Area	Males	Females	Males per 100 Females
City	412,035	445,390	92.5
MSA[1]	1,235,495	1,310,065	94.3
U.S.	159,886,919	164,810,876	97.0

Note: (1) Figures cover the Charlotte-Concord-Gastonia, NC-SC Metropolitan Statistical Area
Source: U.S. Census Bureau, 2015-2019 American Community Survey 5-Year Estimates

Religious Groups by Family

Area	Catholic	Baptist	Non-Den.	Methodist[2]	Lutheran	LDS[3]	Pente-costal	Presby-terian[4]	Muslim[5]	Judaism
MSA[1]	5.9	17.3	6.8	8.6	1.3	0.8	3.3	4.5	0.2	0.3
U.S.	19.1	9.3	4.0	4.0	2.3	2.0	1.9	1.6	0.8	0.7

Note: Figures are the number of adherents as a percentage of the total population; (1) Figures cover the Charlotte-Concord-Gastonia, NC-SC Metropolitan Statistical Area; (2) Methodist/Pietist; (3) Latter Day Saints; (4) Reformed; (5) Figures are estimates
Source: Association of Statisticians of American Religious Bodies, 2010 U.S. Religion Census: Religious Congregations & Membership Study

Religious Groups by Tradition

Area	Catholic	Evangelical Protestant	Mainline Protestant	Other Tradition	Black Protestant	Orthodox
MSA[1]	5.9	27.6	13.3	1.7	2.8	0.5
U.S.	19.1	16.2	7.3	4.3	1.6	0.3

Note: Figures are the number of adherents as a percentage of the total population; (1) Figures cover the Charlotte-Concord-Gastonia, NC-SC Metropolitan Statistical Area
Source: Association of Statisticians of American Religious Bodies, 2010 U.S. Religion Census: Religious Congregations & Membership Study

ECONOMY

Gross Metropolitan Product

Area	2017	2018	2019	2020	Rank[2]
MSA[1]	174.1	185.6	195.5	205.3	20

Note: Figures are in billions of dollars; (1) Figures cover the Charlotte-Concord-Gastonia, NC-SC Metropolitan Statistical Area; (2) Rank is based on 2018 data and ranges from 1 to 381
Source: U.S. Conference of Mayors, U.S. Metro Economies: GMP & Employment 2018-2020, September 2019

Economic Growth

Area	2015-17 (%)	2018 (%)	2019 (%)	2020 (%)	Rank[2]
MSA[1]	3.4	4.2	3.7	2.8	51
U.S.	1.9	2.9	2.3	2.1	—

Note: Figures are real gross metropolitan product (GMP) growth rates and represent average annual percent change; (1) Figures cover the Charlotte-Concord-Gastonia, NC-SC Metropolitan Statistical Area; (2) Rank is based on 2017 2-year average annual percent change and ranges from 1 to 381
Source: U.S. Conference of Mayors, U.S. Metro Economies: GMP & Employment 2018-2020, September 2019

Metropolitan Area Exports

Area	2014	2015	2016	2017	2018	2019	Rank[2]
MSA[1]	12,885.3	13,985.8	11,944.1	13,122.5	14,083.2	13,892.4	27

Note: Figures are in millions of dollars; (1) Figures cover the Charlotte-Concord-Gastonia, NC-SC Metropolitan Statistical Area; (2) Rank is based on 2019 data and ranges from 1 to 386
Source: U.S. Department of Commerce, International Trade Administration, Office of Trade and Economic Analysis, Industry and Analysis, Exports by Metropolitan Area, data extracted March 24, 2021

Building Permits

Area	Single-Family			Multi-Family			Total		
	2018	2019	Pct. Chg.	2018	2019	Pct. Chg.	2018	2019	Pct. Chg.
City	n/a	n/a	n/a	n/a	n/a	n/a	n/a	n/a	n/a
MSA[1]	16,407	16,253	-0.9	9,802	8,384	-14.5	26,209	24,637	-6.0
U.S.	855,300	862,100	0.7	473,500	523,900	10.6	1,328,800	1,386,000	4.3

Note: (1) Figures cover the Charlotte-Concord-Gastonia, NC-SC Metropolitan Statistical Area; Figures represent new, privately-owned housing units authorized (unadjusted data); All permit data are based on estimates with imputation
Source: U.S. Census Bureau, Manufacturing, Mining, and Construction Statistics, Building Permits, 2018, 2019

Bankruptcy Filings

Area	Business Filings			Nonbusiness Filings		
	2019	2020	% Chg.	2019	2020	% Chg.
Mecklenburg County	64	45	-29.7	1,020	639	-37.4
U.S.	22,780	21,655	-4.9	752,160	522,808	-30.5

Note: Business filings include Chapter 7, Chapter 9, Chapter 11, Chapter 12, Chapter 13, Chapter 15, and Section 304; Nonbusiness filings include Chapter 7, Chapter 11, and Chapter 13
Source: Administrative Office of the U.S. Courts, Business and Nonbusiness Bankruptcy, County Cases Commenced by Chapter of the Bankruptcy Code, During the 12-Month Period Ending December 31, 2019 and Business and Nonbusiness Bankruptcy, County Cases Commenced by Chapter of the Bankruptcy Code, During the 12-Month Period Ending December 31, 2020

Housing Vacancy Rates

Area	Gross Vacancy Rate[2] (%)			Year-Round Vacancy Rate[3] (%)			Rental Vacancy Rate[4] (%)			Homeowner Vacancy Rate[5] (%)		
	2018	2019	2020	2018	2019	2020	2018	2019	2020	2018	2019	2020
MSA[1]	8.5	9.3	6.6	8.1	9.0	6.3	5.6	7.6	5.6	1.7	1.8	1.0
U.S.	12.3	12.0	10.6	9.7	9.5	8.2	6.9	6.7	6.3	1.5	1.4	1.0

Note: (1) Figures cover the Charlotte-Concord-Gastonia, NC-SC Metropolitan Statistical Area; (2) The percentage of the total housing inventory that is vacant; (3) The percentage of the housing inventory (excluding seasonal units) that is year-round vacant; (4) The percentage of rental inventory that is vacant for rent; (5) The percentage of homeowner inventory that is vacant for sale
Source: U.S. Census Bureau, Housing Vacancies and Homeownership Annual Statistics: 2018, 2019, 2020

INCOME

Income

Area	Per Capita ($)	Median Household ($)	Average Household ($)
City	38,000	62,817	94,516
MSA[1]	34,558	63,217	89,212
U.S.	34,103	62,843	88,607

Note: (1) Figures cover the Charlotte-Concord-Gastonia, NC-SC Metropolitan Statistical Area
Source: U.S. Census Bureau, 2015-2019 American Community Survey 5-Year Estimates

Household Income Distribution

Area	Percent of Households Earning							
	Under $15,000	$15,000 -$24,999	$25,000 -$34,999	$35,000 -$49,999	$50,000 -$74,999	$75,000 -$99,999	$100,000 -$149,999	$150,000 and up
City	8.6	7.9	9.7	13.3	17.9	12.5	14.6	15.5
MSA[1]	8.9	8.6	9.2	12.7	18.1	13.0	15.1	14.4
U.S.	10.3	8.9	8.9	12.3	17.2	12.7	15.1	14.5

Note: (1) Figures cover the Charlotte-Concord-Gastonia, NC-SC Metropolitan Statistical Area
Source: U.S. Census Bureau, 2015-2019 American Community Survey 5-Year Estimates

Poverty Rate

Area	All Ages	Under 18 Years Old	18 to 64 Years Old	65 Years and Over
City	12.8	18.6	11.4	8.6
MSA[1]	11.7	16.5	10.7	8.2
U.S.	13.4	18.5	12.6	9.3

Note: Figures are percentage of people whose income during the past 12 months was below the poverty level;
(1) Figures cover the Charlotte-Concord-Gastonia, NC-SC Metropolitan Statistical Area
Source: U.S. Census Bureau, 2015-2019 American Community Survey 5-Year Estimates

CITY FINANCES

City Government Finances

Component	2017 ($000)	2017 ($ per capita)
Total Revenues	2,360,169	2,854
Total Expenditures	2,097,059	2,535
Debt Outstanding	4,073,032	4,924
Cash and Securities[1]	812,925	983

Note: (1) Cash and security holdings of a government at the close of its fiscal year,
including those of its dependent agencies, utilities, and liquor stores.
Source: U.S. Census Bureau, State & Local Government Finances 2017

City Government Revenue by Source

Source	2017 ($000)	2017 ($ per capita)	2017 (%)
General Revenue			
From Federal Government	233,550	282	9.9
From State Government	235,017	284	10.0
From Local Governments	33,605	41	1.4
Taxes			
Property	456,176	552	19.3
Sales and Gross Receipts	311,891	377	13.2
Personal Income	0	0	0.0
Corporate Income	0	0	0.0
Motor Vehicle License	34,200	41	1.4
Other Taxes	56,519	68	2.4
Current Charges	646,702	782	27.4
Liquor Store	0	0	0.0
Utility	203,621	246	8.6
Employee Retirement	70,815	86	3.0

Source: U.S. Census Bureau, State & Local Government Finances 2017

City Government Expenditures by Function

Function	2017 ($000)	2017 ($ per capita)	2017 (%)
General Direct Expenditures			
Air Transportation	304,510	368	14.5
Corrections	0	0	0.0
Education	0	0	0.0
Employment Security Administration	0	0	0.0
Financial Administration	29,493	35	1.4
Fire Protection	129,675	156	6.2
General Public Buildings	9,548	11	0.5
Governmental Administration, Other	32,498	39	1.5
Health	0	0	0.0
Highways	119,403	144	5.7
Hospitals	0	0	0.0
Housing and Community Development	68,520	82	3.3
Interest on General Debt	121,800	147	5.8
Judicial and Legal	3,237	3	0.2
Libraries	2	< 1	< 0.1
Parking	626	< 1	< 0.1
Parks and Recreation	110,045	133	5.2
Police Protection	269,884	326	12.9
Public Welfare	334	< 1	< 0.1
Sewerage	203,112	245	9.7
Solid Waste Management	57,943	70	2.8
Veterans' Services	0	0	0.0
Liquor Store	0	0	0.0
Utility	529,608	640	25.3
Employee Retirement	31,145	37	1.5

Source: U.S. Census Bureau, State & Local Government Finances 2017

EMPLOYMENT

Labor Force and Employment

Area	Civilian Labor Force			Workers Employed		
	Dec. 2019	Dec. 2020	% Chg.	Dec. 2019	Dec. 2020	% Chg.
City	499,499	492,206	-1.5	483,932	461,278	-4.7
MSA[1]	1,373,470	1,344,434	-2.1	1,331,441	1,267,112	-4.8
U.S.	164,007,000	160,017,000	-2.4	158,504,000	149,613,000	-5.6

Note: Data is not seasonally adjusted and covers workers 16 years of age and older; (1) Figures cover the Charlotte-Concord-Gastonia, NC-SC Metropolitan Statistical Area
Source: Bureau of Labor Statistics, Local Area Unemployment Statistics

Unemployment Rate

Area	2020											
	Jan.	Feb.	Mar.	Apr.	May	Jun.	Jul.	Aug.	Sep.	Oct.	Nov.	Dec.
City	3.8	3.5	4.0	13.0	13.9	8.8	10.2	8.0	8.1	6.8	6.7	6.3
MSA[1]	3.7	3.4	3.9	12.7	13.2	8.3	9.3	7.1	7.0	5.9	5.9	5.8
U.S.	4.0	3.8	4.5	14.4	13.0	11.2	10.5	8.5	7.7	6.6	6.4	6.5

Note: Data is not seasonally adjusted and covers workers 16 years of age and older; (1) Figures cover the Charlotte-Concord-Gastonia, NC-SC Metropolitan Statistical Area
Source: Bureau of Labor Statistics, Local Area Unemployment Statistics

Average Wages

Occupation	$/Hr.	Occupation	$/Hr.
Accountants and Auditors	42.40	Maintenance and Repair Workers	21.40
Automotive Mechanics	23.40	Marketing Managers	72.20
Bookkeepers	20.70	Network and Computer Systems Admin.	40.30
Carpenters	19.70	Nurses, Licensed Practical	22.80
Cashiers	11.00	Nurses, Registered	33.90
Computer Programmers	48.80	Nursing Assistants	14.10
Computer Systems Analysts	48.00	Office Clerks, General	17.50
Computer User Support Specialists	25.80	Physical Therapists	41.50
Construction Laborers	16.00	Physicians	100.30
Cooks, Restaurant	13.00	Plumbers, Pipefitters and Steamfitters	21.90
Customer Service Representatives	18.80	Police and Sheriff's Patrol Officers	25.90
Dentists	83.90	Postal Service Mail Carriers	25.80
Electricians	22.30	Real Estate Sales Agents	26.80
Engineers, Electrical	48.50	Retail Salespersons	14.40
Fast Food and Counter Workers	10.70	Sales Representatives, Technical/Scientific	45.80
Financial Managers	83.70	Secretaries, Exc. Legal/Medical/Executive	19.40
First-Line Supervisors of Office Workers	28.70	Security Guards	15.20
General and Operations Managers	64.40	Surgeons	n/a
Hairdressers/Cosmetologists	15.60	Teacher Assistants, Exc. Postsecondary*	12.80
Home Health and Personal Care Aides	11.20	Teachers, Secondary School, Exc. Sp. Ed.*	26.00
Janitors and Cleaners	12.30	Telemarketers	16.80
Landscaping/Groundskeeping Workers	15.10	Truck Drivers, Heavy/Tractor-Trailer	23.30
Lawyers	69.60	Truck Drivers, Light/Delivery Services	18.00
Maids and Housekeeping Cleaners	11.70	Waiters and Waitresses	11.80

Note: Wage data covers the Charlotte-Concord-Gastonia, NC-SC Metropolitan Statistical Area; (*) Hourly wages were calculated from annual wage data based on a 40 hour work week; n/a not available.
Source: Bureau of Labor Statistics, Metro Area Occupational Employment & Wage Estimates, May 2020

Employment by Industry

Sector	MSA[1]		U.S.
	Number of Employees	Percent of Total	Percent of Total
Construction, Mining, and Logging	68,700	5.6	5.5
Education and Health Services	123,000	10.1	16.3
Financial Activities	111,400	9.2	6.1
Government	156,300	12.8	15.2
Information	23,200	1.9	1.9
Leisure and Hospitality	114,400	9.4	9.0
Manufacturing	103,800	8.5	8.5
Other Services	42,700	3.5	3.8
Professional and Business Services	212,400	17.4	14.4
Retail Trade	129,700	10.7	10.9
Transportation, Warehousing, and Utilities	74,700	6.1	4.6
Wholesale Trade	57,000	4.7	3.9

Note: Figures are non-farm employment as of December 2020. Figures are not seasonally adjusted and include workers 16 years of age and older; (1) Figures cover the Charlotte-Concord-Gastonia, NC-SC Metropolitan Statistical Area
Source: Bureau of Labor Statistics, Current Employment Statistics, Employment, Hours, and Earnings

Employment by Occupation

Occupation Classification	City (%)	MSA[1] (%)	U.S. (%)
Management, Business, Science, and Arts	43.0	39.4	38.5
Natural Resources, Construction, and Maintenance	7.2	8.4	8.9
Production, Transportation, and Material Moving	11.7	14.2	13.2
Sales and Office	22.2	22.4	21.6
Service	15.9	15.6	17.8

Note: Figures cover employed civilians 16 years of age and older; (1) Figures cover the Charlotte-Concord-Gastonia, NC-SC Metropolitan Statistical Area
Source: U.S. Census Bureau, 2015-2019 American Community Survey 5-Year Estimates

Occupations with Greatest Projected Employment Growth: 2020 – 2022

Occupation[1]	2020 Employment	2022 Projected Employment	Numeric Employment Change	Percent Employment Change
Laborers and Freight, Stock, and Material Movers, Hand	90,950	94,250	3,300	3.6
Stockers and Order Fillers	99,690	102,690	3,000	3.0
Software Developers and Software Quality Assurance Analysts and Testers	74,740	76,850	2,110	2.8
Registered Nurses	87,970	89,970	2,000	2.3
Project Management Specialists and Business Operations Specialists, All Other	62,540	63,660	1,120	1.8
Computer Systems Analysts (SOC 2018)	40,350	41,450	1,100	2.7
Insurance Sales Agents	13,950	14,920	970	7.0
Industrial Truck and Tractor Operators	22,480	23,360	880	3.9
Loan Officers	12,610	13,430	820	6.5
Customer Service Representatives	80,790	81,600	810	1.0

Note: Projections cover North Carolina; (1) Sorted by numeric employment change
Source: www.projectionscentral.com, State Occupational Projections, 2020–2022 Short-Term Projections

Fastest-Growing Occupations: 2020 – 2022

Occupation[1]	2020 Employment	2022 Projected Employment	Numeric Employment Change	Percent Employment Change
Statisticians	1,420	1,540	120	8.5
Operations Research Analysts	2,490	2,700	210	8.4
Butchers and Meat Cutters	2,650	2,860	210	7.9
Insurance Sales Agents	13,950	14,920	970	7.0
Loan Interviewers and Clerks	6,000	6,420	420	7.0
Brokerage Clerks	1,590	1,700	110	6.9
Veterinary Assistants and Laboratory Animal Caretakers	3,590	3,830	240	6.7
Personal Financial Advisors	8,760	9,330	570	6.5
Loan Officers	12,610	13,430	820	6.5
Veterinary Technologists and Technicians	3,040	3,230	190	6.3

Note: Projections cover North Carolina; (1) Sorted by percent employment change and excludes occupations with numeric employment change less than 50
Source: www.projectionscentral.com, State Occupational Projections, 2020–2022 Short-Term Projections

TAXES

State Corporate Income Tax Rates

State	Tax Rate (%)	Income Brackets ($)	Num. of Brackets	Financial Institution Tax Rate (%)[a]	Federal Income Tax Ded.
North Carolina	2.5	Flat rate	1	2.5	No

Note: Tax rates as of January 1, 2021; (a) Rates listed are the corporate income tax rate applied to financial institutions or excise taxes based on income. Some states have other taxes based upon the value of deposits or shares.
Source: Federation of Tax Administrators, State Corporate Income Tax Rates, January 1, 2021

State Individual Income Tax Rates

State	Tax Rate (%)	Income Brackets ($)	Personal Exemptions ($) Single	Personal Exemptions ($) Married	Personal Exemptions ($) Depend.	Standard Ded. ($) Single	Standard Ded. ($) Married
North Carolina	5.25	Flat rate	None	None	None	10,750	21,500

Note: Tax rates as of January 1, 2021; Local- and county-level taxes are not included; Federal income tax is not deductible on state income tax returns
Source: Federation of Tax Administrators, State Individual Income Tax Rates, January 1, 2021

Various State Sales and Excise Tax Rates

State	State Sales Tax (%)	Gasoline[1] (¢/gal.)	Cigarette[2] ($/pack)	Spirits[3] ($/gal.)	Wine[4] ($/gal.)	Beer[5] ($/gal.)	Recreational Marijuana (%)
North Carolina	4.75	36.35	0.45	14.58	1	0.62	Not legal

Note: All tax rates as of January 1, 2021; (1) The American Petroleum Institute has developed a methodology for determining the average tax rate on a gallon of fuel. Rates may include any of the following: excise taxes, environmental fees, storage tank fees, other fees or taxes, general sales tax, and local taxes; (2) The federal excise tax of $1.0066 per pack and local taxes are not included; (3) Rates are those applicable to off-premise sales of 40% alcohol by volume (a.b.v.) distilled spirits in 750ml containers. Local excise taxes are excluded; (4) Rates are those applicable to off-premise sales of 11% a.b.v. non-carbonated wine in 750ml containers; (5) Rates are those applicable to off-premise sales of 4.7% a.b.v. beer in 12 ounce containers.
Source: Tax Foundation, 2021 Facts & Figures: How Does Your State Compare?

State Business Tax Climate Index Rankings

State	Overall Rank	Corporate Tax Rank	Individual Income Tax Rank	Sales Tax Rank	Property Tax Rank	Unemployment Insurance Tax Rank
North Carolina	10	4	16	22	26	10

Note: The index is a measure of how each state's tax laws affect economic performance. The lower the rank, the more favorable a state's tax system is for business. States without a given tax are given a ranking of 1. The scores/rankings for the District of Columbia do not affect other states. The 2021 index represents the tax climate as of July 1, 2020.
Source: Tax Foundation, State Business Tax Climate Index 2021

TRANSPORTATION

Means of Transportation to Work

Area	Car/Truck/Van		Public Transportation			Bicycle	Walked	Other Means	Worked at Home
	Drove Alone	Car-pooled	Bus	Subway	Railroad				
City	76.3	9.3	2.4	0.4	0.2	0.1	2.1	1.5	7.7
MSA[1]	80.4	8.9	1.1	0.2	0.1	0.1	1.4	1.2	6.6
U.S.	76.3	9.0	2.4	1.9	0.6	0.5	2.7	1.4	5.2

Note: Figures are percentages and cover workers 16 years of age and older; (1) Figures cover the Charlotte-Concord-Gastonia, NC-SC Metropolitan Statistical Area
Source: U.S. Census Bureau, 2015-2019 American Community Survey 5-Year Estimates

Travel Time to Work

Area	Less Than 10 Minutes	10 to 19 Minutes	20 to 29 Minutes	30 to 44 Minutes	45 to 59 Minutes	60 to 89 Minutes	90 Minutes or More
City	8.2	28.3	26.6	24.4	7.1	3.5	2.0
MSA[1]	9.3	27.1	22.7	24.0	9.6	5.2	2.1
U.S.	12.2	28.4	20.8	20.8	8.3	6.4	2.9

Note: Note: Figures are percentages and include workers 16 years old and over; (1) Figures cover the Charlotte-Concord-Gastonia, NC-SC Metropolitan Statistical Area
Source: U.S. Census Bureau, 2015-2019 American Community Survey 5-Year Estimates

Key Congestion Measures

Measure	1982	1992	2002	2012	2017
Annual Hours of Delay, Total (000)	3,491	10,967	26,893	39,817	50,641
Annual Hours of Delay, Per Auto Commuter	14	29	41	48	57
Annual Congestion Cost, Total (million $)	26	115	360	706	926
Annual Congestion Cost, Per Auto Commuter ($)	195	423	809	939	1,158

Note: Covers the Charlotte NC-SC urban area
Source: Texas A&M Transportation Institute, 2019 Urban Mobility Report

Freeway Travel Time Index

Measure	1982	1987	1992	1997	2002	2007	2012	2017
Urban Area Index[1]	1.08	1.11	1.15	1.18	1.22	1.25	1.24	1.22
Urban Area Rank[1,2]	28	29	26	28	29	27	26	33

Note: Freeway Travel Time Index—the ratio of travel time in the peak period to the travel time at free-flow conditions. For example, a value of 1.30 indicates a 20-minute free-flow trip takes 26 minutes in the peak (20 minutes x 1.30 = 26 minutes); (1) Covers the Charlotte NC-SC urban area; (2) Rank is based on 101 larger urban areas (#1 = highest travel time index)
Source: Texas A&M Transportation Institute, 2019 Urban Mobility Report

Public Transportation

Agency Name / Mode of Transportation	Vehicles Operated in Maximum Service[1]	Annual Unlinked Passenger Trips[2] (in thous.)	Annual Passenger Miles[3] (in thous.)
Charlotte Area Transit System (CATS)			
Bus (purchased transportation)	187	14,932.7	63,280.3
Commuter Bus (purchased transportation)	65	691.2	9,787.0
Demand Response (directly operated)	73	256.2	2,707.4
Light Rail (directly operated)	36	8,006.9	45,024.7
Streetcar Rail (directly operated)	2	279.7	256.6
Vanpool (directly operated)	48	112.1	5,084.1

Note: (1) Number of revenue vehicles operated by the given mode and type of service to meet the annual maximum service requirement. This is the revenue vehicle count during the peak season of the year; on the week and day that maximum service is provided. Vehicles operated in maximum service (VOMS) exclude atypical days and one-time special events; (2) Number of passengers who boarded public transportation vehicles. Passengers are counted each time they board a vehicle no matter how many vehicles they use to travel from their origin to their destination. (3) Sum of the distances ridden by all passengers during the entire fiscal year.
Source: Federal Transit Administration, National Transit Database, 2019

Air Transportation

Airport Name and Code / Type of Service	Passenger Airlines[1]	Passenger Enplanements	Freight Carriers[2]	Freight (lbs)
Charlotte-Douglas International (CLT)				
Domestic service (U.S. carriers - 2020)	21	12,426,504	15	144,036,362
International service (U.S. carriers - 2019)	10	1,645,906	5	18,153,687

Note: (1) Includes all U.S.-based major, minor and commuter airlines that carried at least one passenger during the year; (2) Includes all U.S.-based airlines and freight carriers that transported at least one pound of freight during the year.
Source: Bureau of Transportation Statistics, The Intermodal Transportation Database, Air Carriers: T-100 Domestic Market (U.S. Carriers), 2020; Bureau of Transportation Statistics, The Intermodal Transportation Database, Air Carriers: T-100 International Market (U.S. Carriers), 2019

BUSINESSES

Major Business Headquarters

Company Name	Industry	Rankings	
		Fortune[1]	Forbes[2]
Bank of America	Commercial Banks	25	-
Belk	Retailing	-	130
Brighthouse Financial	Insurance, Life, Health (Stock)	457	-
Duke Energy	Utilities, Gas and Electric	123	-
Nucor	Metals	139	-
Sonic Automotive	Automotive Retailing, Services	301	-
Truist Financial	Superregional Banks	217	-

Note: (1) Companies that produce a 10-K are ranked 1 to 500 based on 2019 revenue; (2) All private companies with at least $2 billion in annual revenue through the end of their most current fiscal year are ranked 1 to 219; companies listed are headquartered in the city; dashes indicate no ranking
Source: Fortune, "Fortune 500," June/July 2020; Forbes, "America's Largest Private Companies," 2020

Fastest-Growing Businesses

According to *Inc.*, Charlotte is home to four of America's 500 fastest-growing private companies: **BlueDot Cares** (#96); **MedShift** (#185); **Sunlight Financial** (#205); **SeedSpark** (#244). Criteria: must be an independent, privately-held, for-profit, U.S. corporation, proprietorship or partnership as of December 31, 2019; revenues must be at least $100,000 in 2016 and $2 million in 2019; must have four-year operating/sales history. *Inc., "America's 500 Fastest-Growing Private Companies," 2020*

According to Deloitte, Charlotte is home to two of North America's 500 fastest-growing high-technology companies: **Passport** (#246); **Printful** (#254). Companies are ranked by percentage growth in revenue over a four-year period. Criteria for inclusion: company must be headquartered within North America; must own proprietary intellectual property or technology that is sold to customers in products that contributes to a significant portion of the company's operating revenue; must have been in business for a minumum of four years with 2016 operating revenues of at least $50,000 USD/CD and 2019 operating revenues of at least $5 million USD/CD. *Deloitte, 2020 Technology Fast 500*[TM]

Living Environment

COST OF LIVING

Cost of Living Index

Composite Index	Groceries	Housing	Utilities	Trans-portation	Health Care	Misc. Goods/ Services
97.7	102.8	84.2	96.1	101.6	104.2	104.8

Note: The Cost of Living Index measures regional differences in the cost of consumer goods and services, excluding taxes and non-consumer expenditures, for professional and managerial households in the top income quintile. It is based on more than 50,000 prices covering almost 60 different items for which prices are collected three times a year by chambers of commerce, economic development organizations or university applied economic centers in each participating urban area. The numbers shown should be read as a percentage above or below the national average of 100. For example, a value of 115.4 in the groceries column indicates that grocery prices are 15.4% higher than the national average. Small differences in the index numbers should not be interpreted as significant; Figures cover the Charlotte NC urban area.
Source: The Council for Community and Economic Research, Cost of Living Index, 2020

Grocery Prices

Area[1]	T-Bone Steak ($/pound)	Frying Chicken ($/pound)	Whole Milk ($/half gal.)	Eggs ($/dozen)	Orange Juice ($/64 oz.)	Coffee ($/11.5 oz.)
City[2]	12.19	1.46	1.69	1.34	3.54	4.02
Avg.	11.78	1.39	2.05	1.47	3.57	4.34
Min.	8.03	0.94	1.03	0.74	2.94	3.02
Max.	15.86	2.65	4.31	3.77	5.44	8.69

*Note: (1) Values for the local area are compared with the average, minimum and maximum values for all 284 areas in the Cost of Living Index; (2) Figures cover the Charlotte NC urban area; **T-Bone Steak** (price per pound); **Frying Chicken** (price per pound, whole fryer); **Whole Milk** (half gallon carton); **Eggs** (price per dozen, Grade A, large); **Orange Juice** (64 oz. Tropicana or Florida Natural); **Coffee** (11.5 oz. can, vacuum-packed, Maxwell House, Hills Bros, or Folgers).*
Source: The Council for Community and Economic Research, Cost of Living Index, 2020

Housing and Utility Costs

Area[1]	New Home Price ($)	Apartment Rent ($/month)	All Electric ($/month)	Part Electric ($/month)	Other Energy ($/month)	Telephone ($/month)
City[2]	269,325	1,257	158.05	-	-	179.90
Avg.	368,594	1,168	170.86	100.47	65.28	184.30
Min.	190,567	502	91.58	31.42	26.08	169.60
Max.	2,227,806	4,738	470.38	280.31	280.06	206.50

*Note: (1) Values for the local area are compared with the average, minimum and maximum values for all 284 areas in the Cost of Living Index; (2) Figures cover the Charlotte NC urban area; **New Home Price** (2,400 sf living area, 8,000 sf lot, in urban area with full utilities), unfurnished, excluding all utilities except water); **Apartment Rent** (950 sf 2 bedroom/1.5 or 2 bath, unfurnished, excluding all utilities except water); **All Electric** (average monthly cost for an all-electric home); **Part Electric** (average monthly cost for a part-electric home); **Other Energy** (average monthly cost for natural gas, fuel oil, coal, wood, and any other forms of energy except electricity); **Telephone** (price includes the base monthly rate plus taxes and fees for three lines of mobile phone service).*
Source: The Council for Community and Economic Research, Cost of Living Index, 2020

Health Care, Transportation, and Other Costs

Area[1]	Doctor ($/visit)	Dentist ($/visit)	Optometrist ($/visit)	Gasoline ($/gallon)	Beauty Salon ($/visit)	Men's Shirt ($)
City[2]	121.12	112.88	119.06	2.35	39.10	31.86
Avg.	115.44	99.32	108.10	2.21	39.27	31.37
Min.	36.68	59.00	51.36	1.71	19.00	11.00
Max.	219.00	153.10	250.97	3.46	82.05	58.33

*Note: (1) Values for the local area are compared with the average, minimum and maximum values for all 284 areas in the Cost of Living Index; (2) Figures cover the Charlotte NC urban area; **Doctor** (general practitioners routine exam of an established patient); **Dentist** (adult teeth cleaning and periodic oral examination); **Optometrist** (full vision eye exam for established adult patient); **Gasoline** (one gallon regular unleaded, national brand, including all taxes, cash price at self-service pump if available); **Beauty Salon** (woman's shampoo, trim, and blow-dry); **Men's Shirt** (cotton/polyester dress shirt, pinpoint weave, long sleeves).*
Source: The Council for Community and Economic Research, Cost of Living Index, 2020

HOUSING

Homeownership Rate

Area	2012 (%)	2013 (%)	2014 (%)	2015 (%)	2016 (%)	2017 (%)	2018 (%)	2019 (%)	2020 (%)
MSA[1]	58.3	58.9	58.1	62.3	66.2	64.6	67.9	72.3	73.3
U.S.	65.4	65.1	64.5	63.7	63.4	63.9	64.4	64.6	66.6

Note: (1) Figures cover the Charlotte-Concord-Gastonia, NC-SC Metropolitan Statistical Area
Source: U.S. Census Bureau, Housing Vacancies and Homeownership Annual Statistics: 2012-2020

House Price Index (HPI)

Area	National Ranking[2]	Quarterly Change (%)	One-Year Change (%)	Five-Year Change (%)	Since 1991Q1 (%)
MSA[1]	60	2.55	7.46	41.48	183.15
U.S.[3]	–	3.81	10.77	38.99	205.12

Note: The HPI is a weighted repeat sales index. It measures average price changes in repeat sales or refinancings on the same properties. This information is obtained by reviewing repeat mortgage transactions on single-family properties whose mortgages have been purchased or securitized by Fannie Mae or Freddie Mac since January 1975; (1) Figures cover the Charlotte-Concord-Gastonia, NC-SC Metropolitan Statistical Area; (2) Rankings are based on annual percentage change for all metro areas containing at least 15,000 transactions over the last 10 years and ranges from 1 to 253; (3) figures based on a weighted average of Census Division estimates using a seasonally adjusted, purchase-only index; all figures are for the period ending December 31, 2020
Source: Federal Housing Finance Agency, Change in Metropolitan Area House Price Indexes, April 7, 2021

Median Single-Family Home Prices

Area	2018	2019	2020p	Percent Change 2019 to 2020
MSA[1]	241.5	258.6	296.2	14.5
U.S. Average	261.6	274.6	299.9	9.2

Note: Figures are median sales prices of existing single-family homes in thousands of dollars; (p) preliminary; (1) Figures cover the Charlotte-Concord-Gastonia, NC-SC Metropolitan Statistical Area
Source: National Association of Realtors, Median Sales Price of Existing Single-Family Homes for Metropolitan Areas, 4th Quarter 2020

Qualifying Income Based on Median Sales Price of Existing Single-Family Homes

Area	With 5% Down ($)	With 10% Down ($)	With 20% Down ($)
MSA[1]	59,012	55,906	49,695
U.S. Average	59,266	56,147	49,908

Note: Figures are preliminary; Qualifying income is based on a mortgage rate of 2.81%. Monthly principal and interest payment is limited to 25% of income; (1) Figures cover the Charlotte-Concord-Gastonia, NC-SC Metropolitan Statistical Area
Source: National Association of Realtors, Qualifying Income Based on Median Sales Price of Existing Single-Family Homes for Metropolitan Areas, 4th Quarter 2020

Home Value Distribution

Area	Under $50,000	$50,000 -$99,999	$100,000 -$149,999	$150,000 -$199,999	$200,000 -$299,999	$300,000 -$499,999	$500,000 -$999,999	$1,000,000 or more
City	2.1	8.2	17.3	17.6	21.0	19.5	10.9	3.4
MSA[1]	4.8	11.4	16.7	17.1	21.5	18.7	7.8	1.9
U.S.	6.9	12.0	13.3	14.0	19.6	19.3	11.4	3.4

Note: Figures are percentages and cover owner-occupied housing units; (1) Figures cover the Charlotte-Concord-Gastonia, NC-SC Metropolitan Statistical Area
Source: U.S. Census Bureau, 2015-2019 American Community Survey 5-Year Estimates

Year Housing Structure Built

Area	2010 or Later	2000 -2009	1990 -1999	1980 -1989	1970 -1979	1960 -1969	1950 -1959	1940 -1949	Before 1940	Median Year
City	8.9	23.1	19.4	15.1	12.0	9.5	6.6	2.6	2.8	1991
MSA[1]	9.2	24.1	19.5	13.5	11.5	8.4	6.5	3.1	4.2	1991
U.S.	5.2	14.0	13.9	13.4	15.2	10.6	10.3	4.9	12.6	1978

Note: Figures are percentages except for Median Year; Note: (1) Figures cover the Charlotte-Concord-Gastonia, NC-SC Metropolitan Statistical Area
Source: U.S. Census Bureau, 2015-2019 American Community Survey 5-Year Estimates

Gross Monthly Rent

Area	Under $500	$500 -$999	$1,000 -$1,499	$1,500 -$1,999	$2,000 -$2,499	$2,500 -$2,999	$3,000 and up	Median ($)
City	3.8	30.9	46.3	14.5	2.9	0.8	0.7	1,135
MSA[1]	6.1	41.0	37.9	11.2	2.4	0.8	0.6	1,030
U.S.	9.4	36.2	30.0	14.0	5.6	2.4	2.4	1,062

Note: Figures are percentages except for Median; Gross rent is the contract rent plus the estimated average monthly cost of utilities (electricity, gas, and water and sewer) and fuels (oil, coal, kerosene, wood, etc.) if these are paid by the renter (or paid for the renter by someone else); (1) Figures cover the Charlotte-Concord-Gastonia, NC-SC Metropolitan Statistical Area
Source: U.S. Census Bureau, 2015-2019 American Community Survey 5-Year Estimates

HEALTH

Health Risk Factors

Category	MSA[1] (%)	U.S. (%)
Adults aged 18–64 who have any kind of health care coverage	82.6	87.3
Adults who reported being in good or better health	82.1	82.4
Adults who have been told they have high blood cholesterol	35.4	33.0
Adults who have been told they have high blood pressure	32.4	32.3
Adults who are current smokers	14.6	17.1
Adults who currently use E-cigarettes	5.2	4.6
Adults who currently use chewing tobacco, snuff, or snus	3.5	4.0
Adults who are heavy drinkers[2]	7.6	6.3
Adults who are binge drinkers[3]	17.9	17.4
Adults who are overweight (BMI 25.0 - 29.9)	34.0	35.3
Adults who are obese (BMI 30.0 - 99.8)	33.8	31.3
Adults who participated in any physical activities in the past month	74.5	74.4
Adults who always or nearly always wears a seat belt	96.3	94.3

Note: (1) Figures cover the Charlotte-Concord-Gastonia, NC-SC Metropolitan Statistical Area; (2) Heavy drinkers are classified as adult men having more than 14 drinks per week and adult women having more than 7 drinks per week; (3) Binge drinkers are classified as males having five or more drinks on one occasion or females having four or more drinks on one occasion
Source: Centers for Disease Control and Prevention, Behaviorial Risk Factor Surveillance System, SMART: Selected Metropolitan Area Risk Trends, 2017

Acute and Chronic Health Conditions

Category	MSA[1] (%)	U.S. (%)
Adults who have ever been told they had a heart attack	4.0	4.2
Adults who have ever been told they have angina or coronary heart disease	3.2	3.9
Adults who have ever been told they had a stroke	3.7	3.0
Adults who have ever been told they have asthma	13.3	14.2
Adults who have ever been told they have arthritis	22.8	24.9
Adults who have ever been told they have diabetes[2]	11.0	10.5
Adults who have ever been told they had skin cancer	7.1	6.2
Adults who have ever been told they had any other types of cancer	7.4	7.1
Adults who have ever been told they have COPD	7.6	6.5
Adults who have ever been told they have kidney disease	4.1	3.0
Adults who have ever been told they have a form of depression	18.8	20.5

Note: (1) Figures cover the Charlotte-Concord-Gastonia, NC-SC Metropolitan Statistical Area; (2) Figures do not include pregnancy-related, borderline, or pre-diabetes
Source: Centers for Disease Control and Prevention, Behaviorial Risk Factor Surveillance System, SMART: Selected Metropolitan Area Risk Trends, 2017

Health Screening and Vaccination Rates

Category	MSA[1] (%)	U.S. (%)
Adults aged 65+ who have had flu shot within the past year	68.5	60.7
Adults aged 65+ who have ever had a pneumonia vaccination	77.2	75.4
Adults who have ever been tested for HIV	43.9	36.1
Adults who have ever had the shingles or zoster vaccine?	28.1	28.9
Adults who have had their blood cholesterol checked within the last five years	87.9	85.9

Note: n/a not available; (1) Figures cover the Charlotte-Concord-Gastonia, NC-SC Metropolitan Statistical Area.
Source: Centers for Disease Control and Prevention, Behaviorial Risk Factor Surveillance System, SMART: Selected Metropolitan Area Risk Trends, 2017

Disability Status

Category	MSA[1] (%)	U.S. (%)
Adults who reported being deaf	6.5	6.7
Are you blind or have serious difficulty seeing, even when wearing glasses?	4.2	4.5
Are you limited in any way in any of your usual activities due of arthritis?	11.0	12.9
Do you have difficulty doing errands alone?	6.3	6.8
Do you have difficulty dressing or bathing?	3.3	3.6
Do you have serious difficulty concentrating/remembering/making decisions?	10.4	10.7
Do you have serious difficulty walking or climbing stairs?	12.1	13.6

Note: (1) Figures cover the Charlotte-Concord-Gastonia, NC-SC Metropolitan Statistical Area.
Source: Centers for Disease Control and Prevention, Behaviorial Risk Factor Surveillance System, SMART: Selected Metropolitan Area Risk Trends, 2017

Mortality Rates for the Top 10 Causes of Death in the U.S.

ICD-10[a] Sub-Chapter	ICD-10[a] Code	Age-Adjusted Mortality Rate[1] per 100,000 population	
		County[2]	U.S.
Malignant neoplasms	C00-C97	132.8	149.2
Ischaemic heart diseases	I20-I25	48.5	90.5
Other forms of heart disease	I30-I51	58.1	52.2
Chronic lower respiratory diseases	J40-J47	28.9	39.6
Other degenerative diseases of the nervous system	G30-G31	54.2	37.6
Cerebrovascular diseases	I60-I69	38.5	37.2
Other external causes of accidental injury	W00-X59	29.6	36.1
Organic, including symptomatic, mental disorders	F01-F09	29.8	29.4
Hypertensive diseases	I10-I15	15.5	24.1
Diabetes mellitus	E10-E14	19.0	21.5

Note: (a) ICD-10 = International Classification of Diseases 10th Revision; (1) Mortality rates are a three-year average covering 2017-2019; (2) Figures cover Mecklenburg County.
Source: Centers for Disease Control and Prevention, National Center for Health Statistics. Underlying Cause of Death 1999-2019 on CDC WONDER Online Database

Mortality Rates for Selected Causes of Death

ICD-10[a] Sub-Chapter	ICD-10[a] Code	Age-Adjusted Mortality Rate[1] per 100,000 population	
		County[2]	U.S.
Assault	X85-Y09	8.1	6.0
Diseases of the liver	K70-K76	11.2	14.4
Human immunodeficiency virus (HIV) disease	B20-B24	2.6	1.5
Influenza and pneumonia	J09-J18	11.7	13.8
Intentional self-harm	X60-X84	9.4	14.1
Malnutrition	E40-E46	8.8	2.3
Obesity and other hyperalimentation	E65-E68	1.8	2.1
Renal failure	N17-N19	16.2	12.6
Transport accidents	V01-V99	9.6	12.3
Viral hepatitis	B15-B19	1.1	1.2

Note: (a) ICD-10 = International Classification of Diseases 10th Revision; (1) Mortality rates are a three-year average covering 2017-2019; (2) Figures cover Mecklenburg County; Data are suppressed when the data meet the criteria for confidentiality constraints; Mortality rates are flagged as unreliable when the rate would be calculated with a numerator of 20 or less.
Source: Centers for Disease Control and Prevention, National Center for Health Statistics. Underlying Cause of Death 1999-2019 on CDC WONDER Online Database

Health Insurance Coverage

Area	With Health Insurance	With Private Health Insurance	With Public Health Insurance	Without Health Insurance	Population Under Age 19 Without Health Insurance
City	87.5	68.5	26.3	12.5	6.4
MSA[1]	89.8	70.7	29.3	10.2	4.8
U.S.	91.2	67.9	35.1	8.8	5.1

Note: Figures are percentages that cover the civilian noninstitutionalized population; (1) Figures cover the Charlotte-Concord-Gastonia, NC-SC Metropolitan Statistical Area
Source: U.S. Census Bureau, 2015-2019 American Community Survey 5-Year Estimates

Number of Medical Professionals

Area	MDs[3]	DOs[3,4]	Dentists	Podiatrists	Chiropractors	Optometrists
County[1] (number)	3,605	155	776	38	364	156
County[1] (rate[2])	329.6	14.2	69.9	3.4	32.8	14.0
U.S. (rate[2])	282.9	22.7	71.2	6.2	28.1	16.9

37119
Note: Data as of 2019 unless noted; (1) Data covers Mecklenburg County; (2) Rate per 100,000 population; (3) Data as of 2018 and includes all active, non-federal physicians; (4) Doctor of Osteopathic Medicine
Source: U.S. Department of Health and Human Services, Health Resources and Services Administration, Bureau of Health Professions, Area Resource File (ARF) 2019-2020

Best Hospitals

According to *U.S. News,* the Charlotte-Concord-Gastonia, NC-SC metro area is home to one of the best hospitals in the U.S.: **Levine Cancer Institute** (1 adult specialty and 8 pediatric specialties). The hospital listed was nationally ranked in at least one of 16 adult or 10 pediatric specialties. Only 134 hospitals nationwide were nationally ranked in one or more adult or pediatric specialty; this number increases to 178 counting specialized centers within hospitals. Twenty hospitals in the U.S. made the Honor Roll. The Best Hospitals Honor Roll takes both the national rankings and the procedure and condition ratings into account. Hospitals received points if they were nationally ranked in one of the 16 adult specialties—the higher they ranked, the more points they got—and how many ratings of "high performing" they earned in the 10 procedures and conditions. *U.S. News Online, "America's Best Hospitals 2020-21"*

According to *U.S. News*, the Charlotte-Concord-Gastonia, NC-SC metro area is home to one of the best children's hospitals in the U.S.: **Levine Children's Hospital** (8 pediatric specialties). The hospital listed was highly ranked in at least one of 10 pediatric specialties. Eighty-eight children's hospitals in the U.S. were nationally ranked in at least one specialty. Hospitals received points for being ranked in a specialty, and the 10 hospitals with the most points across the 10 specialties make up the Honor Roll. *U.S. News Online, "America's Best Children's Hospitals 2020-21"*

EDUCATION

Public School District Statistics

District Name	Schls	Pupils	Pupil/ Teacher Ratio	Minority Pupils[1] (%)	Free Lunch Eligible[2] (%)	IEP[3] (%)
Charlotte-Mecklenburg Schools	175	147,638	16.2	72.4	54.6	9.8

Note: Table includes school districts with 2,000 or more students; (1) Percentage of students that are not non-Hispanic white; (2) Percentage of students that are eligible for the free lunch program; (3) Percentage of students that have an Individualized Education Program.
Source: U.S. Department of Education, National Center for Education Statistics, Common Core of Data, Local Education Agency (School District) Universe Survey: School Year 2018-2019; U.S. Department of Education, National Center for Education Statistics, Common Core of Data, Public Elementary/Secondary School Universe Survey: School Year 2018-2019

Best High Schools

According to *U.S. News,* Charlotte is home to one of the top 500 high schools in the U.S.: **Cato Middle College High** (#217). Nearly 18,000 public, magnet and charter schools were ranked based on their performance on state assessments and how well they prepare students for college. *U.S. News & World Report, "Best High Schools 2020"*

Highest Level of Education

Area	Less than H.S.	H.S. Diploma	Some College, No Deg.	Associate Degree	Bachelor's Degree	Master's Degree	Prof. School Degree	Doctorate Degree
City	10.9	17.1	20.0	7.7	28.9	11.7	2.6	1.1
MSA[1]	11.0	23.5	21.1	9.2	23.5	9.0	1.8	0.9
U.S.	12.0	27.0	20.4	8.5	19.8	8.8	2.1	1.4

Note: Figures cover persons age 25 and over; (1) Figures cover the Charlotte-Concord-Gastonia, NC-SC Metropolitan Statistical Area
Source: U.S. Census Bureau, 2015-2019 American Community Survey 5-Year Estimates

Educational Attainment by Race

Area	High School Graduate or Higher (%)					Bachelor's Degree or Higher (%)				
	Total	White	Black	Asian	Hisp.[2]	Total	White	Black	Asian	Hisp.[2]
City	89.1	92.7	90.4	81.4	60.0	44.3	55.4	29.4	58.3	17.0
MSA[1]	89.0	90.8	88.4	84.9	63.1	35.1	37.7	25.9	58.1	17.7
U.S.	88.0	89.9	86.0	87.1	68.7	32.1	33.5	21.6	54.3	16.4

Note: Figures shown cover persons 25 years old and over; (1) Figures cover the Charlotte-Concord-Gastonia, NC-SC Metropolitan Statistical Area; (2) People of Hispanic origin can be of any race
Source: U.S. Census Bureau, 2015-2019 American Community Survey 5-Year Estimates

School Enrollment by Grade and Control

Area	Preschool (%)		Kindergarten (%)		Grades 1 - 4 (%)		Grades 5 - 8 (%)		Grades 9 - 12 (%)	
	Public	Private	Public	Private	Public	Private	Public	Private	Public	Private
City	47.5	52.5	90.5	9.5	90.7	9.3	87.6	12.4	89.8	10.2
MSA[1]	50.2	49.8	90.0	10.0	90.5	9.5	88.9	11.1	90.4	9.6
U.S.	59.1	40.9	87.6	12.4	89.5	10.5	89.4	10.6	90.1	9.9

Note: Figures shown cover persons 3 years old and over; (1) Figures cover the Charlotte-Concord-Gastonia, NC-SC Metropolitan Statistical Area
Source: U.S. Census Bureau, 2015-2019 American Community Survey 5-Year Estimates

Higher Education

Four-Year Colleges			Two-Year Colleges			Medical Schools[1]	Law Schools[2]	Voc/ Tech[3]
Public	Private Non-profit	Private For-profit	Public	Private Non-profit	Private For-profit			
2	4	3	1	0	1	0	1	5

Note: Figures cover institutions located within the city limits and include main campuses only; (1) includes schools accredited by the Liaison Committee on Medical Education and the American Osteopathic Association's Commission on Osteopathic College Accreditation; (2) includes ABA-accredited schools, schools with provisional ABA accreditation, and state accredited schools; (3) includes all schools with programs that are less than 2 years.
Source: National Center for Education Statistics, Integrated Postsecondary Education System (IPEDS), 2019-20; Wikipedia, List of Medical Schools in the United States, accessed April 2, 2021; Wikipedia, List of Law Schools in the United States, accessed April 2, 2021

According to *U.S. News & World Report,* the Charlotte-Concord-Gastonia, NC-SC metro area is home to one of the top 100 liberal arts colleges in the U.S.: **Davidson College** (#15 tie). The indicators used to capture academic quality fall into a number of categories: assessment by administrators at peer institutions; retention of students; faculty resources; student selectivity; financial resources; alumni giving; high school counselor ratings of colleges; and graduation rate. *U.S. News & World Report, "America's Best Colleges 2021"*

EMPLOYERS

Major Employers

Company Name	Industry
Bank of America, National Association	National commercial banks
Carlisle Companies Incorporated	Fabricated rubber products
Carolina Medical Center Northeast	General medical & surgical hospitals
Carolina Medical Center Union	General medical & surgical hospitals
Charlotte Mecklenburg Hospital Authority	General medical & surgical hospitals
Compass Group North America	Services
Duke Energy	Electric services
IBM	Office equipment
Insource Performance Solutions	Help supply services
Medcath Incorporated	Specialty hospitals, except psychiatric
Merchandising Corporation of America	Business consulting
Microsoft	Computer peripheral equipment
Polymer Group	Nonwoven fabrics
Presbyterian Hospital	General medical & surgical hospitals
RohrCredit Corporation	Aircraft engines & engine parts
University of NC at Chapel Hill	Colleges & universities
Wachovia Corporation	National commercial banks
Wells Fargo	Banking and financial services

Note: Companies shown are located within the Charlotte-Concord-Gastonia, NC-SC Metropolitan Statistical Area.
Source: Hoovers.com; Wikipedia

Best Companies to Work For

Bank of America, headquartered in Charlotte, is among "The 100 Best Companies to Work For." To pick the best companies, *Fortune* partnered with the Great Place to Work Institute. Two-thirds of a company's score is based on the results of the Institute's Trust Index survey, which is sent to a random sample of employees from each company. The questions related to attitudes about management's credibility, job satisfaction, and camaraderie. The other third of the scoring is based on the company's responses to the Institute's Culture Audit, which includes detailed questions about pay and benefit programs, and a series of open-ended questions about hiring practices, internal communication, training, recognition programs, and diversity efforts. Any company that is at least five years old with more than 1,000 U.S. employees is eligible. *Fortune, "The 100 Best Companies to Work For," 2020*

Bank of America, headquartered in Charlotte, is among the "100 Best Companies for Working Mothers." Criteria: paid time off and leaves; workforce profile; benefits; women's issues and advancement; flexible work; company culture and work life programs. *Working Mother, "100 Best Companies for Working Mothers," 2020*

Bank of America, headquartered in Charlotte, is among the "Best Companies for Multicultural Women." *Working Mother* selected 50 companies based on a detailed application completed by public and private firms based in the United States, excluding government agencies, companies in the human resources field and non-autonomous divisions. Companies supplied data about the hiring, pay, and promotion of multicultural employees. Applications focused on representation of multicultural women, recruitment, retention and advancement programs, and company culture. *Working Mother, "Best Companies for Multicultural Women," 2020*

Atrium Health, headquartered in Charlotte, is among the "100 Best Places to Work in IT." To qualify, companies had to be U.S.-based organizations or be non-U.S.-based employers that met the following criteria: have a minimum of 300 total employees at a U.S. headquarters and a minimum of 30

IT employees in the U.S., with at least 50% of their IT employees based in the U.S. The best places to work were selected based on compensation, benefits, work/life balance, employee morale, and satisfaction with training and development programs. In addition, *InsiderPro* and *Computerworld* looked at retention efforts, programs for recognizing and rewarding outstanding performances, and benefits such as flextime, elder care and child care, and reimbursement for college tuition and the cost of pursuing technology certifications. *InsiderPro and Computerworld, "100 Best Places to Work in IT," 2020*

Bank of America, headquartered in Charlotte, is among the "Top Companies for Executive Women." This list is determined by organizations filling out an in-depth survey that measures female demographics at every level, but with an emphasis on women in senior corporate roles, with profit & loss (P&L) responsibility, and those earning in the top 20 percent of the organization. *Working Mother* defines P&L as having responsibility that involves monitoring the net income after expenses for a department or entire organization, with direct influence on how company resources are allocated. *Working Mother, "Top Companies for Executive Women," 2020+*

Bank of America, headquartered in Charlotte, is among the "Best Companies for Dads." *Working Mother's* newest list recognizes the growing importance companies place on giving dads time off and support for their families. Rankings are determined by measuring gender-neutral or paternity leave offered, as well as actual time taken, phase-back policies, child- and dependent-care benefits, and corporate support groups for men and dads. *Working Mother, "Best Companies for Dads," 2020*

PUBLIC SAFETY

Crime Rate

Area	All Crimes	Violent Crimes				Property Crimes		
		Murder	Rape[3]	Robbery	Aggrav. Assault	Burglary	Larceny -Theft	Motor Vehicle Theft
City	4,665.2	10.9	33.6	209.2	485.8	574.6	2,997.5	353.7
Suburbs[1]	n/a	n/a	n/a	n/a	n/a	n/a	n/a	n/a
Metro[2]	n/a	n/a	n/a	n/a	n/a	n/a	n/a	n/a
U.S.	2,489.3	5.0	42.6	81.6	250.2	340.5	1,549.5	219.9

Note: Figures are crimes per 100,000 population; (1) All areas within the metro area that are located outside the city limits; (2) Figures cover the Charlotte-Concord-Gastonia, NC-SC Metropolitan Statistical Area; n/a not available; (3) All figures shown were reported using the revised Uniform Crime Reporting (UCR) definition of rape.
Source: FBI Uniform Crime Reports, 2019

Hate Crimes

Area	Number of Quarters Reported	Number of Incidents per Bias Motivation					
		Race/Ethnicity/ Ancestry	Religion	Sexual Orientation	Disability	Gender	Gender Identity
City	4	10	7	1	0	0	0
U.S.	4	3,963	1,521	1,195	157	69	198

Source: Federal Bureau of Investigation, Hate Crime Statistics 2019

Identity Theft Consumer Reports

Area	Reports	Reports per 100,000 Population	Rank[2]
MSA[1]	9,522	361	91
U.S.	1,387,615	423	-

Note: (1) Figures cover the Charlotte-Concord-Gastonia, NC-SC Metropolitan Statistical Area; (2) Rank ranges from 1 to 391 where 1 indicates greatest number of identity theft reports per 100,000 population
Source: Federal Trade Commission, Consumer Sentinel Network Data Book 2020

Fraud and Other Consumer Reports

Area	Reports	Reports per 100,000 Population	Rank[2]
MSA[1]	26,802	1,016	19
U.S.	3,385,133	1,031	-

Note: (1) Figures cover the Charlotte-Concord-Gastonia, NC-SC Metropolitan Statistical Area; (2) Rank ranges from 1 to 391 where 1 indicates greatest number of fraud and other consumer reports per 100,000 population
Source: Federal Trade Commission, Consumer Sentinel Network Data Book 2020

POLITICS

2020 Presidential Election Results

Area	Biden	Trump	Jorgensen	Hawkins	Other
Mecklenburg County	66.7	31.6	1.0	0.3	0.5
U.S.	51.3	46.8	1.2	0.3	0.5

Note: Results are percentages and may not add to 100% due to rounding
Source: Dave Leip's Atlas of U.S. Presidential Elections

SPORTS

Professional Sports Teams

Team Name	League	Year Established
Carolina Panthers	National Football League (NFL)	1995
Charlotte FC	Major League Soccer (MLS)	2022
Charlotte Hornets	National Basketball Association (NBA)	2004

Note: Includes teams located in the Charlotte-Concord-Gastonia, NC-SC Metropolitan Statistical Area.
Source: Wikipedia, Major Professional Sports Teams of the United States and Canada, April 6, 2021

CLIMATE

Average and Extreme Temperatures

Temperature	Jan	Feb	Mar	Apr	May	Jun	Jul	Aug	Sep	Oct	Nov	Dec	Yr.
Extreme High (°F)	78	81	86	93	97	103	103	103	104	98	85	77	104
Average High (°F)	51	54	62	72	80	86	89	88	82	72	62	53	71
Average Temp. (°F)	41	44	51	61	69	76	79	78	72	61	51	43	61
Average Low (°F)	31	33	40	48	57	65	69	68	62	50	40	33	50
Extreme Low (°F)	-5	5	4	25	32	45	53	53	39	24	11	2	-5

Note: Figures cover the years 1948-1990
Source: National Climatic Data Center, International Station Meteorological Climate Summary, 9/96

Average Precipitation/Snowfall/Humidity

Precip./Humidity	Jan	Feb	Mar	Apr	May	Jun	Jul	Aug	Sep	Oct	Nov	Dec	Yr.
Avg. Precip. (in.)	3.6	3.8	4.5	3.0	3.7	3.4	3.9	3.9	3.4	3.2	3.1	3.4	42.8
Avg. Snowfall (in.)	2	2	1	Tr	0	0	0	0	0	0	Tr	1	6
Avg. Rel. Hum. 7am (%)	78	77	78	78	82	83	86	89	89	87	83	79	82
Avg. Rel. Hum. 4pm (%)	53	49	46	43	49	51	54	55	54	50	50	54	51

Note: Figures cover the years 1948-1990; Tr = Trace amounts (<0.05 in. of rain; <0.5 in. of snow)
Source: National Climatic Data Center, International Station Meteorological Climate Summary, 9/96

Weather Conditions

Temperature			Daytime Sky			Precipitation		
10°F & below	32°F & below	90°F & above	Clear	Partly cloudy	Cloudy	0.01 inch or more precip.	0.1 inch or more snow/ice	Thunder-storms
1	65	44	98	142	125	113	3	41

Note: Figures are average number of days per year and cover the years 1948-1990
Source: National Climatic Data Center, International Station Meteorological Climate Summary, 9/96

HAZARDOUS WASTE

Superfund Sites

The Charlotte-Concord-Gastonia, NC-SC metro area is home to 12 sites on the EPA's Superfund National Priorities List: **Bypass 601 Ground Water Contamination** (final); **Carolawn, Inc.** (final); **Davis Park Road Tce** (final); **FCX, Inc. (Statesville Plant)** (final); **Hemphill Road Tce** (final); **Jadco-Hughes Facility** (final); **Leonard Chemical Co., Inc.** (final); **National Starch & Chemical Corp.** (final); **North Belmont Pce** (final); **Ram Leather Care Site** (final); **Rock Hill Chemical Co.** (final); **Sigmon's Septic Tank Service** (final). There are a total of 1,375 Superfund sites with a status of proposed or final on the list in the U.S. *U.S. Environmental Protection Agency, National Priorities List, April 7, 2021*

AIR QUALITY

Air Quality Trends: Ozone

	1990	1995	2000	2005	2010	2015	2016	2017	2018	2019
MSA[1]	n/a	n/a	n/a	n/a	n/a	n/a	n/a	n/a	n/a	n/a
U.S.	0.088	0.089	0.082	0.080	0.073	0.068	0.069	0.068	0.069	0.065

Note: (1) Data covers the Charlotte-Concord-Gastonia, NC-SC Metropolitan Statistical Area; n/a not available. The values shown are the composite ozone concentration averages among trend sites based on the highest fourth daily maximum 8-hour concentration in parts per million. These trends are based on sites having an adequate record of monitoring data during the trend period. Data from exceptional events are included.
Source: U.S. Environmental Protection Agency, Air Quality Monitoring Information, "Air Quality Trends by City, 1990-2019"

Air Quality Index

Area	Percent of Days when Air Quality was...[2]					AQI Statistics[2]	
	Good	Moderate	Unhealthy for Sensitive Groups	Unhealthy	Very Unhealthy	Maximum	Median
MSA[1]	54.8	40.3	4.9	0.0	0.0	136	49

Note: (1) Data covers the Charlotte-Concord-Gastonia, NC-SC Metropolitan Statistical Area; (2) Based on 365 days with AQI data in 2019. Air Quality Index (AQI) is an index for reporting daily air quality. EPA calculates the AQI for five major air pollutants regulated by the Clean Air Act: ground-level ozone, particle pollution (aka particulate matter), carbon monoxide, sulfur dioxide, and nitrogen dioxide. The AQI runs from 0 to 500. The higher the AQI value, the greater the level of air pollution and the greater the health concern. There are six AQI categories: "Good" AQI is between 0 and 50. Air quality is considered satisfactory; "Moderate" AQI is between 51 and 100. Air quality is acceptable; "Unhealthy for Sensitive Groups" When AQI values are between 101 and 150, members of sensitive groups may experience health effects; "Unhealthy" When AQI values are between 151 and 200 everyone may begin to experience health effects; "Very Unhealthy" AQI values between 201 and 300 trigger a health alert; "Hazardous" AQI values over 300 trigger warnings of emergency conditions (not shown).
Source: U.S. Environmental Protection Agency, Air Quality Index Report, 2019

Air Quality Index Pollutants

Area	Percent of Days when AQI Pollutant was...[2]					
	Carbon Monoxide	Nitrogen Dioxide	Ozone	Sulfur Dioxide	Particulate Matter 2.5	Particulate Matter 10
MSA[1]	0.0	0.0	66.6	0.0	33.4	0.0

Note: (1) Data covers the Charlotte-Concord-Gastonia, NC-SC Metropolitan Statistical Area; (2) Based on 365 days with AQI data in 2019. The Air Quality Index (AQI) is an index for reporting daily air quality. EPA calculates the AQI for five major air pollutants regulated by the Clean Air Act: ground-level ozone, particle pollution (also known as particulate matter), carbon monoxide, sulfur dioxide, and nitrogen dioxide. The AQI runs from 0 to 500. The higher the AQI value, the greater the level of air pollution and the greater the health concern.
Source: U.S. Environmental Protection Agency, Air Quality Index Report, 2019

Maximum Air Pollutant Concentrations: Particulate Matter, Ozone, CO and Lead

	Particulate Matter 10 (ug/m^3)	Particulate Matter 2.5 Wtd AM (ug/m^3)	Particulate Matter 2.5 24-Hr (ug/m^3)	Ozone (ppm)	Carbon Monoxide (ppm)	Lead (ug/m^3)
MSA[1] Level	36	9.5	18	0.074	1	n/a
NAAQS[2]	150	15	35	0.075	9	0.15
Met NAAQS[2]	Yes	Yes	Yes	Yes	Yes	n/a

Note: (1) Data covers the Charlotte-Concord-Gastonia, NC-SC Metropolitan Statistical Area; Data from exceptional events are included; (2) National Ambient Air Quality Standards; ppm = parts per million; ug/m^3 = micrograms per cubic meter; n/a not available.
Concentrations: Particulate Matter 10 (coarse particulate)—highest second maximum 24-hour concentration; Particulate Matter 2.5 Wtd AM (fine particulate)—highest weighted annual mean concentration; Particulate Matter 2.5 24-Hour (fine particulate)—highest 98th percentile 24-hour concentration; Ozone—highest fourth daily maximum 8-hour concentration; Carbon Monoxide—highest second maximum non-overlapping 8-hour concentration; Lead—maximum running 3-month average
Source: U.S. Environmental Protection Agency, Air Quality Monitoring Information, "Air Quality Statistics by City, 2019"

Maximum Air Pollutant Concentrations: Nitrogen Dioxide and Sulfur Dioxide

	Nitrogen Dioxide AM (ppb)	Nitrogen Dioxide 1-Hr (ppb)	Sulfur Dioxide AM (ppb)	Sulfur Dioxide 1-Hr (ppb)	Sulfur Dioxide 24-Hr (ppb)
MSA[1] Level	11	37	n/a	3	n/a
NAAQS[2]	53	100	30	75	140
Met NAAQS[2]	Yes	Yes	n/a	Yes	n/a

Note: (1) Data covers the Charlotte-Concord-Gastonia, NC-SC Metropolitan Statistical Area; Data from exceptional events are included; (2) National Ambient Air Quality Standards; ppm = parts per million; ug/m^3 = micrograms per cubic meter; n/a not available.
Concentrations: Nitrogen Dioxide AM—highest arithmetic mean concentration; Nitrogen Dioxide 1-Hr—highest 98th percentile 1-hour daily maximum concentration; Sulfur Dioxide AM—highest annual mean concentration; Sulfur Dioxide 1-Hr—highest 99th percentile 1-hour daily maximum concentration; Sulfur Dioxide 24-Hr—highest second maximum 24-hour concentration
Source: U.S. Environmental Protection Agency, Air Quality Monitoring Information, "Air Quality Statistics by City, 2019"

Cincinnati, Ohio

Background

Cincinnati's name has a long history. After the American Revolution, former Continental Army soldiers formed a fraternal organization called the Society of Cincinnati, alluding to the Roman General Lucius Quinctius Cincinnatus. In 1790, General Arthur St. Clair, a member of that society and the first governor of the Northwest Territory, felt that this lovely city overlooking the Ohio River could only be called Cincinnati. As if that were not enough, he had to pay homage to fellow fraternal member Alexander Hamilton, so St. Clair named the county in which Cincinnati lies after him.

Since its incorporation as a city in 1819, the Miami and Erie canals have played great roles in Cincinnati's economic growth. Because of these waterways, farmers had the transportation necessary to sell their produce in town. From there, businesses would process the farmers' wares such as corn, pigs, and wheat into whiskey, pork, and flour.

Incidentally, the South, which was Cincinnati's greatest market for pork, made the city's loyalties difficult to declare during the Civil War. However, Cincinnati finally chose sides when its political climate made it a major station of the Underground Railroad, as well as the haven where Harriet Beecher Stowe could write her classic, *Uncle Tom's Cabin.* The National Underground Railroad Freedom Center here offers programs and exhibits highlighting the Railroad's true stories of courage in the quest for freedom.

Today, the city's major economic sectors include aerospace, automotive, chemistry and plastics, and financial services, although newer sectors are emerging such as advanced energy and consumer products. The city is home to the University of Cincinnati and Xavier University, and its centralized location has attracted Fortune 500 corporate headquarters. Major employers headquartered here include Proctor & Gamble and The Kroger Company. Five interstate highways converge at Cincinnati, providing present-day transportation access just as the canals did early in the city's growth. Additionally, in 2021, Amtrak renewed long-held hopes for the building of a passenger rail line, seeking $300 million in government funding. The project, backed by Cincinnati city council, would connect Cincinnati to other major cities across the state of Ohio.

The city blends Old World charm with modern business savvy. Investments of more than $700 million in the first decades of the 21st century are drawing tourists, conventioneers, and residents downtown—the Cincinnati Center City Development Corp., charged with supporting the area's renaissance, has seen to that. Improvements include new entertainment districts, called The Banks and Over the Rhine that have either opened or undergone gentrification and redevelopment. In addition, multiple new hotels have opened in recent years. They include the 21c Museum Hotel, which has an 8,000 square-foot art museum. On top of that, Horseshoe Casino Cincinnati, which opened in March 2013, boasts a 31-table World

> MLB's Cincinnati Reds offered discounted tickets to COVID-19-vaccinated fans attending home games at the Great American Ballpark.

Series Poker Room in addition to entertainment venues and restaurants. All of these amenities are situated in close proximity to the Duke Energy Convention Center or the city's two professional sports stadiums: the Cincinnati Reds MLB team plays at the Great American Ball Park and the NFL's Cincinnati Bengals call the Paul Brown Stadium home.

The arts thrive in Cincinnati. The Rosenthal Center for Contemporary Art celebrated its 80th anniversary in2019 and is housed in an acclaimed, Zaha Hadid-designed building; she won the Pritzker Architecture Award in 2004, the year after the building opened. The famed Cincinnati Opera, founded in 1920 and the second-oldest opera company in the U.S., features a complete season of productions as well as a summer program. The Cincinnati Symphony Orchestra, founded in 1905, is the nation's fifth-oldest orchestra. Both organizations perform in the historic Music Hall, whose Springer Auditorium is renowned for its acoustics.

To celebrate its German heritage, Cincinnati hosts the second largest Oktoberfest in the world.

But perhaps Cincinnati most celebrated tradition is its chili. "Cincinnati Chili" is unique in that it's served over spaghetti or as a "coney" sauce on a hotdog. It's served in independent restaurants all over the city, but is most famously found in chain restaurants like Skyline Chili, Empress, and Gold Star.

Cincinnati experiences a rather wide range of temperatures from winter to summer. Summers are warm and quite humid, with brief periods of very high temperatures every two or three years. Winters are moderately cold with numerous periods of extensive cloudiness.

Rankings

General Rankings

- In their seventh annual survey, Livability.com looked at data for more than 1,000 small to mid-sized U.S. cities to determine the rankings for Livability's "Top 100 Best Places to Live" in 2020. Cincinnati ranked #42. Criteria: housing and affordable living; vibrant economy; social and civic engagement; education; demographics; health care options; transportation & infrastructure; and abundant lifestyle amenities. *Livability.com, "Top 100 Best Places to Live 2020" October 2020*

Business/Finance Rankings

- Based on metro area social media reviews, the employment opinion group Glassdoor surveyed 50 of the most populous U.S. metro areas and equally weighed cost of living, hiring opportunity, and job satisfaction to compose a list of "25 Best Cities for Jobs." Median pay and home value, and number of active job openings were also factored in. The Cincinnati metro area was ranked #9 in overall job satisfaction. *www.glassdoor.com, "Best Cities for Jobs," February 25, 2020*

- The Brookings Institution ranked the nation's largest cities based on income inequality. Cincinnati was ranked #12 (#1 = greatest inequality). Criteria: the "95/20 ratio," a figure representing the income at which a household earns more than 95 percent of all other households, divided by the income at which a household earns more than only 20 percent of all other households. *Brookings Institution, "Household Income Inequality, Largest Cities of 97 Large U.S. Metro Areas, 2014-2016," February 5, 2018*

- The Brookings Institution ranked the 100 largest metro areas in the U.S. based on income inequality. Cincinnati was ranked #40 (#1 = greatest inequality). Criteria: the "95/20 ratio," a figure representing the income at which a household earns more than 95 percent of all other households, divided by the income at which a household earns more than only 20 percent of all other households. *Brookings Institution, "Household Income Inequality, 100 Largest U.S. Metro Areas, 2014-2016," February 5, 2018*

- Payscale.com ranked the 32 largest metro areas in terms of wage growth. The Cincinnati metro area ranked #11. Criteria: private-sector and education professional wage growth between the 4th quarter of 2019 and the 4th quarter of 2020. *PayScale, "Wage Trends by Metro Area-4th Quarter," January 11, 2021*

- Cincinnati was identified as one of America's most frugal metro areas by *Coupons.com*. The city ranked #24 out of 25. Criteria: digital coupon usage. *Coupons.com, "America's Most Frugal Cities of 2017," March 22, 2018*

- Cincinnati was cited as one of America's top metros for new and expanded facility projects in 2020. The area ranked #9 in the large metro area category (population over 1 million). *Site Selection, "Top Metros of 2020," March 2021*

- Livability.com rated Cincinnati as #7 of ten cities where new college grads' job prospects are brightest. Criteria included: number of 22- to 29-year olds; good job opportunities; affordable housing options; public transportation users; educational attainment; variety of fun things to do. *Livability.com, "2018 Top 10 Best Cities for Recent College Grads," April 26, 2018*

- The Cincinnati metro area appeared on the Milken Institute "2021 Best Performing Cities" list. Rank: #67 out of 200 large metro areas (population over 250,000). Criteria: job growth; wage and salary growth; high-tech output growth; housing affordability; household broadband access. *Milken Institute, "Best-Performing Cities 2021," February 16, 2021*

- *Forbes* ranked the 200 most populous metro areas to determine the nation's "Best Places for Business and Careers." The Cincinnati metro area was ranked #44. Criteria: costs (business and living); job growth (past and projected); income growth; quality of life; educational attainment (college and high school); projected economic growth; cultural and leisure opportunities; workplace tolerance laws; net migration patterns. *Forbes, "The Best Places for Business and Careers 2019: Seattle Still On Top," October 30, 2019*

Children/Family Rankings

- Cincinnati was selected as one of the most playful cities in the U.S. by KaBOOM! The organization's Playful City USA initiative honors cities and towns across the nation that have made their communities more playable. Criteria: pledging to integrate play as a solution to challenges in their communities; making it easy for children to get active and balanced play; creating more family-friendly and innovative communities as a result. *KaBOOM! National Campaign for Play, "2017 Playful City USA Communities"*

Culture/Performing Arts Rankings

- Cincinnati was selected as one of the 25 best cities for moviemakers in North America. COVID-19 has spurred a quest for great film cities that offer more creative space, lower costs, and more great outdoors. NYC & LA were intentionally excluded. Criteria: longstanding reputations as film-friendly communities; efforts to deal with pandemic-specific challenges; and establish appropriate COVID-19 guidelines. The city was ranked #13. *MovieMaker Magazine, "Best Places to Live and Work as a Moviemaker, 2021," January 26, 2021*

Dating/Romance Rankings

- Cincinnati was ranked #5 out of 25 cities that stood out for inspiring romance and attracting diners on the website OpenTable.com. Criteria: percentage of people who dined out on Valentine's Day in 2018; percentage of romantic restaurants as rated by OpenTable diner reviews; and percentage of tables seated for two. *OpenTable, "25 Most Romantic Cities in America for 2019," February 7, 2019*

- Cincinnati was selected as one of the nation's most romantic cities with 100,000 or more residents by Amazon.com. The city ranked #7 of 20. Criteria: per capita sales of romance novels, relationship books, romantic comedy movies, romantic music, and sexual wellness products. *Amazon.com, "Top 20 Most Romantic Cities in the U.S.," February 1, 2017*

Education Rankings

- Personal finance website *WalletHub* analyzed the 150 largest U.S. metropolitan statistical areas to determine where the most educated Americans are putting their degrees to work. Criteria: education levels; percentage of workers with degrees; education quality and attainment gap; public school quality rankings; quality and enrollment of each metro area's universities. Cincinnati was ranked #53 (#1 = most educated city). *www.WalletHub.com, "Most and Least Educated Cities in America," July 20, 2020*

- Cincinnati was selected as one of America's most literate cities. The city ranked #7 out of the 84 largest U.S. cities. Criteria: number of booksellers; library resources; Internet resources; educational attainment; periodical publishing resources; newspaper circulation. *Central Connecticut State University, "America's Most Literate Cities, 2018," February 2019*

Environmental Rankings

- The U.S. Conference of Mayors and Walmart Stores sponsor the Mayors' Climate Protection Awards Program which recognize mayors for outstanding and innovative practices that mayors are taking to increase energy efficiency in their cities, reduce carbon emissions and expand renewable energy. Cincinnati received an Honorable Mention in the large city category. *U.S. Conference of Mayors, "2020 Mayors' Climate Protection Awards," December 18, 2020*

- Cincinnati was highlighted as one of the 25 metro areas most polluted by year-round particle pollution (Annual PM 2.5) in the U.S. during 2016 through 2018. The area ranked #14. *American Lung Association, "State of the Air 2020," April 21, 2020*

- Cincinnati was highlighted as one of the top 98 cleanest metro areas for short-term particle pollution (24-hour PM 2.5) in the U.S. during 2016 through 2018. Monitors in these cities reported no days with unhealthful PM 2.5 levels. *American Lung Association, "State of the Air 2020," April 21, 2020*

Health/Fitness Rankings

- For each of the 100 largest cities in the United States, the American Fitness Index®, published by the American College of Sports Medicine and the Anthem Foundation, evaluated community infrastructure and 33 health behaviors including preventive health, levels of chronic disease conditions, pedestrian safety, air quality, and community resources that support physical activity. Cincinnati ranked #51 for "community fitness." *americanfitnessindex.org, "2020 ACSM American Fitness Index Summary Report," July 14, 2020*

- The Cincinnati metro area was identified as one of the worst cities for bed bugs in America by pest control company Orkin. The area ranked #8 out of 50 based on the number of bed bug treatments Orkin performed from December 2019 to November 2020. *Orkin, "New Year, New Top City on Orkin's 2021 Bed Bug Cities List: Chicago," February 1, 2021*

- Cincinnati was identified as a "2021 Spring Allergy Capital." The area ranked #87 out of 100. Three groups of factors were used to identify the most challenging cities for people with allergies during the spring season: annual spring pollen levels; over the counter medicine use; number of board-certified allergy specialists. *Asthma and Allergy Foundation of America, "Spring Allergy Capitals 2021," February 23, 2021*

- Cincinnati was identified as a "2021 Fall Allergy Capital." The area ranked #79 out of 100. Three groups of factors were used to identify the most challenging cities for people with allergies during the fall season: annual fall pollen levels; over the counter medicine use; number of board-certified allergy specialists. *Asthma and Allergy Foundation of America, "Fall Allergy Capitals 2021," February 23, 2021*

- Cincinnati was identified as a "2019 Asthma Capital." The area ranked #18 out of the nation's 100 largest metropolitan areas. Criteria: estimated asthma prevalence; crude death rate from asthma; and ER visits due to asthma. Risk factors analyzed but not factored in the rankings: annual pollen score; annual air quality; public smoking laws; number of board-certified asthma specialists; rescue medication use; controller medication use; uninsured rate; poverty rate. *Asthma and Allergy Foundation of America, "Asthma Capitals 2019: The Most Challenging Places to Live With Asthma," May 7, 2019*

Real Estate Rankings

- FitSmallBusiness looked at 50 of the largest metropolitan areas in the U.S. to determine which metro was the best to start a real estate business. Data was compiled from such sources as: Zillow, Trulia, U.S. Census Bureau, and the Bureau of Labor Statistics. Criteria: location; inventory; annual wages; median sales price of homes; days on the market; median price cut percentage; and other factors that would influence real estate professional growth. The Cincinnati metro area ranked #50. *fitsmallbusiness.com, "The Best Cities to Become a Real Estate Agent in 2018," January 30, 2018*

- *WalletHub* compared the most populated U.S. cities to determine which had the best markets for real estate agents. Cincinnati ranked #150 where demand was high and pay was the best. Criteria: sales per agent; annual median wage for real-estate agents; monthly average starting salary for real estate agents; real estate job density and competition; unemployment rate; home turnover rate; housing-market health index; and other relevant metrics. *www.WalletHub.com, "2019's Best Places to Be a Real Estate Agent," April 24, 2019*

- Cincinnati was ranked #33 out of 268 metro areas in terms of housing affordability in 2020 by the National Association of Home Builders (#1 = most affordable). Criteria: the share of homes sold in that area affordable to a family earning the local median income, based on standard mortgage underwriting criteria. *National Association of Home Builders®, NAHB-Wells Fargo Housing Opportunity Index, 4th Quarter 2020*

Safety Rankings

- To identify the most dangerous cities in America, 24/7 Wall Street focused on violent crime categories—murder, non-negligent manslaughter, rape, robbery, and aggravated assault—and property crime as reported in the FBI's 2019 annual Uniform Crime Report. Criteria also included median income from American Community Survey and unemployment figures from Bureau of Labor Statistics. For cities with populations over 100,000, Cincinnati was ranked #47. *247wallst.com, "America's 50 Most Dangerous Cities" November 16, 2020*

- Allstate ranked the 200 largest cities in America in terms of driver safety. Cincinnati ranked #173. Criteria: internal property damage claims over a two-year period from January 2016 to December 2017. The report helps increase the importance of safety and awareness behind the wheel. *Allstate, "Allstate America's Best Drivers Report, 2019" June 24, 2019*

- The National Insurance Crime Bureau ranked 384 metro areas in the U.S. in terms of per capita rates of vehicle theft. The Cincinnati metro area ranked #201 (#1 = highest rate). Criteria: number of vehicle theft offenses per 100,000 inhabitants in 2019. *National Insurance Crime Bureau, "Hot Spots 2019," July 21, 2020*

Seniors/Retirement Rankings

- From its Best Cities for Successful Aging indexes, the Milken Institute generated rankings for metropolitan areas, weighing data in nine categories—health care, wellness, living arrangements, transportation and convenience, financial characteristics, education, employment, community engagement, and overall livability. The Cincinnati metro area was ranked #50 overall in the large metro area category. *Milken Institute, "Best Cities for Successful Aging, 2017" March 14, 2017*

Women/Minorities Rankings

- Cincinnati was selected as one of the gayest cities in America by *The Advocate*. The city ranked #7 out of 25. Criteria, among many: Trans Pride parades/festivals; gay rugby teams; lesbian bars; LGBT centers; theater screenings of "Moonlight"; LGBT-inclusive nondiscrimination ordinances; and gay bowling teams. *The Advocate, "Queerest Cities in America 2017" January 12, 2017*

- Personal finance website *WalletHub* compared more than 180 U.S. cities across two key dimensions, "Hispanic Business-Friendliness" and "Hispanic Purchasing Power," to arrive at the most favorable conditions for Hispanic entrepreneurs. Cincinnati was ranked #99 out of 182. Criteria includes: share of Hispanic-Owned Businesses; Hispanic entrepreneurship rate to median annual income of Hispanics; Small Business-Friendliness score; cost of living; and number of Hispanics with at least a bachelor's degree. *WalletHub.com, "2019's Best Cities for Hispanic Entrepreneurs," May 1, 2019*

Miscellaneous Rankings

- The watchdog site, Charity Navigator, conducted a study of charities in major markets both to analyze statistical differences in their financial, accountability, and transparency practices and to track year-to-year variations in individual philanthropic communities. The Cincinnati metro area was ranked #30 among the 30 metro markets in the rating category of Overall Score. *www.charitynavigator.org, "2017 Metro Market Study," May 1, 2017*

- *WalletHub* compared the 150 most populated U.S. cities to determine their operating efficiency. A "Quality of City Services" score was constructed for each city and then divided by the total budget per capita to reveal which were managed the best. Cincinnati ranked #108. Criteria: financial stability; economy; education; safety; health; infrastructure and pollution. *www.WalletHub.com, "2020's Best- & Worst-Run Cities in America," June 29, 2020*

Business Environment

DEMOGRAPHICS

Population Growth

Area	1990 Census	2000 Census	2010 Census	2019* Estimate	Population Growth (%) 1990-2019	2010-2019
City	363,974	331,285	296,943	301,394	-17.2	1.5
MSA[1]	1,844,917	2,009,632	2,130,151	2,201,741	19.3	3.4
U.S.	248,709,873	281,421,906	308,745,538	324,697,795	30.6	5.2

Note: (1) Figures cover the Cincinnati, OH-KY-IN Metropolitan Statistical Area; (*) 2015-2019 5-year estimated population
Source: U.S. Census Bureau, 1990 Census, Census 2000, Census 2010, 2015-2019 American Community Survey 5-Year Estimates

Household Size

Area	Persons in Household (%) One	Two	Three	Four	Five	Six	Seven or More	Average Household Size
City	44.4	30.1	12.1	7.6	3.6	1.4	0.9	2.10
MSA[1]	28.8	34.4	15.2	12.8	5.8	2.0	1.1	2.50
U.S.	27.9	33.9	15.6	12.9	6.0	2.3	1.4	2.60

Note: (1) Figures cover the Cincinnati, OH-KY-IN Metropolitan Statistical Area
Source: U.S. Census Bureau, 2015-2019 American Community Survey 5-Year Estimates

Race

Area	White Alone[2] (%)	Black Alone[2] (%)	Asian Alone[2] (%)	AIAN[3] Alone[2] (%)	NHOPI[4] Alone[2] (%)	Other Race Alone[2] (%)	Two or More Races (%)
City	50.7	42.3	2.2	0.1	0.1	0.9	3.7
MSA[1]	81.8	12.0	2.6	0.1	0.0	0.9	2.6
U.S.	72.5	12.7	5.5	0.8	0.2	4.9	3.3

Note: (1) Figures cover the Cincinnati, OH-KY-IN Metropolitan Statistical Area; (2) Alone is defined as not being in combination with one or more other races; (3) American Indian and Alaska Native; (4) Native Hawaiian and Other Pacific Islander
Source: U.S. Census Bureau, 2015-2019 American Community Survey 5-Year Estimates

Hispanic or Latino Origin

Area	Total (%)	Mexican (%)	Puerto Rican (%)	Cuban (%)	Other (%)
City	3.8	1.2	0.6	0.1	2.0
MSA[1]	3.2	1.5	0.4	0.1	1.2
U.S.	18.0	11.2	1.7	0.7	4.3

Note: Persons of Hispanic or Latino origin can be of any race; (1) Figures cover the Cincinnati, OH-KY-IN Metropolitan Statistical Area
Source: U.S. Census Bureau, 2015-2019 American Community Survey 5-Year Estimates

Ancestry

Area	German	Irish	English	American	Italian	Polish	French[2]	Scottish	Dutch
City	17.7	10.0	5.3	3.9	3.5	1.7	1.6	1.2	0.8
MSA[1]	27.2	13.8	8.3	7.1	4.2	1.6	1.9	1.8	1.2
U.S.	13.3	9.7	7.2	6.2	5.1	2.8	2.3	1.7	1.2

Note: Figures are the percentage of the total population reporting a particular ancestry. The nine most commonly reported ancestries in the U.S. are shown. Figures include multiple ancestries (e.g. if a person reported being Irish and Italian, they were included in both columns); (1) Figures cover the Cincinnati, OH-KY-IN Metropolitan Statistical Area; (2) Excludes Basque
Source: U.S. Census Bureau, 2015-2019 American Community Survey 5-Year Estimates

Foreign-born Population

Area	Percent of Population Born in Any Foreign Country	Asia	Mexico	Europe	Caribbean	Central America[2]	South America	Africa	Canada
City	6.0	1.8	0.3	0.8	0.2	0.9	0.3	1.6	0.2
MSA[1]	4.8	2.1	0.5	0.7	0.1	0.4	0.2	0.7	0.1
U.S.	13.6	4.2	3.5	1.5	1.3	1.1	1.0	0.7	0.2

Note: (1) Figures cover the Cincinnati, OH-KY-IN Metropolitan Statistical Area; (2) Excludes Mexico.
Source: U.S. Census Bureau, 2015-2019 American Community Survey 5-Year Estimates

Marital Status

Area	Never Married	Now Married[2]	Separated	Widowed	Divorced
City	52.0	28.3	2.4	5.1	12.1
MSA[1]	32.3	49.0	1.6	5.7	11.3
U.S.	33.4	48.1	1.9	5.8	10.9

Note: Figures are percentages and cover the population 15 years of age and older; (1) Figures cover the Cincinnati, OH-KY-IN Metropolitan Statistical Area; (2) Excludes separated
Source: U.S. Census Bureau, 2015-2019 American Community Survey 5-Year Estimates

Disability by Age

Area	All Ages	Under 18 Years Old	18 to 64 Years Old	65 Years and Over
City	13.3	5.5	11.9	35.8
MSA[1]	12.4	4.7	10.6	32.7
U.S.	12.6	4.2	10.3	34.5

Note: Figures show percent of the civilian noninstitutionalized population that reported having a disability. Disability status is determined from six types of difficulty: vision, hearing, cognitive, ambulatory, self-care, and independent living. For children under 5 years old, hearing and vision difficulty are used to determine disability status. For children between the ages of 5 and 14, disability status is determined from hearing, vision, cognitive, ambulatory, and self-care difficulties. For people aged 15 years and older, they are considered to have a disability if they have difficulty with any one of the six difficulty types; Note: (1) Figures cover the Cincinnati, OH-KY-IN Metropolitan Statistical Area
Source: U.S. Census Bureau, 2015-2019 American Community Survey 5-Year Estimates

Age

Area	Percent of Population									Median Age
	Under Age 5	Age 5–19	Age 20–34	Age 35–44	Age 45–54	Age 55–64	Age 65–74	Age 75–84	Age 85+	
City	7.1	19.0	28.3	11.3	10.5	11.6	7.0	3.3	1.9	32.2
MSA[1]	6.3	20.1	19.9	12.4	13.2	13.4	8.7	4.2	1.9	37.9
U.S.	6.1	19.1	20.7	12.6	13.0	12.9	9.1	4.6	1.9	38.1

Note: (1) Figures cover the Cincinnati, OH-KY-IN Metropolitan Statistical Area
Source: U.S. Census Bureau, 2015-2019 American Community Survey 5-Year Estimates

Gender

Area	Males	Females	Males per 100 Females
City	145,900	155,494	93.8
MSA[1]	1,079,705	1,122,036	96.2
U.S.	159,886,919	164,810,876	97.0

Note: (1) Figures cover the Cincinnati, OH-KY-IN Metropolitan Statistical Area
Source: U.S. Census Bureau, 2015-2019 American Community Survey 5-Year Estimates

Religious Groups by Family

Area	Catholic	Baptist	Non-Den.	Methodist[2]	Lutheran	LDS[3]	Pentecostal	Presbyterian[4]	Muslim[5]	Judaism
MSA[1]	19.1	9.6	3.7	3.9	1.2	0.6	2.2	1.6	0.2	0.5
U.S.	19.1	9.3	4.0	4.0	2.3	2.0	1.9	1.6	0.8	0.7

Note: Figures are the number of adherents as a percentage of the total population; (1) Figures cover the Cincinnati, OH-KY-IN Metropolitan Statistical Area; (2) Methodist/Pietist; (3) Latter Day Saints; (4) Reformed; (5) Figures are estimates
Source: Association of Statisticians of American Religious Bodies, 2010 U.S. Religion Census: Religious Congregations & Membership Study

Religious Groups by Tradition

Area	Catholic	Evangelical Protestant	Mainline Protestant	Other Tradition	Black Protestant	Orthodox
MSA[1]	19.1	15.5	7.2	1.6	1.2	0.2
U.S.	19.1	16.2	7.3	4.3	1.6	0.3

Note: Figures are the number of adherents as a percentage of the total population; (1) Figures cover the Cincinnati, OH-KY-IN Metropolitan Statistical Area
Source: Association of Statisticians of American Religious Bodies, 2010 U.S. Religion Census: Religious Congregations & Membership Study

ECONOMY

Gross Metropolitan Product

Area	2017	2018	2019	2020	Rank[2]
MSA[1]	137.2	143.5	150.7	156.1	29

Note: Figures are in billions of dollars; (1) Figures cover the Cincinnati, OH-KY-IN Metropolitan Statistical Area; (2) Rank is based on 2018 data and ranges from 1 to 381
Source: U.S. Conference of Mayors, U.S. Metro Economies: GMP & Employment 2018-2020, September 2019

Economic Growth

Area	2015-17 (%)	2018 (%)	2019 (%)	2020 (%)	Rank[2]
MSA[1]	2.0	1.7	3.3	1.4	132
U.S.	1.9	2.9	2.3	2.1	—

Note: Figures are real gross metropolitan product (GMP) growth rates and represent average annual percent change; (1) Figures cover the Cincinnati, OH-KY-IN Metropolitan Statistical Area; (2) Rank is based on 2017 2-year average annual percent change and ranges from 1 to 381
Source: U.S. Conference of Mayors, U.S. Metro Economies: GMP & Employment 2018-2020, September 2019

Metropolitan Area Exports

Area	2014	2015	2016	2017	2018	2019	Rank[2]
MSA[1]	22,280.7	24,127.0	26,326.2	28,581.8	27,396.3	28,778.3	11

Note: Figures are in millions of dollars; (1) Figures cover the Cincinnati, OH-KY-IN Metropolitan Statistical Area; (2) Rank is based on 2019 data and ranges from 1 to 386
Source: U.S. Department of Commerce, International Trade Administration, Office of Trade and Economic Analysis, Industry and Analysis, Exports by Metropolitan Area, data extracted March 24, 2021

Building Permits

Area	Single-Family			Multi-Family			Total		
	2018	2019	Pct. Chg.	2018	2019	Pct. Chg.	2018	2019	Pct. Chg.
City	98	135	37.8	632	992	57.0	730	1,127	54.4
MSA[1]	4,282	4,488	4.8	1,794	1,535	-14.4	6,076	6,023	-0.9
U.S.	855,300	862,100	0.7	473,500	523,900	10.6	1,328,800	1,386,000	4.3

Note: (1) Figures cover the Cincinnati, OH-KY-IN Metropolitan Statistical Area; Figures represent new, privately-owned housing units authorized (unadjusted data); All permit data are based on estimates with imputation
Source: U.S. Census Bureau, Manufacturing, Mining, and Construction Statistics, Building Permits, 2018, 2019

Bankruptcy Filings

Area	Business Filings			Nonbusiness Filings		
	2019	2020	% Chg.	2019	2020	% Chg.
Hamilton County	48	25	-47.9	2,519	1,845	-26.8
U.S.	22,780	21,655	-4.9	752,160	522,808	-30.5

Note: Business filings include Chapter 7, Chapter 9, Chapter 11, Chapter 12, Chapter 13, Chapter 15, and Section 304; Nonbusiness filings include Chapter 7, Chapter 11, and Chapter 13
Source: Administrative Office of the U.S. Courts, Business and Nonbusiness Bankruptcy, County Cases Commenced by Chapter of the Bankruptcy Code, During the 12-Month Period Ending December 31, 2019 and Business and Nonbusiness Bankruptcy, County Cases Commenced by Chapter of the Bankruptcy Code, During the 12-Month Period Ending December 31, 2020

Housing Vacancy Rates

Area	Gross Vacancy Rate[2] (%)			Year-Round Vacancy Rate[3] (%)			Rental Vacancy Rate[4] (%)			Homeowner Vacancy Rate[5] (%)		
	2018	2019	2020	2018	2019	2020	2018	2019	2020	2018	2019	2020
MSA[1]	6.8	8.6	6.6	6.7	8.4	6.2	4.4	10.7	7.9	1.5	1.1	0.7
U.S.	12.3	12.0	10.6	9.7	9.5	8.2	6.9	6.7	6.3	1.5	1.4	1.0

Note: (1) Figures cover the Cincinnati, OH-KY-IN Metropolitan Statistical Area; (2) The percentage of the total housing inventory that is vacant; (3) The percentage of the housing inventory (excluding seasonal units) that is year-round vacant; (4) The percentage of rental inventory that is vacant for rent; (5) The percentage of homeowner inventory that is vacant for sale
Source: U.S. Census Bureau, Housing Vacancies and Homeownership Annual Statistics: 2018, 2019, 2020

INCOME

Income

Area	Per Capita ($)	Median Household ($)	Average Household ($)
City	30,531	40,640	65,213
MSA[1]	34,575	63,987	86,633
U.S.	34,103	62,843	88,607

Note: (1) Figures cover the Cincinnati, OH-KY-IN Metropolitan Statistical Area
Source: U.S. Census Bureau, 2015-2019 American Community Survey 5-Year Estimates

Household Income Distribution

Area	Percent of Households Earning							
	Under $15,000	$15,000 -$24,999	$25,000 -$34,999	$35,000 -$49,999	$50,000 -$74,999	$75,000 -$99,999	$100,000 -$149,999	$150,000 and up
City	21.1	12.6	11.2	12.3	15.6	9.1	9.4	8.7
MSA[1]	10.2	8.7	8.6	11.8	17.6	13.2	16.0	13.8
U.S.	10.3	8.9	8.9	12.3	17.2	12.7	15.1	14.5

Note: (1) Figures cover the Cincinnati, OH-KY-IN Metropolitan Statistical Area
Source: U.S. Census Bureau, 2015-2019 American Community Survey 5-Year Estimates

Poverty Rate

Area	All Ages	Under 18 Years Old	18 to 64 Years Old	65 Years and Over
City	26.3	39.0	24.2	13.9
MSA[1]	12.2	16.8	11.5	7.8
U.S.	13.4	18.5	12.6	9.3

Note: Figures are percentage of people whose income during the past 12 months was below the poverty level;
(1) Figures cover the Cincinnati, OH-KY-IN Metropolitan Statistical Area
Source: U.S. Census Bureau, 2015-2019 American Community Survey 5-Year Estimates

CITY FINANCES

City Government Finances

Component	2017 ($000)	2017 ($ per capita)
Total Revenues	1,538,176	5,152
Total Expenditures	1,183,008	3,963
Debt Outstanding	858,407	2,875
Cash and Securities[1]	2,400,623	8,041

Note: (1) Cash and security holdings of a government at the close of its fiscal year,
including those of its dependent agencies, utilities, and liquor stores.
Source: U.S. Census Bureau, State & Local Government Finances 2017

City Government Revenue by Source

Source	2017 ($000)	2017 ($ per capita)	2017 (%)
General Revenue			
From Federal Government	83,625	280	5.4
From State Government	47,085	158	3.1
From Local Governments	273,230	915	17.8
Taxes			
Property	78,815	264	5.1
Sales and Gross Receipts	8,608	29	0.6
Personal Income	434,701	1,456	28.3
Corporate Income	0	0	0.0
Motor Vehicle License	3,430	11	0.2
Other Taxes	20,370	68	1.3
Current Charges	93,206	312	6.1
Liquor Store	0	0	0.0
Utility	144,932	485	9.4
Employee Retirement	235,180	788	15.3

Source: U.S. Census Bureau, State & Local Government Finances 2017

City Government Expenditures by Function

Function	2017 ($000)	2017 ($ per capita)	2017 (%)
General Direct Expenditures			
Air Transportation	1,736	5	0.1
Corrections	0	0	0.0
Education	5,524	18	0.5
Employment Security Administration	0	0	0.0
Financial Administration	8,991	30	0.8
Fire Protection	106,252	355	9.0
General Public Buildings	30,215	101	2.6
Governmental Administration, Other	10,370	34	0.9
Health	21,123	70	1.8
Highways	114,803	384	9.7
Hospitals	0	0	0.0
Housing and Community Development	24,133	80	2.0
Interest on General Debt	26,243	87	2.2
Judicial and Legal	6,033	20	0.5
Libraries	0	0	0.0
Parking	12,685	42	1.1
Parks and Recreation	55,914	187	4.7
Police Protection	157,515	527	13.3
Public Welfare	0	0	0.0
Sewerage	142,748	478	12.1
Solid Waste Management	0	0	0.0
Veterans' Services	0	0	0.0
Liquor Store	0	0	0.0
Utility	86,855	290	7.3
Employee Retirement	167,461	560	14.2

Source: U.S. Census Bureau, State & Local Government Finances 2017

EMPLOYMENT

Labor Force and Employment

Area	Civilian Labor Force			Workers Employed		
	Dec. 2019	Dec. 2020	% Chg.	Dec. 2019	Dec. 2020	% Chg.
City	147,410	148,764	0.9	142,030	139,857	-1.5
MSA[1]	1,128,063	1,122,791	-0.5	1,090,733	1,069,559	-1.9
U.S.	164,007,000	160,017,000	-2.4	158,504,000	149,613,000	-5.6

Note: Data is not seasonally adjusted and covers workers 16 years of age and older; (1) Figures cover the Cincinnati, OH-KY-IN Metropolitan Statistical Area
Source: Bureau of Labor Statistics, Local Area Unemployment Statistics

Unemployment Rate

Area	2020											
	Jan.	Feb.	Mar.	Apr.	May	Jun.	Jul.	Aug.	Sep.	Oct.	Nov.	Dec.
City	4.7	4.3	4.7	15.1	13.7	12.7	11.1	11.2	10.0	7.5	6.4	6.0
MSA[1]	4.3	4.0	4.4	14.1	11.2	9.0	7.6	7.9	6.8	5.6	4.8	4.7
U.S.	4.0	3.8	4.5	14.4	13.0	11.2	10.5	8.5	7.7	6.6	6.4	6.5

Note: Data is not seasonally adjusted and covers workers 16 years of age and older; (1) Figures cover the Cincinnati, OH-KY-IN Metropolitan Statistical Area
Source: Bureau of Labor Statistics, Local Area Unemployment Statistics

Average Wages

Occupation	$/Hr.	Occupation	$/Hr.
Accountants and Auditors	36.80	Maintenance and Repair Workers	21.30
Automotive Mechanics	22.30	Marketing Managers	66.10
Bookkeepers	20.70	Network and Computer Systems Admin.	38.90
Carpenters	24.10	Nurses, Licensed Practical	23.80
Cashiers	11.70	Nurses, Registered	34.60
Computer Programmers	45.00	Nursing Assistants	15.20
Computer Systems Analysts	47.80	Office Clerks, General	18.70
Computer User Support Specialists	24.70	Physical Therapists	43.00
Construction Laborers	23.00	Physicians	116.50
Cooks, Restaurant	13.00	Plumbers, Pipefitters and Steamfitters	26.10
Customer Service Representatives	18.00	Police and Sheriff's Patrol Officers	33.10
Dentists	103.00	Postal Service Mail Carriers	26.00
Electricians	23.60	Real Estate Sales Agents	23.00
Engineers, Electrical	43.80	Retail Salespersons	14.30
Fast Food and Counter Workers	11.10	Sales Representatives, Technical/Scientific	54.70
Financial Managers	67.70	Secretaries, Exc. Legal/Medical/Executive	19.00
First-Line Supervisors of Office Workers	29.80	Security Guards	17.40
General and Operations Managers	59.60	Surgeons	136.70
Hairdressers/Cosmetologists	14.60	Teacher Assistants, Exc. Postsecondary*	14.30
Home Health and Personal Care Aides	12.30	Teachers, Secondary School, Exc. Sp. Ed.*	30.90
Janitors and Cleaners	15.20	Telemarketers	15.20
Landscaping/Groundskeeping Workers	14.60	Truck Drivers, Heavy/Tractor-Trailer	24.10
Lawyers	67.40	Truck Drivers, Light/Delivery Services	19.10
Maids and Housekeeping Cleaners	12.20	Waiters and Waitresses	11.10

Note: Wage data covers the Cincinnati, OH-KY-IN Metropolitan Statistical Area; (*) Hourly wages were calculated from annual wage data based on a 40 hour work week; n/a not available.
Source: Bureau of Labor Statistics, Metro Area Occupational Employment & Wage Estimates, May 2020

Employment by Industry

Sector	MSA[1]		U.S.
	Number of Employees	Percent of Total	Percent of Total
Construction, Mining, and Logging	45,100	4.2	5.5
Education and Health Services	169,000	15.9	16.3
Financial Activities	74,200	7.0	6.1
Government	125,700	11.8	15.2
Information	13,000	1.2	1.9
Leisure and Hospitality	95,000	8.9	9.0
Manufacturing	111,900	10.5	8.5
Other Services	37,200	3.5	3.8
Professional and Business Services	168,200	15.8	14.4
Retail Trade	108,400	10.2	10.9
Transportation, Warehousing, and Utilities	61,000	5.7	4.6
Wholesale Trade	56,200	5.3	3.9

Note: Figures are non-farm employment as of December 2020. Figures are not seasonally adjusted and include workers 16 years of age and older; (1) Figures cover the Cincinnati, OH-KY-IN Metropolitan Statistical Area
Source: Bureau of Labor Statistics, Current Employment Statistics, Employment, Hours, and Earnings

Employment by Occupation

Occupation Classification	City (%)	MSA[1] (%)	U.S. (%)
Management, Business, Science, and Arts	42.5	40.6	38.5
Natural Resources, Construction, and Maintenance	4.6	6.9	8.9
Production, Transportation, and Material Moving	13.4	14.5	13.2
Sales and Office	19.9	21.9	21.6
Service	19.5	16.0	17.8

Note: Figures cover employed civilians 16 years of age and older; (1) Figures cover the Cincinnati, OH-KY-IN Metropolitan Statistical Area
Source: U.S. Census Bureau, 2015-2019 American Community Survey 5-Year Estimates

Occupations with Greatest Projected Employment Growth: 2020 – 2022

Occupation[1]	2020 Employment	2022 Projected Employment	Numeric Employment Change	Percent Employment Change
Laborers and Freight, Stock, and Material Movers, Hand	119,110	122,880	3,770	3.2
Registered Nurses	129,170	132,090	2,920	2.3
Home Health and Personal Care Aides	94,930	97,520	2,590	2.7
Industrial Truck and Tractor Operators	33,730	35,870	2,140	6.3
Heavy and Tractor-Trailer Truck Drivers	80,440	82,290	1,850	2.3
Construction Laborers	42,520	44,210	1,690	4.0
Electricians	26,990	28,530	1,540	5.7
Medical Assistants	26,150	27,410	1,260	4.8
Light Truck or Delivery Services Drivers	38,160	39,200	1,040	2.7
Heating, Air Conditioning, and Refrigeration Mechanics and Installers	13,410	14,390	980	7.3

Note: Projections cover Ohio; (1) Sorted by numeric employment change
Source: www.projectionscentral.com, State Occupational Projections, 2020–2022 Short-Term Projections

Fastest-Growing Occupations: 2020 – 2022

Occupation[1]	2020 Employment	2022 Projected Employment	Numeric Employment Change	Percent Employment Change
Roofers	5,710	6,240	530	9.3
Helpers—Pipelayers, Plumbers, Pipefitters, and Steamfitters	920	1,000	80	8.7
Brickmasons and Blockmasons	3,790	4,090	300	7.9
Floor Layers, Except Carpet, Wood, and Hard Tiles	1,210	1,300	90	7.4
Heating, Air Conditioning, and Refrigeration Mechanics and Installers	13,410	14,390	980	7.3
Cement Masons and Concrete Finishers	5,580	5,980	400	7.2
Glaziers	1,260	1,350	90	7.1
Structural Iron and Steel Workers	3,210	3,430	220	6.9
Physician Assistants	4,720	5,040	320	6.8
Tile and Marble Setters	910	970	60	6.6

Note: Projections cover Ohio; (1) Sorted by percent employment change and excludes occupations with numeric employment change less than 50
Source: www.projectionscentral.com, State Occupational Projections, 2020–2022 Short-Term Projections

TAXES

State Corporate Income Tax Rates

State	Tax Rate (%)	Income Brackets ($)	Num. of Brackets	Financial Institution Tax Rate (%)[a]	Federal Income Tax Ded.
Ohio	(t)	–	–	(t)	No

Note: Tax rates as of January 1, 2021; (a) Rates listed are the corporate income tax rate applied to financial institutions or excise taxes based on income. Some states have other taxes based upon the value of deposits or shares; (t) Ohio no longer levies a tax based on income (except for a particular subset of corporations), but instead imposes a Commercial Activity Tax (CAT) equal to $150 for gross receipts sitused to Ohio of between $150,000 and $1 million, plus 0.26% of gross receipts over $1 million. Banks continue to pay a franchise tax of 1.3% of net worth. For those few corporations for whom the franchise tax on net worth or net income still applies, a litter tax also applies.
Source: Federation of Tax Administrators, State Corporate Income Tax Rates, January 1, 2021

State Individual Income Tax Rates

State	Tax Rate (%)	Income Brackets ($)	Personal Exemptions ($)			Standard Ded. ($)	
			Single	Married	Depend.	Single	Married
Ohio (a)	0.0 - 4.797	22,150 - 221,300	2,400	4,800 (s)	2,400 (s)	–	–

Note: Tax rates as of January 1, 2021; Local- and county-level taxes are not included; Federal income tax is not deductible on state income tax returns; (a) 19 states have statutory provision for automatically adjusting to the rate of inflation the dollar values of the income tax brackets, standard deductions, and/or personal exemptions. Michigan indexes the personal exemption only. Oregon does not index the income brackets for $125,000 and over; (s) Ohio provides an additional tax credit of $20 per exemption. Exemption amounts reduced for higher income taxpayers. Business income taxes at a flat 3% rate.
Source: Federation of Tax Administrators, State Individual Income Tax Rates, January 1, 2021

Various State Sales and Excise Tax Rates

State	State Sales Tax (%)	Gasoline[1] (¢/gal.)	Cigarette[2] ($/pack)	Spirits[3] ($/gal.)	Wine[4] ($/gal.)	Beer[5] ($/gal.)	Recreational Marijuana (%)
Ohio	5.75	38.51	1.6	9.83	0.32	0.18	Not legal

Note: All tax rates as of January 1, 2021; (1) The American Petroleum Institute has developed a methodology for determining the average tax rate on a gallon of fuel. Rates may include any of the following: excise taxes, environmental fees, storage tank fees, other fees or taxes, general sales tax, and local taxes; (2) The federal excise tax of $1.0066 per pack and local taxes are not included; (3) Rates are those applicable to off-premise sales of 40% alcohol by volume (a.b.v.) distilled spirits in 750ml containers. Local excise taxes are excluded; (4) Rates are those applicable to off-premise sales of 11% a.b.v. non-carbonated wine in 750ml containers; (5) Rates are those applicable to off-premise sales of 4.7% a.b.v. beer in 12 ounce containers.
Source: Tax Foundation, 2021 Facts & Figures: How Does Your State Compare?

State Business Tax Climate Index Rankings

State	Overall Rank	Corporate Tax Rank	Individual Income Tax Rank	Sales Tax Rank	Property Tax Rank	Unemployment Insurance Tax Rank
Ohio	39	42	43	34	6	6

Note: The index is a measure of how each state's tax laws affect economic performance. The lower the rank, the more favorable a state's tax system is for business. States without a given tax are given a ranking of 1. The scores/rankings for the District of Columbia do not affect other states. The 2021 index represents the tax climate as of July 1, 2020.
Source: Tax Foundation, State Business Tax Climate Index 2021

TRANSPORTATION

Means of Transportation to Work

Area	Car/Truck/Van		Public Transportation			Bicycle	Walked	Other Means	Worked at Home
	Drove Alone	Car-pooled	Bus	Subway	Railroad				
City	72.3	8.8	7.0	0.0	0.0	0.4	5.7	1.1	4.7
MSA[1]	82.3	8.0	1.7	0.0	0.0	0.2	2.0	0.8	5.0
U.S.	76.3	9.0	2.4	1.9	0.5	0.6	2.7	1.4	5.2

Note: Figures are percentages and cover workers 16 years of age and older; (1) Figures cover the Cincinnati, OH-KY-IN Metropolitan Statistical Area
Source: U.S. Census Bureau, 2015-2019 American Community Survey 5-Year Estimates

Travel Time to Work

Area	Less Than 10 Minutes	10 to 19 Minutes	20 to 29 Minutes	30 to 44 Minutes	45 to 59 Minutes	60 to 89 Minutes	90 Minutes or More
City	11.0	33.2	27.0	19.2	4.5	3.2	1.9
MSA[1]	10.9	27.5	25.3	23.4	7.8	3.6	1.5
U.S.	12.2	28.4	20.8	20.8	8.3	6.4	2.9

Note: Note: Figures are percentages and include workers 16 years old and over; (1) Figures cover the Cincinnati, OH-KY-IN Metropolitan Statistical Area
Source: U.S. Census Bureau, 2015-2019 American Community Survey 5-Year Estimates

Key Congestion Measures

Measure	1982	1992	2002	2012	2017
Annual Hours of Delay, Total (000)	6,798	22,733	44,590	55,383	64,061
Annual Hours of Delay, Per Auto Commuter	10	28	38	46	52
Annual Congestion Cost, Total (million $)	52	241	605	1,003	1,188
Annual Congestion Cost, Per Auto Commuter ($)	264	607	928	903	1,014

Note: Covers the Cincinnati OH-KY-IN urban area
Source: Texas A&M Transportation Institute, 2019 Urban Mobility Report

Freeway Travel Time Index

Measure	1982	1987	1992	1997	2002	2007	2012	2017
Urban Area Index[1]	1.04	1.07	1.12	1.16	1.17	1.17	1.17	1.17
Urban Area Rank[1,2]	61	55	40	36	41	56	50	49

Note: Freeway Travel Time Index—the ratio of travel time in the peak period to the travel time at free-flow conditions. For example, a value of 1.30 indicates a 20-minute free-flow trip takes 26 minutes in the peak (20 minutes x 1.30 = 26 minutes); (1) Covers the Cincinnati OH-KY-IN urban area; (2) Rank is based on 101 larger urban areas (#1 = highest travel time index)
Source: Texas A&M Transportation Institute, 2019 Urban Mobility Report

Public Transportation

Agency Name / Mode of Transportation	Vehicles Operated in Maximum Service[1]	Annual Unlinked Passenger Trips[2] (in thous.)	Annual Passenger Miles[3] (in thous.)
Southwest Ohio Regional Transit Authority (SORTA/Metro)			
Bus (directly operated)	298	13,244.9	71,291.5
Demand Response (purchased transportation)	46	226.7	2,562.5
Streetcar Rail (purchased transportation)	3	531.6	844.2

Note: (1) Number of revenue vehicles operated by the given mode and type of service to meet the annual maximum service requirement. This is the revenue vehicle count during the peak season of the year; on the week and day that maximum service is provided. Vehicles operated in maximum service (VOMS) exclude atypical days and one-time special events; (2) Number of passengers who boarded public transportation vehicles. Passengers are counted each time they board a vehicle no matter how many vehicles they use to travel from their origin to their destination. (3) Sum of the distances ridden by all passengers during the entire fiscal year.
Source: Federal Transit Administration, National Transit Database, 2019

Air Transportation

Airport Name and Code / Type of Service	Passenger Airlines[1]	Passenger Enplanements	Freight Carriers[2]	Freight (lbs)
Cincinnati-Northern Kentucky International (CVG)				
Domestic service (U.S. carriers - 2020)	24	1,726,634	23	1,232,892,636
International service (U.S. carriers - 2019)	7	94,250	7	296,239,141

Note: (1) Includes all U.S.-based major, minor and commuter airlines that carried at least one passenger during the year; (2) Includes all U.S.-based airlines and freight carriers that transported at least one pound of freight during the year.
Source: Bureau of Transportation Statistics, The Intermodal Transportation Database, Air Carriers: T-100 Domestic Market (U.S. Carriers), 2020; Bureau of Transportation Statistics, The Intermodal Transportation Database, Air Carriers: T-100 International Market (U.S. Carriers), 2019

BUSINESSES

Major Business Headquarters

Company Name	Industry	Rankings Fortune[1]	Rankings Forbes[2]
American Financial Group	Insurance, Property and Casualty (Stock)	383	-
Cintas	Diversified Outsourcing Services	441	-
Fifth Third Bancorp	Commercial Banks	325	-
Kroger	Food and Drug Stores	23	-
Macy's	General Merchandisers	120	-
Procter & Gamble	Household and Personal Products	50	-
Western & Southern Financial Group	Insurance, Life, Health (Mutual)	401	-

Note: (1) Companies that produce a 10-K are ranked 1 to 500 based on 2019 revenue; (2) All private companies with at least $2 billion in annual revenue through the end of their most current fiscal year are ranked 1 to 219; companies listed are headquartered in the city; dashes indicate no ranking
Source: Fortune, "Fortune 500," June/July 2020; Forbes, "America's Largest Private Companies," 2020

Fastest-Growing Businesses

According to *Inc.*, Cincinnati is home to two of America's 500 fastest-growing private companies: **Besomebody** (#49); **SynFiny Advisors** (#302). Criteria: must be an independent, privately-held, for-profit, U.S. corporation, proprietorship or partnership as of December 31, 2019; revenues must be at least $100,000 in 2016 and $2 million in 2019; must have four-year operating/sales history. *Inc., "America's 500 Fastest-Growing Private Companies," 2020*

According to *Fortune*, Cincinnati is home to one of the 100 fastest-growing companies in the world: **Medpace Holdings** (#4). Companies were ranked by their revenue growth rate; their EPS growth rate; and their three-year annualized total return to investors for the period ending June 30, 2020. Criteria for inclusion: a company, foreign or domestic, must trade on a major U.S. stock exchange; must file quarterly reports with the SEC; must have a minimum market capitalization of $250 million; must have a stock price of at least $5 on June 30, 2020; must have been trading continuously since June 30, 2017; must have revenue and net income for the four quarters ended on or before April 30, 2020, of at least $50 million and $10 million, respectively; and must have posted a compound annual growth in revenue and earnings per share of at least 15% annually over the three years ending on or before April 30, 2020. Real estate investment trusts, limited-liability companies, limited parterships, business development companies, closed-end investment firms, companies about to be acquired, and companies that lost money in the quarter ending April 30, 2020 were excluded. *Fortune, "100 Fastest-Growing Companies," 2020*

According to *Initiative for a Competitive Inner City (ICIC)*, Cincinnati is home to one of America's 100 fastest-growing "inner city" companies: **SureFire Innovations** (#19). Criteria for inclusion: company must be headquartered in or have 51 percent or more of its physical operations in an economically distressed urban area; must be an independent, for-profit corporation, partnership or proprietorship; must have 10 or more employees and have a five-year sales history that includes sales of at least $200,000 in the base year and at least $1 million in the current year with no decrease in sales over the two most recent years. Companies were ranked overall by revenue growth over the five-year period between 2015 and 2019. *Initiative for a Competitive Inner City (ICIC), "Inner City 100 Companies," 2020*

Living Environment

COST OF LIVING

Cost of Living Index

Composite Index	Groceries	Housing	Utilities	Trans-portation	Health Care	Misc. Goods/Services
93.4	95.1	80.2	88.0	107.0	99.7	100.4

Note: The Cost of Living Index measures regional differences in the cost of consumer goods and services, excluding taxes and non-consumer expenditures, for professional and managerial households in the top income quintile. It is based on more than 50,000 prices covering almost 60 different items for which prices are collected three times a year by chambers of commerce, economic development organizations or university applied economic centers in each participating urban area. The numbers shown should be read as a percentage above or below the national average of 100. For example, a value of 115.4 in the groceries column indicates that grocery prices are 15.4% higher than the national average. Small differences in the index numbers should not be interpreted as significant; Figures cover the Cincinnati OH urban area.
Source: The Council for Community and Economic Research, Cost of Living Index, 2020

Grocery Prices

Area[1]	T-Bone Steak ($/pound)	Frying Chicken ($/pound)	Whole Milk ($/half gal.)	Eggs ($/dozen)	Orange Juice ($/64 oz.)	Coffee ($/11.5 oz.)
City[2]	13.16	1.25	1.42	1.09	3.61	4.28
Avg.	11.78	1.39	2.05	1.47	3.57	4.34
Min.	8.03	0.94	1.03	0.74	2.94	3.02
Max.	15.86	2.65	4.31	3.77	5.44	8.69

*Note: (1) Values for the local area are compared with the average, minimum and maximum values for all 284 areas in the Cost of Living Index; (2) Figures cover the Cincinnati OH urban area; **T-Bone Steak** (price per pound); **Frying Chicken** (price per pound, whole fryer); **Whole Milk** (half gallon carton); **Eggs** (price per dozen, Grade A, large); **Orange Juice** (64 oz. Tropicana or Florida Natural); **Coffee** (11.5 oz. can, vacuum-packed, Maxwell House, Hills Bros, or Folgers).*
Source: The Council for Community and Economic Research, Cost of Living Index, 2020

Housing and Utility Costs

Area[1]	New Home Price ($)	Apartment Rent ($/month)	All Electric ($/month)	Part Electric ($/month)	Other Energy ($/month)	Telephone ($/month)
City[2]	293,448	944	-	76.98	57.83	179.10
Avg.	368,594	1,168	170.86	100.47	65.28	184.30
Min.	190,567	502	91.58	31.42	26.08	169.60
Max.	2,227,806	4,738	470.38	280.31	280.06	206.50

*Note: (1) Values for the local area are compared with the average, minimum and maximum values for all 284 areas in the Cost of Living Index; (2) Figures cover the Cincinnati OH urban area; **New Home Price** (2,400 sf living area, 8,000 sf lot, in urban area with full utilities); **Apartment Rent** (950 sf 2 bedroom/1.5 or 2 bath, unfurnished, excluding all utilities except water); **All Electric** (average monthly cost for an all-electric home); **Part Electric** (average monthly cost for a part-electric home); **Other Energy** (average monthly cost for natural gas, fuel oil, coal, wood, and any other forms of energy except electricity); **Telephone** (price includes the base monthly rate plus taxes and fees for three lines of mobile phone service).*
Source: The Council for Community and Economic Research, Cost of Living Index, 2020

Health Care, Transportation, and Other Costs

Area[1]	Doctor ($/visit)	Dentist ($/visit)	Optometrist ($/visit)	Gasoline ($/gallon)	Beauty Salon ($/visit)	Men's Shirt ($)
City[2]	109.23	105.08	96.61	2.29	34.80	33.72
Avg.	115.44	99.32	108.10	2.21	39.27	31.37
Min.	36.68	59.00	51.36	1.71	19.00	11.00
Max.	219.00	153.10	250.97	3.46	82.05	58.33

*Note: (1) Values for the local area are compared with the average, minimum and maximum values for all 284 areas in the Cost of Living Index; (2) Figures cover the Cincinnati OH urban area; **Doctor** (general practitioners routine exam of an established patient); **Dentist** (adult teeth cleaning and periodic oral examination); **Optometrist** (full vision eye exam for established adult patient); **Gasoline** (one gallon regular unleaded, national brand, including all taxes, cash price at self-service pump if available); **Beauty Salon** (woman's shampoo, trim, and blow-dry); **Men's Shirt** (cotton/polyester dress shirt, pinpoint weave, long sleeves).*
Source: The Council for Community and Economic Research, Cost of Living Index, 2020

HOUSING

Homeownership Rate

Area	2012 (%)	2013 (%)	2014 (%)	2015 (%)	2016 (%)	2017 (%)	2018 (%)	2019 (%)	2020 (%)
MSA[1]	63.4	63.3	65.5	65.9	64.9	65.7	67.3	67.4	71.1
U.S.	65.4	65.1	64.5	63.7	63.4	63.9	64.4	64.6	66.6

Note: (1) Figures cover the Cincinnati, OH-KY-IN Metropolitan Statistical Area
Source: U.S. Census Bureau, Housing Vacancies and Homeownership Annual Statistics: 2012-2020

House Price Index (HPI)

Area	National Ranking[2]	Quarterly Change (%)	One-Year Change (%)	Five-Year Change (%)	Since 1991Q1 (%)
MSA[1]	98	1.97	6.79	31.23	131.06
U.S.[3]	–	3.81	10.77	38.99	205.12

Note: The HPI is a weighted repeat sales index. It measures average price changes in repeat sales or refinancings on the same properties. This information is obtained by reviewing repeat mortgage transactions on single-family properties whose mortgages have been purchased or securitized by Fannie Mae or Freddie Mac since January 1975; (1) Figures cover the Cincinnati, OH-KY-IN Metropolitan Statistical Area; (2) Rankings are based on annual percentage change for all metro areas containing at least 15,000 transactions over the last 10 years and ranges from 1 to 253; (3) figures based on a weighted average of Census Division estimates using a seasonally adjusted, purchase-only index; all figures are for the period ending December 31, 2020
Source: Federal Housing Finance Agency, Change in Metropolitan Area House Price Indexes, April 7, 2021

Median Single-Family Home Prices

Area	2018	2019	2020[p]	Percent Change 2019 to 2020
MSA[1]	174.3	185.6	208.9	12.6
U.S. Average	261.6	274.6	299.9	9.2

Note: Figures are median sales prices of existing single-family homes in thousands of dollars; (p) preliminary; (1) Figures cover the Cincinnati, OH-KY-IN Metropolitan Statistical Area
Source: National Association of Realtors, Median Sales Price of Existing Single-Family Homes for Metropolitan Areas, 4th Quarter 2020

Qualifying Income Based on Median Sales Price of Existing Single-Family Homes

Area	With 5% Down ($)	With 10% Down ($)	With 20% Down ($)
MSA[1]	40,855	38,704	34,404
U.S. Average	59,266	56,147	49,908

Note: Figures are preliminary; Qualifying income is based on a mortgage rate of 2.81%. Monthly principal and interest payment is limited to 25% of income; (1) Figures cover the Cincinnati, OH-KY-IN Metropolitan Statistical Area
Source: National Association of Realtors, Qualifying Income Based on Median Sales Price of Existing Single-Family Homes for Metropolitan Areas, 4th Quarter 2020

Home Value Distribution

Area	Under $50,000	$50,000 -$99,999	$100,000 -$149,999	$150,000 -$199,999	$200,000 -$299,999	$300,000 -$499,999	$500,000 -$999,999	$1,000,000 or more
City	6.9	25.4	22.2	11.9	14.7	11.5	6.2	1.3
MSA[1]	4.8	15.3	21.4	18.8	21.0	13.6	4.3	0.7
U.S.	6.9	12.0	13.3	14.0	19.6	19.3	11.4	3.4

Note: Figures are percentages and cover owner-occupied housing units; (1) Figures cover the Cincinnati, OH-KY-IN Metropolitan Statistical Area
Source: U.S. Census Bureau, 2015-2019 American Community Survey 5-Year Estimates

Year Housing Structure Built

Area	2010 or Later	2000 -2009	1990 -1999	1980 -1989	1970 -1979	1960 -1969	1950 -1959	1940 -1949	Before 1940	Median Year
City	2.3	3.7	4.2	5.3	9.9	13.0	12.2	8.1	41.2	1951
MSA[1]	3.7	12.4	14.4	10.7	13.8	10.7	11.9	4.9	17.6	1974
U.S.	5.2	14.0	13.9	13.4	15.2	10.6	10.3	4.9	12.6	1978

Note: Figures are percentages except for Median Year; Note: (1) Figures cover the Cincinnati, OH-KY-IN Metropolitan Statistical Area
Source: U.S. Census Bureau, 2015-2019 American Community Survey 5-Year Estimates

Gross Monthly Rent

Area	Under $500	$500 -$999	$1,000 -$1,499	$1,500 -$1,999	$2,000 -$2,499	$2,500 -$2,999	$3,000 and up	Median ($)
City	19.1	56.0	18.0	4.5	1.3	0.4	0.7	738
MSA[1]	12.3	54.7	24.8	5.7	1.5	0.4	0.7	842
U.S.	9.4	36.2	30.0	14.0	5.6	2.4	2.4	1,062

Note: Figures are percentages except for Median; Gross rent is the contract rent plus the estimated average monthly cost of utilities (electricity, gas, and water and sewer) and fuels (oil, coal, kerosene, wood, etc.) if these are paid by the renter (or paid for the renter by someone else); (1) Figures cover the Cincinnati, OH-KY-IN Metropolitan Statistical Area
Source: U.S. Census Bureau, 2015-2019 American Community Survey 5-Year Estimates

HEALTH

Health Risk Factors

Category	MSA[1] (%)	U.S. (%)
Adults aged 18–64 who have any kind of health care coverage	90.1	87.3
Adults who reported being in good or better health	80.5	82.4
Adults who have been told they have high blood cholesterol	33.4	33.0
Adults who have been told they have high blood pressure	33.5	32.3
Adults who are current smokers	23.5	17.1
Adults who currently use E-cigarettes	4.6	4.6
Adults who currently use chewing tobacco, snuff, or snus	4.5	4.0
Adults who are heavy drinkers[2]	7.3	6.3
Adults who are binge drinkers[3]	21.4	17.4
Adults who are overweight (BMI 25.0 - 29.9)	33.1	35.3
Adults who are obese (BMI 30.0 - 99.8)	30.0	31.3
Adults who participated in any physical activities in the past month	73.5	74.4
Adults who always or nearly always wears a seat belt	92.5	94.3

Note: (1) Figures cover the Cincinnati, OH-KY-IN Metropolitan Statistical Area; (2) Heavy drinkers are classified as adult men having more than 14 drinks per week and adult women having more than 7 drinks per week; (3) Binge drinkers are classified as males having five or more drinks on one occasion or females having four or more drinks on one occasion
Source: Centers for Disease Control and Prevention, Behaviorial Risk Factor Surveillance System, SMART: Selected Metropolitan Area Risk Trends, 2017

Acute and Chronic Health Conditions

Category	MSA[1] (%)	U.S. (%)
Adults who have ever been told they had a heart attack	5.2	4.2
Adults who have ever been told they have angina or coronary heart disease	5.1	3.9
Adults who have ever been told they had a stroke	3.4	3.0
Adults who have ever been told they have asthma	11.7	14.2
Adults who have ever been told they have arthritis	28.6	24.9
Adults who have ever been told they have diabetes[2]	9.3	10.5
Adults who have ever been told they had skin cancer	6.1	6.2
Adults who have ever been told they had any other types of cancer	5.7	7.1
Adults who have ever been told they have COPD	8.0	6.5
Adults who have ever been told they have kidney disease	4.1	3.0
Adults who have ever been told they have a form of depression	24.5	20.5

Note: (1) Figures cover the Cincinnati, OH-KY-IN Metropolitan Statistical Area; (2) Figures do not include pregnancy-related, borderline, or pre-diabetes
Source: Centers for Disease Control and Prevention, Behaviorial Risk Factor Surveillance System, SMART: Selected Metropolitan Area Risk Trends, 2017

Health Screening and Vaccination Rates

Category	MSA[1] (%)	U.S. (%)
Adults aged 65+ who have had flu shot within the past year	64.3	60.7
Adults aged 65+ who have ever had a pneumonia vaccination	74.9	75.4
Adults who have ever been tested for HIV	37.1	36.1
Adults who have ever had the shingles or zoster vaccine?	29.7	28.9
Adults who have had their blood cholesterol checked within the last five years	86.7	85.9

Note: n/a not available; (1) Figures cover the Cincinnati, OH-KY-IN Metropolitan Statistical Area.
Source: Centers for Disease Control and Prevention, Behaviorial Risk Factor Surveillance System, SMART: Selected Metropolitan Area Risk Trends, 2017

Disability Status

Category	MSA[1] (%)	U.S. (%)
Adults who reported being deaf	7.6	6.7
Are you blind or have serious difficulty seeing, even when wearing glasses?	4.5	4.5
Are you limited in any way in any of your usual activities due of arthritis?	14.7	12.9
Do you have difficulty doing errands alone?	8.7	6.8
Do you have difficulty dressing or bathing?	4.7	3.6
Do you have serious difficulty concentrating/remembering/making decisions?	14.9	10.7
Do you have serious difficulty walking or climbing stairs?	15.4	13.6

Note: (1) Figures cover the Cincinnati, OH-KY-IN Metropolitan Statistical Area.
Source: Centers for Disease Control and Prevention, Behaviorial Risk Factor Surveillance System, SMART: Selected Metropolitan Area Risk Trends, 2017

Mortality Rates for the Top 10 Causes of Death in the U.S.

ICD-10[a] Sub-Chapter	ICD-10[a] Code	Age-Adjusted Mortality Rate[1] per 100,000 population	
		County[2]	U.S.
Malignant neoplasms	C00-C97	164.6	149.2
Ischaemic heart diseases	I20-I25	84.4	90.5
Other forms of heart disease	I30-I51	70.1	52.2
Chronic lower respiratory diseases	J40-J47	38.5	39.6
Other degenerative diseases of the nervous system	G30-G31	40.5	37.6
Cerebrovascular diseases	I60-I69	48.3	37.2
Other external causes of accidental injury	W00-X59	65.9	36.1
Organic, including symptomatic, mental disorders	F01-F09	39.2	29.4
Hypertensive diseases	I10-I15	25.3	24.1
Diabetes mellitus	E10-E14	23.5	21.5

Note: (a) ICD-10 = International Classification of Diseases 10th Revision; (1) Mortality rates are a three-year average covering 2017-2019; (2) Figures cover Hamilton County.
Source: Centers for Disease Control and Prevention, National Center for Health Statistics. Underlying Cause of Death 1999-2019 on CDC WONDER Online Database

Mortality Rates for Selected Causes of Death

ICD-10[a] Sub-Chapter	ICD-10[a] Code	Age-Adjusted Mortality Rate[1] per 100,000 population	
		County[2]	U.S.
Assault	X85-Y09	10.6	6.0
Diseases of the liver	K70-K76	13.2	14.4
Human immunodeficiency virus (HIV) disease	B20-B24	2.1	1.5
Influenza and pneumonia	J09-J18	14.0	13.8
Intentional self-harm	X60-X84	13.3	14.1
Malnutrition	E40-E46	6.2	2.3
Obesity and other hyperalimentation	E65-E68	1.8	2.1
Renal failure	N17-N19	19.1	12.6
Transport accidents	V01-V99	8.2	12.3
Viral hepatitis	B15-B19	1.0	1.2

Note: (a) ICD-10 = International Classification of Diseases 10th Revision; (1) Mortality rates are a three-year average covering 2017-2019; (2) Figures cover Hamilton County; Data are suppressed when the data meet the criteria for confidentiality constraints; Mortality rates are flagged as unreliable when the rate would be calculated with a numerator of 20 or less.
Source: Centers for Disease Control and Prevention, National Center for Health Statistics. Underlying Cause of Death 1999-2019 on CDC WONDER Online Database

Health Insurance Coverage

Area	With Health Insurance	With Private Health Insurance	With Public Health Insurance	Without Health Insurance	Population Under Age 19 Without Health Insurance
City	92.7	59.1	41.6	7.3	4.5
MSA[1]	94.8	73.1	32.8	5.2	3.1
U.S.	91.2	67.9	35.1	8.8	5.1

Note: Figures are percentages that cover the civilian noninstitutionalized population; (1) Figures cover the Cincinnati, OH-KY-IN Metropolitan Statistical Area
Source: U.S. Census Bureau, 2015-2019 American Community Survey 5-Year Estimates

Number of Medical Professionals

Area	MDs[3]	DOs[3,4]	Dentists	Podiatrists	Chiropractors	Optometrists
County[1] (number)	4,997	205	619	82	166	178
County[1] (rate[2])	612.8	25.1	75.7	10.0	20.3	21.8
U.S. (rate[2])	282.9	22.7	71.2	6.2	28.1	16.9

39061
Note: Data as of 2019 unless noted; (1) Data covers Hamilton County; (2) Rate per 100,000 population; (3) Data as of 2018 and includes all active, non-federal physicians; (4) Doctor of Osteopathic Medicine
Source: U.S. Department of Health and Human Services, Health Resources and Services Administration, Bureau of Health Professions, Area Resource File (ARF) 2019-2020

Best Hospitals

According to *U.S. News,* the Cincinnati, OH-KY-IN metro area is home to one of the best hospitals in the U.S.: **Christ Hospital** (1 adult specialty). The hospital listed was nationally ranked in at least one of 16 adult or 10 pediatric specialties. Only 134 hospitals nationwide were nationally ranked in one or more adult or pediatric specialty; this number increases to 178 counting specialized centers within hospitals. Twenty hospitals in the U.S. made the Honor Roll. The Best Hospitals Honor Roll takes both the national rankings and the procedure and condition ratings into account. Hospitals received points if they were nationally ranked in one of the 16 adult specialties—the higher they ranked, the more points they got—and how many ratings of "high performing" they earned in the 10 procedures and conditions. *U.S. News Online, "America's Best Hospitals 2020-21"*

According to *U.S. News,* the Cincinnati, OH-KY-IN metro area is home to one of the best children's hospitals in the U.S.: **Cincinnati Children's Hospital Medical Center** (Honor Roll/10 pediatric specialties). The hospital listed was highly ranked in at least one of 10 pediatric specialties. Eighty-eight children's hospitals in the U.S. were nationally ranked in at least one specialty. Hospitals received points for being ranked in a specialty, and the 10 hospitals with the most points across the 10 specialties make up the Honor Roll. *U.S. News Online, "America's Best Children's Hospitals 2020-21"*

EDUCATION

Public School District Statistics

District Name	Schls	Pupils	Pupil/ Teacher Ratio	Minority Pupils[1] (%)	Free Lunch Eligible[2] (%)	IEP[3] (%)
Cincinnati Public Schools	62	34,816	15.8	76.5	n/a	20.7

Note: Table includes school districts with 2,000 or more students; (1) Percentage of students that are not non-Hispanic white; (2) Percentage of students that are eligible for the free lunch program; (3) Percentage of students that have an Individualized Education Program.
Source: U.S. Department of Education, National Center for Education Statistics, Common Core of Data, Local Education Agency (School District) Universe Survey: School Year 2018-2019; U.S. Department of Education, National Center for Education Statistics, Common Core of Data, Public Elementary/Secondary School Universe Survey: School Year 2018-2019

Best High Schools

According to *U.S. News,* Cincinnati is home to four of the top 500 high schools in the U.S.: **Walnut Hills High School** (#112); **Indian Hill High School** (#149); **Mariemont High School** (#333); **Turpin High School** (#476). Nearly 18,000 public, magnet and charter schools were ranked based on their performance on state assessments and how well they prepare students for college. *U.S. News & World Report, "Best High Schools 2020"*

Highest Level of Education

Area	Less than H.S.	H.S. Diploma	Some College, No Deg.	Associate Degree	Bachelor's Degree	Master's Degree	Prof. School Degree	Doctorate Degree
City	11.9	24.4	19.1	7.4	21.4	10.4	3.1	2.1
MSA[1]	9.0	29.7	19.2	8.4	21.0	9.3	2.0	1.4
U.S.	12.0	27.0	20.4	8.5	19.8	8.8	2.1	1.4

Note: Figures cover persons age 25 and over; (1) Figures cover the Cincinnati, OH-KY-IN Metropolitan Statistical Area
Source: U.S. Census Bureau, 2015-2019 American Community Survey 5-Year Estimates

Educational Attainment by Race

Area	High School Graduate or Higher (%)					Bachelor's Degree or Higher (%)				
	Total	White	Black	Asian	Hisp.[2]	Total	White	Black	Asian	Hisp.[2]
City	88.1	92.1	83.0	93.1	73.2	37.1	52.6	14.5	80.7	31.0
MSA[1]	91.0	91.9	86.6	88.9	74.1	33.6	34.8	19.2	65.9	24.6
U.S.	88.0	89.9	86.0	87.1	68.7	32.1	33.5	21.6	54.3	16.4

Note: Figures shown cover persons 25 years old and over; (1) Figures cover the Cincinnati, OH-KY-IN Metropolitan Statistical Area; (2) People of Hispanic origin can be of any race
Source: U.S. Census Bureau, 2015-2019 American Community Survey 5-Year Estimates

School Enrollment by Grade and Control

Area	Preschool (%)		Kindergarten (%)		Grades 1 - 4 (%)		Grades 5 - 8 (%)		Grades 9 - 12 (%)	
	Public	Private	Public	Private	Public	Private	Public	Private	Public	Private
City	64.7	35.3	73.1	26.9	77.6	22.4	80.1	19.9	80.8	19.2
MSA[1]	53.4	46.6	78.8	21.2	83.1	16.9	83.9	16.1	82.5	17.5
U.S.	59.1	40.9	87.6	12.4	89.5	10.5	89.4	10.6	90.1	9.9

Note: Figures shown cover persons 3 years old and over; (1) Figures cover the Cincinnati, OH-KY-IN Metropolitan Statistical Area
Source: U.S. Census Bureau, 2015-2019 American Community Survey 5-Year Estimates

Higher Education

Four-Year Colleges			Two-Year Colleges			Medical Schools[1]	Law Schools[2]	Voc/ Tech[3]
Public	Private Non-profit	Private For-profit	Public	Private Non-profit	Private For-profit			
1	10	2	1	0	5	1	1	5

Note: Figures cover institutions located within the city limits and include main campuses only; (1) includes schools accredited by the Liaison Committee on Medical Education and the American Osteopathic Association's Commission on Osteopathic College Accreditation; (2) includes ABA-accredited schools, schools with provisional ABA accreditation, and state accredited schools; (3) includes all schools with programs that are less than 2 years.
Source: National Center for Education Statistics, Integrated Postsecondary Education System (IPEDS), 2019-20; Wikipedia, List of Medical Schools in the United States, accessed April 2, 2021; Wikipedia, List of Law Schools in the United States, accessed April 2, 2021

According to *U.S. News & World Report,* the Cincinnati, OH-KY-IN metro area is home to two of the top 200 national universities in the U.S.: **Miami University—Oxford** (#103 tie); **University of Cincinnati** (#143 tie). The indicators used to capture academic quality fall into a number of categories: assessment by administrators at peer institutions; retention of students; faculty resources; student selectivity; financial resources; alumni giving; high school counselor ratings of colleges; and graduation rate. *U.S. News & World Report, "America's Best Colleges 2021"*

According to *U.S. News & World Report,* the Cincinnati, OH-KY-IN metro area is home to one of the top 100 law schools in the U.S.: **University of Cincinnati** (#81 tie). The rankings are based on a weighted average of 12 measures of quality: peer assessment score; assessment score by lawyers/judges; median LSAT scores; median undergrad GPA; acceptance rate; employment rates for graduates; placement success; bar passage rate; faculty resources; expenditures per student; student/faculty ratio; and library resources. *U.S. News & World Report, "America's Best Graduate Schools, Law, 2022"*

According to *U.S. News & World Report,* the Cincinnati, OH-KY-IN metro area is home to one of the top 75 medical schools for research in the U.S.: **University of Cincinnati** (#42 tie). The rankings are based on a weighted average of 11 measures of quality: quality assessment; peer assessment score; assessment score by residency directors; research activity; total research activity; average research activity per faculty member; student selectivity; median MCAT total score; median undergraduate GPA; acceptance rate; and faculty resources. *U.S. News & World Report, "America's Best Graduate Schools, Medical, 2022"*

EMPLOYERS

Major Employers

Company Name	Industry
Cincinnati Children's Hospital Medical Ctr	Medical
Cleveland Clinic Foundation	Medical
General Electric Company	Conglomerate
Giant Eagle	Grocery stores
Golden Gate Capital LP/Bob Evans	Restaurants
Home Depot	Retail
Honda Motor Co.	Automotive
JP Morgan Chase & Co.	Banking and financial services
Kettering Health Network	Healthcare
Kroger Co.	Grocery stores
Mercy Health	Healthcare
Nationwide Mutual Insurance Company	Insurance
Ohio Health	Healthcare
Ohio State University	Colleges & universities
Premier Health Partners	Healthcare
ProMedica Health System	Healthcare
United Parcel Service	Package delivery services
University Hospitals Health System	Healthcare
Wal-Mart Stores	Retail
Wright-Patterson Air Force Base	Military

Note: Companies shown are located within the Cincinnati, OH-KY-IN Metropolitan Statistical Area.
Source: Hoovers.com; Wikipedia

Best Companies to Work For

Total Quality Logistics, headquartered in Cincinnati, is among "The 100 Best Companies to Work For." To pick the best companies, *Fortune* partnered with the Great Place to Work Institute. Two-thirds of a company's score is based on the results of the Institute's Trust Index survey, which is sent to a random sample of employees from each company. The questions related to attitudes about management's credibility, job satisfaction, and camaraderie. The other third of the scoring is based on the company's responses to the Institute's Culture Audit, which includes detailed questions about pay and benefit programs, and a series of open-ended questions about hiring practices, internal communication, training, recognition programs, and diversity efforts. Any company that is at least five years old with more than 1,000 U.S. employees is eligible. *Fortune, "The 100 Best Companies to Work For," 2020*

Proctor & Gamble, headquartered in Cincinnati, is among the "100 Best Companies for Working Mothers." Criteria: paid time off and leaves; workforce profile; benefits; women's issues and advancement; flexible work; company culture and work life programs. *Working Mother, "100 Best Companies for Working Mothers," 2020*

Proctor & Gamble, headquartered in Cincinnati, is among the "Best Companies for Multicultural Women." *Working Mother* selected 50 companies based on a detailed application completed by public and private firms based in the United States, excluding government agencies, companies in the human resources field and non-autonomous divisions. Companies supplied data about the hiring, pay, and promotion of multicultural employees. Applications focused on representation of multicultural women, recruitment, retention and advancement programs, and company culture. *Working Mother, "Best Companies for Multicultural Women," 2020*

Kroger; Total Quality Logistics, headquartered in Cincinnati, are among the "100 Best Places to Work in IT." To qualify, companies had to be U.S.-based organizations or be non-U.S.-based employers that met the following criteria: have a minimum of 300 total employees at a U.S. headquarters and a minimum of 30 IT employees in the U.S., with at least 50% of their IT employees based in the U.S. The best places to work were selected based on compensation, benefits, work/life balance, employee morale, and satisfaction with training and development programs. In addition, *InsiderPro* and *Computerworld* looked at retention efforts, programs for recognizing and rewarding outstanding performances, and benefits such as flextime, elder care and child care, and reimbursement for college tuition and the cost of pursuing technology certifications. *InsiderPro and Computerworld, "100 Best Places to Work in IT," 2020*

Proctor & Gamble, headquartered in Cincinnati, is among the "Top Companies for Executive Women." This list is determined by organizations filling out an in-depth survey that measures female demographics at every level, but with an emphasis on women in senior corporate roles, with profit & loss (P&L) responsibility, and those earning in the top 20 percent of the organization. *Working Mother* defines P&L as having responsibility that involves monitoring the net income after expenses for a department or entire organization, with direct influence on how company resources are allocated. *Working Mother, "Top Companies for Executive Women," 2020+*

Proctor & Gamble, headquartered in Cincinnati, is among the "Best Companies for Dads." *Working Mother's* newest list recognizes the growing importance companies place on giving dads time off and support for their families. Rankings are determined by measuring gender-neutral or paternity leave offered, as well as actual time taken, phase-back policies, child- and dependent-care benefits, and corporate support groups for men and dads. *Working Mother, "Best Companies for Dads," 2020*

PUBLIC SAFETY

Crime Rate

Area	All Crimes	Violent Crimes				Property Crimes		
		Murder	Rape[3]	Robbery	Aggrav. Assault	Burglary	Larceny -Theft	Motor Vehicle Theft
City	5,147.1	21.1	92.3	287.5	443.7	911.5	2,945.6	445.4
Suburbs[1]	1,749.6	1.5	34.0	32.1	73.6	224.7	1,269.6	114.0
Metro[2]	2,214.3	4.1	42.0	67.0	124.2	318.7	1,498.9	159.4
U.S.	2,489.3	5.0	42.6	81.6	250.2	340.5	1,549.5	219.9

Note: Figures are crimes per 100,000 population; (1) All areas within the metro area that are located outside the city limits; (2) Figures cover the Cincinnati, OH-KY-IN Metropolitan Statistical Area; (3) All figures shown were reported using the revised Uniform Crime Reporting (UCR) definition of rape.
Source: FBI Uniform Crime Reports, 2019

Hate Crimes

Area	Number of Quarters Reported	Number of Incidents per Bias Motivation					
		Race/Ethnicity/ Ancestry	Religion	Sexual Orientation	Disability	Gender	Gender Identity
City	4	24	1	4	3	0	0
U.S.	4	3,963	1,521	1,195	157	69	198

Source: Federal Bureau of Investigation, Hate Crime Statistics 2019

Identity Theft Consumer Reports

Area	Reports	Reports per 100,000 Population	Rank[2]
MSA[1]	4,035	182	241
U.S.	1,387,615	423	-

Note: (1) Figures cover the Cincinnati, OH-KY-IN Metropolitan Statistical Area; (2) Rank ranges from 1 to 391 where 1 indicates greatest number of identity theft reports per 100,000 population
Source: Federal Trade Commission, Consumer Sentinel Network Data Book 2020

Fraud and Other Consumer Reports

Area	Reports	Reports per 100,000 Population	Rank[2]
MSA[1]	16,185	729	161
U.S.	3,385,133	1,031	-

Note: (1) Figures cover the Cincinnati, OH-KY-IN Metropolitan Statistical Area; (2) Rank ranges from 1 to 391 where 1 indicates greatest number of fraud and other consumer reports per 100,000 population
Source: Federal Trade Commission, Consumer Sentinel Network Data Book 2020

POLITICS

2020 Presidential Election Results

Area	Biden	Trump	Jorgensen	Hawkins	Other
Hamilton County	57.1	41.3	1.2	0.3	0.0
U.S.	51.3	46.8	1.2	0.3	0.5

Note: Results are percentages and may not add to 100% due to rounding
Source: Dave Leip's Atlas of U.S. Presidential Elections

SPORTS

Professional Sports Teams

Team Name	League	Year Established
Cincinnati Bengals	National Football League (NFL)	1968
Cincinnati Reds	Major League Baseball (MLB)	1882
FC Cincinnati	Major League Soccer (MLS)	2019

Note: Includes teams located in the Cincinnati, OH-KY-IN Metropolitan Statistical Area.
Source: Wikipedia, Major Professional Sports Teams of the United States and Canada, April 6, 2021

CLIMATE

Average and Extreme Temperatures

Temperature	Jan	Feb	Mar	Apr	May	Jun	Jul	Aug	Sep	Oct	Nov	Dec	Yr.
Extreme High (°F)	74	72	84	89	93	102	103	102	102	89	81	75	103
Average High (°F)	38	42	52	64	74	82	86	85	78	67	53	42	64
Average Temp. (°F)	30	33	43	54	63	72	76	74	68	56	44	34	54
Average Low (°F)	21	24	33	43	52	61	65	63	56	45	35	26	44
Extreme Low (°F)	-25	-15	-11	17	27	39	47	43	33	16	0	-20	-25

Note: Figures cover the years 1948-1990
Source: National Climatic Data Center, International Station Meteorological Climate Summary, 9/96

Average Precipitation/Snowfall/Humidity

Precip./Humidity	Jan	Feb	Mar	Apr	May	Jun	Jul	Aug	Sep	Oct	Nov	Dec	Yr.
Avg. Precip. (in.)	3.2	2.9	3.9	3.5	4.0	3.9	4.2	3.1	2.8	2.8	3.4	3.1	40.9
Avg. Snowfall (in.)	7	5	4	1	Tr	0	0	0	0	Tr	2	4	23
Avg. Rel. Hum. 7am (%)	79	78	77	76	79	82	85	87	87	83	79	79	81
Avg. Rel. Hum. 4pm (%)	65	60	55	50	51	53	54	52	52	51	58	65	55

Note: Figures cover the years 1948-1990; Tr = Trace amounts (<0.05 in. of rain; <0.5 in. of snow)
Source: National Climatic Data Center, International Station Meteorological Climate Summary, 9/96

Weather Conditions

Temperature			Daytime Sky			Precipitation		
10°F & below	32°F & below	90°F & above	Clear	Partly cloudy	Cloudy	0.01 inch or more precip.	0.1 inch or more snow/ice	Thunder-storms
14	107	23	80	126	159	127	25	39

Note: Figures are average number of days per year and cover the years 1948-1990
Source: National Climatic Data Center, International Station Meteorological Climate Summary, 9/96

HAZARDOUS WASTE

Superfund Sites

The Cincinnati, OH-KY-IN metro area is home to six sites on the EPA's Superfund National Priorities List: **Armco Incorporation-Hamilton Plant** (proposed); **Chem-Dyne** (final); **Milford Contaminated Aquifer** (final); **Peters Cartridge Factory** (final); **Pristine, Inc.** (final); **Skinner Landfill** (final). There are a total of 1,375 Superfund sites with a status of proposed or final on the list in the U.S. *U.S. Environmental Protection Agency, National Priorities List, April 7, 2021*

AIR QUALITY

Air Quality Trends: Ozone

	1990	1995	2000	2005	2010	2015	2016	2017	2018	2019
MSA[1]	0.091	0.091	0.081	0.085	0.075	0.068	0.071	0.067	0.074	0.067
U.S.	0.088	0.089	0.082	0.080	0.073	0.068	0.069	0.068	0.069	0.065

Note: (1) Data covers the Cincinnati, OH-KY-IN Metropolitan Statistical Area. The values shown are the composite ozone concentration averages among trend sites based on the highest fourth daily maximum 8-hour concentration in parts per million. These trends are based on sites having an adequate record of monitoring data during the trend period. Data from exceptional events are included.
Source: U.S. Environmental Protection Agency, Air Quality Monitoring Information, "Air Quality Trends by City, 1990-2019"

Air Quality Index

Area	Percent of Days when Air Quality was...[2]					AQI Statistics[2]	
	Good	Moderate	Unhealthy for Sensitive Groups	Unhealthy	Very Unhealthy	Maximum	Median
MSA[1]	38.1	56.4	5.5	0.0	0.0	147	54

Note: (1) Data covers the Cincinnati, OH-KY-IN Metropolitan Statistical Area; (2) Based on 365 days with AQI data in 2019. Air Quality Index (AQI) is an index for reporting daily air quality. EPA calculates the AQI for five major air pollutants regulated by the Clean Air Act: ground-level ozone, particle pollution (aka particulate matter), carbon monoxide, sulfur dioxide, and nitrogen dioxide. The AQI runs from 0 to 500. The higher the AQI value, the greater the level of air pollution and the greater the health concern. There are six AQI categories: "Good" AQI is between 0 and 50. Air quality is considered satisfactory; "Moderate" AQI is between 51 and 100. Air quality is acceptable; "Unhealthy for Sensitive Groups" When AQI values are between 101 and 150, members of sensitive groups may experience health effects; "Unhealthy" When AQI values are between 151 and 200 everyone may begin to experience health effects; "Very Unhealthy" AQI values between 201 and 300 trigger a health alert; "Hazardous" AQI values over 300 trigger warnings of emergency conditions (not shown).
Source: U.S. Environmental Protection Agency, Air Quality Index Report, 2019

Air Quality Index Pollutants

Area	Percent of Days when AQI Pollutant was...[2]					
	Carbon Monoxide	Nitrogen Dioxide	Ozone	Sulfur Dioxide	Particulate Matter 2.5	Particulate Matter 10
MSA[1]	0.0	1.6	41.4	6.0	50.1	0.8

Note: (1) Data covers the Cincinnati, OH-KY-IN Metropolitan Statistical Area; (2) Based on 365 days with AQI data in 2019. The Air Quality Index (AQI) is an index for reporting daily air quality. EPA calculates the AQI for five major air pollutants regulated by the Clean Air Act: ground-level ozone, particle pollution (also known as particulate matter), carbon monoxide, sulfur dioxide, and nitrogen dioxide. The AQI runs from 0 to 500. The higher the AQI value, the greater the level of air pollution and the greater the health concern.
Source: U.S. Environmental Protection Agency, Air Quality Index Report, 2019

Maximum Air Pollutant Concentrations: Particulate Matter, Ozone, CO and Lead

	Particulate Matter 10 (ug/m^3)	Particulate Matter 2.5 Wtd AM (ug/m^3)	Particulate Matter 2.5 24-Hr (ug/m^3)	Ozone (ppm)	Carbon Monoxide (ppm)	Lead (ug/m^3)
MSA[1] Level	108	11.9	26	0.072	2	n/a
NAAQS[2]	150	15	35	0.075	9	0.15
Met NAAQS[2]	Yes	Yes	Yes	Yes	Yes	n/a

Note: (1) Data covers the Cincinnati, OH-KY-IN Metropolitan Statistical Area; Data from exceptional events are included; (2) National Ambient Air Quality Standards; ppm = parts per million; ug/m^3 = micrograms per cubic meter; n/a not available.
Concentrations: Particulate Matter 10 (coarse particulate)—highest second maximum 24-hour concentration; Particulate Matter 2.5 Wtd AM (fine particulate)—highest weighted annual mean concentration; Particulate Matter 2.5 24-Hour (fine particulate)—highest 98th percentile 24-hour concentration; Ozone—highest fourth daily maximum 8-hour concentration; Carbon Monoxide—highest second maximum non-overlapping 8-hour concentration; Lead—maximum running 3-month average
Source: U.S. Environmental Protection Agency, Air Quality Monitoring Information, "Air Quality Statistics by City, 2019"

Maximum Air Pollutant Concentrations: Nitrogen Dioxide and Sulfur Dioxide

	Nitrogen Dioxide AM (ppb)	Nitrogen Dioxide 1-Hr (ppb)	Sulfur Dioxide AM (ppb)	Sulfur Dioxide 1-Hr (ppb)	Sulfur Dioxide 24-Hr (ppb)
MSA[1] Level	18	49	n/a	134	n/a
NAAQS[2]	53	100	30	75	140
Met NAAQS[2]	Yes	Yes	n/a	No	n/a

Note: (1) Data covers the Cincinnati, OH-KY-IN Metropolitan Statistical Area; Data from exceptional events are included; (2) National Ambient Air Quality Standards; ppm = parts per million; ug/m³ = micrograms per cubic meter; n/a not available.
Concentrations: Nitrogen Dioxide AM—highest arithmetic mean concentration; Nitrogen Dioxide 1-Hr—highest 98th percentile 1-hour daily maximum concentration; Sulfur Dioxide AM—highest annual mean concentration; Sulfur Dioxide 1-Hr—highest 99th percentile 1-hour daily maximum concentration; Sulfur Dioxide 24-Hr—highest second maximum 24-hour concentration
Source: U.S. Environmental Protection Agency, Air Quality Monitoring Information, "Air Quality Statistics by City, 2019"

Cleveland, Ohio

Background

Cleveland is located on the south shore of Lake Erie in northeastern Ohio and is bisected by the Cuyahoga River. The metro area has a frontage of 31 miles.

The city began with very modest resources. It was founded in 1796 by General Moses Cleveland, on what was known as the Western Reserve of Connecticut, but of all the people that General Cleveland led on his expedition, only three remained in the area. However, the completion of the Erie and Ohio canals brought people and industry to this city, both of which were sorely needed to keep the area alive. By the 1840s, the population had grown by 500 percent from the prior decade. While neighborhoods fell along racial and ethnic lines, the children of these immigrants intermarried and surpassed their parents on socioeconomic levels. Cleveland was a place where the American dream could be realized.

During World War I, a new wave of job seekers flooded Cleveland. These were largely African Americans from Southern rural areas, and poor whites from Kentucky, Tennessee, and West Virginia filling in for a shortage of workers in war goods production. After the war, the next group of job seekers was unskilled and did not have the same opportunities as did their predecessors, thus making job competition difficult. These collapsing economic conditions set the stage for the urban unrest of the 1960s.

In the 1990s, Cleveland enjoyed an economic renaissance with several projects representing more than $9 billion in capital investment. A public-private partnership was responsible for a new downtown Gateway sports complex (1994) home of the Cleveland Indians, the Rock & Roll Hall of Fame (1998) designed by I.M. Pei, and a vibrant new entertainment district.

The biomed/biotechnology industry has been important in recent years, with the Cleveland Clinic recording more than 7 million patient visits annually and employing 60,000 people, alongside other area universities and foundations. A leading national research center, it receives millions of dollars annually from the National Institutes of Health and in 2018-2019 was ranked by *U.S. News and World Report* as the nation's second best hospital.

The city has set a high priority on redevelopment. Begun in 2005, the Euclid Corridor Transportation Project, designed to improve public transportation between downtown and the University Circle, was completed in 2008. Ridership has steadily increased since its opening.

The Port of Cleveland is the largest for overseas general cargo on Lake Erie, and the third largest on any of the Great Lakes. It generates roughly a billion dollars annually in trade.

Progressive Field is home to the MLB Cleveland Indians, and the Quicken Loans Arena hosts the Cavaliers basketball team. Both venues were extensively improved in the course of an ambitious "Gateway Project." In recent years, both teams have seen success, with the Indians advancing to the World Series in 2016 and the Cavaliers playing in the N.B.A. Finals every year from 2015 to 2018, winning a championship in 2016, behind superstar forward LeBron James.

Increasingly, the northeastern Ohio economy is driven by research and specialized service industries, and Cleveland is considered one of the best metro areas in the U.S. for attracting expanded business facilities. Cleveland is especially prominent in the field of health-related technology. Altogether, nearly 200 tech companies have formed in the Cleveland area. Other fields in which the city's economy thrives include banking, education, insurance, and, healthcare. Cleveland's two largest employers are Cleveland Clinic and University Hospitals.

Few cities of its size offer the array of arts and cultural opportunities afforded by the Greater Cleveland area. The University Circle area is home to more than 70 cultural, educational, science, medical, and religious institutions, including the opulent Severance Hall, home of the renowned Cleveland Orchestra. Playhouse Square offers Broadway shows, plays, opera, ballet, and contemporary performing arts. Cleveland also has one of the six Second City comedy theaters in the nation. At the Cleveland Museum of Natural History you can visit another galaxy at the new Shafran Planetarium or meet "Lucy," one of the oldest skeletons of our earliest known ancestors. The Cleveland Metroparks Zoo houses the biggest collection of primates in North America and has an indoor rainforest. Nearby is the Great Lakes Science center, which features an OMNIMAX® theater, and focuses on science, environment and technology particular to the Great Lakes Region. In 2012, the Museum of Contemporary Art (MoCA) opened its new permanent location in University Circle.

> Cleveland Chamber Choir made a successful leap to virtual programming, performing Mozart's "Ave Verum" and other works by stitching together individual performance videos.

Rankings

General Rankings

- In its eighth annual survey, *Travel + Leisure* readers nominated their favorite small cities and towns in America—those with 100,000 or fewer residents—voting on numerous attractive features in categories including culture, food and drink, quality of life, style, and people. After 50,000 votes, Cleveland was ranked #20 among the proposed favorites. *www.travelandleisure.com, "America's Favorite Cities," October 20, 2017*

Business/Finance Rankings

- Based on metro area social media reviews, the employment opinion group Glassdoor surveyed 50 of the most populous U.S. metro areas and equally weighed cost of living, hiring opportunity, and job satisfaction to compose a list of "25 Best Cities for Jobs." Median pay and home value, and number of active job openings were also factored in. The Cleveland metro area was ranked #5 in overall job satisfaction. *www.glassdoor.com, "Best Cities for Jobs," February 25, 2020*

- The Brookings Institution ranked the nation's largest cities based on income inequality. Cleveland was ranked #23 (#1 = greatest inequality). Criteria: the "95/20 ratio," a figure representing the income at which a household earns more than 95 percent of all other households, divided by the income at which a household earns more than only 20 percent of all other households. *Brookings Institution, "Household Income Inequality, Largest Cities of 97 Large U.S. Metro Areas, 2014-2016," February 5, 2018*

- The Brookings Institution ranked the 100 largest metro areas in the U.S. based on income inequality. Cleveland was ranked #18 (#1 = greatest inequality). Criteria: the "95/20 ratio," a figure representing the income at which a household earns more than 95 percent of all other households, divided by the income at which a household earns more than only 20 percent of all other households. *Brookings Institution, "Household Income Inequality, 100 Largest U.S. Metro Areas, 2014-2016," February 5, 2018*

- Payscale.com ranked the 32 largest metro areas in terms of wage growth. The Cleveland metro area ranked #26. Criteria: private-sector and education professional wage growth between the 4th quarter of 2019 and the 4th quarter of 2020. *PayScale, "Wage Trends by Metro Area-4th Quarter," January 11, 2021*

- Cleveland was identified as one of America's most frugal metro areas by *Coupons.com*. The city ranked #10 out of 25. Criteria: digital coupon usage. *Coupons.com, "America's Most Frugal Cities of 2017," March 22, 2018*

- The Cleveland metro area appeared on the Milken Institute "2021 Best Performing Cities" list. Rank: #173 out of 200 large metro areas (population over 250,000). Criteria: job growth; wage and salary growth; high-tech output growth; housing affordability; household broadband access. *Milken Institute, "Best-Performing Cities 2021," February 16, 2021*

- *Forbes* ranked the 200 most populous metro areas to determine the nation's "Best Places for Business and Careers." The Cleveland metro area was ranked #135. Criteria: costs (business and living); job growth (past and projected); income growth; quality of life; educational attainment (college and high school); projected economic growth; cultural and leisure opportunities; workplace tolerance laws; net migration patterns. *Forbes, "The Best Places for Business and Careers 2019: Seattle Still On Top," October 30, 2019*

- Mercer Human Resources Consulting ranked 209 cities worldwide in terms of cost-of-living. Cleveland ranked #93 (the lower the ranking, the higher the cost-of-living). The survey measured the comparative cost of over 200 items (such as housing, food, clothing, household goods, transportation, and entertainment) in each location. *Mercer, "2020 Cost of Living Survey," June 9, 2020*

Culture/Performing Arts Rankings

- Cleveland was selected as one of the 25 best cities for moviemakers in North America. COVID-19 has spurred a quest for great film cities that offer more creative space, lower costs, and more great outdoors. NYC & LA were intentionally excluded. Criteria: longstanding reputations as film-friendly communities; efforts to deal with pandemic-specific challenges; and establish appropriate COVID-19 guidelines. The city was ranked #14. *MovieMaker Magazine, "Best Places to Live and Work as a Moviemaker, 2021," January 26, 2021*

Education Rankings

- Personal finance website *WalletHub* analyzed the 150 largest U.S. metropolitan statistical areas to determine where the most educated Americans are putting their degrees to work. Criteria: education levels; percentage of workers with degrees; education quality and attainment gap; public school quality rankings; quality and enrollment of each metro area's universities. Cleveland was ranked #84 (#1 = most educated city). *www.WalletHub.com, "Most and Least Educated Cities in America, " July 20, 2020*

- Cleveland was selected as one of America's most literate cities. The city ranked #17 out of the 84 largest U.S. cities. Criteria: number of booksellers; library resources; Internet resources; educational attainment; periodical publishing resources; newspaper circulation. *Central Connecticut State University, "America's Most Literate Cities, 2018," February 2019*

Environmental Rankings

- Niche compiled a list of the nation's snowiest cities, based on the National Oceanic and Atmospheric Administration's 30-year average snowfall data. Among cities with a population of at least 50,000, Cleveland ranked #9. *Niche.com, Top 25 Snowiest Cities in America, December 10, 2018*

- Cleveland was highlighted as one of the 25 metro areas most polluted by year-round particle pollution (Annual PM 2.5) in the U.S. during 2016 through 2018. The area ranked #11. *American Lung Association, "State of the Air 2020," April 21, 2020*

- Cleveland was highlighted as one of the top 98 cleanest metro areas for short-term particle pollution (24-hour PM 2.5) in the U.S. during 2016 through 2018. Monitors in these cities reported no days with unhealthful PM 2.5 levels. *American Lung Association, "State of the Air 2020," April 21, 2020*

Food/Drink Rankings

- Progressive Field was selected as one of PETA's "Top 10 Vegan-Friendly Ballparks" for 2019. The park ranked #5. *People for the Ethical Treatment of Animals, "Top 10 Vegan-Friendly Ballparks, " May 23, 2019*

Health/Fitness Rankings

- For each of the 100 largest cities in the United States, the American Fitness Index®, published by the American College of Sports Medicine and the Anthem Foundation, evaluated community infrastructure and 33 health behaviors including preventive health, levels of chronic disease conditions, pedestrian safety, air quality, and community resources that support physical activity. Cleveland ranked #57 for "community fitness." *americanfitnessindex.org, "2020 ACSM American Fitness Index Summary Report," July 14, 2020*

- The Cleveland metro area was identified as one of the worst cities for bed bugs in America by pest control company Orkin. The area ranked #6 out of 50 based on the number of bed bug treatments Orkin performed from December 2019 to November 2020. *Orkin, "New Year, New Top City on Orkin's 2021 Bed Bug Cities List: Chicago," February 1, 2021*

- Cleveland was identified as a "2021 Spring Allergy Capital." The area ranked #59 out of 100. Three groups of factors were used to identify the most challenging cities for people with allergies during the spring season: annual spring pollen levels; over the counter medicine use; number of board-certified allergy specialists. *Asthma and Allergy Foundation of America, "Spring Allergy Capitals 2021," February 23, 2021*

- Cleveland was identified as a "2021 Fall Allergy Capital." The area ranked #40 out of 100. Three groups of factors were used to identify the most challenging cities for people with allergies during the fall season: annual fall pollen levels; over the counter medicine use; number of board-certified allergy specialists. *Asthma and Allergy Foundation of America, "Fall Allergy Capitals 2021," February 23, 2021*

- Cleveland was identified as a "2019 Asthma Capital." The area ranked #5 out of the nation's 100 largest metropolitan areas. Criteria: estimated asthma prevalence; crude death rate from asthma; and ER visits due to asthma. Risk factors analyzed but not factored in the rankings: annual pollen score; annual air quality; public smoking laws; number of board-certified asthma specialists; rescue medication use; controller medication use; uninsured rate; poverty rate. *Asthma and Allergy Foundation of America, "Asthma Capitals 2019: The Most Challenging Places to Live With Asthma," May 7, 2019*

Real Estate Rankings

- FitSmallBusiness looked at 50 of the largest metropolitan areas in the U.S. to determine which metro was the best to start a real estate business. Data was compiled from such sources as: Zillow, Trulia, U.S. Census Bureau, and the Bureau of Labor Statistics. Criteria: location; inventory; annual wages; median sales price of homes; days on the market; median price cut percentage; and other factors that would influence real estate professional growth. The Cleveland metro area ranked #48. *fitsmallbusiness.com, "The Best Cities to Become a Real Estate Agent in 2018," January 30, 2018*

- *WalletHub* compared the most populated U.S. cities to determine which had the best markets for real estate agents. Cleveland ranked #165 where demand was high and pay was the best. Criteria: sales per agent; annual median wage for real-estate agents; monthly average starting salary for real estate agents; real estate job density and competition; unemployment rate; home turnover rate; housing-market health index; and other relevant metrics. *www.WalletHub.com, "2019's Best Places to Be a Real Estate Agent," April 24, 2019*

- The Cleveland metro area was identified as one of the top 15 housing markets to invest in for 2021 by *Forbes*. Criteria: home price appreciation; percentage of home sales within a 2-week time frame; available inventory; number of home sales; and other factors. *Forbes.com, "Top Housing Markets To Watch In 2021," December 15, 2020*

- Cleveland was ranked #8 in the top 20 out of the 100 largest metro areas in terms of house price appreciation in 2020 (#1 = highest rate). *Federal Housing Finance Agency, House Price Index, 4th Quarter 2020*

- Cleveland was ranked #60 out of 268 metro areas in terms of housing affordability in 2020 by the National Association of Home Builders (#1 = most affordable). Criteria: the share of homes sold in that area affordable to a family earning the local median income, based on standard mortgage underwriting criteria. *National Association of Home Builders®, NAHB-Wells Fargo Housing Opportunity Index, 4th Quarter 2020*

- The nation's largest metro areas were analyzed in terms of the percentage of households entering some stage of foreclosure in 2020. The Cleveland metro area ranked #6 out of 10 (#1 = highest foreclosure rate). *ATTOM Data Solutions, "2020 Year-End U.S. Foreclosure Market Report™," January 14, 2021*

Safety Rankings

- To identify the most dangerous cities in America, 24/7 Wall Street focused on violent crime categories—murder, non-negligent manslaughter, rape, robbery, and aggravated assault—and property crime as reported in the FBI's 2019 annual Uniform Crime Report. Criteria also included median income from American Community Survey and unemployment figures from Bureau of Labor Statistics. For cities with populations over 100,000, Cleveland was ranked #7. *247wallst.com, "America's 50 Most Dangerous Cities" November 16, 2020*

- Allstate ranked the 200 largest cities in America in terms of driver safety. Cleveland ranked #107. Criteria: internal property damage claims over a two-year period from January 2016 to December 2017. The report helps increase the importance of safety and awareness behind the wheel. *Allstate, "Allstate America's Best Drivers Report, 2019" June 24, 2019*

- Cleveland was identified as one of the most dangerous cities in America by NeighborhoodScout. The city ranked #16 out of 100 (#1 = most dangerous). Criteria: number of violent crimes per 1,000 residents. The editors evaluated cities with 25,000 or more residents. *NeighborhoodScout.com, "2021 Top 100 Most Dangerous Cities in the U.S.," January 2, 2021*

- The National Insurance Crime Bureau ranked 384 metro areas in the U.S. in terms of per capita rates of vehicle theft. The Cleveland metro area ranked #118 (#1 = highest rate). Criteria: number of vehicle theft offenses per 100,000 inhabitants in 2019. *National Insurance Crime Bureau, "Hot Spots 2019," July 21, 2020*

Seniors/Retirement Rankings

- From its Best Cities for Successful Aging indexes, the Milken Institute generated rankings for metropolitan areas, weighing data in nine categories—health care, wellness, living arrangements, transportation and convenience, financial characteristics, education, employment, community engagement, and overall livability. The Cleveland metro area was ranked #36 overall in the large metro area category. *Milken Institute, "Best Cities for Successful Aging, 2017" March 14, 2017*

Sports/Recreation Rankings

- Cleveland was chosen as one of America's best cities for bicycling. The city ranked #29 out of 50. Criteria: cycling infrastructure that is safe and friendly for all ages; energy and bike culture. The editors evaluated cities with populations of 100,000 or more. *Bicycling, "The 50 Best Bike Cities in America," October 10, 2018*

Women/Minorities Rankings

- Personal finance website *WalletHub* compared more than 180 U.S. cities across two key dimensions, "Hispanic Business-Friendliness" and "Hispanic Purchasing Power," to arrive at the most favorable conditions for Hispanic entrepreneurs. Cleveland was ranked #178 out of 182. Criteria includes: share of Hispanic-Owned Businesses; Hispanic entrepreneurship rate to median annual income of Hispanics; Small Business-Friendliness score; cost of living; and number of Hispanics with at least a bachelor's degree. *WalletHub.com, "2019's Best Cities for Hispanic Entrepreneurs," May 1, 2019*

Miscellaneous Rankings

- *MoveHub* ranked 446 hipster cities across 20 countries, using its *alternative* Hipster Index and Cleveland came out as #36 among the top 50. Criteria: population over 150,000; number of vintage boutiques; density of tattoo parlors; vegan places to eat; coffee shops; and density of vinyl record stores. *www.movehub.com, "The Hipster Index: Brighton Pips Portland to Global Top Spot," February 20, 2020*

- In its roundup of St. Patrick's Day parades "Gayot" listed the best festivals and parades of all things Irish. The festivities in Cleveland as among the best. *www.gayot.com, "Best St. Patrick's Day Parades," March 2020*

- The watchdog site, Charity Navigator, conducted a study of charities in major markets both to analyze statistical differences in their financial, accountability, and transparency practices and to track year-to-year variations in individual philanthropic communities. The Cleveland metro area was ranked #6 among the 30 metro markets in the rating category of Overall Score. *www.charitynavigator.org, "2017 Metro Market Study," May 1, 2017*

- *WalletHub* compared the 150 most populated U.S. cities to determine their operating efficiency. A "Quality of City Services" score was constructed for each city and then divided by the total budget per capita to reveal which were managed the best. Cleveland ranked #139. Criteria: financial stability; economy; education; safety; health; infrastructure and pollution. *www.WalletHub.com, "2020's Best- & Worst-Run Cities in America," June 29, 2020*

- Cleveland was selected as one of "America's Friendliest Cities." The city ranked #14 in the "Friendliest" category. Respondents to an online survey were asked to rate 38 top urban destinations in the United States as to general friendliness, as well as manners, politeness and warm disposition. *Travel + Leisure, "America's Friendliest Cities," October 20, 2017*

Business Environment

DEMOGRAPHICS

Population Growth

Area	1990 Census	2000 Census	2010 Census	2019* Estimate	Population Growth (%) 1990-2019	Population Growth (%) 2010-2019
City	505,333	478,403	396,815	385,282	-23.8	-2.9
MSA[1]	2,102,219	2,148,143	2,077,240	2,056,898	-2.2	-1.0
U.S.	248,709,873	281,421,906	308,745,538	324,697,795	30.6	5.2

Note: (1) Figures cover the Cleveland-Elyria, OH Metropolitan Statistical Area; (*) 2015-2019 5-year estimated population
Source: U.S. Census Bureau, 1990 Census, Census 2000, Census 2010, 2015-2019 American Community Survey 5-Year Estimates

Household Size

Area	One	Two	Three	Four	Five	Six	Seven or More	Average Household Size
City	44.4	27.5	13.1	8.1	4.2	1.7	1.0	2.20
MSA[1]	34.1	33.8	14.3	10.8	4.6	1.6	0.9	2.30
U.S.	27.9	33.9	15.6	12.9	6.0	2.3	1.4	2.60

Note: (1) Figures cover the Cleveland-Elyria, OH Metropolitan Statistical Area
Source: U.S. Census Bureau, 2015-2019 American Community Survey 5-Year Estimates

Race

Area	White Alone[2] (%)	Black Alone[2] (%)	Asian Alone[2] (%)	AIAN[3] Alone[2] (%)	NHOPI[4] Alone[2] (%)	Other Race Alone[2] (%)	Two or More Races (%)
City	40.0	48.8	2.6	0.5	0.1	3.6	4.4
MSA[1]	73.4	19.9	2.3	0.2	0.0	1.3	2.9
U.S.	72.5	12.7	5.5	0.8	0.2	4.9	3.3

Note: (1) Figures cover the Cleveland-Elyria, OH Metropolitan Statistical Area; (2) Alone is defined as not being in combination with one or more other races; (3) American Indian and Alaska Native; (4) Native Hawaiian and Other Pacific Islander
Source: U.S. Census Bureau, 2015-2019 American Community Survey 5-Year Estimates

Hispanic or Latino Origin

Area	Total (%)	Mexican (%)	Puerto Rican (%)	Cuban (%)	Other (%)
City	11.9	1.3	8.5	0.2	1.9
MSA[1]	5.8	1.3	3.4	0.1	1.0
U.S.	18.0	11.2	1.7	0.7	4.3

Note: Persons of Hispanic or Latino origin can be of any race; (1) Figures cover the Cleveland-Elyria, OH Metropolitan Statistical Area
Source: U.S. Census Bureau, 2015-2019 American Community Survey 5-Year Estimates

Ancestry

Area	German	Irish	English	American	Italian	Polish	French[2]	Scottish	Dutch
City	9.0	8.3	2.6	2.1	4.8	3.8	0.9	0.6	0.5
MSA[1]	18.8	13.4	7.0	3.8	9.8	7.7	1.5	1.5	0.9
U.S.	13.3	9.7	7.2	6.2	5.1	2.8	2.3	1.7	1.2

Note: Figures are the percentage of the total population reporting a particular ancestry. The nine most commonly reported ancestries in the U.S. are shown. Figures include multiple ancestries (e.g. if a person reported being Irish and Italian, they were included in both columns); (1) Figures cover the Cleveland-Elyria, OH Metropolitan Statistical Area; (2) Excludes Basque
Source: U.S. Census Bureau, 2015-2019 American Community Survey 5-Year Estimates

Foreign-born Population

Area	Any Foreign Country	Asia	Mexico	Europe	Caribbean	Central America[2]	South America	Africa	Canada
City	5.9	2.5	0.3	1.0	0.5	0.4	0.3	0.7	0.1
MSA[1]	6.0	2.2	0.3	2.2	0.2	0.2	0.2	0.4	0.2
U.S.	13.6	4.2	3.5	1.5	1.3	1.1	1.0	0.7	0.2

Note: (1) Figures cover the Cleveland-Elyria, OH Metropolitan Statistical Area; (2) Excludes Mexico.
Source: U.S. Census Bureau, 2015-2019 American Community Survey 5-Year Estimates

Marital Status

Area	Never Married	Now Married[2]	Separated	Widowed	Divorced
City	51.4	25.1	3.2	6.2	14.1
MSA[1]	34.9	45.0	1.6	6.6	11.8
U.S.	33.4	48.1	1.9	5.8	10.9

Note: Figures are percentages and cover the population 15 years of age and older; (1) Figures cover the Cleveland-Elyria, OH Metropolitan Statistical Area; (2) Excludes separated
Source: U.S. Census Bureau, 2015-2019 American Community Survey 5-Year Estimates

Disability by Age

Area	All Ages	Under 18 Years Old	18 to 64 Years Old	65 Years and Over
City	20.0	8.6	18.8	44.3
MSA[1]	14.2	5.2	11.7	33.8
U.S.	12.6	4.2	10.3	34.5

Note: Figures show percent of the civilian noninstitutionalized population that reported having a disability. Disability status is determined from six types of difficulty: vision, hearing, cognitive, ambulatory, self-care, and independent living. For children under 5 years old, hearing and vision difficulty are used to determine disability status. For children between the ages of 5 and 14, disability status is determined from hearing, vision, cognitive, ambulatory, and self-care difficulties. For people aged 15 years and older, they are considered to have a disability if they have difficulty with any one of the six difficulty types; Note: (1) Figures cover the Cleveland-Elyria, OH Metropolitan Statistical Area
Source: U.S. Census Bureau, 2015-2019 American Community Survey 5-Year Estimates

Age

Area	Percent of Population									Median Age
	Under Age 5	Age 5–19	Age 20–34	Age 35–44	Age 45–54	Age 55–64	Age 65–74	Age 75–84	Age 85+	
City	6.3	18.3	23.7	11.5	12.4	13.8	8.0	4.2	1.8	36.3
MSA[1]	5.6	18.1	18.9	11.6	13.3	14.5	10.1	5.4	2.5	41.3
U.S.	6.1	19.1	20.7	12.6	13.0	12.9	9.1	4.6	1.9	38.1

Note: (1) Figures cover the Cleveland-Elyria, OH Metropolitan Statistical Area
Source: U.S. Census Bureau, 2015-2019 American Community Survey 5-Year Estimates

Gender

Area	Males	Females	Males per 100 Females
City	185,274	200,008	92.6
MSA[1]	993,227	1,063,671	93.4
U.S.	159,886,919	164,810,876	97.0

Note: (1) Figures cover the Cleveland-Elyria, OH Metropolitan Statistical Area
Source: U.S. Census Bureau, 2015-2019 American Community Survey 5-Year Estimates

Religious Groups by Family

Area	Catholic	Baptist	Non-Den.	Methodist[2]	Lutheran	LDS[3]	Pentecostal	Presbyterian[4]	Muslim[5]	Judaism
MSA[1]	28.9	4.4	3.3	2.9	2.5	0.4	1.1	2.1	0.2	1.5
U.S.	19.1	9.3	4.0	4.0	2.3	2.0	1.9	1.6	0.8	0.7

Note: Figures are the number of adherents as a percentage of the total population; (1) Figures cover the Cleveland-Elyria, OH Metropolitan Statistical Area; (2) Methodist/Pietist; (3) Latter Day Saints; (4) Reformed; (5) Figures are estimates
Source: Association of Statisticians of American Religious Bodies, 2010 U.S. Religion Census: Religious Congregations & Membership Study

Religious Groups by Tradition

Area	Catholic	Evangelical Protestant	Mainline Protestant	Other Tradition	Black Protestant	Orthodox
MSA[1]	28.9	9.1	7.6	2.7	2.1	0.8
U.S.	19.1	16.2	7.3	4.3	1.6	0.3

Note: Figures are the number of adherents as a percentage of the total population; (1) Figures cover the Cleveland-Elyria, OH Metropolitan Statistical Area
Source: Association of Statisticians of American Religious Bodies, 2010 U.S. Religion Census: Religious Congregations & Membership Study

ECONOMY

Gross Metropolitan Product

Area	2017	2018	2019	2020	Rank[2]
MSA[1]	138.3	145.9	152.3	157.1	28

Note: Figures are in billions of dollars; (1) Figures cover the Cleveland-Elyria, OH Metropolitan Statistical Area; (2) Rank is based on 2018 data and ranges from 1 to 381
Source: U.S. Conference of Mayors, U.S. Metro Economies: GMP & Employment 2018-2020, September 2019

Economic Growth

Area	2015-17 (%)	2018 (%)	2019 (%)	2020 (%)	Rank[2]
MSA[1]	1.7	1.9	2.8	0.9	160
U.S.	1.9	2.9	2.3	2.1	—

Note: Figures are real gross metropolitan product (GMP) growth rates and represent average annual percent change; (1) Figures cover the Cleveland-Elyria, OH Metropolitan Statistical Area; (2) Rank is based on 2017 2-year average annual percent change and ranges from 1 to 381
Source: U.S. Conference of Mayors, U.S. Metro Economies: GMP & Employment 2018-2020, September 2019

Metropolitan Area Exports

Area	2014	2015	2016	2017	2018	2019	Rank[2]
MSA[1]	10,706.5	9,629.7	8,752.9	8,944.9	9,382.9	8,829.9	41

Note: Figures are in millions of dollars; (1) Figures cover the Cleveland-Elyria, OH Metropolitan Statistical Area; (2) Rank is based on 2019 data and ranges from 1 to 386
Source: U.S. Department of Commerce, International Trade Administration, Office of Trade and Economic Analysis, Industry and Analysis, Exports by Metropolitan Area, data extracted March 24, 2021

Building Permits

Area	Single-Family			Multi-Family			Total		
	2018	2019	Pct. Chg.	2018	2019	Pct. Chg.	2018	2019	Pct. Chg.
City	114	78	-31.6	34	19	-44.1	148	97	-34.5
MSA[1]	2,733	2,584	-5.5	248	448	80.6	2,981	3,032	1.7
U.S.	855,300	862,100	0.7	473,500	523,900	10.6	1,328,800	1,386,000	4.3

Note: (1) Figures cover the Cleveland-Elyria, OH Metropolitan Statistical Area; Figures represent new, privately-owned housing units authorized (unadjusted data); All permit data are based on estimates with imputation
Source: U.S. Census Bureau, Manufacturing, Mining, and Construction Statistics, Building Permits, 2018, 2019

Bankruptcy Filings

Area	Business Filings			Nonbusiness Filings		
	2019	2020	% Chg.	2019	2020	% Chg.
Cuyahoga County	69	96	39.1	6,013	4,189	-30.3
U.S.	22,780	21,655	-4.9	752,160	522,808	-30.5

Note: Business filings include Chapter 7, Chapter 9, Chapter 11, Chapter 12, Chapter 13, Chapter 15, and Section 304; Nonbusiness filings include Chapter 7, Chapter 11, and Chapter 13
Source: Administrative Office of the U.S. Courts, Business and Nonbusiness Bankruptcy, County Cases Commenced by Chapter of the Bankruptcy Code, During the 12-Month Period Ending December 31, 2019 and Business and Nonbusiness Bankruptcy, County Cases Commenced by Chapter of the Bankruptcy Code, During the 12-Month Period Ending December 31, 2020

Housing Vacancy Rates

Area	Gross Vacancy Rate[2] (%)			Year-Round Vacancy Rate[3] (%)			Rental Vacancy Rate[4] (%)			Homeowner Vacancy Rate[5] (%)		
	2018	2019	2020	2018	2019	2020	2018	2019	2020	2018	2019	2020
MSA[1]	10.4	10.1	9.3	10.3	9.9	8.8	6.9	3.8	5.5	0.9	1.1	0.7
U.S.	12.3	12.0	10.6	9.7	9.5	8.2	6.9	6.7	6.3	1.5	1.4	1.0

Note: (1) Figures cover the Cleveland-Elyria, OH Metropolitan Statistical Area; (2) The percentage of the total housing inventory that is vacant; (3) The percentage of the housing inventory (excluding seasonal units) that is year-round vacant; (4) The percentage of rental inventory that is vacant for rent; (5) The percentage of homeowner inventory that is vacant for sale
Source: U.S. Census Bureau, Housing Vacancies and Homeownership Annual Statistics: 2018, 2019, 2020

INCOME

Income

Area	Per Capita ($)	Median Household ($)	Average Household ($)
City	21,223	30,907	46,137
MSA[1]	33,785	56,008	79,168
U.S.	34,103	62,843	88,607

Note: (1) Figures cover the Cleveland-Elyria, OH Metropolitan Statistical Area
Source: U.S. Census Bureau, 2015-2019 American Community Survey 5-Year Estimates

Household Income Distribution

Area	Percent of Households Earning							
	Under $15,000	$15,000 -$24,999	$25,000 -$34,999	$35,000 -$49,999	$50,000 -$74,999	$75,000 -$99,999	$100,000 -$149,999	$150,000 and up
City	27.1	15.1	12.9	13.7	14.2	7.9	5.7	3.4
MSA[1]	12.6	9.7	9.8	13.0	17.4	12.4	13.9	11.2
U.S.	10.3	8.9	8.9	12.3	17.2	12.7	15.1	14.5

Note: (1) Figures cover the Cleveland-Elyria, OH Metropolitan Statistical Area
Source: U.S. Census Bureau, 2015-2019 American Community Survey 5-Year Estimates

Poverty Rate

Area	All Ages	Under 18 Years Old	18 to 64 Years Old	65 Years and Over
City	32.7	48.2	29.8	20.5
MSA[1]	14.3	20.7	13.6	9.0
U.S.	13.4	18.5	12.6	9.3

Note: Figures are percentage of people whose income during the past 12 months was below the poverty level;
(1) Figures cover the Cleveland-Elyria, OH Metropolitan Statistical Area
Source: U.S. Census Bureau, 2015-2019 American Community Survey 5-Year Estimates

CITY FINANCES

City Government Finances

Component	2017 ($000)	2017 ($ per capita)
Total Revenues	1,488,295	3,835
Total Expenditures	1,490,259	3,840
Debt Outstanding	2,408,888	6,207
Cash and Securities[1]	1,495,196	3,853

Note: (1) Cash and security holdings of a government at the close of its fiscal year,
including those of its dependent agencies, utilities, and liquor stores.
Source: U.S. Census Bureau, State & Local Government Finances 2017

City Government Revenue by Source

Source	2017 ($000)	2017 ($ per capita)	2017 (%)
General Revenue			
From Federal Government	34,261	88	2.3
From State Government	171,591	442	11.5
From Local Governments	0	0	0.0
Taxes			
Property	49,311	127	3.3
Sales and Gross Receipts	43,965	113	3.0
Personal Income	354,162	913	23.8
Corporate Income	0	0	0.0
Motor Vehicle License	4,382	11	0.3
Other Taxes	19,947	51	1.3
Current Charges	238,866	616	16.0
Liquor Store	0	0	0.0
Utility	503,074	1,296	33.8
Employee Retirement	0	0	0.0

Source: U.S. Census Bureau, State & Local Government Finances 2017

City Government Expenditures by Function

Function	2017 ($000)	2017 ($ per capita)	2017 (%)
General Direct Expenditures			
Air Transportation	115,307	297	7.7
Corrections	11,775	30	0.8
Education	0	0	0.0
Employment Security Administration	0	0	0.0
Financial Administration	11,379	29	0.8
Fire Protection	87,428	225	5.9
General Public Buildings	0	0	0.0
Governmental Administration, Other	13,956	36	0.9
Health	41,511	107	2.8
Highways	34,116	87	2.3
Hospitals	0	0	0.0
Housing and Community Development	84,917	218	5.7
Interest on General Debt	64,025	165	4.3
Judicial and Legal	56,781	146	3.8
Libraries	0	0	0.0
Parking	7,294	18	0.5
Parks and Recreation	33,886	87	2.3
Police Protection	240,557	619	16.1
Public Welfare	0	0	0.0
Sewerage	27,490	70	1.8
Solid Waste Management	23,420	60	1.6
Veterans' Services	0	0	0.0
Liquor Store	0	0	0.0
Utility	434,260	1,119	29.1
Employee Retirement	0	0	0.0

Source: U.S. Census Bureau, State & Local Government Finances 2017

EMPLOYMENT

Labor Force and Employment

Area	Civilian Labor Force			Workers Employed		
	Dec. 2019	Dec. 2020	% Chg.	Dec. 2019	Dec. 2020	% Chg.
City	156,471	151,177	-3.4	149,465	137,384	-8.1
MSA[1]	1,049,216	997,566	-4.9	1,009,725	921,287	-8.8
U.S.	164,007,000	160,017,000	-2.4	158,504,000	149,613,000	-5.6

Note: Data is not seasonally adjusted and covers workers 16 years of age and older; (1) Figures cover the Cleveland-Elyria, OH Metropolitan Statistical Area
Source: Bureau of Labor Statistics, Local Area Unemployment Statistics

Unemployment Rate

Area	2020											
	Jan.	Feb.	Mar.	Apr.	May	Jun.	Jul.	Aug.	Sep.	Oct.	Nov.	Dec.
City	5.9	6.4	9.0	26.1	21.9	19.4	17.3	15.9	15.3	10.3	9.0	9.1
MSA[1]	5.0	5.4	6.2	21.8	17.3	12.7	9.2	8.1	8.8	7.2	7.1	7.6
U.S.	4.0	3.8	4.5	14.4	13.0	11.2	10.5	8.5	7.7	6.6	6.4	6.5

Note: Data is not seasonally adjusted and covers workers 16 years of age and older; (1) Figures cover the Cleveland-Elyria, OH Metropolitan Statistical Area
Source: Bureau of Labor Statistics, Local Area Unemployment Statistics

Average Wages

Occupation	$/Hr.	Occupation	$/Hr.
Accountants and Auditors	36.60	Maintenance and Repair Workers	21.10
Automotive Mechanics	22.20	Marketing Managers	66.20
Bookkeepers	20.50	Network and Computer Systems Admin.	42.80
Carpenters	25.80	Nurses, Licensed Practical	23.80
Cashiers	12.10	Nurses, Registered	35.20
Computer Programmers	39.60	Nursing Assistants	14.80
Computer Systems Analysts	40.50	Office Clerks, General	19.50
Computer User Support Specialists	24.40	Physical Therapists	42.90
Construction Laborers	23.80	Physicians	n/a
Cooks, Restaurant	13.10	Plumbers, Pipefitters and Steamfitters	32.20
Customer Service Representatives	19.40	Police and Sheriff's Patrol Officers	31.00
Dentists	101.10	Postal Service Mail Carriers	25.60
Electricians	29.20	Real Estate Sales Agents	25.40
Engineers, Electrical	41.40	Retail Salespersons	13.80
Fast Food and Counter Workers	11.10	Sales Representatives, Technical/Scientific	44.50
Financial Managers	73.40	Secretaries, Exc. Legal/Medical/Executive	18.70
First-Line Supervisors of Office Workers	29.70	Security Guards	15.90
General and Operations Managers	63.10	Surgeons	n/a
Hairdressers/Cosmetologists	15.00	Teacher Assistants, Exc. Postsecondary*	14.60
Home Health and Personal Care Aides	11.50	Teachers, Secondary School, Exc. Sp. Ed.*	34.50
Janitors and Cleaners	14.60	Telemarketers	11.40
Landscaping/Groundskeeping Workers	17.10	Truck Drivers, Heavy/Tractor-Trailer	23.90
Lawyers	71.60	Truck Drivers, Light/Delivery Services	19.80
Maids and Housekeeping Cleaners	12.10	Waiters and Waitresses	10.70

Note: Wage data covers the Cleveland-Elyria, OH Metropolitan Statistical Area; (*) Hourly wages were calculated from annual wage data based on a 40 hour work week; n/a not available.
Source: Bureau of Labor Statistics, Metro Area Occupational Employment & Wage Estimates, May 2020

Employment by Industry

Sector	MSA[1]		U.S.
	Number of Employees	Percent of Total	Percent of Total
Construction, Mining, and Logging	37,400	3.7	5.5
Education and Health Services	195,300	19.4	16.3
Financial Activities	66,300	6.6	6.1
Government	129,500	12.9	15.2
Information	12,200	1.2	1.9
Leisure and Hospitality	83,800	8.3	9.0
Manufacturing	113,300	11.3	8.5
Other Services	34,000	3.4	3.8
Professional and Business Services	150,800	15.0	14.4
Retail Trade	97,500	9.7	10.9
Transportation, Warehousing, and Utilities	36,500	3.6	4.6
Wholesale Trade	48,900	4.9	3.9

Note: Figures are non-farm employment as of December 2020. Figures are not seasonally adjusted and include workers 16 years of age and older; (1) Figures cover the Cleveland-Elyria, OH Metropolitan Statistical Area
Source: Bureau of Labor Statistics, Current Employment Statistics, Employment, Hours, and Earnings

Employment by Occupation

Occupation Classification	City (%)	MSA[1] (%)	U.S. (%)
Management, Business, Science, and Arts	29.0	39.4	38.5
Natural Resources, Construction, and Maintenance	6.1	6.6	8.9
Production, Transportation, and Material Moving	18.8	14.4	13.2
Sales and Office	20.8	22.4	21.6
Service	25.4	17.3	17.8

Note: Figures cover employed civilians 16 years of age and older; (1) Figures cover the Cleveland-Elyria, OH Metropolitan Statistical Area
Source: U.S. Census Bureau, 2015-2019 American Community Survey 5-Year Estimates

Occupations with Greatest Projected Employment Growth: 2020 – 2022

Occupation[1]	2020 Employment	2022 Projected Employment	Numeric Employment Change	Percent Employment Change
Laborers and Freight, Stock, and Material Movers, Hand	119,110	122,880	3,770	3.2
Registered Nurses	129,170	132,090	2,920	2.3
Home Health and Personal Care Aides	94,930	97,520	2,590	2.7
Industrial Truck and Tractor Operators	33,730	35,870	2,140	6.3
Heavy and Tractor-Trailer Truck Drivers	80,440	82,290	1,850	2.3
Construction Laborers	42,520	44,210	1,690	4.0
Electricians	26,990	28,530	1,540	5.7
Medical Assistants	26,150	27,410	1,260	4.8
Light Truck or Delivery Services Drivers	38,160	39,200	1,040	2.7
Heating, Air Conditioning, and Refrigeration Mechanics and Installers	13,410	14,390	980	7.3

Note: Projections cover Ohio; (1) Sorted by numeric employment change
Source: www.projectionscentral.com, State Occupational Projections, 2020–2022 Short-Term Projections

Fastest-Growing Occupations: 2020 – 2022

Occupation[1]	2020 Employment	2022 Projected Employment	Numeric Employment Change	Percent Employment Change
Roofers	5,710	6,240	530	9.3
Helpers—Pipelayers, Plumbers, Pipefitters, and Steamfitters	920	1,000	80	8.7
Brickmasons and Blockmasons	3,790	4,090	300	7.9
Floor Layers, Except Carpet, Wood, and Hard Tiles	1,210	1,300	90	7.4
Heating, Air Conditioning, and Refrigeration Mechanics and Installers	13,410	14,390	980	7.3
Cement Masons and Concrete Finishers	5,580	5,980	400	7.2
Glaziers	1,260	1,350	90	7.1
Structural Iron and Steel Workers	3,210	3,430	220	6.9
Physician Assistants	4,720	5,040	320	6.8
Tile and Marble Setters	910	970	60	6.6

Note: Projections cover Ohio; (1) Sorted by percent employment change and excludes occupations with numeric employment change less than 50
Source: www.projectionscentral.com, State Occupational Projections, 2020–2022 Short-Term Projections

TAXES

State Corporate Income Tax Rates

State	Tax Rate (%)	Income Brackets ($)	Num. of Brackets	Financial Institution Tax Rate (%)[a]	Federal Income Tax Ded.
Ohio	(t)	–	–	(t)	No

Note: Tax rates as of January 1, 2021; (a) Rates listed are the corporate income tax rate applied to financial institutions or excise taxes based on income. Some states have other taxes based upon the value of deposits or shares; (t) Ohio no longer levies a tax based on income (except for a particular subset of corporations), but instead imposes a Commercial Activity Tax (CAT) equal to $150 for gross receipts sitused to Ohio of between $150,000 and $1 million, plus 0.26% of gross receipts over $1 million. Banks continue to pay a franchise tax of 1.3% of net worth. For those few corporations for whom the franchise tax on net worth or net income still applies, a litter tax also applies.
Source: Federation of Tax Administrators, State Corporate Income Tax Rates, January 1, 2021

State Individual Income Tax Rates

State	Tax Rate (%)	Income Brackets ($)	Personal Exemptions ($)			Standard Ded. ($)	
			Single	Married	Depend.	Single	Married
Ohio (a)	0.0 - 4.797	22,150 - 221,300	2,400	4,800 (s)	2,400 (s)	–	–

Note: Tax rates as of January 1, 2021; Local- and county-level taxes are not included; Federal income tax is not deductible on state income tax returns; (a) 19 states have statutory provision for automatically adjusting to the rate of inflation the dollar values of the income tax brackets, standard deductions, and/or personal exemptions. Michigan indexes the personal exemption only. Oregon does not index the income brackets for $125,000 and over; (s) Ohio provides an additional tax credit of $20 per exemption. Exemption amounts reduced for higher income taxpayers. Business income taxes at a flat 3% rate.
Source: Federation of Tax Administrators, State Individual Income Tax Rates, January 1, 2021

Various State Sales and Excise Tax Rates

State	State Sales Tax (%)	Gasoline[1] (¢/gal.)	Cigarette[2] ($/pack)	Spirits[3] ($/gal.)	Wine[4] ($/gal.)	Beer[5] ($/gal.)	Recreational Marijuana (%)
Ohio	5.75	38.51	1.6	9.83	0.32	0.18	Not legal

Note: All tax rates as of January 1, 2021; (1) The American Petroleum Institute has developed a methodology for determining the average tax rate on a gallon of fuel. Rates may include any of the following: excise taxes, environmental fees, storage tank fees, other fees or taxes, general sales tax, and local taxes; (2) The federal excise tax of $1.0066 per pack and local taxes are not included; (3) Rates are those applicable to off-premise sales of 40% alcohol by volume (a.b.v.) distilled spirits in 750ml containers. Local excise taxes are excluded; (4) Rates are those applicable to off-premise sales of 11% a.b.v. non-carbonated wine in 750ml containers; (5) Rates are those applicable to off-premise sales of 4.7% a.b.v. beer in 12 ounce containers.
Source: Tax Foundation, 2021 Facts & Figures: How Does Your State Compare?

State Business Tax Climate Index Rankings

State	Overall Rank	Corporate Tax Rank	Individual Income Tax Rank	Sales Tax Rank	Property Tax Rank	Unemployment Insurance Tax Rank
Ohio	39	42	43	34	6	6

Note: The index is a measure of how each state's tax laws affect economic performance. The lower the rank, the more favorable a state's tax system is for business. States without a given tax are given a ranking of 1. The scores/rankings for the District of Columbia do not affect other states. The 2021 index represents the tax climate as of July 1, 2020.
Source: Tax Foundation, State Business Tax Climate Index 2021

TRANSPORTATION

Means of Transportation to Work

Area	Car/Truck/Van		Public Transportation			Bicycle	Walked	Other Means	Worked at Home
	Drove Alone	Car-pooled	Bus	Subway	Railroad				
City	69.3	10.8	8.9	0.5	0.1	0.6	5.1	1.5	3.2
MSA[1]	81.4	7.7	2.7	0.2	0.1	0.3	2.2	1.1	4.4
U.S.	76.3	9.0	2.4	1.9	0.6	0.5	2.7	1.4	5.2

Note: Figures are percentages and cover workers 16 years of age and older; (1) Figures cover the Cleveland-Elyria, OH Metropolitan Statistical Area
Source: U.S. Census Bureau, 2015-2019 American Community Survey 5-Year Estimates

Travel Time to Work

Area	Less Than 10 Minutes	10 to 19 Minutes	20 to 29 Minutes	30 to 44 Minutes	45 to 59 Minutes	60 to 89 Minutes	90 Minutes or More
City	9.4	33.3	27.0	19.5	5.0	3.7	2.0
MSA[1]	11.2	28.3	25.5	23.1	7.3	3.3	1.4
U.S.	12.2	28.4	20.8	20.8	8.3	6.4	2.9

Note: Note: Figures are percentages and include workers 16 years old and over; (1) Figures cover the Cleveland-Elyria, OH Metropolitan Statistical Area
Source: U.S. Census Bureau, 2015-2019 American Community Survey 5-Year Estimates

Key Congestion Measures

Measure	1982	1992	2002	2012	2017
Annual Hours of Delay, Total (000)	6,210	26,513	39,447	49,805	56,070
Annual Hours of Delay, Per Auto Commuter	6	25	33	41	46
Annual Congestion Cost, Total (million $)	48	283	538	911	1,045
Annual Congestion Cost, Per Auto Commuter ($)	241	707	821	812	886

Note: Covers the Cleveland OH urban area
Source: Texas A&M Transportation Institute, 2019 Urban Mobility Report

Freeway Travel Time Index

Measure	1982	1987	1992	1997	2002	2007	2012	2017
Urban Area Index[1]	1.03	1.04	1.10	1.14	1.13	1.14	1.15	1.15
Urban Area Rank[1,2]	76	89	59	47	75	80	71	71

Note: Freeway Travel Time Index—the ratio of travel time in the peak period to the travel time at free-flow conditions. For example, a value of 1.30 indicates a 20-minute free-flow trip takes 26 minutes in the peak (20 minutes x 1.30 = 26 minutes); (1) Covers the Cleveland OH urban area; (2) Rank is based on 101 larger urban areas (#1 = highest travel time index)
Source: Texas A&M Transportation Institute, 2019 Urban Mobility Report

Public Transportation

Agency Name / Mode of Transportation	Vehicles Operated in Maximum Service[1]	Annual Unlinked Passenger Trips[2] (in thous.)	Annual Passenger Miles[3] (in thous.)
The Greater Cleveland Regional Transit Authority (GCRTA)			
Bus (directly operated)	255	21,787.7	91,902.7
Bus Rapid Transit (directly operated)	11	2,628.5	6,889.6
Demand Response (directly operated)	67	258.8	2,042.3
Demand Response (purchased transportation)	73	317.6	2,552.0
Heavy Rail (directly operated)	24	5,666.7	36,529.7
Light Rail (directly operated)	9	1,484.9	8,974.5
Vanpool (purchased transportation)	22	27.6	887.5

Note: (1) Number of revenue vehicles operated by the given mode and type of service to meet the annual maximum service requirement. This is the revenue vehicle count during the peak season of the year; on the week and day that maximum service is provided. Vehicles operated in maximum service (VOMS) exclude atypical days and one-time special events; (2) Number of passengers who boarded public transportation vehicles. Passengers are counted each time they board a vehicle no matter how many vehicles they use to travel from their origin to their destination. (3) Sum of the distances ridden by all passengers during the entire fiscal year.
Source: Federal Transit Administration, National Transit Database, 2019

Air Transportation

Airport Name and Code / Type of Service	Passenger Airlines[1]	Passenger Enplanements	Freight Carriers[2]	Freight (lbs)
Cleveland-Hopkins International (CLE)				
Domestic service (U.S. carriers - 2020)	26	1,977,474	14	86,886,772
International service (U.S. carriers - 2019)	4	40,477	3	175,966

Note: (1) Includes all U.S.-based major, minor and commuter airlines that carried at least one passenger during the year; (2) Includes all U.S.-based airlines and freight carriers that transported at least one pound of freight during the year.
Source: Bureau of Transportation Statistics, The Intermodal Transportation Database, Air Carriers: T-100 Domestic Market (U.S. Carriers), 2020; Bureau of Transportation Statistics, The Intermodal Transportation Database, Air Carriers: T-100 International Market (U.S. Carriers), 2019

BUSINESSES

Major Business Headquarters

Company Name	Industry	Rankings	
		Fortune[1]	Forbes[2]
Jones Day	Services	-	208
KeyCorp	Commercial Banks	411	-
Parker-Hannifin	Industrial Machinery	224	-
Sherwin-Williams	Chemicals	180	-

Note: (1) Companies that produce a 10-K are ranked 1 to 500 based on 2019 revenue; (2) All private companies with at least $2 billion in annual revenue through the end of their most current fiscal year are ranked 1 to 219; companies listed are headquartered in the city; dashes indicate no ranking
Source: Fortune, "Fortune 500," June/July 2020; Forbes, "America's Largest Private Companies," 2020

Fastest-Growing Businesses

According to *Inc.*, Cleveland is home to two of America's 500 fastest-growing private companies: **Sprinly** (#113); **Clearsulting** (#467). Criteria: must be an independent, privately-held, for-profit, U.S. corporation, proprietorship or partnership as of December 31, 2019; revenues must be at least $100,000 in 2016 and $2 million in 2019; must have four-year operating/sales history. *Inc., "America's 500 Fastest-Growing Private Companies," 2020*

Living Environment

COST OF LIVING

Cost of Living Index

Composite Index	Groceries	Housing	Utilities	Trans-portation	Health Care	Misc. Goods/Services
96.1	103.5	83.6	95.0	99.9	109.9	100.5

Note: The Cost of Living Index measures regional differences in the cost of consumer goods and services, excluding taxes and non-consumer expenditures, for professional and managerial households in the top income quintile. It is based on more than 50,000 prices covering almost 60 different items for which prices are collected three times a year by chambers of commerce, economic development organizations or university applied economic centers in each participating urban area. The numbers shown should be read as a percentage above or below the national average of 100. For example, a value of 115.4 in the groceries column indicates that grocery prices are 15.4% higher than the national average. Small differences in the index numbers should not be interpreted as significant; Figures cover the Cleveland OH urban area.
Source: The Council for Community and Economic Research, Cost of Living Index, 2020

Grocery Prices

Area[1]	T-Bone Steak ($/pound)	Frying Chicken ($/pound)	Whole Milk ($/half gal.)	Eggs ($/dozen)	Orange Juice ($/64 oz.)	Coffee ($/11.5 oz.)
City[2]	14.49	1.83	1.55	1.32	3.72	4.57
Avg.	11.78	1.39	2.05	1.47	3.57	4.34
Min.	8.03	0.94	1.03	0.74	2.94	3.02
Max.	15.86	2.65	4.31	3.77	5.44	8.69

Note: (1) Values for the local area are compared with the average, minimum and maximum values for all 284 areas in the Cost of Living Index; (2) Figures cover the Cleveland OH urban area; **T-Bone Steak** (price per pound); **Frying Chicken** (price per pound, whole fryer); **Whole Milk** (half gallon carton); **Eggs** (price per dozen, Grade A, large); **Orange Juice** (64 oz. Tropicana or Florida Natural); **Coffee** (11.5 oz. can, vacuum-packed, Maxwell House, Hills Bros, or Folgers).
Source: The Council for Community and Economic Research, Cost of Living Index, 2020

Housing and Utility Costs

Area[1]	New Home Price ($)	Apartment Rent ($/month)	All Electric ($/month)	Part Electric ($/month)	Other Energy ($/month)	Telephone ($/month)
City[2]	291,327	1,120	-	84.52	69.85	180.60
Avg.	368,594	1,168	170.86	100.47	65.28	184.30
Min.	190,567	502	91.58	31.42	26.08	169.60
Max.	2,227,806	4,738	470.38	280.31	280.06	206.50

Note: (1) Values for the local area are compared with the average, minimum and maximum values for all 284 areas in the Cost of Living Index; (2) Figures cover the Cleveland OH urban area; **New Home Price** (2,400 sf living area, 8,000 sf lot, in urban area with full utilities); **Apartment Rent** (950 sf 2 bedroom/1.5 or 2 bath, unfurnished, excluding all utilities except water); **All Electric** (average monthly cost for an all-electric home); **Part Electric** (average monthly cost for a part-electric home); **Other Energy** (average monthly cost for natural gas, fuel oil, coal, wood, and any other forms of energy except electricity); **Telephone** (price includes the base monthly rate plus taxes and fees for three lines of mobile phone service).
Source: The Council for Community and Economic Research, Cost of Living Index, 2020

Health Care, Transportation, and Other Costs

Area[1]	Doctor ($/visit)	Dentist ($/visit)	Optometrist ($/visit)	Gasoline ($/gallon)	Beauty Salon ($/visit)	Men's Shirt ($)
City[2]	121.47	119.67	86.00	2.25	31.40	37.72
Avg.	115.44	99.32	108.10	2.21	39.27	31.37
Min.	36.68	59.00	51.36	1.71	19.00	11.00
Max.	219.00	153.10	250.97	3.46	82.05	58.33

Note: (1) Values for the local area are compared with the average, minimum and maximum values for all 284 areas in the Cost of Living Index; (2) Figures cover the Cleveland OH urban area; **Doctor** (general practitioners routine exam of an established patient); **Dentist** (adult teeth cleaning and periodic oral examination); **Optometrist** (full vision eye exam for established adult patient); **Gasoline** (one gallon regular unleaded, national brand, including all taxes, cash price at self-service pump if available); **Beauty Salon** (woman's shampoo, trim, and blow-dry); **Men's Shirt** (cotton/polyester dress shirt, pinpoint weave, long sleeves).
Source: The Council for Community and Economic Research, Cost of Living Index, 2020

HOUSING

Homeownership Rate

Area	2012 (%)	2013 (%)	2014 (%)	2015 (%)	2016 (%)	2017 (%)	2018 (%)	2019 (%)	2020 (%)
MSA[1]	64.2	65.8	69.2	68.4	64.8	66.6	66.7	64.4	66.3
U.S.	65.4	65.1	64.5	63.7	63.4	63.9	64.4	64.6	66.6

Note: (1) Figures cover the Cleveland-Elyria, OH Metropolitan Statistical Area
Source: U.S. Census Bureau, Housing Vacancies and Homeownership Annual Statistics: 2012-2020

House Price Index (HPI)

Area	National Ranking[2]	Quarterly Change (%)	One-Year Change (%)	Five-Year Change (%)	Since 1991Q1 (%)
MSA[1]	50	2.24	7.63	30.38	104.70
U.S.[3]	–	3.81	10.77	38.99	205.12

Note: The HPI is a weighted repeat sales index. It measures average price changes in repeat sales or refinancings on the same properties. This information is obtained by reviewing repeat mortgage transactions on single-family properties whose mortgages have been purchased or securitized by Fannie Mae or Freddie Mac since January 1975; (1) Figures cover the Cleveland-Elyria, OH Metropolitan Statistical Area; (2) Rankings are based on annual percentage change for all metro areas containing at least 15,000 transactions over the last 10 years and ranges from 1 to 253; (3) figures based on a weighted average of Census Division estimates using a seasonally adjusted, purchase-only index; all figures are for the period ending December 31, 2020
Source: Federal Housing Finance Agency, Change in Metropolitan Area House Price Indexes, April 7, 2021

Median Single-Family Home Prices

Area	2018	2019	2020p	Percent Change 2019 to 2020
MSA[1]	153.3	164.1	179.5	9.4
U.S. Average	261.6	274.6	299.9	9.2

Note: Figures are median sales prices of existing single-family homes in thousands of dollars; (p) preliminary; (1) Figures cover the Cleveland-Elyria, OH Metropolitan Statistical Area
Source: National Association of Realtors, Median Sales Price of Existing Single-Family Homes for Metropolitan Areas, 4th Quarter 2020

Qualifying Income Based on Median Sales Price of Existing Single-Family Homes

Area	With 5% Down ($)	With 10% Down ($)	With 20% Down ($)
MSA[1]	35,388	33,526	29,801
U.S. Average	59,266	56,147	49,908

Note: Figures are preliminary; Qualifying income is based on a mortgage rate of 2.81%. Monthly principal and interest payment is limited to 25% of income; (1) Figures cover the Cleveland-Elyria, OH Metropolitan Statistical Area
Source: National Association of Realtors, Qualifying Income Based on Median Sales Price of Existing Single-Family Homes for Metropolitan Areas, 4th Quarter 2020

Home Value Distribution

Area	Under $50,000	$50,000 -$99,999	$100,000 -$149,999	$150,000 -$199,999	$200,000 -$299,999	$300,000 -$499,999	$500,000 -$999,999	$1,000,000 or more
City	28.8	44.0	14.0	5.9	3.6	2.1	1.2	0.4
MSA[1]	7.6	20.0	21.6	17.9	18.4	10.7	3.0	0.7
U.S.	6.9	12.0	13.3	14.0	19.6	19.3	11.4	3.4

Note: Figures are percentages and cover owner-occupied housing units; (1) Figures cover the Cleveland-Elyria, OH Metropolitan Statistical Area
Source: U.S. Census Bureau, 2015-2019 American Community Survey 5-Year Estimates

Year Housing Structure Built

Area	2010 or Later	2000 -2009	1990 -1999	1980 -1989	1970 -1979	1960 -1969	1950 -1959	1940 -1949	Before 1940	Median Year
City	1.7	3.8	3.2	2.4	5.4	7.1	12.5	11.3	52.6	<1940
MSA[1]	2.3	7.1	8.7	6.8	12.4	13.4	18.1	7.6	23.7	1960
U.S.	5.2	14.0	13.9	13.4	15.2	10.6	10.3	4.9	12.6	1978

Note: Figures are percentages except for Median Year; Note: (1) Figures cover the Cleveland-Elyria, OH Metropolitan Statistical Area
Source: U.S. Census Bureau, 2015-2019 American Community Survey 5-Year Estimates

Gross Monthly Rent

Area	Under $500	$500 -$999	$1,000 -$1,499	$1,500 -$1,999	$2,000 -$2,499	$2,500 -$2,999	$3,000 and up	Median ($)
City	21.9	58.1	15.8	2.7	0.9	0.3	0.2	719
MSA[1]	13.0	57.6	23.2	4.3	1.1	0.3	0.5	817
U.S.	9.4	36.2	30.0	14.0	5.6	2.4	2.4	1,062

Note: Figures are percentages except for Median; Gross rent is the contract rent plus the estimated average monthly cost of utilities (electricity, gas, and water and sewer) and fuels (oil, coal, kerosene, wood, etc.) if these are paid by the renter (or paid for the renter by someone else); (1) Figures cover the Cleveland-Elyria, OH Metropolitan Statistical Area
Source: U.S. Census Bureau, 2015-2019 American Community Survey 5-Year Estimates

HEALTH

Health Risk Factors

Category	MSA[1] (%)	U.S. (%)
Adults aged 18–64 who have any kind of health care coverage	92.5	87.3
Adults who reported being in good or better health	81.6	82.4
Adults who have been told they have high blood cholesterol	32.2	33.0
Adults who have been told they have high blood pressure	34.7	32.3
Adults who are current smokers	21.9	17.1
Adults who currently use E-cigarettes	6.5	4.6
Adults who currently use chewing tobacco, snuff, or snus	2.7	4.0
Adults who are heavy drinkers[2]	8.1	6.3
Adults who are binge drinkers[3]	21.9	17.4
Adults who are overweight (BMI 25.0 - 29.9)	35.7	35.3
Adults who are obese (BMI 30.0 - 99.8)	32.7	31.3
Adults who participated in any physical activities in the past month	72.1	74.4
Adults who always or nearly always wears a seat belt	90.8	94.3

Note: (1) Figures cover the Cleveland-Elyria, OH Metropolitan Statistical Area; (2) Heavy drinkers are classified as adult men having more than 14 drinks per week and adult women having more than 7 drinks per week; (3) Binge drinkers are classified as males having five or more drinks on one occasion or females having four or more drinks on one occasion
Source: Centers for Disease Control and Prevention, Behaviorial Risk Factor Surveillance System, SMART: Selected Metropolitan Area Risk Trends, 2017

Acute and Chronic Health Conditions

Category	MSA[1] (%)	U.S. (%)
Adults who have ever been told they had a heart attack	5.2	4.2
Adults who have ever been told they have angina or coronary heart disease	4.2	3.9
Adults who have ever been told they had a stroke	4.1	3.0
Adults who have ever been told they have asthma	14.8	14.2
Adults who have ever been told they have arthritis	30.6	24.9
Adults who have ever been told they have diabetes[2]	11.3	10.5
Adults who have ever been told they had skin cancer	5.5	6.2
Adults who have ever been told they had any other types of cancer	7.2	7.1
Adults who have ever been told they have COPD	7.2	6.5
Adults who have ever been told they have kidney disease	2.0	3.0
Adults who have ever been told they have a form of depression	21.6	20.5

Note: (1) Figures cover the Cleveland-Elyria, OH Metropolitan Statistical Area; (2) Figures do not include pregnancy-related, borderline, or pre-diabetes
Source: Centers for Disease Control and Prevention, Behaviorial Risk Factor Surveillance System, SMART: Selected Metropolitan Area Risk Trends, 2017

Health Screening and Vaccination Rates

Category	MSA[1] (%)	U.S. (%)
Adults aged 65+ who have had flu shot within the past year	63.8	60.7
Adults aged 65+ who have ever had a pneumonia vaccination	79.2	75.4
Adults who have ever been tested for HIV	37.2	36.1
Adults who have ever had the shingles or zoster vaccine?	28.2	28.9
Adults who have had their blood cholesterol checked within the last five years	87.4	85.9

Note: n/a not available; (1) Figures cover the Cleveland-Elyria, OH Metropolitan Statistical Area.
Source: Centers for Disease Control and Prevention, Behaviorial Risk Factor Surveillance System, SMART: Selected Metropolitan Area Risk Trends, 2017

Disability Status

Category	MSA[1] (%)	U.S. (%)
Adults who reported being deaf	5.8	6.7
Are you blind or have serious difficulty seeing, even when wearing glasses?	4.9	4.5
Are you limited in any way in any of your usual activities due of arthritis?	15.3	12.9
Do you have difficulty doing errands alone?	8.2	6.8
Do you have difficulty dressing or bathing?	4.6	3.6
Do you have serious difficulty concentrating/remembering/making decisions?	11.8	10.7
Do you have serious difficulty walking or climbing stairs?	15.4	13.6

Note: (1) Figures cover the Cleveland-Elyria, OH Metropolitan Statistical Area.
Source: Centers for Disease Control and Prevention, Behaviorial Risk Factor Surveillance System, SMART: Selected Metropolitan Area Risk Trends, 2017

Mortality Rates for the Top 10 Causes of Death in the U.S.

ICD-10[a] Sub-Chapter	ICD-10[a] Code	Age-Adjusted Mortality Rate[1] per 100,000 population	
		County[2]	U.S.
Malignant neoplasms	C00-C97	168.1	149.2
Ischaemic heart diseases	I20-I25	107.8	90.5
Other forms of heart disease	I30-I51	68.4	52.2
Chronic lower respiratory diseases	J40-J47	38.4	39.6
Other degenerative diseases of the nervous system	G30-G31	24.5	37.6
Cerebrovascular diseases	I60-I69	36.6	37.2
Other external causes of accidental injury	W00-X59	60.8	36.1
Organic, including symptomatic, mental disorders	F01-F09	44.9	29.4
Hypertensive diseases	I10-I15	30.4	24.1
Diabetes mellitus	E10-E14	22.4	21.5

Note: (a) ICD-10 = International Classification of Diseases 10th Revision; (1) Mortality rates are a three-year average covering 2017-2019; (2) Figures cover Cuyahoga County.
Source: Centers for Disease Control and Prevention, National Center for Health Statistics. Underlying Cause of Death 1999-2019 on CDC WONDER Online Database

Mortality Rates for Selected Causes of Death

ICD-10[a] Sub-Chapter	ICD-10[a] Code	Age-Adjusted Mortality Rate[1] per 100,000 population	
		County[2]	U.S.
Assault	X85-Y09	14.3	6.0
Diseases of the liver	K70-K76	14.0	14.4
Human immunodeficiency virus (HIV) disease	B20-B24	1.3	1.5
Influenza and pneumonia	J09-J18	11.1	13.8
Intentional self-harm	X60-X84	14.0	14.1
Malnutrition	E40-E46	1.8	2.3
Obesity and other hyperalimentation	E65-E68	2.3	2.1
Renal failure	N17-N19	15.0	12.6
Transport accidents	V01-V99	8.0	12.3
Viral hepatitis	B15-B19	0.8	1.2

Note: (a) ICD-10 = International Classification of Diseases 10th Revision; (1) Mortality rates are a three-year average covering 2017-2019; (2) Figures cover Cuyahoga County; Data are suppressed when the data meet the criteria for confidentiality constraints; Mortality rates are flagged as unreliable when the rate would be calculated with a numerator of 20 or less.
Source: Centers for Disease Control and Prevention, National Center for Health Statistics. Underlying Cause of Death 1999-2019 on CDC WONDER Online Database

Health Insurance Coverage

Area	With Health Insurance	With Private Health Insurance	With Public Health Insurance	Without Health Insurance	Population Under Age 19 Without Health Insurance
City	92.3	44.0	57.3	7.7	3.1
MSA[1]	94.7	69.2	38.4	5.3	3.4
U.S.	91.2	67.9	35.1	8.8	5.1

Note: Figures are percentages that cover the civilian noninstitutionalized population; (1) Figures cover the Cleveland-Elyria, OH Metropolitan Statistical Area
Source: U.S. Census Bureau, 2015-2019 American Community Survey 5-Year Estimates

Number of Medical Professionals

Area	MDs[3]	DOs[3,4]	Dentists	Podiatrists	Chiropractors	Optometrists
County[1] (number)	8,869	639	1,354	223	227	213
County[1] (rate[2])	714.3	51.5	109.6	18.1	18.4	17.2
U.S. (rate[2])	282.9	22.7	71.2	6.2	28.1	16.9

39035

Note: Data as of 2019 unless noted; (1) Data covers Cuyahoga County; (2) Rate per 100,000 population; (3) Data as of 2018 and includes all active, non-federal physicians; (4) Doctor of Osteopathic Medicine
Source: U.S. Department of Health and Human Services, Health Resources and Services Administration, Bureau of Health Professions, Area Resource File (ARF) 2019-2020

Best Hospitals

According to *U.S. News,* the Cleveland-Elyria, OH metro area is home to six of the best hospitals in the U.S.: **Cleveland Clinic Fairview Hospital** (4 adult specialties); **Cleveland Clinic Hillcrest Hospital** (4 adult specialties); **Cleveland Clinic** (Honor Roll/14 adult specialties and 10 pediatric specialties); **Cole Eye Institute, Cleveland Clinic** (14 adult specialties and 10 pediatric specialties); **University Hospitals Cleveland Medical Center** (7 adult specialties and 8 pediatric specialties); **University Hospitals Seidman Cancer Center** (7 adult specialties and 8 pediatric specialties). The hospitals listed were nationally ranked in at least one of 16 adult or 10 pediatric specialties. Only 134 hospitals nationwide were nationally ranked in one or more adult or pediatric specialty; this number increases to 178 counting specialized centers within hospitals. Twenty hospitals in the U.S. made the

Honor Roll. The Best Hospitals Honor Roll takes both the national rankings and the procedure and condition ratings into account. Hospitals received points if they were nationally ranked in one of the 16 adult specialties—the higher they ranked, the more points they got—and how many ratings of "high performing" they earned in the 10 procedures and conditions. *U.S. News Online, "America's Best Hospitals 2020-21"*

According to *U.S. News,* the Cleveland-Elyria, OH metro area is home to two of the best children's hospitals in the U.S.: **Cleveland Clinic Children's Hospital** (10 pediatric specialties); **Rainbow Babies and Children's Hospital** (8 pediatric specialties). The hospitals listed were highly ranked in at least one of 10 pediatric specialties. Eighty-eight children's hospitals in the U.S. were nationally ranked in at least one specialty. Hospitals received points for being ranked in a specialty, and the 10 hospitals with the most points across the 10 specialties make up the Honor Roll. *U.S. News Online, "America's Best Children's Hospitals 2020-21"*

EDUCATION

Public School District Statistics

District Name	Schls	Pupils	Pupil/ Teacher Ratio	Minority Pupils[1] (%)	Free Lunch Eligible[2] (%)	IEP[3] (%)
Cleveland Municipal	105	38,012	15.4	84.5	n/a	22.3
Ohio Connections Academy Inc	1	4,969	38.7	26.7	n/a	12.1
Orange City	4	2,047	14.3	32.5	n/a	15.0

Note: Table includes school districts with 2,000 or more students; (1) Percentage of students that are not non-Hispanic white; (2) Percentage of students that are eligible for the free lunch program; (3) Percentage of students that have an Individualized Education Program.
Source: U.S. Department of Education, National Center for Education Statistics, Common Core of Data, Local Education Agency (School District) Universe Survey: School Year 2018-2019; U.S. Department of Education, National Center for Education Statistics, Common Core of Data, Public Elementary/Secondary School Universe Survey: School Year 2018-2019

Highest Level of Education

Area	Less than H.S.	H.S. Diploma	Some College, No Deg.	Associate Degree	Bachelor's Degree	Master's Degree	Prof. School Degree	Doctorate Degree
City	19.2	32.7	23.2	7.4	10.9	4.5	1.4	0.7
MSA[1]	9.4	28.9	21.8	8.7	18.9	8.7	2.4	1.2
U.S.	12.0	27.0	20.4	8.5	19.8	8.8	2.1	1.4

Note: Figures cover persons age 25 and over; (1) Figures cover the Cleveland-Elyria, OH Metropolitan Statistical Area
Source: U.S. Census Bureau, 2015-2019 American Community Survey 5-Year Estimates

Educational Attainment by Race

Area	High School Graduate or Higher (%)					Bachelor's Degree or Higher (%)				
	Total	White	Black	Asian	Hisp.[2]	Total	White	Black	Asian	Hisp.[2]
City	80.8	83.3	80.0	71.5	67.4	17.5	24.9	9.7	39.5	9.0
MSA[1]	90.6	92.3	85.2	86.8	74.6	31.2	34.5	15.1	61.5	15.8
U.S.	88.0	89.9	86.0	87.1	68.7	32.1	33.5	21.6	54.3	16.4

Note: Figures shown cover persons 25 years old and over; (1) Figures cover the Cleveland-Elyria, OH Metropolitan Statistical Area; (2) People of Hispanic origin can be of any race
Source: U.S. Census Bureau, 2015-2019 American Community Survey 5-Year Estimates

School Enrollment by Grade and Control

Area	Preschool (%)		Kindergarten (%)		Grades 1 - 4 (%)		Grades 5 - 8 (%)		Grades 9 - 12 (%)	
	Public	Private	Public	Private	Public	Private	Public	Private	Public	Private
City	74.3	25.7	79.3	20.7	79.6	20.4	77.9	22.1	79.8	20.2
MSA[1]	54.9	45.1	81.2	18.8	81.4	18.6	82.0	18.0	84.1	15.9
U.S.	59.1	40.9	87.6	12.4	89.5	10.5	89.4	10.6	90.1	9.9

Note: Figures shown cover persons 3 years old and over; (1) Figures cover the Cleveland-Elyria, OH Metropolitan Statistical Area
Source: U.S. Census Bureau, 2015-2019 American Community Survey 5-Year Estimates

Higher Education

Four-Year Colleges			Two-Year Colleges			Medical Schools[1]	Law Schools[2]	Voc/ Tech[3]
Public	Private Non-profit	Private For-profit	Public	Private Non-profit	Private For-profit			
1	4	1	1	1	3	3	2	0

Note: Figures cover institutions located within the city limits and include main campuses only; (1) includes schools accredited by the Liaison Committee on Medical Education and the American Osteopathic Association's Commission on Osteopathic College Accreditation; (2) includes ABA-accredited schools, schools with provisional ABA accreditation, and state accredited schools; (3) includes all schools with programs that are less than 2 years.
Source: National Center for Education Statistics, Integrated Postsecondary Education System (IPEDS), 2019-20; Wikipedia, List of Medical Schools in the United States, accessed April 2, 2021; Wikipedia, List of Law Schools in the United States, accessed April 2, 2021

According to *U.S. News & World Report,* the Cleveland-Elyria, OH metro area is home to one of the top 200 national universities in the U.S.: **Case Western Reserve University** (#42 tie). The indicators used to capture academic quality fall into a number of categories: assessment by administrators at peer institutions; retention of students; faculty resources; student selectivity; financial resources; alumni giving; high school counselor ratings of colleges; and graduation rate. *U.S. News & World Report, "America's Best Colleges 2021"*

According to *U.S. News & World Report,* the Cleveland-Elyria, OH metro area is home to one of the top 100 liberal arts colleges in the U.S.: **Oberlin College** (#36 tie). The indicators used to capture academic quality fall into a number of categories: assessment by administrators at peer institutions; retention of students; faculty resources; student selectivity; financial resources; alumni giving; high school counselor ratings of colleges; and graduation rate. *U.S. News & World Report, "America's Best Colleges 2021"*

According to *U.S. News & World Report,* the Cleveland-Elyria, OH metro area is home to one of the top 100 law schools in the U.S.: **Case Western Reserve University** (#72 tie). The rankings are based on a weighted average of 12 measures of quality: peer assessment score; assessment score by lawyers/judges; median LSAT scores; median undergrad GPA; acceptance rate; employment rates for graduates; placement success; bar passage rate; faculty resources; expenditures per student; student/faculty ratio; and library resources. *U.S. News & World Report, "America's Best Graduate Schools, Law, 2022"*

According to *U.S. News & World Report,* the Cleveland-Elyria, OH metro area is home to one of the top 75 medical schools for research in the U.S.: **Case Western Reserve University** (#25). The rankings are based on a weighted average of 11 measures of quality: quality assessment; peer assessment score; assessment score by residency directors; research activity; total research activity; average research activity per faculty member; student selectivity; median MCAT total score; median undergraduate GPA; acceptance rate; and faculty resources. *U.S. News & World Report, "America's Best Graduate Schools, Medical, 2022"*

EMPLOYERS

Major Employers

Company Name	Industry
Case Western Reserve University	Educational services
City of Cleveland	Municipal government
Cleveland Clinic	Health care
Cleveland Metropolitan School District	Educational services
Cuyahoga County	Government
KeyCorp	Finance
Metro Health System	Health care
Sherwin-Williams Co.	Retail
U.S. Office of Personnel Management	Government
University Hospitals	Health care

Note: Companies shown are located within the Cleveland-Elyria, OH Metropolitan Statistical Area.
Source: Hoovers.com; Wikipedia

Best Companies to Work For

Federal Reserve Bank of Cleveland, headquartered in Cleveland, is among the "Top Companies for Executive Women." This list is determined by organizations filling out an in-depth survey that measures female demographics at every level, but with an emphasis on women in senior corporate roles, with profit & loss (P&L) responsibility, and those earning in the top 20 percent of the organization. *Working Mother* defines P&L as having responsibility that involves monitoring the net income after expenses for a department or entire organization, with direct influence on how company resources are allocated. *Working Mother, "Top Companies for Executive Women," 2020+*

PUBLIC SAFETY

Crime Rate

Area	All Crimes	Violent Crimes				Property Crimes		
		Murder	Rape[3]	Robbery	Aggrav. Assault	Burglary	Larceny -Theft	Motor Vehicle Theft
City	5,983.8	24.1	125.4	496.3	870.8	1,129.0	2,610.6	727.6
Suburbs[1]	1,401.7	1.8	21.7	34.6	90.5	189.4	985.7	77.9
Metro[2]	2,254.7	5.9	41.0	120.5	235.8	364.4	1,288.2	198.9
U.S.	2,489.3	5.0	42.6	81.6	250.2	340.5	1,549.5	219.9

Note: Figures are crimes per 100,000 population; (1) All areas within the metro area that are located outside the city limits; (2) Figures cover the Cleveland-Elyria, OH Metropolitan Statistical Area; (3) All figures shown were reported using the revised Uniform Crime Reporting (UCR) definition of rape.
Source: FBI Uniform Crime Reports, 2019

Hate Crimes

Area	Number of Quarters Reported	Number of Incidents per Bias Motivation					
		Race/Ethnicity/ Ancestry	Religion	Sexual Orientation	Disability	Gender	Gender Identity
City	4	20	7	7	4	4	3
U.S.	4	3,963	1,521	1,195	157	69	198

Source: Federal Bureau of Investigation, Hate Crime Statistics 2019

Identity Theft Consumer Reports

Area	Reports	Reports per 100,000 Population	Rank[2]
MSA[1]	7,786	380	81
U.S.	1,387,615	423	-

Note: (1) Figures cover the Cleveland-Elyria, OH Metropolitan Statistical Area; (2) Rank ranges from 1 to 391 where 1 indicates greatest number of identity theft reports per 100,000 population
Source: Federal Trade Commission, Consumer Sentinel Network Data Book 2020

Fraud and Other Consumer Reports

Area	Reports	Reports per 100,000 Population	Rank[2]
MSA[1]	18,854	920	42
U.S.	3,385,133	1,031	-

Note: (1) Figures cover the Cleveland-Elyria, OH Metropolitan Statistical Area; (2) Rank ranges from 1 to 391 where 1 indicates greatest number of fraud and other consumer reports per 100,000 population
Source: Federal Trade Commission, Consumer Sentinel Network Data Book 2020

POLITICS

2020 Presidential Election Results

Area	Biden	Trump	Jorgensen	Hawkins	Other
Cuyahoga County	66.4	32.3	0.7	0.3	0.3
U.S.	51.3	46.8	1.2	0.3	0.5

Note: Results are percentages and may not add to 100% due to rounding
Source: Dave Leip's Atlas of U.S. Presidential Elections

SPORTS

Professional Sports Teams

Team Name	League	Year Established
Cleveland Browns	National Football League (NFL)	1946
Cleveland Cavaliers	National Basketball Association (NBA)	1970
Cleveland Indians	Major League Baseball (MLB)	1900

Note: Includes teams located in the Cleveland-Elyria, OH Metropolitan Statistical Area.
Source: Wikipedia, Major Professional Sports Teams of the United States and Canada, April 6, 2021

CLIMATE

Average and Extreme Temperatures

Temperature	Jan	Feb	Mar	Apr	May	Jun	Jul	Aug	Sep	Oct	Nov	Dec	Yr.
Extreme High (°F)	73	69	82	88	92	104	100	102	101	89	82	77	104
Average High (°F)	33	36	46	58	69	79	83	81	74	63	50	38	59
Average Temp. (°F)	26	28	37	49	59	68	73	71	64	54	43	31	50
Average Low (°F)	19	20	28	38	48	58	62	61	54	44	35	24	41
Extreme Low (°F)	-19	-15	-5	10	25	31	41	38	34	19	3	-15	-19

Note: Figures cover the years 1948-1990
Source: National Climatic Data Center, International Station Meteorological Climate Summary, 9/96

Average Precipitation/Snowfall/Humidity

Precip./Humidity	Jan	Feb	Mar	Apr	May	Jun	Jul	Aug	Sep	Oct	Nov	Dec	Yr.
Avg. Precip. (in.)	2.4	2.3	3.1	3.4	3.5	3.5	3.5	3.4	3.2	2.6	3.2	2.9	37.1
Avg. Snowfall (in.)	13	12	10	2	Tr	0	0	0	0	1	5	12	55
Avg. Rel. Hum. 7am (%)	79	79	78	76	77	78	81	85	84	81	78	78	79
Avg. Rel. Hum. 4pm (%)	70	67	62	56	54	55	55	58	58	58	65	70	61

Note: Figures cover the years 1948-1990; Tr = Trace amounts (<0.05 in. of rain; <0.5 in. of snow)
Source: National Climatic Data Center, International Station Meteorological Climate Summary, 9/96

Weather Conditions

Temperature			Daytime Sky			Precipitation		
5°F & below	32°F & below	90°F & above	Clear	Partly cloudy	Cloudy	0.01 inch or more precip.	0.1 inch or more snow/ice	Thunder-storms
11	123	12	63	127	175	157	48	34

Note: Figures are average number of days per year and cover the years 1948-1990
Source: National Climatic Data Center, International Station Meteorological Climate Summary, 9/96

HAZARDOUS WASTE   Superfund Sites

The Cleveland-Elyria, OH metro area is home to one site on the EPA's Superfund National Priorities List: **Diamond Shamrock Corp. (Painesville Works)** (proposed). There are a total of 1,375 Superfund sites with a status of proposed or final on the list in the U.S. *U.S. Environmental Protection Agency, National Priorities List, April 7, 2021*

AIR QUALITY   Air Quality Trends: Ozone

	1990	1995	2000	2005	2010	2015	2016	2017	2018	2019
MSA[1]	0.085	0.092	0.076	0.083	0.077	0.071	0.072	0.070	0.074	0.070
U.S.	0.088	0.089	0.082	0.073	0.068	0.069	0.069	0.068	0.069	0.065

Note: (1) Data covers the Cleveland-Elyria, OH Metropolitan Statistical Area. The values shown are the composite ozone concentration averages among trend sites based on the highest fourth daily maximum 8-hour concentration in parts per million. These trends are based on sites having an adequate record of monitoring data during the trend period. Data from exceptional events are included.
Source: U.S. Environmental Protection Agency, Air Quality Monitoring Information, "Air Quality Trends by City, 1990-2019"

Air Quality Index

Area	Percent of Days when Air Quality was...[2]					AQI Statistics[2]	
	Good	Moderate	Unhealthy for Sensitive Groups	Unhealthy	Very Unhealthy	Maximum	Median
MSA[1]	50.7	47.4	1.9	0.0	0.0	119	50

Note: (1) Data covers the Cleveland-Elyria, OH Metropolitan Statistical Area; (2) Based on 365 days with AQI data in 2019. Air Quality Index (AQI) is an index for reporting daily air quality. EPA calculates the AQI for five major air pollutants regulated by the Clean Air Act: ground-level ozone, particle pollution (aka particulate matter), carbon monoxide, sulfur dioxide, and nitrogen dioxide. The AQI runs from 0 to 500. The higher the AQI value, the greater the level of air pollution and the greater the health concern. There are six AQI categories: "Good" AQI is between 0 and 50. Air quality is considered satisfactory; "Moderate" AQI is between 51 and 100. Air quality is acceptable; "Unhealthy for Sensitive Groups" When AQI values are between 101 and 150, members of sensitive groups may experience health effects; "Unhealthy" When AQI values are between 151 and 200 everyone may begin to experience health effects; "Very Unhealthy" AQI values between 201 and 300 trigger a health alert; "Hazardous" AQI values over 300 trigger warnings of emergency conditions (not shown).
Source: U.S. Environmental Protection Agency, Air Quality Index Report, 2019

Air Quality Index Pollutants

Area	Percent of Days when AQI Pollutant was...[2]					
	Carbon Monoxide	Nitrogen Dioxide	Ozone	Sulfur Dioxide	Particulate Matter 2.5	Particulate Matter 10
MSA[1]	0.0	0.3	40.5	0.5	55.1	3.6

Note: (1) Data covers the Cleveland-Elyria, OH Metropolitan Statistical Area; (2) Based on 365 days with AQI data in 2019. The Air Quality Index (AQI) is an index for reporting daily air quality. EPA calculates the AQI for five major air pollutants regulated by the Clean Air Act: ground-level ozone, particle pollution (also known as particulate matter), carbon monoxide, sulfur dioxide, and nitrogen dioxide. The AQI runs from 0 to 500. The higher the AQI value, the greater the level of air pollution and the greater the health concern.
Source: U.S. Environmental Protection Agency, Air Quality Index Report, 2019

Maximum Air Pollutant Concentrations: Particulate Matter, Ozone, CO and Lead

	Particulate Matter 10 (ug/m^3)	Particulate Matter 2.5 Wtd AM (ug/m^3)	Particulate Matter 2.5 24-Hr (ug/m^3)	Ozone (ppm)	Carbon Monoxide (ppm)	Lead (ug/m^3)
MSA[1] Level	79	10.8	26	0.071	2	0.01
NAAQS[2]	150	15	35	0.075	9	0.15
Met NAAQS[2]	Yes	Yes	Yes	Yes	Yes	Yes

Note: (1) Data covers the Cleveland-Elyria, OH Metropolitan Statistical Area; Data from exceptional events are included; (2) National Ambient Air Quality Standards; ppm = parts per million; ug/m^3 = micrograms per cubic meter; n/a not available.
Concentrations: Particulate Matter 10 (coarse particulate)—highest second maximum 24-hour concentration; Particulate Matter 2.5 Wtd AM (fine particulate)—highest weighted annual mean concentration; Particulate Matter 2.5 24-Hour (fine particulate)—highest 98th percentile 24-hour concentration; Ozone—highest fourth daily maximum 8-hour concentration; Carbon Monoxide—highest second maximum non-overlapping 8-hour concentration; Lead—maximum running 3-month average
Source: U.S. Environmental Protection Agency, Air Quality Monitoring Information, "Air Quality Statistics by City, 2019"

Maximum Air Pollutant Concentrations: Nitrogen Dioxide and Sulfur Dioxide

	Nitrogen Dioxide AM (ppb)	Nitrogen Dioxide 1-Hr (ppb)	Sulfur Dioxide AM (ppb)	Sulfur Dioxide 1-Hr (ppb)	Sulfur Dioxide 24-Hr (ppb)
MSA[1] Level	10	45	n/a	23	n/a
NAAQS[2]	53	100	30	75	140
Met NAAQS[2]	Yes	Yes	n/a	Yes	n/a

Note: (1) Data covers the Cleveland-Elyria, OH Metropolitan Statistical Area; Data from exceptional events are included; (2) National Ambient Air Quality Standards; ppm = parts per million; ug/m^3 = micrograms per cubic meter; n/a not available.
Concentrations: Nitrogen Dioxide AM—highest arithmetic mean concentration; Nitrogen Dioxide 1-Hr—highest 98th percentile 1-hour daily maximum concentration; Sulfur Dioxide AM—highest annual mean concentration; Sulfur Dioxide 1-Hr—highest 99th percentile 1-hour daily maximum concentration; Sulfur Dioxide 24-Hr—highest second maximum 24-hour concentration
Source: U.S. Environmental Protection Agency, Air Quality Monitoring Information, "Air Quality Statistics by City, 2019"

Columbus, Ohio

Background

Columbus is the capital of Ohio, and centrally located in the watershed of the Ohio River. The largest city in the state, it was not the first choice for the capital, but in 1812, residents of Franklinton, a county seat in the heart of Ohio, offered the government 1,200 acres of land and $50,000 with which to build a capitol building and state penitentiary.

Columbus grew steadily throughout the nineteenth century, its prosperity bolstered by the construction of a feeder link into the Ohio and Erie canals, which connected the town to the Great Lakes system and the Ohio River. By 1834, Columbus had attained a population of about 20,000. The railroad was established in 1850, bringing trade opportunities from the East.

Columbus became a major staging area for Union armies during the Civil War and was also home to Camp Chase, the largest military prison for Rebel soldiers. Both before and after the war, manufacturing in the city developed dramatically, based primarily on agricultural processing and packing, shoes, hardware, and heavy equipment. A specialty of Columbus was the buggy, and the Iron Buggy Company was the largest of its kind in the world.

Ohio State University, originally Ohio Agricultural and Mechanical University (1870), is in Columbus, and other colleges and universities include Franklin University (1902), Capital University (1830), Ohio Dominican University (1911), the Columbus College of Art and Design (1879), and Pontifical College Josephinum (1888). One of the first schools for the blind in the U.S., the Ohio State School for the Blind, was founded in Columbus in 1832.

Cultural resources include the Wexner Center for the Arts of Ohio State University, noted for its innovative architecture, and the Columbus Museum of Art, housing one of the nation's finest collections of 19th and 20th-century paintings. Columbus is also home to a symphony orchestra, and opera and ballet companies. The Columbus Zoo is nationally famous both for its success in the breeding of endangered species and for its large coral reef aquarium. And a National Veteran's Memorial and Museum opened in 2018.

Columbus fans support Ohio State University's Buckeye football, a major league soccer team (Columbus Crew), an expansion National Hockey League franchise (Columbus Blue Jackets), and a minor league baseball team (Columbus Clippers). The Clippers played in Cooper Stadium from 1977 to the 2008 season. April 2009 marked the opening of the new ballpark, Huntington Park. Bodybuilding has long played an important role in Columbus sports. Arnold Fitness Weekend (formerly The Arnold Classic) is a bodybuilding and fitness competition held annually in Columbus, and named for actor/politician Arnold Schwarzenegger.

The largest employers in Columbus are state government and Ohio State University. Other major employers include Nationwide Insurance, and Proctor & Gamble Company. Columbus is a digital city, home to the Online Computer Library Center, CompuServe (a subsidiary of AOL) and the world's largest databases of chemical information. The area's multi-jurisdictional 315 Research + Technology Corridor was designed to achieve national and international recognition similar to Research Triangle Park in North Carolina.

Columbus has a widespread municipal bus service. Port Columbus International Airport, built in the 1920s, today serves national and international carriers. Rickenbacker Airport, named for famed Columbus resident Eddie Rickenbacker, World War I ace and airline pioneer, is a major center for air cargo. Columbus has also been home to other famous Americans, most notably Red Barber, beloved sports announcer, and James Thurber, perhaps the nation's most widely read humorist after Mark Twain. In *More Alarms at Night,* Thurber wrote of Columbus: "It's a town in which almost anything is likely to happen, and in which almost everything has."

Columbus has the usual four seasons associated with a continental climate, but extremes of high and low temperatures are possible. Summers are pleasant and mild. Though variable from year to year, rainfall is slightly in excess of the national average, and flooding is not unusual.

Rankings

General Rankings

- The Columbus metro area was identified as one of America's fastest-growing areas in terms of population and business growth by *MagnifyMoney*. The area ranked #34 out of 35. The 100 most populous metro areas in the U.S. were evaluated on their change from 2011-2016 in the following categories: people and housing; workforce and employment opportunities; growing industry. *www.businessinsider.com, "The 35 Cities in the US with the Biggest Influx of People, the Most Work Opportunities, and the Hottest Business Growth," August 12, 2018*

- In their seventh annual survey, Livability.com looked at data for more than 1,000 small to mid-sized U.S. cities to determine the rankings for Livability's "Top 100 Best Places to Live" in 2020. Columbus ranked #11. Criteria: housing and affordable living; vibrant economy; social and civic engagement; education; demographics; health care options; transportation & infrastructure; and abundant lifestyle amenities. *Livability.com, "Top 100 Best Places to Live 2020" October 2020*

Business/Finance Rankings

- Based on metro area social media reviews, the employment opinion group Glassdoor surveyed 50 of the most populous U.S. metro areas and equally weighed cost of living, hiring opportunity, and job satisfaction to compose a list of "25 Best Cities for Jobs." Median pay and home value, and number of active job openings were also factored in. The Columbus metro area was ranked #14 in overall job satisfaction. *www.glassdoor.com, "Best Cities for Jobs," February 25, 2020*

- The Brookings Institution ranked the nation's largest cities based on income inequality. Columbus was ranked #90 (#1 = greatest inequality). Criteria: the "95/20 ratio," a figure representing the income at which a household earns more than 95 percent of all other households, divided by the income at which a household earns more than only 20 percent of all other households. *Brookings Institution, "Household Income Inequality, Largest Cities of 97 Large U.S. Metro Areas, 2014-2016," February 5, 2018*

- The Brookings Institution ranked the 100 largest metro areas in the U.S. based on income inequality. Columbus was ranked #62 (#1 = greatest inequality). Criteria: the "95/20 ratio," a figure representing the income at which a household earns more than 95 percent of all other households, divided by the income at which a household earns more than only 20 percent of all other households. *Brookings Institution, "Household Income Inequality, 100 Largest U.S. Metro Areas, 2014-2016," February 5, 2018*

- *Forbes* ranked the 100 largest metro areas in the U.S. in terms of the "Best Cities for Young Professionals." The Columbus metro area ranked #9 out of 25. Criteria: median rent of a two-bedroom apartment; job growth and unemployment rate; median salary of college graduates with 5 or less years of work experience; networking opportunities; social outlook; percentage of population 25 years of age and older with college degrees. *Forbes.com, "America's 25 Best Cities for Young Professionals in 2017," May 22, 2017*

- Columbus was identified as one of America's most frugal metro areas by *Coupons.com*. The city ranked #20 out of 25. Criteria: digital coupon usage. *Coupons.com, "America's Most Frugal Cities of 2017," March 22, 2018*

- The Columbus metro area appeared on the Milken Institute "2021 Best Performing Cities" list. Rank: #83 out of 200 large metro areas (population over 250,000). Criteria: job growth; wage and salary growth; high-tech output growth; housing affordability; household broadband access. *Milken Institute, "Best-Performing Cities 2021," February 16, 2021*

- *Forbes* ranked the 200 most populous metro areas to determine the nation's "Best Places for Business and Careers." The Columbus metro area was ranked #28. Criteria: costs (business and living); job growth (past and projected); income growth; quality of life; educational attainment (college and high school); projected economic growth; cultural and leisure opportunities; workplace tolerance laws; net migration patterns. *Forbes, "The Best Places for Business and Careers 2019: Seattle Still On Top," October 30, 2019*

Education Rankings

- Personal finance website *WalletHub* analyzed the 150 largest U.S. metropolitan statistical areas to determine where the most educated Americans are putting their degrees to work. Criteria: education levels; percentage of workers with degrees; education quality and attainment gap; public school quality rankings; quality and enrollment of each metro area's universities. Columbus was ranked #44 (#1 = most educated city). *www.WalletHub.com, "Most and Least Educated Cities in America," July 20, 2020*

- Columbus was selected as one of America's most literate cities. The city ranked #25 out of the 84 largest U.S. cities. Criteria: number of booksellers; library resources; Internet resources; educational attainment; periodical publishing resources; newspaper circulation. *Central Connecticut State University, "America's Most Literate Cities, 2018," February 2019*

Environmental Rankings

- Sperling's BestPlaces assessed the 50 largest metropolitan areas of the United States for the likelihood of dangerously extreme weather events or earthquakes. In general the Southeast and South-Central regions have the highest risk of weather extremes and earthquakes, while the Pacific Northwest enjoys the lowest risk. Of the least risky metropolitan areas, the Columbus metro area was ranked #10. *www.bestplaces.net, "Avoid Natural Disasters: BestPlaces Reveals The Top 10 Safest Places to Live," October 25, 2017*

Food/Drink Rankings

- The U.S. Chamber of Commerce Foundation conducted an in-depth study on local food truck regulations, surveyed 288 food truck owners, and ranked 20 major American cities based on how friendly they are for operating a food truck. The compiled index assessed the following: procedures for obtaining permits and licenses; complying with restrictions; and financial obligations associated with operating a food truck. Columbus ranked #15 overall (1 being the best). *www.foodtrucknation.us, "Food Truck Nation," March 20, 2018*

Health/Fitness Rankings

- For each of the 100 largest cities in the United States, the American Fitness Index®, published by the American College of Sports Medicine and the Anthem Foundation, evaluated community infrastructure and 33 health behaviors including preventive health, levels of chronic disease conditions, pedestrian safety, air quality, and community resources that support physical activity. Columbus ranked #74 for "community fitness." *americanfitnessindex.org, "2020 ACSM American Fitness Index Summary Report," July 14, 2020*

- The Columbus metro area was identified as one of the worst cities for bed bugs in America by pest control company Orkin. The area ranked #5 out of 50 based on the number of bed bug treatments Orkin performed from December 2019 to November 2020. *Orkin, "New Year, New Top City on Orkin's 2021 Bed Bug Cities List: Chicago," February 1, 2021*

- Columbus was identified as a "2021 Spring Allergy Capital." The area ranked #46 out of 100. Three groups of factors were used to identify the most challenging cities for people with allergies during the spring season: annual spring pollen levels; over the counter medicine use; number of board-certified allergy specialists. *Asthma and Allergy Foundation of America, "Spring Allergy Capitals 2021," February 23, 2021*

- Columbus was identified as a "2021 Fall Allergy Capital." The area ranked #29 out of 100. Three groups of factors were used to identify the most challenging cities for people with allergies during the fall season: annual fall pollen levels; over the counter medicine use; number of board-certified allergy specialists. *Asthma and Allergy Foundation of America, "Fall Allergy Capitals 2021," February 23, 2021*

- Columbus was identified as a "2019 Asthma Capital." The area ranked #16 out of the nation's 100 largest metropolitan areas. Criteria: estimated asthma prevalence; crude death rate from asthma; and ER visits due to asthma. Risk factors analyzed but not factored in the rankings: annual pollen score; annual air quality; public smoking laws; number of board-certified asthma specialists; rescue medication use; controller medication use; uninsured rate; poverty rate. *Asthma and Allergy Foundation of America, "Asthma Capitals 2019: The Most Challenging Places to Live With Asthma," May 7, 2019*

Real Estate Rankings

- FitSmallBusiness looked at 50 of the largest metropolitan areas in the U.S. to determine which metro was the best to start a real estate business. Data was compiled from such sources as: Zillow, Trulia, U.S. Census Bureau, and the Bureau of Labor Statistics. Criteria: location; inventory; annual wages; median sales price of homes; days on the market; median price cut percentage; and other factors that would influence real estate professional growth. The Columbus metro area ranked #44. *fitsmallbusiness.com, "The Best Cities to Become a Real Estate Agent in 2018," January 30, 2018*

- *WalletHub* compared the most populated U.S. cities to determine which had the best markets for real estate agents. Columbus ranked #123 where demand was high and pay was the best. Criteria: sales per agent; annual median wage for real-estate agents; monthly average starting salary for real estate agents; real estate job density and competition; unemployment rate; home turnover rate; housing-market health index; and other relevant metrics. *www.WalletHub.com, "2019's Best Places to Be a Real Estate Agent," April 24, 2019*

- The Columbus metro area was identified as one of the nations's 20 hottest housing markets in 2021. Criteria: listing views as an indicator of demand and median days on the market as an indicator of supply. The area ranked #19. *Realtor.com, "January 2021 Top 20 Hottest Housing Markets," February 25, 2021*

- Columbus was ranked #109 out of 268 metro areas in terms of housing affordability in 2020 by the National Association of Home Builders (#1 = most affordable). Criteria: the share of homes sold in that area affordable to a family earning the local median income, based on standard mortgage underwriting criteria. *National Association of Home Builders®, NAHB-Wells Fargo Housing Opportunity Index, 4th Quarter 2020*

Safety Rankings

- Allstate ranked the 200 largest cities in America in terms of driver safety. Columbus ranked #141. Criteria: internal property damage claims over a two-year period from January 2016 to December 2017. The report helps increase the importance of safety and awareness behind the wheel. *Allstate, "Allstate America's Best Drivers Report, 2019" June 24, 2019*

- The National Insurance Crime Bureau ranked 384 metro areas in the U.S. in terms of per capita rates of vehicle theft. The Columbus metro area ranked #108 (#1 = highest rate). Criteria: number of vehicle theft offenses per 100,000 inhabitants in 2019. *National Insurance Crime Bureau, "Hot Spots 2019," July 21, 2020*

Seniors/Retirement Rankings

- From its Best Cities for Successful Aging indexes, the Milken Institute generated rankings for metropolitan areas, weighing data in nine categories—health care, wellness, living arrangements, transportation and convenience, financial characteristics, education, employment, community engagement, and overall livability. The Columbus metro area was ranked #49 overall in the large metro area category. *Milken Institute, "Best Cities for Successful Aging, 2017" March 14, 2017*

- Columbus made the 2020 *Forbes* list of "25 Best Places to Retire." Criteria, focused on high-quality retirement living at an affordable price, include: housing/living costs compared to the national average and state taxes; air quality; crime rates; good economic outlook; home price appreciation; risk associated with climate-change; availability of medical care; bikeability; walkability; healthy living. *Forbes.com, "The Best Places to Retire in 2020," August 14, 2020*

Sports/Recreation Rankings

- Columbus was chosen as one of America's best cities for bicycling. The city ranked #39 out of 50. Criteria: cycling infrastructure that is safe and friendly for all ages; energy and bike culture. The editors evaluated cities with populations of 100,000 or more. *Bicycling, "The 50 Best Bike Cities in America," October 10, 2018*

Women/Minorities Rankings

- Personal finance website *WalletHub* compared more than 180 U.S. cities across two key dimensions, "Hispanic Business-Friendliness" and "Hispanic Purchasing Power," to arrive at the most favorable conditions for Hispanic entrepreneurs. Columbus was ranked #113 out of 182. Criteria includes: share of Hispanic-Owned Businesses; Hispanic entrepreneurship rate to median annual income of Hispanics; Small Business-Friendliness score; cost of living; and number of Hispanics with at least a bachelor's degree. *WalletHub.com, "2019's Best Cities for Hispanic Entrepreneurs," May 1, 2019*

Miscellaneous Rankings

- *WalletHub* compared the 150 most populated U.S. cities to determine their operating efficiency. A "Quality of City Services" score was constructed for each city and then divided by the total budget per capita to reveal which were managed the best. Columbus ranked #94. Criteria: financial stability; economy; education; safety; health; infrastructure and pollution. *www.WalletHub.com, "2020's Best-& Worst-Run Cities in America," June 29, 2020*

Business Environment

DEMOGRAPHICS

Population Growth

Area	1990 Census	2000 Census	2010 Census	2019* Estimate	Population Growth (%) 1990-2019	Population Growth (%) 2010-2019
City	648,656	711,470	787,033	878,553	35.4	11.6
MSA[1]	1,405,176	1,612,694	1,836,536	2,077,761	47.9	13.1
U.S.	248,709,873	281,421,906	308,745,538	324,697,795	30.6	5.2

Note: (1) Figures cover the Columbus, OH Metropolitan Statistical Area; (*) 2015-2019 5-year estimated population
Source: U.S. Census Bureau, 1990 Census, Census 2000, Census 2010, 2015-2019 American Community Survey 5-Year Estimates

Household Size

Area	Persons in Household (%) One	Two	Three	Four	Five	Six	Seven or More	Average Household Size
City	35.6	32.4	14.0	10.1	4.9	1.8	1.2	2.40
MSA[1]	28.5	34.0	15.7	12.9	5.9	2.0	1.1	2.60
U.S.	27.9	33.9	15.6	12.9	6.0	2.3	1.4	2.60

Note: (1) Figures cover the Columbus, OH Metropolitan Statistical Area
Source: U.S. Census Bureau, 2015-2019 American Community Survey 5-Year Estimates

Race

Area	White Alone[2] (%)	Black Alone[2] (%)	Asian Alone[2] (%)	AIAN[3] Alone[2] (%)	NHOPI[4] Alone[2] (%)	Other Race Alone[2] (%)	Two or More Races (%)
City	58.6	29.0	5.8	0.3	0.0	2.1	4.2
MSA[1]	75.3	15.5	4.2	0.2	0.0	1.3	3.4
U.S.	72.5	12.7	5.5	0.8	0.2	4.9	3.3

Note: (1) Figures cover the Columbus, OH Metropolitan Statistical Area; (2) Alone is defined as not being in combination with one or more other races; (3) American Indian and Alaska Native; (4) Native Hawaiian and Other Pacific Islander
Source: U.S. Census Bureau, 2015-2019 American Community Survey 5-Year Estimates

Hispanic or Latino Origin

Area	Total (%)	Mexican (%)	Puerto Rican (%)	Cuban (%)	Other (%)
City	6.2	3.2	0.9	0.1	1.9
MSA[1]	4.2	2.1	0.7	0.1	1.3
U.S.	18.0	11.2	1.7	0.7	4.3

Note: Persons of Hispanic or Latino origin can be of any race; (1) Figures cover the Columbus, OH Metropolitan Statistical Area
Source: U.S. Census Bureau, 2015-2019 American Community Survey 5-Year Estimates

Ancestry

Area	German	Irish	English	American	Italian	Polish	French[2]	Scottish	Dutch
City	16.4	10.1	6.1	4.3	4.9	2.2	1.7	1.7	0.9
MSA[1]	21.8	12.6	8.5	6.3	5.4	2.4	1.9	2.1	1.3
U.S.	13.3	9.7	7.2	6.2	5.1	2.8	2.3	1.7	1.2

Note: Figures are the percentage of the total population reporting a particular ancestry. The nine most commonly reported ancestries in the U.S. are shown. Figures include multiple ancestries (e.g. if a person reported being Irish and Italian, they were included in both columns); (1) Figures cover the Columbus, OH Metropolitan Statistical Area; (2) Excludes Basque
Source: U.S. Census Bureau, 2015-2019 American Community Survey 5-Year Estimates

Foreign-born Population

Area	Any Foreign Country	Asia	Mexico	Europe	Caribbean	Central America[2]	South America	Africa	Canada
City	12.7	5.1	1.2	0.8	0.5	0.5	0.3	4.2	0.1
MSA[1]	8.2	3.6	0.7	0.8	0.3	0.3	0.2	2.2	0.1
U.S.	13.6	4.2	3.5	1.5	1.3	1.1	1.0	0.7	0.2

Note: (1) Figures cover the Columbus, OH Metropolitan Statistical Area; (2) Excludes Mexico.
Source: U.S. Census Bureau, 2015-2019 American Community Survey 5-Year Estimates

Marital Status

Area	Never Married	Now Married[2]	Separated	Widowed	Divorced
City	45.0	36.3	2.1	4.3	12.4
MSA[1]	34.7	47.0	1.7	4.9	11.6
U.S.	33.4	48.1	1.9	5.8	10.9

Note: Figures are percentages and cover the population 15 years of age and older; (1) Figures cover the Columbus, OH Metropolitan Statistical Area; (2) Excludes separated
Source: U.S. Census Bureau, 2015-2019 American Community Survey 5-Year Estimates

Disability by Age

Area	All Ages	Under 18 Years Old	18 to 64 Years Old	65 Years and Over
City	11.7	5.0	10.5	35.3
MSA[1]	12.0	4.7	10.3	33.7
U.S.	12.6	4.2	10.3	34.5

Note: Figures show percent of the civilian noninstitutionalized population that reported having a disability. Disability status is determined from six types of difficulty: vision, hearing, cognitive, ambulatory, self-care, and independent living. For children under 5 years old, hearing and vision difficulty are used to determine disability status. For children between the ages of 5 and 14, disability status is determined from hearing, vision, cognitive, ambulatory, and self-care difficulties. For people aged 15 years and older, they are considered to have a disability if they have difficulty with any one of the six difficulty types; Note: (1) Figures cover the Columbus, OH Metropolitan Statistical Area
Source: U.S. Census Bureau, 2015-2019 American Community Survey 5-Year Estimates

Age

Area	Percent of Population									Median Age
	Under Age 5	Age 5–19	Age 20–34	Age 35–44	Age 45–54	Age 55–64	Age 65–74	Age 75–84	Age 85+	
City	7.3	18.2	29.4	12.9	11.3	10.6	6.2	2.7	1.3	32.2
MSA[1]	6.7	19.8	22.2	13.4	13.0	12.1	7.8	3.6	1.5	36.0
U.S.	6.1	19.1	20.7	12.6	13.0	12.9	9.1	4.6	1.9	38.1

Note: (1) Figures cover the Columbus, OH Metropolitan Statistical Area
Source: U.S. Census Bureau, 2015-2019 American Community Survey 5-Year Estimates

Gender

Area	Males	Females	Males per 100 Females
City	429,868	448,685	95.8
MSA[1]	1,022,627	1,055,134	96.9
U.S.	159,886,919	164,810,876	97.0

Note: (1) Figures cover the Columbus, OH Metropolitan Statistical Area
Source: U.S. Census Bureau, 2015-2019 American Community Survey 5-Year Estimates

Religious Groups by Family

Area	Catholic	Baptist	Non-Den.	Methodist[2]	Lutheran	LDS[3]	Pentecostal	Presbyterian[4]	Muslim[5]	Judaism
MSA[1]	11.8	5.3	3.6	4.7	2.4	0.7	2.0	2.0	0.8	0.5
U.S.	19.1	9.3	4.0	4.0	2.3	2.0	1.9	1.6	0.8	0.7

Note: Figures are the number of adherents as a percentage of the total population; (1) Figures cover the Columbus, OH Metropolitan Statistical Area; (2) Methodist/Pietist; (3) Latter Day Saints; (4) Reformed; (5) Figures are estimates
Source: Association of Statisticians of American Religious Bodies, 2010 U.S. Religion Census: Religious Congregations & Membership Study

Religious Groups by Tradition

Area	Catholic	Evangelical Protestant	Mainline Protestant	Other Tradition	Black Protestant	Orthodox
MSA[1]	11.8	11.9	9.5	3.1	1.1	0.3
U.S.	19.1	16.2	7.3	4.3	1.6	0.3

Note: Figures are the number of adherents as a percentage of the total population; (1) Figures cover the Columbus, OH Metropolitan Statistical Area
Source: Association of Statisticians of American Religious Bodies, 2010 U.S. Religion Census: Religious Congregations & Membership Study

ECONOMY

Gross Metropolitan Product

Area	2017	2018	2019	2020	Rank[2]
MSA[1]	135.6	142.2	148.6	154.7	32

Note: Figures are in billions of dollars; (1) Figures cover the Columbus, OH Metropolitan Statistical Area; (2) Rank is based on 2018 data and ranges from 1 to 381
Source: U.S. Conference of Mayors, U.S. Metro Economies: GMP & Employment 2018-2020, September 2019

Economic Growth

Area	2015-17 (%)	2018 (%)	2019 (%)	2020 (%)	Rank[2]
MSA[1]	2.0	2.1	2.6	1.9	130
U.S.	1.9	2.9	2.3	2.1	–

Note: Figures are real gross metropolitan product (GMP) growth rates and represent average annual percent change; (1) Figures cover the Columbus, OH Metropolitan Statistical Area; (2) Rank is based on 2017 2-year average annual percent change and ranges from 1 to 381
Source: U.S. Conference of Mayors, U.S. Metro Economies: GMP & Employment 2018-2020, September 2019

Metropolitan Area Exports

Area	2014	2015	2016	2017	2018	2019	Rank[2]
MSA[1]	6,245.6	6,201.6	5,675.4	5,962.2	7,529.5	7,296.6	47

Note: Figures are in millions of dollars; (1) Figures cover the Columbus, OH Metropolitan Statistical Area; (2) Rank is based on 2019 data and ranges from 1 to 386
Source: U.S. Department of Commerce, International Trade Administration, Office of Trade and Economic Analysis, Industry and Analysis, Exports by Metropolitan Area, data extracted March 24, 2021

Building Permits

Area	Single-Family			Multi-Family			Total		
	2018	2019	Pct. Chg.	2018	2019	Pct. Chg.	2018	2019	Pct. Chg.
City	555	512	-7.7	3,742	2,258	-39.7	4,297	2,770	-35.5
MSA[1]	4,493	4,389	-2.3	4,947	3,701	-25.2	9,440	8,090	-14.3
U.S.	855,300	862,100	0.7	473,500	523,900	10.6	1,328,800	1,386,000	4.3

Note: (1) Figures cover the Columbus, OH Metropolitan Statistical Area; Figures represent new, privately-owned housing units authorized (unadjusted data); All permit data are based on estimates with imputation
Source: U.S. Census Bureau, Manufacturing, Mining, and Construction Statistics, Building Permits, 2018, 2019

Bankruptcy Filings

Area	Business Filings			Nonbusiness Filings		
	2019	2020	% Chg.	2019	2020	% Chg.
Franklin County	72	86	19.4	4,342	2,960	-31.8
U.S.	22,780	21,655	-4.9	752,160	522,808	-30.5

Note: Business filings include Chapter 7, Chapter 9, Chapter 11, Chapter 12, Chapter 13, Chapter 15, and Section 304; Nonbusiness filings include Chapter 7, Chapter 11, and Chapter 13
Source: Administrative Office of the U.S. Courts, Business and Nonbusiness Bankruptcy, County Cases Commenced by Chapter of the Bankruptcy Code, During the 12-Month Period Ending December 31, 2019 and Business and Nonbusiness Bankruptcy, County Cases Commenced by Chapter of the Bankruptcy Code, During the 12-Month Period Ending December 31, 2020

Housing Vacancy Rates

Area	Gross Vacancy Rate[2] (%)			Year-Round Vacancy Rate[3] (%)			Rental Vacancy Rate[4] (%)			Homeowner Vacancy Rate[5] (%)		
	2018	2019	2020	2018	2019	2020	2018	2019	2020	2018	2019	2020
MSA[1]	7.4	4.5	4.7	7.4	4.2	4.5	8.6	4.3	5.9	1.5	0.8	0.3
U.S.	12.3	12.0	10.6	9.7	9.5	8.2	6.9	6.7	6.3	1.5	1.4	1.0

Note: (1) Figures cover the Columbus, OH Metropolitan Statistical Area; (2) The percentage of the total housing inventory that is vacant; (3) The percentage of the housing inventory (excluding seasonal units) that is year-round vacant; (4) The percentage of rental inventory that is vacant for rent; (5) The percentage of homeowner inventory that is vacant for sale
Source: U.S. Census Bureau, Housing Vacancies and Homeownership Annual Statistics: 2018, 2019, 2020

INCOME

Income

Area	Per Capita ($)	Median Household ($)	Average Household ($)
City	29,322	53,745	69,315
MSA[1]	34,441	65,150	87,472
U.S.	34,103	62,843	88,607

Note: (1) Figures cover the Columbus, OH Metropolitan Statistical Area
Source: U.S. Census Bureau, 2015-2019 American Community Survey 5-Year Estimates

Household Income Distribution

Area	Percent of Households Earning							
	Under $15,000	$15,000 -$24,999	$25,000 -$34,999	$35,000 -$49,999	$50,000 -$74,999	$75,000 -$99,999	$100,000 -$149,999	$150,000 and up
City	12.1	9.7	10.2	14.4	19.5	13.3	13.4	7.3
MSA[1]	9.2	8.1	8.6	12.4	18.2	13.5	16.5	13.5
U.S.	10.3	8.9	8.9	12.3	17.2	12.7	15.1	14.5

Note: (1) Figures cover the Columbus, OH Metropolitan Statistical Area
Source: U.S. Census Bureau, 2015-2019 American Community Survey 5-Year Estimates

Poverty Rate

Area	All Ages	Under 18 Years Old	18 to 64 Years Old	65 Years and Over
City	19.5	29.3	17.4	11.6
MSA[1]	13.2	18.5	12.2	7.9
U.S.	13.4	18.5	12.6	9.3

Note: Figures are percentage of people whose income during the past 12 months was below the poverty level;
(1) Figures cover the Columbus, OH Metropolitan Statistical Area
Source: U.S. Census Bureau, 2015-2019 American Community Survey 5-Year Estimates

CITY FINANCES

City Government Finances

Component	2017 ($000)	2017 ($ per capita)
Total Revenues	1,917,617	2,256
Total Expenditures	2,105,712	2,477
Debt Outstanding	4,294,743	5,052
Cash and Securities[1]	1,751,702	2,061

Note: (1) Cash and security holdings of a government at the close of its fiscal year,
including those of its dependent agencies, utilities, and liquor stores.
Source: U.S. Census Bureau, State & Local Government Finances 2017

City Government Revenue by Source

Source	2017 ($000)	2017 ($ per capita)	2017 (%)
General Revenue			
From Federal Government	93,907	110	4.9
From State Government	52,048	61	2.7
From Local Governments	40,456	48	2.1
Taxes			
Property	43,641	51	2.3
Sales and Gross Receipts	36,918	43	1.9
Personal Income	838,053	986	43.7
Corporate Income	0	0	0.0
Motor Vehicle License	0	0	0.0
Other Taxes	28,543	34	1.5
Current Charges	405,478	477	21.1
Liquor Store	0	0	0.0
Utility	276,990	326	14.4
Employee Retirement	0	0	0.0

Source: U.S. Census Bureau, State & Local Government Finances 2017

City Government Expenditures by Function

Function	2017 ($000)	2017 ($ per capita)	2017 (%)
General Direct Expenditures			
Air Transportation	0	0	0.0
Corrections	0	0	0.0
Education	5,809	6	0.3
Employment Security Administration	0	0	0.0
Financial Administration	54,510	64	2.6
Fire Protection	259,293	305	12.3
General Public Buildings	14,525	17	0.7
Governmental Administration, Other	37,392	44	1.8
Health	51,712	60	2.5
Highways	180,809	212	8.6
Hospitals	0	0	0.0
Housing and Community Development	18,194	21	0.9
Interest on General Debt	110,192	129	5.2
Judicial and Legal	48,471	57	2.3
Libraries	0	0	0.0
Parking	2,735	3	0.1
Parks and Recreation	153,646	180	7.3
Police Protection	311,285	366	14.8
Public Welfare	0	0	0.0
Sewerage	233,528	274	11.1
Solid Waste Management	48,817	57	2.3
Veterans' Services	0	0	0.0
Liquor Store	0	0	0.0
Utility	356,235	419	16.9
Employee Retirement	0	0	0.0

Source: U.S. Census Bureau, State & Local Government Finances 2017

EMPLOYMENT

Labor Force and Employment

Area	Civilian Labor Force			Workers Employed		
	Dec. 2019	Dec. 2020	% Chg.	Dec. 2019	Dec. 2020	% Chg.
City	478,751	473,342	-1.1	463,416	448,688	-3.2
MSA[1]	1,105,853	1,087,829	-1.6	1,070,103	1,037,232	-3.1
U.S.	164,007,000	160,017,000	-2.4	158,504,000	149,613,000	-5.6

Note: Data is not seasonally adjusted and covers workers 16 years of age and older; (1) Figures cover the Columbus, OH Metropolitan Statistical Area
Source: Bureau of Labor Statistics, Local Area Unemployment Statistics

Unemployment Rate

Area	2020											
	Jan.	Feb.	Mar.	Apr.	May	Jun.	Jul.	Aug.	Sep.	Oct.	Nov.	Dec.
City	4.1	3.7	4.1	14.6	12.4	11.3	9.8	9.8	8.8	6.5	5.7	5.2
MSA[1]	4.2	3.8	4.2	13.7	11.0	9.9	8.3	8.3	7.4	5.5	4.9	4.7
U.S.	4.0	3.8	4.5	14.4	13.0	11.2	10.5	8.5	7.7	6.6	6.4	6.5

Note: Data is not seasonally adjusted and covers workers 16 years of age and older; (1) Figures cover the Columbus, OH Metropolitan Statistical Area
Source: Bureau of Labor Statistics, Local Area Unemployment Statistics

Average Wages

Occupation	$/Hr.	Occupation	$/Hr.
Accountants and Auditors	37.00	Maintenance and Repair Workers	21.50
Automotive Mechanics	21.20	Marketing Managers	73.10
Bookkeepers	21.80	Network and Computer Systems Admin.	41.90
Carpenters	24.80	Nurses, Licensed Practical	22.50
Cashiers	12.00	Nurses, Registered	33.40
Computer Programmers	44.60	Nursing Assistants	14.00
Computer Systems Analysts	44.20	Office Clerks, General	19.10
Computer User Support Specialists	26.90	Physical Therapists	42.30
Construction Laborers	24.20	Physicians	108.50
Cooks, Restaurant	13.30	Plumbers, Pipefitters and Steamfitters	28.20
Customer Service Representatives	18.40	Police and Sheriff's Patrol Officers	39.10
Dentists	92.30	Postal Service Mail Carriers	25.60
Electricians	22.90	Real Estate Sales Agents	24.20
Engineers, Electrical	42.70	Retail Salespersons	14.10
Fast Food and Counter Workers	11.00	Sales Representatives, Technical/Scientific	43.50
Financial Managers	68.80	Secretaries, Exc. Legal/Medical/Executive	19.10
First-Line Supervisors of Office Workers	29.80	Security Guards	17.50
General and Operations Managers	58.30	Surgeons	130.80
Hairdressers/Cosmetologists	17.10	Teacher Assistants, Exc. Postsecondary*	14.60
Home Health and Personal Care Aides	12.30	Teachers, Secondary School, Exc. Sp. Ed.*	33.80
Janitors and Cleaners	14.40	Telemarketers	14.40
Landscaping/Groundskeeping Workers	15.70	Truck Drivers, Heavy/Tractor-Trailer	22.70
Lawyers	54.40	Truck Drivers, Light/Delivery Services	19.30
Maids and Housekeeping Cleaners	12.60	Waiters and Waitresses	11.80

Note: Wage data covers the Columbus, OH Metropolitan Statistical Area; (*) Hourly wages were calculated from annual wage data based on a 40 hour work week; n/a not available.
Source: Bureau of Labor Statistics, Metro Area Occupational Employment & Wage Estimates, May 2020

Employment by Industry

Sector	MSA[1]		U.S.
	Number of Employees	Percent of Total	Percent of Total
Construction, Mining, and Logging	45,000	4.2	5.5
Education and Health Services	157,800	14.6	16.3
Financial Activities	86,800	8.0	6.1
Government	178,100	16.4	15.2
Information	14,800	1.4	1.9
Leisure and Hospitality	82,800	7.6	9.0
Manufacturing	72,900	6.7	8.5
Other Services	39,500	3.6	3.8
Professional and Business Services	178,300	16.4	14.4
Retail Trade	101,100	9.3	10.9
Transportation, Warehousing, and Utilities	86,100	7.9	4.6
Wholesale Trade	40,800	3.8	3.9

Note: Figures are non-farm employment as of December 2020. Figures are not seasonally adjusted and include workers 16 years of age and older; (1) Figures cover the Columbus, OH Metropolitan Statistical Area
Source: Bureau of Labor Statistics, Current Employment Statistics, Employment, Hours, and Earnings

Employment by Occupation

Occupation Classification	City (%)	MSA[1] (%)	U.S. (%)
Management, Business, Science, and Arts	40.9	42.6	38.5
Natural Resources, Construction, and Maintenance	4.8	6.0	8.9
Production, Transportation, and Material Moving	14.2	13.6	13.2
Sales and Office	22.5	21.8	21.6
Service	17.6	16.0	17.8

Note: Figures cover employed civilians 16 years of age and older; (1) Figures cover the Columbus, OH Metropolitan Statistical Area
Source: U.S. Census Bureau, 2015-2019 American Community Survey 5-Year Estimates

Occupations with Greatest Projected Employment Growth: 2020 – 2022

Occupation[1]	2020 Employment	2022 Projected Employment	Numeric Employment Change	Percent Employment Change
Laborers and Freight, Stock, and Material Movers, Hand	119,110	122,880	3,770	3.2
Registered Nurses	129,170	132,090	2,920	2.3
Home Health and Personal Care Aides	94,930	97,520	2,590	2.7
Industrial Truck and Tractor Operators	33,730	35,870	2,140	6.3
Heavy and Tractor-Trailer Truck Drivers	80,440	82,290	1,850	2.3
Construction Laborers	42,520	44,210	1,690	4.0
Electricians	26,990	28,530	1,540	5.7
Medical Assistants	26,150	27,410	1,260	4.8
Light Truck or Delivery Services Drivers	38,160	39,200	1,040	2.7
Heating, Air Conditioning, and Refrigeration Mechanics and Installers	13,410	14,390	980	7.3

Note: Projections cover Ohio; (1) Sorted by numeric employment change
Source: www.projectionscentral.com, State Occupational Projections, 2020–2022 Short-Term Projections

Fastest-Growing Occupations: 2020 – 2022

Occupation[1]	2020 Employment	2022 Projected Employment	Numeric Employment Change	Percent Employment Change
Roofers	5,710	6,240	530	9.3
Helpers—Pipelayers, Plumbers, Pipefitters, and Steamfitters	920	1,000	80	8.7
Brickmasons and Blockmasons	3,790	4,090	300	7.9
Floor Layers, Except Carpet, Wood, and Hard Tiles	1,210	1,300	90	7.4
Heating, Air Conditioning, and Refrigeration Mechanics and Installers	13,410	14,390	980	7.3
Cement Masons and Concrete Finishers	5,580	5,980	400	7.2
Glaziers	1,260	1,350	90	7.1
Structural Iron and Steel Workers	3,210	3,430	220	6.9
Physician Assistants	4,720	5,040	320	6.8
Tile and Marble Setters	910	970	60	6.6

Note: Projections cover Ohio; (1) Sorted by percent employment change and excludes occupations with numeric employment change less than 50
Source: www.projectionscentral.com, State Occupational Projections, 2020–2022 Short-Term Projections

TAXES

State Corporate Income Tax Rates

State	Tax Rate (%)	Income Brackets ($)	Num. of Brackets	Financial Institution Tax Rate (%)[a]	Federal Income Tax Ded.
Ohio	(t)	–	–	(t)	No

Note: Tax rates as of January 1, 2021; (a) Rates listed are the corporate income tax rate applied to financial institutions or excise taxes based on income. Some states have other taxes based upon the value of deposits or shares; (t) Ohio no longer levies a tax based on income (except for a particular subset of corporations), but instead imposes a Commercial Activity Tax (CAT) equal to $150 for gross receipts sitused to Ohio of between $150,000 and $1 million, plus 0.26% of gross receipts over $1 million. Banks continue to pay a franchise tax of 1.3% of net worth. For those few corporations for whom the franchise tax on net worth or net income still applies, a litter tax also applies.
Source: Federation of Tax Administrators, State Corporate Income Tax Rates, January 1, 2021

State Individual Income Tax Rates

State	Tax Rate (%)	Income Brackets ($)	Personal Exemptions ($)			Standard Ded. ($)	
			Single	Married	Depend.	Single	Married
Ohio (a)	0.0 - 4.797	22,150 - 221,300	2,400	4,800 (s)	2,400 (s)	–	–

Note: Tax rates as of January 1, 2021; Local- and county-level taxes are not included; Federal income tax is not deductible on state income tax returns; (a) 19 states have statutory provision for automatically adjusting to the rate of inflation the dollar values of the income tax brackets, standard deductions, and/or personal exemptions. Michigan indexes the personal exemption only. Oregon does not index the income brackets for $125,000 and over; (s) Ohio provides an additional tax credit of $20 per exemption. Exemption amounts reduced for higher income taxpayers. Business income taxes at a flat 3% rate.
Source: Federation of Tax Administrators, State Individual Income Tax Rates, January 1, 2021

Various State Sales and Excise Tax Rates

State	State Sales Tax (%)	Gasoline[1] (¢/gal.)	Cigarette[2] ($/pack)	Spirits[3] ($/gal.)	Wine[4] ($/gal.)	Beer[5] ($/gal.)	Recreational Marijuana (%)
Ohio	5.75	38.51	1.6	9.83	0.32	0.18	Not legal

Note: All tax rates as of January 1, 2021; (1) The American Petroleum Institute has developed a methodology for determining the average tax rate on a gallon of fuel. Rates may include any of the following: excise taxes, environmental fees, storage tank fees, other fees or taxes, general sales tax, and local taxes; (2) The federal excise tax of $1.0066 per pack and local taxes are not included; (3) Rates are those applicable to off-premise sales of 40% alcohol by volume (a.b.v.) distilled spirits in 750ml containers. Local excise taxes are excluded; (4) Rates are those applicable to off-premise sales of 11% a.b.v. non-carbonated wine in 750ml containers; (5) Rates are those applicable to off-premise sales of 4.7% a.b.v. beer in 12 ounce containers.
Source: Tax Foundation, 2021 Facts & Figures: How Does Your State Compare?

State Business Tax Climate Index Rankings

State	Overall Rank	Corporate Tax Rank	Individual Income Tax Rank	Sales Tax Rank	Property Tax Rank	Unemployment Insurance Tax Rank
Ohio	39	42	43	34	6	6

Note: The index is a measure of how each state's tax laws affect economic performance. The lower the rank, the more favorable a state's tax system is for business. States without a given tax are given a ranking of 1. The scores/rankings for the District of Columbia do not affect other states. The 2021 index represents the tax climate as of July 1, 2020.
Source: Tax Foundation, State Business Tax Climate Index 2021

TRANSPORTATION

Means of Transportation to Work

Area	Car/Truck/Van		Public Transportation			Bicycle	Walked	Other Means	Worked at Home
	Drove Alone	Car-pooled	Bus	Subway	Railroad				
City	79.4	8.3	3.1	0.0	0.0	0.6	3.1	1.1	4.4
MSA[1]	82.2	7.6	1.6	0.0	0.0	0.4	2.2	1.0	5.0
U.S.	76.3	9.0	2.4	1.9	0.6	0.5	2.7	1.4	5.2

Note: Figures are percentages and cover workers 16 years of age and older; (1) Figures cover the Columbus, OH Metropolitan Statistical Area
Source: U.S. Census Bureau, 2015-2019 American Community Survey 5-Year Estimates

Travel Time to Work

Area	Less Than 10 Minutes	10 to 19 Minutes	20 to 29 Minutes	30 to 44 Minutes	45 to 59 Minutes	60 to 89 Minutes	90 Minutes or More
City	10.0	34.5	29.8	18.8	3.7	2.1	1.1
MSA[1]	11.0	29.7	26.3	21.8	6.6	3.2	1.4
U.S.	12.2	28.4	20.8	20.8	8.3	6.4	2.9

Note: Note: Figures are percentages and include workers 16 years old and over; (1) Figures cover the Columbus, OH Metropolitan Statistical Area
Source: U.S. Census Bureau, 2015-2019 American Community Survey 5-Year Estimates

Key Congestion Measures

Measure	1982	1992	2002	2012	2017
Annual Hours of Delay, Total (000)	7,733	17,345	31,423	43,720	51,381
Annual Hours of Delay, Per Auto Commuter	17	30	40	44	50
Annual Congestion Cost, Total (million $)	59	184	426	789	951
Annual Congestion Cost, Per Auto Commuter ($)	356	549	775	845	963

Note: Covers the Columbus OH urban area
Source: Texas A&M Transportation Institute, 2019 Urban Mobility Report

Freeway Travel Time Index

Measure	1982	1987	1992	1997	2002	2007	2012	2017
Urban Area Index[1]	1.07	1.10	1.14	1.16	1.18	1.18	1.18	1.19
Urban Area Rank[1,2]	35	36	34	36	37	44	40	41

Note: Freeway Travel Time Index—the ratio of travel time in the peak period to the travel time at free-flow conditions. For example, a value of 1.30 indicates a 20-minute free-flow trip takes 26 minutes in the peak (20 minutes x 1.30 = 26 minutes); (1) Covers the Columbus OH urban area; (2) Rank is based on 101 larger urban areas (#1 = highest travel time index)
Source: Texas A&M Transportation Institute, 2019 Urban Mobility Report

Public Transportation

Agency Name / Mode of Transportation	Vehicles Operated in Maximum Service[1]	Annual Unlinked Passenger Trips[2] (in thous.)	Annual Passenger Miles[3] (in thous.)
Central Ohio Transit Authority (COTA)			
Bus (directly operated)	269	19,141.5	74,351.7
Demand Response (purchased transportation)	64	288.7	3,017.3

Note: (1) Number of revenue vehicles operated by the given mode and type of service to meet the annual maximum service requirement. This is the revenue vehicle count during the peak season of the year; on the week and day that maximum service is provided. Vehicles operated in maximum service (VOMS) exclude atypical days and one-time special events; (2) Number of passengers who boarded public transportation vehicles. Passengers are counted each time they board a vehicle no matter how many vehicles they use to travel from their origin to their destination. (3) Sum of the distances ridden by all passengers during the entire fiscal year.
Source: Federal Transit Administration, National Transit Database, 2019

Air Transportation

Airport Name and Code / Type of Service	Passenger Airlines[1]	Passenger Enplanements	Freight Carriers[2]	Freight (lbs)
Port Columbus International (CMH)				
Domestic service (U.S. carriers - 2020)	27	1,568,608	9	1,803,420
International service (U.S. carriers - 2019)	6	12,131	0	0

Note: (1) Includes all U.S.-based major, minor and commuter airlines that carried at least one passenger during the year; (2) Includes all U.S.-based airlines and freight carriers that transported at least one pound of freight during the year.
Source: Bureau of Transportation Statistics, The Intermodal Transportation Database, Air Carriers: T-100 Domestic Market (U.S. Carriers), 2020; Bureau of Transportation Statistics, The Intermodal Transportation Database, Air Carriers: T-100 International Market (U.S. Carriers), 2019

BUSINESSES

Major Business Headquarters

Company Name	Industry	Rankings	
		Fortune[1]	Forbes[2]
American Electric Power	Utilities, Gas and Electric	204	-
Hexion	Chemicals	-	136
Huntington Bancshares	Commercial Banks	500	-
L Brands	Specialty Retailers, Apparel	248	-
Nationwide	Insurance, Property and Casualty (Mutual)	74	-

Note: (1) Companies that produce a 10-K are ranked 1 to 500 based on 2019 revenue; (2) All private companies with at least $2 billion in annual revenue through the end of their most current fiscal year are ranked 1 to 219; companies listed are headquartered in the city; dashes indicate no ranking
Source: Fortune, "Fortune 500," June/July 2020; Forbes, "America's Largest Private Companies," 2020

Fastest-Growing Businesses

According to *Inc.*, Columbus is home to one of America's 500 fastest-growing private companies: **Dash Technologies** (#153). Criteria: must be an independent, privately-held, for-profit, U.S. corporation, proprietorship or partnership as of December 31, 2019; revenues must be at least $100,000 in 2016 and $2 million in 2019; must have four-year operating/sales history. *Inc., "America's 500 Fastest-Growing Private Companies," 2020*

According to *Fortune*, Columbus is home to one of the 100 fastest-growing companies in the world: **Installed Building Products** (#99). Companies were ranked by their revenue growth rate; their EPS growth rate; and their three-year annualized total return to investors for the period ending June 30, 2020. Criteria for inclusion: a company, foreign or domestic, must trade on a major U.S. stock exchange; must file quarterly reports with the SEC; must have a minimum market capitalization of $250 million; must have a stock price of at least $5 on June 30, 2020; must have been trading continuously since June 30, 2017; must have revenue and net income for the four quarters ended on or before April 30, 2020, of at least $50 million and $10 million, respectively; and must have posted a compound annual growth in revenue and earnings per share of at least 15% annually over the three years ending on or before April 30, 2020. Real estate investment trusts, limited-liability companies, limited parterships, business development companies, closed-end investment firms, companies about to be acquired, and companies that lost money in the quarter ending April 30, 2020 were excluded. *Fortune, "100 Fastest-Growing Companies," 2020*

According to *Initiative for a Competitive Inner City (ICIC)*, Columbus is home to two of America's 100 fastest-growing "inner city" companies: **Dos Hermanos Taco Truck** (#22); **Electronic Systems Consultants** (#95). Criteria for inclusion: company must be headquartered in or have 51 percent or more of its physical operations in an economically distressed urban area; must be an independent, for-profit corporation, partnership or proprietorship; must have 10 or more employees and have a five-year sales history that includes sales of at least $200,000 in the base year and at least $1 million in the current year with no decrease in sales over the two most recent years. Companies were ranked overall by revenue growth over the five-year period between 2015 and 2019. *Initiative for a Competitive Inner City (ICIC), "Inner City 100 Companies," 2020*

Minority Business Opportunity

Columbus is home to one company which is on the *Black Enterprise* Industrial/Service list (100 largest companies based on gross sales): **IAP Government Services Group/IAP Design Build** (#66). Criteria: operational in previous calendar year; at least 51% black-owned and manufactures/owns the product it sells or provides industrial or consumer services. Brokerages, real estate firms and firms that provide professional services are not eligible. *Black Enterprise, B.E. 100s, 2019*

Living Environment

COST OF LIVING

Cost of Living Index

Composite Index	Groceries	Housing	Utilities	Trans-portation	Health Care	Misc. Goods/ Services
91.5	98.2	83.0	85.7	100.6	94.1	94.4

Note: The Cost of Living Index measures regional differences in the cost of consumer goods and services, excluding taxes and non-consumer expenditures, for professional and managerial households in the top income quintile. It is based on more than 50,000 prices covering almost 60 different items for which prices are collected three times a year by chambers of commerce, economic development organizations or university applied economic centers in each participating urban area. The numbers shown should be read as a percentage above or below the national average of 100. For example, a value of 115.4 in the groceries column indicates that grocery prices are 15.4% higher than the national average. Small differences in the index numbers should not be interpreted as significant; Figures cover the Columbus OH urban area.
Source: The Council for Community and Economic Research, Cost of Living Index, 2020

Grocery Prices

Area[1]	T-Bone Steak ($/pound)	Frying Chicken ($/pound)	Whole Milk ($/half gal.)	Eggs ($/dozen)	Orange Juice ($/64 oz.)	Coffee ($/11.5 oz.)
City[2]	12.68	1.16	1.58	1.17	3.53	7.19
Avg.	11.78	1.39	2.05	1.47	3.57	4.34
Min.	8.03	0.94	1.03	0.74	2.94	3.02
Max.	15.86	2.65	4.31	3.77	5.44	8.69

*Note: (1) Values for the local area are compared with the average, minimum and maximum values for all 284 areas in the Cost of Living Index; (2) Figures cover the Columbus OH urban area; **T-Bone Steak** (price per pound); **Frying Chicken** (price per pound, whole fryer); **Whole Milk** (half gallon carton); **Eggs** (price per dozen, Grade A, large); **Orange Juice** (64 oz. Tropicana or Florida Natural); **Coffee** (11.5 oz. can, vacuum-packed, Maxwell House, Hills Bros, or Folgers).*
Source: The Council for Community and Economic Research, Cost of Living Index, 2020

Housing and Utility Costs

Area[1]	New Home Price ($)	Apartment Rent ($/month)	All Electric ($/month)	Part Electric ($/month)	Other Energy ($/month)	Telephone ($/month)
City[2]	281,476	1,136	-	68.54	59.10	179.90
Avg.	368,594	1,168	170.86	100.47	65.28	184.30
Min.	190,567	502	91.58	31.42	26.08	169.60
Max.	2,227,806	4,738	470.38	280.31	280.06	206.50

*Note: (1) Values for the local area are compared with the average, minimum and maximum values for all 284 areas in the Cost of Living Index; (2) Figures cover the Columbus OH urban area; **New Home Price** (2,400 sf living area, 8,000 sf lot, in urban area with full utilities); **Apartment Rent** (950 sf 2 bedroom/1.5 or 2 bath, unfurnished, excluding all utilities except water); **All Electric** (average monthly cost for an all-electric home); **Part Electric** (average monthly cost for a part-electric home); **Other Energy** (average monthly cost for natural gas, fuel oil, coal, wood, and any other forms of energy except electricity); **Telephone** (price includes the base monthly rate plus taxes and fees for three lines of mobile phone service).*
Source: The Council for Community and Economic Research, Cost of Living Index, 2020

Health Care, Transportation, and Other Costs

Area[1]	Doctor ($/visit)	Dentist ($/visit)	Optometrist ($/visit)	Gasoline ($/gallon)	Beauty Salon ($/visit)	Men's Shirt ($)
City[2]	130.99	84.54	59.28	2.38	39.83	34.09
Avg.	115.44	99.32	108.10	2.21	39.27	31.37
Min.	36.68	59.00	51.36	1.71	19.00	11.00
Max.	219.00	153.10	250.97	3.46	82.05	58.33

*Note: (1) Values for the local area are compared with the average, minimum and maximum values for all 284 areas in the Cost of Living Index; (2) Figures cover the Columbus OH urban area; **Doctor** (general practitioners routine exam of an established patient); **Dentist** (adult teeth cleaning and periodic oral examination); **Optometrist** (full vision eye exam for established adult patient); **Gasoline** (one gallon regular unleaded, national brand, including all taxes, cash price at self-service pump if available); **Beauty Salon** (woman's shampoo, trim, and blow-dry); **Men's Shirt** (cotton/polyester dress shirt, pinpoint weave, long sleeves).*
Source: The Council for Community and Economic Research, Cost of Living Index, 2020

HOUSING

Homeownership Rate

Area	2012 (%)	2013 (%)	2014 (%)	2015 (%)	2016 (%)	2017 (%)	2018 (%)	2019 (%)	2020 (%)
MSA[1]	60.7	60.5	60.0	59.0	57.5	57.9	64.8	65.7	65.6
U.S.	65.4	65.1	64.5	63.7	63.4	63.9	64.4	64.6	66.6

Note: (1) Figures cover the Columbus, OH Metropolitan Statistical Area
Source: U.S. Census Bureau, Housing Vacancies and Homeownership Annual Statistics: 2012-2020

House Price Index (HPI)

Area	National Ranking[2]	Quarterly Change (%)	One-Year Change (%)	Five-Year Change (%)	Since 1991Q1 (%)
MSA[1]	65	2.05	7.40	37.73	163.06
U.S.[3]	–	3.81	10.77	38.99	205.12

Note: The HPI is a weighted repeat sales index. It measures average price changes in repeat sales or refinancings on the same properties. This information is obtained by reviewing repeat mortgage transactions on single-family properties whose mortgages have been purchased or securitized by Fannie Mae or Freddie Mac since January 1975; (1) Figures cover the Columbus, OH Metropolitan Statistical Area; (2) Rankings are based on annual percentage change for all metro areas containing at least 15,000 transactions over the last 10 years and ranges from 1 to 253; (3) figures based on a weighted average of Census Division estimates using a seasonally adjusted, purchase-only index; all figures are for the period ending December 31, 2020
Source: Federal Housing Finance Agency, Change in Metropolitan Area House Price Indexes, April 7, 2021

Median Single-Family Home Prices

Area	2018	2019	2020[p]	Percent Change 2019 to 2020
MSA[1]	201.8	216.6	240.8	11.2
U.S. Average	261.6	274.6	299.9	9.2

Note: Figures are median sales prices of existing single-family homes in thousands of dollars; (p) preliminary; (1) Figures cover the Columbus, OH Metropolitan Statistical Area
Source: National Association of Realtors, Median Sales Price of Existing Single-Family Homes for Metropolitan Areas, 4th Quarter 2020

Qualifying Income Based on Median Sales Price of Existing Single-Family Homes

Area	With 5% Down ($)	With 10% Down ($)	With 20% Down ($)
MSA[1]	46,605	44,152	39,246
U.S. Average	59,266	56,147	49,908

Note: Figures are preliminary; Qualifying income is based on a mortgage rate of 2.81%. Monthly principal and interest payment is limited to 25% of income; (1) Figures cover the Columbus, OH Metropolitan Statistical Area
Source: National Association of Realtors, Qualifying Income Based on Median Sales Price of Existing Single-Family Homes for Metropolitan Areas, 4th Quarter 2020

Home Value Distribution

Area	Under $50,000	$50,000 -$99,999	$100,000 -$149,999	$150,000 -$199,999	$200,000 -$299,999	$300,000 -$499,999	$500,000 -$999,999	$1,000,000 or more
City	5.9	19.5	23.8	20.7	19.8	7.9	2.0	0.3
MSA[1]	4.8	13.1	18.2	18.8	23.1	16.5	4.9	0.7
U.S.	6.9	12.0	13.3	14.0	19.6	19.3	11.4	3.4

Note: Figures are percentages and cover owner-occupied housing units; (1) Figures cover the Columbus, OH Metropolitan Statistical Area
Source: U.S. Census Bureau, 2015-2019 American Community Survey 5-Year Estimates

Year Housing Structure Built

Area	2010 or Later	2000 -2009	1990 -1999	1980 -1989	1970 -1979	1960 -1969	1950 -1959	1940 -1949	Before 1940	Median Year
City	5.9	11.4	15.4	13.0	15.0	12.0	10.8	5.0	11.6	1977
MSA[1]	5.8	14.2	16.5	11.7	14.4	11.1	10.2	4.1	12.2	1979
U.S.	5.2	14.0	13.9	13.4	15.2	10.6	10.3	4.9	12.6	1978

Note: Figures are percentages except for Median Year; Note: (1) Figures cover the Columbus, OH Metropolitan Statistical Area
Source: U.S. Census Bureau, 2015-2019 American Community Survey 5-Year Estimates

Gross Monthly Rent

Area	Under $500	$500 -$999	$1,000 -$1,499	$1,500 -$1,999	$2,000 -$2,499	$2,500 -$2,999	$3,000 and up	Median ($)
City	6.4	48.7	35.7	7.1	1.5	0.4	0.3	961
MSA[1]	7.6	48.3	34.3	7.3	1.6	0.5	0.4	953
U.S.	9.4	36.2	30.0	14.0	5.6	2.4	2.4	1,062

Note: Figures are percentages except for Median; Gross rent is the contract rent plus the estimated average monthly cost of utilities (electricity, gas, and water and sewer) and fuels (oil, coal, kerosene, wood, etc.) if these are paid by the renter (or paid for the renter by someone else); (1) Figures cover the Columbus, OH Metropolitan Statistical Area
Source: U.S. Census Bureau, 2015-2019 American Community Survey 5-Year Estimates

HEALTH

Health Risk Factors

Category	MSA[1] (%)	U.S. (%)
Adults aged 18–64 who have any kind of health care coverage	90.8	87.3
Adults who reported being in good or better health	83.2	82.4
Adults who have been told they have high blood cholesterol	29.7	33.0
Adults who have been told they have high blood pressure	32.8	32.3
Adults who are current smokers	20.3	17.1
Adults who currently use E-cigarettes	5.3	4.6
Adults who currently use chewing tobacco, snuff, or snus	4.8	4.0
Adults who are heavy drinkers[2]	7.7	6.3
Adults who are binge drinkers[3]	20.1	17.4
Adults who are overweight (BMI 25.0 - 29.9)	35.7	35.3
Adults who are obese (BMI 30.0 - 99.8)	32.5	31.3
Adults who participated in any physical activities in the past month	73.2	74.4
Adults who always or nearly always wears a seat belt	92.7	94.3

Note: (1) Figures cover the Columbus, OH Metropolitan Statistical Area; (2) Heavy drinkers are classified as adult men having more than 14 drinks per week and adult women having more than 7 drinks per week; (3) Binge drinkers are classified as males having five or more drinks on one occasion or females having four or more drinks on one occasion
Source: Centers for Disease Control and Prevention, Behaviorial Risk Factor Surveillance System, SMART: Selected Metropolitan Area Risk Trends, 2017

Acute and Chronic Health Conditions

Category	MSA[1] (%)	U.S. (%)
Adults who have ever been told they had a heart attack	3.7	4.2
Adults who have ever been told they have angina or coronary heart disease	3.1	3.9
Adults who have ever been told they had a stroke	2.9	3.0
Adults who have ever been told they have asthma	13.7	14.2
Adults who have ever been told they have arthritis	25.6	24.9
Adults who have ever been told they have diabetes[2]	9.3	10.5
Adults who have ever been told they had skin cancer	5.9	6.2
Adults who have ever been told they had any other types of cancer	6.4	7.1
Adults who have ever been told they have COPD	7.5	6.5
Adults who have ever been told they have kidney disease	2.3	3.0
Adults who have ever been told they have a form of depression	22.8	20.5

Note: (1) Figures cover the Columbus, OH Metropolitan Statistical Area; (2) Figures do not include pregnancy-related, borderline, or pre-diabetes
Source: Centers for Disease Control and Prevention, Behaviorial Risk Factor Surveillance System, SMART: Selected Metropolitan Area Risk Trends, 2017

Health Screening and Vaccination Rates

Category	MSA[1] (%)	U.S. (%)
Adults aged 65+ who have had flu shot within the past year	65.1	60.7
Adults aged 65+ who have ever had a pneumonia vaccination	82.3	75.4
Adults who have ever been tested for HIV	38.1	36.1
Adults who have ever had the shingles or zoster vaccine?	31.9	28.9
Adults who have had their blood cholesterol checked within the last five years	85.4	85.9

Note: n/a not available; (1) Figures cover the Columbus, OH Metropolitan Statistical Area.
Source: Centers for Disease Control and Prevention, Behaviorial Risk Factor Surveillance System, SMART: Selected Metropolitan Area Risk Trends, 2017

Disability Status

Category	MSA[1] (%)	U.S. (%)
Adults who reported being deaf	5.7	6.7
Are you blind or have serious difficulty seeing, even when wearing glasses?	4.6	4.5
Are you limited in any way in any of your usual activities due of arthritis?	13.3	12.9
Do you have difficulty doing errands alone?	5.9	6.8
Do you have difficulty dressing or bathing?	3.2	3.6
Do you have serious difficulty concentrating/remembering/making decisions?	10.8	10.7
Do you have serious difficulty walking or climbing stairs?	12.9	13.6

Note: (1) Figures cover the Columbus, OH Metropolitan Statistical Area.
Source: Centers for Disease Control and Prevention, Behaviorial Risk Factor Surveillance System, SMART: Selected Metropolitan Area Risk Trends, 2017

Mortality Rates for the Top 10 Causes of Death in the U.S.

ICD-10[a] Sub-Chapter	ICD-10[a] Code	Age-Adjusted Mortality Rate[1] per 100,000 population	
		County[2]	U.S.
Malignant neoplasms	C00-C97	156.3	149.2
Ischaemic heart diseases	I20-I25	78.2	90.5
Other forms of heart disease	I30-I51	69.1	52.2
Chronic lower respiratory diseases	J40-J47	45.8	39.6
Other degenerative diseases of the nervous system	G30-G31	37.6	37.6
Cerebrovascular diseases	I60-I69	45.3	37.2
Other external causes of accidental injury	W00-X59	55.0	36.1
Organic, including symptomatic, mental disorders	F01-F09	46.0	29.4
Hypertensive diseases	I10-I15	26.8	24.1
Diabetes mellitus	E10-E14	24.6	21.5

Note: (a) ICD-10 = International Classification of Diseases 10th Revision; (1) Mortality rates are a three-year average covering 2017-2019; (2) Figures cover Franklin County.
Source: Centers for Disease Control and Prevention, National Center for Health Statistics. Underlying Cause of Death 1999-2019 on CDC WONDER Online Database

Mortality Rates for Selected Causes of Death

ICD-10[a] Sub-Chapter	ICD-10[a] Code	Age-Adjusted Mortality Rate[1] per 100,000 population	
		County[2]	U.S.
Assault	X85-Y09	9.6	6.0
Diseases of the liver	K70-K76	14.2	14.4
Human immunodeficiency virus (HIV) disease	B20-B24	1.3	1.5
Influenza and pneumonia	J09-J18	17.2	13.8
Intentional self-harm	X60-X84	12.3	14.1
Malnutrition	E40-E46	3.1	2.3
Obesity and other hyperalimentation	E65-E68	2.2	2.1
Renal failure	N17-N19	14.6	12.6
Transport accidents	V01-V99	9.8	12.3
Viral hepatitis	B15-B19	1.1	1.2

Note: (a) ICD-10 = International Classification of Diseases 10th Revision; (1) Mortality rates are a three-year average covering 2017-2019; (2) Figures cover Franklin County; Data are suppressed when the data meet the criteria for confidentiality constraints; Mortality rates are flagged as unreliable when the rate would be calculated with a numerator of 20 or less.
Source: Centers for Disease Control and Prevention, National Center for Health Statistics. Underlying Cause of Death 1999-2019 on CDC WONDER Online Database

Health Insurance Coverage

Area	With Health Insurance	With Private Health Insurance	With Public Health Insurance	Without Health Insurance	Population Under Age 19 Without Health Insurance
City	91.0	64.0	34.8	9.0	5.4
MSA[1]	93.3	71.2	32.1	6.7	4.2
U.S.	91.2	67.9	35.1	8.8	5.1

Note: Figures are percentages that cover the civilian noninstitutionalized population; (1) Figures cover the Columbus, OH Metropolitan Statistical Area
Source: U.S. Census Bureau, 2015-2019 American Community Survey 5-Year Estimates

Number of Medical Professionals

Area	MDs[3]	DOs[3,4]	Dentists	Podiatrists	Chiropractors	Optometrists
County[1] (number)	5,553	810	1,226	94	327	357
County[1] (rate[2])	424.6	61.9	93.1	7.1	24.8	27.1
U.S. (rate[2])	282.9	22.7	71.2	6.2	28.1	16.9

39049
Note: Data as of 2019 unless noted; (1) Data covers Franklin County; (2) Rate per 100,000 population; (3) Data as of 2018 and includes all active, non-federal physicians; (4) Doctor of Osteopathic Medicine
Source: U.S. Department of Health and Human Services, Health Resources and Services Administration, Bureau of Health Professions, Area Resource File (ARF) 2019-2020

Best Hospitals

According to *U.S. News,* the Columbus, OH metro area is home to two of the best hospitals in the U.S.: **Ohio State University James Cancer Hospital** (1 adult specialty); **Ohio State University Wexner Medical Center** (9 adult specialties). The hospitals listed were nationally ranked in at least one of 16 adult or 10 pediatric specialties. Only 134 hospitals nationwide were nationally ranked in one or more adult or pediatric specialty; this number increases to 178 counting specialized centers within hospitals. Twenty hospitals in the U.S. made the Honor Roll. The Best Hospitals Honor Roll takes both the national rankings and the procedure and condition ratings into account. Hospitals received points if they were nationally ranked in one of the 16 adult specialties—the higher they ranked, the more points they got—and how many ratings of "high performing" they earned in the 10 procedures and conditions. *U.S. News Online, "America's Best Hospitals 2020-21"*

According to *U.S. News,* the Columbus, OH metro area is home to one of the best children's hospitals in the U.S.: **Nationwide Children's Hospital** (Honor Roll/10 pediatric specialties). The hospital listed was highly ranked in at least one of 10 pediatric specialties. Eighty-eight children's hospitals in the U.S. were nationally ranked in at least one specialty. Hospitals received points for being ranked in a specialty, and the 10 hospitals with the most points across the 10 specialties make up the Honor Roll. *U.S. News Online, "America's Best Children's Hospitals 2020-21"*

EDUCATION

Public School District Statistics

District Name	Schls	Pupils	Pupil/ Teacher Ratio	Minority Pupils[1] (%)	Free Lunch Eligible[2] (%)	IEP[3] (%)
Columbus City School District	115	48,925	16.0	77.5	n/a	18.7
Hamilton Local	5	3,094	20.5	24.5	44.9	11.2
Hilliard City	23	16,367	18.6	27.9	18.7	14.4

Note: Table includes school districts with 2,000 or more students; (1) Percentage of students that are not non-Hispanic white; (2) Percentage of students that are eligible for the free lunch program; (3) Percentage of students that have an Individualized Education Program.
Source: U.S. Department of Education, National Center for Education Statistics, Common Core of Data, Local Education Agency (School District) Universe Survey: School Year 2018-2019; U.S. Department of Education, National Center for Education Statistics, Common Core of Data, Public Elementary/Secondary School Universe Survey: School Year 2018-2019

Highest Level of Education

Area	Less than H.S.	H.S. Diploma	Some College, No Deg.	Associate Degree	Bachelor's Degree	Master's Degree	Prof. School Degree	Doctorate Degree
City	10.2	25.5	20.6	7.2	23.8	9.4	1.9	1.5
MSA[1]	8.5	27.7	19.6	7.5	23.4	9.7	2.2	1.4
U.S.	12.0	27.0	20.4	8.5	19.8	8.8	2.1	1.4

Note: Figures cover persons age 25 and over; (1) Figures cover the Columbus, OH Metropolitan Statistical Area
Source: U.S. Census Bureau, 2015-2019 American Community Survey 5-Year Estimates

Educational Attainment by Race

Area	High School Graduate or Higher (%)					Bachelor's Degree or Higher (%)				
	Total	White	Black	Asian	Hisp.[2]	Total	White	Black	Asian	Hisp.[2]
City	89.8	92.0	86.8	85.3	75.6	36.6	42.3	19.7	57.7	23.2
MSA[1]	91.5	92.7	87.4	88.5	76.6	36.7	38.3	21.5	63.7	25.6
U.S.	88.0	89.9	86.0	87.1	68.7	32.1	33.5	21.6	54.3	16.4

Note: Figures shown cover persons 25 years old and over; (1) Figures cover the Columbus, OH Metropolitan Statistical Area; (2) People of Hispanic origin can be of any race
Source: U.S. Census Bureau, 2015-2019 American Community Survey 5-Year Estimates

School Enrollment by Grade and Control

Area	Preschool (%)		Kindergarten (%)		Grades 1 - 4 (%)		Grades 5 - 8 (%)		Grades 9 - 12 (%)	
	Public	Private	Public	Private	Public	Private	Public	Private	Public	Private
City	60.3	39.7	85.3	14.7	87.7	12.3	87.2	12.8	87.3	12.7
MSA[1]	55.0	45.0	85.2	14.8	88.8	11.2	88.9	11.1	89.3	10.7
U.S.	59.1	40.9	87.6	12.4	89.5	10.5	89.4	10.6	90.1	9.9

Note: Figures shown cover persons 3 years old and over; (1) Figures cover the Columbus, OH Metropolitan Statistical Area
Source: U.S. Census Bureau, 2015-2019 American Community Survey 5-Year Estimates

Higher Education

Four-Year Colleges			Two-Year Colleges			Medical Schools[1]	Law Schools[2]	Voc/ Tech[3]
Public	Private Non-profit	Private For-profit	Public	Private Non-profit	Private For-profit			
1	6	3	1	0	5	1	2	4

Note: Figures cover institutions located within the city limits and include main campuses only; (1) includes schools accredited by the Liaison Committee on Medical Education and the American Osteopathic Association's Commission on Osteopathic College Accreditation; (2) includes ABA-accredited schools, schools with provisional ABA accreditation, and state accredited schools; (3) includes all schools with programs that are less than 2 years.
Source: National Center for Education Statistics, Integrated Postsecondary Education System (IPEDS), 2019-20; Wikipedia, List of Medical Schools in the United States, accessed April 2, 2021; Wikipedia, List of Law Schools in the United States, accessed April 2, 2021

According to *U.S. News & World Report,* the Columbus, OH metro area is home to one of the top 200 national universities in the U.S.: **Ohio State University—Columbus** (#53 tie). The indicators used to capture academic quality fall into a number of categories: assessment by administrators at peer institutions; retention of students; faculty resources; student selectivity; financial resources; alumni giving; high school counselor ratings of colleges; and graduation rate. *U.S. News & World Report, "America's Best Colleges 2021"*

According to *U.S. News & World Report,* the Columbus, OH metro area is home to two of the top 100 liberal arts colleges in the U.S.: **Denison University** (#44 tie); **Ohio Wesleyan University** (#93 tie). The indicators used to capture academic quality fall into a number of categories: assessment by administrators at peer institutions; retention of students; faculty resources; student selectivity; financial resources; alumni giving; high school counselor ratings of colleges; and graduation rate. *U.S. News & World Report, "America's Best Colleges 2021"*

According to *U.S. News & World Report,* the Columbus, OH metro area is home to one of the top 100 law schools in the U.S.: **Ohio State University (Moritz)** (#40). The rankings are based on a weighted average of 12 measures of quality: peer assessment score; assessment score by lawyers/judges; median LSAT scores; median undergrad GPA; acceptance rate; employment rates for graduates; placement success; bar passage rate; faculty resources; expenditures per student; student/faculty ratio; and library resources. *U.S. News & World Report, "America's Best Graduate Schools, Law, 2022"*

According to *U.S. News & World Report,* the Columbus, OH metro area is home to one of the top 75 medical schools for research in the U.S.: **Ohio State University** (#33 tie). The rankings are based on a weighted average of 11 measures of quality: quality assessment; peer assessment score; assessment score by residency directors; research activity; total research activity; average research activity per faculty member; student selectivity; median MCAT total score; median undergraduate GPA; acceptance rate; and faculty resources. *U.S. News & World Report, "America's Best Graduate Schools, Medical, 2022"*

According to *U.S. News & World Report,* the Columbus, OH metro area is home to one of the top 75 business schools in the U.S.: **Ohio State University (Fisher)** (#33 tie). The rankings are based on a weighted average of the following nine measures: quality assessment; peer assessment; recruiter assessment; placement success; mean starting salary and bonus; student selectivity; mean GMAT and GRE scores; mean undergraduate GPA; and acceptance rate. *U.S. News & World Report, "America's Best Graduate Schools, Business, 2022"*

EMPLOYERS

Major Employers

Company Name	Industry
Abbott Labs, Ross Products Division	Manufacturing
American Electric Power	Utilities
AT&T Ohio	Information
Battelle Memorial Institute	Professional services
Big Lots	Corp. mgt./retail trade
City of Columbus	Municipal government
Columbus City Schools	Public education
Franklin County	Government
Honda of America Manufacturing	Manufacturing
Huntington Bancshares	Financial activities
JPMorgan Chase	Financial activities
Kroger Company	Retail grocery
Limited Brands	Corp. mgt./retail trade
Medco Health Solutions	Health care/wholesale trade
Mount Carmel Health System	Health care
Nationwide	Financial activities
Nationwide Children's Hospital	Health care
OhioHealth	Health care
Retail Ventures	Corp. mgt./retail trade
South-Western City School District	Public education
State of Ohio	State government
The Ohio State University	Public education
United States Government	Federal government
Wal-Mart Stores	Retail trade
Wendy's International	Corp. mgt./retail trade

Note: Companies shown are located within the Columbus, OH Metropolitan Statistical Area.
Source: Hoovers.com; Wikipedia

Best Companies to Work For

CoverMyMeds; Nationwide, headquartered in Columbus, are among "The 100 Best Companies to Work For." To pick the best companies, *Fortune* partnered with the Great Place to Work Institute. Two-thirds of a company's score is based on the results of the Institute's Trust Index survey, which is sent to a random sample of employees from each company. The questions related to attitudes about management's credibility, job satisfaction, and camaraderie. The other third of the scoring is based on the company's responses to the Institute's Culture Audit, which includes detailed questions about pay and benefit programs, and a series of open-ended questions about hiring practices, internal communication, training, recognition programs, and diversity efforts. *Any company that is at least five years old with more than 1,000 U.S. employees is eligible. Fortune, "The 100 Best Companies to Work For," 2020*

Nationwide, headquartered in Columbus, is among the "100 Best Companies for Working Mothers." Criteria: paid time off and leaves; workforce profile; benefits; women's issues and advancement; flexible work; company culture and work life programs. *Working Mother, "100 Best Companies for Working Mothers," 2020*

Nationwide Mutual Insurance; Veeam; Worthington Industries, headquartered in Columbus, are among the "100 Best Places to Work in IT." To qualify, companies had to be U.S.-based organizations or be non-U.S.-based employers that met the following criteria: have a minimum of 300 total employees at a U.S. headquarters and a minimum of 30 IT employees in the U.S., with at least 50% of their IT employees based in the U.S. The best places to work were selected based on compensation, benefits, work/life balance, employee morale, and satisfaction with training and development programs. In addition, *InsiderPro* and *Computerworld* looked at retention efforts, programs for recognizing and rewarding outstanding performances, and benefits such as flextime, elder care and child care, and reimbursement for college tuition and the cost of pursuing technology certifications. *InsiderPro and Computerworld, "100 Best Places to Work in IT," 2020*

Nationwide, headquartered in Columbus, is among the "Top Companies for Executive Women." This list is determined by organizations filling out an in-depth survey that measures female demographics at every level, but with an emphasis on women in senior corporate roles, with profit & loss (P&L) responsibility, and those earning in the top 20 percent of the organization. *Working Mother defines P&L as having responsibility that involves monitoring the net income after expenses for a department or entire organization, with direct influence on how company resources are allocated. Working Mother, "Top Companies for Executive Women," 2020+*

PUBLIC SAFETY

Crime Rate

Area	All Crimes	Violent Crimes				Property Crimes		
		Murder	Rape[3]	Robbery	Aggrav. Assault	Burglary	Larceny -Theft	Motor Vehicle Theft
City	3,811.3	8.9	97.3	199.8	197.3	641.1	2,274.1	392.8
Suburbs[1]	1,836.3	2.6	36.4	25.9	60.9	251.9	1,366.9	91.7
Metro[2]	2,676.7	5.3	62.3	99.9	119.0	417.5	1,752.9	219.8
U.S.	2,489.3	5.0	42.6	81.6	250.2	340.5	1,549.5	219.9

Note: Figures are crimes per 100,000 population; (1) All areas within the metro area that are located outside the city limits; (2) Figures cover the Columbus, OH Metropolitan Statistical Area; (3) All figures shown were reported using the revised Uniform Crime Reporting (UCR) definition of rape.
Source: FBI Uniform Crime Reports, 2019

Hate Crimes

Area	Number of Quarters Reported	Number of Incidents per Bias Motivation					
		Race/Ethnicity/ Ancestry	Religion	Sexual Orientation	Disability	Gender	Gender Identity
City	4	35	6	12	5	0	8
U.S.	4	3,963	1,521	1,195	157	69	198

Source: Federal Bureau of Investigation, Hate Crime Statistics 2019

Identity Theft Consumer Reports

Area	Reports	Reports per 100,000 Population	Rank[2]
MSA[1]	5,245	247	165
U.S.	1,387,615	423	-

Note: (1) Figures cover the Columbus, OH Metropolitan Statistical Area; (2) Rank ranges from 1 to 391 where 1 indicates greatest number of identity theft reports per 100,000 population
Source: Federal Trade Commission, Consumer Sentinel Network Data Book 2020

Fraud and Other Consumer Reports

Area	Reports	Reports per 100,000 Population	Rank[2]
MSA[1]	18,599	876	58
U.S.	3,385,133	1,031	-

Note: (1) Figures cover the Columbus, OH Metropolitan Statistical Area; (2) Rank ranges from 1 to 391 where 1 indicates greatest number of fraud and other consumer reports per 100,000 population
Source: Federal Trade Commission, Consumer Sentinel Network Data Book 2020

POLITICS

2020 Presidential Election Results

Area	Biden	Trump	Jorgensen	Hawkins	Other
Franklin County	64.7	33.4	1.2	0.3	0.4
U.S.	51.3	46.8	1.2	0.3	0.5

Note: Results are percentages and may not add to 100% due to rounding
Source: Dave Leip's Atlas of U.S. Presidential Elections

SPORTS

Professional Sports Teams

Team Name	League	Year Established
Columbus Blue Jackets	National Hockey League (NHL)	2000
Columbus Crew	Major League Soccer (MLS)	1996

Note: Includes teams located in the Columbus, OH Metropolitan Statistical Area.
Source: Wikipedia, Major Professional Sports Teams of the United States and Canada, April 6, 2021

CLIMATE

Average and Extreme Temperatures

Temperature	Jan	Feb	Mar	Apr	May	Jun	Jul	Aug	Sep	Oct	Nov	Dec	Yr.
Extreme High (°F)	74	73	82	89	93	101	104	101	100	90	80	76	104
Average High (°F)	36	39	50	62	73	82	85	83	77	65	51	40	62
Average Temp. (°F)	28	31	41	52	62	70	74	73	66	54	43	32	52
Average Low (°F)	20	22	31	40	50	59	63	62	55	43	34	24	42
Extreme Low (°F)	-19	-13	-6	14	25	35	43	39	31	17	-4	-17	-19

Note: Figures cover the years 1948-1990
Source: National Climatic Data Center, International Station Meteorological Climate Summary, 9/96

Average Precipitation/Snowfall/Humidity

Precip./Humidity	Jan	Feb	Mar	Apr	May	Jun	Jul	Aug	Sep	Oct	Nov	Dec	Yr.
Avg. Precip. (in.)	2.8	2.4	3.1	3.3	3.9	4.0	4.3	3.3	2.7	2.1	3.0	2.8	37.9
Avg. Snowfall (in.)	8	6	5	1	Tr	0	0	0	Tr	Tr	2	6	28
Avg. Rel. Hum. 7am (%)	78	78	76	76	79	81	84	87	87	83	80	79	81
Avg. Rel. Hum. 4pm (%)	66	62	55	51	52	53	53	54	53	53	61	68	57

Note: Figures cover the years 1948-1990; Tr = Trace amounts (<0.05 in. of rain; <0.5 in. of snow)
Source: National Climatic Data Center, International Station Meteorological Climate Summary, 9/96

Weather Conditions

Temperature			Daytime Sky			Precipitation		
5°F & below	32°F & below	90°F & above	Clear	Partly cloudy	Cloudy	0.01 inch or more precip.	0.1 inch or more snow/ice	Thunder-storms
10	118	19	72	137	156	136	29	40

Note: Figures are average number of days per year and cover the years 1948-1990
Source: National Climatic Data Center, International Station Meteorological Climate Summary, 9/96

HAZARDOUS WASTE

Superfund Sites

The Columbus, OH metro area is home to one site on the EPA's Superfund National Priorities List: **Air Force Plant 85** (proposed). There are a total of 1,375 Superfund sites with a status of proposed or final on the list in the U.S. *U.S. Environmental Protection Agency, National Priorities List, April 7, 2021*

AIR QUALITY

Air Quality Trends: Ozone

	1990	1995	2000	2005	2010	2015	2016	2017	2018	2019
MSA[1]	0.090	0.091	0.085	0.084	0.073	0.066	0.069	0.065	0.062	0.060
U.S.	0.088	0.089	0.082	0.080	0.073	0.068	0.069	0.068	0.069	0.065

Note: (1) Data covers the Columbus, OH Metropolitan Statistical Area. The values shown are the composite ozone concentration averages among trend sites based on the highest fourth daily maximum 8-hour concentration in parts per million. These trends are based on sites having an adequate record of monitoring data during the trend period. Data from exceptional events are included.
Source: U.S. Environmental Protection Agency, Air Quality Monitoring Information, "Air Quality Trends by City, 1990-2019"

Air Quality Index

Area	Percent of Days when Air Quality was...[2]					AQI Statistics[2]	
	Good	Moderate	Unhealthy for Sensitive Groups	Unhealthy	Very Unhealthy	Maximum	Median
MSA[1]	64.9	34.8	0.3	0.0	0.0	101	46

Note: (1) Data covers the Columbus, OH Metropolitan Statistical Area; (2) Based on 365 days with AQI data in 2019. Air Quality Index (AQI) is an index for reporting daily air quality. EPA calculates the AQI for five major air pollutants regulated by the Clean Air Act: ground-level ozone, particle pollution (aka particulate matter), carbon monoxide, sulfur dioxide, and nitrogen dioxide. The AQI runs from 0 to 500. The higher the AQI value, the greater the level of air pollution and the greater the health concern. There are six AQI categories: "Good" AQI is between 0 and 50. Air quality is considered satisfactory; "Moderate" AQI is between 51 and 100. Air quality is acceptable; "Unhealthy for Sensitive Groups" When AQI values are between 101 and 150, members of sensitive groups may experience health effects; "Unhealthy" When AQI values are between 151 and 200 everyone may begin to experience health effects; "Very Unhealthy" AQI values between 201 and 300 trigger a health alert; "Hazardous" AQI values over 300 trigger warnings of emergency conditions (not shown).
Source: U.S. Environmental Protection Agency, Air Quality Index Report, 2019

Air Quality Index Pollutants

Area	Percent of Days when AQI Pollutant was...[2]					
	Carbon Monoxide	Nitrogen Dioxide	Ozone	Sulfur Dioxide	Particulate Matter 2.5	Particulate Matter 10
MSA[1]	0.0	1.4	49.0	0.0	49.3	0.3

Note: (1) Data covers the Columbus, OH Metropolitan Statistical Area; (2) Based on 365 days with AQI data in 2019. The Air Quality Index (AQI) is an index for reporting daily air quality. EPA calculates the AQI for five major air pollutants regulated by the Clean Air Act: ground-level ozone, particle pollution (also known as particulate matter), carbon monoxide, sulfur dioxide, and nitrogen dioxide. The AQI runs from 0 to 500. The higher the AQI value, the greater the level of air pollution and the greater the health concern.
Source: U.S. Environmental Protection Agency, Air Quality Index Report, 2019

Maximum Air Pollutant Concentrations: Particulate Matter, Ozone, CO and Lead

	Particulate Matter 10 (ug/m^3)	Particulate Matter 2.5 Wtd AM (ug/m^3)	Particulate Matter 2.5 24-Hr (ug/m^3)	Ozone (ppm)	Carbon Monoxide (ppm)	Lead (ug/m^3)
MSA[1] Level	39	9.7	22	0.068	1	n/a
NAAQS[2]	150	15	35	0.075	9	0.15
Met NAAQS[2]	Yes	Yes	Yes	Yes	Yes	n/a

Note: (1) Data covers the Columbus, OH Metropolitan Statistical Area; Data from exceptional events are included; (2) National Ambient Air Quality Standards; ppm = parts per million; ug/m^3 = micrograms per cubic meter; n/a not available.
Concentrations: Particulate Matter 10 (coarse particulate)—highest second maximum 24-hour concentration; Particulate Matter 2.5 Wtd AM (fine particulate)—highest weighted annual mean concentration; Particulate Matter 2.5 24-Hour (fine particulate)—highest 98th percentile 24-hour concentration; Ozone—highest fourth daily maximum 8-hour concentration; Carbon Monoxide—highest second maximum non-overlapping 8-hour concentration; Lead—maximum running 3-month average
Source: U.S. Environmental Protection Agency, Air Quality Monitoring Information, "Air Quality Statistics by City, 2019"

Maximum Air Pollutant Concentrations: Nitrogen Dioxide and Sulfur Dioxide

	Nitrogen Dioxide AM (ppb)	Nitrogen Dioxide 1-Hr (ppb)	Sulfur Dioxide AM (ppb)	Sulfur Dioxide 1-Hr (ppb)	Sulfur Dioxide 24-Hr (ppb)
MSA[1] Level	10	42	n/a	n/a	n/a
NAAQS[2]	53	100	30	75	140
Met NAAQS[2]	Yes	Yes	n/a	n/a	n/a

Note: (1) Data covers the Columbus, OH Metropolitan Statistical Area; Data from exceptional events are included; (2) National Ambient Air Quality Standards; ppm = parts per million; ug/m^3 = micrograms per cubic meter; n/a not available.
Concentrations: Nitrogen Dioxide AM—highest arithmetic mean concentration; Nitrogen Dioxide 1-Hr—highest 98th percentile 1-hour daily maximum concentration; Sulfur Dioxide AM—highest annual mean concentration; Sulfur Dioxide 1-Hr—highest 99th percentile 1-hour daily maximum concentration; Sulfur Dioxide 24-Hr—highest second maximum 24-hour concentration
Source: U.S. Environmental Protection Agency, Air Quality Monitoring Information, "Air Quality Statistics by City, 2019"

Durham, North Carolina

Background

Durham, on the Eno River in north-central North Carolina, is known as the "City of Medicine," and forms a corner of the region's famous Research Triangle, one of the nation's earliest and most successful planned centers for research and development. The economy is deeply interlinked with area universities and businesses specializing in medicine, biopharmaceuticals, computer technology and software, and telecommunications.

The original inhabitants of the area were Eno and Occaneechi Indians, who were mostly settled, horticulturist villagers. An English explorer, John Lawson, visited the site in 1701, and called it the "flower of the Carolinas" for its scenic beauty. By the mid-eighteenth century, Scottish, Irish, and English settlers had established farms in the site of the present city.

Durham began as a station for the North Carolina Railroad, which had been built on land originally owned by the city's namesake, Bartlett Durham. Prior to the Civil War, a number of extensive plantations were established in the area.

Throughout the prewar period and beyond, Durham continued its growth as a center for tobacco farming and processing, with emphasis on "brightleaf" tobacco. One tobacco entrepreneur, Washington Duke, was of particular importance to the growth of Durham, and his own and others' efforts established Durham as a major regional economic center. The textile industry also grew and prospered in the post-Civil War years, giving rise to many clothing innovations: the nation's first denim and sheer hosiery mills were established there.

In 1910, the popular B.C. Headache Powders were produced in Durham; the city's connection with health care deepened considerably when, in 1939, Duke University's Medical School opened. Durham's current economy is both high-tech and broad-based. Hundreds of private companies in the area employ thousands of highly skilled workers in a variety of high-technology enterprises.

Durham boasts a vibrant African-American community, the center of which was an area once known as Hayti, just south of the center of town, where some of the most prominent and successful black-owned businesses in the country were established during the early 20th century. Portions of the Hayti district, along with the loss of large parts of other historic neighborhoods, were demolished for the construction of the Durham Freeway during the late 1960s. Although downtown revitalization heated up in the '70s and '80s, economic progress continues to butt heads with historic preservation.

> "Major the Bull," a 2,5000 pound statue in downtown Durham, celebrated his 17th "birthday" in style, wearing a COVID-19 mask to keep onlookers safe!

Durham's downtown draws many residents and out-of-town visitors for its architecture, shops, and restaurants. Former tobacco warehouses and factories continue to be converted to residential, office, retail or entertainment uses. The American Tobacco Company Historic District now features historic preservation projects, as well as offices, restaurants, stores and residences. At the center of Durham's cultural scene is The Carolina Theatre, a historic building currently owned by the city and maintained by The Carolina Theatre of Durham Inc., a nonprofit. Durham is home to the renowned annual Full Frame Documentary Film Festival, which is more than 20 years old.

Beyond the influence of the historic theater, Durham maintains a vibrant arts scene. Many of Durham's substantial cultural assets are linked to Duke University, including the Nasher Museum of Art at Duke University, whose Rafael Vinoly-designed building hosts traveling exhibitions from cutting-edge contemporary artists. Duke University also hosts The American Dance Festival each summer.

The city is also home to North Carolina Central University (1910), the nation's first publicly supported liberal arts college for African-Americans.

In 2020, Durham residents elected its first Muslim American women to the city commission.

Durham is serviced by the 5,000-acre Raleigh-Durham International Airport, one of the country's fastest-growing terminals, now with two passenger terminals.

Durham lies between coastal plain and piedmont plateau, giving it a moderate climate. The mountains to the west partially protect the area from excess cold winter winds, although temperatures fall below freezing some days. Summers are hot and humid. July and August see the most rain, often in the form of thunderstorms, while October and November see the least amount of rainfall.

Rankings

General Rankings

- The Durham metro area was identified as one of America's fastest-growing areas in terms of population and business growth by *MagnifyMoney*. The area ranked #16 out of 35. The 100 most populous metro areas in the U.S. were evaluated on their change from 2011-2016 in the following categories: people and housing; workforce and employment opportunities; growing industry. *www.businessinsider.com, "The 35 Cities in the US with the Biggest Influx of People, the Most Work Opportunities, and the Hottest Business Growth," August 12, 2018*

- In their seventh annual survey, Livability.com looked at data for more than 1,000 small to mid-sized U.S. cities to determine the rankings for Livability's "Top 100 Best Places to Live" in 2020. Durham ranked #9. Criteria: housing and affordable living; vibrant economy; social and civic engagement; education; demographics; health care options; transportation & infrastructure; and abundant lifestyle amenities. *Livability.com, "Top 100 Best Places to Live 2020" October 2020*

Business/Finance Rankings

- 24/7 Wall Street used metro data from the Bureau of Labor Statistics' Occupational Employment database to identify the cities with the highest percentage of those employed in jobs requiring knowledge in the science, technology, engineering, and math (STEM) fields as well as average wages for STEM jobs. The Durham metro area was #5. *247wallst.com, "15 Cities with the Most High-Tech Jobs," January 11, 2020*

- Durham was cited as one of America's top metros for new and expanded facility projects in 2020. The area ranked #10 in the mid-sized metro area category (population 200,000 to 1 million). *Site Selection, "Top Metros of 2020," March 2021*

- The Durham metro area appeared on the Milken Institute "2021 Best Performing Cities" list. Rank: #42 out of 200 large metro areas (population over 250,000). Criteria: job growth; wage and salary growth; high-tech output growth; housing affordability; household broadband access. *Milken Institute, "Best-Performing Cities 2021," February 16, 2021*

- *Forbes* ranked the 200 most populous metro areas to determine the nation's "Best Places for Business and Careers." The Durham metro area was ranked #17. Criteria: costs (business and living); job growth (past and projected); income growth; quality of life; educational attainment (college and high school); projected economic growth; cultural and leisure opportunities; workplace tolerance laws; net migration patterns. *Forbes, "The Best Places for Business and Careers 2019: Seattle Still On Top," October 30, 2019*

Children/Family Rankings

- Durham was selected as one of the most playful cities in the U.S. by KaBOOM! The organization's Playful City USA initiative honors cities and towns across the nation that have made their communities more playable. Criteria: pledging to integrate play as a solution to challenges in their communities; making it easy for children to get active and balanced play; creating more family-friendly and innovative communities as a result. *KaBOOM! National Campaign for Play, "2017 Playful City USA Communities"*

Education Rankings

- Personal finance website *WalletHub* analyzed the 150 largest U.S. metropolitan statistical areas to determine where the most educated Americans are putting their degrees to work. Criteria: education levels; percentage of workers with degrees; education quality and attainment gap; public school quality rankings; quality and enrollment of each metro area's universities. Durham was ranked #4 (#1 = most educated city). *www.WalletHub.com, "Most and Least Educated Cities in America," July 20, 2020*

- Durham was selected as one of America's most literate cities. The city ranked #16 out of the 84 largest U.S. cities. Criteria: number of booksellers; library resources; Internet resources; educational attainment; periodical publishing resources; newspaper circulation. *Central Connecticut State University, "America's Most Literate Cities, 2018," February 2019*

Health/Fitness Rankings

- For each of the 100 largest cities in the United States, the American Fitness Index®, published by the American College of Sports Medicine and the Anthem Foundation, evaluated community infrastructure and 33 health behaviors including preventive health, levels of chronic disease conditions, pedestrian safety, air quality, and community resources that support physical activity. Durham ranked #34 for "community fitness." *americanfitnessindex.org, "2020 ACSM American Fitness Index Summary Report," July 14, 2020*

- Durham was identified as a "2021 Spring Allergy Capital." The area ranked #100 out of 100. Three groups of factors were used to identify the most challenging cities for people with allergies during the spring season: annual spring pollen levels; over the counter medicine use; number of board-certified allergy specialists. *Asthma and Allergy Foundation of America, "Spring Allergy Capitals 2021," February 23, 2021*

- Durham was identified as a "2021 Fall Allergy Capital." The area ranked #100 out of 100. Three groups of factors were used to identify the most challenging cities for people with allergies during the fall season: annual fall pollen levels; over the counter medicine use; number of board-certified allergy specialists. *Asthma and Allergy Foundation of America, "Fall Allergy Capitals 2021," February 23, 2021*

- Durham was identified as a "2019 Asthma Capital." The area ranked #58 out of the nation's 100 largest metropolitan areas. Criteria: estimated asthma prevalence; crude death rate from asthma; and ER visits due to asthma. Risk factors analyzed but not factored in the rankings: annual pollen score; annual air quality; public smoking laws; number of board-certified asthma specialists; rescue medication use; controller medication use; uninsured rate; poverty rate. *Asthma and Allergy Foundation of America, "Asthma Capitals 2019: The Most Challenging Places to Live With Asthma," May 7, 2019*

Real Estate Rankings

- *WalletHub* compared the most populated U.S. cities to determine which had the best markets for real estate agents. Durham ranked #25 where demand was high and pay was the best. Criteria: sales per agent; annual median wage for real-estate agents; monthly average starting salary for real estate agents; real estate job density and competition; unemployment rate; home turnover rate; housing-market health index; and other relevant metrics. *www.WalletHub.com, "2019's Best Places to Be a Real Estate Agent," April 24, 2019*

- Durham was ranked #109 out of 268 metro areas in terms of housing affordability in 2020 by the National Association of Home Builders (#1 = most affordable). Criteria: the share of homes sold in that area affordable to a family earning the local median income, based on standard mortgage underwriting criteria. *National Association of Home Builders®, NAHB-Wells Fargo Housing Opportunity Index, 4th Quarter 2020*

Safety Rankings

- Allstate ranked the 200 largest cities in America in terms of driver safety. Durham ranked #73. Criteria: internal property damage claims over a two-year period from January 2016 to December 2017. The report helps increase the importance of safety and awareness behind the wheel. *Allstate, "Allstate America's Best Drivers Report, 2019" June 24, 2019*

- The National Insurance Crime Bureau ranked 384 metro areas in the U.S. in terms of per capita rates of vehicle theft. The Durham metro area ranked #183 (#1 = highest rate). Criteria: number of vehicle theft offenses per 100,000 inhabitants in 2019. *National Insurance Crime Bureau, "Hot Spots 2019," July 21, 2020*

Seniors/Retirement Rankings

- From its Best Cities for Successful Aging indexes, the Milken Institute generated rankings for metropolitan areas, weighing data in nine categories—health care, wellness, living arrangements, transportation and convenience, financial characteristics, education, employment, community engagement, and overall livability. The Durham metro area was ranked #3 overall in the large metro area category. *Milken Institute, "Best Cities for Successful Aging, 2017" March 14, 2017*

Women/Minorities Rankings

- NerdWallet examined data for 529 U.S. cities and ranked them based on the environment for working women. Durham ranked #6. Criteria: women's earnings; labor force participation rate; cost of living; unemployment rate. *www.nerdwallet.com, "Best Cities for Women in the Workforce 2016," April 4, 2016*

- *Women's Health*, together with the site Yelp, identified the 15 "Wellthiest" spots in the U.S. Durham appeared among the top for happiest, healthiest, outdoorsiest and Zen-iest. *Women's Health, "The 15 Wellthiest Cities in the U.S." July 5, 2017*

- Durham was selected as one of the gayest cities in America by *The Advocate.* The city ranked #15 out of 25. Criteria, among many: Trans Pride parades/festivals; gay rugby teams; lesbian bars; LGBT centers; theater screenings of "Moonlight"; LGBT-inclusive nondiscrimination ordinances; and gay bowling teams. *The Advocate, "Queerest Cities in America 2017" January 12, 2017*

- Personal finance website *WalletHub* compared more than 180 U.S. cities across two key dimensions, "Hispanic Business-Friendliness" and "Hispanic Purchasing Power," to arrive at the most favorable conditions for Hispanic entrepreneurs. Durham was ranked #64 out of 182. Criteria includes: share of Hispanic-Owned Businesses; Hispanic entrepreneurship rate to median annual income of Hispanics; Small Business-Friendliness score; cost of living; and number of Hispanics with at least a bachelor's degree. *WalletHub.com, "2019's Best Cities for Hispanic Entrepreneurs," May 1, 2019*

Miscellaneous Rankings

- *WalletHub* compared the 150 most populated U.S. cities to determine their operating efficiency. A "Quality of City Services" score was constructed for each city and then divided by the total budget per capita to reveal which were managed the best. Durham ranked #5. Criteria: financial stability; economy; education; safety; health; infrastructure and pollution. *www.WalletHub.com, "2020's Best- & Worst-Run Cities in America," June 29, 2020*

Business Environment

DEMOGRAPHICS

Population Growth

Area	1990 Census	2000 Census	2010 Census	2019* Estimate	Population Growth (%)	
					1990-2019	2010-2019
City	151,737	187,035	228,330	269,702	77.7	18.1
MSA[1]	344,646	426,493	504,357	626,695	81.8	24.3
U.S.	248,709,873	281,421,906	308,745,538	324,697,795	30.6	5.2

Note: (1) Figures cover the Durham-Chapel Hill, NC Metropolitan Statistical Area; (*) 2015-2019 5-year estimated population
Source: U.S. Census Bureau, 1990 Census, Census 2000, Census 2010, 2015-2019 American Community Survey 5-Year Estimates

Household Size

Area	Persons in Household (%)							Average Household Size
	One	Two	Three	Four	Five	Six	Seven or More	
City	33.9	33.5	15.5	10.1	4.5	1.7	0.9	2.40
MSA[1]	30.6	35.8	15.5	11.2	4.8	1.4	0.8	2.40
U.S.	27.9	33.9	15.6	12.9	6.0	2.3	1.4	2.60

Note: (1) Figures cover the Durham-Chapel Hill, NC Metropolitan Statistical Area
Source: U.S. Census Bureau, 2015-2019 American Community Survey 5-Year Estimates

Race

Area	White Alone[2] (%)	Black Alone[2] (%)	Asian Alone[2] (%)	AIAN[3] Alone[2] (%)	NHOPI[4] Alone[2] (%)	Other Race Alone[2] (%)	Two or More Races (%)
City	49.2	38.7	5.4	0.3	0.0	3.4	3.2
MSA[1]	62.5	26.6	4.5	0.4	0.0	3.0	3.1
U.S.	72.5	12.7	5.5	0.8	0.2	4.9	3.3

Note: (1) Figures cover the Durham-Chapel Hill, NC Metropolitan Statistical Area; (2) Alone is defined as not being in combination with one or more other races; (3) American Indian and Alaska Native; (4) Native Hawaiian and Other Pacific Islander
Source: U.S. Census Bureau, 2015-2019 American Community Survey 5-Year Estimates

Hispanic or Latino Origin

Area	Total (%)	Mexican (%)	Puerto Rican (%)	Cuban (%)	Other (%)
City	13.8	6.1	1.1	0.2	6.4
MSA[1]	11.1	5.7	0.9	0.2	4.3
U.S.	18.0	11.2	1.7	0.7	4.3

Note: Persons of Hispanic or Latino origin can be of any race; (1) Figures cover the Durham-Chapel Hill, NC Metropolitan Statistical Area
Source: U.S. Census Bureau, 2015-2019 American Community Survey 5-Year Estimates

Ancestry

Area	German	Irish	English	American	Italian	Polish	French[2]	Scottish	Dutch
City	7.4	5.8	7.0	4.3	2.8	1.7	1.6	1.5	0.6
MSA[1]	8.9	7.4	9.3	6.0	3.1	1.8	1.8	2.3	0.8
U.S.	13.3	9.7	7.2	6.2	5.1	2.8	2.3	1.7	1.2

Note: Figures are the percentage of the total population reporting a particular ancestry. The nine most commonly reported ancestries in the U.S. are shown. Figures include multiple ancestries (e.g. if a person reported being Irish and Italian, they were included in both columns); (1) Figures cover the Durham-Chapel Hill, NC Metropolitan Statistical Area; (2) Excludes Basque
Source: U.S. Census Bureau, 2015-2019 American Community Survey 5-Year Estimates

Foreign-born Population

Area	Percent of Population Born in								
	Any Foreign Country	Asia	Mexico	Europe	Caribbean	Central America[2]	South America	Africa	Canada
City	15.0	4.6	2.8	1.1	0.6	3.2	0.7	1.5	0.4
MSA[1]	11.7	3.6	2.6	1.4	0.4	2.0	0.5	0.9	0.4
U.S.	13.6	4.2	3.5	1.5	1.3	1.1	1.0	0.7	0.2

Note: (1) Figures cover the Durham-Chapel Hill, NC Metropolitan Statistical Area; (2) Excludes Mexico.
Source: U.S. Census Bureau, 2015-2019 American Community Survey 5-Year Estimates

Marital Status

Area	Never Married	Now Married[2]	Separated	Widowed	Divorced
City	43.1	39.9	2.5	4.3	10.2
MSA[1]	36.9	45.4	2.3	5.1	10.2
U.S.	33.4	48.1	1.9	5.8	10.9

Note: Figures are percentages and cover the population 15 years of age and older; (1) Figures cover the Durham-Chapel Hill, NC Metropolitan Statistical Area; (2) Excludes separated
Source: U.S. Census Bureau, 2015-2019 American Community Survey 5-Year Estimates

Disability by Age

Area	All Ages	Under 18 Years Old	18 to 64 Years Old	65 Years and Over
City	9.1	2.9	7.3	31.9
MSA[1]	11.4	3.9	9.1	32.3
U.S.	12.6	4.2	10.3	34.5

Note: Figures show percent of the civilian noninstitutionalized population that reported having a disability. Disability status is determined from six types of difficulty: vision, hearing, cognitive, ambulatory, self-care, and independent living. For children under 5 years old, hearing and vision difficulty are used to determine disability status. For children between the ages of 5 and 14, disability status is determined from hearing, vision, cognitive, ambulatory, and self-care difficulties. For people aged 15 years and older, they are considered to have a disability if they have difficulty with any one of the six difficulty types; Note: (1) Figures cover the Durham-Chapel Hill, NC Metropolitan Statistical Area
Source: U.S. Census Bureau, 2015-2019 American Community Survey 5-Year Estimates

Age

Area	Percent of Population									Median Age
	Under Age 5	Age 5–19	Age 20–34	Age 35–44	Age 45–54	Age 55–64	Age 65–74	Age 75–84	Age 85+	
City	6.8	18.4	26.7	14.0	11.9	10.7	7.1	3.0	1.4	33.9
MSA[1]	5.7	18.6	22.3	13.0	13.0	12.6	9.1	4.0	1.7	37.6
U.S.	6.1	19.1	20.7	12.6	13.0	12.9	9.1	4.6	1.9	38.1

Note: (1) Figures cover the Durham-Chapel Hill, NC Metropolitan Statistical Area
Source: U.S. Census Bureau, 2015-2019 American Community Survey 5-Year Estimates

Gender

Area	Males	Females	Males per 100 Females
City	126,897	142,805	88.9
MSA[1]	301,581	325,114	92.8
U.S.	159,886,919	164,810,876	97.0

Note: (1) Figures cover the Durham-Chapel Hill, NC Metropolitan Statistical Area
Source: U.S. Census Bureau, 2015-2019 American Community Survey 5-Year Estimates

Religious Groups by Family

Area	Catholic	Baptist	Non-Den.	Methodist[2]	Lutheran	LDS[3]	Pentecostal	Presbyterian[4]	Muslim[5]	Judaism
MSA[1]	5.1	13.9	5.6	8.1	0.5	0.8	1.4	2.5	0.5	0.6
U.S.	19.1	9.3	4.0	4.0	2.3	2.0	1.9	1.6	0.8	0.7

Note: Figures are the number of adherents as a percentage of the total population; (1) Figures cover the Durham-Chapel Hill, NC Metropolitan Statistical Area; (2) Methodist/Pietist; (3) Latter Day Saints; (4) Reformed; (5) Figures are estimates
Source: Association of Statisticians of American Religious Bodies, 2010 U.S. Religion Census: Religious Congregations & Membership Study

Religious Groups by Tradition

Area	Catholic	Evangelical Protestant	Mainline Protestant	Other Tradition	Black Protestant	Orthodox
MSA[1]	5.1	19.4	11.7	2.9	3.1	0.1
U.S.	19.1	16.2	7.3	4.3	1.6	0.3

Note: Figures are the number of adherents as a percentage of the total population; (1) Figures cover the Durham-Chapel Hill, NC Metropolitan Statistical Area
Source: Association of Statisticians of American Religious Bodies, 2010 U.S. Religion Census: Religious Congregations & Membership Study

ECONOMY

Gross Metropolitan Product

Area	2017	2018	2019	2020	Rank[2]
MSA[1]	43.4	45.5	48.0	50.7	65

Note: Figures are in billions of dollars; (1) Figures cover the Durham-Chapel Hill, NC Metropolitan Statistical Area; (2) Rank is based on 2018 data and ranges from 1 to 381
Source: U.S. Conference of Mayors, U.S. Metro Economies: GMP & Employment 2018-2020, September 2019

Economic Growth

Area	2015-17 (%)	2018 (%)	2019 (%)	2020 (%)	Rank[2]
MSA[1]	-2.0	2.9	3.7	3.5	363
U.S.	1.9	2.9	2.3	2.1	—

Note: Figures are real gross metropolitan product (GMP) growth rates and represent average annual percent change; (1) Figures cover the Durham-Chapel Hill, NC Metropolitan Statistical Area; (2) Rank is based on 2017 2-year average annual percent change and ranges from 1 to 381
Source: U.S. Conference of Mayors, U.S. Metro Economies: GMP & Employment 2018-2020, September 2019

Metropolitan Area Exports

Area	2014	2015	2016	2017	2018	2019	Rank[2]
MSA[1]	2,934.0	2,807.2	2,937.4	3,128.4	3,945.8	4,452.9	62

Note: Figures are in millions of dollars; (1) Figures cover the Durham-Chapel Hill, NC Metropolitan Statistical Area; (2) Rank is based on 2019 data and ranges from 1 to 386
Source: U.S. Department of Commerce, International Trade Administration, Office of Trade and Economic Analysis, Industry and Analysis, Exports by Metropolitan Area, data extracted March 24, 2021

Building Permits

Area	Single-Family			Multi-Family			Total		
	2018	2019	Pct. Chg.	2018	2019	Pct. Chg.	2018	2019	Pct. Chg.
City	1,894	1,945	2.7	1,336	1,884	41.0	3,230	3,829	18.5
MSA[1]	3,289	3,561	8.3	2,127	2,234	5.0	5,416	5,795	7.0
U.S.	855,300	862,100	0.7	473,500	523,900	10.6	1,328,800	1,386,000	4.3

Note: (1) Figures cover the Durham-Chapel Hill, NC Metropolitan Statistical Area; Figures represent new, privately-owned housing units authorized (unadjusted data); All permit data are based on estimates with imputation
Source: U.S. Census Bureau, Manufacturing, Mining, and Construction Statistics, Building Permits, 2018, 2019

Bankruptcy Filings

Area	Business Filings			Nonbusiness Filings		
	2019	2020	% Chg.	2019	2020	% Chg.
Durham County	16	18	12.5	395	223	-43.5
U.S.	22,780	21,655	-4.9	752,160	522,808	-30.5

Note: Business filings include Chapter 7, Chapter 9, Chapter 11, Chapter 12, Chapter 13, Chapter 15, and Section 304; Nonbusiness filings include Chapter 7, Chapter 11, and Chapter 13
Source: Administrative Office of the U.S. Courts, Business and Nonbusiness Bankruptcy, County Cases Commenced by Chapter of the Bankruptcy Code, During the 12-Month Period Ending December 31, 2019 and Business and Nonbusiness Bankruptcy, County Cases Commenced by Chapter of the Bankruptcy Code, During the 12-Month Period Ending December 31, 2020

Housing Vacancy Rates

Area	Gross Vacancy Rate[2] (%)			Year-Round Vacancy Rate[3] (%)			Rental Vacancy Rate[4] (%)			Homeowner Vacancy Rate[5] (%)		
	2018	2019	2020	2018	2019	2020	2018	2019	2020	2018	2019	2020
MSA[1]	n/a	n/a	n/a	n/a	n/a	n/a	n/a	n/a	n/a	n/a	n/a	n/a
U.S.	12.3	12.0	10.6	9.7	9.5	8.2	6.9	6.7	6.3	1.5	1.4	1.0

Note: (1) Figures cover the Durham-Chapel Hill, NC Metropolitan Statistical Area; (2) The percentage of the total housing inventory that is vacant; (3) The percentage of the housing inventory (excluding seasonal units) that is year-round vacant; (4) The percentage of rental inventory that is vacant for rent; (5) The percentage of homeowner inventory that is vacant for sale; n/a not available
Source: U.S. Census Bureau, Housing Vacancies and Homeownership Annual Statistics: 2018, 2019, 2020

INCOME

Income

Area	Per Capita ($)	Median Household ($)	Average Household ($)
City	34,329	58,905	82,573
MSA[1]	36,322	62,289	90,054
U.S.	34,103	62,843	88,607

Note: (1) Figures cover the Durham-Chapel Hill, NC Metropolitan Statistical Area
Source: U.S. Census Bureau, 2015-2019 American Community Survey 5-Year Estimates

Household Income Distribution

Area	Percent of Households Earning							
	Under $15,000	$15,000 -$24,999	$25,000 -$34,999	$35,000 -$49,999	$50,000 -$74,999	$75,000 -$99,999	$100,000 -$149,999	$150,000 and up
City	10.3	8.4	10.0	13.5	17.4	12.7	14.5	13.2
MSA[1]	10.0	8.6	9.3	12.7	16.8	12.6	14.7	15.3
U.S.	10.3	8.9	8.9	12.3	17.2	12.7	15.1	14.5

Note: (1) Figures cover the Durham-Chapel Hill, NC Metropolitan Statistical Area
Source: U.S. Census Bureau, 2015-2019 American Community Survey 5-Year Estimates

Poverty Rate

Area	All Ages	Under 18 Years Old	18 to 64 Years Old	65 Years and Over
City	15.9	24.5	14.3	8.4
MSA[1]	14.2	20.6	13.6	7.8
U.S.	13.4	18.5	12.6	9.3

Note: Figures are percentage of people whose income during the past 12 months was below the poverty level;
(1) Figures cover the Durham-Chapel Hill, NC Metropolitan Statistical Area
Source: U.S. Census Bureau, 2015-2019 American Community Survey 5-Year Estimates

CITY FINANCES

City Government Finances

Component	2017 ($000)	2017 ($ per capita)
Total Revenues	430,793	1,672
Total Expenditures	358,376	1,391
Debt Outstanding	332,327	1,290
Cash and Securities[1]	3,133	12

Note: (1) Cash and security holdings of a government at the close of its fiscal year,
including those of its dependent agencies, utilities, and liquor stores.
Source: U.S. Census Bureau, State & Local Government Finances 2017

City Government Revenue by Source

Source	2017 ($000)	2017 ($ per capita)	2017 (%)
General Revenue			
From Federal Government	18,835	73	4.4
From State Government	36,197	140	8.4
From Local Governments	3,521	14	0.8
Taxes			
Property	157,484	611	36.6
Sales and Gross Receipts	46,044	179	10.7
Personal Income	0	0	0.0
Corporate Income	0	0	0.0
Motor Vehicle License	3,267	13	0.8
Other Taxes	4,483	17	1.0
Current Charges	97,898	380	22.7
Liquor Store	0	0	0.0
Utility	53,934	209	12.5
Employee Retirement	62	0	0.0

Source: U.S. Census Bureau, State & Local Government Finances 2017

City Government Expenditures by Function

Function	2017 ($000)	2017 ($ per capita)	2017 (%)
General Direct Expenditures			
Air Transportation	13	< 1	< 0.1
Corrections	0	0	0.0
Education	0	0	0.0
Employment Security Administration	0	0	0.0
Financial Administration	6,484	25	1.8
Fire Protection	26,927	104	7.5
General Public Buildings	12,349	47	3.4
Governmental Administration, Other	17,400	67	4.9
Health	0	0	0.0
Highways	22,439	87	6.3
Hospitals	0	0	0.0
Housing and Community Development	27,971	108	7.8
Interest on General Debt	12,027	46	3.4
Judicial and Legal	1,857	7	0.5
Libraries	0	0	0.0
Parking	2,722	10	0.8
Parks and Recreation	18,673	72	5.2
Police Protection	88,000	341	24.6
Public Welfare	0	0	0.0
Sewerage	36,069	140	10.1
Solid Waste Management	17,296	67	4.8
Veterans' Services	0	0	0.0
Liquor Store	0	0	0.0
Utility	49,806	193	13.9
Employee Retirement	0	0	0.0

Source: U.S. Census Bureau, State & Local Government Finances 2017

EMPLOYMENT

Labor Force and Employment

Area	Civilian Labor Force			Workers Employed		
	Dec. 2019	Dec. 2020	% Chg.	Dec. 2019	Dec. 2020	% Chg.
City	150,280	147,613	-1.8	145,981	139,307	-4.6
MSA[1]	305,270	298,535	-2.2	296,522	283,058	-4.5
U.S.	164,007,000	160,017,000	-2.4	158,504,000	149,613,000	-5.6

Note: Data is not seasonally adjusted and covers workers 16 years of age and older; (1) Figures cover the Durham-Chapel Hill, NC Metropolitan Statistical Area
Source: Bureau of Labor Statistics, Local Area Unemployment Statistics

Unemployment Rate

Area	2020											
	Jan.	Feb.	Mar.	Apr.	May	Jun.	Jul.	Aug.	Sep.	Oct.	Nov.	Dec.
City	3.4	3.1	3.7	10.1	11.4	7.6	8.8	6.7	6.8	5.7	5.7	5.6
MSA[1]	3.5	3.1	3.7	9.6	10.6	6.9	7.9	5.9	6.0	5.2	5.2	5.2
U.S.	4.0	3.8	4.5	14.4	13.0	11.2	10.5	8.5	7.7	6.6	6.4	6.5

Note: Data is not seasonally adjusted and covers workers 16 years of age and older; (1) Figures cover the Durham-Chapel Hill, NC Metropolitan Statistical Area
Source: Bureau of Labor Statistics, Local Area Unemployment Statistics

Average Wages

Occupation	$/Hr.	Occupation	$/Hr.
Accountants and Auditors	39.10	Maintenance and Repair Workers	22.30
Automotive Mechanics	22.30	Marketing Managers	74.30
Bookkeepers	21.90	Network and Computer Systems Admin.	46.10
Carpenters	19.70	Nurses, Licensed Practical	24.20
Cashiers	10.90	Nurses, Registered	34.00
Computer Programmers	47.50	Nursing Assistants	15.00
Computer Systems Analysts	45.40	Office Clerks, General	18.40
Computer User Support Specialists	30.20	Physical Therapists	37.70
Construction Laborers	15.70	Physicians	60.20
Cooks, Restaurant	14.30	Plumbers, Pipefitters and Steamfitters	23.40
Customer Service Representatives	19.10	Police and Sheriff's Patrol Officers	25.50
Dentists	109.90	Postal Service Mail Carriers	26.10
Electricians	25.00	Real Estate Sales Agents	23.50
Engineers, Electrical	48.80	Retail Salespersons	12.80
Fast Food and Counter Workers	11.20	Sales Representatives, Technical/Scientific	64.20
Financial Managers	79.50	Secretaries, Exc. Legal/Medical/Executive	20.50
First-Line Supervisors of Office Workers	30.30	Security Guards	24.90
General and Operations Managers	68.80	Surgeons	n/a
Hairdressers/Cosmetologists	15.40	Teacher Assistants, Exc. Postsecondary*	12.80
Home Health and Personal Care Aides	11.60	Teachers, Secondary School, Exc. Sp. Ed.*	26.30
Janitors and Cleaners	14.70	Telemarketers	12.20
Landscaping/Groundskeeping Workers	15.20	Truck Drivers, Heavy/Tractor-Trailer	19.80
Lawyers	59.30	Truck Drivers, Light/Delivery Services	20.80
Maids and Housekeeping Cleaners	13.50	Waiters and Waitresses	12.70

Note: Wage data covers the Durham-Chapel Hill, NC Metropolitan Statistical Area; (*) Hourly wages were calculated from annual wage data based on a 40 hour work week; n/a not available.
Source: Bureau of Labor Statistics, Metro Area Occupational Employment & Wage Estimates, May 2020

Employment by Industry

Sector	MSA[1]		U.S.
	Number of Employees	Percent of Total	Percent of Total
Construction, Mining, and Logging	9,500	3.0	5.5
Education and Health Services	70,900	22.2	16.3
Financial Activities	16,300	5.1	6.1
Government	63,900	20.0	15.2
Information	5,700	1.8	1.9
Leisure and Hospitality	19,900	6.2	9.0
Manufacturing	33,500	10.5	8.5
Other Services	10,800	3.4	3.8
Professional and Business Services	49,100	15.4	14.4
Retail Trade	23,900	7.5	10.9
Transportation, Warehousing, and Utilities	8,000	2.5	4.6
Wholesale Trade	8,300	2.6	3.9

Note: Figures are non-farm employment as of December 2020. Figures are not seasonally adjusted and include workers 16 years of age and older; (1) Figures cover the Durham-Chapel Hill, NC Metropolitan Statistical Area
Source: Bureau of Labor Statistics, Current Employment Statistics, Employment, Hours, and Earnings

Employment by Occupation

Occupation Classification	City (%)	MSA[1] (%)	U.S. (%)
Management, Business, Science, and Arts	50.1	48.5	38.5
Natural Resources, Construction, and Maintenance	6.8	7.5	8.9
Production, Transportation, and Material Moving	9.0	9.9	13.2
Sales and Office	17.3	17.7	21.6
Service	16.8	16.4	17.8

Note: Figures cover employed civilians 16 years of age and older; (1) Figures cover the Durham-Chapel Hill, NC Metropolitan Statistical Area
Source: U.S. Census Bureau, 2015-2019 American Community Survey 5-Year Estimates

Occupations with Greatest Projected Employment Growth: 2020 – 2022

Occupation[1]	2020 Employment	2022 Projected Employment	Numeric Employment Change	Percent Employment Change
Laborers and Freight, Stock, and Material Movers, Hand	90,950	94,250	3,300	3.6
Stockers and Order Fillers	99,690	102,690	3,000	3.0
Software Developers and Software Quality Assurance Analysts and Testers	74,740	76,850	2,110	2.8
Registered Nurses	87,970	89,970	2,000	2.3
Project Management Specialists and Business Operations Specialists, All Other	62,540	63,660	1,120	1.8
Computer Systems Analysts (SOC 2018)	40,350	41,450	1,100	2.7
Insurance Sales Agents	13,950	14,920	970	7.0
Industrial Truck and Tractor Operators	22,480	23,360	880	3.9
Loan Officers	12,610	13,430	820	6.5
Customer Service Representatives	80,790	81,600	810	1.0

Note: Projections cover North Carolina; (1) Sorted by numeric employment change
Source: www.projectionscentral.com, State Occupational Projections, 2020–2022 Short-Term Projections

Fastest-Growing Occupations: 2020 – 2022

Occupation[1]	2020 Employment	2022 Projected Employment	Numeric Employment Change	Percent Employment Change
Statisticians	1,420	1,540	120	8.5
Operations Research Analysts	2,490	2,700	210	8.4
Butchers and Meat Cutters	2,650	2,860	210	7.9
Insurance Sales Agents	13,950	14,920	970	7.0
Loan Interviewers and Clerks	6,000	6,420	420	7.0
Brokerage Clerks	1,590	1,700	110	6.9
Veterinary Assistants and Laboratory Animal Caretakers	3,590	3,830	240	6.7
Personal Financial Advisors	8,760	9,330	570	6.5
Loan Officers	12,610	13,430	820	6.5
Veterinary Technologists and Technicians	3,040	3,230	190	6.3

Note: Projections cover North Carolina; (1) Sorted by percent employment change and excludes occupations with numeric employment change less than 50
Source: www.projectionscentral.com, State Occupational Projections, 2020–2022 Short-Term Projections

TAXES

State Corporate Income Tax Rates

State	Tax Rate (%)	Income Brackets ($)	Num. of Brackets	Financial Institution Tax Rate (%)[a]	Federal Income Tax Ded.
North Carolina	2.5	Flat rate	1	2.5	No

Note: Tax rates as of January 1, 2021; (a) Rates listed are the corporate income tax rate applied to financial institutions or excise taxes based on income. Some states have other taxes based upon the value of deposits or shares.
Source: Federation of Tax Administrators, State Corporate Income Tax Rates, January 1, 2021

State Individual Income Tax Rates

State	Tax Rate (%)	Income Brackets ($)	Personal Exemptions ($)			Standard Ded. ($)	
			Single	Married	Depend.	Single	Married
North Carolina	5.25	Flat rate	None	None	None	10,750	21,500

Note: Tax rates as of January 1, 2021; Local- and county-level taxes are not included; Federal income tax is not deductible on state income tax returns
Source: Federation of Tax Administrators, State Individual Income Tax Rates, January 1, 2021

Various State Sales and Excise Tax Rates

State	State Sales Tax (%)	Gasoline[1] (¢/gal.)	Cigarette[2] ($/pack)	Spirits[3] ($/gal.)	Wine[4] ($/gal.)	Beer[5] ($/gal.)	Recreational Marijuana (%)
North Carolina	4.75	36.35	0.45	14.58	1	0.62	Not legal

Note: All tax rates as of January 1, 2021; (1) The American Petroleum Institute has developed a methodology for determining the average tax rate on a gallon of fuel. Rates may include any of the following: excise taxes, environmental fees, storage tank fees, other fees or taxes, general sales tax, and local taxes; (2) The federal excise tax of $1.0066 per pack and local taxes are not included; (3) Rates are those applicable to off-premise sales of 40% alcohol by volume (a.b.v.) distilled spirits in 750ml containers. Local excise taxes are excluded; (4) Rates are those applicable to off-premise sales of 11% a.b.v. non-carbonated wine in 750ml containers; (5) Rates are those applicable to off-premise sales of 4.7% a.b.v. beer in 12 ounce containers.
Source: Tax Foundation, 2021 Facts & Figures: How Does Your State Compare?

State Business Tax Climate Index Rankings

State	Overall Rank	Corporate Tax Rank	Individual Income Tax Rank	Sales Tax Rank	Property Tax Rank	Unemployment Insurance Tax Rank
North Carolina	10	4	16	22	26	10

Note: The index is a measure of how each state's tax laws affect economic performance. The lower the rank, the more favorable a state's tax system is for business. States without a given tax are given a ranking of 1. The scores/rankings for the District of Columbia do not affect other states. The 2021 index represents the tax climate as of July 1, 2020.
Source: Tax Foundation, State Business Tax Climate Index 2021

TRANSPORTATION

Means of Transportation to Work

Area	Car/Truck/Van Drove Alone	Car-pooled	Public Transportation Bus	Subway	Railroad	Bicycle	Walked	Other Means	Worked at Home
City	76.9	9.3	3.6	0.0	0.0	0.6	2.4	1.3	5.8
MSA[1]	76.5	8.7	3.4	0.0	0.0	0.7	2.8	1.3	6.7
U.S.	76.3	9.0	2.4	1.9	0.6	0.5	2.7	1.4	5.2

Note: Figures are percentages and cover workers 16 years of age and older; (1) Figures cover the Durham-Chapel Hill, NC Metropolitan Statistical Area
Source: U.S. Census Bureau, 2015-2019 American Community Survey 5-Year Estimates

Travel Time to Work

Area	Less Than 10 Minutes	10 to 19 Minutes	20 to 29 Minutes	30 to 44 Minutes	45 to 59 Minutes	60 to 89 Minutes	90 Minutes or More
City	9.4	37.4	26.3	18.0	4.5	3.0	1.6
MSA[1]	9.8	31.6	24.8	21.2	6.8	4.2	1.5
U.S.	12.2	28.4	20.8	20.8	8.3	6.4	2.9

Note: Note: Figures are percentages and include workers 16 years old and over; (1) Figures cover the Durham-Chapel Hill, NC Metropolitan Statistical Area
Source: U.S. Census Bureau, 2015-2019 American Community Survey 5-Year Estimates

Key Congestion Measures

Measure	1982	1992	2002	2012	2017
Annual Hours of Delay, Total (000)	n/a	n/a	n/a	n/a	12,231
Annual Hours of Delay, Per Auto Commuter	n/a	n/a	n/a	n/a	33
Annual Congestion Cost, Total (million $)	n/a	n/a	n/a	n/a	245
Annual Congestion Cost, Per Auto Commuter ($)	n/a	n/a	n/a	n/a	662

Note: n/a not available
Source: Texas A&M Transportation Institute, 2019 Urban Mobility Report

Freeway Travel Time Index

Measure	1982	1987	1992	1997	2002	2007	2012	2017
Urban Area Index[1]	n/a	n/a	n/a	n/a	n/a	n/a	n/a	1.16
Urban Area Rank[1,2]	n/a	n/a	n/a	n/a	n/a	n/a	n/a	n/a

Note: Freeway Travel Time Index—the ratio of travel time in the peak period to the travel time at free-flow conditions. For example, a value of 1.30 indicates a 20-minute free-flow trip takes 26 minutes in the peak (20 minutes x 1.30 = 26 minutes); (1) Covers the Durham NC urban area; (2) Rank is based on 101 larger urban areas (#1 = highest travel time index); n/a not available
Source: Texas A&M Transportation Institute, 2019 Urban Mobility Report

Public Transportation

Agency Name / Mode of Transportation	Vehicles Operated in Maximum Service[1]	Annual Unlinked Passenger Trips[2] (in thous.)	Annual Passenger Miles[3] (in thous.)
Durham Area Transit Authority (DATA)			
Bus (purchased transportation)	47	6,562.5	20,409.4
Demand Response (purchased transportation)	44	202.5	1,804.6

Note: (1) Number of revenue vehicles operated by the given mode and type of service to meet the annual maximum service requirement. This is the revenue vehicle count during the peak season of the year; on the week and day that maximum service is provided. Vehicles operated in maximum service (VOMS) exclude atypical days and one-time special events; (2) Number of passengers who boarded public transportation vehicles. Passengers are counted each time they board a vehicle no matter how many vehicles they use to travel from their origin to their destination. (3) Sum of the distances ridden by all passengers during the entire fiscal year.
Source: Federal Transit Administration, National Transit Database, 2019

Air Transportation

Airport Name and Code / Type of Service	Passenger Airlines[1]	Passenger Enplanements	Freight Carriers[2]	Freight (lbs)
Raleigh-Durham International (RDU)				
Domestic service (U.S. carriers - 2020)	30	2,313,623	15	88,431,187
International service (U.S. carriers - 2019)	8	146,636	3	2,725,471

Note: (1) Includes all U.S.-based major, minor and commuter airlines that carried at least one passenger during the year; (2) Includes all U.S.-based airlines and freight carriers that transported at least one pound of freight during the year.
Source: Bureau of Transportation Statistics, The Intermodal Transportation Database, Air Carriers: T-100 Domestic Market (U.S. Carriers), 2020; Bureau of Transportation Statistics, The Intermodal Transportation Database, Air Carriers: T-100 International Market (U.S. Carriers), 2019

BUSINESSES

Major Business Headquarters

Company Name	Industry	Rankings Fortune[1]	Forbes[2]
IQVIA Holdings	Health Care, Pharmacy and Other Services	290	-

Note: (1) Companies that produce a 10-K are ranked 1 to 500 based on 2019 revenue; (2) All private companies with at least $2 billion in annual revenue through the end of their most current fiscal year are ranked 1 to 219; companies listed are headquartered in the city; dashes indicate no ranking
Source: Fortune, "Fortune 500," June/July 2020; Forbes, "America's Largest Private Companies," 2020

Fastest-Growing Businesses

According to *Inc.*, Durham is home to two of America's 500 fastest-growing private companies: **Esquire Media** (#56); **Sift Media** (#175). Criteria: must be an independent, privately-held, for-profit, U.S. corporation, proprietorship or partnership as of December 31, 2019; revenues must be at least $100,000 in 2016 and $2 million in 2019; must have four-year operating/sales history. *Inc., "America's 500 Fastest-Growing Private Companies," 2020*

According to Deloitte, Durham is home to one of North America's 500 fastest-growing high-technology companies: **Sift Media** (#61). Companies are ranked by percentage growth in revenue over a four-year period. Criteria for inclusion: company must be headquartered within North America; must own proprietary intellectual property or technology that is sold to customers in products that contributes to a significant portion of the company's operating revenue; must have been in business for a minimum of four years with 2016 operating revenues of at least $50,000 USD/CD and 2019 operating revenues of at least $5 million USD/CD. *Deloitte, 2020 Technology Fast 500™*

Minority Business Opportunity

Durham is home to one company which is on the *Black Enterprise* Bank list (15 largest banks based on total assets, capital, deposits and loans, including mortgage-backed securities for the calendar year): **M&F Bancorp (Mechanics & Farmers Bank)** (#9). Only commercial banks or savings and loans that are classified by the Federal Reserve as black institutions and have been fully operational for the previous calendar year were considered. *Black Enterprise, B.E. 100s, 2019*

Living Environment

COST OF LIVING

Cost of Living Index

Composite Index	Groceries	Housing	Utilities	Trans-portation	Health Care	Misc. Goods/Services
n/a	n/a	n/a	n/a	n/a	n/a	n/a

Note: The Cost of Living Index measures regional differences in the cost of consumer goods and services, excluding taxes and non-consumer expenditures, for professional and managerial households in the top income quintile. It is based on more than 50,000 prices covering almost 60 different items for which prices are collected three times a year by chambers of commerce, economic development organizations or university applied economic centers in each participating urban area. The numbers shown should be read as a percentage above or below the national average of 100. For example, a value of 115.4 in the groceries column indicates that grocery prices are 15.4% higher than the national average. Small differences in the index numbers should not be interpreted as significant; n/a not available.
Source: The Council for Community and Economic Research, Cost of Living Index, 2020

Grocery Prices

Area[1]	T-Bone Steak ($/pound)	Frying Chicken ($/pound)	Whole Milk ($/half gal.)	Eggs ($/dozen)	Orange Juice ($/64 oz.)	Coffee ($/11.5 oz.)
City[2]	n/a	n/a	n/a	n/a	n/a	n/a
Avg.	11.78	1.39	2.05	1.47	3.57	4.34
Min.	8.03	0.94	1.03	0.74	2.94	3.02
Max.	15.86	2.65	4.31	3.77	5.44	8.69

*Note: (1) Values for the local area are compared with the average, minimum and maximum values for all 284 areas in the Cost of Living Index; (2) Figures cover the Durham NC urban area; n/a not available; **T-Bone Steak** (price per pound); **Frying Chicken** (price per pound, whole fryer); **Whole Milk** (half gallon carton); **Eggs** (price per dozen, Grade A, large); **Orange Juice** (64 oz. Tropicana or Florida Natural); **Coffee** (11.5 oz. can, vacuum-packed, Maxwell House, Hills Bros, or Folgers).*
Source: The Council for Community and Economic Research, Cost of Living Index, 2020

Housing and Utility Costs

Area[1]	New Home Price ($)	Apartment Rent ($/month)	All Electric ($/month)	Part Electric ($/month)	Other Energy ($/month)	Telephone ($/month)
City[2]	n/a	n/a	n/a	n/a	n/a	n/a
Avg.	368,594	1,168	170.86	100.47	65.28	184.30
Min.	190,567	502	91.58	31.42	26.08	169.60
Max.	2,227,806	4,738	470.38	280.31	280.06	206.50

*Note: (1) Values for the local area are compared with the average, minimum and maximum values for all 284 areas in the Cost of Living Index; (2) Figures cover the Durham NC urban area; n/a not available; **New Home Price** (2,400 sf living area, 8,000 sf lot, in urban area with full utilities); **Apartment Rent** (950 sf 2 bedroom/1.5 or 2 bath, unfurnished, excluding all utilities except water); **All Electric** (average monthly cost for an all-electric home); **Part Electric** (average monthly cost for a part-electric home); **Other Energy** (average monthly cost for natural gas, fuel oil, coal, wood, and any other forms of energy except electricity); **Telephone** (price includes the base monthly rate plus taxes and fees for three lines of mobile phone service).*
Source: The Council for Community and Economic Research, Cost of Living Index, 2020

Health Care, Transportation, and Other Costs

Area[1]	Doctor ($/visit)	Dentist ($/visit)	Optometrist ($/visit)	Gasoline ($/gallon)	Beauty Salon ($/visit)	Men's Shirt ($)
City[2]	n/a	n/a	n/a	n/a	n/a	n/a
Avg.	115.44	99.32	108.10	2.21	39.27	31.37
Min.	36.68	59.00	51.36	1.71	19.00	11.00
Max.	219.00	153.10	250.97	3.46	82.05	58.33

*Note: (1) Values for the local area are compared with the average, minimum and maximum values for all 284 areas in the Cost of Living Index; (2) Figures cover the Durham NC urban area; n/a not available; **Doctor** (general practitioners routine exam of an established patient); **Dentist** (adult teeth cleaning and periodic oral examination); **Optometrist** (full vision eye exam for established adult patient); **Gasoline** (one gallon regular unleaded, national brand, including all taxes, cash price at self-service pump if available); **Beauty Salon** (woman's shampoo, trim, and blow-dry); **Men's Shirt** (cotton/polyester dress shirt, pinpoint weave, long sleeves).*
Source: The Council for Community and Economic Research, Cost of Living Index, 2020

HOUSING

Homeownership Rate

Area	2012 (%)	2013 (%)	2014 (%)	2015 (%)	2016 (%)	2017 (%)	2018 (%)	2019 (%)	2020 (%)
MSA[1]	n/a	n/a	n/a	n/a	n/a	n/a	n/a	n/a	n/a
U.S.	65.4	65.1	64.5	63.7	63.4	63.9	64.4	64.6	66.6

Note: (1) Figures cover the Durham-Chapel Hill, NC Metropolitan Statistical Area; n/a not available
Source: U.S. Census Bureau, Housing Vacancies and Homeownership Annual Statistics: 2012-2020

House Price Index (HPI)

Area	National Ranking[2]	Quarterly Change (%)	One-Year Change (%)	Five-Year Change (%)	Since 1991Q1 (%)
MSA[1]	161	1.51	5.61	34.97	182.89
U.S.[3]	–	3.81	10.77	38.99	205.12

Note: The HPI is a weighted repeat sales index. It measures average price changes in repeat sales or refinancings on the same properties. This information is obtained by reviewing repeat mortgage transactions on single-family properties whose mortgages have been purchased or securitized by Fannie Mae or Freddie Mac since January 1975; (1) Figures cover the Durham-Chapel Hill, NC Metropolitan Statistical Area; (2) Rankings are based on annual percentage change for all metro areas containing at least 15,000 transactions over the last 10 years and ranges from 1 to 253; (3) figures based on a weighted average of Census Division estimates using a seasonally adjusted, purchase-only index; all figures are for the period ending December 31, 2020
Source: Federal Housing Finance Agency, Change in Metropolitan Area House Price Indexes, April 7, 2021

Median Single-Family Home Prices

Area	2018	2019	2020p	Percent Change 2019 to 2020
MSA[1]	279.0	295.9	326.3	10.3
U.S. Average	261.6	274.6	299.9	9.2

Note: Figures are median sales prices of existing single-family homes in thousands of dollars; (p) preliminary; (1) Figures cover the Durham-Chapel Hill, NC Metropolitan Statistical Area
Source: National Association of Realtors, Median Sales Price of Existing Single-Family Homes for Metropolitan Areas, 4th Quarter 2020

Qualifying Income Based on Median Sales Price of Existing Single-Family Homes

Area	With 5% Down ($)	With 10% Down ($)	With 20% Down ($)
MSA[1]	64,308	60,924	54,154
U.S. Average	59,266	56,147	49,908

Note: Figures are preliminary; Qualifying income is based on a mortgage rate of 2.81%. Monthly principal and interest payment is limited to 25% of income; (1) Figures cover the Durham-Chapel Hill, NC Metropolitan Statistical Area
Source: National Association of Realtors, Qualifying Income Based on Median Sales Price of Existing Single-Family Homes for Metropolitan Areas, 4th Quarter 2020

Home Value Distribution

Area	Under $50,000	$50,000 -$99,999	$100,000 -$149,999	$150,000 -$199,999	$200,000 -$299,999	$300,000 -$499,999	$500,000 -$999,999	$1,000,000 or more
City	1.8	5.3	14.5	20.5	30.8	20.3	5.9	1.0
MSA[1]	5.0	7.8	14.2	16.4	23.6	22.0	9.7	1.4
U.S.	6.9	12.0	13.3	14.0	19.6	19.3	11.4	3.4

Note: Figures are percentages and cover owner-occupied housing units; (1) Figures cover the Durham-Chapel Hill, NC Metropolitan Statistical Area
Source: U.S. Census Bureau, 2015-2019 American Community Survey 5-Year Estimates

Year Housing Structure Built

Area	2010 or Later	2000 -2009	1990 -1999	1980 -1989	1970 -1979	1960 -1969	1950 -1959	1940 -1949	Before 1940	Median Year
City	11.6	21.0	16.3	15.4	10.5	8.8	6.6	3.8	6.1	1989
MSA[1]	9.3	19.7	18.7	15.8	12.4	9.2	6.4	3.0	5.6	1989
U.S.	5.2	14.0	13.9	13.4	15.2	10.6	10.3	4.9	12.6	1978

Note: Figures are percentages except for Median Year; Note: (1) Figures cover the Durham-Chapel Hill, NC Metropolitan Statistical Area
Source: U.S. Census Bureau, 2015-2019 American Community Survey 5-Year Estimates

Gross Monthly Rent

Area	Under $500	$500 -$999	$1,000 -$1,499	$1,500 -$1,999	$2,000 -$2,499	$2,500 -$2,999	$3,000 and up	Median ($)
City	7.4	36.4	42.6	10.3	2.0	0.5	0.8	1,058
MSA[1]	7.9	38.7	39.1	10.0	2.5	0.6	1.1	1,033
U.S.	9.4	36.2	30.0	14.0	5.6	2.4	2.4	1,062

Note: Figures are percentages except for Median; Gross rent is the contract rent plus the estimated average monthly cost of utilities (electricity, gas, and water and sewer) and fuels (oil, coal, kerosene, wood, etc.) if these are paid by the renter (or paid for the renter by someone else); (1) Figures cover the Durham-Chapel Hill, NC Metropolitan Statistical Area
Source: U.S. Census Bureau, 2015-2019 American Community Survey 5-Year Estimates

HEALTH

Health Risk Factors

Category	MSA[1] (%)	U.S. (%)
Adults aged 18–64 who have any kind of health care coverage	n/a	87.3
Adults who reported being in good or better health	n/a	82.4
Adults who have been told they have high blood cholesterol	n/a	33.0
Adults who have been told they have high blood pressure	n/a	32.3
Adults who are current smokers	n/a	17.1
Adults who currently use E-cigarettes	n/a	4.6
Adults who currently use chewing tobacco, snuff, or snus	n/a	4.0
Adults who are heavy drinkers[2]	n/a	6.3
Adults who are binge drinkers[3]	n/a	17.4
Adults who are overweight (BMI 25.0 - 29.9)	n/a	35.3
Adults who are obese (BMI 30.0 - 99.8)	n/a	31.3
Adults who participated in any physical activities in the past month	n/a	74.4
Adults who always or nearly always wears a seat belt	n/a	94.3

Note: n/a not available; (1) Figures cover the Durham-Chapel Hill, NC Metropolitan Statistical Area; (2) Heavy drinkers are classified as adult men having more than 14 drinks per week and adult women having more than 7 drinks per week; (3) Binge drinkers are classified as males having five or more drinks on one occasion or females having four or more drinks on one occasion
Source: Centers for Disease Control and Prevention, Behaviorial Risk Factor Surveillance System, SMART: Selected Metropolitan Area Risk Trends, 2017

Acute and Chronic Health Conditions

Category	MSA[1] (%)	U.S. (%)
Adults who have ever been told they had a heart attack	n/a	4.2
Adults who have ever been told they have angina or coronary heart disease	n/a	3.9
Adults who have ever been told they had a stroke	n/a	3.0
Adults who have ever been told they have asthma	n/a	14.2
Adults who have ever been told they have arthritis	n/a	24.9
Adults who have ever been told they have diabetes[2]	n/a	10.5
Adults who have ever been told they had skin cancer	n/a	6.2
Adults who have ever been told they had any other types of cancer	n/a	7.1
Adults who have ever been told they have COPD	n/a	6.5
Adults who have ever been told they have kidney disease	n/a	3.0
Adults who have ever been told they have a form of depression	n/a	20.5

Note: n/a not available; (1) Figures cover the Durham-Chapel Hill, NC Metropolitan Statistical Area; (2) Figures do not include pregnancy-related, borderline, or pre-diabetes
Source: Centers for Disease Control and Prevention, Behaviorial Risk Factor Surveillance System, SMART: Selected Metropolitan Area Risk Trends, 2017

Health Screening and Vaccination Rates

Category	MSA[1] (%)	U.S. (%)
Adults aged 65+ who have had flu shot within the past year	n/a	60.7
Adults aged 65+ who have ever had a pneumonia vaccination	n/a	75.4
Adults who have ever been tested for HIV	n/a	36.1
Adults who have ever had the shingles or zoster vaccine?	n/a	28.9
Adults who have had their blood cholesterol checked within the last five years	n/a	85.9

Note: n/a not available; (1) Figures cover the Durham-Chapel Hill, NC Metropolitan Statistical Area.
Source: Centers for Disease Control and Prevention, Behaviorial Risk Factor Surveillance System, SMART: Selected Metropolitan Area Risk Trends, 2017

Disability Status

Category	MSA[1] (%)	U.S. (%)
Adults who reported being deaf	n/a	6.7
Are you blind or have serious difficulty seeing, even when wearing glasses?	n/a	4.5
Are you limited in any way in any of your usual activities due of arthritis?	n/a	12.9
Do you have difficulty doing errands alone?	n/a	6.8
Do you have difficulty dressing or bathing?	n/a	3.6
Do you have serious difficulty concentrating/remembering/making decisions?	n/a	10.7
Do you have serious difficulty walking or climbing stairs?	n/a	13.6

Note: n/a not available; (1) Figures cover the Durham-Chapel Hill, NC Metropolitan Statistical Area.
Source: Centers for Disease Control and Prevention, Behaviorial Risk Factor Surveillance System, SMART: Selected Metropolitan Area Risk Trends, 2017

Mortality Rates for the Top 10 Causes of Death in the U.S.

ICD-10[a] Sub-Chapter	ICD-10[a] Code	Age-Adjusted Mortality Rate[1] per 100,000 population	
		County[2]	U.S.
Malignant neoplasms	C00-C97	143.8	149.2
Ischaemic heart diseases	I20-I25	58.3	90.5
Other forms of heart disease	I30-I51	51.8	52.2
Chronic lower respiratory diseases	J40-J47	27.6	39.6
Other degenerative diseases of the nervous system	G30-G31	29.9	37.6
Cerebrovascular diseases	I60-I69	29.2	37.2
Other external causes of accidental injury	W00-X59	32.8	36.1
Organic, including symptomatic, mental disorders	F01-F09	58.2	29.4
Hypertensive diseases	I10-I15	17.5	24.1
Diabetes mellitus	E10-E14	18.5	21.5

Note: (a) ICD-10 = International Classification of Diseases 10th Revision; (1) Mortality rates are a three-year average covering 2017-2019; (2) Figures cover Durham County.
Source: Centers for Disease Control and Prevention, National Center for Health Statistics. Underlying Cause of Death 1999-2019 on CDC WONDER Online Database

Mortality Rates for Selected Causes of Death

ICD-10[a] Sub-Chapter	ICD-10[a] Code	Age-Adjusted Mortality Rate[1] per 100,000 population	
		County[2]	U.S.
Assault	X85-Y09	9.6	6.0
Diseases of the liver	K70-K76	9.3	14.4
Human immunodeficiency virus (HIV) disease	B20-B24	2.3	1.5
Influenza and pneumonia	J09-J18	8.0	13.8
Intentional self-harm	X60-X84	8.8	14.1
Malnutrition	E40-E46	2.2	2.3
Obesity and other hyperalimentation	E65-E68	3.5	2.1
Renal failure	N17-N19	14.7	12.6
Transport accidents	V01-V99	12.4	12.3
Viral hepatitis	B15-B19	Suppressed	1.2

Note: (a) ICD-10 = International Classification of Diseases 10th Revision; (1) Mortality rates are a three-year average covering 2017-2019; (2) Figures cover Durham County; Data are suppressed when the data meet the criteria for confidentiality constraints; Mortality rates are flagged as unreliable when the rate would be calculated with a numerator of 20 or less.
Source: Centers for Disease Control and Prevention, National Center for Health Statistics. Underlying Cause of Death 1999-2019 on CDC WONDER Online Database

Health Insurance Coverage

Area	With Health Insurance	With Private Health Insurance	With Public Health Insurance	Without Health Insurance	Population Under Age 19 Without Health Insurance
City	87.5	68.8	28.3	12.5	7.3
MSA[1]	89.7	71.7	29.7	10.3	6.1
U.S.	91.2	67.9	35.1	8.8	5.1

Note: Figures are percentages that cover the civilian noninstitutionalized population; (1) Figures cover the Durham-Chapel Hill, NC Metropolitan Statistical Area
Source: U.S. Census Bureau, 2015-2019 American Community Survey 5-Year Estimates

Number of Medical Professionals

Area	MDs[3]	DOs[3,4]	Dentists	Podiatrists	Chiropractors	Optometrists
County[1] (number)	3,586	50	241	13	62	47
County[1] (rate[2])	1,131.3	15.8	75.0	4.0	19.3	14.6
U.S. (rate[2])	282.9	22.7	71.2	6.2	28.1	16.9

37063
Note: Data as of 2019 unless noted; (1) Data covers Durham County; (2) Rate per 100,000 population; (3) Data as of 2018 and includes all active, non-federal physicians; (4) Doctor of Osteopathic Medicine
Source: U.S. Department of Health and Human Services, Health Resources and Services Administration, Bureau of Health Professions, Area Resource File (ARF) 2019-2020

Best Hospitals

According to *U.S. News,* the Durham-Chapel Hill, NC metro area is home to two of the best hospitals in the U.S.: **Duke University Hospital** (11 adult specialties and 9 pediatric specialties); **University of North Carolina Hospitals** (3 adult specialties and 7 pediatric specialties). The hospitals listed were nationally ranked in at least one of 16 adult or 10 pediatric specialties. Only 134 hospitals nationwide were nationally ranked in one or more adult or pediatric specialty; this number increases to 178 counting specialized centers within hospitals. Twenty hospitals in the U.S. made the Honor Roll. The Best Hospitals Honor Roll takes both the national rankings and the procedure and condition ratings into account. Hospitals received points if they were nationally ranked in one of the 16 adult special-ties—the higher they ranked, the more points they got—and how many ratings of "high performing"

they earned in the 10 procedures and conditions. *U.S. News Online, "America's Best Hospitals 2020-21"*

According to *U.S. News,* the Durham-Chapel Hill, NC metro area is home to two of the best children's hospitals in the U.S.: **Duke Children's Hospital and Health Center** (9 pediatric specialties); **North Carolina Children's Hospital at UNC** (7 pediatric specialties). The hospitals listed were highly ranked in at least one of 10 pediatric specialties. Eighty-eight children's hospitals in the U.S. were nationally ranked in at least one specialty. Hospitals received points for being ranked in a specialty, and the 10 hospitals with the most points across the 10 specialties make up the Honor Roll. *U.S. News Online, "America's Best Children's Hospitals 2020-21"*

EDUCATION

Public School District Statistics

District Name	Schls	Pupils	Pupil/Teacher Ratio	Minority Pupils[1] (%)	Free Lunch Eligible[2] (%)	IEP[3] (%)
Durham Public Schools	54	32,913	14.1	80.9	58.6	14.1
NC Connections Academy	1	2,476	27.5	44.2	17.4	11.8
NC Virtual Academy	1	2,449	26.5	43.2	26.9	12.9

Note: Table includes school districts with 2,000 or more students; (1) Percentage of students that are not non-Hispanic white; (2) Percentage of students that are eligible for the free lunch program; (3) Percentage of students that have an Individualized Education Program.
Source: U.S. Department of Education, National Center for Education Statistics, Common Core of Data, Local Education Agency (School District) Universe Survey: School Year 2018-2019; U.S. Department of Education, National Center for Education Statistics, Common Core of Data, Public Elementary/Secondary School Universe Survey: School Year 2018-2019

Highest Level of Education

Area	Less than H.S.	H.S. Diploma	Some College, No Deg.	Associate Degree	Bachelor's Degree	Master's Degree	Prof. School Degree	Doctorate Degree
City	11.9	16.4	15.5	6.5	25.8	14.7	4.2	4.8
MSA[1]	11.2	19.8	16.1	7.6	23.2	13.2	4.0	4.9
U.S.	12.0	27.0	20.4	8.5	19.8	8.8	2.1	1.4

Note: Figures cover persons age 25 and over; (1) Figures cover the Durham-Chapel Hill, NC Metropolitan Statistical Area
Source: U.S. Census Bureau, 2015-2019 American Community Survey 5-Year Estimates

Educational Attainment by Race

Area	High School Graduate or Higher (%)					Bachelor's Degree or Higher (%)				
	Total	White	Black	Asian	Hisp.[2]	Total	White	Black	Asian	Hisp.[2]
City	88.1	90.1	87.6	90.5	49.4	49.6	60.1	34.2	73.9	13.6
MSA[1]	88.8	91.0	86.3	91.3	52.7	45.3	51.4	28.8	72.3	16.9
U.S.	88.0	89.9	86.0	87.1	68.7	32.1	33.5	21.6	54.3	16.4

Note: Figures shown cover persons 25 years old and over; (1) Figures cover the Durham-Chapel Hill, NC Metropolitan Statistical Area; (2) People of Hispanic origin can be of any race
Source: U.S. Census Bureau, 2015-2019 American Community Survey 5-Year Estimates

School Enrollment by Grade and Control

Area	Preschool (%)		Kindergarten (%)		Grades 1 - 4 (%)		Grades 5 - 8 (%)		Grades 9 - 12 (%)	
	Public	Private	Public	Private	Public	Private	Public	Private	Public	Private
City	52.1	47.9	91.9	8.1	88.8	11.2	87.3	12.7	89.7	10.3
MSA[1]	49.5	50.5	88.6	11.4	89.6	10.4	88.8	11.2	90.8	9.2
U.S.	59.1	40.9	87.6	12.4	89.5	10.5	89.4	10.6	90.1	9.9

Note: Figures shown cover persons 3 years old and over; (1) Figures cover the Durham-Chapel Hill, NC Metropolitan Statistical Area
Source: U.S. Census Bureau, 2015-2019 American Community Survey 5-Year Estimates

Higher Education

Four-Year Colleges			Two-Year Colleges			Medical Schools[1]	Law Schools[2]	Voc/Tech[3]
Public	Private Non-profit	Private For-profit	Public	Private Non-profit	Private For-profit			
1	2	0	1	1	0	1	2	4

Note: Figures cover institutions located within the city limits and include main campuses only; (1) includes schools accredited by the Liaison Committee on Medical Education and the American Osteopathic Association's Commission on Osteopathic College Accreditation; (2) includes ABA-accredited schools, schools with provisional ABA accreditation, and state accredited schools; (3) includes all schools with programs that are less than 2 years.
Source: National Center for Education Statistics, Integrated Postsecondary Education System (IPEDS), 2019-20; Wikipedia, List of Medical Schools in the United States, accessed April 2, 2021; Wikipedia, List of Law Schools in the United States, accessed April 2, 2021

According to *U.S. News & World Report,* the Durham-Chapel Hill, NC metro area is home to two of the top 200 national universities in the U.S.: **Duke University** (#12); **University of North Carolina—Chapel Hill** (#28 tie). The indicators used to capture academic quality fall into a number of categories: assessment by administrators at peer institutions; retention of students; faculty resources; student selectivity; financial resources; alumni giving; high school counselor ratings of colleges; and graduation rate. *U.S. News & World Report, "America's Best Colleges 2021"*

According to *U.S. News & World Report,* the Durham-Chapel Hill, NC metro area is home to two of the top 100 law schools in the U.S.: **Duke University** (#10 tie); **University of North Carolina—Chapel Hill** (#24). The rankings are based on a weighted average of 12 measures of quality: peer assessment score; assessment score by lawyers/judges; median LSAT scores; median undergrad GPA; acceptance rate; employment rates for graduates; placement success; bar passage rate; faculty resources; expenditures per student; student/faculty ratio; and library resources. *U.S. News & World Report, "America's Best Graduate Schools, Law, 2022"*

According to *U.S. News & World Report,* the Durham-Chapel Hill, NC metro area is home to two of the top 75 medical schools for research in the U.S.: **Duke University** (#3); **University of North Carolina—Chapel Hill** (#24). The rankings are based on a weighted average of 11 measures of quality: quality assessment; peer assessment score; assessment score by residency directors; research activity; total research activity; average research activity per faculty member; student selectivity; median MCAT total score; median undergraduate GPA; acceptance rate; and faculty resources. *U.S. News & World Report, "America's Best Graduate Schools, Medical, 2022"*

According to *U.S. News & World Report,* the Durham-Chapel Hill, NC metro area is home to two of the top 75 business schools in the U.S.: **Duke University (Fuqua)** (#12); **University of North Carolina—Chapel Hill (Kenan-Flagler)** (#20). The rankings are based on a weighted average of the following nine measures: quality assessment; peer assessment; recruiter assessment; placement success; mean starting salary and bonus; student selectivity; mean GMAT and GRE scores; mean undergraduate GPA; and acceptance rate. *U.S. News & World Report, "America's Best Graduate Schools, Business, 2022"*

EMPLOYERS

Major Employers

Company Name	Industry
CISCO Systems	Data conversion equipment, media-to-media: computer
City of Durham	Municipal government
Duke University	Colleges & universities
Duke University Health System	General medical & surgical hospitals
Durham County Hospital Corporation	General medical & surgical hospitals
Environmental Protection Agency	Environmental protection agency, government
IBM	Computer peripheral equipment
National Institutes of Health	Environmental health program administration, govt
Netapp	Computer integrated systems design
North Carolina Central University	Colleges & universities
Patheon	Pharmaceutical preparations
Phyamerica Government Services	Hospital management
Research Triangle Institute	Commercial physical research
Sports Endeavors	Sporting goods & bicycle shops
University of NC at Chapel Hill	University
University of North Carolina Hospitals	General medical & surgical hospitals

Note: Companies shown are located within the Durham-Chapel Hill, NC Metropolitan Statistical Area.
Source: Hoovers.com; Wikipedia

Best Companies to Work For

BlueCross BlueShield of North Carolina, headquartered in Durham, is among the "100 Best Companies for Working Mothers." Criteria: paid time off and leaves; workforce profile; benefits; women's issues and advancement; flexible work; company culture and work life programs. *Working Mother, "100 Best Companies for Working Mothers," 2020*

BlueCross BlueShield of North Carolina, headquartered in Durham, is among the "Best Companies for Multicultural Women." *Working Mother* selected 50 companies based on a detailed application completed by public and private firms based in the United States, excluding government agencies, companies in the human resources field and non-autonomous divisions. Companies supplied data about the hiring, pay, and promotion of multicultural employees. Applications focused on representation of multicultural women, recruitment, retention and advancement programs, and company culture. *Working Mother, "Best Companies for Multicultural Women," 2020*

BlueCross and BlueShield of North Carolina, headquartered in Durham, is among the "100 Best Places to Work in IT." To qualify, companies had to be U.S.-based organizations or be non-U.S.-based employers that met the following criteria: have a minimum of 300 total employees at a U.S. headquarters and a minimum of 30 IT employees in the U.S., with at least 50% of their IT employees based in the U.S. The best places to work were selected based on compensation, benefits, work/life balance, employee morale, and satisfaction with training and development programs. In addition, *InsiderPro* and *Computerworld* looked at retention efforts, programs for recognizing and rewarding outstanding performances, and benefits such as flextime, elder care and child care, and reimbursement for college tuition and the cost of pursuing technology certifications. *InsiderPro and Computerworld, "100 Best Places to Work in IT," 2020*

BlueCross BlueShield of North Carolina, headquartered in Durham, is among the "Top Companies for Executive Women." This list is determined by organizations filling out an in-depth survey that measures female demographics at every level, but with an emphasis on women in senior corporate roles, with profit & loss (P&L) responsibility, and those earning in the top 20 percent of the organization. *Working Mother* defines P&L as having responsibility that involves monitoring the net income after expenses for a department or entire organization, with direct influence on how company resources are allocated. *Working Mother, "Top Companies for Executive Women," 2020+*

BlueCross BlueShield of North Carolina, headquartered in Durham, is among the "Best Companies for Dads." *Working Mother's* newest list recognizes the growing importance companies place on giving dads time off and support for their families. Rankings are determined by measuring gender-neutral or paternity leave offered, as well as actual time taken, phase-back policies, child- and dependent-care benefits, and corporate support groups for men and dads. *Working Mother, "Best Companies for Dads," 2020*

PUBLIC SAFETY

Crime Rate

Area	All Crimes	Violent Crimes				Property Crimes		
		Murder	Rape[3]	Robbery	Aggrav. Assault	Burglary	Larceny -Theft	Motor Vehicle Theft
City	4,537.6	13.2	43.2	223.3	450.3	703.6	2,833.6	270.4
Suburbs[1]	1,853.6	2.7	22.5	32.4	157.6	332.5	1,221.8	84.0
Metro[2]	3,020.8	7.3	31.5	115.4	284.9	493.9	1,922.7	165.1
U.S.	2,489.3	5.0	42.6	81.6	250.2	340.5	1,549.5	219.9

Note: Figures are crimes per 100,000 population; (1) All areas within the metro area that are located outside the city limits; (2) Figures cover the Durham-Chapel Hill, NC Metropolitan Statistical Area; (3) All figures shown were reported using the revised Uniform Crime Reporting (UCR) definition of rape.
Source: FBI Uniform Crime Reports, 2019

Hate Crimes

Area	Number of Quarters Reported	Number of Incidents per Bias Motivation					
		Race/Ethnicity/ Ancestry	Religion	Sexual Orientation	Disability	Gender	Gender Identity
City	4	3	0	0	0	0	0
U.S.	4	3,963	1,521	1,195	157	69	198

Source: Federal Bureau of Investigation, Hate Crime Statistics 2019

Identity Theft Consumer Reports

Area	Reports	Reports per 100,000 Population	Rank[2]
MSA[1]	1,481	230	172
U.S.	1,387,615	423	-

Note: (1) Figures cover the Durham-Chapel Hill, NC Metropolitan Statistical Area; (2) Rank ranges from 1 to 391 where 1 indicates greatest number of identity theft reports per 100,000 population
Source: Federal Trade Commission, Consumer Sentinel Network Data Book 2020

Fraud and Other Consumer Reports

Area	Reports	Reports per 100,000 Population	Rank[2]
MSA[1]	4,881	757	131
U.S.	3,385,133	1,031	-

Note: (1) Figures cover the Durham-Chapel Hill, NC Metropolitan Statistical Area; (2) Rank ranges from 1 to 391 where 1 indicates greatest number of fraud and other consumer reports per 100,000 population
Source: Federal Trade Commission, Consumer Sentinel Network Data Book 2020

POLITICS

2020 Presidential Election Results

Area	Biden	Trump	Jorgensen	Hawkins	Other
Durham County	80.4	18.0	0.8	0.3	0.4
U.S.	51.3	46.8	1.2	0.3	0.5

Note: Results are percentages and may not add to 100% due to rounding
Source: Dave Leip's Atlas of U.S. Presidential Elections

SPORTS

Professional Sports Teams

Team Name	League	Year Established
Carolina Hurricanes	National Hockey League (NHL)	1997

Note: Includes teams located in the Durham-Chapel Hill, NC Metropolitan Statistical Area.
Source: Wikipedia, Major Professional Sports Teams of the United States and Canada, April 6, 2021

CLIMATE

Average and Extreme Temperatures

Temperature	Jan	Feb	Mar	Apr	May	Jun	Jul	Aug	Sep	Oct	Nov	Dec	Yr.
Extreme High (°F)	79	84	90	95	97	104	105	105	104	98	88	79	105
Average High (°F)	50	53	61	72	79	86	89	87	81	72	62	53	71
Average Temp. (°F)	40	43	50	59	67	75	78	77	71	60	51	42	60
Average Low (°F)	29	31	38	46	55	63	68	67	60	48	39	32	48
Extreme Low (°F)	-9	5	11	23	29	38	48	46	37	19	11	4	-9

Note: Figures cover the years 1948-1990
Source: National Climatic Data Center, International Station Meteorological Climate Summary, 9/96

Average Precipitation/Snowfall/Humidity

Precip./Humidity	Jan	Feb	Mar	Apr	May	Jun	Jul	Aug	Sep	Oct	Nov	Dec	Yr.
Avg. Precip. (in.)	3.4	3.6	3.6	2.9	3.9	3.6	4.4	4.4	3.2	2.9	3.0	3.1	42.0
Avg. Snowfall (in.)	2	3	1	Tr	0	0	0	0	0	0	Tr	1	8
Avg. Rel. Hum. 7am (%)	79	79	79	80	84	86	88	91	91	90	84	81	84
Avg. Rel. Hum. 4pm (%)	53	49	46	43	51	54	57	59	57	53	51	53	52

Note: Figures cover the years 1948-1990; Tr = Trace amounts (<0.05 in. of rain; <0.5 in. of snow)
Source: National Climatic Data Center, International Station Meteorological Climate Summary, 9/96

Weather Conditions

Temperature			Daytime Sky			Precipitation		
32°F & below	45°F & below	90°F & above	Clear	Partly cloudy	Cloudy	0.01 inch or more precip.	0.1 inch or more snow/ice	Thunder-storms
77	160	39	98	143	124	110	3	42

Note: Figures are average number of days per year and cover the years 1948-1990
Source: National Climatic Data Center, International Station Meteorological Climate Summary, 9/96

HAZARDOUS WASTE

Superfund Sites

The Durham-Chapel Hill, NC metro area is home to one site on the EPA's Superfund National Priorities List: **GMH Electronics** (final). There are a total of 1,375 Superfund sites with a status of proposed or final on the list in the U.S. *U.S. Environmental Protection Agency, National Priorities List, April 7, 2021*

AIR QUALITY

Air Quality Trends: Ozone

	1990	1995	2000	2005	2010	2015	2016	2017	2018	2019
MSA[1]	n/a	n/a	n/a	n/a	n/a	n/a	n/a	n/a	n/a	n/a
U.S.	0.088	0.089	0.082	0.080	0.073	0.068	0.069	0.068	0.069	0.065

Note: (1) Data covers the Durham-Chapel Hill, NC Metropolitan Statistical Area; n/a not available. The values shown are the composite ozone concentration averages among trend sites based on the highest fourth daily maximum 8-hour concentration in parts per million. These trends are based on sites having an adequate record of monitoring data during the trend period. Data from exceptional events are included.
Source: U.S. Environmental Protection Agency, Air Quality Monitoring Information, "Air Quality Trends by City, 1990-2019"

Air Quality Index

Area	Percent of Days when Air Quality was...[2]					AQI Statistics[2]	
	Good	Moderate	Unhealthy for Sensitive Groups	Unhealthy	Very Unhealthy	Maximum	Median
MSA[1]	75.3	24.7	0.0	0.0	0.0	92	44

Note: (1) Data covers the Durham-Chapel Hill, NC Metropolitan Statistical Area; (2) Based on 365 days with AQI data in 2019. Air Quality Index (AQI) is an index for reporting daily air quality. EPA calculates the AQI for five major air pollutants regulated by the Clean Air Act: ground-level ozone, particle pollution (aka particulate matter), carbon monoxide, sulfur dioxide, and nitrogen dioxide. The AQI runs from 0 to 500. The higher the AQI value, the greater the level of air pollution and the greater the health concern. There are six AQI categories: "Good" AQI is between 0 and 50. Air quality is considered satisfactory; "Moderate" AQI is between 51 and 100. Air quality is acceptable; "Unhealthy for Sensitive Groups" When AQI values are between 101 and 150, members of sensitive groups may experience health effects; "Unhealthy" When AQI values are between 151 and 200 everyone may begin to experience health effects; "Very Unhealthy" AQI values between 201 and 300 trigger a health alert; "Hazardous" AQI values over 300 trigger warnings of emergency conditions (not shown).
Source: U.S. Environmental Protection Agency, Air Quality Index Report, 2019

Air Quality Index Pollutants

Area	Percent of Days when AQI Pollutant was...[2]					
	Carbon Monoxide	Nitrogen Dioxide	Ozone	Sulfur Dioxide	Particulate Matter 2.5	Particulate Matter 10
MSA[1]	0.0	0.0	56.7	1.6	41.6	0.0

Note: (1) Data covers the Durham-Chapel Hill, NC Metropolitan Statistical Area; (2) Based on 365 days with AQI data in 2019. The Air Quality Index (AQI) is an index for reporting daily air quality. EPA calculates the AQI for five major air pollutants regulated by the Clean Air Act: ground-level ozone, particle pollution (also known as particulate matter), carbon monoxide, sulfur dioxide, and nitrogen dioxide. The AQI runs from 0 to 500. The higher the AQI value, the greater the level of air pollution and the greater the health concern.
Source: U.S. Environmental Protection Agency, Air Quality Index Report, 2019

Maximum Air Pollutant Concentrations: Particulate Matter, Ozone, CO and Lead

	Particulate Matter 10 (ug/m^3)	Particulate Matter 2.5 Wtd AM (ug/m^3)	Particulate Matter 2.5 24-Hr (ug/m^3)	Ozone (ppm)	Carbon Monoxide (ppm)	Lead (ug/m^3)
MSA[1] Level	27	7.7	15	0.063	n/a	n/a
NAAQS[2]	150	15	35	0.075	9	0.15
Met NAAQS[2]	Yes	Yes	Yes	Yes	n/a	n/a

Note: (1) Data covers the Durham-Chapel Hill, NC Metropolitan Statistical Area; Data from exceptional events are included; (2) National Ambient Air Quality Standards; ppm = parts per million; ug/m^3 = micrograms per cubic meter; n/a not available.
Concentrations: Particulate Matter 10 (coarse particulate)—highest second maximum 24-hour concentration; Particulate Matter 2.5 Wtd AM (fine particulate)—highest weighted annual mean concentration; Particulate Matter 2.5 24-Hour (fine particulate)—highest 98th percentile 24-hour concentration; Ozone—highest fourth daily maximum 8-hour concentration; Carbon Monoxide—highest second maximum non-overlapping 8-hour concentration; Lead—maximum running 3-month average
Source: U.S. Environmental Protection Agency, Air Quality Monitoring Information, "Air Quality Statistics by City, 2019"

Maximum Air Pollutant Concentrations: Nitrogen Dioxide and Sulfur Dioxide

	Nitrogen Dioxide AM (ppb)	Nitrogen Dioxide 1-Hr (ppb)	Sulfur Dioxide AM (ppb)	Sulfur Dioxide 1-Hr (ppb)	Sulfur Dioxide 24-Hr (ppb)
MSA[1] Level	n/a	n/a	n/a	41	n/a
NAAQS[2]	53	100	30	75	140
Met NAAQS[2]	n/a	n/a	n/a	Yes	n/a

Note: (1) Data covers the Durham-Chapel Hill, NC Metropolitan Statistical Area; Data from exceptional events are included; (2) National Ambient Air Quality Standards; ppm = parts per million; ug/m^3 = micrograms per cubic meter; n/a not available.
Concentrations: Nitrogen Dioxide AM—highest arithmetic mean concentration; Nitrogen Dioxide 1-Hr—highest 98th percentile 1-hour daily maximum concentration; Sulfur Dioxide AM—highest annual mean concentration; Sulfur Dioxide 1-Hr—highest 99th percentile 1-hour daily maximum concentration; Sulfur Dioxide 24-Hr—highest second maximum 24-hour concentration
Source: U.S. Environmental Protection Agency, Air Quality Monitoring Information, "Air Quality Statistics by City, 2019"

Edison, New Jersey

Background

Edison, previously known as Raritan Township, earned its eponymous name from the inventor, Thomas Alva Edison. In 1876, Edison set up his home and research laboratory on the site of an unsuccessful real estate development in Raritan Township called Menlo Park. Edison came up with his most famous inventions, including the phonograph and the incandescent light bulb, in his Menlo Park lab. In just over a decade Edison's Menlo Park laboratory had expanded to consume two city blocks. In 1954, town fathers changed the name of the city to honor the inventor. Today, the Thomas Edison Center at Menlo Park includes new and restored exhibits and detailed tours of the surrounding grounds and facilities.

Edison, six miles from New Brunswick and 20 miles from Newark and the surrounding areas of Middlesex County, have a growing Indian community and a number of temples and a large concentration of Indian stores and restaurants to serve the needs of the residents. To reflect Edison's large Indian and Chinese populations, the city has sister-city arrangements with Shijiazhuang, China, and Baroda, India.

In recent years, Edison has been named one of the most livable/best/safest small cities and one of the ten best places to grow up.

Crowded industrial parks, including Raritan Center, the state's largest, help provide Edison with one of the largest municipal tax bases in New Jersey. Majesco Entertainment, Zylog Systems, Boxed, and Bare Necessities all have headquarters in the city, and Italian food producer and importer Colavita, JFK Medical Center, FedEx, UPS and Newegg have warehouse operations in Edison.

> Those wishing to picnic or BBQ at Roosevelt Park can reserve a "picnic grove" online, which are socially distanced.

Edison's Sugarloaf Craft Festivals, operated annually since 1974, showcase the region's diverse culture through the arts, in addition to the many Indian and Chinese events that commemorate the city's Indian and Chinese populations.

The Sergeant Joyce Kilmer U.S. Army Reserve Center is also located in Edison. The township was once home to two large military bases: The Raritan Arsenal and Camp Kilmer, both of which closed in the 1960s. Today Raritan Center and Middlesex County College stand on the Raritan Arsenal land. Camp Kilmer became Rutgers University's Livingston College and the Sutton Industrial Campus. Residents are served by a community college, Middlesex County College, which houses the Middlesex County Academy for Science, Mathematics, and Engineering Technologies. The engineering-based high school is free for all Middlesex County residents, with admission based on grades, and other academic and extra-curricular activities.

The Plainfield Country Club in the city hosted the PGA Tour FedEx Cup playoff most recently in 2015, among other golf events. The 57th Annual Memorial Day Parade celebration took place in 2019. Edison station, located in South Edison, has New Jersey Transit trains to New York City, and the town is connected to nearly every major highway in the state.

Bounded by the Atlantic Ocean and the Delaware River, most of New Jersey has a moderate climate with cold winters and warm, humid summers. Occasional tornadoes, violent spring storms, and floods are not uncommon. A serious drought occurs, on average, about once every 15 years.

Rankings

Business/Finance Rankings

- The Brookings Institution ranked the 100 largest metro areas in the U.S. based on income inequality. New York was ranked #2 (#1 = greatest inequality). Criteria: the "95/20 ratio," a figure representing the income at which a household earns more than 95 percent of all other households, divided by the income at which a household earns more than only 20 percent of all other households. *Brookings Institution, "Household Income Inequality, 100 Largest U.S. Metro Areas, 2014-2016," February 5, 2018*

- Payscale.com ranked the 32 largest metro areas in terms of wage growth. The New York metro area ranked #5. Criteria: private-sector and education professional wage growth between the 4th quarter of 2019 and the 4th quarter of 2020. *PayScale, "Wage Trends by Metro Area-4th Quarter," January 11, 2021*

- The New York metro area was identified as one of the most debt-ridden places in America by the finance site Credit.com. The metro area was ranked #3. Criteria: residents' average credit card debt as well as median income. *Credit.com, "25 Cities With the Most Credit Card Debt," February 28, 2018*

- New York was identified as one of America's most frugal metro areas by *Coupons.com*. The city ranked #15 out of 25. Criteria: digital coupon usage. *Coupons.com, "America's Most Frugal Cities of 2017," March 22, 2018*

- New York was cited as one of America's top metros for new and expanded facility projects in 2020. The area ranked #8 in the large metro area category (population over 1 million). *Site Selection, "Top Metros of 2020," March 2021*

- The New York metro area appeared on the Milken Institute "2021 Best Performing Cities" list. Rank: #106 out of 200 large metro areas (population over 250,000). Criteria: job growth; wage and salary growth; high-tech output growth; housing affordability; household broadband access. *Milken Institute, "Best-Performing Cities 2021," February 16, 2021*

- *Forbes* ranked the 200 most populous metro areas to determine the nation's "Best Places for Business and Careers." The New York metro area was ranked #115. Criteria: costs (business and living); job growth (past and projected); income growth; quality of life; educational attainment (college and high school); projected economic growth; cultural and leisure opportunities; workplace tolerance laws; net migration patterns. *Forbes, "The Best Places for Business and Careers 2019: Seattle Still On Top," October 30, 2019*

Education Rankings

- Personal finance website *WalletHub* analyzed the 150 largest U.S. metropolitan statistical areas to determine where the most educated Americans are putting their degrees to work. Criteria: education levels; percentage of workers with degrees; education quality and attainment gap; public school quality rankings; quality and enrollment of each metro area's universities. New York was ranked #26 (#1 = most educated city). *www.WalletHub.com, "Most and Least Educated Cities in America," July 20, 2020*

Environmental Rankings

- The U.S. Environmental Protection Agency (EPA) released a list of U.S. metropolitan areas with the most ENERGY STAR certified buildings in 2019. The New York metro area was ranked #7 out of 25. *U.S. Environmental Protection Agency, "2020 Energy Star Top Cities," March 2020*

- New York was highlighted as one of the 25 most ozone-polluted metro areas in the U.S. during 2016 through 2018. The area ranked #12. *American Lung Association, "State of the Air 2020," April 21, 2020*

Health/Fitness Rankings

- The Sharecare Community Well-Being Index evaluates 10 individual and social health factors in order to measure what matters to Americans in the communities in which they live. The New York metro area was one of the five communities where social determinants of health were the highest. Criteria: access to food, healthcare, and community resources; housing and transportation; economic security. The area ranked #0. *www.sharecare.com, "Community Well-Being Index: 2019 Metro Area & County Rankings Report," August 31, 2020*

- The New York metro area was identified as one of the worst cities for bed bugs in America by pest control company Orkin. The area ranked #12 out of 50 based on the number of bed bug treatments Orkin performed from December 2019 to November 2020. *Orkin, "New Year, New Top City on Orkin's 2021 Bed Bug Cities List: Chicago," February 1, 2021*

- New York was identified as a "2021 Spring Allergy Capital." The area ranked #45 out of 100. Three groups of factors were used to identify the most challenging cities for people with allergies during the spring season: annual spring pollen levels; over the counter medicine use; number of board-certified allergy specialists. *Asthma and Allergy Foundation of America, "Spring Allergy Capitals 2021," February 23, 2021*

- New York was identified as a "2021 Fall Allergy Capital." The area ranked #66 out of 100. Three groups of factors were used to identify the most challenging cities for people with allergies during the fall season: annual fall pollen levels; over the counter medicine use; number of board-certified allergy specialists. *Asthma and Allergy Foundation of America, "Fall Allergy Capitals 2021," February 23, 2021*

- New York was identified as a "2019 Asthma Capital." The area ranked #39 out of the nation's 100 largest metropolitan areas. Criteria: estimated asthma prevalence; crude death rate from asthma; and ER visits due to asthma. Risk factors analyzed but not factored in the rankings: annual pollen score; annual air quality; public smoking laws; number of board-certified asthma specialists; rescue medication use; controller medication use; uninsured rate; poverty rate. *Asthma and Allergy Foundation of America, "Asthma Capitals 2019: The Most Challenging Places to Live With Asthma," May 7, 2019*

- The Sharecare Community Well-Being Index evaluates 10 individual and social health factors in order to measure what matters to Americans in the communities in which they live. The New York metro area ranked #9 in the top 10 across all 10 domains. Criteria: access to healthcare, food, and community resources; housng and transportation; economic security; feeling of purpose; physical, financial, social, and community well-being. *www.sharecare.com, "Community Well-Being Index: 2019 Metro Area & County Rankings Report," August 31, 2020*

Real Estate Rankings

- FitSmallBusiness looked at 50 of the largest metropolitan areas in the U.S. to determine which metro was the best to start a real estate business. Data was compiled from such sources as: Zillow, Trulia, U.S. Census Bureau, and the Bureau of Labor Statistics. Criteria: location; inventory; annual wages; median sales price of homes; days on the market; median price cut percentage; and other factors that would influence real estate professional growth. The New York metro area ranked #6. *fitsmallbusiness.com, "The Best Cities to Become a Real Estate Agent in 2018," January 30, 2018*

- The New York metro area was identified as one of the 20 best housing markets in the U.S. in 2020. The area ranked #11 out of 180 markets. Criteria: year-over-year change of median sales price of existing single-family homes between the 4th quarter of 2019 and the 4th quarter of 2020. *National Association of Realtors®, Median Sales Price of Existing Single-Family Homes for Metropolitan Areas, 4th Quarter 2020*

- The New York metro area was identified as one of the 10 worst condo markets in the U.S. in 2020. The area ranked #56 out of 63 markets. Criteria: year-over-year change of median sales price of existing apartment condo-coop homes between the 4th quarter of 2019 and the 4th quarter of 2020. *National Association of Realtors®, Median Sales Price of Existing Apartment Condo-Coops Homes for Metropolitan Areas, 4th Quarter 2020*

- The New York metro area was identified as one of the 20 least affordable housing markets in the U.S. in 2020. The area ranked #169 out of 183 markets. Criteria: qualification for a mortgage loan with a 10 percent down payment on a typical home. *National Association of Realtors®, Qualifying Income Based on Sales Price of Existing Single-Family Homes for Metropolitan Areas, 2020*

- New York was ranked #250 out of 268 metro areas in terms of housing affordability in 2020 by the National Association of Home Builders (#1 = most affordable). Criteria: the share of homes sold in that area affordable to a family earning the local median income, based on standard mortgage underwriting criteria. *National Association of Home Builders®, NAHB-Wells Fargo Housing Opportunity Index, 4th Quarter 2020*

Safety Rankings

- To identify the safest cities in America, 24/7 Wall Street focused on violent crime categories—murder, non-negligent manslaughter, rape, robbery, and aggravated assault—and property crime as reported in the FBI's 2018 annual Uniform Crime Report. Criteria also included median income from American Community Survey and unemployment figures from Bureau of Labor Statistics. For cities with populations over 100,000, Edison was ranked #18. *247wallst.com, "America's Safest Cities" January 15, 2020*

- The National Insurance Crime Bureau ranked 384 metro areas in the U.S. in terms of per capita rates of vehicle theft. The New York metro area ranked #300 (#1 = highest rate). Criteria: number of vehicle theft offenses per 100,000 inhabitants in 2019. *National Insurance Crime Bureau, "Hot Spots 2019," July 21, 2020*

Seniors/Retirement Rankings

- From its Best Cities for Successful Aging indexes, the Milken Institute generated rankings for metropolitan areas, weighing data in nine categories—health care, wellness, living arrangements, transportation and convenience, financial characteristics, education, employment, community engagement, and overall livability. The New York metro area was ranked #73 overall in the large metro area category. *Milken Institute, "Best Cities for Successful Aging, 2017" March 14, 2017*

Transportation Rankings

- New York was identified as one of the most congested metro areas in the U.S. The area ranked #4 out of 10. Criteria: yearly delay per auto commuter in hours. *Texas A&M Transportation Institute, "2019 Urban Mobility Report," December 2019*

- According to the INRIX "2019 Global Traffic Scorecard," New York was identified as one of the most congested metro areas in the U.S. The area ranked #4 out of 10. Criteria: average annual time spent in traffic and average cost of congestion per motorist. *Inrix.com, "Congestion Costs Each American Nearly 100 hours, $1,400 A Year," March 9, 2020*

Women/Minorities Rankings

- The *Houston Chronicle* listed the New York metro area as #4 in top places for young Latinos to live in the U.S. Research was largely based on housing and occupational data from the largest metropolitan areas performed by *Forbes* and NBC Universo. Criteria: percentage of 18-34 year-olds; Latino college grad rates; and diversity. *blog.chron.com, "The 15 Best Big Cities for Latino Millenials," January 26, 2016*

Miscellaneous Rankings

- The watchdog site, Charity Navigator, conducted a study of charities in major markets both to analyze statistical differences in their financial, accountability, and transparency practices and to track year-to-year variations in individual philanthropic communities. The New York metro area was ranked #19 among the 30 metro markets in the rating category of Overall Score. *www.charitynavigator.org, "2017 Metro Market Study," May 1, 2017*

- The National Alliance to End Homelessness listed the 25 most populous metro areas with the highest rate of homelessness. The New York metro area had a high rate of homelessness. Criteria: number of homeless people per 10,000 population in 2016. *National Alliance to End Homelessness, "Homelessness in the 25 Most Populous U.S. Metro Areas," September 1, 2017*

Business Environment

DEMOGRAPHICS

Population Growth

Area	1990 Census	2000 Census	2010 Census	2019* Estimate	Population Growth (%) 1990-2019	Population Growth (%) 2010-2019
City	88,680	97,687	99,967	100,447	13.3	0.5
MSA[1]	16,845,992	18,323,002	18,897,109	19,294,236	14.5	2.1
U.S.	248,709,873	281,421,906	308,745,538	324,697,795	30.6	5.2

Note: (1) Figures cover the New York-Newark-Jersey City, NY-NJ-PA Metropolitan Statistical Area; (*) 2015-2019 5-year estimated population
Source: U.S. Census Bureau, 1990 Census, Census 2000, Census 2010, 2015-2019 American Community Survey 5-Year Estimates

Household Size

Area	Persons in Household (%) One	Two	Three	Four	Five	Six	Seven or More	Average Household Size
City	18.9	29.0	21.1	20.4	6.4	2.6	1.6	2.90
MSA[1]	28.1	29.5	16.9	14.6	6.6	2.5	1.9	2.70
U.S.	27.9	33.9	15.6	12.9	6.0	2.3	1.4	2.60

Note: (1) Figures cover the New York-Newark-Jersey City, NY-NJ-PA Metropolitan Statistical Area
Source: U.S. Census Bureau, 2015-2019 American Community Survey 5-Year Estimates

Race

Area	White Alone[2] (%)	Black Alone[2] (%)	Asian Alone[2] (%)	AIAN[3] Alone[2] (%)	NHOPI[4] Alone[2] (%)	Other Race Alone[2] (%)	Two or More Races (%)
City	35.3	8.2	48.7	0.3	0.1	4.0	3.5
MSA[1]	57.5	17.3	11.2	0.3	0.0	10.5	3.1
U.S.	72.5	12.7	5.5	0.8	0.2	4.9	3.3

Note: (1) Figures cover the New York-Newark-Jersey City, NY-NJ-PA Metropolitan Statistical Area; (2) Alone is defined as not being in combination with one or more other races; (3) American Indian and Alaska Native; (4) Native Hawaiian and Other Pacific Islander
Source: U.S. Census Bureau, 2015-2019 American Community Survey 5-Year Estimates

Hispanic or Latino Origin

Area	Total (%)	Mexican (%)	Puerto Rican (%)	Cuban (%)	Other (%)
City	9.9	1.8	2.5	0.8	4.8
MSA[1]	24.6	3.0	6.2	0.8	14.7
U.S.	18.0	11.2	1.7	0.7	4.3

Note: Persons of Hispanic or Latino origin can be of any race; (1) Figures cover the New York-Newark-Jersey City, NY-NJ-PA Metropolitan Statistical Area
Source: U.S. Census Bureau, 2015-2019 American Community Survey 5-Year Estimates

Ancestry

Area	German	Irish	English	American	Italian	Polish	French[2]	Scottish	Dutch
City	4.9	6.8	1.6	1.7	7.8	4.6	0.8	0.6	0.3
MSA[1]	6.2	9.2	2.7	4.4	12.2	3.8	0.9	0.7	0.6
U.S.	13.3	9.7	7.2	6.2	5.1	2.8	2.3	1.7	1.2

Note: Figures are the percentage of the total population reporting a particular ancestry. The nine most commonly reported ancestries in the U.S. are shown. Figures include multiple ancestries (e.g. if a person reported being Irish and Italian, they were included in both columns); (1) Figures cover the New York-Newark-Jersey City, NY-NJ-PA Metropolitan Statistical Area; (2) Excludes Basque
Source: U.S. Census Bureau, 2015-2019 American Community Survey 5-Year Estimates

Foreign-born Population

Area	Percent of Population Born in Any Foreign Country	Asia	Mexico	Europe	Caribbean	Central America[2]	South America	Africa	Canada
City	46.9	37.6	1.0	2.8	1.5	0.3	1.7	1.8	0.2
MSA[1]	29.5	8.7	1.5	4.4	6.9	2.0	4.4	1.4	0.2
U.S.	13.6	4.2	3.5	1.5	1.3	1.1	1.0	0.7	0.2

Note: (1) Figures cover the New York-Newark-Jersey City, NY-NJ-PA Metropolitan Statistical Area; (2) Excludes Mexico.
Source: U.S. Census Bureau, 2015-2019 American Community Survey 5-Year Estimates

Marital Status

Area	Never Married	Now Married[2]	Separated	Widowed	Divorced
City	25.7	61.0	1.0	6.1	6.2
MSA[1]	37.8	46.3	2.3	5.7	7.9
U.S.	33.4	48.1	1.9	5.8	10.9

Note: Figures are percentages and cover the population 15 years of age and older; (1) Figures cover the New York-Newark-Jersey City, NY-NJ-PA Metropolitan Statistical Area; (2) Excludes separated
Source: U.S. Census Bureau, 2015-2019 American Community Survey 5-Year Estimates

Disability by Age

Area	All Ages	Under 18 Years Old	18 to 64 Years Old	65 Years and Over
City	8.2	3.3	5.3	29.0
MSA[1]	10.0	3.2	7.2	31.6
U.S.	12.6	4.2	10.3	34.5

Note: Figures show percent of the civilian noninstitutionalized population that reported having a disability. Disability status is determined from six types of difficulty: vision, hearing, cognitive, ambulatory, self-care, and independent living. For children under 5 years old, hearing and vision difficulty are used to determine disability status. For children between the ages of 5 and 14, disability status is determined from hearing, vision, cognitive, ambulatory, and self-care difficulties. For people aged 15 years and older, they are considered to have a disability if they have difficulty with any one of the six difficulty types; Note: (1) Figures cover the New York-Newark-Jersey City, NY-NJ-PA Metropolitan Statistical Area
Source: U.S. Census Bureau, 2015-2019 American Community Survey 5-Year Estimates

Age

Area	Under Age 5	Age 5–19	Age 20–34	Age 35–44	Age 45–54	Age 55–64	Age 65–74	Age 75–84	Age 85+	Median Age
City	6.1	18.4	17.9	15.7	14.0	13.1	8.4	4.1	2.3	39.6
MSA[1]	6.1	17.8	21.2	13.1	13.6	12.8	8.6	4.6	2.2	38.6
U.S.	6.1	19.1	20.7	12.6	13.0	12.9	9.1	4.6	1.9	38.1

Note: (1) Figures cover the New York-Newark-Jersey City, NY-NJ-PA Metropolitan Statistical Area
Source: U.S. Census Bureau, 2015-2019 American Community Survey 5-Year Estimates

Gender

Area	Males	Females	Males per 100 Females
City	50,210	50,237	99.9
MSA[1]	9,327,459	9,966,777	93.6
U.S.	159,886,919	164,810,876	97.0

Note: (1) Figures cover the New York-Newark-Jersey City, NY-NJ-PA Metropolitan Statistical Area
Source: U.S. Census Bureau, 2015-2019 American Community Survey 5-Year Estimates

Religious Groups by Family

Area	Catholic	Baptist	Non-Den.	Methodist[2]	Lutheran	LDS[3]	Pentecostal	Presbyterian[4]	Muslim[5]	Judaism
MSA[1]	36.9	1.9	1.8	1.3	0.8	0.4	0.9	1.1	2.3	4.8
U.S.	19.1	9.3	4.0	4.0	2.3	2.0	1.9	1.6	0.8	0.7

Note: Figures are the number of adherents as a percentage of the total population; (1) Figures cover the New York-Newark-Jersey City, NY-NJ-PA Metropolitan Statistical Area; (2) Methodist/Pietist; (3) Latter Day Saints; (4) Reformed; (5) Figures are estimates
Source: Association of Statisticians of American Religious Bodies, 2010 U.S. Religion Census: Religious Congregations & Membership Study

Religious Groups by Tradition

Area	Catholic	Evangelical Protestant	Mainline Protestant	Other Tradition	Black Protestant	Orthodox
MSA[1]	36.9	4.0	4.1	8.4	1.2	1.0
U.S.	19.1	16.2	7.3	4.3	1.6	0.3

Note: Figures are the number of adherents as a percentage of the total population; (1) Figures cover the New York-Newark-Jersey City, NY-NJ-PA Metropolitan Statistical Area
Source: Association of Statisticians of American Religious Bodies, 2010 U.S. Religion Census: Religious Congregations & Membership Study

ECONOMY

Gross Metropolitan Product

Area	2017	2018	2019	2020	Rank[2]
MSA[1]	1,765.5	1,851.9	1,932.1	2,007.4	1

Note: Figures are in billions of dollars; (1) Figures cover the New York-Newark-Jersey City, NY-NJ-PA Metropolitan Statistical Area; (2) Rank is based on 2018 data and ranges from 1 to 381
Source: U.S. Conference of Mayors, U.S. Metro Economies: GMP & Employment 2018-2020, September 2019

Economic Growth

Area	2015-17 (%)	2018 (%)	2019 (%)	2020 (%)	Rank[2]
MSA[1]	1.3	2.6	2.6	1.6	196
U.S.	1.9	2.9	2.3	2.1	–

Note: Figures are real gross metropolitan product (GMP) growth rates and represent average annual percent change; (1) Figures cover the New York-Newark-Jersey City, NY-NJ-PA Metropolitan Statistical Area; (2) Rank is based on 2017 2-year average annual percent change and ranges from 1 to 381
Source: U.S. Conference of Mayors, U.S. Metro Economies: GMP & Employment 2018-2020, September 2019

Metropolitan Area Exports

Area	2014	2015	2016	2017	2018	2019	Rank[2]
MSA[1]	105,266.6	95,645.4	89,649.5	93,693.7	97,692.4	87,365.7	2

Note: Figures are in millions of dollars; (1) Figures cover the New York-Newark-Jersey City, NY-NJ-PA Metropolitan Statistical Area; (2) Rank is based on 2019 data and ranges from 1 to 386
Source: U.S. Department of Commerce, International Trade Administration, Office of Trade and Economic Analysis, Industry and Analysis, Exports by Metropolitan Area, data extracted March 24, 2021

Building Permits

Area	Single-Family			Multi-Family			Total		
	2018	2019	Pct. Chg.	2018	2019	Pct. Chg.	2018	2019	Pct. Chg.
City	71	55	-22.5	100	175	75.0	171	230	34.5
MSA[1]	11,077	11,072	0.0	38,615	50,096	29.7	49,692	61,168	23.1
U.S.	855,300	862,100	0.7	473,500	523,900	10.6	1,328,800	1,386,000	4.3

Note: (1) Figures cover the New York-Newark-Jersey City, NY-NJ-PA Metropolitan Statistical Area; Figures represent new, privately-owned housing units authorized (unadjusted data); All permit data are based on estimates with imputation
Source: U.S. Census Bureau, Manufacturing, Mining, and Construction Statistics, Building Permits, 2018, 2019

Bankruptcy Filings

Area	Business Filings			Nonbusiness Filings		
	2019	2020	% Chg.	2019	2020	% Chg.
Middlesex County	46	31	-32.6	1,718	1,097	-36.1
U.S.	22,780	21,655	-4.9	752,160	522,808	-30.5

Note: Business filings include Chapter 7, Chapter 9, Chapter 11, Chapter 12, Chapter 13, Chapter 15, and Section 304; Nonbusiness filings include Chapter 7, Chapter 11, and Chapter 13
Source: Administrative Office of the U.S. Courts, Business and Nonbusiness Bankruptcy, County Cases Commenced by Chapter of the Bankruptcy Code, During the 12-Month Period Ending December 31, 2019 and Business and Nonbusiness Bankruptcy, County Cases Commenced by Chapter of the Bankruptcy Code, During the 12-Month Period Ending December 31, 2020

Housing Vacancy Rates

Area	Gross Vacancy Rate[2] (%)			Year-Round Vacancy Rate[3] (%)			Rental Vacancy Rate[4] (%)			Homeowner Vacancy Rate[5] (%)		
	2018	2019	2020	2018	2019	2020	2018	2019	2020	2018	2019	2020
MSA[1]	10.3	9.2	9.1	9.1	7.8	7.8	4.5	4.3	4.5	1.6	1.4	1.3
U.S.	12.3	12.0	10.6	9.7	9.5	8.2	6.9	6.7	6.3	1.5	1.4	1.0

Note: (1) Figures cover the New York-Newark-Jersey City, NY-NJ-PA Metropolitan Statistical Area; (2) The percentage of the total housing inventory that is vacant; (3) The percentage of the housing inventory (excluding seasonal units) that is year-round vacant; (4) The percentage of rental inventory that is vacant for rent; (5) The percentage of homeowner inventory that is vacant for sale
Source: U.S. Census Bureau, Housing Vacancies and Homeownership Annual Statistics: 2018, 2019, 2020

INCOME

Income

Area	Per Capita ($)	Median Household ($)	Average Household ($)
City	44,667	103,076	127,171
MSA[1]	43,409	78,773	116,604
U.S.	34,103	62,843	88,607

Note: (1) Figures cover the New York-Newark-Jersey City, NY-NJ-PA Metropolitan Statistical Area
Source: U.S. Census Bureau, 2015-2019 American Community Survey 5-Year Estimates

Household Income Distribution

Area	Percent of Households Earning							
	Under $15,000	$15,000 -$24,999	$25,000 -$34,999	$35,000 -$49,999	$50,000 -$74,999	$75,000 -$99,999	$100,000 -$149,999	$150,000 and up
City	4.9	4.3	4.1	8.9	12.6	13.7	21.3	30.1
MSA[1]	10.5	7.5	7.0	9.3	13.9	11.4	16.4	24.1
U.S.	10.3	8.9	8.9	12.3	17.2	12.7	15.1	14.5

Note: (1) Figures cover the New York-Newark-Jersey City, NY-NJ-PA Metropolitan Statistical Area
Source: U.S. Census Bureau, 2015-2019 American Community Survey 5-Year Estimates

Poverty Rate

Area	All Ages	Under 18 Years Old	18 to 64 Years Old	65 Years and Over
City	5.7	6.8	5.1	6.8
MSA[1]	12.8	17.7	11.4	12.0
U.S.	13.4	18.5	12.6	9.3

Note: Figures are percentage of people whose income during the past 12 months was below the poverty level;
(1) Figures cover the New York-Newark-Jersey City, NY-NJ-PA Metropolitan Statistical Area
Source: U.S. Census Bureau, 2015-2019 American Community Survey 5-Year Estimates

CITY FINANCES

City Government Finances

Component	2017 ($000)	2017 ($ per capita)
Total Revenues	292,908	2,852
Total Expenditures	363,747	3,542
Debt Outstanding	51,673	503
Cash and Securities[1]	49,840	485

Note: (1) Cash and security holdings of a government at the close of its fiscal year,
including those of its dependent agencies, utilities, and liquor stores.
Source: U.S. Census Bureau, State & Local Government Finances 2017

City Government Revenue by Source

Source	2017 ($000)	2017 ($ per capita)	2017 (%)
General Revenue			
From Federal Government	0	0	0.0
From State Government	43,674	425	14.9
From Local Governments	327	3	0.1
Taxes			
Property	210,003	2,045	71.7
Sales and Gross Receipts	1,933	19	0.7
Personal Income	0	0	0.0
Corporate Income	0	0	0.0
Motor Vehicle License	0	0	0.0
Other Taxes	6,980	68	2.4
Current Charges	27,225	265	9.3
Liquor Store	0	0	0.0
Utility	90	1	0.0
Employee Retirement	0	0	0.0

Source: U.S. Census Bureau, State & Local Government Finances 2017

City Government Expenditures by Function

Function	2017 ($000)	2017 ($ per capita)	2017 (%)
General Direct Expenditures			
Air Transportation	0	0	0.0
Corrections	0	0	0.0
Education	241,557	2,352	66.4
Employment Security Administration	0	0	0.0
Financial Administration	957	9	0.3
Fire Protection	19,297	187	5.3
General Public Buildings	2,062	20	0.6
Governmental Administration, Other	1,099	10	0.3
Health	1,516	14	0.4
Highways	2,934	28	0.8
Hospitals	0	0	0.0
Housing and Community Development	0	0	0.0
Interest on General Debt	2,117	20	0.6
Judicial and Legal	1,162	11	0.3
Libraries	0	0	0.0
Parking	223	2	0.1
Parks and Recreation	2,686	26	0.7
Police Protection	26,490	257	7.3
Public Welfare	0	0	0.0
Sewerage	18,998	185	5.2
Solid Waste Management	990	9	0.3
Veterans' Services	0	0	0.0
Liquor Store	0	0	0.0
Utility	90	< 1	< 0.1
Employee Retirement	0	0	0.0

Source: U.S. Census Bureau, State & Local Government Finances 2017

EMPLOYMENT

Labor Force and Employment

Area	Civilian Labor Force			Workers Employed		
	Dec. 2019	Dec. 2020	% Chg.	Dec. 2019	Dec. 2020	% Chg.
City	55,345	54,084	-2.3	54,066	51,214	-5.3
MD[1]	7,008,087	6,694,644	-4.5	6,780,009	6,077,482	-10.4
U.S.	164,007,000	160,017,000	-2.4	158,504,000	149,613,000	-5.6

Note: Data is not seasonally adjusted and covers workers 16 years of age and older; (1) Figures cover the New York-Jersey City-White Plains, NY-NJ Metropolitan Division
Source: Bureau of Labor Statistics, Local Area Unemployment Statistics

Unemployment Rate

Area	2020											
	Jan.	Feb.	Mar.	Apr.	May	Jun.	Jul.	Aug.	Sep.	Oct.	Nov.	Dec.
City	2.8	2.7	2.4	11.7	11.3	12.7	11.0	8.4	4.9	5.8	7.4	5.3
MD[1]	3.8	3.6	3.8	15.1	16.3	18.3	17.6	14.0	10.7	10.5	10.4	9.2
U.S.	4.0	3.8	4.5	14.4	13.0	11.2	10.5	8.5	7.7	6.6	6.4	6.5

Note: Data is not seasonally adjusted and covers workers 16 years of age and older; (1) Figures cover the New York-Jersey City-White Plains, NY-NJ Metropolitan Division
Source: Bureau of Labor Statistics, Local Area Unemployment Statistics

Average Wages

Occupation	$/Hr.	Occupation	$/Hr.
Accountants and Auditors	50.80	Maintenance and Repair Workers	24.50
Automotive Mechanics	24.30	Marketing Managers	93.80
Bookkeepers	24.50	Network and Computer Systems Admin.	51.00
Carpenters	34.20	Nurses, Licensed Practical	27.50
Cashiers	14.30	Nurses, Registered	45.60
Computer Programmers	46.30	Nursing Assistants	19.50
Computer Systems Analysts	55.10	Office Clerks, General	19.00
Computer User Support Specialists	31.30	Physical Therapists	47.80
Construction Laborers	29.50	Physicians	99.90
Cooks, Restaurant	17.30	Plumbers, Pipefitters and Steamfitters	35.80
Customer Service Representatives	21.90	Police and Sheriff's Patrol Officers	41.50
Dentists	81.30	Postal Service Mail Carriers	25.80
Electricians	40.50	Real Estate Sales Agents	47.40
Engineers, Electrical	54.50	Retail Salespersons	17.10
Fast Food and Counter Workers	14.00	Sales Representatives, Technical/Scientific	53.90
Financial Managers	103.20	Secretaries, Exc. Legal/Medical/Executive	21.60
First-Line Supervisors of Office Workers	36.50	Security Guards	18.30
General and Operations Managers	82.90	Surgeons	103.30
Hairdressers/Cosmetologists	18.50	Teacher Assistants, Exc. Postsecondary*	17.10
Home Health and Personal Care Aides	15.40	Teachers, Secondary School, Exc. Sp. Ed.*	43.90
Janitors and Cleaners	18.60	Telemarketers	18.00
Landscaping/Groundskeeping Workers	18.60	Truck Drivers, Heavy/Tractor-Trailer	27.40
Lawyers	86.60	Truck Drivers, Light/Delivery Services	21.30
Maids and Housekeeping Cleaners	18.20	Waiters and Waitresses	18.10

Note: Wage data covers the New York-Newark-Jersey City, NY-NJ-PA Metropolitan Statistical Area; (*) Hourly wages were calculated from annual wage data based on a 40 hour work week; n/a not available.
Source: Bureau of Labor Statistics, Metro Area Occupational Employment & Wage Estimates, May 2020

Employment by Industry

Sector	MD[1]		U.S.
	Number of Employees	Percent of Total	Percent of Total
Construction, Mining, and Logging	252,500	3.9	5.5
Education and Health Services	1,478,900	22.7	16.3
Financial Activities	613,100	9.4	6.1
Government	917,900	14.1	15.2
Information	249,000	3.8	1.9
Leisure and Hospitality	390,300	6.0	9.0
Manufacturing	181,400	2.8	8.5
Other Services	248,200	3.8	3.8
Professional and Business Services	1,071,000	16.5	14.4
Retail Trade	580,800	8.9	10.9
Transportation, Warehousing, and Utilities	275,900	4.2	4.6
Wholesale Trade	246,700	3.8	3.9

Note: Figures are non-farm employment as of December 2020. Figures are not seasonally adjusted and include workers 16 years of age and older; (1) Figures cover the New York-Jersey City-White Plains, NY-NJ Metropolitan Division
Source: Bureau of Labor Statistics, Current Employment Statistics, Employment, Hours, and Earnings

Employment by Occupation

Occupation Classification	City (%)	MSA[1] (%)	U.S. (%)
Management, Business, Science, and Arts	54.8	43.2	38.5
Natural Resources, Construction, and Maintenance	4.9	6.7	8.9
Production, Transportation, and Material Moving	10.2	9.7	13.2
Sales and Office	19.1	21.4	21.6
Service	10.9	19.0	17.8

Note: Figures cover employed civilians 16 years of age and older; (1) Figures cover the New York-Newark-Jersey City, NY-NJ-PA Metropolitan Statistical Area
Source: U.S. Census Bureau, 2015-2019 American Community Survey 5-Year Estimates

Occupations with Greatest Projected Employment Growth: 2018 – 2028

Occupation[1]	2018 Employment	2028 Projected Employment	Numeric Employment Change	Percent Employment Change
Home Health Aides	42,660	60,110	17,450	40.9
Laborers and Freight, Stock, and Material Movers, Hand	141,760	156,860	15,100	10.7
Registered Nurses	85,470	95,090	9,620	11.3
Combined Food Preparation and Serving Workers, Including Fast Food	46,070	55,560	9,490	20.6
Software Developers, Applications	48,110	57,100	8,990	18.7
Waiters and Waitresses	60,280	66,560	6,280	10.4
Personal Care Aides	16,270	22,140	5,870	36.1
Heavy and Tractor-Trailer Truck Drivers	52,200	57,540	5,340	10.2
Cooks, Restaurant	21,220	26,490	5,270	24.8
Hairdressers, Hairstylists, and Cosmetologists	31,540	36,780	5,240	16.6

Note: Projections cover New Jersey; Short-term projections for 2020-2022 were not available at time of publication; (1) Sorted by numeric employment change
Source: www.projectionscentral.com, State Occupational Projections, 2018–2028 Long-Term Projections

Fastest-Growing Occupations: 2018 – 2028

Occupation[1]	2018 Employment	2028 Projected Employment	Numeric Employment Change	Percent Employment Change
Solar Photovoltaic Installers	780	1,150	370	47.4
Home Health Aides	42,660	60,110	17,450	40.9
Occupational Therapy Assistants	680	930	250	36.8
Personal Care Aides	16,270	22,140	5,870	36.1
Mathematicians	290	390	100	34.5
Physician Assistants	2,920	3,860	940	32.2
Statisticians	1,300	1,700	400	30.8
Tank Car, Truck, and Ship Loaders	470	610	140	29.8
Nurse Practitioners	6,250	8,010	1,760	28.2
Massage Therapists	4,150	5,300	1,150	27.7

Note: Projections cover New Jersey; Short-term projections for 2020-2022 were not available at time of publication; (1) Sorted by percent employment change and excludes occupations with numeric employment change less than 50
Source: www.projectionscentral.com, State Occupational Projections, 2018–2028 Long-Term Projections

TAXES

State Corporate Income Tax Rates

State	Tax Rate (%)	Income Brackets ($)	Num. of Brackets	Financial Institution Tax Rate (%)[a]	Federal Income Tax Ded.
New Jersey	9.0 (q)	Flat rate	1	9.0 (q)	No

Note: Tax rates as of January 1, 2021; (a) Rates listed are the corporate income tax rate applied to financial institutions or excise taxes based on income. Some states have other taxes based upon the value of deposits or shares; (q) New Jersey also imposes a 2.5% surtax on taxpayers with income over $1 million in tax year 2021. Small businesses with annual entire net income under $100,000 pay a tax rate of 7.5%; businesses with income under $50,000 pay 6.5%. The minimum Corporation Business Tax is based on New Jersey gross receipts. It ranges from $500 for a corporation with gross receipts less than $100,000, to $2,000 for a corporation with gross receipts of $1 million or more.
Source: Federation of Tax Administrators, State Corporate Income Tax Rates, January 1, 2021

State Individual Income Tax Rates

| State | Tax Rate (%) | Income Brackets ($) | Personal Exemptions ($) | | | Standard Ded. ($) | |
			Single	Married	Depend.	Single	Married
New Jersey	1.4 - 10.75	20,000 - 1 million (p)	1,000	2,000	1,500	–	–

Note: Tax rates as of January 1, 2021; Local- and county-level taxes are not included; Federal income tax is not deductible on state income tax returns; (p) The New Jersey rates reported are for single individuals. For married couples filing jointly, the tax rates also range from 1.4% to 10.75%, with 8 brackets and the same high and low income ranges.
Source: Federation of Tax Administrators, State Individual Income Tax Rates, January 1, 2021

Various State Sales and Excise Tax Rates

State	State Sales Tax (%)	Gasoline[1] (¢/gal.)	Cigarette[2] ($/pack)	Spirits[3] ($/gal.)	Wine[4] ($/gal.)	Beer[5] ($/gal.)	Recreational Marijuana (%)
New Jersey	6.625	50.7	2.7	5.5	0.88	0.12	(k)

Note: All tax rates as of January 1, 2021; (1) The American Petroleum Institute has developed a methodology for determining the average tax rate on a gallon of fuel. Rates may include any of the following: excise taxes, environmental fees, storage tank fees, other fees or taxes, general sales tax, and local taxes; (2) The federal excise tax of $1.0066 per pack and local taxes are not included; (3) Rates are those applicable to off-premise sales of 40% alcohol by volume (a.b.v.) distilled spirits in 750ml containers. Local excise taxes are excluded; (4) Rates are those applicable to off-premise sales of 11% a.b.v. non-carbonated wine in 750ml containers; (5) Rates are those applicable to off-premise sales of 4.7% a.b.v. beer in 12 ounce containers; (k) Up to $10 per ounce, if the average retail price of an ounce of usable cannabis was $350 or more; up to $30 per ounce, if the average retail price of an ounce of usable cannabis was less than $350 but at least $250; up to $40 per ounce, if the average retail price of an ounce of usable cannabis was less than $250 but at least $200; up to $60 per ounce, if the average retail price of an ounce of usable cannabis was less than $200.
Source: Tax Foundation, 2021 Facts & Figures: How Does Your State Compare?

State Business Tax Climate Index Rankings

State	Overall Rank	Corporate Tax Rank	Individual Income Tax Rank	Sales Tax Rank	Property Tax Rank	Unemployment Insurance Tax Rank
New Jersey	50	48	50	42	46	31

Note: The index is a measure of how each state's tax laws affect economic performance. The lower the rank, the more favorable a state's tax system is for business. States without a given tax are given a ranking of 1. The scores/rankings for the District of Columbia do not affect other states. The 2021 index represents the tax climate as of July 1, 2020.
Source: Tax Foundation, State Business Tax Climate Index 2021

TRANSPORTATION

Means of Transportation to Work

| Area | Car/Truck/Van | | Public Transportation | | | Bicycle | Walked | Other Means | Worked at Home |
	Drove Alone	Car-pooled	Bus	Subway	Railroad				
City	69.4	9.0	0.5	0.5	12.6	0.3	1.7	1.2	4.8
MSA[1]	49.2	6.3	7.5	20.0	3.9	0.7	5.9	2.0	4.5
U.S.	76.3	9.0	2.4	1.9	0.6	0.5	2.7	1.4	5.2

Note: Figures are percentages and cover workers 16 years of age and older; (1) Figures cover the New York-Newark-Jersey City, NY-NJ-PA Metropolitan Statistical Area
Source: U.S. Census Bureau, 2015-2019 American Community Survey 5-Year Estimates

Travel Time to Work

Area	Less Than 10 Minutes	10 to 19 Minutes	20 to 29 Minutes	30 to 44 Minutes	45 to 59 Minutes	60 to 89 Minutes	90 Minutes or More
City	6.4	23.1	17.4	18.1	11.2	14.0	9.7
MSA[1]	6.7	18.2	16.1	23.9	12.7	15.3	7.1
U.S.	12.2	28.4	20.8	20.8	8.3	6.4	2.9

Note: Note: Figures are percentages and include workers 16 years old and over; (1) Figures cover the New York-Newark-Jersey City, NY-NJ-PA Metropolitan Statistical Area
Source: U.S. Census Bureau, 2015-2019 American Community Survey 5-Year Estimates

Key Congestion Measures

Measure	1982	1992	2002	2012	2017
Annual Hours of Delay, Total (000)	190,419	298,115	536,526	727,659	811,609
Annual Hours of Delay, Per Auto Commuter	32	45	66	81	92
Annual Congestion Cost, Total (million $)	1,441	3,158	7,282	13,149	15,040
Annual Congestion Cost, Per Auto Commuter ($)	1,024	1,102	1,547	1,644	1,778

Note: Covers the New York-Newark NY-NJ-CT urban area
Source: Texas A&M Transportation Institute, 2019 Urban Mobility Report

Freeway Travel Time Index

Measure	1982	1987	1992	1997	2002	2007	2012	2017
Urban Area Index[1]	1.15	1.18	1.21	1.26	1.31	1.34	1.34	1.35
Urban Area Rank[1,2]	8	11	11	8	6	7	8	7

Note: Freeway Travel Time Index—the ratio of travel time in the peak period to the travel time at free-flow conditions. For example, a value of 1.30 indicates a 20-minute free-flow trip takes 26 minutes in the peak (20 minutes x 1.30 = 26 minutes); (1) Covers the New York-Newark NY-NJ-CT urban area; (2) Rank is based on 101 larger urban areas (#1 = highest travel time index)
Source: Texas A&M Transportation Institute, 2019 Urban Mobility Report

Public Transportation

Agency Name / Mode of Transportation	Vehicles Operated in Maximum Service[1]	Annual Unlinked Passenger Trips[2] (in thous.)	Annual Passenger Miles[3] (in thous.)
New Jersey Transit Corporation			
Bus (directly operated)	1,871	141,247.4	975,132.9
Bus (purchased transportation)	181	9,818.2	42,195.9
Commuter Rail (directly operated)	923	89,562.9	2,006,197.8
Demand Response (purchased transportation)	427	1,711.3	10,751.0
Hybrid Rail (purchased transportation)	16	2,744.9	40,925.5
Light Rail (directly operated)	14	5,417.4	12,445.5
Light Rail (purchased transportation)	42	16,133.0	61,258.6
Vanpool (purchased transportation)	171	635.2	22,289.8

Note: (1) Number of revenue vehicles operated by the given mode and type of service to meet the annual maximum service requirement. This is the revenue vehicle count during the peak season of the year; on the week and day that maximum service is provided. Vehicles operated in maximum service (VOMS) exclude atypical days and one-time special events; (2) Number of passengers who boarded public transportation vehicles. Passengers are counted each time they board a vehicle no matter how many vehicles they use to travel from their origin to their destination. (3) Sum of the distances ridden by all passengers during the entire fiscal year.
Source: Federal Transit Administration, National Transit Database, 2019

Air Transportation

Airport Name and Code / Type of Service	Passenger Airlines[1]	Passenger Enplanements	Freight Carriers[2]	Freight (lbs)
Newark International (EWR)				
Domestic service (U.S. carriers - 2020)	27	6,116,356	15	557,955,905
International service (U.S. carriers - 2019)	13	4,413,093	4	96,542,501

Note: (1) Includes all U.S.-based major, minor and commuter airlines that carried at least one passenger during the year; (2) Includes all U.S.-based airlines and freight carriers that transported at least one pound of freight during the year.
Source: Bureau of Transportation Statistics, The Intermodal Transportation Database, Air Carriers: T-100 Domestic Market (U.S. Carriers), 2020; Bureau of Transportation Statistics, The Intermodal Transportation Database, Air Carriers: T-100 International Market (U.S. Carriers), 2019

BUSINESSES

Major Business Headquarters

Company Name	Industry	Rankings	
		Fortune[1]	Forbes[2]
No companies listed	-	-	-

Note: (1) Companies that produce a 10-K are ranked 1 to 500 based on 2019 revenue; (2) All private companies with at least $2 billion in annual revenue through the end of their most current fiscal year are ranked 1 to 219; companies listed are headquartered in the city; dashes indicate no ranking
Source: Fortune, "Fortune 500," June/July 2020; Forbes, "America's Largest Private Companies," 2020

Fastest-Growing Businesses

According to Deloitte, Edison is home to one of North America's 500 fastest-growing high-technology companies: **Mentour Corp** (#215). Companies are ranked by percentage growth in revenue over a four-year period. Criteria for inclusion: company must be headquartered within North America; must own proprietary intellectual property or technology that is sold to customers in products that contributes to a significant portion of the company's operating revenue; must have been in business for a minumum of four years with 2016 operating revenues of at least $50,000 USD/CD and 2019 operating revenues of at least $5 million USD/CD. *Deloitte, 2020 Technology Fast 500*[TM]

Living Environment

COST OF LIVING

Cost of Living Index

Composite Index	Groceries	Housing	Utilities	Trans-portation	Health Care	Misc. Goods/ Services
118.3	106.7	143.7	101.6	105.8	101.8	112.5

Note: The Cost of Living Index measures regional differences in the cost of consumer goods and services, excluding taxes and non-consumer expenditures, for professional and managerial households in the top income quintile. It is based on more than 50,000 prices covering almost 60 different items for which prices are collected three times a year by chambers of commerce, economic development organizations or university applied economic centers in each participating urban area. The numbers shown should be read as a percentage above or below the national average of 100. For example, a value of 115.4 in the groceries column indicates that grocery prices are 15.4% higher than the national average. Small differences in the index numbers should not be interpreted as significant; Figures cover the Middlesex-Monmouth NJ urban area.
Source: The Council for Community and Economic Research, Cost of Living Index, 2020

Grocery Prices

Area[1]	T-Bone Steak ($/pound)	Frying Chicken ($/pound)	Whole Milk ($/half gal.)	Eggs ($/dozen)	Orange Juice ($/64 oz.)	Coffee ($/11.5 oz.)
City[2]	13.96	1.67	2.41	1.60	3.51	4.06
Avg.	11.78	1.39	2.05	1.47	3.57	4.34
Min.	8.03	0.94	1.03	0.74	2.94	3.02
Max.	15.86	2.65	4.31	3.77	5.44	8.69

Note: (1) Values for the local area are compared with the average, minimum and maximum values for all 284 areas in the Cost of Living Index; (2) Figures cover the Middlesex-Monmouth NJ urban area; T-Bone Steak (price per pound); Frying Chicken (price per pound, whole fryer); Whole Milk (half gallon carton); Eggs (price per dozen, Grade A, large); Orange Juice (64 oz. Tropicana or Florida Natural); Coffee (11.5 oz. can, vacuum-packed, Maxwell House, Hills Bros, or Folgers).
Source: The Council for Community and Economic Research, Cost of Living Index, 2020

Housing and Utility Costs

Area[1]	New Home Price ($)	Apartment Rent ($/month)	All Electric ($/month)	Part Electric ($/month)	Other Energy ($/month)	Telephone ($/month)
City[2]	532,983	1,597	-	102.88	71.38	179.90
Avg.	368,594	1,168	170.86	100.47	65.28	184.30
Min.	190,567	502	91.58	31.42	26.08	169.60
Max.	2,227,806	4,738	470.38	280.31	280.06	206.50

Note: (1) Values for the local area are compared with the average, minimum and maximum values for all 284 areas in the Cost of Living Index; (2) Figures cover the Middlesex-Monmouth NJ urban area; New Home Price (2,400 sf living area, 8,000 sf lot, in urban area with full utilities); Apartment Rent (950 sf 2 bedroom/1.5 or 2 bath, unfurnished, excluding all utilities except water); All Electric (average monthly cost for an all-electric home); Part Electric (average monthly cost for a part-electric home); Other Energy (average monthly cost for natural gas, fuel oil, coal, wood, and any other forms of energy except electricity); Telephone (price includes the base monthly rate plus taxes and fees for three lines of mobile phone service).
Source: The Council for Community and Economic Research, Cost of Living Index, 2020

Health Care, Transportation, and Other Costs

Area[1]	Doctor ($/visit)	Dentist ($/visit)	Optometrist ($/visit)	Gasoline ($/gallon)	Beauty Salon ($/visit)	Men's Shirt ($)
City[2]	94.50	113.15	101.33	2.26	36.40	41.77
Avg.	115.44	99.32	108.10	2.21	39.27	31.37
Min.	36.68	59.00	51.36	1.71	19.00	11.00
Max.	219.00	153.10	250.97	3.46	82.05	58.33

Note: (1) Values for the local area are compared with the average, minimum and maximum values for all 284 areas in the Cost of Living Index; (2) Figures cover the Middlesex-Monmouth NJ urban area; Doctor (general practitioners routine exam of an established patient); Dentist (adult teeth cleaning and periodic oral examination); Optometrist (full vision eye exam for established adult patient); Gasoline (one gallon regular unleaded, national brand, including all taxes, cash price at self-service pump if available); Beauty Salon (woman's shampoo, trim, and blow-dry); Men's Shirt (cotton/polyester dress shirt, pinpoint weave, long sleeves).
Source: The Council for Community and Economic Research, Cost of Living Index, 2020

HOUSING

Homeownership Rate

Area	2012 (%)	2013 (%)	2014 (%)	2015 (%)	2016 (%)	2017 (%)	2018 (%)	2019 (%)	2020 (%)
MSA[1]	51.5	50.6	50.7	49.9	50.4	49.9	49.7	50.4	50.9
U.S.	65.4	65.1	64.5	63.7	63.4	63.9	64.4	64.6	66.6

Note: (1) Figures cover the New York-Newark-Jersey City, NY-NJ-PA Metropolitan Statistical Area
Source: U.S. Census Bureau, Housing Vacancies and Homeownership Annual Statistics: 2012-2020

House Price Index (HPI)

Area	National Ranking[2]	Quarterly Change (%)	One-Year Change (%)	Five-Year Change (%)	Since 1991Q1 (%)
MD[1]	220	1.50	3.91	23.15	199.59
U.S.[3]	–	3.81	10.77	38.99	205.12

Note: The HPI is a weighted repeat sales index. It measures average price changes in repeat sales or refinancings on the same properties. This information is obtained by reviewing repeat mortgage transactions on single-family properties whose mortgages have been purchased or securitized by Fannie Mae or Freddie Mac since January 1975; (1) Figures cover the New York-Jersey City-White Plains, NY-NJ Metropolitan Division; (2) Rankings are based on annual percentage change for all metro areas containing at least 15,000 transactions over the last 10 years and ranges from 1 to 253; (3) figures based on a weighted average of Census Division estimates using a seasonally adjusted, purchase-only index; all figures are for the period ending December 31, 2020
Source: Federal Housing Finance Agency, Change in Metropolitan Area House Price Indexes, April 7, 2021

Median Single-Family Home Prices

Area	2018	2019	2020p	Percent Change 2019 to 2020
MD[1]	377.8	386.5	442.0	14.4
U.S. Average	261.6	274.6	299.9	9.2

Note: Figures are median sales prices of existing single-family homes in thousands of dollars; (p) preliminary; (1) Figures cover the New York-Jersey City-White Plains, NY-NJ Metropolitan Division
Source: National Association of Realtors, Median Sales Price of Existing Single-Family Homes for Metropolitan Areas, 4th Quarter 2020

Qualifying Income Based on Median Sales Price of Existing Single-Family Homes

Area	With 5% Down ($)	With 10% Down ($)	With 20% Down ($)
MD[1]	90,977	86,189	76,613
U.S. Average	59,266	56,147	49,908

Note: Figures are preliminary; Qualifying income is based on a mortgage rate of 2.81%. Monthly principal and interest payment is limited to 25% of income; (1) Figures cover the New York-Jersey City-White Plains, NY-NJ Metropolitan Division
Source: National Association of Realtors, Qualifying Income Based on Median Sales Price of Existing Single-Family Homes for Metropolitan Areas, 4th Quarter 2020

Home Value Distribution

Area	Under $50,000	$50,000 -$99,999	$100,000 -$149,999	$150,000 -$199,999	$200,000 -$299,999	$300,000 -$499,999	$500,000 -$999,999	$1,000,000 or more
City	2.1	1.8	1.9	2.7	17.0	47.4	25.4	1.6
MSA[1]	2.0	1.4	2.4	3.9	13.2	35.1	32.1	9.9
U.S.	6.9	12.0	13.3	14.0	19.6	19.3	11.4	3.4

Note: Figures are percentages and cover owner-occupied housing units; (1) Figures cover the New York-Newark-Jersey City, NY-NJ-PA Metropolitan Statistical Area
Source: U.S. Census Bureau, 2015-2019 American Community Survey 5-Year Estimates

Year Housing Structure Built

Area	2010 or Later	2000 -2009	1990 -1999	1980 -1989	1970 -1979	1960 -1969	1950 -1959	1940 -1949	Before 1940	Median Year
City	1.7	4.7	9.3	23.3	13.6	20.3	17.4	4.5	5.1	1972
MSA[1]	2.8	6.7	6.1	7.7	9.8	13.7	15.9	8.8	28.6	1958
U.S.	5.2	14.0	13.9	13.4	15.2	10.6	10.3	4.9	12.6	1978

Note: Figures are percentages except for Median Year; Note: (1) Figures cover the New York-Newark-Jersey City, NY-NJ-PA Metropolitan Statistical Area
Source: U.S. Census Bureau, 2015-2019 American Community Survey 5-Year Estimates

Gross Monthly Rent

Area	Under $500	$500 -$999	$1,000 -$1,499	$1,500 -$1,999	$2,000 -$2,499	$2,500 -$2,999	$3,000 and up	Median ($)
City	2.8	5.8	39.4	35.3	13.2	2.6	0.9	1,528
MSA[1]	9.4	13.9	30.7	23.1	11.0	5.3	6.7	1,439
U.S.	9.4	36.2	30.0	14.0	5.6	2.4	2.4	1,062

Note: Figures are percentages except for Median; Gross rent is the contract rent plus the estimated average monthly cost of utilities (electricity, gas, and water and sewer) and fuels (oil, coal, kerosene, wood, etc.) if these are paid by the renter (or paid for the renter by someone else); (1) Figures cover the New York-Newark-Jersey City, NY-NJ-PA Metropolitan Statistical Area
Source: U.S. Census Bureau, 2015-2019 American Community Survey 5-Year Estimates

HEALTH

Health Risk Factors

Category	MD[1] (%)	U.S. (%)
Adults aged 18–64 who have any kind of health care coverage	86.1	87.3
Adults who reported being in good or better health	81.6	82.4
Adults who have been told they have high blood cholesterol	32.6	33.0
Adults who have been told they have high blood pressure	28.9	32.3
Adults who are current smokers	12.3	17.1
Adults who currently use E-cigarettes	3.5	4.6
Adults who currently use chewing tobacco, snuff, or snus	2.2	4.0
Adults who are heavy drinkers[2]	5.2	6.3
Adults who are binge drinkers[3]	16.5	17.4
Adults who are overweight (BMI 25.0 - 29.9)	35.5	35.3
Adults who are obese (BMI 30.0 - 99.8)	23.6	31.3
Adults who participated in any physical activities in the past month	71.5	74.4
Adults who always or nearly always wears a seat belt	92.1	94.3

Note: (1) Figures cover the New York-Jersey City-White Plains, NY-NJ Metropolitan Division; (2) Heavy drinkers are classified as adult men having more than 14 drinks per week and adult women having more than 7 drinks per week; (3) Binge drinkers are classified as males having five or more drinks on one occasion or females having four or more drinks on one occasion
Source: Centers for Disease Control and Prevention, Behaviorial Risk Factor Surveillance System, SMART: Selected Metropolitan Area Risk Trends, 2017

Acute and Chronic Health Conditions

Category	MD[1] (%)	U.S. (%)
Adults who have ever been told they had a heart attack	3.3	4.2
Adults who have ever been told they have angina or coronary heart disease	3.4	3.9
Adults who have ever been told they had a stroke	2.0	3.0
Adults who have ever been told they have asthma	12.5	14.2
Adults who have ever been told they have arthritis	19.2	24.9
Adults who have ever been told they have diabetes[2]	10.5	10.5
Adults who have ever been told they had skin cancer	3.5	6.2
Adults who have ever been told they had any other types of cancer	5.4	7.1
Adults who have ever been told they have COPD	4.5	6.5
Adults who have ever been told they have kidney disease	2.5	3.0
Adults who have ever been told they have a form of depression	13.8	20.5

Note: (1) Figures cover the New York-Jersey City-White Plains, NY-NJ Metropolitan Division; (2) Figures do not include pregnancy-related, borderline, or pre-diabetes
Source: Centers for Disease Control and Prevention, Behaviorial Risk Factor Surveillance System, SMART: Selected Metropolitan Area Risk Trends, 2017

Health Screening and Vaccination Rates

Category	MD[1] (%)	U.S. (%)
Adults aged 65+ who have had flu shot within the past year	55.7	60.7
Adults aged 65+ who have ever had a pneumonia vaccination	67.1	75.4
Adults who have ever been tested for HIV	50.9	36.1
Adults who have ever had the shingles or zoster vaccine?	21.8	28.9
Adults who have had their blood cholesterol checked within the last five years	91.0	85.9

Note: n/a not available; (1) Figures cover the New York-Jersey City-White Plains, NY-NJ Metropolitan Division.
Source: Centers for Disease Control and Prevention, Behaviorial Risk Factor Surveillance System, SMART: Selected Metropolitan Area Risk Trends, 2017

Disability Status

Category	MD[1] (%)	U.S. (%)
Adults who reported being deaf	4.3	6.7
Are you blind or have serious difficulty seeing, even when wearing glasses?	5.0	4.5
Are you limited in any way in any of your usual activities due of arthritis?	10.0	12.9
Do you have difficulty doing errands alone?	6.2	6.8
Do you have difficulty dressing or bathing?	3.8	3.6
Do you have serious difficulty concentrating/remembering/making decisions?	9.2	10.7
Do you have serious difficulty walking or climbing stairs?	12.9	13.6

Note: (1) Figures cover the New York-Jersey City-White Plains, NY-NJ Metropolitan Division.
Source: Centers for Disease Control and Prevention, Behaviorial Risk Factor Surveillance System, SMART: Selected Metropolitan Area Risk Trends, 2017

Mortality Rates for the Top 10 Causes of Death in the U.S.

ICD-10[a] Sub-Chapter	ICD-10[a] Code	Age-Adjusted Mortality Rate[1] per 100,000 population	
		County[2]	U.S.
Malignant neoplasms	C00-C97	131.7	149.2
Ischaemic heart diseases	I20-I25	82.7	90.5
Other forms of heart disease	I30-I51	52.9	52.2
Chronic lower respiratory diseases	J40-J47	23.8	39.6
Other degenerative diseases of the nervous system	G30-G31	20.2	37.6
Cerebrovascular diseases	I60-I69	27.6	37.2
Other external causes of accidental injury	W00-X59	33.6	36.1
Organic, including symptomatic, mental disorders	F01-F09	26.6	29.4
Hypertensive diseases	I10-I15	15.4	24.1
Diabetes mellitus	E10-E14	16.5	21.5

Note: (a) ICD-10 = International Classification of Diseases 10th Revision; (1) Mortality rates are a three-year average covering 2017-2019; (2) Figures cover Middlesex County.
Source: Centers for Disease Control and Prevention, National Center for Health Statistics. Underlying Cause of Death 1999-2019 on CDC WONDER Online Database

Mortality Rates for Selected Causes of Death

ICD-10[a] Sub-Chapter	ICD-10[a] Code	Age-Adjusted Mortality Rate[1] per 100,000 population	
		County[2]	U.S.
Assault	X85-Y09	1.8	6.0
Diseases of the liver	K70-K76	9.0	14.4
Human immunodeficiency virus (HIV) disease	B20-B24	0.9	1.5
Influenza and pneumonia	J09-J18	12.5	13.8
Intentional self-harm	X60-X84	7.5	14.1
Malnutrition	E40-E46	1.3	2.3
Obesity and other hyperalimentation	E65-E68	1.8	2.1
Renal failure	N17-N19	13.8	12.6
Transport accidents	V01-V99	5.1	12.3
Viral hepatitis	B15-B19	Unreliable	1.2

Note: (a) ICD-10 = International Classification of Diseases 10th Revision; (1) Mortality rates are a three-year average covering 2017-2019; (2) Figures cover Middlesex County; Data are suppressed when the data meet the criteria for confidentiality constraints; Mortality rates are flagged as unreliable when the rate would be calculated with a numerator of 20 or less.
Source: Centers for Disease Control and Prevention, National Center for Health Statistics. Underlying Cause of Death 1999-2019 on CDC WONDER Online Database

Health Insurance Coverage

Area	With Health Insurance	With Private Health Insurance	With Public Health Insurance	Without Health Insurance	Population Under Age 19 Without Health Insurance
City	94.6	81.1	22.8	5.4	1.3
MSA[1]	92.8	67.2	36.0	7.2	2.9
U.S.	91.2	67.9	35.1	8.8	5.1

Note: Figures are percentages that cover the civilian noninstitutionalized population; (1) Figures cover the New York-Newark-Jersey City, NY-NJ-PA Metropolitan Statistical Area
Source: U.S. Census Bureau, 2015-2019 American Community Survey 5-Year Estimates

Number of Medical Professionals

Area	MDs[3]	DOs[3,4]	Dentists	Podiatrists	Chiropractors	Optometrists
County[1] (number)	3,098	161	750	82	210	165
County[1] (rate[2])	375.0	19.5	90.9	9.9	25.5	20.0
U.S. (rate[2])	282.9	22.7	71.2	6.2	28.1	16.9

34023
Note: Data as of 2019 unless noted; (1) Data covers Middlesex County; (2) Rate per 100,000 population; (3) Data as of 2018 and includes all active, non-federal physicians; (4) Doctor of Osteopathic Medicine
Source: U.S. Department of Health and Human Services, Health Resources and Services Administration, Bureau of Health Professions, Area Resource File (ARF) 2019-2020

Best Hospitals

According to *U.S. News,* the New York-Jersey City-White Plains, NY-NJ metro area is home to 15 of the best hospitals in the U.S.: **Hackensack University Medical Center** (2 pediatric specialties); **Hospital for Special Surgery** (2 adult specialties and 1 pediatric specialty); **Lenox Hill Hospital** (3 adult specialties); **Manhattan Eye, Ear & Throat Hospital** (3 adult specialties); **Memorial Sloan Kettering Cancer Center** (9 adult specialties and 1 pediatric specialty); **Montefiore Medical Center** (7 adult specialties and 5 pediatric specialties); **Mount Sinai Beth Israel Hospital** (1 adult specialty); **Mount Sinai Hospital** (Honor Roll/11 adult specialties and 4 pediatric specialties); **Mount Sinai Morningside and Mount Sinai West Hospitals** (2 adult specialties); **NYU Langone Hospi-**

tals (Honor Roll/15 adult specialties); **New York Eye and Ear Infirmary of Mount Sinai** (1 adult specialty); **New York-Presbyterian Hospital-Columbia and Cornell** (Honor Roll/15 adult specialties and 8 pediatric specialties); **NYU Langone Orthopedic Hospital** (Honor Roll/15 adult specialties); **Perlmutter Cancer Center at NYU Langone Hospitals** (Honor Roll/15 adult specialties); **Rusk Rehabilitation at NYU Langone Hospitals** (Honor Roll/15 adult specialties). The hospitals listed were nationally ranked in at least one of 16 adult or 10 pediatric specialties. Only 134 hospitals nationwide were nationally ranked in one or more adult or pediatric specialty; this number increases to 178 counting specialized centers within hospitals. Twenty hospitals in the U.S. made the Honor Roll. The Best Hospitals Honor Roll takes both the national rankings and the procedure and condition ratings into account. Hospitals received points if they were nationally ranked in one of the 16 adult specialties—the higher they ranked, the more points they got—and how many ratings of "high performing" they earned in the 10 procedures and conditions. *U.S. News Online, "America's Best Hospitals 2020-21"*

According to *U.S. News,* the New York-Jersey City-White Plains, NY-NJ metro area is home to seven of the best children's hospitals in the U.S.: **Children's Hospital at Montefiore** (5 pediatric specialties); **Children's Hospital at St. Peter's University Hospital** (1 pediatric specialty); **Joseph M. Sanzari Children's Hospital at Hackensack University Medical Center** (2 pediatric specialties); **Lerner Children's Pavilion-Hospital for Special Surgery** (1 pediatric specialty); **Memorial Sloan Kettering Children's Cancer Center** (1 pediatric specialty); **Mount Sinai Kravis Children's Hospital** (4 pediatric specialties); **New York-Presbyterian Hospital-Columbia and Cornell** (8 pediatric specialties). The hospitals listed were highly ranked in at least one of 10 pediatric specialties. Eighty-eight children's hospitals in the U.S. were nationally ranked in at least one specialty. Hospitals received points for being ranked in a specialty, and the 10 hospitals with the most points across the 10 specialties make up the Honor Roll. *U.S. News Online, "America's Best Children's Hospitals 2020-21"*

EDUCATION

Public School District Statistics

District Name	Schls	Pupils	Pupil/ Teacher Ratio	Minority Pupils[1] (%)	Free Lunch Eligible[2] (%)	IEP[3] (%)
Edison Township School District	19	16,494	14.2	86.7	8.8	11.6

Note: Table includes school districts with 2,000 or more students; (1) Percentage of students that are not non-Hispanic white; (2) Percentage of students that are eligible for the free lunch program; (3) Percentage of students that have an Individualized Education Program.
Source: U.S. Department of Education, National Center for Education Statistics, Common Core of Data, Local Education Agency (School District) Universe Survey: School Year 2018-2019; U.S. Department of Education, National Center for Education Statistics, Common Core of Data, Public Elementary/Secondary School Universe Survey: School Year 2018-2019

Best High Schools

According to *U.S. News,* Edison is home to one of the top 500 high schools in the U.S.: **Middlesex County Academy for Science, Mathematics and Engineering Technologies** (#33). Nearly 18,000 public, magnet and charter schools were ranked based on their performance on state assessments and how well they prepare students for college. *U.S. News & World Report, "Best High Schools 2020"*

Highest Level of Education

Area	Less than H.S.	H.S. Diploma	Some College, No Deg.	Associate Degree	Bachelor's Degree	Master's Degree	Prof. School Degree	Doctorate Degree
City	7.9	19.5	11.7	5.4	30.0	20.3	2.8	2.5
MSA[1]	13.5	24.7	14.8	6.7	23.4	12.1	3.3	1.6
U.S.	12.0	27.0	20.4	8.5	19.8	8.8	2.1	1.4

Note: Figures cover persons age 25 and over; (1) Figures cover the New York-Newark-Jersey City, NY-NJ-PA Metropolitan Statistical Area
Source: U.S. Census Bureau, 2015-2019 American Community Survey 5-Year Estimates

Educational Attainment by Race

Area	High School Graduate or Higher (%)					Bachelor's Degree or Higher (%)				
	Total	White	Black	Asian	Hisp.[2]	Total	White	Black	Asian	Hisp.[2]
City	92.1	92.8	94.7	93.0	82.0	55.5	37.2	35.0	77.0	24.1
MSA[1]	86.5	90.8	85.4	83.5	71.4	40.4	46.0	25.6	54.5	19.6
U.S.	88.0	89.9	86.0	87.1	68.7	32.1	33.5	21.6	54.3	16.4

Note: Figures shown cover persons 25 years old and over; (1) Figures cover the New York-Newark-Jersey City, NY-NJ-PA Metropolitan Statistical Area; (2) People of Hispanic origin can be of any race
Source: U.S. Census Bureau, 2015-2019 American Community Survey 5-Year Estimates

School Enrollment by Grade and Control

Area	Preschool (%)		Kindergarten (%)		Grades 1 - 4 (%)		Grades 5 - 8 (%)		Grades 9 - 12 (%)	
	Public	Private	Public	Private	Public	Private	Public	Private	Public	Private
City	30.2	69.8	67.7	32.3	90.1	9.9	90.0	10.0	91.6	8.4
MSA[1]	54.8	45.2	82.3	17.7	85.6	14.4	85.7	14.3	85.1	14.9
U.S.	59.1	40.9	87.6	12.4	89.5	10.5	89.4	10.6	90.1	9.9

Note: Figures shown cover persons 3 years old and over; (1) Figures cover the New York-Newark-Jersey City, NY-NJ-PA Metropolitan Statistical Area
Source: U.S. Census Bureau, 2015-2019 American Community Survey 5-Year Estimates

Higher Education

Four-Year Colleges			Two-Year Colleges			Medical Schools[1]	Law Schools[2]	Voc/ Tech[3]
Public	Private Non-profit	Private For-profit	Public	Private Non-profit	Private For-profit			
0	1	0	1	0	0	0	0	1

Note: Figures cover institutions located within the city limits and include main campuses only; (1) includes schools accredited by the Liaison Committee on Medical Education and the American Osteopathic Association's Commission on Osteopathic College Accreditation; (2) includes ABA-accredited schools, schools with provisional ABA accreditation, and state accredited schools; (3) includes all schools with programs that are less than 2 years.
Source: National Center for Education Statistics, Integrated Postsecondary Education System (IPEDS), 2019-20; Wikipedia, List of Medical Schools in the United States, accessed April 2, 2021; Wikipedia, List of Law Schools in the United States, accessed April 2, 2021

According to *U.S. News & World Report,* the New York-Jersey City-White Plains, NY-NJ metro division is home to nine of the top 200 national universities in the U.S.: **Columbia University** (#3); **New York University** (#30 tie); **Rutgers University—New Brunswick** (#63 tie); **Fordham University** (#66 tie); **Yeshiva University** (#76 tie); **Stevens Institute of Technology** (#80 tie); **The New School** (#133 tie); **St. John's University (NY)** (#170 tie); **CUNY—City College** (#176 tie). The indicators used to capture academic quality fall into a number of categories: assessment by administrators at peer institutions; retention of students; faculty resources; student selectivity; financial resources; alumni giving; high school counselor ratings of colleges; and graduation rate. *U.S. News & World Report, "America's Best Colleges 2021"*

According to *U.S. News & World Report,* the New York-Jersey City-White Plains, NY-NJ metro division is home to three of the top 100 liberal arts colleges in the U.S.: **United States Military Academy** (#15 tie); **Barnard College** (#22 tie); **Sarah Lawrence College** (#63 tie). The indicators used to capture academic quality fall into a number of categories: assessment by administrators at peer institutions; retention of students; faculty resources; student selectivity; financial resources; alumni giving; high school counselor ratings of colleges; and graduation rate. *U.S. News & World Report, "America's Best Colleges 2021"*

According to *U.S. News & World Report,* the New York-Jersey City-White Plains, NY-NJ metro division is home to five of the top 100 law schools in the U.S.: **Columbia University** (#4 tie); **New York University** (#6 tie); **Fordham University** (#35 tie); **Yeshiva University (Cardozo)** (#53 tie); **Brooklyn Law School** (#81 tie). The rankings are based on a weighted average of 12 measures of quality: peer assessment score; assessment score by lawyers/judges; median LSAT scores; median undergrad GPA; acceptance rate; employment rates for graduates; placement success; bar passage rate; faculty resources; expenditures per student; student/faculty ratio; and library resources. *U.S. News & World Report, "America's Best Graduate Schools, Law, 2022"*

According to *U.S. News & World Report,* the New York-Jersey City-White Plains, NY-NJ metro division is home to six of the top 75 medical schools for research in the U.S.: **New York University (Grossman)** (#2); **Columbia University** (#4 tie); **Icahn School of Medicine at Mount Sinai** (#17 tie); **Cornell University (Weill)** (#19 tie); **Albert Einstein College of Medicine** (#39 tie); **Rutgers Robert Wood Johnson Medical School—New Brunswick** (#70). The rankings are based on a weighted average of 11 measures of quality: quality assessment; peer assessment score; assessment score by residency directors; research activity; total research activity; average research activity per faculty member; student selectivity; median MCAT total score; median undergraduate GPA; acceptance rate; and faculty resources. *U.S. News & World Report, "America's Best Graduate Schools, Medical, 2022"*

According to *U.S. News & World Report,* the New York-Jersey City-White Plains, NY-NJ metro division is home to four of the top 75 business schools in the U.S.: **Columbia University** (#7 tie); **New York University (Stern)** (#10 tie); **Fordham University (Gabelli)** (#64 tie); **Stevens Institute of Technology** (#68 tie). The rankings are based on a weighted average of the following nine measures: quality assessment; peer assessment; recruiter assessment; placement success; mean starting salary and bonus; student selectivity; mean GMAT and GRE scores; mean undergraduate GPA; and acceptance rate. *U.S. News & World Report, "America's Best Graduate Schools, Business, 2022"*

EMPLOYERS

Major Employers

Company Name	Industry
American Express Company	Personal credit institutions
American International Group	Life insurance
Deloitte Consulting	Management consulting services
Hackensack University Medical Center	University
Merrill Lynch and Co	Security brokers & dealers
Mount Sinai Hospital	General medical & surgical hospitals
Mount Sinai School of Medicine	Medical training services
New York-Presbyterian Hospital	General medical & surgical hospitals
NYC Health and Hospitals Corp	Psychiatric hospitals
NYU School of Medicine	Offices & clinics of medical doctors
Paramount Comm Acq Corp	Investment holding companies, except banks
Patriarch Partners	Investment offices
Rutgers, The State Univ of NJ	Colleges & universities
Standard Americas	Agencies of foreign banks
The Long Island Rail Road Company	Local & suburban transit
UMASS Memorial Health Care	Psychiatrist
United States Postal Service	U.S. postal service
University of Med and Dentistry of NJ	Colleges & universities
Wellchoice	Health insurance carriers

Note: Companies shown are located within the New York-Newark-Jersey City, NY-NJ-PA Metropolitan Statistical Area.
Source: Hoovers.com; Wikipedia

Best Companies to Work For

Avaap USA, headquartered in Edison, is among the "100 Best Places to Work in IT." To qualify, companies had to be U.S.-based organizations or be non-U.S.-based employers that met the following criteria: have a minimum of 300 total employees at a U.S. headquarters and a minimum of 30 IT employees in the U.S., with at least 50% of their IT employees based in the U.S. The best places to work were selected based on compensation, benefits, work/life balance, employee morale, and satisfaction with training and development programs. In addition, *InsiderPro* and *Computerworld* looked at retention efforts, programs for recognizing and rewarding outstanding performances, and benefits such as flextime, elder care and child care, and reimbursement for college tuition and the cost of pursuing technology certifications. *InsiderPro and Computerworld, "100 Best Places to Work in IT," 2020*

PUBLIC SAFETY

Crime Rate

Area	All Crimes	Violent Crimes				Property Crimes		
		Murder	Rape[3]	Robbery	Aggrav. Assault	Burglary	Larceny -Theft	Motor Vehicle Theft
City	1,450.9	1.0	9.0	18.9	54.8	137.6	1,139.8	89.7
Suburbs[1]	n/a	n/a	n/a	n/a	n/a	n/a	n/a	n/a
Metro[2]	n/a	n/a	n/a	n/a	n/a	n/a	n/a	n/a
U.S.	2,489.3	5.0	42.6	81.6	250.2	340.5	1,549.5	219.9

Note: Figures are crimes per 100,000 population; (1) All areas within the metro area that are located outside the city limits; (2) Figures cover the New York-Jersey City-White Plains, NY-NJ Metropolitan Division; n/a not available; (3) All figures shown were reported using the revised Uniform Crime Reporting (UCR) definition of rape.
Source: FBI Uniform Crime Reports, 2019

Hate Crimes

Area	Number of Quarters Reported	Number of Incidents per Bias Motivation					
		Race/Ethnicity/ Ancestry	Religion	Sexual Orientation	Disability	Gender	Gender Identity
City[1]	4	2	3	0	1	0	0
U.S.	4	3,963	1,521	1,195	157	69	198

Note: (1) Figures include one incident reported with more than one bias motivation.
Source: Federal Bureau of Investigation, Hate Crime Statistics 2019

Identity Theft Consumer Reports

Area	Reports	Reports per 100,000 Population	Rank[2]
MSA[1]	77,363	403	71
U.S.	1,387,615	423	-

Note: (1) Figures cover the New York-Newark-Jersey City, NY-NJ-PA Metropolitan Statistical Area; (2) Rank ranges from 1 to 391 where 1 indicates greatest number of identity theft reports per 100,000 population
Source: Federal Trade Commission, Consumer Sentinel Network Data Book 2020

Fraud and Other Consumer Reports

Area	Reports	Reports per 100,000 Population	Rank[2]
MSA[1]	172,473	898	49
U.S.	3,385,133	1,031	-

Note: (1) Figures cover the New York-Newark-Jersey City, NY-NJ-PA Metropolitan Statistical Area; (2) Rank ranges from 1 to 391 where 1 indicates greatest number of fraud and other consumer reports per 100,000 population
Source: Federal Trade Commission, Consumer Sentinel Network Data Book 2020

POLITICS

2020 Presidential Election Results

Area	Biden	Trump	Jorgensen	Hawkins	Other
Middlesex County	60.2	38.2	0.7	0.3	0.6
U.S.	51.3	46.8	1.2	0.3	0.5

Note: Results are percentages and may not add to 100% due to rounding
Source: Dave Leip's Atlas of U.S. Presidential Elections

SPORTS

Professional Sports Teams

Team Name	League	Year Established
Brooklyn Nets	National Basketball Association (NBA)	1967
New Jersey Devils	National Hockey League (NHL)	1982
New York City FC	Major League Soccer (MLS)	2015
New York Giants	National Football League (NFL)	1925
New York Islanders	National Hockey League (NHL)	1972
New York Jets	National Football League (NFL)	1960
New York Knicks	National Basketball Association (NBA)	1946
New York Mets	Major League Baseball (MLB)	1962
New York Rangers	National Hockey League (NHL)	1926
New York Red Bulls	Major League Soccer (MLS)	1996
New York Yankees	Major League Baseball (MLB)	1903

Note: Includes teams located in the New York-Newark-Jersey City, NY-NJ-PA Metropolitan Statistical Area.
Source: Wikipedia, Major Professional Sports Teams of the United States and Canada, April 6, 2021

CLIMATE

Average and Extreme Temperatures

Temperature	Jan	Feb	Mar	Apr	May	Jun	Jul	Aug	Sep	Oct	Nov	Dec	Yr.
Extreme High (°F)	74	76	89	94	98	102	105	103	105	93	85	72	105
Average High (°F)	38	41	50	61	72	81	86	84	77	66	54	42	63
Average Temp. (°F)	32	33	42	52	63	72	77	76	68	57	47	36	55
Average Low (°F)	24	25	33	43	53	62	68	67	59	48	39	28	46
Extreme Low (°F)	-8	-7	6	16	33	41	52	45	35	25	15	-1	-8

Note: Figures cover the years 1935-1995
Source: National Climatic Data Center, International Station Meteorological Climate Summary, 9/96

Average Precipitation/Snowfall/Humidity

Precip./Humidity	Jan	Feb	Mar	Apr	May	Jun	Jul	Aug	Sep	Oct	Nov	Dec	Yr.
Avg. Precip. (in.)	3.4	3.0	4.0	3.7	3.9	3.3	4.2	4.1	3.6	3.0	3.8	3.4	43.5
Avg. Snowfall (in.)	8	8	5	1	Tr	0	0	0	0	Tr	1	5	27
Avg. Rel. Hum. 7am (%)	73	71	69	67	70	71	72	76	79	78	76	74	73
Avg. Rel. Hum. 4pm (%)	58	54	51	48	51	51	52	54	55	53	57	59	54

Note: Figures cover the years 1935-1995; Tr = Trace amounts (<0.05 in. of rain; <0.5 in. of snow)
Source: National Climatic Data Center, International Station Meteorological Climate Summary, 9/96

Weather Conditions

Temperature			Daytime Sky			Precipitation		
5°F & below	32°F & below	90°F & above	Clear	Partly cloudy	Cloudy	0.01 inch or more precip.	0.1 inch or more snow/ice	Thunderstorms
2	90	24	80	146	139	122	16	46

Note: Figures are average number of days per year and cover the years 1935-1995
Source: National Climatic Data Center, International Station Meteorological Climate Summary, 9/96

HAZARDOUS WASTE

Superfund Sites

The New York-Jersey City-White Plains, NY-NJ metro division is home to 49 sites on the EPA's Superfund National Priorities List: **Atlantic Resources** (final); **Bog Creek Farm** (final); **Brick Township Landfill** (final); **Burnt Fly Bog** (final); **Carroll & Dubies Sewage Disposal** (final); **Chemical Insecticide Corp.** (final); **Chemsol, Inc.** (final); **Ciba-Geigy Corp.** (final); **Cornell Dubilier Electronics Inc.** (final); **CPS/Madison Industries** (final); **Curcio Scrap Metal, Inc.** (final); **Diamond Head Oil Refinery Division** (final); **Evor Phillips Leasing** (final); **Fair Lawn Well**

Field (final); **Fried Industries** (final); **Garfield Ground Water Contamination** (final); **Global Sanitary Landfill** (final); **Goose Farm** (final); **Gowanus Canal** (final); **Horseshoe Road** (final); **Hudson Technologies, Inc.** (proposed); **Imperial Oil Co., Inc./Champion Chemicals** (final); **JIS Landfill** (final); **Kin-Buc Landfill** (final); **Lone Pine Landfill** (final); **Magna Metals** (final); **Maywood Chemical Co.** (final); **Middlesex Sampling Plant (USDOE)** (final); **Monitor Devices, Inc./Intercircuits, Inc.** (final); **Naval Air Engineering Center** (final); **Naval Weapons Station Earle (Site A)** (final); **Nepera Chemical Co., Inc.** (final); **Newtown Creek** (final); **PJP Landfill** (final); **Quanta Resources** (final); **Ramapo Landfill** (final); **Raritan Bay Slag** (final); **Reich Farms** (final); **Ringwood Mines/Landfill** (final); **Scientific Chemical Processing** (final); **Standard Chlorine** (final); **Syncon Resins** (final); **Universal Oil Products (Chemical Division)** (final); **Ventron/Velsicol** (final); **Waldick Aerospace Devices, Inc.** (final); **White Swan Laundry and Cleaner Inc.** (final); **Wolff-Alport Chemical Company** (final); **Woodbrook Road Dump** (final); **Zschiegner Refining** (final). There are a total of 1,375 Superfund sites with a status of proposed or final on the list in the U.S. *U.S. Environmental Protection Agency, National Priorities List, April 7, 2021*

AIR QUALITY

Air Quality Trends: Ozone

	1990	1995	2000	2005	2010	2015	2016	2017	2018	2019
MSA[1]	0.101	0.106	0.090	0.091	0.081	0.075	0.073	0.070	0.073	0.067
U.S.	0.088	0.089	0.082	0.080	0.073	0.068	0.069	0.068	0.069	0.065

Note: (1) Data covers the New York-Newark-Jersey City, NY-NJ-PA Metropolitan Statistical Area. The values shown are the composite ozone concentration averages among trend sites based on the highest fourth daily maximum 8-hour concentration in parts per million. These trends are based on sites having an adequate record of monitoring data during the trend period. Data from exceptional events are included.
Source: U.S. Environmental Protection Agency, Air Quality Monitoring Information, "Air Quality Trends by City, 1990-2019"

Air Quality Index

Area	Percent of Days when Air Quality was...[2]					AQI Statistics[2]	
	Good	Moderate	Unhealthy for Sensitive Groups	Unhealthy	Very Unhealthy	Maximum	Median
MSA[1]	46.3	49.3	4.4	0.0	0.0	150	51

Note: (1) Data covers the New York-Newark-Jersey City, NY-NJ-PA Metropolitan Statistical Area; (2) Based on 365 days with AQI data in 2019. Air Quality Index (AQI) is an index for reporting daily air quality. EPA calculates the AQI for five major air pollutants regulated by the Clean Air Act: ground-level ozone, particle pollution (aka particulate matter), carbon monoxide, sulfur dioxide, and nitrogen dioxide. The AQI runs from 0 to 500. The higher the AQI value, the greater the level of air pollution and the greater the health concern. There are six AQI categories: "Good" AQI is between 0 and 50. Air quality is considered satisfactory; "Moderate" AQI is between 51 and 100. Air quality is acceptable; "Unhealthy for Sensitive Groups" When AQI values are between 101 and 150, members of sensitive groups may experience health effects; "Unhealthy" When AQI values are between 151 and 200 everyone may begin to experience health effects; "Very Unhealthy" AQI values between 201 and 300 trigger a health alert; "Hazardous" AQI values over 300 trigger warnings of emergency conditions (not shown).
Source: U.S. Environmental Protection Agency, Air Quality Index Report, 2019

Air Quality Index Pollutants

Area	Percent of Days when AQI Pollutant was...[2]					
	Carbon Monoxide	Nitrogen Dioxide	Ozone	Sulfur Dioxide	Particulate Matter 2.5	Particulate Matter 10
MSA[1]	0.0	17.5	39.2	0.0	43.3	0.0

Note: (1) Data covers the New York-Newark-Jersey City, NY-NJ-PA Metropolitan Statistical Area; (2) Based on 365 days with AQI data in 2019. The Air Quality Index (AQI) is an index for reporting daily air quality. EPA calculates the AQI for five major air pollutants regulated by the Clean Air Act: ground-level ozone, particle pollution (also known as particulate matter), carbon monoxide, sulfur dioxide, and nitrogen dioxide. The AQI runs from 0 to 500. The higher the AQI value, the greater the level of air pollution and the greater the health concern.
Source: U.S. Environmental Protection Agency, Air Quality Index Report, 2019

Maximum Air Pollutant Concentrations: Particulate Matter, Ozone, CO and Lead

	Particulate Matter 10 (ug/m^3)	Particulate Matter 2.5 Wtd AM (ug/m^3)	Particulate Matter 2.5 24-Hr (ug/m^3)	Ozone (ppm)	Carbon Monoxide (ppm)	Lead (ug/m^3)
MSA[1] Level	34	11.0	24	0.073	2	n/a
NAAQS[2]	150	15	35	0.075	9	0.15
Met NAAQS[2]	Yes	Yes	Yes	Yes	Yes	n/a

Note: (1) Data covers the New York-Newark-Jersey City, NY-NJ-PA Metropolitan Statistical Area; Data from exceptional events are included; (2) National Ambient Air Quality Standards; ppm = parts per million; ug/m^3 = micrograms per cubic meter; n/a not available.
Concentrations: Particulate Matter 10 (coarse particulate)—highest second maximum 24-hour concentration; Particulate Matter 2.5 Wtd AM (fine particulate)—highest weighted annual mean concentration; Particulate Matter 2.5 24-Hour (fine particulate)—highest 98th percentile 24-hour concentration; Ozone—highest fourth daily maximum 8-hour concentration; Carbon Monoxide—highest second maximum non-overlapping 8-hour concentration; Lead—maximum running 3-month average
Source: U.S. Environmental Protection Agency, Air Quality Monitoring Information, "Air Quality Statistics by City, 2019"

Maximum Air Pollutant Concentrations: Nitrogen Dioxide and Sulfur Dioxide

	Nitrogen Dioxide AM (ppb)	Nitrogen Dioxide 1-Hr (ppb)	Sulfur Dioxide AM (ppb)	Sulfur Dioxide 1-Hr (ppb)	Sulfur Dioxide 24-Hr (ppb)
MSA[1] Level	21	66	n/a	11	n/a
NAAQS[2]	53	100	30	75	140
Met NAAQS[2]	Yes	Yes	n/a	Yes	n/a

Note: (1) Data covers the New York-Newark-Jersey City, NY-NJ-PA Metropolitan Statistical Area; Data from exceptional events are included; (2) National Ambient Air Quality Standards; ppm = parts per million; ug/m^3 = micrograms per cubic meter; n/a not available.
Concentrations: Nitrogen Dioxide AM—highest arithmetic mean concentration; Nitrogen Dioxide 1-Hr—highest 98th percentile 1-hour daily maximum concentration; Sulfur Dioxide AM—highest annual mean concentration; Sulfur Dioxide 1-Hr—highest 99th percentile 1-hour daily maximum concentration; Sulfur Dioxide 24-Hr—highest second maximum 24-hour concentration
Source: U.S. Environmental Protection Agency, Air Quality Monitoring Information, "Air Quality Statistics by City, 2019"

Fayetteville, North Carolina

Background

Fayetteville, the first town named after a revolutionary war hero—Marquis de Lafayette—is located on the Cape Fear River, about 100 miles from the coast. Most rivers in North Carolina flow south into South Carolina, but the Cape Fear flows in a more easterly direction, making it an important inland port of entry for North Carolina. Originally established as a trading post, Fayetteville's location and rich river-bottom soil made the area an important place for early settlement—evidenced by shiploads of Scottish Highlanders who settled in the area around 1739. Later, the community of Scots had divided loyalties with men fighting on either side during the American Revolution. With the *Liberty Point Resolve* of 1775, the local population pledged its allegiance to the revolutionary cause.

In 1793, George Washington chartered the Fayetteville Independent Light Infantry, one of the oldest military units in continuous service in the south, though today its role is largely ceremonial. The FILI sparked great controversy in the Spanish-American War by refusing to retire the Confederate Grey—an action that would preclude them from entering the North Carolina state guard. To this day, the military is still the heart and soul of the Fayetteville community.

Following the American Revolution, Fayetteville experienced a boom, both politically and economically. The state Constitution was ratified in Fayetteville, and many thought the city would become the new state capital. In addition, the charter for the University of North Carolina was created, the first of its kind in the country. During these years, free black minister Henry Evans fathered Fayetteville's first church, as he preached to black slaves.

North Carolina had a southern, agrarian culture and, as such, supported the Confederacy during the Civil War. General William Sherman's troop spent two days in Fayetteville, destroying the Confederacy's arsenal manufacturing facilities, as well as the town's foundries, cotton factories, and news organizations. During Reconstruction, Fayetteville created one of three schools dedicated to educating freed slaves. One of these, the Howard School, evolved into today's Fayetteville State University.

The military remains integral, both economically and socially, in Fayetteville. Fort Bragg, named after Confederate commander General Braxton Bragg, was established in 1918 as an artillery training ground. The fort was nearly closed following World War I, but a visit from the Secretary of War, Newton Baker, saved the base. In 1922, the Field Artillery Board was relocated there, and in 1952, the Army established the Psychological Warfare Center at Fort Bragg. Today, Bragg is the largest Army base in the country, absorbing in 2005 the base at McPherson, GA and in 2011, the Pope Air Force Base. Since 2000, Fort Bragg's population has increased over 65 percent. Fort Bragg remains one of the largest military complexes in the world, employing over 68,000: 57,000 military personnel; 11,000 civilian employees; and 23,000 family members. It occupies nearly 250 square miles.

Following World War II, Fayetteville began a cultural initiative with the Fayetteville Symphony. The Fayetteville Art Museum was established in 1972. It is also home of the Cape Fear Museum of history. In recent years, Fayetteville has honored its past by painstakingly restoring its historic districts—nine in all. The Cape Fear Botanical Garden sits atop land where Fayetteville's early settlers first built their homes. The gardens include two children's gardens. The Lilliput Labyrinth features giant-sized sculptures. A recent addition to Fayetteville's cultural landscape is the Airborne and Special Operations Museum. In addition, Fayetteville is home to three universities—Fayetteville State University, Methodist College, and Fayetteville Technical Community College.

Fayetteville has a subtropical climate, with mostly moderate temperatures year round. Winters are mild, but can get cool with snow occurring a few days per year. Summers are hot and humid with a risk of thunderstorms and rain showers. Temperatures range from -5 °F on January 21, 1985 to 110 °F on August 21, 1983, the highest temperature ever recorded in the State of North Carolina. In April, 2011, Fayetteville was struck by an EF3 tornado during North Carolina's largest tornado outbreak.

Rankings

General Rankings

- For its "Best for Vets: Places to Live 2019" rankings, *Military Times* evaluated 599 cities (83 large, 234 medium, 282 small) and compared the locations across three broad categories: veteran and military culture/services; economic indicators; and livability factors such as health, crime, traffic, and school quality. Fayetteville ranked #50 out of the top 50, in the medium-sized city category (population of 100,000-249,999). Data points more specific to veterans and the military weighed more heavily than others. *rebootcamp.militarytimes.com, "Military Times Best Places to Live 2019," September 10, 2018*

Business/Finance Rankings

- The Fayetteville metro area appeared on the Milken Institute "2021 Best Performing Cities" list. Rank: #183 out of 200 large metro areas (population over 250,000). Criteria: job growth; wage and salary growth; high-tech output growth; housing affordability; household broadband access. *Milken Institute, "Best-Performing Cities 2021," February 16, 2021*

- *Forbes* ranked the 200 most populous metro areas to determine the nation's "Best Places for Business and Careers." The Fayetteville metro area was ranked #186. Criteria: costs (business and living); job growth (past and projected); income growth; quality of life; educational attainment (college and high school); projected economic growth; cultural and leisure opportunities; workplace tolerance laws; net migration patterns. *Forbes, "The Best Places for Business and Careers 2019: Seattle Still On Top," October 30, 2019*

Education Rankings

- Personal finance website *WalletHub* analyzed the 150 largest U.S. metropolitan statistical areas to determine where the most educated Americans are putting their degrees to work. Criteria: education levels; percentage of workers with degrees; education quality and attainment gap; public school quality rankings; quality and enrollment of each metro area's universities. Fayetteville was ranked #101 (#1 = most educated city). *www.WalletHub.com, "Most and Least Educated Cities in America, " July 20, 2020*

Environmental Rankings

- Fayetteville was highlighted as one of the cleanest metro areas for ozone air pollution in the U.S. during 2016 through 2018. The list represents cities with no monitored ozone air pollution in unhealthful ranges. *American Lung Association, "State of the Air 2020," April 21, 2020*

- Fayetteville was highlighted as one of the top 98 cleanest metro areas for short-term particle pollution (24-hour PM 2.5) in the U.S. during 2016 through 2018. Monitors in these cities reported no days with unhealthful PM 2.5 levels. *American Lung Association, "State of the Air 2020," April 21, 2020*

Real Estate Rankings

- *WalletHub* compared the most populated U.S. cities to determine which had the best markets for real estate agents. Fayetteville ranked #174 where demand was high and pay was the best. Criteria: sales per agent; annual median wage for real-estate agents; monthly average starting salary for real estate agents; real estate job density and competition; unemployment rate; home turnover rate; housing-market health index; and other relevant metrics. *www.WalletHub.com, "2019's Best Places to Be a Real Estate Agent," April 24, 2019*

- Fayetteville was ranked #105 out of 268 metro areas in terms of housing affordability in 2020 by the National Association of Home Builders (#1 = most affordable). Criteria: the share of homes sold in that area affordable to a family earning the local median income, based on standard mortgage underwriting criteria. *National Association of Home Builders®, NAHB-Wells Fargo Housing Opportunity Index, 4th Quarter 2020*

Safety Rankings

- To identify the most dangerous cities in America, 24/7 Wall Street focused on violent crime categories—murder, non-negligent manslaughter, rape, robbery, and aggravated assault—and property crime as reported in the FBI's 2019 annual Uniform Crime Report. Criteria also included median income from American Community Survey and unemployment figures from Bureau of Labor Statistics. For cities with populations over 100,000, Fayetteville was ranked #40. *247wallst.com, "America's 50 Most Dangerous Cities" November 16, 2020*

- Allstate ranked the 200 largest cities in America in terms of driver safety. Fayetteville ranked #43. Criteria: internal property damage claims over a two-year period from January 2016 to December 2017. The report helps increase the importance of safety and awareness behind the wheel. *Allstate, "Allstate America's Best Drivers Report, 2019" June 24, 2019*

- Fayetteville was identified as one of the most dangerous cities in America by NeighborhoodScout. The city ranked #91 out of 100 (#1 = most dangerous). Criteria: number of violent crimes per 1,000 residents. The editors evaluated cities with 25,000 or more residents. *NeighborhoodScout.com, "2021 Top 100 Most Dangerous Cities in the U.S.," January 2, 2021*

- The National Insurance Crime Bureau ranked 384 metro areas in the U.S. in terms of per capita rates of vehicle theft. The Fayetteville metro area ranked #170 (#1 = highest rate). Criteria: number of vehicle theft offenses per 100,000 inhabitants in 2019. *National Insurance Crime Bureau, "Hot Spots 2019," July 21, 2020*

Seniors/Retirement Rankings

- From its Best Cities for Successful Aging indexes, the Milken Institute generated rankings for metropolitan areas, weighing data in nine categories—health care, wellness, living arrangements, transportation and convenience, financial characteristics, education, employment, community engagement, and overall livability. The Fayetteville metro area was ranked #165 overall in the small metro area category. *Milken Institute, "Best Cities for Successful Aging, 2017" March 14, 2017*

Women/Minorities Rankings

- Personal finance website *WalletHub* compared more than 180 U.S. cities across two key dimensions, "Hispanic Business-Friendliness" and "Hispanic Purchasing Power," to arrive at the most favorable conditions for Hispanic entrepreneurs. Fayetteville was ranked #140 out of 182. Criteria includes: share of Hispanic-Owned Businesses; Hispanic entrepreneurship rate to median annual income of Hispanics; Small Business-Friendliness score; cost of living; and number of Hispanics with at least a bachelor's degree. *WalletHub.com, "2019's Best Cities for Hispanic Entrepreneurs," May 1, 2019*

Business Environment

DEMOGRAPHICS

Population Growth

Area	1990 Census	2000 Census	2010 Census	2019* Estimate	Population Growth (%) 1990-2019	Population Growth (%) 2010-2019
City	118,247	121,015	200,564	210,432	78.0	4.9
MSA[1]	297,422	336,609	366,383	519,101	74.5	41.7
U.S.	248,709,873	281,421,906	308,745,538	324,697,795	30.6	5.2

Note: (1) Figures cover the Fayetteville, NC Metropolitan Statistical Area; (*) 2015-2019 5-year estimated population
Source: U.S. Census Bureau, 1990 Census, Census 2000, Census 2010, 2015-2019 American Community Survey 5-Year Estimates

Household Size

Area	One	Two	Three	Four	Five	Six	Seven or More	Average Household Size
City	35.6	31.4	15.3	10.7	4.3	1.9	0.8	2.40
MSA[1]	30.7	31.6	16.1	12.5	5.8	2.3	1.1	2.60
U.S.	27.9	33.9	15.6	12.9	6.0	2.3	1.4	2.60

Note: (1) Figures cover the Fayetteville, NC Metropolitan Statistical Area
Source: U.S. Census Bureau, 2015-2019 American Community Survey 5-Year Estimates

Race

Area	White Alone[2] (%)	Black Alone[2] (%)	Asian Alone[2] (%)	AIAN[3] Alone[2] (%)	NHOPI[4] Alone[2] (%)	Other Race Alone[2] (%)	Two or More Races (%)
City	44.6	42.1	2.9	1.1	0.4	2.9	6.1
MSA[1]	53.8	32.6	2.0	2.0	0.3	4.1	5.3
U.S.	72.5	12.7	5.5	0.8	0.2	4.9	3.3

Note: (1) Figures cover the Fayetteville, NC Metropolitan Statistical Area; (2) Alone is defined as not being in combination with one or more other races; (3) American Indian and Alaska Native; (4) Native Hawaiian and Other Pacific Islander
Source: U.S. Census Bureau, 2015-2019 American Community Survey 5-Year Estimates

Hispanic or Latino Origin

Area	Total (%)	Mexican (%)	Puerto Rican (%)	Cuban (%)	Other (%)
City	12.4	4.2	4.1	0.4	3.7
MSA[1]	12.1	5.3	3.5	0.3	2.9
U.S.	18.0	11.2	1.7	0.7	4.3

Note: Persons of Hispanic or Latino origin can be of any race; (1) Figures cover the Fayetteville, NC Metropolitan Statistical Area
Source: U.S. Census Bureau, 2015-2019 American Community Survey 5-Year Estimates

Ancestry

Area	German	Irish	English	American	Italian	Polish	French[2]	Scottish	Dutch
City	8.8	6.9	6.6	3.9	2.8	1.4	1.5	1.8	0.6
MSA[1]	8.7	7.0	6.6	5.6	3.0	1.4	1.5	2.2	0.6
U.S.	13.3	9.7	7.2	6.2	5.1	2.8	2.3	1.7	1.2

Note: Figures are the percentage of the total population reporting a particular ancestry. The nine most commonly reported ancestries in the U.S. are shown. Figures include multiple ancestries (e.g. if a person reported being Irish and Italian, they were included in both columns); (1) Figures cover the Fayetteville, NC Metropolitan Statistical Area; (2) Excludes Basque
Source: U.S. Census Bureau, 2015-2019 American Community Survey 5-Year Estimates

Foreign-born Population

Area	Any Foreign Country	Asia	Mexico	Europe	Caribbean	Central America[2]	South America	Africa	Canada
City	7.1	2.3	0.6	1.0	0.9	0.8	0.6	0.6	0.1
MSA[1]	6.2	1.6	1.4	0.9	0.7	0.8	0.4	0.3	0.1
U.S.	13.6	4.2	3.5	1.5	1.3	1.1	1.0	0.7	0.2

Note: (1) Figures cover the Fayetteville, NC Metropolitan Statistical Area; (2) Excludes Mexico.
Source: U.S. Census Bureau, 2015-2019 American Community Survey 5-Year Estimates

Marital Status

Area	Never Married	Now Married[2]	Separated	Widowed	Divorced
City	38.4	40.7	3.6	5.5	11.8
MSA[1]	33.8	46.1	3.2	5.8	11.2
U.S.	33.4	48.1	1.9	5.8	10.9

Note: Figures are percentages and cover the population 15 years of age and older; (1) Figures cover the Fayetteville, NC Metropolitan Statistical Area; (2) Excludes separated
Source: U.S. Census Bureau, 2015-2019 American Community Survey 5-Year Estimates

Disability by Age

Area	All Ages	Under 18 Years Old	18 to 64 Years Old	65 Years and Over
City	17.5	6.7	16.6	44.5
MSA[1]	16.4	6.0	15.7	43.7
U.S.	12.6	4.2	10.3	34.5

Note: Figures show percent of the civilian noninstitutionalized population that reported having a disability. Disability status is determined from six types of difficulty: vision, hearing, cognitive, ambulatory, self-care, and independent living. For children under 5 years old, hearing and vision difficulty are used to determine disability status. For children between the ages of 5 and 14, disability status is determined from hearing, vision, cognitive, ambulatory, and self-care difficulties. For people aged 15 years and older, they are considered to have a disability if they have difficulty with any one of the six difficulty types; Note: (1) Figures cover the Fayetteville, NC Metropolitan Statistical Area
Source: U.S. Census Bureau, 2015-2019 American Community Survey 5-Year Estimates

Age

Area	Percent of Population									Median Age
	Under Age 5	Age 5–19	Age 20–34	Age 35–44	Age 45–54	Age 55–64	Age 65–74	Age 75–84	Age 85+	
City	7.7	18.9	30.9	11.0	9.8	10.1	6.7	3.5	1.4	30.0
MSA[1]	7.7	20.7	25.7	12.5	11.4	10.6	7.0	3.4	1.1	32.3
U.S.	6.1	19.1	20.7	12.6	13.0	12.9	9.1	4.6	1.9	38.1

Note: (1) Figures cover the Fayetteville, NC Metropolitan Statistical Area
Source: U.S. Census Bureau, 2015-2019 American Community Survey 5-Year Estimates

Gender

Area	Males	Females	Males per 100 Females
City	105,869	104,563	101.2
MSA[1]	257,939	261,162	98.8
U.S.	159,886,919	164,810,876	97.0

Note: (1) Figures cover the Fayetteville, NC Metropolitan Statistical Area
Source: U.S. Census Bureau, 2015-2019 American Community Survey 5-Year Estimates

Religious Groups by Family

Area	Catholic	Baptist	Non-Den.	Methodist[2]	Lutheran	LDS[3]	Pente-costal	Presby-terian[4]	Muslim[5]	Judaism
MSA[1]	2.6	14.1	10.5	6.2	0.2	1.4	4.9	2.1	0.2	<0.1
U.S.	19.1	9.3	4.0	4.0	2.3	1.9	1.9	1.6	0.8	0.7

Note: Figures are the number of adherents as a percentage of the total population; (1) Figures cover the Fayetteville, NC Metropolitan Statistical Area; (2) Methodist/Pietist; (3) Latter Day Saints; (4) Reformed; (5) Figures are estimates
Source: Association of Statisticians of American Religious Bodies, 2010 U.S. Religion Census: Religious Congregations & Membership Study

Religious Groups by Tradition

Area	Catholic	Evangelical Protestant	Mainline Protestant	Other Tradition	Black Protestant	Orthodox
MSA[1]	2.6	26.7	7.9	1.8	4.3	0.1
U.S.	19.1	16.2	7.3	4.3	1.6	0.3

Note: Figures are the number of adherents as a percentage of the total population; (1) Figures cover the Fayetteville, NC Metropolitan Statistical Area
Source: Association of Statisticians of American Religious Bodies, 2010 U.S. Religion Census: Religious Congregations & Membership Study

ECONOMY

Gross Metropolitan Product

Area	2017	2018	2019	2020	Rank[2]
MSA[1]	17.2	17.6	18.1	18.8	149

Note: Figures are in billions of dollars; (1) Figures cover the Fayetteville, NC Metropolitan Statistical Area; (2) Rank is based on 2018 data and ranges from 1 to 381
Source: U.S. Conference of Mayors, U.S. Metro Economies: GMP & Employment 2018-2020, September 2019

Economic Growth

Area	2015-17 (%)	2018 (%)	2019 (%)	2020 (%)	Rank[2]
MSA[1]	-1.0	0.0	1.2	1.5	343
U.S.	1.9	2.9	2.3	2.1	—

Note: Figures are real gross metropolitan product (GMP) growth rates and represent average annual percent change; (1) Figures cover the Fayetteville, NC Metropolitan Statistical Area; (2) Rank is based on 2017 2-year average annual percent change and ranges from 1 to 381
Source: U.S. Conference of Mayors, U.S. Metro Economies: GMP & Employment 2018-2020, September 2019

Metropolitan Area Exports

Area	2014	2015	2016	2017	2018	2019	Rank[2]
MSA[1]	375.8	256.3	179.8	231.6	260.5	287.8	263

Note: Figures are in millions of dollars; (1) Figures cover the Fayetteville, NC Metropolitan Statistical Area; (2) Rank is based on 2019 data and ranges from 1 to 386
Source: U.S. Department of Commerce, International Trade Administration, Office of Trade and Economic Analysis, Industry and Analysis, Exports by Metropolitan Area, data extracted March 24, 2021

Building Permits

Area	Single-Family			Multi-Family			Total		
	2018	2019	Pct. Chg.	2018	2019	Pct. Chg.	2018	2019	Pct. Chg.
City	241	240	-0.4	0	282	—	241	522	116.6
MSA[1]	803	1,547	92.7	16	292	1,725.0	819	1,839	124.5
U.S.	855,300	862,100	0.7	473,500	523,900	10.6	1,328,800	1,386,000	4.3

Note: (1) Figures cover the Fayetteville, NC Metropolitan Statistical Area; Figures represent new, privately-owned housing units authorized (unadjusted data); All permit data are based on estimates with imputation
Source: U.S. Census Bureau, Manufacturing, Mining, and Construction Statistics, Building Permits, 2018, 2019

Bankruptcy Filings

Area	Business Filings			Nonbusiness Filings		
	2019	2020	% Chg.	2019	2020	% Chg.
Cumberland County	8	8	0.0	795	506	-36.4
U.S.	22,780	21,655	-4.9	752,160	522,808	-30.5

Note: Business filings include Chapter 7, Chapter 9, Chapter 11, Chapter 12, Chapter 13, Chapter 15, and Section 304; Nonbusiness filings include Chapter 7, Chapter 11, and Chapter 13
Source: Administrative Office of the U.S. Courts, Business and Nonbusiness Bankruptcy, County Cases Commenced by Chapter of the Bankruptcy Code, During the 12-Month Period Ending December 31, 2019 and Business and Nonbusiness Bankruptcy, County Cases Commenced by Chapter of the Bankruptcy Code, During the 12-Month Period Ending December 31, 2020

Housing Vacancy Rates

Area	Gross Vacancy Rate[2] (%)			Year-Round Vacancy Rate[3] (%)			Rental Vacancy Rate[4] (%)			Homeowner Vacancy Rate[5] (%)		
	2018	2019	2020	2018	2019	2020	2018	2019	2020	2018	2019	2020
MSA[1]	n/a	n/a	n/a	n/a	n/a	n/a	n/a	n/a	n/a	n/a	n/a	n/a
U.S.	12.3	12.0	10.6	9.7	9.5	8.2	6.9	6.7	6.3	1.5	1.4	1.0

Note: (1) Figures cover the Fayetteville, NC Metropolitan Statistical Area; (2) The percentage of the total housing inventory that is vacant; (3) The percentage of the housing inventory (excluding seasonal units) that is year-round vacant; (4) The percentage of rental inventory that is vacant for rent; (5) The percentage of homeowner inventory that is vacant for sale; n/a not available
Source: U.S. Census Bureau, Housing Vacancies and Homeownership Annual Statistics: 2018, 2019, 2020

INCOME

Income

Area	Per Capita ($)	Median Household ($)	Average Household ($)
City	24,823	45,024	58,752
MSA[1]	24,228	48,459	61,989
U.S.	34,103	62,843	88,607

Note: (1) Figures cover the Fayetteville, NC Metropolitan Statistical Area
Source: U.S. Census Bureau, 2015-2019 American Community Survey 5-Year Estimates

Household Income Distribution

Area	Percent of Households Earning							
	Under $15,000	$15,000 -$24,999	$25,000 -$34,999	$35,000 -$49,999	$50,000 -$74,999	$75,000 -$99,999	$100,000 -$149,999	$150,000 and up
City	14.5	12.0	12.4	16.4	19.2	11.1	9.3	5.2
MSA[1]	13.8	11.1	11.2	15.5	18.9	12.5	11.5	5.6
U.S.	10.3	8.9	8.9	12.3	17.2	12.7	15.1	14.5

Note: (1) Figures cover the Fayetteville, NC Metropolitan Statistical Area
Source: U.S. Census Bureau, 2015-2019 American Community Survey 5-Year Estimates

Poverty Rate

Area	All Ages	Under 18 Years Old	18 to 64 Years Old	65 Years and Over
City	19.3	28.0	17.4	11.6
MSA[1]	17.9	24.8	16.3	11.4
U.S.	13.4	18.5	12.6	9.3

Note: Figures are percentage of people whose income during the past 12 months was below the poverty level;
(1) Figures cover the Fayetteville, NC Metropolitan Statistical Area
Source: U.S. Census Bureau, 2015-2019 American Community Survey 5-Year Estimates

CITY FINANCES

City Government Finances

Component	2017 ($000)	2017 ($ per capita)
Total Revenues	202,619	1,003
Total Expenditures	207,666	1,028
Debt Outstanding	312,500	1,547
Cash and Securities[1]	4,689	23

Note: (1) Cash and security holdings of a government at the close of its fiscal year,
including those of its dependent agencies, utilities, and liquor stores.
Source: U.S. Census Bureau, State & Local Government Finances 2017

City Government Revenue by Source

Source	2017 ($000)	2017 ($ per capita)	2017 (%)
General Revenue			
From Federal Government	22,165	110	10.9
From State Government	27,720	137	13.7
From Local Governments	14,960	74	7.4
Taxes			
Property	71,975	356	35.5
Sales and Gross Receipts	32,233	160	15.9
Personal Income	0	0	0.0
Corporate Income	0	0	0.0
Motor Vehicle License	1,974	10	1.0
Other Taxes	2,093	10	1.0
Current Charges	19,711	98	9.7
Liquor Store	0	0	0.0
Utility	1,374	7	0.7
Employee Retirement	443	2	0.2

Source: U.S. Census Bureau, State & Local Government Finances 2017

City Government Expenditures by Function

Function	2017 ($000)	2017 ($ per capita)	2017 (%)
General Direct Expenditures			
Air Transportation	7,782	38	3.7
Corrections	0	0	0.0
Education	0	0	0.0
Employment Security Administration	0	0	0.0
Financial Administration	2,917	14	1.4
Fire Protection	26,835	132	12.9
General Public Buildings	1,552	7	0.7
Governmental Administration, Other	10,481	51	5.0
Health	0	0	0.0
Highways	15,523	76	7.5
Hospitals	0	0	0.0
Housing and Community Development	5,451	27	2.6
Interest on General Debt	13,292	65	6.4
Judicial and Legal	1,340	6	0.6
Libraries	0	0	0.0
Parking	330	1	0.2
Parks and Recreation	14,346	71	6.9
Police Protection	53,474	264	25.8
Public Welfare	361	1	0.2
Sewerage	5,661	28	2.7
Solid Waste Management	10,189	50	4.9
Veterans' Services	0	0	0.0
Liquor Store	0	0	0.0
Utility	14,683	72	7.1
Employee Retirement	763	3	0.4

Source: U.S. Census Bureau, State & Local Government Finances 2017

EMPLOYMENT

Labor Force and Employment

Area	Civilian Labor Force			Workers Employed		
	Dec. 2019	Dec. 2020	% Chg.	Dec. 2019	Dec. 2020	% Chg.
City	76,883	75,832	-1.4	73,263	69,057	-5.7
MSA[1]	148,437	145,648	-1.9	141,883	133,739	-5.7
U.S.	164,007,000	160,017,000	-2.4	158,504,000	149,613,000	-5.6

Note: Data is not seasonally adjusted and covers workers 16 years of age and older; (1) Figures cover the Fayetteville, NC Metropolitan Statistical Area
Source: Bureau of Labor Statistics, Local Area Unemployment Statistics

Unemployment Rate

Area	2020											
	Jan.	Feb.	Mar.	Apr.	May	Jun.	Jul.	Aug.	Sep.	Oct.	Nov.	Dec.
City	5.8	5.2	6.0	15.7	16.8	10.8	12.9	10.1	10.4	9.0	9.0	8.9
MSA[1]	5.4	4.9	5.6	14.6	15.4	9.8	11.6	9.1	9.3	8.2	8.3	8.2
U.S.	4.0	3.8	4.5	14.4	13.0	11.2	10.5	8.5	7.7	6.6	6.4	6.5

Note: Data is not seasonally adjusted and covers workers 16 years of age and older; (1) Figures cover the Fayetteville, NC Metropolitan Statistical Area
Source: Bureau of Labor Statistics, Local Area Unemployment Statistics

Average Wages

Occupation	$/Hr.	Occupation	$/Hr.
Accountants and Auditors	35.70	Maintenance and Repair Workers	19.80
Automotive Mechanics	18.00	Marketing Managers	54.50
Bookkeepers	17.80	Network and Computer Systems Admin.	41.90
Carpenters	19.90	Nurses, Licensed Practical	22.70
Cashiers	10.60	Nurses, Registered	36.30
Computer Programmers	31.00	Nursing Assistants	12.70
Computer Systems Analysts	38.40	Office Clerks, General	15.80
Computer User Support Specialists	23.80	Physical Therapists	41.90
Construction Laborers	15.30	Physicians	125.80
Cooks, Restaurant	11.80	Plumbers, Pipefitters and Steamfitters	21.50
Customer Service Representatives	16.50	Police and Sheriff's Patrol Officers	22.20
Dentists	92.30	Postal Service Mail Carriers	25.40
Electricians	21.10	Real Estate Sales Agents	31.80
Engineers, Electrical	41.80	Retail Salespersons	12.90
Fast Food and Counter Workers	10.20	Sales Representatives, Technical/Scientific	n/a
Financial Managers	62.00	Secretaries, Exc. Legal/Medical/Executive	17.40
First-Line Supervisors of Office Workers	24.70	Security Guards	19.90
General and Operations Managers	57.50	Surgeons	n/a
Hairdressers/Cosmetologists	12.40	Teacher Assistants, Exc. Postsecondary*	11.90
Home Health and Personal Care Aides	10.50	Teachers, Secondary School, Exc. Sp. Ed.*	22.90
Janitors and Cleaners	12.80	Telemarketers	n/a
Landscaping/Groundskeeping Workers	12.90	Truck Drivers, Heavy/Tractor-Trailer	18.00
Lawyers	59.60	Truck Drivers, Light/Delivery Services	17.40
Maids and Housekeeping Cleaners	10.40	Waiters and Waitresses	9.30

Note: Wage data covers the Fayetteville, NC Metropolitan Statistical Area; (*) Hourly wages were calculated from annual wage data based on a 40 hour work week; n/a not available.
Source: Bureau of Labor Statistics, Metro Area Occupational Employment & Wage Estimates, May 2020

Employment by Industry

Sector	MSA[1]		U.S.
	Number of Employees	Percent of Total	Percent of Total
Construction, Mining, and Logging	4,800	3.8	5.5
Education and Health Services	14,800	11.6	16.3
Financial Activities	3,800	3.0	6.1
Government	40,700	31.9	15.2
Information	900	0.7	1.9
Leisure and Hospitality	14,800	11.6	9.0
Manufacturing	8,000	6.3	8.5
Other Services	4,300	3.4	3.8
Professional and Business Services	11,100	8.7	14.4
Retail Trade	17,400	13.6	10.9
Transportation, Warehousing, and Utilities	5,100	4.0	4.6
Wholesale Trade	2,000	1.6	3.9

Note: Figures are non-farm employment as of December 2020. Figures are not seasonally adjusted and include workers 16 years of age and older; (1) Figures cover the Fayetteville, NC Metropolitan Statistical Area
Source: Bureau of Labor Statistics, Current Employment Statistics, Employment, Hours, and Earnings

Employment by Occupation

Occupation Classification	City (%)	MSA[1] (%)	U.S. (%)
Management, Business, Science, and Arts	32.8	33.3	38.5
Natural Resources, Construction, and Maintenance	7.9	9.9	8.9
Production, Transportation, and Material Moving	13.5	14.6	13.2
Sales and Office	23.8	22.9	21.6
Service	22.1	19.3	17.8

Note: Figures cover employed civilians 16 years of age and older; (1) Figures cover the Fayetteville, NC Metropolitan Statistical Area
Source: U.S. Census Bureau, 2015-2019 American Community Survey 5-Year Estimates

Occupations with Greatest Projected Employment Growth: 2020 – 2022

Occupation[1]	2020 Employment	2022 Projected Employment	Numeric Employment Change	Percent Employment Change
Laborers and Freight, Stock, and Material Movers, Hand	90,950	94,250	3,300	3.6
Stockers and Order Fillers	99,690	102,690	3,000	3.0
Software Developers and Software Quality Assurance Analysts and Testers	74,740	76,850	2,110	2.8
Registered Nurses	87,970	89,970	2,000	2.3
Project Management Specialists and Business Operations Specialists, All Other	62,540	63,660	1,120	1.8
Computer Systems Analysts (SOC 2018)	40,350	41,450	1,100	2.7
Insurance Sales Agents	13,950	14,920	970	7.0
Industrial Truck and Tractor Operators	22,480	23,360	880	3.9
Loan Officers	12,610	13,430	820	6.5
Customer Service Representatives	80,790	81,600	810	1.0

Note: Projections cover North Carolina; (1) Sorted by numeric employment change
Source: www.projectionscentral.com, State Occupational Projections, 2020–2022 Short-Term Projections

Fastest-Growing Occupations: 2020 – 2022

Occupation[1]	2020 Employment	2022 Projected Employment	Numeric Employment Change	Percent Employment Change
Statisticians	1,420	1,540	120	8.5
Operations Research Analysts	2,490	2,700	210	8.4
Butchers and Meat Cutters	2,650	2,860	210	7.9
Insurance Sales Agents	13,950	14,920	970	7.0
Loan Interviewers and Clerks	6,000	6,420	420	7.0
Brokerage Clerks	1,590	1,700	110	6.9
Veterinary Assistants and Laboratory Animal Caretakers	3,590	3,830	240	6.7
Personal Financial Advisors	8,760	9,330	570	6.5
Loan Officers	12,610	13,430	820	6.5
Veterinary Technologists and Technicians	3,040	3,230	190	6.3

Note: Projections cover North Carolina; (1) Sorted by percent employment change and excludes occupations with numeric employment change less than 50
Source: www.projectionscentral.com, State Occupational Projections, 2020–2022 Short-Term Projections

TAXES

State Corporate Income Tax Rates

State	Tax Rate (%)	Income Brackets ($)	Num. of Brackets	Financial Institution Tax Rate (%)[a]	Federal Income Tax Ded.
North Carolina	2.5	Flat rate	1	2.5	No

Note: Tax rates as of January 1, 2021; (a) Rates listed are the corporate income tax rate applied to financial institutions or excise taxes based on income. Some states have other taxes based upon the value of deposits or shares.
Source: Federation of Tax Administrators, State Corporate Income Tax Rates, January 1, 2021

State Individual Income Tax Rates

State	Tax Rate (%)	Income Brackets ($)	Personal Exemptions ($) Single	Personal Exemptions ($) Married	Personal Exemptions ($) Depend.	Standard Ded. ($) Single	Standard Ded. ($) Married
North Carolina	5.25	Flat rate	None	None	None	10,750	21,500

Note: Tax rates as of January 1, 2021; Local- and county-level taxes are not included; Federal income tax is not deductible on state income tax returns
Source: Federation of Tax Administrators, State Individual Income Tax Rates, January 1, 2021

Various State Sales and Excise Tax Rates

State	State Sales Tax (%)	Gasoline[1] (¢/gal.)	Cigarette[2] ($/pack)	Spirits[3] ($/gal.)	Wine[4] ($/gal.)	Beer[5] ($/gal.)	Recreational Marijuana (%)
North Carolina	4.75	36.35	0.45	14.58	1	0.62	Not legal

Note: All tax rates as of January 1, 2021; (1) The American Petroleum Institute has developed a methodology for determining the average tax rate on a gallon of fuel. Rates may include any of the following: excise taxes, environmental fees, storage tank fees, other fees or taxes, general sales tax, and local taxes; (2) The federal excise tax of $1.0066 per pack and local taxes are not included; (3) Rates are those applicable to off-premise sales of 40% alcohol by volume (a.b.v.) distilled spirits in 750ml containers. Local excise taxes are excluded; (4) Rates are those applicable to off-premise sales of 11% a.b.v. non-carbonated wine in 750ml containers; (5) Rates are those applicable to off-premise sales of 4.7% a.b.v. beer in 12 ounce containers.
Source: Tax Foundation, 2021 Facts & Figures: How Does Your State Compare?

State Business Tax Climate Index Rankings

State	Overall Rank	Corporate Tax Rank	Individual Income Tax Rank	Sales Tax Rank	Property Tax Rank	Unemployment Insurance Tax Rank
North Carolina	10	4	16	22	26	10

Note: The index is a measure of how each state's tax laws affect economic performance. The lower the rank, the more favorable a state's tax system is for business. States without a given tax are given a ranking of 1. The scores/rankings for the District of Columbia do not affect other states. The 2021 index represents the tax climate as of July 1, 2020.
Source: Tax Foundation, State Business Tax Climate Index 2021

TRANSPORTATION

Means of Transportation to Work

Area	Car/Truck/Van		Public Transportation			Bicycle	Walked	Other Means	Worked at Home
	Drove Alone	Car-pooled	Bus	Subway	Railroad				
City	77.2	9.4	0.6	0.0	0.0	0.2	7.8	1.7	3.1
MSA[1]	81.3	9.2	0.3	0.0	0.0	0.1	4.2	1.4	3.4
U.S.	76.3	9.0	2.4	1.9	0.6	0.5	2.7	1.4	5.2

Note: Figures are percentages and cover workers 16 years of age and older; (1) Figures cover the Fayetteville, NC Metropolitan Statistical Area
Source: U.S. Census Bureau, 2015-2019 American Community Survey 5-Year Estimates

Travel Time to Work

Area	Less Than 10 Minutes	10 to 19 Minutes	20 to 29 Minutes	30 to 44 Minutes	45 to 59 Minutes	60 to 89 Minutes	90 Minutes or More
City	20.6	37.5	22.3	12.5	3.3	2.1	1.6
MSA[1]	14.4	29.4	23.3	20.1	6.6	4.1	2.1
U.S.	12.2	28.4	20.8	20.8	8.3	6.4	2.9

Note: Note: Figures are percentages and include workers 16 years old and over; (1) Figures cover the Fayetteville, NC Metropolitan Statistical Area
Source: U.S. Census Bureau, 2015-2019 American Community Survey 5-Year Estimates

Key Congestion Measures

Measure	1982	1992	2002	2012	2017
Annual Hours of Delay, Total (000)	n/a	n/a	n/a	n/a	6,624
Annual Hours of Delay, Per Auto Commuter	n/a	n/a	n/a	n/a	20
Annual Congestion Cost, Total (million $)	n/a	n/a	n/a	n/a	133
Annual Congestion Cost, Per Auto Commuter ($)	n/a	n/a	n/a	n/a	397

Note: n/a not available
Source: Texas A&M Transportation Institute, 2019 Urban Mobility Report

Freeway Travel Time Index

Measure	1982	1987	1992	1997	2002	2007	2012	2017
Urban Area Index[1]	n/a	n/a	n/a	n/a	n/a	n/a	n/a	1.09
Urban Area Rank[1,2]	n/a	n/a	n/a	n/a	n/a	n/a	n/a	n/a

Note: Freeway Travel Time Index—the ratio of travel time in the peak period to the travel time at free-flow conditions. For example, a value of 1.30 indicates a 20-minute free-flow trip takes 26 minutes in the peak (20 minutes x 1.30 = 26 minutes); (1) Covers the Fayetteville NC urban area; (2) Rank is based on 101 larger urban areas (#1 = highest travel time index); n/a not available
Source: Texas A&M Transportation Institute, 2019 Urban Mobility Report

Public Transportation

Agency Name / Mode of Transportation	Vehicles Operated in Maximum Service[1]	Annual Unlinked Passenger Trips[2] (in thous.)	Annual Passenger Miles[3] (in thous.)
Fayetteville Area System of Transit			
Bus (directly operated)	22	1,389.4	5,706.1
Demand Response (directly operated)	15	63.4	540.9

Note: (1) Number of revenue vehicles operated by the given mode and type of service to meet the annual maximum service requirement. This is the revenue vehicle count during the peak season of the year; on the week and day that maximum service is provided. Vehicles operated in maximum service (VOMS) exclude atypical days and one-time special events; (2) Number of passengers who boarded public transportation vehicles. Passengers are counted each time they board a vehicle no matter how many vehicles they use to travel from their origin to their destination. (3) Sum of the distances ridden by all passengers during the entire fiscal year. Source: Federal Transit Administration, National Transit Database, 2019

Air Transportation

Airport Name and Code / Type of Service	Passenger Airlines[1]	Passenger Enplanements	Freight Carriers[2]	Freight (lbs)
Fayetteville Regional Airport (FAY)				
Domestic service (U.S. carriers - 2020)	7	117,211	1	703
International service (U.S. carriers - 2019)	0	0	0	0

Note: (1) Includes all U.S.-based major, minor and commuter airlines that carried at least one passenger during the year; (2) Includes all U.S.-based airlines and freight carriers that transported at least one pound of freight during the year. Source: Bureau of Transportation Statistics, The Intermodal Transportation Database, Air Carriers: T-100 Domestic Market (U.S. Carriers), 2020; Bureau of Transportation Statistics, The Intermodal Transportation Database, Air Carriers: T-100 International Market (U.S. Carriers), 2019

BUSINESSES

Major Business Headquarters

Company Name	Industry	Rankings	
		Fortune[1]	Forbes[2]
No companies listed	-	-	-

Note: (1) Companies that produce a 10-K are ranked 1 to 500 based on 2019 revenue; (2) All private companies with at least $2 billion in annual revenue through the end of their most current fiscal year are ranked 1 to 219; companies listed are headquartered in the city; dashes indicate no ranking Source: Fortune, "Fortune 500," June/July 2020; Forbes, "America's Largest Private Companies," 2020

Minority Business Opportunity

Fayetteville is home to one company which is on the *Black Enterprise* Auto Dealer list (45 largest dealers based on gross sales): **Cross Creek Subaru** (#36). Criteria: company must be operational in previous calendar year and be at least 51% black-owned. *Black Enterprise, B.E. 100s, 2019*

Living Environment

COST OF LIVING

Cost of Living Index

Composite Index	Groceries	Housing	Utilities	Trans-portation	Health Care	Misc. Goods/ Services
n/a	n/a	n/a	n/a	n/a	n/a	n/a

Note: The Cost of Living Index measures regional differences in the cost of consumer goods and services, excluding taxes and non-consumer expenditures, for professional and managerial households in the top income quintile. It is based on more than 50,000 prices covering almost 60 different items for which prices are collected three times a year by chambers of commerce, economic development organizations or university applied economic centers in each participating urban area. The numbers shown should be read as a percentage above or below the national average of 100. For example, a value of 115.4 in the groceries column indicates that grocery prices are 15.4% higher than the national average. Small differences in the index numbers should not be interpreted as significant; n/a not available.
Source: The Council for Community and Economic Research, Cost of Living Index, 2020

Grocery Prices

Area[1]	T-Bone Steak ($/pound)	Frying Chicken ($/pound)	Whole Milk ($/half gal.)	Eggs ($/dozen)	Orange Juice ($/64 oz.)	Coffee ($/11.5 oz.)
City[2]	n/a	n/a	n/a	n/a	n/a	n/a
Avg.	11.78	1.39	2.05	1.47	3.57	4.34
Min.	8.03	0.94	1.03	0.74	2.94	3.02
Max.	15.86	2.65	4.31	3.77	5.44	8.69

*Note: (1) Values for the local area are compared with the average, minimum and maximum values for all 284 areas in the Cost of Living Index; (2) Figures cover the Fayetteville NC urban area; n/a not available; **T-Bone Steak** (price per pound); **Frying Chicken** (price per pound, whole fryer); **Whole Milk** (half gallon carton); **Eggs** (price per dozen, Grade A, large); **Orange Juice** (64 oz. Tropicana or Florida Natural); **Coffee** (11.5 oz. can, vacuum-packed, Maxwell House, Hills Bros, or Folgers).*
Source: The Council for Community and Economic Research, Cost of Living Index, 2020

Housing and Utility Costs

Area[1]	New Home Price ($)	Apartment Rent ($/month)	All Electric ($/month)	Part Electric ($/month)	Other Energy ($/month)	Telephone ($/month)
City[2]	n/a	n/a	n/a	n/a	n/a	n/a
Avg.	368,594	1,168	170.86	100.47	65.28	184.30
Min.	190,567	502	91.58	31.42	26.08	169.60
Max.	2,227,806	4,738	470.38	280.31	280.06	206.50

*Note: (1) Values for the local area are compared with the average, minimum and maximum values for all 284 areas in the Cost of Living Index; (2) Figures cover the Fayetteville NC urban area; n/a not available; **New Home Price** (2,400 sf living area, 8,000 sf lot, in urban area with full utilities); **Apartment Rent** (950 sf 2 bedroom/1.5 or 2 bath, unfurnished, excluding all utilities except water); **All Electric** (average monthly cost for an all-electric home); **Part Electric** (average monthly cost for a part-electric home); **Other Energy** (average monthly cost for natural gas, fuel oil, coal, wood, and any other forms of energy except electricity); **Telephone** (price includes the base monthly rate plus taxes and fees for three lines of mobile phone service).*
Source: The Council for Community and Economic Research, Cost of Living Index, 2020

Health Care, Transportation, and Other Costs

Area[1]	Doctor ($/visit)	Dentist ($/visit)	Optometrist ($/visit)	Gasoline ($/gallon)	Beauty Salon ($/visit)	Men's Shirt ($)
City[2]	n/a	n/a	n/a	n/a	n/a	n/a
Avg.	115.44	99.32	108.10	2.21	39.27	31.37
Min.	36.68	59.00	51.36	1.71	19.00	11.00
Max.	219.00	153.10	250.97	3.46	82.05	58.33

*Note: (1) Values for the local area are compared with the average, minimum and maximum values for all 284 areas in the Cost of Living Index; (2) Figures cover the Fayetteville NC urban area; n/a not available; **Doctor** (general practitioners routine exam of an established patient); **Dentist** (adult teeth cleaning and periodic oral examination); **Optometrist** (full vision eye exam for established adult patient); **Gasoline** (one gallon regular unleaded, national brand, including all taxes, cash price at self-service pump if available); **Beauty Salon** (woman's shampoo, trim, and blow-dry); **Men's Shirt** (cotton/polyester dress shirt, pinpoint weave, long sleeves).*
Source: The Council for Community and Economic Research, Cost of Living Index, 2020

HOUSING

Homeownership Rate

Area	2012 (%)	2013 (%)	2014 (%)	2015 (%)	2016 (%)	2017 (%)	2018 (%)	2019 (%)	2020 (%)
MSA[1]	n/a	n/a	n/a	n/a	n/a	n/a	n/a	n/a	n/a
U.S.	65.4	65.1	64.5	63.7	63.4	63.9	64.4	64.6	66.6

Note: (1) Figures cover the Fayetteville, NC Metropolitan Statistical Area; n/a not available
Source: U.S. Census Bureau, Housing Vacancies and Homeownership Annual Statistics: 2012-2020

House Price Index (HPI)

Area	National Ranking[2]	Quarterly Change (%)	One-Year Change (%)	Five-Year Change (%)	Since 1991Q1 (%)
MSA[1]	n/a	n/a	n/a	n/a	n/a
U.S.[3]	–	3.81	10.77	38.99	205.12

Note: The HPI is a weighted repeat sales index. It measures average price changes in repeat sales or refinancings on the same properties. This information is obtained by reviewing repeat mortgage transactions on single-family properties whose mortgages have been purchased or securitized by Fannie Mae or Freddie Mac since January 1975; (1) Figures cover the , Metropolitan Statistical Area; (2) Rankings are based on annual percentage change for all metro areas containing at least 15,000 transactions over the last 10 years and ranges from 1 to 253; (3) figures based on a weighted average of Census Division estimates using a seasonally adjusted, purchase-only index; all figures are for the period ending December 31, 2020; n/a not available
Source: Federal Housing Finance Agency, Change in Metropolitan Area House Price Indexes, April 7, 2021

Median Single-Family Home Prices

Area	2018	2019	2020p	Percent Change 2019 to 2020
MSA[1]	137.1	144.4	163.2	13.0
U.S. Average	261.6	274.6	299.9	9.2

Note: Figures are median sales prices of existing single-family homes in thousands of dollars; (p) preliminary; (1) Figures cover the Fayetteville, NC Metropolitan Statistical Area
Source: National Association of Realtors, Median Sales Price of Existing Single-Family Homes for Metropolitan Areas, 4th Quarter 2020

Qualifying Income Based on Median Sales Price of Existing Single-Family Homes

Area	With 5% Down ($)	With 10% Down ($)	With 20% Down ($)
MSA[1]	32,608	30,892	27,459
U.S. Average	59,266	56,147	49,908

Note: Figures are preliminary; Qualifying income is based on a mortgage rate of 2.81%. Monthly principal and interest payment is limited to 25% of income; (1) Figures cover the Fayetteville, NC Metropolitan Statistical Area
Source: National Association of Realtors, Qualifying Income Based on Median Sales Price of Existing Single-Family Homes for Metropolitan Areas, 4th Quarter 2020

Home Value Distribution

Area	Under $50,000	$50,000 -$99,999	$100,000 -$149,999	$150,000 -$199,999	$200,000 -$299,999	$300,000 -$499,999	$500,000 -$999,999	$1,000,000 or more
City	5.0	26.2	28.2	19.3	13.7	5.5	1.7	0.3
MSA[1]	8.8	21.8	23.2	20.1	18.1	6.2	1.5	0.4
U.S.	6.9	12.0	13.3	14.0	19.6	19.3	11.4	3.4

Note: Figures are percentages and cover owner-occupied housing units; (1) Figures cover the Fayetteville, NC Metropolitan Statistical Area
Source: U.S. Census Bureau, 2015-2019 American Community Survey 5-Year Estimates

Year Housing Structure Built

Area	2010 or Later	2000 -2009	1990 -1999	1980 -1989	1970 -1979	1960 -1969	1950 -1959	1940 -1949	Before 1940	Median Year
City	6.9	11.9	18.1	16.9	21.6	13.2	6.6	2.9	1.8	1982
MSA[1]	9.3	17.9	21.7	14.5	16.4	9.6	5.6	2.4	2.5	1989
U.S.	5.2	14.0	13.9	13.4	15.2	10.6	10.3	4.9	12.6	1978

Note: Figures are percentages except for Median Year; Note: (1) Figures cover the Fayetteville, NC Metropolitan Statistical Area
Source: U.S. Census Bureau, 2015-2019 American Community Survey 5-Year Estimates

Gross Monthly Rent

Area	Under $500	$500 -$999	$1,000 -$1,499	$1,500 -$1,999	$2,000 -$2,499	$2,500 -$2,999	$3,000 and up	Median ($)
City	5.6	51.7	36.6	5.2	0.7	0.2	0.1	947
MSA[1]	7.3	50.9	33.4	7.2	1.1	0.1	0.1	932
U.S.	9.4	36.2	30.0	14.0	5.6	2.4	2.4	1,062

Note: Figures are percentages except for Median; Gross rent is the contract rent plus the estimated average monthly cost of utilities (electricity, gas, and water and sewer) and fuels (oil, coal, kerosene, wood, etc.) if these are paid by the renter (or paid for the renter by someone else); (1) Figures cover the Fayetteville, NC Metropolitan Statistical Area
Source: U.S. Census Bureau, 2015-2019 American Community Survey 5-Year Estimates

HEALTH

Health Risk Factors

Category	MSA[1] (%)	U.S. (%)
Adults aged 18–64 who have any kind of health care coverage	n/a	87.3
Adults who reported being in good or better health	n/a	82.4
Adults who have been told they have high blood cholesterol	n/a	33.0
Adults who have been told they have high blood pressure	n/a	32.3
Adults who are current smokers	n/a	17.1
Adults who currently use E-cigarettes	n/a	4.6
Adults who currently use chewing tobacco, snuff, or snus	n/a	4.0
Adults who are heavy drinkers[2]	n/a	6.3
Adults who are binge drinkers[3]	n/a	17.4
Adults who are overweight (BMI 25.0 - 29.9)	n/a	35.3
Adults who are obese (BMI 30.0 - 99.8)	n/a	31.3
Adults who participated in any physical activities in the past month	n/a	74.4
Adults who always or nearly always wears a seat belt	n/a	94.3

Note: n/a not available; (1) Figures cover the Fayetteville, NC Metropolitan Statistical Area; (2) Heavy drinkers are classified as adult men having more than 14 drinks per week and adult women having more than 7 drinks per week; (3) Binge drinkers are classified as males having five or more drinks on one occasion or females having four or more drinks on one occasion
Source: Centers for Disease Control and Prevention, Behaviorial Risk Factor Surveillance System, SMART: Selected Metropolitan Area Risk Trends, 2017

Acute and Chronic Health Conditions

Category	MSA[1] (%)	U.S. (%)
Adults who have ever been told they had a heart attack	n/a	4.2
Adults who have ever been told they have angina or coronary heart disease	n/a	3.9
Adults who have ever been told they had a stroke	n/a	3.0
Adults who have ever been told they have asthma	n/a	14.2
Adults who have ever been told they have arthritis	n/a	24.9
Adults who have ever been told they have diabetes[2]	n/a	10.5
Adults who have ever been told they had skin cancer	n/a	6.2
Adults who have ever been told they had any other types of cancer	n/a	7.1
Adults who have ever been told they have COPD	n/a	6.5
Adults who have ever been told they have kidney disease	n/a	3.0
Adults who have ever been told they have a form of depression	n/a	20.5

Note: n/a not available; (1) Figures cover the Fayetteville, NC Metropolitan Statistical Area; (2) Figures do not include pregnancy-related, borderline, or pre-diabetes
Source: Centers for Disease Control and Prevention, Behaviorial Risk Factor Surveillance System, SMART: Selected Metropolitan Area Risk Trends, 2017

Health Screening and Vaccination Rates

Category	MSA[1] (%)	U.S. (%)
Adults aged 65+ who have had flu shot within the past year	n/a	60.7
Adults aged 65+ who have ever had a pneumonia vaccination	n/a	75.4
Adults who have ever been tested for HIV	n/a	36.1
Adults who have ever had the shingles or zoster vaccine?	n/a	28.9
Adults who have had their blood cholesterol checked within the last five years	n/a	85.9

Note: n/a not available; (1) Figures cover the Fayetteville, NC Metropolitan Statistical Area.
Source: Centers for Disease Control and Prevention, Behaviorial Risk Factor Surveillance System, SMART: Selected Metropolitan Area Risk Trends, 2017

Disability Status

Category	MSA[1] (%)	U.S. (%)
Adults who reported being deaf	n/a	6.7
Are you blind or have serious difficulty seeing, even when wearing glasses?	n/a	4.5
Are you limited in any way in any of your usual activities due of arthritis?	n/a	12.9
Do you have difficulty doing errands alone?	n/a	6.8
Do you have difficulty dressing or bathing?	n/a	3.6
Do you have serious difficulty concentrating/remembering/making decisions?	n/a	10.7
Do you have serious difficulty walking or climbing stairs?	n/a	13.6

Note: n/a not available; (1) Figures cover the Fayetteville, NC Metropolitan Statistical Area.
Source: Centers for Disease Control and Prevention, Behaviorial Risk Factor Surveillance System, SMART: Selected Metropolitan Area Risk Trends, 2017

Mortality Rates for the Top 10 Causes of Death in the U.S.

ICD-10[a] Sub-Chapter	ICD-10[a] Code	Age-Adjusted Mortality Rate[1] per 100,000 population	
		County[2]	U.S.
Malignant neoplasms	C00-C97	168.0	149.2
Ischaemic heart diseases	I20-I25	104.5	90.5
Other forms of heart disease	I30-I51	46.7	52.2
Chronic lower respiratory diseases	J40-J47	50.6	39.6
Other degenerative diseases of the nervous system	G30-G31	47.2	37.6
Cerebrovascular diseases	I60-I69	37.3	37.2
Other external causes of accidental injury	W00-X59	42.6	36.1
Organic, including symptomatic, mental disorders	F01-F09	26.9	29.4
Hypertensive diseases	I10-I15	36.9	24.1
Diabetes mellitus	E10-E14	39.6	21.5

Note: (a) ICD-10 = International Classification of Diseases 10th Revision; (1) Mortality rates are a three-year average covering 2017-2019; (2) Figures cover Cumberland County.
Source: Centers for Disease Control and Prevention, National Center for Health Statistics. Underlying Cause of Death 1999-2019 on CDC WONDER Online Database

Mortality Rates for Selected Causes of Death

ICD-10[a] Sub-Chapter	ICD-10[a] Code	Age-Adjusted Mortality Rate[1] per 100,000 population	
		County[2]	U.S.
Assault	X85-Y09	9.0	6.0
Diseases of the liver	K70-K76	13.4	14.4
Human immunodeficiency virus (HIV) disease	B20-B24	3.8	1.5
Influenza and pneumonia	J09-J18	17.9	13.8
Intentional self-harm	X60-X84	16.6	14.1
Malnutrition	E40-E46	6.5	2.3
Obesity and other hyperalimentation	E65-E68	2.6	2.1
Renal failure	N17-N19	13.8	12.6
Transport accidents	V01-V99	17.3	12.3
Viral hepatitis	B15-B19	1.9	1.2

Note: (a) ICD-10 = International Classification of Diseases 10th Revision; (1) Mortality rates are a three-year average covering 2017-2019; (2) Figures cover Cumberland County; Data are suppressed when the data meet the criteria for confidentiality constraints; Mortality rates are flagged as unreliable when the rate would be calculated with a numerator of 20 or less.
Source: Centers for Disease Control and Prevention, National Center for Health Statistics. Underlying Cause of Death 1999-2019 on CDC WONDER Online Database

Health Insurance Coverage

Area	With Health Insurance	With Private Health Insurance	With Public Health Insurance	Without Health Insurance	Population Under Age 19 Without Health Insurance
City	90.0	65.3	40.4	10.0	3.3
MSA[1]	89.3	64.6	38.7	10.7	3.6
U.S.	91.2	67.9	35.1	8.8	5.1

Note: Figures are percentages that cover the civilian noninstitutionalized population; (1) Figures cover the Fayetteville, NC Metropolitan Statistical Area
Source: U.S. Census Bureau, 2015-2019 American Community Survey 5-Year Estimates

Number of Medical Professionals

Area	MDs[3]	DOs[3,4]	Dentists	Podiatrists	Chiropractors	Optometrists
County[1] (number)	668	77	352	20	33	61
County[1] (rate[2])	200.3	23.1	104.9	6.0	9.8	18.2
U.S. (rate[2])	282.9	22.7	71.2	6.2	28.1	16.9

37051
Note: Data as of 2019 unless noted; (1) Data covers Cumberland County; (2) Rate per 100,000 population; (3) Data as of 2018 and includes all active, non-federal physicians; (4) Doctor of Osteopathic Medicine
Source: U.S. Department of Health and Human Services, Health Resources and Services Administration, Bureau of Health Professions, Area Resource File (ARF) 2019-2020

EDUCATION

Public School District Statistics

District Name	Schls	Pupils	Pupil/ Teacher Ratio	Minority Pupils[1] (%)	Free Lunch Eligible[2] (%)	IEP[3] (%)
Cumberland County Schools	87	50,879	15.1	71.5	73.5	14.3

Note: Table includes school districts with 2,000 or more students; (1) Percentage of students that are not non-Hispanic white; (2) Percentage of students that are eligible for the free lunch program; (3) Percentage of students that have an Individualized Education Program.
Source: U.S. Department of Education, National Center for Education Statistics, Common Core of Data, Local Education Agency (School District) Universe Survey: School Year 2018-2019; U.S. Department of Education, National Center for Education Statistics, Common Core of Data, Public Elementary/Secondary School Universe Survey: School Year 2018-2019

Highest Level of Education

Area	Less than H.S.	H.S. Diploma	Some College, No Deg.	Associate Degree	Bachelor's Degree	Master's Degree	Prof. School Degree	Doctorate Degree
City	8.3	24.4	29.4	10.6	18.0	6.7	1.5	1.0
MSA[1]	10.4	27.3	27.5	11.1	15.7	6.2	1.0	0.8
U.S.	12.0	27.0	20.4	8.5	19.8	8.8	2.1	1.4

Note: Figures cover persons age 25 and over; (1) Figures cover the Fayetteville, NC Metropolitan Statistical Area
Source: U.S. Census Bureau, 2015-2019 American Community Survey 5-Year Estimates

Educational Attainment by Race

Area	High School Graduate or Higher (%)					Bachelor's Degree or Higher (%)				
	Total	White	Black	Asian	Hisp.[2]	Total	White	Black	Asian	Hisp.[2]
City	91.7	93.7	90.6	86.3	88.5	27.2	31.3	22.9	43.0	21.7
MSA[1]	89.6	91.5	89.7	84.8	80.2	23.7	25.6	21.5	39.3	19.3
U.S.	88.0	89.9	86.0	87.1	68.7	32.1	33.5	21.6	54.3	16.4

Note: Figures shown cover persons 25 years old and over; (1) Figures cover the Fayetteville, NC Metropolitan Statistical Area; (2) People of Hispanic origin can be of any race
Source: U.S. Census Bureau, 2015-2019 American Community Survey 5-Year Estimates

School Enrollment by Grade and Control

Area	Preschool (%)		Kindergarten (%)		Grades 1 - 4 (%)		Grades 5 - 8 (%)		Grades 9 - 12 (%)	
	Public	Private	Public	Private	Public	Private	Public	Private	Public	Private
City	63.5	36.5	88.7	11.3	87.2	12.8	87.4	12.6	89.7	10.3
MSA[1]	63.5	36.5	88.7	11.3	87.7	12.3	88.9	11.1	89.4	10.6
U.S.	59.1	40.9	87.6	12.4	89.5	10.5	89.4	10.6	90.1	9.9

Note: Figures shown cover persons 3 years old and over; (1) Figures cover the Fayetteville, NC Metropolitan Statistical Area
Source: U.S. Census Bureau, 2015-2019 American Community Survey 5-Year Estimates

Higher Education

Four-Year Colleges			Two-Year Colleges			Medical Schools[1]	Law Schools[2]	Voc/ Tech[3]
Public	Private Non-profit	Private For-profit	Public	Private Non-profit	Private For-profit			
1	3	0	1	0	1	0	0	1

Note: Figures cover institutions located within the city limits and include main campuses only; (1) includes schools accredited by the Liaison Committee on Medical Education and the American Osteopathic Association's Commission on Osteopathic College Accreditation; (2) includes ABA-accredited schools, schools with provisional ABA accreditation, and state accredited schools; (3) includes all schools with programs that are less than 2 years.
Source: National Center for Education Statistics, Integrated Postsecondary Education System (IPEDS), 2019-20; Wikipedia, List of Medical Schools in the United States, accessed April 2, 2021; Wikipedia, List of Law Schools in the United States, accessed April 2, 2021

EMPLOYERS

Major Employers

Company Name	Industry
Army & Air Force Exchange Service	Public administration
AT&T Services	Information
Cape Fear Valley Health Systems	Education & health services
City of Fayetteville	Municipal government
County of Cumberland	County government
Cumberland County Board of Education	Education & health services
Department of Defense	Public administration
E.I. du Pont de Nemours and Company	Professional & business services
Eaton Corporation	Manufacturing
Fayetteville State University	Education & health services
Fayetteville Technical Community College	Education & health services
Food Lion	Trade, transportation & utilities
Goodyear Tire and Rubber Company	Manufacturing
ITT Systems Corporation	Other services
Linc Government Services	Construction
Lowes Home Centers	Trade, transportation & utilities
Methodist University	Education & health services
National Security Solutions	Professional & business services
Public Works Commission	Public administration
Purolator Filters	Manufacturing
U.S. Postal Service	Trade, transportation & utilities
Veterans Administration	Public administration
Wal-Mart Associates	Trade, transportation & utilities
Worldwide Language Resources	Professional & business services

Note: Companies shown are located within the Fayetteville, NC Metropolitan Statistical Area.
Source: Hoovers.com; Wikipedia

PUBLIC SAFETY

Crime Rate

Area	All Crimes	Violent Crimes				Property Crimes		
		Murder	Rape[3]	Robbery	Aggrav. Assault	Burglary	Larceny -Theft	Motor Vehicle Theft
City	4,401.4	11.4	55.8	134.1	674.1	651.2	2,691.1	183.7
Suburbs[1]	n/a	n/a	n/a	n/a	n/a	n/a	n/a	n/a
Metro[2]	n/a	n/a	n/a	n/a	n/a	n/a	n/a	n/a
U.S.	2,489.3	5.0	42.6	81.6	250.2	340.5	1,549.5	219.9

Note: Figures are crimes per 100,000 population; (1) All areas within the metro area that are located outside the city limits; (2) Figures cover the Fayetteville, NC Metropolitan Statistical Area; n/a not available; (3) All figures shown were reported using the revised Uniform Crime Reporting (UCR) definition of rape.
Source: FBI Uniform Crime Reports, 2019

Hate Crimes

Area	Number of Quarters Reported	Number of Incidents per Bias Motivation					
		Race/Ethnicity/ Ancestry	Religion	Sexual Orientation	Disability	Gender	Gender Identity
City	4	8	1	2	0	0	0
U.S.	4	3,963	1,521	1,195	157	69	198

Source: Federal Bureau of Investigation, Hate Crime Statistics 2019

Identity Theft Consumer Reports

Area	Reports	Reports per 100,000 Population	Rank[2]
MSA[1]	2,327	442	61
U.S.	1,387,615	423	-

Note: (1) Figures cover the Fayetteville, NC Metropolitan Statistical Area; (2) Rank ranges from 1 to 391 where 1 indicates greatest number of identity theft reports per 100,000 population
Source: Federal Trade Commission, Consumer Sentinel Network Data Book 2020

Fraud and Other Consumer Reports

Area	Reports	Reports per 100,000 Population	Rank[2]
MSA[1]	4,399	835	84
U.S.	3,385,133	1,031	-

Note: (1) Figures cover the Fayetteville, NC Metropolitan Statistical Area; (2) Rank ranges from 1 to 391 where 1 indicates greatest number of fraud and other consumer reports per 100,000 population
Source: Federal Trade Commission, Consumer Sentinel Network Data Book 2020

POLITICS

2020 Presidential Election Results

Area	Biden	Trump	Jorgensen	Hawkins	Other
Cumberland County	57.4	40.8	1.1	0.3	0.4
U.S.	51.3	46.8	1.2	0.3	0.5

Note: Results are percentages and may not add to 100% due to rounding
Source: Dave Leip's Atlas of U.S. Presidential Elections

SPORTS

Professional Sports Teams

Team Name	League	Year Established
No teams are located in the metro area		

Source: Wikipedia, Major Professional Sports Teams of the United States and Canada, April 6, 2021

CLIMATE

Average and Extreme Temperatures

Temperature	Jan	Feb	Mar	Apr	May	Jun	Jul	Aug	Sep	Oct	Nov	Dec	Yr.
Extreme High (°F)	79	84	90	95	97	104	105	105	104	98	88	79	105
Average High (°F)	50	53	61	72	79	86	89	87	81	72	62	53	71
Average Temp. (°F)	40	43	50	59	67	75	78	77	71	60	51	42	60
Average Low (°F)	29	31	38	46	55	63	68	67	60	48	39	32	48
Extreme Low (°F)	-9	5	11	23	29	38	48	46	37	19	11	4	-9

Note: Figures cover the years 1948-1990
Source: National Climatic Data Center, International Station Meteorological Climate Summary, 9/96

Average Precipitation/Snowfall/Humidity

Precip./Humidity	Jan	Feb	Mar	Apr	May	Jun	Jul	Aug	Sep	Oct	Nov	Dec	Yr.
Avg. Precip. (in.)	3.4	3.6	3.6	2.9	3.9	3.6	4.4	4.4	3.2	2.9	3.0	3.1	42.0
Avg. Snowfall (in.)	2	3	1	Tr	0	0	0	0	0	0	Tr	1	8
Avg. Rel. Hum. 7am (%)	79	79	79	80	84	86	88	91	91	90	84	81	84
Avg. Rel. Hum. 4pm (%)	53	49	46	43	51	54	57	59	57	53	51	53	52

Note: Figures cover the years 1948-1990; Tr = Trace amounts (<0.05 in. of rain; <0.5 in. of snow)
Source: National Climatic Data Center, International Station Meteorological Climate Summary, 9/96

Weather Conditions

Temperature			Daytime Sky			Precipitation		
32°F & below	45°F & below	90°F & above	Clear	Partly cloudy	Cloudy	0.01 inch or more precip.	0.1 inch or more snow/ice	Thunder-storms
77	160	39	98	143	124	110	3	42

Note: Figures are average number of days per year and cover the years 1948-1990
Source: National Climatic Data Center, International Station Meteorological Climate Summary, 9/96

HAZARDOUS WASTE

Superfund Sites

The Fayetteville, NC metro area is home to two sites on the EPA's Superfund National Priorities List: **Cape Fear Wood Preserving** (final); **Carolina Transformer Co.** (final). There are a total of 1,375 Superfund sites with a status of proposed or final on the list in the U.S. *U.S. Environmental Protection Agency, National Priorities List, April 7, 2021*

AIR QUALITY

Air Quality Trends: Ozone

	1990	1995	2000	2005	2010	2015	2016	2017	2018	2019
MSA[1]	0.087	0.081	0.086	0.084	0.071	0.060	0.064	0.063	0.064	0.061
U.S.	0.088	0.089	0.082	0.080	0.073	0.068	0.069	0.068	0.069	0.065

Note: (1) Data covers the Fayetteville, NC Metropolitan Statistical Area. The values shown are the composite ozone concentration averages among trend sites based on the highest fourth daily maximum 8-hour concentration in parts per million. These trends are based on sites having an adequate record of monitoring data during the trend period. Data from exceptional events are included.
Source: U.S. Environmental Protection Agency, Air Quality Monitoring Information, "Air Quality Trends by City, 1990-2019"

Air Quality Index

Area	Percent of Days when Air Quality was...[2]					AQI Statistics[2]	
	Good	Moderate	Unhealthy for Sensitive Groups	Unhealthy	Very Unhealthy	Maximum	Median
MSA[1]	77.7	22.3	0.0	0.0	0.0	84	41

Note: (1) Data covers the Fayetteville, NC Metropolitan Statistical Area; (2) Based on 363 days with AQI data in 2019. Air Quality Index (AQI) is an index for reporting daily air quality. EPA calculates the AQI for five major air pollutants regulated by the Clean Air Act: ground-level ozone, particle pollution (aka particulate matter), carbon monoxide, sulfur dioxide, and nitrogen dioxide. The AQI runs from 0 to 500. The higher the AQI value, the greater the level of air pollution and the greater the health concern. There are six AQI categories: "Good" AQI is between 0 and 50. Air quality is considered satisfactory; "Moderate" AQI is between 51 and 100. Air quality is acceptable; "Unhealthy for Sensitive Groups" When AQI values are between 101 and 150, members of sensitive groups may experience health effects; "Unhealthy" When AQI values are between 151 and 200 everyone may begin to experience health effects; "Very Unhealthy" AQI values between 201 and 300 trigger a health alert; "Hazardous" AQI values over 300 trigger warnings of emergency conditions (not shown).
Source: U.S. Environmental Protection Agency, Air Quality Index Report, 2019

Air Quality Index Pollutants

Area	Percent of Days when AQI Pollutant was...[2]					
	Carbon Monoxide	Nitrogen Dioxide	Ozone	Sulfur Dioxide	Particulate Matter 2.5	Particulate Matter 10
MSA[1]	0.0	0.0	56.7	0.0	42.1	1.1

Note: (1) Data covers the Fayetteville, NC Metropolitan Statistical Area; (2) Based on 363 days with AQI data in 2019. The Air Quality Index (AQI) is an index for reporting daily air quality. EPA calculates the AQI for five major air pollutants regulated by the Clean Air Act: ground-level ozone, particle pollution (also known as particulate matter), carbon monoxide, sulfur dioxide, and nitrogen dioxide. The AQI runs from 0 to 500. The higher the AQI value, the greater the level of air pollution and the greater the health concern.
Source: U.S. Environmental Protection Agency, Air Quality Index Report, 2019

Maximum Air Pollutant Concentrations: Particulate Matter, Ozone, CO and Lead

	Particulate Matter 10 (ug/m^3)	Particulate Matter 2.5 Wtd AM (ug/m^3)	Particulate Matter 2.5 24-Hr (ug/m^3)	Ozone (ppm)	Carbon Monoxide (ppm)	Lead (ug/m^3)
MSA[1] Level	30	7.4	16	0.061	n/a	n/a
NAAQS[2]	150	15	35	0.075	9	0.15
Met NAAQS[2]	Yes	Yes	Yes	Yes	n/a	n/a

Note: (1) Data covers the Fayetteville, NC Metropolitan Statistical Area; Data from exceptional events are included; (2) National Ambient Air Quality Standards; ppm = parts per million; ug/m³ = micrograms per cubic meter; n/a not available.
Concentrations: Particulate Matter 10 (coarse particulate)—highest second maximum 24-hour concentration; Particulate Matter 2.5 Wtd AM (fine particulate)—highest weighted annual mean concentration; Particulate Matter 2.5 24-Hour (fine particulate)—highest 98th percentile 24-hour concentration; Ozone—highest fourth daily maximum 8-hour concentration; Carbon Monoxide—highest second maximum non-overlapping 8-hour concentration; Lead—maximum running 3-month average
Source: U.S. Environmental Protection Agency, Air Quality Monitoring Information, "Air Quality Statistics by City, 2019"

Maximum Air Pollutant Concentrations: Nitrogen Dioxide and Sulfur Dioxide

	Nitrogen Dioxide AM (ppb)	Nitrogen Dioxide 1-Hr (ppb)	Sulfur Dioxide AM (ppb)	Sulfur Dioxide 1-Hr (ppb)	Sulfur Dioxide 24-Hr (ppb)
MSA[1] Level	n/a	n/a	n/a	n/a	n/a
NAAQS[2]	53	100	30	75	140
Met NAAQS[2]	n/a	n/a	n/a	n/a	n/a

Note: (1) Data covers the Fayetteville, NC Metropolitan Statistical Area; Data from exceptional events are included; (2) National Ambient Air Quality Standards; ppm = parts per million; ug/m³ = micrograms per cubic meter; n/a not available.
Concentrations: Nitrogen Dioxide AM—highest arithmetic mean concentration; Nitrogen Dioxide 1-Hr—highest 98th percentile 1-hour daily maximum concentration; Sulfur Dioxide AM—highest annual mean concentration; Sulfur Dioxide 1-Hr—highest 99th percentile 1-hour daily maximum concentration; Sulfur Dioxide 24-Hr—highest second maximum 24-hour concentration
Source: U.S. Environmental Protection Agency, Air Quality Monitoring Information, "Air Quality Statistics by City, 2019"

Greensboro, North Carolina

Background

Greensboro is a quiet community in northern North Carolina. It, along with Winston-Salem and High Point, is part of an urban triangle. The city was the site of the Battle of Guilford Courthouse on March 15, 1781, during the American Revolution, as well as the birthplace of such notable Americans as Dolly Madison, wife of James Madison, the fourth president of the United States, and William Sydney Porter, otherwise known as author O. Henry.

During the mid- to late nineteenth century, the economy of the city was largely based upon textile production. While that still remains a vital role in Greensboro, petroleum, pharmaceutical products, and furniture have come into prominence as well.

The birth of the American Civil Rights movement can be traced to 1960 in Greensboro when four students from the historically black North Carolina A&T State sat at the white-only lunch counter at Greensboro's downtown Woolworth's department store. Their violent removal led to sit-ins all over the south. In 1979, several Ku Klux Klan (KKK) members traded gunfire with members of the Communist Workers Party (CWP) who were holding an anti-KKK rally. Five CWP members were killed and the event became known as the Greensboro Massacre. Today, the former Woolworth Building houses the Civil Rights Center and Museum.

Greensboro is one of the anchors of the center for business opportunities in North Carolina, the Piedmont Triad. Along with Winston-Salem and High Point, it has become a major metro area for attracting new plants and facilities. FedEx has a Mid-Atlantic air-cargo package-sorting hub in Greensboro, which is also home to the Gateway University Research Park, consisting of two 75-acre campuses focusing on nanotechnology, biotechnology, biochemistry, electronics, artificial intelligence, environmental sciences, food and nutrition, health genetics, materials science and engineering, alternate and renewable energy and social sciences.

Greensboro has a thriving cultural scene. The Green Hill Center for North Carolina Art Gallery promotes the visual arts and includes ArtQuest, an interactive gallery. The Greensboro Ballet provides performances, educational programs, the Summer Ballet Festival, and houses student and professional studios. The Greensboro Symphony Orchestra's Masterworks and Chamber Series concerts feature guest artists from around the world.

Greensboro College, Guilford College, University of North Carolina at Greensboro, North Carolina A&T State, and Bennett College for Women all reside in Greensboro. The Eastern Music Festival and School, part of Guilford College, offers a summer concert series. Elon University School of Law is in the heart of downtown.

In the past 30 years, Greensboro has grown into an internationally diverse community. Today, the city is home to large populations of Vietnamese, West African and Latino immigrants. Such diverse communities have contributed to the local cuisine and flavor, and authentic international specialty stores and restaurants are not hard to come by.

Downtown development, such as the NewBridge Bank Park minor league baseball stadium, and a variety of residential options, have helped transform the city center. The revitalized Southside neighborhood is touted as one of the best planned re-developments in the U.S. The city is famous to college sports fans as the home to the Atlantic Coast Conference. The annual ACC basketball tournament in March often airs from the Greensboro Coliseum Complex.

The Greensboro Parks & Recreation Department has acquired over 3,200 acres of land, with more than 170 parks and special facilities recognized internationally for their culturally diverse athletic, historical, and arts programs. The Bog Garden features more than 8,000 individually labeled trees, shrubs, ferns, bamboo, and wildflowers. Wet 'n' Wild Emerald Pointe Water Park offers one of only four tsunami (giant wave) pools in the U.S. Greensboro Historical Museum, located downtown in a building dating back to 1900, is listed on the National Register of Historic Places. The Battle of Guilford Courthouse National Military Park, with 220 acres of historic fields and forests, monuments, and graves, was the first national park established at a Revolutionary War site.

For children, Greensboro hosts a Science Center and Zoo, and a Children's Museum with a 30-foot climbing structure.

Greensboro is the largest city in the Piedmont Triad region. Both winter temperatures and rainfall are modified by the Blue Ridge Mountain barrier on the northwest. The summer temperatures vary with cloudiness and shower activity, but are generally mild. Northwesterly winds rarely bring heavy or prolonged winter rain or snow. Damaging storms are infrequent, as are tornadoes.

Rankings

Business/Finance Rankings

- The Brookings Institution ranked the nation's largest cities based on income inequality. Greensboro was ranked #32 (#1 = greatest inequality). Criteria: the "95/20 ratio," a figure representing the income at which a household earns more than 95 percent of all other households, divided by the income at which a household earns more than only 20 percent of all other households. *Brookings Institution, "Household Income Inequality, Largest Cities of 97 Large U.S. Metro Areas, 2014-2016," February 5, 2018*

- The Brookings Institution ranked the 100 largest metro areas in the U.S. based on income inequality. Greensboro was ranked #25 (#1 = greatest inequality). Criteria: the "95/20 ratio," a figure representing the income at which a household earns more than 95 percent of all other households, divided by the income at which a household earns more than only 20 percent of all other households. *Brookings Institution, "Household Income Inequality, 100 Largest U.S. Metro Areas, 2014-2016," February 5, 2018*

- Greensboro was cited as one of America's top metros for new and expanded facility projects in 2020. The area ranked #4 in the mid-sized metro area category (population 200,000 to 1 million). *Site Selection, "Top Metros of 2020," March 2021*

- Greensboro was identified as one of the unhappiest cities to work in by CareerBliss.com, an online community for career advancement. The city ranked #3 out of 5. Criteria: an employee's relationship with his or her boss and co-workers; general work environment; compensation; opportunities for advancement; company culture and job reputation; and resources. *Businesswire.com, "CareerBliss Unhappiest Cities to Work 2019," February 12, 2019*

- The Greensboro metro area appeared on the Milken Institute "2021 Best Performing Cities" list. Rank: #147 out of 200 large metro areas (population over 250,000). Criteria: job growth; wage and salary growth; high-tech output growth; housing affordability; household broadband access. *Milken Institute, "Best-Performing Cities 2021," February 16, 2021*

- *Forbes* ranked the 200 most populous metro areas to determine the nation's "Best Places for Business and Careers." The Greensboro metro area was ranked #66. Criteria: costs (business and living); job growth (past and projected); income growth; quality of life; educational attainment (college and high school); projected economic growth; cultural and leisure opportunities; workplace tolerance laws; net migration patterns. *Forbes, "The Best Places for Business and Careers 2019: Seattle Still On Top," October 30, 2019*

Dating/Romance Rankings

- Greensboro was ranked #8 out of 25 cities that stood out for inspiring romance and attracting diners on the website OpenTable.com. Criteria: percentage of people who dined out on Valentine's Day in 2018; percentage of romantic restaurants as rated by OpenTable diner reviews; and percentage of tables seated for two. *OpenTable, "25 Most Romantic Cities in America for 2019," February 7, 2019*

Education Rankings

- Personal finance website *WalletHub* analyzed the 150 largest U.S. metropolitan statistical areas to determine where the most educated Americans are putting their degrees to work. Criteria: education levels; percentage of workers with degrees; education quality and attainment gap; public school quality rankings; quality and enrollment of each metro area's universities. Greensboro was ranked #97 (#1 = most educated city). *www.WalletHub.com, "Most and Least Educated Cities in America," July 20, 2020*

- Greensboro was selected as one of America's most literate cities. The city ranked #45 out of the 84 largest U.S. cities. Criteria: number of booksellers; library resources; Internet resources; educational attainment; periodical publishing resources; newspaper circulation. *Central Connecticut State University, "America's Most Literate Cities, 2018," February 2019*

Health/Fitness Rankings

- For each of the 100 largest cities in the United States, the American Fitness Index®, published by the American College of Sports Medicine and the Anthem Foundation, evaluated community infrastructure and 33 health behaviors including preventive health, levels of chronic disease conditions, pedestrian safety, air quality, and community resources that support physical activity. Greensboro ranked #60 for "community fitness." *americanfitnessindex.org, "2020 ACSM American Fitness Index Summary Report," July 14, 2020*

- The Greensboro metro area was identified as one of the worst cities for bed bugs in America by pest control company Orkin. The area ranked #34 out of 50 based on the number of bed bug treatments Orkin performed from December 2019 to November 2020. *Orkin, "New Year, New Top City on Orkin's 2021 Bed Bug Cities List: Chicago," February 1, 2021*

- Greensboro was identified as a "2021 Spring Allergy Capital." The area ranked #35 out of 100. Three groups of factors were used to identify the most challenging cities for people with allergies during the spring season: annual spring pollen levels; over the counter medicine use; number of board-certified allergy specialists. *Asthma and Allergy Foundation of America, "Spring Allergy Capitals 2021," February 23, 2021*

- Greensboro was identified as a "2021 Fall Allergy Capital." The area ranked #56 out of 100. Three groups of factors were used to identify the most challenging cities for people with allergies during the fall season: annual fall pollen levels; over the counter medicine use; number of board-certified allergy specialists. *Asthma and Allergy Foundation of America, "Fall Allergy Capitals 2021," February 23, 2021*

- Greensboro was identified as a "2019 Asthma Capital." The area ranked #3 out of the nation's 100 largest metropolitan areas. Criteria: estimated asthma prevalence; crude death rate from asthma; and ER visits due to asthma. Risk factors analyzed but not factored in the rankings: annual pollen score; annual air quality; public smoking laws; number of board-certified asthma specialists; rescue medication use; controller medication use; uninsured rate; poverty rate. *Asthma and Allergy Foundation of America, "Asthma Capitals 2019: The Most Challenging Places to Live With Asthma," May 7, 2019*

Real Estate Rankings

- *WalletHub* compared the most populated U.S. cities to determine which had the best markets for real estate agents. Greensboro ranked #130 where demand was high and pay was the best. Criteria: sales per agent; annual median wage for real-estate agents; monthly average starting salary for real estate agents; real estate job density and competition; unemployment rate; home turnover rate; housing-market health index; and other relevant metrics. *www.WalletHub.com, "2019's Best Places to Be a Real Estate Agent," April 24, 2019*

- The Greensboro metro area was identified as one of the 10 best condo markets in the U.S. in 2020. The area ranked #8 out of 63 markets. Criteria: year-over-year change of median sales price of existing apartment condo-coop homes between the 4th quarter of 2019 and the 4th quarter of 2020. *National Association of Realtors®, Median Sales Price of Existing Apartment Condo-Coops Homes for Metropolitan Areas, 4th Quarter 2020*

- Greensboro was ranked #109 out of 268 metro areas in terms of housing affordability in 2020 by the National Association of Home Builders (#1 = most affordable). Criteria: the share of homes sold in that area affordable to a family earning the local median income, based on standard mortgage underwriting criteria. *National Association of Home Builders®, NAHB-Wells Fargo Housing Opportunity Index, 4th Quarter 2020*

Safety Rankings

- To identify the most dangerous cities in America, 24/7 Wall Street focused on violent crime categories—murder, non-negligent manslaughter, rape, robbery, and aggravated assault—and property crime as reported in the FBI's 2019 annual Uniform Crime Report. Criteria also included median income from American Community Survey and unemployment figures from Bureau of Labor Statistics. For cities with populations over 100,000, Greensboro was ranked #49. *247wallst.com, "America's 50 Most Dangerous Cities" November 16, 2020*

- Statistics drawn from the FBI's Uniform Crime Report were used to rank the metropolitan statistical areas where violent crime rose the most between the years 2014–2019. 24/7 Wall Street found that the Greensboro metro area placed #4 of those with an increase of at least 32.5 percent in violent crime. *247wallst.com, "25 Cities Where Crime Is Soaring," February 18, 2021*

- Allstate ranked the 200 largest cities in America in terms of driver safety. Greensboro ranked #77. Criteria: internal property damage claims over a two-year period from January 2016 to December 2017. The report helps increase the importance of safety and awareness behind the wheel. *Allstate, "Allstate America's Best Drivers Report, 2019" June 24, 2019*

- The National Insurance Crime Bureau ranked 384 metro areas in the U.S. in terms of per capita rates of vehicle theft. The Greensboro metro area ranked #110 (#1 = highest rate). Criteria: number of vehicle theft offenses per 100,000 inhabitants in 2019. *National Insurance Crime Bureau, "Hot Spots 2019," July 21, 2020*

Seniors/Retirement Rankings

- From its Best Cities for Successful Aging indexes, the Milken Institute generated rankings for metropolitan areas, weighing data in nine categories—health care, wellness, living arrangements, transportation and convenience, financial characteristics, education, employment, community engagement, and overall livability. The Greensboro metro area was ranked #92 overall in the large metro area category. *Milken Institute, "Best Cities for Successful Aging, 2017" March 14, 2017*

Women/Minorities Rankings

- Greensboro was selected as one of the gayest cities in America by *The Advocate.* The city ranked #18 out of 25. Criteria, among many: Trans Pride parades/festivals; gay rugby teams; lesbian bars; LGBT centers; theater screenings of "Moonlight"; LGBT-inclusive nondiscrimination ordinances; and gay bowling teams. *The Advocate, "Queerest Cities in America 2017" January 12, 2017*

- Personal finance website *WalletHub* compared more than 180 U.S. cities across two key dimensions, "Hispanic Business-Friendliness" and "Hispanic Purchasing Power," to arrive at the most favorable conditions for Hispanic entrepreneurs. Greensboro was ranked #88 out of 182. Criteria includes: share of Hispanic-Owned Businesses; Hispanic entrepreneurship rate to median annual income of Hispanics; Small Business-Friendliness score; cost of living; and number of Hispanics with at least a bachelor's degree. *WalletHub.com, "2019's Best Cities for Hispanic Entrepreneurs," May 1, 2019*

Miscellaneous Rankings

- Greensboro was selected as a 2020 Digital Cities Survey winner. The city ranked #3 in the large city (250,000 to 499,999 population) category. The survey examined and assessed how city governments are utilizing technology to improve transparency, enhance cybersecurity, and respond to the pandemic. Survey questions focused on ten initiatives: cybersecurity, citizen experience, disaster recovery, business intelligence, IT personnel, data governance, collaboration, infrastructure modernization, cloud computing, and mobile applications. *Center for Digital Government, "2020 Digital Cities Survey," November 10, 2020*

- *WalletHub* compared the 150 most populated U.S. cities to determine their operating efficiency. A "Quality of City Services" score was constructed for each city and then divided by the total budget per capita to reveal which were managed the best. Greensboro ranked #12. Criteria: financial stability; economy; education; safety; health; infrastructure and pollution. *www.WalletHub.com, "2020's Best- & Worst-Run Cities in America," June 29, 2020*

Business Environment

DEMOGRAPHICS

Population Growth

Area	1990 Census	2000 Census	2010 Census	2019* Estimate	Population Growth (%)	
					1990-2019	2010-2019
City	193,389	223,891	269,666	291,303	50.6	8.0
MSA[1]	540,257	643,430	723,801	762,063	41.1	5.3
U.S.	248,709,873	281,421,906	308,745,538	324,697,795	30.6	5.2

Note: (1) Figures cover the Greensboro-High Point, NC Metropolitan Statistical Area; (*) 2015-2019 5-year estimated population
Source: U.S. Census Bureau, 1990 Census, Census 2000, Census 2010, 2015-2019 American Community Survey 5-Year Estimates

Household Size

Area	Persons in Household (%)							Average Household Size
	One	Two	Three	Four	Five	Six	Seven or More	
City	34.3	33.2	15.4	10.2	4.6	1.5	0.8	2.40
MSA[1]	29.4	35.0	16.2	11.4	5.1	1.8	1.0	2.50
U.S.	27.9	33.9	15.6	12.9	6.0	2.3	1.4	2.60

Note: (1) Figures cover the Greensboro-High Point, NC Metropolitan Statistical Area
Source: U.S. Census Bureau, 2015-2019 American Community Survey 5-Year Estimates

Race

Area	White Alone[2] (%)	Black Alone[2] (%)	Asian Alone[2] (%)	AIAN[3] Alone[2] (%)	NHOPI[4] Alone[2] (%)	Other Race Alone[2] (%)	Two or More Races (%)
City	47.3	41.4	5.0	0.5	0.1	2.7	3.0
MSA[1]	63.0	26.8	3.7	0.5	0.1	3.3	2.6
U.S.	72.5	12.7	5.5	0.8	0.2	4.9	3.3

Note: (1) Figures cover the Greensboro-High Point, NC Metropolitan Statistical Area; (2) Alone is defined as not being in combination with one or more other races; (3) American Indian and Alaska Native; (4) Native Hawaiian and Other Pacific Islander
Source: U.S. Census Bureau, 2015-2019 American Community Survey 5-Year Estimates

Hispanic or Latino Origin

Area	Total (%)	Mexican (%)	Puerto Rican (%)	Cuban (%)	Other (%)
City	7.9	4.7	0.7	0.2	2.2
MSA[1]	8.4	5.5	0.7	0.2	1.9
U.S.	18.0	11.2	1.7	0.7	4.3

Note: Persons of Hispanic or Latino origin can be of any race; (1) Figures cover the Greensboro-High Point, NC Metropolitan Statistical Area
Source: U.S. Census Bureau, 2015-2019 American Community Survey 5-Year Estimates

Ancestry

Area	German	Irish	English	American	Italian	Polish	French[2]	Scottish	Dutch
City	7.0	5.5	7.3	4.8	2.4	1.1	1.1	1.7	0.7
MSA[1]	8.0	6.6	8.2	8.3	2.3	1.1	1.2	1.9	0.8
U.S.	13.3	9.7	7.2	6.2	5.1	2.8	2.3	1.7	1.2

Note: Figures are the percentage of the total population reporting a particular ancestry. The nine most commonly reported ancestries in the U.S. are shown. Figures include multiple ancestries (e.g. if a person reported being Irish and Italian, they were included in both columns); (1) Figures cover the Greensboro-High Point, NC Metropolitan Statistical Area; (2) Excludes Basque
Source: U.S. Census Bureau, 2015-2019 American Community Survey 5-Year Estimates

Foreign-born Population

Area	Percent of Population Born in								
	Any Foreign Country	Asia	Mexico	Europe	Caribbean	Central America[2]	South America	Africa	Canada
City	11.0	3.9	2.0	1.2	0.6	0.6	0.5	2.0	0.2
MSA[1]	8.8	2.9	2.5	0.8	0.4	0.6	0.4	1.0	0.2
U.S.	13.6	4.2	3.5	1.5	1.3	1.1	1.0	0.7	0.2

Note: (1) Figures cover the Greensboro-High Point, NC Metropolitan Statistical Area; (2) Excludes Mexico.
Source: U.S. Census Bureau, 2015-2019 American Community Survey 5-Year Estimates

Marital Status

Area	Never Married	Now Married[2]	Separated	Widowed	Divorced
City	42.2	38.4	2.6	5.7	11.0
MSA[1]	33.6	46.1	2.7	6.3	11.3
U.S.	33.4	48.1	1.9	5.8	10.9

Note: Figures are percentages and cover the population 15 years of age and older; (1) Figures cover the Greensboro-High Point, NC Metropolitan Statistical Area; (2) Excludes separated
Source: U.S. Census Bureau, 2015-2019 American Community Survey 5-Year Estimates

Disability by Age

Area	All Ages	Under 18 Years Old	18 to 64 Years Old	65 Years and Over
City	10.7	4.3	8.7	30.9
MSA[1]	12.7	4.5	10.7	32.5
U.S.	12.6	4.2	10.3	34.5

Note: Figures show percent of the civilian noninstitutionalized population that reported having a disability. Disability status is determined from six types of difficulty: vision, hearing, cognitive, ambulatory, self-care, and independent living. For children under 5 years old, hearing and vision difficulty are used to determine disability status. For children between the ages of 5 and 14, disability status is determined from hearing, vision, cognitive, ambulatory, and self-care difficulties. For people aged 15 years and older, they are considered to have a disability if they have difficulty with any one of the six difficulty types; Note: (1) Figures cover the Greensboro-High Point, NC Metropolitan Statistical Area
Source: U.S. Census Bureau, 2015-2019 American Community Survey 5-Year Estimates

Age

Area	Percent of Population									Median Age
	Under Age 5	Age 5–19	Age 20–34	Age 35–44	Age 45–54	Age 55–64	Age 65–74	Age 75–84	Age 85+	
City	6.0	19.9	24.0	12.5	12.4	11.5	8.0	3.9	1.8	35.1
MSA[1]	5.8	19.7	19.8	12.1	13.7	13.0	9.3	4.7	1.9	38.8
U.S.	6.1	19.1	20.7	12.6	13.0	12.9	9.1	4.6	1.9	38.1

Note: (1) Figures cover the Greensboro-High Point, NC Metropolitan Statistical Area
Source: U.S. Census Bureau, 2015-2019 American Community Survey 5-Year Estimates

Gender

Area	Males	Females	Males per 100 Females
City	135,572	155,731	87.1
MSA[1]	364,321	397,742	91.6
U.S.	159,886,919	164,810,876	97.0

Note: (1) Figures cover the Greensboro-High Point, NC Metropolitan Statistical Area
Source: U.S. Census Bureau, 2015-2019 American Community Survey 5-Year Estimates

Religious Groups by Family

Area	Catholic	Baptist	Non-Den.	Methodist[2]	Lutheran	LDS[3]	Pentecostal	Presbyterian[4]	Muslim[5]	Judaism
MSA[1]	2.7	12.8	7.4	9.9	0.7	0.8	2.5	3.2	0.6	0.4
U.S.	19.1	9.3	4.0	4.0	2.3	2.0	1.9	1.6	0.8	0.7

Note: Figures are the number of adherents as a percentage of the total population; (1) Figures cover the Greensboro-High Point, NC Metropolitan Statistical Area; (2) Methodist/Pietist; (3) Latter Day Saints; (4) Reformed; (5) Figures are estimates
Source: Association of Statisticians of American Religious Bodies, 2010 U.S. Religion Census: Religious Congregations & Membership Study

Religious Groups by Tradition

Area	Catholic	Evangelical Protestant	Mainline Protestant	Other Tradition	Black Protestant	Orthodox
MSA[1]	2.7	23.2	14.0	2.2	2.6	0.1
U.S.	19.1	16.2	7.3	4.3	1.6	0.3

Note: Figures are the number of adherents as a percentage of the total population; (1) Figures cover the Greensboro-High Point, NC Metropolitan Statistical Area
Source: Association of Statisticians of American Religious Bodies, 2010 U.S. Religion Census: Religious Congregations & Membership Study

ECONOMY

Gross Metropolitan Product

Area	2017	2018	2019	2020	Rank[2]
MSA[1]	41.5	43.0	44.3	45.7	71

Note: Figures are in billions of dollars; (1) Figures cover the Greensboro-High Point, NC Metropolitan Statistical Area; (2) Rank is based on 2018 data and ranges from 1 to 381
Source: U.S. Conference of Mayors, U.S. Metro Economies: GMP & Employment 2018-2020, September 2019

Economic Growth

Area	2015-17 (%)	2018 (%)	2019 (%)	2020 (%)	Rank[2]
MSA[1]	-0.2	1.5	1.2	1.2	312
U.S.	1.9	2.9	2.3	2.1	—

Note: Figures are real gross metropolitan product (GMP) growth rates and represent average annual percent change; (1) Figures cover the Greensboro-High Point, NC Metropolitan Statistical Area; (2) Rank is based on 2017 2-year average annual percent change and ranges from 1 to 381
Source: U.S. Conference of Mayors, U.S. Metro Economies: GMP & Employment 2018-2020, September 2019

Metropolitan Area Exports

Area	2014	2015	2016	2017	2018	2019	Rank[2]
MSA[1]	3,505.5	3,286.1	3,730.4	3,537.9	3,053.5	2,561.8	87

Note: Figures are in millions of dollars; (1) Figures cover the Greensboro-High Point, NC Metropolitan Statistical Area; (2) Rank is based on 2019 data and ranges from 1 to 386
Source: U.S. Department of Commerce, International Trade Administration, Office of Trade and Economic Analysis, Industry and Analysis, Exports by Metropolitan Area, data extracted March 24, 2021

Building Permits

Area	Single-Family			Multi-Family			Total		
	2018	2019	Pct. Chg.	2018	2019	Pct. Chg.	2018	2019	Pct. Chg.
City	597	548	-8.2	249	385	54.6	846	933	10.3
MSA[1]	1,949	2,002	2.7	275	421	53.1	2,224	2,423	8.9
U.S.	855,300	862,100	0.7	473,500	523,900	10.6	1,328,800	1,386,000	4.3

Note: (1) Figures cover the Greensboro-High Point, NC Metropolitan Statistical Area; Figures represent new, privately-owned housing units authorized (unadjusted data); All permit data are based on estimates with imputation
Source: U.S. Census Bureau, Manufacturing, Mining, and Construction Statistics, Building Permits, 2018, 2019

Bankruptcy Filings

Area	Business Filings			Nonbusiness Filings		
	2019	2020	% Chg.	2019	2020	% Chg.
Guilford County	25	21	-16.0	758	471	-37.9
U.S.	22,780	21,655	-4.9	752,160	522,808	-30.5

Note: Business filings include Chapter 7, Chapter 9, Chapter 11, Chapter 12, Chapter 13, Chapter 15, and Section 304; Nonbusiness filings include Chapter 7, Chapter 11, and Chapter 13
Source: Administrative Office of the U.S. Courts, Business and Nonbusiness Bankruptcy, County Cases Commenced by Chapter of the Bankruptcy Code, During the 12-Month Period Ending December 31, 2019 and Business and Nonbusiness Bankruptcy, County Cases Commenced by Chapter of the Bankruptcy Code, During the 12-Month Period Ending December 31, 2020

Housing Vacancy Rates

Area	Gross Vacancy Rate[2] (%)			Year-Round Vacancy Rate[3] (%)			Rental Vacancy Rate[4] (%)			Homeowner Vacancy Rate[5] (%)		
	2018	2019	2020	2018	2019	2020	2018	2019	2020	2018	2019	2020
MSA[1]	11.6	9.9	8.3	11.5	9.5	8.2	11.4	8.1	7.2	1.0	0.7	0.7
U.S.	12.3	12.0	10.6	9.7	9.5	8.2	6.9	6.7	6.3	1.5	1.4	1.0

Note: (1) Figures cover the Greensboro-High Point, NC Metropolitan Statistical Area; (2) The percentage of the total housing inventory that is vacant; (3) The percentage of the housing inventory (excluding seasonal units) that is year-round vacant; (4) The percentage of rental inventory that is vacant for rent; (5) The percentage of homeowner inventory that is vacant for sale
Source: U.S. Census Bureau, Housing Vacancies and Homeownership Annual Statistics: 2018, 2019, 2020

INCOME

Income

Area	Per Capita ($)	Median Household ($)	Average Household ($)
City	29,628	48,964	71,453
MSA[1]	28,787	50,891	71,256
U.S.	34,103	62,843	88,607

Note: (1) Figures cover the Greensboro-High Point, NC Metropolitan Statistical Area
Source: U.S. Census Bureau, 2015-2019 American Community Survey 5-Year Estimates

Household Income Distribution

Area	Percent of Households Earning							
	Under $15,000	$15,000 -$24,999	$25,000 -$34,999	$35,000 -$49,999	$50,000 -$74,999	$75,000 -$99,999	$100,000 -$149,999	$150,000 and up
City	13.5	10.9	11.5	15.1	18.0	11.2	11.3	8.4
MSA[1]	12.4	10.8	11.3	14.7	18.2	12.2	11.9	8.6
U.S.	10.3	8.9	8.9	12.3	17.2	12.7	15.1	14.5

Note: (1) Figures cover the Greensboro-High Point, NC Metropolitan Statistical Area
Source: U.S. Census Bureau, 2015-2019 American Community Survey 5-Year Estimates

Poverty Rate

Area	All Ages	Under 18 Years Old	18 to 64 Years Old	65 Years and Over
City	18.5	26.7	17.1	11.5
MSA[1]	16.0	23.2	14.9	10.0
U.S.	13.4	18.5	12.6	9.3

Note: Figures are percentage of people whose income during the past 12 months was below the poverty level;
(1) Figures cover the Greensboro-High Point, NC Metropolitan Statistical Area
Source: U.S. Census Bureau, 2015-2019 American Community Survey 5-Year Estimates

CITY FINANCES

City Government Finances

Component	2017 ($000)	2017 ($ per capita)
Total Revenues	482,194	1,690
Total Expenditures	513,041	1,798
Debt Outstanding	496,855	1,741
Cash and Securities[1]	62	0

Note: (1) Cash and security holdings of a government at the close of its fiscal year,
including those of its dependent agencies, utilities, and liquor stores.
Source: U.S. Census Bureau, State & Local Government Finances 2017

City Government Revenue by Source

Source	2017 ($000)	2017 ($ per capita)	2017 (%)
General Revenue			
From Federal Government	10,161	36	2.1
From State Government	39,015	137	8.1
From Local Governments	3,452	12	0.7
Taxes			
Property	143,876	504	29.8
Sales and Gross Receipts	58,433	205	12.1
Personal Income	0	0	0.0
Corporate Income	0	0	0.0
Motor Vehicle License	1,119	4	0.2
Other Taxes	3,405	12	0.7
Current Charges	113,065	396	23.4
Liquor Store	36,101	127	7.5
Utility	61,113	214	12.7
Employee Retirement	0	0	0.0

Source: U.S. Census Bureau, State & Local Government Finances 2017

City Government Expenditures by Function

Function	2017 ($000)	2017 ($ per capita)	2017 (%)
General Direct Expenditures			
Air Transportation	0	0	0.0
Corrections	0	0	0.0
Education	0	0	0.0
Employment Security Administration	0	0	0.0
Financial Administration	7,333	25	1.4
Fire Protection	49,901	174	9.7
General Public Buildings	14,232	49	2.8
Governmental Administration, Other	4,793	16	0.9
Health	184	< 1	< 0.1
Highways	49,107	172	9.6
Hospitals	0	0	0.0
Housing and Community Development	15,314	53	3.0
Interest on General Debt	8,974	31	1.7
Judicial and Legal	1,234	4	0.2
Libraries	8,439	29	1.6
Parking	4,703	16	0.9
Parks and Recreation	61,640	216	12.0
Police Protection	77,197	270	15.0
Public Welfare	0	0	0.0
Sewerage	64,877	227	12.6
Solid Waste Management	31,981	112	6.2
Veterans' Services	0	0	0.0
Liquor Store	30,948	108	6.0
Utility	67,111	235	13.1
Employee Retirement	0	0	0.0

Source: U.S. Census Bureau, State & Local Government Finances 2017

EMPLOYMENT

Labor Force and Employment

Area	Civilian Labor Force			Workers Employed		
	Dec. 2019	Dec. 2020	% Chg.	Dec. 2019	Dec. 2020	% Chg.
City	147,165	143,483	-2.5	141,957	132,895	-6.4
MSA[1]	371,920	360,292	-3.1	359,136	336,201	-6.4
U.S.	164,007,000	160,017,000	-2.4	158,504,000	149,613,000	-5.6

Note: Data is not seasonally adjusted and covers workers 16 years of age and older; (1) Figures cover the Greensboro-High Point, NC Metropolitan Statistical Area
Source: Bureau of Labor Statistics, Local Area Unemployment Statistics

Unemployment Rate

Area	2020											
	Jan.	Feb.	Mar.	Apr.	May	Jun.	Jul.	Aug.	Sep.	Oct.	Nov.	Dec.
City	4.4	4.0	4.6	15.3	15.8	10.0	11.6	9.1	9.0	7.7	7.7	7.4
MSA[1]	4.3	3.9	4.5	14.8	14.5	9.0	10.2	7.8	7.9	6.9	6.9	6.7
U.S.	4.0	3.8	4.5	14.4	13.0	11.2	10.5	8.5	7.7	6.6	6.4	6.5

Note: Data is not seasonally adjusted and covers workers 16 years of age and older; (1) Figures cover the Greensboro-High Point, NC Metropolitan Statistical Area
Source: Bureau of Labor Statistics, Local Area Unemployment Statistics

Average Wages

Occupation	$/Hr.	Occupation	$/Hr.
Accountants and Auditors	38.60	Maintenance and Repair Workers	20.20
Automotive Mechanics	22.10	Marketing Managers	69.80
Bookkeepers	19.90	Network and Computer Systems Admin.	41.10
Carpenters	17.70	Nurses, Licensed Practical	22.20
Cashiers	10.60	Nurses, Registered	33.80
Computer Programmers	40.70	Nursing Assistants	13.30
Computer Systems Analysts	45.50	Office Clerks, General	16.50
Computer User Support Specialists	24.50	Physical Therapists	43.40
Construction Laborers	15.50	Physicians	133.50
Cooks, Restaurant	12.60	Plumbers, Pipefitters and Steamfitters	24.90
Customer Service Representatives	18.30	Police and Sheriff's Patrol Officers	24.40
Dentists	72.10	Postal Service Mail Carriers	26.00
Electricians	23.30	Real Estate Sales Agents	21.10
Engineers, Electrical	49.10	Retail Salespersons	14.00
Fast Food and Counter Workers	9.90	Sales Representatives, Technical/Scientific	47.50
Financial Managers	69.80	Secretaries, Exc. Legal/Medical/Executive	18.20
First-Line Supervisors of Office Workers	27.40	Security Guards	14.10
General and Operations Managers	63.60	Surgeons	n/a
Hairdressers/Cosmetologists	12.90	Teacher Assistants, Exc. Postsecondary*	12.40
Home Health and Personal Care Aides	11.00	Teachers, Secondary School, Exc. Sp. Ed.*	24.20
Janitors and Cleaners	12.70	Telemarketers	n/a
Landscaping/Groundskeeping Workers	13.70	Truck Drivers, Heavy/Tractor-Trailer	24.60
Lawyers	59.40	Truck Drivers, Light/Delivery Services	17.90
Maids and Housekeeping Cleaners	10.60	Waiters and Waitresses	10.40

Note: Wage data covers the Greensboro-High Point, NC Metropolitan Statistical Area; (*) Hourly wages were calculated from annual wage data based on a 40 hour work week; n/a not available.
Source: Bureau of Labor Statistics, Metro Area Occupational Employment & Wage Estimates, May 2020

Employment by Industry

Sector	MSA[1]		U.S.
	Number of Employees	Percent of Total	Percent of Total
Construction, Mining, and Logging	15,700	4.5	5.5
Education and Health Services	49,800	14.4	16.3
Financial Activities	18,100	5.2	6.1
Government	42,200	12.2	15.2
Information	4,300	1.2	1.9
Leisure and Hospitality	29,700	8.6	9.0
Manufacturing	50,400	14.6	8.5
Other Services	11,500	3.3	3.8
Professional and Business Services	45,100	13.0	14.4
Retail Trade	38,400	11.1	10.9
Transportation, Warehousing, and Utilities	22,400	6.5	4.6
Wholesale Trade	18,500	5.3	3.9

Note: Figures are non-farm employment as of December 2020. Figures are not seasonally adjusted and include workers 16 years of age and older; (1) Figures cover the Greensboro-High Point, NC Metropolitan Statistical Area
Source: Bureau of Labor Statistics, Current Employment Statistics, Employment, Hours, and Earnings

Employment by Occupation

Occupation Classification	City (%)	MSA[1] (%)	U.S. (%)
Management, Business, Science, and Arts	38.3	35.3	38.5
Natural Resources, Construction, and Maintenance	5.8	8.4	8.9
Production, Transportation, and Material Moving	14.9	17.4	13.2
Sales and Office	22.5	22.4	21.6
Service	18.4	16.6	17.8

Note: Figures cover employed civilians 16 years of age and older; (1) Figures cover the Greensboro-High Point, NC Metropolitan Statistical Area
Source: U.S. Census Bureau, 2015-2019 American Community Survey 5-Year Estimates

Occupations with Greatest Projected Employment Growth: 2020 – 2022

Occupation[1]	2020 Employment	2022 Projected Employment	Numeric Employment Change	Percent Employment Change
Laborers and Freight, Stock, and Material Movers, Hand	90,950	94,250	3,300	3.6
Stockers and Order Fillers	99,690	102,690	3,000	3.0
Software Developers and Software Quality Assurance Analysts and Testers	74,740	76,850	2,110	2.8
Registered Nurses	87,970	89,970	2,000	2.3
Project Management Specialists and Business Operations Specialists, All Other	62,540	63,660	1,120	1.8
Computer Systems Analysts (SOC 2018)	40,350	41,450	1,100	2.7
Insurance Sales Agents	13,950	14,920	970	7.0
Industrial Truck and Tractor Operators	22,480	23,360	880	3.9
Loan Officers	12,610	13,430	820	6.5
Customer Service Representatives	80,790	81,600	810	1.0

Note: Projections cover North Carolina; (1) Sorted by numeric employment change
Source: www.projectionscentral.com, State Occupational Projections, 2020–2022 Short-Term Projections

Fastest-Growing Occupations: 2020 – 2022

Occupation[1]	2020 Employment	2022 Projected Employment	Numeric Employment Change	Percent Employment Change
Statisticians	1,420	1,540	120	8.5
Operations Research Analysts	2,490	2,700	210	8.4
Butchers and Meat Cutters	2,650	2,860	210	7.9
Insurance Sales Agents	13,950	14,920	970	7.0
Loan Interviewers and Clerks	6,000	6,420	420	7.0
Brokerage Clerks	1,590	1,700	110	6.9
Veterinary Assistants and Laboratory Animal Caretakers	3,590	3,830	240	6.7
Personal Financial Advisors	8,760	9,330	570	6.5
Loan Officers	12,610	13,430	820	6.5
Veterinary Technologists and Technicians	3,040	3,230	190	6.3

Note: Projections cover North Carolina; (1) Sorted by percent employment change and excludes occupations with numeric employment change less than 50
Source: www.projectionscentral.com, State Occupational Projections, 2020–2022 Short-Term Projections

TAXES

State Corporate Income Tax Rates

State	Tax Rate (%)	Income Brackets ($)	Num. of Brackets	Financial Institution Tax Rate (%)[a]	Federal Income Tax Ded.
North Carolina	2.5	Flat rate	1	2.5	No

Note: Tax rates as of January 1, 2021; (a) Rates listed are the corporate income tax rate applied to financial institutions or excise taxes based on income. Some states have other taxes based upon the value of deposits or shares.
Source: Federation of Tax Administrators, State Corporate Income Tax Rates, January 1, 2021

State Individual Income Tax Rates

State	Tax Rate (%)	Income Brackets ($)	Personal Exemptions ($) Single	Personal Exemptions ($) Married	Personal Exemptions ($) Depend.	Standard Ded. ($) Single	Standard Ded. ($) Married
North Carolina	5.25	Flat rate	None	None	None	10,750	21,500

Note: Tax rates as of January 1, 2021; Local- and county-level taxes are not included; Federal income tax is not deductible on state income tax returns
Source: Federation of Tax Administrators, State Individual Income Tax Rates, January 1, 2021

Various State Sales and Excise Tax Rates

State	State Sales Tax (%)	Gasoline[1] (¢/gal.)	Cigarette[2] ($/pack)	Spirits[3] ($/gal.)	Wine[4] ($/gal.)	Beer[5] ($/gal.)	Recreational Marijuana (%)
North Carolina	4.75	36.35	0.45	14.58	1	0.62	Not legal

Note: All tax rates as of January 1, 2021; (1) The American Petroleum Institute has developed a methodology for determining the average tax rate on a gallon of fuel. Rates may include any of the following: excise taxes, environmental fees, storage tank fees, other fees or taxes, general sales tax, and local taxes; (2) The federal excise tax of $1.0066 per pack and local taxes are not included; (3) Rates are those applicable to off-premise sales of 40% alcohol by volume (a.b.v.) distilled spirits in 750ml containers. Local excise taxes are excluded; (4) Rates are those applicable to off-premise sales of 11% a.b.v. non-carbonated wine in 750ml containers; (5) Rates are those applicable to off-premise sales of 4.7% a.b.v. beer in 12 ounce containers.
Source: Tax Foundation, 2021 Facts & Figures: How Does Your State Compare?

State Business Tax Climate Index Rankings

State	Overall Rank	Corporate Tax Rank	Individual Income Tax Rank	Sales Tax Rank	Property Tax Rank	Unemployment Insurance Tax Rank
North Carolina	10	4	16	22	26	10

Note: The index is a measure of how each state's tax laws affect economic performance. The lower the rank, the more favorable a state's tax system is for business. States without a given tax are given a ranking of 1. The scores/rankings for the District of Columbia do not affect other states. The 2021 index represents the tax climate as of July 1, 2020.
Source: Tax Foundation, State Business Tax Climate Index 2021

TRANSPORTATION

Means of Transportation to Work

Area	Car/Truck/Van		Public Transportation			Bicycle	Walked	Other Means	Worked at Home
	Drove Alone	Car-pooled	Bus	Subway	Railroad				
City	81.9	7.6	1.9	0.0	0.0	0.2	1.9	0.9	5.6
MSA[1]	82.7	9.0	0.9	0.0	0.0	0.1	1.4	0.9	4.9
U.S.	76.3	9.0	2.4	1.9	0.6	0.5	2.7	1.4	5.2

Note: Figures are percentages and cover workers 16 years of age and older; (1) Figures cover the Greensboro-High Point, NC Metropolitan Statistical Area
Source: U.S. Census Bureau, 2015-2019 American Community Survey 5-Year Estimates

Travel Time to Work

Area	Less Than 10 Minutes	10 to 19 Minutes	20 to 29 Minutes	30 to 44 Minutes	45 to 59 Minutes	60 to 89 Minutes	90 Minutes or More
City	12.1	41.4	24.1	14.7	3.5	2.6	1.6
MSA[1]	12.2	34.8	25.3	18.4	5.0	2.6	1.7
U.S.	12.2	28.4	20.8	20.8	8.3	6.4	2.9

Note: Note: Figures are percentages and include workers 16 years old and over; (1) Figures cover the Greensboro-High Point, NC Metropolitan Statistical Area
Source: U.S. Census Bureau, 2015-2019 American Community Survey 5-Year Estimates

Key Congestion Measures

Measure	1982	1992	2002	2012	2017
Annual Hours of Delay, Total (000)	447	1,972	5,055	6,969	7,896
Annual Hours of Delay, Per Auto Commuter	5	16	29	34	38
Annual Congestion Cost, Total (million $)	3	21	68	124	145
Annual Congestion Cost, Per Auto Commuter ($)	81	244	488	528	579

Note: Covers the Greensboro NC urban area
Source: Texas A&M Transportation Institute, 2019 Urban Mobility Report

Freeway Travel Time Index

Measure	1982	1987	1992	1997	2002	2007	2012	2017
Urban Area Index[1]	1.02	1.02	1.05	1.07	1.09	1.10	1.11	1.13
Urban Area Rank[1,2]	90	96	92	94	96	97	94	83

Note: Freeway Travel Time Index—the ratio of travel time in the peak period to the travel time at free-flow conditions. For example, a value of 1.30 indicates a 20-minute free-flow trip takes 26 minutes in the peak (20 minutes x 1.30 = 26 minutes); (1) Covers the Greensboro NC urban area; (2) Rank is based on 101 larger urban areas (#1 = highest travel time index)
Source: Texas A&M Transportation Institute, 2019 Urban Mobility Report

Public Transportation

Agency Name / Mode of Transportation	Vehicles Operated in Maximum Service[1]	Annual Unlinked Passenger Trips[2] (in thous.)	Annual Passenger Miles[3] (in thous.)
Greensboro Transit Authority (GTA)			
Bus (purchased transportation)	41	3,191.2	7,255.1
Demand Response (purchased transportation)	45	274.8	2,052.8

Note: (1) Number of revenue vehicles operated by the given mode and type of service to meet the annual maximum service requirement. This is the revenue vehicle count during the peak season of the year; on the week and day that maximum service is provided. Vehicles operated in maximum service (VOMS) exclude atypical days and one-time special events; (2) Number of passengers who boarded public transportation vehicles. Passengers are counted each time they board a vehicle no matter how many vehicles they use to travel from their origin to their destination. (3) Sum of the distances ridden by all passengers during the entire fiscal year. Source: Federal Transit Administration, National Transit Database, 2019

Air Transportation

Airport Name and Code / Type of Service	Passenger Airlines[1]	Passenger Enplanements	Freight Carriers[2]	Freight (lbs)
Piedmont Triad International (GSO)				
Domestic service (U.S. carriers - 2020)	23	379,379	18	107,216,252
International service (U.S. carriers - 2019)	1	12	1	60,916

Note: (1) Includes all U.S.-based major, minor and commuter airlines that carried at least one passenger during the year; (2) Includes all U.S.-based airlines and freight carriers that transported at least one pound of freight during the year. Source: Bureau of Transportation Statistics, The Intermodal Transportation Database, Air Carriers: T-100 Domestic Market (U.S. Carriers), 2020; Bureau of Transportation Statistics, The Intermodal Transportation Database, Air Carriers: T-100 International Market (U.S. Carriers), 2019

BUSINESSES

Major Business Headquarters

Company Name	Industry	Rankings	
		Fortune[1]	Forbes[2]
VF	Apparel	233	-

Note: (1) Companies that produce a 10-K are ranked 1 to 500 based on 2019 revenue; (2) All private companies with at least $2 billion in annual revenue through the end of their most current fiscal year are ranked 1 to 219; companies listed are headquartered in the city; dashes indicate no ranking Source: Fortune, "Fortune 500," June/July 2020; Forbes, "America's Largest Private Companies," 2020

Fastest-Growing Businesses

According to *Inc.*, Greensboro is home to one of America's 500 fastest-growing private companies: **Guerrilla Rf** (#421). Criteria: must be an independent, privately-held, for-profit, U.S. corporation, proprietorship or partnership as of December 31, 2019; revenues must be at least $100,000 in 2016 and $2 million in 2019; must have four-year operating/sales history. *Inc., "America's 500 Fastest-Growing Private Companies," 2020*

Living Environment

COST OF LIVING

Cost of Living Index

Composite Index	Groceries	Housing	Utilities	Trans-portation	Health Care	Misc. Goods/ Services
94.3	101.1	79.9	93.7	99.7	116.7	98.8

Note: The Cost of Living Index measures regional differences in the cost of consumer goods and services, excluding taxes and non-consumer expenditures, for professional and managerial households in the top income quintile. It is based on more than 50,000 prices covering almost 60 different items for which prices are collected three times a year by chambers of commerce, economic development organizations or university applied economic centers in each participating urban area. The numbers shown should be read as a percentage above or below the national average of 100. For example, a value of 115.4 in the groceries column indicates that grocery prices are 15.4% higher than the national average. Small differences in the index numbers should not be interpreted as significant; Figures cover the Winston-Salem NC urban area.
Source: The Council for Community and Economic Research, Cost of Living Index, 2020

Grocery Prices

Area[1]	T-Bone Steak ($/pound)	Frying Chicken ($/pound)	Whole Milk ($/half gal.)	Eggs ($/dozen)	Orange Juice ($/64 oz.)	Coffee ($/11.5 oz.)
City[2]	11.86	1.27	1.55	1.45	3.94	4.03
Avg.	11.78	1.39	2.05	1.47	3.57	4.34
Min.	8.03	0.94	1.03	0.74	2.94	3.02
Max.	15.86	2.65	4.31	3.77	5.44	8.69

Note: (1) Values for the local area are compared with the average, minimum and maximum values for all 284 areas in the Cost of Living Index; (2) Figures cover the Winston-Salem NC urban area; T-Bone Steak (price per pound); Frying Chicken (price per pound, whole fryer); Whole Milk (half gallon carton); Eggs (price per dozen, Grade A, large); Orange Juice (64 oz. Tropicana or Florida Natural); Coffee (11.5 oz. can, vacuum-packed, Maxwell House, Hills Bros, or Folgers).
Source: The Council for Community and Economic Research, Cost of Living Index, 2020

Housing and Utility Costs

Area[1]	New Home Price ($)	Apartment Rent ($/month)	All Electric ($/month)	Part Electric ($/month)	Other Energy ($/month)	Telephone ($/month)
City[2]	248,204	1,242	158.18	-	-	169.60
Avg.	368,594	1,168	170.86	100.47	65.28	184.30
Min.	190,567	502	91.58	31.42	26.08	169.60
Max.	2,227,806	4,738	470.38	280.31	280.06	206.50

Note: (1) Values for the local area are compared with the average, minimum and maximum values for all 284 areas in the Cost of Living Index; (2) Figures cover the Winston-Salem NC urban area; New Home Price (2,400 sf living area, 8,000 sf lot, in urban area with full utilities); Apartment Rent (950 sf 2 bedroom/1.5 or 2 bath, unfurnished, excluding all utilities except water); All Electric (average monthly cost for an all-electric home); Part Electric (average monthly cost for a part-electric home); Other Energy (average monthly cost for natural gas, fuel oil, coal, wood, and any other forms of energy except electricity); Telephone (price includes the base monthly rate plus taxes and fees for three lines of mobile phone service).
Source: The Council for Community and Economic Research, Cost of Living Index, 2020

Health Care, Transportation, and Other Costs

Area[1]	Doctor ($/visit)	Dentist ($/visit)	Optometrist ($/visit)	Gasoline ($/gallon)	Beauty Salon ($/visit)	Men's Shirt ($)
City[2]	124.74	139.81	109.70	2.12	35.48	39.18
Avg.	115.44	99.32	108.10	2.21	39.27	31.37
Min.	36.68	59.00	51.36	1.71	19.00	11.00
Max.	219.00	153.10	250.97	3.46	82.05	58.33

Note: (1) Values for the local area are compared with the average, minimum and maximum values for all 284 areas in the Cost of Living Index; (2) Figures cover the Winston-Salem NC urban area; Doctor (general practitioners routine exam of an established patient); Dentist (adult teeth cleaning and periodic oral examination); Optometrist (full vision eye exam for established adult patient); Gasoline (one gallon regular unleaded, national brand, including all taxes, cash price at self-service pump if available); Beauty Salon (woman's shampoo, trim, and blow-dry); Men's Shirt (cotton/polyester dress shirt, pinpoint weave, long sleeves).
Source: The Council for Community and Economic Research, Cost of Living Index, 2020

HOUSING

Homeownership Rate

Area	2012 (%)	2013 (%)	2014 (%)	2015 (%)	2016 (%)	2017 (%)	2018 (%)	2019 (%)	2020 (%)
MSA[1]	64.9	67.9	68.1	65.4	62.9	61.9	63.2	61.7	65.8
U.S.	65.4	65.1	64.5	63.7	63.4	63.9	64.4	64.6	66.6

Note: (1) Figures cover the Greensboro-High Point, NC Metropolitan Statistical Area
Source: U.S. Census Bureau, Housing Vacancies and Homeownership Annual Statistics: 2012-2020

House Price Index (HPI)

Area	National Ranking[2]	Quarterly Change (%)	One-Year Change (%)	Five-Year Change (%)	Since 1991Q1 (%)
MSA[1]	128	1.99	6.14	27.91	106.32
U.S.[3]	–	3.81	10.77	38.99	205.12

Note: The HPI is a weighted repeat sales index. It measures average price changes in repeat sales or refinancings on the same properties. This information is obtained by reviewing repeat mortgage transactions on single-family properties whose mortgages have been purchased or securitized by Fannie Mae or Freddie Mac since January 1975; (1) Figures cover the Greensboro-High Point, NC Metropolitan Statistical Area; (2) Rankings are based on annual percentage change for all metro areas containing at least 15,000 transactions over the last 10 years and ranges from 1 to 253; (3) figures based on a weighted average of Census Division estimates using a seasonally adjusted, purchase-only index; all figures are for the period ending December 31, 2020
Source: Federal Housing Finance Agency, Change in Metropolitan Area House Price Indexes, April 7, 2021

Median Single-Family Home Prices

Area	2018	2019	2020[p]	Percent Change 2019 to 2020
MSA[1]	164.1	176.2	199.2	13.1
U.S. Average	261.6	274.6	299.9	9.2

Note: Figures are median sales prices of existing single-family homes in thousands of dollars; (p) preliminary; (1) Figures cover the Greensboro-High Point, NC Metropolitan Statistical Area
Source: National Association of Realtors, Median Sales Price of Existing Single-Family Homes for Metropolitan Areas, 4th Quarter 2020

Qualifying Income Based on Median Sales Price of Existing Single-Family Homes

Area	With 5% Down ($)	With 10% Down ($)	With 20% Down ($)
MSA[1]	39,209	37,146	33,018
U.S. Average	59,266	56,147	49,908

Note: Figures are preliminary; Qualifying income is based on a mortgage rate of 2.81%. Monthly principal and interest payment is limited to 25% of income; (1) Figures cover the Greensboro-High Point, NC Metropolitan Statistical Area
Source: National Association of Realtors, Qualifying Income Based on Median Sales Price of Existing Single-Family Homes for Metropolitan Areas, 4th Quarter 2020

Home Value Distribution

Area	Under $50,000	$50,000 -$99,999	$100,000 -$149,999	$150,000 -$199,999	$200,000 -$299,999	$300,000 -$499,999	$500,000 -$999,999	$1,000,000 or more
City	3.5	19.2	24.5	18.3	18.2	11.4	3.7	1.2
MSA[1]	7.0	19.7	23.7	17.7	17.2	10.7	3.4	0.7
U.S.	6.9	12.0	13.3	14.0	19.6	19.3	11.4	3.4

Note: Figures are percentages and cover owner-occupied housing units; (1) Figures cover the Greensboro-High Point, NC Metropolitan Statistical Area
Source: U.S. Census Bureau, 2015-2019 American Community Survey 5-Year Estimates

Year Housing Structure Built

Area	2010 or Later	2000 -2009	1990 -1999	1980 -1989	1970 -1979	1960 -1969	1950 -1959	1940 -1949	Before 1940	Median Year
City	5.2	15.0	17.9	16.6	14.4	11.2	10.2	3.8	5.5	1983
MSA[1]	5.0	15.9	18.9	14.5	14.7	10.9	9.5	4.5	6.1	1983
U.S.	5.2	14.0	13.9	13.4	15.2	10.6	10.3	4.9	12.6	1978

Note: Figures are percentages except for Median Year; Note: (1) Figures cover the Greensboro-High Point, NC Metropolitan Statistical Area
Source: U.S. Census Bureau, 2015-2019 American Community Survey 5-Year Estimates

Gross Monthly Rent

Area	Under $500	$500 -$999	$1,000 -$1,499	$1,500 -$1,999	$2,000 -$2,499	$2,500 -$2,999	$3,000 and up	Median ($)
City	6.8	61.7	26.0	3.4	1.2	0.4	0.5	877
MSA[1]	9.6	63.4	22.4	2.9	1.0	0.3	0.5	834
U.S.	9.4	36.2	30.0	14.0	5.6	2.4	2.4	1,062

Note: Figures are percentages except for Median; Gross rent is the contract rent plus the estimated average monthly cost of utilities (electricity, gas, and water and sewer) and fuels (oil, coal, kerosene, wood, etc.) if these are paid by the renter (or paid for the renter by someone else); (1) Figures cover the Greensboro-High Point, NC Metropolitan Statistical Area
Source: U.S. Census Bureau, 2015-2019 American Community Survey 5-Year Estimates

HEALTH

Health Risk Factors

Category	MSA[1] (%)	U.S. (%)
Adults aged 18–64 who have any kind of health care coverage	n/a	87.3
Adults who reported being in good or better health	n/a	82.4
Adults who have been told they have high blood cholesterol	n/a	33.0
Adults who have been told they have high blood pressure	n/a	32.3
Adults who are current smokers	n/a	17.1
Adults who currently use E-cigarettes	n/a	4.6
Adults who currently use chewing tobacco, snuff, or snus	n/a	4.0
Adults who are heavy drinkers[2]	n/a	6.3
Adults who are binge drinkers[3]	n/a	17.4
Adults who are overweight (BMI 25.0 - 29.9)	n/a	35.3
Adults who are obese (BMI 30.0 - 99.8)	n/a	31.3
Adults who participated in any physical activities in the past month	n/a	74.4
Adults who always or nearly always wears a seat belt	n/a	94.3

Note: n/a not available; (1) Figures cover the Greensboro-High Point, NC Metropolitan Statistical Area; (2) Heavy drinkers are classified as adult men having more than 14 drinks per week and adult women having more than 7 drinks per week; (3) Binge drinkers are classified as males having five or more drinks on one occasion or females having four or more drinks on one occasion
Source: Centers for Disease Control and Prevention, Behaviorial Risk Factor Surveillance System, SMART: Selected Metropolitan Area Risk Trends, 2017

Acute and Chronic Health Conditions

Category	MSA[1] (%)	U.S. (%)
Adults who have ever been told they had a heart attack	n/a	4.2
Adults who have ever been told they have angina or coronary heart disease	n/a	3.9
Adults who have ever been told they had a stroke	n/a	3.0
Adults who have ever been told they have asthma	n/a	14.2
Adults who have ever been told they have arthritis	n/a	24.9
Adults who have ever been told they have diabetes[2]	n/a	10.5
Adults who have ever been told they had skin cancer	n/a	6.2
Adults who have ever been told they had any other types of cancer	n/a	7.1
Adults who have ever been told they have COPD	n/a	6.5
Adults who have ever been told they have kidney disease	n/a	3.0
Adults who have ever been told they have a form of depression	n/a	20.5

Note: n/a not available; (1) Figures cover the Greensboro-High Point, NC Metropolitan Statistical Area; (2) Figures do not include pregnancy-related, borderline, or pre-diabetes
Source: Centers for Disease Control and Prevention, Behaviorial Risk Factor Surveillance System, SMART: Selected Metropolitan Area Risk Trends, 2017

Health Screening and Vaccination Rates

Category	MSA[1] (%)	U.S. (%)
Adults aged 65+ who have had flu shot within the past year	n/a	60.7
Adults aged 65+ who have ever had a pneumonia vaccination	n/a	75.4
Adults who have ever been tested for HIV	n/a	36.1
Adults who have ever had the shingles or zoster vaccine?	n/a	28.9
Adults who have had their blood cholesterol checked within the last five years	n/a	85.9

Note: n/a not available; (1) Figures cover the Greensboro-High Point, NC Metropolitan Statistical Area.
Source: Centers for Disease Control and Prevention, Behaviorial Risk Factor Surveillance System, SMART: Selected Metropolitan Area Risk Trends, 2017

Disability Status

Category	MSA[1] (%)	U.S. (%)
Adults who reported being deaf	n/a	6.7
Are you blind or have serious difficulty seeing, even when wearing glasses?	n/a	4.5
Are you limited in any way in any of your usual activities due of arthritis?	n/a	12.9
Do you have difficulty doing errands alone?	n/a	6.8
Do you have difficulty dressing or bathing?	n/a	3.6
Do you have serious difficulty concentrating/remembering/making decisions?	n/a	10.7
Do you have serious difficulty walking or climbing stairs?	n/a	13.6

Note: n/a not available; (1) Figures cover the Greensboro-High Point, NC Metropolitan Statistical Area.
Source: Centers for Disease Control and Prevention, Behaviorial Risk Factor Surveillance System, SMART: Selected Metropolitan Area Risk Trends, 2017

Mortality Rates for the Top 10 Causes of Death in the U.S.

ICD-10[a] Sub-Chapter	ICD-10[a] Code	Age-Adjusted Mortality Rate[1] per 100,000 population	
		County[2]	U.S.
Malignant neoplasms	C00-C97	150.5	149.2
Ischaemic heart diseases	I20-I25	67.2	90.5
Other forms of heart disease	I30-I51	52.0	52.2
Chronic lower respiratory diseases	J40-J47	32.0	39.6
Other degenerative diseases of the nervous system	G30-G31	42.3	37.6
Cerebrovascular diseases	I60-I69	43.4	37.2
Other external causes of accidental injury	W00-X59	43.6	36.1
Organic, including symptomatic, mental disorders	F01-F09	45.0	29.4
Hypertensive diseases	I10-I15	20.2	24.1
Diabetes mellitus	E10-E14	25.6	21.5

Note: (a) ICD-10 = International Classification of Diseases 10th Revision; (1) Mortality rates are a three-year average covering 2017-2019; (2) Figures cover Guilford County.
Source: Centers for Disease Control and Prevention, National Center for Health Statistics. Underlying Cause of Death 1999-2019 on CDC WONDER Online Database

Mortality Rates for Selected Causes of Death

ICD-10[a] Sub-Chapter	ICD-10[a] Code	Age-Adjusted Mortality Rate[1] per 100,000 population	
		County[2]	U.S.
Assault	X85-Y09	10.0	6.0
Diseases of the liver	K70-K76	14.6	14.4
Human immunodeficiency virus (HIV) disease	B20-B24	1.8	1.5
Influenza and pneumonia	J09-J18	19.4	13.8
Intentional self-harm	X60-X84	11.5	14.1
Malnutrition	E40-E46	3.6	2.3
Obesity and other hyperalimentation	E65-E68	3.5	2.1
Renal failure	N17-N19	19.4	12.6
Transport accidents	V01-V99	14.0	12.3
Viral hepatitis	B15-B19	1.3	1.2

Note: (a) ICD-10 = International Classification of Diseases 10th Revision; (1) Mortality rates are a three-year average covering 2017-2019; (2) Figures cover Guilford County; Data are suppressed when the data meet the criteria for confidentiality constraints; Mortality rates are flagged as unreliable when the rate would be calculated with a numerator of 20 or less.
Source: Centers for Disease Control and Prevention, National Center for Health Statistics. Underlying Cause of Death 1999-2019 on CDC WONDER Online Database

Health Insurance Coverage

Area	With Health Insurance	With Private Health Insurance	With Public Health Insurance	Without Health Insurance	Population Under Age 19 Without Health Insurance
City	89.7	65.9	34.1	10.3	4.5
MSA[1]	89.6	65.5	35.2	10.4	4.7
U.S.	91.2	67.9	35.1	8.8	5.1

Note: Figures are percentages that cover the civilian noninstitutionalized population; (1) Figures cover the Greensboro-High Point, NC Metropolitan Statistical Area
Source: U.S. Census Bureau, 2015-2019 American Community Survey 5-Year Estimates

Number of Medical Professionals

Area	MDs[3]	DOs[3,4]	Dentists	Podiatrists	Chiropractors	Optometrists
County[1] (number)	1,347	75	306	27	76	55
County[1] (rate[2])	252.9	14.1	57.0	5.0	14.1	10.2
U.S. (rate[2])	282.9	22.7	71.2	6.2	28.1	16.9

37081
Note: Data as of 2019 unless noted; (1) Data covers Guilford County; (2) Rate per 100,000 population; (3) Data as of 2018 and includes all active, non-federal physicians; (4) Doctor of Osteopathic Medicine
Source: U.S. Department of Health and Human Services, Health Resources and Services Administration, Bureau of Health Professions, Area Resource File (ARF) 2019-2020

EDUCATION

Public School District Statistics

District Name	Schls	Pupils	Pupil/ Teacher Ratio	Minority Pupils[1] (%)	Free Lunch Eligible[2] (%)	IEP[3] (%)
Guilford County Schools	125	72,950	15.6	68.8	61.7	13.7

Note: Table includes school districts with 2,000 or more students; (1) Percentage of students that are not non-Hispanic white; (2) Percentage of students that are eligible for the free lunch program; (3) Percentage of students that have an Individualized Education Program.
Source: U.S. Department of Education, National Center for Education Statistics, Common Core of Data, Local Education Agency (School District) Universe Survey: School Year 2018-2019; U.S. Department of Education, National Center for Education Statistics, Common Core of Data, Public Elementary/Secondary School Universe Survey: School Year 2018-2019

Best High Schools

According to *U.S. News,* Greensboro is home to three of the top 500 high schools in the U.S.: **The Early College at Guilford** (#31); **Philip J. Weaver Ed Center** (#141); **STEM Early College at N.C. A&T** (#194). Nearly 18,000 public, magnet and charter schools were ranked based on their performance on state assessments and how well they prepare students for college. *U.S. News & World Report, "Best High Schools 2020"*

Highest Level of Education

Area	Less than H.S.	H.S. Diploma	Some College, No Deg.	Associate Degree	Bachelor's Degree	Master's Degree	Prof. School Degree	Doctorate Degree
City	10.2	21.5	21.7	8.4	24.1	10.0	2.3	1.8
MSA[1]	13.2	26.7	21.7	8.9	19.2	7.5	1.5	1.3
U.S.	12.0	27.0	20.4	8.5	19.8	8.8	2.1	1.4

Note: Figures cover persons age 25 and over; (1) Figures cover the Greensboro-High Point, NC Metropolitan Statistical Area
Source: U.S. Census Bureau, 2015-2019 American Community Survey 5-Year Estimates

Educational Attainment by Race

Area	High School Graduate or Higher (%)					Bachelor's Degree or Higher (%)				
	Total	White	Black	Asian	Hisp.[2]	Total	White	Black	Asian	Hisp.[2]
City	89.8	93.4	88.5	75.2	64.2	38.2	49.1	24.5	41.9	18.2
MSA[1]	86.8	88.9	86.1	76.4	57.6	29.5	32.0	23.0	42.6	13.7
U.S.	88.0	89.9	86.0	87.1	68.7	32.1	33.5	21.6	54.3	16.4

Note: Figures shown cover persons 25 years old and over; (1) Figures cover the Greensboro-High Point, NC Metropolitan Statistical Area; (2) People of Hispanic origin can be of any race
Source: U.S. Census Bureau, 2015-2019 American Community Survey 5-Year Estimates

School Enrollment by Grade and Control

Area	Preschool (%)		Kindergarten (%)		Grades 1 - 4 (%)		Grades 5 - 8 (%)		Grades 9 - 12 (%)	
	Public	Private	Public	Private	Public	Private	Public	Private	Public	Private
City	53.2	46.8	89.5	10.5	93.4	6.6	90.2	9.8	91.6	8.4
MSA[1]	50.5	49.5	89.4	10.6	90.3	9.7	89.1	10.9	90.3	9.7
U.S.	59.1	40.9	87.6	12.4	89.5	10.5	89.4	10.6	90.1	9.9

Note: Figures shown cover persons 3 years old and over; (1) Figures cover the Greensboro-High Point, NC Metropolitan Statistical Area
Source: U.S. Census Bureau, 2015-2019 American Community Survey 5-Year Estimates

Higher Education

Four-Year Colleges			Two-Year Colleges			Medical Schools[1]	Law Schools[2]	Voc/ Tech[3]
Public	Private Non-profit	Private For-profit	Public	Private Non-profit	Private For-profit			
2	3	0	0	0	1	0	1	3

Note: Figures cover institutions located within the city limits and include main campuses only; (1) includes schools accredited by the Liaison Committee on Medical Education and the American Osteopathic Association's Commission on Osteopathic College Accreditation; (2) includes ABA-accredited schools, schools with provisional ABA accreditation, and state accredited schools; (3) includes all schools with programs that are less than 2 years.
Source: National Center for Education Statistics, Integrated Postsecondary Education System (IPEDS), 2019-20; Wikipedia, List of Medical Schools in the United States, accessed April 2, 2021; Wikipedia, List of Law Schools in the United States, accessed April 2, 2021

EMPLOYERS

Major Employers

Company Name	Industry
Bank of America	Financial services
CitiGroup	Financial services
City of Greensboro	Municipal government
City of High Point	Municipal government
Cone Denim	Denims
County of Guilford	County government
Daimler Trucks North America	Motor vehicles & car bodies
Gilbarco	Electronic computers
High Point Regional Health System	General medical & surgical hospitals
ITG Holdings	Denims
Kayser- Roth Corporation	Mens, boys, girls, hosiery
Klaussner Furniture Industries	Upholstered/household furniture
Lorillard Tobbacco Co	Cigarettes
NC Ag & Technical State University	University
Piedmont Express	Airline ticket offices
Ralph Lauren Corporation	Distribution/customer service
RF Micro Devices	Semiconductors & related devices
Technimark	Injection-molded plastics
The Fresh Market	Grocery stores
The Moses H Cone Memorial Hospital	General medical & surgical hospitals
The University of NC at Greensboro	Colleges & universities
Thomas Built Buses	Truck and bus bodies
Zen Hro	Employee leasing services

Note: Companies shown are located within the Greensboro-High Point, NC Metropolitan Statistical Area.
Source: Hoovers.com; Wikipedia

PUBLIC SAFETY

Crime Rate

Area	All Crimes	Violent Crimes				Property Crimes		
		Murder	Rape[3]	Robbery	Aggrav. Assault	Burglary	Larceny -Theft	Motor Vehicle Theft
City	4,507.7	14.4	37.9	208.4	558.0	743.2	2,614.5	331.2
Suburbs[1]	2,421.7	6.7	29.9	53.7	258.8	475.5	1,421.1	175.9
Metro[2]	3,226.1	9.7	33.0	113.3	374.2	578.8	1,881.3	235.7
U.S.	2,489.3	5.0	42.6	81.6	250.2	340.5	1,549.5	219.9

Note: Figures are crimes per 100,000 population; (1) All areas within the metro area that are located outside the city limits; (2) Figures cover the Greensboro-High Point, NC Metropolitan Statistical Area; (3) All figures shown were reported using the revised Uniform Crime Reporting (UCR) definition of rape.
Source: FBI Uniform Crime Reports, 2019

Hate Crimes

Area	Number of Quarters Reported	Number of Incidents per Bias Motivation					
		Race/Ethnicity/ Ancestry	Religion	Sexual Orientation	Disability	Gender	Gender Identity
City	4	8	1	0	1	0	0
U.S.	4	3,963	1,521	1,195	157	69	198

Source: Federal Bureau of Investigation, Hate Crime Statistics 2019

Identity Theft Consumer Reports

Area	Reports	Reports per 100,000 Population	Rank[2]
MSA[1]	2,580	334	101
U.S.	1,387,615	423	-

Note: (1) Figures cover the Greensboro-High Point, NC Metropolitan Statistical Area; (2) Rank ranges from 1 to 391 where 1 indicates greatest number of identity theft reports per 100,000 population
Source: Federal Trade Commission, Consumer Sentinel Network Data Book 2020

Fraud and Other Consumer Reports

Area	Reports	Reports per 100,000 Population	Rank[2]
MSA[1]	6,078	787	111
U.S.	3,385,133	1,031	-

Note: (1) Figures cover the Greensboro-High Point, NC Metropolitan Statistical Area; (2) Rank ranges from 1 to 391 where 1 indicates greatest number of fraud and other consumer reports per 100,000 population
Source: Federal Trade Commission, Consumer Sentinel Network Data Book 2020

POLITICS

2020 Presidential Election Results

Area	Biden	Trump	Jorgensen	Hawkins	Other
Guilford County	60.8	37.7	0.8	0.2	0.4
U.S.	51.3	46.8	1.2	0.3	0.5

Note: Results are percentages and may not add to 100% due to rounding
Source: Dave Leip's Atlas of U.S. Presidential Elections

SPORTS

Professional Sports Teams

Team Name	League	Year Established

No teams are located in the metro area
Source: Wikipedia, Major Professional Sports Teams of the United States and Canada, April 6, 2021

CLIMATE

Average and Extreme Temperatures

Temperature	Jan	Feb	Mar	Apr	May	Jun	Jul	Aug	Sep	Oct	Nov	Dec	Yr.
Extreme High (°F)	78	81	89	91	96	102	102	103	100	95	85	78	103
Average High (°F)	48	51	60	70	78	84	87	86	80	70	60	50	69
Average Temp. (°F)	38	41	49	58	67	74	78	76	70	59	49	40	58
Average Low (°F)	28	30	37	46	55	63	67	66	59	47	37	30	47
Extreme Low (°F)	-8	-1	5	23	32	42	49	45	37	20	10	0	-8

Note: Figures cover the years 1948-1990
Source: National Climatic Data Center, International Station Meteorological Climate Summary, 9/96

Average Precipitation/Snowfall/Humidity

Precip./Humidity	Jan	Feb	Mar	Apr	May	Jun	Jul	Aug	Sep	Oct	Nov	Dec	Yr.
Avg. Precip. (in.)	3.2	3.4	3.7	3.1	3.7	3.8	4.5	4.2	3.4	3.4	2.9	3.3	42.5
Avg. Snowfall (in.)	4	3	2	Tr	0	0	0	0	0	0	Tr	1	10
Avg. Rel. Hum. 7am (%)	80	78	78	77	82	84	87	90	90	88	83	80	83
Avg. Rel. Hum. 4pm (%)	53	50	47	44	51	54	57	58	56	51	51	54	52

Note: Figures cover the years 1948-1990; Tr = Trace amounts (<0.05 in. of rain; <0.5 in. of snow)
Source: National Climatic Data Center, International Station Meteorological Climate Summary, 9/96

Weather Conditions

Temperature			Daytime Sky			Precipitation		
10°F & below	32°F & below	90°F & above	Clear	Partly cloudy	Cloudy	0.01 inch or more precip.	0.1 inch or more snow/ice	Thunder-storms
3	85	32	94	143	128	113	5	43

Note: Figures are average number of days per year and cover the years 1948-1990
Source: National Climatic Data Center, International Station Meteorological Climate Summary, 9/96

HAZARDOUS WASTE

Superfund Sites

The Greensboro-High Point, NC metro area has no sites on the EPA's Superfund Final National Priorities List. There are a total of 1,375 Superfund sites with a status of proposed or final on the list in the U.S. *U.S. Environmental Protection Agency, National Priorities List, April 7, 2021*

AIR QUALITY

Air Quality Trends: Ozone

	1990	1995	2000	2005	2010	2015	2016	2017	2018	2019
MSA[1]	n/a	n/a	n/a	n/a	n/a	n/a	n/a	n/a	n/a	n/a
U.S.	0.088	0.089	0.082	0.080	0.073	0.068	0.069	0.068	0.069	0.065

Note: (1) Data covers the Greensboro-High Point, NC Metropolitan Statistical Area; n/a not available. The values shown are the composite ozone concentration averages among trend sites based on the highest fourth daily maximum 8-hour concentration in parts per million. These trends are based on sites having an adequate record of monitoring data during the trend period. Data from exceptional events are included.
Source: U.S. Environmental Protection Agency, Air Quality Monitoring Information, "Air Quality Trends by City, 1990-2019"

Air Quality Index

Area	Percent of Days when Air Quality was...[2]					AQI Statistics[2]	
	Good	Moderate	Unhealthy for Sensitive Groups	Unhealthy	Very Unhealthy	Maximum	Median
MSA[1]	79.7	20.3	0.0	0.0	0.0	90	43

Note: (1) Data covers the Greensboro-High Point, NC Metropolitan Statistical Area; (2) Based on 365 days with AQI data in 2019. Air Quality Index (AQI) is an index for reporting daily air quality. EPA calculates the AQI for five major air pollutants regulated by the Clean Air Act: ground-level ozone, particle pollution (aka particulate matter), carbon monoxide, sulfur dioxide, and nitrogen dioxide. The AQI runs from 0 to 500. The higher the AQI value, the greater the level of air pollution and the greater the health concern. There are six AQI categories: "Good" AQI is between 0 and 50. Air quality is considered satisfactory; "Moderate" AQI is between 51 and 100. Air quality is acceptable; "Unhealthy for Sensitive Groups" When AQI values are between 101 and 150, members of sensitive groups may experience health effects; "Unhealthy" When AQI values are between 151 and 200 everyone may begin to experience health effects; "Very Unhealthy" AQI values between 201 and 300 trigger a health alert; "Hazardous" AQI values over 300 trigger warnings of emergency conditions (not shown).
Source: U.S. Environmental Protection Agency, Air Quality Index Report, 2019

Air Quality Index Pollutants

Area	Percent of Days when AQI Pollutant was...[2]					
	Carbon Monoxide	Nitrogen Dioxide	Ozone	Sulfur Dioxide	Particulate Matter 2.5	Particulate Matter 10
MSA[1]	0.0	0.0	63.6	0.0	29.3	7.1

Note: (1) Data covers the Greensboro-High Point, NC Metropolitan Statistical Area; (2) Based on 365 days with AQI data in 2019. The Air Quality Index (AQI) is an index for reporting daily air quality. EPA calculates the AQI for five major air pollutants regulated by the Clean Air Act: ground-level ozone, particle pollution (also known as particulate matter), carbon monoxide, sulfur dioxide, and nitrogen dioxide. The AQI runs from 0 to 500. The higher the AQI value, the greater the level of air pollution and the greater the health concern.
Source: U.S. Environmental Protection Agency, Air Quality Index Report, 2019

Maximum Air Pollutant Concentrations: Particulate Matter, Ozone, CO and Lead

	Particulate Matter 10 (ug/m^3)	Particulate Matter 2.5 Wtd AM (ug/m^3)	Particulate Matter 2.5 24-Hr (ug/m^3)	Ozone (ppm)	Carbon Monoxide (ppm)	Lead (ug/m^3)
MSA[1] Level	33	6.8	15	0.064	n/a	n/a
NAAQS[2]	150	15	35	0.075	9	0.15
Met NAAQS[2]	Yes	Yes	Yes	Yes	n/a	n/a

Note: (1) Data covers the Greensboro-High Point, NC Metropolitan Statistical Area; Data from exceptional events are included; (2) National Ambient Air Quality Standards; ppm = parts per million; ug/m^3 = micrograms per cubic meter; n/a not available.
Concentrations: Particulate Matter 10 (coarse particulate)—highest second maximum 24-hour concentration; Particulate Matter 2.5 Wtd AM (fine particulate)—highest weighted annual mean concentration; Particulate Matter 2.5 24-Hour (fine particulate)—highest 98th percentile 24-hour concentration; Ozone—highest fourth daily maximum 8-hour concentration; Carbon Monoxide—highest second maximum non-overlapping 8-hour concentration; Lead—maximum running 3-month average
Source: U.S. Environmental Protection Agency, Air Quality Monitoring Information, "Air Quality Statistics by City, 2019"

Maximum Air Pollutant Concentrations: Nitrogen Dioxide and Sulfur Dioxide

	Nitrogen Dioxide AM (ppb)	Nitrogen Dioxide 1-Hr (ppb)	Sulfur Dioxide AM (ppb)	Sulfur Dioxide 1-Hr (ppb)	Sulfur Dioxide 24-Hr (ppb)
MSA[1] Level	n/a	n/a	n/a	n/a	n/a
NAAQS[2]	53	100	30	75	140
Met NAAQS[2]	n/a	n/a	n/a	n/a	n/a

Note: (1) Data covers the Greensboro-High Point, NC Metropolitan Statistical Area; Data from exceptional events are included; (2) National Ambient Air Quality Standards; ppm = parts per million; ug/m^3 = micrograms per cubic meter; n/a not available.
Concentrations: Nitrogen Dioxide AM—highest arithmetic mean concentration; Nitrogen Dioxide 1-Hr—highest 98th percentile 1-hour daily maximum concentration; Sulfur Dioxide AM—highest annual mean concentration; Sulfur Dioxide 1-Hr—highest 99th percentile 1-hour daily maximum concentration; Sulfur Dioxide 24-Hr—highest second maximum 24-hour concentration
Source: U.S. Environmental Protection Agency, Air Quality Monitoring Information, "Air Quality Statistics by City, 2019"

Lexington, Kentucky

Background

Lexington has managed to combine the frenzied pace of a major city with the slow tempo of a small town without losing the traditions and gentility of its Southern heritage. It is located in a scenic area of rolling plateaus and small creeks flowing into the Kentucky River.

Since its settlement in 1775, Lexington has grown to become Kentucky's second-largest city and the commercial center of the Bluegrass Region. The town was founded in 1779 and incorporated in 1832. Hemp was Lexington's major antebellum crop until the rope from which it was made was no longer used for ship rigging. After the Civil War the farmers in the area switched to tobacco as their primary crop. The city is also the chief producer of bluegrass seed and white barley in the United States.

Other products manufactured in Lexington include paper products, air-conditioning and heating equipment, electric typewriters, metal products, and bourbon whiskey.

Lexington was once known as the "Athens of the West" when a large number of early American artists, poets, musicians, and architects settled here, all leaving their imprint on the city. The Actor's Guild of Lexington and the Studio Players, Lexington's oldest community theater (1953) reside there, as does the Chamber Music Society of Kentucky. The 1898 Fayette County Courthouse, which operated from 1901 to 2001, has been transformed into the Lexington History Museum.

No discussion of Lexington would be complete without mention of horse racing. Kentucky is synonymous with horses, especially the American Saddlebred—Kentucky's only native breed. The region, with its fertile soil and excellent pastureland, is perfectly suited for breeding horses. Horse racing in Kentucky dates back to 1789, when the first course was laid out in Lexington. In 1787, The Commons, a park-like block near Race Street in Lexington, was used for horse racing, but complaints by citizens led to the formal development of a race meet, organized by Kentucky statesman Henry Clay, who also helped form the commonwealth's first jockey club, now known as the Kentucky Jockey Club. The Kentucky Horse Park, a 1,200-acre educational theme park, highlights 50 different horse breeds and allows visitors the opportunity to pet and ride the horses and talk with riders, while the International Museum of the Horse traces the history of the horse with exhibits and artifacts, and includes online exhibits. Finally, the American Saddle Horse Museum offers exciting exhibits showing the role of the saddle horse in American history.

In addition to race courses, Lexington has its share of fine golf courses, and there are plenty of blues, country, and dance clubs for those who prefer musical nightlife. Lexington is also home to many thriving arts organizations including a professional orchestra, two ballet companies, and several museums including a basketball museum, several choral organizations and a highly respected opera program at the University of Kentucky. There are more than 200 churches and synagogues in Lexington, representing 38 denominations.

Regarding education in and around the city, Lexington built two new elementary schools in 2016 and a new high school in 2017. Institutions of higher learning include the University of Kentucky, Lexington Theological Seminary, the National College of Business and Technology, Georgetown College, Kentucky State University, and Transylvania University. Since its opening in 1982, the Kentucky World Trade Center has organized high-profile trade programs featuring business and political leaders from Asia, Europe, and the Middle East. The Commonwealth of Kentucky has emerged as a leader among the 50 states in expanding its international trade.

> Lexington pharmaceutical company partnered with Altimmune to develop a COVID-19 vaccine that could be administered as a nasal spray, for hopeful release in 2022.

Every June, the Gay and Lesbian Services Organization hosts the Lexington Pride Festival, which celebrates the lesbian, gay, bisexual, and transgender communities and welcomes allies. The festival offers live music, crafts, food, and informational booths from diverse service organizations. Mayor Jim Gray, elected in 2010 and the first openly gay mayor of Lexington, proclaimed June 29, 2013, as Pride Day. Lexington has one of the highest concentrations of gay and lesbian couples in the United States for a city its size.

Lexington has a definite continental climate, temperate and well-suited to a varied plant and animal life. The area is subject to sudden and sweeping temperature changes, generally of short duration. Temperatures below zero and above 100 degrees are relatively rare.

Rankings

Business/Finance Rankings

- Lexington was the #7-ranked city for savers, according to a study by the finance site GOBankingRates, which considered the prospects for people trying to save money. Criteria: average monthly cost of grocery items; median home listing price; median rent; median income; transportation costs; gas prices; and the cost of eating out for an inexpensive and mid-range meal in 100 U.S. cities. *www.gobankingrates.com, "The 20 Best (and Worst) Places to Live If You're Trying to Save Money," August 27, 2019*

- Lexington was ranked #7 among 100 U.S. cities for most difficult conditions for savers, according to a study by the finance site GOBankingRates. Criteria: average monthly cost of grocery items; median home listing price; median rent; median income; transportation costs; gas prices; and the cost of eating out for an inexpensive and mid-range meal. *www.gobankingrates.com, "The 20 Best (and Worst) Places to Live If You're Trying to Save Money," August 27, 2019*

- Lexington was cited as one of America's top metros for new and expanded facility projects in 2020. The area ranked #10 in the mid-sized metro area category (population 200,000 to 1 million). *Site Selection, "Top Metros of 2020," March 2021*

- The Lexington metro area appeared on the Milken Institute "2021 Best Performing Cities" list. Rank: #146 out of 200 large metro areas (population over 250,000). Criteria: job growth; wage and salary growth; high-tech output growth; housing affordability; household broadband access. *Milken Institute, "Best-Performing Cities 2021," February 16, 2021*

- *Forbes* ranked the 200 most populous metro areas to determine the nation's "Best Places for Business and Careers." The Lexington metro area was ranked #33. Criteria: costs (business and living); job growth (past and projected); income growth; quality of life; educational attainment (college and high school); projected economic growth; cultural and leisure opportunities; workplace tolerance laws; net migration patterns. *Forbes, "The Best Places for Business and Careers 2019: Seattle Still On Top," October 30, 2019*

Children/Family Rankings

- Lexington was selected as one of the most playful cities in the U.S. by KaBOOM! The organization's Playful City USA initiative honors cities and towns across the nation that have made their communities more playable. Criteria: pledging to integrate play as a solution to challenges in their communities; making it easy for children to get active and balanced play; creating more family-friendly and innovative communities as a result. *KaBOOM! National Campaign for Play, "2017 Playful City USA Communities"*

- Lexington was selected as one of the best cities for newlyweds by *Rent.com*. The city ranked #14 of 15. Criteria: cost of living; availability of affordable rental inventory; annual household income; activities and restaurant options; percentage of married couples; concentration of millennials; safety. *Rent.com, "The 15 Best Cities for Newlyweds," December 11, 2018*

Education Rankings

- Personal finance website *WalletHub* analyzed the 150 largest U.S. metropolitan statistical areas to determine where the most educated Americans are putting their degrees to work. Criteria: education levels; percentage of workers with degrees; education quality and attainment gap; public school quality rankings; quality and enrollment of each metro area's universities. Lexington was ranked #25 (#1 = most educated city). *www.WalletHub.com, "Most and Least Educated Cities in America," July 20, 2020*

- Lexington was selected as one of America's most literate cities. The city ranked #26 out of the 84 largest U.S. cities. Criteria: number of booksellers; library resources; Internet resources; educational attainment; periodical publishing resources; newspaper circulation. *Central Connecticut State University, "America's Most Literate Cities, 2018," February 2019*

Environmental Rankings

- Lexington was highlighted as one of the top 98 cleanest metro areas for short-term particle pollution (24-hour PM 2.5) in the U.S. during 2016 through 2018. Monitors in these cities reported no days with unhealthful PM 2.5 levels. *American Lung Association, "State of the Air 2020," April 21, 2020*

Health/Fitness Rankings

- For each of the 100 largest cities in the United States, the American Fitness Index®, published by the American College of Sports Medicine and the Anthem Foundation, evaluated community infrastructure and 33 health behaviors including preventive health, levels of chronic disease conditions, pedestrian safety, air quality, and community resources that support physical activity. Lexington ranked #86 for "community fitness." *americanfitnessindex.org, "2020 ACSM American Fitness Index Summary Report," July 14, 2020*

- The Lexington metro area was identified as one of the worst cities for bed bugs in America by pest control company Orkin. The area ranked #43 out of 50 based on the number of bed bug treatments Orkin performed from December 2019 to November 2020. *Orkin, "New Year, New Top City on Orkin's 2021 Bed Bug Cities List: Chicago," February 1, 2021*

Real Estate Rankings

- *WalletHub* compared the most populated U.S. cities to determine which had the best markets for real estate agents. Lexington ranked #115 where demand was high and pay was the best. Criteria: sales per agent; annual median wage for real-estate agents; monthly average starting salary for real estate agents; real estate job density and competition; unemployment rate; home turnover rate; housing-market health index; and other relevant metrics. *www.WalletHub.com, "2019's Best Places to Be a Real Estate Agent," April 24, 2019*

Safety Rankings

- Allstate ranked the 200 largest cities in America in terms of driver safety. Lexington ranked #29. Criteria: internal property damage claims over a two-year period from January 2016 to December 2017. The report helps increase the importance of safety and awareness behind the wheel. *Allstate, "Allstate America's Best Drivers Report, 2019" June 24, 2019*

- The National Insurance Crime Bureau ranked 384 metro areas in the U.S. in terms of per capita rates of vehicle theft. The Lexington metro area ranked #148 (#1 = highest rate). Criteria: number of vehicle theft offenses per 100,000 inhabitants in 2019. *National Insurance Crime Bureau, "Hot Spots 2019," July 21, 2020*

Seniors/Retirement Rankings

- From its Best Cities for Successful Aging indexes, the Milken Institute generated rankings for metropolitan areas, weighing data in nine categories—health care, wellness, living arrangements, transportation and convenience, financial characteristics, education, employment, community engagement, and overall livability. The Lexington metro area was ranked #60 overall in the small metro area category. *Milken Institute, "Best Cities for Successful Aging, 2017" March 14, 2017*

Women/Minorities Rankings

- *Travel + Leisure* listed the best cities in and around the US for a memorable and fun girls' trip, even on a budget. Whether it is for a special occasion or just to get away, Lexington is sure to have something for all the ladies in your tribe. *Travel + Leisure, "25 Girls' Weekend Getaways That Won't Break the Bank," June 8, 2020*

- Personal finance website *WalletHub* compared more than 180 U.S. cities across two key dimensions, "Hispanic Business-Friendliness" and "Hispanic Purchasing Power," to arrive at the most favorable conditions for Hispanic entrepreneurs. Lexington was ranked #142 out of 182. Criteria includes: share of Hispanic-Owned Businesses; Hispanic entrepreneurship rate to median annual income of Hispanics; Small Business-Friendliness score; cost of living; and number of Hispanics with at least a bachelor's degree. *WalletHub.com, "2019's Best Cities for Hispanic Entrepreneurs," May 1, 2019*

Miscellaneous Rankings

- *WalletHub* compared the 150 most populated U.S. cities to determine their operating efficiency. A "Quality of City Services" score was constructed for each city and then divided by the total budget per capita to reveal which were managed the best. Lexington ranked #6. Criteria: financial stability; economy; education; safety; health; infrastructure and pollution. *www.WalletHub.com, "2020's Best-& Worst-Run Cities in America," June 29, 2020*

Business Environment

DEMOGRAPHICS

Population Growth

Area	1990 Census	2000 Census	2010 Census	2019* Estimate	Population Growth (%) 1990-2019	Population Growth (%) 2010-2019
City	225,366	260,512	295,803	320,601	42.3	8.4
MSA[1]	348,428	408,326	472,099	510,647	46.6	8.2
U.S.	248,709,873	281,421,906	308,745,538	324,697,795	30.6	5.2

Note: (1) Figures cover the Lexington-Fayette, KY Metropolitan Statistical Area; (*) 2015-2019 5-year estimated population
Source: U.S. Census Bureau, 1990 Census, Census 2000, Census 2010, 2015-2019 American Community Survey 5-Year Estimates

Household Size

Area	Persons in Household (%) One	Two	Three	Four	Five	Six	Seven or More	Average Household Size
City	31.6	35.1	15.2	11.2	4.6	1.6	0.7	2.40
MSA[1]	28.5	35.6	16.0	12.4	5.0	1.7	0.8	2.40
U.S.	27.9	33.9	15.6	12.9	6.0	2.3	1.4	2.60

Note: (1) Figures cover the Lexington-Fayette, KY Metropolitan Statistical Area
Source: U.S. Census Bureau, 2015-2019 American Community Survey 5-Year Estimates

Race

Area	White Alone[2] (%)	Black Alone[2] (%)	Asian Alone[2] (%)	AIAN[3] Alone[2] (%)	NHOPI[4] Alone[2] (%)	Other Race Alone[2] (%)	Two or More Races (%)
City	74.9	14.6	3.8	0.2	0.0	2.8	3.8
MSA[1]	80.7	11.0	2.7	0.2	0.0	2.3	3.1
U.S.	72.5	12.7	5.5	0.8	0.2	4.9	3.3

Note: (1) Figures cover the Lexington-Fayette, KY Metropolitan Statistical Area; (2) Alone is defined as not being in combination with one or more other races; (3) American Indian and Alaska Native; (4) Native Hawaiian and Other Pacific Islander
Source: U.S. Census Bureau, 2015-2019 American Community Survey 5-Year Estimates

Hispanic or Latino Origin

Area	Total (%)	Mexican (%)	Puerto Rican (%)	Cuban (%)	Other (%)
City	7.2	4.8	0.7	0.2	1.5
MSA[1]	6.2	4.2	0.5	0.1	1.3
U.S.	18.0	11.2	1.7	0.7	4.3

Note: Persons of Hispanic or Latino origin can be of any race; (1) Figures cover the Lexington-Fayette, KY Metropolitan Statistical Area
Source: U.S. Census Bureau, 2015-2019 American Community Survey 5-Year Estimates

Ancestry

Area	German	Irish	English	American	Italian	Polish	French[2]	Scottish	Dutch
City	13.7	11.8	10.8	9.2	2.9	1.7	1.9	2.9	1.1
MSA[1]	13.0	11.8	10.9	13.6	2.6	1.5	1.8	2.7	1.1
U.S.	13.3	9.7	7.2	6.2	5.1	2.8	2.3	1.7	1.2

Note: Figures are the percentage of the total population reporting a particular ancestry. The nine most commonly reported ancestries in the U.S. are shown. Figures include multiple ancestries (e.g. if a person reported being Irish and Italian, they were included in both columns); (1) Figures cover the Lexington-Fayette, KY Metropolitan Statistical Area; (2) Excludes Basque
Source: U.S. Census Bureau, 2015-2019 American Community Survey 5-Year Estimates

Foreign-born Population

Area	Percent of Population Born in Any Foreign Country	Asia	Mexico	Europe	Caribbean	Central America[2]	South America	Africa	Canada
City	9.7	3.7	2.4	1.0	0.2	0.5	0.3	1.2	0.2
MSA[1]	7.5	2.6	2.1	0.9	0.2	0.5	0.2	0.8	0.1
U.S.	13.6	4.2	3.5	1.5	1.3	1.1	1.0	0.7	0.2

Note: (1) Figures cover the Lexington-Fayette, KY Metropolitan Statistical Area; (2) Excludes Mexico.
Source: U.S. Census Bureau, 2015-2019 American Community Survey 5-Year Estimates

Marital Status

Area	Never Married	Now Married[2]	Separated	Widowed	Divorced
City	38.8	43.1	1.7	4.6	11.8
MSA[1]	34.3	46.5	1.7	5.1	12.3
U.S.	33.4	48.1	1.9	5.8	10.9

Note: Figures are percentages and cover the population 15 years of age and older; (1) Figures cover the Lexington-Fayette, KY Metropolitan Statistical Area; (2) Excludes separated
Source: U.S. Census Bureau, 2015-2019 American Community Survey 5-Year Estimates

Disability by Age

Area	All Ages	Under 18 Years Old	18 to 64 Years Old	65 Years and Over
City	12.4	4.5	10.7	34.3
MSA[1]	13.5	5.1	11.8	35.5
U.S.	12.6	4.2	10.3	34.5

Note: Figures show percent of the civilian noninstitutionalized population that reported having a disability. Disability status is determined from six types of difficulty: vision, hearing, cognitive, ambulatory, self-care, and independent living. For children under 5 years old, hearing and vision difficulty are used to determine disability status. For children between the ages of 5 and 14, disability status is determined from hearing, vision, cognitive, ambulatory, and self-care difficulties. For people aged 15 years and older, they are considered to have a disability if they have difficulty with any one of the six difficulty types; Note: (1) Figures cover the Lexington-Fayette, KY Metropolitan Statistical Area
Source: U.S. Census Bureau, 2015-2019 American Community Survey 5-Year Estimates

Age

Area	Under Age 5	Age 5–19	Age 20–34	Age 35–44	Age 45–54	Age 55–64	Age 65–74	Age 75–84	Age 85+	Median Age
City	6.1	18.4	26.0	13.1	11.8	11.5	7.8	3.7	1.5	34.6
MSA[1]	6.2	19.0	23.2	13.0	12.6	12.1	8.3	4.0	1.5	36.1
U.S.	6.1	19.1	20.7	12.6	13.0	12.9	9.1	4.6	1.9	38.1

Note: (1) Figures cover the Lexington-Fayette, KY Metropolitan Statistical Area
Source: U.S. Census Bureau, 2015-2019 American Community Survey 5-Year Estimates

Gender

Area	Males	Females	Males per 100 Females
City	157,231	163,370	96.2
MSA[1]	249,429	261,218	95.5
U.S.	159,886,919	164,810,876	97.0

Note: (1) Figures cover the Lexington-Fayette, KY Metropolitan Statistical Area
Source: U.S. Census Bureau, 2015-2019 American Community Survey 5-Year Estimates

Religious Groups by Family

Area	Catholic	Baptist	Non-Den.	Methodist[2]	Lutheran	LDS[3]	Pentecostal	Presbyterian[4]	Muslim[5]	Judaism
MSA[1]	6.8	24.9	2.4	5.9	0.4	1.1	2.1	1.4	0.1	0.3
U.S.	19.1	9.3	4.0	4.0	2.3	2.0	1.9	1.6	0.8	0.7

Note: Figures are the number of adherents as a percentage of the total population; (1) Figures cover the Lexington-Fayette, KY Metropolitan Statistical Area; (2) Methodist/Pietist; (3) Latter Day Saints; (4) Reformed; (5) Figures are estimates
Source: Association of Statisticians of American Religious Bodies, 2010 U.S. Religion Census: Religious Congregations & Membership Study

Religious Groups by Tradition

Area	Catholic	Evangelical Protestant	Mainline Protestant	Other Tradition	Black Protestant	Orthodox
MSA[1]	6.8	28.3	10.3	1.7	2.1	0.2
U.S.	19.1	16.2	7.3	4.3	1.6	0.3

Note: Figures are the number of adherents as a percentage of the total population; (1) Figures cover the Lexington-Fayette, KY Metropolitan Statistical Area
Source: Association of Statisticians of American Religious Bodies, 2010 U.S. Religion Census: Religious Congregations & Membership Study

ECONOMY

Gross Metropolitan Product

Area	2017	2018	2019	2020	Rank[2]
MSA[1]	29.7	30.8	31.9	33.0	90

Note: Figures are in billions of dollars; (1) Figures cover the Lexington-Fayette, KY Metropolitan Statistical Area; (2) Rank is based on 2018 data and ranges from 1 to 381
Source: U.S. Conference of Mayors, U.S. Metro Economies: GMP & Employment 2018-2020, September 2019

Economic Growth

Area	2015-17 (%)	2018 (%)	2019 (%)	2020 (%)	Rank[2]
MSA[1]	1.6	1.3	2.0	1.1	167
U.S.	1.9	2.9	2.3	2.1	—

Note: Figures are real gross metropolitan product (GMP) growth rates and represent average annual percent change; (1) Figures cover the Lexington-Fayette, KY Metropolitan Statistical Area; (2) Rank is based on 2017 2-year average annual percent change and ranges from 1 to 381
Source: U.S. Conference of Mayors, U.S. Metro Economies: GMP & Employment 2018-2020, September 2019

Metropolitan Area Exports

Area	2014	2015	2016	2017	2018	2019	Rank[2]
MSA[1]	2,191.4	2,065.7	2,069.6	2,119.8	2,148.0	2,093.8	100

Note: Figures are in millions of dollars; (1) Figures cover the Lexington-Fayette, KY Metropolitan Statistical Area; (2) Rank is based on 2019 data and ranges from 1 to 386
Source: U.S. Department of Commerce, International Trade Administration, Office of Trade and Economic Analysis, Industry and Analysis, Exports by Metropolitan Area, data extracted March 24, 2021

Building Permits

Area	Single-Family			Multi-Family			Total		
	2018	2019	Pct. Chg.	2018	2019	Pct. Chg.	2018	2019	Pct. Chg.
City	733	579	-21.0	1,056	804	-23.9	1,789	1,383	-22.7
MSA[1]	1,404	1,308	-6.8	1,368	938	-31.4	2,772	2,246	-19.0
U.S.	855,300	862,100	0.7	473,500	523,900	10.6	1,328,800	1,386,000	4.3

Note: (1) Figures cover the Lexington-Fayette, KY Metropolitan Statistical Area; Figures represent new, privately-owned housing units authorized (unadjusted data); All permit data are based on estimates with imputation
Source: U.S. Census Bureau, Manufacturing, Mining, and Construction Statistics, Building Permits, 2018, 2019

Bankruptcy Filings

Area	Business Filings			Nonbusiness Filings		
	2019	2020	% Chg.	2019	2020	% Chg.
Fayette County	56	54	-3.6	749	520	-30.6
U.S.	22,780	21,655	-4.9	752,160	522,808	-30.5

Note: Business filings include Chapter 7, Chapter 9, Chapter 11, Chapter 12, Chapter 13, Chapter 15, and Section 304; Nonbusiness filings include Chapter 7, Chapter 11, and Chapter 13
Source: Administrative Office of the U.S. Courts, Business and Nonbusiness Bankruptcy, County Cases Commenced by Chapter of the Bankruptcy Code, During the 12-Month Period Ending December 31, 2019 and Business and Nonbusiness Bankruptcy, County Cases Commenced by Chapter of the Bankruptcy Code, During the 12-Month Period Ending December 31, 2020

Housing Vacancy Rates

Area	Gross Vacancy Rate[2] (%)			Year-Round Vacancy Rate[3] (%)			Rental Vacancy Rate[4] (%)			Homeowner Vacancy Rate[5] (%)		
	2018	2019	2020	2018	2019	2020	2018	2019	2020	2018	2019	2020
MSA[1]	n/a	n/a	n/a	n/a	n/a	n/a	n/a	n/a	n/a	n/a	n/a	n/a
U.S.	12.3	12.0	10.6	9.7	9.5	8.2	6.9	6.7	6.3	1.5	1.4	1.0

Note: (1) Figures cover the Lexington-Fayette, KY Metropolitan Statistical Area; (2) The percentage of the total housing inventory that is vacant; (3) The percentage of the housing inventory (excluding seasonal units) that is year-round vacant; (4) The percentage of rental inventory that is vacant for rent; (5) The percentage of homeowner inventory that is vacant for sale; n/a not available
Source: U.S. Census Bureau, Housing Vacancies and Homeownership Annual Statistics: 2018, 2019, 2020

INCOME

Income

Area	Per Capita ($)	Median Household ($)	Average Household ($)
City	34,442	57,291	83,111
MSA[1]	33,153	58,685	82,094
U.S.	34,103	62,843	88,607

Note: (1) Figures cover the Lexington-Fayette, KY Metropolitan Statistical Area
Source: U.S. Census Bureau, 2015-2019 American Community Survey 5-Year Estimates

Household Income Distribution

Area	Percent of Households Earning							
	Under $15,000	$15,000 -$24,999	$25,000 -$34,999	$35,000 -$49,999	$50,000 -$74,999	$75,000 -$99,999	$100,000 -$149,999	$150,000 and up
City	11.5	9.6	9.9	13.0	17.6	12.2	14.2	12.1
MSA[1]	10.9	9.4	9.7	13.1	17.5	13.1	14.7	11.5
U.S.	10.3	8.9	8.9	12.3	17.2	12.7	15.1	14.5

Note: (1) Figures cover the Lexington-Fayette, KY Metropolitan Statistical Area
Source: U.S. Census Bureau, 2015-2019 American Community Survey 5-Year Estimates

Poverty Rate

Area	All Ages	Under 18 Years Old	18 to 64 Years Old	65 Years and Over
City	16.8	20.4	17.5	7.4
MSA[1]	15.8	20.9	15.9	7.6
U.S.	13.4	18.5	12.6	9.3

Note: Figures are percentage of people whose income during the past 12 months was below the poverty level;
(1) Figures cover the Lexington-Fayette, KY Metropolitan Statistical Area
Source: U.S. Census Bureau, 2015-2019 American Community Survey 5-Year Estimates

CITY FINANCES

City Government Finances

Component	2017 ($000)	2017 ($ per capita)
Total Revenues	800,827	2,546
Total Expenditures	688,204	2,188
Debt Outstanding	919,417	2,924
Cash and Securities[1]	1,454,685	4,626

Note: (1) Cash and security holdings of a government at the close of its fiscal year,
including those of its dependent agencies, utilities, and liquor stores.
Source: U.S. Census Bureau, State & Local Government Finances 2017

City Government Revenue by Source

Source	2017 ($000)	2017 ($ per capita)	2017 (%)
General Revenue			
From Federal Government	58,409	186	7.3
From State Government	20,379	65	2.5
From Local Governments	8,030	26	1.0
Taxes			
Property	104,238	331	13.0
Sales and Gross Receipts	68,952	219	8.6
Personal Income	194,106	617	24.2
Corporate Income	39,198	125	4.9
Motor Vehicle License	221	1	0.0
Other Taxes	4,474	14	0.6
Current Charges	179,898	572	22.5
Liquor Store	0	0	0.0
Utility	3,796	12	0.5
Employee Retirement	106,849	340	13.3

Source: U.S. Census Bureau, State & Local Government Finances 2017

City Government Expenditures by Function

Function	2017 ($000)	2017 ($ per capita)	2017 (%)
General Direct Expenditures			
Air Transportation	27,518	87	4.0
Corrections	32,505	103	4.7
Education	0	0	0.0
Employment Security Administration	0	0	0.0
Financial Administration	4,483	14	0.7
Fire Protection	70,351	223	10.2
General Public Buildings	0	0	0.0
Governmental Administration, Other	90,877	289	13.2
Health	15,853	50	2.3
Highways	16,590	52	2.4
Hospitals	0	0	0.0
Housing and Community Development	8,138	25	1.2
Interest on General Debt	23,613	75	3.4
Judicial and Legal	10,462	33	1.5
Libraries	14,427	45	2.1
Parking	0	0	0.0
Parks and Recreation	59,134	188	8.6
Police Protection	60,094	191	8.7
Public Welfare	10,985	34	1.6
Sewerage	71,908	228	10.4
Solid Waste Management	49,739	158	7.2
Veterans' Services	0	0	0.0
Liquor Store	0	0	0.0
Utility	31,887	101	4.6
Employee Retirement	66,425	211	9.7

Source: U.S. Census Bureau, State & Local Government Finances 2017

EMPLOYMENT

Labor Force and Employment

Area	Civilian Labor Force			Workers Employed		
	Dec. 2019	Dec. 2020	% Chg.	Dec. 2019	Dec. 2020	% Chg.
City	175,216	173,151	-1.2	170,118	164,394	-3.4
MSA[1]	273,326	269,822	-1.3	265,044	256,418	-3.3
U.S.	164,007,000	160,017,000	-2.4	158,504,000	149,613,000	-5.6

Note: Data is not seasonally adjusted and covers workers 16 years of age and older; (1) Figures cover the Lexington-Fayette, KY Metropolitan Statistical Area
Source: Bureau of Labor Statistics, Local Area Unemployment Statistics

Unemployment Rate

Area	2020											
	Jan.	Feb.	Mar.	Apr.	May	Jun.	Jul.	Aug.	Sep.	Oct.	Nov.	Dec.
City	3.5	3.1	4.1	14.1	9.0	4.5	4.6	6.7	4.8	6.2	4.5	5.1
MSA[1]	3.7	3.3	4.2	15.2	9.1	4.4	4.5	6.5	4.7	6.1	4.4	5.0
U.S.	4.0	3.8	4.5	14.4	13.0	11.2	10.5	8.5	7.7	6.6	6.4	6.5

Note: Data is not seasonally adjusted and covers workers 16 years of age and older; (1) Figures cover the Lexington-Fayette, KY Metropolitan Statistical Area
Source: Bureau of Labor Statistics, Local Area Unemployment Statistics

Average Wages

Occupation	$/Hr.	Occupation	$/Hr.
Accountants and Auditors	34.10	Maintenance and Repair Workers	20.50
Automotive Mechanics	20.10	Marketing Managers	50.10
Bookkeepers	19.10	Network and Computer Systems Admin.	30.80
Carpenters	22.60	Nurses, Licensed Practical	21.40
Cashiers	11.20	Nurses, Registered	30.90
Computer Programmers	37.20	Nursing Assistants	14.30
Computer Systems Analysts	39.30	Office Clerks, General	16.80
Computer User Support Specialists	25.90	Physical Therapists	41.60
Construction Laborers	18.60	Physicians	117.60
Cooks, Restaurant	13.50	Plumbers, Pipefitters and Steamfitters	30.50
Customer Service Representatives	16.60	Police and Sheriff's Patrol Officers	23.70
Dentists	n/a	Postal Service Mail Carriers	25.60
Electricians	24.00	Real Estate Sales Agents	21.40
Engineers, Electrical	41.50	Retail Salespersons	13.50
Fast Food and Counter Workers	9.90	Sales Representatives, Technical/Scientific	40.80
Financial Managers	57.30	Secretaries, Exc. Legal/Medical/Executive	18.80
First-Line Supervisors of Office Workers	28.00	Security Guards	13.30
General and Operations Managers	48.40	Surgeons	n/a
Hairdressers/Cosmetologists	12.00	Teacher Assistants, Exc. Postsecondary*	15.30
Home Health and Personal Care Aides	12.60	Teachers, Secondary School, Exc. Sp. Ed.*	28.70
Janitors and Cleaners	13.90	Telemarketers	n/a
Landscaping/Groundskeeping Workers	15.40	Truck Drivers, Heavy/Tractor-Trailer	25.20
Lawyers	51.90	Truck Drivers, Light/Delivery Services	22.50
Maids and Housekeeping Cleaners	11.20	Waiters and Waitresses	10.80

Note: Wage data covers the Lexington-Fayette, KY Metropolitan Statistical Area; (*) Hourly wages were calculated from annual wage data based on a 40 hour work week; n/a not available.
Source: Bureau of Labor Statistics, Metro Area Occupational Employment & Wage Estimates, May 2020

Employment by Industry

Sector	MSA[1]		U.S.
	Number of Employees	Percent of Total	Percent of Total
Construction, Mining, and Logging	13,600	5.1	5.5
Education and Health Services	34,800	13.0	16.3
Financial Activities	10,000	3.7	6.1
Government	52,100	19.5	15.2
Information	2,600	1.0	1.9
Leisure and Hospitality	23,600	8.8	9.0
Manufacturing	28,200	10.5	8.5
Other Services	9,700	3.6	3.8
Professional and Business Services	39,800	14.9	14.4
Retail Trade	30,100	11.2	10.9
Transportation, Warehousing, and Utilities	12,600	4.7	4.6
Wholesale Trade	10,500	3.9	3.9

Note: Figures are non-farm employment as of December 2020. Figures are not seasonally adjusted and include workers 16 years of age and older; (1) Figures cover the Lexington-Fayette, KY Metropolitan Statistical Area
Source: Bureau of Labor Statistics, Current Employment Statistics, Employment, Hours, and Earnings

Employment by Occupation

Occupation Classification	City (%)	MSA[1] (%)	U.S. (%)
Management, Business, Science, and Arts	43.5	40.6	38.5
Natural Resources, Construction, and Maintenance	5.8	7.4	8.9
Production, Transportation, and Material Moving	11.5	13.7	13.2
Sales and Office	21.8	21.3	21.6
Service	17.5	17.0	17.8

Note: Figures cover employed civilians 16 years of age and older; (1) Figures cover the Lexington-Fayette, KY Metropolitan Statistical Area
Source: U.S. Census Bureau, 2015-2019 American Community Survey 5-Year Estimates

Occupations with Greatest Projected Employment Growth: 2020 – 2022

Occupation[1]	2020 Employment	2022 Projected Employment	Numeric Employment Change	Percent Employment Change
Combined Food Preparation and Serving Workers, Including Fast Food	56,290	64,080	7,790	13.8
Waiters and Waitresses	26,910	30,230	3,320	12.3
Laborers and Freight, Stock, and Material Movers, Hand	61,690	64,690	3,000	4.9
Cooks, Restaurant	17,120	19,830	2,710	15.8
Personal Care Aides	19,850	21,690	1,840	9.3
Registered Nurses	46,830	48,380	1,550	3.3
Retail Salespersons	50,950	52,470	1,520	3.0
First-Line Supervisors of Food Preparation and Serving Workers	12,550	14,060	1,510	12.0
Maids and Housekeeping Cleaners	19,820	21,220	1,400	7.1
Industrial Truck and Tractor Operators	14,190	15,250	1,060	7.5

Note: Projections cover Kentucky; (1) Sorted by numeric employment change
Source: www.projectionscentral.com, State Occupational Projections, 2020–2022 Short-Term Projections

Fastest-Growing Occupations: 2020 – 2022

Occupation[1]	2020 Employment	2022 Projected Employment	Numeric Employment Change	Percent Employment Change
Hotel, Motel, and Resort Desk Clerks	2,960	3,940	980	33.1
Lodging Managers	220	290	70	31.8
Gaming and Sports Book Writers and Runners	300	360	60	20.0
Animal Trainers	470	560	90	19.1
Ushers, Lobby Attendants, and Ticket Takers	860	1,020	160	18.6
Cooks, Restaurant	17,120	19,830	2,710	15.8
Dining Room and Cafeteria Attendants and Bartender Helpers	2,850	3,290	440	15.4
Hosts and Hostesses, Restaurant, Lounge, and Coffee Shop	4,100	4,670	570	13.9
Taxi Drivers and Chauffeurs	2,590	2,950	360	13.9
Combined Food Preparation and Serving Workers, Including Fast Food	56,290	64,080	7,790	13.8

Note: Projections cover Kentucky; (1) Sorted by percent employment change and excludes occupations with numeric employment change less than 50
Source: www.projectionscentral.com, State Occupational Projections, 2020–2022 Short-Term Projections

TAXES

State Corporate Income Tax Rates

State	Tax Rate (%)	Income Brackets ($)	Num. of Brackets	Financial Institution Tax Rate (%)[a]	Federal Income Tax Ded.
Kentucky	5.0	Flat rate	1	5.0	No

Note: Tax rates as of January 1, 2021; (a) Rates listed are the corporate income tax rate applied to financial institutions or excise taxes based on income. Some states have other taxes based upon the value of deposits or shares.
Source: Federation of Tax Administrators, State Corporate Income Tax Rates, January 1, 2021

State Individual Income Tax Rates

State	Tax Rate (%)	Income Brackets ($)	Personal Exemptions ($) Single	Married	Depend.	Standard Ded. ($) Single	Married
Kentucky	5.0	Flat rate	None	None	None	2,690	2,690

Note: Tax rates as of January 1, 2021; Local- and county-level taxes are not included; Federal income tax is not deductible on state income tax returns
Source: Federation of Tax Administrators, State Individual Income Tax Rates, January 1, 2021

Various State Sales and Excise Tax Rates

State	State Sales Tax (%)	Gasoline[1] (¢/gal.)	Cigarette[2] ($/pack)	Spirits[3] ($/gal.)	Wine[4] ($/gal.)	Beer[5] ($/gal.)	Recreational Marijuana (%)
Kentucky	6	26	1.1	8.41	3.23	0.89	Not legal

Note: All tax rates as of January 1, 2021; (1) The American Petroleum Institute has developed a methodology for determining the average tax rate on a gallon of fuel. Rates may include any of the following: excise taxes, environmental fees, storage tank fees, other fees or taxes, general sales tax, and local taxes; (2) The federal excise tax of $1.0066 per pack and local taxes are not included; (3) Rates are those applicable to off-premise sales of 40% alcohol by volume (a.b.v.) distilled spirits in 750ml containers. Local excise taxes are excluded; (4) Rates are those applicable to off-premise sales of 11% a.b.v. non-carbonated wine in 750ml containers; (5) Rates are those applicable to off-premise sales of 4.7% a.b.v. beer in 12 ounce containers.
Source: Tax Foundation, 2021 Facts & Figures: How Does Your State Compare?

State Business Tax Climate Index Rankings

State	Overall Rank	Corporate Tax Rank	Individual Income Tax Rank	Sales Tax Rank	Property Tax Rank	Unemployment Insurance Tax Rank
Kentucky	19	19	18	13	21	49

Note: The index is a measure of how each state's tax laws affect economic performance. The lower the rank, the more favorable a state's tax system is for business. States without a given tax are given a ranking of 1. The scores/rankings for the District of Columbia do not affect other states. The 2021 index represents the tax climate as of July 1, 2020.
Source: Tax Foundation, State Business Tax Climate Index 2021

TRANSPORTATION

Means of Transportation to Work

Area	Car/Truck/Van		Public Transportation			Bicycle	Walked	Other Means	Worked at Home
	Drove Alone	Car-pooled	Bus	Subway	Railroad				
City	78.5	9.3	1.9	0.0	0.0	0.6	3.7	1.5	4.4
MSA[1]	79.9	9.3	1.3	0.0	0.0	0.4	3.1	1.3	4.6
U.S.	76.3	9.0	2.4	1.9	0.6	0.5	2.7	1.4	5.2

Note: Figures are percentages and cover workers 16 years of age and older; (1) Figures cover the Lexington-Fayette, KY Metropolitan Statistical Area
Source: U.S. Census Bureau, 2015-2019 American Community Survey 5-Year Estimates

Travel Time to Work

Area	Less Than 10 Minutes	10 to 19 Minutes	20 to 29 Minutes	30 to 44 Minutes	45 to 59 Minutes	60 to 89 Minutes	90 Minutes or More
City	12.4	38.0	27.6	14.9	3.2	2.5	1.4
MSA[1]	14.3	34.6	25.1	17.7	4.5	2.5	1.3
U.S.	12.2	28.4	20.8	20.8	8.3	6.4	2.9

Note: Note: Figures are percentages and include workers 16 years old and over; (1) Figures cover the Lexington-Fayette, KY Metropolitan Statistical Area
Source: U.S. Census Bureau, 2015-2019 American Community Survey 5-Year Estimates

Key Congestion Measures

Measure	1982	1992	2002	2012	2017
Annual Hours of Delay, Total (000)	n/a	n/a	n/a	n/a	11,318
Annual Hours of Delay, Per Auto Commuter	n/a	n/a	n/a	n/a	37
Annual Congestion Cost, Total (million $)	n/a	n/a	n/a	n/a	240
Annual Congestion Cost, Per Auto Commuter ($)	n/a	n/a	n/a	n/a	790

Note: n/a not available
Source: Texas A&M Transportation Institute, 2019 Urban Mobility Report

Freeway Travel Time Index

Measure	1982	1987	1992	1997	2002	2007	2012	2017
Urban Area Index[1]	n/a	n/a	n/a	n/a	n/a	n/a	n/a	1.19
Urban Area Rank[1,2]	n/a	n/a	n/a	n/a	n/a	n/a	n/a	n/a

Note: Freeway Travel Time Index—the ratio of travel time in the peak period to the travel time at free-flow conditions. For example, a value of 1.30 indicates a 20-minute free-flow trip takes 26 minutes in the peak (20 minutes x 1.30 = 26 minutes); (1) Covers the Lexington-Fayette KY urban area; (2) Rank is based on 101 larger urban areas (#1 = highest travel time index); n/a not available
Source: Texas A&M Transportation Institute, 2019 Urban Mobility Report

Public Transportation

Agency Name / Mode of Transportation	Vehicles Operated in Maximum Service[1]	Annual Unlinked Passenger Trips[2] (in thous.)	Annual Passenger Miles[3] (in thous.)
Lexington Transit Authority (LexTran)			
Bus (directly operated)	52	4,364.6	18,227.7
Demand Response (purchased transportation)	51	227.1	1,632.8
Vanpool (purchased transportation)	8	21.0	798.8

Note: (1) Number of revenue vehicles operated by the given mode and type of service to meet the annual maximum service requirement. This is the revenue vehicle count during the peak season of the year; on the week and day that maximum service is provided. Vehicles operated in maximum service (VOMS) exclude atypical days and one-time special events; (2) Number of passengers who boarded public transportation vehicles. Passengers are counted each time they board a vehicle no matter how many vehicles they use to travel from their origin to their destination. (3) Sum of the distances ridden by all passengers during the entire fiscal year.
Source: Federal Transit Administration, National Transit Database, 2019

Air Transportation

Airport Name and Code / Type of Service	Passenger Airlines[1]	Passenger Enplanements	Freight Carriers[2]	Freight (lbs)
Bluegrass Airport (LEX)				
Domestic service (U.S. carriers - 2020)	21	290,994	6	596,294
International service (U.S. carriers - 2019)	0	0	1	1,060

Note: (1) Includes all U.S.-based major, minor and commuter airlines that carried at least one passenger during the year; (2) Includes all U.S.-based airlines and freight carriers that transported at least one pound of freight during the year.
Source: Bureau of Transportation Statistics, The Intermodal Transportation Database, Air Carriers: T-100 Domestic Market (U.S. Carriers), 2020; Bureau of Transportation Statistics, The Intermodal Transportation Database, Air Carriers: T-100 International Market (U.S. Carriers), 2019

BUSINESSES

Major Business Headquarters

Company Name	Industry	Rankings	
		Fortune[1]	Forbes[2]
No companies listed	-	-	-

Note: (1) Companies that produce a 10-K are ranked 1 to 500 based on 2019 revenue; (2) All private companies with at least $2 billion in annual revenue through the end of their most current fiscal year are ranked 1 to 219; companies listed are headquartered in the city; dashes indicate no ranking
Source: Fortune, "Fortune 500," June/July 2020; Forbes, "America's Largest Private Companies," 2020

Living Environment

COST OF LIVING

Cost of Living Index

Composite Index	Groceries	Housing	Utilities	Trans-portation	Health Care	Misc. Goods/Services
93.2	89.4	83.7	102.2	92.8	80.7	101.7

Note: The Cost of Living Index measures regional differences in the cost of consumer goods and services, excluding taxes and non-consumer expenditures, for professional and managerial households in the top income quintile. It is based on more than 50,000 prices covering almost 60 different items for which prices are collected three times a year by chambers of commerce, economic development organizations or university applied economic centers in each participating urban area. The numbers shown should be read as a percentage above or below the national average of 100. For example, a value of 115.4 in the groceries column indicates that grocery prices are 15.4% higher than the national average. Small differences in the index numbers should not be interpreted as significant; Figures cover the Lexington KY urban area.
Source: The Council for Community and Economic Research, Cost of Living Index, 2020

Grocery Prices

Area[1]	T-Bone Steak ($/pound)	Frying Chicken ($/pound)	Whole Milk ($/half gal.)	Eggs ($/dozen)	Orange Juice ($/64 oz.)	Coffee ($/11.5 oz.)
City[2]	10.82	1.11	1.64	1.16	3.18	3.69
Avg.	11.78	1.39	2.05	1.47	3.57	4.34
Min.	8.03	0.94	1.03	0.74	2.94	3.02
Max.	15.86	2.65	4.31	3.77	5.44	8.69

*Note: (1) Values for the local area are compared with the average, minimum and maximum values for all 284 areas in the Cost of Living Index; (2) Figures cover the Lexington KY urban area; **T-Bone Steak** (price per pound); **Frying Chicken** (price per pound, whole fryer); **Whole Milk** (half gallon carton); **Eggs** (price per dozen, Grade A, large); **Orange Juice** (64 oz. Tropicana or Florida Natural); **Coffee** (11.5 oz. can, vacuum-packed, Maxwell House, Hills Bros, or Folgers).*
Source: The Council for Community and Economic Research, Cost of Living Index, 2020

Housing and Utility Costs

Area[1]	New Home Price ($)	Apartment Rent ($/month)	All Electric ($/month)	Part Electric ($/month)	Other Energy ($/month)	Telephone ($/month)
City[2]	309,955	976	-	79.97	77.60	206.50
Avg.	368,594	1,168	170.86	100.47	65.28	184.30
Min.	190,567	502	91.58	31.42	26.08	169.60
Max.	2,227,806	4,738	470.38	280.31	280.06	206.50

*Note: (1) Values for the local area are compared with the average, minimum and maximum values for all 284 areas in the Cost of Living Index; (2) Figures cover the Lexington KY urban area; **New Home Price** (2,400 sf living area, 8,000 sf lot, in urban area with full utilities); **Apartment Rent** (950 sf 2 bedroom/1.5 or 2 bath, unfurnished, excluding all utilities except water); **All Electric** (average monthly cost for an all-electric home); **Part Electric** (average monthly cost for a part-electric home); **Other Energy** (average monthly cost for natural gas, fuel oil, coal, wood, and any other forms of energy except electricity); **Telephone** (price includes the base monthly rate plus taxes and fees for three lines of mobile phone service).*
Source: The Council for Community and Economic Research, Cost of Living Index, 2020

Health Care, Transportation, and Other Costs

Area[1]	Doctor ($/visit)	Dentist ($/visit)	Optometrist ($/visit)	Gasoline ($/gallon)	Beauty Salon ($/visit)	Men's Shirt ($)
City[2]	82.39	76.80	74.07	2.08	37.90	38.67
Avg.	115.44	99.32	108.10	2.21	39.27	31.37
Min.	36.68	59.00	51.36	1.71	19.00	11.00
Max.	219.00	153.10	250.97	3.46	82.05	58.33

*Note: (1) Values for the local area are compared with the average, minimum and maximum values for all 284 areas in the Cost of Living Index; (2) Figures cover the Lexington KY urban area; **Doctor** (general practitioners routine exam of an established patient); **Dentist** (adult teeth cleaning and periodic oral examination); **Optometrist** (full vision eye exam for established adult patient); **Gasoline** (one gallon regular unleaded, national brand, including all taxes, cash price at self-service pump if available); **Beauty Salon** (woman's shampoo, trim, and blow-dry); **Men's Shirt** (cotton/polyester dress shirt, pinpoint weave, long sleeves).*
Source: The Council for Community and Economic Research, Cost of Living Index, 2020

HOUSING

Homeownership Rate

Area	2012 (%)	2013 (%)	2014 (%)	2015 (%)	2016 (%)	2017 (%)	2018 (%)	2019 (%)	2020 (%)
MSA[1]	n/a	n/a	n/a	n/a	n/a	n/a	n/a	n/a	n/a
U.S.	65.4	65.1	64.5	63.7	63.4	63.9	64.4	64.6	66.6

Note: (1) Figures cover the Lexington-Fayette, KY Metropolitan Statistical Area; n/a not available
Source: U.S. Census Bureau, Housing Vacancies and Homeownership Annual Statistics: 2012-2020

House Price Index (HPI)

Area	National Ranking[2]	Quarterly Change (%)	One-Year Change (%)	Five-Year Change (%)	Since 1991Q1 (%)
MSA[1]	200	1.46	5.04	28.47	155.18
U.S.[3]	–	3.81	10.77	38.99	205.12

Note: The HPI is a weighted repeat sales index. It measures average price changes in repeat sales or refinancings on the same properties. This information is obtained by reviewing repeat mortgage transactions on single-family properties whose mortgages have been purchased or securitized by Fannie Mae or Freddie Mac since January 1975; (1) Figures cover the Lexington-Fayette, KY Metropolitan Statistical Area; (2) Rankings are based on annual percentage change for all metro areas containing at least 15,000 transactions over the last 10 years and ranges from 1 to 253; (3) figures based on a weighted average of Census Division estimates using a seasonally adjusted, purchase-only index; all figures are for the period ending December 31, 2020
Source: Federal Housing Finance Agency, Change in Metropolitan Area House Price Indexes, April 7, 2021

Median Single-Family Home Prices

Area	2018	2019	2020p	Percent Change 2019 to 2020
MSA[1]	171.2	180.0	201.2	11.8
U.S. Average	261.6	274.6	299.9	9.2

Note: Figures are median sales prices of existing single-family homes in thousands of dollars; (p) preliminary; (1) Figures cover the Lexington-Fayette, KY Metropolitan Statistical Area
Source: National Association of Realtors, Median Sales Price of Existing Single-Family Homes for Metropolitan Areas, 4th Quarter 2020

Qualifying Income Based on Median Sales Price of Existing Single-Family Homes

Area	With 5% Down ($)	With 10% Down ($)	With 20% Down ($)
MSA[1]	38,963	36,913	32,811
U.S. Average	59,266	56,147	49,908

Note: Figures are preliminary; Qualifying income is based on a mortgage rate of 2.81%. Monthly principal and interest payment is limited to 25% of income; (1) Figures cover the Lexington-Fayette, KY Metropolitan Statistical Area
Source: National Association of Realtors, Qualifying Income Based on Median Sales Price of Existing Single-Family Homes for Metropolitan Areas, 4th Quarter 2020

Home Value Distribution

Area	Under $50,000	$50,000-$99,999	$100,000-$149,999	$150,000-$199,999	$200,000-$299,999	$300,000-$499,999	$500,000-$999,999	$1,000,000 or more
City	2.6	8.8	21.0	21.1	22.4	16.6	6.0	1.4
MSA[1]	3.5	9.9	22.0	20.7	21.4	15.4	5.9	1.3
U.S.	6.9	12.0	13.3	14.0	19.6	19.3	11.4	3.4

Note: Figures are percentages and cover owner-occupied housing units; (1) Figures cover the Lexington-Fayette, KY Metropolitan Statistical Area
Source: U.S. Census Bureau, 2015-2019 American Community Survey 5-Year Estimates

Year Housing Structure Built

Area	2010 or Later	2000-2009	1990-1999	1980-1989	1970-1979	1960-1969	1950-1959	1940-1949	Before 1940	Median Year
City	6.1	15.5	15.8	14.0	15.0	13.5	9.7	3.1	7.3	1981
MSA[1]	6.4	17.2	17.0	13.9	14.8	11.5	8.0	3.3	7.9	1983
U.S.	5.2	14.0	13.9	13.4	15.2	10.6	10.3	4.9	12.6	1978

Note: Figures are percentages except for Median Year; Note: (1) Figures cover the Lexington-Fayette, KY Metropolitan Statistical Area
Source: U.S. Census Bureau, 2015-2019 American Community Survey 5-Year Estimates

Gross Monthly Rent

Area	Under $500	$500-$999	$1,000-$1,499	$1,500-$1,999	$2,000-$2,499	$2,500-$2,999	$3,000 and up	Median ($)
City	8.1	52.5	30.6	5.8	2.2	0.4	0.3	896
MSA[1]	9.6	55.1	28.1	4.9	1.7	0.3	0.3	867
U.S.	9.4	36.2	30.0	14.0	5.6	2.4	2.4	1,062

Note: Figures are percentages except for Median; Gross rent is the contract rent plus the estimated average monthly cost of utilities (electricity, gas, and water and sewer) and fuels (oil, coal, kerosene, wood, etc.) if these are paid by the renter (or paid for the renter by someone else); (1) Figures cover the Lexington-Fayette, KY Metropolitan Statistical Area
Source: U.S. Census Bureau, 2015-2019 American Community Survey 5-Year Estimates

HEALTH

Health Risk Factors

Category	MSA[1] (%)	U.S. (%)
Adults aged 18–64 who have any kind of health care coverage	92.8	87.3
Adults who reported being in good or better health	84.5	82.4
Adults who have been told they have high blood cholesterol	30.9	33.0
Adults who have been told they have high blood pressure	35.2	32.3
Adults who are current smokers	18.6	17.1
Adults who currently use E-cigarettes	8.7	4.6
Adults who currently use chewing tobacco, snuff, or snus	7.3	4.0
Adults who are heavy drinkers[2]	6.6	6.3
Adults who are binge drinkers[3]	18.0	17.4
Adults who are overweight (BMI 25.0 - 29.9)	32.7	35.3
Adults who are obese (BMI 30.0 - 99.8)	32.0	31.3
Adults who participated in any physical activities in the past month	70.7	74.4
Adults who always or nearly always wears a seat belt	93.5	94.3

Note: (1) Figures cover the Lexington-Fayette, KY Metropolitan Statistical Area; (2) Heavy drinkers are classified as adult men having more than 14 drinks per week and adult women having more than 7 drinks per week; (3) Binge drinkers are classified as males having five or more drinks on one occasion or females having four or more drinks on one occasion
Source: Centers for Disease Control and Prevention, Behaviorial Risk Factor Surveillance System, SMART: Selected Metropolitan Area Risk Trends, 2017

Acute and Chronic Health Conditions

Category	MSA[1] (%)	U.S. (%)
Adults who have ever been told they had a heart attack	5.7	4.2
Adults who have ever been told they have angina or coronary heart disease	4.4	3.9
Adults who have ever been told they had a stroke	n/a	3.0
Adults who have ever been told they have asthma	15.9	14.2
Adults who have ever been told they have arthritis	25.6	24.9
Adults who have ever been told they have diabetes[2]	9.8	10.5
Adults who have ever been told they had skin cancer	8.8	6.2
Adults who have ever been told they had any other types of cancer	8.3	7.1
Adults who have ever been told they have COPD	7.3	6.5
Adults who have ever been told they have kidney disease	3.2	3.0
Adults who have ever been told they have a form of depression	16.5	20.5

Note: n/a not available; (1) Figures cover the Lexington-Fayette, KY Metropolitan Statistical Area; (2) Figures do not include pregnancy-related, borderline, or pre-diabetes
Source: Centers for Disease Control and Prevention, Behaviorial Risk Factor Surveillance System, SMART: Selected Metropolitan Area Risk Trends, 2017

Health Screening and Vaccination Rates

Category	MSA[1] (%)	U.S. (%)
Adults aged 65+ who have had flu shot within the past year	66.1	60.7
Adults aged 65+ who have ever had a pneumonia vaccination	76.2	75.4
Adults who have ever been tested for HIV	35.1	36.1
Adults who have ever had the shingles or zoster vaccine?	26.6	28.9
Adults who have had their blood cholesterol checked within the last five years	85.7	85.9

Note: n/a not available; (1) Figures cover the Lexington-Fayette, KY Metropolitan Statistical Area.
Source: Centers for Disease Control and Prevention, Behaviorial Risk Factor Surveillance System, SMART: Selected Metropolitan Area Risk Trends, 2017

Disability Status

Category	MSA[1] (%)	U.S. (%)
Adults who reported being deaf	7.8	6.7
Are you blind or have serious difficulty seeing, even when wearing glasses?	6.9	4.5
Are you limited in any way in any of your usual activities due of arthritis?	12.5	12.9
Do you have difficulty doing errands alone?	6.0	6.8
Do you have difficulty dressing or bathing?	4.6	3.6
Do you have serious difficulty concentrating/remembering/making decisions?	10.6	10.7
Do you have serious difficulty walking or climbing stairs?	15.3	13.6

Note: (1) Figures cover the Lexington-Fayette, KY Metropolitan Statistical Area.
Source: Centers for Disease Control and Prevention, Behaviorial Risk Factor Surveillance System, SMART: Selected Metropolitan Area Risk Trends, 2017

Mortality Rates for the Top 10 Causes of Death in the U.S.

ICD-10[a] Sub-Chapter	ICD-10[a] Code	Age-Adjusted Mortality Rate[1] per 100,000 population	
		County[2]	U.S.
Malignant neoplasms	C00-C97	149.8	149.2
Ischaemic heart diseases	I20-I25	57.0	90.5
Other forms of heart disease	I30-I51	59.8	52.2
Chronic lower respiratory diseases	J40-J47	42.4	39.6
Other degenerative diseases of the nervous system	G30-G31	41.0	37.6
Cerebrovascular diseases	I60-I69	35.4	37.2
Other external causes of accidental injury	W00-X59	55.0	36.1
Organic, including symptomatic, mental disorders	F01-F09	43.1	29.4
Hypertensive diseases	I10-I15	26.6	24.1
Diabetes mellitus	E10-E14	22.8	21.5

Note: (a) ICD-10 = International Classification of Diseases 10th Revision; (1) Mortality rates are a three-year average covering 2017-2019; (2) Figures cover Fayette County.
Source: Centers for Disease Control and Prevention, National Center for Health Statistics. Underlying Cause of Death 1999-2019 on CDC WONDER Online Database

Mortality Rates for Selected Causes of Death

ICD-10[a] Sub-Chapter	ICD-10[a] Code	Age-Adjusted Mortality Rate[1] per 100,000 population	
		County[2]	U.S.
Assault	X85-Y09	6.7	6.0
Diseases of the liver	K70-K76	14.1	14.4
Human immunodeficiency virus (HIV) disease	B20-B24	Unreliable	1.5
Influenza and pneumonia	J09-J18	13.2	13.8
Intentional self-harm	X60-X84	11.0	14.1
Malnutrition	E40-E46	Unreliable	2.3
Obesity and other hyperalimentation	E65-E68	2.9	2.1
Renal failure	N17-N19	11.2	12.6
Transport accidents	V01-V99	7.9	12.3
Viral hepatitis	B15-B19	Unreliable	1.2

Note: (a) ICD-10 = International Classification of Diseases 10th Revision; (1) Mortality rates are a three-year average covering 2017-2019; (2) Figures cover Fayette County; Data are suppressed when the data meet the criteria for confidentiality constraints; Mortality rates are flagged as unreliable when the rate would be calculated with a numerator of 20 or less.
Source: Centers for Disease Control and Prevention, National Center for Health Statistics. Underlying Cause of Death 1999-2019 on CDC WONDER Online Database

Health Insurance Coverage

Area	With Health Insurance	With Private Health Insurance	With Public Health Insurance	Without Health Insurance	Population Under Age 19 Without Health Insurance
City	93.2	71.6	32.5	6.8	4.3
MSA[1]	93.7	70.8	34.5	6.3	4.0
U.S.	91.2	67.9	35.1	8.8	5.1

Note: Figures are percentages that cover the civilian noninstitutionalized population; (1) Figures cover the Lexington-Fayette, KY Metropolitan Statistical Area
Source: U.S. Census Bureau, 2015-2019 American Community Survey 5-Year Estimates

Number of Medical Professionals

Area	MDs[3]	DOs[3,4]	Dentists	Podiatrists	Chiropractors	Optometrists
County[1] (number)	2,350	118	480	24	73	75
County[1] (rate[2])	728.8	36.6	148.5	7.4	22.6	23.2
U.S. (rate[2])	282.9	22.7	71.2	6.2	28.1	16.9

21067
Note: Data as of 2019 unless noted; (1) Data covers Fayette County; (2) Rate per 100,000 population; (3) Data as of 2018 and includes all active, non-federal physicians; (4) Doctor of Osteopathic Medicine
Source: U.S. Department of Health and Human Services, Health Resources and Services Administration, Bureau of Health Professions, Area Resource File (ARF) 2019-2020

Best Hospitals

According to *U.S. News,* the Lexington-Fayette, KY metro area is home to one of the best hospitals in the U.S.: **University of Kentucky Albert B. Chandler Hospital** (1 adult specialty and 2 pediatric specialties). The hospital listed was nationally ranked in at least one of 16 adult or 10 pediatric specialties. Only 134 hospitals nationwide were nationally ranked in one or more adult or pediatric specialty; this number increases to 178 counting specialized centers within hospitals. Twenty hospitals in the U.S. made the Honor Roll. The Best Hospitals Honor Roll takes both the national rankings and the procedure and condition ratings into account. Hospitals received points if they were nationally ranked in one of the 16 adult specialties—the higher they ranked, the more points they got—and how many ratings of "high performing" they earned in the 10 procedures and conditions. *U.S. News Online, "America's Best Hospitals 2020-21"*

According to *U.S. News,* the Lexington-Fayette, KY metro area is home to one of the best children's hospitals in the U.S.: **Kentucky Children's Hospital-Shriners Hospitals for Children** (2 pediatric specialties). The hospital listed was highly ranked in at least one of 10 pediatric specialties. Eighty-eight children's hospitals in the U.S. were nationally ranked in at least one specialty. Hospitals received points for being ranked in a specialty, and the 10 hospitals with the most points across the 10 specialties make up the Honor Roll. *U.S. News Online, "America's Best Children's Hospitals 2020-21"*

EDUCATION

Public School District Statistics

District Name	Schls	Pupils	Pupil/ Teacher Ratio	Minority Pupils[1] (%)	Free Lunch Eligible[2] (%)	IEP[3] (%)
Fayette County	80	41,987	14.8	50.1	43.6	12.0

Note: Table includes school districts with 2,000 or more students; (1) Percentage of students that are not non-Hispanic white; (2) Percentage of students that are eligible for the free lunch program; (3) Percentage of students that have an Individualized Education Program.
Source: U.S. Department of Education, National Center for Education Statistics, Common Core of Data, Local Education Agency (School District) Universe Survey: School Year 2018-2019; U.S. Department of Education, National Center for Education Statistics, Common Core of Data, Public Elementary/Secondary School Universe Survey: School Year 2018-2019

Highest Level of Education

Area	Less than H.S.	H.S. Diploma	Some College, No Deg.	Associate Degree	Bachelor's Degree	Master's Degree	Prof. School Degree	Doctorate Degree
City	8.8	19.6	20.5	7.5	24.4	12.0	4.1	3.2
MSA[1]	9.9	24.2	20.8	7.9	21.3	10.3	3.2	2.4
U.S.	12.0	27.0	20.4	8.5	19.8	8.8	2.1	1.4

Note: Figures cover persons age 25 and over; (1) Figures cover the Lexington-Fayette, KY Metropolitan Statistical Area
Source: U.S. Census Bureau, 2015-2019 American Community Survey 5-Year Estimates

Educational Attainment by Race

Area	High School Graduate or Higher (%)					Bachelor's Degree or Higher (%)				
	Total	White	Black	Asian	Hisp.[2]	Total	White	Black	Asian	Hisp.[2]
City	91.2	93.4	85.4	91.1	61.0	43.6	47.7	19.5	68.5	19.2
MSA[1]	90.1	91.6	85.1	91.1	60.8	37.3	39.2	19.0	64.5	16.9
U.S.	88.0	89.9	86.0	87.1	68.7	32.1	33.5	21.6	54.3	16.4

Note: Figures shown cover persons 25 years old and over; (1) Figures cover the Lexington-Fayette, KY Metropolitan Statistical Area; (2) People of Hispanic origin can be of any race
Source: U.S. Census Bureau, 2015-2019 American Community Survey 5-Year Estimates

School Enrollment by Grade and Control

Area	Preschool (%)		Kindergarten (%)		Grades 1 - 4 (%)		Grades 5 - 8 (%)		Grades 9 - 12 (%)	
	Public	Private	Public	Private	Public	Private	Public	Private	Public	Private
City	44.2	55.8	86.4	13.6	87.2	12.8	86.6	13.4	86.1	13.9
MSA[1]	47.1	52.9	83.9	16.1	88.1	11.9	86.9	13.1	86.8	13.2
U.S.	59.1	40.9	87.6	12.4	89.5	10.5	89.4	10.6	90.1	9.9

Note: Figures shown cover persons 3 years old and over; (1) Figures cover the Lexington-Fayette, KY Metropolitan Statistical Area
Source: U.S. Census Bureau, 2015-2019 American Community Survey 5-Year Estimates

Higher Education

Four-Year Colleges			Two-Year Colleges			Medical Schools[1]	Law Schools[2]	Voc/ Tech[3]
Public	Private Non-profit	Private For-profit	Public	Private Non-profit	Private For-profit			
1	2	1	1	0	0	1	1	4

Note: Figures cover institutions located within the city limits and include main campuses only; (1) includes schools accredited by the Liaison Committee on Medical Education and the American Osteopathic Association's Commission on Osteopathic College Accreditation; (2) includes ABA-accredited schools, schools with provisional ABA accreditation, and state accredited schools; (3) includes all schools with programs that are less than 2 years.
Source: National Center for Education Statistics, Integrated Postsecondary Education System (IPEDS), 2019-20; Wikipedia, List of Medical Schools in the United States, accessed April 2, 2021; Wikipedia, List of Law Schools in the United States, accessed April 2, 2021

According to *U.S. News & World Report,* the Lexington-Fayette, KY metro area is home to one of the top 200 national universities in the U.S.: **University of Kentucky** (#133 tie). The indicators used to capture academic quality fall into a number of categories: assessment by administrators at peer institutions; retention of students; faculty resources; student selectivity; financial resources; alumni giving; high school counselor ratings of colleges; and graduation rate. *U.S. News & World Report, "America's Best Colleges 2021"*

According to *U.S. News & World Report,* the Lexington-Fayette, KY metro area is home to one of the top 100 liberal arts colleges in the U.S.: **Transylvania University** (#84 tie). The indicators used to capture academic quality fall into a number of categories: assessment by administrators at peer institutions; retention of students; faculty resources; student selectivity; financial resources; alumni giving; high school counselor ratings of colleges; and graduation rate. *U.S. News & World Report, "America's Best Colleges 2021"*

According to *U.S. News & World Report,* the Lexington-Fayette, KY metro area is home to one of the top 100 law schools in the U.S.: **University of Kentucky** (#81 tie). The rankings are based on a weighted average of 12 measures of quality: peer assessment score; assessment score by lawyers/judges; median LSAT scores; median undergrad GPA; acceptance rate; employment rates for graduates; placement success; bar passage rate; faculty resources; expenditures per student; student/faculty ratio; and library resources. *U.S. News & World Report, "America's Best Graduate Schools, Law, 2022"*

According to *U.S. News & World Report,* the Lexington-Fayette, KY metro area is home to one of the top 75 medical schools for research in the U.S.: **University of Kentucky** (#70 tie). The rankings are based on a weighted average of 11 measures of quality: quality assessment; peer assessment score; assessment score by residency directors; research activity; total research activity; average research activity per faculty member; student selectivity; median MCAT total score; median undergraduate GPA; acceptance rate; and faculty resources. *U.S. News & World Report, "America's Best Graduate Schools, Medical, 2022"*

EMPLOYERS

Major Employers

Company Name	Industry
Amazon.com	Distribution
Baptist Health	Healthcare
Cardinal Hill Rehabilitation Hospital	Healthcare
Eastern Kentucky University	Education
Fayette County Public Schools	Education
Kentucky Health & Family Svcs Cabinet	Government
KentuckyOne Health	Healthcare
KY Dept for Workforce Inv	Government
Lexington-Fayette Urban County Govt	Government
Lexmark International	Enterprise software, hardware and services
Lockheed Martin	Manufacturing
Osram Sylvania	Manufacturing
Scott County Public Schools	Education
Tokico (USA) (Hitachi)	Manufacturing
Toyota Motor Manufacturing	Manufacturing
Transportation Cabinet of Kentucky	Government
University of Kentucky	Education
Veterans Medical Center	Healthcare
Wal-Mart Stores	Retail
Xerox	Outsourcing

Note: Companies shown are located within the Lexington-Fayette, KY Metropolitan Statistical Area.
Source: Hoovers.com; Wikipedia

Best Companies to Work For

Lexmark, headquartered in Lexington, is among the "100 Best Companies for Working Mothers." Criteria: paid time off and leaves; workforce profile; benefits; women's issues and advancement; flexible work; company culture and work life programs. *Working Mother, "100 Best Companies for Working Mothers," 2020*

Lexmark, headquartered in Lexington, is among the "Top Companies for Executive Women." This list is determined by organizations filling out an in-depth survey that measures female demographics at every level, but with an emphasis on women in senior corporate roles, with profit & loss (P&L) responsibility, and those earning in the top 20 percent of the organization. *Working Mother* defines P&L as having responsibility that involves monitoring the net income after expenses for a department or entire organization, with direct influence on how company resources are allocated. *Working Mother, "Top Companies for Executive Women," 2020+*

Lexmark, headquartered in Lexington, is among the "Best Companies for Dads." *Working Mother's* newest list recognizes the growing importance companies place on giving dads time off and support for their families. Rankings are determined by measuring gender-neutral or paternity leave offered, as well as actual time taken, phase-back policies, child- and dependent-care benefits, and corporate support groups for men and dads. *Working Mother, "Best Companies for Dads," 2020*

PUBLIC SAFETY

Crime Rate

Area	All Crimes	Violent Crimes				Property Crimes		
		Murder	Rape[3]	Robbery	Aggrav. Assault	Burglary	Larceny -Theft	Motor Vehicle Theft
City	3,294.7	8.0	53.7	111.0	123.9	471.4	2,248.9	277.9
Suburbs[1]	2,369.2	0.5	30.9	28.3	60.2	318.5	1,748.7	182.1
Metro[2]	2,949.0	5.2	45.2	80.1	100.1	414.3	2,062.1	242.1
U.S.	2,489.3	5.0	42.6	81.6	250.2	340.5	1,549.5	219.9

Note: Figures are crimes per 100,000 population; (1) All areas within the metro area that are located outside the city limits; (2) Figures cover the Lexington-Fayette, KY Metropolitan Statistical Area; (3) All figures shown were reported using the revised Uniform Crime Reporting (UCR) definition of rape.
Source: FBI Uniform Crime Reports, 2019

Hate Crimes

Area	Number of Quarters Reported	Number of Incidents per Bias Motivation					
		Race/Ethnicity/ Ancestry	Religion	Sexual Orientation	Disability	Gender	Gender Identity
City[1]	4	15	1	2	0	0	0
U.S.	4	3,963	1,521	1,195	157	69	198

Note: (1) Figures include one incident reported with more than one bias motivation.
Source: Federal Bureau of Investigation, Hate Crime Statistics 2019

Identity Theft Consumer Reports

Area	Reports	Reports per 100,000 Population	Rank[2]
MSA[1]	707	137	317
U.S.	1,387,615	423	-

Note: (1) Figures cover the Lexington-Fayette, KY Metropolitan Statistical Area; (2) Rank ranges from 1 to 391 where 1 indicates greatest number of identity theft reports per 100,000 population
Source: Federal Trade Commission, Consumer Sentinel Network Data Book 2020

Fraud and Other Consumer Reports

Area	Reports	Reports per 100,000 Population	Rank[2]
MSA[1]	3,843	743	149
U.S.	3,385,133	1,031	-

Note: (1) Figures cover the Lexington-Fayette, KY Metropolitan Statistical Area; (2) Rank ranges from 1 to 391 where 1 indicates greatest number of fraud and other consumer reports per 100,000 population
Source: Federal Trade Commission, Consumer Sentinel Network Data Book 2020

POLITICS

2020 Presidential Election Results

Area	Biden	Trump	Jorgensen	Hawkins	Other
Fayette County	59.2	38.5	1.6	0.1	0.6
U.S.	51.3	46.8	1.2	0.3	0.5

Note: Results are percentages and may not add to 100% due to rounding
Source: Dave Leip's Atlas of U.S. Presidential Elections

SPORTS

Professional Sports Teams

Team Name	League	Year Established

No teams are located in the metro area
Source: Wikipedia, Major Professional Sports Teams of the United States and Canada, April 6, 2021

CLIMATE

Average and Extreme Temperatures

Temperature	Jan	Feb	Mar	Apr	May	Jun	Jul	Aug	Sep	Oct	Nov	Dec	Yr.
Extreme High (°F)	76	75	82	88	92	101	103	103	103	91	83	75	103
Average High (°F)	40	44	54	66	75	83	86	85	79	68	55	44	65
Average Temp. (°F)	32	36	45	55	64	73	76	75	69	57	46	36	55
Average Low (°F)	24	26	34	44	54	62	66	65	58	46	36	28	45
Extreme Low (°F)	-21	-15	-2	18	26	39	47	42	35	20	-3	-19	-21

Note: Figures cover the years 1948-1990
Source: National Climatic Data Center, International Station Meteorological Climate Summary, 9/96

Average Precipitation/Snowfall/Humidity

Precip./Humidity	Jan	Feb	Mar	Apr	May	Jun	Jul	Aug	Sep	Oct	Nov	Dec	Yr.
Avg. Precip. (in.)	3.6	3.4	4.4	3.9	4.3	4.0	4.8	3.7	3.0	2.4	3.5	3.9	45.1
Avg. Snowfall (in.)	6	5	3	Tr	Tr	0	0	0	0	Tr	1	3	17
Avg. Rel. Hum. 7am (%)	81	80	77	75	78	80	83	85	85	83	81	81	81
Avg. Rel. Hum. 4pm (%)	67	61	55	51	54	54	56	55	54	53	60	66	57

Note: Figures cover the years 1948-1990; Tr = Trace amounts (<0.05 in. of rain; <0.5 in. of snow)
Source: National Climatic Data Center, International Station Meteorological Climate Summary, 9/96

Weather Conditions

Temperature			Daytime Sky			Precipitation		
10°F & below	32°F & below	90°F & above	Clear	Partly cloudy	Cloudy	0.01 inch or more precip.	0.1 inch or more snow/ice	Thunder-storms
11	96	22	86	136	143	129	17	44

Note: Figures are average number of days per year and cover the years 1948-1990
Source: National Climatic Data Center, International Station Meteorological Climate Summary, 9/96

HAZARDOUS WASTE

Superfund Sites

The Lexington-Fayette, KY metro area has no sites on the EPA's Superfund Final National Priorities List. There are a total of 1,375 Superfund sites with a status of proposed or final on the list in the U.S.
U.S. Environmental Protection Agency, National Priorities List, April 7, 2021

AIR QUALITY

Air Quality Trends: Ozone

	1990	1995	2000	2005	2010	2015	2016	2017	2018	2019
MSA[1]	0.078	0.088	0.077	0.078	0.070	0.069	0.066	0.063	0.063	0.059
U.S.	0.088	0.089	0.082	0.080	0.073	0.068	0.069	0.068	0.069	0.065

Note: (1) Data covers the Lexington-Fayette, KY Metropolitan Statistical Area. The values shown are the composite ozone concentration averages among trend sites based on the highest fourth daily maximum 8-hour concentration in parts per million. These trends are based on sites having an adequate record of monitoring data during the trend period. Data from exceptional events are included.
Source: U.S. Environmental Protection Agency, Air Quality Monitoring Information, "Air Quality Trends by City, 1990-2019"

Air Quality Index

Area	Percent of Days when Air Quality was...[2]					AQI Statistics[2]	
	Good	Moderate	Unhealthy for Sensitive Groups	Unhealthy	Very Unhealthy	Maximum	Median
MSA[1]	83.0	17.0	0.0	0.0	0.0	80	42

Note: (1) Data covers the Lexington-Fayette, KY Metropolitan Statistical Area; (2) Based on 365 days with AQI data in 2019. Air Quality Index (AQI) is an index for reporting daily air quality. EPA calculates the AQI for five major air pollutants regulated by the Clean Air Act: ground-level ozone, particle pollution (aka particulate matter), carbon monoxide, sulfur dioxide, and nitrogen dioxide. The AQI runs from 0 to 500. The higher the AQI value, the greater the level of air pollution and the greater the health concern. There are six AQI categories: "Good" AQI is between 0 and 50. Air quality is considered satisfactory; "Moderate" AQI is between 51 and 100. Air quality is acceptable; "Unhealthy for Sensitive Groups" When AQI values are between 101 and 150, members of sensitive groups may experience health effects; "Unhealthy" When AQI values are between 151 and 200 everyone may begin to experience health effects; "Very Unhealthy" AQI values between 201 and 300 trigger a health alert; "Hazardous" AQI values over 300 trigger warnings of emergency conditions (not shown).
Source: U.S. Environmental Protection Agency, Air Quality Index Report, 2019

Air Quality Index Pollutants

Area	Percent of Days when AQI Pollutant was...[2]					
	Carbon Monoxide	Nitrogen Dioxide	Ozone	Sulfur Dioxide	Particulate Matter 2.5	Particulate Matter 10
MSA[1]	0.0	2.7	52.9	0.0	44.4	0.0

Note: (1) Data covers the Lexington-Fayette, KY Metropolitan Statistical Area; (2) Based on 365 days with AQI data in 2019. The Air Quality Index (AQI) is an index for reporting daily air quality. EPA calculates the AQI for five major air pollutants regulated by the Clean Air Act: ground-level ozone, particle pollution (also known as particulate matter), carbon monoxide, sulfur dioxide, and nitrogen dioxide. The AQI runs from 0 to 500. The higher the AQI value, the greater the level of air pollution and the greater the health concern.
Source: U.S. Environmental Protection Agency, Air Quality Index Report, 2019

Maximum Air Pollutant Concentrations: Particulate Matter, Ozone, CO and Lead

	Particulate Matter 10 (ug/m³)	Particulate Matter 2.5 Wtd AM (ug/m³)	Particulate Matter 2.5 24-Hr (ug/m³)	Ozone (ppm)	Carbon Monoxide (ppm)	Lead (ug/m³)
MSA[1] Level	28	8.0	17	0.059	n/a	n/a
NAAQS[2]	150	15	35	0.075	9	0.15
Met NAAQS[2]	Yes	Yes	Yes	Yes	n/a	n/a

Note: (1) Data covers the Lexington-Fayette, KY Metropolitan Statistical Area; Data from exceptional events are included; (2) National Ambient Air Quality Standards; ppm = parts per million; ug/m³ = micrograms per cubic meter; n/a not available.
Concentrations: Particulate Matter 10 (coarse particulate)—highest second maximum 24-hour concentration; Particulate Matter 2.5 Wtd AM (fine particulate)—highest weighted annual mean concentration; Particulate Matter 2.5 24-Hour (fine particulate)—highest 98th percentile 24-hour concentration; Ozone—highest fourth daily maximum 8-hour concentration; Carbon Monoxide—highest second maximum non-overlapping 8-hour concentration; Lead—maximum running 3-month average
Source: U.S. Environmental Protection Agency, Air Quality Monitoring Information, "Air Quality Statistics by City, 2019"

Maximum Air Pollutant Concentrations: Nitrogen Dioxide and Sulfur Dioxide

	Nitrogen Dioxide AM (ppb)	Nitrogen Dioxide 1-Hr (ppb)	Sulfur Dioxide AM (ppb)	Sulfur Dioxide 1-Hr (ppb)	Sulfur Dioxide 24-Hr (ppb)
MSA[1] Level	6	42	n/a	4	n/a
NAAQS[2]	53	100	30	75	140
Met NAAQS[2]	Yes	Yes	n/a	Yes	n/a

Note: (1) Data covers the Lexington-Fayette, KY Metropolitan Statistical Area; Data from exceptional events are included; (2) National Ambient Air Quality Standards; ppm = parts per million; ug/m³ = micrograms per cubic meter; n/a not available.
Concentrations: Nitrogen Dioxide AM—highest arithmetic mean concentration; Nitrogen Dioxide 1-Hr—highest 98th percentile 1-hour daily maximum concentration; Sulfur Dioxide AM—highest annual mean concentration; Sulfur Dioxide 1-Hr—highest 99th percentile 1-hour daily maximum concentration; Sulfur Dioxide 24-Hr—highest second maximum 24-hour concentration
Source: U.S. Environmental Protection Agency, Air Quality Monitoring Information, "Air Quality Statistics by City, 2019"

Louisville, Kentucky

Background

Louisville was founded in 1778, when George Rogers Clark, on his way to capture British Fort Vincennes, established a base on an island above the Falls of the Ohio River. Shortly thereafter a settlement grew on the south side of the river. Two years later the Virginia state legislature named the town Louisville to pay homage to King Louis XVI of France, who had allied his country with America during the American Revolution.

The Falls forced people traveling down the Ohio to use the portage of Louisville, which helped the town grow in the early nineteenth century. Kentucky incorporated the town as a city in 1828. Two years later, the Portland Canal opened, allowing boats to go around the rapids, thereby increasing river traffic and assisting the city's growth. In the next several years, the arrival of the railroad would link the town to much of the rest of the South. The cultivation of tobacco became important to the state in the 1830s, when Louisville became a prominent processing site.

The Civil War was an interesting period in the city's history, as adherents to both the North and the South walked the city's streets. Yet the North had the upper hand, and Louisville quickly became a supply center for Union armies marching south.

The postwar period saw boom times for Louisville, and by the end of the nineteenth century the population topped 200,000. In 1937, after the Ohio River flooded the city's environs, a floodwall was built to prevent such a catastrophe from recurring. World War II saw Louisville rebound as it became an important center for munitions production. After the war, the city desegregated its schools in a calm fashion, without the trouble seen in so many other areas.

The Kentucky Derby horserace—the annual Run for the Roses—has been held at Churchill Downs in Louisville since 1875, earning the city the nickname, "Derby Town." The fabled track now includes the Grandstand Terrace and Rooftop Garden and close to 2,400 new seats. A new stadium for the city's pro soccer team opened in 2020.

The city serves as an important corporate command post, hosting the headquarters of several major companies. Louisville also produces one third of all bourbon whiskey, with major bourbon maker Brown-Forman headquartered there.

Louisville has maintained its importance as a vital center of transportation. The metropolitan area has two ports on the Ohio River and three interstate highways intersecting the city. The Louisville International Airport, serves as the international hub for United Parcel Service with a 10,000-foot taxiway. The Louisville metro area has many incentives to offer new businesses, including a foreign trade zone.

The "NuLu" District, formally called the East Market District, is hopping with shops, restaurants and breweries established in the old warehouse district. City attractions include the Kentucky Science Center with interactive exhibits and Science Education Wing, the Louisville Zoo, the Kentucky Derby Museum, Kentucky Kingdom and Hurricane Bay, the Louisville Slugger Museum & Factor (with the world's largest bat), and the Kentucky Exposition Center. The Speed Art Museum, the oldest (1927) and largest art museum in the state, reopened in 2016 with 220,000 of renovated space after a 3-year closure.

> Organizers of the Kentucky Derby's annual fireworks show encouraged the public to watch from home, keeping the exact location secret to prevent large gatherings.

The city's climate is a typical continental one. Look for cool winters, warm summers, and thunderstorms with intense rainfall during spring and summer. Fall tends to be the driest, and snow can arrive anytime from November through March, although all precipitation varies from year to year.

Rankings

General Rankings

- For its "Best for Vets: Places to Live 2019" rankings, *Military Times* evaluated 599 cities (83 large, 234 medium, 282 small) and compared the locations across three broad categories: veteran and military culture/services; economic indicators; and livability factors such as health, crime, traffic, and school quality. Louisville ranked #19 out of the top 25, in the large city category (population of more than 250,000). Data points more specific to veterans and the military weighed more heavily than others. *rebootcamp.militarytimes.com, "Military Times Best Places to Live 2019," September 10, 2018*

- In its eighth annual survey, *Travel + Leisure* readers nominated their favorite small cities and towns in America—those with 100,000 or fewer residents—voting on numerous attractive features in categories including culture, food and drink, quality of life, style, and people. After 50,000 votes, Louisville was ranked #13 among the proposed favorites. *www.travelandleisure.com, "America's Favorite Cities," October 20, 2017*

Business/Finance Rankings

- Based on metro area social media reviews, the employment opinion group Glassdoor surveyed 50 of the most populous U.S. metro areas and equally weighed cost of living, hiring opportunity, and job satisfaction to compose a list of "25 Best Cities for Jobs." Median pay and home value, and number of active job openings were also factored in. The Louisville metro area was ranked #13 in overall job satisfaction. *www.glassdoor.com, "Best Cities for Jobs," February 25, 2020*

- The Brookings Institution ranked the nation's largest cities based on income inequality. Louisville was ranked #74 (#1 = greatest inequality). Criteria: the "95/20 ratio," a figure representing the income at which a household earns more than 95 percent of all other households, divided by the income at which a household earns more than only 20 percent of all other households. *Brookings Institution, "Household Income Inequality, Largest Cities of 97 Large U.S. Metro Areas, 2014-2016," February 5, 2018*

- The Brookings Institution ranked the 100 largest metro areas in the U.S. based on income inequality. Louisville was ranked #74 (#1 = greatest inequality). Criteria: the "95/20 ratio," a figure representing the income at which a household earns more than 95 percent of all other households, divided by the income at which a household earns more than only 20 percent of all other households. *Brookings Institution, "Household Income Inequality, 100 Largest U.S. Metro Areas, 2014-2016," February 5, 2018*

- The Louisville metro area appeared on the Milken Institute "2021 Best Performing Cities" list. Rank: #110 out of 200 large metro areas (population over 250,000). Criteria: job growth; wage and salary growth; high-tech output growth; housing affordability; household broadband access. *Milken Institute, "Best-Performing Cities 2021," February 16, 2021*

- *Forbes* ranked the 200 most populous metro areas to determine the nation's "Best Places for Business and Careers." The Louisville metro area was ranked #92. Criteria: costs (business and living); job growth (past and projected); income growth; quality of life; educational attainment (college and high school); projected economic growth; cultural and leisure opportunities; workplace tolerance laws; net migration patterns. *Forbes, "The Best Places for Business and Careers 2019: Seattle Still On Top," October 30, 2019*

Dating/Romance Rankings

- Louisville was ranked #14 out of 25 cities that stood out for inspiring romance and attracting diners on the website OpenTable.com. Criteria: percentage of people who dined out on Valentine's Day in 2018; percentage of romantic restaurants as rated by OpenTable diner reviews; and percentage of tables seated for two. *OpenTable, "25 Most Romantic Cities in America for 2019," February 7, 2019*

Education Rankings

- Personal finance website *WalletHub* analyzed the 150 largest U.S. metropolitan statistical areas to determine where the most educated Americans are putting their degrees to work. Criteria: education levels; percentage of workers with degrees; education quality and attainment gap; public school quality rankings; quality and enrollment of each metro area's universities. Louisville was ranked #95 (#1 = most educated city). *www.WalletHub.com, "Most and Least Educated Cities in America," July 20, 2020*

- Louisville was selected as one of America's most literate cities. The city ranked #44 out of the 84 largest U.S. cities. Criteria: number of booksellers; library resources; Internet resources; educational attainment; periodical publishing resources; newspaper circulation. *Central Connecticut State University, "America's Most Literate Cities, 2018," February 2019*

Environmental Rankings

- The U.S. Environmental Protection Agency (EPA) released a list of mid-size U.S. metropolitan areas with the most ENERGY STAR certified buildings in 2019. The Louisville metro area was ranked #4 out of 10. *U.S. Environmental Protection Agency, "2020 Energy Star Top Cities," March 2020*

- Louisville was highlighted as one of the top 98 cleanest metro areas for short-term particle pollution (24-hour PM 2.5) in the U.S. during 2016 through 2018. Monitors in these cities reported no days with unhealthful PM 2.5 levels. *American Lung Association, "State of the Air 2020," April 21, 2020*

Health/Fitness Rankings

- For each of the 100 largest cities in the United States, the American Fitness Index®, published by the American College of Sports Medicine and the Anthem Foundation, evaluated community infrastructure and 33 health behaviors including preventive health, levels of chronic disease conditions, pedestrian safety, air quality, and community resources that support physical activity. Louisville ranked #89 for "community fitness." *americanfitnessindex.org, "2020 ACSM American Fitness Index Summary Report," July 14, 2020*

- The Louisville metro area was identified as one of the worst cities for bed bugs in America by pest control company Orkin. The area ranked #46 out of 50 based on the number of bed bug treatments Orkin performed from December 2019 to November 2020. *Orkin, "New Year, New Top City on Orkin's 2021 Bed Bug Cities List: Chicago," February 1, 2021*

- Louisville was identified as a "2021 Spring Allergy Capital." The area ranked #21 out of 100. Three groups of factors were used to identify the most challenging cities for people with allergies during the spring season: annual spring pollen levels; over the counter medicine use; number of board-certified allergy specialists. *Asthma and Allergy Foundation of America, "Spring Allergy Capitals 2021," February 23, 2021*

- Louisville was identified as a "2021 Fall Allergy Capital." The area ranked #20 out of 100. Three groups of factors were used to identify the most challenging cities for people with allergies during the fall season: annual fall pollen levels; over the counter medicine use; number of board-certified allergy specialists. *Asthma and Allergy Foundation of America, "Fall Allergy Capitals 2021," February 23, 2021*

- Louisville was identified as a "2019 Asthma Capital." The area ranked #7 out of the nation's 100 largest metropolitan areas. Criteria: estimated asthma prevalence; crude death rate from asthma; and ER visits due to asthma. Risk factors analyzed but not factored in the rankings: annual pollen score; annual air quality; public smoking laws; number of board-certified asthma specialists; rescue medication use; controller medication use; uninsured rate; poverty rate. *Asthma and Allergy Foundation of America, "Asthma Capitals 2019: The Most Challenging Places to Live With Asthma," May 7, 2019*

Real Estate Rankings

- FitSmallBusiness looked at 50 of the largest metropolitan areas in the U.S. to determine which metro was the best to start a real estate business. Data was compiled from such sources as: Zillow, Trulia, U.S. Census Bureau, and the Bureau of Labor Statistics. Criteria: location; inventory; annual wages; median sales price of homes; days on the market; median price cut percentage; and other factors that would influence real estate professional growth. The Louisville metro area ranked #46. *fitsmallbusiness.com, "The Best Cities to Become a Real Estate Agent in 2018," January 30, 2018*

- *WalletHub* compared the most populated U.S. cities to determine which had the best markets for real estate agents. Louisville ranked #93 where demand was high and pay was the best. Criteria: sales per agent; annual median wage for real-estate agents; monthly average starting salary for real estate agents; real estate job density and competition; unemployment rate; home turnover rate; housing-market health index; and other relevant metrics. *www.WalletHub.com, "2019's Best Places to Be a Real Estate Agent," April 24, 2019*

- Louisville was ranked #73 out of 268 metro areas in terms of housing affordability in 2020 by the National Association of Home Builders (#1 = most affordable). Criteria: the share of homes sold in that area affordable to a family earning the local median income, based on standard mortgage underwriting criteria. *National Association of Home Builders®, NAHB-Wells Fargo Housing Opportunity Index, 4th Quarter 2020*

Safety Rankings

- Allstate ranked the 200 largest cities in America in terms of driver safety. Louisville ranked #98. Criteria: internal property damage claims over a two-year period from January 2016 to December 2017. The report helps increase the importance of safety and awareness behind the wheel. *Allstate, "Allstate America's Best Drivers Report, 2019" June 24, 2019*

- The National Insurance Crime Bureau ranked 384 metro areas in the U.S. in terms of per capita rates of vehicle theft. The Louisville metro area ranked #39 (#1 = highest rate). Criteria: number of vehicle theft offenses per 100,000 inhabitants in 2019. *National Insurance Crime Bureau, "Hot Spots 2019," July 21, 2020*

Seniors/Retirement Rankings

- From its Best Cities for Successful Aging indexes, the Milken Institute generated rankings for metropolitan areas, weighing data in nine categories—health care, wellness, living arrangements, transportation and convenience, financial characteristics, education, employment, community engagement, and overall livability. The Louisville metro area was ranked #79 overall in the large metro area category. *Milken Institute, "Best Cities for Successful Aging, 2017" March 14, 2017*

Sports/Recreation Rankings

- Louisville was chosen as one of America's best cities for bicycling. The city ranked #37 out of 50. Criteria: cycling infrastructure that is safe and friendly for all ages; energy and bike culture. The editors evaluated cities with populations of 100,000 or more. *Bicycling, "The 50 Best Bike Cities in America," October 10, 2018*

Women/Minorities Rankings

- Personal finance website *WalletHub* compared more than 180 U.S. cities across two key dimensions, "Hispanic Business-Friendliness" and "Hispanic Purchasing Power," to arrive at the most favorable conditions for Hispanic entrepreneurs. Louisville was ranked #138 out of 182. Criteria includes: share of Hispanic-Owned Businesses; Hispanic entrepreneurship rate to median annual income of Hispanics; Small Business-Friendliness score; cost of living; and number of Hispanics with at least a bachelor's degree. *WalletHub.com, "2019's Best Cities for Hispanic Entrepreneurs," May 1, 2019*

Miscellaneous Rankings

- *WalletHub* compared the 150 most populated U.S. cities to determine their operating efficiency. A "Quality of City Services" score was constructed for each city and then divided by the total budget per capita to reveal which were managed the best. Louisville ranked #21. Criteria: financial stability; economy; education; safety; health; infrastructure and pollution. *www.WalletHub.com, "2020's Best- & Worst-Run Cities in America," June 29, 2020*

- Louisville was selected as one of "America's Friendliest Cities." The city ranked #8 in the "Friendliest" category. Respondents to an online survey were asked to rate 38 top urban destinations in the United States as to general friendliness, as well as manners, politeness and warm disposition. *Travel + Leisure, "America's Friendliest Cities," October 20, 2017*

Business Environment

DEMOGRAPHICS

Population Growth

Area	1990 Census	2000 Census	2010 Census	2019* Estimate	Population Growth (%) 1990-2019	Population Growth (%) 2010-2019
City	269,160	256,231	597,337	617,790	129.5	3.4
MSA[1]	1,055,973	1,161,975	1,283,566	1,257,088	19.0	-2.1
U.S.	248,709,873	281,421,906	308,745,538	324,697,795	30.6	5.2

Note: (1) Figures cover the Louisville/Jefferson County, KY-IN Metropolitan Statistical Area; (*) 2015-2019 5-year estimated population
Source: U.S. Census Bureau, 1990 Census, Census 2000, Census 2010, 2015-2019 American Community Survey 5-Year Estimates

Household Size

Area	Persons in Household (%) One	Two	Three	Four	Five	Six	Seven or More	Average Household Size
City	33.4	33.0	15.3	10.6	4.9	1.8	1.0	2.40
MSA[1]	30.3	34.1	15.8	11.8	5.2	1.9	0.9	2.50
U.S.	27.9	33.9	15.6	12.9	6.0	2.3	1.4	2.60

Note: (1) Figures cover the Louisville/Jefferson County, KY-IN Metropolitan Statistical Area
Source: U.S. Census Bureau, 2015-2019 American Community Survey 5-Year Estimates

Race

Area	White Alone[2] (%)	Black Alone[2] (%)	Asian Alone[2] (%)	AIAN[3] Alone[2] (%)	NHOPI[4] Alone[2] (%)	Other Race Alone[2] (%)	Two or More Races (%)
City	69.9	23.6	2.7	0.2	0.1	1.0	2.6
MSA[1]	79.4	14.8	2.1	0.2	0.0	0.9	2.5
U.S.	72.5	12.7	5.5	0.8	0.2	4.9	3.3

Note: (1) Figures cover the Louisville/Jefferson County, KY-IN Metropolitan Statistical Area; (2) Alone is defined as not being in combination with one or more other races; (3) American Indian and Alaska Native; (4) Native Hawaiian and Other Pacific Islander
Source: U.S. Census Bureau, 2015-2019 American Community Survey 5-Year Estimates

Hispanic or Latino Origin

Area	Total (%)	Mexican (%)	Puerto Rican (%)	Cuban (%)	Other (%)
City	5.6	2.0	0.5	1.9	1.2
MSA[1]	4.9	2.4	0.4	1.1	1.1
U.S.	18.0	11.2	1.7	0.7	4.3

Note: Persons of Hispanic or Latino origin can be of any race; (1) Figures cover the Louisville/Jefferson County, KY-IN Metropolitan Statistical Area
Source: U.S. Census Bureau, 2015-2019 American Community Survey 5-Year Estimates

Ancestry

Area	German	Irish	English	American	Italian	Polish	French[2]	Scottish	Dutch
City	15.1	11.5	7.8	8.7	2.5	1.0	1.9	1.6	0.9
MSA[1]	17.2	12.4	9.1	10.1	2.4	1.1	2.1	1.9	1.0
U.S.	13.3	9.7	7.2	6.2	5.1	2.8	2.3	1.7	1.2

Note: Figures are the percentage of the total population reporting a particular ancestry. The nine most commonly reported ancestries in the U.S. are shown. Figures include multiple ancestries (e.g. if a person reported being Irish and Italian, they were included in both columns); (1) Figures cover the Louisville/Jefferson County, KY-IN Metropolitan Statistical Area; (2) Excludes Basque
Source: U.S. Census Bureau, 2015-2019 American Community Survey 5-Year Estimates

Foreign-born Population

Area	Percent of Population Born in Any Foreign Country	Asia	Mexico	Europe	Caribbean	Central America[2]	South America	Africa	Canada
City	7.7	2.5	0.7	0.9	1.6	0.4	0.3	1.2	0.1
MSA[1]	5.9	1.9	0.9	0.7	0.9	0.3	0.2	0.7	0.1
U.S.	13.6	4.2	3.5	1.5	1.3	1.1	1.0	0.7	0.2

Note: (1) Figures cover the Louisville/Jefferson County, KY-IN Metropolitan Statistical Area; (2) Excludes Mexico.
Source: U.S. Census Bureau, 2015-2019 American Community Survey 5-Year Estimates

Marital Status

Area	Never Married	Now Married[2]	Separated	Widowed	Divorced
City	36.3	42.1	2.1	6.1	13.4
MSA[1]	31.6	47.4	1.9	6.1	13.0
U.S.	33.4	48.1	1.9	5.8	10.9

Note: Figures are percentages and cover the population 15 years of age and older; (1) Figures cover the Louisville/Jefferson County, KY-IN Metropolitan Statistical Area; (2) Excludes separated
Source: U.S. Census Bureau, 2015-2019 American Community Survey 5-Year Estimates

Disability by Age

Area	All Ages	Under 18 Years Old	18 to 64 Years Old	65 Years and Over
City	14.8	4.6	13.4	36.4
MSA[1]	14.1	4.2	12.4	35.5
U.S.	12.6	4.2	10.3	34.5

Note: Figures show percent of the civilian noninstitutionalized population that reported having a disability. Disability status is determined from six types of difficulty: vision, hearing, cognitive, ambulatory, self-care, and independent living. For children under 5 years old, hearing and vision difficulty are used to determine disability status. For children between the ages of 5 and 14, disability status is determined from hearing, vision, cognitive, ambulatory, and self-care difficulties. For people aged 15 years and older, they are considered to have a disability if they have difficulty with any one of the six difficulty types; Note: (1) Figures cover the Louisville/Jefferson County, KY-IN Metropolitan Statistical Area
Source: U.S. Census Bureau, 2015-2019 American Community Survey 5-Year Estimates

Age

Area	Percent of Population									Median Age
	Under Age 5	Age 5–19	Age 20–34	Age 35–44	Age 45–54	Age 55–64	Age 65–74	Age 75–84	Age 85+	
City	6.5	18.5	21.5	12.4	12.8	13.4	8.7	4.3	1.9	37.6
MSA[1]	6.1	18.7	19.9	12.8	13.3	13.6	9.3	4.4	1.8	39.0
U.S.	6.1	19.1	20.7	12.6	13.0	12.9	9.1	4.6	1.9	38.1

Note: (1) Figures cover the Louisville/Jefferson County, KY-IN Metropolitan Statistical Area
Source: U.S. Census Bureau, 2015-2019 American Community Survey 5-Year Estimates

Gender

Area	Males	Females	Males per 100 Females
City	299,406	318,384	94.0
MSA[1]	613,822	643,266	95.4
U.S.	159,886,919	164,810,876	97.0

Note: (1) Figures cover the Louisville/Jefferson County, KY-IN Metropolitan Statistical Area
Source: U.S. Census Bureau, 2015-2019 American Community Survey 5-Year Estimates

Religious Groups by Family

Area	Catholic	Baptist	Non-Den.	Methodist[2]	Lutheran	LDS[3]	Pentecostal	Presbyterian[4]	Muslim[5]	Judaism
MSA[1]	13.7	25.1	1.7	3.7	0.6	0.8	1.0	1.2	0.5	0.4
U.S.	19.1	9.3	4.0	4.0	2.3	2.0	1.9	1.6	0.8	0.7

Note: Figures are the number of adherents as a percentage of the total population; (1) Figures cover the Louisville/Jefferson County, KY-IN Metropolitan Statistical Area; (2) Methodist/Pietist; (3) Latter Day Saints; (4) Reformed; (5) Figures are estimates
Source: Association of Statisticians of American Religious Bodies, 2010 U.S. Religion Census: Religious Congregations & Membership Study

Religious Groups by Tradition

Area	Catholic	Evangelical Protestant	Mainline Protestant	Other Tradition	Black Protestant	Orthodox
MSA[1]	13.7	24.5	7.1	2.0	3.0	0.1
U.S.	19.1	16.2	7.3	4.3	1.6	0.3

Note: Figures are the number of adherents as a percentage of the total population; (1) Figures cover the Louisville/Jefferson County, KY-IN Metropolitan Statistical Area
Source: Association of Statisticians of American Religious Bodies, 2010 U.S. Religion Census: Religious Congregations & Membership Study

ECONOMY

Gross Metropolitan Product

Area	2017	2018	2019	2020	Rank[2]
MSA[1]	75.3	78.1	81.3	83.9	48

Note: Figures are in billions of dollars; (1) Figures cover the Louisville/Jefferson County, KY-IN Metropolitan Statistical Area; (2) Rank is based on 2018 data and ranges from 1 to 381
Source: U.S. Conference of Mayors, U.S. Metro Economies: GMP & Employment 2018-2020, September 2019

Economic Growth

Area	2015-17 (%)	2018 (%)	2019 (%)	2020 (%)	Rank[2]
MSA[1]	0.7	1.4	2.3	1.2	254
U.S.	1.9	2.9	2.3	2.1	–

Note: Figures are real gross metropolitan product (GMP) growth rates and represent average annual percent change; (1) Figures cover the Louisville/Jefferson County, KY-IN Metropolitan Statistical Area; (2) Rank is based on 2017 2-year average annual percent change and ranges from 1 to 381
Source: U.S. Conference of Mayors, U.S. Metro Economies: GMP & Employment 2018-2020, September 2019

Metropolitan Area Exports

Area	2014	2015	2016	2017	2018	2019	Rank[2]
MSA[1]	8,877.3	8,037.9	7,793.3	8,925.9	8,987.0	9,105.5	39

Note: Figures are in millions of dollars; (1) Figures cover the Louisville/Jefferson County, KY-IN Metropolitan Statistical Area; (2) Rank is based on 2019 data and ranges from 1 to 386
Source: U.S. Department of Commerce, International Trade Administration, Office of Trade and Economic Analysis, Industry and Analysis, Exports by Metropolitan Area, data extracted March 24, 2021

Building Permits

Area	Single-Family			Multi-Family			Total		
	2018	2019	Pct. Chg.	2018	2019	Pct. Chg.	2018	2019	Pct. Chg.
City	1,183	1,207	2.0	2,080	2,204	6.0	3,263	3,411	4.5
MSA[1]	3,104	3,122	0.6	2,409	2,644	9.8	5,513	5,766	4.6
U.S.	855,300	862,100	0.7	473,500	523,900	10.6	1,328,800	1,386,000	4.3

Note: (1) Figures cover the Louisville/Jefferson County, KY-IN Metropolitan Statistical Area; Figures represent new, privately-owned housing units authorized (unadjusted data); All permit data are based on estimates with imputation
Source: U.S. Census Bureau, Manufacturing, Mining, and Construction Statistics, Building Permits, 2018, 2019

Bankruptcy Filings

Area	Business Filings			Nonbusiness Filings		
	2019	2020	% Chg.	2019	2020	% Chg.
Jefferson County	50	39	-22.0	2,893	2,174	-24.9
U.S.	22,780	21,655	-4.9	752,160	522,808	-30.5

Note: Business filings include Chapter 7, Chapter 9, Chapter 11, Chapter 12, Chapter 13, Chapter 15, and Section 304; Nonbusiness filings include Chapter 7, Chapter 11, and Chapter 13
Source: Administrative Office of the U.S. Courts, Business and Nonbusiness Bankruptcy, County Cases Commenced by Chapter of the Bankruptcy Code, During the 12-Month Period Ending December 31, 2019 and Business and Nonbusiness Bankruptcy, County Cases Commenced by Chapter of the Bankruptcy Code, During the 12-Month Period Ending December 31, 2020

Housing Vacancy Rates

Area	Gross Vacancy Rate[2] (%)			Year-Round Vacancy Rate[3] (%)			Rental Vacancy Rate[4] (%)			Homeowner Vacancy Rate[5] (%)		
	2018	2019	2020	2018	2019	2020	2018	2019	2020	2018	2019	2020
MSA[1]	7.6	7.9	6.9	7.4	7.8	6.9	7.7	10.6	6.4	1.4	0.7	1.4
U.S.	12.3	12.0	10.6	9.7	9.5	8.2	6.9	6.7	6.3	1.5	1.4	1.0

Note: (1) Figures cover the Louisville/Jefferson County, KY-IN Metropolitan Statistical Area; (2) The percentage of the total housing inventory that is vacant; (3) The percentage of the housing inventory (excluding seasonal units) that is year-round vacant; (4) The percentage of rental inventory that is vacant for rent; (5) The percentage of homeowner inventory that is vacant for sale
Source: U.S. Census Bureau, Housing Vacancies and Homeownership Annual Statistics: 2018, 2019, 2020

INCOME

Income

Area	Per Capita ($)	Median Household ($)	Average Household ($)
City	30,943	53,436	74,580
MSA[1]	32,630	59,158	80,682
U.S.	34,103	62,843	88,607

Note: (1) Figures cover the Louisville/Jefferson County, KY-IN Metropolitan Statistical Area
Source: U.S. Census Bureau, 2015-2019 American Community Survey 5-Year Estimates

Household Income Distribution

Area	Percent of Households Earning							
	Under $15,000	$15,000 -$24,999	$25,000 -$34,999	$35,000 -$49,999	$50,000 -$74,999	$75,000 -$99,999	$100,000 -$149,999	$150,000 and up
City	12.4	10.3	10.2	13.9	17.8	12.5	12.7	10.1
MSA[1]	10.2	9.3	9.4	13.6	18.4	13.4	14.4	11.4
U.S.	10.3	8.9	8.9	12.3	17.2	12.7	15.1	14.5

Note: (1) Figures cover the Louisville/Jefferson County, KY-IN Metropolitan Statistical Area
Source: U.S. Census Bureau, 2015-2019 American Community Survey 5-Year Estimates

Poverty Rate

Area	All Ages	Under 18 Years Old	18 to 64 Years Old	65 Years and Over
City	15.9	24.0	14.6	9.4
MSA[1]	12.5	18.2	11.6	7.9
U.S.	13.4	18.5	12.6	9.3

Note: Figures are percentage of people whose income during the past 12 months was below the poverty level;
(1) Figures cover the Louisville/Jefferson County, KY-IN Metropolitan Statistical Area
Source: U.S. Census Bureau, 2015-2019 American Community Survey 5-Year Estimates

CITY FINANCES

City Government Finances

Component	2017 ($000)	2017 ($ per capita)
Total Revenues	1,321,039	1,730
Total Expenditures	1,536,301	2,012
Debt Outstanding	2,142,653	2,806
Cash and Securities[1]	1,795,010	2,351

Note: (1) Cash and security holdings of a government at the close of its fiscal year,
including those of its dependent agencies, utilities, and liquor stores.
Source: U.S. Census Bureau, State & Local Government Finances 2017

City Government Revenue by Source

Source	2017 ($000)	2017 ($ per capita)	2017 (%)
General Revenue			
From Federal Government	95,008	124	7.2
From State Government	72,946	96	5.5
From Local Governments	24,748	32	1.9
Taxes			
Property	156,760	205	11.9
Sales and Gross Receipts	85,722	112	6.5
Personal Income	321,245	421	24.3
Corporate Income	70,046	92	5.3
Motor Vehicle License	597	1	0.0
Other Taxes	10,856	14	0.8
Current Charges	228,395	299	17.3
Liquor Store	0	0	0.0
Utility	190,734	250	14.4
Employee Retirement	2,696	4	0.2

Source: U.S. Census Bureau, State & Local Government Finances 2017

City Government Expenditures by Function

Function	2017 ($000)	2017 ($ per capita)	2017 (%)
General Direct Expenditures			
Air Transportation	51,237	67	3.3
Corrections	68,189	89	4.4
Education	53,347	69	3.5
Employment Security Administration	0	0	0.0
Financial Administration	60,787	79	4.0
Fire Protection	61,045	79	4.0
General Public Buildings	0	0	0.0
Governmental Administration, Other	43,401	56	2.8
Health	97,397	127	6.3
Highways	82,648	108	5.4
Hospitals	0	0	0.0
Housing and Community Development	53,878	70	3.5
Interest on General Debt	121,382	159	7.9
Judicial and Legal	9,703	12	0.6
Libraries	23,962	31	1.6
Parking	27,136	35	1.8
Parks and Recreation	59,412	77	3.9
Police Protection	184,257	241	12.0
Public Welfare	14,639	19	1.0
Sewerage	0	0	0.0
Solid Waste Management	26,750	35	1.7
Veterans' Services	0	0	0.0
Liquor Store	0	0	0.0
Utility	315,869	413	20.6
Employee Retirement	5,148	6	0.3

Source: U.S. Census Bureau, State & Local Government Finances 2017

EMPLOYMENT

Labor Force and Employment

Area	Civilian Labor Force			Workers Employed		
	Dec. 2019	Dec. 2020	% Chg.	Dec. 2019	Dec. 2020	% Chg.
City	402,027	394,489	-1.9	388,284	371,824	-4.2
MSA[1]	674,729	662,325	-1.8	652,752	628,916	-3.7
U.S.	164,007,000	160,017,000	-2.4	158,504,000	149,613,000	-5.6

Note: Data is not seasonally adjusted and covers workers 16 years of age and older; (1) Figures cover the Louisville/Jefferson County, KY-IN Metropolitan Statistical Area
Source: Bureau of Labor Statistics, Local Area Unemployment Statistics

Unemployment Rate

Area	2020											
	Jan.	Feb.	Mar.	Apr.	May	Jun.	Jul.	Aug.	Sep.	Oct.	Nov.	Dec.
City	4.1	3.7	4.7	16.5	11.7	5.3	5.3	7.7	5.6	7.4	5.4	5.7
MSA[1]	3.9	3.5	4.3	16.8	11.8	6.5	5.6	7.0	5.3	6.5	4.9	5.0
U.S.	4.0	3.8	4.5	14.4	13.0	11.2	10.5	8.5	7.7	6.6	6.4	6.5

Note: Data is not seasonally adjusted and covers workers 16 years of age and older; (1) Figures cover the Louisville/Jefferson County, KY-IN Metropolitan Statistical Area
Source: Bureau of Labor Statistics, Local Area Unemployment Statistics

Average Wages

Occupation	$/Hr.	Occupation	$/Hr.
Accountants and Auditors	36.50	Maintenance and Repair Workers	22.00
Automotive Mechanics	20.20	Marketing Managers	68.50
Bookkeepers	19.70	Network and Computer Systems Admin.	37.60
Carpenters	26.00	Nurses, Licensed Practical	21.90
Cashiers	11.30	Nurses, Registered	31.90
Computer Programmers	36.60	Nursing Assistants	14.50
Computer Systems Analysts	41.10	Office Clerks, General	17.30
Computer User Support Specialists	25.00	Physical Therapists	41.20
Construction Laborers	18.90	Physicians	119.20
Cooks, Restaurant	13.50	Plumbers, Pipefitters and Steamfitters	28.30
Customer Service Representatives	17.70	Police and Sheriff's Patrol Officers	25.30
Dentists	61.30	Postal Service Mail Carriers	25.70
Electricians	28.10	Real Estate Sales Agents	31.10
Engineers, Electrical	42.60	Retail Salespersons	13.30
Fast Food and Counter Workers	10.30	Sales Representatives, Technical/Scientific	42.70
Financial Managers	58.60	Secretaries, Exc. Legal/Medical/Executive	18.50
First-Line Supervisors of Office Workers	28.00	Security Guards	13.20
General and Operations Managers	50.00	Surgeons	134.50
Hairdressers/Cosmetologists	15.10	Teacher Assistants, Exc. Postsecondary*	15.10
Home Health and Personal Care Aides	14.10	Teachers, Secondary School, Exc. Sp. Ed.*	27.30
Janitors and Cleaners	13.60	Telemarketers	n/a
Landscaping/Groundskeeping Workers	15.80	Truck Drivers, Heavy/Tractor-Trailer	25.60
Lawyers	57.00	Truck Drivers, Light/Delivery Services	20.40
Maids and Housekeeping Cleaners	12.20	Waiters and Waitresses	11.00

Note: Wage data covers the Louisville/Jefferson County, KY-IN Metropolitan Statistical Area; (*) Hourly wages were calculated from annual wage data based on a 40 hour work week; n/a not available.
Source: Bureau of Labor Statistics, Metro Area Occupational Employment & Wage Estimates, May 2020

Employment by Industry

Sector	MSA[1]		U.S.
	Number of Employees	Percent of Total	Percent of Total
Construction, Mining, and Logging	28,000	4.3	5.5
Education and Health Services	92,500	14.3	16.3
Financial Activities	47,300	7.3	6.1
Government	69,800	10.8	15.2
Information	8,300	1.3	1.9
Leisure and Hospitality	50,600	7.8	9.0
Manufacturing	81,800	12.7	8.5
Other Services	23,000	3.6	3.8
Professional and Business Services	84,600	13.1	14.4
Retail Trade	64,500	10.0	10.9
Transportation, Warehousing, and Utilities	65,900	10.2	4.6
Wholesale Trade	28,900	4.5	3.9

Note: Figures are non-farm employment as of December 2020. Figures are not seasonally adjusted and include workers 16 years of age and older; (1) Figures cover the Louisville/Jefferson County, KY-IN Metropolitan Statistical Area
Source: Bureau of Labor Statistics, Current Employment Statistics, Employment, Hours, and Earnings

Employment by Occupation

Occupation Classification	City (%)	MSA[1] (%)	U.S. (%)
Management, Business, Science, and Arts	35.6	36.7	38.5
Natural Resources, Construction, and Maintenance	6.5	7.6	8.9
Production, Transportation, and Material Moving	19.0	18.2	13.2
Sales and Office	22.3	22.0	21.6
Service	16.5	15.5	17.8

Note: Figures cover employed civilians 16 years of age and older; (1) Figures cover the Louisville/Jefferson County, KY-IN Metropolitan Statistical Area
Source: U.S. Census Bureau, 2015-2019 American Community Survey 5-Year Estimates

Occupations with Greatest Projected Employment Growth: 2020 – 2022

Occupation[1]	2020 Employment	2022 Projected Employment	Numeric Employment Change	Percent Employment Change
Combined Food Preparation and Serving Workers, Including Fast Food	56,290	64,080	7,790	13.8
Waiters and Waitresses	26,910	30,230	3,320	12.3
Laborers and Freight, Stock, and Material Movers, Hand	61,690	64,690	3,000	4.9
Cooks, Restaurant	17,120	19,830	2,710	15.8
Personal Care Aides	19,850	21,690	1,840	9.3
Registered Nurses	46,830	48,380	1,550	3.3
Retail Salespersons	50,950	52,470	1,520	3.0
First-Line Supervisors of Food Preparation and Serving Workers	12,550	14,060	1,510	12.0
Maids and Housekeeping Cleaners	19,820	21,220	1,400	7.1
Industrial Truck and Tractor Operators	14,190	15,250	1,060	7.5

Note: Projections cover Kentucky; (1) Sorted by numeric employment change
Source: www.projectionscentral.com, State Occupational Projections, 2020–2022 Short-Term Projections

Fastest-Growing Occupations: 2020 – 2022

Occupation[1]	2020 Employment	2022 Projected Employment	Numeric Employment Change	Percent Employment Change
Hotel, Motel, and Resort Desk Clerks	2,960	3,940	980	33.1
Lodging Managers	220	290	70	31.8
Gaming and Sports Book Writers and Runners	300	360	60	20.0
Animal Trainers	470	560	90	19.1
Ushers, Lobby Attendants, and Ticket Takers	860	1,020	160	18.6
Cooks, Restaurant	17,120	19,830	2,710	15.8
Dining Room and Cafeteria Attendants and Bartender Helpers	2,850	3,290	440	15.4
Hosts and Hostesses, Restaurant, Lounge, and Coffee Shop	4,100	4,670	570	13.9
Taxi Drivers and Chauffeurs	2,590	2,950	360	13.9
Combined Food Preparation and Serving Workers, Including Fast Food	56,290	64,080	7,790	13.8

Note: Projections cover Kentucky; (1) Sorted by percent employment change and excludes occupations with numeric employment change less than 50
Source: www.projectionscentral.com, State Occupational Projections, 2020–2022 Short-Term Projections

TAXES

State Corporate Income Tax Rates

State	Tax Rate (%)	Income Brackets ($)	Num. of Brackets	Financial Institution Tax Rate (%)[a]	Federal Income Tax Ded.
Kentucky	5.0	Flat rate	1	5.0	No

Note: Tax rates as of January 1, 2021; (a) Rates listed are the corporate income tax rate applied to financial institutions or excise taxes based on income. Some states have other taxes based upon the value of deposits or shares.
Source: Federation of Tax Administrators, State Corporate Income Tax Rates, January 1, 2021

State Individual Income Tax Rates

State	Tax Rate (%)	Income Brackets ($)	Personal Exemptions ($)			Standard Ded. ($)	
			Single	Married	Depend.	Single	Married
Kentucky	5.0	Flat rate	None	None	None	2,690	2,690

Note: Tax rates as of January 1, 2021; Local- and county-level taxes are not included; Federal income tax is not deductible on state income tax returns
Source: Federation of Tax Administrators, State Individual Income Tax Rates, January 1, 2021

Various State Sales and Excise Tax Rates

State	State Sales Tax (%)	Gasoline[1] (¢/gal.)	Cigarette[2] ($/pack)	Spirits[3] ($/gal.)	Wine[4] ($/gal.)	Beer[5] ($/gal.)	Recreational Marijuana (%)
Kentucky	6	26	1.1	8.41	3.23	0.89	Not legal

Note: All tax rates as of January 1, 2021; (1) The American Petroleum Institute has developed a methodology for determining the average tax rate on a gallon of fuel. Rates may include any of the following: excise taxes, environmental fees, storage tank fees, other fees or taxes, general sales tax, and local taxes; (2) The federal excise tax of $1.0066 per pack and local taxes are not included; (3) Rates are those applicable to off-premise sales of 40% alcohol by volume (a.b.v.) distilled spirits in 750ml containers. Local excise taxes are excluded; (4) Rates are those applicable to off-premise sales of 11% a.b.v. non-carbonated wine in 750ml containers; (5) Rates are those applicable to off-premise sales of 4.7% a.b.v. beer in 12 ounce containers.
Source: Tax Foundation, 2021 Facts & Figures: How Does Your State Compare?

State Business Tax Climate Index Rankings

State	Overall Rank	Corporate Tax Rank	Individual Income Tax Rank	Sales Tax Rank	Property Tax Rank	Unemployment Insurance Tax Rank
Kentucky	19	19	18	13	21	49

Note: The index is a measure of how each state's tax laws affect economic performance. The lower the rank, the more favorable a state's tax system is for business. States without a given tax are given a ranking of 1. The scores/rankings for the District of Columbia do not affect other states. The 2021 index represents the tax climate as of July 1, 2020.
Source: Tax Foundation, State Business Tax Climate Index 2021

TRANSPORTATION

Means of Transportation to Work

Area	Car/Truck/Van		Public Transportation			Bicycle	Walked	Other Means	Worked at Home
	Drove Alone	Car-pooled	Bus	Subway	Railroad				
City	79.6	8.9	3.1	0.0	0.0	0.4	2.0	1.8	4.3
MSA[1]	82.0	8.5	1.8	0.0	0.0	0.2	1.6	1.3	4.6
U.S.	76.3	9.0	2.4	1.9	0.6	0.5	2.7	1.4	5.2

Note: Figures are percentages and cover workers 16 years of age and older; (1) Figures cover the Louisville/Jefferson County, KY-IN Metropolitan Statistical Area
Source: U.S. Census Bureau, 2015-2019 American Community Survey 5-Year Estimates

Travel Time to Work

Area	Less Than 10 Minutes	10 to 19 Minutes	20 to 29 Minutes	30 to 44 Minutes	45 to 59 Minutes	60 to 89 Minutes	90 Minutes or More
City	9.3	32.4	30.1	20.3	4.4	2.2	1.4
MSA[1]	9.7	29.9	27.3	22.6	6.4	2.6	1.5
U.S.	12.2	28.4	20.8	20.8	8.3	6.4	2.9

Note: Note: Figures are percentages and include workers 16 years old and over; (1) Figures cover the Louisville/Jefferson County, KY-IN Metropolitan Statistical Area
Source: U.S. Census Bureau, 2015-2019 American Community Survey 5-Year Estimates

Key Congestion Measures

Measure	1982	1992	2002	2012	2017
Annual Hours of Delay, Total (000)	5,501	11,479	18,950	25,811	29,392
Annual Hours of Delay, Per Auto Commuter	17	31	33	40	46
Annual Congestion Cost, Total (million $)	42	121	256	465	544
Annual Congestion Cost, Per Auto Commuter ($)	304	437	562	600	663

Note: Covers the Louisville-Jefferson County KY-IN urban area
Source: Texas A&M Transportation Institute, 2019 Urban Mobility Report

Freeway Travel Time Index

Measure	1982	1987	1992	1997	2002	2007	2012	2017
Urban Area Index[1]	1.08	1.10	1.15	1.16	1.17	1.18	1.18	1.18
Urban Area Rank[1,2]	28	36	26	36	41	44	40	45

Note: Freeway Travel Time Index—the ratio of travel time in the peak period to the travel time at free-flow conditions. For example, a value of 1.30 indicates a 20-minute free-flow trip takes 26 minutes in the peak (20 minutes x 1.30 = 26 minutes); (1) Covers the Louisville-Jefferson County KY-IN urban area; (2) Rank is based on 101 larger urban areas (#1 = highest travel time index)
Source: Texas A&M Transportation Institute, 2019 Urban Mobility Report

Public Transportation

Agency Name / Mode of Transportation	Vehicles Operated in Maximum Service[1]	Annual Unlinked Passenger Trips[2] (in thous.)	Annual Passenger Miles[3] (in thous.)
Transit Authority of River City (TARC)			
Bus (directly operated)	180	10,762.7	45,741.7
Bus (purchased transportation)	2	70.1	197.7
Demand Response (directly operated)	1	1.0	5.5
Demand Response (purchased transportation)	86	365.4	3,307.4
Demand Response Taxi (purchased transportation)	61	257.7	2,517.1

Note: (1) Number of revenue vehicles operated by the given mode and type of service to meet the annual maximum service requirement. This is the revenue vehicle count during the peak season of the year; on the week and day that maximum service is provided. Vehicles operated in maximum service (VOMS) exclude atypical days and one-time special events; (2) Number of passengers who boarded public transportation vehicles. Passengers are counted each time they board a vehicle no matter how many vehicles they use to travel from their origin to their destination. (3) Sum of the distances ridden by all passengers during the entire fiscal year. Source: Federal Transit Administration, National Transit Database, 2019

Air Transportation

Airport Name and Code / Type of Service	Passenger Airlines[1]	Passenger Enplanements	Freight Carriers[2]	Freight (lbs)
Louisville International-Standiford Field (SDF)				
Domestic service (U.S. carriers - 2020)	24	788,280	21	3,009,689,912
International service (U.S. carriers - 2019)	2	7	5	172,791,481

Note: (1) Includes all U.S.-based major, minor and commuter airlines that carried at least one passenger during the year; (2) Includes all U.S.-based airlines and freight carriers that transported at least one pound of freight during the year. Source: Bureau of Transportation Statistics, The Intermodal Transportation Database, Air Carriers: T-100 Domestic Market (U.S. Carriers), 2020; Bureau of Transportation Statistics, The Intermodal Transportation Database, Air Carriers: T-100 International Market (U.S. Carriers), 2019

BUSINESSES

Major Business Headquarters

Company Name	Industry	Rankings	
		Fortune[1]	Forbes[2]
Humana	Health Care, Insurance and Managed Care	52	-

Note: (1) Companies that produce a 10-K are ranked 1 to 500 based on 2019 revenue; (2) All private companies with at least $2 billion in annual revenue through the end of their most current fiscal year are ranked 1 to 219; companies listed are headquartered in the city; dashes indicate no ranking Source: Fortune, "Fortune 500," June/July 2020; Forbes, "America's Largest Private Companies," 2020

Fastest-Growing Businesses

According to *Inc.*, Louisville is home to two of America's 500 fastest-growing private companies: **TKT** (#20); **New Source Medical** (#280). Criteria: must be an independent, privately-held, for-profit, U.S. corporation, proprietorship or partnership as of December 31, 2019; revenues must be at least $100,000 in 2016 and $2 million in 2019; must have four-year operating/sales history. *Inc., "America's 500 Fastest-Growing Private Companies," 2020*

Minority Business Opportunity

Louisville is home to one company which is on the *Black Enterprise* Industrial/Service list (100 largest companies based on gross sales): **Bridgeman Foods** (#6). Criteria: operational in previous calendar year; at least 51% black-owned and manufactures/owns the product it sells or provides industrial or consumer services. Brokerages, real estate firms and firms that provide professional services are not eligible. *Black Enterprise, B.E. 100s, 2019*

Louisville is home to one company which is on the *Black Enterprise* Auto Dealer list (45 largest dealers based on gross sales): **Pittman Enterprise** (#8). Criteria: company must be operational in previous calendar year and be at least 51% black-owned. *Black Enterprise, B.E. 100s, 2019*

Living Environment

COST OF LIVING

Cost of Living Index

Composite Index	Groceries	Housing	Utilities	Trans-portation	Health Care	Misc. Goods/ Services
94.2	92.3	78.4	96.1	103.3	95.5	104.5

Note: The Cost of Living Index measures regional differences in the cost of consumer goods and services, excluding taxes and non-consumer expenditures, for professional and managerial households in the top income quintile. It is based on more than 50,000 prices covering almost 60 different items for which prices are collected three times a year by chambers of commerce, economic development organizations or university applied economic centers in each participating urban area. The numbers shown should be read as a percentage above or below the national average of 100. For example, a value of 115.4 in the groceries column indicates that grocery prices are 15.4% higher than the national average. Small differences in the index numbers should not be interpreted as significant; Figures cover the Louisville KY urban area.
Source: The Council for Community and Economic Research, Cost of Living Index, 2020

Grocery Prices

Area[1]	T-Bone Steak ($/pound)	Frying Chicken ($/pound)	Whole Milk ($/half gal.)	Eggs ($/dozen)	Orange Juice ($/64 oz.)	Coffee ($/11.5 oz.)
City[2]	12.70	1.09	1.15	1.02	3.13	4.01
Avg.	11.78	1.39	2.05	1.47	3.57	4.34
Min.	8.03	0.94	1.03	0.74	2.94	3.02
Max.	15.86	2.65	4.31	3.77	5.44	8.69

*Note: (1) Values for the local area are compared with the average, minimum and maximum values for all 284 areas in the Cost of Living Index; (2) Figures cover the Louisville KY urban area; **T-Bone Steak** (price per pound); **Frying Chicken** (price per pound, whole fryer); **Whole Milk** (half gallon carton); **Eggs** (price per dozen, Grade A, large); **Orange Juice** (64 oz. Tropicana or Florida Natural); **Coffee** (11.5 oz. can, vacuum-packed, Maxwell House, Hills Bros, or Folgers).*
Source: The Council for Community and Economic Research, Cost of Living Index, 2020

Housing and Utility Costs

Area[1]	New Home Price ($)	Apartment Rent ($/month)	All Electric ($/month)	Part Electric ($/month)	Other Energy ($/month)	Telephone ($/month)
City[2]	273,187	1,038	-	80.02	77.60	180.80
Avg.	368,594	1,168	170.86	100.47	65.28	184.30
Min.	190,567	502	91.58	31.42	26.08	169.60
Max.	2,227,806	4,738	470.38	280.31	280.06	206.50

*Note: (1) Values for the local area are compared with the average, minimum and maximum values for all 284 areas in the Cost of Living Index; (2) Figures cover the Louisville KY urban area; **New Home Price** (2,400 sf living area, 8,000 sf lot, in urban area with full utilities); **Apartment Rent** (950 sf 2 bedroom/1.5 or 2 bath, unfurnished, excluding all utilities except water); **All Electric** (average monthly cost for an all-electric home); **Part Electric** (average monthly cost for a part-electric home); **Other Energy** (average monthly cost for natural gas, fuel oil, coal, wood, and any other forms of energy except electricity); **Telephone** (price includes the base monthly rate plus taxes and fees for three lines of mobile phone service).*
Source: The Council for Community and Economic Research, Cost of Living Index, 2020

Health Care, Transportation, and Other Costs

Area[1]	Doctor ($/visit)	Dentist ($/visit)	Optometrist ($/visit)	Gasoline ($/gallon)	Beauty Salon ($/visit)	Men's Shirt ($)
City[2]	133.98	82.89	71.56	2.28	49.58	32.27
Avg.	115.44	99.32	108.10	2.21	39.27	31.37
Min.	36.68	59.00	51.36	1.71	19.00	11.00
Max.	219.00	153.10	250.97	3.46	82.05	58.33

*Note: (1) Values for the local area are compared with the average, minimum and maximum values for all 284 areas in the Cost of Living Index; (2) Figures cover the Louisville KY urban area; **Doctor** (general practitioners routine exam of an established patient); **Dentist** (adult teeth cleaning and periodic oral examination); **Optometrist** (full vision eye exam for established adult patient); **Gasoline** (one gallon regular unleaded, national brand, including all taxes, cash price at self-service pump if available); **Beauty Salon** (woman's shampoo, trim, and blow-dry); **Men's Shirt** (cotton/polyester dress shirt, pinpoint weave, long sleeves).*
Source: The Council for Community and Economic Research, Cost of Living Index, 2020

HOUSING

Homeownership Rate

Area	2012 (%)	2013 (%)	2014 (%)	2015 (%)	2016 (%)	2017 (%)	2018 (%)	2019 (%)	2020 (%)
MSA[1]	63.3	64.5	68.9	67.7	67.6	71.7	67.9	64.9	69.3
U.S.	65.4	65.1	64.5	63.7	63.4	63.9	64.4	64.6	66.6

Note: (1) Figures cover the Louisville/Jefferson County, KY-IN Metropolitan Statistical Area
Source: U.S. Census Bureau, Housing Vacancies and Homeownership Annual Statistics: 2012-2020

House Price Index (HPI)

Area	National Ranking[2]	Quarterly Change (%)	One-Year Change (%)	Five-Year Change (%)	Since 1991Q1 (%)
MSA[1]	111	2.46	6.56	29.08	178.89
U.S.[3]	–	3.81	10.77	38.99	205.12

Note: The HPI is a weighted repeat sales index. It measures average price changes in repeat sales or refinancings on the same properties. This information is obtained by reviewing repeat mortgage transactions on single-family properties whose mortgages have been purchased or securitized by Fannie Mae or Freddie Mac since January 1975; (1) Figures cover the Louisville/Jefferson County, KY-IN Metropolitan Statistical Area; (2) Rankings are based on annual percentage change for all metro areas containing at least 15,000 transactions over the last 10 years and ranges from 1 to 253; (3) figures based on a weighted average of Census Division estimates using a seasonally adjusted, purchase-only index; all figures are for the period ending December 31, 2020
Source: Federal Housing Finance Agency, Change in Metropolitan Area House Price Indexes, April 7, 2021

Median Single-Family Home Prices

Area	2018	2019	2020p	Percent Change 2019 to 2020
MSA[1]	180.1	192.7	212.1	10.1
U.S. Average	261.6	274.6	299.9	9.2

Note: Figures are median sales prices of existing single-family homes in thousands of dollars; (p) preliminary; (1) Figures cover the Louisville/Jefferson County, KY-IN Metropolitan Statistical Area
Source: National Association of Realtors, Median Sales Price of Existing Single-Family Homes for Metropolitan Areas, 4th Quarter 2020

Qualifying Income Based on Median Sales Price of Existing Single-Family Homes

Area	With 5% Down ($)	With 10% Down ($)	With 20% Down ($)
MSA[1]	41,479	39,296	34,930
U.S. Average	59,266	56,147	49,908

Note: Figures are preliminary; Qualifying income is based on a mortgage rate of 2.81%. Monthly principal and interest payment is limited to 25% of income; (1) Figures cover the Louisville/Jefferson County, KY-IN Metropolitan Statistical Area
Source: National Association of Realtors, Qualifying Income Based on Median Sales Price of Existing Single-Family Homes for Metropolitan Areas, 4th Quarter 2020

Home Value Distribution

Area	Under $50,000	$50,000 -$99,999	$100,000 -$149,999	$150,000 -$199,999	$200,000 -$299,999	$300,000 -$499,999	$500,000 -$999,999	$1,000,000 or more
City	5.5	15.7	24.8	18.2	17.6	13.0	4.4	0.8
MSA[1]	4.8	13.7	22.6	18.9	20.8	13.6	4.5	0.9
U.S.	6.9	12.0	13.3	14.0	19.6	19.3	11.4	3.4

Note: Figures are percentages and cover owner-occupied housing units; (1) Figures cover the Louisville/Jefferson County, KY-IN Metropolitan Statistical Area
Source: U.S. Census Bureau, 2015-2019 American Community Survey 5-Year Estimates

Year Housing Structure Built

Area	2010 or Later	2000 -2009	1990 -1999	1980 -1989	1970 -1979	1960 -1969	1950 -1959	1940 -1949	Before 1940	Median Year
City	4.3	11.0	11.7	6.9	12.7	13.8	14.8	7.4	17.4	1968
MSA[1]	4.4	13.1	14.2	9.2	15.2	12.4	12.6	6.2	12.8	1974
U.S.	5.2	14.0	13.9	13.4	15.2	10.6	10.3	4.9	12.6	1978

Note: Figures are percentages except for Median Year; Note: (1) Figures cover the Louisville/Jefferson County, KY-IN Metropolitan Statistical Area
Source: U.S. Census Bureau, 2015-2019 American Community Survey 5-Year Estimates

Gross Monthly Rent

Area	Under $500	$500 -$999	$1,000 -$1,499	$1,500 -$1,999	$2,000 -$2,499	$2,500 -$2,999	$3,000 and up	Median ($)
City	13.7	54.1	25.9	4.9	0.7	0.4	0.3	846
MSA[1]	13.1	54.3	26.6	4.6	0.8	0.4	0.3	854
U.S.	9.4	36.2	30.0	14.0	5.6	2.4	2.4	1,062

Note: Figures are percentages except for Median; Gross rent is the contract rent plus the estimated average monthly cost of utilities (electricity, gas, and water and sewer) and fuels (oil, coal, kerosene, wood, etc.) if these are paid by the renter (or paid for the renter by someone else); (1) Figures cover the Louisville/Jefferson County, KY-IN Metropolitan Statistical Area
Source: U.S. Census Bureau, 2015-2019 American Community Survey 5-Year Estimates

HEALTH

Health Risk Factors

Category	MSA[1] (%)	U.S. (%)
Adults aged 18–64 who have any kind of health care coverage	89.0	87.3
Adults who reported being in good or better health	77.6	82.4
Adults who have been told they have high blood cholesterol	37.0	33.0
Adults who have been told they have high blood pressure	34.6	32.3
Adults who are current smokers	22.7	17.1
Adults who currently use E-cigarettes	5.8	4.6
Adults who currently use chewing tobacco, snuff, or snus	6.5	4.0
Adults who are heavy drinkers[2]	5.9	6.3
Adults who are binge drinkers[3]	15.6	17.4
Adults who are overweight (BMI 25.0 - 29.9)	34.1	35.3
Adults who are obese (BMI 30.0 - 99.8)	30.1	31.3
Adults who participated in any physical activities in the past month	69.9	74.4
Adults who always or nearly always wears a seat belt	93.3	94.3

Note: (1) Figures cover the Louisville/Jefferson County, KY-IN Metropolitan Statistical Area; (2) Heavy drinkers are classified as adult men having more than 14 drinks per week and adult women having more than 7 drinks per week; (3) Binge drinkers are classified as males having five or more drinks on one occasion or females having four or more drinks on one occasion
Source: Centers for Disease Control and Prevention, Behaviorial Risk Factor Surveillance System, SMART: Selected Metropolitan Area Risk Trends, 2017

Acute and Chronic Health Conditions

Category	MSA[1] (%)	U.S. (%)
Adults who have ever been told they had a heart attack	5.5	4.2
Adults who have ever been told they have angina or coronary heart disease	5.4	3.9
Adults who have ever been told they had a stroke	4.9	3.0
Adults who have ever been told they have asthma	16.5	14.2
Adults who have ever been told they have arthritis	26.5	24.9
Adults who have ever been told they have diabetes[2]	12.4	10.5
Adults who have ever been told they had skin cancer	6.6	6.2
Adults who have ever been told they had any other types of cancer	7.9	7.1
Adults who have ever been told they have COPD	10.9	6.5
Adults who have ever been told they have kidney disease	4.1	3.0
Adults who have ever been told they have a form of depression	21.9	20.5

Note: (1) Figures cover the Louisville/Jefferson County, KY-IN Metropolitan Statistical Area; (2) Figures do not include pregnancy-related, borderline, or pre-diabetes
Source: Centers for Disease Control and Prevention, Behaviorial Risk Factor Surveillance System, SMART: Selected Metropolitan Area Risk Trends, 2017

Health Screening and Vaccination Rates

Category	MSA[1] (%)	U.S. (%)
Adults aged 65+ who have had flu shot within the past year	60.5	60.7
Adults aged 65+ who have ever had a pneumonia vaccination	75.3	75.4
Adults who have ever been tested for HIV	38.7	36.1
Adults who have ever had the shingles or zoster vaccine?	29.9	28.9
Adults who have had their blood cholesterol checked within the last five years	85.1	85.9

Note: n/a not available; (1) Figures cover the Louisville/Jefferson County, KY-IN Metropolitan Statistical Area.
Source: Centers for Disease Control and Prevention, Behaviorial Risk Factor Surveillance System, SMART: Selected Metropolitan Area Risk Trends, 2017

Disability Status

Category	MSA[1] (%)	U.S. (%)
Adults who reported being deaf	6.9	6.7
Are you blind or have serious difficulty seeing, even when wearing glasses?	4.9	4.5
Are you limited in any way in any of your usual activities due of arthritis?	14.3	12.9
Do you have difficulty doing errands alone?	8.1	6.8
Do you have difficulty dressing or bathing?	5.1	3.6
Do you have serious difficulty concentrating/remembering/making decisions?	11.4	10.7
Do you have serious difficulty walking or climbing stairs?	17.0	13.6

Note: (1) Figures cover the Louisville/Jefferson County, KY-IN Metropolitan Statistical Area.
Source: Centers for Disease Control and Prevention, Behaviorial Risk Factor Surveillance System, SMART: Selected Metropolitan Area Risk Trends, 2017

Mortality Rates for the Top 10 Causes of Death in the U.S.

ICD-10[a] Sub-Chapter	ICD-10[a] Code	Age-Adjusted Mortality Rate[1] per 100,000 population	
		County[2]	U.S.
Malignant neoplasms	C00-C97	166.0	149.2
Ischaemic heart diseases	I20-I25	58.4	90.5
Other forms of heart disease	I30-I51	75.6	52.2
Chronic lower respiratory diseases	J40-J47	47.8	39.6
Other degenerative diseases of the nervous system	G30-G31	45.8	37.6
Cerebrovascular diseases	I60-I69	36.3	37.2
Other external causes of accidental injury	W00-X59	57.9	36.1
Organic, including symptomatic, mental disorders	F01-F09	54.9	29.4
Hypertensive diseases	I10-I15	39.2	24.1
Diabetes mellitus	E10-E14	20.7	21.5

Note: (a) ICD-10 = International Classification of Diseases 10th Revision; (1) Mortality rates are a three-year average covering 2017-2019; (2) Figures cover Jefferson County.
Source: Centers for Disease Control and Prevention, National Center for Health Statistics. Underlying Cause of Death 1999-2019 on CDC WONDER Online Database

Mortality Rates for Selected Causes of Death

ICD-10[a] Sub-Chapter	ICD-10[a] Code	Age-Adjusted Mortality Rate[1] per 100,000 population	
		County[2]	U.S.
Assault	X85-Y09	13.6	6.0
Diseases of the liver	K70-K76	16.4	14.4
Human immunodeficiency virus (HIV) disease	B20-B24	2.4	1.5
Influenza and pneumonia	J09-J18	14.7	13.8
Intentional self-harm	X60-X84	16.3	14.1
Malnutrition	E40-E46	4.7	2.3
Obesity and other hyperalimentation	E65-E68	1.8	2.1
Renal failure	N17-N19	18.5	12.6
Transport accidents	V01-V99	13.2	12.3
Viral hepatitis	B15-B19	1.6	1.2

Note: (a) ICD-10 = International Classification of Diseases 10th Revision; (1) Mortality rates are a three-year average covering 2017-2019; (2) Figures cover Jefferson County; Data are suppressed when the data meet the criteria for confidentiality constraints; Mortality rates are flagged as unreliable when the rate would be calculated with a numerator of 20 or less.
Source: Centers for Disease Control and Prevention, National Center for Health Statistics. Underlying Cause of Death 1999-2019 on CDC WONDER Online Database

Health Insurance Coverage

Area	With Health Insurance	With Private Health Insurance	With Public Health Insurance	Without Health Insurance	Population Under Age 19 Without Health Insurance
City	94.6	67.1	40.3	5.4	2.7
MSA[1]	94.6	71.4	36.4	5.4	3.3
U.S.	91.2	67.9	35.1	8.8	5.1

Note: Figures are percentages that cover the civilian noninstitutionalized population; (1) Figures cover the Louisville/Jefferson County, KY-IN Metropolitan Statistical Area
Source: U.S. Census Bureau, 2015-2019 American Community Survey 5-Year Estimates

Number of Medical Professionals

Area	MDs[3]	DOs[3,4]	Dentists	Podiatrists	Chiropractors	Optometrists
County[1] (number)	3,661	102	840	60	221	119
County[1] (rate[2])	476.6	13.3	109.6	7.8	28.8	15.5
U.S. (rate[2])	282.9	22.7	71.2	6.2	28.1	16.9

21111
Note: Data as of 2019 unless noted; (1) Data covers Jefferson County; (2) Rate per 100,000 population; (3) Data as of 2018 and includes all active, non-federal physicians; (4) Doctor of Osteopathic Medicine
Source: U.S. Department of Health and Human Services, Health Resources and Services Administration, Bureau of Health Professions, Area Resource File (ARF) 2019-2020

Best Hospitals

According to *U.S. News,* the Louisville/Jefferson County, KY-IN metro area is home to one of the best children's hospitals in the U.S.: **Norton Children's Hospital** (2 pediatric specialties). The hospital listed was highly ranked in at least one of 10 pediatric specialties. Eighty-eight children's hospitals in the U.S. were nationally ranked in at least one specialty. Hospitals received points for being ranked in a specialty, and the 10 hospitals with the most points across the 10 specialties make up the Honor Roll. *U.S. News Online, "America's Best Children's Hospitals 2020-21"*

EDUCATION

Public School District Statistics

District Name	Schls	Pupils	Pupil/ Teacher Ratio	Minority Pupils[1] (%)	Free Lunch Eligible[2] (%)	IEP[3] (%)
Jefferson County	170	97,936	15.8	57.6	53.1	13.0

Note: Table includes school districts with 2,000 or more students; (1) Percentage of students that are not non-Hispanic white; (2) Percentage of students that are eligible for the free lunch program; (3) Percentage of students that have an Individualized Education Program.
Source: U.S. Department of Education, National Center for Education Statistics, Common Core of Data, Local Education Agency (School District) Universe Survey: School Year 2018-2019; U.S. Department of Education, National Center for Education Statistics, Common Core of Data, Public Elementary/Secondary School Universe Survey: School Year 2018-2019

Best High Schools

According to *U.S. News,* Louisville is home to three of the top 500 high schools in the U.S.: **Dupont Manual High** (#45); **J. Graham Brown School** (#348); **Atherton High School** (#435). Nearly 18,000 public, magnet and charter schools were ranked based on their performance on state assessments and how well they prepare students for college. *U.S. News & World Report, "Best High Schools 2020"*

Highest Level of Education

Area	Less than H.S.	H.S. Diploma	Some College, No Deg.	Associate Degree	Bachelor's Degree	Master's Degree	Prof. School Degree	Doctorate Degree
City	10.4	28.6	22.9	8.1	17.9	8.5	2.3	1.2
MSA[1]	9.9	29.6	22.3	8.6	17.9	8.4	2.2	1.1
U.S.	12.0	27.0	20.4	8.5	19.8	8.8	2.1	1.4

Note: Figures cover persons age 25 and over; (1) Figures cover the Louisville/Jefferson County, KY-IN Metropolitan Statistical Area
Source: U.S. Census Bureau, 2015-2019 American Community Survey 5-Year Estimates

Educational Attainment by Race

Area	High School Graduate or Higher (%)					Bachelor's Degree or Higher (%)				
	Total	White	Black	Asian	Hisp.[2]	Total	White	Black	Asian	Hisp.[2]
City	89.6	90.7	86.9	81.4	80.2	29.9	32.9	17.8	49.0	25.8
MSA[1]	90.1	90.9	87.2	86.3	74.0	29.6	31.0	18.3	54.2	22.7
U.S.	88.0	89.9	86.0	87.1	68.7	32.1	33.5	21.6	54.3	16.4

Note: Figures shown cover persons 25 years old and over; (1) Figures cover the Louisville/Jefferson County, KY-IN Metropolitan Statistical Area; (2) People of Hispanic origin can be of any race
Source: U.S. Census Bureau, 2015-2019 American Community Survey 5-Year Estimates

School Enrollment by Grade and Control

Area	Preschool (%)		Kindergarten (%)		Grades 1 - 4 (%)		Grades 5 - 8 (%)		Grades 9 - 12 (%)	
	Public	Private	Public	Private	Public	Private	Public	Private	Public	Private
City	51.1	48.9	80.2	19.8	83.4	16.6	79.9	20.1	79.3	20.7
MSA[1]	49.2	50.8	82.9	17.1	84.2	15.8	81.4	18.6	81.3	18.7
U.S.	59.1	40.9	87.6	12.4	89.5	10.5	89.4	10.6	90.1	9.9

Note: Figures shown cover persons 3 years old and over; (1) Figures cover the Louisville/Jefferson County, KY-IN Metropolitan Statistical Area
Source: U.S. Census Bureau, 2015-2019 American Community Survey 5-Year Estimates

Higher Education

Four-Year Colleges			Two-Year Colleges			Medical Schools[1]	Law Schools[2]	Voc/ Tech[3]
Public	Private Non-profit	Private For-profit	Public	Private Non-profit	Private For-profit			
1	5	2	1	0	2	1	1	8

Note: Figures cover institutions located within the city limits and include main campuses only; (1) includes schools accredited by the Liaison Committee on Medical Education and the American Osteopathic Association's Commission on Osteopathic College Accreditation; (2) includes ABA-accredited schools, schools with provisional ABA accreditation, and state accredited schools; (3) includes all schools with programs that are less than 2 years.
Source: National Center for Education Statistics, Integrated Postsecondary Education System (IPEDS), 2019-20; Wikipedia, List of Medical Schools in the United States, accessed April 2, 2021; Wikipedia, List of Law Schools in the United States, accessed April 2, 2021

According to *U.S. News & World Report,* the Louisville/Jefferson County, KY-IN metro area is home to one of the top 200 national universities in the U.S.: **University of Louisville** (#176 tie). The indicators used to capture academic quality fall into a number of categories: assessment by administrators at peer institutions; retention of students; faculty resources; student selectivity; financial resources; alumni giving; high school counselor ratings of colleges; and graduation rate. *U.S. News & World Report, "America's Best Colleges 2021"*

According to *U.S. News & World Report,* the Louisville/Jefferson County, KY-IN metro area is home to one of the top 100 law schools in the U.S.: **University of Louisville (Brandeis)** (#98 tie). The rankings are based on a weighted average of 12 measures of quality: peer assessment score; assessment score by lawyers/judges; median LSAT scores; median undergrad GPA; acceptance rate; employment rates for graduates; placement success; bar passage rate; faculty resources; expenditures per student; student/faculty ratio; and library resources. *U.S. News & World Report, "America's Best Graduate Schools, Law, 2022"*

According to *U.S. News & World Report,* the Louisville/Jefferson County, KY-IN metro area is home to one of the top 75 medical schools for research in the U.S.: **University of Louisville** (#75 tie). The rankings are based on a weighted average of 11 measures of quality: quality assessment; peer assessment score; assessment score by residency directors; research activity; total research activity; average research activity per faculty member; student selectivity; median MCAT total score; median undergraduate GPA; acceptance rate; and faculty resources. *U.S. News & World Report, "America's Best Graduate Schools, Medical, 2022"*

EMPLOYERS

Major Employers

Company Name	Industry
Baptist Healthcare Systems	Healthcare
BF Cos./ERJ Dining	Restaurants
Catholic Archdiocese of Louisville	Schools/churches/related activities
Clark Memorial Hospital	Healthcare
Floyd Memorial Hospital & Health Services	Healthcare
Ford Motor Co.	Automotive manufacturer
GE Appliances & Lighting	Home appliance/lighting products
Horseshoe Southern Indiana	Entertainment
Humana	Health insurance
Jefferson County Public Schools	K-12 public education
Kentucky State Government	Government
KentuckyOne Health	Healthcare
Kindred Healthcare	Healthcare
LG&E and KU Energy	Utility
Louisville/Jefferson County Metro Govt	Government
New Albany-Floyd County School Corp	K-12 public education
Norton Healthcare	Healthcare
Publishers Printing Co.	Printer
Robley Rex VA Medical Center	Healthcare
Securitas Security Services USA	Security services
U.S. Government	Government
United Parcel Services	Package delivery services
University of Louisville	Higher education
University of Louisville Hospital	Healthcare
Yum! Brands	Quick-service restaurants

Note: Companies shown are located within the Louisville/Jefferson County, KY-IN Metropolitan Statistical Area.
Source: Hoovers.com; Wikipedia

Best Companies to Work For

Humana; Norton Healthcare, headquartered in Louisville, are among the "100 Best Places to Work in IT." To qualify, companies had to be U.S.-based organizations or be non-U.S.-based employers that met the following criteria: have a minimum of 300 total employees at a U.S. headquarters and a minimum of 30 IT employees in the U.S., with at least 50% of their IT employees based in the U.S. The best places to work were selected based on compensation, benefits, work/life balance, employee morale, and satisfaction with training and development programs. In addition, *InsiderPro* and *Computerworld* looked at retention efforts, programs for recognizing and rewarding outstanding performances, and benefits such as flextime, elder care and child care, and reimbursement for college tuition and the cost of pursuing technology certifications. *InsiderPro and Computerworld, "100 Best Places to Work in IT," 2020*

Brown Forman, headquartered in Louisville, is among the "Top Companies for Executive Women." This list is determined by organizations filling out an in-depth survey that measures female demographics at every level, but with an emphasis on women in senior corporate roles, with profit & loss (P&L) responsibility, and those earning in the top 20 percent of the organization. *Working Mother* defines P&L as having responsibility that involves monitoring the net income after expenses for a department or entire organization, with direct influence on how company resources are allocated. *Working Mother, "Top Companies for Executive Women," 2020+*

PUBLIC SAFETY

Crime Rate

Area	All Crimes	Violent Crimes				Property Crimes		
		Murder	Rape[3]	Robbery	Aggrav. Assault	Burglary	Larceny -Theft	Motor Vehicle Theft
City	4,578.4	13.9	29.8	149.2	494.0	638.9	2,670.2	582.4
Suburbs[1]	1,847.8	1.9	21.7	30.8	98.0	230.7	1,263.0	201.7
Metro[2]	3,300.8	8.3	26.0	93.8	308.7	447.9	2,011.8	404.3
U.S.	2,489.3	5.0	42.6	81.6	250.2	340.5	1,549.5	219.9

Note: Figures are crimes per 100,000 population; (1) All areas within the metro area that are located outside the city limits; (2) Figures cover the Louisville/Jefferson County, KY-IN Metropolitan Statistical Area; (3) All figures shown were reported using the revised Uniform Crime Reporting (UCR) definition of rape.
Source: FBI Uniform Crime Reports, 2019

Hate Crimes

Area	Number of Quarters Reported	Number of Incidents per Bias Motivation					
		Race/Ethnicity/ Ancestry	Religion	Sexual Orientation	Disability	Gender	Gender Identity
City	4	4	4	2	0	0	1
U.S.	4	3,963	1,521	1,195	157	69	198

Source: Federal Bureau of Investigation, Hate Crime Statistics 2019

Identity Theft Consumer Reports

Area	Reports	Reports per 100,000 Population	Rank[2]
MSA[1]	2,397	189	228
U.S.	1,387,615	423	-

Note: (1) Figures cover the Louisville/Jefferson County, KY-IN Metropolitan Statistical Area; (2) Rank ranges from 1 to 391 where 1 indicates greatest number of identity theft reports per 100,000 population
Source: Federal Trade Commission, Consumer Sentinel Network Data Book 2020

Fraud and Other Consumer Reports

Area	Reports	Reports per 100,000 Population	Rank[2]
MSA[1]	10,219	808	93
U.S.	3,385,133	1,031	-

Note: (1) Figures cover the Louisville/Jefferson County, KY-IN Metropolitan Statistical Area; (2) Rank ranges from 1 to 391 where 1 indicates greatest number of fraud and other consumer reports per 100,000 population
Source: Federal Trade Commission, Consumer Sentinel Network Data Book 2020

POLITICS

2020 Presidential Election Results

Area	Biden	Trump	Jorgensen	Hawkins	Other
Jefferson County	59.1	39.0	1.2	0.1	0.7
U.S.	51.3	46.8	1.2	0.3	0.5

Note: Results are percentages and may not add to 100% due to rounding
Source: Dave Leip's Atlas of U.S. Presidential Elections

SPORTS

Professional Sports Teams

Team Name	League	Year Established

No teams are located in the metro area
Source: Wikipedia, Major Professional Sports Teams of the United States and Canada, April 6, 2021

CLIMATE

Average and Extreme Temperatures

Temperature	Jan	Feb	Mar	Apr	May	Jun	Jul	Aug	Sep	Oct	Nov	Dec	Yr.
Extreme High (°F)	77	77	86	91	95	102	105	101	104	92	84	76	105
Average High (°F)	41	46	56	68	77	85	88	87	80	69	56	45	67
Average Temp. (°F)	33	37	46	57	66	74	78	77	70	58	47	37	57
Average Low (°F)	25	27	36	46	55	64	68	66	59	47	37	29	46
Extreme Low (°F)	-20	-9	-1	22	31	42	50	46	33	23	-1	-15	-20

Note: Figures cover the years 1948-1990
Source: National Climatic Data Center, International Station Meteorological Climate Summary, 9/96

Average Precipitation/Snowfall/Humidity

Precip./Humidity	Jan	Feb	Mar	Apr	May	Jun	Jul	Aug	Sep	Oct	Nov	Dec	Yr.
Avg. Precip. (in.)	3.4	3.5	4.5	4.0	4.5	3.7	4.2	3.2	3.0	2.6	3.7	3.6	43.9
Avg. Snowfall (in.)	5	4	3	Tr	Tr	0	0	0	0	Tr	1	2	17
Avg. Rel. Hum. 7am (%)	78	78	75	75	79	80	82	85	86	84	79	78	80
Avg. Rel. Hum. 4pm (%)	62	58	52	49	52	53	55	53	53	51	57	62	55

Note: Figures cover the years 1948-1990; Tr = Trace amounts (<0.05 in. of rain; <0.5 in. of snow)
Source: National Climatic Data Center, International Station Meteorological Climate Summary, 9/96

Weather Conditions

Temperature			Daytime Sky			Precipitation		
10°F & below	32°F & below	90°F & above	Clear	Partly cloudy	Cloudy	0.01 inch or more precip.	0.1 inch or more snow/ice	Thunder-storms
8	90	35	82	143	140	125	15	45

Note: Figures are average number of days per year and cover the years 1948-1990
Source: National Climatic Data Center, International Station Meteorological Climate Summary, 9/96

HAZARDOUS WASTE

Superfund Sites

The Louisville/Jefferson County, KY-IN metro area is home to three sites on the EPA's Superfund National Priorities List: **Distler Farm** (final); **Smith's Farm** (final); **Tri-City Disposal Co.** (final). There are a total of 1,375 Superfund sites with a status of proposed or final on the list in the U.S. *U.S. Environmental Protection Agency, National Priorities List, April 7, 2021*

AIR QUALITY

Air Quality Trends: Ozone

	1990	1995	2000	2005	2010	2015	2016	2017	2018	2019
MSA[1]	0.075	0.087	0.088	0.083	0.076	0.070	0.070	0.064	0.067	0.064
U.S.	0.088	0.089	0.082	0.080	0.073	0.068	0.069	0.068	0.069	0.065

Note: (1) Data covers the Louisville/Jefferson County, KY-IN Metropolitan Statistical Area. The values shown are the composite ozone concentration averages among trend sites based on the highest fourth daily maximum 8-hour concentration in parts per million. These trends are based on sites having an adequate record of monitoring data during the trend period. Data from exceptional events are included.
Source: U.S. Environmental Protection Agency, Air Quality Monitoring Information, "Air Quality Trends by City, 1990-2019"

Air Quality Index

Area	Percent of Days when Air Quality was...[2]					AQI Statistics[2]	
	Good	Moderate	Unhealthy for Sensitive Groups	Unhealthy	Very Unhealthy	Maximum	Median
MSA[1]	53.4	45.5	1.1	0.0	0.0	136	49

Note: (1) Data covers the Louisville/Jefferson County, KY-IN Metropolitan Statistical Area; (2) Based on 365 days with AQI data in 2019. Air Quality Index (AQI) is an index for reporting daily air quality. EPA calculates the AQI for five major air pollutants regulated by the Clean Air Act: ground-level ozone, particle pollution (aka particulate matter), carbon monoxide, sulfur dioxide, and nitrogen dioxide. The AQI runs from 0 to 500. The higher the AQI value, the greater the level of air pollution and the greater the health concern. There are six AQI categories: "Good" AQI is between 0 and 50. Air quality is considered satisfactory; "Moderate" AQI is between 51 and 100. Air quality is acceptable; "Unhealthy for Sensitive Groups" When AQI values are between 101 and 150, members of sensitive groups may experience health effects; "Unhealthy" When AQI values are between 151 and 200 everyone may begin to experience health effects; "Very Unhealthy" AQI values between 201 and 300 trigger a health alert; "Hazardous" AQI values over 300 trigger warnings of emergency conditions (not shown).
Source: U.S. Environmental Protection Agency, Air Quality Index Report, 2019

Air Quality Index Pollutants

Area	Percent of Days when AQI Pollutant was...[2]					
	Carbon Monoxide	Nitrogen Dioxide	Ozone	Sulfur Dioxide	Particulate Matter 2.5	Particulate Matter 10
MSA[1]	0.0	2.7	45.8	0.0	51.5	0.0

Note: (1) Data covers the Louisville/Jefferson County, KY-IN Metropolitan Statistical Area; (2) Based on 365 days with AQI data in 2019. The Air Quality Index (AQI) is an index for reporting daily air quality. EPA calculates the AQI for five major air pollutants regulated by the Clean Air Act: ground-level ozone, particle pollution (also known as particulate matter), carbon monoxide, sulfur dioxide, and nitrogen dioxide. The AQI runs from 0 to 500. The higher the AQI value, the greater the level of air pollution and the greater the health concern.
Source: U.S. Environmental Protection Agency, Air Quality Index Report, 2019

Maximum Air Pollutant Concentrations: Particulate Matter, Ozone, CO and Lead

	Particulate Matter 10 (ug/m^3)	Particulate Matter 2.5 Wtd AM (ug/m^3)	Particulate Matter 2.5 24-Hr (ug/m^3)	Ozone (ppm)	Carbon Monoxide (ppm)	Lead (ug/m^3)
MSA[1] Level	40	10.5	23	0.068	2	n/a
NAAQS[2]	150	15	35	0.075	9	0.15
Met NAAQS[2]	Yes	Yes	Yes	Yes	Yes	n/a

Note: (1) Data covers the Louisville/Jefferson County, KY-IN Metropolitan Statistical Area; Data from exceptional events are included; (2) National Ambient Air Quality Standards; ppm = parts per million; ug/m^3 = micrograms per cubic meter; n/a not available.
Concentrations: Particulate Matter 10 (coarse particulate)—highest second maximum 24-hour concentration; Particulate Matter 2.5 Wtd AM (fine particulate)—highest weighted annual mean concentration; Particulate Matter 2.5 24-Hour (fine particulate)—highest 98th percentile 24-hour concentration; Ozone—highest fourth daily maximum 8-hour concentration; Carbon Monoxide—highest second maximum non-overlapping 8-hour concentration; Lead—maximum running 3-month average
Source: U.S. Environmental Protection Agency, Air Quality Monitoring Information, "Air Quality Statistics by City, 2019"

Maximum Air Pollutant Concentrations: Nitrogen Dioxide and Sulfur Dioxide

	Nitrogen Dioxide AM (ppb)	Nitrogen Dioxide 1-Hr (ppb)	Sulfur Dioxide AM (ppb)	Sulfur Dioxide 1-Hr (ppb)	Sulfur Dioxide 24-Hr (ppb)
MSA[1] Level	15	49	n/a	15	n/a
NAAQS[2]	53	100	30	75	140
Met NAAQS[2]	Yes	Yes	n/a	Yes	n/a

Note: (1) Data covers the Louisville/Jefferson County, KY-IN Metropolitan Statistical Area; Data from exceptional events are included; (2) National Ambient Air Quality Standards; ppm = parts per million; ug/m^3 = micrograms per cubic meter; n/a not available.
Concentrations: Nitrogen Dioxide AM—highest arithmetic mean concentration; Nitrogen Dioxide 1-Hr—highest 98th percentile 1-hour daily maximum concentration; Sulfur Dioxide AM—highest annual mean concentration; Sulfur Dioxide 1-Hr—highest 99th percentile 1-hour daily maximum concentration; Sulfur Dioxide 24-Hr—highest second maximum 24-hour concentration
Source: U.S. Environmental Protection Agency, Air Quality Monitoring Information, "Air Quality Statistics by City, 2019"

Manchester, New Hampshire

Background

Manchester, the largest city in northern New England, lies along the Merrimack River in the southern part of the "Live Free or Die" state. Fifty-one miles northwest of Boston, Manchester is a major financial and manufacturing center in its region and a main stop along the way to New Hampshire's many vacation resorts.

Amoskeag Falls, on the Merrimack, had been an important Penacook Indian fishing site for many years prior to the arrival of the first Europeans, who came in 1636 on instructions from Massachusetts Governor John Winthrop. A schoolhouse was built in 1650 by the missionary John Elliot, but for many years the European population was limited to a small number of hunters, trappers, and fishermen. The first permanent settlement was established in 1722 by a tiny group from the Massachusetts Bay Colony. The town was known by a variety of names, including Old Harrytown, Tyngstown, and Derryfield.

For many years "Derryfield's" fortunes depended on lumber and fishing, but in 1810, cotton mills relying on water power from the Merrimack River became an economic mainstay. Though the town's population was then only 615, a local resident, Judge Samuel Blodgett, predicted that it would eventually grow to become a mighty center of industry, like England's Manchester. The name change was a result of this unlikely prediction, and by 1846, the new American Manchester had grown to a population of more than 10,000.

Manchester's early industrial history is inextricably linked to the history of the Amoskeag Manufacturing Company, whose 64 mills lined the banks of the river with what came to be the world's largest cotton milling operation. As Amoskeag thrived, so did Manchester. By the 1920s, however, Amoskeag had lost its leading edge, with obsolete machinery and alternatives to cotton, like silk and rayon. It declared bankruptcy in 1935, paving the way for cheaper facilities, particularly in the Southern states, and causing a decline in Manchester's jobs and population.

By the mid-1990s, Manchester recovered from its Depression-era difficulties to become the nation's fastest-growing city. A development company bought up the old mill buildings, restoring and adapting them to new commercial and residential uses. But the changes were not merely cosmetic; in light of a lesson well-learned from its single-industry past, Manchester's economic renaissance was finely calibrated to fit in with regional and national trends.

In recent years the ongoing Neighborhood Initiative program has included streetscapes, infrastructure improvements and continued development of the Amoskeag Mill into high end condominiums. The city's downtown include the tallest buildings north of Cambridge, MA.

The economic attractiveness of the city today, and its overall affordability, is enhanced by New Hampshire's unique reluctance to institute any sales or income tax. Manchester has been recognized as "tax friendly" and one of the best places in America to launch a business. The city is home to Segway, Inc., manufacturers of the two-wheeled, self balancing electric vehicle, as well as headquarters for Bank of America and Citizens Bank.

The city is served by the Manchester-Boston Regional Airport, one of the nation's fastest-growing. With its recent 74,000-square-foot addition, airport traffic continues to increase. A downtown rail loop continues to be on the table.

The cultural assets of Manchester include the Currier Museum of Art, and the New Hampshire Institute of Art. Another major attraction is the Manchester Historical Association's Millyard Museum founded in 1896. Institutions of higher education convenient to Manchester include St. Anselm College, Southern New Hampshire University, Franklin Pierce College, and the University of New Hampshire at Manchester, as well as a community college. SNHU's Arena is the centerpiece of the city's downtown, hosting concerts and other events.

> Saint Anselm College reported an uptick in applicants to their nursing program for the fall of 2021, indicating an interest in the medical profession in the wake of COVID-19.

There are four seasons in Manchester, and the climate can be characterized as typical of northern New England. Long winters with considerable snow are to be expected, as are lovely, cool springs and summers.

Rankings

General Rankings

- In their seventh annual survey, Livability.com looked at data for more than 1,000 small to mid-sized U.S. cities to determine the rankings for Livability's "Top 100 Best Places to Live" in 2020. Manchester ranked #57. Criteria: housing and affordable living; vibrant economy; social and civic engagement; education; demographics; health care options; transportation & infrastructure; and abundant lifestyle amenities. *Livability.com, "Top 100 Best Places to Live 2020" October 2020*

Business/Finance Rankings

- According to *Business Insider*, the Manchester metro area is a prime place to run a startup or move an existing business to. The area ranked #12. Nearly 190 metro areas were analyzed on overall economic health and investments. Data was based on the 2019 U.S. Census Bureau American Community Survey, the marketing company PitchBook, Bureau of Labor Statistics employment report, and Zillow. Criteria: percentage of change in typical home values and employment rates; quarterly venture capital investment activity; and median household income. *www.businessinsider.com, "The 25 Best Cities to Start a Business-Or Move Your Current One," January 12, 2021*

- The Manchester metro area appeared on the Milken Institute "2021 Best Performing Cities" list. Rank: #99 out of 200 large metro areas (population over 250,000). Criteria: job growth; wage and salary growth; high-tech output growth; housing affordability; household broadband access. *Milken Institute, "Best-Performing Cities 2021," February 16, 2021*

- *Forbes* ranked the 200 most populous metro areas to determine the nation's "Best Places for Business and Careers." The Manchester metro area was ranked #133. Criteria: costs (business and living); job growth (past and projected); income growth; quality of life; educational attainment (college and high school); projected economic growth; cultural and leisure opportunities; workplace tolerance laws; net migration patterns. *Forbes, "The Best Places for Business and Careers 2019: Seattle Still On Top," October 30, 2019*

Education Rankings

- Personal finance website *WalletHub* analyzed the 150 largest U.S. metropolitan statistical areas to determine where the most educated Americans are putting their degrees to work. Criteria: education levels; percentage of workers with degrees; education quality and attainment gap; public school quality rankings; quality and enrollment of each metro area's universities. Manchester was ranked #46 (#1 = most educated city). *www.WalletHub.com, "Most and Least Educated Cities in America," July 20, 2020*

Environmental Rankings

- Niche compiled a list of the nation's snowiest cities, based on the National Oceanic and Atmospheric Administration's 30-year average snowfall data. Among cities with a population of at least 50,000, Manchester ranked #23. *Niche.com, Top 25 Snowiest Cities in America, December 10, 2018*

Real Estate Rankings

- *WalletHub* compared the most populated U.S. cities to determine which had the best markets for real estate agents. Manchester ranked #51 where demand was high and pay was the best. Criteria: sales per agent; annual median wage for real-estate agents; monthly average starting salary for real estate agents; real estate job density and competition; unemployment rate; home turnover rate; housing-market health index; and other relevant metrics. *www.WalletHub.com, "2019's Best Places to Be a Real Estate Agent," April 24, 2019*

- Manchester was ranked #150 out of 268 metro areas in terms of housing affordability in 2020 by the National Association of Home Builders (#1 = most affordable). Criteria: the share of homes sold in that area affordable to a family earning the local median income, based on standard mortgage underwriting criteria. *National Association of Home Builders®, NAHB-Wells Fargo Housing Opportunity Index, 4th Quarter 2020*

Safety Rankings

- The National Insurance Crime Bureau ranked 384 metro areas in the U.S. in terms of per capita rates of vehicle theft. The Manchester metro area ranked #350 (#1 = highest rate). Criteria: number of vehicle theft offenses per 100,000 inhabitants in 2019. *National Insurance Crime Bureau, "Hot Spots 2019," July 21, 2020*

Seniors/Retirement Rankings

- From its Best Cities for Successful Aging indexes, the Milken Institute generated rankings for metropolitan areas, weighing data in nine categories—health care, wellness, living arrangements, transportation and convenience, financial characteristics, education, employment, community engagement, and overall livability. The Manchester metro area was ranked #181 overall in the small metro area category. *Milken Institute, "Best Cities for Successful Aging, 2017" March 14, 2017*

Women/Minorities Rankings

- Personal finance website *WalletHub* compared more than 180 U.S. cities across two key dimensions, "Hispanic Business-Friendliness" and "Hispanic Purchasing Power," to arrive at the most favorable conditions for Hispanic entrepreneurs. Manchester was ranked #163 out of 182. Criteria includes: share of Hispanic-Owned Businesses; Hispanic entrepreneurship rate to median annual income of Hispanics; Small Business-Friendliness score; cost of living; and number of Hispanics with at least a bachelor's degree. *WalletHub.com, "2019's Best Cities for Hispanic Entrepreneurs," May 1, 2019*

Miscellaneous Rankings

- *WalletHub* compared the 150 most populated U.S. cities to determine their operating efficiency. A "Quality of City Services" score was constructed for each city and then divided by the total budget per capita to reveal which were managed the best. Manchester ranked #39. Criteria: financial stability; economy; education; safety; health; infrastructure and pollution. *www.WalletHub.com, "2020's Best-& Worst-Run Cities in America," June 29, 2020*

Business Environment

DEMOGRAPHICS

Population Growth

Area	1990 Census	2000 Census	2010 Census	2019* Estimate	Population Growth (%) 1990-2019	Population Growth (%) 2010-2019
City	99,567	107,006	109,565	112,109	12.6	2.3
MSA[1]	336,073	380,841	400,721	413,035	22.9	3.1
U.S.	248,709,873	281,421,906	308,745,538	324,697,795	30.6	5.2

Note: (1) Figures cover the Manchester-Nashua, NH Metropolitan Statistical Area; (*) 2015-2019 5-year estimated population
Source: U.S. Census Bureau, 1990 Census, Census 2000, Census 2010, 2015-2019 American Community Survey 5-Year Estimates

Household Size

Area	Persons in Household (%) One	Two	Three	Four	Five	Six	Seven or More	Average Household Size
City	31.4	34.1	16.6	10.8	4.5	1.6	1.0	2.40
MSA[1]	25.6	36.3	16.5	13.5	5.2	1.9	1.0	2.50
U.S.	27.9	33.9	15.6	12.9	6.0	2.3	1.4	2.60

Note: (1) Figures cover the Manchester-Nashua, NH Metropolitan Statistical Area
Source: U.S. Census Bureau, 2015-2019 American Community Survey 5-Year Estimates

Race

Area	White Alone[2] (%)	Black Alone[2] (%)	Asian Alone[2] (%)	AIAN[3] Alone[2] (%)	NHOPI[4] Alone[2] (%)	Other Race Alone[2] (%)	Two or More Races (%)
City	84.8	6.1	5.1	0.1	0.0	0.9	3.0
MSA[1]	89.4	2.9	4.0	0.1	0.1	0.9	2.5
U.S.	72.5	12.7	5.5	0.8	0.2	4.9	3.3

Note: (1) Figures cover the Manchester-Nashua, NH Metropolitan Statistical Area; (2) Alone is defined as not being in combination with one or more other races; (3) American Indian and Alaska Native; (4) Native Hawaiian and Other Pacific Islander
Source: U.S. Census Bureau, 2015-2019 American Community Survey 5-Year Estimates

Hispanic or Latino Origin

Area	Total (%)	Mexican (%)	Puerto Rican (%)	Cuban (%)	Other (%)
City	10.4	1.5	4.4	0.1	4.4
MSA[1]	6.8	1.0	2.5	0.2	3.0
U.S.	18.0	11.2	1.7	0.7	4.3

Note: Persons of Hispanic or Latino origin can be of any race; (1) Figures cover the Manchester-Nashua, NH Metropolitan Statistical Area
Source: U.S. Census Bureau, 2015-2019 American Community Survey 5-Year Estimates

Ancestry

Area	German	Irish	English	American	Italian	Polish	French[2]	Scottish	Dutch
City	6.6	19.3	9.0	2.9	8.2	3.9	13.5	3.2	0.5
MSA[1]	8.4	20.8	13.0	3.5	10.0	4.4	12.4	3.4	0.8
U.S.	13.3	9.7	7.2	6.2	5.1	2.8	2.3	1.7	1.2

Note: Figures are the percentage of the total population reporting a particular ancestry. The nine most commonly reported ancestries in the U.S. are shown. Figures include multiple ancestries (e.g. if a person reported being Irish and Italian, they were included in both columns); (1) Figures cover the Manchester-Nashua, NH Metropolitan Statistical Area; (2) Excludes Basque
Source: U.S. Census Bureau, 2015-2019 American Community Survey 5-Year Estimates

Foreign-born Population

Area	Percent of Population Born in Any Foreign Country	Asia	Mexico	Europe	Caribbean	Central America[2]	South America	Africa	Canada
City	14.5	5.1	0.5	2.5	1.6	1.2	0.8	1.9	0.8
MSA[1]	9.7	3.6	0.4	1.8	1.0	0.5	0.8	0.9	0.8
U.S.	13.6	4.2	3.5	1.5	1.3	1.1	1.0	0.7	0.2

Note: (1) Figures cover the Manchester-Nashua, NH Metropolitan Statistical Area; (2) Excludes Mexico.
Source: U.S. Census Bureau, 2015-2019 American Community Survey 5-Year Estimates

Marital Status

Area	Never Married	Now Married[2]	Separated	Widowed	Divorced
City	38.8	39.9	2.0	5.8	13.4
MSA[1]	30.4	51.3	1.4	5.3	11.6
U.S.	33.4	48.1	1.9	5.8	10.9

Note: Figures are percentages and cover the population 15 years of age and older; (1) Figures cover the Manchester-Nashua, NH Metropolitan Statistical Area; (2) Excludes separated
Source: U.S. Census Bureau, 2015-2019 American Community Survey 5-Year Estimates

Disability by Age

Area	All Ages	Under 18 Years Old	18 to 64 Years Old	65 Years and Over
City	14.1	6.0	11.7	39.8
MSA[1]	11.8	4.7	9.5	31.8
U.S.	12.6	4.2	10.3	34.5

Note: Figures show percent of the civilian noninstitutionalized population that reported having a disability. Disability status is determined from six types of difficulty: vision, hearing, cognitive, ambulatory, self-care, and independent living. For children under 5 years old, hearing and vision difficulty are used to determine disability status. For children between the ages of 5 and 14, disability status is determined from hearing, vision, cognitive, ambulatory, and self-care difficulties. For people aged 15 years and older, they are considered to have a disability if they have difficulty with any one of the six difficulty types; Note: (1) Figures cover the Manchester-Nashua, NH Metropolitan Statistical Area
Source: U.S. Census Bureau, 2015-2019 American Community Survey 5-Year Estimates

Age

Area	Percent of Population									Median Age
	Under Age 5	Age 5–19	Age 20–34	Age 35–44	Age 45–54	Age 55–64	Age 65–74	Age 75–84	Age 85+	
City	6.0	15.7	26.6	12.8	13.2	12.4	7.2	3.7	2.3	36.0
MSA[1]	5.2	17.8	19.8	12.3	14.9	14.7	9.0	4.3	1.9	40.7
U.S.	6.1	19.1	20.7	12.6	13.0	12.9	9.1	4.6	1.9	38.1

Note: (1) Figures cover the Manchester-Nashua, NH Metropolitan Statistical Area
Source: U.S. Census Bureau, 2015-2019 American Community Survey 5-Year Estimates

Gender

Area	Males	Females	Males per 100 Females
City	56,510	55,599	101.6
MSA[1]	205,394	207,641	98.9
U.S.	159,886,919	164,810,876	97.0

Note: (1) Figures cover the Manchester-Nashua, NH Metropolitan Statistical Area
Source: U.S. Census Bureau, 2015-2019 American Community Survey 5-Year Estimates

Religious Groups by Family

Area	Catholic	Baptist	Non-Den.	Methodist[2]	Lutheran	LDS[3]	Pentecostal	Presbyterian[4]	Muslim[5]	Judaism
MSA[1]	31.2	1.4	2.4	1.2	0.5	0.6	0.5	2.0	0.3	0.5
U.S.	19.1	9.3	4.0	4.0	2.3	2.0	1.9	1.6	0.8	0.7

Note: Figures are the number of adherents as a percentage of the total population; (1) Figures cover the Manchester-Nashua, NH Metropolitan Statistical Area; (2) Methodist/Pietist; (3) Latter Day Saints; (4) Reformed; (5) Figures are estimates
Source: Association of Statisticians of American Religious Bodies, 2010 U.S. Religion Census: Religious Congregations & Membership Study

Religious Groups by Tradition

Area	Catholic	Evangelical Protestant	Mainline Protestant	Other Tradition	Black Protestant	Orthodox
MSA[1]	31.2	5.1	4.4	1.8	<0.1	0.7
U.S.	19.1	16.2	7.3	4.3	1.6	0.3

Note: Figures are the number of adherents as a percentage of the total population; (1) Figures cover the Manchester-Nashua, NH Metropolitan Statistical Area
Source: Association of Statisticians of American Religious Bodies, 2010 U.S. Religion Census: Religious Congregations & Membership Study

ECONOMY

Gross Metropolitan Product

Area	2017	2018	2019	2020	Rank[2]
MSA[1]	28.7	30.0	31.2	32.5	94

Note: Figures are in billions of dollars; (1) Figures cover the Manchester-Nashua, NH Metropolitan Statistical Area; (2) Rank is based on 2018 data and ranges from 1 to 381
Source: U.S. Conference of Mayors, U.S. Metro Economies: GMP & Employment 2018-2020, September 2019

Economic Growth

Area	2015-17 (%)	2018 (%)	2019 (%)	2020 (%)	Rank[2]
MSA[1]	2.7	2.6	2.3	1.8	84
U.S.	1.9	2.9	2.3	2.1	—

Note: Figures are real gross metropolitan product (GMP) growth rates and represent average annual percent change; (1) Figures cover the Manchester-Nashua, NH Metropolitan Statistical Area; (2) Rank is based on 2017 2-year average annual percent change and ranges from 1 to 381
Source: U.S. Conference of Mayors, U.S. Metro Economies: GMP & Employment 2018-2020, September 2019

Metropolitan Area Exports

Area	2014	2015	2016	2017	2018	2019	Rank[2]
MSA[1]	1,575.4	1,556.6	1,465.2	1,714.7	1,651.4	1,587.1	118

Note: Figures are in millions of dollars; (1) Figures cover the Manchester-Nashua, NH Metropolitan Statistical Area; (2) Rank is based on 2019 data and ranges from 1 to 386
Source: U.S. Department of Commerce, International Trade Administration, Office of Trade and Economic Analysis, Industry and Analysis, Exports by Metropolitan Area, data extracted March 24, 2021

Building Permits

Area	Single-Family			Multi-Family			Total		
	2018	2019	Pct. Chg.	2018	2019	Pct. Chg.	2018	2019	Pct. Chg.
City	151	106	-29.8	59	26	-55.9	210	132	-37.1
MSA[1]	709	691	-2.5	697	561	-19.5	1,406	1,252	-11.0
U.S.	855,300	862,100	0.7	473,500	523,900	10.6	1,328,800	1,386,000	4.3

Note: (1) Figures cover the Manchester-Nashua, NH Metropolitan Statistical Area; Figures represent new, privately-owned housing units authorized (unadjusted data); All permit data are based on estimates with imputation
Source: U.S. Census Bureau, Manufacturing, Mining, and Construction Statistics, Building Permits, 2018, 2019

Bankruptcy Filings

Area	Business Filings			Nonbusiness Filings		
	2019	2020	% Chg.	2019	2020	% Chg.
Hillsborough County	25	27	8.0	519	339	-34.7
U.S.	22,780	21,655	-4.9	752,160	522,808	-30.5

Note: Business filings include Chapter 7, Chapter 9, Chapter 11, Chapter 12, Chapter 13, Chapter 15, and Section 304; Nonbusiness filings include Chapter 7, Chapter 11, and Chapter 13
Source: Administrative Office of the U.S. Courts, Business and Nonbusiness Bankruptcy, County Cases Commenced by Chapter of the Bankruptcy Code, During the 12-Month Period Ending December 31, 2019 and Business and Nonbusiness Bankruptcy, County Cases Commenced by Chapter of the Bankruptcy Code, During the 12-Month Period Ending December 31, 2020

Housing Vacancy Rates

Area	Gross Vacancy Rate[2] (%)			Year-Round Vacancy Rate[3] (%)			Rental Vacancy Rate[4] (%)			Homeowner Vacancy Rate[5] (%)		
	2018	2019	2020	2018	2019	2020	2018	2019	2020	2018	2019	2020
MSA[1]	n/a	n/a	n/a	n/a	n/a	n/a	n/a	n/a	n/a	n/a	n/a	n/a
U.S.	12.3	12.0	10.6	9.7	9.5	8.2	6.9	6.7	6.3	1.5	1.4	1.0

Note: (1) Figures cover the Manchester-Nashua, NH Metropolitan Statistical Area; (2) The percentage of the total housing inventory that is vacant; (3) The percentage of the housing inventory (excluding seasonal units) that is year-round vacant; (4) The percentage of rental inventory that is vacant for rent; (5) The percentage of homeowner inventory that is vacant for sale; n/a not available
Source: U.S. Census Bureau, Housing Vacancies and Homeownership Annual Statistics: 2018, 2019, 2020

INCOME

Income

Area	Per Capita ($)	Median Household ($)	Average Household ($)
City	31,951	60,711	75,665
MSA[1]	40,955	81,460	103,090
U.S.	34,103	62,843	88,607

Note: (1) Figures cover the Manchester-Nashua, NH Metropolitan Statistical Area
Source: U.S. Census Bureau, 2015-2019 American Community Survey 5-Year Estimates

Household Income Distribution

Area	Percent of Households Earning							
	Under $15,000	$15,000 -$24,999	$25,000 -$34,999	$35,000 -$49,999	$50,000 -$74,999	$75,000 -$99,999	$100,000 -$149,999	$150,000 and up
City	10.1	8.6	9.9	12.5	19.8	13.3	16.3	9.3
MSA[1]	6.3	6.3	7.3	9.8	16.1	13.8	19.9	20.5
U.S.	10.3	8.9	8.9	12.3	17.2	12.7	15.1	14.5

Note: (1) Figures cover the Manchester-Nashua, NH Metropolitan Statistical Area
Source: U.S. Census Bureau, 2015-2019 American Community Survey 5-Year Estimates

Poverty Rate

Area	All Ages	Under 18 Years Old	18 to 64 Years Old	65 Years and Over
City	14.1	19.8	13.2	10.1
MSA[1]	7.8	9.4	7.6	6.1
U.S.	13.4	18.5	12.6	9.3

Note: Figures are percentage of people whose income during the past 12 months was below the poverty level;
(1) Figures cover the Manchester-Nashua, NH Metropolitan Statistical Area
Source: U.S. Census Bureau, 2015-2019 American Community Survey 5-Year Estimates

CITY FINANCES

City Government Finances

Component	2017 ($000)	2017 ($ per capita)
Total Revenues	468,494	4,250
Total Expenditures	416,319	3,777
Debt Outstanding	437,653	3,970
Cash and Securities[1]	388,956	3,529

Note: (1) Cash and security holdings of a government at the close of its fiscal year,
including those of its dependent agencies, utilities, and liquor stores.
Source: U.S. Census Bureau, State & Local Government Finances 2017

City Government Revenue by Source

Source	2017 ($000)	2017 ($ per capita)	2017 (%)
General Revenue			
From Federal Government	9,395	85	2.0
From State Government	127,143	1,153	27.1
From Local Governments	7,432	67	1.6
Taxes			
Property	193,073	1,752	41.2
Sales and Gross Receipts	1,963	18	0.4
Personal Income	0	0	0.0
Corporate Income	0	0	0.0
Motor Vehicle License	0	0	0.0
Other Taxes	3,506	32	0.7
Current Charges	78,714	714	16.8
Liquor Store	0	0	0.0
Utility	21,024	191	4.5
Employee Retirement	15,929	145	3.4

Source: U.S. Census Bureau, State & Local Government Finances 2017

City Government Expenditures by Function

Function	2017 ($000)	2017 ($ per capita)	2017 (%)
General Direct Expenditures			
Air Transportation	34,341	311	8.2
Corrections	0	0	0.0
Education	172,935	1,568	41.5
Employment Security Administration	0	0	0.0
Financial Administration	3,556	32	0.9
Fire Protection	19,705	178	4.7
General Public Buildings	6,654	60	1.6
Governmental Administration, Other	4,168	37	1.0
Health	2,685	24	0.6
Highways	16,202	147	3.9
Hospitals	0	0	0.0
Housing and Community Development	0	0	0.0
Interest on General Debt	18,615	168	4.5
Judicial and Legal	1,287	11	0.3
Libraries	2,003	18	0.5
Parking	2,313	21	0.6
Parks and Recreation	6,573	59	1.6
Police Protection	22,989	208	5.5
Public Welfare	935	8	0.2
Sewerage	10,072	91	2.4
Solid Waste Management	2,685	24	0.6
Veterans' Services	0	0	0.0
Liquor Store	0	0	0.0
Utility	21,909	198	5.3
Employee Retirement	17,755	161	4.3

Source: U.S. Census Bureau, State & Local Government Finances 2017

EMPLOYMENT

Labor Force and Employment

Area	Civilian Labor Force			Workers Employed		
	Dec. 2019	Dec. 2020	% Chg.	Dec. 2019	Dec. 2020	% Chg.
City	66,041	64,338	-2.6	64,553	61,492	-4.7
NECTA[1]	123,691	119,789	-3.2	121,082	115,342	-4.7
U.S.	164,007,000	160,017,000	-2.4	158,504,000	149,613,000	-5.6

Note: Data is not seasonally adjusted and covers workers 16 years of age and older; (1) Figures cover the Manchester, NH New England City and Town Area
Source: Bureau of Labor Statistics, Local Area Unemployment Statistics

Unemployment Rate

Area	2020											
	Jan.	Feb.	Mar.	Apr.	May	Jun.	Jul.	Aug.	Sep.	Oct.	Nov.	Dec.
City	3.0	3.0	2.7	20.0	18.4	10.5	9.2	7.8	6.7	4.5	4.3	4.4
NECTA[1]	2.8	2.8	2.5	17.4	15.8	9.0	7.9	6.5	5.6	3.8	3.7	3.7
U.S.	4.0	3.8	4.5	14.4	13.0	11.2	10.5	8.5	7.7	6.6	6.4	6.5

Note: Data is not seasonally adjusted and covers workers 16 years of age and older; (1) Figures cover the Manchester, NH New England City and Town Area
Source: Bureau of Labor Statistics, Local Area Unemployment Statistics

Average Wages

Occupation	$/Hr.	Occupation	$/Hr.
Accountants and Auditors	36.20	Maintenance and Repair Workers	23.20
Automotive Mechanics	23.60	Marketing Managers	75.30
Bookkeepers	20.50	Network and Computer Systems Admin.	41.60
Carpenters	22.50	Nurses, Licensed Practical	27.50
Cashiers	11.60	Nurses, Registered	36.90
Computer Programmers	33.10	Nursing Assistants	16.60
Computer Systems Analysts	45.30	Office Clerks, General	19.90
Computer User Support Specialists	27.50	Physical Therapists	40.60
Construction Laborers	19.30	Physicians	145.30
Cooks, Restaurant	15.60	Plumbers, Pipefitters and Steamfitters	27.60
Customer Service Representatives	20.30	Police and Sheriff's Patrol Officers	30.40
Dentists	112.00	Postal Service Mail Carriers	25.30
Electricians	26.40	Real Estate Sales Agents	23.80
Engineers, Electrical	52.50	Retail Salespersons	14.30
Fast Food and Counter Workers	11.90	Sales Representatives, Technical/Scientific	48.60
Financial Managers	67.80	Secretaries, Exc. Legal/Medical/Executive	18.80
First-Line Supervisors of Office Workers	32.10	Security Guards	17.10
General and Operations Managers	65.40	Surgeons	n/a
Hairdressers/Cosmetologists	13.20	Teacher Assistants, Exc. Postsecondary*	15.10
Home Health and Personal Care Aides	14.40	Teachers, Secondary School, Exc. Sp. Ed.*	28.80
Janitors and Cleaners	14.10	Telemarketers	n/a
Landscaping/Groundskeeping Workers	16.70	Truck Drivers, Heavy/Tractor-Trailer	24.60
Lawyers	66.90	Truck Drivers, Light/Delivery Services	18.30
Maids and Housekeeping Cleaners	12.80	Waiters and Waitresses	13.50

Note: Wage data covers the Manchester, NH New England City and Town Area; (*) Hourly wages were calculated from annual wage data based on a 40 hour work week; n/a not available.
Source: Bureau of Labor Statistics, Metro Area Occupational Employment & Wage Estimates, May 2020

Employment by Industry

Sector	NECTA[1]		U.S.
	Number of Employees	Percent of Total	Percent of Total
Construction, Mining, and Logging	5,400	5.0	5.5
Education and Health Services	24,500	22.7	16.3
Financial Activities	7,800	7.2	6.1
Government	11,500	10.6	15.2
Information	3,100	2.9	1.9
Leisure and Hospitality	7,300	6.8	9.0
Manufacturing	7,600	7.0	8.5
Other Services	4,000	3.7	3.8
Professional and Business Services	16,500	15.3	14.4
Retail Trade	12,500	11.6	10.9
Transportation, Warehousing, and Utilities	3,500	3.2	4.6
Wholesale Trade	4,400	4.1	3.9

Note: Figures are non-farm employment as of December 2020. Figures are not seasonally adjusted and include workers 16 years of age and older; (1) Figures cover the Manchester, NH New England City and Town Area
Source: Bureau of Labor Statistics, Current Employment Statistics, Employment, Hours, and Earnings

Employment by Occupation

Occupation Classification	City (%)	MSA[1] (%)	U.S. (%)
Management, Business, Science, and Arts	34.9	42.4	38.5
Natural Resources, Construction, and Maintenance	7.2	7.6	8.9
Production, Transportation, and Material Moving	15.5	12.4	13.2
Sales and Office	23.0	22.4	21.6
Service	19.4	15.3	17.8

Note: Figures cover employed civilians 16 years of age and older; (1) Figures cover the Manchester-Nashua, NH Metropolitan Statistical Area
Source: U.S. Census Bureau, 2015-2019 American Community Survey 5-Year Estimates

Occupations with Greatest Projected Employment Growth: 2020 – 2022

Occupation[1]	2020 Employment	2022 Projected Employment	Numeric Employment Change	Percent Employment Change
Fast Food and Counter Workers	9,540	14,310	4,770	50.0
Waiters and Waitresses	7,490	12,200	4,710	62.9
Cooks, Restaurant	3,760	6,460	2,700	71.8
Retail Salespersons	18,650	20,820	2,170	11.6
Bartenders	2,860	4,310	1,450	50.7
Passenger Vehicle Drivers, Except Bus Drivers, Transit and Intercity	3,080	4,380	1,300	42.2
First-Line Supervisors of Food Preparation and Serving Workers	2,620	3,870	1,250	47.7
Landscaping and Groundskeeping Workers	6,480	7,620	1,140	17.6
Cashiers	18,970	20,110	1,140	6.0
General and Operations Managers	12,160	13,290	1,130	9.3

Note: Projections cover New Hampshire; (1) Sorted by numeric employment change
Source: www.projectionscentral.com, State Occupational Projections, 2020–2022 Short-Term Projections

Fastest-Growing Occupations: 2020 – 2022

Occupation[1]	2020 Employment	2022 Projected Employment	Numeric Employment Change	Percent Employment Change
Hotel, Motel, and Resort Desk Clerks	730	1,370	640	87.7
Gaming Dealers	170	310	140	82.4
Ushers, Lobby Attendants, and Ticket Takers	80	140	60	75.0
Amusement and Recreation Attendants	920	1,610	690	75.0
Cooks, Restaurant	3,760	6,460	2,700	71.8
Bus Drivers, Transit and Intercity (SOC 2018)	240	410	170	70.8
Reservation and Transportation Ticket Agents and Travel Clerks	160	270	110	68.8
Hosts and Hostesses, Restaurant, Lounge, and Coffee Shop	1,160	1,940	780	67.2
Lodging Managers	150	250	100	66.7
Waiters and Waitresses	7,490	12,200	4,710	62.9

Note: Projections cover New Hampshire; (1) Sorted by percent employment change and excludes occupations with numeric employment change less than 50
Source: www.projectionscentral.com, State Occupational Projections, 2020–2022 Short-Term Projections

TAXES

State Corporate Income Tax Rates

State	Tax Rate (%)	Income Brackets ($)	Num. of Brackets	Financial Institution Tax Rate (%)[a]	Federal Income Tax Ded.
New Hampshire	7.7 (p)	Flat rate	1	7.7 (p)	No

Note: Tax rates as of January 1, 2021; (a) Rates listed are the corporate income tax rate applied to financial institutions or excise taxes based on income. Some states have other taxes based upon the value of deposits or shares; (p) New Hampshire's 7.7% Business Profits Tax is imposed on both corporations and unincorporated associations with gross income over $50,000. In addition, New Hampshire levies a Business Enterprise Tax of 0.60% on the enterprise base (total compensation, interest and dividends paid) for businesses with gross receipts over $222,000 or enterprise base over $111,000, adjusted every biennium for CPI. The Business Profits Tax is scheduled to decrease to 7.5% for tax year 2022, if revenue targets are
Source: Federation of Tax Administrators, State Corporate Income Tax Rates, January 1, 2021

State Individual Income Tax Rates

State	Tax Rate (%)	Income Brackets ($)	Personal Exemptions ($)			Standard Ded. ($)	
			Single	Married	Depend.	Single	Married
New Hampshire	– State income tax of 5% on dividends and interest income only –						

Note: Tax rates as of January 1, 2021; Local- and county-level taxes are not included; Federal income tax is not deductible on state income tax returns
Source: Federation of Tax Administrators, State Individual Income Tax Rates, January 1, 2021

Various State Sales and Excise Tax Rates

State	State Sales Tax (%)	Gasoline[1] (¢/gal.)	Cigarette[2] ($/pack)	Spirits[3] ($/gal.)	Wine[4] ($/gal.)	Beer[5] ($/gal.)	Recreational Marijuana (%)
New Hampshire	None	23.83	1.78	0.00	0.00	0.3	(q)

Note: All tax rates as of January 1, 2021; (1) The American Petroleum Institute has developed a methodology for determining the average tax rate on a gallon of fuel. Rates may include any of the following: excise taxes, environmental fees, storage tank fees, other fees or taxes, general sales tax, and local taxes; (2) The federal excise tax of $1.0066 per pack and local taxes are not included; (3) Rates are those applicable to off-premise sales of 40% alcohol by volume (a.b.v.) distilled spirits in 750ml containers. Local excise taxes are excluded; (4) Rates are those applicable to off-premise sales of 11% a.b.v. non-carbonated wine in 750ml containers; (5) Rates are those applicable to off-premise sales of 4.7% a.b.v. beer in 12 ounce containers; (q) In 2018, the New Hampshire legislature voted to legalize the possession and growing of marijuana, but sales are not permitted.
Source: Tax Foundation, 2021 Facts & Figures: How Does Your State Compare?

State Business Tax Climate Index Rankings

State	Overall Rank	Corporate Tax Rank	Individual Income Tax Rank	Sales Tax Rank	Property Tax Rank	Unemployment Insurance Tax Rank
New Hampshire	6	41	9	1	47	44

Note: The index is a measure of how each state's tax laws affect economic performance. The lower the rank, the more favorable a state's tax system is for business. States without a given tax are given a ranking of 1. The scores/rankings for the District of Columbia do not affect other states. The 2021 index represents the tax climate as of July 1, 2020.
Source: Tax Foundation, State Business Tax Climate Index 2021

TRANSPORTATION

Means of Transportation to Work

Area	Car/Truck/Van		Public Transportation			Bicycle	Walked	Other Means	Worked at Home
	Drove Alone	Car-pooled	Bus	Subway	Railroad				
City	79.1	11.0	0.7	0.0	0.1	0.3	3.2	1.3	4.2
MSA[1]	81.4	8.1	0.8	0.0	0.1	0.1	2.1	0.9	6.4
U.S.	76.3	9.0	2.4	1.9	0.6	0.5	2.7	1.4	5.2

Note: Figures are percentages and cover workers 16 years of age and older; (1) Figures cover the Manchester-Nashua, NH Metropolitan Statistical Area
Source: U.S. Census Bureau, 2015-2019 American Community Survey 5-Year Estimates

Travel Time to Work

Area	Less Than 10 Minutes	10 to 19 Minutes	20 to 29 Minutes	30 to 44 Minutes	45 to 59 Minutes	60 to 89 Minutes	90 Minutes or More
City	14.1	38.3	19.2	14.5	5.9	4.8	3.2
MSA[1]	11.1	29.7	19.7	19.8	8.6	7.2	3.9
U.S.	12.2	28.4	20.8	20.8	8.3	6.4	2.9

Note: Note: Figures are percentages and include workers 16 years old and over; (1) Figures cover the Manchester-Nashua, NH Metropolitan Statistical Area
Source: U.S. Census Bureau, 2015-2019 American Community Survey 5-Year Estimates

Key Congestion Measures

Measure	1982	1992	2002	2012	2017
Annual Hours of Delay, Total (000)	n/a	n/a	n/a	n/a	3,750
Annual Hours of Delay, Per Auto Commuter	n/a	n/a	n/a	n/a	22
Annual Congestion Cost, Total (million $)	n/a	n/a	n/a	n/a	77
Annual Congestion Cost, Per Auto Commuter ($)	n/a	n/a	n/a	n/a	453

Note: n/a not available
Source: Texas A&M Transportation Institute, 2019 Urban Mobility Report

Freeway Travel Time Index

Measure	1982	1987	1992	1997	2002	2007	2012	2017
Urban Area Index[1]	n/a	n/a	n/a	n/a	n/a	n/a	n/a	1.07
Urban Area Rank[1,2]	n/a	n/a	n/a	n/a	n/a	n/a	n/a	n/a

Note: Freeway Travel Time Index—the ratio of travel time in the peak period to the travel time at free-flow conditions. For example, a value of 1.30 indicates a 20-minute free-flow trip takes 26 minutes in the peak (20 minutes x 1.30 = 26 minutes); (1) Covers the Manchester NH urban area; (2) Rank is based on 101 larger urban areas (#1 = highest travel time index); n/a not available
Source: Texas A&M Transportation Institute, 2019 Urban Mobility Report

Public Transportation

Agency Name / Mode of Transportation	Vehicles Operated in Maximum Service[1]	Annual Unlinked Passenger Trips[2] (in thous.)	Annual Passenger Miles[3] (in thous.)
Manchester Transit Authority (MTA)			
Bus (directly operated)	14	399.1	n/a
Demand Response (directly operated)	5	10.2	n/a

Note: (1) Number of revenue vehicles operated by the given mode and type of service to meet the annual maximum service requirement. This is the revenue vehicle count during the peak season of the year; on the week and day that maximum service is provided. Vehicles operated in maximum service (VOMS) exclude atypical days and one-time special events; (2) Number of passengers who boarded public transportation vehicles. Passengers are counted each time they board a vehicle no matter how many vehicles they use to travel from their origin to their destination. (3) Sum of the distances ridden by all passengers during the entire fiscal year.
Source: Federal Transit Administration, National Transit Database, 2019

Air Transportation

Airport Name and Code / Type of Service	Passenger Airlines[1]	Passenger Enplanements	Freight Carriers[2]	Freight (lbs)
Manchester Municipal (MHT)				
Domestic service (U.S. carriers - 2020)	13	305,895	5	84,759,551
International service (U.S. carriers - 2019)	1	11	0	0

Note: (1) Includes all U.S.-based major, minor and commuter airlines that carried at least one passenger during the year; (2) Includes all U.S.-based airlines and freight carriers that transported at least one pound of freight during the year.
Source: Bureau of Transportation Statistics, The Intermodal Transportation Database, Air Carriers: T-100 Domestic Market (U.S. Carriers), 2020; Bureau of Transportation Statistics, The Intermodal Transportation Database, Air Carriers: T-100 International Market (U.S. Carriers), 2019

BUSINESSES

Major Business Headquarters

Company Name	Industry	Rankings	
		Fortune[1]	Forbes[2]
No companies listed	-	-	-

Note: (1) Companies that produce a 10-K are ranked 1 to 500 based on 2019 revenue; (2) All private companies with at least $2 billion in annual revenue through the end of their most current fiscal year are ranked 1 to 219; companies listed are headquartered in the city; dashes indicate no ranking
Source: Fortune, "Fortune 500," June/July 2020; Forbes, "America's Largest Private Companies," 2020

Fastest-Growing Businesses

According to *Inc.*, Manchester is home to one of America's 500 fastest-growing private companies: **Forcivity** (#157). Criteria: must be an independent, privately-held, for-profit, U.S. corporation, proprietorship or partnership as of December 31, 2019; revenues must be at least $100,000 in 2016 and $2 million in 2019; must have four-year operating/sales history. *Inc., "America's 500 Fastest-Growing Private Companies," 2020*

Living Environment

COST OF LIVING

Cost of Living Index

Composite Index	Groceries	Housing	Utilities	Trans-portation	Health Care	Misc. Goods/ Services
108.6	98.5	112.1	112.3	94.7	114.3	111.6

Note: The Cost of Living Index measures regional differences in the cost of consumer goods and services, excluding taxes and non-consumer expenditures, for professional and managerial households in the top income quintile. It is based on more than 50,000 prices covering almost 60 different items for which prices are collected three times a year by chambers of commerce, economic development organizations or university applied economic centers in each participating urban area. The numbers shown should be read as a percentage above or below the national average of 100. For example, a value of 115.4 in the groceries column indicates that grocery prices are 15.4% higher than the national average. Small differences in the index numbers should not be interpreted as significant; Figures cover the Manchester NH urban area.
Source: The Council for Community and Economic Research, Cost of Living Index, 2020

Grocery Prices

Area[1]	T-Bone Steak ($/pound)	Frying Chicken ($/pound)	Whole Milk ($/half gal.)	Eggs ($/dozen)	Orange Juice ($/64 oz.)	Coffee ($/11.5 oz.)
City[2]	13.66	1.19	2.79	1.52	3.41	3.66
Avg.	11.78	1.39	2.05	1.47	3.57	4.34
Min.	8.03	0.94	1.03	0.74	2.94	3.02
Max.	15.86	2.65	4.31	3.77	5.44	8.69

*Note: (1) Values for the local area are compared with the average, minimum and maximum values for all 284 areas in the Cost of Living Index; (2) Figures cover the Manchester NH urban area; **T-Bone Steak** (price per pound); **Frying Chicken** (price per pound, whole fryer); **Whole Milk** (half gallon carton); **Eggs** (price per dozen, Grade A, large); **Orange Juice** (64 oz. Tropicana or Florida Natural); **Coffee** (11.5 oz. can, vacuum-packed, Maxwell House, Hills Bros, or Folgers).*
Source: The Council for Community and Economic Research, Cost of Living Index, 2020

Housing and Utility Costs

Area[1]	New Home Price ($)	Apartment Rent ($/month)	All Electric ($/month)	Part Electric ($/month)	Other Energy ($/month)	Telephone ($/month)
City[2]	362,551	1,625	-	117.62	88.11	180.00
Avg.	368,594	1,168	170.86	100.47	65.28	184.30
Min.	190,567	502	91.58	31.42	26.08	169.60
Max.	2,227,806	4,738	470.38	280.31	280.06	206.50

*Note: (1) Values for the local area are compared with the average, minimum and maximum values for all 284 areas in the Cost of Living Index; (2) Figures cover the Manchester NH urban area; **New Home Price** (2,400 sf living area, 8,000 sf lot, in urban area with full utilities); **Apartment Rent** (950 sf 2 bedroom/1.5 or 2 bath, unfurnished, excluding all utilities except water); **All Electric** (average monthly cost for an all-electric home); **Part Electric** (average monthly cost for a part-electric home); **Other Energy** (average monthly cost for natural gas, fuel oil, coal, wood, and any other forms of energy except electricity); **Telephone** (price includes the base monthly rate plus taxes and fees for three lines of mobile phone service).*
Source: The Council for Community and Economic Research, Cost of Living Index, 2020

Health Care, Transportation, and Other Costs

Area[1]	Doctor ($/visit)	Dentist ($/visit)	Optometrist ($/visit)	Gasoline ($/gallon)	Beauty Salon ($/visit)	Men's Shirt ($)
City[2]	152.49	121.64	101.89	2.00	41.18	34.23
Avg.	115.44	99.32	108.10	2.21	39.27	31.37
Min.	36.68	59.00	51.36	1.71	19.00	11.00
Max.	219.00	153.10	250.97	3.46	82.05	58.33

*Note: (1) Values for the local area are compared with the average, minimum and maximum values for all 284 areas in the Cost of Living Index; (2) Figures cover the Manchester NH urban area; **Doctor** (general practitioners routine exam of an established patient); **Dentist** (adult teeth cleaning and periodic oral examination); **Optometrist** (full vision eye exam for established adult patient); **Gasoline** (one gallon regular unleaded, national brand, including all taxes, cash price at self-service pump if available); **Beauty Salon** (woman's shampoo, trim, and blow-dry); **Men's Shirt** (cotton/polyester dress shirt, pinpoint weave, long sleeves).*
Source: The Council for Community and Economic Research, Cost of Living Index, 2020

HOUSING

Homeownership Rate

Area	2012 (%)	2013 (%)	2014 (%)	2015 (%)	2016 (%)	2017 (%)	2018 (%)	2019 (%)	2020 (%)
MSA[1]	n/a	n/a	n/a	n/a	n/a	n/a	n/a	n/a	n/a
U.S.	65.4	65.1	64.5	63.7	63.4	63.9	64.4	64.6	66.6

Note: (1) Figures cover the Manchester-Nashua, NH Metropolitan Statistical Area; n/a not available
Source: U.S. Census Bureau, Housing Vacancies and Homeownership Annual Statistics: 2012-2020

House Price Index (HPI)

Area	National Ranking[2]	Quarterly Change (%)	One-Year Change (%)	Five-Year Change (%)	Since 1991Q1 (%)
MSA[1]	17	3.48	9.02	33.95	167.53
U.S.[3]	–	3.81	10.77	38.99	205.12

Note: The HPI is a weighted repeat sales index. It measures average price changes in repeat sales or refinancings on the same properties. This information is obtained by reviewing repeat mortgage transactions on single-family properties whose mortgages have been purchased or securitized by Fannie Mae or Freddie Mac since January 1975; (1) Figures cover the Manchester-Nashua, NH Metropolitan Statistical Area; (2) Rankings are based on annual percentage change for all metro areas containing at least 15,000 transactions over the last 10 years and ranges from 1 to 253; (3) figures based on a weighted average of Census Division estimates using a seasonally adjusted, purchase-only index; all figures are for the period ending December 31, 2020
Source: Federal Housing Finance Agency, Change in Metropolitan Area House Price Indexes, April 7, 2021

Median Single-Family Home Prices

Area	2018	2019	2020p	Percent Change 2019 to 2020
MSA[1]	294.9	317.4	357.8	12.7
U.S. Average	261.6	274.6	299.9	9.2

Note: Figures are median sales prices of existing single-family homes in thousands of dollars; (p) preliminary; (1) Figures cover the Manchester-Nashua, NH Metropolitan Statistical Area
Source: National Association of Realtors, Median Sales Price of Existing Single-Family Homes for Metropolitan Areas, 4th Quarter 2020

Qualifying Income Based on Median Sales Price of Existing Single-Family Homes

Area	With 5% Down ($)	With 10% Down ($)	With 20% Down ($)
MSA[1]	69,661	65,995	58,662
U.S. Average	59,266	56,147	49,908

Note: Figures are preliminary; Qualifying income is based on a mortgage rate of 2.81%. Monthly principal and interest payment is limited to 25% of income; (1) Figures cover the Manchester-Nashua, NH Metropolitan Statistical Area
Source: National Association of Realtors, Qualifying Income Based on Median Sales Price of Existing Single-Family Homes for Metropolitan Areas, 4th Quarter 2020

Home Value Distribution

Area	Under $50,000	$50,000 -$99,999	$100,000 -$149,999	$150,000 -$199,999	$200,000 -$299,999	$300,000 -$499,999	$500,000 -$999,999	$1,000,000 or more
City	1.9	3.0	8.3	21.6	47.9	15.7	1.4	0.2
MSA[1]	1.9	2.5	5.9	12.0	37.5	32.8	6.7	0.7
U.S.	6.9	12.0	13.3	14.0	19.6	19.3	11.4	3.4

Note: Figures are percentages and cover owner-occupied housing units; (1) Figures cover the Manchester-Nashua, NH Metropolitan Statistical Area
Source: U.S. Census Bureau, 2015-2019 American Community Survey 5-Year Estimates

Year Housing Structure Built

Area	2010 or Later	2000 -2009	1990 -1999	1980 -1989	1970 -1979	1960 -1969	1950 -1959	1940 -1949	Before 1940	Median Year
City	1.9	6.7	8.1	15.9	10.4	7.9	10.3	6.1	32.6	1961
MSA[1]	3.0	10.1	10.3	20.9	15.3	9.6	7.1	3.7	19.9	1976
U.S.	5.2	14.0	13.9	13.4	15.2	10.6	10.3	4.9	12.6	1978

Note: Figures are percentages except for Median Year; Note: (1) Figures cover the Manchester-Nashua, NH Metropolitan Statistical Area
Source: U.S. Census Bureau, 2015-2019 American Community Survey 5-Year Estimates

Gross Monthly Rent

Area	Under $500	$500 -$999	$1,000 -$1,499	$1,500 -$1,999	$2,000 -$2,499	$2,500 -$2,999	$3,000 and up	Median ($)
City	7.4	28.2	45.1	15.4	2.5	0.7	0.6	1,135
MSA[1]	6.9	24.7	42.8	19.9	4.2	0.9	0.5	1,191
U.S.	9.4	36.2	30.0	14.0	5.6	2.4	2.4	1,062

Note: Figures are percentages except for Median; Gross rent is the contract rent plus the estimated average monthly cost of utilities (electricity, gas, and water and sewer) and fuels (oil, coal, kerosene, wood, etc.) if these are paid by the renter (or paid for the renter by someone else); (1) Figures cover the Manchester-Nashua, NH Metropolitan Statistical Area
Source: U.S. Census Bureau, 2015-2019 American Community Survey 5-Year Estimates

HEALTH

Health Risk Factors

Category	MSA[1] (%)	U.S. (%)
Adults aged 18–64 who have any kind of health care coverage	n/a	87.3
Adults who reported being in good or better health	n/a	82.4
Adults who have been told they have high blood cholesterol	n/a	33.0
Adults who have been told they have high blood pressure	n/a	32.3
Adults who are current smokers	n/a	17.1
Adults who currently use E-cigarettes	n/a	4.6
Adults who currently use chewing tobacco, snuff, or snus	n/a	4.0
Adults who are heavy drinkers[2]	n/a	6.3
Adults who are binge drinkers[3]	n/a	17.4
Adults who are overweight (BMI 25.0 - 29.9)	n/a	35.3
Adults who are obese (BMI 30.0 - 99.8)	n/a	31.3
Adults who participated in any physical activities in the past month	n/a	74.4
Adults who always or nearly always wears a seat belt	n/a	94.3

Note: n/a not available; (1) Figures cover the Manchester-Nashua, NH Metropolitan Statistical Area; (2) Heavy drinkers are classified as adult men having more than 14 drinks per week and adult women having more than 7 drinks per week; (3) Binge drinkers are classified as males having five or more drinks on one occasion or females having four or more drinks on one occasion
Source: Centers for Disease Control and Prevention, Behaviorial Risk Factor Surveillance System, SMART: Selected Metropolitan Area Risk Trends, 2017

Acute and Chronic Health Conditions

Category	MSA[1] (%)	U.S. (%)
Adults who have ever been told they had a heart attack	n/a	4.2
Adults who have ever been told they have angina or coronary heart disease	n/a	3.9
Adults who have ever been told they had a stroke	n/a	3.0
Adults who have ever been told they have asthma	n/a	14.2
Adults who have ever been told they have arthritis	n/a	24.9
Adults who have ever been told they have diabetes[2]	n/a	10.5
Adults who have ever been told they had skin cancer	n/a	6.2
Adults who have ever been told they had any other types of cancer	n/a	7.1
Adults who have ever been told they have COPD	n/a	6.5
Adults who have ever been told they have kidney disease	n/a	3.0
Adults who have ever been told they have a form of depression	n/a	20.5

Note: n/a not available; (1) Figures cover the Manchester-Nashua, NH Metropolitan Statistical Area; (2) Figures do not include pregnancy-related, borderline, or pre-diabetes
Source: Centers for Disease Control and Prevention, Behaviorial Risk Factor Surveillance System, SMART: Selected Metropolitan Area Risk Trends, 2017

Health Screening and Vaccination Rates

Category	MSA[1] (%)	U.S. (%)
Adults aged 65+ who have had flu shot within the past year	n/a	60.7
Adults aged 65+ who have ever had a pneumonia vaccination	n/a	75.4
Adults who have ever been tested for HIV	n/a	36.1
Adults who have ever had the shingles or zoster vaccine?	n/a	28.9
Adults who have had their blood cholesterol checked within the last five years	n/a	85.9

Note: n/a not available; (1) Figures cover the Manchester-Nashua, NH Metropolitan Statistical Area.
Source: Centers for Disease Control and Prevention, Behaviorial Risk Factor Surveillance System, SMART: Selected Metropolitan Area Risk Trends, 2017

Disability Status

Category	MSA[1] (%)	U.S. (%)
Adults who reported being deaf	n/a	6.7
Are you blind or have serious difficulty seeing, even when wearing glasses?	n/a	4.5
Are you limited in any way in any of your usual activities due of arthritis?	n/a	12.9
Do you have difficulty doing errands alone?	n/a	6.8
Do you have difficulty dressing or bathing?	n/a	3.6
Do you have serious difficulty concentrating/remembering/making decisions?	n/a	10.7
Do you have serious difficulty walking or climbing stairs?	n/a	13.6

Note: n/a not available; (1) Figures cover the Manchester-Nashua, NH Metropolitan Statistical Area.
Source: Centers for Disease Control and Prevention, Behaviorial Risk Factor Surveillance System, SMART: Selected Metropolitan Area Risk Trends, 2017

Mortality Rates for the Top 10 Causes of Death in the U.S.

ICD-10[a] Sub-Chapter	ICD-10[a] Code	Age-Adjusted Mortality Rate[1] per 100,000 population	
		County[2]	U.S.
Malignant neoplasms	C00-C97	141.8	149.2
Ischaemic heart diseases	I20-I25	75.4	90.5
Other forms of heart disease	I30-I51	57.6	52.2
Chronic lower respiratory diseases	J40-J47	41.9	39.6
Other degenerative diseases of the nervous system	G30-G31	27.4	37.6
Cerebrovascular diseases	I60-I69	25.7	37.2
Other external causes of accidental injury	W00-X59	56.6	36.1
Organic, including symptomatic, mental disorders	F01-F09	48.7	29.4
Hypertensive diseases	I10-I15	16.7	24.1
Diabetes mellitus	E10-E14	18.9	21.5

Note: (a) ICD-10 = International Classification of Diseases 10th Revision; (1) Mortality rates are a three-year average covering 2017-2019; (2) Figures cover Hillsborough County.
Source: Centers for Disease Control and Prevention, National Center for Health Statistics. Underlying Cause of Death 1999-2019 on CDC WONDER Online Database

Mortality Rates for Selected Causes of Death

ICD-10[a] Sub-Chapter	ICD-10[a] Code	Age-Adjusted Mortality Rate[1] per 100,000 population	
		County[2]	U.S.
Assault	X85-Y09	Unreliable	6.0
Diseases of the liver	K70-K76	13.0	14.4
Human immunodeficiency virus (HIV) disease	B20-B24	Suppressed	1.5
Influenza and pneumonia	J09-J18	13.1	13.8
Intentional self-harm	X60-X84	18.7	14.1
Malnutrition	E40-E46	1.5	2.3
Obesity and other hyperalimentation	E65-E68	3.6	2.1
Renal failure	N17-N19	10.3	12.6
Transport accidents	V01-V99	6.6	12.3
Viral hepatitis	B15-B19	Unreliable	1.2

Note: (a) ICD-10 = International Classification of Diseases 10th Revision; (1) Mortality rates are a three-year average covering 2017-2019; (2) Figures cover Hillsborough County; Data are suppressed when the data meet the criteria for confidentiality constraints; Mortality rates are flagged as unreliable when the rate would be calculated with a numerator of 20 or less.
Source: Centers for Disease Control and Prevention, National Center for Health Statistics. Underlying Cause of Death 1999-2019 on CDC WONDER Online Database

Health Insurance Coverage

Area	With Health Insurance	With Private Health Insurance	With Public Health Insurance	Without Health Insurance	Population Under Age 19 Without Health Insurance
City	90.1	64.0	36.3	9.9	3.7
MSA[1]	93.8	76.9	28.9	6.2	2.6
U.S.	91.2	67.9	35.1	8.8	5.1

Note: Figures are percentages that cover the civilian noninstitutionalized population; (1) Figures cover the Manchester-Nashua, NH Metropolitan Statistical Area
Source: U.S. Census Bureau, 2015-2019 American Community Survey 5-Year Estimates

Number of Medical Professionals

Area	MDs[3]	DOs[3,4]	Dentists	Podiatrists	Chiropractors	Optometrists
County[1] (number)	986	105	345	23	108	84
County[1] (rate[2])	237.8	25.3	82.7	5.5	25.9	20.1
U.S. (rate[2])	282.9	22.7	71.2	6.2	28.1	16.9

33011
Note: Data as of 2019 unless noted; (1) Data covers Hillsborough County; (2) Rate per 100,000 population; (3) Data as of 2018 and includes all active, non-federal physicians; (4) Doctor of Osteopathic Medicine
Source: U.S. Department of Health and Human Services, Health Resources and Services Administration, Bureau of Health Professions, Area Resource File (ARF) 2019-2020

EDUCATION

Public School District Statistics

District Name	Schls	Pupils	Pupil/ Teacher Ratio	Minority Pupils[1] (%)	Free Lunch Eligible[2] (%)	IEP[3] (%)
Manchester School District	22	13,522	13.9	44.0	52.9	19.8

Note: Table includes school districts with 2,000 or more students; (1) Percentage of students that are not non-Hispanic white; (2) Percentage of students that are eligible for the free lunch program; (3) Percentage of students that have an Individualized Education Program.
Source: U.S. Department of Education, National Center for Education Statistics, Common Core of Data, Local Education Agency (School District) Universe Survey: School Year 2018-2019; U.S. Department of Education, National Center for Education Statistics, Common Core of Data, Public Elementary/Secondary School Universe Survey: School Year 2018-2019

Highest Level of Education

Area	Less than H.S.	H.S. Diploma	Some College, No Deg.	Associate Degree	Bachelor's Degree	Master's Degree	Prof. School Degree	Doctorate Degree
City	12.7	29.1	18.9	9.3	20.3	7.3	1.7	0.9
MSA[1]	7.9	25.8	18.2	10.0	24.3	10.9	1.6	1.3
U.S.	12.0	27.0	20.4	8.5	19.8	8.8	2.1	1.4

Note: Figures cover persons age 25 and over; (1) Figures cover the Manchester-Nashua, NH Metropolitan Statistical Area
Source: U.S. Census Bureau, 2015-2019 American Community Survey 5-Year Estimates

Educational Attainment by Race

Area	High School Graduate or Higher (%)					Bachelor's Degree or Higher (%)				
	Total	White	Black	Asian	Hisp.[2]	Total	White	Black	Asian	Hisp.[2]
City	87.3	88.4	79.2	76.4	67.0	30.1	29.7	22.1	44.6	14.9
MSA[1]	92.1	92.6	83.7	88.3	71.7	38.1	37.4	24.0	64.8	19.4
U.S.	88.0	89.9	86.0	87.1	68.7	32.1	33.5	21.6	54.3	16.4

Note: Figures shown cover persons 25 years old and over; (1) Figures cover the Manchester-Nashua, NH Metropolitan Statistical Area; (2) People of Hispanic origin can be of any race
Source: U.S. Census Bureau, 2015-2019 American Community Survey 5-Year Estimates

School Enrollment by Grade and Control

Area	Preschool (%)		Kindergarten (%)		Grades 1 - 4 (%)		Grades 5 - 8 (%)		Grades 9 - 12 (%)	
	Public	Private	Public	Private	Public	Private	Public	Private	Public	Private
City	52.6	47.4	86.1	13.9	89.9	10.1	93.1	6.9	89.5	10.5
MSA[1]	42.4	57.6	83.7	16.3	87.1	12.9	89.9	10.1	88.9	11.1
U.S.	59.1	40.9	87.6	12.4	89.5	10.5	89.4	10.6	90.1	9.9

Note: Figures shown cover persons 3 years old and over; (1) Figures cover the Manchester-Nashua, NH Metropolitan Statistical Area
Source: U.S. Census Bureau, 2015-2019 American Community Survey 5-Year Estimates

Higher Education

Four-Year Colleges			Two-Year Colleges			Medical Schools[1]	Law Schools[2]	Voc/ Tech[3]
Public	Private Non-profit	Private For-profit	Public	Private Non-profit	Private For-profit			
1	3	0	1	0	0	0	0	2

Note: Figures cover institutions located within the city limits and include main campuses only; (1) includes schools accredited by the Liaison Committee on Medical Education and the American Osteopathic Association's Commission on Osteopathic College Accreditation; (2) includes ABA-accredited schools, schools with provisional ABA accreditation, and state accredited schools; (3) includes all schools with programs that are less than 2 years.
Source: National Center for Education Statistics, Integrated Postsecondary Education System (IPEDS), 2019-20; Wikipedia, List of Medical Schools in the United States, accessed April 2, 2021; Wikipedia, List of Law Schools in the United States, accessed April 2, 2021

EMPLOYERS

Major Employers

Company Name	Industry
C & S Wholesale Grocers Inc	Grocery stores
Concord Hospital	Healthcare
Dartmouth-Hitchcock Medical Center	Healthcare
Elliot Hospital	Healthcare
Fidelity Investments	Financial services
Freudenberg-Nok	Healthcare
Hypertherm	Technology
J Jill	Retailer
Liberty Life Assurance Co	Insurance companies/services
Southern New Hampshire Health	Healthcare
St. Joseph's Hospital	Healthcare
Sturm Ruger & Co. Inc	Firearms
Trustees of Dartmouth College	Education
UA Local 788 Marine Pipefitter	Union
United Physical Therapy	Healthcare
University of New Hampshire	Education
University System of NH	Education

Note: Companies shown are located within the Manchester-Nashua, NH Metropolitan Statistical Area.
Source: Hoovers.com; Wikipedia

PUBLIC SAFETY

Crime Rate

Area	All Crimes	Violent Crimes				Property Crimes		
		Murder	Rape[3]	Robbery	Aggrav. Assault	Burglary	Larceny -Theft	Motor Vehicle Theft
City	2,972.7	5.3	54.9	117.8	422.5	264.8	1,970.9	136.4
Suburbs[1]	1,000.0	1.6	42.2	12.2	35.9	81.4	789.2	37.5
Metro[2]	1,534.7	2.6	45.6	40.8	140.7	131.1	1,109.5	64.3
U.S.	2,489.3	5.0	42.6	81.6	250.2	340.5	1,549.5	219.9

Note: Figures are crimes per 100,000 population; (1) All areas within the metro area that are located outside the city limits; (2) Figures cover the Manchester-Nashua, NH Metropolitan Statistical Area; (3) All figures shown were reported using the revised Uniform Crime Reporting (UCR) definition of rape.
Source: FBI Uniform Crime Reports, 2019

Hate Crimes

Area	Number of Quarters Reported	Number of Incidents per Bias Motivation					
		Race/Ethnicity/ Ancestry	Religion	Sexual Orientation	Disability	Gender	Gender Identity
City	4	0	0	0	0	0	0
U.S.	4	3,963	1,521	1,195	157	69	198

Source: Federal Bureau of Investigation, Hate Crime Statistics 2019

Identity Theft Consumer Reports

Area	Reports	Reports per 100,000 Population	Rank[2]
MSA[1]	829	199	214
U.S.	1,387,615	423	-

Note: (1) Figures cover the Manchester-Nashua, NH Metropolitan Statistical Area; (2) Rank ranges from 1 to 391 where 1 indicates greatest number of identity theft reports per 100,000 population
Source: Federal Trade Commission, Consumer Sentinel Network Data Book 2020

Fraud and Other Consumer Reports

Area	Reports	Reports per 100,000 Population	Rank[2]
MSA[1]	3,155	757	135
U.S.	3,385,133	1,031	-

Note: (1) Figures cover the Manchester-Nashua, NH Metropolitan Statistical Area; (2) Rank ranges from 1 to 391 where 1 indicates greatest number of fraud and other consumer reports per 100,000 population
Source: Federal Trade Commission, Consumer Sentinel Network Data Book 2020

POLITICS

2020 Presidential Election Results

Area	Biden	Trump	Jorgensen	Hawkins	Other
Hillsborough County	52.8	45.2	1.7	0.0	0.3
U.S.	51.3	46.8	1.2	0.3	0.5

Note: Results are percentages and may not add to 100% due to rounding
Source: Dave Leip's Atlas of U.S. Presidential Elections

SPORTS

Professional Sports Teams

Team Name	League	Year Established
No teams are located in the metro area		

Source: Wikipedia, Major Professional Sports Teams of the United States and Canada, April 6, 2021

CLIMATE

Average and Extreme Temperatures

Temperature	Jan	Feb	Mar	Apr	May	Jun	Jul	Aug	Sep	Oct	Nov	Dec	Yr.
Extreme High (°F)	68	66	85	95	97	98	102	101	98	90	80	68	102
Average High (°F)	31	34	43	57	69	77	83	80	72	61	48	35	57
Average Temp. (°F)	20	23	33	44	56	65	70	68	59	48	38	25	46
Average Low (°F)	9	11	22	32	42	51	57	55	46	35	28	15	34
Extreme Low (°F)	-33	-27	-16	8	21	30	35	29	22	10	-5	-22	-33

Note: Figures cover the years 1948-1990
Source: National Climatic Data Center, International Station Meteorological Climate Summary, 9/96

Average Precipitation/Snowfall/Humidity

Precip./Humidity	Jan	Feb	Mar	Apr	May	Jun	Jul	Aug	Sep	Oct	Nov	Dec	Yr.
Avg. Precip. (in.)	2.8	2.5	2.9	3.1	3.2	3.1	3.1	3.3	2.9	3.1	3.8	3.2	36.9
Avg. Snowfall (in.)	18	15	11	2	Tr	0	0	0	0	Tr	4	14	63
Avg. Rel. Hum. 7am (%)	76	76	76	75	75	80	82	87	89	86	83	79	80
Avg. Rel. Hum. 4pm (%)	59	55	52	46	47	52	51	53	55	53	61	63	54

Note: Figures cover the years 1948-1990; Tr = Trace amounts (<0.05 in. of rain; <0.5 in. of snow)
Source: National Climatic Data Center, International Station Meteorological Climate Summary, 9/96

Weather Conditions

Temperature			Daytime Sky			Precipitation		
5°F & below	32°F & below	90°F & above	Clear	Partly cloudy	Cloudy	0.01 inch or more precip.	0.1 inch or more snow/ice	Thunder-storms
32	171	12	87	131	147	125	32	19

Note: Figures are average number of days per year and cover the years 1948-1990
Source: National Climatic Data Center, International Station Meteorological Climate Summary, 9/96

HAZARDOUS WASTE

Superfund Sites

The Manchester-Nashua, NH metro area is home to six sites on the EPA's Superfund National Priorities List: **Fletcher's Paint Works & Storage** (final); **Mohawk Tannery** (proposed); **New Hampshire Plating Co.** (final); **Savage Municipal Water Supply** (final); **South Municipal Water Supply Well** (final); **Sylvester** (final). There are a total of 1,375 Superfund sites with a status of proposed or final on the list in the U.S. *U.S. Environmental Protection Agency, National Priorities List, April 7, 2021*

AIR QUALITY

Air Quality Trends: Ozone

	1990	1995	2000	2005	2010	2015	2016	2017	2018	2019
MSA[1]	n/a	n/a	n/a	n/a	n/a	n/a	n/a	n/a	n/a	n/a
U.S.	0.088	0.089	0.082	0.080	0.073	0.068	0.069	0.068	0.069	0.065

Note: (1) Data covers the Manchester-Nashua, NH Metropolitan Statistical Area; n/a not available. The values shown are the composite ozone concentration averages among trend sites based on the highest fourth daily maximum 8-hour concentration in parts per million. These trends are based on sites having an adequate record of monitoring data during the trend period. Data from exceptional events are included.
Source: U.S. Environmental Protection Agency, Air Quality Monitoring Information, "Air Quality Trends by City, 1990-2019"

Air Quality Index

| Area | Percent of Days when Air Quality was...[2] | | | | | AQI Statistics[2] | |
	Good	Moderate	Unhealthy for Sensitive Groups	Unhealthy	Very Unhealthy	Maximum	Median
MSA[1]	96.7	3.3	0.0	0.0	0.0	80	37

Note: (1) Data covers the Manchester-Nashua, NH Metropolitan Statistical Area; (2) Based on 365 days with AQI data in 2019. Air Quality Index (AQI) is an index for reporting daily air quality. EPA calculates the AQI for five major air pollutants regulated by the Clean Air Act: ground-level ozone, particle pollution (aka particulate matter), carbon monoxide, sulfur dioxide, and nitrogen dioxide. The AQI runs from 0 to 500. The higher the AQI value, the greater the level of air pollution and the greater the health concern. There are six AQI categories: "Good" AQI is between 0 and 50. Air quality is considered satisfactory; "Moderate" AQI is between 51 and 100. Air quality is acceptable; "Unhealthy for Sensitive Groups" When AQI values are between 101 and 150, members of sensitive groups may experience health effects; "Unhealthy" When AQI values are between 151 and 200 everyone may begin to experience health effects; "Very Unhealthy" AQI values between 201 and 300 trigger a health alert; "Hazardous" AQI values over 300 trigger warnings of emergency conditions (not shown).
Source: U.S. Environmental Protection Agency, Air Quality Index Report, 2019

Air Quality Index Pollutants

| Area | Percent of Days when AQI Pollutant was...[2] | | | | | |
	Carbon Monoxide	Nitrogen Dioxide	Ozone	Sulfur Dioxide	Particulate Matter 2.5	Particulate Matter 10
MSA[1]	0.0	0.0	97.5	0.0	2.5	0.0

Note: (1) Data covers the Manchester-Nashua, NH Metropolitan Statistical Area; (2) Based on 365 days with AQI data in 2019. The Air Quality Index (AQI) is an index for reporting daily air quality. EPA calculates the AQI for five major air pollutants regulated by the Clean Air Act: ground-level ozone, particle pollution (also known as particulate matter), carbon monoxide, sulfur dioxide, and nitrogen dioxide. The AQI runs from 0 to 500. The higher the AQI value, the greater the level of air pollution and the greater the health concern.
Source: U.S. Environmental Protection Agency, Air Quality Index Report, 2019

Maximum Air Pollutant Concentrations: Particulate Matter, Ozone, CO and Lead

	Particulate Matter 10 (ug/m³)	Particulate Matter 2.5 Wtd AM (ug/m³)	Particulate Matter 2.5 24-Hr (ug/m³)	Ozone (ppm)	Carbon Monoxide (ppm)	Lead (ug/m³)
MSA[1] Level	n/a	3.0	10	0.057	0	n/a
NAAQS[2]	150	15	35	0.075	9	0.15
Met NAAQS[2]	n/a	Yes	Yes	Yes	Yes	n/a

Note: (1) Data covers the Manchester-Nashua, NH Metropolitan Statistical Area; Data from exceptional events are included; (2) National Ambient Air Quality Standards; ppm = parts per million; ug/m³ = micrograms per cubic meter; n/a not available.
Concentrations: Particulate Matter 10 (coarse particulate)—highest second maximum 24-hour concentration; Particulate Matter 2.5 Wtd AM (fine particulate)—highest weighted annual mean concentration; Particulate Matter 2.5 24-Hour (fine particulate)—highest 98th percentile 24-hour concentration; Ozone—highest fourth daily maximum 8-hour concentration; Carbon Monoxide—highest second maximum non-overlapping 8-hour concentration; Lead—maximum running 3-month average
Source: U.S. Environmental Protection Agency, Air Quality Monitoring Information, "Air Quality Statistics by City, 2019"

Maximum Air Pollutant Concentrations: Nitrogen Dioxide and Sulfur Dioxide

	Nitrogen Dioxide AM (ppb)	Nitrogen Dioxide 1-Hr (ppb)	Sulfur Dioxide AM (ppb)	Sulfur Dioxide 1-Hr (ppb)	Sulfur Dioxide 24-Hr (ppb)
MSA[1] Level	n/a	n/a	n/a	1	n/a
NAAQS[2]	53	100	30	75	140
Met NAAQS[2]	n/a	n/a	n/a	Yes	n/a

Note: (1) Data covers the Manchester-Nashua, NH Metropolitan Statistical Area; Data from exceptional events are included; (2) National Ambient Air Quality Standards; ppm = parts per million; ug/m³ = micrograms per cubic meter; n/a not available.
Concentrations: Nitrogen Dioxide AM—highest arithmetic mean concentration; Nitrogen Dioxide 1-Hr—highest 98th percentile 1-hour daily maximum concentration; Sulfur Dioxide AM—highest annual mean concentration; Sulfur Dioxide 1-Hr—highest 99th percentile 1-hour daily maximum concentration; Sulfur Dioxide 24-Hr—highest second maximum 24-hour concentration
Source: U.S. Environmental Protection Agency, Air Quality Monitoring Information, "Air Quality Statistics by City, 2019"

New Haven, Connecticut

Background

New Haven is located along on the northern shore of Long Island Sound in central Connecticut. One of the main cities in New Haven County, it is the principal municipality of the Greater New Haven area, as well part of the larger New York City metropolitan area. The city is drained by three rivers, the West, the Mill, and the Quinnipiac, which flow into the New Haven and West Haven Harbors.

Originally home to the Quinnipiac tribe, the area that became New Haven was first visited by Dutch traders in 1614 and then in 1637 by a group of English Puritans who had left the Massachusetts Bay Colony. These Puritans purchased the land occupied by the Quinnipiacs in exchange for protection against the rival Pequot tribe, and set up a theocratic government in what was called the New Haven Colony and which, in 1664, became part of the Connecticut Colony. In 1716, the city received a major cultural boost when the Collegiate School moved from Old Saybrook to New Haven. Two years later, it took on its current name, Yale, when a wealthy merchant named Elihu Yale made a large donation to the school that set it on its current path.

Incorporated as a city in 1784, New Haven quickly became a leading industrial center thanks largely to the efforts of Yale alumni Eli Whitney who developed the cotton gin and established a gun-making factory in the city. New Haven's status as a gun manufacturing center was cemented during the Civil War when demand for firearms significantly increased and the New Haven Arms Company (later the Winchester Repeating Arms Company) was founded. The number of residents grew steadily after the war, with increased immigration from Italy and Eastern Europe swelling the population, which doubled between 1870 and 1900.

New Haven continued to grow throughout the first half of the 20th century with large populations of African Americans and Puerto Ricans moving to the city. During the 1950s, New Haven suffered from a mass exodus of white middle-class workers, and thanks to policies such as redlining and rezoning, as well as the departure of the city's industrial base, the conditions for the remaining population began to deteriorate.

Since 2000, a number of revitalization projects have brought new life to downtown New Haven and made it a newly desirable place for people to live. In addition, policies such as community policing resulted in crime rates dropping during the 2000s. In 2018, the city instituted Bike New Haven bike share program.

Economically, New Haven is dominated by Yale University. The largest employer and taxpayer in the city, Yale's rapid growth during the late 20th and 21st century has helped make New Haven's economy largely reliant on the service sector, particularly education and health services. After Yale, the city's other largest employers include Yale-New Haven Hospital, Southern Connecticut State University, and Alexion Pharmaceuticals. Once an industrial center, New Haven has largely moved away from its manufacturing tradition, with the field accounting for less than 3 percent of the economy. In recent years, New Haven has become a burgeoning center for tech startups.

Culturally, New Haven is extraordinarily rich, largely thanks again to Yale University. Among the numerous world-class museums are the Beinecke Rare Book and Manuscript Library and the Yale University Art Gallery, both associated with Yale, and the New Haven Museum and Historical Society. The Yale Repertory Theater, the Long Wharf Theater, and the Shubert Theater are among the city's numerous venues for attending plays and other performances, while the city is served musically by the New Haven Symphony Orchestra which occasionally performs for free on the New Haven Green. The Yale School of Music also offers many free concerts to residents. New Haven is also a culinary hotspot, excelling in both fine dining and lowbrow treats, the latter embodied by its signature New Haven style pizza, served up in classic neighborhood joints like the legendary Pepe's.

New Haven experiences a temperate climate, marked by hot, humid summers and moderately cold winters. Average temperatures exceed 80 degrees Fahrenheit 70 days a year. In January, the average high is 37.8 degrees and the average low 22.2 degrees. Although extreme weather is rare, hurricanes have struck New Haven on several occasions.

Rankings

General Rankings

- In their seventh annual survey, Livability.com looked at data for more than 1,000 small to mid-sized U.S. cities to determine the rankings for Livability's "Top 100 Best Places to Live" in 2020. New Haven ranked #62. Criteria: housing and affordable living; vibrant economy; social and civic engagement; education; demographics; health care options; transportation & infrastructure; and abundant lifestyle amenities. *Livability.com, "Top 100 Best Places to Live 2020" October 2020*

Business/Finance Rankings

- The Brookings Institution ranked the nation's largest cities based on income inequality. New Haven was ranked #35 (#1 = greatest inequality). Criteria: the "95/20 ratio," a figure representing the income at which a household earns more than 95 percent of all other households, divided by the income at which a household earns more than only 20 percent of all other households. *Brookings Institution, "Household Income Inequality, Largest Cities of 97 Large U.S. Metro Areas, 2014-2016," February 5, 2018*

- The Brookings Institution ranked the 100 largest metro areas in the U.S. based on income inequality. New Haven was ranked #30 (#1 = greatest inequality). Criteria: the "95/20 ratio," a figure representing the income at which a household earns more than 95 percent of all other households, divided by the income at which a household earns more than only 20 percent of all other households. *Brookings Institution, "Household Income Inequality, 100 Largest U.S. Metro Areas, 2014-2016," February 5, 2018*

- The New Haven metro area appeared on the Milken Institute "2021 Best Performing Cities" list. Rank: #185 out of 200 large metro areas (population over 250,000). Criteria: job growth; wage and salary growth; high-tech output growth; housing affordability; household broadband access. *Milken Institute, "Best-Performing Cities 2021," February 16, 2021*

- *Forbes* ranked the 200 most populous metro areas to determine the nation's "Best Places for Business and Careers." The New Haven metro area was ranked #169. Criteria: costs (business and living); job growth (past and projected); income growth; quality of life; educational attainment (college and high school); projected economic growth; cultural and leisure opportunities; workplace tolerance laws; net migration patterns. *Forbes, "The Best Places for Business and Careers 2019: Seattle Still On Top," October 30, 2019*

Dating/Romance Rankings

- *Apartment List* conducted its annual survey of renters to for cities that have the best opportunities for dating. More than 11,000 single respondents rated their current city or neighborhood for opportunities to date. New Haven ranked #4 out of 86 where single residents were very satisfied or somewhat satisfied, making it among the ten worst areas for dating opportunities. Other criteria analyzed included gender and education levels of renters. *Apartment List, "The Best & Worst Metros for Dating 2020," February 4, 2020*

Education Rankings

- Personal finance website *WalletHub* analyzed the 150 largest U.S. metropolitan statistical areas to determine where the most educated Americans are putting their degrees to work. Criteria: education levels; percentage of workers with degrees; education quality and attainment gap; public school quality rankings; quality and enrollment of each metro area's universities. New Haven was ranked #45 (#1 = most educated city). *www.WalletHub.com, "Most and Least Educated Cities in America," July 20, 2020*

Health/Fitness Rankings

- New Haven was identified as a "2021 Spring Allergy Capital." The area ranked #11 out of 100. Three groups of factors were used to identify the most challenging cities for people with allergies during the spring season: annual spring pollen levels; over the counter medicine use; number of board-certified allergy specialists. *Asthma and Allergy Foundation of America, "Spring Allergy Capitals 2021," February 23, 2021*

- New Haven was identified as a "2021 Fall Allergy Capital." The area ranked #9 out of 100. Three groups of factors were used to identify the most challenging cities for people with allergies during the fall season: annual fall pollen levels; over the counter medicine use; number of board-certified allergy specialists. *Asthma and Allergy Foundation of America, "Fall Allergy Capitals 2021," February 23, 2021*

- New Haven was identified as a "2019 Asthma Capital." The area ranked #11 out of the nation's 100 largest metropolitan areas. Criteria: estimated asthma prevalence; crude death rate from asthma; and ER visits due to asthma. Risk factors analyzed but not factored in the rankings: annual pollen score; annual air quality; public smoking laws; number of board-certified asthma specialists; rescue medication use; controller medication use; uninsured rate; poverty rate. *Asthma and Allergy Foundation of America, "Asthma Capitals 2019: The Most Challenging Places to Live With Asthma," May 7, 2019*

Real Estate Rankings

- *WalletHub* compared the most populated U.S. cities to determine which had the best markets for real estate agents. New Haven ranked #154 where demand was high and pay was the best. Criteria: sales per agent; annual median wage for real-estate agents; monthly average starting salary for real estate agents; real estate job density and competition; unemployment rate; home turnover rate; housing-market health index; and other relevant metrics. *www.WalletHub.com, "2019's Best Places to Be a Real Estate Agent," April 24, 2019*

- New Haven was ranked #14 in the top 20 out of the 100 largest metro areas in terms of house price appreciation in 2020 (#1 = highest rate). *Federal Housing Finance Agency, House Price Index, 4th Quarter 2020*

- New Haven was ranked #108 out of 268 metro areas in terms of housing affordability in 2020 by the National Association of Home Builders (#1 = most affordable). Criteria: the share of homes sold in that area affordable to a family earning the local median income, based on standard mortgage underwriting criteria. *National Association of Home Builders®, NAHB-Wells Fargo Housing Opportunity Index, 4th Quarter 2020*

Safety Rankings

- To identify the most dangerous cities in America, 24/7 Wall Street focused on violent crime categories—murder, non-negligent manslaughter, rape, robbery, and aggravated assault—and property crime as reported in the FBI's 2019 annual Uniform Crime Report. Criteria also included median income from American Community Survey and unemployment figures from Bureau of Labor Statistics. For cities with populations over 100,000, New Haven was ranked #39. *247wallst.com, "America's 50 Most Dangerous Cities" November 16, 2020*

- New Haven was identified as one of the most dangerous cities in America by NeighborhoodScout. The city ranked #85 out of 100 (#1 = most dangerous). Criteria: number of violent crimes per 1,000 residents. The editors evaluated cities with 25,000 or more residents. *NeighborhoodScout.com, "2021 Top 100 Most Dangerous Cities in the U.S.," January 2, 2021*

- The National Insurance Crime Bureau ranked 384 metro areas in the U.S. in terms of per capita rates of vehicle theft. The New Haven metro area ranked #109 (#1 = highest rate). Criteria: number of vehicle theft offenses per 100,000 inhabitants in 2019. *National Insurance Crime Bureau, "Hot Spots 2019," July 21, 2020*

Seniors/Retirement Rankings

- From its Best Cities for Successful Aging indexes, the Milken Institute generated rankings for metropolitan areas, weighing data in nine categories—health care, wellness, living arrangements, transportation and convenience, financial characteristics, education, employment, community engagement, and overall livability. The New Haven metro area was ranked #78 overall in the large metro area category. *Milken Institute, "Best Cities for Successful Aging, 2017" March 14, 2017*

Transportation Rankings

- The business website 24/7 Wall Street reviewed U.S. Census data to identify the 25 cities where the largest share of households do not own a vehicle. New Haven held the #7 position. *247wallst.com, "Cities Where No One Wants to Drive," February 15, 2017*

Women/Minorities Rankings

- Personal finance website *WalletHub* compared more than 180 U.S. cities across two key dimensions, "Hispanic Business-Friendliness" and "Hispanic Purchasing Power," to arrive at the most favorable conditions for Hispanic entrepreneurs. New Haven was ranked #179 out of 182. Criteria includes: share of Hispanic-Owned Businesses; Hispanic entrepreneurship rate to median annual income of Hispanics; Small Business-Friendliness score; cost of living; and number of Hispanics with at least a bachelor's degree. *WalletHub.com, "2019's Best Cities for Hispanic Entrepreneurs," May 1, 2019*

Miscellaneous Rankings

- *WalletHub* compared the 150 most populated U.S. cities to determine their operating efficiency. A "Quality of City Services" score was constructed for each city and then divided by the total budget per capita to reveal which were managed the best. New Haven ranked #127. Criteria: financial stability; economy; education; safety; health; infrastructure and pollution. *www.WalletHub.com, "2020's Best- & Worst-Run Cities in America," June 29, 2020*

Business Environment

DEMOGRAPHICS

Population Growth

Area	1990 Census	2000 Census	2010 Census	2019* Estimate	Population Growth (%) 1990-2019	Population Growth (%) 2010-2019
City	130,474	123,626	129,779	130,331	-0.1	0.4
MSA[1]	804,219	824,008	862,477	857,513	6.6	-0.6
U.S.	248,709,873	281,421,906	308,745,538	324,697,795	30.6	5.2

Note: (1) Figures cover the New Haven-Milford, CT Metropolitan Statistical Area; (*) 2015-2019 5-year estimated population
Source: U.S. Census Bureau, 1990 Census, Census 2000, Census 2010, 2015-2019 American Community Survey 5-Year Estimates

Household Size

Area	Persons in Household (%) One	Two	Three	Four	Five	Six	Seven or More	Average Household Size
City	38.4	27.4	15.4	9.9	5.4	2.4	1.1	2.50
MSA[1]	31.2	33.0	16.2	12.3	4.8	1.7	0.8	2.50
U.S.	27.9	33.9	15.6	12.9	6.0	2.3	1.4	2.60

Note: (1) Figures cover the New Haven-Milford, CT Metropolitan Statistical Area
Source: U.S. Census Bureau, 2015-2019 American Community Survey 5-Year Estimates

Race

Area	White Alone[2] (%)	Black Alone[2] (%)	Asian Alone[2] (%)	AIAN[3] Alone[2] (%)	NHOPI[4] Alone[2] (%)	Other Race Alone[2] (%)	Two or More Races (%)
City	44.4	32.6	5.0	0.4	0.0	13.1	4.4
MSA[1]	73.3	13.5	4.0	0.2	0.0	5.7	3.3
U.S.	72.5	12.7	5.5	0.8	0.2	4.9	3.3

Note: (1) Figures cover the New Haven-Milford, CT Metropolitan Statistical Area; (2) Alone is defined as not being in combination with one or more other races; (3) American Indian and Alaska Native; (4) Native Hawaiian and Other Pacific Islander
Source: U.S. Census Bureau, 2015-2019 American Community Survey 5-Year Estimates

Hispanic or Latino Origin

Area	Total (%)	Mexican (%)	Puerto Rican (%)	Cuban (%)	Other (%)
City	31.2	5.6	17.6	0.3	7.7
MSA[1]	18.1	1.9	10.6	0.4	5.3
U.S.	18.0	11.2	1.7	0.7	4.3

Note: Persons of Hispanic or Latino origin can be of any race; (1) Figures cover the New Haven-Milford, CT Metropolitan Statistical Area
Source: U.S. Census Bureau, 2015-2019 American Community Survey 5-Year Estimates

Ancestry

Area	German	Irish	English	American	Italian	Polish	French[2]	Scottish	Dutch
City	4.1	6.5	3.2	1.1	7.7	2.1	1.3	0.6	0.5
MSA[1]	7.9	14.9	6.8	2.7	20.6	6.2	3.5	1.2	0.6
U.S.	13.3	9.7	7.2	6.2	5.1	2.8	2.3	1.7	1.2

Note: Figures are the percentage of the total population reporting a particular ancestry. The nine most commonly reported ancestries in the U.S. are shown. Figures include multiple ancestries (e.g. if a person reported being Irish and Italian, they were included in both columns); (1) Figures cover the New Haven-Milford, CT Metropolitan Statistical Area; (2) Excludes Basque
Source: U.S. Census Bureau, 2015-2019 American Community Survey 5-Year Estimates

Foreign-born Population

Area	Percent of Population Born in Any Foreign Country	Asia	Mexico	Europe	Caribbean	Central America[2]	South America	Africa	Canada
City	17.8	4.6	3.1	1.9	2.5	1.0	2.9	1.2	0.5
MSA[1]	12.7	3.3	1.0	2.8	1.9	0.5	1.9	0.9	0.3
U.S.	13.6	4.2	3.5	1.5	1.3	1.1	1.0	0.7	0.2

Note: (1) Figures cover the New Haven-Milford, CT Metropolitan Statistical Area; (2) Excludes Mexico.
Source: U.S. Census Bureau, 2015-2019 American Community Survey 5-Year Estimates

Marital Status

Area	Never Married	Now Married[2]	Separated	Widowed	Divorced
City	57.8	26.1	1.9	4.3	9.9
MSA[1]	37.9	43.6	1.3	6.2	10.9
U.S.	33.4	48.1	1.9	5.8	10.9

Note: Figures are percentages and cover the population 15 years of age and older; (1) Figures cover the New Haven-Milford, CT Metropolitan Statistical Area; (2) Excludes separated
Source: U.S. Census Bureau, 2015-2019 American Community Survey 5-Year Estimates

Disability by Age

Area	All Ages	Under 18 Years Old	18 to 64 Years Old	65 Years and Over
City	10.2	5.2	8.6	31.9
MSA[1]	11.6	4.0	8.8	31.5
U.S.	12.6	4.2	10.3	34.5

Note: Figures show percent of the civilian noninstitutionalized population that reported having a disability. Disability status is determined from six types of difficulty: vision, hearing, cognitive, ambulatory, self-care, and independent living. For children under 5 years old, hearing and vision difficulty are used to determine disability status. For children between the ages of 5 and 14, disability status is determined from hearing, vision, cognitive, ambulatory, and self-care difficulties. For people aged 15 years and older, they are considered to have a disability if they have difficulty with any one of the six difficulty types; Note: (1) Figures cover the New Haven-Milford, CT Metropolitan Statistical Area
Source: U.S. Census Bureau, 2015-2019 American Community Survey 5-Year Estimates

Age

Area	Percent of Population									Median Age
	Under Age 5	Age 5–19	Age 20–34	Age 35–44	Age 45–54	Age 55–64	Age 65–74	Age 75–84	Age 85+	
City	6.3	21.2	29.6	12.6	11.1	8.9	6.4	2.7	1.2	30.8
MSA[1]	5.2	18.2	20.2	11.8	13.7	13.8	9.5	4.9	2.6	40.3
U.S.	6.1	19.1	20.7	12.6	13.0	12.9	9.1	4.6	1.9	38.1

Note: (1) Figures cover the New Haven-Milford, CT Metropolitan Statistical Area
Source: U.S. Census Bureau, 2015-2019 American Community Survey 5-Year Estimates

Gender

Area	Males	Females	Males per 100 Females
City	61,926	68,405	90.5
MSA[1]	413,519	443,994	93.1
U.S.	159,886,919	164,810,876	97.0

Note: (1) Figures cover the New Haven-Milford, CT Metropolitan Statistical Area
Source: U.S. Census Bureau, 2015-2019 American Community Survey 5-Year Estimates

Religious Groups by Family

Area	Catholic	Baptist	Non-Den.	Methodist[2]	Lutheran	LDS[3]	Pentecostal	Presbyterian[4]	Muslim[5]	Judaism
MSA[1]	35.3	1.5	2.0	1.5	0.7	0.3	1.0	2.3	0.5	1.3
U.S.	19.1	9.3	4.0	4.0	2.3	2.0	1.9	1.6	0.8	0.7

Note: Figures are the number of adherents as a percentage of the total population; (1) Figures cover the New Haven-Milford, CT Metropolitan Statistical Area; (2) Methodist/Pietist; (3) Latter Day Saints; (4) Reformed; (5) Figures are estimates
Source: Association of Statisticians of American Religious Bodies, 2010 U.S. Religion Census: Religious Congregations & Membership Study

Religious Groups by Tradition

Area	Catholic	Evangelical Protestant	Mainline Protestant	Other Tradition	Black Protestant	Orthodox
MSA[1]	35.3	3.9	6.1	2.3	0.8	0.4
U.S.	19.1	16.2	7.3	4.3	1.6	0.3

Note: Figures are the number of adherents as a percentage of the total population; (1) Figures cover the New Haven-Milford, CT Metropolitan Statistical Area
Source: Association of Statisticians of American Religious Bodies, 2010 U.S. Religion Census: Religious Congregations & Membership Study

ECONOMY

Gross Metropolitan Product

Area	2017	2018	2019	2020	Rank[2]
MSA[1]	46.1	47.8	49.7	51.2	62

Note: Figures are in billions of dollars; (1) Figures cover the New Haven-Milford, CT Metropolitan Statistical Area; (2) Rank is based on 2018 data and ranges from 1 to 381
Source: U.S. Conference of Mayors, U.S. Metro Economies: GMP & Employment 2018-2020, September 2019

Economic Growth

Area	2015-17 (%)	2018 (%)	2019 (%)	2020 (%)	Rank[2]
MSA[1]	1.2	1.7	2.1	0.9	204
U.S.	1.9	2.9	2.3	2.1	—

Note: Figures are real gross metropolitan product (GMP) growth rates and represent average annual percent change; (1) Figures cover the New Haven-Milford, CT Metropolitan Statistical Area; (2) Rank is based on 2017 2-year average annual percent change and ranges from 1 to 381
Source: U.S. Conference of Mayors, U.S. Metro Economies: GMP & Employment 2018-2020, September 2019

Metropolitan Area Exports

Area	2014	2015	2016	2017	2018	2019	Rank[2]
MSA[1]	1,834.5	1,756.3	1,819.8	1,876.3	2,082.3	2,133.8	98

Note: Figures are in millions of dollars; (1) Figures cover the New Haven-Milford, CT Metropolitan Statistical Area; (2) Rank is based on 2019 data and ranges from 1 to 386
Source: U.S. Department of Commerce, International Trade Administration, Office of Trade and Economic Analysis, Industry and Analysis, Exports by Metropolitan Area, data extracted March 24, 2021

Building Permits

Area	Single-Family			Multi-Family			Total		
	2018	2019	Pct. Chg.	2018	2019	Pct. Chg.	2018	2019	Pct. Chg.
City	4	4	0.0	456	695	52.4	460	699	52.0
MSA[1]	406	399	-1.7	760	1,054	38.7	1,166	1,453	24.6
U.S.	855,300	862,100	0.7	473,500	523,900	10.6	1,328,800	1,386,000	4.3

Note: (1) Figures cover the New Haven-Milford, CT Metropolitan Statistical Area; Figures represent new, privately-owned housing units authorized (unadjusted data); All permit data are based on estimates with imputation
Source: U.S. Census Bureau, Manufacturing, Mining, and Construction Statistics, Building Permits, 2018, 2019

Bankruptcy Filings

Area	Business Filings			Nonbusiness Filings		
	2019	2020	% Chg.	2019	2020	% Chg.
New Haven County	47	33	-29.8	1,884	1,258	-33.2
U.S.	22,780	21,655	-4.9	752,160	522,808	-30.5

Note: Business filings include Chapter 7, Chapter 9, Chapter 11, Chapter 12, Chapter 13, Chapter 15, and Section 304; Nonbusiness filings include Chapter 7, Chapter 11, and Chapter 13
Source: Administrative Office of the U.S. Courts, Business and Nonbusiness Bankruptcy, County Cases Commenced by Chapter of the Bankruptcy Code, During the 12-Month Period Ending December 31, 2019 and Business and Nonbusiness Bankruptcy, County Cases Commenced by Chapter of the Bankruptcy Code, During the 12-Month Period Ending December 31, 2020

Housing Vacancy Rates

Area	Gross Vacancy Rate[2] (%)			Year-Round Vacancy Rate[3] (%)			Rental Vacancy Rate[4] (%)			Homeowner Vacancy Rate[5] (%)		
	2018	2019	2020	2018	2019	2020	2018	2019	2020	2018	2019	2020
MSA[1]	10.9	11.9	9.4	10.0	11.1	8.4	5.6	8.3	7.8	1.4	1.5	0.2
U.S.	12.3	12.0	10.6	9.7	9.5	8.2	6.9	6.7	6.3	1.5	1.4	1.0

Note: (1) Figures cover the New Haven-Milford, CT Metropolitan Statistical Area; (2) The percentage of the total housing inventory that is vacant; (3) The percentage of the housing inventory (excluding seasonal units) that is year-round vacant; (4) The percentage of rental inventory that is vacant for rent; (5) The percentage of homeowner inventory that is vacant for sale
Source: U.S. Census Bureau, Housing Vacancies and Homeownership Annual Statistics: 2018, 2019, 2020

INCOME

Income

Area	Per Capita ($)	Median Household ($)	Average Household ($)
City	26,429	42,222	65,362
MSA[1]	38,009	69,905	94,740
U.S.	34,103	62,843	88,607

Note: (1) Figures cover the New Haven-Milford, CT Metropolitan Statistical Area
Source: U.S. Census Bureau, 2015-2019 American Community Survey 5-Year Estimates

Household Income Distribution

Area	Percent of Households Earning							
	Under $15,000	$15,000 -$24,999	$25,000 -$34,999	$35,000 -$49,999	$50,000 -$74,999	$75,000 -$99,999	$100,000 -$149,999	$150,000 and up
City	20.2	11.9	11.1	12.5	15.8	9.6	9.7	9.4
MSA[1]	10.0	8.2	7.6	11.1	16.2	12.5	16.5	17.9
U.S.	10.3	8.9	8.9	12.3	17.2	12.7	15.1	14.5

Note: (1) Figures cover the New Haven-Milford, CT Metropolitan Statistical Area
Source: U.S. Census Bureau, 2015-2019 American Community Survey 5-Year Estimates

Poverty Rate

Area	All Ages	Under 18 Years Old	18 to 64 Years Old	65 Years and Over
City	26.5	36.2	24.7	16.3
MSA[1]	11.7	17.3	11.0	7.6
U.S.	13.4	18.5	12.6	9.3

Note: Figures are percentage of people whose income during the past 12 months was below the poverty level;
(1) Figures cover the New Haven-Milford, CT Metropolitan Statistical Area
Source: U.S. Census Bureau, 2015-2019 American Community Survey 5-Year Estimates

CITY FINANCES

City Government Finances

Component	2017 ($000)	2017 ($ per capita)
Total Revenues	920,312	7,062
Total Expenditures	942,679	7,233
Debt Outstanding	604,976	4,642
Cash and Securities[1]	660,535	5,068

Note: (1) Cash and security holdings of a government at the close of its fiscal year,
including those of its dependent agencies, utilities, and liquor stores.
Source: U.S. Census Bureau, State & Local Government Finances 2017

City Government Revenue by Source

Source	2017 ($000)	2017 ($ per capita)	2017 (%)
General Revenue			
From Federal Government	37,367	287	4.1
From State Government	464,749	3,566	50.5
From Local Governments	4,194	32	0.5
Taxes			
Property	252,390	1,937	27.4
Sales and Gross Receipts	0	0	0.0
Personal Income	0	0	0.0
Corporate Income	0	0	0.0
Motor Vehicle License	0	0	0.0
Other Taxes	15,526	119	1.7
Current Charges	51,051	392	5.5
Liquor Store	0	0	0.0
Utility	0	0	0.0
Employee Retirement	74,279	570	8.1

Source: U.S. Census Bureau, State & Local Government Finances 2017

City Government Expenditures by Function

Function	2017 ($000)	2017 ($ per capita)	2017 (%)
General Direct Expenditures			
Air Transportation	0	0	0.0
Corrections	0	0	0.0
Education	423,501	3,249	44.9
Employment Security Administration	0	0	0.0
Financial Administration	8,091	62	0.9
Fire Protection	31,813	244	3.4
General Public Buildings	0	0	0.0
Governmental Administration, Other	15,520	119	1.6
Health	3,562	27	0.4
Highways	21,235	162	2.3
Hospitals	0	0	0.0
Housing and Community Development	11,456	87	1.2
Interest on General Debt	23,446	179	2.5
Judicial and Legal	2,007	15	0.2
Libraries	4,113	31	0.4
Parking	23,339	179	2.5
Parks and Recreation	5,891	45	0.6
Police Protection	41,376	317	4.4
Public Welfare	0	0	0.0
Sewerage	0	0	0.0
Solid Waste Management	7,165	55	0.8
Veterans' Services	0	0	0.0
Liquor Store	0	0	0.0
Utility	0	0	0.0
Employee Retirement	70,514	541	7.5

Source: U.S. Census Bureau, State & Local Government Finances 2017

EMPLOYMENT

Labor Force and Employment

Area	Civilian Labor Force			Workers Employed		
	Dec. 2019	Dec. 2020	% Chg.	Dec. 2019	Dec. 2020	% Chg.
City	65,459	65,774	0.5	63,121	59,553	-5.7
NECTA[1]	331,537	326,637	-1.5	321,457	303,291	-5.7
U.S.	164,007,000	160,017,000	-2.4	158,504,000	149,613,000	-5.6

Note: Data is not seasonally adjusted and covers workers 16 years of age and older; (1) Figures cover the New Haven, CT New England City and Town Area
Source: Bureau of Labor Statistics, Local Area Unemployment Statistics

Unemployment Rate

Area	2020											
	Jan.	Feb.	Mar.	Apr.	May	Jun.	Jul.	Aug.	Sep.	Oct.	Nov.	Dec.
City	4.9	4.8	4.0	7.0	8.8	10.6	11.8	9.7	9.1	7.5	10.0	9.5
NECTA[1]	4.2	4.1	3.4	7.2	8.5	9.3	9.7	7.7	7.1	5.5	7.4	7.1
U.S.	4.0	3.8	4.5	14.4	13.0	11.2	10.5	8.5	7.7	6.6	6.4	6.5

Note: Data is not seasonally adjusted and covers workers 16 years of age and older; (1) Figures cover the New Haven, CT New England City and Town Area
Source: Bureau of Labor Statistics, Local Area Unemployment Statistics

Average Wages

Occupation	$/Hr.	Occupation	$/Hr.
Accountants and Auditors	40.00	Maintenance and Repair Workers	24.80
Automotive Mechanics	23.80	Marketing Managers	62.80
Bookkeepers	23.80	Network and Computer Systems Admin.	46.00
Carpenters	29.30	Nurses, Licensed Practical	27.80
Cashiers	12.80	Nurses, Registered	41.60
Computer Programmers	47.30	Nursing Assistants	17.50
Computer Systems Analysts	46.10	Office Clerks, General	19.50
Computer User Support Specialists	28.50	Physical Therapists	49.00
Construction Laborers	22.10	Physicians	109.60
Cooks, Restaurant	15.50	Plumbers, Pipefitters and Steamfitters	38.00
Customer Service Representatives	20.30	Police and Sheriff's Patrol Officers	36.20
Dentists	120.40	Postal Service Mail Carriers	25.60
Electricians	34.70	Real Estate Sales Agents	n/a
Engineers, Electrical	50.30	Retail Salespersons	15.80
Fast Food and Counter Workers	13.20	Sales Representatives, Technical/Scientific	51.90
Financial Managers	67.40	Secretaries, Exc. Legal/Medical/Executive	23.40
First-Line Supervisors of Office Workers	33.60	Security Guards	16.80
General and Operations Managers	71.10	Surgeons	n/a
Hairdressers/Cosmetologists	15.80	Teacher Assistants, Exc. Postsecondary*	15.40
Home Health and Personal Care Aides	14.00	Teachers, Secondary School, Exc. Sp. Ed.*	37.70
Janitors and Cleaners	17.90	Telemarketers	18.00
Landscaping/Groundskeeping Workers	21.10	Truck Drivers, Heavy/Tractor-Trailer	24.70
Lawyers	73.00	Truck Drivers, Light/Delivery Services	19.10
Maids and Housekeeping Cleaners	14.40	Waiters and Waitresses	13.90

Note: Wage data covers the New Haven, CT New England City and Town Area; (*) Hourly wages were calculated from annual wage data based on a 40 hour work week; n/a not available.
Source: Bureau of Labor Statistics, Metro Area Occupational Employment & Wage Estimates, May 2020

Employment by Industry

Sector	NECTA[1]		U.S.
	Number of Employees	Percent of Total	Percent of Total
Construction, Mining, and Logging	10,200	3.6	5.5
Education and Health Services	81,200	28.5	16.3
Financial Activities	11,600	4.1	6.1
Government	36,500	12.8	15.2
Information	3,700	1.3	1.9
Leisure and Hospitality	18,800	6.6	9.0
Manufacturing	23,400	8.2	8.5
Other Services	10,000	3.5	3.8
Professional and Business Services	31,100	10.9	14.4
Retail Trade	27,600	9.7	10.9
Transportation, Warehousing, and Utilities	20,300	7.1	4.6
Wholesale Trade	10,900	3.8	3.9

Note: Figures are non-farm employment as of December 2020. Figures are not seasonally adjusted and include workers 16 years of age and older; (1) Figures cover the New Haven, CT New England City and Town Area
Source: Bureau of Labor Statistics, Current Employment Statistics, Employment, Hours, and Earnings

Employment by Occupation

Occupation Classification	City (%)	MSA[1] (%)	U.S. (%)
Management, Business, Science, and Arts	39.1	42.3	38.5
Natural Resources, Construction, and Maintenance	6.4	7.3	8.9
Production, Transportation, and Material Moving	12.3	11.2	13.2
Sales and Office	17.4	21.6	21.6
Service	24.8	17.6	17.8

Note: Figures cover employed civilians 16 years of age and older; (1) Figures cover the New Haven-Milford, CT Metropolitan Statistical Area
Source: U.S. Census Bureau, 2015-2019 American Community Survey 5-Year Estimates

Occupations with Greatest Projected Employment Growth: 2020 – 2022

Occupation[1]	2020 Employment	2022 Projected Employment	Numeric Employment Change	Percent Employment Change
Waiters and Waitresses	16,820	31,440	14,620	86.9
Fast Food and Counter Workers	19,280	33,430	14,150	73.4
Retail Salespersons	27,890	35,800	7,910	28.4
Cooks, Restaurant	7,040	13,830	6,790	96.4
Childcare Workers	9,540	16,130	6,590	69.1
Maids and Housekeeping Cleaners	6,890	12,760	5,870	85.2
Passenger Vehicle Drivers, Except Bus Drivers, Transit and Intercity	9,320	14,620	5,300	56.9
Laborers and Freight, Stock, and Material Movers, Hand	27,090	31,880	4,790	17.7
Janitors and Cleaners, Except Maids and Housekeeping Cleaners	28,790	32,540	3,750	13.0
Food Preparation Workers	8,920	12,630	3,710	41.6

Note: Projections cover Connecticut; (1) Sorted by numeric employment change
Source: www.projectionscentral.com, State Occupational Projections, 2020–2022 Short-Term Projections

Fastest-Growing Occupations: 2020 – 2022

Occupation[1]	2020 Employment	2022 Projected Employment	Numeric Employment Change	Percent Employment Change
Gaming Service Workers, All Other	50	140	90	180.0
Gaming Dealers	850	2,210	1,360	160.0
Hotel, Motel, and Resort Desk Clerks	540	1,310	770	142.6
Locker Room, Coatroom, and Dressing Room Attendants	100	230	130	130.0
Funeral Attendants	460	1,010	550	119.6
Morticians, Undertakers, and Funeral Directors	290	620	330	113.8
Pressers, Textile, Garment, and Related Materials	380	800	420	110.5
Agents and Business Managers of Artists, Performers, and Athletes	120	240	120	100.0
Shampooers	50	100	50	100.0
Baggage Porters and Bellhops	80	160	80	100.0

Note: Projections cover Connecticut; (1) Sorted by percent employment change and excludes occupations with numeric employment change less than 50
Source: www.projectionscentral.com, State Occupational Projections, 2020–2022 Short-Term Projections

TAXES

State Corporate Income Tax Rates

State	Tax Rate (%)	Income Brackets ($)	Num. of Brackets	Financial Institution Tax Rate (%)[a]	Federal Income Tax Ded.
Connecticut	7.5 (c)	Flat rate	1	7.5 (c)	No

Note: Tax rates as of January 1, 2021; (a) Rates listed are the corporate income tax rate applied to financial institutions or excise taxes based on income. Some states have other taxes based upon the value of deposits or shares; (c) Connecticut's tax is the greater of the 7.5% tax on net income, a 0.26% tax on capital stock and surplus (maximum tax of $1 million), or $250 (the minimum tax).
Source: Federation of Tax Administrators, State Corporate Income Tax Rates, January 1, 2021

State Individual Income Tax Rates

State	Tax Rate (%)	Income Brackets ($)	Personal Exemptions ($)			Standard Ded. ($)	
			Single	Married	Depend.	Single	Married
Connecticut	3.0 - 6.99	10,000 - 500,000 (b)	15,000	24,000 (h)	0	(h)	(h)

Note: Tax rates as of January 1, 2021; Local- and county-level taxes are not included; Federal income tax is not deductible on state income tax returns; (b) For joint returns, taxes are twice the tax on half the couple's income; (h) Connecticut's personal exemption incorporates a standard deduction. An additional tax credit is allowed ranging from 75% to 0% based on state adjusted gross income. Exemption amounts and 3% rate are phased out for higher income taxpayers until they are eliminated for households earning over $78,500.
Source: Federation of Tax Administrators, State Individual Income Tax Rates, January 1, 2021

Various State Sales and Excise Tax Rates

State	State Sales Tax (%)	Gasoline[1] (¢/gal.)	Cigarette[2] ($/pack)	Spirits[3] ($/gal.)	Wine[4] ($/gal.)	Beer[5] ($/gal.)	Recreational Marijuana (%)
Connecticut	6.35	35.75	4.35	5.94	0.792	0.23	Not legal

Note: All tax rates as of January 1, 2021; (1) The American Petroleum Institute has developed a methodology for determining the average tax rate on a gallon of fuel. Rates may include any of the following: excise taxes, environmental fees, storage tank fees, other fees or taxes, general sales tax, and local taxes; (2) The federal excise tax of $1.0066 per pack and local taxes are not included; (3) Rates are those applicable to off-premise sales of 40% alcohol by volume (a.b.v.) distilled spirits in 750ml containers. Local excise taxes are excluded; (4) Rates are those applicable to off-premise sales of 11% a.b.v. non-carbonated wine in 750ml containers; (5) Rates are those applicable to off-premise sales of 4.7% a.b.v. beer in 12 ounce containers.
Source: Tax Foundation, 2021 Facts & Figures: How Does Your State Compare?

State Business Tax Climate Index Rankings

State	Overall Rank	Corporate Tax Rank	Individual Income Tax Rank	Sales Tax Rank	Property Tax Rank	Unemployment Insurance Tax Rank
Connecticut	47	27	44	26	50	22

Note: The index is a measure of how each state's tax laws affect economic performance. The lower the rank, the more favorable a state's tax system is for business. States without a given tax are given a ranking of 1. The scores/rankings for the District of Columbia do not affect other states. The 2021 index represents the tax climate as of July 1, 2020.
Source: Tax Foundation, State Business Tax Climate Index 2021

TRANSPORTATION

Means of Transportation to Work

Area	Car/Truck/Van		Public Transportation			Bicycle	Walked	Other Means	Worked at Home
	Drove Alone	Car-pooled	Bus	Subway	Railroad				
City	58.7	9.1	10.5	0.1	1.1	3.1	11.4	1.2	4.7
MSA[1]	78.3	8.4	2.8	0.1	0.9	0.5	3.3	1.0	4.7
U.S.	76.3	9.0	2.4	1.9	0.6	0.5	2.7	1.4	5.2

Note: Figures are percentages and cover workers 16 years of age and older; (1) Figures cover the New Haven-Milford, CT Metropolitan Statistical Area
Source: U.S. Census Bureau, 2015-2019 American Community Survey 5-Year Estimates

Travel Time to Work

Area	Less Than 10 Minutes	10 to 19 Minutes	20 to 29 Minutes	30 to 44 Minutes	45 to 59 Minutes	60 to 89 Minutes	90 Minutes or More
City	13.6	40.4	20.1	13.1	4.7	4.7	3.4
MSA[1]	11.5	31.8	22.9	19.5	6.6	4.8	2.9
U.S.	12.2	28.4	20.8	20.8	8.3	6.4	2.9

Note: Note: Figures are percentages and include workers 16 years old and over; (1) Figures cover the New Haven-Milford, CT Metropolitan Statistical Area
Source: U.S. Census Bureau, 2015-2019 American Community Survey 5-Year Estimates

Key Congestion Measures

Measure	1982	1992	2002	2012	2017
Annual Hours of Delay, Total (000)	2,050	5,928	11,840	13,778	15,574
Annual Hours of Delay, Per Auto Commuter	10	25	37	42	45
Annual Congestion Cost, Total (million $)	16	63	161	250	289
Annual Congestion Cost, Per Auto Commuter ($)	227	451	702	640	701

Note: Covers the New Haven CT urban area
Source: Texas A&M Transportation Institute, 2019 Urban Mobility Report

Freeway Travel Time Index

Measure	1982	1987	1992	1997	2002	2007	2012	2017
Urban Area Index[1]	1.04	1.08	1.10	1.14	1.16	1.17	1.16	1.16
Urban Area Rank[1,2]	61	44	59	47	54	56	60	61

Note: Freeway Travel Time Index—the ratio of travel time in the peak period to the travel time at free-flow conditions. For example, a value of 1.30 indicates a 20-minute free-flow trip takes 26 minutes in the peak (20 minutes x 1.30 = 26 minutes); (1) Covers the New Haven CT urban area; (2) Rank is based on 101 larger urban areas (#1 = highest travel time index)
Source: Texas A&M Transportation Institute, 2019 Urban Mobility Report

Public Transportation

Agency Name / Mode of Transportation	Vehicles Operated in Maximum Service[1]	Annual Unlinked Passenger Trips[2] (in thous.)	Annual Passenger Miles[3] (in thous.)
CTTRANSIT New Haven Division			
Bus (directly operated)	98	7,567.6	25,128.8
The Greater New Haven Transit District			
Demand Response (directly operated)	53	232.3	1,770.8

Note: (1) Number of revenue vehicles operated by the given mode and type of service to meet the annual maximum service requirement. This is the revenue vehicle count during the peak season of the year; on the week and day that maximum service is provided. Vehicles operated in maximum service (VOMS) exclude atypical days and one-time special events; (2) Number of passengers who boarded public transportation vehicles. Passengers are counted each time they board a vehicle no matter how many vehicles they use to travel from their origin to their destination. (3) Sum of the distances ridden by all passengers during the entire fiscal year.
Source: Federal Transit Administration, National Transit Database, 2019

Air Transportation

Airport Name and Code / Type of Service	Passenger Airlines[1]	Passenger Enplanements	Freight Carriers[2]	Freight (lbs)
Bradley International Airport (BDL)				
Domestic service (U.S. carriers - 2020)	23	1,139,615	15	158,968,008
International service (U.S. carriers - 2019)	3	3,443	1	6,810
Tweed New Haven Airport (HVN)				
Domestic service (U.S. carriers - 2020)	5	11,419	0	0
International service (U.S. carriers - 2019)	1	6	0	0

Note: (1) Includes all U.S.-based major, minor and commuter airlines that carried at least one passenger during the year; (2) Includes all U.S.-based airlines and freight carriers that transported at least one pound of freight during the year.
Source: Bureau of Transportation Statistics, The Intermodal Transportation Database, Air Carriers: T-100 Domestic Market (U.S. Carriers), 2020; Bureau of Transportation Statistics, The Intermodal Transportation Database, Air Carriers: T-100 International Market (U.S. Carriers), 2019

BUSINESSES

Major Business Headquarters

Company Name	Industry	Rankings	
		Fortune[1]	Forbes[2]
No companies listed	-	-	-

Note: (1) Companies that produce a 10-K are ranked 1 to 500 based on 2019 revenue; (2) All private companies with at least $2 billion in annual revenue through the end of their most current fiscal year are ranked 1 to 219; companies listed are headquartered in the city; dashes indicate no ranking
Source: Fortune, "Fortune 500," June/July 2020; Forbes, "America's Largest Private Companies," 2020

Fastest-Growing Businesses

According to Deloitte, New Haven is home to one of North America's 500 fastest-growing high-technology companies: **Arvinas, Inc.** (#216). Companies are ranked by percentage growth in revenue over a four-year period. Criteria for inclusion: company must be headquartered within North America; must own proprietary intellectual property or technology that is sold to customers in products that contributes to a significant portion of the company's operating revenue; must have been in business for a minumum of four years with 2016 operating revenues of at least $50,000 USD/CD and 2019 operating revenues of at least $5 million USD/CD. *Deloitte, 2020 Technology Fast 500*[TM]

Living Environment

COST OF LIVING

Cost of Living Index

Composite Index	Groceries	Housing	Utilities	Trans-portation	Health Care	Misc. Goods/ Services
119.5	105.7	126.3	144.9	106.6	109.7	117.4

Note: The Cost of Living Index measures regional differences in the cost of consumer goods and services, excluding taxes and non-consumer expenditures, for professional and managerial households in the top income quintile. It is based on more than 50,000 prices covering almost 60 different items for which prices are collected three times a year by chambers of commerce, economic development organizations or university applied economic centers in each participating urban area. The numbers shown should be read as a percentage above or below the national average of 100. For example, a value of 115.4 in the groceries column indicates that grocery prices are 15.4% higher than the national average. Small differences in the index numbers should not be interpreted as significant; Figures cover the New Haven CT urban area.
Source: The Council for Community and Economic Research, Cost of Living Index, 2020

Grocery Prices

Area[1]	T-Bone Steak ($/pound)	Frying Chicken ($/pound)	Whole Milk ($/half gal.)	Eggs ($/dozen)	Orange Juice ($/64 oz.)	Coffee ($/11.5 oz.)
City[2]	10.42	1.51	2.52	1.73	3.32	4.03
Avg.	11.78	1.39	2.05	1.47	3.57	4.34
Min.	8.03	0.94	1.03	0.74	2.94	3.02
Max.	15.86	2.65	4.31	3.77	5.44	8.69

*Note: (1) Values for the local area are compared with the average, minimum and maximum values for all 284 areas in the Cost of Living Index; (2) Figures cover the New Haven CT urban area; **T-Bone Steak** (price per pound); **Frying Chicken** (price per pound, whole fryer); **Whole Milk** (half gallon carton); **Eggs** (price per dozen, Grade A, large); **Orange Juice** (64 oz. Tropicana or Florida Natural); **Coffee** (11.5 oz. can, vacuum-packed, Maxwell House, Hills Bros, or Folgers).*
Source: The Council for Community and Economic Research, Cost of Living Index, 2020

Housing and Utility Costs

Area[1]	New Home Price ($)	Apartment Rent ($/month)	All Electric ($/month)	Part Electric ($/month)	Other Energy ($/month)	Telephone ($/month)
City[2]	393,588	1,995	-	170.80	131.69	178.60
Avg.	368,594	1,168	170.86	100.47	65.28	184.30
Min.	190,567	502	91.58	31.42	26.08	169.60
Max.	2,227,806	4,738	470.38	280.31	280.06	206.50

*Note: (1) Values for the local area are compared with the average, minimum and maximum values for all 284 areas in the Cost of Living Index; (2) Figures cover the New Haven CT urban area; **New Home Price** (2,400 sf living area, 8,000 sf lot, in urban area with full utilities); **Apartment Rent** (950 sf 2 bedroom/1.5 or 2 bath, unfurnished, excluding all utilities except water); **All Electric** (average monthly cost for an all-electric home); **Part Electric** (average monthly cost for a part-electric home); **Other Energy** (average monthly cost for natural gas, fuel oil, coal, wood, and any other forms of energy except electricity); **Telephone** (price includes the base monthly rate plus taxes and fees for three lines of mobile phone service).*
Source: The Council for Community and Economic Research, Cost of Living Index, 2020

Health Care, Transportation, and Other Costs

Area[1]	Doctor ($/visit)	Dentist ($/visit)	Optometrist ($/visit)	Gasoline ($/gallon)	Beauty Salon ($/visit)	Men's Shirt ($)
City[2]	130.27	107.76	112.13	2.30	47.72	35.60
Avg.	115.44	99.32	108.10	2.21	39.27	31.37
Min.	36.68	59.00	51.36	1.71	19.00	11.00
Max.	219.00	153.10	250.97	3.46	82.05	58.33

*Note: (1) Values for the local area are compared with the average, minimum and maximum values for all 284 areas in the Cost of Living Index; (2) Figures cover the New Haven CT urban area; **Doctor** (general practitioners routine exam of an established patient); **Dentist** (adult teeth cleaning and periodic oral examination); **Optometrist** (full vision eye exam for established adult patient); **Gasoline** (one gallon regular unleaded, national brand, including all taxes, cash price at self-service pump if available); **Beauty Salon** (woman's shampoo, trim, and blow-dry); **Men's Shirt** (cotton/polyester dress shirt, pinpoint weave, long sleeves).*
Source: The Council for Community and Economic Research, Cost of Living Index, 2020

HOUSING

Homeownership Rate

Area	2012 (%)	2013 (%)	2014 (%)	2015 (%)	2016 (%)	2017 (%)	2018 (%)	2019 (%)	2020 (%)
MSA[1]	62.2	62.0	62.4	64.6	59.4	58.7	65.0	65.1	63.4
U.S.	65.4	65.1	64.5	63.7	63.4	63.9	64.4	64.6	66.6

Note: (1) Figures cover the New Haven-Milford, CT Metropolitan Statistical Area
Source: U.S. Census Bureau, Housing Vacancies and Homeownership Annual Statistics: 2012-2020

House Price Index (HPI)

Area	National Ranking[2]	Quarterly Change (%)	One-Year Change (%)	Five-Year Change (%)	Since 1991Q1 (%)
MSA[1]	99	2.80	6.78	15.33	80.58
U.S.[3]	–	3.81	10.77	38.99	205.12

Note: The HPI is a weighted repeat sales index. It measures average price changes in repeat sales or refinancings on the same properties. This information is obtained by reviewing repeat mortgage transactions on single-family properties whose mortgages have been purchased or securitized by Fannie Mae or Freddie Mac since January 1975; (1) Figures cover the New Haven-Milford, CT Metropolitan Statistical Area; (2) Rankings are based on annual percentage change for all metro areas containing at least 15,000 transactions over the last 10 years and ranges from 1 to 253; (3) figures based on a weighted average of Census Division estimates using a seasonally adjusted, purchase-only index; all figures are for the period ending December 31, 2020
Source: Federal Housing Finance Agency, Change in Metropolitan Area House Price Indexes, April 7, 2021

Median Single-Family Home Prices

Area	2018	2019	2020p	Percent Change 2019 to 2020
MSA[1]	232.9	237.4	265.9	12.0
U.S. Average	261.6	274.6	299.9	9.2

Note: Figures are median sales prices of existing single-family homes in thousands of dollars; (p) preliminary; (1) Figures cover the New Haven-Milford, CT Metropolitan Statistical Area
Source: National Association of Realtors, Median Sales Price of Existing Single-Family Homes for Metropolitan Areas, 4th Quarter 2020

Qualifying Income Based on Median Sales Price of Existing Single-Family Homes

Area	With 5% Down ($)	With 10% Down ($)	With 20% Down ($)
MSA[1]	51,995	49,259	43,785
U.S. Average	59,266	56,147	49,908

Note: Figures are preliminary; Qualifying income is based on a mortgage rate of 2.81%. Monthly principal and interest payment is limited to 25% of income; (1) Figures cover the New Haven-Milford, CT Metropolitan Statistical Area
Source: National Association of Realtors, Qualifying Income Based on Median Sales Price of Existing Single-Family Homes for Metropolitan Areas, 4th Quarter 2020

Home Value Distribution

Area	Under $50,000	$50,000 -$99,999	$100,000 -$149,999	$150,000 -$199,999	$200,000 -$299,999	$300,000 -$499,999	$500,000 -$999,999	$1,000,000 or more
City	2.7	7.9	14.1	25.8	28.0	14.9	6.0	0.7
MSA[1]	2.0	4.9	10.6	17.0	29.8	26.8	7.6	1.2
U.S.	6.9	12.0	13.3	14.0	19.6	19.3	11.4	3.4

Note: Figures are percentages and cover owner-occupied housing units; (1) Figures cover the New Haven-Milford, CT Metropolitan Statistical Area
Source: U.S. Census Bureau, 2015-2019 American Community Survey 5-Year Estimates

Year Housing Structure Built

Area	2010 or Later	2000 -2009	1990 -1999	1980 -1989	1970 -1979	1960 -1969	1950 -1959	1940 -1949	Before 1940	Median Year
City	3.1	4.8	2.6	7.1	8.0	9.7	9.4	7.5	47.7	1943
MSA[1]	1.8	5.6	7.1	12.3	13.3	12.3	15.2	7.1	25.2	1962
U.S.	5.2	14.0	13.9	13.4	15.2	10.6	10.3	4.9	12.6	1978

Note: Figures are percentages except for Median Year; Note: (1) Figures cover the New Haven-Milford, CT Metropolitan Statistical Area
Source: U.S. Census Bureau, 2015-2019 American Community Survey 5-Year Estimates

Gross Monthly Rent

Area	Under $500	$500 -$999	$1,000 -$1,499	$1,500 -$1,999	$2,000 -$2,499	$2,500 -$2,999	$3,000 and up	Median ($)
City	13.3	18.7	41.2	19.5	5.1	1.5	0.8	1,196
MSA[1]	10.4	24.6	41.3	17.0	4.6	1.2	1.0	1,153
U.S.	9.4	36.2	30.0	14.0	5.6	2.4	2.4	1,062

Note: Figures are percentages except for Median; Gross rent is the contract rent plus the estimated average monthly cost of utilities (electricity, gas, and water and sewer) and fuels (oil, coal, kerosene, wood, etc.) if these are paid by the renter (or paid for the renter by someone else); (1) Figures cover the New Haven-Milford, CT Metropolitan Statistical Area
Source: U.S. Census Bureau, 2015-2019 American Community Survey 5-Year Estimates

HEALTH

Health Risk Factors

Category	MSA[1] (%)	U.S. (%)
Adults aged 18–64 who have any kind of health care coverage	n/a	87.3
Adults who reported being in good or better health	n/a	82.4
Adults who have been told they have high blood cholesterol	n/a	33.0
Adults who have been told they have high blood pressure	n/a	32.3
Adults who are current smokers	n/a	17.1
Adults who currently use E-cigarettes	n/a	4.6
Adults who currently use chewing tobacco, snuff, or snus	n/a	4.0
Adults who are heavy drinkers[2]	n/a	6.3
Adults who are binge drinkers[3]	n/a	17.4
Adults who are overweight (BMI 25.0 - 29.9)	n/a	35.3
Adults who are obese (BMI 30.0 - 99.8)	n/a	31.3
Adults who participated in any physical activities in the past month	n/a	74.4
Adults who always or nearly always wears a seat belt	n/a	94.3

Note: n/a not available; (1) Figures cover the New Haven-Milford, CT Metropolitan Statistical Area; (2) Heavy drinkers are classified as adult men having more than 14 drinks per week and adult women having more than 7 drinks per week; (3) Binge drinkers are classified as males having five or more drinks on one occasion or females having four or more drinks on one occasion
Source: Centers for Disease Control and Prevention, Behaviorial Risk Factor Surveillance System, SMART: Selected Metropolitan Area Risk Trends, 2017

Acute and Chronic Health Conditions

Category	MSA[1] (%)	U.S. (%)
Adults who have ever been told they had a heart attack	n/a	4.2
Adults who have ever been told they have angina or coronary heart disease	n/a	3.9
Adults who have ever been told they had a stroke	n/a	3.0
Adults who have ever been told they have asthma	n/a	14.2
Adults who have ever been told they have arthritis	n/a	24.9
Adults who have ever been told they have diabetes[2]	n/a	10.5
Adults who have ever been told they had skin cancer	n/a	6.2
Adults who have ever been told they had any other types of cancer	n/a	7.1
Adults who have ever been told they have COPD	n/a	6.5
Adults who have ever been told they have kidney disease	n/a	3.0
Adults who have ever been told they have a form of depression	n/a	20.5

Note: n/a not available; (1) Figures cover the New Haven-Milford, CT Metropolitan Statistical Area; (2) Figures do not include pregnancy-related, borderline, or pre-diabetes
Source: Centers for Disease Control and Prevention, Behaviorial Risk Factor Surveillance System, SMART: Selected Metropolitan Area Risk Trends, 2017

Health Screening and Vaccination Rates

Category	MSA[1] (%)	U.S. (%)
Adults aged 65+ who have had flu shot within the past year	n/a	60.7
Adults aged 65+ who have ever had a pneumonia vaccination	n/a	75.4
Adults who have ever been tested for HIV	n/a	36.1
Adults who have ever had the shingles or zoster vaccine?	n/a	28.9
Adults who have had their blood cholesterol checked within the last five years	n/a	85.9

Note: n/a not available; (1) Figures cover the New Haven-Milford, CT Metropolitan Statistical Area.
Source: Centers for Disease Control and Prevention, Behaviorial Risk Factor Surveillance System, SMART: Selected Metropolitan Area Risk Trends, 2017

Disability Status

Category	MSA[1] (%)	U.S. (%)
Adults who reported being deaf	n/a	6.7
Are you blind or have serious difficulty seeing, even when wearing glasses?	n/a	4.5
Are you limited in any way in any of your usual activities due of arthritis?	n/a	12.9
Do you have difficulty doing errands alone?	n/a	6.8
Do you have difficulty dressing or bathing?	n/a	3.6
Do you have serious difficulty concentrating/remembering/making decisions?	n/a	10.7
Do you have serious difficulty walking or climbing stairs?	n/a	13.6

Note: n/a not available; (1) Figures cover the New Haven-Milford, CT Metropolitan Statistical Area.
Source: Centers for Disease Control and Prevention, Behaviorial Risk Factor Surveillance System, SMART: Selected Metropolitan Area Risk Trends, 2017

Mortality Rates for the Top 10 Causes of Death in the U.S.

ICD-10[a] Sub-Chapter	ICD-10[a] Code	Age-Adjusted Mortality Rate[1] per 100,000 population	
		County[2]	U.S.
Malignant neoplasms	C00-C97	140.1	149.2
Ischaemic heart diseases	I20-I25	74.1	90.5
Other forms of heart disease	I30-I51	59.7	52.2
Chronic lower respiratory diseases	J40-J47	30.5	39.6
Other degenerative diseases of the nervous system	G30-G31	21.7	37.6
Cerebrovascular diseases	I60-I69	30.8	37.2
Other external causes of accidental injury	W00-X59	50.9	36.1
Organic, including symptomatic, mental disorders	F01-F09	44.3	29.4
Hypertensive diseases	I10-I15	15.9	24.1
Diabetes mellitus	E10-E14	15.9	21.5

Note: (a) ICD-10 = International Classification of Diseases 10th Revision; (1) Mortality rates are a three-year average covering 2017-2019; (2) Figures cover New Haven County.
Source: Centers for Disease Control and Prevention, National Center for Health Statistics. Underlying Cause of Death 1999-2019 on CDC WONDER Online Database

Mortality Rates for Selected Causes of Death

ICD-10[a] Sub-Chapter	ICD-10[a] Code	Age-Adjusted Mortality Rate[1] per 100,000 population	
		County[2]	U.S.
Assault	X85-Y09	3.5	6.0
Diseases of the liver	K70-K76	12.5	14.4
Human immunodeficiency virus (HIV) disease	B20-B24	1.4	1.5
Influenza and pneumonia	J09-J18	11.2	13.8
Intentional self-harm	X60-X84	11.1	14.1
Malnutrition	E40-E46	1.2	2.3
Obesity and other hyperalimentation	E65-E68	2.9	2.1
Renal failure	N17-N19	13.2	12.6
Transport accidents	V01-V99	8.6	12.3
Viral hepatitis	B15-B19	0.9	1.2

Note: (a) ICD-10 = International Classification of Diseases 10th Revision; (1) Mortality rates are a three-year average covering 2017-2019; (2) Figures cover New Haven County; Data are suppressed when the data meet the criteria for confidentiality constraints; Mortality rates are flagged as unreliable when the rate would be calculated with a numerator of 20 or less.
Source: Centers for Disease Control and Prevention, National Center for Health Statistics. Underlying Cause of Death 1999-2019 on CDC WONDER Online Database

Health Insurance Coverage

Area	With Health Insurance	With Private Health Insurance	With Public Health Insurance	Without Health Insurance	Population Under Age 19 Without Health Insurance
City	91.1	50.8	46.7	8.9	2.8
MSA[1]	95.0	68.2	38.7	5.0	2.2
U.S.	91.2	67.9	35.1	8.8	5.1

Note: Figures are percentages that cover the civilian noninstitutionalized population; (1) Figures cover the New Haven-Milford, CT Metropolitan Statistical Area
Source: U.S. Census Bureau, 2015-2019 American Community Survey 5-Year Estimates

Number of Medical Professionals

Area	MDs[3]	DOs[3,4]	Dentists	Podiatrists	Chiropractors	Optometrists
County[1] (number)	4,771	92	683	86	230	148
County[1] (rate[2])	556.7	10.7	79.9	10.1	26.9	17.3
U.S. (rate[2])	282.9	22.7	71.2	6.2	28.1	16.9

09009
Note: Data as of 2019 unless noted; (1) Data covers New Haven County; (2) Rate per 100,000 population; (3) Data as of 2018 and includes all active, non-federal physicians; (4) Doctor of Osteopathic Medicine
Source: U.S. Department of Health and Human Services, Health Resources and Services Administration, Bureau of Health Professions, Area Resource File (ARF) 2019-2020

Best Hospitals

According to *U.S. News*, the New Haven-Milford, CT metro area is home to two of the best hospitals in the U.S.: **Smilow Cancer Hospital at Yale New Haven** (9 adult specialties and 7 pediatric specialties); **Yale New Haven Hospital** (9 adult specialties and 7 pediatric specialties). The hospitals listed were nationally ranked in at least one of 16 adult or 10 pediatric specialties. Only 134 hospitals nationwide were nationally ranked in one or more adult or pediatric specialty; this number increases to 178 counting specialized centers within hospitals. Twenty hospitals in the U.S. made the Honor Roll. The Best Hospitals Honor Roll takes both the national rankings and the procedure and condition ratings into account. Hospitals received points if they were nationally ranked in one of the 16 adult specialties—the higher they ranked, the more points they got—and how many ratings of "high performing" they earned in the 10 procedures and conditions. *U.S. News Online, "America's Best Hospitals 2020-21"*

According to *U.S. News,* the New Haven-Milford, CT metro area is home to one of the best children's hospitals in the U.S.: **Yale New Haven Children's Hospital** (7 pediatric specialties). The hospital listed was highly ranked in at least one of 10 pediatric specialties. Eighty-eight children's hospitals in the U.S. were nationally ranked in at least one specialty. Hospitals received points for being ranked in a specialty, and the 10 hospitals with the most points across the 10 specialties make up the Honor Roll. *U.S. News Online, "America's Best Children's Hospitals 2020-21"*

EDUCATION

Public School District Statistics

District Name	Schls	Pupils	Pupil/ Teacher Ratio	Minority Pupils[1] (%)	Free Lunch Eligible[2] (%)	IEP[3] (%)
New Haven School District	39	21,075	13.4	87.1	53.9	15.7

Note: Table includes school districts with 2,000 or more students; (1) Percentage of students that are not non-Hispanic white; (2) Percentage of students that are eligible for the free lunch program; (3) Percentage of students that have an Individualized Education Program.
Source: U.S. Department of Education, National Center for Education Statistics, Common Core of Data, Local Education Agency (School District) Universe Survey: School Year 2018-2019; U.S. Department of Education, National Center for Education Statistics, Common Core of Data, Public Elementary/Secondary School Universe Survey: School Year 2018-2019

Highest Level of Education

Area	Less than H.S.	H.S. Diploma	Some College, No Deg.	Associate Degree	Bachelor's Degree	Master's Degree	Prof. School Degree	Doctorate Degree
City	14.4	32.2	14.0	4.5	15.7	10.7	4.2	4.3
MSA[1]	9.9	30.7	17.1	7.3	18.6	11.2	3.1	2.1
U.S.	12.0	27.0	20.4	8.5	19.8	8.8	2.1	1.4

Note: Figures cover persons age 25 and over; (1) Figures cover the New Haven-Milford, CT Metropolitan Statistical Area
Source: U.S. Census Bureau, 2015-2019 American Community Survey 5-Year Estimates

Educational Attainment by Race

Area	High School Graduate or Higher (%)					Bachelor's Degree or Higher (%)				
	Total	White	Black	Asian	Hisp.[2]	Total	White	Black	Asian	Hisp.[2]
City	85.6	87.5	87.2	96.8	70.9	34.9	46.6	19.9	78.7	13.6
MSA[1]	90.1	91.8	87.6	90.1	74.4	35.0	37.4	20.2	65.3	15.6
U.S.	88.0	89.9	86.0	87.1	68.7	32.1	33.5	21.6	54.3	16.4

Note: Figures shown cover persons 25 years old and over; (1) Figures cover the New Haven-Milford, CT Metropolitan Statistical Area; (2) People of Hispanic origin can be of any race
Source: U.S. Census Bureau, 2015-2019 American Community Survey 5-Year Estimates

School Enrollment by Grade and Control

Area	Preschool (%)		Kindergarten (%)		Grades 1 - 4 (%)		Grades 5 - 8 (%)		Grades 9 - 12 (%)	
	Public	Private	Public	Private	Public	Private	Public	Private	Public	Private
City	83.6	16.4	94.0	6.0	94.8	5.2	93.8	6.2	92.2	7.8
MSA[1]	65.1	34.9	90.7	9.3	92.2	7.8	90.5	9.5	89.3	10.7
U.S.	59.1	40.9	87.6	12.4	89.5	10.5	89.4	10.6	90.1	9.9

Note: Figures shown cover persons 3 years old and over; (1) Figures cover the New Haven-Milford, CT Metropolitan Statistical Area
Source: U.S. Census Bureau, 2015-2019 American Community Survey 5-Year Estimates

Higher Education

Four-Year Colleges			Two-Year Colleges			Medical Schools[1]	Law Schools[2]	Voc/ Tech[3]
Public	Private Non-profit	Private For-profit	Public	Private Non-profit	Private For-profit			
1	2	0	1	0	0	1	1	0

Note: Figures cover institutions located within the city limits and include main campuses only; (1) includes schools accredited by the Liaison Committee on Medical Education and the American Osteopathic Association's Commission on Osteopathic College Accreditation; (2) includes ABA-accredited schools, schools with provisional ABA accreditation, and state accredited schools; (3) includes all schools with programs that are less than 2 years.
Source: National Center for Education Statistics, Integrated Postsecondary Education System (IPEDS), 2019-20; Wikipedia, List of Medical Schools in the United States, accessed April 2, 2021; Wikipedia, List of Law Schools in the United States, accessed April 2, 2021

According to *U.S. News & World Report,* the New Haven-Milford, CT metro area is home to two of the top 200 national universities in the U.S.: **Yale University** (#4 tie); **Quinnipiac University** (#153 tie). The indicators used to capture academic quality fall into a number of categories: assessment by administrators at peer institutions; retention of students; faculty resources; student selectivity; financial resources; alumni giving; high school counselor ratings of colleges; and graduation rate. *U.S. News & World Report, "America's Best Colleges 2021"*

According to *U.S. News & World Report,* the New Haven-Milford, CT metro area is home to one of the top 100 law schools in the U.S.: **Yale University** (#1). The rankings are based on a weighted average of 12 measures of quality: peer assessment score; assessment score by lawyers/judges; median LSAT scores; median undergrad GPA; acceptance rate; employment rates for graduates; placement success; bar passage rate; faculty resources; expenditures per student; student/faculty ratio; and library resources. *U.S. News & World Report, "America's Best Graduate Schools, Law, 2022"*

According to *U.S. News & World Report,* the New Haven-Milford, CT metro area is home to one of the top 75 medical schools for research in the U.S.: **Yale University** (#10). The rankings are based on a weighted average of 11 measures of quality: quality assessment; peer assessment score; assessment score by residency directors; research activity; total research activity; average research activity per faculty member; student selectivity; median MCAT total score; median undergraduate GPA; acceptance rate; and faculty resources. *U.S. News & World Report, "America's Best Graduate Schools, Medical, 2022"*

According to *U.S. News & World Report,* the New Haven-Milford, CT metro area is home to one of the top 75 business schools in the U.S.: **Yale University** (#9). The rankings are based on a weighted average of the following nine measures: quality assessment; peer assessment; recruiter assessment; placement success; mean starting salary and bonus; student selectivity; mean GMAT and GRE scores; mean undergraduate GPA; and acceptance rate. *U.S. News & World Report, "America's Best Graduate Schools, Business, 2022"*

EMPLOYERS

Major Employers

Company Name	Industry
Bozzuto's	Distribution centers, wholesale
Connecticut Education Association	Schools
Covidien-Surgical Devices	Physicians & surgeons equip & supls-whls
General Counselors Office	Business services nec
Grandview Adult Behavioral Health	Mental health services
Griffin Hospital	Hospitals
LATICRETE International	Adhesives & glues, wholesale
Masonicare Health Center	Hospitals
Medtronic	Hospital equipment & supplies, wholesale
Saint Mary's Hospital	Hospitals
Southbury Training School	Junior-community college-tech institutes
Southern CT State University	Schools-universities & colleges academic
VA Connecticut Healthcare System	Health care management
Waterbury Board of Education	Boards of education
Waterbury Hospital	Hospitals
Yale New Haven Health System	Health care management

Note: Companies shown are located within the New Haven-Milford, CT Metropolitan Statistical Area.
Source: Hoovers.com; Wikipedia

PUBLIC SAFETY

Crime Rate

Area	All Crimes	Violent Crimes				Property Crimes		
		Murder	Rape[3]	Robbery	Aggrav. Assault	Burglary	Larceny -Theft	Motor Vehicle Theft
City	4,694.5	10.0	34.5	246.0	604.6	505.0	2,743.4	551.0
Suburbs[1]	1,934.6	2.2	24.3	47.9	77.5	206.4	1,361.4	214.9
Metro[2]	2,383.4	3.5	25.9	80.1	163.2	255.0	1,586.2	269.5
U.S.	2,489.3	5.0	42.6	81.6	250.2	340.5	1,549.5	219.9

Note: Figures are crimes per 100,000 population; (1) All areas within the metro area that are located outside the city limits; (2) Figures cover the New Haven-Milford, CT Metropolitan Statistical Area; (3) All figures shown were reported using the revised Uniform Crime Reporting (UCR) definition of rape.
Source: FBI Uniform Crime Reports, 2019

Hate Crimes

Area	Number of Quarters Reported	Number of Incidents per Bias Motivation					
		Race/Ethnicity/ Ancestry	Religion	Sexual Orientation	Disability	Gender	Gender Identity
City	4	5	2	2	0	0	0
U.S.	4	3,963	1,521	1,195	157	69	198

Source: Federal Bureau of Investigation, Hate Crime Statistics 2019

Identity Theft Consumer Reports

Area	Reports	Reports per 100,000 Population	Rank[2]
MSA[1]	1,716	201	210
U.S.	1,387,615	423	-

Note: (1) Figures cover the New Haven-Milford, CT Metropolitan Statistical Area; (2) Rank ranges from 1 to 391 where 1 indicates greatest number of identity theft reports per 100,000 population
Source: Federal Trade Commission, Consumer Sentinel Network Data Book 2020

Fraud and Other Consumer Reports

Area	Reports	Reports per 100,000 Population	Rank[2]
MSA[1]	6,872	804	94
U.S.	3,385,133	1,031	-

Note: (1) Figures cover the New Haven-Milford, CT Metropolitan Statistical Area; (2) Rank ranges from 1 to 391 where 1 indicates greatest number of fraud and other consumer reports per 100,000 population
Source: Federal Trade Commission, Consumer Sentinel Network Data Book 2020

POLITICS

2020 Presidential Election Results

Area	Biden	Trump	Jorgensen	Hawkins	Other
New Haven County	58.0	40.6	0.9	0.4	0.0
U.S.	51.3	46.8	1.2	0.3	0.5

Note: Results are percentages and may not add to 100% due to rounding
Source: Dave Leip's Atlas of U.S. Presidential Elections

SPORTS

Professional Sports Teams

Team Name	League	Year Established
No teams are located in the metro area		

Source: Wikipedia, Major Professional Sports Teams of the United States and Canada, April 6, 2021

CLIMATE

Average and Extreme Temperatures

Temperature	Jan	Feb	Mar	Apr	May	Jun	Jul	Aug	Sep	Oct	Nov	Dec	Yr.
Extreme High (°F)	65	67	84	91	92	96	103	100	99	85	78	65	103
Average High (°F)	37	38	46	57	67	76	82	81	74	64	53	41	60
Average Temp. (°F)	30	32	39	49	59	68	74	73	66	56	46	35	52
Average Low (°F)	23	24	31	40	50	59	65	65	57	47	38	27	44
Extreme Low (°F)	-7	-5	4	18	31	41	49	44	36	26	16	-4	-7

Note: Figures cover the years 1948-1992
Source: National Climatic Data Center, International Station Meteorological Climate Summary, 9/96

Average Precipitation/Snowfall/Humidity

Precip./Humidity	Jan	Feb	Mar	Apr	May	Jun	Jul	Aug	Sep	Oct	Nov	Dec	Yr.
Avg. Precip. (in.)	3.2	2.9	3.7	3.7	3.7	3.1	3.7	3.8	3.0	3.2	3.8	3.5	41.4
Avg. Snowfall (in.)	7	7	5	1	Tr	0	0	0	0	Tr	1	5	25
Avg. Rel. Hum. 7am (%)	73	72	72	72	76	77	79	80	81	79	77	74	76
Avg. Rel. Hum. 4pm (%)	61	59	56	55	59	60	60	61	61	60	62	63	60

Note: Figures cover the years 1948-1992; Tr = Trace amounts (<0.05 in. of rain; <0.5 in. of snow)
Source: National Climatic Data Center, International Station Meteorological Climate Summary, 9/96

Weather Conditions

Temperature			Daytime Sky			Precipitation		
32°F & below	45°F & below	90°F & above	Clear	Partly cloudy	Cloudy	0.01 inch or more precip.	0.1 inch or more snow/ice	Thunder-storms
100	193	7	80	146	139	118	17	22

Note: Figures are average number of days per year and cover the years 1948-1992
Source: National Climatic Data Center, International Station Meteorological Climate Summary, 9/96

HAZARDOUS WASTE

Superfund Sites

The New Haven-Milford, CT metro area is home to three sites on the EPA's Superfund National Priorities List: **Beacon Heights Landfill** (final); **Laurel Park, Inc.** (final); **Scovill Industrial Landfill** (final). There are a total of 1,375 Superfund sites with a status of proposed or final on the list in the U.S. *U.S. Environmental Protection Agency, National Priorities List, April 7, 2021*

AIR QUALITY

Air Quality Trends: Ozone

	1990	1995	2000	2005	2010	2015	2016	2017	2018	2019
MSA[1]	n/a	n/a	n/a	n/a	n/a	n/a	n/a	n/a	n/a	n/a
U.S.	0.088	0.089	0.082	0.080	0.073	0.068	0.069	0.068	0.069	0.065

Note: (1) Data covers the New Haven-Milford, CT Metropolitan Statistical Area; n/a not available. The values shown are the composite ozone concentration averages among trend sites based on the highest fourth daily maximum 8-hour concentration in parts per million. These trends are based on sites having an adequate record of monitoring data during the trend period. Data from exceptional events are included.
Source: U.S. Environmental Protection Agency, Air Quality Monitoring Information, "Air Quality Trends by City, 1990-2019"

Air Quality Index

Area	Percent of Days when Air Quality was...[2]					AQI Statistics[2]	
	Good	Moderate	Unhealthy for Sensitive Groups	Unhealthy	Very Unhealthy	Maximum	Median
MSA[1]	76.7	19.5	3.3	0.5	0.0	159	41

Note: (1) Data covers the New Haven-Milford, CT Metropolitan Statistical Area; (2) Based on 365 days with AQI data in 2019. Air Quality Index (AQI) is an index for reporting daily air quality. EPA calculates the AQI for five major air pollutants regulated by the Clean Air Act: ground-level ozone, particle pollution (aka particulate matter), carbon monoxide, sulfur dioxide, and nitrogen dioxide. The AQI runs from 0 to 500. The higher the AQI value, the greater the level of air pollution and the greater the health concern. There are six AQI categories: "Good" AQI is between 0 and 50. Air quality is considered satisfactory; "Moderate" AQI is between 51 and 100. Air quality is acceptable; "Unhealthy for Sensitive Groups" When AQI values are between 101 and 150, members of sensitive groups may experience health effects; "Unhealthy" When AQI values are between 151 and 200 everyone may begin to experience health effects; "Very Unhealthy" AQI values between 201 and 300 trigger a health alert; "Hazardous" AQI values over 300 trigger warnings of emergency conditions (not shown).
Source: U.S. Environmental Protection Agency, Air Quality Index Report, 2019

Air Quality Index Pollutants

Area	Percent of Days when AQI Pollutant was...[2]					
	Carbon Monoxide	Nitrogen Dioxide	Ozone	Sulfur Dioxide	Particulate Matter 2.5	Particulate Matter 10
MSA[1]	0.0	4.1	67.7	0.0	27.1	1.1

Note: (1) Data covers the New Haven-Milford, CT Metropolitan Statistical Area; (2) Based on 365 days with AQI data in 2019. The Air Quality Index (AQI) is an index for reporting daily air quality. EPA calculates the AQI for five major air pollutants regulated by the Clean Air Act: ground-level ozone, particle pollution (also known as particulate matter), carbon monoxide, sulfur dioxide, and nitrogen dioxide. The AQI runs from 0 to 500. The higher the AQI value, the greater the level of air pollution and the greater the health concern.
Source: U.S. Environmental Protection Agency, Air Quality Index Report, 2019

Maximum Air Pollutant Concentrations: Particulate Matter, Ozone, CO and Lead

	Particulate Matter 10 (ug/m^3)	Particulate Matter 2.5 Wtd AM (ug/m^3)	Particulate Matter 2.5 24-Hr (ug/m^3)	Ozone (ppm)	Carbon Monoxide (ppm)	Lead (ug/m^3)
MSA[1] Level	67	7.7	18	0.084	1	n/a
NAAQS[2]	150	15	35	0.075	9	0.15
Met NAAQS[2]	Yes	Yes	Yes	No	Yes	n/a

Note: (1) Data covers the New Haven-Milford, CT Metropolitan Statistical Area; Data from exceptional events are included; (2) National Ambient Air Quality Standards; ppm = parts per million; ug/m³ = micrograms per cubic meter; n/a not available.
Concentrations: Particulate Matter 10 (coarse particulate)—highest second maximum 24-hour concentration; Particulate Matter 2.5 Wtd AM (fine particulate)—highest weighted annual mean concentration; Particulate Matter 2.5 24-Hour (fine particulate)—highest 98th percentile 24-hour concentration; Ozone—highest fourth daily maximum 8-hour concentration; Carbon Monoxide—highest second maximum non-overlapping 8-hour concentration; Lead—maximum running 3-month average
Source: U.S. Environmental Protection Agency, Air Quality Monitoring Information, "Air Quality Statistics by City, 2019"

Maximum Air Pollutant Concentrations: Nitrogen Dioxide and Sulfur Dioxide

	Nitrogen Dioxide AM (ppb)	Nitrogen Dioxide 1-Hr (ppb)	Sulfur Dioxide AM (ppb)	Sulfur Dioxide 1-Hr (ppb)	Sulfur Dioxide 24-Hr (ppb)
MSA[1] Level	12	46	n/a	2	n/a
NAAQS[2]	53	100	30	75	140
Met NAAQS[2]	Yes	Yes	n/a	Yes	n/a

Note: (1) Data covers the New Haven-Milford, CT Metropolitan Statistical Area; Data from exceptional events are included; (2) National Ambient Air Quality Standards; ppm = parts per million; ug/m³ = micrograms per cubic meter; n/a not available.
Concentrations: Nitrogen Dioxide AM—highest arithmetic mean concentration; Nitrogen Dioxide 1-Hr—highest 98th percentile 1-hour daily maximum concentration; Sulfur Dioxide AM—highest annual mean concentration; Sulfur Dioxide 1-Hr—highest 99th percentile 1-hour daily maximum concentration; Sulfur Dioxide 24-Hr—highest second maximum 24-hour concentration
Source: U.S. Environmental Protection Agency, Air Quality Monitoring Information, "Air Quality Statistics by City, 2019"

New York, New York

Background

Few cities in the world can compare with New York's frenetic excitement. Known for its dramatic skyline and world-famous bridges and historic buildings, the city is beautiful, mighty, inspiring, loaded with attitude and home to more than 8 million people living within its five boroughs—Bronx, Brooklyn, Queens, Manhattan, and Staten Island.

New York is the largest city in New York State, in the U.S., and one of the largest cities in the world. Located at the mouth of the Hudson River, the area was first explored by Giovanni da Verrazzano in 1524, and then by Henry Hudson in 1609. In The 1625, it became New Amsterdam and a year later, as the story goes, Peter Minuit purchased the island of Manhattan from local Native Americans for the equivalent of $24.00.

The city offers the best in the arts—Metropolitan Museum of Art, Museum of Modern Art, Guggenheim Museum, among thousands of others; education—New York University and Columbia University; finance—the New York and the American stock exchanges; plus fashion, theaters, restaurants, political activism, and more.

New York is home to The Alvin Ailey American Dance Theater, American Ballet Theater, Brooklyn Academy of Music, Carnegie Hall, and Cunningham Dance Company, among many other world-famous artistic centers.

Professional sports abound in the city, including New York Giants and Jets football teams, New York Red Bulls soccer team, Knicks basketball team, and New York Yankees and Mets baseball teams. The Giants' MetLife Stadium hosted the Super Bowl in 2014, the first outdoor, cold-weather Super Bowl. In addition, Barclays Arena in Brooklyn is home to the New Jersey Nets basketball team, the New York Islanders hockey team, and hosts world-class entertainment.

New York City is also an international business capital, with its entrepreneurial spirit, highly educated workforce, first-rate transportation system, unequaled telecommunications infrastructure and lowest crime rate of any big city in America.

On September 11, 2001, New York became the site of the deadliest terrorist attack ever to occur in the United States. Two hijacked commercial airplanes were flown into the Twin Towers demolished the complex of seven buildings at the World Trade Center and killed more than 3,500 people. The grieving city immediately began the monumental task of moving forward. The new 8-acre World Trade Center Complex consists of seven office buildings, a Memorial, and Museum. The Memorial, which opened on the 10th anniversary of the attacks, consists of two massive pools in the footprints of the Twin Towers, with the largest manmade waterfalls in the country.

> The annual Macy's Thanksgiving Day Parade was confined to a single city block, down from its traditional 2.5-mile route. There were no high school bands, and 130 balloon handlers instead of the usual 2,000.

The New York metropolitan area is home to a prominent LBGTQ+ community. At about 600,000 strong, it's the largest in the country. The annual New York City Pride March traverses southward down Fifth Avenue and ends at Greenwich Village in Lower Manhattan; the parade attracts tens of thousands of participants and millions of sidewalk spectators each June.

The New York metro area is close to the path of most storm and frontal systems which move across the continent. The city can experience very high temperatures in summer and very low in winter, despite its coastal location. The passage of many weather systems helps to reduce the duration of both cold and warm spells, circulate the air, and reduce stagnation. The most recent major weather event occurred in 2012, as Hurricane Sandy flooded subways and tunnels, shut down hospitals and the NYSE.

Rankings

General Rankings

- In its eighth annual survey, *Travel + Leisure* readers nominated their favorite small cities and towns in America—those with 100,000 or fewer residents—voting on numerous attractive features in categories including culture, food and drink, quality of life, style, and people. After 50,000 votes, New York was ranked #11 among the proposed favorites. *www.travelandleisure.com, "America's Favorite Cities," October 20, 2017*

- New York was selected as one of the best places to live in America by *Outside Magazine*. Criteria included population, park acreage, neighborhood and resident diversity, new and upcoming things of interest, and opportunities for outdoor adventure. *Outside Magazine, "The 12 Best Places to Live in 2019," July 11, 2019*

- The human resources consulting firm Mercer ranked 231 major cities worldwide in terms of overall quality of life. New York ranked #44. Criteria: political, social, economic, and socio-cultural factors; medical and health considerations; schools and education; public services and transportation; recreation; consumer goods; housing; and natural environment. *Mercer, "Mercer 2019 Quality of Living Survey," March 13, 2019*

- New York appeared on *Travel + Leisure's* list of the 15 best cities in the United States. The city was ranked #6. Criteria: sights/landmarks; culture; food; friendliness; shopping; and overall value. *Travel + Leisure, "The World's Best Awards 2020" July 8, 2020*

- For its 33rd annual "Readers' Choice Awards" survey, *Condé Nast Traveler* ranked its readers' favorite cities in the U.S. These places brought feelings of comfort in a time of limited travel. The list was broken into large cities and cities under 250,000. New York ranked #6 in the big city category. *Condé Nast Traveler, Readers' Choice Awards 2020, "Best Big Cities in the U.S." October 6, 2020*

Business/Finance Rankings

- The Brookings Institution ranked the nation's largest cities based on income inequality. New York was ranked #8 (#1 = greatest inequality). Criteria: the "95/20 ratio," a figure representing the income at which a household earns more than 95 percent of all other households, divided by the income at which a household earns more than only 20 percent of all other households. *Brookings Institution, "Household Income Inequality, Largest Cities of 97 Large U.S. Metro Areas, 2014-2016," February 5, 2018*

- The Brookings Institution ranked the 100 largest metro areas in the U.S. based on income inequality. New York was ranked #2 (#1 = greatest inequality). Criteria: the "95/20 ratio," a figure representing the income at which a household earns more than 95 percent of all other households, divided by the income at which a household earns more than only 20 percent of all other households. *Brookings Institution, "Household Income Inequality, 100 Largest U.S. Metro Areas, 2014-2016," February 5, 2018*

- Payscale.com ranked the 32 largest metro areas in terms of wage growth. The New York metro area ranked #5. Criteria: private-sector and education professional wage growth between the 4th quarter of 2019 and the 4th quarter of 2020. *PayScale, "Wage Trends by Metro Area-4th Quarter," January 11, 2021*

- The New York metro area was identified as one of the most debt-ridden places in America by the finance site Credit.com. The metro area was ranked #3. Criteria: residents' average credit card debt as well as median income. *Credit.com, "25 Cities With the Most Credit Card Debt," February 28, 2018*

- For its annual survey of the "Most Expensive U.S. Cities to Live In," Kiplinger applied Cost of Living Index statistics developed by the Council for Community and Economic Research to U.S. Census Bureau population and median household income data for 256 urban areas. New York was among the 20 most expensive in the country. *Kiplinger.com, "The 20 Most Expensive Cities in the U.S.," July 29, 2020*

- New York was identified as one of America's most frugal metro areas by *Coupons.com*. The city ranked #15 out of 25. Criteria: digital coupon usage. *Coupons.com, "America's Most Frugal Cities of 2017," March 22, 2018*

- New York was cited as one of America's top metros for new and expanded facility projects in 2020. The area ranked #8 in the large metro area category (population over 1 million). *Site Selection, "Top Metros of 2020," March 2021*

- New York was identified as one of the happiest cities to work in by CareerBliss.com, an online community for career advancement. The city ranked #5 out of 10. Criteria: an employee's relationship with his or her boss and co-workers; daily tasks; general work environment; compensation; opportunities for advancement; company culture and job reputation; and resources. *Businesswire.com, "CareerBliss Happiest Cities to Work 2019," February 12, 2019*

- The New York metro area appeared on the Milken Institute "2021 Best Performing Cities" list. Rank: #106 out of 200 large metro areas (population over 250,000). Criteria: job growth; wage and salary growth; high-tech output growth; housing affordability; household broadband access. *Milken Institute, "Best-Performing Cities 2021," February 16, 2021*

- *Forbes* ranked the 200 most populous metro areas to determine the nation's "Best Places for Business and Careers." The New York metro area was ranked #115. Criteria: costs (business and living); job growth (past and projected); income growth; quality of life; educational attainment (college and high school); projected economic growth; cultural and leisure opportunities; workplace tolerance laws; net migration patterns. *Forbes, "The Best Places for Business and Careers 2019: Seattle Still On Top," October 30, 2019*

- Mercer Human Resources Consulting ranked 209 cities worldwide in terms of cost-of-living. New York ranked #6 (the lower the ranking, the higher the cost-of-living). The survey measured the comparative cost of over 200 items (such as housing, food, clothing, household goods, transportation, and entertainment) in each location. *Mercer, "2020 Cost of Living Survey," June 9, 2020*

Dating/Romance Rankings

- New York was ranked #17 out of 25 cities that stood out for inspiring romance and attracting diners on the website OpenTable.com. Criteria: percentage of people who dined out on Valentine's Day in 2018; percentage of romantic restaurants as rated by OpenTable diner reviews; and percentage of tables seated for two. *OpenTable, "25 Most Romantic Cities in America for 2019," February 7, 2019*

Education Rankings

- Personal finance website *WalletHub* analyzed the 150 largest U.S. metropolitan statistical areas to determine where the most educated Americans are putting their degrees to work. Criteria: education levels; percentage of workers with degrees; education quality and attainment gap; public school quality rankings; quality and enrollment of each metro area's universities. New York was ranked #26 (#1 = most educated city). *www.WalletHub.com, "Most and Least Educated Cities in America," July 20, 2020*

- New York was selected as one of America's most literate cities. The city ranked #22 out of the 84 largest U.S. cities. Criteria: number of booksellers; library resources; Internet resources; educational attainment; periodical publishing resources; newspaper circulation. *Central Connecticut State University, "America's Most Literate Cities, 2018," February 2019*

Environmental Rankings

- The U.S. Environmental Protection Agency (EPA) released a list of U.S. metropolitan areas with the most ENERGY STAR certified buildings in 2019. The New York metro area was ranked #7 out of 25. *U.S. Environmental Protection Agency, "2020 Energy Star Top Cities," March 2020*

- New York was highlighted as one of the 25 most ozone-polluted metro areas in the U.S. during 2016 through 2018. The area ranked #12. *American Lung Association, "State of the Air 2020," April 21, 2020*

Food/Drink Rankings

- The U.S. Chamber of Commerce Foundation conducted an in-depth study on local food truck regulations, surveyed 288 food truck owners, and ranked 20 major American cities based on how friendly they are for operating a food truck. The compiled index assessed the following: procedures for obtaining permits and licenses; complying with restrictions; and financial obligations associated with operating a food truck. New York ranked #9 overall (1 being the best). *www.foodtrucknation.us, "Food Truck Nation," March 20, 2018*

- New York was identified as one of the cities in America ordering the most vegan food options by GrubHub.com. The city ranked #1 out of 5. Criteria: percentage of vegan, vegetarian and plant-based food orders compared to the overall number of orders. *GrubHub.com, "State of the Plate Report 2020: Top Vegan-Friendly Cities," July 9, 2020*

- Yankee Stadium was selected as one of PETA's "Top 10 Vegan-Friendly Ballparks" for 2019. The park ranked #6. *People for the Ethical Treatment of Animals, "Top 10 Vegan-Friendly Ballparks," May 23, 2019*

Health/Fitness Rankings

- The Sharecare Community Well-Being Index evaluates 10 individual and social health factors in order to measure what matters to Americans in the co mmunities in which they live. The New York metro area was one of the five communities where social determinants of health were the highest. Criteria: access to food, healthcare, and community resources; housing and transportation; economic security. The area ranked #0. *www.sharecare.com, "Community Well-Being Index: 2019 Metro Area & County Rankings Report," August 31, 2020*

- For each of the 100 largest cities in the United States, the American Fitness Index®, published by the American College of Sports Medicine and the Anthem Foundation, evaluated community infrastructure and 33 health behaviors including preventive health, levels of chronic disease conditions, pedestrian safety, air quality, and community resources that support physical activity. New York ranked #21 for "community fitness." *americanfitnessindex.org, "2020 ACSM American Fitness Index Summary Report," July 14, 2020*

- New York was identified as one of the 10 most walkable cities in the U.S. by Walk Score. The city ranked #1. Walk Score measures walkability by analyzing hundreds of walking routes to nearby amenities, and also measures pedestrian friendliness by analyzing population density and road metrics such as block length and intersection density. *WalkScore.com, April 13, 2021*

- The New York metro area was identified as one of the worst cities for bed bugs in America by pest control company Orkin. The area ranked #12 out of 50 based on the number of bed bug treatments Orkin performed from December 2019 to November 2020. *Orkin, "New Year, New Top City on Orkin's 2021 Bed Bug Cities List: Chicago," February 1, 2021*

- New York was identified as a "2021 Spring Allergy Capital." The area ranked #45 out of 100. Three groups of factors were used to identify the most challenging cities for people with allergies during the spring season: annual spring pollen levels; over the counter medicine use; number of board-certified allergy specialists. *Asthma and Allergy Foundation of America, "Spring Allergy Capitals 2021," February 23, 2021*

- New York was identified as a "2021 Fall Allergy Capital." The area ranked #66 out of 100. Three groups of factors were used to identify the most challenging cities for people with allergies during the fall season: annual fall pollen levels; over the counter medicine use; number of board-certified allergy specialists. *Asthma and Allergy Foundation of America, "Fall Allergy Capitals 2021," February 23, 2021*

- New York was identified as a "2019 Asthma Capital." The area ranked #39 out of the nation's 100 largest metropolitan areas. Criteria: estimated asthma prevalence; crude death rate from asthma; and ER visits due to asthma. Risk factors analyzed but not factored in the rankings: annual pollen score; annual air quality; public smoking laws; number of board-certified asthma specialists; rescue medication use; controller medication use; uninsured rate; poverty rate. *Asthma and Allergy Foundation of America, "Asthma Capitals 2019: The Most Challenging Places to Live With Asthma," May 7, 2019*

- The Sharecare Community Well-Being Index evaluates 10 individual and social health factors in order to measure what matters to Americans in the communities in which they live. The New York metro area ranked #9 in the top 10 across all 10 domains. Criteria: access to healthcare, food, and community resources; housng and transportation; economic security; feeling of purpose; physical, financial, social, and community well-being. *www.sharecare.com, "Community Well-Being Index: 2019 Metro Area & County Rankings Report," August 31, 2020*

Real Estate Rankings

- FitSmallBusiness looked at 50 of the largest metropolitan areas in the U.S. to determine which metro was the best to start a real estate business. Data was compiled from such sources as: Zillow, Trulia, U.S. Census Bureau, and the Bureau of Labor Statistics. Criteria: location; inventory; annual wages; median sales price of homes; days on the market; median price cut percentage; and other factors that would influence real estate professional growth. The New York metro area ranked #6. *fitsmallbusiness.com, "The Best Cities to Become a Real Estate Agent in 2018," January 30, 2018*

- *WalletHub* compared the most populated U.S. cities to determine which had the best markets for real estate agents. New York ranked #33 where demand was high and pay was the best. Criteria: sales per agent; annual median wage for real-estate agents; monthly average starting salary for real estate agents; real estate job density and competition; unemployment rate; home turnover rate; housing-market health index; and other relevant metrics. *www.WalletHub.com, "2019's Best Places to Be a Real Estate Agent," April 24, 2019*

- The New York metro area was identified as one of the 20 best housing markets in the U.S. in 2020. The area ranked #11 out of 180 markets. Criteria: year-over-year change of median sales price of existing single-family homes between the 4th quarter of 2019 and the 4th quarter of 2020. *National Association of Realtors®, Median Sales Price of Existing Single-Family Homes for Metropolitan Areas, 4th Quarter 2020*

- The New York metro area was identified as one of the 10 worst condo markets in the U.S. in 2020. The area ranked #56 out of 63 markets. Criteria: year-over-year change of median sales price of existing apartment condo-coop homes between the 4th quarter of 2019 and the 4th quarter of 2020. *National Association of Realtors®, Median Sales Price of Existing Apartment Condo-Coops Homes for Metropolitan Areas, 4th Quarter 2020*

- The New York metro area was identified as one of the 20 least affordable housing markets in the U.S. in 2020. The area ranked #169 out of 183 markets. Criteria: qualification for a mortgage loan with a 10 percent down payment on a typical home. *National Association of Realtors®, Qualifying Income Based on Sales Price of Existing Single-Family Homes for Metropolitan Areas, 2020*

- New York was ranked #250 out of 268 metro areas in terms of housing affordability in 2020 by the National Association of Home Builders (#1 = most affordable). Criteria: the share of homes sold in that area affordable to a family earning the local median income, based on standard mortgage underwriting criteria. *National Association of Home Builders®, NAHB-Wells Fargo Housing Opportunity Index, 4th Quarter 2020*

Safety Rankings

- Allstate ranked the 200 largest cities in America in terms of driver safety. New York ranked #111. Criteria: internal property damage claims over a two-year period from January 2016 to December 2017. The report helps increase the importance of safety and awareness behind the wheel. *Allstate, "Allstate America's Best Drivers Report, 2019" June 24, 2019*

- The National Insurance Crime Bureau ranked 384 metro areas in the U.S. in terms of per capita rates of vehicle theft. The New York metro area ranked #300 (#1 = highest rate). Criteria: number of vehicle theft offenses per 100,000 inhabitants in 2019. *National Insurance Crime Bureau, "Hot Spots 2019," July 21, 2020*

Seniors/Retirement Rankings

- From its Best Cities for Successful Aging indexes, the Milken Institute generated rankings for metropolitan areas, weighing data in nine categories—health care, wellness, living arrangements, transportation and convenience, financial characteristics, education, employment, community engagement, and overall livability. The New York metro area was ranked #73 overall in the large metro area category. *Milken Institute, "Best Cities for Successful Aging, 2017" March 14, 2017*

Sports/Recreation Rankings

- New York was chosen as one of America's best cities for bicycling. The city ranked #9 out of 50. Criteria: cycling infrastructure that is safe and friendly for all ages; energy and bike culture. The editors evaluated cities with populations of 100,000 or more. *Bicycling, "The 50 Best Bike Cities in America," October 10, 2018*

Transportation Rankings

- Business Insider presented an AllTransit Performance Score ranking of public transportation in major U.S. cities and towns, with populations over 250,000, in which New York earned the #2-ranked "Transit Score," awarded for frequency of service, access to jobs, quality and number of stops, and affordability. *www.businessinsider.com, "The 17 Major U.S. Cities with the Best Public Transportation," April 17, 2018*

- The business website 24/7 Wall Street reviewed U.S. Census data to identify the 25 cities where the largest share of households do not own a vehicle. New York held the #1 position. *247wallst.com, "Cities Where No One Wants to Drive," February 15, 2017*

- New York was identified as one of the most congested metro areas in the U.S. The area ranked #4 out of 10. Criteria: yearly delay per auto commuter in hours. *Texas A&M Transportation Institute, "2019 Urban Mobility Report," December 2019*

- According to the INRIX "2019 Global Traffic Scorecard," New York was identified as one of the most congested metro areas in the U.S. The area ranked #4 out of 10. Criteria: average annual time spent in traffic and average cost of congestion per motorist. *Inrix.com, "Congestion Costs Each American Nearly 100 hours, $1,400 A Year," March 9, 2020*

Women/Minorities Rankings

- *Travel + Leisure* listed the best cities in and around the US for a memorable and fun girls' trip, even on a budget. Whether it is for a special occasion or just to get away, New York is sure to have something for all the ladies in your tribe. *Travel + Leisure, "25 Girls' Weekend Getaways That Won't Break the Bank," June 8, 2020*

- The *Houston Chronicle* listed the New York metro area as #4 in top places for young Latinos to live in the U.S. Research was largely based on housing and occupational data from the largest metropolitan areas performed by *Forbes* and NBC Universo. Criteria: percentage of 18-34 year-olds; Latino college grad rates; and diversity. *blog.chron.com, "The 15 Best Big Cities for Latino Millenials," January 26, 2016*

- Personal finance website *WalletHub* compared more than 180 U.S. cities across two key dimensions, "Hispanic Business-Friendliness" and "Hispanic Purchasing Power," to arrive at the most favorable conditions for Hispanic entrepreneurs. New York was ranked #160 out of 182. Criteria includes: share of Hispanic-Owned Businesses; Hispanic entrepreneurship rate to median annual income of Hispanics; Small Business-Friendliness score; cost of living; and number of Hispanics with at least a bachelor's degree. *WalletHub.com, "2019's Best Cities for Hispanic Entrepreneurs," May 1, 2019*

Miscellaneous Rankings

- While the majority of travel ground to a halt in 2020, plugged-in travel influencers and experts were able to rediscover their local regions. New York appeared on a *Forbes* list of 15 U.S. cities that provided solace as well as local inspiration. Whether it be quirky things to see and do, delicious take out, outdoor exploring and daytrips, these places are must-see destinations. *Forbes, "Bucket List Travel: The 15 Best U.S. Destinations For 2021," January 1, 2021*

- In its roundup of St. Patrick's Day parades "Gayot" listed the best festivals and parades of all things Irish. The festivities in New York as among the best. *www.gayot.com, "Best St. Patrick's Day Parades," March 2020*

- The watchdog site, Charity Navigator, conducted a study of charities in major markets both to analyze statistical differences in their financial, accountability, and transparency practices and to track year-to-year variations in individual philanthropic communities. The New York metro area was ranked #19 among the 30 metro markets in the rating category of Overall Score. *www.charitynavigator.org, "2017 Metro Market Study," May 1, 2017*

- *WalletHub* compared the 150 most populated U.S. cities to determine their operating efficiency. A "Quality of City Services" score was constructed for each city and then divided by the total budget per capita to reveal which were managed the best. New York ranked #146. Criteria: financial stability; economy; education; safety; health; infrastructure and pollution. *www.WalletHub.com, "2020's Best- & Worst-Run Cities in America," June 29, 2020*

- The National Alliance to End Homelessness listed the 25 most populous metro areas with the highest rate of homelessness. The New York metro area had a high rate of homelessness. Criteria: number of homeless people per 10,000 population in 2016. *National Alliance to End Homelessness, "Homelessness in the 25 Most Populous U.S. Metro Areas," September 1, 2017*

Business Environment

DEMOGRAPHICS

Population Growth

Area	1990 Census	2000 Census	2010 Census	2019* Estimate	Population Growth (%) 1990-2019	Population Growth (%) 2010-2019
City	7,322,552	8,008,278	8,175,133	8,419,316	15.0	3.0
MSA[1]	16,845,992	18,323,002	18,897,109	19,294,236	14.5	2.1
U.S.	248,709,873	281,421,906	308,745,538	324,697,795	30.6	5.2

Note: (1) Figures cover the New York-Newark-Jersey City, NY-NJ-PA Metropolitan Statistical Area;
(*) 2015-2019 5-year estimated population
Source: U.S. Census Bureau, 1990 Census, Census 2000, Census 2010, 2015-2019 American Community Survey 5-Year Estimates

Household Size

Area	Persons in Household (%) One	Two	Three	Four	Five	Six	Seven or More	Average Household Size
City	32.3	28.5	16.2	12.5	5.9	2.5	2.1	2.60
MSA[1]	28.1	29.5	16.9	14.6	6.6	2.5	1.9	2.70
U.S.	27.9	33.9	15.6	12.9	6.0	2.3	1.4	2.60

Note: (1) Figures cover the New York-Newark-Jersey City, NY-NJ-PA Metropolitan Statistical Area
Source: U.S. Census Bureau, 2015-2019 American Community Survey 5-Year Estimates

Race

Area	White Alone[2] (%)	Black Alone[2] (%)	Asian Alone[2] (%)	AIAN[3] Alone[2] (%)	NHOPI[4] Alone[2] (%)	Other Race Alone[2] (%)	Two or More Races (%)
City	42.7	24.3	14.1	0.4	0.1	14.7	3.6
MSA[1]	57.5	17.3	11.2	0.3	0.0	10.5	3.1
U.S.	72.5	12.7	5.5	0.8	0.2	4.9	3.3

Note: (1) Figures cover the New York-Newark-Jersey City, NY-NJ-PA Metropolitan Statistical Area; (2) Alone is defined as not being in combination with one or more other races; (3) American Indian and Alaska Native; (4) Native Hawaiian and Other Pacific Islander
Source: U.S. Census Bureau, 2015-2019 American Community Survey 5-Year Estimates

Hispanic or Latino Origin

Area	Total (%)	Mexican (%)	Puerto Rican (%)	Cuban (%)	Other (%)
City	29.1	4.0	8.1	0.5	16.5
MSA[1]	24.6	3.0	6.2	0.8	14.7
U.S.	18.0	11.2	1.7	0.7	4.3

Note: Persons of Hispanic or Latino origin can be of any race; (1) Figures cover the New York-Newark-Jersey City, NY-NJ-PA Metropolitan Statistical Area
Source: U.S. Census Bureau, 2015-2019 American Community Survey 5-Year Estimates

Ancestry

Area	German	Irish	English	American	Italian	Polish	French[2]	Scottish	Dutch
City	2.9	4.4	1.6	4.2	6.2	2.4	0.8	0.5	0.3
MSA[1]	6.2	9.2	2.7	4.4	12.2	3.8	0.9	0.7	0.6
U.S.	13.3	9.7	7.2	6.2	5.1	2.8	2.3	1.7	1.2

Note: Figures are the percentage of the total population reporting a particular ancestry. The nine most commonly reported ancestries in the U.S. are shown. Figures include multiple ancestries (e.g. if a person reported being Irish and Italian, they were included in both columns); (1) Figures cover the New York-Newark-Jersey City, NY-NJ-PA Metropolitan Statistical Area; (2) Excludes Basque
Source: U.S. Census Bureau, 2015-2019 American Community Survey 5-Year Estimates

Foreign-born Population

Area	Percent of Population Born in Any Foreign Country	Asia	Mexico	Europe	Caribbean	Central America[2]	South America	Africa	Canada
City	36.8	10.9	2.0	5.3	10.2	1.4	4.8	1.7	0.3
MSA[1]	29.5	8.7	1.5	4.4	6.9	2.0	4.4	1.4	0.2
U.S.	13.6	4.2	3.5	1.5	1.3	1.1	1.0	0.7	0.2

Note: (1) Figures cover the New York-Newark-Jersey City, NY-NJ-PA Metropolitan Statistical Area;
(2) Excludes Mexico.
Source: U.S. Census Bureau, 2015-2019 American Community Survey 5-Year Estimates

Marital Status

Area	Never Married	Now Married[2]	Separated	Widowed	Divorced
City	43.4	40.4	3.0	5.4	7.8
MSA[1]	37.8	46.3	2.3	5.7	7.9
U.S.	33.4	48.1	1.9	5.8	10.9

Note: Figures are percentages and cover the population 15 years of age and older; (1) Figures cover the New York-Newark-Jersey City, NY-NJ-PA Metropolitan Statistical Area; (2) Excludes separated
Source: U.S. Census Bureau, 2015-2019 American Community Survey 5-Year Estimates

Disability by Age

Area	All Ages	Under 18 Years Old	18 to 64 Years Old	65 Years and Over
City	10.8	3.4	7.9	35.1
MSA[1]	10.0	3.2	7.2	31.6
U.S.	12.6	4.2	10.3	34.5

Note: Figures show percent of the civilian noninstitutionalized population that reported having a disability. Disability status is determined from six types of difficulty: vision, hearing, cognitive, ambulatory, self-care, and independent living. For children under 5 years old, hearing and vision difficulty are used to determine disability status. For children between the ages of 5 and 14, disability status is determined from hearing, vision, cognitive, ambulatory, and self-care difficulties. For people aged 15 years and older, they are considered to have a disability if they have difficulty with any one of the six difficulty types; Note: (1) Figures cover the New York-Newark-Jersey City, NY-NJ-PA Metropolitan Statistical Area
Source: U.S. Census Bureau, 2015-2019 American Community Survey 5-Year Estimates

Age

Area	Percent of Population									Median Age
	Under Age 5	Age 5–19	Age 20–34	Age 35–44	Age 45–54	Age 55–64	Age 65–74	Age 75–84	Age 85+	
City	6.5	16.5	24.3	13.7	12.7	11.8	8.1	4.4	2.0	36.7
MSA[1]	6.1	17.8	21.2	13.1	13.6	12.8	8.6	4.6	2.2	38.6
U.S.	6.1	19.1	20.7	12.6	13.0	12.9	9.1	4.6	1.9	38.1

Note: (1) Figures cover the New York-Newark-Jersey City, NY-NJ-PA Metropolitan Statistical Area
Source: U.S. Census Bureau, 2015-2019 American Community Survey 5-Year Estimates

Gender

Area	Males	Females	Males per 100 Females
City	4,015,982	4,403,334	91.2
MSA[1]	9,327,459	9,966,777	93.6
U.S.	159,886,919	164,810,876	97.0

Note: (1) Figures cover the New York-Newark-Jersey City, NY-NJ-PA Metropolitan Statistical Area
Source: U.S. Census Bureau, 2015-2019 American Community Survey 5-Year Estimates

Religious Groups by Family

Area	Catholic	Baptist	Non-Den.	Methodist[2]	Lutheran	LDS[3]	Pente-costal	Presby-terian[4]	Muslim[5]	Judaism
MSA[1]	36.9	1.9	1.8	1.3	0.8	0.4	0.9	1.1	2.3	4.8
U.S.	19.1	9.3	4.0	2.3	2.0	1.0	1.9	0.8	0.8	0.7

Note: Figures are the number of adherents as a percentage of the total population; (1) Figures cover the New York-Newark-Jersey City, NY-NJ-PA Metropolitan Statistical Area; (2) Methodist/Pietist; (3) Latter Day Saints; (4) Reformed; (5) Figures are estimates
Source: Association of Statisticians of American Religious Bodies, 2010 U.S. Religion Census: Religious Congregations & Membership Study

Religious Groups by Tradition

Area	Catholic	Evangelical Protestant	Mainline Protestant	Other Tradition	Black Protestant	Orthodox
MSA[1]	36.9	4.0	4.1	8.4	1.2	1.0
U.S.	19.1	16.2	7.3	4.3	1.6	0.3

Note: Figures are the number of adherents as a percentage of the total population; (1) Figures cover the New York-Newark-Jersey City, NY-NJ-PA Metropolitan Statistical Area
Source: Association of Statisticians of American Religious Bodies, 2010 U.S. Religion Census: Religious Congregations & Membership Study

ECONOMY

Gross Metropolitan Product

Area	2017	2018	2019	2020	Rank[2]
MSA[1]	1,765.5	1,851.9	1,932.1	2,007.4	1

Note: Figures are in billions of dollars; (1) Figures cover the New York-Newark-Jersey City, NY-NJ-PA Metropolitan Statistical Area; (2) Rank is based on 2018 data and ranges from 1 to 381
Source: U.S. Conference of Mayors, U.S. Metro Economies: GMP & Employment 2018-2020, September 2019

Economic Growth

Area	2015-17 (%)	2018 (%)	2019 (%)	2020 (%)	Rank[2]
MSA[1]	1.3	2.6	2.6	1.6	196
U.S.	1.9	2.9	2.3	2.1	—

Note: Figures are real gross metropolitan product (GMP) growth rates and represent average annual percent change; (1) Figures cover the New York-Newark-Jersey City, NY-NJ-PA Metropolitan Statistical Area; (2) Rank is based on 2017 2-year average annual percent change and ranges from 1 to 381
Source: U.S. Conference of Mayors, U.S. Metro Economies: GMP & Employment 2018-2020, September 2019

Metropolitan Area Exports

Area	2014	2015	2016	2017	2018	2019	Rank[2]
MSA[1]	105,266.6	95,645.4	89,649.5	93,693.7	97,692.4	87,365.7	2

Note: Figures are in millions of dollars; (1) Figures cover the New York-Newark-Jersey City, NY-NJ-PA Metropolitan Statistical Area; (2) Rank is based on 2019 data and ranges from 1 to 386
Source: U.S. Department of Commerce, International Trade Administration, Office of Trade and Economic Analysis, Industry and Analysis, Exports by Metropolitan Area, data extracted March 24, 2021

Building Permits

Area	Single-Family			Multi-Family			Total		
	2018	2019	Pct. Chg.	2018	2019	Pct. Chg.	2018	2019	Pct. Chg.
City	417	332	-20.4	20,493	26,215	27.9	20,910	26,547	27.0
MSA[1]	11,077	11,072	0.0	38,615	50,096	29.7	49,692	61,168	23.1
U.S.	855,300	862,100	0.7	473,500	523,900	10.6	1,328,800	1,386,000	4.3

Note: (1) Figures cover the New York-Newark-Jersey City, NY-NJ-PA Metropolitan Statistical Area; Figures represent new, privately-owned housing units authorized (unadjusted data); All permit data are based on estimates with imputation
Source: U.S. Census Bureau, Manufacturing, Mining, and Construction Statistics, Building Permits, 2018, 2019

Bankruptcy Filings

Area	Business Filings			Nonbusiness Filings		
	2019	2020	% Chg.	2019	2020	% Chg.
Bronx County	44	24	-45.5	2,486	1,498	-39.7
Kings County	327	182	-44.3	2,743	1,710	-37.7
New York County	244	480	96.7	1,210	854	-29.4
Queens County	206	127	-38.3	3,708	1,990	-46.3
Richmond County	22	19	-13.6	835	459	-45.0
U.S.	22,780	21,655	-4.9	752,160	522,808	-30.5

Note: Business filings include Chapter 7, Chapter 9, Chapter 11, Chapter 12, Chapter 13, Chapter 15, and Section 304; Nonbusiness filings include Chapter 7, Chapter 11, and Chapter 13
Source: Administrative Office of the U.S. Courts, Business and Nonbusiness Bankruptcy, County Cases Commenced by Chapter of the Bankruptcy Code, During the 12-Month Period Ending December 31, 2019 and Business and Nonbusiness Bankruptcy, County Cases Commenced by Chapter of the Bankruptcy Code, During the 12-Month Period Ending December 31, 2020

Housing Vacancy Rates

Area	Gross Vacancy Rate[2] (%)			Year-Round Vacancy Rate[3] (%)			Rental Vacancy Rate[4] (%)			Homeowner Vacancy Rate[5] (%)		
	2018	2019	2020	2018	2019	2020	2018	2019	2020	2018	2019	2020
MSA[1]	10.3	9.2	9.1	9.1	7.8	7.8	4.5	4.3	4.5	1.6	1.4	1.3
U.S.	12.3	12.0	10.6	9.7	9.5	8.2	6.9	6.7	6.3	1.5	1.4	1.0

Note: (1) Figures cover the New York-Newark-Jersey City, NY-NJ-PA Metropolitan Statistical Area; (2) The percentage of the total housing inventory that is vacant; (3) The percentage of the housing inventory (excluding seasonal units) that is year-round vacant; (4) The percentage of rental inventory that is vacant for rent; (5) The percentage of homeowner inventory that is vacant for sale
Source: U.S. Census Bureau, Housing Vacancies and Homeownership Annual Statistics: 2018, 2019, 2020

INCOME

Income

Area	Per Capita ($)	Median Household ($)	Average Household ($)
City	39,828	63,998	102,946
MSA[1]	43,409	78,773	116,604
U.S.	34,103	62,843	88,607

Note: (1) Figures cover the New York-Newark-Jersey City, NY-NJ-PA Metropolitan Statistical Area
Source: U.S. Census Bureau, 2015-2019 American Community Survey 5-Year Estimates

Household Income Distribution

Area	Percent of Households Earning							
	Under $15,000	$15,000 -$24,999	$25,000 -$34,999	$35,000 -$49,999	$50,000 -$74,999	$75,000 -$99,999	$100,000 -$149,999	$150,000 and up
City	14.3	9.0	7.9	10.2	14.3	11.1	14.3	18.9
MSA[1]	10.5	7.5	7.0	9.3	13.9	11.4	16.4	24.1
U.S.	10.3	8.9	8.9	12.3	17.2	12.7	15.1	14.5

Note: (1) Figures cover the New York-Newark-Jersey City, NY-NJ-PA Metropolitan Statistical Area
Source: U.S. Census Bureau, 2015-2019 American Community Survey 5-Year Estimates

Poverty Rate

Area	All Ages	Under 18 Years Old	18 to 64 Years Old	65 Years and Over
City	17.9	25.1	15.6	18.2
MSA[1]	12.8	17.7	11.4	12.0
U.S.	13.4	18.5	12.6	9.3

Note: Figures are percentage of people whose income during the past 12 months was below the poverty level;
(1) Figures cover the New York-Newark-Jersey City, NY-NJ-PA Metropolitan Statistical Area
Source: U.S. Census Bureau, 2015-2019 American Community Survey 5-Year Estimates

CITY FINANCES

City Government Finances

Component	2017 ($000)	2017 ($ per capita)
Total Revenues	136,203,360	15,929
Total Expenditures	129,468,995	15,142
Debt Outstanding	140,617,849	16,446
Cash and Securities[1]	237,417,811	27,767

Note: (1) Cash and security holdings of a government at the close of its fiscal year,
including those of its dependent agencies, utilities, and liquor stores.
Source: U.S. Census Bureau, State & Local Government Finances 2017

City Government Expenditures by Function

Function	2017 ($000)	2017 ($ per capita)	2017 (%)
General Direct Expenditures			
Air Transportation	0	0	0.0
Corrections	1,879,858	219	1.5
Education	31,702,430	3,707	24.5
Employment Security Administration	0	0	0.0
Financial Administration	568,070	66	0.4
Fire Protection	2,155,415	252	1.7
General Public Buildings	665,367	77	0.5
Governmental Administration, Other	314,683	36	0.2
Health	1,225,993	143	0.9
Highways	2,550,538	298	2.0
Hospitals	8,876,511	1,038	6.9
Housing and Community Development	5,825,736	681	4.5
Interest on General Debt	6,228,816	728	4.8
Judicial and Legal	793,153	92	0.6
Libraries	379,871	44	0.3
Parking	43,482	5	0.0
Parks and Recreation	1,287,569	150	1.0
Police Protection	5,685,111	664	4.4
Public Welfare	8,232,954	962	6.4
Sewerage	1,929,901	225	1.5
Solid Waste Management	1,719,569	201	1.3
Veterans' Services	0	0	0.0
Liquor Store	0	0	0.0
Utility	14,070,571	1,645	10.9
Employee Retirement	12,847,241	1,502	9.9

Source: U.S. Census Bureau, State & Local Government Finances 2017

City Government Revenue by Source

Source	2017 ($000)	2017 ($ per capita)	2017 (%)
General Revenue			
From Federal Government	6,187,516	724	4.5
From State Government	30,559,408	3,574	22.4
From Local Governments	906,557	106	0.7
Taxes			
Property	24,746,286	2,894	18.2
Sales and Gross Receipts	9,132,981	1,068	6.7
Personal Income	11,690,220	1,367	8.6
Corporate Income	6,560,104	767	4.8
Motor Vehicle License	108,908	13	0.1
Other Taxes	3,071,900	359	2.3
Current Charges	9,729,641	1,138	7.1
Liquor Store	0	0	0.0
Utility	6,003,382	702	4.4
Employee Retirement	23,604,864	2,761	17.3

Source: U.S. Census Bureau, State & Local Government Finances 2017

EMPLOYMENT

Labor Force and Employment

Area	Civilian Labor Force			Workers Employed		
	Dec. 2019	Dec. 2020	% Chg.	Dec. 2019	Dec. 2020	% Chg.
City	4,055,234	3,856,031	-4.9	3,932,458	3,408,146	-13.3
MD[1]	7,008,087	6,694,644	-4.5	6,780,009	6,077,482	-10.4
U.S.	164,007,000	160,017,000	-2.4	158,504,000	149,613,000	-5.6

Note: Data is not seasonally adjusted and covers workers 16 years of age and older; (1) Figures cover the New York-Jersey City-White Plains, NY-NJ Metropolitan Division
Source: Bureau of Labor Statistics, Local Area Unemployment Statistics

Unemployment Rate

Area	2020											
	Jan.	Feb.	Mar.	Apr.	May	Jun.	Jul.	Aug.	Sep.	Oct.	Nov.	Dec.
City	3.8	3.8	4.2	15.5	20.2	18.7	18.8	14.9	14.7	11.7	11.7	11.6
MD[1]	3.8	3.6	3.8	15.1	16.3	18.3	17.6	14.0	10.7	10.5	10.4	9.2
U.S.	4.0	3.8	4.5	14.4	13.0	11.2	10.5	8.5	7.7	6.6	6.4	6.5

Note: Data is not seasonally adjusted and covers workers 16 years of age and older; (1) Figures cover the New York-Jersey City-White Plains, NY-NJ Metropolitan Division
Source: Bureau of Labor Statistics, Local Area Unemployment Statistics

Average Wages

Occupation	$/Hr.	Occupation	$/Hr.
Accountants and Auditors	50.80	Maintenance and Repair Workers	24.50
Automotive Mechanics	24.30	Marketing Managers	93.80
Bookkeepers	24.50	Network and Computer Systems Admin.	51.00
Carpenters	34.20	Nurses, Licensed Practical	27.50
Cashiers	14.30	Nurses, Registered	45.60
Computer Programmers	46.30	Nursing Assistants	19.50
Computer Systems Analysts	55.10	Office Clerks, General	19.00
Computer User Support Specialists	31.30	Physical Therapists	47.80
Construction Laborers	29.50	Physicians	99.90
Cooks, Restaurant	17.30	Plumbers, Pipefitters and Steamfitters	35.80
Customer Service Representatives	21.90	Police and Sheriff's Patrol Officers	41.50
Dentists	81.30	Postal Service Mail Carriers	25.80
Electricians	40.50	Real Estate Sales Agents	47.40
Engineers, Electrical	54.50	Retail Salespersons	17.10
Fast Food and Counter Workers	14.00	Sales Representatives, Technical/Scientific	53.90
Financial Managers	103.20	Secretaries, Exc. Legal/Medical/Executive	21.60
First-Line Supervisors of Office Workers	36.50	Security Guards	18.30
General and Operations Managers	82.90	Surgeons	103.30
Hairdressers/Cosmetologists	18.50	Teacher Assistants, Exc. Postsecondary*	17.10
Home Health and Personal Care Aides	15.40	Teachers, Secondary School, Exc. Sp. Ed.*	43.90
Janitors and Cleaners	18.60	Telemarketers	18.00
Landscaping/Groundskeeping Workers	18.60	Truck Drivers, Heavy/Tractor-Trailer	27.40
Lawyers	86.60	Truck Drivers, Light/Delivery Services	21.30
Maids and Housekeeping Cleaners	18.20	Waiters and Waitresses	18.10

Note: Wage data covers the New York-Newark-Jersey City, NY-NJ-PA Metropolitan Statistical Area; (*) Hourly wages were calculated from annual wage data based on a 40 hour work week; n/a not available.
Source: Bureau of Labor Statistics, Metro Area Occupational Employment & Wage Estimates, May 2020

Employment by Industry

Sector	MD[1]		U.S.
	Number of Employees	Percent of Total	Percent of Total
Construction, Mining, and Logging	252,500	3.9	5.5
Education and Health Services	1,478,900	22.7	16.3
Financial Activities	613,100	9.4	6.1
Government	917,900	14.1	15.2
Information	249,000	3.8	1.9
Leisure and Hospitality	390,300	6.0	9.0
Manufacturing	181,400	2.8	8.5
Other Services	248,200	3.8	3.8
Professional and Business Services	1,071,000	16.5	14.4
Retail Trade	580,800	8.9	10.9
Transportation, Warehousing, and Utilities	275,900	4.2	4.6
Wholesale Trade	246,700	3.8	3.9

Note: Figures are non-farm employment as of December 2020. Figures are not seasonally adjusted and include workers 16 years of age and older; (1) Figures cover the New York-Jersey City-White Plains, NY-NJ Metropolitan Division
Source: Bureau of Labor Statistics, Current Employment Statistics, Employment, Hours, and Earnings

Employment by Occupation

Occupation Classification	City (%)	MSA[1] (%)	U.S. (%)
Management, Business, Science, and Arts	42.0	43.2	38.5
Natural Resources, Construction, and Maintenance	6.0	6.7	8.9
Production, Transportation, and Material Moving	9.1	9.7	13.2
Sales and Office	20.3	21.4	21.6
Service	22.6	19.0	17.8

Note: Figures cover employed civilians 16 years of age and older; (1) Figures cover the New York-Newark-Jersey City, NY-NJ-PA Metropolitan Statistical Area
Source: U.S. Census Bureau, 2015-2019 American Community Survey 5-Year Estimates

Occupations with Greatest Projected Employment Growth: 2020 – 2022

Occupation[1]	2020 Employment	2022 Projected Employment	Numeric Employment Change	Percent Employment Change
Retail Salespersons	197,790	284,450	86,660	43.8
Fast Food and Counter Workers	105,620	180,900	75,280	71.3
Home Health and Personal Care Aides	429,720	494,210	64,490	15.0
Waiters and Waitresses	72,540	131,730	59,190	81.6
Janitors and Cleaners, Except Maids and Housekeeping Cleaners	170,290	200,580	30,290	17.8
Cashiers	160,190	189,810	29,620	18.5
Cooks, Restaurant	31,170	59,920	28,750	92.2
General and Operations Managers	141,420	170,010	28,590	20.2
Laborers and Freight, Stock, and Material Movers, Hand	113,850	139,380	25,530	22.4
Security Guards	97,380	119,070	21,690	22.3

Note: Projections cover New York; (1) Sorted by numeric employment change
Source: www.projectionscentral.com, State Occupational Projections, 2020–2022 Short-Term Projections

Fastest-Growing Occupations: 2020 – 2022

Occupation[1]	2020 Employment	2022 Projected Employment	Numeric Employment Change	Percent Employment Change
Gaming Change Persons and Booth Cashiers	210	490	280	133.3
Manicurists and Pedicurists	13,970	30,930	16,960	121.4
Gaming Dealers	1,240	2,720	1,480	119.4
Shampooers	470	1,020	550	117.0
Morticians, Undertakers, and Funeral Directors	650	1,390	740	113.8
First-Line Supervisors of Gambling Services Workers	710	1,440	730	102.8
Gaming and Sports Book Writers and Runners	230	450	220	95.7
Barbers	2,730	5,330	2,600	95.2
Cooks, Restaurant	31,170	59,920	28,750	92.2
Skincare Specialists	3,950	7,520	3,570	90.4

Note: Projections cover New York; (1) Sorted by percent employment change and excludes occupations with numeric employment change less than 50
Source: www.projectionscentral.com, State Occupational Projections, 2020–2022 Short-Term Projections

TAXES

State Corporate Income Tax Rates

State	Tax Rate (%)	Income Brackets ($)	Num. of Brackets	Financial Institution Tax Rate (%)[a]	Federal Income Tax Ded.
New York	6.5 (r)	Flat rate	1	6.5 (r)	No

Note: Tax rates as of January 1, 2021; (a) Rates listed are the corporate income tax rate applied to financial institutions or excise taxes based on income. Some states have other taxes based upon the value of deposits or shares; (r) New York's General business corporate rate shown. The Corporate Stocks Tax was eliminated for tax year 2021. A minimum tax ranges from $25 to $200,000, depending on receipts ($250 minimum for banks). Certain qualified New York manufacturers pay 0%.
Source: Federation of Tax Administrators, State Corporate Income Tax Rates, January 1, 2021

State Individual Income Tax Rates

State	Tax Rate (%)	Income Brackets ($)	Personal Exemptions ($) Single	Married	Depend.	Standard Ded. ($) Single	Married
New York (a)	4.0 - 8.82	8,500 - 1,077,550 (b)	0	0	1,000	8,000	16,050

Note: Tax rates as of January 1, 2021; Local- and county-level taxes are not included; Federal income tax is not deductible on state income tax returns; (a) 19 states have statutory provision for automatically adjusting to the rate of inflation the dollar values of the income tax brackets, standard deductions, and/or personal exemptions. Michigan indexes the personal exemption only. Oregon does not index the income brackets for $125,000 and over; (b) For joint returns, taxes are twice the tax on half the couple's income.
Source: Federation of Tax Administrators, State Individual Income Tax Rates, January 1, 2021

Various State Sales and Excise Tax Rates

State	State Sales Tax (%)	Gasoline[1] (¢/gal.)	Cigarette[2] ($/pack)	Spirits[3] ($/gal.)	Wine[4] ($/gal.)	Beer[5] ($/gal.)	Recreational Marijuana (%)
New York	4	42.7	4.35	6.44	0.3	0.14	(r)

Note: All tax rates as of January 1, 2021; (1) The American Petroleum Institute has developed a methodology for determining the average tax rate on a gallon of fuel. Rates may include any of the following: excise taxes, environmental fees, storage tank fees, other fees or taxes, general sales tax, and local taxes; (2) The federal excise tax of $1.0066 per pack and local taxes are not included; (3) Rates are those applicable to off-premise sales of 40% alcohol by volume (a.b.v.) distilled spirits in 750ml containers. Local excise taxes are excluded; (4) Rates are those applicable to off-premise sales of 11% a.b.v. non-carbonated wine in 750ml containers; (5) Rates are those applicable to off-premise sales of 4.7% a.b.v. beer in 12 ounce containers; (r) 9% state tax; 4% local tax
Source: Tax Foundation, 2021 Facts & Figures: How Does Your State Compare?

State Business Tax Climate Index Rankings

State	Overall Rank	Corporate Tax Rank	Individual Income Tax Rank	Sales Tax Rank	Property Tax Rank	Unemployment Insurance Tax Rank
New York	48	15	48	43	45	38

Note: The index is a measure of how each state's tax laws affect economic performance. The lower the rank, the more favorable a state's tax system is for business. States without a given tax are given a ranking of 1. The scores/rankings for the District of Columbia do not affect other states. The 2021 index represents the tax climate as of July 1, 2020.
Source: Tax Foundation, State Business Tax Climate Index 2021

TRANSPORTATION

Means of Transportation to Work

Area	Car/Truck/Van Drove Alone	Car-pooled	Public Transportation Bus	Subway	Railroad	Bicycle	Walked	Other Means	Worked at Home
City	22.3	4.5	10.1	43.9	1.5	1.3	10.0	2.2	4.3
MSA[1]	49.2	6.3	7.5	20.0	3.9	0.7	5.9	2.0	4.5
U.S.	76.3	9.0	2.4	1.9	0.6	0.5	2.7	1.4	5.2

Note: Figures are percentages and cover workers 16 years of age and older; (1) Figures cover the New York-Newark-Jersey City, NY-NJ-PA Metropolitan Statistical Area
Source: U.S. Census Bureau, 2015-2019 American Community Survey 5-Year Estimates

Travel Time to Work

Area	Less Than 10 Minutes	10 to 19 Minutes	20 to 29 Minutes	30 to 44 Minutes	45 to 59 Minutes	60 to 89 Minutes	90 Minutes or More
City	3.8	12.1	13.4	27.1	16.4	19.5	7.7
MSA[1]	6.7	18.2	16.1	23.9	12.7	15.3	7.1
U.S.	12.2	28.4	20.8	20.8	8.3	6.4	2.9

Note: Note: Figures are percentages and include workers 16 years old and over; (1) Figures cover the New York-Newark-Jersey City, NY-NJ-PA Metropolitan Statistical Area
Source: U.S. Census Bureau, 2015-2019 American Community Survey 5-Year Estimates

Key Congestion Measures

Measure	1982	1992	2002	2012	2017
Annual Hours of Delay, Total (000)	190,419	298,115	536,526	727,659	811,609
Annual Hours of Delay, Per Auto Commuter	32	45	66	81	92
Annual Congestion Cost, Total (million $)	1,441	3,158	7,282	13,149	15,040
Annual Congestion Cost, Per Auto Commuter ($)	1,024	1,102	1,547	1,644	1,778

Note: Covers the New York-Newark NY-NJ-CT urban area
Source: Texas A&M Transportation Institute, 2019 Urban Mobility Report

Freeway Travel Time Index

Measure	1982	1987	1992	1997	2002	2007	2012	2017
Urban Area Index[1]	1.15	1.18	1.21	1.26	1.31	1.34	1.34	1.35
Urban Area Rank[1,2]	8	11	11	8	6	7	8	7

Note: Freeway Travel Time Index—the ratio of travel time in the peak period to the travel time at free-flow conditions. For example, a value of 1.30 indicates a 20-minute free-flow trip takes 26 minutes in the peak (20 minutes x 1.30 = 26 minutes); (1) Covers the New York-Newark NY-NJ-CT urban area; (2) Rank is based on 101 larger urban areas (#1 = highest travel time index)
Source: Texas A&M Transportation Institute, 2019 Urban Mobility Report

Public Transportation

Agency Name / Mode of Transportation	Vehicles Operated in Maximum Service[1]	Annual Unlinked Passenger Trips[2] (in thous.)	Annual Passenger Miles[3] (in thous.)
MTA New York City Transit (NYCT)			
Bus (directly operated)	3,262	691,616.6	1,478,429.6
Bus Rapid Transit (directly operated)	146	30,695.7	57,076.2
Commuter Bus (directly operated)	437	11,477.2	153,389.1
Demand Response (purchased transportation)	1,627	4,828.4	43,330.2
Heavy Rail (directly operated)	5,413	2,712,521.7	10,462,782.6
MTA Metro-North Railroad (MTA-MNCR)			
Bus (purchased transportation)	9	406.2	488.5
Commuter Rail (directly operated)	1,135	91,433.8	2,034,489.6
Ferryboat (purchased transportation)	2	172.8	707.2
MTA Long Island Railroad (MTA-LIRR)			
Commuter Rail (directly operated)	1,026	114,241.4	3,929,860.0
MTA Staten Island Railway (SIRTOA)			
Heavy Rail (directly operated)	44	7,731.8	48,222.7
New York City Department of Transportation (NYCDOT)			
Commuter Bus (purchased transportation)	24	396.0	13,374.2
Ferryboat (directly operated)	4	25,222.0	131,154.3
Port Authority Trans-Hudson Corporation (PATH)			
Ferryboat (purchased transportation)	6	1,397.0	3,483.1
Heavy Rail (directly operated)	303	90,275.2	447,020.7

Note: (1) Number of revenue vehicles operated by the given mode and type of service to meet the annual maximum service requirement. This is the revenue vehicle count during the peak season of the year; on the week and day that maximum service is provided. Vehicles operated in maximum service (VOMS) exclude atypical days and one-time special events; (2) Number of passengers who boarded public transportation vehicles. Passengers are counted each time they board a vehicle no matter how many vehicles they use to travel from their origin to their destination. (3) Sum of the distances ridden by all passengers during the entire fiscal year.
Source: Federal Transit Administration, National Transit Database, 2019

Air Transportation

Airport Name and Code / Type of Service	Passenger Airlines[1]	Passenger Enplanements	Freight Carriers[2]	Freight (lbs)
John F. Kennedy International (JFK)				
Domestic service (U.S. carriers - 2020)	16	4,111,005	20	354,024,442
International service (U.S. carriers - 2019)	13	6,077,264	10	103,269,622
La Guardia International (LGA)				
Domestic service (U.S. carriers - 2020)	18	3,945,827	5	5,366,681
International service (U.S. carriers - 2019)	9	227,804	3	5,749
Newark International (EWR)				
Domestic service (U.S. carriers - 2020)	27	6,116,356	15	557,955,905
International service (U.S. carriers - 2019)	13	4,413,093	4	96,542,501

Note: (1) Includes all U.S.-based major, minor and commuter airlines that carried at least one passenger during the year; (2) Includes all U.S.-based airlines and freight carriers that transported at least one pound of freight during the year.
Source: Bureau of Transportation Statistics, The Intermodal Transportation Database, Air Carriers: T-100 Domestic Market (U.S. Carriers), 2020; Bureau of Transportation Statistics, The Intermodal Transportation Database, Air Carriers: T-100 International Market (U.S. Carriers), 2019

BUSINESSES

Major Business Headquarters

Company Name	Industry	Rankings	
		Fortune[1]	Forbes[2]
ABM Industries	Diversified Outsourcing Services	462	-
Alcoa	Metals	302	-
Alleghany	Insurance, Property and Casualty (Stock)	351	-
Altice USA	Telecommunications	327	-
AmTrust Financial Services	Insurance	-	72
American Express	Commercial Banks	67	-
American International Group	Insurance: Property and Casualty (Stock)	66	-
Assurant	Insurance, Property and Casualty (Stock)	315	-
Bank of New York Mellon	Commercial Banks	159	-
BlackRock	Securities	219	-
Blackstone Group	Diversified Financials	420	-
Bloomberg	Business Services & Supplies	-	33
Breakthru Beverage Group	Food, Drink & Tobacco	-	76
Bristol-Myers Squibb	Pharmaceuticals	115	-
Citigroup	Commercial Banks	31	-
Colgate-Palmolive	Household and Personal Products	203	-
Consolidated Edison	Utilities, Gas and Electric	256	-
Continental Grain	Food, Drink & Tobacco	-	174
Coty	Household and Personal Products	366	-
Deloitte	Business Services & Supplies	-	3
Equitable Holdings	Insurance: Life, Health (stock)	333	-
Ernst & Young	Business Services & Supplies	-	6
Estée Lauder	Soaps and Cosmetics	215	-
Foot Locker	Specialty Retailers, Apparel	397	-
Fox	Entertainment	280	-
Goldman Sachs Group	Commercial Banks	60	-
Guardian Life Ins. Co. of America	Insurance, Life, Health (Mutual)	238	-
Hearst	Media	-	28
Hess	Mining, Crude Oil Production	461	-
Icahn Enterprises	Petroleum Refining	352	-
Interpublic Group	Advertising, Marketing	308	-
J. Crew	Retailing	-	176
JPMorgan Chase	Commercial Banks	17	-
JetBlue Airways	Airlines	394	-
KKR	Securities	349	-
Latham & Watkins	Services	-	120
Loews	Insurance, Property and Casualty (Stock)	212	-
Marsh & McLennan	Diversified Financials	195	-
McKinsey & Company	Business Services & Supplies	-	35
MetLife	Insurance, Life, Health (Stock)	48	-
Morgan Stanley	Commercial Banks	61	-
New York Life Insurance	Insurance, Life, Health (Mutual)	73	-
News Corp.	Publishing, Printing	318	-
Omnicom Group	Advertising, Marketing	211	-
PVH	Apparel	322	-
Pfizer	Pharmaceuticals	64	-
Philip Morris International	Tobacco	107	-
PricewaterhouseCoopers	Business Services & Supplies	-	4
Ralph Lauren	Apparel	469	-
Red Apple Group	Oil & Gas Operations	-	100
Renco Group	Materials	-	85
S&P Global	Financial Data Services	451	-
STO Building Group	Construction	-	51
Skadden, Arps, Slate, Meagher & Flom	Services	-	171
Standard Industries	Manufacturing	-	69
StoneX Group	Diversified Financials	100	-
TIAA	Insurance, Life, Health (Mutual)	81	-
Tapestry	Apparel	485	-
Trammo	Trading Companies	-	202
Travelers Cos.	Insurance: Property and Casualty	106	-
Univision Communications	Media	-	161
Verizon Communications	Telecommunications	20	-
ViacomCBS	Entertainment	111	-

| Voya Financial | Insurance, Life, Health (Stock) | 353 | - |
| White & Case | Services | - | 207 |

Note: (1) Companies that produce a 10-K are ranked 1 to 500 based on 2019 revenue; (2) All private companies with at least $2 billion in annual revenue through the end of their most current fiscal year are ranked 1 to 219; companies listed are headquartered in the city; dashes indicate no ranking
Source: Fortune, "Fortune 500," June/July 2020; Forbes, "America's Largest Private Companies," 2020

Fastest-Growing Businesses

According to *Inc.*, New York is home to 29 of America's 500 fastest-growing private companies: **Kitu Life Super Coffee** (#18); **Ocrolus** (#30); **Noom** (#45); **Yieldstreet** (#46); **Constellation Agency** (#65); **Stadiumred Group** (#84); **Henson Group** (#132); **Glow Global Events** (#145); **Remesh** (#152); **GovernmentOfficeFurniture.com** (#162); **Silverback Development** (#168); **Qloo** (#187); **Siddhi Ops** (#197); **Andium** (#200); **Swag.com** (#218); **HireArt** (#223); **Stojo** (#245); **Jackson Hedden** (#251); **Experiture** (#283); **VetMed Group** (#306); **Bambridge Accountants New York** (#353); **Better.com** (#359); **McVeigh Global Meetings and Events** (#382); **Wachsman** (#405); **A Non-Agency** (#413); **Splendid Spoon** (#449); **GAN Integrity** (#458); **Industrious** (#489); **Venture Home Solar** (#497). Criteria: must be an independent, privately-held, for-profit, U.S. corporation, proprietorship or partnership as of December 31, 2019; revenues must be at least $100,000 in 2016 and $2 million in 2019; must have four-year operating/sales history. *Inc., "America's 500 Fastest-Growing Private Companies," 2020*

According to *Fortune*, New York is home to five of the 100 fastest-growing companies in the world: **Etsy** (#8); **Take-Two Interactive Software** (#20); **Virtu Financial** (#33); **StoneX Group** (#37); **Ubiquiti** (#72). Companies were ranked by their revenue growth rate; their EPS growth rate; and their three-year annualized total return to investors for the period ending June 30, 2020. Criteria for inclusion: a company, foreign or domestic, must trade on a major U.S. stock exchange; must file quarterly reports with the SEC; must have a minimum market capitalization of $250 million; must have a stock price of at least $5 on June 30, 2020; must have been trading continuously since June 30, 2017; must have revenue and net income for the four quarters ended on or before April 30, 2020, of at least $50 million and $10 million, respectively; and must have posted a compound annual growth in revenue and earnings per share of at least 15% annually over the three years ending on or before April 30, 2020. Real estate investment trusts, limited-liability companies, limited parterships, business development companies, closed-end investment firms, companies about to be acquired, and companies that lost money in the quarter ending April 30, 2020 were excluded. *Fortune, "100 Fastest-Growing Companies," 2020*

According to *Initiative for a Competitive Inner City (ICIC)*, New York is home to eight of America's 100 fastest-growing "inner city" companies: **JSD Holdings (dba Salon 718)** (#36); **Tempco Glass Fabrication** (#62); **UrbanTech Consulting Engineering PC** (#68); **Ombligo** (#77); **Creative Business** (#82); **InfoPeople Corporation** (#83); **The Crabby Shack** (#93); **Red Table Catering** (#100). Criteria for inclusion: company must be headquartered in or have 51 percent or more of its physical operations in an economically distressed urban area; must be an independent, for-profit corporation, partnership or proprietorship; must have 10 or more employees and have a five-year sales history that includes sales of at least $200,000 in the base year and at least $1 million in the current year with no decrease in sales over the two most recent years. Companies were ranked overall by revenue growth over the five-year period between 2015 and 2019. *Initiative for a Competitive Inner City (ICIC), "Inner City 100 Companies," 2020*

According to Deloitte, New York is home to 45 of North America's 500 fastest-growing high-technology companies: **Nanit** (#19); **Ocrolus** (#28); **Semperis** (#35); **Noom** (#40); **Even Financial** (#41); **Remesh** (#57); **HireArt** (#66); **Socure** (#70); **KeyMe** (#78); **Better.com** (#93); **DataCamp** (#94); **Freshly** (#98); **Cuebiq Inc.** (#107); **Aircall** (#117); **Hyperscience** (#130); **Intercept Pharmaceuticals, Inc.** (#133); **Fortress Biotech, Inc.** (#135); **dv01** (#144); **Avanan** (#171); **Dataminr** (#176); **Prove (formerly Payfone)** (#178); **Datadog, Inc.** (#186); **TripleLift** (#202); **SecurityScorecard** (#218); **Glia** (#223); **iTechArt Group** (#225); **Mohawk Group Holdings, Inc.** (#226); **Connatix** (#232); **Fundera** (#237); **Insticator** (#247); **Unite Us** (#264); **Fund That Flip** (#297); **Kasisto** (#302); **Slice** (#311); **BioCatch** (#312); **TickPick** (#323); **MongoDB** (#326); **Dashlane Inc.** (#331); **TodayTix** (#342); **LeagueApps** (#360); **Health-E Commerce** (#365); **Diligent** (#433); **Ambra Health** (#435); **Greenhouse Software** (#450); **Unbound Tech** (#465). Companies are ranked by percentage growth in revenue over a four-year period. Criteria for inclusion: company must be headquartered within North America; must own proprietary intellectual property or technology that is sold to customers in products that contributes to a significant portion of the company's operating revenue; must have been in business for a minumum of four years with 2016 operating revenues of at least $50,000 USD/CD and 2019 operating revenues of at least $5 million USD/CD. *Deloitte, 2020 Technology Fast 500™*

Minority Business Opportunity

New York is home to five companies which are on the *Black Enterprise* Industrial/Service list (100 largest companies based on gross sales): **McKissack & McKissack** (#64); **Golden Krust Franchis-**

ing (#76); **Bithgroup Technologies** (#89); **Black Enterprise** (#90); **Skyline Industries** (#95). Criteria: operational in previous calendar year; at least 51% black-owned and manufactures/owns the product it sells or provides industrial or consumer services. Brokerages, real estate firms and firms that provide professional services are not eligible. *Black Enterprise, B.E. 100s, 2019*

New York is home to one company which is on the *Black Enterprise* Auto Dealer list (45 largest dealers based on gross sales): **Bical Auto Mall (Brooklyn)** (#26). Criteria: company must be operational in previous calendar year and be at least 51% black-owned. *Black Enterprise, B.E. 100s, 2019*

New York is home to one company which is on the *Black Enterprise* Bank list (15 largest banks based on total assets, capital, deposits and loans, including mortgage-backed securities for the calendar year): **Carver Bancorp. (Carver Federal Savings Bank)** (#3). Only commercial banks or savings and loans that are classified by the Federal Reserve as black institutions and have been fully operational for the previous calendar year were considered. *Black Enterprise, B.E. 100s, 2019*

New York is home to two companies which are on the *Black Enterprise* Asset Manager list (10 largest asset management firms based on assets under management): **Advent Capital Management** (#3); **Semper Capital Management** (#8). Criteria: company must have been operational in previous calendar year and be at least 51% black-owned. *Black Enterprise, B.E. 100s, 2019*

New York is home to two companies which are on the *Black Enterprise* Private Equity list (10 largest private equity firms based on capital under management): **GenNx360 Capital Partners** (#5); **ICV Partners** (#5). Criteria: company must be operational in previous calendar year and be at least 51% black-owned. *Black Enterprise, B.E. 100s, 2019*

Living Environment

COST OF LIVING

Cost of Living Index

Composite Index	Groceries	Housing	Utilities	Trans-portation	Health Care	Misc. Goods/ Services
179.3	134.4	334.3	103.8	109.0	106.0	121.8

Note: The Cost of Living Index measures regional differences in the cost of consumer goods and services, excluding taxes and non-consumer expenditures, for professional and managerial households in the top income quintile. It is based on more than 50,000 prices covering almost 60 different items for which prices are collected three times a year by chambers of commerce, economic development organizations or university applied economic centers in each participating urban area. The numbers shown should be read as a percentage above or below the national average of 100. For example, a value of 115.4 in the groceries column indicates that grocery prices are 15.4% higher than the national average. Small differences in the index numbers should not be interpreted as significant; Figures cover the Brooklyn NY urban area.
Source: The Council for Community and Economic Research, Cost of Living Index, 2020

Grocery Prices

Area[1]	T-Bone Steak ($/pound)	Frying Chicken ($/pound)	Whole Milk ($/half gal.)	Eggs ($/dozen)	Orange Juice ($/64 oz.)	Coffee ($/11.5 oz.)
City[2]	15.20	2.36	2.82	2.78	4.36	4.74
Avg.	11.78	1.39	2.05	1.47	3.57	4.34
Min.	8.03	0.94	1.03	0.74	2.94	3.02
Max.	15.86	2.65	4.31	3.77	5.44	8.69

Note: (1) Values for the local area are compared with the average, minimum and maximum values for all 284 areas in the Cost of Living Index; (2) Figures cover the Brooklyn NY urban area; T-Bone Steak (price per pound); Frying Chicken (price per pound, whole fryer); Whole Milk (half gallon carton); Eggs (price per dozen, Grade A, large); Orange Juice (64 oz. Tropicana or Florida Natural); Coffee (11.5 oz. can, vacuum-packed, Maxwell House, Hills Bros, or Folgers).
Source: The Council for Community and Economic Research, Cost of Living Index, 2020

Housing and Utility Costs

Area[1]	New Home Price ($)	Apartment Rent ($/month)	All Electric ($/month)	Part Electric ($/month)	Other Energy ($/month)	Telephone ($/month)
City[2]	1,278,996	3,486	-	95.03	78.96	189.50
Avg.	368,594	1,168	170.86	100.47	65.28	184.30
Min.	190,567	502	91.58	31.42	26.08	169.60
Max.	2,227,806	4,738	470.38	280.31	280.06	206.50

Note: (1) Values for the local area are compared with the average, minimum and maximum values for all 284 areas in the Cost of Living Index; (2) Figures cover the Brooklyn NY urban area; New Home Price (2,400 sf living area, 8,000 sf lot, in urban area with full utilities); Apartment Rent (950 sf 2 bedroom/1.5 or 2 bath, unfurnished, excluding all utilities except water); All Electric (average monthly cost for an all-electric home); Part Electric (average monthly cost for a part-electric home); Other Energy (average monthly cost for natural gas, fuel oil, coal, wood, and any other forms of energy except electricity); Telephone (price includes the base monthly rate plus taxes and fees for three lines of mobile phone service).
Source: The Council for Community and Economic Research, Cost of Living Index, 2020

Health Care, Transportation, and Other Costs

Area[1]	Doctor ($/visit)	Dentist ($/visit)	Optometrist ($/visit)	Gasoline ($/gallon)	Beauty Salon ($/visit)	Men's Shirt ($)
City[2]	116.89	116.47	100.16	2.32	70.14	49.22
Avg.	115.44	99.32	108.10	2.21	39.27	31.37
Min.	36.68	59.00	51.36	1.71	19.00	11.00
Max.	219.00	153.10	250.97	3.46	82.05	58.33

Note: (1) Values for the local area are compared with the average, minimum and maximum values for all 284 areas in the Cost of Living Index; (2) Figures cover the Brooklyn NY urban area; Doctor (general practitioners routine exam of an established patient); Dentist (adult teeth cleaning and periodic oral examination); Optometrist (full vision eye exam for established adult patient); Gasoline (one gallon regular unleaded, national brand, including all taxes, cash price at self-service pump if available); Beauty Salon (woman's shampoo, trim, and blow-dry); Men's Shirt (cotton/polyester dress shirt, pinpoint weave, long sleeves).
Source: The Council for Community and Economic Research, Cost of Living Index, 2020

HOUSING

Homeownership Rate

Area	2012 (%)	2013 (%)	2014 (%)	2015 (%)	2016 (%)	2017 (%)	2018 (%)	2019 (%)	2020 (%)
MSA[1]	51.5	50.6	50.7	49.9	50.4	49.9	49.7	50.4	50.9
U.S.	65.4	65.1	64.5	63.7	63.4	63.9	64.4	64.6	66.6

Note: (1) Figures cover the New York-Newark-Jersey City, NY-NJ-PA Metropolitan Statistical Area
Source: U.S. Census Bureau, Housing Vacancies and Homeownership Annual Statistics: 2012-2020

House Price Index (HPI)

Area	National Ranking[2]	Quarterly Change (%)	One-Year Change (%)	Five-Year Change (%)	Since 1991Q1 (%)
MD[1]	220	1.50	3.91	23.15	199.59
U.S.[3]	–	3.81	10.77	38.99	205.12

Note: The HPI is a weighted repeat sales index. It measures average price changes in repeat sales or refinancings on the same properties. This information is obtained by reviewing repeat mortgage transactions on single-family properties whose mortgages have been purchased or securitized by Fannie Mae or Freddie Mac since January 1975; (1) Figures cover the New York-Jersey City-White Plains, NY-NJ Metropolitan Division; (2) Rankings are based on annual percentage change for all metro areas containing at least 15,000 transactions over the last 10 years and ranges from 1 to 253; (3) figures based on a weighted average of Census Division estimates using a seasonally adjusted, purchase-only index; all figures are for the period ending December 31, 2020
Source: Federal Housing Finance Agency, Change in Metropolitan Area House Price Indexes, April 7, 2021

Median Single-Family Home Prices

Area	2018	2019	2020p	Percent Change 2019 to 2020
MD[1]	377.8	386.5	442.0	14.4
U.S. Average	261.6	274.6	299.9	9.2

Note: Figures are median sales prices of existing single-family homes in thousands of dollars; (p) preliminary; (1) Figures cover the New York-Jersey City-White Plains, NY-NJ Metropolitan Division
Source: National Association of Realtors, Median Sales Price of Existing Single-Family Homes for Metropolitan Areas, 4th Quarter 2020

Qualifying Income Based on Median Sales Price of Existing Single-Family Homes

Area	With 5% Down ($)	With 10% Down ($)	With 20% Down ($)
MD[1]	90,977	86,189	76,613
U.S. Average	59,266	56,147	49,908

Note: Figures are preliminary; Qualifying income is based on a mortgage rate of 2.81%. Monthly principal and interest payment is limited to 25% of income; (1) Figures cover the New York-Jersey City-White Plains, NY-NJ Metropolitan Division
Source: National Association of Realtors, Qualifying Income Based on Median Sales Price of Existing Single-Family Homes for Metropolitan Areas, 4th Quarter 2020

Home Value Distribution

Area	Under $50,000	$50,000 -$99,999	$100,000 -$149,999	$150,000 -$199,999	$200,000 -$299,999	$300,000 -$499,999	$500,000 -$999,999	$1,000,000 or more
City	2.9	1.3	1.9	2.4	6.6	23.7	41.4	19.9
MSA[1]	2.0	1.4	2.4	3.9	13.2	35.1	32.1	9.9
U.S.	6.9	12.0	13.3	14.0	19.6	19.3	11.4	3.4

Note: Figures are percentages and cover owner-occupied housing units; (1) Figures cover the New York-Newark-Jersey City, NY-NJ-PA Metropolitan Statistical Area
Source: U.S. Census Bureau, 2015-2019 American Community Survey 5-Year Estimates

Year Housing Structure Built

Area	2010 or Later	2000 -2009	1990 -1999	1980 -1989	1970 -1979	1960 -1969	1950 -1959	1940 -1949	Before 1940	Median Year
City	2.8	5.6	3.7	4.8	7.1	12.5	13.0	9.9	40.6	1949
MSA[1]	2.8	6.7	6.1	7.7	9.8	13.7	15.9	8.8	28.6	1958
U.S.	5.2	14.0	13.9	13.4	15.2	10.6	10.3	4.9	12.6	1978

Note: Figures are percentages except for Median Year; Note: (1) Figures cover the New York-Newark-Jersey City, NY-NJ-PA Metropolitan Statistical Area
Source: U.S. Census Bureau, 2015-2019 American Community Survey 5-Year Estimates

Gross Monthly Rent

Area	Under $500	$500 -$999	$1,000 -$1,499	$1,500 -$1,999	$2,000 -$2,499	$2,500 -$2,999	$3,000 and up	Median ($)
City	10.6	14.6	28.1	22.1	11.0	5.6	8.0	1,443
MSA[1]	9.4	13.9	30.7	23.1	11.0	5.3	6.7	1,439
U.S.	9.4	36.2	30.0	14.0	5.6	2.4	2.4	1,062

Note: Figures are percentages except for Median; Gross rent is the contract rent plus the estimated average monthly cost of utilities (electricity, gas, and water and sewer) and fuels (oil, coal, kerosene, wood, etc.) if these are paid by the renter (or paid for the renter by someone else); (1) Figures cover the New York-Newark-Jersey City, NY-NJ-PA Metropolitan Statistical Area
Source: U.S. Census Bureau, 2015-2019 American Community Survey 5-Year Estimates

HEALTH

Health Risk Factors

Category	MD[1] (%)	U.S. (%)
Adults aged 18–64 who have any kind of health care coverage	86.1	87.3
Adults who reported being in good or better health	81.6	82.4
Adults who have been told they have high blood cholesterol	32.6	33.0
Adults who have been told they have high blood pressure	28.9	32.3
Adults who are current smokers	12.3	17.1
Adults who currently use E-cigarettes	3.5	4.6
Adults who currently use chewing tobacco, snuff, or snus	2.2	4.0
Adults who are heavy drinkers[2]	5.2	6.3
Adults who are binge drinkers[3]	16.5	17.4
Adults who are overweight (BMI 25.0 - 29.9)	35.5	35.3
Adults who are obese (BMI 30.0 - 99.8)	23.6	31.3
Adults who participated in any physical activities in the past month	71.5	74.4
Adults who always or nearly always wears a seat belt	92.1	94.3

Note: (1) Figures cover the New York-Jersey City-White Plains, NY-NJ Metropolitan Division; (2) Heavy drinkers are classified as adult men having more than 14 drinks per week and adult women having more than 7 drinks per week; (3) Binge drinkers are classified as males having five or more drinks on one occasion or females having four or more drinks on one occasion
Source: Centers for Disease Control and Prevention, Behaviorial Risk Factor Surveillance System, SMART: Selected Metropolitan Area Risk Trends, 2017

Acute and Chronic Health Conditions

Category	MD[1] (%)	U.S. (%)
Adults who have ever been told they had a heart attack	3.3	4.2
Adults who have ever been told they have angina or coronary heart disease	3.4	3.9
Adults who have ever been told they had a stroke	2.0	3.0
Adults who have ever been told they have asthma	12.5	14.2
Adults who have ever been told they have arthritis	19.2	24.9
Adults who have ever been told they have diabetes[2]	10.5	10.5
Adults who have ever been told they had skin cancer	3.5	6.2
Adults who have ever been told they had any other types of cancer	5.4	7.1
Adults who have ever been told they have COPD	4.5	6.5
Adults who have ever been told they have kidney disease	2.5	3.0
Adults who have ever been told they have a form of depression	13.8	20.5

Note: (1) Figures cover the New York-Jersey City-White Plains, NY-NJ Metropolitan Division; (2) Figures do not include pregnancy-related, borderline, or pre-diabetes
Source: Centers for Disease Control and Prevention, Behaviorial Risk Factor Surveillance System, SMART: Selected Metropolitan Area Risk Trends, 2017

Health Screening and Vaccination Rates

Category	MD[1] (%)	U.S. (%)
Adults aged 65+ who have had flu shot within the past year	55.7	60.7
Adults aged 65+ who have ever had a pneumonia vaccination	67.1	75.4
Adults who have ever been tested for HIV	50.9	36.1
Adults who have ever had the shingles or zoster vaccine?	21.8	28.9
Adults who have had their blood cholesterol checked within the last five years	91.0	85.9

Note: n/a not available; (1) Figures cover the New York-Jersey City-White Plains, NY-NJ Metropolitan Division.
Source: Centers for Disease Control and Prevention, Behaviorial Risk Factor Surveillance System, SMART: Selected Metropolitan Area Risk Trends, 2017

Disability Status

Category	MD[1] (%)	U.S. (%)
Adults who reported being deaf	4.3	6.7
Are you blind or have serious difficulty seeing, even when wearing glasses?	5.0	4.5
Are you limited in any way in any of your usual activities due of arthritis?	10.0	12.9
Do you have difficulty doing errands alone?	6.2	6.8
Do you have difficulty dressing or bathing?	3.8	3.6
Do you have serious difficulty concentrating/remembering/making decisions?	9.2	10.7
Do you have serious difficulty walking or climbing stairs?	12.9	13.6

Note: (1) Figures cover the New York-Jersey City-White Plains, NY-NJ Metropolitan Division.
Source: Centers for Disease Control and Prevention, Behaviorial Risk Factor Surveillance System, SMART: Selected Metropolitan Area Risk Trends, 2017

Mortality Rates for the Top 10 Causes of Death in the U.S. (Bronx)

ICD-10[a] Sub-Chapter	ICD-10[a] Code	Age-Adjusted Mortality Rate[1] per 100,000 population	
		County[2]	U.S.
Malignant neoplasms	C00-C97	134.4	149.2
Ischaemic heart diseases	I20-I25	135.4	90.5
Other forms of heart disease	I30-I51	17.0	52.2
Chronic lower respiratory diseases	J40-J47	23.5	39.6
Cerebrovascular diseases	I60-I69	25.4	37.2
Other degenerative diseases of the nervous system	G30-G31	17.5	37.6
Other external causes of accidental injury	W00-X59	34.5	36.1
Hypertensive diseases	I10-I15	51.6	24.1
Organic, including symptomatic, mental disorders	F01-F09	18.8	29.4
Diabetes mellitus	E10-E14	25.6	21.5

Note: (a) ICD-10 = International Classification of Diseases 10th Revision; (1) Mortality rates are a three-year average covering 2017-2019; (2) Figures cover Bronx County
Source: Centers for Disease Control and Prevention, National Center for Health Statistics. Underlying Cause of Death 1999-2019 on CDC WONDER Online Database

Mortality Rates for the Top 10 Causes of Death in the U.S. (Brooklyn)

ICD-10[a] Sub-Chapter	ICD-10[a] Code	Age-Adjusted Mortality Rate[1] per 100,000 population	
		County[2]	U.S.
Malignant neoplasms	C00-C97	127.2	149.2
Ischaemic heart diseases	I20-I25	144.2	90.5
Other forms of heart disease	I30-I51	14.4	52.2
Chronic lower respiratory diseases	J40-J47	16.5	39.6
Cerebrovascular diseases	I60-I69	18.5	37.2
Other degenerative diseases of the nervous system	G30-G31	11.9	37.6
Other external causes of accidental injury	W00-X59	19.3	36.1
Hypertensive diseases	I10-I15	42.0	24.1
Organic, including symptomatic, mental disorders	F01-F09	11.9	29.4
Diabetes mellitus	E10-E14	23.4	21.5

Note: (a) ICD-10 = International Classification of Diseases 10th Revision; (1) Mortality rates are a three-year average covering 2017-2019; (2) Figures cover Kings County
Source: Centers for Disease Control and Prevention, National Center for Health Statistics. Underlying Cause of Death 1999-2019 on CDC WONDER Online Database

Mortality Rates for the Top 10 Causes of Death in the U.S. (Manhattan)

ICD-10[a] Sub-Chapter	ICD-10[a] Code	Age-Adjusted Mortality Rate[1] per 100,000 population	
		County[2]	U.S.
Malignant neoplasms	C00-C97	114.8	149.2
Ischaemic heart diseases	I20-I25	92.3	90.5
Other forms of heart disease	I30-I51	15.6	52.2
Chronic lower respiratory diseases	J40-J47	15.9	39.6
Cerebrovascular diseases	I60-I69	16.6	37.2
Other degenerative diseases of the nervous system	G30-G31	17.5	37.6
Other external causes of accidental injury	W00-X59	22.6	36.1
Hypertensive diseases	I10-I15	33.3	24.1
Organic, including symptomatic, mental disorders	F01-F09	18.3	29.4
Diabetes mellitus	E10-E14	13.5	21.5

Note: (a) ICD-10 = International Classification of Diseases 10th Revision; (1) Mortality rates are a three-year average covering 2017-2019; (2) Figures cover New York County
Source: Centers for Disease Control and Prevention, National Center for Health Statistics. Underlying Cause of Death 1999-2019 on CDC WONDER Online Database

Mortality Rates for the Top 10 Causes of Death in the U.S. (Queens)

ICD-10[a] Sub-Chapter	ICD-10[a] Code	Age-Adjusted Mortality Rate[1] per 100,000 population	
		County[2]	U.S.
Malignant neoplasms	C00-C97	117.1	149.2
Ischaemic heart diseases	I20-I25	138.2	90.5
Other forms of heart disease	I30-I51	13.6	52.2
Chronic lower respiratory diseases	J40-J47	16.3	39.6
Cerebrovascular diseases	I60-I69	20.0	37.2
Other degenerative diseases of the nervous system	G30-G31	16.7	37.6
Other external causes of accidental injury	W00-X59	18.8	36.1
Hypertensive diseases	I10-I15	30.0	24.1
Organic, including symptomatic, mental disorders	F01-F09	11.5	29.4
Diabetes mellitus	E10-E14	15.6	21.5

Note: (a) ICD-10 = International Classification of Diseases 10th Revision; (1) Mortality rates are a three-year average covering 2017-2019; (2) Figures cover Queens County
Source: Centers for Disease Control and Prevention, National Center for Health Statistics. Underlying Cause of Death 1999-2019 on CDC WONDER Online Database

Mortality Rates for the Top 10 Causes of Death in the U.S. (Staten Island)

ICD-10[a] Sub-Chapter	ICD-10[a] Code	Age-Adjusted Mortality Rate[1] per 100,000 population	
		County[2]	U.S.
Malignant neoplasms	C00-C97	147.6	149.2
Ischaemic heart diseases	I20-I25	197.0	90.5
Other forms of heart disease	I30-I51	12.8	52.2
Chronic lower respiratory diseases	J40-J47	27.5	39.6
Cerebrovascular diseases	I60-I69	14.7	37.2
Other degenerative diseases of the nervous system	G30-G31	21.8	37.6
Other external causes of accidental injury	W00-X59	31.2	36.1
Hypertensive diseases	I10-I15	35.9	24.1
Organic, including symptomatic, mental disorders	F01-F09	13.0	29.4
Diabetes mellitus	E10-E14	22.1	21.5

Note: (a) ICD-10 = International Classification of Diseases 10th Revision; (1) Mortality rates are a three-year average covering 2017-2019; (2) Figures cover Richmond County
Source: Centers for Disease Control and Prevention, National Center for Health Statistics. Underlying Cause of Death 1999-2019 on CDC WONDER Online Database

Mortality Rates for Selected Causes of Death (Bronx)

ICD-10[a] Sub-Chapter	ICD-10[a] Code	Age-Adjusted Mortality Rate[1] per 100,000 population	
		County[2]	U.S.
Assault	X85-Y09	5.7	6.0
Diseases of the liver	K70-K76	9.8	14.4
Human immunodeficiency virus (HIV) disease	B20-B24	7.0	1.5
Influenza and pneumonia	J09-J18	27.2	13.8
Intentional self-harm	X60-X84	5.0	14.1
Malnutrition	E40-E46	Suppressed	2.3
Obesity and other hyperalimentation	E65-E68	2.3	2.1
Renal failure	N17-N19	4.8	12.6
Transport accidents	V01-V99	3.6	12.3
Viral hepatitis	B15-B19	3.0	1.2

Note: (a) ICD-10 = International Classification of Diseases 10th Revision; (1) Mortality rates are a three-year average covering 2017-2019; (2) Figures cover Bronx County; Data are suppressed when the data meet the criteria for confidentiality constraints; Mortality rates are flagged as unreliable when the rate would be calculated with a numerator of 20 or less.
Source: Centers for Disease Control and Prevention, National Center for Health Statistics. Underlying Cause of Death 1999-2019 on CDC WONDER Online Database

Mortality Rates for Selected Causes of Death (Brooklyn)

ICD-10[a] Sub-Chapter	ICD-10[a] Code	Age-Adjusted Mortality Rate[1] per 100,000 population	
		County[2]	U.S.
Assault	X85-Y09	4.1	6.0
Diseases of the liver	K70-K76	6.8	14.4
Human immunodeficiency virus (HIV) disease	B20-B24	4.2	1.5
Influenza and pneumonia	J09-J18	21.1	13.8
Intentional self-harm	X60-X84	5.5	14.1
Malnutrition	E40-E46	0.3	2.3
Obesity and other hyperalimentation	E65-E68	2.0	2.1
Renal failure	N17-N19	6.7	12.6
Transport accidents	V01-V99	3.5	12.3
Viral hepatitis	B15-B19	1.7	1.2

Note: (a) ICD-10 = International Classification of Diseases 10th Revision; (1) Mortality rates are a three-year average covering 2017-2019; (2) Figures cover Kings County; Data are suppressed when the data meet the criteria for confidentiality constraints; Mortality rates are flagged as unreliable when the rate would be calculated with a numerator of 20 or less.
Source: Centers for Disease Control and Prevention, National Center for Health Statistics. Underlying Cause of Death 1999-2019 on CDC WONDER Online Database

Mortality Rates for Selected Causes of Death (Manhattan)

ICD-10[a] Sub-Chapter	ICD-10[a] Code	Age-Adjusted Mortality Rate[1] per 100,000 population	
		County[2]	U.S.
Assault	X85-Y09	1.8	6.0
Diseases of the liver	K70-K76	5.5	14.4
Human immunodeficiency virus (HIV) disease	B20-B24	3.4	1.5
Influenza and pneumonia	J09-J18	12.6	13.8
Intentional self-harm	X60-X84	7.4	14.1
Malnutrition	E40-E46	0.5	2.3
Obesity and other hyperalimentation	E65-E68	1.4	2.1
Renal failure	N17-N19	4.1	12.6
Transport accidents	V01-V99	2.2	12.3
Viral hepatitis	B15-B19	1.3	1.2

Note: (a) ICD-10 = International Classification of Diseases 10th Revision; (1) Mortality rates are a three-year average covering 2017-2019; (2) Figures cover New York County; Data are suppressed when the data meet the criteria for confidentiality constraints; Mortality rates are flagged as unreliable when the rate would be calculated with a numerator of 20 or less.
Source: Centers for Disease Control and Prevention, National Center for Health Statistics. Underlying Cause of Death 1999-2019 on CDC WONDER Online Database

Mortality Rates for Selected Causes of Death (Queens)

ICD-10[a] Sub-Chapter	ICD-10[a] Code	Age-Adjusted Mortality Rate[1] per 100,000 population	
		County[2]	U.S.
Assault	X85-Y09	2.6	6.0
Diseases of the liver	K70-K76	6.4	14.4
Human immunodeficiency virus (HIV) disease	B20-B24	1.5	1.5
Influenza and pneumonia	J09-J18	17.3	13.8
Intentional self-harm	X60-X84	6.1	14.1
Malnutrition	E40-E46	0.2	2.3
Obesity and other hyperalimentation	E65-E68	1.4	2.1
Renal failure	N17-N19	3.8	12.6
Transport accidents	V01-V99	4.0	12.3
Viral hepatitis	B15-B19	0.8	1.2

Note: (a) ICD-10 = International Classification of Diseases 10th Revision; (1) Mortality rates are a three-year average covering 2017-2019; (2) Figures cover Queens County; Data are suppressed when the data meet the criteria for confidentiality constraints; Mortality rates are flagged as unreliable when the rate would be calculated with a numerator of 20 or less.
Source: Centers for Disease Control and Prevention, National Center for Health Statistics. Underlying Cause of Death 1999-2019 on CDC WONDER Online Database

Mortality Rates for Selected Causes of Death (Staten Island)

ICD-10[a] Sub-Chapter	ICD-10[a] Code	Age-Adjusted Mortality Rate[1] per 100,000 population	
		County[2]	U.S.
Assault	X85-Y09	2.8	6.0
Diseases of the liver	K70-K76	6.7	14.4
Human immunodeficiency virus (HIV) disease	B20-B24	2.1	1.5
Influenza and pneumonia	J09-J18	16.4	13.8
Intentional self-harm	X60-X84	7.1	14.1
Malnutrition	E40-E46	Suppressed	2.3
Obesity and other hyperalimentation	E65-E68	2.4	2.1
Renal failure	N17-N19	4.1	12.6
Transport accidents	V01-V99	3.8	12.3
Viral hepatitis	B15-B19	Unreliable	1.2

Note: (a) ICD-10 = International Classification of Diseases 10th Revision; (1) Mortality rates are a three-year average covering 2017-2019; (2) Figures cover Richmond County; Data are suppressed when the data meet the criteria for confidentiality constraints; Mortality rates are flagged as unreliable when the rate would be calculated with a numerator of 20 or less.
Source: Centers for Disease Control and Prevention, National Center for Health Statistics. Underlying Cause of Death 1999-2019 on CDC WONDER Online Database

Health Insurance Coverage

Area	With Health Insurance	With Private Health Insurance	With Public Health Insurance	Without Health Insurance	Population Under Age 19 Without Health Insurance
City	92.5	58.3	43.0	7.5	2.4
MSA[1]	92.8	67.2	36.0	7.2	2.9
U.S.	91.2	67.9	35.1	8.8	5.1

Note: Figures are percentages that cover the civilian noninstitutionalized population; (1) Figures cover the New York-Newark-Jersey City, NY-NJ-PA Metropolitan Statistical Area
Source: U.S. Census Bureau, 2015-2019 American Community Survey 5-Year Estimates

Number of Medical Professionals

Area	MDs[3]	DOs[3,4]	Dentists	Podiatrists	Chiropractors	Optometrists
City[1] (number)	40,597	1,395	7,583	1,134	1,377	1,469
City[1] (rate[2])	483.9	16.6	91.0	13.6	16.5	17.6
U.S. (rate[2])	282.9	22.7	71.2	6.2	28.1	16.9

36999
Note: Data as of 2019 unless noted; (1) Data covers New York City; (2) Rate per 100,000 population; (3) Data as of 2018 and includes all active, non-federal physicians; (4) Doctor of Osteopathic Medicine
Source: U.S. Department of Health and Human Services, Health Resources and Services Administration, Bureau of Health Professions, Area Resource File (ARF) 2019-2020

Best Hospitals

According to *U.S. News,* the New York-Jersey City-White Plains, NY-NJ metro area is home to 15 of the best hospitals in the U.S.: **Hackensack University Medical Center** (2 pediatric specialties); **Hospital for Special Surgery** (2 adult specialties and 1 pediatric specialty); **Lenox Hill Hospital** (3 adult specialties); **Manhattan Eye, Ear & Throat Hospital** (3 adult specialties); **Memorial Sloan Kettering Cancer Center** (9 adult specialties and 1 pediatric specialty); **Montefiore Medical Center** (7 adult specialties and 5 pediatric specialties); **Mount Sinai Beth Israel Hospital** (1 adult specialty); **Mount Sinai Hospital** (Honor Roll/11 adult specialties and 4 pediatric specialties); **Mount Sinai Morningside and Mount Sinai West Hospitals** (2 adult specialties); **NYU Langone Hospitals** (Honor Roll/15 adult specialties); **New York Eye and Ear Infirmary of Mount Sinai** (1 adult specialty); **New York-Presbyterian Hospital-Columbia and Cornell** (Honor Roll/15 adult specialties and 8 pediatric specialties); **NYU Langone Orthopedic Hospital** (Honor Roll/15 adult specialties); **Perlmutter Cancer Center at NYU Langone Hospitals** (Honor Roll/15 adult specialties); **Rusk Rehabilitation at NYU Langone Hospitals** (Honor Roll/15 adult specialties). The hospitals listed were nationally ranked in at least one of 16 adult or 10 pediatric specialties. Only 134 hospitals nationwide were nationally ranked in one or more adult or pediatric specialty; this number increases to 178 counting specialized centers within hospitals. Twenty hospitals in the U.S. made the Honor Roll. The Best Hospitals Honor Roll takes both the national rankings and the procedure and condition ratings into account. Hospitals received points if they were nationally ranked in one of the 16 adult specialties—the higher they ranked, the more points they got—and how many ratings of "high performing" they earned in the 10 procedures and conditions. *U.S. News Online, "America's Best Hospitals 2020-21"*

According to *U.S. News,* the New York-Jersey City-White Plains, NY-NJ metro area is home to seven of the best children's hospitals in the U.S.: **Children's Hospital at Montefiore** (5 pediatric specialties); **Children's Hospital at St. Peter's University Hospital** (1 pediatric specialty); **Joseph M. Sanzari Children's Hospital at Hackensack University Medical Center** (2 pediatric specialties); **Lerner Children's Pavilion-Hospital for Special Surgery** (1 pediatric specialty); **Memorial Sloan**

Kettering Children's Cancer Center (1 pediatric specialty); **Mount Sinai Kravis Children's Hospital** (4 pediatric specialties); **New York-Presbyterian Hospital-Columbia and Cornell** (8 pediatric specialties). The hospitals listed were highly ranked in at least one of 10 pediatric specialties. Eighty-eight children's hospitals in the U.S. were nationally ranked in at least one specialty. Hospitals received points for being ranked in a specialty, and the 10 hospitals with the most points across the 10 specialties make up the Honor Roll. *U.S. News Online, "America's Best Children's Hospitals 2020-21"*

EDUCATION

Public School District Statistics

District Name	Schls	Pupils	Pupil/ Teacher Ratio	Minority Pupils[1] (%)	Free Lunch Eligible[2] (%)	IEP[3] (%)
NYC Geo Dist #1 (Manhattan)	28	10,900	12.5	81.7	59.9	24.1
NYC Geo Dist #10 (Bronx)	85	54,036	14.2	94.2	80.6	26.3
NYC Geo Dist #11 (Bronx)	62	39,126	15.2	91.3	75.1	28.8
NYC Geo Dist #12 (Bronx)	47	22,350	14.0	98.4	89.8	32.0
NYC Geo Dist #13 (Brooklyn)	40	21,148	15.7	82.6	59.2	18.7
NYC Geo Dist #14 (Brooklyn)	38	17,699	13.9	84.7	69.1	28.2
NYC Geo Dist #15 (Brooklyn)	48	32,661	13.9	69.9	54.5	23.8
NYC Geo Dist #16 (Brooklyn)	25	6,759	13.2	96.4	81.4	41.3
NYC Geo Dist #17 (Brooklyn)	48	21,389	15.2	96.5	77.0	35.5
NYC Geo Dist #18 (Brooklyn)	33	14,699	14.1	96.6	74.7	30.0
NYC Geo Dist #19 (Brooklyn)	49	22,363	14.3	97.9	85.7	33.8
NYC Geo Dist #2 (Manhattan)	119	62,417	14.9	73.2	49.1	19.2
NYC Geo Dist #20 (Brooklyn)	43	51,578	15.7	74.6	72.6	27.2
NYC Geo Dist #21 (Brooklyn)	40	35,325	15.2	67.8	69.4	31.6
NYC Geo Dist #22 (Brooklyn)	40	35,075	16.1	68.7	65.3	31.8
NYC Geo Dist #23 (Brooklyn)	29	9,526	13.9	98.4	87.4	38.5
NYC Geo Dist #24 (Corona)	56	58,483	15.6	86.7	71.3	21.0
NYC Geo Dist #25 (Flushing)	46	37,349	14.9	88.1	62.6	18.2
NYC Geo Dist #26 (Bayside)	33	31,911	16.6	84.1	49.8	16.6
NYC Geo Dist #27 (Ozone Park)	63	45,389	15.2	89.5	70.3	25.0
NYC Geo Dist #28 (Jamaica)	50	41,465	16.7	84.2	64.0	19.9
NYC Geo Dist #29 (Queens Village)	46	27,024	16.2	97.8	67.4	24.2
NYC Geo Dist #3 (Manhattan)	44	21,820	14.4	66.2	45.2	22.4
NYC Geo Dist #30 (Long Island City)	49	39,782	15.3	83.5	67.0	19.2
NYC Geo Dist #31 (Staten Island)	72	62,125	14.9	55.2	52.6	30.4
NYC Geo Dist #32 (Brooklyn)	27	10,553	13.2	97.3	86.3	29.3
NYC Geo Dist #4 (Manhattan)	28	12,842	12.5	95.3	77.3	32.6
NYC Geo Dist #5 (Manhattan)	27	11,689	13.6	94.2	78.9	44.1
NYC Geo Dist #6 (Manhattan)	46	21,186	13.1	94.3	82.6	29.0
NYC Geo Dist #7 (Bronx)	40	19,324	13.6	98.4	90.2	34.2
NYC Geo Dist #8 (Bronx)	52	27,939	13.8	94.3	80.4	34.3
NYC Geo Dist #9 (Bronx)	69	34,552	13.4	98.5	90.4	32.5

Note: Table includes school districts with 2,000 or more students; (1) Percentage of students that are not non-Hispanic white; (2) Percentage of students that are eligible for the free lunch program; (3) Percentage of students that have an Individualized Education Program.
Source: U.S. Department of Education, National Center for Education Statistics, Common Core of Data, Local Education Agency (School District) Universe Survey: School Year 2018-2019; U.S. Department of Education, National Center for Education Statistics, Common Core of Data, Public Elementary/Secondary School Universe Survey: School Year 2018-2019

Best High Schools

According to *U.S. News,* New York is home to 22 of the top 500 high schools in the U.S.: **Townsend Harris High School-Flushing** (#5); **Stuyvesant High School** (#25); **Queens High School for the Sciences at York College-Jamaica** (#28); **Staten Island Technical High School** (#35); **Bronx High School of Science** (#36); **High School Math Science and Engineering at CCNY** (#41); **Brooklyn Technical High School** (#47); **High School for Dual Language and Asian Studies** (#54); **High School of American Studies at Lehman College-Bronx** (#58); **Brooklyn Latin School** (#59); **Baccalaureate School for Global Education-Long Island City** (#65); **Eleanor Roosevelt High School** (#162); **New Explorations Into Science, Tech and Math High School** (#178); **Fiorello H Laguardia High School** (#181); **Columbia Secondary School** (#204); **Millennium High School** (#259); **Manhattan Village Academy** (#268); **Leon M. Goldstein High School for the Sciences-Brooklyn** (#300); **Manhattan Bridges High School** (#363); **All City Leadership Secondary School-Brooklyn** (#434); **NYC iSchool** (#468); **Beacon High School** (#479). Nearly 18,000 public, magnet and charter schools were ranked based on their performance on state assessments and how well they prepare students for college. *U.S. News & World Report, "Best High Schools 2020"*

Highest Level of Education

Area	Less than H.S.	H.S. Diploma	Some College, No Deg.	Associate Degree	Bachelor's Degree	Master's Degree	Prof. School Degree	Doctorate Degree
City	17.8	24.0	13.7	6.3	22.2	11.2	3.2	1.5
MSA[1]	13.5	24.7	14.8	6.7	23.4	12.1	3.3	1.6
U.S.	12.0	27.0	20.4	8.5	19.8	8.8	2.1	1.4

Note: Figures cover persons age 25 and over; (1) Figures cover the New York-Newark-Jersey City, NY-NJ-PA Metropolitan Statistical Area
Source: U.S. Census Bureau, 2015-2019 American Community Survey 5-Year Estimates

Educational Attainment by Race

Area	High School Graduate or Higher (%)					Bachelor's Degree or Higher (%)				
	Total	White	Black	Asian	Hisp.[2]	Total	White	Black	Asian	Hisp.[2]
City	82.2	88.7	83.5	76.1	68.9	38.1	51.0	24.4	42.4	18.6
MSA[1]	86.5	90.8	85.4	83.5	71.4	40.4	46.0	25.6	54.5	19.6
U.S.	88.0	89.9	86.0	87.1	68.7	32.1	33.5	21.6	54.3	16.4

Note: Figures shown cover persons 25 years old and over; (1) Figures cover the New York-Newark-Jersey City, NY-NJ-PA Metropolitan Statistical Area; (2) People of Hispanic origin can be of any race
Source: U.S. Census Bureau, 2015-2019 American Community Survey 5-Year Estimates

School Enrollment by Grade and Control

Area	Preschool (%)		Kindergarten (%)		Grades 1 - 4 (%)		Grades 5 - 8 (%)		Grades 9 - 12 (%)	
	Public	Private	Public	Private	Public	Private	Public	Private	Public	Private
City	60.9	39.1	79.2	20.8	82.7	17.3	82.2	17.8	82.3	17.7
MSA[1]	54.8	45.2	82.3	17.7	85.6	14.4	85.7	14.3	85.1	14.9
U.S.	59.1	40.9	87.6	12.4	89.5	10.5	89.4	10.6	90.1	9.9

Note: Figures shown cover persons 3 years old and over; (1) Figures cover the New York-Newark-Jersey City, NY-NJ-PA Metropolitan Statistical Area
Source: U.S. Census Bureau, 2015-2019 American Community Survey 5-Year Estimates

Higher Education

Four-Year Colleges			Two-Year Colleges			Medical Schools[1]	Law Schools[2]	Voc/ Tech[3]
Public	Private Non-profit	Private For-profit	Public	Private Non-profit	Private For-profit			
17	82	10	7	12	14	7	8	41

Note: Figures cover institutions located within the city limits and include main campuses only; (1) includes schools accredited by the Liaison Committee on Medical Education and the American Osteopathic Association's Commission on Osteopathic College Accreditation; (2) includes ABA-accredited schools, schools with provisional ABA accreditation, and state accredited schools; (3) includes all schools with programs that are less than 2 years.
Source: National Center for Education Statistics, Integrated Postsecondary Education System (IPEDS), 2019-20; Wikipedia, List of Medical Schools in the United States, accessed April 2, 2021; Wikipedia, List of Law Schools in the United States, accessed April 2, 2021

According to *U.S. News & World Report,* the New York-Jersey City-White Plains, NY-NJ metro division is home to nine of the top 200 national universities in the U.S.: **Columbia University** (#3); **New York University** (#30 tie); **Rutgers University—New Brunswick** (#63 tie); **Fordham University** (#66 tie); **Yeshiva University** (#76 tie); **Stevens Institute of Technology** (#80 tie); **The New School** (#133 tie); **St. John's University (NY)** (#170 tie); **CUNY—City College** (#176 tie). The indicators used to capture academic quality fall into a number of categories: assessment by administrators at peer institutions; retention of students; faculty resources; student selectivity; financial resources; alumni giving; high school counselor ratings of colleges; and graduation rate. *U.S. News & World Report, "America's Best Colleges 2021"*

According to *U.S. News & World Report,* the New York-Jersey City-White Plains, NY-NJ metro division is home to three of the top 100 liberal arts colleges in the U.S.: **United States Military Academy** (#15 tie); **Barnard College** (#22 tie); **Sarah Lawrence College** (#63 tie). The indicators used to capture academic quality fall into a number of categories: assessment by administrators at peer institutions; retention of students; faculty resources; student selectivity; financial resources; alumni giving; high school counselor ratings of colleges; and graduation rate. *U.S. News & World Report, "America's Best Colleges 2021"*

According to *U.S. News & World Report,* the New York-Jersey City-White Plains, NY-NJ metro division is home to five of the top 100 law schools in the U.S.: **Columbia University** (#4 tie); **New York University** (#6 tie); **Fordham University** (#35 tie); **Yeshiva University (Cardozo)** (#53 tie); **Brooklyn Law School** (#81 tie). The rankings are based on a weighted average of 12 measures of quality: peer assessment score; assessment score by lawyers/judges; median LSAT scores; median undergrad GPA; acceptance rate; employment rates for graduates; placement success; bar passage rate; faculty resources; expenditures per student; student/faculty ratio; and library resources. *U.S. News & World Report, "America's Best Graduate Schools, Law, 2022"*

According to *U.S. News & World Report,* the New York-Jersey City-White Plains, NY-NJ metro division is home to six of the top 75 medical schools for research in the U.S.: **New York University (Grossman)** (#2); **Columbia University** (#4 tie); **Icahn School of Medicine at Mount Sinai** (#17 tie); **Cornell University (Weill)** (#19 tie); **Albert Einstein College of Medicine** (#39 tie); **Rutgers Robert Wood Johnson Medical School—New Brunswick** (#70). The rankings are based on a weighted average of 11 measures of quality: quality assessment; peer assessment score; assessment score by residency directors; research activity; total research activity; average research activity per faculty member; student selectivity; median MCAT total score; median undergraduate GPA; acceptance rate; and faculty resources. *U.S. News & World Report, "America's Best Graduate Schools, Medical, 2022"*

According to *U.S. News & World Report,* the New York-Jersey City-White Plains, NY-NJ metro division is home to four of the top 75 business schools in the U.S.: **Columbia University** (#7 tie); **New York University (Stern)** (#10 tie); **Fordham University (Gabelli)** (#64 tie); **Stevens Institute of Technology** (#68 tie). The rankings are based on a weighted average of the following nine measures: quality assessment; peer assessment; recruiter assessment; placement success; mean starting salary and bonus; student selectivity; mean GMAT and GRE scores; mean undergraduate GPA; and acceptance rate. *U.S. News & World Report, "America's Best Graduate Schools, Business, 2022"*

EMPLOYERS

Major Employers

Company Name	Industry
American Express Company	Personal credit institutions
American International Group	Life insurance
Deloitte Consulting	Management consulting services
Hackensack University Medical Center	University
Merrill Lynch and Co	Security brokers & dealers
Mount Sinai Hospital	General medical & surgical hospitals
Mount Sinai School of Medicine	Medical training services
New York-Presbyterian Hospital	General medical & surgical hospitals
NYC Health and Hospitals Corp	Psychiatric hospitals
NYU School of Medicine	Offices & clinics of medical doctors
Paramount Comm Acq Corp	Investment holding companies, except banks
Patriarch Partners	Investment offices
Rutgers, The State Univ of NJ	Colleges & universities
Standard Americas	Agencies of foreign banks
The Long Island Rail Road Company	Local & suburban transit
UMASS Memorial Health Care	Psychiatrist
United States Postal Service	U.S. postal service
University of Med and Dentistry of NJ	Colleges & universities
Wellchoice	Health insurance carriers

Note: Companies shown are located within the New York-Newark-Jersey City, NY-NJ-PA Metropolitan Statistical Area.
Source: Hoovers.com; Wikipedia

Best Companies to Work For

Accenture; American Express; Deloitte; EY; Goldman Sachs Group; KPMG; Pricewaterhouse-Coopers, headquartered in New York, are among "The 100 Best Companies to Work For." To pick the best companies, *Fortune* partnered with the Great Place to Work Institute. Two-thirds of a company's score is based on the results of the Institute's Trust Index survey, which is sent to a random sample of employees from each company. The questions related to attitudes about management's credibility, job satisfaction, and camaraderie. The other third of the scoring is based on the company's responses to the Institute's Culture Audit, which includes detailed questions about pay and benefit programs, and a series of open-ended questions about hiring practices, internal communication, training, recognition programs, and diversity efforts. Any company that is at least five years old with more than 1,000 U.S. employees is eligible. *Fortune, "The 100 Best Companies to Work For," 2020*

Accenture; American Express; Barclays; Bristol Myers Squibb; Colgate-Palmolive; Deloitte; Dow Jones & Co; Ernst & Young; Goldman Sachs; HSBC USA; JPMorgan Chase; KPMG; L'Oréal; Mckinsey & Company; Metlife; Moody's; Morgan Stanley; New York Life; New York-Presbyterian; NYU Langone; Pillsbury Winthrop Shaw Pittman; PwC; S&P Global; The New York Times Company; TIAA; UBS; Verizon; Viacom, headquartered in New York, are among the "100 Best Companies for Working Mothers." Criteria: paid time off and leaves; workforce profile; benefits; women's issues and advancement; flexible work; company culture and work life programs. *Working Mother, "100 Best Companies for Working Mothers," 2020*

Accenture; Colgate-Palmolive; Ernst & Young; Estée Lauder; HSBC USA; JPMorgan Chase; KPMG; L'Oréal; New York Life; New York-Presbyterian; NYU Langone; Pillsbury Winthrop Shaw Pittman; PVH; PWC; Verizon, headquartered in New York, are among the "Best Companies for Multicultural Women." *Working Mother* selected 50 companies based on a detailed application completed by public and private firms based in the United States, excluding government agencies, companies in the human resources field and non-autonomous divisions. Companies supplied data about the hiring, pay, and promotion of multicultural employees. Applications focused on representation of multicultural women, recruitment, retention and advancement programs, and company culture. *Working Mother, "Best Companies for Multicultural Women," 2020*

Memorial Sloan Kettering Cancer Center; Sprinklr, headquartered in New York, are among the "100 Best Places to Work in IT." To qualify, companies had to be U.S.-based organizations or be non-U.S.-based employers that met the following criteria: have a minimum of 300 total employees at a U.S. headquarters and a minimum of 30 IT employees in the U.S., with at least 50% of their IT employees based in the U.S. The best places to work were selected based on compensation, benefits, work/life balance, employee morale, and satisfaction with training and development programs. In addition, *InsiderPro* and *Computerworld* looked at retention efforts, programs for recognizing and rewarding outstanding performances, and benefits such as flextime, elder care and child care, and reimbursement for college tuition and the cost of pursuing technology certifications. *InsiderPro and Computerworld, "100 Best Places to Work in IT," 2020*

Accenture; American Express; Bristol Myers Squibb; Capgemini America; Colgate-Palmolive; Deloitte; Diageo North America; Ernst & Young; Estée Lauder; KPMG; L'Oréal; Metlife; Moody's; New York Life; New York-Presbyterian; Pillsbury Winthrop Shaw Pittman; ViacomCBS, headquartered in New York, are among the "Top Companies for Executive Women." This list is determined by organizations filling out an in-depth survey that measures female demographics at every level, but with an emphasis on women in senior corporate roles, with profit & loss (P&L) responsibility, and those earning in the top 20 percent of the organization. *Working Mother* defines P&L as having responsibility that involves monitoring the net income after expenses for a department or entire organization, with direct influence on how company resources are allocated. *Working Mother, "Top Companies for Executive Women," 2020+*

Accenture; American Express; Barclays; Capgemini America; Colgate-Palmolive; Deloitte; Dow Jones & Co; Ernst & Young; KPMG; L'Oréal; Marsh & Mclennon; McKinsey & Company; Moody's; Morgan Stanley; New York Life; Pillsbury Winthrop Shaw Pittman; PWC; S&P Global; Verizon; Viacom, headquartered in New York, are among the "Best Companies for Dads." *Working Mother's* newest list recognizes the growing importance companies place on giving dads time off and support for their families. Rankings are determined by measuring gender-neutral or paternity leave offered, as well as actual time taken, phase-back policies, child- and dependent-care benefits, and corporate support groups for men and dads. *Working Mother, "Best Companies for Dads," 2020*

PUBLIC SAFETY

Crime Rate

Area	All Crimes	Violent Crimes				Property Crimes		
		Murder	Rape[3]	Robbery	Aggrav. Assault	Burglary	Larceny -Theft	Motor Vehicle Theft
City	2,030.3	3.8	33.1	159.9	374.0	117.5	1,276.2	65.9
Suburbs[1]	n/a	n/a	n/a	n/a	n/a	n/a	n/a	n/a
Metro[2]	n/a	n/a	n/a	n/a	n/a	n/a	n/a	n/a
U.S.	2,489.3	5.0	42.6	81.6	250.2	340.5	1,549.5	219.9

Note: Figures are crimes per 100,000 population; (1) All areas within the metro area that are located outside the city limits; (2) Figures cover the New York-Jersey City-White Plains, NY-NJ Metropolitan Division; n/a not available; (3) All figures shown were reported using the revised Uniform Crime Reporting (UCR) definition of rape.
Source: FBI Uniform Crime Reports, 2019

Hate Crimes

Area	Number of Quarters Reported	Number of Incidents per Bias Motivation					
		Race/Ethnicity/ Ancestry	Religion	Sexual Orientation	Disability	Gender	Gender Identity
City	4	90	266	53	1	0	13
U.S.	4	3,963	1,521	1,195	157	69	198

Source: Federal Bureau of Investigation, Hate Crime Statistics 2019

Identity Theft Consumer Reports

Area	Reports	Reports per 100,000 Population	Rank[2]
MSA[1]	77,363	403	71
U.S.	1,387,615	423	-

Note: (1) Figures cover the New York-Newark-Jersey City, NY-NJ-PA Metropolitan Statistical Area; (2) Rank ranges from 1 to 391 where 1 indicates greatest number of identity theft reports per 100,000 population
Source: Federal Trade Commission, Consumer Sentinel Network Data Book 2020

Fraud and Other Consumer Reports

Area	Reports	Reports per 100,000 Population	Rank[2]
MSA[1]	172,473	898	49
U.S.	3,385,133	1,031	-

Note: (1) Figures cover the New York-Newark-Jersey City, NY-NJ-PA Metropolitan Statistical Area; (2) Rank ranges from 1 to 391 where 1 indicates greatest number of fraud and other consumer reports per 100,000 population
Source: Federal Trade Commission, Consumer Sentinel Network Data Book 2020

POLITICS

2020 Presidential Election Results

Area	Biden	Trump	Jorgensen	Hawkins	Other
Bronx County	83.3	15.9	0.2	0.3	0.3
Kings County	76.8	22.1	0.3	0.4	0.4
New York County	86.4	12.2	0.5	0.4	0.5
Queens County	72.0	26.9	0.3	0.4	0.4
Richmond County	42.0	56.9	0.4	0.3	0.4
U.S.	51.3	46.8	1.2	0.3	0.5

Note: Results are percentages and may not add to 100% due to rounding
Source: Dave Leip's Atlas of U.S. Presidential Elections

SPORTS

Professional Sports Teams

Team Name	League	Year Established
Brooklyn Nets	National Basketball Association (NBA)	1967
New Jersey Devils	National Hockey League (NHL)	1982
New York City FC	Major League Soccer (MLS)	2015
New York Giants	National Football League (NFL)	1925
New York Islanders	National Hockey League (NHL)	1972
New York Jets	National Football League (NFL)	1960
New York Knicks	National Basketball Association (NBA)	1946
New York Mets	Major League Baseball (MLB)	1962
New York Rangers	National Hockey League (NHL)	1926
New York Red Bulls	Major League Soccer (MLS)	1996
New York Yankees	Major League Baseball (MLB)	1903

Note: Includes teams located in the New York-Newark-Jersey City, NY-NJ-PA Metropolitan Statistical Area.
Source: Wikipedia, Major Professional Sports Teams of the United States and Canada, April 6, 2021

CLIMATE

Average and Extreme Temperatures

Temperature	Jan	Feb	Mar	Apr	May	Jun	Jul	Aug	Sep	Oct	Nov	Dec	Yr.
Extreme High (°F)	68	75	85	96	97	101	104	99	99	88	81	72	104
Average High (°F)	38	41	50	61	72	80	85	84	76	65	54	43	62
Average Temp. (°F)	32	34	43	53	63	72	77	76	68	58	48	37	55
Average Low (°F)	26	27	35	44	54	63	68	67	60	49	41	31	47
Extreme Low (°F)	-2	-2	8	21	36	46	53	50	40	29	17	-1	-2

Note: Figures cover the years 1962-1992
Source: National Climatic Data Center, International Station Meteorological Climate Summary, 9/96

Average Precipitation/Snowfall/Humidity

Precip./Humidity	Jan	Feb	Mar	Apr	May	Jun	Jul	Aug	Sep	Oct	Nov	Dec	Yr.
Avg. Precip. (in.)	3.5	3.1	4.0	3.9	4.5	3.8	4.5	4.1	4.1	3.3	4.5	3.8	47.0
Avg. Snowfall (in.)	7	8	4	Tr	Tr	0	0	0	0	Tr	Tr	3	23
Avg. Rel. Hum. 7am (%)	67	67	66	64	72	74	74	76	78	75	72	69	71
Avg. Rel. Hum. 4pm (%)	55	53	50	45	52	55	53	54	56	55	57	58	53

Note: Figures cover the years 1962-1992; Tr = Trace amounts (<0.05 in. of rain; <0.5 in. of snow)
Source: National Climatic Data Center, International Station Meteorological Climate Summary, 9/96

Weather Conditions

Temperature			Daytime Sky			Precipitation		
32°F & below	45°F & below	90°F & above	Clear	Partly cloudy	Cloudy	0.01 inch or more precip.	0.1 inch or more snow/ice	Thunder-storms
75	170	18	85	166	114	120	11	20

Note: Figures are average number of days per year and cover the years 1962-1992
Source: National Climatic Data Center, International Station Meteorological Climate Summary, 9/96

HAZARDOUS WASTE

Superfund Sites

The New York-Jersey City-White Plains, NY-NJ metro division is home to 49 sites on the EPA's Superfund National Priorities List: **Atlantic Resources** (final); **Bog Creek Farm** (final); **Brick**

Township Landfill (final); **Burnt Fly Bog** (final); **Carroll & Dubies Sewage Disposal** (final); **Chemical Insecticide Corp.** (final); **Chemsol, Inc.** (final); **Ciba-Geigy Corp.** (final); **Cornell Dubilier Electronics Inc.** (final); **CPS/Madison Industries** (final); **Curcio Scrap Metal, Inc.** (final); **Diamond Head Oil Refinery Division** (final); **Evor Phillips Leasing** (final); **Fair Lawn Well Field** (final); **Fried Industries** (final); **Garfield Ground Water Contamination** (final); **Global Sanitary Landfill** (final); **Goose Farm** (final); **Gowanus Canal** (final); **Horseshoe Road** (final); **Hudson Technologies, Inc.** (proposed); **Imperial Oil Co., Inc./Champion Chemicals** (final); **JIS Landfill** (final); **Kin-Buc Landfill** (final); **Lone Pine Landfill** (final); **Magna Metals** (final); **Maywood Chemical Co.** (final); **Middlesex Sampling Plant (USDOE)** (final); **Monitor Devices, Inc./Intercircuits, Inc.** (final); **Naval Air Engineering Center** (final); **Naval Weapons Station Earle (Site A)** (final); **Nepera Chemical Co., Inc.** (final); **Newtown Creek** (final); **PJP Landfill** (final); **Quanta Resources** (final); **Ramapo Landfill** (final); **Raritan Bay Slag** (final); **Reich Farms** (final); **Ringwood Mines/Landfill** (final); **Scientific Chemical Processing** (final); **Standard Chlorine** (final); **Syncon Resins** (final); **Universal Oil Products (Chemical Division)** (final); **Ventron/Velsicol** (final); **Waldick Aerospace Devices, Inc.** (final); **White Swan Laundry and Cleaner Inc.** (final); **Wolff-Alport Chemical Company** (final); **Woodbrook Road Dump** (final); **Zschiegner Refining** (final). There are a total of 1,375 Superfund sites with a status of proposed or final on the list in the U.S. *U.S. Environmental Protection Agency, National Priorities List, April 7, 2021*

AIR QUALITY

Air Quality Trends: Ozone

	1990	1995	2000	2005	2010	2015	2016	2017	2018	2019
MSA[1]	0.101	0.106	0.090	0.091	0.081	0.075	0.073	0.070	0.073	0.067
U.S.	0.088	0.089	0.082	0.080	0.073	0.068	0.069	0.068	0.069	0.065

Note: (1) Data covers the New York-Newark-Jersey City, NY-NJ-PA Metropolitan Statistical Area. The values shown are the composite ozone concentration averages among trend sites based on the highest fourth daily maximum 8-hour concentration in parts per million. These trends are based on sites having an adequate record of monitoring data during the trend period. Data from exceptional events are included.
Source: U.S. Environmental Protection Agency, Air Quality Monitoring Information, "Air Quality Trends by City, 1990-2019"

Air Quality Index

Area	Percent of Days when Air Quality was...[2]					AQI Statistics[2]	
	Good	Moderate	Unhealthy for Sensitive Groups	Unhealthy	Very Unhealthy	Maximum	Median
MSA[1]	46.3	49.3	4.4	0.0	0.0	150	51

Note: (1) Data covers the New York-Newark-Jersey City, NY-NJ-PA Metropolitan Statistical Area; (2) Based on 365 days with AQI data in 2019. Air Quality Index (AQI) is an index for reporting daily air quality. EPA calculates the AQI for five major air pollutants regulated by the Clean Air Act: ground-level ozone, particle pollution (aka particulate matter), carbon monoxide, sulfur dioxide, and nitrogen dioxide. The AQI runs from 0 to 500. The higher the AQI value, the greater the level of air pollution and the greater the health concern. There are six AQI categories: "Good" AQI is between 0 and 50. Air quality is considered satisfactory; "Moderate" AQI is between 51 and 100. Air quality is acceptable; "Unhealthy for Sensitive Groups" When AQI values are between 101 and 150, members of sensitive groups may experience health effects; "Unhealthy" When AQI values are between 151 and 200 everyone may begin to experience health effects; "Very Unhealthy" AQI values between 201 and 300 trigger a health alert; "Hazardous" AQI values over 300 trigger warnings of emergency conditions (not shown).
Source: U.S. Environmental Protection Agency, Air Quality Index Report, 2019

Air Quality Index Pollutants

Area	Percent of Days when AQI Pollutant was...[2]					
	Carbon Monoxide	Nitrogen Dioxide	Ozone	Sulfur Dioxide	Particulate Matter 2.5	Particulate Matter 10
MSA[1]	0.0	17.5	39.2	0.0	43.3	0.0

Note: (1) Data covers the New York-Newark-Jersey City, NY-NJ-PA Metropolitan Statistical Area; (2) Based on 365 days with AQI data in 2019. The Air Quality Index (AQI) is an index for reporting daily air quality. EPA calculates the AQI for five major air pollutants regulated by the Clean Air Act: ground-level ozone, particle pollution (also known as particulate matter), carbon monoxide, sulfur dioxide, and nitrogen dioxide. The AQI runs from 0 to 500. The higher the AQI value, the greater the level of air pollution and the greater the health concern.
Source: U.S. Environmental Protection Agency, Air Quality Index Report, 2019

Maximum Air Pollutant Concentrations: Particulate Matter, Ozone, CO and Lead

	Particulate Matter 10 (ug/m³)	Particulate Matter 2.5 Wtd AM (ug/m³)	Particulate Matter 2.5 24-Hr (ug/m³)	Ozone (ppm)	Carbon Monoxide (ppm)	Lead (ug/m³)
MSA[1] Level	34	11.0	24	0.073	2	n/a
NAAQS[2]	150	15	35	0.075	9	0.15
Met NAAQS[2]	Yes	Yes	Yes	Yes	Yes	n/a

Note: (1) Data covers the New York-Newark-Jersey City, NY-NJ-PA Metropolitan Statistical Area; Data from exceptional events are included; (2) National Ambient Air Quality Standards; ppm = parts per million; ug/m³ = micrograms per cubic meter; n/a not available.
Concentrations: Particulate Matter 10 (coarse particulate)—highest second maximum 24-hour concentration; Particulate Matter 2.5 Wtd AM (fine particulate)—highest weighted annual mean concentration; Particulate Matter 2.5 24-Hour (fine particulate)—highest 98th percentile 24-hour concentration; Ozone—highest fourth daily maximum 8-hour concentration; Carbon Monoxide—highest second maximum non-overlapping 8-hour concentration; Lead—maximum running 3-month average
Source: U.S. Environmental Protection Agency, Air Quality Monitoring Information, "Air Quality Statistics by City, 2019"

Maximum Air Pollutant Concentrations: Nitrogen Dioxide and Sulfur Dioxide

	Nitrogen Dioxide AM (ppb)	Nitrogen Dioxide 1-Hr (ppb)	Sulfur Dioxide AM (ppb)	Sulfur Dioxide 1-Hr (ppb)	Sulfur Dioxide 24-Hr (ppb)
MSA[1] Level	21	66	n/a	11	n/a
NAAQS[2]	53	100	30	75	140
Met NAAQS[2]	Yes	Yes	n/a	Yes	n/a

Note: (1) Data covers the New York-Newark-Jersey City, NY-NJ-PA Metropolitan Statistical Area; Data from exceptional events are included; (2) National Ambient Air Quality Standards; ppm = parts per million; ug/m³ = micrograms per cubic meter; n/a not available.
Concentrations: Nitrogen Dioxide AM—highest arithmetic mean concentration; Nitrogen Dioxide 1-Hr—highest 98th percentile 1-hour daily maximum concentration; Sulfur Dioxide AM—highest annual mean concentration; Sulfur Dioxide 1-Hr—highest 99th percentile 1-hour daily maximum concentration; Sulfur Dioxide 24-Hr—highest second maximum 24-hour concentration
Source: U.S. Environmental Protection Agency, Air Quality Monitoring Information, "Air Quality Statistics by City, 2019"

Philadelphia, Pennsylvania

Background

Philadelphia, "The City of Brotherly Love," was not founded upon brotherly love at all. The largest city in Pennsylvania was settled by Swedes and Finns in 1638, in a settlement known as New Sweden, seized in 1655 by Peter Stuyvesant, director general of New Amsterdam for the Dutch crown. Inconsiderate of any previous claims by the Dutch, King Charles II of England conferred land between the Connecticut and Delaware rivers upon his brother, the duke of York. Naturally, the two countries went to war. However, thanks to a generous loan by Admiral Sir William Penn, the land fell permanently into English hands. To repay the loan, the king gave Sir William's son, also named William, sole proprietorship of the state of present-day Pennsylvania. At the same time, he was probably glad to be rid of a subject heavily influenced by a dissenting religious sect known as the Society of Friends, or the Quakers.

Pennsylvania's landlord had the vision and the financial means with which to carry out a simple but radical experiment for the times: a city built upon religious tolerance. Amazingly enough, the place of religious outcasts prospered. Thanks to forests abundant in natural resources, and ports busy with international trade, Philadelphia, in the state's southeast corner, was a bustling, ideal American city.

The service sector has emerged as the predominant economic force driving current and future growth in the city. Greater Philadelphia has one of the largest health care industries in the nation. It has also become a major materials development and processing center, with about 100,000 or more individuals involved in the manufacture of chemicals, advanced materials, glass, plastics, industrial gases, metals, composites, and textiles. Philadelphia is also a national leader in the biotech field. Its "knowledge industry," with over 80 colleges and universities helps to supply a skilled workforce for the growing technical and bio-industries. Because of Philadelphia's importance as a mecca for medical research, the region is a major center for the pharmaceutical industry.

The city claimed firsts in many cultural, educational, and political arenas. The Pennsylvania Academy of Fine Arts is the oldest museum and fine arts school in the country. The University of Pennsylvania, which Benjamin Franklin helped found, is the oldest university in the country. And, of course, on July 4, 1776, the United States was born when "longhaired radicals" such as Thomas Jefferson, George Washington, and John Hancock signed the Declaration of Independence in Philadelphia, breaking away from the mother country forever.

The city offers a thriving cultural scene with something for everyone, from chamber music to jazz, from historic Society Hill to South Philadelphia, home of the open-air Italian Market and famous Philly cheesesteak. The historic and waterfront district has many colonial-era homes and cobblestone streets, as well as the Liberty Bell, Independence Hall and Independence National Historic Park.

The Avenue of the Arts is home to several theaters, the Kimmel Center for the Performing Arts and the Academy of Music serve as home to a number of Resident Company performing arts organizations, including The Philadelphia Orchestra, Opera Company of Philadelphia, Pennsylvania Ballet, Chamber Orchestra of Philadelphia, American Theater Arts for Youth, PHILADANCO, Philadelphia Chamber Music Society and Peter Nero and the Philly Pops. The Walnut Street Theater, a National Historical Landmark and the oldest and most subscribed theater in the English-speaking world, recently announced a major expansion.

The National Constitution Center Museum, devoted to exploring the role and meaning of the United States Constitution, is a glass, steel, and limestone building designed by Pei, Cobb Freed and Partners, built in 2003. That same year, a new Liberty Bell Center, designed to enhance the viewing of the nation's iconic Liberty Bell, also opened.

Sports venues include Lincoln Financial Field for the Philadelphia Eagles NFL football team, who won Super Bowl LI in 2018, and Citizens Bank Park for Major League Baseball's Philadelphia Phillies, who won the World Series in 2008. These replace the 33-year-old Veterans Stadium, which was razed in a sentimental farewell ceremony. The Wells Fargo Center along the Delaware River hosts the Philadelphia Flyers professional ice hockey team and the Philadelphia 76ers professional basketball team.

The Appalachian Mountains to the west and the Atlantic Ocean to the east have a moderating effect on the city's climate and temperatures. Summer does bring humid days, owing to proximity to the ocean. Precipitation is fairly evenly distributed throughout the year, but there are variations within the city. Summer rains and winter snows are sometimes heavier in suburbs to the north and west, with their higher elevations, than in the south and east.

Rankings

General Rankings

- As part of its *Next Stop* series, *Insider* listed 10 places in the U.S. that were either a classic vacation destination experiencing a renaissance or a new up-and-coming hot spot. That could mean the exploding food scene, experiencing the great outdoors, where cool people are moving to, or not overrun with tourists, according to the website insider.com Philadelphia is a place to visit in 2020. *Insider, "10 Places in the U.S. You Need to Visit in 2020," December 23, 2019*

- In its eighth annual survey, *Travel + Leisure* readers nominated their favorite small cities and towns in America—those with 100,000 or fewer residents—voting on numerous attractive features in categories including culture, food and drink, quality of life, style, and people. After 50,000 votes, Philadelphia was ranked #19 among the proposed favorites. *www.travelandleisure.com, "America's Favorite Cities," October 20, 2017*

- The human resources consulting firm Mercer ranked 231 major cities worldwide in terms of overall quality of life. Philadelphia ranked #54. Criteria: political, social, economic, and socio-cultural factors; medical and health considerations; schools and education; public services and transportation; recreation; consumer goods; housing; and natural environment. *Mercer, "Mercer 2019 Quality of Living Survey," March 13, 2019*

Business/Finance Rankings

- The Brookings Institution ranked the nation's largest cities based on income inequality. Philadelphia was ranked #20 (#1 = greatest inequality). Criteria: the "95/20 ratio," a figure representing the income at which a household earns more than 95 percent of all other households, divided by the income at which a household earns more than only 20 percent of all other households. *Brookings Institution, "Household Income Inequality, Largest Cities of 97 Large U.S. Metro Areas, 2014-2016," February 5, 2018*

- The Brookings Institution ranked the 100 largest metro areas in the U.S. based on income inequality. Philadelphia was ranked #12 (#1 = greatest inequality). Criteria: the "95/20 ratio," a figure representing the income at which a household earns more than 95 percent of all other households, divided by the income at which a household earns more than only 20 percent of all other households. *Brookings Institution, "Household Income Inequality, 100 Largest U.S. Metro Areas, 2014-2016," February 5, 2018*

- The Philadelphia metro area was identified as one of the most debt-ridden places in America by the finance site Credit.com. The metro area was ranked #11. Criteria: residents' average credit card debt as well as median income. *Credit.com, "25 Cities With the Most Credit Card Debt," February 28, 2018*

- Philadelphia was identified as one of America's most frugal metro areas by *Coupons.com*. The city ranked #6 out of 25. Criteria: digital coupon usage. *Coupons.com, "America's Most Frugal Cities of 2017," March 22, 2018*

- Philadelphia was identified as one of the happiest cities to work in by CareerBliss.com, an online community for career advancement. The city ranked #8 out of 10. Criteria: an employee's relationship with his or her boss and co-workers; daily tasks; general work environment; compensation; opportunities for advancement; company culture and job reputation; and resources. *Businesswire.com, "CareerBliss Happiest Cities to Work 2019," February 12, 2019*

- *Forbes* ranked the 200 most populous metro areas to determine the nation's "Best Places for Business and Careers." The Philadelphia metro area was ranked #88. Criteria: costs (business and living); job growth (past and projected); income growth; quality of life; educational attainment (college and high school); projected economic growth; cultural and leisure opportunities; workplace tolerance laws; net migration patterns. *Forbes, "The Best Places for Business and Careers 2019: Seattle Still On Top," October 30, 2019*

Culture/Performing Arts Rankings

- Philadelphia was selected as one of the 25 best cities for moviemakers in North America. COVID-19 has spurred a quest for great film cities that offer more creative space, lower costs, and more great outdoors. NYC & LA were intentionally excluded. Criteria: longstanding reputations as film-friendly communities; efforts to deal with pandemic-specific challenges; and establish appropriate COVID-19 guidelines. The city was ranked #6. *MovieMaker Magazine, "Best Places to Live and Work as a Moviemaker, 2021," January 26, 2021*

- Philadelphia was selected as one of "America's Favorite Cities." The city ranked #9 in the "Architecture" category. Respondents to an online survey were asked to rate their favorite place (population over 100,000) in over 65 categories. *Travelandleisure.com, "America's Favorite Cities for Architecture 2016," March 2, 2017*

Education Rankings

- Philadelphia was selected as one of America's most literate cities. The city ranked #26 out of the 84 largest U.S. cities. Criteria: number of booksellers; library resources; Internet resources; educational attainment; periodical publishing resources; newspaper circulation. *Central Connecticut State University, "America's Most Literate Cities, 2018," February 2019*

Environmental Rankings

- The U.S. Environmental Protection Agency (EPA) released a list of U.S. metropolitan areas with the most ENERGY STAR certified buildings in 2019. The Philadelphia metro area was ranked #20 out of 25. *U.S. Environmental Protection Agency, "2020 Energy Star Top Cities," March 2020*

- Philadelphia was highlighted as one of the 25 most ozone-polluted metro areas in the U.S. during 2016 through 2018. The area ranked #23. *American Lung Association, "State of the Air 2020," April 21, 2020*

- Philadelphia was highlighted as one of the 25 metro areas most polluted by year-round particle pollution (Annual PM 2.5) in the U.S. during 2016 through 2018. The area ranked #12. *American Lung Association, "State of the Air 2020," April 21, 2020*

Food/Drink Rankings

- The U.S. Chamber of Commerce Foundation conducted an in-depth study on local food truck regulations, surveyed 288 food truck owners, and ranked 20 major American cities based on how friendly they are for operating a food truck. The compiled index assessed the following: procedures for obtaining permits and licenses; complying with restrictions; and financial obligations associated with operating a food truck. Philadelphia ranked #4 overall (1 being the best). *www.foodtrucknation.us, "Food Truck Nation," March 20, 2018*

Health/Fitness Rankings

- For each of the 100 largest cities in the United States, the American Fitness Index®, published by the American College of Sports Medicine and the Anthem Foundation, evaluated community infrastructure and 33 health behaviors including preventive health, levels of chronic disease conditions, pedestrian safety, air quality, and community resources that support physical activity. Philadelphia ranked #52 for "community fitness." *americanfitnessindex.org, "2020 ACSM American Fitness Index Summary Report," July 14, 2020*

- Philadelphia was identified as one of the 10 most walkable cities in the U.S. by Walk Score. The city ranked #4. Walk Score measures walkability by analyzing hundreds of walking routes to nearby amenities, and also measures pedestrian friendliness by analyzing population density and road metrics such as block length and intersection density. *WalkScore.com, April 13, 2021*

- Philadelphia was identified as a "2021 Spring Allergy Capital." The area ranked #27 out of 100. Three groups of factors were used to identify the most challenging cities for people with allergies during the spring season: annual spring pollen levels; over the counter medicine use; number of board-certified allergy specialists. *Asthma and Allergy Foundation of America, "Spring Allergy Capitals 2021," February 23, 2021*

- Philadelphia was identified as a "2021 Fall Allergy Capital." The area ranked #30 out of 100. Three groups of factors were used to identify the most challenging cities for people with allergies during the fall season: annual fall pollen levels; over the counter medicine use; number of board-certified allergy specialists. *Asthma and Allergy Foundation of America, "Fall Allergy Capitals 2021," February 23, 2021*

- Philadelphia was identified as a "2019 Asthma Capital." The area ranked #4 out of the nation's 100 largest metropolitan areas. Criteria: estimated asthma prevalence; crude death rate from asthma; and ER visits due to asthma. Risk factors analyzed but not factored in the rankings: annual pollen score; annual air quality; public smoking laws; number of board-certified asthma specialists; rescue medication use; controller medication use; uninsured rate; poverty rate. *Asthma and Allergy Foundation of America, "Asthma Capitals 2019: The Most Challenging Places to Live With Asthma," May 7, 2019*

Pet Rankings

- Philadelphia appeared on *The Dogington Post* site as one of the top cities for dog lovers, ranking #11 out of 20. The real estate brokerage, Redfin and Rover, the largest pet sitter and dog walker network, compiled a list from over 14,000 U.S. cities to come up with a "Rover Rank." Criteria: highest count of dog walks, the city's Walk Score®, for-sale home listings that mention "dog," number of dog walkers and pet sitters and the hours spent and distance logged. *www.dogingtonpost.com, "The 20 Most Dog-Friendly Cities of 2019," April 4, 2019*

Real Estate Rankings

- FitSmallBusiness looked at 50 of the largest metropolitan areas in the U.S. to determine which metro was the best to start a real estate business. Data was compiled from such sources as: Zillow, Trulia, U.S. Census Bureau, and the Bureau of Labor Statistics. Criteria: location; inventory; annual wages; median sales price of homes; days on the market; median price cut percentage; and other factors that would influence real estate professional growth. The Philadelphia metro area ranked #17. *fitsmallbusiness.com, "The Best Cities to Become a Real Estate Agent in 2018," January 30, 2018*

- *WalletHub* compared the most populated U.S. cities to determine which had the best markets for real estate agents. Philadelphia ranked #71 where demand was high and pay was the best. Criteria: sales per agent; annual median wage for real-estate agents; monthly average starting salary for real estate agents; real estate job density and competition; unemployment rate; home turnover rate; housing-market health index; and other relevant metrics. *www.WalletHub.com, "2019's Best Places to Be a Real Estate Agent," April 24, 2019*

Safety Rankings

- Allstate ranked the 200 largest cities in America in terms of driver safety. Philadelphia ranked #190. Criteria: internal property damage claims over a two-year period from January 2016 to December 2017. The report helps increase the importance of safety and awareness behind the wheel. *Allstate, "Allstate America's Best Drivers Report, 2019" June 24, 2019*

Sports/Recreation Rankings

- Philadelphia was chosen as one of America's best cities for bicycling. The city ranked #26 out of 50. Criteria: cycling infrastructure that is safe and friendly for all ages; energy and bike culture. The editors evaluated cities with populations of 100,000 or more. *Bicycling, "The 50 Best Bike Cities in America," October 10, 2018*

Transportation Rankings

- Business Insider presented an AllTransit Performance Score ranking of public transportation in major U.S. cities and towns, with populations over 250,000, in which Philadelphia earned the #7-ranked "Transit Score," awarded for frequency of service, access to jobs, quality and number of stops, and affordability. *www.businessinsider.com, "The 17 Major U.S. Cities with the Best Public Transportation," April 17, 2018*

- The business website 24/7 Wall Street reviewed U.S. Census data to identify the 25 cities where the largest share of households do not own a vehicle. Philadelphia held the #6 position. *247wallst.com, "Cities Where No One Wants to Drive," February 15, 2017*

- According to the INRIX "2019 Global Traffic Scorecard," Philadelphia was identified as one of the most congested metro areas in the U.S. The area ranked #3 out of 10. Criteria: average annual time spent in traffic and average cost of congestion per motorist. *Inrix.com, "Congestion Costs Each American Nearly 100 hours, $1,400 A Year," March 9, 2020*

Women/Minorities Rankings

- Personal finance website *WalletHub* compared more than 180 U.S. cities across two key dimensions, "Hispanic Business-Friendliness" and "Hispanic Purchasing Power," to arrive at the most favorable conditions for Hispanic entrepreneurs. Philadelphia was ranked #174 out of 182. Criteria includes: share of Hispanic-Owned Businesses; Hispanic entrepreneurship rate to median annual income of Hispanics; Small Business-Friendliness score; cost of living; and number of Hispanics with at least a bachelor's degree. *WalletHub.com, "2019's Best Cities for Hispanic Entrepreneurs," May 1, 2019*

Miscellaneous Rankings

- In its roundup of St. Patrick's Day parades "Gayot" listed the best festivals and parades of all things Irish. The festivities in Philadelphia as among the best. *www.gayot.com, "Best St. Patrick's Day Parades," March 2020*

- The watchdog site, Charity Navigator, conducted a study of charities in major markets both to analyze statistical differences in their financial, accountability, and transparency practices and to track year-to-year variations in individual philanthropic communities. The Philadelphia metro area was ranked #20 among the 30 metro markets in the rating category of Overall Score. *www.charitynavigator.org, "2017 Metro Market Study," May 1, 2017*

- *WalletHub* compared the 150 most populated U.S. cities to determine their operating efficiency. A "Quality of City Services" score was constructed for each city and then divided by the total budget per capita to reveal which were managed the best. Philadelphia ranked #135. Criteria: financial stability; economy; education; safety; health; infrastructure and pollution. *www.WalletHub.com, "2020's Best- & Worst-Run Cities in America," June 29, 2020*

Business Environment

DEMOGRAPHICS

Population Growth

Area	1990 Census	2000 Census	2010 Census	2019* Estimate	Population Growth (%) 1990-2019	Population Growth (%) 2010-2019
City	1,585,577	1,517,550	1,526,006	1,579,075	-0.4	3.5
MSA[1]	5,435,470	5,687,147	5,965,343	6,079,130	11.8	1.9
U.S.	248,709,873	281,421,906	308,745,538	324,697,795	30.6	5.2

Note: (1) Figures cover the Philadelphia-Camden-Wilmington, PA-NJ-DE-MD Metropolitan Statistical Area; (*) 2015-2019 5-year estimated population
Source: U.S. Census Bureau, 1990 Census, Census 2000, Census 2010, 2015-2019 American Community Survey 5-Year Estimates

Household Size

Area	Persons in Household (%) One	Two	Three	Four	Five	Six	Seven or More	Average Household Size
City	37.5	29.2	14.8	10.4	4.8	1.9	1.3	2.60
MSA[1]	29.1	32.3	16.3	13.5	5.7	1.9	1.1	2.60
U.S.	27.9	33.9	15.6	12.9	6.0	2.3	1.4	2.60

Note: (1) Figures cover the Philadelphia-Camden-Wilmington, PA-NJ-DE-MD Metropolitan Statistical Area
Source: U.S. Census Bureau, 2015-2019 American Community Survey 5-Year Estimates

Race

Area	White Alone[2] (%)	Black Alone[2] (%)	Asian Alone[2] (%)	AIAN[3] Alone[2] (%)	NHOPI[4] Alone[2] (%)	Other Race Alone[2] (%)	Two or More Races (%)
City	40.7	42.1	7.2	0.4	0.0	6.5	3.1
MSA[1]	66.6	21.0	5.9	0.2	0.0	3.4	2.8
U.S.	72.5	12.7	5.5	0.8	0.2	4.9	3.3

Note: (1) Figures cover the Philadelphia-Camden-Wilmington, PA-NJ-DE-MD Metropolitan Statistical Area; (2) Alone is defined as not being in combination with one or more other races; (3) American Indian and Alaska Native; (4) Native Hawaiian and Other Pacific Islander
Source: U.S. Census Bureau, 2015-2019 American Community Survey 5-Year Estimates

Hispanic or Latino Origin

Area	Total (%)	Mexican (%)	Puerto Rican (%)	Cuban (%)	Other (%)
City	14.7	1.3	8.8	0.3	4.3
MSA[1]	9.4	1.9	4.6	0.3	2.7
U.S.	18.0	11.2	1.7	0.7	4.3

Note: Persons of Hispanic or Latino origin can be of any race; (1) Figures cover the Philadelphia-Camden-Wilmington, PA-NJ-DE-MD Metropolitan Statistical Area
Source: U.S. Census Bureau, 2015-2019 American Community Survey 5-Year Estimates

Ancestry

Area	German	Irish	English	American	Italian	Polish	French[2]	Scottish	Dutch
City	6.4	10.4	2.6	2.3	7.4	3.3	0.7	0.5	0.3
MSA[1]	14.6	18.0	7.0	3.2	13.0	5.0	1.4	1.3	0.8
U.S.	13.3	9.7	7.2	6.2	5.1	2.8	2.3	1.7	1.2

Note: Figures are the percentage of the total population reporting a particular ancestry. The nine most commonly reported ancestries in the U.S. are shown. Figures include multiple ancestries (e.g. if a person reported being Irish and Italian, they were included in both columns); (1) Figures cover the Philadelphia-Camden-Wilmington, PA-NJ-DE-MD Metropolitan Statistical Area; (2) Excludes Basque
Source: U.S. Census Bureau, 2015-2019 American Community Survey 5-Year Estimates

Foreign-born Population

Area	Percent of Population Born in Any Foreign Country	Asia	Mexico	Europe	Caribbean	Central America[2]	South America	Africa	Canada
City	14.1	5.5	0.5	2.2	2.7	0.6	0.9	1.6	0.1
MSA[1]	11.0	4.5	0.9	1.9	1.3	0.4	0.6	1.1	0.2
U.S.	13.6	4.2	3.5	1.5	1.3	1.1	1.0	0.7	0.2

Note: (1) Figures cover the Philadelphia-Camden-Wilmington, PA-NJ-DE-MD Metropolitan Statistical Area; (2) Excludes Mexico.
Source: U.S. Census Bureau, 2015-2019 American Community Survey 5-Year Estimates

Marital Status

Area	Never Married	Now Married[2]	Separated	Widowed	Divorced
City	50.7	30.6	3.3	6.2	9.3
MSA[1]	37.2	45.5	2.1	6.0	9.2
U.S.	33.4	48.1	1.9	5.8	10.9

Note: Figures are percentages and cover the population 15 years of age and older; (1) Figures cover the Philadelphia-Camden-Wilmington, PA-NJ-DE-MD Metropolitan Statistical Area; (2) Excludes separated
Source: U.S. Census Bureau, 2015-2019 American Community Survey 5-Year Estimates

Disability by Age

Area	All Ages	Under 18 Years Old	18 to 64 Years Old	65 Years and Over
City	16.7	6.0	15.0	43.2
MSA[1]	12.7	4.6	10.5	33.4
U.S.	12.6	4.2	10.3	34.5

Note: Figures show percent of the civilian noninstitutionalized population that reported having a disability. Disability status is determined from six types of difficulty: vision, hearing, cognitive, ambulatory, self-care, and independent living. For children under 5 years old, hearing and vision difficulty are used to determine disability status. For children between the ages of 5 and 14, disability status is determined from hearing, vision, cognitive, ambulatory, and self-care difficulties. For people aged 15 years and older, they are considered to have a disability if they have difficulty with any one of the six difficulty types; Note: (1) Figures cover the Philadelphia-Camden-Wilmington, PA-NJ-DE-MD Metropolitan Statistical Area
Source: U.S. Census Bureau, 2015-2019 American Community Survey 5-Year Estimates

Age

Area	Percent of Population									Median Age
	Under Age 5	Age 5–19	Age 20–34	Age 35–44	Age 45–54	Age 55–64	Age 65–74	Age 75–84	Age 85+	
City	6.7	18.0	26.2	12.4	11.7	11.6	7.7	4.0	1.8	34.4
MSA[1]	5.9	18.6	20.7	12.3	13.4	13.5	8.9	4.6	2.1	38.8
U.S.	6.1	19.1	20.7	12.6	13.0	12.9	9.1	4.6	1.9	38.1

Note: (1) Figures cover the Philadelphia-Camden-Wilmington, PA-NJ-DE-MD Metropolitan Statistical Area
Source: U.S. Census Bureau, 2015-2019 American Community Survey 5-Year Estimates

Gender

Area	Males	Females	Males per 100 Females
City	747,479	831,596	89.9
MSA[1]	2,939,397	3,139,733	93.6
U.S.	159,886,919	164,810,876	97.0

Note: (1) Figures cover the Philadelphia-Camden-Wilmington, PA-NJ-DE-MD Metropolitan Statistical Area
Source: U.S. Census Bureau, 2015-2019 American Community Survey 5-Year Estimates

Religious Groups by Family

Area	Catholic	Baptist	Non-Den.	Methodist[2]	Lutheran	LDS[3]	Pentecostal	Presbyterian[4]	Muslim[5]	Judaism
MSA[1]	33.5	3.9	2.9	3.0	1.9	0.3	0.9	2.1	1.3	1.4
U.S.	19.1	9.3	4.0	4.0	2.3	2.0	1.9	1.6	0.8	0.7

Note: Figures are the number of adherents as a percentage of the total population; (1) Figures cover the Philadelphia-Camden-Wilmington, PA-NJ-DE-MD Metropolitan Statistical Area; (2) Methodist/Pietist; (3) Latter Day Saints; (4) Reformed; (5) Figures are estimates
Source: Association of Statisticians of American Religious Bodies, 2010 U.S. Religion Census: Religious Congregations & Membership Study

Religious Groups by Tradition

Area	Catholic	Evangelical Protestant	Mainline Protestant	Other Tradition	Black Protestant	Orthodox
MSA[1]	33.5	6.3	8.9	3.7	1.8	0.4
U.S.	19.1	16.2	7.3	4.3	1.6	0.3

Note: Figures are the number of adherents as a percentage of the total population; (1) Figures cover the Philadelphia-Camden-Wilmington, PA-NJ-DE-MD Metropolitan Statistical Area
Source: Association of Statisticians of American Religious Bodies, 2010 U.S. Religion Census: Religious Congregations & Membership Study

ECONOMY

Gross Metropolitan Product

Area	2017	2018	2019	2020	Rank[2]
MSA[1]	445.1	465.5	485.8	504.6	9

Note: Figures are in billions of dollars; (1) Figures cover the Philadelphia-Camden-Wilmington, PA-NJ-DE-MD Metropolitan Statistical Area; (2) Rank is based on 2018 data and ranges from 1 to 381
Source: U.S. Conference of Mayors, U.S. Metro Economies: GMP & Employment 2018-2020, September 2019

Economic Growth

Area	2015-17 (%)	2018 (%)	2019 (%)	2020 (%)	Rank[2]
MSA[1]	1.4	1.9	2.7	1.7	188
U.S.	1.9	2.9	2.3	2.1	–

Note: Figures are real gross metropolitan product (GMP) growth rates and represent average annual percent change; (1) Figures cover the Philadelphia-Camden-Wilmington, PA-NJ-DE-MD Metropolitan Statistical Area; (2) Rank is based on 2017 2-year average annual percent change and ranges from 1 to 381
Source: U.S. Conference of Mayors, U.S. Metro Economies: GMP & Employment 2018-2020, September 2019

Metropolitan Area Exports

Area	2014	2015	2016	2017	2018	2019	Rank[2]
MSA[1]	26,321.3	24,236.1	21,359.9	21,689.7	23,663.2	24,721.3	15

Note: Figures are in millions of dollars; (1) Figures cover the Philadelphia-Camden-Wilmington, PA-NJ-DE-MD Metropolitan Statistical Area; (2) Rank is based on 2019 data and ranges from 1 to 386
Source: U.S. Department of Commerce, International Trade Administration, Office of Trade and Economic Analysis, Industry and Analysis, Exports by Metropolitan Area, data extracted March 24, 2021

Building Permits

Area	Single-Family			Multi-Family			Total		
	2018	2019	Pct. Chg.	2018	2019	Pct. Chg.	2018	2019	Pct. Chg.
City	683	894	30.9	2,556	3,672	43.7	3,239	4,566	41.0
MSA[1]	6,875	6,963	1.3	6,281	8,644	37.6	13,156	15,607	18.6
U.S.	855,300	862,100	0.7	473,500	523,900	10.6	1,328,800	1,386,000	4.3

Note: (1) Figures cover the Philadelphia-Camden-Wilmington, PA-NJ-DE-MD Metropolitan Statistical Area; Figures represent new, privately-owned housing units authorized (unadjusted data); All permit data are based on estimates with imputation
Source: U.S. Census Bureau, Manufacturing, Mining, and Construction Statistics, Building Permits, 2018, 2019

Bankruptcy Filings

Area	Business Filings			Nonbusiness Filings		
	2019	2020	% Chg.	2019	2020	% Chg.
Philadelphia County	88	116	31.8	2,222	1,162	-47.7
U.S.	22,780	21,655	-4.9	752,160	522,808	-30.5

Note: Business filings include Chapter 7, Chapter 9, Chapter 11, Chapter 12, Chapter 13, Chapter 15, and Section 304; Nonbusiness filings include Chapter 7, Chapter 11, and Chapter 13
Source: Administrative Office of the U.S. Courts, Business and Nonbusiness Bankruptcy, County Cases Commenced by Chapter of the Bankruptcy Code, During the 12-Month Period Ending December 31, 2019 and Business and Nonbusiness Bankruptcy, County Cases Commenced by Chapter of the Bankruptcy Code, During the 12-Month Period Ending December 31, 2020

Housing Vacancy Rates

Area	Gross Vacancy Rate[2] (%)			Year-Round Vacancy Rate[3] (%)			Rental Vacancy Rate[4] (%)			Homeowner Vacancy Rate[5] (%)		
	2018	2019	2020	2018	2019	2020	2018	2019	2020	2018	2019	2020
MSA[1]	9.0	8.3	6.0	8.9	8.1	5.8	6.4	7.1	5.4	1.2	1.3	0.7
U.S.	12.3	12.0	10.6	9.7	9.5	8.2	6.9	6.7	6.3	1.5	1.4	1.0

Note: (1) Figures cover the Philadelphia-Camden-Wilmington, PA-NJ-DE-MD Metropolitan Statistical Area; (2) The percentage of the total housing inventory that is vacant; (3) The percentage of the housing inventory (excluding seasonal units) that is year-round vacant; (4) The percentage of rental inventory that is vacant for rent; (5) The percentage of homeowner inventory that is vacant for sale
Source: U.S. Census Bureau, Housing Vacancies and Homeownership Annual Statistics: 2018, 2019, 2020

INCOME

Income

Area	Per Capita ($)	Median Household ($)	Average Household ($)
City	27,924	45,927	68,379
MSA[1]	39,091	72,343	100,889
U.S.	34,103	62,843	88,607

Note: (1) Figures cover the Philadelphia-Camden-Wilmington, PA-NJ-DE-MD Metropolitan Statistical Area
Source: U.S. Census Bureau, 2015-2019 American Community Survey 5-Year Estimates

Household Income Distribution

Area	Percent of Households Earning							
	Under $15,000	$15,000 -$24,999	$25,000 -$34,999	$35,000 -$49,999	$50,000 -$74,999	$75,000 -$99,999	$100,000 -$149,999	$150,000 and up
City	19.1	11.2	10.2	12.7	15.8	10.5	11.0	9.4
MSA[1]	10.0	7.8	7.7	10.4	15.6	12.6	16.6	19.3
U.S.	10.3	8.9	8.9	12.3	17.2	12.7	15.1	14.5

Note: (1) Figures cover the Philadelphia-Camden-Wilmington, PA-NJ-DE-MD Metropolitan Statistical Area
Source: U.S. Census Bureau, 2015-2019 American Community Survey 5-Year Estimates

Poverty Rate

Area	All Ages	Under 18 Years Old	18 to 64 Years Old	65 Years and Over
City	24.3	34.8	22.2	17.6
MSA[1]	12.4	16.9	11.7	8.6
U.S.	13.4	18.5	12.6	9.3

Note: Figures are percentage of people whose income during the past 12 months was below the poverty level;
(1) Figures cover the Philadelphia-Camden-Wilmington, PA-NJ-DE-MD Metropolitan Statistical Area
Source: U.S. Census Bureau, 2015-2019 American Community Survey 5-Year Estimates

CITY FINANCES

City Government Finances

Component	2017 ($000)	2017 ($ per capita)
Total Revenues	8,304,929	5,298
Total Expenditures	8,487,838	5,415
Debt Outstanding	4,997,930	3,189
Cash and Securities[1]	7,333,644	4,679

Note: (1) Cash and security holdings of a government at the close of its fiscal year,
including those of its dependent agencies, utilities, and liquor stores.
Source: U.S. Census Bureau, State & Local Government Finances 2017

City Government Revenue by Source

Source	2017 ($000)	2017 ($ per capita)	2017 (%)
General Revenue			
From Federal Government	714,812	456	8.6
From State Government	1,547,207	987	18.6
From Local Governments	56,613	36	0.7
Taxes			
Property	571,648	365	6.9
Sales and Gross Receipts	606,036	387	7.3
Personal Income	1,819,689	1,161	21.9
Corporate Income	417,526	266	5.0
Motor Vehicle License	0	0	0.0
Other Taxes	293,387	187	3.5
Current Charges	1,017,133	649	12.2
Liquor Store	0	0	0.0
Utility	953,730	608	11.5
Employee Retirement	201,716	129	2.4

Source: U.S. Census Bureau, State & Local Government Finances 2017

City Government Expenditures by Function

Function	2017 ($000)	2017 ($ per capita)	2017 (%)
General Direct Expenditures			
Air Transportation	394,127	251	4.6
Corrections	372,653	237	4.4
Education	0	0	0.0
Employment Security Administration	0	0	0.0
Financial Administration	95,420	60	1.1
Fire Protection	255,215	162	3.0
General Public Buildings	192,772	123	2.3
Governmental Administration, Other	115,642	73	1.4
Health	1,685,635	1,075	19.9
Highways	206,455	131	2.4
Hospitals	0	0	0.0
Housing and Community Development	396,925	253	4.7
Interest on General Debt	232,819	148	2.7
Judicial and Legal	339,570	216	4.0
Libraries	49,181	31	0.6
Parking	0	0	0.0
Parks and Recreation	102,017	65	1.2
Police Protection	673,356	429	7.9
Public Welfare	200,592	128	2.4
Sewerage	327,401	208	3.9
Solid Waste Management	154,253	98	1.8
Veterans' Services	0	0	0.0
Liquor Store	0	0	0.0
Utility	821,855	524	9.7
Employee Retirement	804,614	513	9.5

Source: U.S. Census Bureau, State & Local Government Finances 2017

EMPLOYMENT

Labor Force and Employment

Area	Civilian Labor Force			Workers Employed		
	Dec. 2019	Dec. 2020	% Chg.	Dec. 2019	Dec. 2020	% Chg.
City	729,738	699,455	-4.1	690,247	634,633	-8.1
MD[1]	1,031,591	989,425	-4.1	980,295	906,853	-7.5
U.S.	164,007,000	160,017,000	-2.4	158,504,000	149,613,000	-5.6

Note: Data is not seasonally adjusted and covers workers 16 years of age and older; (1) Figures cover the Philadelphia, PA Metropolitan Division
Source: Bureau of Labor Statistics, Local Area Unemployment Statistics

Unemployment Rate

Area	2020											
	Jan.	Feb.	Mar.	Apr.	May	Jun.	Jul.	Aug.	Sep.	Oct.	Nov.	Dec.
City	6.0	5.9	7.0	17.0	16.4	18.2	18.1	15.8	12.0	10.8	9.7	9.3
MD[1]	5.5	5.4	6.4	16.3	15.5	17.0	16.7	14.5	10.9	9.8	8.8	8.3
U.S.	4.0	3.8	4.5	14.4	13.0	11.2	10.5	8.5	7.7	6.6	6.4	6.5

Note: Data is not seasonally adjusted and covers workers 16 years of age and older; (1) Figures cover the Philadelphia, PA Metropolitan Division
Source: Bureau of Labor Statistics, Local Area Unemployment Statistics

Average Wages

Occupation	$/Hr.	Occupation	$/Hr.
Accountants and Auditors	41.20	Maintenance and Repair Workers	22.60
Automotive Mechanics	22.50	Marketing Managers	75.70
Bookkeepers	22.30	Network and Computer Systems Admin.	41.50
Carpenters	30.90	Nurses, Licensed Practical	27.70
Cashiers	11.80	Nurses, Registered	38.50
Computer Programmers	48.80	Nursing Assistants	15.80
Computer Systems Analysts	50.50	Office Clerks, General	19.60
Computer User Support Specialists	29.10	Physical Therapists	45.60
Construction Laborers	24.80	Physicians	110.80
Cooks, Restaurant	14.80	Plumbers, Pipefitters and Steamfitters	33.20
Customer Service Representatives	20.20	Police and Sheriff's Patrol Officers	36.70
Dentists	81.40	Postal Service Mail Carriers	25.80
Electricians	37.00	Real Estate Sales Agents	23.80
Engineers, Electrical	53.00	Retail Salespersons	15.40
Fast Food and Counter Workers	11.80	Sales Representatives, Technical/Scientific	39.40
Financial Managers	82.20	Secretaries, Exc. Legal/Medical/Executive	20.80
First-Line Supervisors of Office Workers	33.40	Security Guards	15.80
General and Operations Managers	74.60	Surgeons	127.70
Hairdressers/Cosmetologists	16.20	Teacher Assistants, Exc. Postsecondary*	14.30
Home Health and Personal Care Aides	13.00	Teachers, Secondary School, Exc. Sp. Ed.*	35.00
Janitors and Cleaners	15.30	Telemarketers	17.40
Landscaping/Groundskeeping Workers	16.90	Truck Drivers, Heavy/Tractor-Trailer	25.10
Lawyers	73.10	Truck Drivers, Light/Delivery Services	20.10
Maids and Housekeeping Cleaners	14.50	Waiters and Waitresses	13.00

Note: Wage data covers the Philadelphia-Camden-Wilmington, PA-NJ-DE-MD Metropolitan Statistical Area; (*) Hourly wages were calculated from annual wage data based on a 40 hour work week; n/a not available.
Source: Bureau of Labor Statistics, Metro Area Occupational Employment & Wage Estimates, May 2020

Employment by Industry

Sector	MD[1]		U.S.
	Number of Employees	Percent of Total	Percent of Total
Construction, Mining, and Logging	23,400	2.6	5.5
Education and Health Services	287,900	32.2	16.3
Financial Activities	56,900	6.4	6.1
Government	129,500	14.5	15.2
Information	17,200	1.9	1.9
Leisure and Hospitality	54,400	6.1	9.0
Manufacturing	31,300	3.5	8.5
Other Services	33,400	3.7	3.8
Professional and Business Services	131,900	14.7	14.4
Retail Trade	69,500	7.8	10.9
Transportation, Warehousing, and Utilities	37,500	4.2	4.6
Wholesale Trade	22,100	2.5	3.9

Note: Figures are non-farm employment as of December 2020. Figures are not seasonally adjusted and include workers 16 years of age and older; (1) Figures cover the Philadelphia, PA Metropolitan Division
Source: Bureau of Labor Statistics, Current Employment Statistics, Employment, Hours, and Earnings

Employment by Occupation

Occupation Classification	City (%)	MSA[1] (%)	U.S. (%)
Management, Business, Science, and Arts	39.3	44.2	38.5
Natural Resources, Construction, and Maintenance	5.8	6.9	8.9
Production, Transportation, and Material Moving	12.1	10.6	13.2
Sales and Office	20.1	21.5	21.6
Service	22.8	16.8	17.8

Note: Figures cover employed civilians 16 years of age and older; (1) Figures cover the Philadelphia-Camden-Wilmington, PA-NJ-DE-MD Metropolitan Statistical Area
Source: U.S. Census Bureau, 2015-2019 American Community Survey 5-Year Estimates

Occupations with Greatest Projected Employment Growth: 2020 – 2022

Occupation[1]	2020 Employment	2022 Projected Employment	Numeric Employment Change	Percent Employment Change
Fast Food and Counter Workers	99,390	133,800	34,410	34.6
Retail Salespersons	114,460	140,170	25,710	22.5
Waiters and Waitresses	50,420	71,990	21,570	42.8
Home Health and Personal Care Aides	167,300	188,640	21,340	12.8
Laborers and Freight, Stock, and Material Movers, Hand	136,300	150,840	14,540	10.7
Cooks, Restaurant	30,330	44,850	14,520	47.9
Janitors and Cleaners, Except Maids and Housekeeping Cleaners	84,010	95,320	11,310	13.5
Office Clerks, General	142,930	154,180	11,250	7.9
Cashiers	119,300	129,290	9,990	8.4
First-Line Supervisors of Food Preparation and Serving Workers	24,060	32,140	8,080	33.6

Note: Projections cover Pennsylvania; (1) Sorted by numeric employment change
Source: www.projectionscentral.com, State Occupational Projections, 2020–2022 Short-Term Projections

Fastest-Growing Occupations: 2020 – 2022

Occupation[1]	2020 Employment	2022 Projected Employment	Numeric Employment Change	Percent Employment Change
Motion Picture Projectionists	160	310	150	93.8
Gaming Dealers	1,960	3,610	1,650	84.2
Gaming Change Persons and Booth Cashiers	210	380	170	81.0
Amusement and Recreation Attendants	5,330	9,600	4,270	80.1
Ushers, Lobby Attendants, and Ticket Takers	2,460	4,340	1,880	76.4
Athletes and Sports Competitors	580	1,010	430	74.1
Hotel, Motel, and Resort Desk Clerks	4,010	6,860	2,850	71.1
Funeral Attendants	1,150	1,820	670	58.3
Pressers, Textile, Garment, and Related Materials	780	1,190	410	52.6
Locker Room, Coatroom, and Dressing Room Attendants	570	860	290	50.9

Note: Projections cover Pennsylvania; (1) Sorted by percent employment change and excludes occupations with numeric employment change less than 50
Source: www.projectionscentral.com, State Occupational Projections, 2020–2022 Short-Term Projections

TAXES

State Corporate Income Tax Rates

State	Tax Rate (%)	Income Brackets ($)	Num. of Brackets	Financial Institution Tax Rate (%)[a]	Federal Income Tax Ded.
Pennsylvania	9.99	Flat rate	1	(a)	No

Note: Tax rates as of January 1, 2021; (a) Rates listed are the corporate income tax rate applied to financial institutions or excise taxes based on income. Some states have other taxes based upon the value of deposits or shares.
Source: Federation of Tax Administrators, State Corporate Income Tax Rates, January 1, 2021

State Individual Income Tax Rates

State	Tax Rate (%)	Income Brackets ($)	Personal Exemptions ($) Single	Married	Depend.	Standard Ded. ($) Single	Married
Pennsylvania	3.07	Flat rate	None	None	None	–	–

Note: Tax rates as of January 1, 2021; Local- and county-level taxes are not included; Federal income tax is not deductible on state income tax returns
Source: Federation of Tax Administrators, State Individual Income Tax Rates, January 1, 2021

Various State Sales and Excise Tax Rates

State	State Sales Tax (%)	Gasoline[1] (¢/gal.)	Cigarette[2] ($/pack)	Spirits[3] ($/gal.)	Wine[4] ($/gal.)	Beer[5] ($/gal.)	Recreational Marijuana (%)
Pennsylvania	6	58.7	2.6	7.41	0.00	0.08	Not legal

Note: All tax rates as of January 1, 2021; (1) The American Petroleum Institute has developed a methodology for determining the average tax rate on a gallon of fuel. Rates may include any of the following: excise taxes, environmental fees, storage tank fees, other fees or taxes, general sales tax, and local taxes; (2) The federal excise tax of $1.0066 per pack and local taxes are not included; (3) Rates are those applicable to off-premise sales of 40% alcohol by volume (a.b.v.) distilled spirits in 750ml containers. Local excise taxes are excluded; (4) Rates are those applicable to off-premise sales of 11% a.b.v. non-carbonated wine in 750ml containers; (5) Rates are those applicable to off-premise sales of 4.7% a.b.v. beer in 12 ounce containers.
Source: Tax Foundation, 2021 Facts & Figures: How Does Your State Compare?

State Business Tax Climate Index Rankings

State	Overall Rank	Corporate Tax Rank	Individual Income Tax Rank	Sales Tax Rank	Property Tax Rank	Unemployment Insurance Tax Rank
Pennsylvania	27	43	19	17	15	40

Note: The index is a measure of how each state's tax laws affect economic performance. The lower the rank, the more favorable a state's tax system is for business. States without a given tax are given a ranking of 1. The scores/rankings for the District of Columbia do not affect other states. The 2021 index represents the tax climate as of July 1, 2020.
Source: Tax Foundation, State Business Tax Climate Index 2021

TRANSPORTATION

Means of Transportation to Work

Area	Car/Truck/Van		Public Transportation			Bicycle	Walked	Other Means	Worked at Home
	Drove Alone	Car-pooled	Bus	Subway	Railroad				
City	50.3	8.2	16.0	5.6	2.8	2.1	8.5	2.3	4.2
MSA[1]	72.5	7.6	5.0	1.9	2.3	0.6	3.6	1.3	5.2
U.S.	76.3	9.0	2.4	1.9	0.6	0.5	2.7	1.4	5.2

Note: Figures are percentages and cover workers 16 years of age and older; (1) Figures cover the Philadelphia-Camden-Wilmington, PA-NJ-DE-MD Metropolitan Statistical Area
Source: U.S. Census Bureau, 2015-2019 American Community Survey 5-Year Estimates

Travel Time to Work

Area	Less Than 10 Minutes	10 to 19 Minutes	20 to 29 Minutes	30 to 44 Minutes	45 to 59 Minutes	60 to 89 Minutes	90 Minutes or More
City	6.1	18.7	19.7	28.0	12.6	10.6	4.4
MSA[1]	9.2	23.6	20.3	24.0	11.1	8.5	3.3
U.S.	12.2	28.4	20.8	20.8	8.3	6.4	2.9

Note: Note: Figures are percentages and include workers 16 years old and over; (1) Figures cover the Philadelphia-Camden-Wilmington, PA-NJ-DE-MD Metropolitan Statistical Area
Source: U.S. Census Bureau, 2015-2019 American Community Survey 5-Year Estimates

Key Congestion Measures

Measure	1982	1992	2002	2012	2017
Annual Hours of Delay, Total (000)	41,664	77,912	151,525	174,990	194,655
Annual Hours of Delay, Per Auto Commuter	19	32	46	52	62
Annual Congestion Cost, Total (million $)	315	826	2,052	3,159	3,625
Annual Congestion Cost, Per Auto Commuter ($)	577	742	1,125	1,018	1,099

Note: Covers the Philadelphia PA-NJ-DE-MD urban area
Source: Texas A&M Transportation Institute, 2019 Urban Mobility Report

Freeway Travel Time Index

Measure	1982	1987	1992	1997	2002	2007	2012	2017
Urban Area Index[1]	1.10	1.15	1.16	1.19	1.23	1.25	1.24	1.25
Urban Area Rank[1,2]	19	17	23	26	26	27	26	25

Note: Freeway Travel Time Index—the ratio of travel time in the peak period to the travel time at free-flow conditions. For example, a value of 1.30 indicates a 20-minute free-flow trip takes 26 minutes in the peak (20 minutes x 1.30 = 26 minutes); (1) Covers the Philadelphia PA-NJ-DE-MD urban area; (2) Rank is based on 101 larger urban areas (#1 = highest travel time index)
Source: Texas A&M Transportation Institute, 2019 Urban Mobility Report

Public Transportation

Agency Name / Mode of Transportation	Vehicles Operated in Maximum Service[1]	Annual Unlinked Passenger Trips[2] (in thous.)	Annual Passenger Miles[3] (in thous.)
Southeastern Pennsylvania Transportation Authority (SEPTA)			
Bus (directly operated)	1,185	153,878.8	479,341.9
Bus (purchased transportation)	6	77.6	440.7
Commuter Rail (directly operated)	348	34,730.1	465,744.5
Demand Response (purchased transportation)	415	1,513.1	10,507.1
Heavy Rail (directly operated)	287	90,754.2	399,537.4
Streetcar Rail (directly operated)	120	22,816.9	58,270.4
Trolleybus (directly operated)	29	4,495.9	9,169.2

Note: (1) Number of revenue vehicles operated by the given mode and type of service to meet the annual maximum service requirement. This is the revenue vehicle count during the peak season of the year; on the week and day that maximum service is provided. Vehicles operated in maximum service (VOMS) exclude atypical days and one-time special events; (2) Number of passengers who boarded public transportation vehicles. Passengers are counted each time they board a vehicle no matter how many vehicles they use to travel from their origin to their destination. (3) Sum of the distances ridden by all passengers during the entire fiscal year. Source: Federal Transit Administration, National Transit Database, 2019

Air Transportation

Airport Name and Code / Type of Service	Passenger Airlines[1]	Passenger Enplanements	Freight Carriers[2]	Freight (lbs)
Philadelphia International (PHL)				
Domestic service (U.S. carriers - 2020)	30	5,417,483	19	464,285,548
International service (U.S. carriers - 2019)	8	1,542,593	5	127,546,543

*Note: (1) Includes all U.S.-based major, minor and commuter airlines that carried at least one passenger during the year; (2) Includes all U.S.-based airlines and freight carriers that transported at least one pound of freight during the year.
Source: Bureau of Transportation Statistics, The Intermodal Transportation Database, Air Carriers: T-100 Domestic Market (U.S. Carriers), 2020; Bureau of Transportation Statistics, The Intermodal Transportation Database, Air Carriers: T-100 International Market (U.S. Carriers), 2019*

BUSINESSES

Major Business Headquarters

Company Name	Industry	Rankings	
		Fortune[1]	Forbes[2]
Aramark	Diversified Outsourcing Services	200	-
Comcast	Telecommunications	28	-
Crown Holdings	Packaging, Containers	272	-
Day & Zimmermann	Construction	-	188
Morgan Lewis & Bockius	Services	-	196

*Note: (1) Companies that produce a 10-K are ranked 1 to 500 based on 2019 revenue; (2) All private companies with at least $2 billion in annual revenue through the end of their most current fiscal year are ranked 1 to 219; companies listed are headquartered in the city; dashes indicate no ranking
Source: Fortune, "Fortune 500," June/July 2020; Forbes, "America's Largest Private Companies," 2020*

Fastest-Growing Businesses

According to *Inc.*, Philadelphia is home to two of America's 500 fastest-growing private companies: **Dropps** (#289); **Double Wood** (#367). Criteria: must be an independent, privately-held, for-profit, U.S. corporation, proprietorship or partnership as of December 31, 2019; revenues must be at least $100,000 in 2016 and $2 million in 2019; must have four-year operating/sales history. *Inc., "America's 500 Fastest-Growing Private Companies," 2020*

According to *Fortune*, Philadelphia is home to one of the 100 fastest-growing companies in the world: **FMC** (#19). Companies were ranked by their revenue growth rate; their EPS growth rate; and their three-year annualized total return to investors for the period ending June 30, 2020. Criteria for inclusion: a company, foreign or domestic, must trade on a major U.S. stock exchange; must file quarterly reports with the SEC; must have a minimum market capitalization of $250 million; must have a stock price of at least $5 on June 30, 2020; must have been trading continuously since June 30, 2017; must have revenue and net income for the four quarters ended on or before April 30, 2020, of at least $50 million and $10 million, respectively; and must have posted a compound annual growth in revenue and earnings per share of at least 15% annually over the three years ending on or before April 30, 2020. Real estate investment trusts, limited-liability companies, limited parterships, business development companies, closed-end investment firms, companies about to be acquired, and companies that lost money in the quarter ending April 30, 2020 were excluded. *Fortune, "100 Fastest-Growing Companies," 2020*

According to *Initiative for a Competitive Inner City (ICIC)*, Philadelphia is home to three of America's 100 fastest-growing "inner city" companies: **STRATIS IoT** (#4); **Seer Interactive** (#38); **Erec-**

tor Sets (#88). Criteria for inclusion: company must be headquartered in or have 51 percent or more of its physical operations in an economically distressed urban area; must be an independent, for-profit corporation, partnership or proprietorship; must have 10 or more employees and have a five-year sales history that includes sales of at least $200,000 in the base year and at least $1 million in the current year with no decrease in sales over the two most recent years. Companies were ranked overall by revenue growth over the five-year period between 2015 and 2019. *Initiative for a Competitive Inner City (ICIC), "Inner City 100 Companies," 2020*

According to Deloitte, Philadelphia is home to four of North America's 500 fastest-growing high-technology companies: **Piano** (#258); **Health Union** (#271); **Sidecar** (#399); **Vici Media** (#404). Companies are ranked by percentage growth in revenue over a four-year period. Criteria for inclusion: company must be headquartered within North America; must own proprietary intellectual property or technology that is sold to customers in products that contributes to a significant portion of the company's operating revenue; must have been in business for a minumum of four years with 2016 operating revenues of at least $50,000 USD/CD and 2019 operating revenues of at least $5 million USD/CD. *Deloitte, 2020 Technology Fast 500*™

Minority Business Opportunity

Philadelphia is home to one company which is on the *Black Enterprise* Industrial/Service list (100 largest companies based on gross sales): **PRWT Services** (#34). Criteria: operational in previous calendar year; at least 51% black-owned and manufactures/owns the product it sells or provides industrial or consumer services. Brokerages, real estate firms and firms that provide professional services are not eligible. *Black Enterprise, B.E. 100s, 2019*

Living Environment

COST OF LIVING

Cost of Living Index

Composite Index	Groceries	Housing	Utilities	Trans-portation	Health Care	Misc. Goods/ Services
111.9	119.8	117.4	111.2	113.6	100.6	105.7

Note: The Cost of Living Index measures regional differences in the cost of consumer goods and services, excluding taxes and non-consumer expenditures, for professional and managerial households in the top income quintile. It is based on more than 50,000 prices covering almost 60 different items for which prices are collected three times a year by chambers of commerce, economic development organizations or university applied economic centers in each participating urban area. The numbers shown should be read as a percentage above or below the national average of 100. For example, a value of 115.4 in the groceries column indicates that grocery prices are 15.4% higher than the national average. Small differences in the index numbers should not be interpreted as significant; Figures cover the Philadelphia PA urban area.
Source: The Council for Community and Economic Research, Cost of Living Index, 2020

Grocery Prices

Area[1]	T-Bone Steak ($/pound)	Frying Chicken ($/pound)	Whole Milk ($/half gal.)	Eggs ($/dozen)	Orange Juice ($/64 oz.)	Coffee ($/11.5 oz.)
City[2]	13.82	1.60	2.18	1.99	4.08	4.54
Avg.	11.78	1.39	2.05	1.47	3.57	4.34
Min.	8.03	0.94	1.03	0.74	2.94	3.02
Max.	15.86	2.65	4.31	3.77	5.44	8.69

*Note: (1) Values for the local area are compared with the average, minimum and maximum values for all 284 areas in the Cost of Living Index; (2) Figures cover the Philadelphia PA urban area; **T-Bone Steak** (price per pound); **Frying Chicken** (price per pound, whole fryer); **Whole Milk** (half gallon carton); **Eggs** (price per dozen, Grade A, large); **Orange Juice** (64 oz. Tropicana or Florida Natural); **Coffee** (11.5 oz. can, vacuum-packed, Maxwell House, Hills Bros, or Folgers).*
Source: The Council for Community and Economic Research, Cost of Living Index, 2020

Housing and Utility Costs

Area[1]	New Home Price ($)	Apartment Rent ($/month)	All Electric ($/month)	Part Electric ($/month)	Other Energy ($/month)	Telephone ($/month)
City[2]	426,075	1,517	-	100.69	93.28	192.10
Avg.	368,594	1,168	170.86	100.47	65.28	184.30
Min.	190,567	502	91.58	31.42	26.08	169.60
Max.	2,227,806	4,738	470.38	280.31	280.06	206.50

*Note: (1) Values for the local area are compared with the average, minimum and maximum values for all 284 areas in the Cost of Living Index; (2) Figures cover the Philadelphia PA urban area; **New Home Price** (2,400 sf living area, 8,000 sf lot, in urban area with full utilities); **Apartment Rent** (950 sf 2 bedroom/1.5 or 2 bath, unfurnished, excluding all utilities except water); **All Electric** (average monthly cost for an all-electric home); **Part Electric** (average monthly cost for a part-electric home); **Other Energy** (average monthly cost for natural gas, fuel oil, coal, wood, and any other forms of energy except electricity); **Telephone** (price includes the base monthly rate plus taxes and fees for three lines of mobile phone service).*
Source: The Council for Community and Economic Research, Cost of Living Index, 2020

Health Care, Transportation, and Other Costs

Area[1]	Doctor ($/visit)	Dentist ($/visit)	Optometrist ($/visit)	Gasoline ($/gallon)	Beauty Salon ($/visit)	Men's Shirt ($)
City[2]	133.89	96.86	108.61	2.43	60.55	31.89
Avg.	115.44	99.32	108.10	2.21	39.27	31.37
Min.	36.68	59.00	51.36	1.71	19.00	11.00
Max.	219.00	153.10	250.97	3.46	82.05	58.33

*Note: (1) Values for the local area are compared with the average, minimum and maximum values for all 284 areas in the Cost of Living Index; (2) Figures cover the Philadelphia PA urban area; **Doctor** (general practitioners routine exam of an established patient); **Dentist** (adult teeth cleaning and periodic oral examination); **Optometrist** (full vision eye exam for established adult patient); **Gasoline** (one gallon regular unleaded, national brand, including all taxes, cash price at self-service pump if available); **Beauty Salon** (woman's shampoo, trim, and blow-dry); **Men's Shirt** (cotton/polyester dress shirt, pinpoint weave, long sleeves).*
Source: The Council for Community and Economic Research, Cost of Living Index, 2020

HOUSING

Homeownership Rate

Area	2012 (%)	2013 (%)	2014 (%)	2015 (%)	2016 (%)	2017 (%)	2018 (%)	2019 (%)	2020 (%)
MSA[1]	69.5	69.1	67.0	67.0	64.7	65.6	67.4	67.4	69.2
U.S.	65.4	65.1	64.5	63.7	63.4	63.9	64.4	64.6	66.6

Note: (1) Figures cover the Philadelphia-Camden-Wilmington, PA-NJ-DE-MD Metropolitan Statistical Area
Source: U.S. Census Bureau, Housing Vacancies and Homeownership Annual Statistics: 2012-2020

House Price Index (HPI)

Area	National Ranking[2]	Quarterly Change (%)	One-Year Change (%)	Five-Year Change (%)	Since 1991Q1 (%)
MD[1]	145	1.50	5.90	33.20	191.57
U.S.[3]	–	3.81	10.77	38.99	205.12

Note: The HPI is a weighted repeat sales index. It measures average price changes in repeat sales or refinancings on the same properties. This information is obtained by reviewing repeat mortgage transactions on single-family properties whose mortgages have been purchased or securitized by Fannie Mae or Freddie Mac since January 1975; (1) Figures cover the Philadelphia, PA Metropolitan Division; (2) Rankings are based on annual percentage change for all metro areas containing at least 15,000 transactions over the last 10 years and ranges from 1 to 253; (3) figures based on a weighted average of Census Division estimates using a seasonally adjusted, purchase-only index; all figures are for the period ending December 31, 2020
Source: Federal Housing Finance Agency, Change in Metropolitan Area House Price Indexes, April 7, 2021

Median Single-Family Home Prices

Area	2018	2019	2020p	Percent Change 2019 to 2020
MSA[1]	229.0	246.2	272.9	10.8
U.S. Average	261.6	274.6	299.9	9.2

Note: Figures are median sales prices of existing single-family homes in thousands of dollars; (p) preliminary; (1) Figures cover the Philadelphia-Camden-Wilmington, PA-NJ-DE-MD Metropolitan Statistical Area
Source: National Association of Realtors, Median Sales Price of Existing Single-Family Homes for Metropolitan Areas, 4th Quarter 2020

Qualifying Income Based on Median Sales Price of Existing Single-Family Homes

Area	With 5% Down ($)	With 10% Down ($)	With 20% Down ($)
MSA[1]	53,470	50,656	45,028
U.S. Average	59,266	56,147	49,908

Note: Figures are preliminary; Qualifying income is based on a mortgage rate of 2.81%. Monthly principal and interest payment is limited to 25% of income; (1) Figures cover the Philadelphia-Camden-Wilmington, PA-NJ-DE-MD Metropolitan Statistical Area
Source: National Association of Realtors, Qualifying Income Based on Median Sales Price of Existing Single-Family Homes for Metropolitan Areas, 4th Quarter 2020

Home Value Distribution

Area	Under $50,000	$50,000 -$99,999	$100,000 -$149,999	$150,000 -$199,999	$200,000 -$299,999	$300,000 -$499,999	$500,000 -$999,999	$1,000,000 or more
City	6.7	19.4	18.6	18.0	19.6	11.3	5.1	1.3
MSA[1]	3.4	7.3	10.2	14.8	26.3	26.2	10.1	1.7
U.S.	6.9	12.0	13.3	14.0	19.6	19.3	11.4	3.4

Note: Figures are percentages and cover owner-occupied housing units; (1) Figures cover the Philadelphia-Camden-Wilmington, PA-NJ-DE-MD Metropolitan Statistical Area
Source: U.S. Census Bureau, 2015-2019 American Community Survey 5-Year Estimates

Year Housing Structure Built

Area	2010 or Later	2000 -2009	1990 -1999	1980 -1989	1970 -1979	1960 -1969	1950 -1959	1940 -1949	Before 1940	Median Year
City	2.7	3.0	3.2	3.7	7.1	10.7	16.3	11.6	41.7	1947
MSA[1]	3.1	7.8	9.6	10.0	12.1	11.9	15.7	7.5	22.2	1964
U.S.	5.2	14.0	13.9	13.4	15.2	10.6	10.3	4.9	12.6	1978

Note: Figures are percentages except for Median Year; Note: (1) Figures cover the Philadelphia-Camden-Wilmington, PA-NJ-DE-MD Metropolitan Statistical Area
Source: U.S. Census Bureau, 2015-2019 American Community Survey 5-Year Estimates

Gross Monthly Rent

Area	Under $500	$500 -$999	$1,000 -$1,499	$1,500 -$1,999	$2,000 -$2,499	$2,500 -$2,999	$3,000 and up	Median ($)
City	11.0	35.4	34.7	11.6	4.4	1.5	1.3	1,042
MSA[1]	8.1	29.1	38.4	15.9	5.4	1.7	1.4	1,143
U.S.	9.4	36.2	30.0	14.0	5.6	2.4	2.4	1,062

Note: Figures are percentages except for Median; Gross rent is the contract rent plus the estimated average monthly cost of utilities (electricity, gas, and water and sewer) and fuels (oil, coal, kerosene, wood, etc.) if these are paid by the renter (or paid for the renter by someone else); (1) Figures cover the Philadelphia-Camden-Wilmington, PA-NJ-DE-MD Metropolitan Statistical Area
Source: U.S. Census Bureau, 2015-2019 American Community Survey 5-Year Estimates

HEALTH

Health Risk Factors

Category	MD[1] (%)	U.S. (%)
Adults aged 18–64 who have any kind of health care coverage	89.2	87.3
Adults who reported being in good or better health	79.2	82.4
Adults who have been told they have high blood cholesterol	28.1	33.0
Adults who have been told they have high blood pressure	31.3	32.3
Adults who are current smokers	19.8	17.1
Adults who currently use E-cigarettes	3.9	4.6
Adults who currently use chewing tobacco, snuff, or snus	1.3	4.0
Adults who are heavy drinkers[2]	7.4	6.3
Adults who are binge drinkers[3]	21.7	17.4
Adults who are overweight (BMI 25.0 - 29.9)	35.6	35.3
Adults who are obese (BMI 30.0 - 99.8)	32.0	31.3
Adults who participated in any physical activities in the past month	74.4	74.4
Adults who always or nearly always wears a seat belt	88.4	94.3

Note: (1) Figures cover the Philadelphia, PA Metropolitan Division; (2) Heavy drinkers are classified as adult men having more than 14 drinks per week and adult women having more than 7 drinks per week; (3) Binge drinkers are classified as males having five or more drinks on one occasion or females having four or more drinks on one occasion
Source: Centers for Disease Control and Prevention, Behaviorial Risk Factor Surveillance System, SMART: Selected Metropolitan Area Risk Trends, 2017

Acute and Chronic Health Conditions

Category	MD[1] (%)	U.S. (%)
Adults who have ever been told they had a heart attack	3.3	4.2
Adults who have ever been told they have angina or coronary heart disease	4.6	3.9
Adults who have ever been told they had a stroke	3.7	3.0
Adults who have ever been told they have asthma	16.8	14.2
Adults who have ever been told they have arthritis	26.1	24.9
Adults who have ever been told they have diabetes[2]	11.4	10.5
Adults who have ever been told they had skin cancer	3.3	6.2
Adults who have ever been told they had any other types of cancer	7.3	7.1
Adults who have ever been told they have COPD	6.7	6.5
Adults who have ever been told they have kidney disease	2.3	3.0
Adults who have ever been told they have a form of depression	21.3	20.5

Note: (1) Figures cover the Philadelphia, PA Metropolitan Division; (2) Figures do not include pregnancy-related, borderline, or pre-diabetes
Source: Centers for Disease Control and Prevention, Behaviorial Risk Factor Surveillance System, SMART: Selected Metropolitan Area Risk Trends, 2017

Health Screening and Vaccination Rates

Category	MD[1] (%)	U.S. (%)
Adults aged 65+ who have had flu shot within the past year	64.5	60.7
Adults aged 65+ who have ever had a pneumonia vaccination	78.9	75.4
Adults who have ever been tested for HIV	52.7	36.1
Adults who have ever had the shingles or zoster vaccine?	25.4	28.9
Adults who have had their blood cholesterol checked within the last five years	86.8	85.9

Note: n/a not available; (1) Figures cover the Philadelphia, PA Metropolitan Division.
Source: Centers for Disease Control and Prevention, Behaviorial Risk Factor Surveillance System, SMART: Selected Metropolitan Area Risk Trends, 2017

Disability Status

Category	MD[1] (%)	U.S. (%)
Adults who reported being deaf	4.7	6.7
Are you blind or have serious difficulty seeing, even when wearing glasses?	4.5	4.5
Are you limited in any way in any of your usual activities due of arthritis?	12.7	12.9
Do you have difficulty doing errands alone?	9.4	6.8
Do you have difficulty dressing or bathing?	4.3	3.6
Do you have serious difficulty concentrating/remembering/making decisions?	12.3	10.7
Do you have serious difficulty walking or climbing stairs?	17.2	13.6

Note: (1) Figures cover the Philadelphia, PA Metropolitan Division.
Source: Centers for Disease Control and Prevention, Behaviorial Risk Factor Surveillance System, SMART: Selected Metropolitan Area Risk Trends, 2017

Mortality Rates for the Top 10 Causes of Death in the U.S.

ICD-10[a] Sub-Chapter	ICD-10[a] Code	Age-Adjusted Mortality Rate[1] per 100,000 population	
		County[2]	U.S.
Malignant neoplasms	C00-C97	172.6	149.2
Ischaemic heart diseases	I20-I25	107.7	90.5
Other forms of heart disease	I30-I51	61.0	52.2
Chronic lower respiratory diseases	J40-J47	33.1	39.6
Other degenerative diseases of the nervous system	G30-G31	17.8	37.6
Cerebrovascular diseases	I60-I69	42.2	37.2
Other external causes of accidental injury	W00-X59	76.7	36.1
Organic, including symptomatic, mental disorders	F01-F09	32.7	29.4
Hypertensive diseases	I10-I15	31.7	24.1
Diabetes mellitus	E10-E14	20.4	21.5

Note: (a) ICD-10 = International Classification of Diseases 10th Revision; (1) Mortality rates are a three-year average covering 2017-2019; (2) Figures cover Philadelphia County.
Source: Centers for Disease Control and Prevention, National Center for Health Statistics. Underlying Cause of Death 1999-2019 on CDC WONDER Online Database

Mortality Rates for Selected Causes of Death

ICD-10[a] Sub-Chapter	ICD-10[a] Code	Age-Adjusted Mortality Rate[1] per 100,000 population	
		County[2]	U.S.
Assault	X85-Y09	21.0	6.0
Diseases of the liver	K70-K76	12.3	14.4
Human immunodeficiency virus (HIV) disease	B20-B24	2.8	1.5
Influenza and pneumonia	J09-J18	12.6	13.8
Intentional self-harm	X60-X84	10.3	14.1
Malnutrition	E40-E46	2.3	2.3
Obesity and other hyperalimentation	E65-E68	2.6	2.1
Renal failure	N17-N19	20.3	12.6
Transport accidents	V01-V99	7.7	12.3
Viral hepatitis	B15-B19	1.8	1.2

Note: (a) ICD-10 = International Classification of Diseases 10th Revision; (1) Mortality rates are a three-year average covering 2017-2019; (2) Figures cover Philadelphia County; Data are suppressed when the data meet the criteria for confidentiality constraints; Mortality rates are flagged as unreliable when the rate would be calculated with a numerator of 20 or less.
Source: Centers for Disease Control and Prevention, National Center for Health Statistics. Underlying Cause of Death 1999-2019 on CDC WONDER Online Database

Health Insurance Coverage

Area	With Health Insurance	With Private Health Insurance	With Public Health Insurance	Without Health Insurance	Population Under Age 19 Without Health Insurance
City	91.9	56.9	45.2	8.1	3.5
MSA[1]	94.4	73.2	34.0	5.6	2.9
U.S.	91.2	67.9	35.1	8.8	5.1

Note: Figures are percentages that cover the civilian noninstitutionalized population; (1) Figures cover the Philadelphia-Camden-Wilmington, PA-NJ-DE-MD Metropolitan Statistical Area
Source: U.S. Census Bureau, 2015-2019 American Community Survey 5-Year Estimates

Number of Medical Professionals

Area	MDs[3]	DOs[3,4]	Dentists	Podiatrists	Chiropractors	Optometrists
County[1] (number)	9,057	710	1,285	272	247	280
County[1] (rate[2])	571.9	44.8	81.1	17.2	15.6	17.7
U.S. (rate[2])	282.9	22.7	71.2	6.2	28.1	16.9

42101
Note: Data as of 2019 unless noted; (1) Data covers Philadelphia County; (2) Rate per 100,000 population; (3) Data as of 2018 and includes all active, non-federal physicians; (4) Doctor of Osteopathic Medicine
Source: U.S. Department of Health and Human Services, Health Resources and Services Administration, Bureau of Health Professions, Area Resource File (ARF) 2019-2020

Best Hospitals

According to *U.S. News,* the Philadelphia, PA metro area is home to eight of the best hospitals in the U.S.: **Chester County Hospital** (1 adult specialty); **Fox Chase Cancer Center** (1 adult specialty); **Hospitals of the University of Pennsylvania-Penn Presbyterian** (Honor Roll/12 adult specialties); **MossRehab** (1 adult specialty); **Pennsylvania Hospital** (1 adult specialty); **Scheie Eye Institute, Hospitals of the University of Pennsylvania** (12 adult specialties); **Thomas Jefferson University Hospitals** (9 adult specialties); **Wills Eye Hospital, Thomas Jefferson University Hospitals** (1 adult specialty). The hospitals listed were nationally ranked in at least one of 16 adult or 10 pediatric specialties. Only 134 hospitals nationwide were nationally ranked in one or more adult or pediatric specialty; this number increases to 178 counting specialized centers within hospitals. Twenty hospitals in the U.S. made the Honor Roll. The Best Hospitals Honor Roll takes both the national rankings and the procedure and condition ratings into account. Hospitals received points if they were nationally ranked in one of the 16 adult specialties—the higher they ranked, the more points they got—and how many ratings of "high performing" they earned in the 10 procedures and conditions. *U.S. News Online, "America's Best Hospitals 2020-21"*

According to *U.S. News,* the Philadelphia, PA metro area is home to one of the best children's hospitals in the U.S.: **Children's Hospital of Philadelphia** (Honor Roll/10 pediatric specialties). The hospital listed was highly ranked in at least one of 10 pediatric specialties. Eighty-eight children's hospitals in the U.S. were nationally ranked in at least one specialty. Hospitals received points for being ranked in a specialty, and the 10 hospitals with the most points across the 10 specialties make up the Honor Roll. *U.S. News Online, "America's Best Children's Hospitals 2020-21"*

EDUCATION

Public School District Statistics

District Name	Schls	Pupils	Pupil/ Teacher Ratio	Minority Pupils[1] (%)	Free Lunch Eligible[2] (%)	IEP[3] (%)
Philadelphia City SD	217	132,520	16.7	86.0	99.9	17.6
Philadelphia Performing Arts CS	1	2,446	16.3	55.2	56.4	15.9

Note: Table includes school districts with 2,000 or more students; (1) Percentage of students that are not non-Hispanic white; (2) Percentage of students that are eligible for the free lunch program; (3) Percentage of students that have an Individualized Education Program.
Source: U.S. Department of Education, National Center for Education Statistics, Common Core of Data, Local Education Agency (School District) Universe Survey: School Year 2018-2019; U.S. Department of Education, National Center for Education Statistics, Common Core of Data, Public Elementary/Secondary School Universe Survey: School Year 2018-2019

Best High Schools

According to *U.S. News,* Philadelphia is home to two of the top 500 high schools in the U.S.: **Julia R. Masterman Secondary School** (#16); **Central High School** (#275). Nearly 18,000 public, magnet and charter schools were ranked based on their performance on state assessments and how well they prepare students for college. *U.S. News & World Report, "Best High Schools 2020"*

Highest Level of Education

Area	Less than H.S.	H.S. Diploma	Some College, No Deg.	Associate Degree	Bachelor's Degree	Master's Degree	Prof. School Degree	Doctorate Degree
City	15.3	32.6	16.7	5.7	17.3	8.1	2.6	1.6
MSA[1]	9.3	29.0	16.7	7.1	22.4	10.8	2.7	1.9
U.S.	12.0	27.0	20.4	8.5	19.8	8.8	2.1	1.4

Note: Figures cover persons age 25 and over; (1) Figures cover the Philadelphia-Camden-Wilmington, PA-NJ-DE-MD Metropolitan Statistical Area
Source: U.S. Census Bureau, 2015-2019 American Community Survey 5-Year Estimates

Educational Attainment by Race

Area	High School Graduate or Higher (%)					Bachelor's Degree or Higher (%)				
	Total	White	Black	Asian	Hisp.[2]	Total	White	Black	Asian	Hisp.[2]
City	84.7	89.2	84.6	73.0	67.2	29.7	41.6	17.3	40.3	14.6
MSA[1]	90.7	93.2	87.5	84.6	70.1	37.9	42.1	21.4	57.1	17.8
U.S.	88.0	89.9	86.0	87.1	68.7	32.1	33.5	21.6	54.3	16.4

Note: Figures shown cover persons 25 years old and over; (1) Figures cover the Philadelphia-Camden-Wilmington, PA-NJ-DE-MD Metropolitan Statistical Area; (2) People of Hispanic origin can be of any race
Source: U.S. Census Bureau, 2015-2019 American Community Survey 5-Year Estimates

School Enrollment by Grade and Control

Area	Preschool (%)		Kindergarten (%)		Grades 1 - 4 (%)		Grades 5 - 8 (%)		Grades 9 - 12 (%)	
	Public	Private	Public	Private	Public	Private	Public	Private	Public	Private
City	56.8	43.2	79.1	20.9	79.1	20.9	80.6	19.4	80.1	19.9
MSA[1]	46.0	54.0	81.8	18.2	84.9	15.1	84.9	15.1	83.3	16.7
U.S.	59.1	40.9	87.6	12.4	89.5	10.5	89.4	10.6	90.1	9.9

Note: Figures shown cover persons 3 years old and over; (1) Figures cover the Philadelphia-Camden-Wilmington, PA-NJ-DE-MD Metropolitan Statistical Area
Source: U.S. Census Bureau, 2015-2019 American Community Survey 5-Year Estimates

Higher Education

Four-Year Colleges			Two-Year Colleges			Medical Schools[1]	Law Schools[2]	Voc/ Tech[3]
Public	Private Non-profit	Private For-profit	Public	Private Non-profit	Private For-profit			
1	17	3	1	3	4	4	3	6

Note: Figures cover institutions located within the city limits and include main campuses only; (1) includes schools accredited by the Liaison Committee on Medical Education and the American Osteopathic Association's Commission on Osteopathic College Accreditation; (2) includes ABA-accredited schools, schools with provisional ABA accreditation, and state accredited schools; (3) includes all schools with programs that are less than 2 years.
Source: National Center for Education Statistics, Integrated Postsecondary Education System (IPEDS), 2019-20; Wikipedia, List of Medical Schools in the United States, accessed April 2, 2021; Wikipedia, List of Law Schools in the United States, accessed April 2, 2021

According to *U.S. News & World Report,* the Philadelphia, PA metro division is home to five of the top 200 national universities in the U.S.: **University of Pennsylvania** (#8); **Villanova University** (#53 tie); **Temple University** (#103 tie); **Drexel University** (#133 tie); **Thomas Jefferson University** (#176 tie). The indicators used to capture academic quality fall into a number of categories: assessment by administrators at peer institutions; retention of students; faculty resources; student selectivity; financial resources; alumni giving; high school counselor ratings of colleges; and graduation rate. *U.S. News & World Report, "America's Best Colleges 2021"*

According to *U.S. News & World Report,* the Philadelphia, PA metro division is home to two of the top 100 liberal arts colleges in the U.S.: **Swarthmore College** (#3); **Haverford College** (#15 tie). The indicators used to capture academic quality fall into a number of categories: assessment by administrators at peer institutions; retention of students; faculty resources; student selectivity; financial resources; alumni giving; high school counselor ratings of colleges; and graduation rate. *U.S. News & World Report, "America's Best Colleges 2021"*

According to *U.S. News & World Report,* the Philadelphia, PA metro division is home to four of the top 100 law schools in the U.S.: **University of Pennsylvania (Carey)** (#6 tie); **Temple University (Beasley)** (#53 tie); **Villanova University** (#53 tie); **Drexel University (Kline)** (#81 tie). The rankings are based on a weighted average of 12 measures of quality: peer assessment score; assessment score by lawyers/judges; median LSAT scores; median undergrad GPA; acceptance rate; employment rates for graduates; placement success; bar passage rate; faculty resources; expenditures per student; student/faculty ratio; and library resources. *U.S. News & World Report, "America's Best Graduate Schools, Law, 2022"*

According to *U.S. News & World Report,* the Philadelphia, PA metro division is home to three of the top 75 medical schools for research in the U.S.: **University of Pennsylvania (Perelman)** (#9); **Thomas Jefferson University (Kimmel)** (#55 tie); **Temple University (Katz)** (#61 tie). The rankings are based on a weighted average of 11 measures of quality: quality assessment; peer assessment score; assessment score by residency directors; research activity; total research activity; average research activity per faculty member; student selectivity; median MCAT total score; median undergraduate GPA; acceptance rate; and faculty resources. *U.S. News & World Report, "America's Best Graduate Schools, Medical, 2022"*

According to *U.S. News & World Report,* the Philadelphia, PA metro division is home to one of the top 75 business schools in the U.S.: **University of Pennsylvania (Wharton) 1** (#2). The rankings are based on a weighted average of the following nine measures: quality assessment; peer assessment; recruiter assessment; placement success; mean starting salary and bonus; student selectivity; mean GMAT and GRE scores; mean undergraduate GPA; and acceptance rate. *U.S. News & World Report, "America's Best Graduate Schools, Business, 2022"*

EMPLOYERS

Major Employers

Company Name	Industry
Abington Memorial Hospital	General medical & surgical hospitals
AstraZeneca Pharmaceuticals	Pharmaceutical preparations
City of Philadelphia	Municipal government
Comcast Holdings Corporation	Cable & other pay television services
Cooper Health Care	Hospital management
E.I. du Pont de Nemours and Company	Agricultural chemicals
Einstein Community Health Associates	Offices & clinics of medical doctors
Glaxosmithkline	Commerical physical research
Lockheed Martin Corporation	Defense systems & equipment
Mercy Health System of SE Pennsylvania	General medical & surgical hospitals
On Time Staffing	Employment agencies
Richlieu Associates	Apartment building operators
Temple University	General medical & surgical hospitals
The University of Pennsylvania	Colleges & universities
The Vanguard Group	Management, investment, open-end
Thomas Jefferson University Hospital	General medical & surgical hospitals
Trustees of the University of Penn	General medical & surgical hospitals
U.S. Navy	U.S. military
Unisys Corporation	Computer integrated systems design
University of Delaware	Colleges & universities

Note: Companies shown are located within the Philadelphia-Camden-Wilmington, PA-NJ-DE-MD Metropolitan Statistical Area.
Source: Hoovers.com; Wikipedia

Best Companies to Work For

Comcast NBCUniversal, headquartered in Philadelphia, is among "The 100 Best Companies to Work For." To pick the best companies, *Fortune* partnered with the Great Place to Work Institute. Two-thirds of a company's score is based on the results of the Institute's Trust Index survey, which is sent to a random sample of employees from each company. The questions related to attitudes about management's credibility, job satisfaction, and camaraderie. The other third of the scoring is based on the company's responses to the Institute's Culture Audit, which includes detailed questions about pay and benefit programs, and a series of open-ended questions about hiring practices, internal communication, training, recognition programs, and diversity efforts. Any company that is at least five years old with more than 1,000 U.S. employees is eligible. *Fortune, "The 100 Best Companies to Work For," 2020*

Dechert; GlaxoSmithKline, headquartered in Philadelphia, are among the "100 Best Companies for Working Mothers." Criteria: paid time off and leaves; workforce profile; benefits; women's issues and advancement; flexible work; company culture and work life programs. *Working Mother, "100 Best Companies for Working Mothers," 2020*

Children's Hospital of Philadelphia; Janney Montgomery Scott, headquartered in Philadelphia, are among the "100 Best Places to Work in IT." To qualify, companies had to be U.S.-based organizations or be non-U.S.-based employers that met the following criteria: have a minimum of 300 total employees at a U.S. headquarters and a minimum of 30 IT employees in the U.S., with at least 50% of their IT employees based in the U.S. The best places to work were selected based on compensation, benefits, work/life balance, employee morale, and satisfaction with training and development programs. In addition, *InsiderPro* and *Computerworld* looked at retention efforts, programs for recognizing and rewarding outstanding performances, and benefits such as flextime, elder care and child care, and reimbursement for college tuition and the cost of pursuing technology certifications. *InsiderPro and Computerworld, "100 Best Places to Work in IT," 2020*

Dechert, headquartered in Philadelphia, is among the "Top Companies for Executive Women." This list is determined by organizations filling out an in-depth survey that measures female demographics at every level, but with an emphasis on women in senior corporate roles, with profit & loss (P&L) responsibility, and those earning in the top 20 percent of the organization. *Working Mother* defines P&L as having responsibility that involves monitoring the net income after expenses for a department or entire organization, with direct influence on how company resources are allocated. *Working Mother, "Top Companies for Executive Women," 2020+*

Dechert, headquartered in Philadelphia, is among the "Best Companies for Dads." *Working Mother's* newest list recognizes the growing importance companies place on giving dads time off and support for their families. Rankings are determined by measuring gender-neutral or paternity leave offered, as well as actual time taken, phase-back policies, child- and dependent-care benefits, and corporate support groups for men and dads. *Working Mother, "Best Companies for Dads," 2020*

PUBLIC SAFETY

Crime Rate

Area	All Crimes	Violent Crimes				Property Crimes		
		Murder	Rape[3]	Robbery	Aggrav. Assault	Burglary	Larceny -Theft	Motor Vehicle Theft
City	4,005.6	22.1	69.0	331.6	486.0	409.4	2,329.5	357.9
Suburbs[1]	1,935.5	7.6	16.3	96.8	235.8	202.8	1,235.3	140.9
Metro[2]	3,462.1	18.3	55.2	270.0	420.3	355.2	2,042.3	300.9
U.S.	2,593.1	5.0	44.0	86.1	248.2	378.0	1,601.6	230.2

Note: Figures are crimes per 100,000 population; (1) All areas within the metro area that are located outside the city limits; (2) Figures cover the Philadelphia, PA Metropolitan Division; (3) All figures shown were reported using the revised Uniform Crime Reporting (UCR) definition of rape.
Source: FBI Uniform Crime Reports, 2018 (data for 2019 was not available)

Hate Crimes

Area	Number of Quarters Reported	Number of Incidents per Bias Motivation					
		Race/Ethnicity/ Ancestry	Religion	Sexual Orientation	Disability	Gender	Gender Identity
City	4	7	4	1	0	0	0
U.S.	4	3,963	1,521	1,195	157	69	198

Source: Federal Bureau of Investigation, Hate Crime Statistics 2019

Identity Theft Consumer Reports

Area	Reports	Reports per 100,000 Population	Rank[2]
MSA[1]	26,563	435	63
U.S.	1,387,615	423	-

Note: (1) Figures cover the Philadelphia-Camden-Wilmington, PA-NJ-DE-MD Metropolitan Statistical Area; (2) Rank ranges from 1 to 391 where 1 indicates greatest number of identity theft reports per 100,000 population
Source: Federal Trade Commission, Consumer Sentinel Network Data Book 2020

Fraud and Other Consumer Reports

Area	Reports	Reports per 100,000 Population	Rank[2]
MSA[1]	65,226	1,069	15
U.S.	3,385,133	1,031	-

Note: (1) Figures cover the Philadelphia-Camden-Wilmington, PA-NJ-DE-MD Metropolitan Statistical Area; (2) Rank ranges from 1 to 391 where 1 indicates greatest number of fraud and other consumer reports per 100,000 population
Source: Federal Trade Commission, Consumer Sentinel Network Data Book 2020

POLITICS

2020 Presidential Election Results

Area	Biden	Trump	Jorgensen	Hawkins	Other
Philadelphia County	81.2	17.9	0.7	0.1	0.2
U.S.	51.3	46.8	1.2	0.3	0.5

Note: Results are percentages and may not add to 100% due to rounding
Source: Dave Leip's Atlas of U.S. Presidential Elections

SPORTS

Professional Sports Teams

Team Name	League	Year Established
Philadelphia 76ers	National Basketball Association (NBA)	1963
Philadelphia Eagles	National Football League (NFL)	1933
Philadelphia Flyers	National Hockey League (NHL)	1967
Philadelphia Phillies	Major League Baseball (MLB)	1883
Philadelphia Union	Major League Soccer (MLS)	2010

Note: Includes teams located in the Philadelphia-Camden-Wilmington, PA-NJ-DE-MD Metropolitan Statistical Area.
Source: Wikipedia, Major Professional Sports Teams of the United States and Canada, April 6, 2021

CLIMATE

Average and Extreme Temperatures

Temperature	Jan	Feb	Mar	Apr	May	Jun	Jul	Aug	Sep	Oct	Nov	Dec	Yr.
Extreme High (°F)	74	74	85	94	96	100	104	101	100	89	84	72	104
Average High (°F)	39	42	51	63	73	82	86	85	78	67	55	43	64
Average Temp. (°F)	32	34	42	53	63	72	77	76	68	57	47	36	55
Average Low (°F)	24	26	33	43	53	62	67	66	59	47	38	28	45
Extreme Low (°F)	-7	-4	7	19	28	44	51	44	35	25	15	1	-7

Note: Figures cover the years 1948-1990
Source: National Climatic Data Center, International Station Meteorological Climate Summary, 9/96

Average Precipitation/Snowfall/Humidity

Precip./Humidity	Jan	Feb	Mar	Apr	May	Jun	Jul	Aug	Sep	Oct	Nov	Dec	Yr.
Avg. Precip. (in.)	3.2	2.8	3.7	3.5	3.7	3.6	4.1	4.0	3.3	2.7	3.4	3.3	41.4
Avg. Snowfall (in.)	7	7	4	Tr	Tr	0	0	0	0	Tr	1	4	22
Avg. Rel. Hum. 7am (%)	74	73	73	72	75	77	80	82	84	83	79	75	77
Avg. Rel. Hum. 4pm (%)	60	55	51	48	51	52	54	55	55	54	57	60	54

Note: Figures cover the years 1948-1990; Tr = Trace amounts (<0.05 in. of rain; <0.5 in. of snow)
Source: National Climatic Data Center, International Station Meteorological Climate Summary, 9/96

Weather Conditions

Temperature			Daytime Sky			Precipitation		
10°F & below	32°F & below	90°F & above	Clear	Partly cloudy	Cloudy	0.01 inch or more precip.	0.1 inch or more snow/ice	Thunder-storms
5	94	23	81	146	138	117	14	27

Note: Figures are average number of days per year and cover the years 1948-1990
Source: National Climatic Data Center, International Station Meteorological Climate Summary, 9/96

HAZARDOUS WASTE

Superfund Sites

The Philadelphia, PA metro division is home to six sites on the EPA's Superfund National Priorities List: **East Tenth Street** (proposed); **Franklin Slag Pile (MDC)** (final); **Havertown Pcp** (final); **Lower Darby Creek Area** (final); **Metal Bank** (final); **Metro Container Corporation** (final). There are a total of 1,375 Superfund sites with a status of proposed or final on the list in the U.S. *U.S. Environmental Protection Agency, National Priorities List, April 7, 2021*

AIR QUALITY

Air Quality Trends: Ozone

	1990	1995	2000	2005	2010	2015	2016	2017	2018	2019
MSA[1]	0.102	0.109	0.099	0.091	0.083	0.074	0.075	0.073	0.075	0.067
U.S.	0.088	0.089	0.082	0.080	0.073	0.068	0.069	0.068	0.069	0.065

Note: (1) Data covers the Philadelphia-Camden-Wilmington, PA-NJ-DE-MD Metropolitan Statistical Area. The values shown are the composite ozone concentration averages among trend sites based on the highest fourth daily maximum 8-hour concentration in parts per million. These trends are based on sites having an adequate record of monitoring data during the trend period. Data from exceptional events are included.
Source: U.S. Environmental Protection Agency, Air Quality Monitoring Information, "Air Quality Trends by City, 1990-2019"

Air Quality Index

Area	Percent of Days when Air Quality was...[2]					AQI Statistics[2]	
	Good	Moderate	Unhealthy for Sensitive Groups	Unhealthy	Very Unhealthy	Maximum	Median
MSA[1]	49.3	46.3	4.4	0.0	0.0	150	51

Note: (1) Data covers the Philadelphia-Camden-Wilmington, PA-NJ-DE-MD Metropolitan Statistical Area; (2) Based on 365 days with AQI data in 2019. Air Quality Index (AQI) is an index for reporting daily air quality. EPA calculates the AQI for five major air pollutants regulated by the Clean Air Act: ground-level ozone, particle pollution (aka particulate matter), carbon monoxide, sulfur dioxide, and nitrogen dioxide. The AQI runs from 0 to 500. The higher the AQI value, the greater the level of air pollution and the greater the health concern. There are six AQI categories: "Good" AQI is between 0 and 50. Air quality is considered satisfactory; "Moderate" AQI is between 51 and 100. Air quality is acceptable; "Unhealthy for Sensitive Groups" When AQI values are between 101 and 150, members of sensitive groups may experience health effects; "Unhealthy" When AQI values are between 151 and 200 everyone may begin to experience health effects; "Very Unhealthy" AQI values between 201 and 300 trigger a health alert; "Hazardous" AQI values over 300 trigger warnings of emergency conditions (not shown).
Source: U.S. Environmental Protection Agency, Air Quality Index Report, 2019

Air Quality Index Pollutants

Area	Percent of Days when AQI Pollutant was...[2]					
	Carbon Monoxide	Nitrogen Dioxide	Ozone	Sulfur Dioxide	Particulate Matter 2.5	Particulate Matter 10
MSA[1]	0.0	3.6	50.1	0.0	46.3	0.0

Note: (1) Data covers the Philadelphia-Camden-Wilmington, PA-NJ-DE-MD Metropolitan Statistical Area; (2) Based on 365 days with AQI data in 2019. The Air Quality Index (AQI) is an index for reporting daily air quality. EPA calculates the AQI for five major air pollutants regulated by the Clean Air Act: ground-level ozone, particle pollution (also known as particulate matter), carbon monoxide, sulfur dioxide, and nitrogen dioxide. The AQI runs from 0 to 500. The higher the AQI value, the greater the level of air pollution and the greater the health concern.
Source: U.S. Environmental Protection Agency, Air Quality Index Report, 2019

Maximum Air Pollutant Concentrations: Particulate Matter, Ozone, CO and Lead

	Particulate Matter 10 (ug/m^3)	Particulate Matter 2.5 Wtd AM (ug/m^3)	Particulate Matter 2.5 24-Hr (ug/m^3)	Ozone (ppm)	Carbon Monoxide (ppm)	Lead (ug/m^3)
MSA[1] Level	49	9.8	26	0.072	2	0
NAAQS[2]	150	15	35	0.075	9	0.15
Met NAAQS[2]	Yes	Yes	Yes	Yes	Yes	Yes

Note: (1) Data covers the Philadelphia-Camden-Wilmington, PA-NJ-DE-MD Metropolitan Statistical Area; Data from exceptional events are included; (2) National Ambient Air Quality Standards; ppm = parts per million; ug/m^3 = micrograms per cubic meter; n/a not available.
Concentrations: Particulate Matter 10 (coarse particulate)—highest second maximum 24-hour concentration; Particulate Matter 2.5 Wtd AM (fine particulate)—highest weighted annual mean concentration; Particulate Matter 2.5 24-Hour (fine particulate)—highest 98th percentile 24-hour concentration; Ozone—highest fourth daily maximum 8-hour concentration; Carbon Monoxide—highest second maximum non-overlapping 8-hour concentration; Lead—maximum running 3-month average
Source: U.S. Environmental Protection Agency, Air Quality Monitoring Information, "Air Quality Statistics by City, 2019"

Maximum Air Pollutant Concentrations: Nitrogen Dioxide and Sulfur Dioxide

	Nitrogen Dioxide AM (ppb)	Nitrogen Dioxide 1-Hr (ppb)	Sulfur Dioxide AM (ppb)	Sulfur Dioxide 1-Hr (ppb)	Sulfur Dioxide 24-Hr (ppb)
MSA[1] Level	13	52	n/a	17	n/a
NAAQS[2]	53	100	30	75	140
Met NAAQS[2]	Yes	Yes	n/a	Yes	n/a

Note: (1) Data covers the Philadelphia-Camden-Wilmington, PA-NJ-DE-MD Metropolitan Statistical Area; Data from exceptional events are included; (2) National Ambient Air Quality Standards; ppm = parts per million; ug/m^3 = micrograms per cubic meter; n/a not available.
Concentrations: Nitrogen Dioxide AM—highest arithmetic mean concentration; Nitrogen Dioxide 1-Hr—highest 98th percentile 1-hour daily maximum concentration; Sulfur Dioxide AM—highest annual mean concentration; Sulfur Dioxide 1-Hr—highest 99th percentile 1-hour daily maximum concentration; Sulfur Dioxide 24-Hr—highest second maximum 24-hour concentration
Source: U.S. Environmental Protection Agency, Air Quality Monitoring Information, "Air Quality Statistics by City, 2019"

Pittsburgh, Pennsylvania

Background

Pittsburgh was once the creaking, croaking, belching giant of heavy industry. Thanks to a plentiful supply of bituminous coal beds and limestone deposits nearby, the city had forged a prosperous economy based upon steel, glass, rubber, petroleum, and machinery. However, unregulated spews of soot into the air by these factories earned Pittsburgh the title of "Smoky City," prompting concerned citizens and politicians to pass smoke-control laws. Today, Pittsburgh's renaissance is a result of its citizens' unflagging faith.

In the eighteenth century, the area in and around the Ohio Valley and the Allegheny River, where present-day Pittsburgh lies, was claimed by both the British and the French. After being lobbed back and forth between the two, the land finally fell into British hands. The city was named Pittsborough, for the British prime minister at the time, William Pitt.

Almost immediately, the city showed signs of what it was to become. In 1792, the first blast furnace was built by George Anschulz. In 1797, the first glass factory was opened, and in 1804, the first cotton factory. Irish, Scottish, and a smattering of English immigrants provided the labor pool for these factories. During the Civil War, a wave of German immigrants workers swept in. Finally, during the late nineteenth century, Poles, Czechs, Slovaks, Italians, Russians, and Hungarians completed the picture in the colorful quilt of Pittsburgh's workforce. The last wave particularly contributed their sweat and toil to the fortunes of captains of industry such as Andrew Carnegie, Henry Clay Frick, and Charles M. Schwab.

Fortunately for Pittsburgh, these industrialists gave back to the city in the form of their cultural and educational patronage. The Carnegie Museum of Natural History has an extensive dinosaur collection and ancient Egypt wing. The Frick Art & Historical Center holds a noted private collection featuring such artists as Rubens, Tintoretto, Fragonard, and Boucher. Other educational and cultural attractions include the Pittsburgh Ballet Theatre, Pittsburgh Opera, Pittsburgh Civic Light Opera, Pittsburgh Symphony Orchestra, Pittsburgh Broadway Across America series, Carnegie Science Center, Phipps Conservatory and Botanical Gardens, Pittsburgh Zoo and PPG Aquarium, Children's Museum of Pittsburgh, Johnstown Flood Museum, Rachel Carson Homestead and the Andy Warhol Museum.

By the late 1990s, Pittsburgh was showing tremendous growth. Technology and health care services, their manufacturing counterparts, and financial institutions were dominant forces behind a steadily diversifying economy. New Internet software and computer software companies set up operations in or near Pittsburgh, and many major corporations have their headquarters in the city.

An incredible amount of downtown building has occurred in recent years. Two downtown stadiums were opened in 2001: PNC Park for the Pittsburgh Pirates baseball team, and Heinz Field for the Steelers football team, 2009 Superbowl XLII champions. PNC Park is built along the lines of traditional two-tier ballparks, providing spectators intimate contact with the game. Heinz Field is an open, natural-turf field with stands in a horseshoe shape, the open end affording visitors a magnificent view of the Pittsburgh skyline.

Filmed at Pittsburgh's Center for Vaccine Research, "Chasing Covid" was created for educators to help demystify the process through which vaccines are made.

In September 2003, the city inaugurated its handsome riverfront David L. Lawrence Convention Center, the first and largest certified "green" convention center, which provides 330,000 square feet of exhibition space, meeting rooms, two lecture halls, and a 35,000 square-foot ballroom. The Pittsburgh Cultural Trust completed 700 residential units and multiple towers. This area is home to the PPG Place gothic glass skyscraper complex as well as residents, as condo towers have been constructed and historic office towers have been converted to residential use. Downtown is serviced by a subway, buses and multiple bridges leading north and south.

Pittsburgh has ranked high in several "Most Livable City" lists since the mid-80s. Livability rankings typically consider factors such as cost of living, crime, and cultural opportunities. Pittsburgh has a low cost of living compared to other northeastern U.S. cities. Pittsburgh has five city parks and several others managed by the Nature Conservancy. Birding enthusiasts love to visit the Clayton Hill area of Frick Park, where well over 100 species of birds have been recorded

Pittsburgh is a little over 100 miles southeast of Lake Erie. Its nearness to the Great Lakes and to the Atlantic Seaboard helps to modify its humid, continental climate. Winter is influenced primarily by Canadian air masses that are infrequently tempered by air from the Gulf of Mexico. During the summer, Gulf air brings warm, humid weather. Once every four years, the Monongahela and Ohio rivers combine, causing the Ohio River to reach flood stage.

Rankings

General Rankings

- The human resources consulting firm Mercer ranked 231 major cities worldwide in terms of overall quality of life. Pittsburgh ranked #59. Criteria: political, social, economic, and socio-cultural factors; medical and health considerations; schools and education; public services and transportation; recreation; consumer goods; housing; and natural environment. *Mercer, "Mercer 2019 Quality of Living Survey," March 13, 2019*

- In their seventh annual survey, Livability.com looked at data for more than 1,000 small to mid-sized U.S. cities to determine the rankings for Livability's "Top 100 Best Places to Live" in 2020. Pittsburgh ranked #51. Criteria: housing and affordable living; vibrant economy; social and civic engagement; education; demographics; health care options; transportation & infrastructure; and abundant lifestyle amenities. *Livability.com, "Top 100 Best Places to Live 2020" October 2020*

Business/Finance Rankings

- Based on metro area social media reviews, the employment opinion group Glassdoor surveyed 50 of the most populous U.S. metro areas and equally weighed cost of living, hiring opportunity, and job satisfaction to compose a list of "25 Best Cities for Jobs." Median pay and home value, and number of active job openings were also factored in. The Pittsburgh metro area was ranked #2 in overall job satisfaction. *www.glassdoor.com, "Best Cities for Jobs," February 25, 2020*

- The Brookings Institution ranked the nation's largest cities based on income inequality. Pittsburgh was ranked #27 (#1 = greatest inequality). Criteria: the "95/20 ratio," a figure representing the income at which a household earns more than 95 percent of all other households, divided by the income at which a household earns more than only 20 percent of all other households. *Brookings Institution, "Household Income Inequality, Largest Cities of 97 Large U.S. Metro Areas, 2014-2016," February 5, 2018*

- The Brookings Institution ranked the 100 largest metro areas in the U.S. based on income inequality. Pittsburgh was ranked #34 (#1 = greatest inequality). Criteria: the "95/20 ratio," a figure representing the income at which a household earns more than 95 percent of all other households, divided by the income at which a household earns more than only 20 percent of all other households. *Brookings Institution, "Household Income Inequality, 100 Largest U.S. Metro Areas, 2014-2016," February 5, 2018*

- Payscale.com ranked the 32 largest metro areas in terms of wage growth. The Pittsburgh metro area ranked #15. Criteria: private-sector and education professional wage growth between the 4th quarter of 2019 and the 4th quarter of 2020. *PayScale, "Wage Trends by Metro Area-4th Quarter," January 11, 2021*

- Pittsburgh was identified as one of America's most frugal metro areas by *Coupons.com.* The city ranked #25 out of 25. Criteria: digital coupon usage. *Coupons.com, "America's Most Frugal Cities of 2017," March 22, 2018*

- The Pittsburgh metro area appeared on the Milken Institute "2021 Best Performing Cities" list. Rank: #127 out of 200 large metro areas (population over 250,000). Criteria: job growth; wage and salary growth; high-tech output growth; housing affordability; household broadband access. *Milken Institute, "Best-Performing Cities 2021," February 16, 2021*

- *Forbes* ranked the 200 most populous metro areas to determine the nation's "Best Places for Business and Careers." The Pittsburgh metro area was ranked #114. Criteria: costs (business and living); job growth (past and projected); income growth; quality of life; educational attainment (college and high school); projected economic growth; cultural and leisure opportunities; workplace tolerance laws; net migration patterns. *Forbes, "The Best Places for Business and Careers 2019: Seattle Still On Top," October 30, 2019*

- Mercer Human Resources Consulting ranked 209 cities worldwide in terms of cost-of-living. Pittsburgh ranked #91 (the lower the ranking, the higher the cost-of-living). The survey measured the comparative cost of over 200 items (such as housing, food, clothing, household goods, transportation, and entertainment) in each location. *Mercer, "2020 Cost of Living Survey," June 9, 2020*

Children/Family Rankings

- Pittsburgh was selected as one of the most playful cities in the U.S. by KaBOOM! The organization's Playful City USA initiative honors cities and towns across the nation that have made their communities more playable. Criteria: pledging to integrate play as a solution to challenges in their communities; making it easy for children to get active and balanced play; creating more family-friendly and innovative communities as a result. *KaBOOM! National Campaign for Play, "2017 Playful City USA Communities"*

Culture/Performing Arts Rankings

- Pittsburgh was selected as one of the ten best small North American cities and towns for moviemakers. Of cities with smaller populations, the area ranked #3. As with the 2021 list for bigger cities, pandemic challenges and COVID-19 guidelines were factored in. Other criteria: film community and culture; access to equipment and facilities; tax incentives; and standard of living. *MovieMaker Magazine, "Best Places to Live and Work as a Moviemaker, 2021," January 26, 2021*

- Pittsburgh was selected as one of "America's Favorite Cities." The city ranked #11 in the "Architecture " category. Respondents to an online survey were asked to rate their favorite place (population over 100,000) in over 65 categories. *Travelandleisure.com, "America's Favorite Cities for Architecture 2016," March 2, 2017*

Dating/Romance Rankings

- *Apartment List* conducted its annual survey of renters for cities that have the best opportunities for dating. More than 11,000 single respondents rated their current city or neighborhood for opportunities to date. Pittsburgh ranked #6 out of 86 where single residents were very satisfied or somewhat satisfied, making it among the ten best areas for dating opportunities. Other criteria analyzed included gender and education levels of renters. *Apartment List, "The Best & Worst Metros for Dating 2020," February 4, 2020*

- Pittsburgh was selected as one of the nation's most romantic cities with 100,000 or more residents by Amazon.com. The city ranked #8 of 20. Criteria: per capita sales of romance novels, relationship books, romantic comedy movies, romantic music, and sexual wellness products. *Amazon.com, "Top 20 Most Romantic Cities in the U.S.," February 1, 2017*

Education Rankings

- Personal finance website *WalletHub* analyzed the 150 largest U.S. metropolitan statistical areas to determine where the most educated Americans are putting their degrees to work. Criteria: education levels; percentage of workers with degrees; education quality and attainment gap; public school quality rankings; quality and enrollment of each metro area's universities. Pittsburgh was ranked #39 (#1 = most educated city). *www.WalletHub.com, "Most and Least Educated Cities in America, " July 20, 2020*

- Pittsburgh was selected as one of America's most literate cities. The city ranked #9 out of the 84 largest U.S. cities. Criteria: number of booksellers; library resources; Internet resources; educational attainment; periodical publishing resources; newspaper circulation. *Central Connecticut State University, "America's Most Literate Cities, 2018," February 2019*

Environmental Rankings

- The U.S. Conference of Mayors and Walmart Stores sponsor the Mayors' Climate Protection Awards Program which recognize mayors for outstanding and innovative practices that mayors are taking to increase energy efficiency in their cities, reduce carbon emissions and expand renewable energy. Pittsburgh received First Place Honors in the large city category. *U.S. Conference of Mayors, "2020 Mayors' Climate Protection Awards," December 18, 2020*

- Pittsburgh was highlighted as one of the 25 metro areas most polluted by year-round particle pollution (Annual PM 2.5) in the U.S. during 2016 through 2018. The area ranked #8. *American Lung Association, "State of the Air 2020," April 21, 2020*

- Pittsburgh was highlighted as one of the 25 metro areas most polluted by short-term particle pollution (24-hour PM 2.5) in the U.S. during 2016 through 2018. The area ranked #16. *American Lung Association, "State of the Air 2020," April 21, 2020*

Health/Fitness Rankings

- For each of the 100 largest cities in the United States, the American Fitness Index®, published by the American College of Sports Medicine and the Anthem Foundation, evaluated community infrastructure and 33 health behaviors including preventive health, levels of chronic disease conditions, pedestrian safety, air quality, and community resources that support physical activity. Pittsburgh ranked #22 for "community fitness." *americanfitnessindex.org, "2020 ACSM American Fitness Index Summary Report," July 14, 2020*

- The Pittsburgh metro area was identified as one of the worst cities for bed bugs in America by pest control company Orkin. The area ranked #19 out of 50 based on the number of bed bug treatments Orkin performed from December 2019 to November 2020. *Orkin, "New Year, New Top City on Orkin's 2021 Bed Bug Cities List: Chicago," February 1, 2021*

- Pittsburgh was identified as a "2021 Spring Allergy Capital." The area ranked #5 out of 100. Three groups of factors were used to identify the most challenging cities for people with allergies during the spring season: annual spring pollen levels; over the counter medicine use; number of board-certified allergy specialists. *Asthma and Allergy Foundation of America, "Spring Allergy Capitals 2021," February 23, 2021*

- Pittsburgh was identified as a "2021 Fall Allergy Capital." The area ranked #5 out of 100. Three groups of factors were used to identify the most challenging cities for people with allergies during the fall season: annual fall pollen levels; over the counter medicine use; number of board-certified allergy specialists. *Asthma and Allergy Foundation of America, "Fall Allergy Capitals 2021," February 23, 2021*

- Pittsburgh was identified as a "2019 Asthma Capital." The area ranked #54 out of the nation's 100 largest metropolitan areas. Criteria: estimated asthma prevalence; crude death rate from asthma; and ER visits due to asthma. Risk factors analyzed but not factored in the rankings: annual pollen score; annual air quality; public smoking laws; number of board-certified asthma specialists; rescue medication use; controller medication use; uninsured rate; poverty rate. *Asthma and Allergy Foundation of America, "Asthma Capitals 2019: The Most Challenging Places to Live With Asthma," May 7, 2019*

Real Estate Rankings

- FitSmallBusiness looked at 50 of the largest metropolitan areas in the U.S. to determine which metro was the best to start a real estate business. Data was compiled from such sources as: Zillow, Trulia, U.S. Census Bureau, and the Bureau of Labor Statistics. Criteria: location; inventory; annual wages; median sales price of homes; days on the market; median price cut percentage; and other factors that would influence real estate professional growth. The Pittsburgh metro area ranked #49. *fitsmallbusiness.com, "The Best Cities to Become a Real Estate Agent in 2018," January 30, 2018*

- *WalletHub* compared the most populated U.S. cities to determine which had the best markets for real estate agents. Pittsburgh ranked #128 where demand was high and pay was the best. Criteria: sales per agent; annual median wage for real-estate agents; monthly average starting salary for real estate agents; real estate job density and competition; unemployment rate; home turnover rate; housing-market health index; and other relevant metrics. *www.WalletHub.com, "2019's Best Places to Be a Real Estate Agent," April 24, 2019*

- Pittsburgh was ranked #13 out of 268 metro areas in terms of housing affordability in 2020 by the National Association of Home Builders (#1 = most affordable). Criteria: the share of homes sold in that area affordable to a family earning the local median income, based on standard mortgage underwriting criteria. *National Association of Home Builders®, NAHB-Wells Fargo Housing Opportunity Index, 4th Quarter 2020*

Safety Rankings

- Allstate ranked the 200 largest cities in America in terms of driver safety. Pittsburgh ranked #167. Criteria: internal property damage claims over a two-year period from January 2016 to December 2017. The report helps increase the importance of safety and awareness behind the wheel. *Allstate, "Allstate America's Best Drivers Report, 2019" June 24, 2019*

- The National Insurance Crime Bureau ranked 384 metro areas in the U.S. in terms of per capita rates of vehicle theft. The Pittsburgh metro area ranked #308 (#1 = highest rate). Criteria: number of vehicle theft offenses per 100,000 inhabitants in 2019. *National Insurance Crime Bureau, "Hot Spots 2019," July 21, 2020*

Seniors/Retirement Rankings

- From its Best Cities for Successful Aging indexes, the Milken Institute generated rankings for metropolitan areas, weighing data in nine categories—health care, wellness, living arrangements, transportation and convenience, financial characteristics, education, employment, community engagement, and overall livability. The Pittsburgh metro area was ranked #44 overall in the large metro area category. *Milken Institute, "Best Cities for Successful Aging, 2017" March 14, 2017*

- Pittsburgh made the 2020 *Forbes* list of "25 Best Places to Retire." Criteria, focused on high-quality retirement living at an affordable price, include: housing/living costs compared to the national average and state taxes; air quality; crime rates; good economic outlook; home price appreciation; risk associated with climate-change; availability of medical care; bikeability; walkability; healthy living. *Forbes.com, "The Best Places to Retire in 2020," August 14, 2020*

Sports/Recreation Rankings

- Pittsburgh was chosen as one of America's best cities for bicycling. The city ranked #40 out of 50. Criteria: cycling infrastructure that is safe and friendly for all ages; energy and bike culture. The editors evaluated cities with populations of 100,000 or more. *Bicycling, "The 50 Best Bike Cities in America," October 10, 2018*

Transportation Rankings

- Business Insider presented an AllTransit Performance Score ranking of public transportation in major U.S. cities and towns, with populations over 250,000, in which Pittsburgh earned the #15-ranked "Transit Score," awarded for frequency of service, access to jobs, quality and number of stops, and affordability. *www.businessinsider.com, "The 17 Major U.S. Cities with the Best Public Transportation," April 17, 2018*

Women/Minorities Rankings

- Pittsburgh was selected as one of the gayest cities in America by *The Advocate*. The city ranked #8 out of 25. Criteria, among many: Trans Pride parades/festivals; gay rugby teams; lesbian bars; LGBT centers; theater screenings of "Moonlight"; LGBT-inclusive nondiscrimination ordinances; and gay bowling teams. *The Advocate, "Queerest Cities in America 2017" January 12, 2017*

- Personal finance website *WalletHub* compared more than 180 U.S. cities across two key dimensions, "Hispanic Business-Friendliness" and "Hispanic Purchasing Power," to arrive at the most favorable conditions for Hispanic entrepreneurs. Pittsburgh was ranked #97 out of 182. Criteria includes: share of Hispanic-Owned Businesses; Hispanic entrepreneurship rate to median annual income of Hispanics; Small Business-Friendliness score; cost of living; and number of Hispanics with at least a bachelor's degree. *WalletHub.com, "2019's Best Cities for Hispanic Entrepreneurs," May 1, 2019*

Miscellaneous Rankings

- The watchdog site, Charity Navigator, conducted a study of charities in major markets both to analyze statistical differences in their financial, accountability, and transparency practices and to track year-to-year variations in individual philanthropic communities. The Pittsburgh metro area was ranked #27 among the 30 metro markets in the rating category of Overall Score. *www.charitynavigator.org, "2017 Metro Market Study," May 1, 2017*

- *WalletHub* compared the 150 most populated U.S. cities to determine their operating efficiency. A "Quality of City Services" score was constructed for each city and then divided by the total budget per capita to reveal which were managed the best. Pittsburgh ranked #115. Criteria: financial stability; economy; education; safety; health; infrastructure and pollution. *www.WalletHub.com, "2020's Best- & Worst-Run Cities in America," June 29, 2020*

- Pittsburgh was selected as one of "America's Friendliest Cities." The city ranked #12 in the "Friendliest" category. Respondents to an online survey were asked to rate 38 top urban destinations in the United States as to general friendliness, as well as manners, politeness and warm disposition. *Travel + Leisure, "America's Friendliest Cities," October 20, 2017*

Business Environment

DEMOGRAPHICS

Population Growth

Area	1990 Census	2000 Census	2010 Census	2019* Estimate	Population Growth (%) 1990-2019	Population Growth (%) 2010-2019
City	369,785	334,563	305,704	302,205	-18.3	-1.1
MSA[1]	2,468,289	2,431,087	2,356,285	2,331,447	-5.5	-1.1
U.S.	248,709,873	281,421,906	308,745,538	324,697,795	30.6	5.2

Note: (1) Figures cover the Pittsburgh, PA Metropolitan Statistical Area; (*) 2015-2019 5-year estimated population
Source: U.S. Census Bureau, 1990 Census, Census 2000, Census 2010, 2015-2019 American Community Survey 5-Year Estimates

Household Size

Area	One	Two	Three	Four	Five	Six	Seven or More	Average Household Size
City	43.6	32.4	12.9	6.8	2.5	1.1	0.6	2.00
MSA[1]	33.2	35.5	14.3	10.9	4.1	1.3	0.6	2.30
U.S.	27.9	33.9	15.6	12.9	6.0	2.3	1.4	2.60

Note: (1) Figures cover the Pittsburgh, PA Metropolitan Statistical Area
Source: U.S. Census Bureau, 2015-2019 American Community Survey 5-Year Estimates

Race

Area	White Alone[2] (%)	Black Alone[2] (%)	Asian Alone[2] (%)	AIAN[3] Alone[2] (%)	NHOPI[4] Alone[2] (%)	Other Race Alone[2] (%)	Two or More Races (%)
City	66.8	23.0	5.8	0.2	0.0	0.6	3.5
MSA[1]	86.6	8.1	2.3	0.1	0.0	0.4	2.5
U.S.	72.5	12.7	5.5	0.8	0.2	4.9	3.3

Note: (1) Figures cover the Pittsburgh, PA Metropolitan Statistical Area; (2) Alone is defined as not being in combination with one or more other races; (3) American Indian and Alaska Native; (4) Native Hawaiian and Other Pacific Islander
Source: U.S. Census Bureau, 2015-2019 American Community Survey 5-Year Estimates

Hispanic or Latino Origin

Area	Total (%)	Mexican (%)	Puerto Rican (%)	Cuban (%)	Other (%)
City	3.2	1.0	0.7	0.2	1.3
MSA[1]	1.8	0.5	0.5	0.1	0.7
U.S.	18.0	11.2	1.7	0.7	4.3

Note: Persons of Hispanic or Latino origin can be of any race; (1) Figures cover the Pittsburgh, PA Metropolitan Statistical Area
Source: U.S. Census Bureau, 2015-2019 American Community Survey 5-Year Estimates

Ancestry

Area	German	Irish	English	American	Italian	Polish	French[2]	Scottish	Dutch
City	18.7	14.6	5.1	3.6	12.3	6.9	1.6	1.4	0.6
MSA[1]	26.1	17.3	8.0	3.7	15.6	8.4	1.8	1.9	1.1
U.S.	13.3	9.7	7.2	6.2	5.1	2.8	2.3	1.7	1.2

Note: Figures are the percentage of the total population reporting a particular ancestry. The nine most commonly reported ancestries in the U.S. are shown. Figures include multiple ancestries (e.g. if a person reported being Irish and Italian, they were included in both columns); (1) Figures cover the Pittsburgh, PA Metropolitan Statistical Area; (2) Excludes Basque
Source: U.S. Census Bureau, 2015-2019 American Community Survey 5-Year Estimates

Foreign-born Population

Area	Any Foreign Country	Asia	Mexico	Europe	Caribbean	Central America[2]	South America	Africa	Canada
City	9.0	4.8	0.3	1.9	0.3	0.1	0.5	0.8	0.2
MSA[1]	3.9	2.0	0.1	1.0	0.1	0.1	0.2	0.3	0.1
U.S.	13.6	4.2	3.5	1.5	1.3	1.1	1.0	0.7	0.2

Note: (1) Figures cover the Pittsburgh, PA Metropolitan Statistical Area; (2) Excludes Mexico.
Source: U.S. Census Bureau, 2015-2019 American Community Survey 5-Year Estimates

Marital Status

Area	Never Married	Now Married[2]	Separated	Widowed	Divorced
City	52.4	30.7	1.9	5.8	9.3
MSA[1]	31.7	49.4	1.7	7.3	9.9
U.S.	33.4	48.1	1.9	5.8	10.9

Note: Figures are percentages and cover the population 15 years of age and older; (1) Figures cover the Pittsburgh, PA Metropolitan Statistical Area; (2) Excludes separated
Source: U.S. Census Bureau, 2015-2019 American Community Survey 5-Year Estimates

Disability by Age

Area	All Ages	Under 18 Years Old	18 to 64 Years Old	65 Years and Over
City	13.9	6.9	10.7	36.8
MSA[1]	14.5	5.4	11.4	33.8
U.S.	12.6	4.2	10.3	34.5

Note: Figures show percent of the civilian noninstitutionalized population that reported having a disability. Disability status is determined from six types of difficulty: vision, hearing, cognitive, ambulatory, self-care, and independent living. For children under 5 years old, hearing and vision difficulty are used to determine disability status. For children between the ages of 5 and 14, disability status is determined from hearing, vision, cognitive, ambulatory, and self-care difficulties. For people aged 15 years and older, they are considered to have a disability if they have difficulty with any one of the six difficulty types; Note: (1) Figures cover the Pittsburgh, PA Metropolitan Statistical Area
Source: U.S. Census Bureau, 2015-2019 American Community Survey 5-Year Estimates

Age

Area	Percent of Population									Median Age
	Under Age 5	Age 5–19	Age 20–34	Age 35–44	Age 45–54	Age 55–64	Age 65–74	Age 75–84	Age 85+	
City	4.7	15.4	33.3	10.6	9.5	11.8	8.1	4.3	2.3	32.9
MSA[1]	5.1	16.5	19.2	11.5	13.1	15.2	10.8	5.8	3.0	43.1
U.S.	6.1	19.1	20.7	12.6	13.0	12.9	9.1	4.6	1.9	38.1

Note: (1) Figures cover the Pittsburgh, PA Metropolitan Statistical Area
Source: U.S. Census Bureau, 2015-2019 American Community Survey 5-Year Estimates

Gender

Area	Males	Females	Males per 100 Females
City	147,776	154,429	95.7
MSA[1]	1,135,076	1,196,371	94.9
U.S.	159,886,919	164,810,876	97.0

Note: (1) Figures cover the Pittsburgh, PA Metropolitan Statistical Area
Source: U.S. Census Bureau, 2015-2019 American Community Survey 5-Year Estimates

Religious Groups by Family

Area	Catholic	Baptist	Non-Den.	Methodist[2]	Lutheran	LDS[3]	Pentecostal	Presbyterian[4]	Muslim[5]	Judaism
MSA[1]	32.8	2.3	2.8	5.7	3.4	0.4	1.1	4.7	0.3	0.7
U.S.	19.1	9.3	4.0	4.0	2.3	2.0	1.9	1.6	0.8	0.7

Note: Figures are the number of adherents as a percentage of the total population; (1) Figures cover the Pittsburgh, PA Metropolitan Statistical Area; (2) Methodist/Pietist; (3) Latter Day Saints; (4) Reformed; (5) Figures are estimates
Source: Association of Statisticians of American Religious Bodies, 2010 U.S. Religion Census: Religious Congregations & Membership Study

Religious Groups by Tradition

Area	Catholic	Evangelical Protestant	Mainline Protestant	Other Tradition	Black Protestant	Orthodox
MSA[1]	32.8	7.4	13.8	2.1	0.9	0.7
U.S.	19.1	16.2	7.3	4.3	1.6	0.3

Note: Figures are the number of adherents as a percentage of the total population; (1) Figures cover the Pittsburgh, PA Metropolitan Statistical Area
Source: Association of Statisticians of American Religious Bodies, 2010 U.S. Religion Census: Religious Congregations & Membership Study

ECONOMY

Gross Metropolitan Product

Area	2017	2018	2019	2020	Rank[2]
MSA[1]	147.4	156.4	162.8	168.5	26

Note: Figures are in billions of dollars; (1) Figures cover the Pittsburgh, PA Metropolitan Statistical Area; (2) Rank is based on 2018 data and ranges from 1 to 381
Source: U.S. Conference of Mayors, U.S. Metro Economies: GMP & Employment 2018-2020, September 2019

Economic Growth

Area	2015-17 (%)	2018 (%)	2019 (%)	2020 (%)	Rank[2]
MSA[1]	2.0	2.6	2.5	1.3	137
U.S.	1.9	2.9	2.3	2.1	—

Note: Figures are real gross metropolitan product (GMP) growth rates and represent average annual percent change; (1) Figures cover the Pittsburgh, PA Metropolitan Statistical Area; (2) Rank is based on 2017 2-year average annual percent change and ranges from 1 to 381
Source: U.S. Conference of Mayors, U.S. Metro Economies: GMP & Employment 2018-2020, September 2019

Metropolitan Area Exports

Area	2014	2015	2016	2017	2018	2019	Rank[2]
MSA[1]	10,015.8	9,137.1	7,971.0	9,322.7	9,824.2	9,672.9	38

Note: Figures are in millions of dollars; (1) Figures cover the Pittsburgh, PA Metropolitan Statistical Area; (2) Rank is based on 2019 data and ranges from 1 to 386
Source: U.S. Department of Commerce, International Trade Administration, Office of Trade and Economic Analysis, Industry and Analysis, Exports by Metropolitan Area, data extracted March 24, 2021

Building Permits

Area	Single-Family			Multi-Family			Total		
	2018	2019	Pct. Chg.	2018	2019	Pct. Chg.	2018	2019	Pct. Chg.
City	90	78	-13.3	553	582	5.2	643	660	2.6
MSA[1]	2,977	2,830	-4.9	1,060	1,154	8.9	4,037	3,984	-1.3
U.S.	855,300	862,100	0.7	473,500	523,900	10.6	1,328,800	1,386,000	4.3

Note: (1) Figures cover the Pittsburgh, PA Metropolitan Statistical Area; Figures represent new, privately-owned housing units authorized (unadjusted data); All permit data are based on estimates with imputation
Source: U.S. Census Bureau, Manufacturing, Mining, and Construction Statistics, Building Permits, 2018, 2019

Bankruptcy Filings

Area	Business Filings			Nonbusiness Filings		
	2019	2020	% Chg.	2019	2020	% Chg.
Allegheny County	140	116	-17.1	2,280	1,700	-25.4
U.S.	22,780	21,655	-4.9	752,160	522,808	-30.5

Note: Business filings include Chapter 7, Chapter 9, Chapter 11, Chapter 12, Chapter 13, Chapter 15, and Section 304; Nonbusiness filings include Chapter 7, Chapter 11, and Chapter 13
Source: Administrative Office of the U.S. Courts, Business and Nonbusiness Bankruptcy, County Cases Commenced by Chapter of the Bankruptcy Code, During the 12-Month Period Ending December 31, 2019 and Business and Nonbusiness Bankruptcy, County Cases Commenced by Chapter of the Bankruptcy Code, During the 12-Month Period Ending December 31, 2020

Housing Vacancy Rates

Area	Gross Vacancy Rate[2] (%)			Year-Round Vacancy Rate[3] (%)			Rental Vacancy Rate[4] (%)			Homeowner Vacancy Rate[5] (%)		
	2018	2019	2020	2018	2019	2020	2018	2019	2020	2018	2019	2020
MSA[1]	10.2	10.6	11.5	9.9	10.3	11.3	6.3	7.3	9.3	2.2	1.2	1.0
U.S.	12.3	12.0	10.6	9.7	9.5	8.2	6.9	6.7	6.3	1.5	1.4	1.0

Note: (1) Figures cover the Pittsburgh, PA Metropolitan Statistical Area; (2) The percentage of the total housing inventory that is vacant; (3) The percentage of the housing inventory (excluding seasonal units) that is year-round vacant; (4) The percentage of rental inventory that is vacant for rent; (5) The percentage of homeowner inventory that is vacant for sale
Source: U.S. Census Bureau, Housing Vacancies and Homeownership Annual Statistics: 2018, 2019, 2020

INCOME

Income

Area	Per Capita ($)	Median Household ($)	Average Household ($)
City	34,083	48,711	72,981
MSA[1]	36,208	60,535	82,754
U.S.	34,103	62,843	88,607

Note: (1) Figures cover the Pittsburgh, PA Metropolitan Statistical Area
Source: U.S. Census Bureau, 2015-2019 American Community Survey 5-Year Estimates

Household Income Distribution

Area	Percent of Households Earning							
	Under $15,000	$15,000 -$24,999	$25,000 -$34,999	$35,000 -$49,999	$50,000 -$74,999	$75,000 -$99,999	$100,000 -$149,999	$150,000 and up
City	17.5	11.6	10.0	11.8	15.9	11.3	11.2	10.6
MSA[1]	10.6	9.7	9.3	12.3	17.4	12.9	15.5	12.3
U.S.	10.3	8.9	8.9	12.3	17.2	12.7	15.1	14.5

Note: (1) Figures cover the Pittsburgh, PA Metropolitan Statistical Area
Source: U.S. Census Bureau, 2015-2019 American Community Survey 5-Year Estimates

Poverty Rate

Area	All Ages	Under 18 Years Old	18 to 64 Years Old	65 Years and Over
City	20.5	27.2	20.7	12.8
MSA[1]	11.2	14.9	11.0	8.0
U.S.	13.4	18.5	12.6	9.3

Note: Figures are percentage of people whose income during the past 12 months was below the poverty level;
(1) Figures cover the Pittsburgh, PA Metropolitan Statistical Area
Source: U.S. Census Bureau, 2015-2019 American Community Survey 5-Year Estimates

CITY FINANCES

City Government Finances

Component	2017 ($000)	2017 ($ per capita)
Total Revenues	691,465	2,272
Total Expenditures	849,799	2,792
Debt Outstanding	473,216	1,555
Cash and Securities[1]	816,663	2,683

Note: (1) Cash and security holdings of a government at the close of its fiscal year,
including those of its dependent agencies, utilities, and liquor stores.
Source: U.S. Census Bureau, State & Local Government Finances 2017

City Government Revenue by Source

Source	2017 ($000)	2017 ($ per capita)	2017 (%)
General Revenue			
From Federal Government	32,711	107	4.7
From State Government	74,336	244	10.8
From Local Governments	8,710	29	1.3
Taxes			
Property	141,649	465	20.5
Sales and Gross Receipts	141,154	464	20.4
Personal Income	92,272	303	13.3
Corporate Income	0	0	0.0
Motor Vehicle License	0	0	0.0
Other Taxes	42,473	140	6.1
Current Charges	50,797	167	7.3
Liquor Store	0	0	0.0
Utility	0	0	0.0
Employee Retirement	62,879	207	9.1

Source: U.S. Census Bureau, State & Local Government Finances 2017

City Government Expenditures by Function

Function	2017 ($000)	2017 ($ per capita)	2017 (%)
General Direct Expenditures			
Air Transportation	0	0	0.0
Corrections	0	0	0.0
Education	0	0	0.0
Employment Security Administration	0	0	0.0
Financial Administration	18,215	59	2.1
Fire Protection	68,804	226	8.1
General Public Buildings	4,095	13	0.5
Governmental Administration, Other	74,717	245	8.8
Health	19,162	63	2.3
Highways	106,954	351	12.6
Hospitals	0	0	0.0
Housing and Community Development	13,237	43	1.6
Interest on General Debt	24,569	80	2.9
Judicial and Legal	5,347	17	0.6
Libraries	0	0	0.0
Parking	0	0	0.0
Parks and Recreation	10,015	32	1.2
Police Protection	94,372	310	11.1
Public Welfare	0	0	0.0
Sewerage	0	0	0.0
Solid Waste Management	17,247	56	2.0
Veterans' Services	0	0	0.0
Liquor Store	0	0	0.0
Utility	0	0	0.0
Employee Retirement	92,658	304	10.9

Source: U.S. Census Bureau, State & Local Government Finances 2017

EMPLOYMENT

Labor Force and Employment

Area	Civilian Labor Force			Workers Employed		
	Dec. 2019	Dec. 2020	% Chg.	Dec. 2019	Dec. 2020	% Chg.
City	157,702	150,397	-4.6	151,169	140,388	-7.1
MSA[1]	1,217,975	1,157,008	-5.0	1,162,800	1,080,640	-7.1
U.S.	164,007,000	160,017,000	-2.4	158,504,000	149,613,000	-5.6

Note: Data is not seasonally adjusted and covers workers 16 years of age and older; (1) Figures cover the Pittsburgh, PA Metropolitan Statistical Area
Source: Bureau of Labor Statistics, Local Area Unemployment Statistics

Unemployment Rate

Area	2020											
	Jan.	Feb.	Mar.	Apr.	May	Jun.	Jul.	Aug.	Sep.	Oct.	Nov.	Dec.
City	4.7	4.6	5.6	15.2	13.6	13.8	14.6	12.2	8.9	7.7	6.9	6.7
MSA[1]	5.2	5.2	6.1	16.4	13.6	12.9	13.1	10.9	7.9	6.9	6.3	6.6
U.S.	4.0	3.8	4.5	14.4	13.0	11.2	10.5	8.5	7.7	6.6	6.4	6.5

Note: Data is not seasonally adjusted and covers workers 16 years of age and older; (1) Figures cover the Pittsburgh, PA Metropolitan Statistical Area
Source: Bureau of Labor Statistics, Local Area Unemployment Statistics

Average Wages

Occupation	$/Hr.	Occupation	$/Hr.
Accountants and Auditors	35.70	Maintenance and Repair Workers	21.00
Automotive Mechanics	20.60	Marketing Managers	67.30
Bookkeepers	19.40	Network and Computer Systems Admin.	38.20
Carpenters	28.40	Nurses, Licensed Practical	22.00
Cashiers	11.00	Nurses, Registered	33.70
Computer Programmers	41.90	Nursing Assistants	15.30
Computer Systems Analysts	41.20	Office Clerks, General	17.80
Computer User Support Specialists	25.00	Physical Therapists	41.00
Construction Laborers	21.30	Physicians	61.90
Cooks, Restaurant	13.00	Plumbers, Pipefitters and Steamfitters	31.40
Customer Service Representatives	18.00	Police and Sheriff's Patrol Officers	32.40
Dentists	71.80	Postal Service Mail Carriers	25.30
Electricians	31.50	Real Estate Sales Agents	35.60
Engineers, Electrical	47.10	Retail Salespersons	14.10
Fast Food and Counter Workers	10.90	Sales Representatives, Technical/Scientific	41.10
Financial Managers	70.80	Secretaries, Exc. Legal/Medical/Executive	18.30
First-Line Supervisors of Office Workers	29.30	Security Guards	14.50
General and Operations Managers	62.40	Surgeons	n/a
Hairdressers/Cosmetologists	13.20	Teacher Assistants, Exc. Postsecondary*	14.10
Home Health and Personal Care Aides	12.80	Teachers, Secondary School, Exc. Sp. Ed.*	34.50
Janitors and Cleaners	14.90	Telemarketers	12.80
Landscaping/Groundskeeping Workers	15.20	Truck Drivers, Heavy/Tractor-Trailer	26.00
Lawyers	60.20	Truck Drivers, Light/Delivery Services	17.60
Maids and Housekeeping Cleaners	12.70	Waiters and Waitresses	13.60

Note: Wage data covers the Pittsburgh, PA Metropolitan Statistical Area; (*) Hourly wages were calculated from annual wage data based on a 40 hour work week; n/a not available.
Source: Bureau of Labor Statistics, Metro Area Occupational Employment & Wage Estimates, May 2020

Employment by Industry

Sector	MSA[1]		U.S.
	Number of Employees	Percent of Total	Percent of Total
Construction	56,400	5.1	5.1
Education and Health Services	251,000	22.9	16.3
Financial Activities	75,200	6.9	6.1
Government	112,000	10.2	15.2
Information	17,800	1.6	1.9
Leisure and Hospitality	82,700	7.5	9.0
Manufacturing	79,500	7.2	8.5
Mining and Logging	7,600	0.7	0.4
Other Services	41,600	3.8	3.8
Professional and Business Services	171,100	15.6	14.4
Retail Trade	116,400	10.6	10.9
Transportation, Warehousing, and Utilities	48,700	4.4	4.6
Wholesale Trade	37,600	3.4	3.9

Note: Figures are non-farm employment as of December 2020. Figures are not seasonally adjusted and include workers 16 years of age and older; (1) Figures cover the Pittsburgh, PA Metropolitan Statistical Area
Source: Bureau of Labor Statistics, Current Employment Statistics, Employment, Hours, and Earnings

Employment by Occupation

Occupation Classification	City (%)	MSA[1] (%)	U.S. (%)
Management, Business, Science, and Arts	50.1	41.7	38.5
Natural Resources, Construction, and Maintenance	4.4	7.8	8.9
Production, Transportation, and Material Moving	7.9	12.0	13.2
Sales and Office	18.6	21.8	21.6
Service	19.0	16.7	17.8

Note: Figures cover employed civilians 16 years of age and older; (1) Figures cover the Pittsburgh, PA Metropolitan Statistical Area
Source: U.S. Census Bureau, 2015-2019 American Community Survey 5-Year Estimates

Occupations with Greatest Projected Employment Growth: 2020 – 2022

Occupation[1]	2020 Employment	2022 Projected Employment	Numeric Employment Change	Percent Employment Change
Fast Food and Counter Workers	99,390	133,800	34,410	34.6
Retail Salespersons	114,460	140,170	25,710	22.5
Waiters and Waitresses	50,420	71,990	21,570	42.8
Home Health and Personal Care Aides	167,300	188,640	21,340	12.8
Laborers and Freight, Stock, and Material Movers, Hand	136,300	150,840	14,540	10.7
Cooks, Restaurant	30,330	44,850	14,520	47.9
Janitors and Cleaners, Except Maids and Housekeeping Cleaners	84,010	95,320	11,310	13.5
Office Clerks, General	142,930	154,180	11,250	7.9
Cashiers	119,300	129,290	9,990	8.4
First-Line Supervisors of Food Preparation and Serving Workers	24,060	32,140	8,080	33.6

Note: Projections cover Pennsylvania; (1) Sorted by numeric employment change
Source: www.projectionscentral.com, State Occupational Projections, 2020–2022 Short-Term Projections

Fastest-Growing Occupations: 2020 – 2022

Occupation[1]	2020 Employment	2022 Projected Employment	Numeric Employment Change	Percent Employment Change
Motion Picture Projectionists	160	310	150	93.8
Gaming Dealers	1,960	3,610	1,650	84.2
Gaming Change Persons and Booth Cashiers	210	380	170	81.0
Amusement and Recreation Attendants	5,330	9,600	4,270	80.1
Ushers, Lobby Attendants, and Ticket Takers	2,460	4,340	1,880	76.4
Athletes and Sports Competitors	580	1,010	430	74.1
Hotel, Motel, and Resort Desk Clerks	4,010	6,860	2,850	71.1
Funeral Attendants	1,150	1,820	670	58.3
Pressers, Textile, Garment, and Related Materials	780	1,190	410	52.6
Locker Room, Coatroom, and Dressing Room Attendants	570	860	290	50.9

Note: Projections cover Pennsylvania; (1) Sorted by percent employment change and excludes occupations with numeric employment change less than 50
Source: www.projectionscentral.com, State Occupational Projections, 2020–2022 Short-Term Projections

TAXES

State Corporate Income Tax Rates

State	Tax Rate (%)	Income Brackets ($)	Num. of Brackets	Financial Institution Tax Rate (%)[a]	Federal Income Tax Ded.
Pennsylvania	9.99	Flat rate	1	(a)	No

Note: Tax rates as of January 1, 2021; (a) Rates listed are the corporate income tax rate applied to financial institutions or excise taxes based on income. Some states have other taxes based upon the value of deposits or shares.
Source: Federation of Tax Administrators, State Corporate Income Tax Rates, January 1, 2021

State Individual Income Tax Rates

State	Tax Rate (%)	Income Brackets ($)	Personal Exemptions ($)			Standard Ded. ($)	
			Single	Married	Depend.	Single	Married
Pennsylvania	3.07	Flat rate	None	None	None	–	–

Note: Tax rates as of January 1, 2021; Local- and county-level taxes are not included; Federal income tax is not deductible on state income tax returns
Source: Federation of Tax Administrators, State Individual Income Tax Rates, January 1, 2021

Various State Sales and Excise Tax Rates

State	State Sales Tax (%)	Gasoline[1] (¢/gal.)	Cigarette[2] ($/pack)	Spirits[3] ($/gal.)	Wine[4] ($/gal.)	Beer[5] ($/gal.)	Recreational Marijuana (%)
Pennsylvania	6	58.7	2.6	7.41	0.00	0.08	Not legal

Note: All tax rates as of January 1, 2021; (1) The American Petroleum Institute has developed a methodology for determining the average tax rate on a gallon of fuel. Rates may include any of the following: excise taxes, environmental fees, storage tank fees, other fees or taxes, general sales tax, and local taxes; (2) The federal excise tax of $1.0066 per pack and local taxes are not included; (3) Rates are those applicable to off-premise sales of 40% alcohol by volume (a.b.v.) distilled spirits in 750ml containers. Local excise taxes are excluded; (4) Rates are those applicable to off-premise sales of 11% a.b.v. non-carbonated wine in 750ml containers; (5) Rates are those applicable to off-premise sales of 4.7% a.b.v. beer in 12 ounce containers.
Source: Tax Foundation, 2021 Facts & Figures: How Does Your State Compare?

State Business Tax Climate Index Rankings

State	Overall Rank	Corporate Tax Rank	Individual Income Tax Rank	Sales Tax Rank	Property Tax Rank	Unemployment Insurance Tax Rank
Pennsylvania	27	43	19	17	15	40

Note: The index is a measure of how each state's tax laws affect economic performance. The lower the rank, the more favorable a state's tax system is for business. States without a given tax are given a ranking of 1. The scores/rankings for the District of Columbia do not affect other states. The 2021 index represents the tax climate as of July 1, 2020.
Source: Tax Foundation, State Business Tax Climate Index 2021

TRANSPORTATION

Means of Transportation to Work

Area	Car/Truck/Van		Public Transportation			Bicycle	Walked	Other Means	Worked at Home
	Drove Alone	Car-pooled	Bus	Subway	Railroad				
City	55.3	8.1	16.9	0.4	0.0	1.8	10.7	1.2	5.6
MSA[1]	76.6	8.3	5.1	0.2	0.0	0.3	3.4	1.1	5.0
U.S.	76.3	9.0	2.4	1.9	0.6	0.5	2.7	1.4	5.2

Note: Figures are percentages and cover workers 16 years of age and older; (1) Figures cover the Pittsburgh, PA Metropolitan Statistical Area
Source: U.S. Census Bureau, 2015-2019 American Community Survey 5-Year Estimates

Travel Time to Work

Area	Less Than 10 Minutes	10 to 19 Minutes	20 to 29 Minutes	30 to 44 Minutes	45 to 59 Minutes	60 to 89 Minutes	90 Minutes or More
City	9.4	31.5	25.8	22.9	5.1	3.7	1.6
MSA[1]	11.8	26.6	21.0	22.8	9.5	6.2	2.1
U.S.	12.2	28.4	20.8	20.8	8.3	6.4	2.9

Note: Note: Figures are percentages and include workers 16 years old and over; (1) Figures cover the Pittsburgh, PA Metropolitan Statistical Area
Source: U.S. Census Bureau, 2015-2019 American Community Survey 5-Year Estimates

Key Congestion Measures

Measure	1982	1992	2002	2012	2017
Annual Hours of Delay, Total (000)	9,396	25,547	37,147	45,502	51,370
Annual Hours of Delay, Per Auto Commuter	11	28	34	41	46
Annual Congestion Cost, Total (million $)	72	272	505	828	962
Annual Congestion Cost, Per Auto Commuter ($)	373	697	790	758	830

Note: Covers the Pittsburgh PA urban area
Source: Texas A&M Transportation Institute, 2019 Urban Mobility Report

Freeway Travel Time Index

Measure	1982	1987	1992	1997	2002	2007	2012	2017
Urban Area Index[1]	1.05	1.09	1.14	1.15	1.17	1.18	1.18	1.19
Urban Area Rank[1,2]	51	40	34	41	41	44	40	41

Note: Freeway Travel Time Index—the ratio of travel time in the peak period to the travel time at free-flow conditions. For example, a value of 1.30 indicates a 20-minute free-flow trip takes 26 minutes in the peak (20 minutes x 1.30 = 26 minutes); (1) Covers the Pittsburgh PA urban area; (2) Rank is based on 101 larger urban areas (#1 = highest travel time index)
Source: Texas A&M Transportation Institute, 2019 Urban Mobility Report

Public Transportation

Agency Name / Mode of Transportation	Vehicles Operated in Maximum Service[1]	Annual Unlinked Passenger Trips[2] (in thous.)	Annual Passenger Miles[3] (in thous.)
Port Authority of Allegheny County			
Bus (directly operated)	603	55,016.6	231,734.1
Demand Response (purchased transportation)	279	1,397.5	11,406.1
Inclined Plane (directly operated)	2	431.0	50.4
Light Rail (directly operated)	58	7,162.8	28,888.0

Note: (1) Number of revenue vehicles operated by the given mode and type of service to meet the annual maximum service requirement. This is the revenue vehicle count during the peak season of the year; on the week and day that maximum service is provided. Vehicles operated in maximum service (VOMS) exclude atypical days and one-time special events; (2) Number of passengers who boarded public transportation vehicles. Passengers are counted each time they board a vehicle no matter how many vehicles they use to travel from their origin to their destination. (3) Sum of the distances ridden by all passengers during the entire fiscal year.
Source: Federal Transit Administration, National Transit Database, 2019

Air Transportation

Airport Name and Code / Type of Service	Passenger Airlines[1]	Passenger Enplanements	Freight Carriers[2]	Freight (lbs)
Pittsburgh International Airport (PIT)				
Domestic service (U.S. carriers - 2020)	30	1,734,901	13	79,312,843
International service (U.S. carriers - 2019)	8	28,152	3	292,591

Note: (1) Includes all U.S.-based major, minor and commuter airlines that carried at least one passenger during the year; (2) Includes all U.S.-based airlines and freight carriers that transported at least one pound of freight during the year.
Source: Bureau of Transportation Statistics, The Intermodal Transportation Database, Air Carriers: T-100 Domestic Market (U.S. Carriers), 2020; Bureau of Transportation Statistics, The Intermodal Transportation Database, Air Carriers: T-100 International Market (U.S. Carriers), 2019

BUSINESSES

Major Business Headquarters

Company Name	Industry	Rankings	
		Fortune[1]	Forbes[2]
Armada	Business Services & Supplies	-	116
Giant Eagle	Food Markets	-	41
Howmet Aerospace	Aerospace & Defense	226	-
Kraft Heinz	Food Consumer Products	122	-
PNC Financial Services Group	Superregional Banks	151	-
PPG Industries	Chemicals	209	-
United States Steel	Metals	247	-
WESCO International	Wholesalers, Diversified	379	-
Westinghouse Air Brake	Industrial Machinery	388	-

Note: (1) Companies that produce a 10-K are ranked 1 to 500 based on 2019 revenue; (2) All private companies with at least $2 billion in annual revenue through the end of their most current fiscal year are ranked 1 to 219; companies listed are headquartered in the city; dashes indicate no ranking
Source: Fortune, "Fortune 500," June/July 2020; Forbes, "America's Largest Private Companies," 2020

Living Environment

COST OF LIVING

Cost of Living Index

Composite Index	Groceries	Housing	Utilities	Trans-portation	Health Care	Misc. Goods/Services
104.1	109.0	103.5	116.5	117.5	95.8	97.1

Note: The Cost of Living Index measures regional differences in the cost of consumer goods and services, excluding taxes and non-consumer expenditures, for professional and managerial households in the top income quintile. It is based on more than 50,000 prices covering almost 60 different items for which prices are collected three times a year by chambers of commerce, economic development organizations or university applied economic centers in each participating urban area. The numbers shown should be read as a percentage above or below the national average of 100. For example, a value of 115.4 in the groceries column indicates that grocery prices are 15.4% higher than the national average. Small differences in the index numbers should not be interpreted as significant; Figures cover the Pittsburgh PA urban area.
Source: The Council for Community and Economic Research, Cost of Living Index, 2020

Grocery Prices

Area[1]	T-Bone Steak ($/pound)	Frying Chicken ($/pound)	Whole Milk ($/half gal.)	Eggs ($/dozen)	Orange Juice ($/64 oz.)	Coffee ($/11.5 oz.)
City[2]	13.64	1.61	2.03	1.35	3.36	4.62
Avg.	11.78	1.39	2.05	1.47	3.57	4.34
Min.	8.03	0.94	1.03	0.74	2.94	3.02
Max.	15.86	2.65	4.31	3.77	5.44	8.69

*Note: (1) Values for the local area are compared with the average, minimum and maximum values for all 284 areas in the Cost of Living Index; (2) Figures cover the Pittsburgh PA urban area; **T-Bone Steak** (price per pound); **Frying Chicken** (price per pound, whole fryer); **Whole Milk** (half gallon carton); **Eggs** (price per dozen, Grade A, large); **Orange Juice** (64 oz. Tropicana or Florida Natural); **Coffee** (11.5 oz. can, vacuum-packed, Maxwell House, Hills Bros, or Folgers).*
Source: The Council for Community and Economic Research, Cost of Living Index, 2020

Housing and Utility Costs

Area[1]	New Home Price ($)	Apartment Rent ($/month)	All Electric ($/month)	Part Electric ($/month)	Other Energy ($/month)	Telephone ($/month)
City[2]	378,703	1,232	-	108.94	101.72	190.60
Avg.	368,594	1,168	170.86	100.47	65.28	184.30
Min.	190,567	502	91.58	31.42	26.08	169.60
Max.	2,227,806	4,738	470.38	280.31	280.06	206.50

*Note: (1) Values for the local area are compared with the average, minimum and maximum values for all 284 areas in the Cost of Living Index; (2) Figures cover the Pittsburgh PA urban area; **New Home Price** (2,400 sf living area, 8,000 sf lot, in urban area with full utilities); **Apartment Rent** (950 sf 2 bedroom/1.5 or 2 bath, unfurnished, excluding all utilities except water); **All Electric** (average monthly cost for an all-electric home); **Part Electric** (average monthly cost for a part-electric home); **Other Energy** (average monthly cost for natural gas, fuel oil, coal, wood, and any other forms of energy except electricity); **Telephone** (price includes the base monthly rate plus taxes and fees for three lines of mobile phone service).*
Source: The Council for Community and Economic Research, Cost of Living Index, 2020

Health Care, Transportation, and Other Costs

Area[1]	Doctor ($/visit)	Dentist ($/visit)	Optometrist ($/visit)	Gasoline ($/gallon)	Beauty Salon ($/visit)	Men's Shirt ($)
City[2]	93.55	102.37	90.39	2.55	34.18	22.73
Avg.	115.44	99.32	108.10	2.21	39.27	31.37
Min.	36.68	59.00	51.36	1.71	19.00	11.00
Max.	219.00	153.10	250.97	3.46	82.05	58.33

*Note: (1) Values for the local area are compared with the average, minimum and maximum values for all 284 areas in the Cost of Living Index; (2) Figures cover the Pittsburgh PA urban area; **Doctor** (general practitioners routine exam of an established patient); **Dentist** (adult teeth cleaning and periodic oral examination); **Optometrist** (full vision eye exam for established adult patient); **Gasoline** (one gallon regular unleaded, national brand, including all taxes, cash price at self-service pump if available); **Beauty Salon** (woman's shampoo, trim, and blow-dry); **Men's Shirt** (cotton/polyester dress shirt, pinpoint weave, long sleeves).*
Source: The Council for Community and Economic Research, Cost of Living Index, 2020

HOUSING

Homeownership Rate

Area	2012 (%)	2013 (%)	2014 (%)	2015 (%)	2016 (%)	2017 (%)	2018 (%)	2019 (%)	2020 (%)
MSA[1]	67.9	68.3	69.1	71.0	72.2	72.7	71.7	71.5	69.8
U.S.	65.4	65.1	64.5	63.7	63.4	63.9	64.4	64.6	66.6

Note: (1) Figures cover the Pittsburgh, PA Metropolitan Statistical Area
Source: U.S. Census Bureau, Housing Vacancies and Homeownership Annual Statistics: 2012-2020

House Price Index (HPI)

Area	National Ranking[2]	Quarterly Change (%)	One-Year Change (%)	Five-Year Change (%)	Since 1991Q1 (%)
MSA[1]	123	1.67	6.33	26.47	167.39
U.S.[3]	–	3.81	10.77	38.99	205.12

Note: The HPI is a weighted repeat sales index. It measures average price changes in repeat sales or refinancings on the same properties. This information is obtained by reviewing repeat mortgage transactions on single-family properties whose mortgages have been purchased or securitized by Fannie Mae or Freddie Mac since January 1975; (1) Figures cover the Pittsburgh, PA Metropolitan Statistical Area; (2) Rankings are based on annual percentage change for all metro areas containing at least 15,000 transactions over the last 10 years and ranges from 1 to 253; (3) figures based on a weighted average of Census Division estimates using a seasonally adjusted, purchase-only index; all figures are for the period ending December 31, 2020
Source: Federal Housing Finance Agency, Change in Metropolitan Area House Price Indexes, April 7, 2021

Median Single-Family Home Prices

Area	2018	2019	2020[p]	Percent Change 2019 to 2020
MSA[1]	n/a	n/a	n/a	n/a
U.S. Average	261.6	274.6	299.9	9.2

Note: Figures are median sales prices of existing single-family homes in thousands of dollars; (p) preliminary; n/a not available; (1) Figures cover the Pittsburgh, PA Metropolitan Statistical Area
Source: National Association of Realtors, Median Sales Price of Existing Single-Family Homes for Metropolitan Areas, 4th Quarter 2020

Qualifying Income Based on Median Sales Price of Existing Single-Family Homes

Area	With 5% Down ($)	With 10% Down ($)	With 20% Down ($)
MSA[1]	n/a	n/a	n/a
U.S. Average	59,266	56,147	49,908

Note: Figures are preliminary; Qualifying income is based on a mortgage rate of 2.81%. Monthly principal and interest payment is limited to 25% of income; n/a not available; (1) Figures cover the Pittsburgh, PA Metropolitan Statistical Area
Source: National Association of Realtors, Qualifying Income Based on Median Sales Price of Existing Single-Family Homes for Metropolitan Areas, 4th Quarter 2020

Home Value Distribution

Area	Under $50,000	$50,000 -$99,999	$100,000 -$149,999	$150,000 -$199,999	$200,000 -$299,999	$300,000 -$499,999	$500,000 -$999,999	$1,000,000 or more
City	11.8	27.6	18.0	12.8	12.4	10.6	5.7	1.0
MSA[1]	8.8	20.3	19.2	17.8	17.5	12.0	3.6	0.7
U.S.	6.9	12.0	13.3	14.0	19.6	19.3	11.4	3.4

Note: Figures are percentages and cover owner-occupied housing units; (1) Figures cover the Pittsburgh, PA Metropolitan Statistical Area
Source: U.S. Census Bureau, 2015-2019 American Community Survey 5-Year Estimates

Year Housing Structure Built

Area	2010 or Later	2000 -2009	1990 -1999	1980 -1989	1970 -1979	1960 -1969	1950 -1959	1940 -1949	Before 1940	Median Year
City	2.3	3.0	3.5	4.4	6.7	8.7	12.6	8.9	49.8	1940
MSA[1]	2.8	6.5	7.7	7.5	11.9	11.5	16.7	8.9	26.4	1959
U.S.	5.2	14.0	13.9	13.4	15.2	10.6	10.3	4.9	12.6	1978

Note: Figures are percentages except for Median Year; Note: (1) Figures cover the Pittsburgh, PA Metropolitan Statistical Area
Source: U.S. Census Bureau, 2015-2019 American Community Survey 5-Year Estimates

Gross Monthly Rent

Area	Under $500	$500 -$999	$1,000 -$1,499	$1,500 -$1,999	$2,000 -$2,499	$2,500 -$2,999	$3,000 and up	Median ($)
City	13.6	40.7	28.8	11.2	4.0	1.0	0.7	958
MSA[1]	15.6	51.9	23.2	6.0	1.9	0.6	0.8	831
U.S.	9.4	36.2	30.0	14.0	5.6	2.4	2.4	1,062

Note: Figures are percentages except for Median; Gross rent is the contract rent plus the estimated average monthly cost of utilities (electricity, gas, and water and sewer) and fuels (oil, coal, kerosene, wood, etc.) if these are paid by the renter (or paid for the renter by someone else); (1) Figures cover the Pittsburgh, PA Metropolitan Statistical Area
Source: U.S. Census Bureau, 2015-2019 American Community Survey 5-Year Estimates

HEALTH

Health Risk Factors

Category	MSA[1] (%)	U.S. (%)
Adults aged 18–64 who have any kind of health care coverage	93.3	87.3
Adults who reported being in good or better health	83.6	82.4
Adults who have been told they have high blood cholesterol	35.1	33.0
Adults who have been told they have high blood pressure	34.9	32.3
Adults who are current smokers	21.3	17.1
Adults who currently use E-cigarettes	4.7	4.6
Adults who currently use chewing tobacco, snuff, or snus	5.7	4.0
Adults who are heavy drinkers[2]	7.4	6.3
Adults who are binge drinkers[3]	19.4	17.4
Adults who are overweight (BMI 25.0 - 29.9)	35.6	35.3
Adults who are obese (BMI 30.0 - 99.8)	31.1	31.3
Adults who participated in any physical activities in the past month	75.0	74.4
Adults who always or nearly always wears a seat belt	90.2	94.3

Note: (1) Figures cover the Pittsburgh, PA Metropolitan Statistical Area; (2) Heavy drinkers are classified as adult men having more than 14 drinks per week and adult women having more than 7 drinks per week; (3) Binge drinkers are classified as males having five or more drinks on one occasion or females having four or more drinks on one occasion
Source: Centers for Disease Control and Prevention, Behaviorial Risk Factor Surveillance System, SMART: Selected Metropolitan Area Risk Trends, 2017

Acute and Chronic Health Conditions

Category	MSA[1] (%)	U.S. (%)
Adults who have ever been told they had a heart attack	4.4	4.2
Adults who have ever been told they have angina or coronary heart disease	5.3	3.9
Adults who have ever been told they had a stroke	3.0	3.0
Adults who have ever been told they have asthma	11.0	14.2
Adults who have ever been told they have arthritis	30.2	24.9
Adults who have ever been told they have diabetes[2]	10.3	10.5
Adults who have ever been told they had skin cancer	6.3	6.2
Adults who have ever been told they had any other types of cancer	7.7	7.1
Adults who have ever been told they have COPD	7.1	6.5
Adults who have ever been told they have kidney disease	1.9	3.0
Adults who have ever been told they have a form of depression	18.9	20.5

Note: (1) Figures cover the Pittsburgh, PA Metropolitan Statistical Area; (2) Figures do not include pregnancy-related, borderline, or pre-diabetes
Source: Centers for Disease Control and Prevention, Behaviorial Risk Factor Surveillance System, SMART: Selected Metropolitan Area Risk Trends, 2017

Health Screening and Vaccination Rates

Category	MSA[1] (%)	U.S. (%)
Adults aged 65+ who have had flu shot within the past year	65.8	60.7
Adults aged 65+ who have ever had a pneumonia vaccination	81.1	75.4
Adults who have ever been tested for HIV	29.9	36.1
Adults who have ever had the shingles or zoster vaccine?	33.3	28.9
Adults who have had their blood cholesterol checked within the last five years	87.7	85.9

Note: n/a not available; (1) Figures cover the Pittsburgh, PA Metropolitan Statistical Area.
Source: Centers for Disease Control and Prevention, Behaviorial Risk Factor Surveillance System, SMART: Selected Metropolitan Area Risk Trends, 2017

Disability Status

Category	MSA[1] (%)	U.S. (%)
Adults who reported being deaf	5.3	6.7
Are you blind or have serious difficulty seeing, even when wearing glasses?	2.7	4.5
Are you limited in any way in any of your usual activities due of arthritis?	14.2	12.9
Do you have difficulty doing errands alone?	6.4	6.8
Do you have difficulty dressing or bathing?	3.5	3.6
Do you have serious difficulty concentrating/remembering/making decisions?	9.9	10.7
Do you have serious difficulty walking or climbing stairs?	11.0	13.6

Note: (1) Figures cover the Pittsburgh, PA Metropolitan Statistical Area.
Source: Centers for Disease Control and Prevention, Behaviorial Risk Factor Surveillance System, SMART: Selected Metropolitan Area Risk Trends, 2017

Mortality Rates for the Top 10 Causes of Death in the U.S.

ICD-10[a] Sub-Chapter	ICD-10[a] Code	Age-Adjusted Mortality Rate[1] per 100,000 population	
		County[2]	U.S.
Malignant neoplasms	C00-C97	159.0	149.2
Ischaemic heart diseases	I20-I25	114.5	90.5
Other forms of heart disease	I30-I51	58.4	52.2
Chronic lower respiratory diseases	J40-J47	37.6	39.6
Other degenerative diseases of the nervous system	G30-G31	26.6	37.6
Cerebrovascular diseases	I60-I69	33.5	37.2
Other external causes of accidental injury	W00-X59	67.9	36.1
Organic, including symptomatic, mental disorders	F01-F09	40.5	29.4
Hypertensive diseases	I10-I15	13.9	24.1
Diabetes mellitus	E10-E14	17.4	21.5

Note: (a) ICD-10 = International Classification of Diseases 10th Revision; (1) Mortality rates are a three-year average covering 2017-2019; (2) Figures cover Allegheny County.
Source: Centers for Disease Control and Prevention, National Center for Health Statistics. Underlying Cause of Death 1999-2019 on CDC WONDER Online Database

Mortality Rates for Selected Causes of Death

ICD-10[a] Sub-Chapter	ICD-10[a] Code	Age-Adjusted Mortality Rate[1] per 100,000 population	
		County[2]	U.S.
Assault	X85-Y09	8.3	6.0
Diseases of the liver	K70-K76	15.5	14.4
Human immunodeficiency virus (HIV) disease	B20-B24	0.7	1.5
Influenza and pneumonia	J09-J18	14.9	13.8
Intentional self-harm	X60-X84	15.2	14.1
Malnutrition	E40-E46	1.7	2.3
Obesity and other hyperalimentation	E65-E68	1.5	2.1
Renal failure	N17-N19	14.7	12.6
Transport accidents	V01-V99	6.5	12.3
Viral hepatitis	B15-B19	0.7	1.2

Note: (a) ICD-10 = International Classification of Diseases 10th Revision; (1) Mortality rates are a three-year average covering 2017-2019; (2) Figures cover Allegheny County; Data are suppressed when the data meet the criteria for confidentiality constraints; Mortality rates are flagged as unreliable when the rate would be calculated with a numerator of 20 or less.
Source: Centers for Disease Control and Prevention, National Center for Health Statistics. Underlying Cause of Death 1999-2019 on CDC WONDER Online Database

Health Insurance Coverage

Area	With Health Insurance	With Private Health Insurance	With Public Health Insurance	Without Health Insurance	Population Under Age 19 Without Health Insurance
City	94.7	73.5	33.4	5.3	3.3
MSA[1]	96.2	77.0	35.8	3.8	1.7
U.S.	91.2	67.9	35.1	8.8	5.1

Note: Figures are percentages that cover the civilian noninstitutionalized population; (1) Figures cover the Pittsburgh, PA Metropolitan Statistical Area
Source: U.S. Census Bureau, 2015-2019 American Community Survey 5-Year Estimates

Number of Medical Professionals

Area	MDs[3]	DOs[3,4]	Dentists	Podiatrists	Chiropractors	Optometrists
County[1] (number)	7,824	534	1,193	133	544	254
County[1] (rate[2])	642.7	43.9	98.1	10.9	44.7	20.9
U.S. (rate[2])	282.9	22.7	71.2	6.2	28.1	16.9

42003
Note: Data as of 2019 unless noted; (1) Data covers Allegheny County; (2) Rate per 100,000 population; (3) Data as of 2018 and includes all active, non-federal physicians; (4) Doctor of Osteopathic Medicine
Source: U.S. Department of Health and Human Services, Health Resources and Services Administration, Bureau of Health Professions, Area Resource File (ARF) 2019-2020

Best Hospitals

According to *U.S. News,* the Pittsburgh, PA metro area is home to two of the best hospitals in the U.S.: **UPMC Magee-Womens Hospital** (1 adult specialty); **UPMC Presbyterian Shadyside** (11 adult specialties). The hospitals listed were nationally ranked in at least one of 16 adult or 10 pediatric specialties. Only 134 hospitals nationwide were nationally ranked in one or more adult or pediatric specialty; this number increases to 178 counting specialized centers within hospitals. Twenty hospitals in the U.S. made the Honor Roll. The Best Hospitals Honor Roll takes both the national rankings and the procedure and condition ratings into account. Hospitals received points if they were nationally ranked in one of the 16 adult specialties—the higher they ranked, the more points they got—and how many ratings of "high performing" they earned in the 10 procedures and conditions. *U.S. News Online, "America's Best Hospitals 2020-21"*

According to *U.S. News,* the Pittsburgh, PA metro area is home to one of the best children's hospitals in the U.S.: **UPMC Children's Hospital of Pittsburgh-Shriners Hospitals for Children Erie** (Honor Roll/10 pediatric specialties). The hospital listed was highly ranked in at least one of 10 pediatric specialties. Eighty-eight children's hospitals in the U.S. were nationally ranked in at least one specialty. Hospitals received points for being ranked in a specialty, and the 10 hospitals with the most points across the 10 specialties make up the Honor Roll. *U.S. News Online, "America's Best Children's Hospitals 2020-21"*

EDUCATION

Public School District Statistics

District Name	Schls	Pupils	Pupil/ Teacher Ratio	Minority Pupils[1] (%)	Free Lunch Eligible[2] (%)	IEP[3] (%)
Baldwin-Whitehall SD	5	4,364	17.9	27.3	35.7	13.5
Chartiers Valley SD	4	3,283	13.9	19.4	26.1	13.8
Fox Chapel Area SD	6	4,016	11.7	18.9	18.9	13.1
Mount Lebanon SD	10	5,521	14.2	14.3	11.6	13.3
North Allegheny SD	11	8,493	14.9	22.2	4.7	13.1
North Hills SD	6	4,481	13.5	14.3	20.0	15.0
Penn Hills SD	3	3,360	15.3	72.3	81.6	26.8
Pittsburgh SD	58	22,934	11.8	68.4	96.4	22.2
Upper Saint Clair SD	6	4,055	15.5	18.0	7.0	13.2

Note: Table includes school districts with 2,000 or more students; (1) Percentage of students that are not non-Hispanic white; (2) Percentage of students that are eligible for the free lunch program; (3) Percentage of students that have an Individualized Education Program.
Source: U.S. Department of Education, National Center for Education Statistics, Common Core of Data, Local Education Agency (School District) Universe Survey: School Year 2018-2019; U.S. Department of Education, National Center for Education Statistics, Common Core of Data, Public Elementary/Secondary School Universe Survey: School Year 2018-2019

Highest Level of Education

Area	Less than H.S.	H.S. Diploma	Some College, No Deg.	Associate Degree	Bachelor's Degree	Master's Degree	Prof. School Degree	Doctorate Degree
City	7.1	25.5	15.1	7.9	23.2	13.1	4.3	3.9
MSA[1]	6.1	32.4	16.4	10.2	21.3	9.8	2.3	1.7
U.S.	12.0	27.0	20.4	8.5	19.8	8.8	2.1	1.4

Note: Figures cover persons age 25 and over; (1) Figures cover the Pittsburgh, PA Metropolitan Statistical Area
Source: U.S. Census Bureau, 2015-2019 American Community Survey 5-Year Estimates

Educational Attainment by Race

Area	High School Graduate or Higher (%)					Bachelor's Degree or Higher (%)				
	Total	White	Black	Asian	Hisp.[2]	Total	White	Black	Asian	Hisp.[2]
City	92.9	94.5	88.6	90.9	87.1	44.6	50.2	18.4	78.3	48.4
MSA[1]	93.9	94.4	89.7	88.2	88.0	34.9	35.3	20.2	70.7	36.8
U.S.	88.0	89.9	86.0	87.1	68.7	32.1	33.5	21.6	54.3	16.4

Note: Figures shown cover persons 25 years old and over; (1) Figures cover the Pittsburgh, PA Metropolitan Statistical Area; (2) People of Hispanic origin can be of any race
Source: U.S. Census Bureau, 2015-2019 American Community Survey 5-Year Estimates

School Enrollment by Grade and Control

Area	Preschool (%)		Kindergarten (%)		Grades 1 - 4 (%)		Grades 5 - 8 (%)		Grades 9 - 12 (%)	
	Public	Private	Public	Private	Public	Private	Public	Private	Public	Private
City	48.0	52.0	77.1	22.9	73.1	26.9	75.8	24.2	81.5	18.5
MSA[1]	49.3	50.7	85.0	15.0	88.0	12.0	88.3	11.7	89.8	10.2
U.S.	59.1	40.9	87.6	12.4	89.5	10.5	89.4	10.6	90.1	9.9

Note: Figures shown cover persons 3 years old and over; (1) Figures cover the Pittsburgh, PA Metropolitan Statistical Area
Source: U.S. Census Bureau, 2015-2019 American Community Survey 5-Year Estimates

Higher Education

Four-Year Colleges			Two-Year Colleges			Medical Schools[1]	Law Schools[2]	Voc/ Tech[3]
Public	Private Non-profit	Private For-profit	Public	Private Non-profit	Private For-profit			
1	9	0	1	7	6	1	2	4

Note: Figures cover institutions located within the city limits and include main campuses only; (1) includes schools accredited by the Liaison Committee on Medical Education and the American Osteopathic Association's Commission on Osteopathic College Accreditation; (2) includes ABA-accredited schools, schools with provisional ABA accreditation, and state accredited schools; (3) includes all schools with programs that are less than 2 years.
Source: National Center for Education Statistics, Integrated Postsecondary Education System (IPEDS), 2019-20; Wikipedia, List of Medical Schools in the United States, accessed April 2, 2021; Wikipedia, List of Law Schools in the United States, accessed April 2, 2021

According to *U.S. News & World Report*, the Pittsburgh, PA metro area is home to five of the top 200 national universities in the U.S.: **Carnegie Mellon University** (#26 tie); **University of Pittsburgh—Pittsburgh Campus** (#58 tie); **Duquesne University** (#143 tie); **Chatham University** (#187 tie); **Robert Morris University** (#196 tie). The indicators used to capture academic quality fall into a number of categories: assessment by administrators at peer institutions; retention of students; faculty resources; student selectivity; financial resources; alumni giving; high school counselor ratings of colleges; and graduation rate. *U.S. News & World Report, "America's Best Colleges 2021"*

According to *U.S. News & World Report*, the Pittsburgh, PA metro area is home to one of the top 100 liberal arts colleges in the U.S.: **Washington and Jefferson College** (#96 tie). The indicators used to capture academic quality fall into a number of categories: assessment by administrators at peer institutions; retention of students; faculty resources; student selectivity; financial resources; alumni giving; high school counselor ratings of colleges; and graduation rate. *U.S. News & World Report, "America's Best Colleges 2021"*

According to *U.S. News & World Report*, the Pittsburgh, PA metro area is home to one of the top 100 law schools in the U.S.: **University of Pittsburgh** (#67 tie). The rankings are based on a weighted average of 12 measures of quality: peer assessment score; assessment score by lawyers/judges; median LSAT scores; median undergrad GPA; acceptance rate; employment rates for graduates; placement success; bar passage rate; faculty resources; expenditures per student; student/faculty ratio; and library resources. *U.S. News & World Report, "America's Best Graduate Schools, Law, 2022"*

According to *U.S. News & World Report*, the Pittsburgh, PA metro area is home to one of the top 75 medical schools for research in the U.S.: **University of Pittsburgh** (#13 tie). The rankings are based on a weighted average of 11 measures of quality: quality assessment; peer assessment score; assessment score by residency directors; research activity; total research activity; average research activity per faculty member; student selectivity; median MCAT total score; median undergraduate GPA; acceptance rate; and faculty resources. *U.S. News & World Report, "America's Best Graduate Schools, Medical, 2022"*

According to *U.S. News & World Report*, the Pittsburgh, PA metro area is home to two of the top 75 business schools in the U.S.: **Carnegie Mellon University (Tepper)** (#16 tie); **University of Pittsburgh (Katz)** (#52). The rankings are based on a weighted average of the following nine measures: quality assessment; peer assessment; recruiter assessment; placement success; mean starting salary and bonus; student selectivity; mean GMAT and GRE scores; mean undergraduate GPA; and acceptance rate. *U.S. News & World Report, "America's Best Graduate Schools, Business, 2022"*

EMPLOYERS

Major Employers

Company Name	Industry
Allegheny General Hospital	Extended care facility
Associated Cleaning Consultants	Janitorial service, contract basis
Bayer Corporation	Pharmaceutical preparations
Children's Hospital of Pittsburgh	Specialty hospitals, except psychiatric
Duquesne University of the Holy Spirit	Colleges & universities
Highmark	Hospital & medical services plans
Jefferson Regional Medical Center	General medical & surgical hospitals
Magee-Womens Hospital of UPMC	Hospital, affiliated with ama residency
Mercy Life Center Corporation	Mental health clinic, outpatient
PNC Bank	National trust companies with deposits, commercial
U.S. Dept of Energy	Noncommercial research organizations
United States Steel Corporation	Blast furnaces & steel mills
United States Steel International	Steel
University of Pittsburgh	Colleges & universities
UPMC Mercy	General medical & surgical hospitals
UPMC Shadyside	General medical & surgical hospitals
Veterans Health Administration	Administration of veterans' affairs
West Penn Allegheny Health System	Management services

Note: Companies shown are located within the Pittsburgh, PA Metropolitan Statistical Area.
Source: Hoovers.com; Wikipedia

Best Companies to Work For

PNC Bank, headquartered in Pittsburgh, is among the "100 Best Companies for Working Mothers." Criteria: paid time off and leaves; workforce profile; benefits; women's issues and advancement; flexible work; company culture and work life programs. *Working Mother, "100 Best Companies for Working Mothers," 2020*

PPG, headquartered in Pittsburgh, is among the "100 Best Places to Work in IT." To qualify, companies had to be U.S.-based organizations or be non-U.S.-based employers that met the following criteria: have a minimum of 300 total employees at a U.S. headquarters and a minimum of 30 IT employees in the U.S., with at least 50% of their IT employees based in the U.S. The best places to work were selected based on compensation, benefits, work/life balance, employee morale, and satisfaction with training and development programs. In addition, *InsiderPro* and *Computerworld* looked at retention efforts, programs for recognizing and rewarding outstanding performances, and benefits such as flextime, elder care and child care, and reimbursement for college tuition and the cost of pursuing technology certifications. *InsiderPro and Computerworld, "100 Best Places to Work in IT," 2020*

PNC Financial Services Group, headquartered in Pittsburgh, is among the "Top Companies for Executive Women." This list is determined by organizations filling out an in-depth survey that measures female demographics at every level, but with an emphasis on women in senior corporate roles, with profit & loss (P&L) responsibility, and those earning in the top 20 percent of the organization. *Working Mother* defines P&L as having responsibility that involves monitoring the net income after expenses for a department or entire organization, with direct influence on how company resources are allocated. *Working Mother, "Top Companies for Executive Women," 2020+*

PUBLIC SAFETY

Crime Rate

Area	All Crimes	Violent Crimes				Property Crimes		
		Murder	Rape[3]	Robbery	Aggrav. Assault	Burglary	Larceny-Theft	Motor Vehicle Theft
City	3,594.8	18.8	40.0	230.0	289.9	443.2	2,331.9	241.0
Suburbs[1]	1,402.7	3.5	23.7	33.2	168.7	159.1	958.5	55.9
Metro[2]	1,687.7	5.5	25.8	58.8	184.5	196.1	1,137.0	80.0
U.S.	2,593.1	5.0	44.0	86.1	248.2	378.0	1,601.6	230.2

Note: Figures are crimes per 100,000 population; (1) All areas within the metro area that are located outside the city limits; (2) Figures cover the Pittsburgh, PA Metropolitan Statistical Area; (3) All figures shown were reported using the revised Uniform Crime Reporting (UCR) definition of rape.
Source: FBI Uniform Crime Reports, 2018 (data for 2019 was not available)

Hate Crimes

Area	Number of Quarters Reported	Number of Incidents per Bias Motivation					
		Race/Ethnicity/ Ancestry	Religion	Sexual Orientation	Disability	Gender	Gender Identity
City	4	5	2	3	0	0	0
U.S.	4	3,963	1,521	1,195	157	69	198

Source: Federal Bureau of Investigation, Hate Crime Statistics 2019

Identity Theft Consumer Reports

Area	Reports	Reports per 100,000 Population	Rank[2]
MSA[1]	4,500	194	220
U.S.	1,387,615	423	-

Note: (1) Figures cover the Pittsburgh, PA Metropolitan Statistical Area; (2) Rank ranges from 1 to 391 where 1 indicates greatest number of identity theft reports per 100,000 population
Source: Federal Trade Commission, Consumer Sentinel Network Data Book 2020

Fraud and Other Consumer Reports

Area	Reports	Reports per 100,000 Population	Rank[2]
MSA[1]	19,291	832	85
U.S.	3,385,133	1,031	-

Note: (1) Figures cover the Pittsburgh, PA Metropolitan Statistical Area; (2) Rank ranges from 1 to 391 where 1 indicates greatest number of fraud and other consumer reports per 100,000 population
Source: Federal Trade Commission, Consumer Sentinel Network Data Book 2020

POLITICS

2020 Presidential Election Results

Area	Biden	Trump	Jorgensen	Hawkins	Other
Allegheny County	59.4	39.0	1.2	0.0	0.4
U.S.	51.3	46.8	1.2	0.3	0.5

Note: Results are percentages and may not add to 100% due to rounding
Source: Dave Leip's Atlas of U.S. Presidential Elections

SPORTS

Professional Sports Teams

Team Name	League	Year Established
Pittsburgh Penguins	National Hockey League (NHL)	1967
Pittsburgh Pirates	Major League Baseball (MLB)	1882
Pittsburgh Steelers	National Football League (NFL)	1933

Note: Includes teams located in the Pittsburgh, PA Metropolitan Statistical Area.
Source: Wikipedia, Major Professional Sports Teams of the United States and Canada, April 6, 2021

CLIMATE

Average and Extreme Temperatures

Temperature	Jan	Feb	Mar	Apr	May	Jun	Jul	Aug	Sep	Oct	Nov	Dec	Yr.
Extreme High (°F)	75	69	83	89	91	98	103	100	97	89	82	74	103
Average High (°F)	35	38	48	61	71	79	83	81	75	63	50	39	60
Average Temp. (°F)	28	30	39	50	60	68	73	71	64	53	42	32	51
Average Low (°F)	20	22	29	39	49	57	62	61	54	43	34	25	41
Extreme Low (°F)	-18	-12	-1	14	26	34	42	39	31	16	-1	-12	-18

Note: Figures cover the years 1948-1990
Source: National Climatic Data Center, International Station Meteorological Climate Summary, 9/96

Average Precipitation/Snowfall/Humidity

Precip./Humidity	Jan	Feb	Mar	Apr	May	Jun	Jul	Aug	Sep	Oct	Nov	Dec	Yr.
Avg. Precip. (in.)	2.8	2.4	3.4	3.3	3.6	3.9	3.8	3.2	2.8	2.4	2.7	2.8	37.1
Avg. Snowfall (in.)	11	9	8	2	Tr	0	0	0	0	Tr	4	8	43
Avg. Rel. Hum. 7am (%)	76	75	75	73	76	79	82	86	85	81	78	77	79
Avg. Rel. Hum. 4pm (%)	64	60	54	49	50	51	53	54	55	53	60	66	56

Note: Figures cover the years 1948-1990; Tr = Trace amounts (<0.05 in. of rain; <0.5 in. of snow)
Source: National Climatic Data Center, International Station Meteorological Climate Summary, 9/96

Weather Conditions

Temperature			Daytime Sky			Precipitation		
5°F & below	32°F & below	90°F & above	Clear	Partly cloudy	Cloudy	0.01 inch or more precip.	0.1 inch or more snow/ice	Thunder-storms
9	121	8	62	137	166	154	42	35

Note: Figures are average number of days per year and cover the years 1948-1990
Source: National Climatic Data Center, International Station Meteorological Climate Summary, 9/96

HAZARDOUS WASTE

Superfund Sites

The Pittsburgh, PA metro area is home to three sites on the EPA's Superfund National Priorities List: **Breslube-Penn, Inc.** (final); **Lindane Dump** (final); **Ohio River Park** (final). There are a total of 1,375 Superfund sites with a status of proposed or final on the list in the U.S. *U.S. Environmental Protection Agency, National Priorities List, April 7, 2021*

AIR QUALITY

Air Quality Trends: Ozone

	1990	1995	2000	2005	2010	2015	2016	2017	2018	2019
MSA[1]	0.080	0.095	0.082	0.082	0.075	0.069	0.068	0.066	0.068	0.062
U.S.	0.088	0.089	0.082	0.080	0.073	0.068	0.069	0.068	0.069	0.065

Note: (1) Data covers the Pittsburgh, PA Metropolitan Statistical Area. The values shown are the composite ozone concentration averages among trend sites based on the highest fourth daily maximum 8-hour concentration in parts per million. These trends are based on sites having an adequate record of monitoring data during the trend period. Data from exceptional events are included.
Source: U.S. Environmental Protection Agency, Air Quality Monitoring Information, "Air Quality Trends by City, 1990-2019"

Air Quality Index

Area	Percent of Days when Air Quality was...[2]					AQI Statistics[2]	
	Good	Moderate	Unhealthy for Sensitive Groups	Unhealthy	Very Unhealthy	Maximum	Median
MSA[1]	35.3	60.3	3.3	1.1	0.0	161	56

Note: (1) Data covers the Pittsburgh, PA Metropolitan Statistical Area; (2) Based on 365 days with AQI data in 2019. Air Quality Index (AQI) is an index for reporting daily air quality. EPA calculates the AQI for five major air pollutants regulated by the Clean Air Act: particle pollution (aka particulate matter), carbon monoxide, sulfur dioxide, and nitrogen dioxide. The AQI runs from 0 to 500. The higher the AQI value, the greater the level of air pollution and the greater the health concern. There are six AQI categories: "Good" AQI is between 0 and 50. Air quality is considered satisfactory; "Moderate" AQI is between 51 and 100. Air quality is acceptable; "Unhealthy for Sensitive Groups" When AQI values are between 101 and 150, members of sensitive groups may experience health effects; "Unhealthy" When AQI values are between 151 and 200 everyone may begin to experience health effects; "Very Unhealthy" AQI values between 201 and 300 trigger a health alert; "Hazardous" AQI values over 300 trigger warnings of emergency conditions (not shown).
Source: U.S. Environmental Protection Agency, Air Quality Index Report, 2019

Air Quality Index Pollutants

Area	Percent of Days when AQI Pollutant was...[2]					
	Carbon Monoxide	Nitrogen Dioxide	Ozone	Sulfur Dioxide	Particulate Matter 2.5	Particulate Matter 10
MSA[1]	0.0	0.0	29.3	6.3	64.4	0.0

Note: (1) Data covers the Pittsburgh, PA Metropolitan Statistical Area; (2) Based on 365 days with AQI data in 2019. The Air Quality Index (AQI) is an index for reporting daily air quality. EPA calculates the AQI for five major air pollutants regulated by the Clean Air Act: ground-level ozone, particle pollution (also known as particulate matter), carbon monoxide, sulfur dioxide, and nitrogen dioxide. The AQI runs from 0 to 500. The higher the AQI value, the greater the level of air pollution and the greater the health concern.
Source: U.S. Environmental Protection Agency, Air Quality Index Report, 2019

Maximum Air Pollutant Concentrations: Particulate Matter, Ozone, CO and Lead

	Particulate Matter 10 (ug/m^3)	Particulate Matter 2.5 Wtd AM (ug/m^3)	Particulate Matter 2.5 24-Hr (ug/m^3)	Ozone (ppm)	Carbon Monoxide (ppm)	Lead (ug/m^3)
MSA[1] Level	86	12.2	39	0.064	3	0
NAAQS[2]	150	15	35	0.075	9	0.15
Met NAAQS[2]	Yes	Yes	No	Yes	Yes	Yes

Note: (1) Data covers the Pittsburgh, PA Metropolitan Statistical Area; Data from exceptional events are included; (2) National Ambient Air Quality Standards; ppm = parts per million; ug/m^3 = micrograms per cubic meter; n/a not available.
Concentrations: Particulate Matter 10 (coarse particulate)—highest second maximum 24-hour concentration; Particulate Matter 2.5 Wtd AM (fine particulate)—highest weighted annual mean concentration; Particulate Matter 2.5 24-Hour (fine particulate)—highest 98th percentile 24-hour concentration; Ozone—highest fourth daily maximum 8-hour concentration; Carbon Monoxide—highest second maximum non-overlapping 8-hour concentration; Lead—maximum running 3-month average
Source: U.S. Environmental Protection Agency, Air Quality Monitoring Information, "Air Quality Statistics by City, 2019"

Maximum Air Pollutant Concentrations: Nitrogen Dioxide and Sulfur Dioxide

	Nitrogen Dioxide AM (ppb)	Nitrogen Dioxide 1-Hr (ppb)	Sulfur Dioxide AM (ppb)	Sulfur Dioxide 1-Hr (ppb)	Sulfur Dioxide 24-Hr (ppb)
MSA[1] Level	10	37	n/a	80	n/a
NAAQS[2]	53	100	30	75	140
Met NAAQS[2]	Yes	Yes	n/a	No	n/a

Note: (1) Data covers the Pittsburgh, PA Metropolitan Statistical Area; Data from exceptional events are included; (2) National Ambient Air Quality Standards; ppm = parts per million; ug/m³ = micrograms per cubic meter; n/a not available.
Concentrations: Nitrogen Dioxide AM—highest arithmetic mean concentration; Nitrogen Dioxide 1-Hr—highest 98th percentile 1-hour daily maximum concentration; Sulfur Dioxide AM—highest annual mean concentration; Sulfur Dioxide 1-Hr—highest 99th percentile 1-hour daily maximum concentration; Sulfur Dioxide 24-Hr—highest second maximum 24-hour concentration
Source: U.S. Environmental Protection Agency, Air Quality Monitoring Information, "Air Quality Statistics by City, 2019"

Providence, Rhode Island

Background

Providence is the capital of Rhode Island. At the head of Narragansett Bay, it's one of the nation's most historic cities as well as one of its most fashionable and inviting, recognized as having great city qualities on a small city scale.

Providence was founded in 1636 by Roger Williams, the Massachusetts preacher exiled by the Puritans for his radical religious ideas. In a reversal of the usual procedure, Williams first obtained title to the land directly from the Narragansett tribe, and subsequently, in 1644, received a Royal Charter from London for the settlement.

Though the economy originally depended on agriculture, trade soon dominated. Whaling, a related maritime activity, was as important in Providence as it was to all of Rhode Island's ports. In the course of this trade, a number of Rhode Islanders naturally amassed considerable wealth and endowed many of Providence's enduring public and cultural institutions, including Brown University, one of the nation's oldest.

After the Revolution, Providence industrialized and became a major center for the textile, silver, and jewelry trades. Innovations born from Providence workshops include plating base metals with gold or silver. By the time of the Civil War, the economy had shifted from mercantile shipping to the fully industrial, making the city a major economic resource to the Union during the Civil War.

By the mid-twentieth century, Providence's population had declined and government mismanagement, along with the national decline of heavy industry, combined to blemish the city. Since the 1980s, however, reforms and improvements have brought to Providence a renaissance of jobs, city services, downtown revitalization, and cultural assets. The city is now regarded, particularly by younger professionals, as one of the most desirable urban locations on the East Coast. Educational and cultural assets include museums, theaters, an award-winning zoo, highly acclaimed restaurants, and renowned venues for arts and entertainment. Providence and the surrounding areas have been a backdrop for several movies and television series and the city remains invested in luring filmmakers by offering a tax credit to motion picture companies.

A living testament to Providence's renaissance is WaterFire, a fire sculpture installation by Barnaby Evans which burns anew each spring on downtown Providence's three rivers. Waterplace Park and Riverwalk was perhaps the most important revitalization project to happen in Providence for many years. Parts of the river that had long been paved over with streets were reopened, and park areas were created along the banks. The picturesque river is now used routinely for boating and sculling and by the Brown University rowing crews.

> A bill introduced by Democrat Thomas Noret would make vaccination status a protected class under the state law that currently defends against discrimination based on race, gender or sexual orientation.

Downtown Providence offers the Providence Place Mall, a state-of-the-art emporium that mirrors the historically mercantile character of the city, the Arcade, built in 1828 and America's first indoor shopping mall, and famous landmark, the 1922 Biltmore Hotel. Another favorite Providence neighborhood is College Hill, which connects the campuses of Brown University and the Rhode Island School of Design with cafes, restaurants, shops, and street vendors.

Getting around Providence is getting easier. In 2020, Providence's public transit system expanded service in the city. Also in 2020, plans were unveiled to develop 60 miles of bike paths, bike lanes, and greenways.

The city is considered one of the most active gay communities in the Northeast. Former mayor David Cicilline ran as openly gay, and former Mayor Cianci instituted the position of Mayor's Liaison to the Gay and Lesbian community in the 1990s.

The energy of Providence is apparent in its choice of sports. The city is home to the American Hockey League's Providence Bruins, and it competed successfully against other cities to host the Gravity Games. Providence is also the birthplace of ESPN's X Games.

Providence enjoys variable southern New England weather with temperatures slightly moderated by the city's proximity to Narragansett Bay and the Atlantic Ocean. The weather is changeable, due to the convergence of weather systems from the west, the Gulf of Mexico, and the North Atlantic. Precipitation is evenly distributed throughout the year. In October 2012, the city was hit by Hurricane Sandy, resulting in storm surges, power outages, and interrupted transportation.

Rankings

General Rankings

- In their seventh annual survey, Livability.com looked at data for more than 1,000 small to mid-sized U.S. cities to determine the rankings for Livability's "Top 100 Best Places to Live" in 2020. Providence ranked #71. Criteria: housing and affordable living; vibrant economy; social and civic engagement; education; demographics; health care options; transportation & infrastructure; and abundant lifestyle amenities. *Livability.com, "Top 100 Best Places to Live 2020" October 2020*

Business/Finance Rankings

- The Brookings Institution ranked the nation's largest cities based on income inequality. Providence was ranked #3 (#1 = greatest inequality). Criteria: the "95/20 ratio," a figure representing the income at which a household earns more than 95 percent of all other households, divided by the income at which a household earns more than only 20 percent of all other households. *Brookings Institution, "Household Income Inequality, Largest Cities of 97 Large U.S. Metro Areas, 2014-2016," February 5, 2018*

- The Brookings Institution ranked the 100 largest metro areas in the U.S. based on income inequality. Providence was ranked #20 (#1 = greatest inequality). Criteria: the "95/20 ratio," a figure representing the income at which a household earns more than 95 percent of all other households, divided by the income at which a household earns more than only 20 percent of all other households. *Brookings Institution, "Household Income Inequality, 100 Largest U.S. Metro Areas, 2014-2016," February 5, 2018*

- Providence was identified as one of America's most frugal metro areas by *Coupons.com*. The city ranked #22 out of 25. Criteria: digital coupon usage. *Coupons.com, "America's Most Frugal Cities of 2017," March 22, 2018*

- The Providence metro area appeared on the Milken Institute "2021 Best Performing Cities" list. Rank: #156 out of 200 large metro areas (population over 250,000). Criteria: job growth; wage and salary growth; high-tech output growth; housing affordability; household broadband access. *Milken Institute, "Best-Performing Cities 2021," February 16, 2021*

- *Forbes* ranked the 200 most populous metro areas to determine the nation's "Best Places for Business and Careers." The Providence metro area was ranked #124. Criteria: costs (business and living); job growth (past and projected); income growth; quality of life; educational attainment (college and high school); projected economic growth; cultural and leisure opportunities; workplace tolerance laws; net migration patterns. *Forbes, "The Best Places for Business and Careers 2019: Seattle Still On Top," October 30, 2019*

Children/Family Rankings

- Providence was selected as one of the most playful cities in the U.S. by KaBOOM! The organization's Playful City USA initiative honors cities and towns across the nation that have made their communities more playable. Criteria: pledging to integrate play as a solution to challenges in their communities; making it easy for children to get active and balanced play; creating more family-friendly and innovative communities as a result. *KaBOOM! National Campaign for Play, "2017 Playful City USA Communities"*

Culture/Performing Arts Rankings

- Providence was selected as one of the ten best small North American cities and towns for moviemakers. Of cities with smaller populations, the area ranked #6. As with the 2021 list for bigger cities, pandemic challenges and COVID-19 guidelines were factored in. Other criteria: film community and culture; access to equipment and facilities; tax incentives; and standard of living. *MovieMaker Magazine, "Best Places to Live and Work as a Moviemaker, 2021," January 26, 2021*

- Providence was selected as one of "America's Favorite Cities." The city ranked #4 in the "Architecture " category. Respondents to an online survey were asked to rate their favorite place (population over 100,000) in over 65 categories. *Travelandleisure.com, "America's Favorite Cities for Architecture 2016," March 2, 2017*

Dating/Romance Rankings

- Providence was ranked #20 out of 25 cities that stood out for inspiring romance and attracting diners on the website OpenTable.com. Criteria: percentage of people who dined out on Valentine's Day in 2018; percentage of romantic restaurants as rated by OpenTable diner reviews; and percentage of tables seated for two. *OpenTable, "25 Most Romantic Cities in America for 2019," February 7, 2019*

Education Rankings

- Personal finance website *WalletHub* analyzed the 150 largest U.S. metropolitan statistical areas to determine where the most educated Americans are putting their degrees to work. Criteria: education levels; percentage of workers with degrees; education quality and attainment gap; public school quality rankings; quality and enrollment of each metro area's universities. Providence was ranked #93 (#1 = most educated city). *www.WalletHub.com, "Most and Least Educated Cities in America," July 20, 2020*

Environmental Rankings

- Sperling's BestPlaces assessed the 50 largest metropolitan areas of the United States for the likelihood of dangerously extreme weather events or earthquakes. In general the Southeast and South-Central regions have the highest risk of weather extremes and earthquakes, while the Pacific Northwest enjoys the lowest risk. Of the least risky metropolitan areas, the Providence metro area was ranked #9. *www.bestplaces.net, "Avoid Natural Disasters: BestPlaces Reveals The Top 10 Safest Places to Live," October 25, 2017*

Health/Fitness Rankings

- Providence was identified as a "2021 Spring Allergy Capital." The area ranked #29 out of 100. Three groups of factors were used to identify the most challenging cities for people with allergies during the spring season: annual spring pollen levels; over the counter medicine use; number of board-certified allergy specialists. *Asthma and Allergy Foundation of America, "Spring Allergy Capitals 2021," February 23, 2021*

- Providence was identified as a "2021 Fall Allergy Capital." The area ranked #36 out of 100. Three groups of factors were used to identify the most challenging cities for people with allergies during the fall season: annual fall pollen levels; over the counter medicine use; number of board-certified allergy specialists. *Asthma and Allergy Foundation of America, "Fall Allergy Capitals 2021," February 23, 2021*

- Providence was identified as a "2019 Asthma Capital." The area ranked #65 out of the nation's 100 largest metropolitan areas. Criteria: estimated asthma prevalence; crude death rate from asthma; and ER visits due to asthma. Risk factors analyzed but not factored in the rankings: annual pollen score; annual air quality; public smoking laws; number of board-certified asthma specialists; rescue medication use; controller medication use; uninsured rate; poverty rate. *Asthma and Allergy Foundation of America, "Asthma Capitals 2019: The Most Challenging Places to Live With Asthma," May 7, 2019*

Real Estate Rankings

- FitSmallBusiness looked at 50 of the largest metropolitan areas in the U.S. to determine which metro was the best to start a real estate business. Data was compiled from such sources as: Zillow, Trulia, U.S. Census Bureau, and the Bureau of Labor Statistics. Criteria: location; inventory; annual wages; median sales price of homes; days on the market; median price cut percentage; and other factors that would influence real estate professional growth. The Providence metro area ranked #11. *fitsmallbusiness.com, "The Best Cities to Become a Real Estate Agent in 2018," January 30, 2018*

- *WalletHub* compared the most populated U.S. cities to determine which had the best markets for real estate agents. Providence ranked #131 where demand was high and pay was the best. Criteria: sales per agent; annual median wage for real-estate agents; monthly average starting salary for real estate agents; real estate job density and competition; unemployment rate; home turnover rate; housing-market health index; and other relevant metrics. *www.WalletHub.com, "2019's Best Places to Be a Real Estate Agent," April 24, 2019*

- Providence was ranked #20 in the top 20 out of the 100 largest metro areas in terms of house price appreciation in 2020 (#1 = highest rate). *Federal Housing Finance Agency, House Price Index, 4th Quarter 2020*

- Providence was ranked #172 out of 268 metro areas in terms of housing affordability in 2020 by the National Association of Home Builders (#1 = most affordable). Criteria: the share of homes sold in that area affordable to a family earning the local median income, based on standard mortgage underwriting criteria. *National Association of Home Builders®, NAHB-Wells Fargo Housing Opportunity Index, 4th Quarter 2020*

Safety Rankings

- Allstate ranked the 200 largest cities in America in terms of driver safety. Providence ranked #193. Criteria: internal property damage claims over a two-year period from January 2016 to December 2017. The report helps increase the importance of safety and awareness behind the wheel. *Allstate, "Allstate America's Best Drivers Report, 2019" June 24, 2019*

- The National Insurance Crime Bureau ranked 384 metro areas in the U.S. in terms of per capita rates of vehicle theft. The Providence metro area ranked #270 (#1 = highest rate). Criteria: number of vehicle theft offenses per 100,000 inhabitants in 2019. *National Insurance Crime Bureau, "Hot Spots 2019," July 21, 2020*

Seniors/Retirement Rankings

- From its Best Cities for Successful Aging indexes, the Milken Institute generated rankings for metropolitan areas, weighing data in nine categories—health care, wellness, living arrangements, transportation and convenience, financial characteristics, education, employment, community engagement, and overall livability. The Providence metro area was ranked #70 overall in the large metro area category. *Milken Institute, "Best Cities for Successful Aging, 2017" March 14, 2017*

Women/Minorities Rankings

- Personal finance website *WalletHub* compared more than 180 U.S. cities across two key dimensions, "Hispanic Business-Friendliness" and "Hispanic Purchasing Power," to arrive at the most favorable conditions for Hispanic entrepreneurs. Providence was ranked #182 out of 182. Criteria includes: share of Hispanic-Owned Businesses; Hispanic entrepreneurship rate to median annual income of Hispanics; Small Business-Friendliness score; cost of living; and number of Hispanics with at least a bachelor's degree. *WalletHub.com, "2019's Best Cities for Hispanic Entrepreneurs," May 1, 2019*

Miscellaneous Rankings

- *MoveHub* ranked 446 hipster cities across 20 countries, using its *alternative* Hipster Index and Providence came out as #33 among the top 50. Criteria: population over 150,000; number of vintage boutiques; density of tattoo parlors; vegan places to eat; coffee shops; and density of vinyl record stores. *www.movehub.com, "The Hipster Index: Brighton Pips Portland to Global Top Spot," February 20, 2020*

- *WalletHub* compared the 150 most populated U.S. cities to determine their operating efficiency. A "Quality of City Services" score was constructed for each city and then divided by the total budget per capita to reveal which were managed the best. Providence ranked #93. Criteria: financial stability; economy; education; safety; health; infrastructure and pollution. *www.WalletHub.com, "2020's Best-& Worst-Run Cities in America," June 29, 2020*

Business Environment

DEMOGRAPHICS

Population Growth

Area	1990 Census	2000 Census	2010 Census	2019* Estimate	Population Growth (%)	
					1990-2019	2010-2019
City	160,734	173,618	178,042	179,494	11.7	0.8
MSA[1]	1,509,789	1,582,997	1,600,852	1,618,268	7.2	1.1
U.S.	248,709,873	281,421,906	308,745,538	324,697,795	30.6	5.2

Note: (1) Figures cover the Providence-Warwick, RI-MA Metropolitan Statistical Area; (*) 2015-2019 5-year estimated population
Source: U.S. Census Bureau, 1990 Census, Census 2000, Census 2010, 2015-2019 American Community Survey 5-Year Estimates

Household Size

Area	Persons in Household (%)							Average Household Size
	One	Two	Three	Four	Five	Six	Seven or More	
City	33.3	29.0	15.6	11.8	7.1	1.7	1.5	2.70
MSA[1]	29.9	33.3	16.6	12.8	5.1	1.5	0.8	2.50
U.S.	27.9	33.9	15.6	12.9	6.0	2.3	1.4	2.60

Note: (1) Figures cover the Providence-Warwick, RI-MA Metropolitan Statistical Area
Source: U.S. Census Bureau, 2015-2019 American Community Survey 5-Year Estimates

Race

Area	White Alone[2] (%)	Black Alone[2] (%)	Asian Alone[2] (%)	AIAN[3] Alone[2] (%)	NHOPI[4] Alone[2] (%)	Other Race Alone[2] (%)	Two or More Races (%)
City	55.1	16.8	6.0	1.0	0.1	16.3	4.7
MSA[1]	81.7	5.9	3.0	0.4	0.1	5.7	3.2
U.S.	72.5	12.7	5.5	0.8	0.2	4.9	3.3

Note: (1) Figures cover the Providence-Warwick, RI-MA Metropolitan Statistical Area; (2) Alone is defined as not being in combination with one or more other races; (3) American Indian and Alaska Native; (4) Native Hawaiian and Other Pacific Islander
Source: U.S. Census Bureau, 2015-2019 American Community Survey 5-Year Estimates

Hispanic or Latino Origin

Area	Total (%)	Mexican (%)	Puerto Rican (%)	Cuban (%)	Other (%)
City	43.3	1.8	9.3	0.3	31.9
MSA[1]	12.9	0.9	4.3	0.2	7.4
U.S.	18.0	11.2	1.7	0.7	4.3

Note: Persons of Hispanic or Latino origin can be of any race; (1) Figures cover the Providence-Warwick, RI-MA Metropolitan Statistical Area
Source: U.S. Census Bureau, 2015-2019 American Community Survey 5-Year Estimates

Ancestry

Area	German	Irish	English	American	Italian	Polish	French[2]	Scottish	Dutch
City	3.2	7.6	3.9	2.9	7.2	1.9	2.9	0.8	0.3
MSA[1]	4.5	17.6	10.6	3.4	13.6	3.7	9.4	1.6	0.4
U.S.	13.3	9.7	7.2	6.2	5.1	2.8	2.3	1.7	1.2

Note: Figures are the percentage of the total population reporting a particular ancestry. The nine most commonly reported ancestries in the U.S. are shown. Figures include multiple ancestries (e.g. if a person reported being Irish and Italian, they were included in both columns); (1) Figures cover the Providence-Warwick, RI-MA Metropolitan Statistical Area; (2) Excludes Basque
Source: U.S. Census Bureau, 2015-2019 American Community Survey 5-Year Estimates

Foreign-born Population

Area	Percent of Population Born in								
	Any Foreign Country	Asia	Mexico	Europe	Caribbean	Central America[2]	South America	Africa	Canada
City	28.7	4.2	0.6	2.2	12.3	5.0	1.4	2.7	0.2
MSA[1]	13.3	2.3	0.2	4.2	2.3	1.4	1.0	1.6	0.2
U.S.	13.6	4.2	3.5	1.5	1.3	1.1	1.0	0.7	0.2

Note: (1) Figures cover the Providence-Warwick, RI-MA Metropolitan Statistical Area; (2) Excludes Mexico.
Source: U.S. Census Bureau, 2015-2019 American Community Survey 5-Year Estimates

Marital Status

Area	Never Married	Now Married[2]	Separated	Widowed	Divorced
City	54.4	30.6	2.3	4.2	8.5
MSA[1]	36.0	45.2	1.6	6.1	11.0
U.S.	33.4	48.1	1.9	5.8	10.9

Note: Figures are percentages and cover the population 15 years of age and older; (1) Figures cover the Providence-Warwick, RI-MA Metropolitan Statistical Area; (2) Excludes separated
Source: U.S. Census Bureau, 2015-2019 American Community Survey 5-Year Estimates

Disability by Age

Area	All Ages	Under 18 Years Old	18 to 64 Years Old	65 Years and Over
City	13.3	5.5	12.2	38.5
MSA[1]	13.6	5.2	11.2	33.3
U.S.	12.6	4.2	10.3	34.5

Note: Figures show percent of the civilian noninstitutionalized population that reported having a disability. Disability status is determined from six types of difficulty: vision, hearing, cognitive, ambulatory, self-care, and independent living. For children under 5 years old, hearing and vision difficulty are used to determine disability status. For children between the ages of 5 and 14, disability status is determined from hearing, vision, cognitive, ambulatory, and self-care difficulties. For people aged 15 years and older, they are considered to have a disability if they have difficulty with any one of the six difficulty types; Note: (1) Figures cover the Providence-Warwick, RI-MA Metropolitan Statistical Area
Source: U.S. Census Bureau, 2015-2019 American Community Survey 5-Year Estimates

Age

Area	Percent of Population									Median Age
	Under Age 5	Age 5–19	Age 20–34	Age 35–44	Age 45–54	Age 55–64	Age 65–74	Age 75–84	Age 85+	
City	6.3	21.9	28.3	12.3	10.9	9.4	5.9	3.2	1.7	30.6
MSA[1]	5.2	17.9	20.5	11.9	13.9	13.9	9.5	4.8	2.5	40.3
U.S.	6.1	19.1	20.7	12.6	13.0	12.9	9.1	4.6	1.9	38.1

Note: (1) Figures cover the Providence-Warwick, RI-MA Metropolitan Statistical Area
Source: U.S. Census Bureau, 2015-2019 American Community Survey 5-Year Estimates

Gender

Area	Males	Females	Males per 100 Females
City	86,874	92,620	93.8
MSA[1]	785,383	832,885	94.3
U.S.	159,886,919	164,810,876	97.0

Note: (1) Figures cover the Providence-Warwick, RI-MA Metropolitan Statistical Area
Source: U.S. Census Bureau, 2015-2019 American Community Survey 5-Year Estimates

Religious Groups by Family

Area	Catholic	Baptist	Non-Den.	Methodist[2]	Lutheran	LDS[3]	Pentecostal	Presbyterian[4]	Muslim[5]	Judaism
MSA[1]	47.0	1.4	1.2	0.8	0.5	0.3	0.6	1.0	0.1	0.7
U.S.	19.1	9.3	4.0	4.0	2.3	2.0	1.9	1.6	0.8	0.7

Note: Figures are the number of adherents as a percentage of the total population; (1) Figures cover the Providence-Warwick, RI-MA Metropolitan Statistical Area; (2) Methodist/Pietist; (3) Latter Day Saints; (4) Reformed; (5) Figures are estimates
Source: Association of Statisticians of American Religious Bodies, 2010 U.S. Religion Census: Religious Congregations & Membership Study

Religious Groups by Tradition

Area	Catholic	Evangelical Protestant	Mainline Protestant	Other Tradition	Black Protestant	Orthodox
MSA[1]	47.0	2.8	4.7	1.6	0.1	0.6
U.S.	19.1	16.2	7.3	4.3	1.6	0.3

Note: Figures are the number of adherents as a percentage of the total population; (1) Figures cover the Providence-Warwick, RI-MA Metropolitan Statistical Area
Source: Association of Statisticians of American Religious Bodies, 2010 U.S. Religion Census: Religious Congregations & Membership Study

ECONOMY

Gross Metropolitan Product

Area	2017	2018	2019	2020	Rank[2]
MSA[1]	84.0	86.8	89.5	93.0	44

Note: Figures are in billions of dollars; (1) Figures cover the Providence-Warwick, RI-MA Metropolitan Statistical Area; (2) Rank is based on 2018 data and ranges from 1 to 381
Source: U.S. Conference of Mayors, U.S. Metro Economies: GMP & Employment 2018-2020, September 2019

Economic Growth

Area	2015-17 (%)	2018 (%)	2019 (%)	2020 (%)	Rank[2]
MSA[1]	0.7	1.0	1.3	1.7	262
U.S.	1.9	2.9	2.3	2.1	–

Note: Figures are real gross metropolitan product (GMP) growth rates and represent average annual percent change; (1) Figures cover the Providence-Warwick, RI-MA Metropolitan Statistical Area; (2) Rank is based on 2017 2-year average annual percent change and ranges from 1 to 381
Source: U.S. Conference of Mayors, U.S. Metro Economies: GMP & Employment 2018-2020, September 2019

Metropolitan Area Exports

Area	2014	2015	2016	2017	2018	2019	Rank[2]
MSA[1]	6,595.1	5,048.8	6,595.7	7,125.4	6,236.6	7,424.8	46

Note: Figures are in millions of dollars; (1) Figures cover the Providence-Warwick, RI-MA Metropolitan Statistical Area; (2) Rank is based on 2019 data and ranges from 1 to 386
Source: U.S. Department of Commerce, International Trade Administration, Office of Trade and Economic Analysis, Industry and Analysis, Exports by Metropolitan Area, data extracted March 24, 2021

Building Permits

Area	Single-Family			Multi-Family			Total		
	2018	2019	Pct. Chg.	2018	2019	Pct. Chg.	2018	2019	Pct. Chg.
City	1	14	1,300.0	0	183	–	1	197	19,600.0
MSA[1]	1,553	1,592	2.5	410	456	11.2	1,963	2,048	4.3
U.S.	855,300	862,100	0.7	473,500	523,900	10.6	1,328,800	1,386,000	4.3

Note: (1) Figures cover the Providence-Warwick, RI-MA Metropolitan Statistical Area; Figures represent new, privately-owned housing units authorized (unadjusted data); All permit data are based on estimates with imputation
Source: U.S. Census Bureau, Manufacturing, Mining, and Construction Statistics, Building Permits, 2018, 2019

Bankruptcy Filings

Area	Business Filings			Nonbusiness Filings		
	2019	2020	% Chg.	2019	2020	% Chg.
Providence County	38	29	-23.7	1,246	887	-28.8
U.S.	22,780	21,655	-4.9	752,160	522,808	-30.5

Note: Business filings include Chapter 7, Chapter 9, Chapter 11, Chapter 12, Chapter 13, Chapter 15, and Section 304; Nonbusiness filings include Chapter 7, Chapter 11, and Chapter 13
Source: Administrative Office of the U.S. Courts, Business and Nonbusiness Bankruptcy, County Cases Commenced by Chapter of the Bankruptcy Code, During the 12-Month Period Ending December 31, 2019 and Business and Nonbusiness Bankruptcy, County Cases Commenced by Chapter of the Bankruptcy Code, During the 12-Month Period Ending December 31, 2020

Housing Vacancy Rates

Area	Gross Vacancy Rate[2] (%)			Year-Round Vacancy Rate[3] (%)			Rental Vacancy Rate[4] (%)			Homeowner Vacancy Rate[5] (%)		
	2018	2019	2020	2018	2019	2020	2018	2019	2020	2018	2019	2020
MSA[1]	10.3	9.8	8.7	8.5	8.2	6.6	5.0	4.2	3.5	1.1	0.9	0.8
U.S.	12.3	12.0	10.6	9.7	9.5	8.2	6.9	6.7	6.3	1.5	1.4	1.0

Note: (1) Figures cover the Providence-Warwick, RI-MA Metropolitan Statistical Area; (2) The percentage of the total housing inventory that is vacant; (3) The percentage of the housing inventory (excluding seasonal units) that is year-round vacant; (4) The percentage of rental inventory that is vacant for rent; (5) The percentage of homeowner inventory that is vacant for sale
Source: U.S. Census Bureau, Housing Vacancies and Homeownership Annual Statistics: 2018, 2019, 2020

INCOME

Income

Area	Per Capita ($)	Median Household ($)	Average Household ($)
City	26,560	45,610	71,136
MSA[1]	35,991	67,818	89,281
U.S.	34,103	62,843	88,607

Note: (1) Figures cover the Providence-Warwick, RI-MA Metropolitan Statistical Area
Source: U.S. Census Bureau, 2015-2019 American Community Survey 5-Year Estimates

Household Income Distribution

Area	Percent of Households Earning							
	Under $15,000	$15,000 -$24,999	$25,000 -$34,999	$35,000 -$49,999	$50,000 -$74,999	$75,000 -$99,999	$100,000 -$149,999	$150,000 and up
City	20.2	12.0	9.0	11.4	16.7	11.1	10.0	9.7
MSA[1]	11.0	8.8	7.9	10.8	15.9	13.2	17.0	15.4
U.S.	10.3	8.9	8.9	12.3	17.2	12.7	15.1	14.5

Note: (1) Figures cover the Providence-Warwick, RI-MA Metropolitan Statistical Area
Source: U.S. Census Bureau, 2015-2019 American Community Survey 5-Year Estimates

Poverty Rate

Area	All Ages	Under 18 Years Old	18 to 64 Years Old	65 Years and Over
City	25.5	34.7	23.0	20.6
MSA[1]	12.0	16.9	11.1	9.6
U.S.	13.4	18.5	12.6	9.3

Note: Figures are percentage of people whose income during the past 12 months was below the poverty level;
(1) Figures cover the Providence-Warwick, RI-MA Metropolitan Statistical Area
Source: U.S. Census Bureau, 2015-2019 American Community Survey 5-Year Estimates

CITY FINANCES

City Government Finances

Component	2017 ($000)	2017 ($ per capita)
Total Revenues	1,001,556	5,589
Total Expenditures	996,207	5,559
Debt Outstanding	711,118	3,968
Cash and Securities[1]	454,202	2,535

Note: (1) Cash and security holdings of a government at the close of its fiscal year,
including those of its dependent agencies, utilities, and liquor stores.
Source: U.S. Census Bureau, State & Local Government Finances 2017

City Government Revenue by Source

Source	2017 ($000)	2017 ($ per capita)	2017 (%)
General Revenue			
From Federal Government	11,055	62	1.1
From State Government	375,423	2,095	37.5
From Local Governments	15,035	84	1.5
Taxes			
Property	356,050	1,987	35.5
Sales and Gross Receipts	7,497	42	0.7
Personal Income	0	0	0.0
Corporate Income	0	0	0.0
Motor Vehicle License	0	0	0.0
Other Taxes	8,316	46	0.8
Current Charges	96,349	538	9.6
Liquor Store	0	0	0.0
Utility	73,404	410	7.3
Employee Retirement	30,185	168	3.0

Source: U.S. Census Bureau, State & Local Government Finances 2017

City Government Expenditures by Function

Function	2017 ($000)	2017 ($ per capita)	2017 (%)
General Direct Expenditures			
Air Transportation	0	0	0.0
Corrections	0	0	0.0
Education	438,314	2,445	44.0
Employment Security Administration	0	0	0.0
Financial Administration	7,231	40	0.7
Fire Protection	72,596	405	7.3
General Public Buildings	13,066	72	1.3
Governmental Administration, Other	11,965	66	1.2
Health	0	0	0.0
Highways	9,286	51	0.9
Hospitals	0	0	0.0
Housing and Community Development	15,590	87	1.6
Interest on General Debt	33,451	186	3.4
Judicial and Legal	18,386	102	1.8
Libraries	3,770	21	0.4
Parking	0	0	0.0
Parks and Recreation	10,822	60	1.1
Police Protection	94,872	529	9.5
Public Welfare	0	0	0.0
Sewerage	960	5	0.1
Solid Waste Management	10,681	59	1.1
Veterans' Services	0	0	0.0
Liquor Store	0	0	0.0
Utility	87,170	486	8.8
Employee Retirement	118,427	660	11.9

Source: U.S. Census Bureau, State & Local Government Finances 2017

EMPLOYMENT

Labor Force and Employment

Area	Civilian Labor Force			Workers Employed		
	Dec. 2019	Dec. 2020	% Chg.	Dec. 2019	Dec. 2020	% Chg.
City	86,891	84,686	-2.5	83,544	77,341	-7.4
NECTA[1]	695,900	674,373	-3.1	673,941	622,895	-7.6
U.S.	164,007,000	160,017,000	-2.4	158,504,000	149,613,000	-5.6

Note: Data is not seasonally adjusted and covers workers 16 years of age and older; (1) Figures cover the Providence-Warwick, RI-MA New England City and Town Area
Source: Bureau of Labor Statistics, Local Area Unemployment Statistics

Unemployment Rate

Area	2020											
	Jan.	Feb.	Mar.	Apr.	May	Jun.	Jul.	Aug.	Sep.	Oct.	Nov.	Dec.
City	4.7	4.7	5.9	19.5	18.7	15.2	14.9	16.7	13.3	8.5	8.5	8.7
NECTA[1]	4.1	4.1	4.7	18.2	16.7	13.7	12.7	12.7	10.1	6.5	6.8	7.6
U.S.	4.0	3.8	4.5	14.4	13.0	11.2	10.5	8.5	7.7	6.6	6.4	6.5

Note: Data is not seasonally adjusted and covers workers 16 years of age and older; (1) Figures cover the Providence-Warwick, RI-MA New England City and Town Area
Source: Bureau of Labor Statistics, Local Area Unemployment Statistics

Average Wages

Occupation	$/Hr.	Occupation	$/Hr.
Accountants and Auditors	41.50	Maintenance and Repair Workers	24.00
Automotive Mechanics	21.90	Marketing Managers	78.20
Bookkeepers	22.70	Network and Computer Systems Admin.	44.50
Carpenters	25.80	Nurses, Licensed Practical	28.40
Cashiers	13.20	Nurses, Registered	39.80
Computer Programmers	51.80	Nursing Assistants	16.40
Computer Systems Analysts	47.50	Office Clerks, General	19.50
Computer User Support Specialists	30.00	Physical Therapists	41.70
Construction Laborers	26.80	Physicians	101.60
Cooks, Restaurant	15.10	Plumbers, Pipefitters and Steamfitters	29.90
Customer Service Representatives	19.40	Police and Sheriff's Patrol Officers	31.90
Dentists	120.20	Postal Service Mail Carriers	25.40
Electricians	28.90	Real Estate Sales Agents	34.40
Engineers, Electrical	52.30	Retail Salespersons	16.60
Fast Food and Counter Workers	13.20	Sales Representatives, Technical/Scientific	43.30
Financial Managers	78.90	Secretaries, Exc. Legal/Medical/Executive	22.00
First-Line Supervisors of Office Workers	33.60	Security Guards	15.80
General and Operations Managers	71.70	Surgeons	136.00
Hairdressers/Cosmetologists	16.30	Teacher Assistants, Exc. Postsecondary*	17.30
Home Health and Personal Care Aides	15.40	Teachers, Secondary School, Exc. Sp. Ed.*	37.00
Janitors and Cleaners	15.80	Telemarketers	16.70
Landscaping/Groundskeeping Workers	17.80	Truck Drivers, Heavy/Tractor-Trailer	24.10
Lawyers	61.80	Truck Drivers, Light/Delivery Services	20.20
Maids and Housekeeping Cleaners	15.60	Waiters and Waitresses	14.10

Note: Wage data covers the Providence-Warwick, RI-MA New England City and Town Area; (*) Hourly wages were calculated from annual wage data based on a 40 hour work week; n/a not available.
Source: Bureau of Labor Statistics, Metro Area Occupational Employment & Wage Estimates, May 2020

Employment by Industry

Sector	NECTA[1]		U.S.
	Number of Employees	Percent of Total	Percent of Total
Construction	25,000	4.5	5.1
Education and Health Services	118,200	21.5	16.3
Financial Activities	36,400	6.6	6.1
Government	73,100	13.3	15.2
Information	5,900	1.1	1.9
Leisure and Hospitality	47,400	8.6	9.0
Manufacturing	48,300	8.8	8.5
Mining and Logging	200	<0.1	0.4
Other Services	22,500	4.1	3.8
Professional and Business Services	72,100	13.1	14.4
Retail Trade	63,800	11.6	10.9
Transportation, Warehousing, and Utilities	19,000	3.5	4.6
Wholesale Trade	18,100	3.3	3.9

Note: Figures are non-farm employment as of December 2020. Figures are not seasonally adjusted and include workers 16 years of age and older; (1) Figures cover the Providence-Warwick, RI-MA New England City and Town Area
Source: Bureau of Labor Statistics, Current Employment Statistics, Employment, Hours, and Earnings

Employment by Occupation

Occupation Classification	City (%)	MSA[1] (%)	U.S. (%)
Management, Business, Science, and Arts	36.2	39.1	38.5
Natural Resources, Construction, and Maintenance	4.8	8.1	8.9
Production, Transportation, and Material Moving	16.1	12.4	13.2
Sales and Office	19.4	21.8	21.6
Service	23.5	18.7	17.8

Note: Figures cover employed civilians 16 years of age and older; (1) Figures cover the Providence-Warwick, RI-MA Metropolitan Statistical Area
Source: U.S. Census Bureau, 2015-2019 American Community Survey 5-Year Estimates

Occupations with Greatest Projected Employment Growth: 2020 – 2022

Occupation[1]	2020 Employment	2022 Projected Employment	Numeric Employment Change	Percent Employment Change
Financial Managers	2,540	2,570	30	1.2
Home Health and Personal Care Aides	7,630	7,660	30	0.4
Market Research Analysts and Marketing Specialists	2,570	2,590	20	0.8
Social and Human Service Assistants	2,580	2,600	20	0.8
Paralegals and Legal Assistants	1,230	1,250	20	1.6
Health Specialties Teachers, Postsecondary	370	390	20	5.4
Secondary School Teachers, Except Special and Career/Technical Education	4,810	4,830	20	0.4
Teaching Assistants, Except Postsecondary	4,110	4,130	20	0.5
Veterinary Technologists and Technicians	640	660	20	3.1
Education Administrators, Elementary and Secondary School	1,040	1,050	10	1.0

Note: Projections cover Rhode Island; (1) Sorted by numeric employment change
Source: www.projectionscentral.com, State Occupational Projections, 2020–2022 Short-Term Projections

Fastest-Growing Occupations: 2020 – 2022

Projections not available at time of publication.

TAXES

State Corporate Income Tax Rates

State	Tax Rate (%)	Income Brackets ($)	Num. of Brackets	Financial Institution Tax Rate (%)[a]	Federal Income Tax Ded.
Rhode Island	7.0 (b)	Flat rate	1	9.0 (b)	No

Note: Tax rates as of January 1, 2021; (a) Rates listed are the corporate income tax rate applied to financial institutions or excise taxes based on income. Some states have other taxes based upon the value of deposits or shares; (b) Minimum tax is $800 in California, $250 in District of Columbia, $50 in Arizona and North Dakota (banks), $400 ($100 banks) in Rhode Island, $200 per location in South Dakota (banks), $100 in Utah, $300 in Vermont.
Source: Federation of Tax Administrators, State Corporate Income Tax Rates, January 1, 2021

State Individual Income Tax Rates

State	Tax Rate (%)	Income Brackets ($)	Personal Exemptions ($)			Standard Ded. ($)	
			Single	Married	Depend.	Single	Married
Rhode Island (a)	3.75 - 5.99	66,200 - 150,550	4,250	8,500	4,250	9,050	18,100 (y)

Note: Tax rates as of January 1, 2021; Local- and county-level taxes are not included; Federal income tax is not deductible on state income tax returns; (a) 19 states have statutory provision for automatically adjusting to the rate of inflation the dollar values of the income tax brackets, standard deductions, and/or personal exemptions. Michigan indexes the personal exemption only. Oregon does not index the income brackets for $125,000 and over; (y) Alabama standard deduction is phased out for incomes over $23,000. Rhode Island exemptions & standard deductions phased out for incomes over $207,700; Wisconsin standard deduciton phases out for income over $16,149.
Source: Federation of Tax Administrators, State Individual Income Tax Rates, January 1, 2021

Various State Sales and Excise Tax Rates

State	State Sales Tax (%)	Gasoline[1] (¢/gal.)	Cigarette[2] ($/pack)	Spirits[3] ($/gal.)	Wine[4] ($/gal.)	Beer[5] ($/gal.)	Recreational Marijuana (%)
Rhode Island	7	35	4.25	5.4	1.4	0.12	Not legal

Note: All tax rates as of January 1, 2021; (1) The American Petroleum Institute has developed a methodology for determining the average tax rate on a gallon of fuel. Rates may include any of the following: excise taxes, environmental fees, storage tank fees, other fees or taxes, general sales tax, and local taxes; (2) The federal excise tax of $1.0066 per pack and local taxes are not included; (3) Rates are those applicable to off-premise sales of 40% alcohol by volume (a.b.v.) distilled spirits in 750ml containers. Local excise taxes are excluded; (4) Rates are those applicable to off-premise sales of 11% a.b.v. non-carbonated wine in 750ml containers; (5) Rates are those applicable to off-premise sales of 4.7% a.b.v. beer in 12 ounce containers.
Source: Tax Foundation, 2021 Facts & Figures: How Does Your State Compare?

State Business Tax Climate Index Rankings

State	Overall Rank	Corporate Tax Rank	Individual Income Tax Rank	Sales Tax Rank	Property Tax Rank	Unemployment Insurance Tax Rank
Rhode Island	37	39	29	25	42	30

Note: The index is a measure of how each state's tax laws affect economic performance. The lower the rank, the more favorable a state's tax system is for business. States without a given tax are given a ranking of 1. The scores/rankings for the District of Columbia do not affect other states. The 2021 index represents the tax climate as of July 1, 2020.
Source: Tax Foundation, State Business Tax Climate Index 2021

TRANSPORTATION

Means of Transportation to Work

Area	Car/Truck/Van		Public Transportation			Bicycle	Walked	Other Means	Worked at Home
	Drove Alone	Car-pooled	Bus	Subway	Railroad				
City	64.5	12.0	5.2	0.1	1.2	0.7	9.5	1.3	5.5
MSA[1]	80.7	8.6	1.5	0.2	1.0	0.2	3.1	0.8	3.9
U.S.	76.3	9.0	2.4	1.9	0.6	0.5	2.7	1.4	5.2

Note: Figures are percentages and cover workers 16 years of age and older; (1) Figures cover the Providence-Warwick, RI-MA Metropolitan Statistical Area
Source: U.S. Census Bureau, 2015-2019 American Community Survey 5-Year Estimates

Travel Time to Work

Area	Less Than 10 Minutes	10 to 19 Minutes	20 to 29 Minutes	30 to 44 Minutes	45 to 59 Minutes	60 to 89 Minutes	90 Minutes or More
City	12.2	39.9	20.8	14.3	5.6	4.1	3.1
MSA[1]	11.9	29.9	21.9	19.6	7.6	5.9	3.2
U.S.	12.2	28.4	20.8	20.8	8.3	6.4	2.9

Note: Note: Figures are percentages and include workers 16 years old and over; (1) Figures cover the Providence-Warwick, RI-MA Metropolitan Statistical Area
Source: U.S. Census Bureau, 2015-2019 American Community Survey 5-Year Estimates

Key Congestion Measures

Measure	1982	1992	2002	2012	2017
Annual Hours of Delay, Total (000)	3,618	11,786	25,786	31,694	36,273
Annual Hours of Delay, Per Auto Commuter	7	21	38	43	48
Annual Congestion Cost, Total (million $)	27	125	350	573	672
Annual Congestion Cost, Per Auto Commuter ($)	185	415	707	681	756

Note: Covers the Providence RI-MA urban area
Source: Texas A&M Transportation Institute, 2019 Urban Mobility Report

Freeway Travel Time Index

Measure	1982	1987	1992	1997	2002	2007	2012	2017
Urban Area Index[1]	1.03	1.05	1.10	1.13	1.18	1.19	1.18	1.17
Urban Area Rank[1,2]	76	79	59	62	37	40	40	49

Note: Freeway Travel Time Index—the ratio of travel time in the peak period to the travel time at free-flow conditions. For example, a value of 1.30 indicates a 20-minute free-flow trip takes 26 minutes in the peak (20 minutes x 1.30 = 26 minutes); (1) Covers the Providence RI-MA urban area; (2) Rank is based on 101 larger urban areas (#1 = highest travel time index)
Source: Texas A&M Transportation Institute, 2019 Urban Mobility Report

Public Transportation

Agency Name / Mode of Transportation	Vehicles Operated in Maximum Service[1]	Annual Unlinked Passenger Trips[2] (in thous.)	Annual Passenger Miles[3] (in thous.)
Rhode Island Public Transit Authority (RIPTA)			
Bus (directly operated)	196	16,029.4	70,301.7
Demand Response (directly operated)	80	332.0	3,375.8
Demand Response Taxi (purchased transportation)	7	52.2	1,425.2
Vanpool (purchased transportation)	8	18.0	885.5

Note: (1) Number of revenue vehicles operated by the given mode and type of service to meet the annual maximum service requirement. This is the revenue vehicle count during the peak season of the year; on the week and day that maximum service is provided. Vehicles operated in maximum service (VOMS) exclude atypical days and one-time special events; (2) Number of passengers who boarded public transportation vehicles. Passengers are counted each time they board a vehicle no matter how many vehicles they use to travel from their origin to their destination. (3) Sum of the distances ridden by all passengers during the entire fiscal year.
Source: Federal Transit Administration, National Transit Database, 2019

Air Transportation

Airport Name and Code / Type of Service	Passenger Airlines[1]	Passenger Enplanements	Freight Carriers[2]	Freight (lbs)
Theodore Francis Green State Airport (PVD)				
Domestic service (U.S. carriers - 2020)	24	642,131	10	14,193,768
International service (U.S. carriers - 2019)	2	225	1	24,762

Note: (1) Includes all U.S.-based major, minor and commuter airlines that carried at least one passenger during the year; (2) Includes all U.S.-based airlines and freight carriers that transported at least one pound of freight during the year.
Source: Bureau of Transportation Statistics, The Intermodal Transportation Database, Air Carriers: T-100 Domestic Market (U.S. Carriers), 2020; Bureau of Transportation Statistics, The Intermodal Transportation Database, Air Carriers: T-100 International Market (U.S. Carriers), 2019

BUSINESSES

Major Business Headquarters

Company Name	Industry	Rankings	
		Fortune[1]	Forbes[2]
Citizens Financial Group	Commercial Banks	395	-
Gilbane	Construction	-	65
Textron	Aerospace and Defense	236	-
United Natural Foods	Wholesalers, Food and Grocery	133	-

Note: (1) Companies that produce a 10-K are ranked 1 to 500 based on 2019 revenue; (2) All private companies with at least $2 billion in annual revenue through the end of their most current fiscal year are ranked 1 to 219; companies listed are headquartered in the city; dashes indicate no ranking
Source: Fortune, "Fortune 500," June/July 2020; Forbes, "America's Largest Private Companies," 2020

Living Environment

COST OF LIVING

Cost of Living Index

Composite Index	Groceries	Housing	Utilities	Trans-portation	Health Care	Misc. Goods/ Services
119.8	110.1	130.4	126.3	105.6	106.5	119.0

Note: The Cost of Living Index measures regional differences in the cost of consumer goods and services, excluding taxes and non-consumer expenditures, for professional and managerial households in the top income quintile. It is based on more than 50,000 prices covering almost 60 different items for which prices are collected three times a year by chambers of commerce, economic development organizations or university applied economic centers in each participating urban area. The numbers shown should be read as a percentage above or below the national average of 100. For example, a value of 115.4 in the groceries column indicates that grocery prices are 15.4% higher than the national average. Small differences in the index numbers should not be interpreted as significant; Figures cover the Providence RI urban area.
Source: The Council for Community and Economic Research, Cost of Living Index, 2020

Grocery Prices

Area[1]	T-Bone Steak ($/pound)	Frying Chicken ($/pound)	Whole Milk ($/half gal.)	Eggs ($/dozen)	Orange Juice ($/64 oz.)	Coffee ($/11.5 oz.)
City[2]	12.73	1.75	2.52	2.17	3.57	4.42
Avg.	11.78	1.39	2.05	1.47	3.57	4.34
Min.	8.03	0.94	1.03	0.74	2.94	3.02
Max.	15.86	2.65	4.31	3.77	5.44	8.69

*Note: (1) Values for the local area are compared with the average, minimum and maximum values for all 284 areas in the Cost of Living Index; (2) Figures cover the Providence RI urban area; **T-Bone Steak** (price per pound); **Frying Chicken** (price per pound, whole fryer); **Whole Milk** (half gallon carton); **Eggs** (price per dozen, Grade A, large); **Orange Juice** (64 oz. Tropicana or Florida Natural); **Coffee** (11.5 oz. can, vacuum-packed, Maxwell House, Hills Bros, or Folgers).*
Source: The Council for Community and Economic Research, Cost of Living Index, 2020

Housing and Utility Costs

Area[1]	New Home Price ($)	Apartment Rent ($/month)	All Electric ($/month)	Part Electric ($/month)	Other Energy ($/month)	Telephone ($/month)
City[2]	430,197	1,800	-	125.74	114.83	189.00
Avg.	368,594	1,168	170.86	100.47	65.28	184.30
Min.	190,567	502	91.58	31.42	26.08	169.60
Max.	2,227,806	4,738	470.38	280.31	280.06	206.50

*Note: (1) Values for the local area are compared with the average, minimum and maximum values for all 284 areas in the Cost of Living Index; (2) Figures cover the Providence RI urban area; **New Home Price** (2,400 sf living area, 8,000 sf lot, in urban area with full utilities); **Apartment Rent** (950 sf 2 bedroom/1.5 or 2 bath, unfurnished, excluding all utilities except water); **All Electric** (average monthly cost for an all-electric home); **Part Electric** (average monthly cost for a part-electric home); **Other Energy** (average monthly cost for natural gas, fuel oil, coal, wood, and any other forms of energy except electricity); **Telephone** (price includes the base monthly rate plus taxes and fees for three lines of mobile phone service).*
Source: The Council for Community and Economic Research, Cost of Living Index, 2020

Health Care, Transportation, and Other Costs

Area[1]	Doctor ($/visit)	Dentist ($/visit)	Optometrist ($/visit)	Gasoline ($/gallon)	Beauty Salon ($/visit)	Men's Shirt ($)
City[2]	157.87	92.75	131.39	2.15	48.53	38.26
Avg.	115.44	99.32	108.10	2.21	39.27	31.37
Min.	36.68	59.00	51.36	1.71	19.00	11.00
Max.	219.00	153.10	250.97	3.46	82.05	58.33

*Note: (1) Values for the local area are compared with the average, minimum and maximum values for all 284 areas in the Cost of Living Index; (2) Figures cover the Providence RI urban area; **Doctor** (general practitioners routine exam of an established patient); **Dentist** (adult teeth cleaning and periodic oral examination); **Optometrist** (full vision eye exam for established adult patient); **Gasoline** (one gallon regular unleaded, national brand, including all taxes, cash price at self-service pump if available); **Beauty Salon** (woman's shampoo, trim, and blow-dry); **Men's Shirt** (cotton/polyester dress shirt, pinpoint weave, long sleeves).*
Source: The Council for Community and Economic Research, Cost of Living Index, 2020

HOUSING

Homeownership Rate

Area	2012 (%)	2013 (%)	2014 (%)	2015 (%)	2016 (%)	2017 (%)	2018 (%)	2019 (%)	2020 (%)
MSA[1]	61.7	60.1	61.6	60.0	57.5	58.6	61.3	63.5	64.8
U.S.	65.4	65.1	64.5	63.7	63.4	63.9	64.4	64.6	66.6

Note: (1) Figures cover the Providence-Warwick, RI-MA Metropolitan Statistical Area
Source: U.S. Census Bureau, Housing Vacancies and Homeownership Annual Statistics: 2012-2020

House Price Index (HPI)

Area	National Ranking[2]	Quarterly Change (%)	One-Year Change (%)	Five-Year Change (%)	Since 1991Q1 (%)
MSA[1]	89	2.66	6.95	31.83	154.93
U.S.[3]	–	3.81	10.77	38.99	205.12

Note: The HPI is a weighted repeat sales index. It measures average price changes in repeat sales or refinancings on the same properties. This information is obtained by reviewing repeat mortgage transactions on single-family properties whose mortgages have been purchased or securitized by Fannie Mae or Freddie Mac since January 1975; (1) Figures cover the Providence-Warwick, RI-MA Metropolitan Statistical Area; (2) Rankings are based on annual percentage change for all metro areas containing at least 15,000 transactions over the last 10 years and ranges from 1 to 253; (3) figures based on a weighted average of Census Division estimates using a seasonally adjusted, purchase-only index; all figures are for the period ending December 31, 2020
Source: Federal Housing Finance Agency, Change in Metropolitan Area House Price Indexes, April 7, 2021

Median Single-Family Home Prices

Area	2018	2019	2020[p]	Percent Change 2019 to 2020
MSA[1]	292.5	311.1	347.3	11.6
U.S. Average	261.6	274.6	299.9	9.2

Note: Figures are median sales prices of existing single-family homes in thousands of dollars; (p) preliminary; (1) Figures cover the Providence-Warwick, RI-MA Metropolitan Statistical Area
Source: National Association of Realtors, Median Sales Price of Existing Single-Family Homes for Metropolitan Areas, 4th Quarter 2020

Qualifying Income Based on Median Sales Price of Existing Single-Family Homes

Area	With 5% Down ($)	With 10% Down ($)	With 20% Down ($)
MSA[1]	68,545	64,937	57,722
U.S. Average	59,266	56,147	49,908

Note: Figures are preliminary; Qualifying income is based on a mortgage rate of 2.81%. Monthly principal and interest payment is limited to 25% of income; (1) Figures cover the Providence-Warwick, RI-MA Metropolitan Statistical Area
Source: National Association of Realtors, Qualifying Income Based on Median Sales Price of Existing Single-Family Homes for Metropolitan Areas, 4th Quarter 2020

Home Value Distribution

Area	Under $50,000	$50,000 -$99,999	$100,000 -$149,999	$150,000 -$199,999	$200,000 -$299,999	$300,000 -$499,999	$500,000 -$999,999	$1,000,000 or more
City	2.1	5.3	16.9	25.7	23.9	15.6	8.6	1.9
MSA[1]	2.1	2.0	5.7	14.1	33.3	31.2	10.0	1.7
U.S.	6.9	12.0	13.3	14.0	19.6	19.3	11.4	3.4

Note: Figures are percentages and cover owner-occupied housing units; (1) Figures cover the Providence-Warwick, RI-MA Metropolitan Statistical Area
Source: U.S. Census Bureau, 2015-2019 American Community Survey 5-Year Estimates

Year Housing Structure Built

Area	2010 or Later	2000 -2009	1990 -1999	1980 -1989	1970 -1979	1960 -1969	1950 -1959	1940 -1949	Before 1940	Median Year
City	0.6	4.5	3.7	5.5	9.2	5.9	7.6	6.8	56.2	<1940
MSA[1]	1.9	6.3	8.1	11.1	12.2	11.0	11.6	6.6	31.4	1960
U.S.	5.2	14.0	13.9	13.4	15.2	10.6	10.3	4.9	12.6	1978

Note: Figures are percentages except for Median Year; Note: (1) Figures cover the Providence-Warwick, RI-MA Metropolitan Statistical Area
Source: U.S. Census Bureau, 2015-2019 American Community Survey 5-Year Estimates

Gross Monthly Rent

Area	Under $500	$500 -$999	$1,000 -$1,499	$1,500 -$1,999	$2,000 -$2,499	$2,500 -$2,999	$3,000 and up	Median ($)
City	19.5	31.1	35.2	9.8	2.6	0.7	1.1	994
MSA[1]	16.0	37.6	31.8	10.3	2.8	0.6	0.7	968
U.S.	9.4	36.2	30.0	14.0	5.6	2.4	2.4	1,062

Note: Figures are percentages except for Median; Gross rent is the contract rent plus the estimated average monthly cost of utilities (electricity, gas, and water and sewer) and fuels (oil, coal, kerosene, wood, etc.) if these are paid by the renter (or paid for the renter by someone else); (1) Figures cover the Providence-Warwick, RI-MA Metropolitan Statistical Area
Source: U.S. Census Bureau, 2015-2019 American Community Survey 5-Year Estimates

HEALTH

Health Risk Factors

Category	MSA[1] (%)	U.S. (%)
Adults aged 18–64 who have any kind of health care coverage	93.0	87.3
Adults who reported being in good or better health	82.5	82.4
Adults who have been told they have high blood cholesterol	33.7	33.0
Adults who have been told they have high blood pressure	31.9	32.3
Adults who are current smokers	15.3	17.1
Adults who currently use E-cigarettes	5.3	4.6
Adults who currently use chewing tobacco, snuff, or snus	1.7	4.0
Adults who are heavy drinkers[2]	6.5	6.3
Adults who are binge drinkers[3]	17.2	17.4
Adults who are overweight (BMI 25.0 - 29.9)	35.0	35.3
Adults who are obese (BMI 30.0 - 99.8)	31.6	31.3
Adults who participated in any physical activities in the past month	72.7	74.4
Adults who always or nearly always wears a seat belt	94.5	94.3

Note: (1) Figures cover the Providence-Warwick, RI-MA Metropolitan Statistical Area; (2) Heavy drinkers are classified as adult men having more than 14 drinks per week and adult women having more than 7 drinks per week; (3) Binge drinkers are classified as males having five or more drinks on one occasion or females having four or more drinks on one occasion
Source: Centers for Disease Control and Prevention, Behaviorial Risk Factor Surveillance System, SMART: Selected Metropolitan Area Risk Trends, 2017

Acute and Chronic Health Conditions

Category	MSA[1] (%)	U.S. (%)
Adults who have ever been told they had a heart attack	4.9	4.2
Adults who have ever been told they have angina or coronary heart disease	4.6	3.9
Adults who have ever been told they had a stroke	3.1	3.0
Adults who have ever been told they have asthma	17.6	14.2
Adults who have ever been told they have arthritis	27.5	24.9
Adults who have ever been told they have diabetes[2]	9.9	10.5
Adults who have ever been told they had skin cancer	6.3	6.2
Adults who have ever been told they had any other types of cancer	7.9	7.1
Adults who have ever been told they have COPD	8.2	6.5
Adults who have ever been told they have kidney disease	2.6	3.0
Adults who have ever been told they have a form of depression	23.7	20.5

Note: (1) Figures cover the Providence-Warwick, RI-MA Metropolitan Statistical Area; (2) Figures do not include pregnancy-related, borderline, or pre-diabetes
Source: Centers for Disease Control and Prevention, Behaviorial Risk Factor Surveillance System, SMART: Selected Metropolitan Area Risk Trends, 2017

Health Screening and Vaccination Rates

Category	MSA[1] (%)	U.S. (%)
Adults aged 65+ who have had flu shot within the past year	63.6	60.7
Adults aged 65+ who have ever had a pneumonia vaccination	82.8	75.4
Adults who have ever been tested for HIV	37.9	36.1
Adults who have ever had the shingles or zoster vaccine?	30.4	28.9
Adults who have had their blood cholesterol checked within the last five years	88.9	85.9

Note: n/a not available; (1) Figures cover the Providence-Warwick, RI-MA Metropolitan Statistical Area.
Source: Centers for Disease Control and Prevention, Behaviorial Risk Factor Surveillance System, SMART: Selected Metropolitan Area Risk Trends, 2017

Disability Status

Category	MSA[1] (%)	U.S. (%)
Adults who reported being deaf	5.8	6.7
Are you blind or have serious difficulty seeing, even when wearing glasses?	4.7	4.5
Are you limited in any way in any of your usual activities due of arthritis?	14.1	12.9
Do you have difficulty doing errands alone?	8.2	6.8
Do you have difficulty dressing or bathing?	4.0	3.6
Do you have serious difficulty concentrating/remembering/making decisions?	12.1	10.7
Do you have serious difficulty walking or climbing stairs?	13.8	13.6

Note: (1) Figures cover the Providence-Warwick, RI-MA Metropolitan Statistical Area.
Source: Centers for Disease Control and Prevention, Behaviorial Risk Factor Surveillance System, SMART: Selected Metropolitan Area Risk Trends, 2017

Mortality Rates for the Top 10 Causes of Death in the U.S.

ICD-10[a] Sub-Chapter	ICD-10[a] Code	Age-Adjusted Mortality Rate[1] per 100,000 population	
		County[2]	U.S.
Malignant neoplasms	C00-C97	152.2	149.2
Ischaemic heart diseases	I20-I25	105.8	90.5
Other forms of heart disease	I30-I51	38.7	52.2
Chronic lower respiratory diseases	J40-J47	34.8	39.6
Other degenerative diseases of the nervous system	G30-G31	34.7	37.6
Cerebrovascular diseases	I60-I69	29.0	37.2
Other external causes of accidental injury	W00-X59	53.8	36.1
Organic, including symptomatic, mental disorders	F01-F09	46.5	29.4
Hypertensive diseases	I10-I15	22.0	24.1
Diabetes mellitus	E10-E14	20.8	21.5

Note: (a) ICD-10 = International Classification of Diseases 10th Revision; (1) Mortality rates are a three-year average covering 2017-2019; (2) Figures cover Providence County.
Source: Centers for Disease Control and Prevention, National Center for Health Statistics. Underlying Cause of Death 1999-2019 on CDC WONDER Online Database

Mortality Rates for Selected Causes of Death

ICD-10[a] Sub-Chapter	ICD-10[a] Code	Age-Adjusted Mortality Rate[1] per 100,000 population	
		County[2]	U.S.
Assault	X85-Y09	2.5	6.0
Diseases of the liver	K70-K76	14.6	14.4
Human immunodeficiency virus (HIV) disease	B20-B24	1.1	1.5
Influenza and pneumonia	J09-J18	13.0	13.8
Intentional self-harm	X60-X84	9.7	14.1
Malnutrition	E40-E46	Unreliable	2.3
Obesity and other hyperalimentation	E65-E68	2.7	2.1
Renal failure	N17-N19	10.9	12.6
Transport accidents	V01-V99	8.0	12.3
Viral hepatitis	B15-B19	1.2	1.2

Note: (a) ICD-10 = International Classification of Diseases 10th Revision; (1) Mortality rates are a three-year average covering 2017-2019; (2) Figures cover Providence County; Data are suppressed when the data meet the criteria for confidentiality constraints; Mortality rates are flagged as unreliable when the rate would be calculated with a numerator of 20 or less.
Source: Centers for Disease Control and Prevention, National Center for Health Statistics. Underlying Cause of Death 1999-2019 on CDC WONDER Online Database

Health Insurance Coverage

Area	With Health Insurance	With Private Health Insurance	With Public Health Insurance	Without Health Insurance	Population Under Age 19 Without Health Insurance
City	92.5	53.2	46.4	7.5	3.1
MSA[1]	96.1	70.9	38.8	3.9	2.1
U.S.	91.2	67.9	35.1	8.8	5.1

Note: Figures are percentages that cover the civilian noninstitutionalized population; (1) Figures cover the Providence-Warwick, RI-MA Metropolitan Statistical Area
Source: U.S. Census Bureau, 2015-2019 American Community Survey 5-Year Estimates

Number of Medical Professionals

Area	MDs[3]	DOs[3,4]	Dentists	Podiatrists	Chiropractors	Optometrists
County[1] (number)	3,161	115	387	63	130	132
County[1] (rate[2])	496.3	18.1	60.6	9.9	20.3	20.7
U.S. (rate[2])	282.9	22.7	71.2	6.2	28.1	16.9

44007
Note: Data as of 2019 unless noted; (1) Data covers Providence County; (2) Rate per 100,000 population; (3) Data as of 2018 and includes all active, non-federal physicians; (4) Doctor of Osteopathic Medicine
Source: U.S. Department of Health and Human Services, Health Resources and Services Administration, Bureau of Health Professions, Area Resource File (ARF) 2019-2020

Best Hospitals

According to *U.S. News,* the Providence-Warwick, RI-MA metro area is home to one of the best hospitals in the U.S.: **Miriam Hospital** (1 adult specialty). The hospital listed was nationally ranked in at least one of 16 adult or 10 pediatric specialties. Only 134 hospitals nationwide were nationally ranked in one or more adult or pediatric specialty; this number increases to 178 counting specialized centers within hospitals. Twenty hospitals in the U.S. made the Honor Roll. The Best Hospitals Honor Roll takes both the national rankings and the procedure and condition ratings into account. Hospitals received points if they were nationally ranked in one of the 16 adult specialties—the higher they ranked, the more points they got—and how many ratings of "high performing" they earned in the 10 procedures and conditions. *U.S. News Online, "America's Best Hospitals 2020-21"*

EDUCATION

Public School District Statistics

District Name	Schls	Pupils	Pupil/ Teacher Ratio	Minority Pupils[1] (%)	Free Lunch Eligible[2] (%)	IEP[3] (%)
Providence	42	23,955	14.4	91.4	77.9	16.8

Note: Table includes school districts with 2,000 or more students; (1) Percentage of students that are not non-Hispanic white; (2) Percentage of students that are eligible for the free lunch program; (3) Percentage of students that have an Individualized Education Program.
Source: U.S. Department of Education, National Center for Education Statistics, Common Core of Data, Local Education Agency (School District) Universe Survey: School Year 2018-2019; U.S. Department of Education, National Center for Education Statistics, Common Core of Data, Public Elementary/Secondary School Universe Survey: School Year 2018-2019

Best High Schools

According to *U.S. News,* Providence is home to one of the top 500 high schools in the U.S.: **Classical High School** (#132). Nearly 18,000 public, magnet and charter schools were ranked based on their performance on state assessments and how well they prepare students for college. *U.S. News & World Report, "Best High Schools 2020"*

Highest Level of Education

Area	Less than H.S.	H.S. Diploma	Some College, No Deg.	Associate Degree	Bachelor's Degree	Master's Degree	Prof. School Degree	Doctorate Degree
City	18.4	31.4	15.2	5.0	16.1	8.6	2.9	2.5
MSA[1]	12.3	28.8	18.0	8.6	19.6	9.2	1.9	1.5
U.S.	12.0	27.0	20.4	8.5	19.8	8.8	2.1	1.4

Note: Figures cover persons age 25 and over; (1) Figures cover the Providence-Warwick, RI-MA Metropolitan Statistical Area
Source: U.S. Census Bureau, 2015-2019 American Community Survey 5-Year Estimates

Educational Attainment by Race

Area	High School Graduate or Higher (%)					Bachelor's Degree or Higher (%)				
	Total	White	Black	Asian	Hisp.[2]	Total	White	Black	Asian	Hisp.[2]
City	81.6	86.4	84.4	79.3	71.9	30.1	38.0	19.1	48.1	10.4
MSA[1]	87.7	89.2	85.5	85.5	73.3	32.3	33.7	22.3	51.6	14.0
U.S.	88.0	89.9	86.0	87.1	68.7	32.1	33.5	21.6	54.3	16.4

Note: Figures shown cover persons 25 years old and over; (1) Figures cover the Providence-Warwick, RI-MA Metropolitan Statistical Area; (2) People of Hispanic origin can be of any race
Source: U.S. Census Bureau, 2015-2019 American Community Survey 5-Year Estimates

School Enrollment by Grade and Control

Area	Preschool (%)		Kindergarten (%)		Grades 1 - 4 (%)		Grades 5 - 8 (%)		Grades 9 - 12 (%)	
	Public	Private	Public	Private	Public	Private	Public	Private	Public	Private
City	51.6	48.4	87.8	12.2	86.0	14.0	85.4	14.6	88.6	11.4
MSA[1]	53.8	46.2	89.9	10.1	90.4	9.6	89.6	10.4	88.5	11.5
U.S.	59.1	40.9	87.6	12.4	89.5	10.5	89.4	10.6	90.1	9.9

Note: Figures shown cover persons 3 years old and over; (1) Figures cover the Providence-Warwick, RI-MA Metropolitan Statistical Area
Source: U.S. Census Bureau, 2015-2019 American Community Survey 5-Year Estimates

Higher Education

Four-Year Colleges			Two-Year Colleges			Medical Schools[1]	Law Schools[2]	Voc/ Tech[3]
Public	Private Non-profit	Private For-profit	Public	Private Non-profit	Private For-profit			
1	6	0	0	0	0	1	0	1

Note: Figures cover institutions located within the city limits and include main campuses only; (1) includes schools accredited by the Liaison Committee on Medical Education and the American Osteopathic Association's Commission on Osteopathic College Accreditation; (2) includes ABA-accredited schools, schools with provisional ABA accreditation, and state accredited schools; (3) includes all schools with programs that are less than 2 years.
Source: National Center for Education Statistics, Integrated Postsecondary Education System (IPEDS), 2019-20; Wikipedia, List of Medical Schools in the United States, accessed April 2, 2021; Wikipedia, List of Law Schools in the United States, accessed April 2, 2021

According to *U.S. News & World Report,* the Providence-Warwick, RI-MA metro area is home to two of the top 200 national universities in the U.S.: **Brown University** (#14 tie); **University of Rhode Island** (#170 tie). The indicators used to capture academic quality fall into a number of categories: assessment by administrators at peer institutions; retention of students; faculty resources; student selectivity; financial resources; alumni giving; high school counselor ratings of colleges; and graduation rate. *U.S. News & World Report, "America's Best Colleges 2021"*

According to *U.S. News & World Report,* the Providence-Warwick, RI-MA metro area is home to one of the top 100 liberal arts colleges in the U.S.: **Wheaton College (MA)** (#84 tie). The indicators used to capture academic quality fall into a number of categories: assessment by administrators at peer institutions; retention of students; faculty resources; student selectivity; financial resources; alumni giving; high school counselor ratings of colleges; and graduation rate. *U.S. News & World Report, "America's Best Colleges 2021"*

According to *U.S. News & World Report,* the Providence-Warwick, RI-MA metro area is home to one of the top 75 medical schools for research in the U.S.: **Brown University (Alpert)** (#36 tie). The rankings are based on a weighted average of 11 measures of quality: quality assessment; peer assessment score; assessment score by residency directors; research activity; total research activity; average research activity per faculty member; student selectivity; median MCAT total score; median undergraduate GPA; acceptance rate; and faculty resources. *U.S. News & World Report, "America's Best Graduate Schools, Medical, 2022"*

EMPLOYERS

Major Employers

Company Name	Industry
A&M Special Purchasing	Payroll accounting service
Acushnet Company	Sporting & recreation goods
Brown University	Colleges & universities
Charlton Memorial Hospital	General medical & surgical hospitals
City of Fall River	Public elementary & secondary schools
City of Providence	Municipal government
CVS Pharmacy	Drug stores
Hasbro	Games, toys, & children's vehicles
Hasbro Managerial Services	Management services
Kent Hospital	General medical & surgical hospitals
Providence School Department	Public elementary & secondary schools
Rhode Island Hospital	General medical & surgical hospitals
Roman Catholic Diocese of Fall River	Catholic church
Saint Luke's Hospital of New Bedford	General medical & surgical hospitals
Samsonite International S.A.	Luggage
Southcoast Hospitals Group	General medical & surgical hospitals
U.S. Navy	U.S. military
University of Rhode Island	Colleges & universities
Women & Infants Hospital of Rhode Island	Specialty outpatient clinics, nec

Note: Companies shown are located within the Providence-Warwick, RI-MA Metropolitan Statistical Area.
Source: Hoovers.com; Wikipedia

PUBLIC SAFETY

Crime Rate

Area	All Crimes	Violent Crimes				Property Crimes		
		Murder	Rape[3]	Robbery	Aggrav. Assault	Burglary	Larceny -Theft	Motor Vehicle Theft
City	3,507.4	7.2	59.0	134.1	295.9	397.7	2,349.8	263.7
Suburbs[1]	1,466.1	1.7	43.0	37.4	173.7	203.4	912.5	94.2
Metro[2]	1,692.5	2.3	44.8	48.1	187.3	225.0	1,071.9	113.0
U.S.	2,489.3	5.0	42.6	81.6	250.2	340.5	1,549.5	219.9

Note: Figures are crimes per 100,000 population; (1) All areas within the metro area that are located outside the city limits; (2) Figures cover the Providence-Warwick, RI-MA Metropolitan Statistical Area; (3) All figures shown were reported using the revised Uniform Crime Reporting (UCR) definition of rape.
Source: FBI Uniform Crime Reports, 2019

Hate Crimes

Area	Number of Quarters Reported	Number of Incidents per Bias Motivation					
		Race/Ethnicity/ Ancestry	Religion	Sexual Orientation	Disability	Gender	Gender Identity
City	4	1	2	1	0	0	0
U.S.	4	3,963	1,521	1,195	157	69	198

Source: Federal Bureau of Investigation, Hate Crime Statistics 2019

Identity Theft Consumer Reports

Area	Reports	Reports per 100,000 Population	Rank[2]
MSA[1]	15,751	970	10
U.S.	1,387,615	423	-

Note: (1) Figures cover the Providence-Warwick, RI-MA Metropolitan Statistical Area; (2) Rank ranges from 1 to 391 where 1 indicates greatest number of identity theft reports per 100,000 population
Source: Federal Trade Commission, Consumer Sentinel Network Data Book 2020

Fraud and Other Consumer Reports

Area	Reports	Reports per 100,000 Population	Rank[2]
MSA[1]	11,958	736	154
U.S.	3,385,133	1,031	-

Note: (1) Figures cover the Providence-Warwick, RI-MA Metropolitan Statistical Area; (2) Rank ranges from 1 to 391 where 1 indicates greatest number of fraud and other consumer reports per 100,000 population
Source: Federal Trade Commission, Consumer Sentinel Network Data Book 2020

POLITICS

2020 Presidential Election Results

Area	Biden	Trump	Jorgensen	Hawkins	Other
Providence County	60.5	37.6	0.8	0.0	1.0
U.S.	51.3	46.8	1.2	0.3	0.5

Note: Results are percentages and may not add to 100% due to rounding
Source: Dave Leip's Atlas of U.S. Presidential Elections

SPORTS

Professional Sports Teams

Team Name	League	Year Established

No teams are located in the metro area
Source: Wikipedia, Major Professional Sports Teams of the United States and Canada, April 6, 2021

CLIMATE

Average and Extreme Temperatures

Temperature	Jan	Feb	Mar	Apr	May	Jun	Jul	Aug	Sep	Oct	Nov	Dec	Yr.
Extreme High (°F)	66	72	80	98	94	97	102	104	100	88	81	70	104
Average High (°F)	37	39	46	58	68	77	82	80	73	63	52	41	60
Average Temp. (°F)	29	30	38	48	58	67	73	71	64	54	44	33	51
Average Low (°F)	20	22	29	39	48	57	63	62	54	43	35	25	42
Extreme Low (°F)	-13	-7	1	14	29	41	48	40	32	20	6	-10	-13

Note: Figures cover the years 1948-1992
Source: National Climatic Data Center, International Station Meteorological Climate Summary, 9/96

Average Precipitation/Snowfall/Humidity

Precip./Humidity	Jan	Feb	Mar	Apr	May	Jun	Jul	Aug	Sep	Oct	Nov	Dec	Yr.
Avg. Precip. (in.)	3.9	3.6	4.2	4.1	3.7	2.9	3.2	4.0	3.5	3.6	4.5	4.3	45.3
Avg. Snowfall (in.)	10	10	7	1	Tr	0	0	0	0	Tr	1	7	35
Avg. Rel. Hum. 7am (%)	71	71	71	70	73	75	78	81	83	81	78	74	75
Avg. Rel. Hum. 4pm (%)	58	56	54	51	55	58	58	60	60	58	60	60	57

Note: Figures cover the years 1948-1992; Tr = Trace amounts (<0.05 in. of rain; <0.5 in. of snow)
Source: National Climatic Data Center, International Station Meteorological Climate Summary, 9/96

Weather Conditions

Temperature			Daytime Sky			Precipitation		
5°F & below	32°F & below	90°F & above	Clear	Partly cloudy	Cloudy	0.01 inch or more precip.	0.1 inch or more snow/ice	Thunderstorms
6	117	9	85	134	146	123	21	21

Note: Figures are average number of days per year and cover the years 1948-1992
Source: National Climatic Data Center, International Station Meteorological Climate Summary, 9/96

HAZARDOUS WASTE

Superfund Sites

The Providence-Warwick, RI-MA metro area is home to 17 sites on the EPA's Superfund National Priorities List: **Atlas Tack Corp.** (final); **Central Landfill** (final); **Centredale Manor Restoration Project** (final); **Davis Liquid Waste** (final); **Davisville Naval Construction Battalion Center** (final); **Landfill & Resource Recovery, Inc. (L&RR)** (final); **New Bedford** (final); **Newport Naval Education & Training Center** (final); **Peterson/Puritan, Inc.** (final); **Picillo Farm** (final); **Re-Solve, Inc.** (final); **Rose Hill Regional Landfill** (final); **Stamina Mills, Inc.** (final); **Sullivan's Ledge** (final); **Walton & Lonsbury Inc.** (final); **West Kingston Town Dump/URI Disposal Area** (final); **Western Sand & Gravel** (final). There are a total of 1,375 Superfund sites with a status of proposed or final on the list in the U.S. *U.S. Environmental Protection Agency, National Priorities List, April 7, 2021*

AIR QUALITY

Air Quality Trends: Ozone

	1990	1995	2000	2005	2010	2015	2016	2017	2018	2019
MSA[1]	0.106	0.107	0.087	0.090	0.072	0.070	0.075	0.076	0.074	0.064
U.S.	0.088	0.089	0.082	0.080	0.073	0.068	0.069	0.068	0.069	0.065

Note: (1) Data covers the Providence-Warwick, RI-MA Metropolitan Statistical Area. The values shown are the composite ozone concentration averages among trend sites based on the highest fourth daily maximum 8-hour concentration in parts per million. These trends are based on sites having an adequate record of monitoring data during the trend period. Data from exceptional events are included.
Source: U.S. Environmental Protection Agency, Air Quality Monitoring Information, "Air Quality Trends by City, 1990-2019"

Air Quality Index

Area	Percent of Days when Air Quality was...[2]					AQI Statistics[2]	
	Good	Moderate	Unhealthy for Sensitive Groups	Unhealthy	Very Unhealthy	Maximum	Median
MSA[1]	79.2	20.3	0.5	0.0	0.0	126	44

Note: (1) Data covers the Providence-Warwick, RI-MA Metropolitan Statistical Area; (2) Based on 365 days with AQI data in 2019. Air Quality Index (AQI) is an index for reporting daily air quality. EPA calculates the AQI for five major air pollutants regulated by the Clean Air Act: ground-level ozone, particle pollution (aka particulate matter), carbon monoxide, sulfur dioxide, and nitrogen dioxide. The AQI runs from 0 to 500. The higher the AQI value, the greater the level of air pollution and the greater the health concern. There are six AQI categories: "Good" AQI is between 0 and 50. Air quality is considered satisfactory; "Moderate" AQI is between 51 and 100. Air quality is acceptable; "Unhealthy for Sensitive Groups" When AQI values are between 101 and 150, members of sensitive groups may experience health effects; "Unhealthy" When AQI values are between 151 and 200 everyone may begin to experience health effects; "Very Unhealthy" AQI values between 201 and 300 trigger a health alert; "Hazardous" AQI values over 300 trigger warnings of emergency conditions (not shown).
Source: U.S. Environmental Protection Agency, Air Quality Index Report, 2019

Air Quality Index Pollutants

Area	Percent of Days when AQI Pollutant was...[2]					
	Carbon Monoxide	Nitrogen Dioxide	Ozone	Sulfur Dioxide	Particulate Matter 2.5	Particulate Matter 10
MSA[1]	0.0	2.2	70.7	0.0	26.8	0.3

Note: (1) Data covers the Providence-Warwick, RI-MA Metropolitan Statistical Area; (2) Based on 365 days with AQI data in 2019. The Air Quality Index (AQI) is an index for reporting daily air quality. EPA calculates the AQI for five major air pollutants regulated by the Clean Air Act: ground-level ozone, particle pollution (also known as particulate matter), carbon monoxide, sulfur dioxide, and nitrogen dioxide. The AQI runs from 0 to 500. The higher the AQI value, the greater the level of air pollution and the greater the health concern.
Source: U.S. Environmental Protection Agency, Air Quality Index Report, 2019

Maximum Air Pollutant Concentrations: Particulate Matter, Ozone, CO and Lead

	Particulate Matter 10 (ug/m³)	Particulate Matter 2.5 Wtd AM (ug/m³)	Particulate Matter 2.5 24-Hr (ug/m³)	Ozone (ppm)	Carbon Monoxide (ppm)	Lead (ug/m³)
MSA[1] Level	37	8.3	18	0.066	2	n/a
NAAQS[2]	150	15	35	0.075	9	0.15
Met NAAQS[2]	Yes	Yes	Yes	Yes	Yes	n/a

Note: (1) Data covers the Providence-Warwick, RI-MA Metropolitan Statistical Area; Data from exceptional events are included; (2) National Ambient Air Quality Standards; ppm = parts per million; ug/m³ = micrograms per cubic meter; n/a not available.
Concentrations: Particulate Matter 10 (coarse particulate)—highest second maximum 24-hour concentration; Particulate Matter 2.5 Wtd AM (fine particulate)—highest weighted annual mean concentration; Particulate Matter 2.5 24-Hour (fine particulate)—highest 98th percentile 24-hour concentration; Ozone—highest fourth daily maximum 8-hour concentration; Carbon Monoxide—highest second maximum non-overlapping 8-hour concentration; Lead—maximum running 3-month average
Source: U.S. Environmental Protection Agency, Air Quality Monitoring Information, "Air Quality Statistics by City, 2019"

Maximum Air Pollutant Concentrations: Nitrogen Dioxide and Sulfur Dioxide

	Nitrogen Dioxide AM (ppb)	Nitrogen Dioxide 1-Hr (ppb)	Sulfur Dioxide AM (ppb)	Sulfur Dioxide 1-Hr (ppb)	Sulfur Dioxide 24-Hr (ppb)
MSA[1] Level	17	52	n/a	2	n/a
NAAQS[2]	53	100	30	75	140
Met NAAQS[2]	Yes	Yes	n/a	Yes	n/a

Note: (1) Data covers the Providence-Warwick, RI-MA Metropolitan Statistical Area; Data from exceptional events are included; (2) National Ambient Air Quality Standards; ppm = parts per million; ug/m^3 = micrograms per cubic meter; n/a not available.
Concentrations: Nitrogen Dioxide AM—highest arithmetic mean concentration; Nitrogen Dioxide 1-Hr—highest 98th percentile 1-hour daily maximum concentration; Sulfur Dioxide AM—highest annual mean concentration; Sulfur Dioxide 1-Hr—highest 99th percentile 1-hour daily maximum concentration; Sulfur Dioxide 24-Hr—highest second maximum 24-hour concentration
Source: U.S. Environmental Protection Agency, Air Quality Monitoring Information, "Air Quality Statistics by City, 2019"

Raleigh, North Carolina

Background

Raleigh is named for Queen Elizabeth I's swashbuckling favorite, Sir Walter Raleigh. In her name, he plundered Spanish ships for gold in the New World and founded the first English settlement along the North Carolina coast. His excessive piracy led to his execution in 1618.

Raleigh is the capital of North Carolina, and its cultural and educational center. Located 120 miles west of the Atlantic Ocean, Raleigh is the retail and wholesale center of eastern North Carolina. Its numerous federal, state, and local government offices provide jobs for the economy of the surrounding area. The Research Triangle Park—a complex of research laboratories among the cities of Raleigh, Durham, and Chapel Hill—continues to pump money into the local economy.

The city is home to high-tech businesses, including information technology, telecommunications, biomedicine, pharmaceuticals and computer software and hardware. It also boasts first-rate universities such as North Carolina State, Duke University and the University of North Carolina.

The region has a high business startup rate, a low unemployment rate, and average wages above the state level. Research Triangle Park is one of the largest university-affiliated research parks in the world. North Carolina State University's Centennial Campus has also brought major corporate re-locators and thousands of jobs to the area.

Called the "City of Oaks," for its tree-lined streets, architecture in Raleigh ranges from the modern architecture of the North Carolina Museum of Art, designed by Edward Durrell Stone (architect of Washington DC's John F. Kennedy Center), to the antebellum structures such as the Greek Revival Capitol Building. The city's street grid simplifies exploration of Raleigh's downtown, with continues to prosper and develop. In 2009, Raleigh became one of three United States cities participating in Project Get Ready—a non-profit program led by the Rocky Mountain Institute (RMI) to advance Electric Vehicle policies, and Raleigh leads the East Coast in Electric Vehicle (EV) readiness. Now that factory-made electric cars are being purchased by consumers, RMI looks forward to the day when at least 50 percent of all registered vehicles are plug-ins.

Cultural attractions include the North Carolina Symphony, the Opera Company of North Carolina, and the Carolina Ballet, all of which perform at the Progress Energy Center for the Performing Arts. There are numerous other musical, dance and theater groups in the city and the City of Raleigh Arts Commission actively supports the arts. Children enjoy the Marbles Kids Museum & Wachovia IMAX® Theatre.

> The 2020 North Carolina State Fair was canceled due to COVID-19, marking the first time since World War II that the fair did not take place.

The Coastal Credit Union Music Park at Walnut Creek hosts major international touring acts. The Downtown Raleigh Amphitheater (aka the Red Hat Amphitheater), hosts numerous concerts in the summer months. An additional amphitheater sits on the grounds of the North Carolina Museum of Art, which hosts a summer concert series and outdoor movies.

Because it is centrally located between the mountains on the west and the coast on the south and east, the Raleigh area enjoys a pleasant climate. The mountains form a partial barrier to cold air masses moving from the west. As a result, there are few winter days when the temperature gets seriously cold. In the summer, tropical air is present over the eastern and central sections of North Carolina, bringing warm temperatures and rather high humidity to the area. Raleigh is situated far enough from the coast so that the effects of coastal storms are usually reduced. In April 2011, however, a devastating tornado hit the city, killing 24 people. While snow and sleet usually occur each year, excessive accumulations of snow are rare.

Rankings

General Rankings

- For its "Best for Vets: Places to Live 2019" rankings, *Military Times* evaluated 599 cities (83 large, 234 medium, 282 small) and compared the locations across three broad categories: veteran and military culture/services; economic indicators; and livability factors such as health, crime, traffic, and school quality. Raleigh ranked #23 out of the top 25, in the large city category (population of more than 250,000). Data points more specific to veterans and the military weighed more heavily than others. *rebootcamp.militarytimes.com, "Military Times Best Places to Live 2019," September 10, 2018*

- *US News & World Report* conducted a survey of more than 3,000 people and analyzed the 150 largest metropolitan areas to determine what matters most when selecting the next place to live. Raleigh ranked #11 out of the top 25 as having the best combination of desirable factors. Criteria: cost of living; quality of life; net migration; job market; desirability; and other factors. *realestate.usnews.com, "The 25 Best Places to Live in the U.S. in 2020-21," October 13, 2020*

- The Raleigh metro area was identified as one of America's fastest-growing areas in terms of population and business growth by *MagnifyMoney*. The area ranked #3 out of 35. The 100 most populous metro areas in the U.S. were evaluated on their change from 2011-2016 in the following categories: people and housing; workforce and employment opportunities; growing industry. *www.businessinsider.com, "The 35 Cities in the US with the Biggest Influx of People, the Most Work Opportunities, and the Hottest Business Growth," August 12, 2018*

- The Raleigh metro area was identified as one of America's fastest-growing areas in terms of population and economy by *Forbes*. The area ranked #15 out of 25. The 100 most populous metro areas in the U.S. were evaluated on the following criteria: estimated population growth; employment; economic output; wages; home values. *Forbes, "America's Fastest-Growing Cities 2018," February 28, 2018*

Business/Finance Rankings

- 24/7 Wall Street used metro data from the Bureau of Labor Statistics' Occupational Employment database to identify the cities with the highest percentage of those employed in jobs requiring knowledge in the science, technology, engineering, and math (STEM) fields as well as average wages for STEM jobs. The Raleigh metro area was #8. *247wallst.com, "15 Cities with the Most High-Tech Jobs," January 11, 2020*

- Based on metro area social media reviews, the employment opinion group Glassdoor surveyed 50 of the most populous U.S. metro areas and equally weighed cost of living, hiring opportunity, and job satisfaction to compose a list of "25 Best Cities for Jobs." Median pay and home value, and number of active job openings were also factored in. The Raleigh metro area was ranked #1 in overall job satisfaction. *www.glassdoor.com, "Best Cities for Jobs," February 25, 2020*

- The Brookings Institution ranked the nation's largest cities based on income inequality. Raleigh was ranked #84 (#1 = greatest inequality). Criteria: the "95/20 ratio," a figure representing the income at which a household earns more than 95 percent of all other households, divided by the income at which a household earns more than only 20 percent of all other households. *Brookings Institution, "Household Income Inequality, Largest Cities of 97 Large U.S. Metro Areas, 2014-2016," February 5, 2018*

- The Brookings Institution ranked the 100 largest metro areas in the U.S. based on income inequality. Raleigh was ranked #80 (#1 = greatest inequality). Criteria: the "95/20 ratio," a figure representing the income at which a household earns more than 95 percent of all other households, divided by the income at which a household earns more than only 20 percent of all other households. *Brookings Institution, "Household Income Inequality, 100 Largest U.S. Metro Areas, 2014-2016," February 5, 2018*

- *Forbes* ranked the 100 largest metro areas in the U.S. in terms of the "Best Cities for Young Professionals." The Raleigh metro area ranked #10 out of 25. Criteria: median rent of a two-bedroom apartment; job growth and unemployment rate; median salary of college graduates with 5 or less years of work experience; networking opportunities; social outlook; percentage of population 25 years of age and older with college degrees. *Forbes.com, "America's 25 Best Cities for Young Professionals in 2017," May 22, 2017*

- Payscale.com ranked the 32 largest metro areas in terms of wage growth. The Raleigh metro area ranked #21. Criteria: private-sector and education professional wage growth between the 4th quarter of 2019 and the 4th quarter of 2020. *PayScale, "Wage Trends by Metro Area-4th Quarter," January 11, 2021*

- Raleigh was identified as one of America's most frugal metro areas by *Coupons.com*. The city ranked #3 out of 25. Criteria: digital coupon usage. *Coupons.com, "America's Most Frugal Cities of 2017," March 22, 2018*

- The Raleigh metro area appeared on the Milken Institute "2021 Best Performing Cities" list. Rank: #5 out of 200 large metro areas (population over 250,000). Criteria: job growth; wage and salary growth; high-tech output growth; housing affordability; household broadband access. *Milken Institute, "Best-Performing Cities 2021," February 16, 2021*

- *Forbes* ranked the 200 most populous metro areas to determine the nation's "Best Places for Business and Careers." The Raleigh metro area was ranked #3. Criteria: costs (business and living); job growth (past and projected); income growth; quality of life; educational attainment (college and high school); projected economic growth; cultural and leisure opportunities; workplace tolerance laws; net migration patterns. *Forbes, "The Best Places for Business and Careers 2019: Seattle Still On Top," October 30, 2019*

Children/Family Rankings

- Raleigh was selected as one of the most playful cities in the U.S. by KaBOOM! The organization's Playful City USA initiative honors cities and towns across the nation that have made their communities more playable. Criteria: pledging to integrate play as a solution to challenges in their communities; making it easy for children to get active and balanced play; creating more family-friendly and innovative communities as a result. *KaBOOM! National Campaign for Play, "2017 Playful City USA Communities"*

Dating/Romance Rankings

- *Apartment List* conducted its annual survey of renters for cities that have the best opportunities for dating. More than 11,000 single respondents rated their current city or neighborhood for opportunities to date. Raleigh ranked #3 out of 86 where single residents were very satisfied or somewhat satisfied, making it among the ten best areas for dating opportunities. Other criteria analyzed included gender and education levels of renters. *Apartment List, "The Best & Worst Metros for Dating 2020," February 4, 2020*

- Raleigh was selected as one of the best cities for post grads by *Rent.com*. The city ranked among the top 10. Criteria: jobs per capita; unemployment rate; mean annual income; cost of living; rental inventory. *Rent.com, "Best Cities for College Grads," December 11, 2018*

Education Rankings

- Personal finance website *WalletHub* analyzed the 150 largest U.S. metropolitan statistical areas to determine where the most educated Americans are putting their degrees to work. Criteria: education levels; percentage of workers with degrees; education quality and attainment gap; public school quality rankings; quality and enrollment of each metro area's universities. Raleigh was ranked #12 (#1 = most educated city). *www.WalletHub.com, "Most and Least Educated Cities in America, " July 20, 2020*

- Raleigh was selected as one of America's most literate cities. The city ranked #14 out of the 84 largest U.S. cities. Criteria: number of booksellers; library resources; Internet resources; educational attainment; periodical publishing resources; newspaper circulation. *Central Connecticut State University, "America's Most Literate Cities, 2018," February 2019*

Environmental Rankings

- The U.S. Environmental Protection Agency (EPA) released a list of mid-size U.S. metropolitan areas with the most ENERGY STAR certified buildings in 2019. The Raleigh metro area was ranked #4 out of 10. *U.S. Environmental Protection Agency, "2020 Energy Star Top Cities," March 2020*

Food/Drink Rankings

- The U.S. Chamber of Commerce Foundation conducted an in-depth study on local food truck regulations, surveyed 288 food truck owners, and ranked 20 major American cities based on how friendly they are for operating a food truck. The compiled index assessed the following: procedures for obtaining permits and licenses; complying with restrictions; and financial obligations associated with operating a food truck. Raleigh ranked #11 overall (1 being the best). *www.foodtrucknation.us, "Food Truck Nation," March 20, 2018*

Health/Fitness Rankings

- For each of the 100 largest cities in the United States, the American Fitness Index®, published by the American College of Sports Medicine and the Anthem Foundation, evaluated community infrastructure and 33 health behaviors including preventive health, levels of chronic disease conditions, pedestrian safety, air quality, and community resources that support physical activity. Raleigh ranked #36 for "community fitness." *americanfitnessindex.org, "2020 ACSM American Fitness Index Summary Report," July 14, 2020*

- The Raleigh metro area was identified as one of the worst cities for bed bugs in America by pest control company Orkin. The area ranked #17 out of 50 based on the number of bed bug treatments Orkin performed from December 2019 to November 2020. *Orkin, "New Year, New Top City on Orkin's 2021 Bed Bug Cities List: Chicago," February 1, 2021*

- Raleigh was identified as a "2021 Spring Allergy Capital." The area ranked #80 out of 100. Three groups of factors were used to identify the most challenging cities for people with allergies during the spring season: annual spring pollen levels; over the counter medicine use; number of board-certified allergy specialists. *Asthma and Allergy Foundation of America, "Spring Allergy Capitals 2021," February 23, 2021*

- Raleigh was identified as a "2021 Fall Allergy Capital." The area ranked #84 out of 100. Three groups of factors were used to identify the most challenging cities for people with allergies during the fall season: annual fall pollen levels; over the counter medicine use; number of board-certified allergy specialists. *Asthma and Allergy Foundation of America, "Fall Allergy Capitals 2021," February 23, 2021*

- Raleigh was identified as a "2019 Asthma Capital." The area ranked #70 out of the nation's 100 largest metropolitan areas. Criteria: estimated asthma prevalence; crude death rate from asthma; and ER visits due to asthma. Risk factors analyzed but not factored in the rankings: annual pollen score; annual air quality; public smoking laws; number of board-certified asthma specialists; rescue medication use; controller medication use; uninsured rate; poverty rate. *Asthma and Allergy Foundation of America, "Asthma Capitals 2019: The Most Challenging Places to Live With Asthma," May 7, 2019*

Real Estate Rankings

- FitSmallBusiness looked at 50 of the largest metropolitan areas in the U.S. to determine which metro was the best to start a real estate business. Data was compiled from such sources as: Zillow, Trulia, U.S. Census Bureau, and the Bureau of Labor Statistics. Criteria: location; inventory; annual wages; median sales price of homes; days on the market; median price cut percentage; and other factors that would influence real estate professional growth. The Raleigh metro area ranked #29. *fitsmallbusiness.com, "The Best Cities to Become a Real Estate Agent in 2018," January 30, 2018*

- *WalletHub* compared the most populated U.S. cities to determine which had the best markets for real estate agents. Raleigh ranked #122 where demand was high and pay was the best. Criteria: sales per agent; annual median wage for real-estate agents; monthly average starting salary for real estate agents; real estate job density and competition; unemployment rate; home turnover rate; housing-market health index; and other relevant metrics. *www.WalletHub.com, "2019's Best Places to Be a Real Estate Agent," April 24, 2019*

- According to Penske Truck Rental, the Raleigh metro area was named the #8 moving destination in 2019, based on one-way consumer truck rental reservations made through Penske's website, rental locations, and reservations call center. *gopenske.com/blog, "Penske Truck Rental's 2019 Top Moving Destinations," January 22, 2020*

- Raleigh was ranked #129 out of 268 metro areas in terms of housing affordability in 2020 by the National Association of Home Builders (#1 = most affordable). Criteria: the share of homes sold in that area affordable to a family earning the local median income, based on standard mortgage underwriting criteria. *National Association of Home Builders®, NAHB-Wells Fargo Housing Opportunity Index, 4th Quarter 2020*

Safety Rankings

- Allstate ranked the 200 largest cities in America in terms of driver safety. Raleigh ranked #81. Criteria: internal property damage claims over a two-year period from January 2016 to December 2017. The report helps increase the importance of safety and awareness behind the wheel. *Allstate, "Allstate America's Best Drivers Report, 2019" June 24, 2019*

- The National Insurance Crime Bureau ranked 384 metro areas in the U.S. in terms of per capita rates of vehicle theft. The Raleigh metro area ranked #262 (#1 = highest rate). Criteria: number of vehicle theft offenses per 100,000 inhabitants in 2019. *National Insurance Crime Bureau, "Hot Spots 2019," July 21, 2020*

Seniors/Retirement Rankings

- From its Best Cities for Successful Aging indexes, the Milken Institute generated rankings for metropolitan areas, weighing data in nine categories—health care, wellness, living arrangements, transportation and convenience, financial characteristics, education, employment, community engagement, and overall livability. The Raleigh metro area was ranked #42 overall in the large metro area category. *Milken Institute, "Best Cities for Successful Aging, 2017" March 14, 2017*

- Raleigh made the 2020 *Forbes* list of "25 Best Places to Retire." Criteria, focused on high-quality retirement living at an affordable price, include: housing/living costs compared to the national average and state taxes; air quality; crime rates; good economic outlook; home price appreciation; risk associated with climate-change; availability of medical care; bikeability; walkability; healthy living. *Forbes.com, "The Best Places to Retire in 2020," August 14, 2020*

Women/Minorities Rankings

- Personal finance website *WalletHub* compared more than 180 U.S. cities across two key dimensions, "Hispanic Business-Friendliness" and "Hispanic Purchasing Power," to arrive at the most favorable conditions for Hispanic entrepreneurs. Raleigh was ranked #56 out of 182. Criteria includes: share of Hispanic-Owned Businesses; Hispanic entrepreneurship rate to median annual income of Hispanics; Small Business-Friendliness score; cost of living; and number of Hispanics with at least a bachelor's degree. *WalletHub.com, "2019's Best Cities for Hispanic Entrepreneurs," May 1, 2019*

Miscellaneous Rankings

- *WalletHub* compared the 150 most populated U.S. cities to determine their operating efficiency. A "Quality of City Services" score was constructed for each city and then divided by the total budget per capita to reveal which were managed the best. Raleigh ranked #22. Criteria: financial stability; economy; education; safety; health; infrastructure and pollution. *www.WalletHub.com, "2020's Best- & Worst-Run Cities in America," June 29, 2020*

Business Environment

DEMOGRAPHICS

Population Growth

Area	1990 Census	2000 Census	2010 Census	2019* Estimate	Population Growth (%) 1990-2019	2010-2019
City	226,841	276,093	403,892	464,485	104.8	15.0
MSA[1]	541,081	797,071	1,130,490	1,332,311	146.2	17.9
U.S.	248,709,873	281,421,906	308,745,538	324,697,795	30.6	5.2

Note: (1) Figures cover the Raleigh, NC Metropolitan Statistical Area; (*) 2015-2019 5-year estimated population
Source: U.S. Census Bureau, 1990 Census, Census 2000, Census 2010, 2015-2019 American Community Survey 5-Year Estimates

Household Size

Area	One	Two	Three	Four	Five	Six	Seven or More	Average Household Size
City	33.1	32.5	15.2	12.5	4.8	1.3	0.7	2.40
MSA[1]	25.1	33.1	17.7	15.3	6.1	1.8	0.9	2.60
U.S.	27.9	33.9	15.6	12.9	6.0	2.3	1.4	2.60

Note: (1) Figures cover the Raleigh, NC Metropolitan Statistical Area
Source: U.S. Census Bureau, 2015-2019 American Community Survey 5-Year Estimates

Race

Area	White Alone[2] (%)	Black Alone[2] (%)	Asian Alone[2] (%)	AIAN[3] Alone[2] (%)	NHOPI[4] Alone[2] (%)	Other Race Alone[2] (%)	Two or More Races (%)
City	58.3	29.0	4.6	0.4	0.0	4.8	2.9
MSA[1]	67.2	20.0	5.7	0.4	0.0	3.7	2.9
U.S.	72.5	12.7	5.5	0.8	0.2	4.9	3.3

Note: (1) Figures cover the Raleigh, NC Metropolitan Statistical Area; (2) Alone is defined as not being in combination with one or more other races; (3) American Indian and Alaska Native; (4) Native Hawaiian and Other Pacific Islander
Source: U.S. Census Bureau, 2015-2019 American Community Survey 5-Year Estimates

Hispanic or Latino Origin

Area	Total (%)	Mexican (%)	Puerto Rican (%)	Cuban (%)	Other (%)
City	11.2	5.1	1.2	0.4	4.5
MSA[1]	10.6	5.5	1.3	0.4	3.4
U.S.	18.0	11.2	1.7	0.7	4.3

Note: Persons of Hispanic or Latino origin can be of any race; (1) Figures cover the Raleigh, NC Metropolitan Statistical Area
Source: U.S. Census Bureau, 2015-2019 American Community Survey 5-Year Estimates

Ancestry

Area	German	Irish	English	American	Italian	Polish	French[2]	Scottish	Dutch
City	8.9	7.5	9.0	12.2	4.0	2.2	1.7	2.3	0.6
MSA[1]	10.3	9.0	10.1	10.3	4.8	2.2	1.9	2.5	0.9
U.S.	13.3	9.7	7.2	6.2	5.1	2.8	2.3	1.7	1.2

Note: Figures are the percentage of the total population reporting a particular ancestry. The nine most commonly reported ancestries in the U.S. are shown. Figures include multiple ancestries (e.g. if a person reported being Irish and Italian, they were included in both columns); (1) Figures cover the Raleigh, NC Metropolitan Statistical Area; (2) Excludes Basque
Source: U.S. Census Bureau, 2015-2019 American Community Survey 5-Year Estimates

Foreign-born Population

Area	Any Foreign Country	Asia	Mexico	Europe	Caribbean	Central America[2]	South America	Africa	Canada
City	13.4	3.9	2.7	1.4	0.9	1.4	0.7	2.1	0.3
MSA[1]	12.3	4.4	2.6	1.4	0.6	1.1	0.6	1.2	0.4
U.S.	13.6	4.2	3.5	1.5	1.3	1.1	1.0	0.7	0.2

Note: (1) Figures cover the Raleigh, NC Metropolitan Statistical Area; (2) Excludes Mexico.
Source: U.S. Census Bureau, 2015-2019 American Community Survey 5-Year Estimates

Marital Status

Area	Never Married	Now Married[2]	Separated	Widowed	Divorced
City	42.7	40.3	2.5	3.7	10.8
MSA[1]	32.0	51.7	2.3	4.2	9.9
U.S.	33.4	48.1	1.9	5.8	10.9

Note: Figures are percentages and cover the population 15 years of age and older; (1) Figures cover the Raleigh, NC Metropolitan Statistical Area; (2) Excludes separated
Source: U.S. Census Bureau, 2015-2019 American Community Survey 5-Year Estimates

Disability by Age

Area	All Ages	Under 18 Years Old	18 to 64 Years Old	65 Years and Over
City	9.0	4.7	6.8	31.6
MSA[1]	9.6	3.8	7.7	32.1
U.S.	12.6	4.2	10.3	34.5

Note: Figures show percent of the civilian noninstitutionalized population that reported having a disability. Disability status is determined from six types of difficulty: vision, hearing, cognitive, ambulatory, self-care, and independent living. For children under 5 years old, hearing and vision difficulty are used to determine disability status. For children between the ages of 5 and 14, disability status is determined from hearing, vision, cognitive, ambulatory, and self-care difficulties. For people aged 15 years and older, they are considered to have a disability if they have difficulty with any one of the six difficulty types; Note: (1) Figures cover the Raleigh, NC Metropolitan Statistical Area
Source: U.S. Census Bureau, 2015-2019 American Community Survey 5-Year Estimates

Age

Area	Percent of Population									Median Age
	Under Age 5	Age 5–19	Age 20–34	Age 35–44	Age 45–54	Age 55–64	Age 65–74	Age 75–84	Age 85+	
City	5.9	18.9	27.5	14.5	12.7	9.9	6.4	2.9	1.3	33.6
MSA[1]	6.2	20.8	20.4	14.8	14.5	11.6	7.4	3.2	1.2	36.7
U.S.	6.1	19.1	20.7	12.6	13.0	12.9	9.1	4.6	1.9	38.1

Note: (1) Figures cover the Raleigh, NC Metropolitan Statistical Area
Source: U.S. Census Bureau, 2015-2019 American Community Survey 5-Year Estimates

Gender

Area	Males	Females	Males per 100 Females
City	223,942	240,543	93.1
MSA[1]	649,577	682,734	95.1
U.S.	159,886,919	164,810,876	97.0

Note: (1) Figures cover the Raleigh, NC Metropolitan Statistical Area
Source: U.S. Census Bureau, 2015-2019 American Community Survey 5-Year Estimates

Religious Groups by Family

Area	Catholic	Baptist	Non-Den.	Methodist[2]	Lutheran	LDS[3]	Pentecostal	Presbyterian[4]	Muslim[5]	Judaism
MSA[1]	9.2	12.1	6.0	6.7	0.9	0.9	2.3	2.3	0.9	0.3
U.S.	19.1	9.3	4.0	4.0	2.3	2.0	1.9	1.6	0.8	0.7

Note: Figures are the number of adherents as a percentage of the total population; (1) Figures cover the Raleigh, NC Metropolitan Statistical Area; (2) Methodist/Pietist; (3) Latter Day Saints; (4) Reformed; (5) Figures are estimates
Source: Association of Statisticians of American Religious Bodies, 2010 U.S. Religion Census: Religious Congregations & Membership Study

Religious Groups by Tradition

Area	Catholic	Evangelical Protestant	Mainline Protestant	Other Tradition	Black Protestant	Orthodox
MSA[1]	9.2	19.9	10.1	3.3	1.7	0.2
U.S.	19.1	16.2	7.3	4.3	1.6	0.3

Note: Figures are the number of adherents as a percentage of the total population; (1) Figures cover the Raleigh, NC Metropolitan Statistical Area
Source: Association of Statisticians of American Religious Bodies, 2010 U.S. Religion Census: Religious Congregations & Membership Study

ECONOMY

Gross Metropolitan Product

Area	2017	2018	2019	2020	Rank[2]
MSA[1]	83.2	88.3	92.8	97.8	42

Note: Figures are in billions of dollars; (1) Figures cover the Raleigh, NC Metropolitan Statistical Area; (2) Rank is based on 2018 data and ranges from 1 to 381
Source: U.S. Conference of Mayors, U.S. Metro Economies: GMP & Employment 2018-2020, September 2019

Economic Growth

Area	2015-17 (%)	2018 (%)	2019 (%)	2020 (%)	Rank[2]
MSA[1]	3.1	3.9	3.4	3.3	62
U.S.	1.9	2.9	2.3	2.1	—

Note: Figures are real gross metropolitan product (GMP) growth rates and represent average annual percent change; (1) Figures cover the Raleigh, NC Metropolitan Statistical Area; (2) Rank is based on 2017 2-year average annual percent change and ranges from 1 to 381
Source: U.S. Conference of Mayors, U.S. Metro Economies: GMP & Employment 2018-2020, September 2019

Metropolitan Area Exports

Area	2014	2015	2016	2017	2018	2019	Rank[2]
MSA[1]	2,713.1	2,553.4	2,620.4	2,865.8	3,193.2	3,546.8	70

Note: Figures are in millions of dollars; (1) Figures cover the Raleigh, NC Metropolitan Statistical Area; (2) Rank is based on 2019 data and ranges from 1 to 386
Source: U.S. Department of Commerce, International Trade Administration, Office of Trade and Economic Analysis, Industry and Analysis, Exports by Metropolitan Area, data extracted March 24, 2021

Building Permits

Area	Single-Family			Multi-Family			Total		
	2018	2019	Pct. Chg.	2018	2019	Pct. Chg.	2018	2019	Pct. Chg.
City	1,304	380	-70.9	2,907	827	-71.6	4,211	1,207	-71.3
MSA[1]	11,160	11,142	-0.2	4,790	2,178	-54.5	15,950	13,320	-16.5
U.S.	855,300	862,100	0.7	473,500	523,900	10.6	1,328,800	1,386,000	4.3

Note: (1) Figures cover the Raleigh, NC Metropolitan Statistical Area; Figures represent new, privately-owned housing units authorized (unadjusted data); All permit data are based on estimates with imputation
Source: U.S. Census Bureau, Manufacturing, Mining, and Construction Statistics, Building Permits, 2018, 2019

Bankruptcy Filings

Area	Business Filings			Nonbusiness Filings		
	2019	2020	% Chg.	2019	2020	% Chg.
Wake County	91	75	-17.6	1,314	882	-32.9
U.S.	22,780	21,655	-4.9	752,160	522,808	-30.5

Note: Business filings include Chapter 7, Chapter 9, Chapter 11, Chapter 12, Chapter 13, Chapter 15, and Section 304; Nonbusiness filings include Chapter 7, Chapter 11, and Chapter 13
Source: Administrative Office of the U.S. Courts, Business and Nonbusiness Bankruptcy, County Cases Commenced by Chapter of the Bankruptcy Code, During the 12-Month Period Ending December 31, 2019 and Business and Nonbusiness Bankruptcy, County Cases Commenced by Chapter of the Bankruptcy Code, During the 12-Month Period Ending December 31, 2020

Housing Vacancy Rates

Area	Gross Vacancy Rate[2] (%)			Year-Round Vacancy Rate[3] (%)			Rental Vacancy Rate[4] (%)			Homeowner Vacancy Rate[5] (%)		
	2018	2019	2020	2018	2019	2020	2018	2019	2020	2018	2019	2020
MSA[1]	6.7	6.6	4.6	6.6	6.5	4.5	6.4	7.0	2.3	0.9	0.8	0.4
U.S.	12.3	12.0	10.6	9.7	9.5	8.2	6.9	6.7	6.3	1.5	1.4	1.0

Note: (1) Figures cover the Raleigh, NC Metropolitan Statistical Area; (2) The percentage of the total housing inventory that is vacant; (3) The percentage of the housing inventory (excluding seasonal units) that is year-round vacant; (4) The percentage of rental inventory that is vacant for rent; (5) The percentage of homeowner inventory that is vacant for sale
Source: U.S. Census Bureau, Housing Vacancies and Homeownership Annual Statistics: 2018, 2019, 2020

INCOME

Income

Area	Per Capita ($)	Median Household ($)	Average Household ($)
City	38,494	67,266	94,359
MSA[1]	38,370	75,851	100,551
U.S.	34,103	62,843	88,607

Note: (1) Figures cover the Raleigh, NC Metropolitan Statistical Area
Source: U.S. Census Bureau, 2015-2019 American Community Survey 5-Year Estimates

Household Income Distribution

Area	Percent of Households Earning							
	Under $15,000	$15,000 -$24,999	$25,000 -$34,999	$35,000 -$49,999	$50,000 -$74,999	$75,000 -$99,999	$100,000 -$149,999	$150,000 and up
City	7.3	7.3	8.9	13.2	18.4	13.5	15.8	15.6
MSA[1]	6.5	6.6	7.6	11.7	17.1	13.7	18.2	18.6
U.S.	10.3	8.9	8.9	12.3	17.2	12.7	15.1	14.5

Note: (1) Figures cover the Raleigh, NC Metropolitan Statistical Area
Source: U.S. Census Bureau, 2015-2019 American Community Survey 5-Year Estimates

Poverty Rate

Area	All Ages	Under 18 Years Old	18 to 64 Years Old	65 Years and Over
City	12.6	17.8	11.9	6.7
MSA[1]	9.8	13.4	9.1	6.3
U.S.	13.4	18.5	12.6	9.3

Note: Figures are percentage of people whose income during the past 12 months was below the poverty level;
(1) Figures cover the Raleigh, NC Metropolitan Statistical Area
Source: U.S. Census Bureau, 2015-2019 American Community Survey 5-Year Estimates

CITY FINANCES

City Government Finances

Component	2017 ($000)	2017 ($ per capita)
Total Revenues	835,411	1,852
Total Expenditures	822,681	1,824
Debt Outstanding	1,680,353	3,725
Cash and Securities[1]	0	0

Note: (1) Cash and security holdings of a government at the close of its fiscal year,
including those of its dependent agencies, utilities, and liquor stores.
Source: U.S. Census Bureau, State & Local Government Finances 2017

City Government Revenue by Source

Source	2017 ($000)	2017 ($ per capita)	2017 (%)
General Revenue			
From Federal Government	20,361	45	2.4
From State Government	59,131	131	7.1
From Local Governments	29,555	66	3.5
Taxes			
Property	243,503	540	29.1
Sales and Gross Receipts	93,559	207	11.2
Personal Income	0	0	0.0
Corporate Income	0	0	0.0
Motor Vehicle License	10,732	24	1.3
Other Taxes	8,329	18	1.0
Current Charges	248,266	550	29.7
Liquor Store	0	0	0.0
Utility	111,249	247	13.3
Employee Retirement	0	0	0.0

Source: U.S. Census Bureau, State & Local Government Finances 2017

City Government Expenditures by Function

Function	2017 ($000)	2017 ($ per capita)	2017 (%)
General Direct Expenditures			
Air Transportation	0	0	0.0
Corrections	0	0	0.0
Education	0	0	0.0
Employment Security Administration	0	0	0.0
Financial Administration	4,976	11	0.6
Fire Protection	63,135	140	7.7
General Public Buildings	9,206	20	1.1
Governmental Administration, Other	19,420	43	2.4
Health	0	0	0.0
Highways	52,166	115	6.3
Hospitals	0	0	0.0
Housing and Community Development	20,974	46	2.5
Interest on General Debt	32,030	71	3.9
Judicial and Legal	3,189	7	0.4
Libraries	0	0	0.0
Parking	9,237	20	1.1
Parks and Recreation	92,256	204	11.2
Police Protection	103,922	230	12.6
Public Welfare	1,543	3	0.2
Sewerage	61,739	136	7.5
Solid Waste Management	31,387	69	3.8
Veterans' Services	0	0	0.0
Liquor Store	0	0	0.0
Utility	270,283	599	32.9
Employee Retirement	0	0	0.0

Source: U.S. Census Bureau, State & Local Government Finances 2017

EMPLOYMENT

Labor Force and Employment

Area	Civilian Labor Force			Workers Employed		
	Dec. 2019	Dec. 2020	% Chg.	Dec. 2019	Dec. 2020	% Chg.
City	260,153	256,088	-1.6	252,404	241,439	-4.3
MSA[1]	731,065	715,982	-2.1	709,901	678,982	-4.4
U.S.	164,007,000	160,017,000	-2.4	158,504,000	149,613,000	-5.6

Note: Data is not seasonally adjusted and covers workers 16 years of age and older; (1) Figures cover the Raleigh, NC Metropolitan Statistical Area
Source: Bureau of Labor Statistics, Local Area Unemployment Statistics

Unemployment Rate

Area	2020											
	Jan.	Feb.	Mar.	Apr.	May	Jun.	Jul.	Aug.	Sep.	Oct.	Nov.	Dec.
City	3.6	3.3	3.9	12.4	13.2	8.2	9.1	6.9	6.9	5.9	5.9	5.7
MSA[1]	3.5	3.2	3.7	11.0	11.5	7.0	7.9	6.0	6.1	5.2	5.2	5.2
U.S.	4.0	3.8	4.5	14.4	13.0	11.2	10.5	8.5	7.7	6.6	6.4	6.5

Note: Data is not seasonally adjusted and covers workers 16 years of age and older; (1) Figures cover the Raleigh, NC Metropolitan Statistical Area
Source: Bureau of Labor Statistics, Local Area Unemployment Statistics

Average Wages

Occupation	$/Hr.	Occupation	$/Hr.
Accountants and Auditors	36.20	Maintenance and Repair Workers	21.70
Automotive Mechanics	23.90	Marketing Managers	71.50
Bookkeepers	20.20	Network and Computer Systems Admin.	43.80
Carpenters	20.60	Nurses, Licensed Practical	23.20
Cashiers	11.20	Nurses, Registered	33.70
Computer Programmers	47.70	Nursing Assistants	14.30
Computer Systems Analysts	47.60	Office Clerks, General	17.60
Computer User Support Specialists	27.30	Physical Therapists	40.50
Construction Laborers	16.80	Physicians	131.20
Cooks, Restaurant	15.70	Plumbers, Pipefitters and Steamfitters	21.80
Customer Service Representatives	18.50	Police and Sheriff's Patrol Officers	25.40
Dentists	95.70	Postal Service Mail Carriers	26.00
Electricians	21.80	Real Estate Sales Agents	25.90
Engineers, Electrical	48.20	Retail Salespersons	13.70
Fast Food and Counter Workers	10.00	Sales Representatives, Technical/Scientific	53.80
Financial Managers	68.50	Secretaries, Exc. Legal/Medical/Executive	18.80
First-Line Supervisors of Office Workers	28.10	Security Guards	16.10
General and Operations Managers	70.90	Surgeons	n/a
Hairdressers/Cosmetologists	14.20	Teacher Assistants, Exc. Postsecondary*	11.90
Home Health and Personal Care Aides	11.50	Teachers, Secondary School, Exc. Sp. Ed.*	27.20
Janitors and Cleaners	12.30	Telemarketers	n/a
Landscaping/Groundskeeping Workers	15.40	Truck Drivers, Heavy/Tractor-Trailer	22.00
Lawyers	66.00	Truck Drivers, Light/Delivery Services	17.00
Maids and Housekeeping Cleaners	12.10	Waiters and Waitresses	11.80

Note: Wage data covers the Raleigh, NC Metropolitan Statistical Area; (*) Hourly wages were calculated from annual wage data based on a 40 hour work week; n/a not available.
Source: Bureau of Labor Statistics, Metro Area Occupational Employment & Wage Estimates, May 2020

Employment by Industry

Sector	MSA[1]		U.S.
	Number of Employees	Percent of Total	Percent of Total
Construction, Mining, and Logging	42,300	6.6	5.5
Education and Health Services	80,100	12.5	16.3
Financial Activities	33,200	5.2	6.1
Government	96,100	15.0	15.2
Information	22,200	3.5	1.9
Leisure and Hospitality	57,800	9.0	9.0
Manufacturing	30,100	4.7	8.5
Other Services	25,500	4.0	3.8
Professional and Business Services	131,700	20.5	14.4
Retail Trade	74,800	11.7	10.9
Transportation, Warehousing, and Utilities	21,800	3.4	4.6
Wholesale Trade	25,900	4.0	3.9

Note: Figures are non-farm employment as of December 2020. Figures are not seasonally adjusted and include workers 16 years of age and older; (1) Figures cover the Raleigh, NC Metropolitan Statistical Area
Source: Bureau of Labor Statistics, Current Employment Statistics, Employment, Hours, and Earnings

Employment by Occupation

Occupation Classification	City (%)	MSA[1] (%)	U.S. (%)
Management, Business, Science, and Arts	48.0	48.7	38.5
Natural Resources, Construction, and Maintenance	6.2	7.2	8.9
Production, Transportation, and Material Moving	8.6	8.7	13.2
Sales and Office	22.0	21.3	21.6
Service	15.1	14.0	17.8

Note: Figures cover employed civilians 16 years of age and older; (1) Figures cover the Raleigh, NC Metropolitan Statistical Area
Source: U.S. Census Bureau, 2015-2019 American Community Survey 5-Year Estimates

Occupations with Greatest Projected Employment Growth: 2020 – 2022

Occupation[1]	2020 Employment	2022 Projected Employment	Numeric Employment Change	Percent Employment Change
Laborers and Freight, Stock, and Material Movers, Hand	90,950	94,250	3,300	3.6
Stockers and Order Fillers	99,690	102,690	3,000	3.0
Software Developers and Software Quality Assurance Analysts and Testers	74,740	76,850	2,110	2.8
Registered Nurses	87,970	89,970	2,000	2.3
Project Management Specialists and Business Operations Specialists, All Other	62,540	63,660	1,120	1.8
Computer Systems Analysts (SOC 2018)	40,350	41,450	1,100	2.7
Insurance Sales Agents	13,950	14,920	970	7.0
Industrial Truck and Tractor Operators	22,480	23,360	880	3.9
Loan Officers	12,610	13,430	820	6.5
Customer Service Representatives	80,790	81,600	810	1.0

Note: Projections cover North Carolina; (1) Sorted by numeric employment change
Source: www.projectionscentral.com, State Occupational Projections, 2020–2022 Short-Term Projections

Fastest-Growing Occupations: 2020 – 2022

Occupation[1]	2020 Employment	2022 Projected Employment	Numeric Employment Change	Percent Employment Change
Statisticians	1,420	1,540	120	8.5
Operations Research Analysts	2,490	2,700	210	8.4
Butchers and Meat Cutters	2,650	2,860	210	7.9
Insurance Sales Agents	13,950	14,920	970	7.0
Loan Interviewers and Clerks	6,000	6,420	420	7.0
Brokerage Clerks	1,590	1,700	110	6.9
Veterinary Assistants and Laboratory Animal Caretakers	3,590	3,830	240	6.7
Personal Financial Advisors	8,760	9,330	570	6.5
Loan Officers	12,610	13,430	820	6.5
Veterinary Technologists and Technicians	3,040	3,230	190	6.3

Note: Projections cover North Carolina; (1) Sorted by percent employment change and excludes occupations with numeric employment change less than 50
Source: www.projectionscentral.com, State Occupational Projections, 2020–2022 Short-Term Projections

TAXES

State Corporate Income Tax Rates

State	Tax Rate (%)	Income Brackets ($)	Num. of Brackets	Financial Institution Tax Rate (%)[a]	Federal Income Tax Ded.
North Carolina	2.5	Flat rate	1	2.5	No

Note: Tax rates as of January 1, 2021; (a) Rates listed are the corporate income tax rate applied to financial institutions or excise taxes based on income. Some states have other taxes based upon the value of deposits or shares.
Source: Federation of Tax Administrators, State Corporate Income Tax Rates, January 1, 2021

State Individual Income Tax Rates

State	Tax Rate (%)	Income Brackets ($)	Personal Exemptions ($)			Standard Ded. ($)	
			Single	Married	Depend.	Single	Married
North Carolina	5.25	Flat rate	None	None	None	10,750	21,500

Note: Tax rates as of January 1, 2021; Local- and county-level taxes are not included; Federal income tax is not deductible on state income tax returns
Source: Federation of Tax Administrators, State Individual Income Tax Rates, January 1, 2021

Various State Sales and Excise Tax Rates

State	State Sales Tax (%)	Gasoline[1] (¢/gal.)	Cigarette[2] ($/pack)	Spirits[3] ($/gal.)	Wine[4] ($/gal.)	Beer[5] ($/gal.)	Recreational Marijuana (%)
North Carolina	4.75	36.35	0.45	14.58	1	0.62	Not legal

Note: All tax rates as of January 1, 2021; (1) The American Petroleum Institute has developed a methodology for determining the average tax rate on a gallon of fuel. Rates may include any of the following: excise taxes, environmental fees, storage tank fees, other fees or taxes, general sales tax, and local taxes; (2) The federal excise tax of $1.0066 per pack and local taxes are not included; (3) Rates are those applicable to off-premise sales of 40% alcohol by volume (a.b.v.) distilled spirits in 750ml containers. Local excise taxes are excluded; (4) Rates are those applicable to off-premise sales of 11% a.b.v. non-carbonated wine in 750ml containers; (5) Rates are those applicable to off-premise sales of 4.7% a.b.v. beer in 12 ounce containers.
Source: Tax Foundation, 2021 Facts & Figures: How Does Your State Compare?

State Business Tax Climate Index Rankings

State	Overall Rank	Corporate Tax Rank	Individual Income Tax Rank	Sales Tax Rank	Property Tax Rank	Unemployment Insurance Tax Rank
North Carolina	10	4	16	22	26	10

Note: The index is a measure of how each state's tax laws affect economic performance. The lower the rank, the more favorable a state's tax system is for business. States without a given tax are given a ranking of 1. The scores/rankings for the District of Columbia do not affect other states. The 2021 index represents the tax climate as of July 1, 2020.
Source: Tax Foundation, State Business Tax Climate Index 2021

TRANSPORTATION

Means of Transportation to Work

Area	Car/Truck/Van Drove Alone	Car/Truck/Van Car-pooled	Public Transportation Bus	Public Transportation Subway	Public Transportation Railroad	Bicycle	Walked	Other Means	Worked at Home
City	78.2	8.0	1.9	0.1	0.0	0.4	1.6	1.3	8.5
MSA[1]	79.7	8.3	0.8	0.0	0.0	0.2	1.1	0.9	8.9
U.S.	76.3	9.0	2.4	1.9	0.6	0.5	2.7	1.4	5.2

Note: Figures are percentages and cover workers 16 years of age and older; (1) Figures cover the Raleigh, NC Metropolitan Statistical Area
Source: U.S. Census Bureau, 2015-2019 American Community Survey 5-Year Estimates

Travel Time to Work

Area	Less Than 10 Minutes	10 to 19 Minutes	20 to 29 Minutes	30 to 44 Minutes	45 to 59 Minutes	60 to 89 Minutes	90 Minutes or More
City	9.8	33.0	25.8	21.0	5.7	3.1	1.7
MSA[1]	8.9	27.5	24.4	23.9	8.7	4.8	1.9
U.S.	12.2	28.4	20.8	20.8	8.3	6.4	2.9

Note: Note: Figures are percentages and include workers 16 years old and over; (1) Figures cover the Raleigh, NC Metropolitan Statistical Area
Source: U.S. Census Bureau, 2015-2019 American Community Survey 5-Year Estimates

Key Congestion Measures

Measure	1982	1992	2002	2012	2017
Annual Hours of Delay, Total (000)	1,304	6,421	16,115	22,446	27,243
Annual Hours of Delay, Per Auto Commuter	7	20	31	35	42
Annual Congestion Cost, Total (million $)	10	67	216	397	498
Annual Congestion Cost, Per Auto Commuter ($)	85	289	565	616	725

Note: Covers the Raleigh NC urban area
Source: Texas A&M Transportation Institute, 2019 Urban Mobility Report

Freeway Travel Time Index

Measure	1982	1987	1992	1997	2002	2007	2012	2017
Urban Area Index[1]	1.03	1.07	1.10	1.13	1.16	1.16	1.16	1.17
Urban Area Rank[1,2]	76	55	59	62	54	63	60	49

Note: Freeway Travel Time Index—the ratio of travel time in the peak period to the travel time at free-flow conditions. For example, a value of 1.30 indicates a 20-minute free-flow trip takes 26 minutes in the peak (20 minutes x 1.30 = 26 minutes); (1) Covers the Raleigh NC urban area; (2) Rank is based on 101 larger urban areas (#1 = highest travel time index)
Source: Texas A&M Transportation Institute, 2019 Urban Mobility Report

Public Transportation

Agency Name / Mode of Transportation	Vehicles Operated in Maximum Service[1]	Annual Unlinked Passenger Trips[2] (in thous.)	Annual Passenger Miles[3] (in thous.)
Capital Area Transit (CAT)			
Bus (directly operated)	71	5,271.4	19,651.5
Demand Response Taxi (purchased transportation)	224	493.5	3,444.3

Note: (1) Number of revenue vehicles operated by the given mode and type of service to meet the annual maximum service requirement. This is the revenue vehicle count during the peak season of the year; on the week and day that maximum service is provided. Vehicles operated in maximum service (VOMS) exclude atypical days and one-time special events; (2) Number of passengers who boarded public transportation vehicles. Passengers are counted each time they board a vehicle no matter how many vehicles they use to travel from their origin to their destination. (3) Sum of the distances ridden by all passengers during the entire fiscal year.
Source: Federal Transit Administration, National Transit Database, 2019

Air Transportation

Airport Name and Code / Type of Service	Passenger Airlines[1]	Passenger Enplanements	Freight Carriers[2]	Freight (lbs)
Raleigh-Durham International (RDU)				
Domestic service (U.S. carriers - 2020)	30	2,313,623	15	88,431,187
International service (U.S. carriers - 2019)	8	146,636	3	2,725,471

Note: (1) Includes all U.S.-based major, minor and commuter airlines that carried at least one passenger during the year; (2) Includes all U.S.-based airlines and freight carriers that transported at least one pound of freight during the year.
Source: Bureau of Transportation Statistics, The Intermodal Transportation Database, Air Carriers: T-100 Domestic Market (U.S. Carriers), 2020; Bureau of Transportation Statistics, The Intermodal Transportation Database, Air Carriers: T-100 International Market (U.S. Carriers), 2019

BUSINESSES

Major Business Headquarters

Company Name	Industry	Rankings	
		Fortune[1]	Forbes[2]
No companies listed	-	-	-

Note: (1) Companies that produce a 10-K are ranked 1 to 500 based on 2019 revenue; (2) All private companies with at least $2 billion in annual revenue through the end of their most current fiscal year are ranked 1 to 219; companies listed are headquartered in the city; dashes indicate no ranking
Source: Fortune, "Fortune 500," June/July 2020; Forbes, "America's Largest Private Companies," 2020

Fastest-Growing Businesses

According to *Inc.*, Raleigh is home to two of America's 500 fastest-growing private companies: **Pendo** (#26); **AURA Technologies** (#125). Criteria: must be an independent, privately-held, for-profit, U.S. corporation, proprietorship or partnership as of December 31, 2019; revenues must be at least $100,000 in 2016 and $2 million in 2019; must have four-year operating/sales history. *Inc., "America's 500 Fastest-Growing Private Companies," 2020*

According to *Fortune*, Raleigh is home to one of the 100 fastest-growing companies in the world: **PRA Health Sciences** (#65). Companies were ranked by their revenue growth rate; their EPS growth rate; and their three-year annualized total return to investors for the period ending June 30, 2020. Criteria for inclusion: a company, foreign or domestic, must trade on a major U.S. stock exchange; must file quarterly reports with the SEC; must have a minimum market capitalization of $250 million; must have a stock price of at least $5 on June 30, 2020; must have been trading continuously since June 30, 2017; must have revenue and net income for the four quarters ended on or before April 30, 2020, of at least $50 million and $10 million, respectively; and must have posted a compound annual growth in revenue and earnings per share of at least 15% annually over the three years ending on or before April 30, 2020. Real estate investment trusts, limited-liability companies, limited parterships, business development companies, closed-end investment firms, companies about to be acquired, and companies that lost money in the quarter ending April 30, 2020 were excluded. *Fortune, "100 Fastest-Growing Companies," 2020*

According to Deloitte, Raleigh is home to two of North America's 500 fastest-growing high-technology companies: **Pendo** (#74); **BioDelivery Sciences International Inc.** (#198). Companies are ranked by percentage growth in revenue over a four-year period. Criteria for inclusion: company must be headquartered within North America; must own proprietary intellectual property or technology that is sold to customers in products that contributes to a significant portion of the company's operating revenue; must have been in business for a minumum of four years with 2016 operating revenues of at least $50,000 USD/CD and 2019 operating revenues of at least $5 million USD/CD. *Deloitte, 2020 Technology Fast 500*[TM]

Minority Business Opportunity

Raleigh is home to one company which is on the *Black Enterprise* Industrial/Service list (100 largest companies based on gross sales): **Brodie Contractors** (#77). Criteria: operational in previous calendar year; at least 51% black-owned and manufactures/owns the product it sells or provides industrial or consumer services. Brokerages, real estate firms and firms that provide professional services are not eligible. *Black Enterprise, B.E. 100s, 2019*

Living Environment

COST OF LIVING

Cost of Living Index

Composite Index	Groceries	Housing	Utilities	Trans-portation	Health Care	Misc. Goods/Services
97.1	91.1	92.5	97.7	93.7	104.8	102.8

Note: The Cost of Living Index measures regional differences in the cost of consumer goods and services, excluding taxes and non-consumer expenditures, for professional and managerial households in the top income quintile. It is based on more than 50,000 prices covering almost 60 different items for which prices are collected three times a year by chambers of commerce, economic development organizations or university applied economic centers in each participating urban area. The numbers shown should be read as a percentage above or below the national average of 100. For example, a value of 115.4 in the groceries column indicates that grocery prices are 15.4% higher than the national average. Small differences in the index numbers should not be interpreted as significant; Figures cover the Raleigh NC urban area.
Source: The Council for Community and Economic Research, Cost of Living Index, 2020

Grocery Prices

Area[1]	T-Bone Steak ($/pound)	Frying Chicken ($/pound)	Whole Milk ($/half gal.)	Eggs ($/dozen)	Orange Juice ($/64 oz.)	Coffee ($/11.5 oz.)
City[2]	10.15	0.97	1.61	1.19	3.79	3.83
Avg.	11.78	1.39	2.05	1.47	3.57	4.34
Min.	8.03	0.94	1.03	0.74	2.94	3.02
Max.	15.86	2.65	4.31	3.77	5.44	8.69

*Note: (1) Values for the local area are compared with the average, minimum and maximum values for all 284 areas in the Cost of Living Index; (2) Figures cover the Raleigh NC urban area; **T-Bone Steak** (price per pound); **Frying Chicken** (price per pound, whole fryer); **Whole Milk** (half gallon carton); **Eggs** (price per dozen, Grade A, large); **Orange Juice** (64 oz. Tropicana or Florida Natural); **Coffee** (11.5 oz. can, vacuum-packed, Maxwell House, Hills Bros, or Folgers).*
Source: The Council for Community and Economic Research, Cost of Living Index, 2020

Housing and Utility Costs

Area[1]	New Home Price ($)	Apartment Rent ($/month)	All Electric ($/month)	Part Electric ($/month)	Other Energy ($/month)	Telephone ($/month)
City[2]	308,897	1,309	-	103.82	58.98	179.90
Avg.	368,594	1,168	170.86	100.47	65.28	184.30
Min.	190,567	502	91.58	31.42	26.08	169.60
Max.	2,227,806	4,738	470.38	280.31	280.06	206.50

*Note: (1) Values for the local area are compared with the average, minimum and maximum values for all 284 areas in the Cost of Living Index; (2) Figures cover the Raleigh NC urban area; **New Home Price** (2,400 sf living area, 8,000 sf lot, in urban area with full utilities); **Apartment Rent** (950 sf 2 bedroom/1.5 or 2 bath, unfurnished, excluding all utilities except water); **All Electric** (average monthly cost for an all-electric home); **Part Electric** (average monthly cost for a part-electric home); **Other Energy** (average monthly cost for natural gas, fuel oil, coal, wood, and any other forms of energy except electricity); **Telephone** (price includes the base monthly rate plus taxes and fees for three lines of mobile phone service).*
Source: The Council for Community and Economic Research, Cost of Living Index, 2020

Health Care, Transportation, and Other Costs

Area[1]	Doctor ($/visit)	Dentist ($/visit)	Optometrist ($/visit)	Gasoline ($/gallon)	Beauty Salon ($/visit)	Men's Shirt ($)
City[2]	145.22	99.00	98.89	2.27	48.42	30.33
Avg.	115.44	99.32	108.10	2.21	39.27	31.37
Min.	36.68	59.00	51.36	1.71	19.00	11.00
Max.	219.00	153.10	250.97	3.46	82.05	58.33

*Note: (1) Values for the local area are compared with the average, minimum and maximum values for all 284 areas in the Cost of Living Index; (2) Figures cover the Raleigh NC urban area; **Doctor** (general practitioners routine exam of an established patient); **Dentist** (adult teeth cleaning and periodic oral examination); **Optometrist** (full vision eye exam for established adult patient); **Gasoline** (one gallon regular unleaded, national brand, including all taxes, cash price at self-service pump if available); **Beauty Salon** (woman's shampoo, trim, and blow-dry); **Men's Shirt** (cotton/polyester dress shirt, pinpoint weave, long sleeves).*
Source: The Council for Community and Economic Research, Cost of Living Index, 2020

HOUSING

Homeownership Rate

Area	2012 (%)	2013 (%)	2014 (%)	2015 (%)	2016 (%)	2017 (%)	2018 (%)	2019 (%)	2020 (%)
MSA[1]	67.7	65.5	65.5	67.4	65.9	68.2	64.9	63.0	68.2
U.S.	65.4	65.1	64.5	63.7	63.4	63.9	64.4	64.6	66.6

Note: (1) Figures cover the Raleigh, NC Metropolitan Statistical Area
Source: U.S. Census Bureau, Housing Vacancies and Homeownership Annual Statistics: 2012-2020

House Price Index (HPI)

Area	National Ranking[2]	Quarterly Change (%)	One-Year Change (%)	Five-Year Change (%)	Since 1991Q1 (%)
MSA[1]	159	1.84	5.67	34.46	180.65
U.S.[3]	–	3.81	10.77	38.99	205.12

Note: The HPI is a weighted repeat sales index. It measures average price changes in repeat sales or refinancings on the same properties. This information is obtained by reviewing repeat mortgage transactions on single-family properties whose mortgages have been purchased or securitized by Fannie Mae or Freddie Mac since January 1975; (1) Figures cover the Raleigh, NC Metropolitan Statistical Area; (2) Rankings are based on annual percentage change for all metro areas containing at least 15,000 transactions over the last 10 years and ranges from 1 to 253; (3) figures based on a weighted average of Census Division estimates using a seasonally adjusted, purchase-only index; all figures are for the period ending December 31, 2020
Source: Federal Housing Finance Agency, Change in Metropolitan Area House Price Indexes, April 7, 2021

Median Single-Family Home Prices

Area	2018	2019	2020[p]	Percent Change 2019 to 2020
MSA[1]	283.6	291.5	325.2	11.6
U.S. Average	261.6	274.6	299.9	9.2

Note: Figures are median sales prices of existing single-family homes in thousands of dollars; (p) preliminary; (1) Figures cover the Raleigh, NC Metropolitan Statistical Area
Source: National Association of Realtors, Median Sales Price of Existing Single-Family Homes for Metropolitan Areas, 4th Quarter 2020

Qualifying Income Based on Median Sales Price of Existing Single-Family Homes

Area	With 5% Down ($)	With 10% Down ($)	With 20% Down ($)
MSA[1]	64,422	61,031	54,250
U.S. Average	59,266	56,147	49,908

Note: Figures are preliminary; Qualifying income is based on a mortgage rate of 2.81%. Monthly principal and interest payment is limited to 25% of income; (1) Figures cover the Raleigh, NC Metropolitan Statistical Area
Source: National Association of Realtors, Qualifying Income Based on Median Sales Price of Existing Single-Family Homes for Metropolitan Areas, 4th Quarter 2020

Home Value Distribution

Area	Under $50,000	$50,000 -$99,999	$100,000 -$149,999	$150,000 -$199,999	$200,000 -$299,999	$300,000 -$499,999	$500,000 -$999,999	$1,000,000 or more
City	2.0	2.7	11.4	19.4	27.1	24.8	10.8	1.8
MSA[1]	3.5	5.0	11.9	15.5	25.7	27.6	9.6	1.3
U.S.	6.9	12.0	13.3	14.0	19.6	19.3	11.4	3.4

Note: Figures are percentages and cover owner-occupied housing units; (1) Figures cover the Raleigh, NC Metropolitan Statistical Area
Source: U.S. Census Bureau, 2015-2019 American Community Survey 5-Year Estimates

Year Housing Structure Built

Area	2010 or Later	2000 -2009	1990 -1999	1980 -1989	1970 -1979	1960 -1969	1950 -1959	1940 -1949	Before 1940	Median Year
City	10.7	25.0	19.0	17.3	10.6	7.7	4.5	2.1	3.1	1992
MSA[1]	12.7	25.9	23.0	15.2	9.3	5.9	3.7	1.6	2.8	1995
U.S.	5.2	14.0	13.9	13.4	15.2	10.6	10.3	4.9	12.6	1978

Note: Figures are percentages except for Median Year; Note: (1) Figures cover the Raleigh, NC Metropolitan Statistical Area
Source: U.S. Census Bureau, 2015-2019 American Community Survey 5-Year Estimates

Gross Monthly Rent

Area	Under $500	$500 -$999	$1,000 -$1,499	$1,500 -$1,999	$2,000 -$2,499	$2,500 -$2,999	$3,000 and up	Median ($)
City	3.9	31.6	47.0	13.2	3.0	0.5	0.8	1,121
MSA[1]	4.9	32.8	43.7	13.4	3.4	0.8	1.0	1,113
U.S.	9.4	36.2	30.0	14.0	5.6	2.4	2.4	1,062

Note: Figures are percentages except for Median; Gross rent is the contract rent plus the estimated average monthly cost of utilities (electricity, gas, and water and sewer) and fuels (oil, coal, kerosene, wood, etc.) if these are paid by the renter (or paid for the renter by someone else); (1) Figures cover the Raleigh, NC Metropolitan Statistical Area
Source: U.S. Census Bureau, 2015-2019 American Community Survey 5-Year Estimates

HEALTH

Health Risk Factors

Category	MSA[1] (%)	U.S. (%)
Adults aged 18–64 who have any kind of health care coverage	n/a	87.3
Adults who reported being in good or better health	n/a	82.4
Adults who have been told they have high blood cholesterol	n/a	33.0
Adults who have been told they have high blood pressure	n/a	32.3
Adults who are current smokers	n/a	17.1
Adults who currently use E-cigarettes	n/a	4.6
Adults who currently use chewing tobacco, snuff, or snus	n/a	4.0
Adults who are heavy drinkers[2]	n/a	6.3
Adults who are binge drinkers[3]	n/a	17.4
Adults who are overweight (BMI 25.0 - 29.9)	n/a	35.3
Adults who are obese (BMI 30.0 - 99.8)	n/a	31.3
Adults who participated in any physical activities in the past month	n/a	74.4
Adults who always or nearly always wears a seat belt	n/a	94.3

Note: n/a not available; (1) Figures cover the Raleigh, NC Metropolitan Statistical Area; (2) Heavy drinkers are classified as adult men having more than 14 drinks per week and adult women having more than 7 drinks per week; (3) Binge drinkers are classified as males having five or more drinks on one occasion or females having four or more drinks on one occasion
Source: Centers for Disease Control and Prevention, Behaviorial Risk Factor Surveillance System, SMART: Selected Metropolitan Area Risk Trends, 2017

Acute and Chronic Health Conditions

Category	MSA[1] (%)	U.S. (%)
Adults who have ever been told they had a heart attack	n/a	4.2
Adults who have ever been told they have angina or coronary heart disease	n/a	3.9
Adults who have ever been told they had a stroke	n/a	3.0
Adults who have ever been told they have asthma	n/a	14.2
Adults who have ever been told they have arthritis	n/a	24.9
Adults who have ever been told they have diabetes[2]	n/a	10.5
Adults who have ever been told they had skin cancer	n/a	6.2
Adults who have ever been told they had any other types of cancer	n/a	7.1
Adults who have ever been told they have COPD	n/a	6.5
Adults who have ever been told they have kidney disease	n/a	3.0
Adults who have ever been told they have a form of depression	n/a	20.5

Note: n/a not available; (1) Figures cover the Raleigh, NC Metropolitan Statistical Area; (2) Figures do not include pregnancy-related, borderline, or pre-diabetes
Source: Centers for Disease Control and Prevention, Behaviorial Risk Factor Surveillance System, SMART: Selected Metropolitan Area Risk Trends, 2017

Health Screening and Vaccination Rates

Category	MSA[1] (%)	U.S. (%)
Adults aged 65+ who have had flu shot within the past year	n/a	60.7
Adults aged 65+ who have ever had a pneumonia vaccination	n/a	75.4
Adults who have ever been tested for HIV	n/a	36.1
Adults who have ever had the shingles or zoster vaccine?	n/a	28.9
Adults who have had their blood cholesterol checked within the last five years	n/a	85.9

Note: n/a not available; (1) Figures cover the Raleigh, NC Metropolitan Statistical Area.
Source: Centers for Disease Control and Prevention, Behaviorial Risk Factor Surveillance System, SMART: Selected Metropolitan Area Risk Trends, 2017

Disability Status

Category	MSA[1] (%)	U.S. (%)
Adults who reported being deaf	n/a	6.7
Are you blind or have serious difficulty seeing, even when wearing glasses?	n/a	4.5
Are you limited in any way in any of your usual activities due of arthritis?	n/a	12.9
Do you have difficulty doing errands alone?	n/a	6.8
Do you have difficulty dressing or bathing?	n/a	3.6
Do you have serious difficulty concentrating/remembering/making decisions?	n/a	10.7
Do you have serious difficulty walking or climbing stairs?	n/a	13.6

Note: n/a not available; (1) Figures cover the Raleigh, NC Metropolitan Statistical Area.
Source: Centers for Disease Control and Prevention, Behaviorial Risk Factor Surveillance System, SMART: Selected Metropolitan Area Risk Trends, 2017

Mortality Rates for the Top 10 Causes of Death in the U.S.

ICD-10[a] Sub-Chapter	ICD-10[a] Code	Age-Adjusted Mortality Rate[1] per 100,000 population	
		County[2]	U.S.
Malignant neoplasms	C00-C97	132.1	149.2
Ischaemic heart diseases	I20-I25	55.4	90.5
Other forms of heart disease	I30-I51	49.1	52.2
Chronic lower respiratory diseases	J40-J47	26.8	39.6
Other degenerative diseases of the nervous system	G30-G31	36.3	37.6
Cerebrovascular diseases	I60-I69	42.6	37.2
Other external causes of accidental injury	W00-X59	28.0	36.1
Organic, including symptomatic, mental disorders	F01-F09	40.6	29.4
Hypertensive diseases	I10-I15	15.9	24.1
Diabetes mellitus	E10-E14	16.0	21.5

Note: (a) ICD-10 = International Classification of Diseases 10th Revision; (1) Mortality rates are a three-year average covering 2017-2019; (2) Figures cover Wake County.
Source: Centers for Disease Control and Prevention, National Center for Health Statistics. Underlying Cause of Death 1999-2019 on CDC WONDER Online Database

Mortality Rates for Selected Causes of Death

ICD-10[a] Sub-Chapter	ICD-10[a] Code	Age-Adjusted Mortality Rate[1] per 100,000 population	
		County[2]	U.S.
Assault	X85-Y09	2.4	6.0
Diseases of the liver	K70-K76	9.1	14.4
Human immunodeficiency virus (HIV) disease	B20-B24	1.1	1.5
Influenza and pneumonia	J09-J18	9.7	13.8
Intentional self-harm	X60-X84	9.6	14.1
Malnutrition	E40-E46	2.1	2.3
Obesity and other hyperalimentation	E65-E68	1.4	2.1
Renal failure	N17-N19	12.7	12.6
Transport accidents	V01-V99	7.1	12.3
Viral hepatitis	B15-B19	0.6	1.2

Note: (a) ICD-10 = International Classification of Diseases 10th Revision; (1) Mortality rates are a three-year average covering 2017-2019; (2) Figures cover Wake County; Data are suppressed when the data meet the criteria for confidentiality constraints; Mortality rates are flagged as unreliable when the rate would be calculated with a numerator of 20 or less.
Source: Centers for Disease Control and Prevention, National Center for Health Statistics. Underlying Cause of Death 1999-2019 on CDC WONDER Online Database

Health Insurance Coverage

Area	With Health Insurance	With Private Health Insurance	With Public Health Insurance	Without Health Insurance	Population Under Age 19 Without Health Insurance
City	89.8	74.2	24.5	10.2	5.4
MSA[1]	91.0	75.9	24.8	9.0	4.6
U.S.	91.2	67.9	35.1	8.8	5.1

Note: Figures are percentages that cover the civilian noninstitutionalized population; (1) Figures cover the Raleigh, NC Metropolitan Statistical Area
Source: U.S. Census Bureau, 2015-2019 American Community Survey 5-Year Estimates

Number of Medical Professionals

Area	MDs[3]	DOs[3,4]	Dentists	Podiatrists	Chiropractors	Optometrists
County[1] (number)	3,022	124	796	39	295	185
County[1] (rate[2])	276.9	11.4	71.6	3.5	26.5	16.6
U.S. (rate[2])	282.9	22.7	71.2	6.2	28.1	16.9

37183
Note: Data as of 2019 unless noted; (1) Data covers Wake County; (2) Rate per 100,000 population; (3) Data as of 2018 and includes all active, non-federal physicians; (4) Doctor of Osteopathic Medicine
Source: U.S. Department of Health and Human Services, Health Resources and Services Administration, Bureau of Health Professions, Area Resource File (ARF) 2019-2020

EDUCATION

Public School District Statistics

District Name	Schls	Pupils	Pupil/ Teacher Ratio	Minority Pupils[1] (%)	Free Lunch Eligible[2] (%)	IEP[3] (%)
Wake County Schools	187	161,784	15.8	54.2	27.7	12.4

Note: Table includes school districts with 2,000 or more students; (1) Percentage of students that are not non-Hispanic white; (2) Percentage of students that are eligible for the free lunch program; (3) Percentage of students that have an Individualized Education Program.
Source: U.S. Department of Education, National Center for Education Statistics, Common Core of Data, Local Education Agency (School District) Universe Survey: School Year 2018-2019; U.S. Department of Education, National Center for Education Statistics, Common Core of Data, Public Elementary/Secondary School Universe Survey: School Year 2018-2019

Best High Schools

According to *U.S. News*, Raleigh is home to two of the top 500 high schools in the U.S.: **Raleigh Charter High School** (#116); **Wake NCSU STEM Early College High School** (#226). Nearly 18,000 public, magnet and charter schools were ranked based on their performance on state assessments and how well they prepare students for college. *U.S. News & World Report, "Best High Schools 2020"*

Highest Level of Education

Area	Less than H.S.	H.S. Diploma	Some College, No Deg.	Associate Degree	Bachelor's Degree	Master's Degree	Prof. School Degree	Doctorate Degree
City	8.2	15.6	17.8	7.5	32.4	13.1	3.1	2.3
MSA[1]	8.3	17.7	18.2	9.0	29.6	12.6	2.4	2.2
U.S.	12.0	27.0	20.4	8.5	19.8	8.8	2.1	1.4

Note: Figures cover persons age 25 and over; (1) Figures cover the Raleigh, NC Metropolitan Statistical Area
Source: U.S. Census Bureau, 2015-2019 American Community Survey 5-Year Estimates

Educational Attainment by Race

Area	High School Graduate or Higher (%)					Bachelor's Degree or Higher (%)				
	Total	White	Black	Asian	Hisp.[2]	Total	White	Black	Asian	Hisp.[2]
City	91.8	95.9	89.7	86.8	61.2	50.9	61.8	31.0	60.0	21.9
MSA[1]	91.7	94.1	89.0	92.4	62.5	46.8	50.5	30.8	73.2	20.1
U.S.	88.0	89.9	86.0	87.1	68.7	32.1	33.5	21.6	54.3	16.4

Note: Figures shown cover persons 25 years old and over; (1) Figures cover the Raleigh, NC Metropolitan Statistical Area; (2) People of Hispanic origin can be of any race
Source: U.S. Census Bureau, 2015-2019 American Community Survey 5-Year Estimates

School Enrollment by Grade and Control

Area	Preschool (%)		Kindergarten (%)		Grades 1 - 4 (%)		Grades 5 - 8 (%)		Grades 9 - 12 (%)	
	Public	Private	Public	Private	Public	Private	Public	Private	Public	Private
City	43.5	56.5	89.3	10.7	90.6	9.4	89.2	10.8	90.6	9.4
MSA[1]	38.9	61.1	88.2	11.8	89.0	11.0	87.8	12.2	89.9	10.1
U.S.	59.1	40.9	87.6	12.4	89.5	10.5	89.4	10.6	90.1	9.9

Note: Figures shown cover persons 3 years old and over; (1) Figures cover the Raleigh, NC Metropolitan Statistical Area
Source: U.S. Census Bureau, 2015-2019 American Community Survey 5-Year Estimates

Higher Education

Four-Year Colleges			Two-Year Colleges			Medical Schools[1]	Law Schools[2]	Voc/ Tech[3]
Public	Private Non-profit	Private For-profit	Public	Private Non-profit	Private For-profit			
1	4	1	1	0	1	0	1	5

Note: Figures cover institutions located within the city limits and include main campuses only; (1) includes schools accredited by the Liaison Committee on Medical Education and the American Osteopathic Association's Commission on Osteopathic College Accreditation; (2) includes ABA-accredited schools, schools with provisional ABA accreditation, and state accredited schools; (3) includes all schools with programs that are less than 2 years.
Source: National Center for Education Statistics, Integrated Postsecondary Education System (IPEDS), 2019-20; Wikipedia, List of Medical Schools in the United States, accessed April 2, 2021; Wikipedia, List of Law Schools in the United States, accessed April 2, 2021

According to *U.S. News & World Report*, the Raleigh, NC metro area is home to one of the top 200 national universities in the U.S.: **North Carolina State University** (#80 tie). The indicators used to capture academic quality fall into a number of categories: assessment by administrators at peer institutions; retention of students; faculty resources; student selectivity; financial resources; alumni giving; high school counselor ratings of colleges; and graduation rate. *U.S. News & World Report, "America's Best Colleges 2021"*

According to *U.S. News & World Report,* the Raleigh, NC metro area is home to one of the top 75 business schools in the U.S.: **North Carolina State University (Poole)** (#64 tie). The rankings are based on a weighted average of the following nine measures: quality assessment; peer assessment; recruiter assessment; placement success; mean starting salary and bonus; student selectivity; mean GMAT and GRE scores; mean undergraduate GPA; and acceptance rate. *U.S. News & World Report, "America's Best Graduate Schools, Business, 2022"*

EMPLOYERS

Major Employers

Company Name	Industry
Cisco Systems	Software
City of Raleigh	Municipal government
Duke Energy	Electric services
Fidelity Investments	Financial services
GlaxoSmithKline	Healthcare
IBM	Technology
Lenovo	Technology
N.C. DHHS	Government
North Carolina State University	Education
Rex Healthcare	Healthcare
RTI International	Research & development
SAS Institute	Data management
State of North Carolina	State government
Wake County Government	Government
Wake County Public School System	Education
Wake Technical Community College	Education
WakeMed Health & Hospitals	Education
Wells Fargo	Financial services

Note: Companies shown are located within the Raleigh, NC Metropolitan Statistical Area.
Source: Hoovers.com; Wikipedia

Best Companies to Work For

Kimley-Horn; Red Hat, headquartered in Raleigh, are among "The 100 Best Companies to Work For." To pick the best companies, *Fortune* partnered with the Great Place to Work Institute. Two-thirds of a company's score is based on the results of the Institute's Trust Index survey, which is sent to a random sample of employees from each company. The questions related to attitudes about management's credibility, job satisfaction, and camaraderie. The other third of the scoring is based on the company's responses to the Institute's Culture Audit, which includes detailed questions about pay and benefit programs, and a series of open-ended questions about hiring practices, internal communication, training, recognition programs, and diversity efforts. Any company that is at least five years old with more than 1,000 U.S. employees is eligible. *Fortune, "The 100 Best Companies to Work For," 2020*

PUBLIC SAFETY

Crime Rate

Area	All Crimes	Violent Crimes				Property Crimes		
		Murder	Rape[3]	Robbery	Aggrav. Assault	Burglary	Larceny -Theft	Motor Vehicle Theft
City	2,038.8	1.0	34.3	67.4	153.0	251.1	1,375.4	156.5
Suburbs[1]	1,325.7	2.1	14.8	21.7	90.6	209.5	912.4	74.6
Metro[2]	1,570.3	1.7	21.5	37.4	112.0	223.8	1,071.2	102.7
U.S.	2,489.3	5.0	42.6	81.6	250.2	340.5	1,549.5	219.9

Note: Figures are crimes per 100,000 population; (1) All areas within the metro area that are located outside the city limits; (2) Figures cover the Raleigh, NC Metropolitan Statistical Area; (3) All figures shown were reported using the revised Uniform Crime Reporting (UCR) definition of rape.
Source: FBI Uniform Crime Reports, 2019

Hate Crimes

Area	Number of Quarters Reported	Number of Incidents per Bias Motivation					
		Race/Ethnicity/ Ancestry	Religion	Sexual Orientation	Disability	Gender	Gender Identity
City	4	7	2	5	0	0	0
U.S.	4	3,963	1,521	1,195	157	69	198

Source: Federal Bureau of Investigation, Hate Crime Statistics 2019

Identity Theft Consumer Reports

Area	Reports	Reports per 100,000 Population	Rank[2]
MSA[1]	5,036	362	90
U.S.	1,387,615	423	-

Note: (1) Figures cover the Raleigh, NC Metropolitan Statistical Area; (2) Rank ranges from 1 to 391 where 1 indicates greatest number of identity theft reports per 100,000 population
Source: Federal Trade Commission, Consumer Sentinel Network Data Book 2020

Fraud and Other Consumer Reports

Area	Reports	Reports per 100,000 Population	Rank[2]
MSA[1]	12,460	896	51
U.S.	3,385,133	1,031	-

Note: (1) Figures cover the Raleigh, NC Metropolitan Statistical Area; (2) Rank ranges from 1 to 391 where 1 indicates greatest number of fraud and other consumer reports per 100,000 population
Source: Federal Trade Commission, Consumer Sentinel Network Data Book 2020

POLITICS

2020 Presidential Election Results

Area	Biden	Trump	Jorgensen	Hawkins	Other
Wake County	62.3	35.8	1.2	0.3	0.5
U.S.	51.3	46.8	1.2	0.3	0.5

Note: Results are percentages and may not add to 100% due to rounding
Source: Dave Leip's Atlas of U.S. Presidential Elections

SPORTS

Professional Sports Teams

Team Name	League	Year Established
Carolina Hurricanes	National Hockey League (NHL)	1997

Note: Includes teams located in the Raleigh, NC Metropolitan Statistical Area.
Source: Wikipedia, Major Professional Sports Teams of the United States and Canada, April 6, 2021

CLIMATE

Average and Extreme Temperatures

Temperature	Jan	Feb	Mar	Apr	May	Jun	Jul	Aug	Sep	Oct	Nov	Dec	Yr.
Extreme High (°F)	79	84	90	95	97	104	105	105	104	98	88	79	105
Average High (°F)	50	53	61	72	79	86	89	87	81	72	62	53	71
Average Temp. (°F)	40	43	50	59	67	75	78	77	71	60	51	42	60
Average Low (°F)	29	31	38	46	55	63	68	67	60	48	39	32	48
Extreme Low (°F)	-9	5	11	23	29	38	48	46	37	19	11	4	-9

Note: Figures cover the years 1948-1990
Source: National Climatic Data Center, International Station Meteorological Climate Summary, 9/96

Average Precipitation/Snowfall/Humidity

Precip./Humidity	Jan	Feb	Mar	Apr	May	Jun	Jul	Aug	Sep	Oct	Nov	Dec	Yr.
Avg. Precip. (in.)	3.4	3.6	3.6	2.9	3.9	3.6	4.4	4.4	3.2	2.9	3.0	3.1	42.0
Avg. Snowfall (in.)	2	3	1	Tr	0	0	0	0	0	0	Tr	1	8
Avg. Rel. Hum. 7am (%)	79	79	79	80	84	86	88	91	91	90	84	81	84
Avg. Rel. Hum. 4pm (%)	53	49	46	43	51	54	57	59	57	53	51	53	52

Note: Figures cover the years 1948-1990; Tr = Trace amounts (<0.05 in. of rain; <0.5 in. of snow)
Source: National Climatic Data Center, International Station Meteorological Climate Summary, 9/96

Weather Conditions

Temperature			Daytime Sky			Precipitation		
32°F & below	45°F & below	90°F & above	Clear	Partly cloudy	Cloudy	0.01 inch or more precip.	0.1 inch or more snow/ice	Thunder-storms
77	160	39	98	143	124	110	3	42

Note: Figures are average number of days per year and cover the years 1948-1990
Source: National Climatic Data Center, International Station Meteorological Climate Summary, 9/96

HAZARDOUS WASTE

Superfund Sites

The Raleigh, NC metro area is home to three sites on the EPA's Superfund National Priorities List: **Koppers Co., Inc. (Morrisville Plant)** (final); **North Carolina State University (Lot 86, Farm Unit #1)** (final); **Ward Transformer** (final). There are a total of 1,375 Superfund sites with a status of proposed or final on the list in the U.S. *U.S. Environmental Protection Agency, National Priorities List, April 7, 2021*

AIR QUALITY

Air Quality Trends: Ozone

	1990	1995	2000	2005	2010	2015	2016	2017	2018	2019
MSA[1]	0.093	0.081	0.087	0.082	0.071	0.065	0.069	0.066	0.063	0.064
U.S.	0.088	0.089	0.082	0.080	0.073	0.068	0.069	0.068	0.069	0.065

Note: (1) Data covers the Raleigh, NC Metropolitan Statistical Area. The values shown are the composite ozone concentration averages among trend sites based on the highest fourth daily maximum 8-hour concentration in parts per million. These trends are based on sites having an adequate record of monitoring data during the trend period. Data from exceptional events are included.
Source: U.S. Environmental Protection Agency, Air Quality Monitoring Information, "Air Quality Trends by City, 1990-2019"

Air Quality Index

Area	Percent of Days when Air Quality was...[2]					AQI Statistics[2]	
	Good	Moderate	Unhealthy for Sensitive Groups	Unhealthy	Very Unhealthy	Maximum	Median
MSA[1]	65.5	34.5	0.0	0.0	0.0	93	46

Note: (1) Data covers the Raleigh, NC Metropolitan Statistical Area; (2) Based on 365 days with AQI data in 2019. Air Quality Index (AQI) is an index for reporting daily air quality. EPA calculates the AQI for five major air pollutants regulated by the Clean Air Act: ground-level ozone, particle pollution (aka particulate matter), carbon monoxide, sulfur dioxide, and nitrogen dioxide. The AQI runs from 0 to 500. The higher the AQI value, the greater the level of air pollution and the greater the health concern. There are six AQI categories: "Good" AQI is between 0 and 50. Air quality is considered satisfactory; "Moderate" AQI is between 51 and 100. Air quality is acceptable; "Unhealthy for Sensitive Groups" When AQI values are between 101 and 150, members of sensitive groups may experience health effects; "Unhealthy" When AQI values are between 151 and 200 everyone may begin to experience health effects; "Very Unhealthy" AQI values between 201 and 300 trigger a health alert; "Hazardous" AQI values over 300 trigger warnings of emergency conditions (not shown).
Source: U.S. Environmental Protection Agency, Air Quality Index Report, 2019

Air Quality Index Pollutants

Area	Percent of Days when AQI Pollutant was...[2]					
	Carbon Monoxide	Nitrogen Dioxide	Ozone	Sulfur Dioxide	Particulate Matter 2.5	Particulate Matter 10
MSA[1]	0.3	0.3	46.8	0.0	52.6	0.0

Note: (1) Data covers the Raleigh, NC Metropolitan Statistical Area; (2) Based on 365 days with AQI data in 2019. The Air Quality Index (AQI) is an index for reporting daily air quality. EPA calculates the AQI for five major air pollutants regulated by the Clean Air Act: ground-level ozone, particle pollution (also known as particulate matter), carbon monoxide, sulfur dioxide, and nitrogen dioxide. The AQI runs from 0 to 500. The higher the AQI value, the greater the level of air pollution and the greater the health concern.
Source: U.S. Environmental Protection Agency, Air Quality Index Report, 2019

Maximum Air Pollutant Concentrations: Particulate Matter, Ozone, CO and Lead

	Particulate Matter 10 (ug/m^3)	Particulate Matter 2.5 Wtd AM (ug/m^3)	Particulate Matter 2.5 24-Hr (ug/m^3)	Ozone (ppm)	Carbon Monoxide (ppm)	Lead (ug/m^3)
MSA[1] Level	30	8.9	17	0.064	1	n/a
NAAQS[2]	150	15	35	0.075	9	0.15
Met NAAQS[2]	Yes	Yes	Yes	Yes	Yes	n/a

Note: (1) Data covers the Raleigh, NC Metropolitan Statistical Area; Data from exceptional events are included; (2) National Ambient Air Quality Standards; ppm = parts per million; ug/m^3 = micrograms per cubic meter; n/a not available.
Concentrations: Particulate Matter 10 (coarse particulate)—highest second maximum 24-hour concentration; Particulate Matter 2.5 Wtd AM (fine particulate)—highest weighted annual mean concentration; Particulate Matter 2.5 24-Hour (fine particulate)—highest 98th percentile 24-hour concentration; Ozone—highest fourth daily maximum 8-hour concentration; Carbon Monoxide—highest second maximum non-overlapping 8-hour concentration; Lead—maximum running 3-month average
Source: U.S. Environmental Protection Agency, Air Quality Monitoring Information, "Air Quality Statistics by City, 2019"

Maximum Air Pollutant Concentrations: Nitrogen Dioxide and Sulfur Dioxide

	Nitrogen Dioxide AM (ppb)	Nitrogen Dioxide 1-Hr (ppb)	Sulfur Dioxide AM (ppb)	Sulfur Dioxide 1-Hr (ppb)	Sulfur Dioxide 24-Hr (ppb)
MSA[1] Level	9	34	n/a	2	n/a
NAAQS[2]	53	100	30	75	140
Met NAAQS[2]	Yes	Yes	n/a	Yes	n/a

Note: (1) Data covers the Raleigh, NC Metropolitan Statistical Area; Data from exceptional events are included; (2) National Ambient Air Quality Standards; ppm = parts per million; ug/m³ = micrograms per cubic meter; n/a not available.
Concentrations: Nitrogen Dioxide AM—highest arithmetic mean concentration; Nitrogen Dioxide 1-Hr—highest 98th percentile 1-hour daily maximum concentration; Sulfur Dioxide AM—highest annual mean concentration; Sulfur Dioxide 1-Hr—highest 99th percentile 1-hour daily maximum concentration; Sulfur Dioxide 24-Hr—highest second maximum 24-hour concentration
Source: U.S. Environmental Protection Agency, Air Quality Monitoring Information, "Air Quality Statistics by City, 2019"

Richmond, Virginia

Background

Richmond is the capital of Virginia and is located on the James River. Home to blue-blooded old families such as the Byrds and Lees, the city played a central role in both U.S. and Confederate histories.

John Smith (of Pocahontas fame) and Christopher Newport first claimed Richmond in 1607 as English territory. In 1679, the area was granted to William Byrd I, with the understanding that he establish a settlement. His son, William Byrd II, continued his father's work, and, along with William Mayo, surveyed lots for what was to be named Richmond. During the Revolutionary War, Richmond played host to two Virginia Conventions. These conventions, which gathered founding fathers such as George Washington, Thomas Jefferson, and Patrick Henry in the same room, ratified the Constitution as the law of the land for the emerging nation. In 1775, Patrick Henry delivered his famous "Give me Liberty or Give me Death" speech in the city's St. John's Church.

Not long after the United States congealed as a nation, however, dissension caused fragmentation and Richmond became the Confederate States' capital. From its Roman temple-inspired capitol designed by Thomas Jefferson, Jefferson Davis presided over the Confederacy.

Not surprisingly, today Richmond is home to authoritative repositories of both Southern and Virginia history, which include the Virginia State Library, the Museum of the Confederacy, and the Virginia Historical Society.

Today, government and higher education are economic mainstays for the city, with Virginia Commonwealth University, the Medical College of Virginia, the University of Richmond, and Virginia Union University all located within the city limits. The Virginia BioTechnology Research Park houses more than 60 life sciences organizations in 1.3 million square feet of research and office space adjacent to the VCU Medical Center. Companies located there include government and VCU labs, young companies nearing mid-stage, international bioscience companies, and headquarters of several major companies. Banking and telecommunications sectors are also well represented in the city's economy.

The city's James River waterfront, with a multimillion-dollar flood wall to protect it from the frequent rising waters of the river, is now home to much of Richmond's entertainment, dining and nightlife activity, bolstered by the creation of a Canal Walk along the city's former industrial canals. In 2018, the city's first rapid transit system began operating.

> The Jackson Ward neighborhood celebrated its 150th anniversary with virtual and socially-distanced events —music, poetry, architectural appreciation—to honor its historic African American heritage.

Richmond's cultural offerings include the Richmond Symphony, Richmond Ballet, and the Virginia Museum of Fine Arts, known for its fine Faberge collection that travels for exhibitions. A variety of murals from internationally recognized street artists have appeared throughout the city as a result of the efforts of Art Whino and RVA Magazine with The Richmond Mural Project and the RVA Street Art Festival. And, after some controversy, a bronze statue of African American Richmond native and tennis star Arthur Ashe was completed on the city's Monument Avenue.

Richmond's Northside is home to a number of listed historic districts, including Chestnut Hill-Plateau and Barton Heights. The affluent West End is home to the University of Richmond and the Country Club of Virginia.

Richmond's climate is classified as modified continental with its warm summer and humid, mild winters. Snow only remains on the ground for a day or so. Ice storms are not uncommon, but are not usually severe enough to cause considerable damage. Hurricanes and tropical storms, when they occur, are responsible for flooding during the summer and early fall months. Tornadoes are infrequent, but some notable occurrences have been observed in the Richmond area.

Rankings

Business/Finance Rankings

- Based on metro area social media reviews, the employment opinion group Glassdoor surveyed 50 of the most populous U.S. metro areas and equally weighed cost of living, hiring opportunity, and job satisfaction to compose a list of "25 Best Cities for Jobs." Median pay and home value, and number of active job openings were also factored in. The Richmond metro area was ranked #22 in overall job satisfaction. *www.glassdoor.com, "Best Cities for Jobs," February 25, 2020*

- The Brookings Institution ranked the nation's largest cities based on income inequality. Richmond was ranked #14 (#1 = greatest inequality). Criteria: the "95/20 ratio," a figure representing the income at which a household earns more than 95 percent of all other households, divided by the income at which a household earns more than only 20 percent of all other households. *Brookings Institution, "Household Income Inequality, Largest Cities of 97 Large U.S. Metro Areas, 2014-2016," February 5, 2018*

- The Brookings Institution ranked the 100 largest metro areas in the U.S. based on income inequality. Richmond was ranked #75 (#1 = greatest inequality). Criteria: the "95/20 ratio," a figure representing the income at which a household earns more than 95 percent of all other households, divided by the income at which a household earns more than only 20 percent of all other households. *Brookings Institution, "Household Income Inequality, 100 Largest U.S. Metro Areas, 2014-2016," February 5, 2018*

- The Richmond metro area appeared on the Milken Institute "2021 Best Performing Cities" list. Rank: #117 out of 200 large metro areas (population over 250,000). Criteria: job growth; wage and salary growth; high-tech output growth; housing affordability; household broadband access. *Milken Institute, "Best-Performing Cities 2021," February 16, 2021*

- *Forbes* ranked the 200 most populous metro areas to determine the nation's "Best Places for Business and Careers." The Richmond metro area was ranked #55. Criteria: costs (business and living); job growth (past and projected); income growth; quality of life; educational attainment (college and high school); projected economic growth; cultural and leisure opportunities; workplace tolerance laws; net migration patterns. *Forbes, "The Best Places for Business and Careers 2019: Seattle Still On Top," October 30, 2019*

Children/Family Rankings

- Richmond was selected as one of the most playful cities in the U.S. by KaBOOM! The organization's Playful City USA initiative honors cities and towns across the nation that have made their communities more playable. Criteria: pledging to integrate play as a solution to challenges in their communities; making it easy for children to get active and balanced play; creating more family-friendly and innovative communities as a result. *KaBOOM! National Campaign for Play, "2017 Playful City USA Communities"*

Culture/Performing Arts Rankings

- Richmond was selected as one of the ten best small North American cities and towns for moviemakers. Of cities with smaller populations, the area ranked #8. As with the 2021 list for bigger cities, pandemic challenges and COVID-19 guidelines were factored in. Other criteria: film community and culture; access to equipment and facilities; tax incentives; and standard of living. *MovieMaker Magazine, "Best Places to Live and Work as a Moviemaker, 2021," January 26, 2021*

- Richmond was selected as one of "America's Favorite Cities." The city ranked #12 in the "Architecture" category. Respondents to an online survey were asked to rate their favorite place (population over 100,000) in over 65 categories. *Travelandleisure.com, "America's Favorite Cities for Architecture 2016," March 2, 2017*

Dating/Romance Rankings

- *Apartment List* conducted its annual survey of renters for cities that have the best opportunities for dating. More than 11,000 single respondents rated their current city or neighborhood for opportunities to date. Richmond ranked #2 out of 86 where single residents were very satisfied or somewhat satisfied, making it among the ten best areas for dating opportunities. Other criteria analyzed included gender and education levels of renters. *Apartment List, "The Best & Worst Metros for Dating 2020," February 4, 2020*

Education Rankings

- Personal finance website *WalletHub* analyzed the 150 largest U.S. metropolitan statistical areas to determine where the most educated Americans are putting their degrees to work. Criteria: education levels; percentage of workers with degrees; education quality and attainment gap; public school quality rankings; quality and enrollment of each metro area's universities. Richmond was ranked #38 (#1 = most educated city). *www.WalletHub.com, "Most and Least Educated Cities in America," July 20, 2020*

Environmental Rankings

- Sperling's BestPlaces assessed the 50 largest metropolitan areas of the United States for the likelihood of dangerously extreme weather events or earthquakes. In general the Southeast and South-Central regions have the highest risk of weather extremes and earthquakes, while the Pacific Northwest enjoys the lowest risk. Of the least risky metropolitan areas, the Richmond metro area was ranked #8. *www.bestplaces.net, "Avoid Natural Disasters: BestPlaces Reveals The Top 10 Safest Places to Live," October 25, 2017*

- Richmond was highlighted as one of the top 98 cleanest metro areas for short-term particle pollution (24-hour PM 2.5) in the U.S. during 2016 through 2018. Monitors in these cities reported no days with unhealthful PM 2.5 levels. *American Lung Association, "State of the Air 2020," April 21, 2020*

Health/Fitness Rankings

- For each of the 100 largest cities in the United States, the American Fitness Index®, published by the American College of Sports Medicine and the Anthem Foundation, evaluated community infrastructure and 33 health behaviors including preventive health, levels of chronic disease conditions, pedestrian safety, air quality, and community resources that support physical activity. Richmond ranked #46 for "community fitness." *americanfitnessindex.org, "2020 ACSM American Fitness Index Summary Report," July 14, 2020*

- The Richmond metro area was identified as one of the worst cities for bed bugs in America by pest control company Orkin. The area ranked #26 out of 50 based on the number of bed bug treatments Orkin performed from December 2019 to November 2020. *Orkin, "New Year, New Top City on Orkin's 2021 Bed Bug Cities List: Chicago," February 1, 2021*

- Richmond was identified as a "2021 Spring Allergy Capital." The area ranked #1 out of 100. Three groups of factors were used to identify the most challenging cities for people with allergies during the spring season: annual spring pollen levels; over the counter medicine use; number of board-certified allergy specialists. *Asthma and Allergy Foundation of America, "Spring Allergy Capitals 2021," February 23, 2021*

- Richmond was identified as a "2021 Fall Allergy Capital." The area ranked #2 out of 100. Three groups of factors were used to identify the most challenging cities for people with allergies during the fall season: annual fall pollen levels; over the counter medicine use; number of board-certified allergy specialists. *Asthma and Allergy Foundation of America, "Fall Allergy Capitals 2021," February 23, 2021*

- Richmond was identified as a "2019 Asthma Capital." The area ranked #12 out of the nation's 100 largest metropolitan areas. Criteria: estimated asthma prevalence; crude death rate from asthma; and ER visits due to asthma. Risk factors analyzed but not factored in the rankings: annual pollen score; annual air quality; public smoking laws; number of board-certified asthma specialists; rescue medication use; controller medication use; uninsured rate; poverty rate. *Asthma and Allergy Foundation of America, "Asthma Capitals 2019: The Most Challenging Places to Live With Asthma," May 7, 2019*

Real Estate Rankings

- FitSmallBusiness looked at 50 of the largest metropolitan areas in the U.S. to determine which metro was the best to start a real estate business. Data was compiled from such sources as: Zillow, Trulia, U.S. Census Bureau, and the Bureau of Labor Statistics. Criteria: location; inventory; annual wages; median sales price of homes; days on the market; median price cut percentage; and other factors that would influence real estate professional growth. The Richmond metro area ranked #31. *fitsmallbusiness.com, "The Best Cities to Become a Real Estate Agent in 2018," January 30, 2018*

- *WalletHub* compared the most populated U.S. cities to determine which had the best markets for real estate agents. Richmond ranked #35 where demand was high and pay was the best. Criteria: sales per agent; annual median wage for real-estate agents; monthly average starting salary for real estate agents; real estate job density and competition; unemployment rate; home turnover rate; housing-market health index; and other relevant metrics. *www.WalletHub.com, "2019's Best Places to Be a Real Estate Agent," April 24, 2019*

- The Richmond metro area was identified as one of the top 15 housing markets to invest in for 2021 by *Forbes*. Criteria: home price appreciation; percentage of home sales within a 2-week time frame; available inventory; number of home sales; and other factors. *Forbes.com, "Top Housing Markets To Watch In 2021," December 15, 2020*

- The Richmond metro area was identified as one of the 10 best condo markets in the U.S. in 2020. The area ranked #7 out of 63 markets. Criteria: year-over-year change of median sales price of existing apartment condo-coop homes between the 4th quarter of 2019 and the 4th quarter of 2020. *National Association of Realtors®, Median Sales Price of Existing Apartment Condo-Coops Homes for Metropolitan Areas, 4th Quarter 2020*

- Richmond was ranked #90 out of 268 metro areas in terms of housing affordability in 2020 by the National Association of Home Builders (#1 = most affordable). Criteria: the share of homes sold in that area affordable to a family earning the local median income, based on standard mortgage underwriting criteria. *National Association of Home Builders®, NAHB-Wells Fargo Housing Opportunity Index, 4th Quarter 2020*

Safety Rankings

- Allstate ranked the 200 largest cities in America in terms of driver safety. Richmond ranked #113. Criteria: internal property damage claims over a two-year period from January 2016 to December 2017. The report helps increase the importance of safety and awareness behind the wheel. *Allstate, "Allstate America's Best Drivers Report, 2019" June 24, 2019*

- The National Insurance Crime Bureau ranked 384 metro areas in the U.S. in terms of per capita rates of vehicle theft. The Richmond metro area ranked #153 (#1 = highest rate). Criteria: number of vehicle theft offenses per 100,000 inhabitants in 2019. *National Insurance Crime Bureau, "Hot Spots 2019," July 21, 2020*

Seniors/Retirement Rankings

- From its Best Cities for Successful Aging indexes, the Milken Institute generated rankings for metropolitan areas, weighing data in nine categories—health care, wellness, living arrangements, transportation and convenience, financial characteristics, education, employment, community engagement, and overall livability. The Richmond metro area was ranked #32 overall in the large metro area category. *Milken Institute, "Best Cities for Successful Aging, 2017" March 14, 2017*

Sports/Recreation Rankings

- Richmond was chosen as one of America's best cities for bicycling. The city ranked #34 out of 50. Criteria: cycling infrastructure that is safe and friendly for all ages; energy and bike culture. The editors evaluated cities with populations of 100,000 or more. *Bicycling, "The 50 Best Bike Cities in America," October 10, 2018*

Women/Minorities Rankings

- Personal finance website *WalletHub* compared more than 180 U.S. cities across two key dimensions, "Hispanic Business-Friendliness" and "Hispanic Purchasing Power," to arrive at the most favorable conditions for Hispanic entrepreneurs. Richmond was ranked #152 out of 182. Criteria includes: share of Hispanic-Owned Businesses; Hispanic entrepreneurship rate to median annual income of Hispanics; Small Business-Friendliness score; cost of living; and number of Hispanics with at least a bachelor's degree. *WalletHub.com, "2019's Best Cities for Hispanic Entrepreneurs," May 1, 2019*

Miscellaneous Rankings

- *MoveHub* ranked 446 hipster cities across 20 countries, using its *alternative* Hipster Index and Richmond came out as #20 among the top 50. Criteria: population over 150,000; number of vintage boutiques; density of tattoo parlors; vegan places to eat; coffee shops; and density of vinyl record stores. *www.movehub.com, "The Hipster Index: Brighton Pips Portland to Global Top Spot," February 20, 2020*

- *WalletHub* compared the 150 most populated U.S. cities to determine their operating efficiency. A "Quality of City Services" score was constructed for each city and then divided by the total budget per capita to reveal which were managed the best. Richmond ranked #98. Criteria: financial stability; economy; education; safety; health; infrastructure and pollution. *www.WalletHub.com, "2020's Best- & Worst-Run Cities in America," June 29, 2020*

Business Environment

DEMOGRAPHICS

Population Growth

Area	1990 Census	2000 Census	2010 Census	2019* Estimate	Population Growth (%) 1990-2019	Population Growth (%) 2010-2019
City	202,783	197,790	204,214	226,622	11.8	11.0
MSA[1]	949,244	1,096,957	1,258,251	1,269,530	33.7	0.9
U.S.	248,709,873	281,421,906	308,745,538	324,697,795	30.6	5.2

Note: (1) Figures cover the Richmond, VA Metropolitan Statistical Area; (*) 2015-2019 5-year estimated population
Source: U.S. Census Bureau, 1990 Census, Census 2000, Census 2010, 2015-2019 American Community Survey 5-Year Estimates

Household Size

Area	Persons in Household (%) One	Two	Three	Four	Five	Six	Seven or More	Average Household Size
City	43.4	32.8	12.0	6.8	3.0	1.3	0.6	2.40
MSA[1]	29.4	34.2	16.0	12.4	5.3	1.8	0.8	2.60
U.S.	27.9	33.9	15.6	12.9	6.0	2.3	1.4	2.60

Note: (1) Figures cover the Richmond, VA Metropolitan Statistical Area
Source: U.S. Census Bureau, 2015-2019 American Community Survey 5-Year Estimates

Race

Area	White Alone[2] (%)	Black Alone[2] (%)	Asian Alone[2] (%)	AIAN[3] Alone[2] (%)	NHOPI[4] Alone[2] (%)	Other Race Alone[2] (%)	Two or More Races (%)
City	45.5	46.9	2.1	0.4	0.0	1.7	3.4
MSA[1]	61.1	29.7	3.8	0.3	0.1	1.8	3.1
U.S.	72.5	12.7	5.5	0.8	0.2	4.9	3.3

Note: (1) Figures cover the Richmond, VA Metropolitan Statistical Area; (2) Alone is defined as not being in combination with one or more other races; (3) American Indian and Alaska Native; (4) Native Hawaiian and Other Pacific Islander
Source: U.S. Census Bureau, 2015-2019 American Community Survey 5-Year Estimates

Hispanic or Latino Origin

Area	Total (%)	Mexican (%)	Puerto Rican (%)	Cuban (%)	Other (%)
City	6.9	1.7	0.7	0.2	4.3
MSA[1]	6.3	1.6	1.0	0.2	3.5
U.S.	18.0	11.2	1.7	0.7	4.3

Note: Persons of Hispanic or Latino origin can be of any race; (1) Figures cover the Richmond, VA Metropolitan Statistical Area
Source: U.S. Census Bureau, 2015-2019 American Community Survey 5-Year Estimates

Ancestry

Area	German	Irish	English	American	Italian	Polish	French[2]	Scottish	Dutch
City	6.9	6.3	7.4	4.2	3.5	1.3	1.4	2.1	0.5
MSA[1]	9.2	7.9	10.7	6.7	3.7	1.6	1.6	2.1	0.7
U.S.	13.3	9.7	7.2	6.2	5.1	2.8	2.3	1.7	1.2

Note: Figures are the percentage of the total population reporting a particular ancestry. The nine most commonly reported ancestries in the U.S. are shown. Figures include multiple ancestries (e.g. if a person reported being Irish and Italian, they were included in both columns); (1) Figures cover the Richmond, VA Metropolitan Statistical Area; (2) Excludes Basque
Source: U.S. Census Bureau, 2015-2019 American Community Survey 5-Year Estimates

Foreign-born Population

Area	Percent of Population Born in Any Foreign Country	Asia	Mexico	Europe	Caribbean	Central America[2]	South America	Africa	Canada
City	7.0	1.5	0.8	0.7	0.4	2.5	0.4	0.6	0.2
MSA[1]	7.9	3.2	0.6	1.0	0.4	1.4	0.5	0.6	0.1
U.S.	13.6	4.2	3.5	1.5	1.3	1.1	1.0	0.7	0.2

Note: (1) Figures cover the Richmond, VA Metropolitan Statistical Area; (2) Excludes Mexico.
Source: U.S. Census Bureau, 2015-2019 American Community Survey 5-Year Estimates

Marital Status

Area	Never Married	Now Married[2]	Separated	Widowed	Divorced
City	52.7	27.3	3.0	5.4	11.6
MSA[1]	34.9	46.0	2.5	5.8	10.9
U.S.	33.4	48.1	1.9	5.8	10.9

Note: Figures are percentages and cover the population 15 years of age and older; (1) Figures cover the Richmond, VA Metropolitan Statistical Area; (2) Excludes separated
Source: U.S. Census Bureau, 2015-2019 American Community Survey 5-Year Estimates

Disability by Age

Area	All Ages	Under 18 Years Old	18 to 64 Years Old	65 Years and Over
City	15.2	6.7	13.2	38.0
MSA[1]	12.6	5.0	10.4	32.6
U.S.	12.6	4.2	10.3	34.5

Note: Figures show percent of the civilian noninstitutionalized population that reported having a disability. Disability status is determined from six types of difficulty: vision, hearing, cognitive, ambulatory, self-care, and independent living. For children under 5 years old, hearing and vision difficulty are used to determine disability status. For children between the ages of 5 and 14, disability status is determined from hearing, vision, cognitive, ambulatory, and self-care difficulties. For people aged 15 years and older, they are considered to have a disability if they have difficulty with any one of the six difficulty types; Note: (1) Figures cover the Richmond, VA Metropolitan Statistical Area
Source: U.S. Census Bureau, 2015-2019 American Community Survey 5-Year Estimates

Age

Area	Under Age 5	Age 5–19	Age 20–34	Age 35–44	Age 45–54	Age 55–64	Age 65–74	Age 75–84	Age 85+	Median Age
City	5.9	15.6	30.2	11.8	11.2	12.4	7.7	3.3	1.8	34.0
MSA[1]	5.8	18.7	20.7	12.8	13.6	13.5	9.2	4.1	1.8	38.8
U.S.	6.1	19.1	20.7	12.6	13.0	12.9	9.1	4.6	1.9	38.1

Note: (1) Figures cover the Richmond, VA Metropolitan Statistical Area
Source: U.S. Census Bureau, 2015-2019 American Community Survey 5-Year Estimates

Gender

Area	Males	Females	Males per 100 Females
City	107,430	119,192	90.1
MSA[1]	613,475	656,055	93.5
U.S.	159,886,919	164,810,876	97.0

Note: (1) Figures cover the Richmond, VA Metropolitan Statistical Area
Source: U.S. Census Bureau, 2015-2019 American Community Survey 5-Year Estimates

Religious Groups by Family

Area	Catholic	Baptist	Non-Den.	Methodist[2]	Lutheran	LDS[3]	Pentecostal	Presbyterian[4]	Muslim[5]	Judaism
MSA[1]	6.0	19.9	5.5	6.1	0.6	1.0	1.8	2.1	2.8	0.4
U.S.	19.1	9.3	4.0	4.0	2.3	2.0	1.9	1.6	0.8	0.7

Note: Figures are the number of adherents as a percentage of the total population; (1) Figures cover the Richmond, VA Metropolitan Statistical Area; (2) Methodist/Pietist; (3) Latter Day Saints; (4) Reformed; (5) Figures are estimates
Source: Association of Statisticians of American Religious Bodies, 2010 U.S. Religion Census: Religious Congregations & Membership Study

Religious Groups by Tradition

Area	Catholic	Evangelical Protestant	Mainline Protestant	Other Tradition	Black Protestant	Orthodox
MSA[1]	6.0	23.7	13.3	4.6	2.4	0.2
U.S.	19.1	16.2	7.3	4.3	1.6	0.3

Note: Figures are the number of adherents as a percentage of the total population; (1) Figures cover the Richmond, VA Metropolitan Statistical Area
Source: Association of Statisticians of American Religious Bodies, 2010 U.S. Religion Census: Religious Congregations & Membership Study

ECONOMY

Gross Metropolitan Product

Area	2017	2018	2019	2020	Rank[2]
MSA[1]	83.0	87.2	91.0	94.7	43

Note: Figures are in billions of dollars; (1) Figures cover the Richmond, VA Metropolitan Statistical Area; (2) Rank is based on 2018 data and ranges from 1 to 381
Source: U.S. Conference of Mayors, U.S. Metro Economies: GMP & Employment 2018-2020, September 2019

Economic Growth

Area	2015-17 (%)	2018 (%)	2019 (%)	2020 (%)	Rank[2]
MSA[1]	1.5	3.0	2.6	1.8	179
U.S.	1.9	2.9	2.3	2.1	–

Note: Figures are real gross metropolitan product (GMP) growth rates and represent average annual percent change; (1) Figures cover the Richmond, VA Metropolitan Statistical Area; (2) Rank is based on 2017 2-year average annual percent change and ranges from 1 to 381
Source: U.S. Conference of Mayors, U.S. Metro Economies: GMP & Employment 2018-2020, September 2019

Metropolitan Area Exports

Area	2014	2015	2016	2017	2018	2019	Rank[2]
MSA[1]	3,307.0	3,325.9	3,525.7	3,663.7	3,535.0	3,203.2	76

Note: Figures are in millions of dollars; (1) Figures cover the Richmond, VA Metropolitan Statistical Area; (2) Rank is based on 2019 data and ranges from 1 to 386
Source: U.S. Department of Commerce, International Trade Administration, Office of Trade and Economic Analysis, Industry and Analysis, Exports by Metropolitan Area, data extracted March 24, 2021

Building Permits

Area	Single-Family			Multi-Family			Total		
	2018	2019	Pct. Chg.	2018	2019	Pct. Chg.	2018	2019	Pct. Chg.
City	273	353	29.3	290	887	205.9	563	1,240	120.2
MSA[1]	4,498	4,481	-0.4	1,563	3,859	146.9	6,061	8,340	37.6
U.S.	855,300	862,100	0.7	473,500	523,900	10.6	1,328,800	1,386,000	4.3

Note: (1) Figures cover the Richmond, VA Metropolitan Statistical Area; Figures represent new, privately-owned housing units authorized (unadjusted data); All permit data are based on estimates with imputation
Source: U.S. Census Bureau, Manufacturing, Mining, and Construction Statistics, Building Permits, 2018, 2019

Bankruptcy Filings

Area	Business Filings			Nonbusiness Filings		
	2019	2020	% Chg.	2019	2020	% Chg.
Richmond city	18	21	16.7	897	695	-22.5
U.S.	22,780	21,655	-4.9	752,160	522,808	-30.5

Note: Business filings include Chapter 7, Chapter 9, Chapter 11, Chapter 12, Chapter 13, Chapter 15, and Section 304; Nonbusiness filings include Chapter 7, Chapter 11, and Chapter 13
Source: Administrative Office of the U.S. Courts, Business and Nonbusiness Bankruptcy, County Cases Commenced by Chapter of the Bankruptcy Code, During the 12-Month Period Ending December 31, 2019 and Business and Nonbusiness Bankruptcy, County Cases Commenced by Chapter of the Bankruptcy Code, During the 12-Month Period Ending December 31, 2020

Housing Vacancy Rates

Area	Gross Vacancy Rate[2] (%)			Year-Round Vacancy Rate[3] (%)			Rental Vacancy Rate[4] (%)			Homeowner Vacancy Rate[5] (%)		
	2018	2019	2020	2018	2019	2020	2018	2019	2020	2018	2019	2020
MSA[1]	8.0	8.5	6.0	8.0	8.5	6.0	5.4	9.5	2.7	2.1	1.3	0.9
U.S.	12.3	12.0	10.6	9.7	9.5	8.2	6.9	6.7	6.3	1.5	1.4	1.0

Note: (1) Figures cover the Richmond, VA Metropolitan Statistical Area; (2) The percentage of the total housing inventory that is vacant; (3) The percentage of the housing inventory (excluding seasonal units) that is year-round vacant; (4) The percentage of rental inventory that is vacant for rent; (5) The percentage of homeowner inventory that is vacant for sale
Source: U.S. Census Bureau, Housing Vacancies and Homeownership Annual Statistics: 2018, 2019, 2020

INCOME

Income

Area	Per Capita ($)	Median Household ($)	Average Household ($)
City	33,549	47,250	76,182
MSA[1]	36,413	68,529	92,171
U.S.	34,103	62,843	88,607

Note: (1) Figures cover the Richmond, VA Metropolitan Statistical Area
Source: U.S. Census Bureau, 2015-2019 American Community Survey 5-Year Estimates

Household Income Distribution

Area	Percent of Households Earning							
	Under $15,000	$15,000 -$24,999	$25,000 -$34,999	$35,000 -$49,999	$50,000 -$74,999	$75,000 -$99,999	$100,000 -$149,999	$150,000 and up
City	17.6	11.0	10.1	13.3	16.2	10.2	10.5	11.0
MSA[1]	9.0	7.4	8.0	12.4	17.2	13.4	17.3	15.3
U.S.	10.3	8.9	8.9	12.3	17.2	12.7	15.1	14.5

Note: (1) Figures cover the Richmond, VA Metropolitan Statistical Area
Source: U.S. Census Bureau, 2015-2019 American Community Survey 5-Year Estimates

Poverty Rate

Area	All Ages	Under 18 Years Old	18 to 64 Years Old	65 Years and Over
City	23.2	37.0	21.5	13.2
MSA[1]	11.2	15.8	10.5	7.6
U.S.	13.4	18.5	12.6	9.3

Note: Figures are percentage of people whose income during the past 12 months was below the poverty level;
(1) Figures cover the Richmond, VA Metropolitan Statistical Area
Source: U.S. Census Bureau, 2015-2019 American Community Survey 5-Year Estimates

CITY FINANCES

City Government Finances

Component	2017 ($000)	2017 ($ per capita)
Total Revenues	1,556,352	7,065
Total Expenditures	1,525,695	6,926
Debt Outstanding	1,610,298	7,310
Cash and Securities[1]	1,113,108	5,053

Note: (1) Cash and security holdings of a government at the close of its fiscal year,
including those of its dependent agencies, utilities, and liquor stores.
Source: U.S. Census Bureau, State & Local Government Finances 2017

City Government Revenue by Source

Source	2017 ($000)	2017 ($ per capita)	2017 (%)
General Revenue			
From Federal Government	90,101	409	5.8
From State Government	432,155	1,962	27.8
From Local Governments	22,728	103	1.5
Taxes			
Property	329,786	1,497	21.2
Sales and Gross Receipts	141,989	645	9.1
Personal Income	0	0	0.0
Corporate Income	0	0	0.0
Motor Vehicle License	6,032	27	0.4
Other Taxes	47,453	215	3.0
Current Charges	185,832	844	11.9
Liquor Store	0	0	0.0
Utility	218,924	994	14.1
Employee Retirement	48,656	221	3.1

Source: U.S. Census Bureau, State & Local Government Finances 2017

City Government Expenditures by Function

Function	2017 ($000)	2017 ($ per capita)	2017 (%)
General Direct Expenditures			
Air Transportation	0	0	0.0
Corrections	35,455	160	2.3
Education	377,042	1,711	24.7
Employment Security Administration	0	0	0.0
Financial Administration	25,654	116	1.7
Fire Protection	45,823	208	3.0
General Public Buildings	3,919	17	0.3
Governmental Administration, Other	19,553	88	1.3
Health	77,698	352	5.1
Highways	48,378	219	3.2
Hospitals	0	0	0.0
Housing and Community Development	128,979	585	8.5
Interest on General Debt	39,858	180	2.6
Judicial and Legal	21,997	99	1.4
Libraries	5,040	22	0.3
Parking	6,507	29	0.4
Parks and Recreation	26,604	120	1.7
Police Protection	103,295	468	6.8
Public Welfare	71,227	323	4.7
Sewerage	88,567	402	5.8
Solid Waste Management	34,529	156	2.3
Veterans' Services	0	0	0.0
Liquor Store	0	0	0.0
Utility	269,243	1,222	17.6
Employee Retirement	38,775	176	2.5

Source: U.S. Census Bureau, State & Local Government Finances 2017

EMPLOYMENT

Labor Force and Employment

Area	Civilian Labor Force			Workers Employed		
	Dec. 2019	Dec. 2020	% Chg.	Dec. 2019	Dec. 2020	% Chg.
City	119,856	116,571	-2.7	116,483	108,936	-6.5
MSA[1]	692,884	665,116	-4.0	675,329	631,884	-6.4
U.S.	164,007,000	160,017,000	-2.4	158,504,000	149,613,000	-5.6

Note: Data is not seasonally adjusted and covers workers 16 years of age and older; (1) Figures cover the Richmond, VA Metropolitan Statistical Area
Source: Bureau of Labor Statistics, Local Area Unemployment Statistics

Unemployment Rate

Area	2020											
	Jan.	Feb.	Mar.	Apr.	May	Jun.	Jul.	Aug.	Sep.	Oct.	Nov.	Dec.
City	3.5	3.2	3.8	14.1	12.1	11.8	12.1	9.5	9.3	7.6	6.5	6.5
MSA[1]	3.1	2.8	3.4	11.2	9.4	8.9	8.8	6.9	6.8	5.5	4.9	5.0
U.S.	4.0	3.8	4.5	14.4	13.0	11.2	10.5	8.5	7.7	6.6	6.4	6.5

Note: Data is not seasonally adjusted and covers workers 16 years of age and older; (1) Figures cover the Richmond, VA Metropolitan Statistical Area
Source: Bureau of Labor Statistics, Local Area Unemployment Statistics

Average Wages

Occupation	$/Hr.	Occupation	$/Hr.
Accountants and Auditors	39.90	Maintenance and Repair Workers	21.90
Automotive Mechanics	24.50	Marketing Managers	74.20
Bookkeepers	21.30	Network and Computer Systems Admin.	43.80
Carpenters	22.30	Nurses, Licensed Practical	23.80
Cashiers	11.10	Nurses, Registered	38.20
Computer Programmers	45.10	Nursing Assistants	14.30
Computer Systems Analysts	47.10	Office Clerks, General	17.50
Computer User Support Specialists	26.70	Physical Therapists	48.20
Construction Laborers	15.20	Physicians	100.10
Cooks, Restaurant	13.00	Plumbers, Pipefitters and Steamfitters	24.50
Customer Service Representatives	18.00	Police and Sheriff's Patrol Officers	28.10
Dentists	79.00	Postal Service Mail Carriers	25.30
Electricians	27.00	Real Estate Sales Agents	31.10
Engineers, Electrical	47.90	Retail Salespersons	14.10
Fast Food and Counter Workers	10.60	Sales Representatives, Technical/Scientific	52.20
Financial Managers	75.80	Secretaries, Exc. Legal/Medical/Executive	19.20
First-Line Supervisors of Office Workers	29.90	Security Guards	13.70
General and Operations Managers	63.10	Surgeons	129.70
Hairdressers/Cosmetologists	17.50	Teacher Assistants, Exc. Postsecondary*	12.70
Home Health and Personal Care Aides	10.70	Teachers, Secondary School, Exc. Sp. Ed.*	n/a
Janitors and Cleaners	11.90	Telemarketers	15.00
Landscaping/Groundskeeping Workers	15.80	Truck Drivers, Heavy/Tractor-Trailer	23.70
Lawyers	67.90	Truck Drivers, Light/Delivery Services	21.30
Maids and Housekeeping Cleaners	12.10	Waiters and Waitresses	12.00

Note: Wage data covers the Richmond, VA Metropolitan Statistical Area; (*) Hourly wages were calculated from annual wage data based on a 40 hour work week; n/a not available.
Source: Bureau of Labor Statistics, Metro Area Occupational Employment & Wage Estimates, May 2020

Employment by Industry

Sector	MSA[1]		U.S.
	Number of Employees	Percent of Total	Percent of Total
Construction, Mining, and Logging	40,100	6.1	5.5
Education and Health Services	96,600	14.8	16.3
Financial Activities	52,800	8.1	6.1
Government	107,600	16.4	15.2
Information	6,100	0.9	1.9
Leisure and Hospitality	52,300	8.0	9.0
Manufacturing	30,400	4.6	8.5
Other Services	28,000	4.3	3.8
Professional and Business Services	112,800	17.2	14.4
Retail Trade	67,400	10.3	10.9
Transportation, Warehousing, and Utilities	35,000	5.3	4.6
Wholesale Trade	25,200	3.9	3.9

Note: Figures are non-farm employment as of December 2020. Figures are not seasonally adjusted and include workers 16 years of age and older; (1) Figures cover the Richmond, VA Metropolitan Statistical Area
Source: Bureau of Labor Statistics, Current Employment Statistics, Employment, Hours, and Earnings

Employment by Occupation

Occupation Classification	City (%)	MSA[1] (%)	U.S. (%)
Management, Business, Science, and Arts	42.0	42.0	38.5
Natural Resources, Construction, and Maintenance	6.7	7.8	8.9
Production, Transportation, and Material Moving	10.3	11.3	13.2
Sales and Office	20.2	22.6	21.6
Service	20.9	16.2	17.8

Note: Figures cover employed civilians 16 years of age and older; (1) Figures cover the Richmond, VA Metropolitan Statistical Area
Source: U.S. Census Bureau, 2015-2019 American Community Survey 5-Year Estimates

Occupations with Greatest Projected Employment Growth: 2020 – 2022

Occupation[1]	2020 Employment	2022 Projected Employment	Numeric Employment Change	Percent Employment Change
Retail Salespersons	81,130	93,780	12,650	15.6
Combined Food Preparation and Serving Workers, Including Fast Food	66,410	75,450	9,040	13.6
Cashiers	105,090	113,180	8,090	7.7
Waiters and Waitresses	46,090	53,400	7,310	15.9
Fitness Trainers and Aerobics Instructors	8,900	15,470	6,570	73.8
Laborers and Freight, Stock, and Material Movers, Hand	55,200	60,910	5,710	10.3
Childcare Workers	18,440	24,050	5,610	30.4
Customer Service Representatives	67,210	72,440	5,230	7.8
Management Analysts	62,240	67,200	4,960	8.0
Software Developers, Applications	40,250	44,610	4,360	10.8

Note: Projections cover Virginia; (1) Sorted by numeric employment change
Source: www.projectionscentral.com, State Occupational Projections, 2020–2022 Short-Term Projections

Fastest-Growing Occupations: 2020 – 2022

Occupation[1]	2020 Employment	2022 Projected Employment	Numeric Employment Change	Percent Employment Change
Fitness Trainers and Aerobics Instructors	8,900	15,470	6,570	73.8
Education Administrators, Preschool and Childcare Center/Program	830	1,180	350	42.2
Locker Room, Coatroom, and Dressing Room Attendants	130	180	50	38.5
Preschool Teachers, Except Special Education	7,830	10,600	2,770	35.4
Childcare Workers	18,440	24,050	5,610	30.4
Ushers, Lobby Attendants, and Ticket Takers	1,070	1,390	320	29.9
First-Line Supervisors of Personal Service Workers	5,310	6,750	1,440	27.1
Funeral Service Managers	300	380	80	26.7
Jewelers and Precious Stone and Metal Workers	300	380	80	26.7
Shampooers	800	1,010	210	26.3

Note: Projections cover Virginia; (1) Sorted by percent employment change and excludes occupations with numeric employment change less than 50
Source: www.projectionscentral.com, State Occupational Projections, 2020–2022 Short-Term Projections

TAXES

State Corporate Income Tax Rates

State	Tax Rate (%)	Income Brackets ($)	Num. of Brackets	Financial Institution Tax Rate (%)[a]	Federal Income Tax Ded.
Virginia	6.0	Flat rate	1	6.0	No

Note: Tax rates as of January 1, 2021; (a) Rates listed are the corporate income tax rate applied to financial institutions or excise taxes based on income. Some states have other taxes based upon the value of deposits or shares.
Source: Federation of Tax Administrators, State Corporate Income Tax Rates, January 1, 2021

State Individual Income Tax Rates

State	Tax Rate (%)	Income Brackets ($)	Personal Exemptions ($)			Standard Ded. ($)	
			Single	Married	Depend.	Single	Married
Virginia	2.0 - 5.75	3,000 - 17,001	930	1,860	930	4,500	9,000

Note: Tax rates as of January 1, 2021; Local- and county-level taxes are not included; Federal income tax is not deductible on state income tax returns
Source: Federation of Tax Administrators, State Individual Income Tax Rates, January 1, 2021

Various State Sales and Excise Tax Rates

State	State Sales Tax (%)	Gasoline[1] (¢/gal.)	Cigarette[2] ($/pack)	Spirits[3] ($/gal.)	Wine[4] ($/gal.)	Beer[5] ($/gal.)	Recreational Marijuana (%)
Virginia	5.3	29.4	0.6	19.89	1.51	0.26	(s)

Note: All tax rates as of January 1, 2021; (1) The American Petroleum Institute has developed a methodology for determining the average tax rate on a gallon of fuel. Rates may include any of the following: excise taxes, environmental fees, storage tank fees, other fees or taxes, general sales tax, and local taxes; (2) The federal excise tax of $1.0066 per pack and local taxes are not included; (3) Rates are those applicable to off-premise sales of 40% alcohol by volume (a.b.v.) distilled spirits in 750ml containers. Local excise taxes are excluded; (4) Rates are those applicable to off-premise sales of 11% a.b.v. non-carbonated wine in 750ml containers; (5) Rates are those applicable to off-premise sales of 4.7% a.b.v. beer in 12 ounce containers; (s) The Virginia legislature passed a bill in 2021 that would legalize recreational marijuana sales starting in 2024
Source: Tax Foundation, 2021 Facts & Figures: How Does Your State Compare?

State Business Tax Climate Index Rankings

State	Overall Rank	Corporate Tax Rank	Individual Income Tax Rank	Sales Tax Rank	Property Tax Rank	Unemployment Insurance Tax Rank
Virginia	26	16	35	11	27	46

Note: The index is a measure of how each state's tax laws affect economic performance. The lower the rank, the more favorable a state's tax system is for business. States without a given tax are given a ranking of 1. The scores/rankings for the District of Columbia do not affect other states. The 2021 index represents the tax climate as of July 1, 2020.
Source: Tax Foundation, State Business Tax Climate Index 2021

TRANSPORTATION

Means of Transportation to Work

Area	Car/Truck/Van		Public Transportation			Bicycle	Walked	Other Means	Worked at Home
	Drove Alone	Car-pooled	Bus	Subway	Railroad				
City	71.1	9.5	5.5	0.1	0.1	2.1	5.2	1.8	4.6
MSA[1]	81.1	8.6	1.4	0.0	0.1	0.5	1.7	1.3	5.3
U.S.	76.3	9.0	2.4	1.9	0.6	0.5	2.7	1.4	5.2

Note: Figures are percentages and cover workers 16 years of age and older; (1) Figures cover the Richmond, VA Metropolitan Statistical Area
Source: U.S. Census Bureau, 2015-2019 American Community Survey 5-Year Estimates

Travel Time to Work

Area	Less Than 10 Minutes	10 to 19 Minutes	20 to 29 Minutes	30 to 44 Minutes	45 to 59 Minutes	60 to 89 Minutes	90 Minutes or More
City	9.8	37.9	28.5	16.4	3.2	2.6	1.5
MSA[1]	8.7	29.1	27.4	23.2	6.3	3.1	2.0
U.S.	12.2	28.4	20.8	20.8	8.3	6.4	2.9

Note: Note: Figures are percentages and include workers 16 years old and over; (1) Figures cover the Richmond, VA Metropolitan Statistical Area
Source: U.S. Census Bureau, 2015-2019 American Community Survey 5-Year Estimates

Key Congestion Measures

Measure	1982	1992	2002	2012	2017
Annual Hours of Delay, Total (000)	2,607	6,978	12,190	21,100	24,461
Annual Hours of Delay, Per Auto Commuter	9	19	24	28	35
Annual Congestion Cost, Total (million $)	19	73	163	374	447
Annual Congestion Cost, Per Auto Commuter ($)	153	282	383	520	584

Note: Covers the Richmond VA urban area
Source: Texas A&M Transportation Institute, 2019 Urban Mobility Report

Freeway Travel Time Index

Measure	1982	1987	1992	1997	2002	2007	2012	2017
Urban Area Index[1]	1.03	1.05	1.07	1.08	1.09	1.12	1.12	1.12
Urban Area Rank[1,2]	76	79	82	88	96	90	91	93

Note: Freeway Travel Time Index—the ratio of travel time in the peak period to the travel time at free-flow conditions. For example, a value of 1.30 indicates a 20-minute free-flow trip takes 26 minutes in the peak (20 minutes x 1.30 = 26 minutes); (1) Covers the Richmond VA urban area; (2) Rank is based on 101 larger urban areas (#1 = highest travel time index)
Source: Texas A&M Transportation Institute, 2019 Urban Mobility Report

Public Transportation

Agency Name / Mode of Transportation	Vehicles Operated in Maximum Service[1]	Annual Unlinked Passenger Trips[2] (in thous.)	Annual Passenger Miles[3] (in thous.)
Greater Richmond Transit Company (GRTC)			
Bus (directly operated)	111	6,635.0	35,539.7
Bus Rapid Transit (directly operated)	9	1,951.4	5,817.1
Demand Response (purchased transportation)	53	309.9	2,823.9
Vanpool (purchased transportation)	143	387.2	27,910.8

Note: (1) Number of revenue vehicles operated by the given mode and type of service to meet the annual maximum service requirement. This is the revenue vehicle count during the peak season of the year; on the week and day that maximum service is provided. Vehicles operated in maximum service (VOMS) exclude atypical days and one-time special events; (2) Number of passengers who boarded public transportation vehicles. Passengers are counted each time they board a vehicle no matter how many vehicles they use to travel from their origin to their destination. (3) Sum of the distances ridden by all passengers during the entire fiscal year. Source: Federal Transit Administration, National Transit Database, 2019

Air Transportation

Airport Name and Code / Type of Service	Passenger Airlines[1]	Passenger Enplanements	Freight Carriers[2]	Freight (lbs)
Richmond International (RIC)				
Domestic service (U.S. carriers - 2020)	24	844,145	14	67,493,184
International service (U.S. carriers - 2019)	3	26	0	0

Note: (1) Includes all U.S.-based major, minor and commuter airlines that carried at least one passenger during the year; (2) Includes all U.S.-based airlines and freight carriers that transported at least one pound of freight during the year. Source: Bureau of Transportation Statistics, The Intermodal Transportation Database, Air Carriers: T-100 Domestic Market (U.S. Carriers), 2020; Bureau of Transportation Statistics, The Intermodal Transportation Database, Air Carriers: T-100 International Market (U.S. Carriers), 2019

BUSINESSES

Major Business Headquarters

Company Name	Industry	Rankings Fortune[1]	Rankings Forbes[2]
Altria Group	Tobacco	167	-
CarMax	Automotive Retailing, Services	173	-
Carpenter	Materials	-	212
Dominion Energy	Utilities, Gas and Electric	197	-
Estes Express Lines	Transportation	-	140
Genworth Financial	Insurance, Life, Health (Stock)	364	-
Performance Food Group	Wholesalers, Food and Grocery	168	-

Note: (1) Companies that produce a 10-K are ranked 1 to 500 based on 2019 revenue; (2) All private companies with at least $2 billion in annual revenue through the end of their most current fiscal year are ranked 1 to 219; companies listed are headquartered in the city; dashes indicate no ranking Source: Fortune, "Fortune 500," June/July 2020; Forbes, "America's Largest Private Companies," 2020

Fastest-Growing Businesses

According to *Inc.*, Richmond is home to two of America's 500 fastest-growing private companies: **Sassy Jones** (#75); **Spinnaker Consulting Group** (#160). Criteria: must be an independent, privately-held, for-profit, U.S. corporation, proprietorship or partnership as of December 31, 2019; revenues must be at least $100,000 in 2016 and $2 million in 2019; must have four-year operating/sales history. *Inc., "America's 500 Fastest-Growing Private Companies," 2020*

According to *Fortune*, Richmond is home to one of the 100 fastest-growing companies in the world: **Kinsale Capital Group** (#7). Companies were ranked by their revenue growth rate; their EPS growth rate; and their three-year annualized total return to investors for the period ending June 30, 2020. Criteria for inclusion: a company, foreign or domestic, must trade on a major U.S. stock exchange; must file quarterly reports with the SEC; must have a minimum market capitalization of $250 million; must have a stock price of at least $5 on June 30, 2020; must have been trading continuously since June 30, 2017; must have revenue and net income for the four quarters ended on or before April 30, 2020, of at least $50 million and $10 million, respectively; and must have posted a compound annual growth in revenue and earnings per share of at least 15% annually over the three years ending on or before April 30, 2020. Real estate investment trusts, limited-liability companies, limited parterships, business development companies, closed-end investment firms, companies about to be acquired, and companies that lost money in the quarter ending April 30, 2020 were excluded. *Fortune, "100 Fastest-Growing Companies," 2020*

According to *Initiative for a Competitive Inner City (ICIC)*, Richmond is home to one of America's 100 fastest-growing "inner city" companies: **W. E. Bowman Construction** (#97). Criteria for inclusion: company must be headquartered in or have 51 percent or more of its physical operations in an economically distressed urban area; must be an independent, for-profit corporation, partnership or proprietorship; must have 10 or more employees and have a five-year sales history that includes sales of at least $200,000 in the base year and at least $1 million in the current year with no decrease in sales over the two most recent years. Companies were ranked overall by revenue growth over the five-year period between 2015 and 2019. *Initiative for a Competitive Inner City (ICIC), "Inner City 100 Companies," 2020*

Living Environment

COST OF LIVING

Cost of Living Index

Composite Index	Groceries	Housing	Utilities	Trans-portation	Health Care	Misc. Goods/ Services
96.6	92.6	88.6	101.9	91.8	104.6	103.4

Note: The Cost of Living Index measures regional differences in the cost of consumer goods and services, excluding taxes and non-consumer expenditures, for professional and managerial households in the top income quintile. It is based on more than 50,000 prices covering almost 60 different items for which prices are collected three times a year by chambers of commerce, economic development organizations or university applied economic centers in each participating urban area. The numbers shown should be read as a percentage above or below the national average of 100. For example, a value of 115.4 in the groceries column indicates that grocery prices are 15.4% higher than the national average. Small differences in the index numbers should not be interpreted as significant; Figures cover the Richmond VA urban area.
Source: The Council for Community and Economic Research, Cost of Living Index, 2020

Grocery Prices

Area[1]	T-Bone Steak ($/pound)	Frying Chicken ($/pound)	Whole Milk ($/half gal.)	Eggs ($/dozen)	Orange Juice ($/64 oz.)	Coffee ($/11.5 oz.)
City[2]	11.36	1.05	1.58	0.86	3.20	3.78
Avg.	11.78	1.39	2.05	1.47	3.57	4.34
Min.	8.03	0.94	1.03	0.74	2.94	3.02
Max.	15.86	2.65	4.31	3.77	5.44	8.69

*Note: (1) Values for the local area are compared with the average, minimum and maximum values for all 284 areas in the Cost of Living Index; (2) Figures cover the Richmond VA urban area; **T-Bone Steak** (price per pound); **Frying Chicken** (price per pound, whole fryer); **Whole Milk** (half gallon carton); **Eggs** (price per dozen, Grade A, large); **Orange Juice** (64 oz. Tropicana or Florida Natural); **Coffee** (11.5 oz. can, vacuum-packed, Maxwell House, Hills Bros, or Folgers).*
Source: The Council for Community and Economic Research, Cost of Living Index, 2020

Housing and Utility Costs

Area[1]	New Home Price ($)	Apartment Rent ($/month)	All Electric ($/month)	Part Electric ($/month)	Other Energy ($/month)	Telephone ($/month)
City[2]	318,880	1,135	-	94.98	81.43	178.00
Avg.	368,594	1,168	170.86	100.47	65.28	184.30
Min.	190,567	502	91.58	31.42	26.08	169.60
Max.	2,227,806	4,738	470.38	280.31	280.06	206.50

*Note: (1) Values for the local area are compared with the average, minimum and maximum values for all 284 areas in the Cost of Living Index; (2) Figures cover the Richmond VA urban area; **New Home Price** (2,400 sf living area, 8,000 sf lot, in urban area with full utilities); **Apartment Rent** (950 sf 2 bedroom/1.5 or 2 bath, unfurnished, excluding all utilities except water); **All Electric** (average monthly cost for an all-electric home); **Part Electric** (average monthly cost for a part-electric home); **Other Energy** (average monthly cost for natural gas, fuel oil, coal, wood, and any other forms of energy except electricity); **Telephone** (price includes the base monthly rate plus taxes and fees for three lines of mobile phone service).*
Source: The Council for Community and Economic Research, Cost of Living Index, 2020

Health Care, Transportation, and Other Costs

Area[1]	Doctor ($/visit)	Dentist ($/visit)	Optometrist ($/visit)	Gasoline ($/gallon)	Beauty Salon ($/visit)	Men's Shirt ($)
City[2]	139.74	99.40	116.20	2.01	44.43	29.26
Avg.	115.44	99.32	108.10	2.21	39.27	31.37
Min.	36.68	59.00	51.36	1.71	19.00	11.00
Max.	219.00	153.10	250.97	3.46	82.05	58.33

*Note: (1) Values for the local area are compared with the average, minimum and maximum values for all 284 areas in the Cost of Living Index; (2) Figures cover the Richmond VA urban area; **Doctor** (general practitioners routine exam of an established patient); **Dentist** (adult teeth cleaning and periodic oral examination); **Optometrist** (full vision eye exam for established adult patient); **Gasoline** (one gallon regular unleaded, national brand, including all taxes, cash price at self-service pump if available); **Beauty Salon** (woman's shampoo, trim, and blow-dry); **Men's Shirt** (cotton/polyester dress shirt, pinpoint weave, long sleeves).*
Source: The Council for Community and Economic Research, Cost of Living Index, 2020

HOUSING

Homeownership Rate

Area	2012 (%)	2013 (%)	2014 (%)	2015 (%)	2016 (%)	2017 (%)	2018 (%)	2019 (%)	2020 (%)
MSA[1]	67.0	65.4	72.6	67.4	61.7	63.1	62.9	66.4	66.5
U.S.	65.4	65.1	64.5	63.7	63.4	63.9	64.4	64.6	66.6

Note: (1) Figures cover the Richmond, VA Metropolitan Statistical Area
Source: U.S. Census Bureau, Housing Vacancies and Homeownership Annual Statistics: 2012-2020

House Price Index (HPI)

Area	National Ranking[2]	Quarterly Change (%)	One-Year Change (%)	Five-Year Change (%)	Since 1991Q1 (%)
MSA[1]	134	2.05	6.10	28.56	172.25
U.S.[3]	—	3.81	10.77	38.99	205.12

Note: The HPI is a weighted repeat sales index. It measures average price changes in repeat sales or refinancings on the same properties. This information is obtained by reviewing repeat mortgage transactions on single-family properties whose mortgages have been purchased or securitized by Fannie Mae or Freddie Mac since January 1975; (1) Figures cover the Richmond, VA Metropolitan Statistical Area; (2) Rankings are based on annual percentage change for all metro areas containing at least 15,000 transactions over the last 10 years and ranges from 1 to 253; (3) figures based on a weighted average of Census Division estimates using a seasonally adjusted, purchase-only index; all figures are for the period ending December 31, 2020
Source: Federal Housing Finance Agency, Change in Metropolitan Area House Price Indexes, April 7, 2021

Median Single-Family Home Prices

Area	2018	2019	2020[p]	Percent Change 2019 to 2020
MSA[1]	258.8	264.0	273.2	3.5
U.S. Average	261.6	274.6	299.9	9.2

Note: Figures are median sales prices of existing single-family homes in thousands of dollars; (p) preliminary; (1) Figures cover the Richmond, VA Metropolitan Statistical Area
Source: National Association of Realtors, Median Sales Price of Existing Single-Family Homes for Metropolitan Areas, 4th Quarter 2020

Qualifying Income Based on Median Sales Price of Existing Single-Family Homes

Area	With 5% Down ($)	With 10% Down ($)	With 20% Down ($)
MSA[1]	60,166	56,999	50,666
U.S. Average	59,266	56,147	49,908

Note: Figures are preliminary; Qualifying income is based on a mortgage rate of 2.81%. Monthly principal and interest payment is limited to 25% of income; (1) Figures cover the Richmond, VA Metropolitan Statistical Area
Source: National Association of Realtors, Qualifying Income Based on Median Sales Price of Existing Single-Family Homes for Metropolitan Areas, 4th Quarter 2020

Home Value Distribution

Area	Under $50,000	$50,000 -$99,999	$100,000 -$149,999	$150,000 -$199,999	$200,000 -$299,999	$300,000 -$499,999	$500,000 -$999,999	$1,000,000 or more
City	2.0	11.4	13.9	15.4	20.8	21.7	11.5	3.3
MSA[1]	2.4	5.3	11.7	18.2	29.4	23.7	8.2	1.2
U.S.	6.9	12.0	13.3	14.0	19.6	19.3	11.4	3.4

Note: Figures are percentages and cover owner-occupied housing units; (1) Figures cover the Richmond, VA Metropolitan Statistical Area
Source: U.S. Census Bureau, 2015-2019 American Community Survey 5-Year Estimates

Year Housing Structure Built

Area	2010 or Later	2000 -2009	1990 -1999	1980 -1989	1970 -1979	1960 -1969	1950 -1959	1940 -1949	Before 1940	Median Year
City	4.0	5.4	4.9	6.3	11.3	12.4	15.0	9.1	31.7	1956
MSA[1]	5.9	14.9	15.3	16.1	15.1	9.7	9.4	4.3	9.2	1981
U.S.	5.2	14.0	13.9	13.4	15.2	10.6	10.3	4.9	12.6	1978

Note: Figures are percentages except for Median Year; Note: (1) Figures cover the Richmond, VA Metropolitan Statistical Area
Source: U.S. Census Bureau, 2015-2019 American Community Survey 5-Year Estimates

Gross Monthly Rent

Area	Under $500	$500 -$999	$1,000 -$1,499	$1,500 -$1,999	$2,000 -$2,499	$2,500 -$2,999	$3,000 and up	Median ($)
City	12.6	35.0	37.0	11.7	2.7	0.3	0.6	1,025
MSA[1]	7.3	30.2	44.1	13.9	2.9	0.8	0.8	1,117
U.S.	9.4	36.2	30.0	14.0	5.6	2.4	2.4	1,062

Note: Figures are percentages except for Median; Gross rent is the contract rent plus the estimated average monthly cost of utilities (electricity, gas, and water and sewer) and fuels (oil, coal, kerosene, wood, etc.) if these are paid by the renter (or paid for the renter by someone else); (1) Figures cover the Richmond, VA Metropolitan Statistical Area
Source: U.S. Census Bureau, 2015-2019 American Community Survey 5-Year Estimates

HEALTH

Health Risk Factors

Category	MSA[1] (%)	U.S. (%)
Adults aged 18–64 who have any kind of health care coverage	87.7	87.3
Adults who reported being in good or better health	85.5	82.4
Adults who have been told they have high blood cholesterol	35.4	33.0
Adults who have been told they have high blood pressure	34.0	32.3
Adults who are current smokers	17.4	17.1
Adults who currently use E-cigarettes	4.7	4.6
Adults who currently use chewing tobacco, snuff, or snus	2.1	4.0
Adults who are heavy drinkers[2]	6.6	6.3
Adults who are binge drinkers[3]	18.6	17.4
Adults who are overweight (BMI 25.0 - 29.9)	33.2	35.3
Adults who are obese (BMI 30.0 - 99.8)	31.6	31.3
Adults who participated in any physical activities in the past month	74.2	74.4
Adults who always or nearly always wears a seat belt	93.7	94.3

Note: (1) Figures cover the Richmond, VA Metropolitan Statistical Area; (2) Heavy drinkers are classified as adult men having more than 14 drinks per week and adult women having more than 7 drinks per week; (3) Binge drinkers are classified as males having five or more drinks on one occasion or females having four or more drinks on one occasion
Source: Centers for Disease Control and Prevention, Behaviorial Risk Factor Surveillance System, SMART: Selected Metropolitan Area Risk Trends, 2017

Acute and Chronic Health Conditions

Category	MSA[1] (%)	U.S. (%)
Adults who have ever been told they had a heart attack	4.8	4.2
Adults who have ever been told they have angina or coronary heart disease	4.6	3.9
Adults who have ever been told they had a stroke	3.6	3.0
Adults who have ever been told they have asthma	12.9	14.2
Adults who have ever been told they have arthritis	22.5	24.9
Adults who have ever been told they have diabetes[2]	10.9	10.5
Adults who have ever been told they had skin cancer	6.3	6.2
Adults who have ever been told they had any other types of cancer	5.7	7.1
Adults who have ever been told they have COPD	7.4	6.5
Adults who have ever been told they have kidney disease	3.1	3.0
Adults who have ever been told they have a form of depression	20.8	20.5

Note: (1) Figures cover the Richmond, VA Metropolitan Statistical Area; (2) Figures do not include pregnancy-related, borderline, or pre-diabetes
Source: Centers for Disease Control and Prevention, Behaviorial Risk Factor Surveillance System, SMART: Selected Metropolitan Area Risk Trends, 2017

Health Screening and Vaccination Rates

Category	MSA[1] (%)	U.S. (%)
Adults aged 65+ who have had flu shot within the past year	60.8	60.7
Adults aged 65+ who have ever had a pneumonia vaccination	79.0	75.4
Adults who have ever been tested for HIV	45.1	36.1
Adults who have ever had the shingles or zoster vaccine?	31.2	28.9
Adults who have had their blood cholesterol checked within the last five years	86.1	85.9

Note: n/a not available; (1) Figures cover the Richmond, VA Metropolitan Statistical Area.
Source: Centers for Disease Control and Prevention, Behaviorial Risk Factor Surveillance System, SMART: Selected Metropolitan Area Risk Trends, 2017

Disability Status

Category	MSA[1] (%)	U.S. (%)
Adults who reported being deaf	5.3	6.7
Are you blind or have serious difficulty seeing, even when wearing glasses?	4.0	4.5
Are you limited in any way in any of your usual activities due of arthritis?	10.9	12.9
Do you have difficulty doing errands alone?	7.4	6.8
Do you have difficulty dressing or bathing?	3.6	3.6
Do you have serious difficulty concentrating/remembering/making decisions?	9.6	10.7
Do you have serious difficulty walking or climbing stairs?	13.6	13.6

Note: (1) Figures cover the Richmond, VA Metropolitan Statistical Area.
Source: Centers for Disease Control and Prevention, Behaviorial Risk Factor Surveillance System, SMART: Selected Metropolitan Area Risk Trends, 2017

Mortality Rates for the Top 10 Causes of Death in the U.S.

ICD-10[a] Sub-Chapter	ICD-10[a] Code	Age-Adjusted Mortality Rate[1] per 100,000 population	
		County[2]	U.S.
Malignant neoplasms	C00-C97	155.1	149.2
Ischaemic heart diseases	I20-I25	78.7	90.5
Other forms of heart disease	I30-I51	73.3	52.2
Chronic lower respiratory diseases	J40-J47	37.1	39.6
Other degenerative diseases of the nervous system	G30-G31	31.3	37.6
Cerebrovascular diseases	I60-I69	41.6	37.2
Other external causes of accidental injury	W00-X59	54.1	36.1
Organic, including symptomatic, mental disorders	F01-F09	34.1	29.4
Hypertensive diseases	I10-I15	23.0	24.1
Diabetes mellitus	E10-E14	24.1	21.5

Note: (a) ICD-10 = International Classification of Diseases 10th Revision; (1) Mortality rates are a three-year average covering 2017-2019; (2) Figures cover Richmond city.
Source: Centers for Disease Control and Prevention, National Center for Health Statistics. Underlying Cause of Death 1999-2019 on CDC WONDER Online Database

Mortality Rates for Selected Causes of Death

ICD-10[a] Sub-Chapter	ICD-10[a] Code	Age-Adjusted Mortality Rate[1] per 100,000 population	
		County[2]	U.S.
Assault	X85-Y09	17.1	6.0
Diseases of the liver	K70-K76	13.2	14.4
Human immunodeficiency virus (HIV) disease	B20-B24	3.4	1.5
Influenza and pneumonia	J09-J18	9.6	13.8
Intentional self-harm	X60-X84	11.6	14.1
Malnutrition	E40-E46	3.1	2.3
Obesity and other hyperalimentation	E65-E68	Unreliable	2.1
Renal failure	N17-N19	24.2	12.6
Transport accidents	V01-V99	11.1	12.3
Viral hepatitis	B15-B19	Suppressed	1.2

Note: (a) ICD-10 = International Classification of Diseases 10th Revision; (1) Mortality rates are a three-year average covering 2017-2019; (2) Figures cover Richmond city; Data are suppressed when the data meet the criteria for confidentiality constraints; Mortality rates are flagged as unreliable when the rate would be calculated with a numerator of 20 or less.
Source: Centers for Disease Control and Prevention, National Center for Health Statistics. Underlying Cause of Death 1999-2019 on CDC WONDER Online Database

Health Insurance Coverage

Area	With Health Insurance	With Private Health Insurance	With Public Health Insurance	Without Health Insurance	Population Under Age 19 Without Health Insurance
City	88.0	62.6	34.9	12.0	6.5
MSA[1]	91.8	75.2	29.4	8.2	4.6
U.S.	91.2	67.9	35.1	8.8	5.1

Note: Figures are percentages that cover the civilian noninstitutionalized population; (1) Figures cover the Richmond, VA Metropolitan Statistical Area
Source: U.S. Census Bureau, 2015-2019 American Community Survey 5-Year Estimates

Number of Medical Professionals

Area	MDs[3]	DOs[3,4]	Dentists	Podiatrists	Chiropractors	Optometrists
Ind. City[1] (number)	1,697	65	330	25	17	38
Ind. City[1] (rate[2])	740.3	28.4	143.2	10.8	7.4	16.5
U.S. (rate[2])	282.9	22.7	71.2	6.2	28.1	16.9
51760						

Note: Data as of 2019 unless noted; (1) Data covers Richmond independent city; (2) Rate per 100,000 population; (3) Data as of 2018 and includes all active, non-federal physicians; (4) Doctor of Osteopathic Medicine
Source: U.S. Department of Health and Human Services, Health Resources and Services Administration, Bureau of Health Professions, Area Resource File (ARF) 2019-2020

Best Hospitals

According to *U.S. News,* the Richmond, VA metro area is home to one of the best hospitals in the U.S.: **VCU Medical Center** (2 adult specialties and 4 pediatric specialties). The hospital listed was nationally ranked in at least one of 16 adult or 10 pediatric specialties. Only 134 hospitals nationwide were nationally ranked in one or more adult or pediatric specialty; this number increases to 178 counting specialized centers within hospitals. Twenty hospitals in the U.S. made the Honor Roll. The Best Hospitals Honor Roll takes both the national rankings and the procedure and condition ratings into account. Hospitals received points if they were nationally ranked in one of the 16 adult specialties—the higher they ranked, the more points they got—and how many ratings of "high performing"

they earned in the 10 procedures and conditions. *U.S. News Online, "America's Best Hospitals 2020-21"*

According to *U.S. News,* the Richmond, VA metro area is home to one of the best children's hospitals in the U.S.: **Children's Hospital of Richmond at VCU** (4 pediatric specialties). The hospital listed was highly ranked in at least one of 10 pediatric specialties. Eighty-eight children's hospitals in the U.S. were nationally ranked in at least one specialty. Hospitals received points for being ranked in a specialty, and the 10 hospitals with the most points across the 10 specialties make up the Honor Roll. *U.S. News Online, "America's Best Children's Hospitals 2020-21"*

EDUCATION

Public School District Statistics

District Name	Schls	Pupils	Pupil/ Teacher Ratio	Minority Pupils[1] (%)	Free Lunch Eligible[2] (%)	IEP[3] (%)
Richmond City Public Schools	54	24,763	16.0	86.6	87.6	16.0

Note: Table includes school districts with 2,000 or more students; (1) Percentage of students that are not non-Hispanic white; (2) Percentage of students that are eligible for the free lunch program; (3) Percentage of students that have an Individualized Education Program.
Source: U.S. Department of Education, National Center for Education Statistics, Common Core of Data, Local Education Agency (School District) Universe Survey: School Year 2018-2019; U.S. Department of Education, National Center for Education Statistics, Common Core of Data, Public Elementary/Secondary School Universe Survey: School Year 2018-2019

Best High Schools

According to *U.S. News,* Richmond is home to one of the top 500 high schools in the U.S.: **Open High School** (#493). Nearly 18,000 public, magnet and charter schools were ranked based on their performance on state assessments and how well they prepare students for college. *U.S. News & World Report, "Best High Schools 2020"*

Highest Level of Education

Area	Less than H.S.	H.S. Diploma	Some College, No Deg.	Associate Degree	Bachelor's Degree	Master's Degree	Prof. School Degree	Doctorate Degree
City	14.6	21.8	18.4	5.6	23.5	11.0	3.1	2.0
MSA[1]	10.1	25.1	20.0	7.4	23.1	10.5	2.3	1.6
U.S.	12.0	27.0	20.4	8.5	19.8	8.8	2.1	1.4

Note: Figures cover persons age 25 and over; (1) Figures cover the Richmond, VA Metropolitan Statistical Area
Source: U.S. Census Bureau, 2015-2019 American Community Survey 5-Year Estimates

Educational Attainment by Race

Area	High School Graduate or Higher (%)					Bachelor's Degree or Higher (%)				
	Total	White	Black	Asian	Hisp.[2]	Total	White	Black	Asian	Hisp.[2]
City	85.4	92.3	78.8	81.7	50.8	39.6	61.8	15.5	62.5	14.3
MSA[1]	89.9	92.8	85.0	88.8	67.3	37.4	43.4	21.8	64.0	21.3
U.S.	88.0	89.9	86.0	87.1	68.7	32.1	33.5	21.6	54.3	16.4

Note: Figures shown cover persons 25 years old and over; (1) Figures cover the Richmond, VA Metropolitan Statistical Area; (2) People of Hispanic origin can be of any race
Source: U.S. Census Bureau, 2015-2019 American Community Survey 5-Year Estimates

School Enrollment by Grade and Control

Area	Preschool (%)		Kindergarten (%)		Grades 1 - 4 (%)		Grades 5 - 8 (%)		Grades 9 - 12 (%)	
	Public	Private	Public	Private	Public	Private	Public	Private	Public	Private
City	58.6	41.4	91.1	8.9	87.8	12.2	80.8	19.2	87.1	12.9
MSA[1]	41.9	58.1	89.0	11.0	89.8	10.2	88.6	11.4	90.3	9.7
U.S.	59.1	40.9	87.6	12.4	89.5	10.5	89.4	10.6	90.1	9.9

Note: Figures shown cover persons 3 years old and over; (1) Figures cover the Richmond, VA Metropolitan Statistical Area
Source: U.S. Census Bureau, 2015-2019 American Community Survey 5-Year Estimates

Higher Education

Four-Year Colleges			Two-Year Colleges			Medical Schools[1]	Law Schools[2]	Voc/ Tech[3]
Public	Private Non-profit	Private For-profit	Public	Private Non-profit	Private For-profit			
1	3	0	1	1	2	1	1	1

Note: Figures cover institutions located within the city limits and include main campuses only; (1) includes schools accredited by the Liaison Committee on Medical Education and the American Osteopathic Association's Commission on Osteopathic College Accreditation; (2) includes ABA-accredited schools, schools with provisional ABA accreditation, and state accredited schools; (3) includes all schools with programs that are less than 2 years.
Source: National Center for Education Statistics, Integrated Postsecondary Education System (IPEDS), 2019-20; Wikipedia, List of Medical Schools in the United States, accessed April 2, 2021; Wikipedia, List of Law Schools in the United States, accessed April 2, 2021

According to *U.S. News & World Report,* the Richmond, VA metro area is home to one of the top 200 national universities in the U.S.: **Virginia Commonwealth University** (#160 tie). The indicators used to capture academic quality fall into a number of categories: assessment by administrators at peer institutions; retention of students; faculty resources; student selectivity; financial resources; alumni giving; high school counselor ratings of colleges; and graduation rate. *U.S. News & World Report, "America's Best Colleges 2021"*

According to *U.S. News & World Report,* the Richmond, VA metro area is home to one of the top 100 liberal arts colleges in the U.S.: **University of Richmond** (#22 tie). The indicators used to capture academic quality fall into a number of categories: assessment by administrators at peer institutions; retention of students; faculty resources; student selectivity; financial resources; alumni giving; high school counselor ratings of colleges; and graduation rate. *U.S. News & World Report, "America's Best Colleges 2021"*

According to *U.S. News & World Report,* the Richmond, VA metro area is home to one of the top 100 law schools in the U.S.: **University of Richmond** (#53 tie). The rankings are based on a weighted average of 12 measures of quality: peer assessment score; assessment score by lawyers/judges; median LSAT scores; median undergrad GPA; acceptance rate; employment rates for graduates; placement success; bar passage rate; faculty resources; expenditures per student; student/faculty ratio; and library resources. *U.S. News & World Report, "America's Best Graduate Schools, Law, 2022"*

According to *U.S. News & World Report,* the Richmond, VA metro area is home to one of the top 75 medical schools for research in the U.S.: **Virginia Commonwealth University** (#61 tie). The rankings are based on a weighted average of 11 measures of quality: quality assessment; peer assessment score; assessment score by residency directors; research activity; total research activity; average research activity per faculty member; student selectivity; median MCAT total score; median undergraduate GPA; acceptance rate; and faculty resources. *U.S. News & World Report, "America's Best Graduate Schools, Medical, 2022"*

EMPLOYERS

Major Employers

Company Name	Industry
Altria Group	Cigarettes
Amazon.com	Retail
Anthem Blue Cross and Blue Shield	Insurance
Bank of America	Financial services
Bon Secours Richmond	Healthcare
Capital One Financial Corp.	Financial services
Dominion Resources	Power & energy
DuPont	Conglomerate
Federal Reserve Bank of Richmond	Financial services
Food Lion	Grocery stores
HCA	General medical & surgical hospitals
Markel Corporation	Specialty insurance products
SunTrust Banks	Financial services
The Kroger Co.	Grocery stores
United Parcel Service	Package delivery services
University of Richmond	Education
VCU Health System	Healthcare
Verizon Communications	Communications
Wal-Mart Stores	Retail
Wells Fargo	Financial services

Note: Companies shown are located within the Richmond, VA Metropolitan Statistical Area.
Source: Hoovers.com; Wikipedia

Best Companies to Work For

CarMax, headquartered in Richmond, is among "The 100 Best Companies to Work For." To pick the best companies, *Fortune* partnered with the Great Place to Work Institute. Two-thirds of a company's score is based on the results of the Institute's Trust Index survey, which is sent to a random sample of employees from each company. The questions related to attitudes about management's credibility, job satisfaction, and camaraderie. The other third of the scoring is based on the company's responses to the Institute's Culture Audit, which includes detailed questions about pay and benefit programs, and a series of open-ended questions about hiring practices, internal communication, training, recognition programs, and diversity efforts. Any company that is at least five years old with more than 1,000 U.S. employees is eligible. *Fortune, "The 100 Best Companies to Work For," 2020*

Bon Secours Health System, headquartered in Richmond, is among the "Top Companies for Executive Women." This list is determined by organizations filling out an in-depth survey that measures female demographics at every level, but with an emphasis on women in senior corporate roles, with profit & loss (P&L) responsibility, and those earning in the top 20 percent of the organization. *Working Mother* defines P&L as having responsibility that involves monitoring the net income after expenses for a department or entire organization, with direct influence on how company resources are allocated. *Working Mother, "Top Companies for Executive Women," 2020+*

PUBLIC SAFETY

Crime Rate

Area	All Crimes	Violent Crimes				Property Crimes		
		Murder	Rape[3]	Robbery	Aggrav. Assault	Burglary	Larceny -Theft	Motor Vehicle Theft
City	3,962.4	23.8	19.5	166.9	252.7	427.4	2,702.0	370.1
Suburbs[1]	2,045.4	4.9	28.3	37.0	106.2	170.5	1,580.8	117.6
Metro[2]	2,388.9	8.3	26.7	60.3	132.4	216.6	1,781.7	162.9
U.S.	2,489.3	5.0	42.6	81.6	250.2	340.5	1,549.5	219.9

Note: Figures are crimes per 100,000 population; (1) All areas within the metro area that are located outside the city limits; (2) Figures cover the Richmond, VA Metropolitan Statistical Area; (3) All figures shown were reported using the revised Uniform Crime Reporting (UCR) definition of rape.
Source: FBI Uniform Crime Reports, 2019

Hate Crimes

Area	Number of Quarters Reported	Number of Incidents per Bias Motivation					
		Race/Ethnicity/ Ancestry	Religion	Sexual Orientation	Disability	Gender	Gender Identity
City	4	3	0	2	0	0	0
U.S.	4	3,963	1,521	1,195	157	69	198

Source: Federal Bureau of Investigation, Hate Crime Statistics 2019

Identity Theft Consumer Reports

Area	Reports	Reports per 100,000 Population	Rank[2]
MSA[1]	2,985	231	171
U.S.	1,387,615	423	-

Note: (1) Figures cover the Richmond, VA Metropolitan Statistical Area; (2) Rank ranges from 1 to 391 where 1 indicates greatest number of identity theft reports per 100,000 population
Source: Federal Trade Commission, Consumer Sentinel Network Data Book 2020

Fraud and Other Consumer Reports

Area	Reports	Reports per 100,000 Population	Rank[2]
MSA[1]	12,131	939	35
U.S.	3,385,133	1,031	-

Note: (1) Figures cover the Richmond, VA Metropolitan Statistical Area; (2) Rank ranges from 1 to 391 where 1 indicates greatest number of fraud and other consumer reports per 100,000 population
Source: Federal Trade Commission, Consumer Sentinel Network Data Book 2020

POLITICS

2020 Presidential Election Results

Area	Biden	Trump	Jorgensen	Hawkins	Other
Richmond City	82.9	14.9	1.5	0.0	0.6
U.S.	51.3	46.8	1.2	0.3	0.5

Note: Results are percentages and may not add to 100% due to rounding
Source: Dave Leip's Atlas of U.S. Presidential Elections

SPORTS

Professional Sports Teams

Team Name	League	Year Established
No teams are located in the metro area		

Source: Wikipedia, Major Professional Sports Teams of the United States and Canada, April 6, 2021

CLIMATE

Average and Extreme Temperatures

Temperature	Jan	Feb	Mar	Apr	May	Jun	Jul	Aug	Sep	Oct	Nov	Dec	Yr.
Extreme High (°F)	80	82	91	96	98	104	105	103	103	99	86	80	105
Average High (°F)	47	50	59	69	78	85	88	86	81	71	60	50	69
Average Temp. (°F)	38	40	48	58	66	75	78	77	71	60	50	41	58
Average Low (°F)	28	30	37	45	55	63	68	67	60	48	38	31	48
Extreme Low (°F)	-6	-8	11	19	31	40	51	47	35	21	14	1	-8

Note: Figures cover the years 1921-1990
Source: National Climatic Data Center, International Station Meteorological Climate Summary, 9/96

Average Precipitation/Snowfall/Humidity

Precip./Humidity	Jan	Feb	Mar	Apr	May	Jun	Jul	Aug	Sep	Oct	Nov	Dec	Yr.
Avg. Precip. (in.)	3.3	3.0	3.5	3.1	3.7	3.7	5.2	4.9	3.3	3.1	2.9	3.1	43.0
Avg. Snowfall (in.)	5	4	2	Tr	0	0	0	0	0	Tr	1	2	13
Avg. Rel. Hum. 7am (%)	79	79	78	76	81	82	85	89	90	89	84	80	83
Avg. Rel. Hum. 4pm (%)	54	51	46	43	51	53	56	58	57	53	51	55	52

Note: Figures cover the years 1921-1990; Tr = Trace amounts (<0.05 in. of rain; <0.5 in. of snow)
Source: National Climatic Data Center, International Station Meteorological Climate Summary, 9/96

Weather Conditions

Temperature			Daytime Sky			Precipitation		
10°F & below	32°F & below	90°F & above	Clear	Partly cloudy	Cloudy	0.01 inch or more precip.	0.1 inch or more snow/ice	Thunder-storms
3	79	41	90	147	128	115	7	43

Note: Figures are average number of days per year and cover the years 1921-1990
Source: National Climatic Data Center, International Station Meteorological Climate Summary, 9/96

HAZARDOUS WASTE

Superfund Sites

The Richmond, VA metro area is home to four sites on the EPA's Superfund National Priorities List: **C & R Battery Co.** (final); **Defense General Supply Center (DLA)** (final); **H & H Inc., Burn Pit** (final); **Rentokil, Inc. (Virginia Wood Preserving Division)** (final). There are a total of 1,375 Superfund sites with a status of proposed or final on the list in the U.S. *U.S. Environmental Protection Agency, National Priorities List, April 7, 2021*

AIR QUALITY

Air Quality Trends: Ozone

	1990	1995	2000	2005	2010	2015	2016	2017	2018	2019
MSA[1]	0.083	0.089	0.080	0.082	0.079	0.062	0.065	0.063	0.062	0.061
U.S.	0.088	0.089	0.082	0.080	0.073	0.068	0.069	0.068	0.069	0.065

Note: (1) Data covers the Richmond, VA Metropolitan Statistical Area. The values shown are the composite ozone concentration averages among trend sites based on the highest fourth daily maximum 8-hour concentration in parts per million. These trends are based on sites having an adequate record of monitoring data during the trend period. Data from exceptional events are included.
Source: U.S. Environmental Protection Agency, Air Quality Monitoring Information, "Air Quality Trends by City, 1990-2019"

Air Quality Index

Area	Percent of Days when Air Quality was...[2]					AQI Statistics[2]	
	Good	Moderate	Unhealthy for Sensitive Groups	Unhealthy	Very Unhealthy	Maximum	Median
MSA[1]	74.5	25.5	0.0	0.0	0.0	100	44

Note: (1) Data covers the Richmond, VA Metropolitan Statistical Area; (2) Based on 365 days with AQI data in 2019. Air Quality Index (AQI) is an index for reporting daily air quality. EPA calculates the AQI for five major air pollutants regulated by the Clean Air Act: ground-level ozone, particle pollution (aka particulate matter), carbon monoxide, sulfur dioxide, and nitrogen dioxide. The AQI runs from 0 to 500. The higher the AQI value, the greater the level of air pollution and the greater the health concern. There are six AQI categories: "Good" AQI is between 0 and 50. Air quality is considered satisfactory; "Moderate" AQI is between 51 and 100. Air quality is acceptable; "Unhealthy for Sensitive Groups" When AQI values are between 101 and 150, members of sensitive groups may experience health effects; "Unhealthy" When AQI values are between 151 and 200 everyone may begin to experience health effects; "Very Unhealthy" AQI values between 201 and 300 trigger a health alert; "Hazardous" AQI values over 300 trigger warnings of emergency conditions (not shown).
Source: U.S. Environmental Protection Agency, Air Quality Index Report, 2019

Air Quality Index Pollutants

Area	Percent of Days when AQI Pollutant was...[2]					
	Carbon Monoxide	Nitrogen Dioxide	Ozone	Sulfur Dioxide	Particulate Matter 2.5	Particulate Matter 10
MSA[1]	0.0	4.4	67.4	0.0	28.2	0.0

Note: (1) Data covers the Richmond, VA Metropolitan Statistical Area; (2) Based on 365 days with AQI data in 2019. The Air Quality Index (AQI) is an index for reporting daily air quality. EPA calculates the AQI for five major air pollutants regulated by the Clean Air Act: ground-level ozone, particle pollution (also known as particulate matter), carbon monoxide, sulfur dioxide, and nitrogen dioxide. The AQI runs from 0 to 500. The higher the AQI value, the greater the level of air pollution and the greater the health concern.
Source: U.S. Environmental Protection Agency, Air Quality Index Report, 2019

Maximum Air Pollutant Concentrations: Particulate Matter, Ozone, CO and Lead

	Particulate Matter 10 (ug/m^3)	Particulate Matter 2.5 Wtd AM (ug/m^3)	Particulate Matter 2.5 24-Hr (ug/m^3)	Ozone (ppm)	Carbon Monoxide (ppm)	Lead (ug/m^3)
MSA[1] Level	27	8.4	20	0.064	1	n/a
NAAQS[2]	150	15	35	0.075	9	0.15
Met NAAQS[2]	Yes	Yes	Yes	Yes	Yes	n/a

Note: (1) Data covers the Richmond, VA Metropolitan Statistical Area; Data from exceptional events are included; (2) National Ambient Air Quality Standards; ppm = parts per million; ug/m^3 = micrograms per cubic meter; n/a not available.
Concentrations: Particulate Matter 10 (coarse particulate)—highest second maximum 24-hour concentration; Particulate Matter 2.5 Wtd AM (fine particulate)—highest weighted annual mean concentration; Particulate Matter 2.5 24-Hour (fine particulate)—highest 98th percentile 24-hour concentration; Ozone—highest fourth daily maximum 8-hour concentration; Carbon Monoxide—highest second maximum non-overlapping 8-hour concentration; Lead—maximum running 3-month average
Source: U.S. Environmental Protection Agency, Air Quality Monitoring Information, "Air Quality Statistics by City, 2019"

Maximum Air Pollutant Concentrations: Nitrogen Dioxide and Sulfur Dioxide

	Nitrogen Dioxide AM (ppb)	Nitrogen Dioxide 1-Hr (ppb)	Sulfur Dioxide AM (ppb)	Sulfur Dioxide 1-Hr (ppb)	Sulfur Dioxide 24-Hr (ppb)
MSA[1] Level	12	43	n/a	14	n/a
NAAQS[2]	53	100	30	75	140
Met NAAQS[2]	Yes	Yes	n/a	Yes	n/a

Note: (1) Data covers the Richmond, VA Metropolitan Statistical Area; Data from exceptional events are included; (2) National Ambient Air Quality Standards; ppm = parts per million; ug/m^3 = micrograms per cubic meter; n/a not available.
Concentrations: Nitrogen Dioxide AM—highest arithmetic mean concentration; Nitrogen Dioxide 1-Hr—highest 98th percentile 1-hour daily maximum concentration; Sulfur Dioxide AM—highest annual mean concentration; Sulfur Dioxide 1-Hr—highest 99th percentile 1-hour daily maximum concentration; Sulfur Dioxide 24-Hr—highest second maximum 24-hour concentration
Source: U.S. Environmental Protection Agency, Air Quality Monitoring Information, "Air Quality Statistics by City, 2019"

Virginia Beach, Virginia

Background

Virginia Beach, on the shores of the Chesapeake Bay and the Atlantic Ocean, is a paradise for beach lovers. With nearly half a million residents, it is also one of the fastest-growing cities on the East Coast.

The history of Virginia Beach began in 1607 when English settlers led by Captain John Smith first reached Virginia's shore at Cape Henry aboard the *Susan Constant,* the *Godspeed,* and the *Discovery.* The 100 colonists, sent by the Virginia Company to investigate trade possibilities, shortly moved up the James River to found the first permanent English settlement in America at Jamestown. The first actual settlement within the Virginia Beach city limits was at Lynnhaven Bay in 1621. It was at Cape Henry that the French Admiral Comte de Grassein, during the Revolutionary War, came to the aid of American patriots by blockading the British fleet during the final and decisive Battle of Yorktown, and the area to this day has been home to strategically important military bases.

With the connection of a railway to Norfolk in the late nineteenth century, Virginia Beach became a popular shore resort and was incorporated as a town in 1906, then as a city in 1952. In 1963, all of neighboring Princess Ann County merged with the city, and today's Virginia Beach covers a territory of 310 square miles, with 38 miles of shoreline. It is the largest city in Virginia and the largest resort city in the world, with tourism still the economic mainstay. It hosts the East Coast Surfing Championship and the North American Sand Soccer Championship every year.

Virginia Beach is listed in the *Guinness Book of World Records* as having the longest pleasure beach in the world, and is located at the southern end of the Chesapeake Bay Bridge Tunnel—which was the longest bridge-tunnel in the world until 2018, when it was surpassed by a tunnel in China.

The city naturally enjoys a lifestyle oriented to the water, with 28 miles of public beaches and 79 miles of scenic waterways. The beaches are enjoyed most of the year, while sailing and fishing opportunities are varied and virtually inexhaustible. There are three state and regional parks and three national wildlife refuges in the city, with 208 city parks, making it a municipality with a unique mix of urban, natural, and ecotourist attractions.

Agribusiness also contributes to the vitality of the area, with more than 32,700 acres of land under cultivation, and the construction and real estate industries are robust. Convention and trade shows annually produce millions of dollars in revenues. The labor force is abundant, productive, and energetic, offering a rich range of professional, technical, blue-collar, and clerical skills. Local government receives high grades from residents and visitors alike, and the city received the American Society of Public Administration's first-ever Innovation Recognition Award for excellence in organizational development, strategic planning, quality initiatives, and process improvements.

Virginia Beach is located alongside the Port of Hampton Roads, one of the world's finest harbors. Rail service serves major industrial centers, and nearby Norfolk International Airport serves seven major and seven commuter airlines. Twenty internationally-based companies are headquartered in the city, including Busch, Amerigroup and the Christian Broadcasting Network.

Virginia Beach and its environs are home to 11 colleges and universities, including the Virginia Beach Higher Education Center, the College of William and Mary, Old Dominion University, Norfolk State University, Virginia Wesleyan College, Eastern Virginia Medical School, and Tidewater Community College.

There are more than 200 art and cultural organizations based in the city, including a symphony, opera, theater groups, and many museums. The Virginia Marine Science Museum hosts one of the most attended aquariums in the nation.

Virginia Beach enjoys a temperate maritime climate influenced by the Gulf Stream. Winters are mild, rarely freezing, and splendid beach weather characterizes the area from spring through fall.

Rankings

General Rankings

- For its "Best for Vets: Places to Live 2019" rankings, *Military Times* evaluated 599 cities (83 large, 234 medium, 282 small) and compared the locations across three broad categories: veteran and military culture/services; economic indicators; and livability factors such as health, crime, traffic, and school quality. Virginia Beach ranked #2 out of the top 25, in the large city category (population of more than 250,000). Data points more specific to veterans and the military weighed more heavily than others. *rebootcamp.militarytimes.com, "Military Times Best Places to Live 2019," September 10, 2018*

Business/Finance Rankings

- The Brookings Institution ranked the nation's largest cities based on income inequality. Virginia Beach was ranked #96 (#1 = greatest inequality). Criteria: the "95/20 ratio," a figure representing the income at which a household earns more than 95 percent of all other households, divided by the income at which a household earns more than only 20 percent of all other households. *Brookings Institution, "Household Income Inequality, Largest Cities of 97 Large U.S. Metro Areas, 2014-2016," February 5, 2018*

- The Brookings Institution ranked the 100 largest metro areas in the U.S. based on income inequality. Virginia Beach was ranked #91 (#1 = greatest inequality). Criteria: the "95/20 ratio," a figure representing the income at which a household earns more than 95 percent of all other households, divided by the income at which a household earns more than only 20 percent of all other households. *Brookings Institution, "Household Income Inequality, 100 Largest U.S. Metro Areas, 2014-2016," February 5, 2018*

- Virginia Beach was identified as one of America's most frugal metro areas by *Coupons.com*. The city ranked #13 out of 25. Criteria: digital coupon usage. *Coupons.com, "America's Most Frugal Cities of 2017," March 22, 2018*

- The Virginia Beach metro area appeared on the Milken Institute "2021 Best Performing Cities" list. Rank: #140 out of 200 large metro areas (population over 250,000). Criteria: job growth; wage and salary growth; high-tech output growth; housing affordability; household broadband access. *Milken Institute, "Best-Performing Cities 2021," February 16, 2021*

- *Forbes* ranked the 200 most populous metro areas to determine the nation's "Best Places for Business and Careers." The Virginia Beach metro area was ranked #79. Criteria: costs (business and living); job growth (past and projected); income growth; quality of life; educational attainment (college and high school); projected economic growth; cultural and leisure opportunities; workplace tolerance laws; net migration patterns. *Forbes, "The Best Places for Business and Careers 2019: Seattle Still On Top," October 30, 2019*

Dating/Romance Rankings

- Virginia Beach was ranked #25 out of 25 cities that stood out for inspiring romance and attracting diners on the website OpenTable.com. Criteria: percentage of people who dined out on Valentine's Day in 2018; percentage of romantic restaurants as rated by OpenTable diner reviews; and percentage of tables seated for two. *OpenTable, "25 Most Romantic Cities in America for 2019," February 7, 2019*

Education Rankings

- Personal finance website *WalletHub* analyzed the 150 largest U.S. metropolitan statistical areas to determine where the most educated Americans are putting their degrees to work. Criteria: education levels; percentage of workers with degrees; education quality and attainment gap; public school quality rankings; quality and enrollment of each metro area's universities. Virginia Beach was ranked #36 (#1 = most educated city). *www.WalletHub.com, "Most and Least Educated Cities in America," July 20, 2020*

- Virginia Beach was selected as one of America's most literate cities. The city ranked #46 out of the 84 largest U.S. cities. Criteria: number of booksellers; library resources; Internet resources; educational attainment; periodical publishing resources; newspaper circulation. *Central Connecticut State University, "America's Most Literate Cities, 2018," February 2019*

Environmental Rankings

- Virginia Beach was highlighted as one of the top 98 cleanest metro areas for short-term particle pollution (24-hour PM 2.5) in the U.S. during 2016 through 2018. Monitors in these cities reported no days with unhealthful PM 2.5 levels. *American Lung Association, "State of the Air 2020," April 21, 2020*

Health/Fitness Rankings

- For each of the 100 largest cities in the United States, the American Fitness Index®, published by the American College of Sports Medicine and the Anthem Foundation, evaluated community infrastructure and 33 health behaviors including preventive health, levels of chronic disease conditions, pedestrian safety, air quality, and community resources that support physical activity. Virginia Beach ranked #28 for "community fitness." *americanfitnessindex.org, "2020 ACSM American Fitness Index Summary Report," July 14, 2020*

- Virginia Beach was identified as a "2021 Spring Allergy Capital." The area ranked #4 out of 100. Three groups of factors were used to identify the most challenging cities for people with allergies during the spring season: annual spring pollen levels; over the counter medicine use; number of board-certified allergy specialists. *Asthma and Allergy Foundation of America, "Spring Allergy Capitals 2021," February 23, 2021*

- Virginia Beach was identified as a "2021 Fall Allergy Capital." The area ranked #15 out of 100. Three groups of factors were used to identify the most challenging cities for people with allergies during the fall season: annual fall pollen levels; over the counter medicine use; number of board-certified allergy specialists. *Asthma and Allergy Foundation of America, "Fall Allergy Capitals 2021," February 23, 2021*

- Virginia Beach was identified as a "2019 Asthma Capital." The area ranked #47 out of the nation's 100 largest metropolitan areas. Criteria: estimated asthma prevalence; crude death rate from asthma; and ER visits due to asthma. Risk factors analyzed but not factored in the rankings: annual pollen score; annual air quality; public smoking laws; number of board-certified asthma specialists; rescue medication use; controller medication use; uninsured rate; poverty rate. *Asthma and Allergy Foundation of America, "Asthma Capitals 2019: The Most Challenging Places to Live With Asthma," May 7, 2019*

Real Estate Rankings

- FitSmallBusiness looked at 50 of the largest metropolitan areas in the U.S. to determine which metro was the best to start a real estate business. Data was compiled from such sources as: Zillow, Trulia, U.S. Census Bureau, and the Bureau of Labor Statistics. Criteria: location; inventory; annual wages; median sales price of homes; days on the market; median price cut percentage; and other factors that would influence real estate professional growth. The Virginia Beach metro area ranked #26. *fitsmallbusiness.com, "The Best Cities to Become a Real Estate Agent in 2018," January 30, 2018*

- *WalletHub* compared the most populated U.S. cities to determine which had the best markets for real estate agents. Virginia Beach ranked #93 where demand was high and pay was the best. Criteria: sales per agent; annual median wage for real-estate agents; monthly average starting salary for real estate agents; real estate job density and competition; unemployment rate; home turnover rate; housing-market health index; and other relevant metrics. *www.WalletHub.com, "2019's Best Places to Be a Real Estate Agent," April 24, 2019*

- Virginia Beach was ranked #91 out of 268 metro areas in terms of housing affordability in 2020 by the National Association of Home Builders (#1 = most affordable). Criteria: the share of homes sold in that area affordable to a family earning the local median income, based on standard mortgage underwriting criteria. *National Association of Home Builders®, NAHB-Wells Fargo Housing Opportunity Index, 4th Quarter 2020*

Safety Rankings

- To identify the safest cities in America, 24/7 Wall Street focused on violent crime categories—murder, non-negligent manslaughter, rape, robbery, and aggravated assault—and property crime as reported in the FBI's 2018 annual Uniform Crime Report. Criteria also included median income from American Community Survey and unemployment figures from Bureau of Labor Statistics. For cities with populations over 100,000, Virginia Beach was ranked #16. *247wallst.com, "America's Safest Cities" January 15, 2020*

- Allstate ranked the 200 largest cities in America in terms of driver safety. Virginia Beach ranked #66. Criteria: internal property damage claims over a two-year period from January 2016 to December 2017. The report helps increase the importance of safety and awareness behind the wheel. *Allstate, "Allstate America's Best Drivers Report, 2019" June 24, 2019*

- The National Insurance Crime Bureau ranked 384 metro areas in the U.S. in terms of per capita rates of vehicle theft. The Virginia Beach metro area ranked #179 (#1 = highest rate). Criteria: number of vehicle theft offenses per 100,000 inhabitants in 2019. *National Insurance Crime Bureau, "Hot Spots 2019," July 21, 2020*

Seniors/Retirement Rankings

- From its Best Cities for Successful Aging indexes, the Milken Institute generated rankings for metropolitan areas, weighing data in nine categories—health care, wellness, living arrangements, transportation and convenience, financial characteristics, education, employment, community engagement, and overall livability. The Virginia Beach metro area was ranked #61 overall in the large metro area category. *Milken Institute, "Best Cities for Successful Aging, 2017" March 14, 2017*

- Virginia Beach made the 2020 *Forbes* list of "25 Best Places to Retire." Criteria, focused on high-quality retirement living at an affordable price, include: housing/living costs compared to the national average and state taxes; air quality; crime rates; good economic outlook; home price appreciation; risk associated with climate-change; availability of medical care; bikeability; walkability; healthy living. *Forbes.com, "The Best Places to Retire in 2020," August 14, 2020*

Women/Minorities Rankings

- *Women's Health*, together with the site Yelp, identified the 15 "Wellthiest" spots in the U.S. Virginia Beach appeared among the top for happiest, healthiest, outdoorsiest and Zen-iest. *Women's Health, "The 15 Wellthiest Cities in the U.S." July 5, 2017*

- Personal finance website *WalletHub* compared more than 180 U.S. cities across two key dimensions, "Hispanic Business-Friendliness" and "Hispanic Purchasing Power," to arrive at the most favorable conditions for Hispanic entrepreneurs. Virginia Beach was ranked #96 out of 182. Criteria includes: share of Hispanic-Owned Businesses; Hispanic entrepreneurship rate to median annual income of Hispanics; Small Business-Friendliness score; cost of living; and number of Hispanics with at least a bachelor's degree. *WalletHub.com, "2019's Best Cities for Hispanic Entrepreneurs," May 1, 2019*

Miscellaneous Rankings

- Virginia Beach was selected as a 2020 Digital Cities Survey winner. The city ranked #1 in the large city (250,000 to 499,999 population) category. The survey examined and assessed how city governments are utilizing technology to improve transparency, enhance cybersecurity, and respond to the pandemic. Survey questions focused on ten initiatives: cybersecurity, citizen experience, disaster recovery, business intelligence, IT personnel, data governance, collaboration, infrastructure modernization, cloud computing, and mobile applications. *Center for Digital Government, "2020 Digital Cities Survey," November 10, 2020*

- *WalletHub* compared the 150 most populated U.S. cities to determine their operating efficiency. A "Quality of City Services" score was constructed for each city and then divided by the total budget per capita to reveal which were managed the best. Virginia Beach ranked #9. Criteria: financial stability; economy; education; safety; health; infrastructure and pollution. *www.WalletHub.com, "2020's Best- & Worst-Run Cities in America," June 29, 2020*

Business Environment

DEMOGRAPHICS

Population Growth

Area	1990 Census	2000 Census	2010 Census	2019* Estimate	Population Growth (%) 1990-2019	Population Growth (%) 2010-2019
City	393,069	425,257	437,994	450,201	14.5	2.8
MSA[1]	1,449,389	1,576,370	1,671,683	1,761,729	21.5	5.4
U.S.	248,709,873	281,421,906	308,745,538	324,697,795	30.6	5.2

Note: (1) Figures cover the Virginia Beach-Norfolk-Newport News, VA-NC Metropolitan Statistical Area; (*) 2015-2019 5-year estimated population
Source: U.S. Census Bureau, 1990 Census, Census 2000, Census 2010, 2015-2019 American Community Survey 5-Year Estimates

Household Size

Area	Persons in Household (%) One	Two	Three	Four	Five	Six	Seven or More	Average Household Size
City	24.5	34.4	17.6	14.9	5.9	2.0	0.8	2.60
MSA[1]	27.3	34.2	17.4	13.1	5.3	1.8	0.9	2.60
U.S.	27.9	33.9	15.6	12.9	6.0	2.3	1.4	2.60

Note: (1) Figures cover the Virginia Beach-Norfolk-Newport News, VA-NC Metropolitan Statistical Area
Source: U.S. Census Bureau, 2015-2019 American Community Survey 5-Year Estimates

Race

Area	White Alone[2] (%)	Black Alone[2] (%)	Asian Alone[2] (%)	AIAN[3] Alone[2] (%)	NHOPI[4] Alone[2] (%)	Other Race Alone[2] (%)	Two or More Races (%)
City	66.3	19.0	6.7	0.3	0.1	2.1	5.6
MSA[1]	59.0	30.6	3.8	0.3	0.1	1.8	4.5
U.S.	72.5	12.7	5.5	0.8	0.2	4.9	3.3

Note: (1) Figures cover the Virginia Beach-Norfolk-Newport News, VA-NC Metropolitan Statistical Area; (2) Alone is defined as not being in combination with one or more other races; (3) American Indian and Alaska Native; (4) Native Hawaiian and Other Pacific Islander
Source: U.S. Census Bureau, 2015-2019 American Community Survey 5-Year Estimates

Hispanic or Latino Origin

Area	Total (%)	Mexican (%)	Puerto Rican (%)	Cuban (%)	Other (%)
City	8.2	2.5	2.4	0.3	3.0
MSA[1]	6.7	2.2	2.0	0.3	2.3
U.S.	18.0	11.2	1.7	0.7	4.3

Note: Persons of Hispanic or Latino origin can be of any race; (1) Figures cover the Virginia Beach-Norfolk-Newport News, VA-NC Metropolitan Statistical Area
Source: U.S. Census Bureau, 2015-2019 American Community Survey 5-Year Estimates

Ancestry

Area	German	Irish	English	American	Italian	Polish	French[2]	Scottish	Dutch
City	11.7	11.0	9.1	9.4	5.6	2.4	2.3	2.3	0.9
MSA[1]	9.8	8.8	8.7	9.3	4.1	1.8	1.9	1.9	0.8
U.S.	13.3	9.7	7.2	6.2	5.1	2.8	2.3	1.7	1.2

Note: Figures are the percentage of the total population reporting a particular ancestry. The nine most commonly reported ancestries in the U.S. are shown. Figures include multiple ancestries (e.g. if a person reported being Irish and Italian, they were included in both columns); (1) Figures cover the Virginia Beach-Norfolk-Newport News, VA-NC Metropolitan Statistical Area; (2) Excludes Basque
Source: U.S. Census Bureau, 2015-2019 American Community Survey 5-Year Estimates

Foreign-born Population

Area	Percent of Population Born in Any Foreign Country	Asia	Mexico	Europe	Caribbean	Central America[2]	South America	Africa	Canada
City	9.4	4.9	0.5	1.6	0.7	0.6	0.5	0.4	0.1
MSA[1]	6.5	2.8	0.4	1.1	0.6	0.7	0.4	0.4	0.1
U.S.	13.6	4.2	3.5	1.5	1.3	1.1	1.0	0.7	0.2

Note: (1) Figures cover the Virginia Beach-Norfolk-Newport News, VA-NC Metropolitan Statistical Area; (2) Excludes Mexico.
Source: U.S. Census Bureau, 2015-2019 American Community Survey 5-Year Estimates

Marital Status

Area	Never Married	Now Married[2]	Separated	Widowed	Divorced
City	30.4	51.1	2.4	5.0	11.1
MSA[1]	33.5	47.3	2.7	5.6	11.0
U.S.	33.4	48.1	1.9	5.8	10.9

Note: Figures are percentages and cover the population 15 years of age and older; (1) Figures cover the Virginia Beach-Norfolk-Newport News, VA-NC Metropolitan Statistical Area; (2) Excludes separated
Source: U.S. Census Bureau, 2015-2019 American Community Survey 5-Year Estimates

Disability by Age

Area	All Ages	Under 18 Years Old	18 to 64 Years Old	65 Years and Over
City	11.2	3.5	9.4	31.6
MSA[1]	13.1	4.7	11.1	34.4
U.S.	12.6	4.2	10.3	34.5

Note: Figures show percent of the civilian noninstitutionalized population that reported having a disability. Disability status is determined from six types of difficulty: vision, hearing, cognitive, ambulatory, self-care, and independent living. For children under 5 years old, hearing and vision difficulty are used to determine disability status. For children between the ages of 5 and 14, disability status is determined from hearing, vision, cognitive, ambulatory, and self-care difficulties. For people aged 15 years and older, they are considered to have a disability if they have difficulty with any one of the six difficulty types; Note: (1) Figures cover the Virginia Beach-Norfolk-Newport News, VA-NC Metropolitan Statistical Area
Source: U.S. Census Bureau, 2015-2019 American Community Survey 5-Year Estimates

Age

Area	Percent of Population									Median Age
	Under Age 5	Age 5–19	Age 20–34	Age 35–44	Age 45–54	Age 55–64	Age 65–74	Age 75–84	Age 85+	
City	6.3	18.2	23.7	13.0	12.7	12.1	8.1	4.0	1.6	36.2
MSA[1]	6.3	18.6	23.4	12.3	12.4	12.7	8.5	4.2	1.7	36.3
U.S.	6.1	19.1	20.7	12.6	13.0	12.9	9.1	4.6	1.9	38.1

Note: (1) Figures cover the Virginia Beach-Norfolk-Newport News, VA-NC Metropolitan Statistical Area
Source: U.S. Census Bureau, 2015-2019 American Community Survey 5-Year Estimates

Gender

Area	Males	Females	Males per 100 Females
City	221,324	228,877	96.7
MSA[1]	867,843	893,886	97.1
U.S.	159,886,919	164,810,876	97.0

Note: (1) Figures cover the Virginia Beach-Norfolk-Newport News, VA-NC Metropolitan Statistical Area
Source: U.S. Census Bureau, 2015-2019 American Community Survey 5-Year Estimates

Religious Groups by Family

Area	Catholic	Baptist	Non-Den.	Methodist[2]	Lutheran	LDS[3]	Pentecostal	Presbyterian[4]	Muslim[5]	Judaism
MSA[1]	6.4	11.6	6.2	5.3	0.7	0.9	1.9	2.0	2.1	0.4
U.S.	19.1	9.3	4.0	4.0	2.3	2.0	1.9	1.6	0.8	0.7

Note: Figures are the number of adherents as a percentage of the total population; (1) Figures cover the Virginia Beach-Norfolk-Newport News, VA-NC Metropolitan Statistical Area; (2) Methodist/Pietist; (3) Latter Day Saints; (4) Reformed; (5) Figures are estimates
Source: Association of Statisticians of American Religious Bodies, 2010 U.S. Religion Census: Religious Congregations & Membership Study

Religious Groups by Tradition

Area	Catholic	Evangelical Protestant	Mainline Protestant	Other Tradition	Black Protestant	Orthodox
MSA[1]	6.4	18.0	9.4	4.0	2.3	0.3
U.S.	19.1	16.2	7.3	4.3	1.6	0.3

Note: Figures are the number of adherents as a percentage of the total population; (1) Figures cover the Virginia Beach-Norfolk-Newport News, VA-NC Metropolitan Statistical Area
Source: Association of Statisticians of American Religious Bodies, 2010 U.S. Religion Census: Religious Congregations & Membership Study

ECONOMY

Gross Metropolitan Product

Area	2017	2018	2019	2020	Rank[2]
MSA[1]	95.2	99.3	103.6	107.4	39

Note: Figures are in billions of dollars; (1) Figures cover the Virginia Beach-Norfolk-Newport News, VA-NC Metropolitan Statistical Area; (2) Rank is based on 2018 data and ranges from 1 to 381
Source: U.S. Conference of Mayors, U.S. Metro Economies: GMP & Employment 2018-2020, September 2019

Economic Growth

Area	2015-17 (%)	2018 (%)	2019 (%)	2020 (%)	Rank[2]
MSA[1]	-0.4	2.2	2.5	1.4	323
U.S.	1.9	2.9	2.3	2.1	—

Note: Figures are real gross metropolitan product (GMP) growth rates and represent average annual percent change; (1) Figures cover the Virginia Beach-Norfolk-Newport News, VA-NC Metropolitan Statistical Area; (2) Rank is based on 2017 2-year average annual percent change and ranges from 1 to 381
Source: U.S. Conference of Mayors, U.S. Metro Economies: GMP & Employment 2018-2020, September 2019

Metropolitan Area Exports

Area	2014	2015	2016	2017	2018	2019	Rank[2]
MSA[1]	3,573.2	3,556.4	3,291.1	3,307.2	3,950.6	3,642.4	69

Note: Figures are in millions of dollars; (1) Figures cover the Virginia Beach-Norfolk-Newport News, VA-NC Metropolitan Statistical Area; (2) Rank is based on 2019 data and ranges from 1 to 386
Source: U.S. Department of Commerce, International Trade Administration, Office of Trade and Economic Analysis, Industry and Analysis, Exports by Metropolitan Area, data extracted March 24, 2021

Building Permits

Area	Single-Family			Multi-Family			Total		
	2018	2019	Pct. Chg.	2018	2019	Pct. Chg.	2018	2019	Pct. Chg.
City	534	667	24.9	245	683	178.8	779	1,350	73.3
MSA[1]	4,168	4,345	4.2	1,436	1,563	8.8	5,604	5,908	5.4
U.S.	855,300	862,100	0.7	473,500	523,900	10.6	1,328,800	1,386,000	4.3

Note: (1) Figures cover the Virginia Beach-Norfolk-Newport News, VA-NC Metropolitan Statistical Area; Figures represent new, privately-owned housing units authorized (unadjusted data); All permit data are based on estimates with imputation
Source: U.S. Census Bureau, Manufacturing, Mining, and Construction Statistics, Building Permits, 2018, 2019

Bankruptcy Filings

Area	Business Filings			Nonbusiness Filings		
	2019	2020	% Chg.	2019	2020	% Chg.
Virginia Beach city	18	14	-22.2	1,606	1,206	-24.9
U.S.	22,780	21,655	-4.9	752,160	522,808	-30.5

Note: Business filings include Chapter 7, Chapter 9, Chapter 11, Chapter 12, Chapter 13, Chapter 15, and Section 304; Nonbusiness filings include Chapter 7, Chapter 11, and Chapter 13
Source: Administrative Office of the U.S. Courts, Business and Nonbusiness Bankruptcy, County Cases Commenced by Chapter of the Bankruptcy Code, During the 12-Month Period Ending December 31, 2019 and Business and Nonbusiness Bankruptcy, County Cases Commenced by Chapter of the Bankruptcy Code, During the 12-Month Period Ending December 31, 2020

Housing Vacancy Rates

Area	Gross Vacancy Rate[2] (%)			Year-Round Vacancy Rate[3] (%)			Rental Vacancy Rate[4] (%)			Homeowner Vacancy Rate[5] (%)		
	2018	2019	2020	2018	2019	2020	2018	2019	2020	2018	2019	2020
MSA[1]	8.9	10.4	7.9	7.6	9.3	7.0	7.1	7.1	5.5	1.2	2.2	0.6
U.S.	12.3	12.0	10.6	9.7	9.5	8.2	6.9	6.7	6.3	1.5	1.4	1.0

Note: (1) Figures cover the Virginia Beach-Norfolk-Newport News, VA-NC Metropolitan Statistical Area; (2) The percentage of the total housing inventory that is vacant; (3) The percentage of the housing inventory (excluding seasonal units) that is year-round vacant; (4) The percentage of rental inventory that is vacant for rent; (5) The percentage of homeowner inventory that is vacant for sale
Source: U.S. Census Bureau, Housing Vacancies and Homeownership Annual Statistics: 2018, 2019, 2020

INCOME

Income

Area	Per Capita ($)	Median Household ($)	Average Household ($)
City	37,776	76,610	96,936
MSA[1]	33,907	66,759	86,062
U.S.	34,103	62,843	88,607

Note: (1) Figures cover the Virginia Beach-Norfolk-Newport News, VA-NC Metropolitan Statistical Area
Source: U.S. Census Bureau, 2015-2019 American Community Survey 5-Year Estimates

Household Income Distribution

Area	Percent of Households Earning							
	Under $15,000	$15,000 -$24,999	$25,000 -$34,999	$35,000 -$49,999	$50,000 -$74,999	$75,000 -$99,999	$100,000 -$149,999	$150,000 and up
City	5.3	5.4	7.4	11.7	19.1	15.8	19.9	15.4
MSA[1]	8.7	7.7	8.2	12.3	18.8	14.4	17.1	12.7
U.S.	10.3	8.9	8.9	12.3	17.2	12.7	15.1	14.5

Note: (1) Figures cover the Virginia Beach-Norfolk-Newport News, VA-NC Metropolitan Statistical Area
Source: U.S. Census Bureau, 2015-2019 American Community Survey 5-Year Estimates

Poverty Rate

Area	All Ages	Under 18 Years Old	18 to 64 Years Old	65 Years and Over
City	7.3	10.2	6.9	4.5
MSA[1]	11.3	17.1	10.2	6.9
U.S.	13.4	18.5	12.6	9.3

Note: Figures are percentage of people whose income during the past 12 months was below the poverty level;
(1) Figures cover the Virginia Beach-Norfolk-Newport News, VA-NC Metropolitan Statistical Area
Source: U.S. Census Bureau, 2015-2019 American Community Survey 5-Year Estimates

CITY FINANCES

City Government Finances

Component	2017 ($000)	2017 ($ per capita)
Total Revenues	2,022,034	4,466
Total Expenditures	1,945,207	4,296
Debt Outstanding	1,484,008	3,278
Cash and Securities[1]	1,259,067	2,781

Note: (1) Cash and security holdings of a government at the close of its fiscal year,
including those of its dependent agencies, utilities, and liquor stores.
Source: U.S. Census Bureau, State & Local Government Finances 2017

City Government Revenue by Source

Source	2017 ($000)	2017 ($ per capita)	2017 (%)
General Revenue			
From Federal Government	121,179	268	6.0
From State Government	599,168	1,323	29.6
From Local Governments	20,076	44	1.0
Taxes			
Property	644,378	1,423	31.9
Sales and Gross Receipts	231,204	511	11.4
Personal Income	0	0	0.0
Corporate Income	0	0	0.0
Motor Vehicle License	9,325	21	0.5
Other Taxes	63,219	140	3.1
Current Charges	205,301	453	10.2
Liquor Store	0	0	0.0
Utility	89,648	198	4.4
Employee Retirement	0	0	0.0

Source: U.S. Census Bureau, State & Local Government Finances 2017

City Government Expenditures by Function

Function	2017 ($000)	2017 ($ per capita)	2017 (%)
General Direct Expenditures			
Air Transportation	0	0	0.0
Corrections	50,626	111	2.6
Education	837,469	1,849	43.1
Employment Security Administration	0	0	0.0
Financial Administration	19,247	42	1.0
Fire Protection	55,117	121	2.8
General Public Buildings	40,469	89	2.1
Governmental Administration, Other	27,709	61	1.4
Health	66,095	146	3.4
Highways	108,860	240	5.6
Hospitals	0	0	0.0
Housing and Community Development	32,731	72	1.7
Interest on General Debt	22,343	49	1.1
Judicial and Legal	19,694	43	1.0
Libraries	17,334	38	0.9
Parking	9,406	20	0.5
Parks and Recreation	136,701	301	7.0
Police Protection	97,551	215	5.0
Public Welfare	58,587	129	3.0
Sewerage	110,866	244	5.7
Solid Waste Management	40,826	90	2.1
Veterans' Services	0	0	0.0
Liquor Store	0	0	0.0
Utility	86,179	190	4.4
Employee Retirement	0	0	0.0

Source: U.S. Census Bureau, State & Local Government Finances 2017

EMPLOYMENT

Labor Force and Employment

Area	Civilian Labor Force			Workers Employed		
	Dec. 2019	Dec. 2020	% Chg.	Dec. 2019	Dec. 2020	% Chg.
City	234,164	226,000	-3.5	228,643	216,261	-5.4
MSA[1]	858,173	834,317	-2.8	834,872	790,145	-5.4
U.S.	164,007,000	160,017,000	-2.4	158,504,000	149,613,000	-5.6

Note: Data is not seasonally adjusted and covers workers 16 years of age and older; (1) Figures cover the Virginia Beach-Norfolk-Newport News, VA-NC Metropolitan Statistical Area
Source: Bureau of Labor Statistics, Local Area Unemployment Statistics

Unemployment Rate

Area	2020											
	Jan.	Feb.	Mar.	Apr.	May	Jun.	Jul.	Aug.	Sep.	Oct.	Nov.	Dec.
City	2.9	2.6	3.1	12.2	9.4	8.2	7.7	6.0	5.9	4.6	4.2	4.3
MSA[1]	3.3	3.0	3.6	12.1	10.0	9.2	9.2	7.4	7.2	5.8	5.1	5.3
U.S.	4.0	3.8	4.5	14.4	13.0	11.2	10.5	8.5	7.7	6.6	6.4	6.5

Note: Data is not seasonally adjusted and covers workers 16 years of age and older; (1) Figures cover the Virginia Beach-Norfolk-Newport News, VA-NC Metropolitan Statistical Area
Source: Bureau of Labor Statistics, Local Area Unemployment Statistics

Average Wages

Occupation	$/Hr.	Occupation	$/Hr.
Accountants and Auditors	36.20	Maintenance and Repair Workers	19.60
Automotive Mechanics	25.60	Marketing Managers	70.10
Bookkeepers	20.20	Network and Computer Systems Admin.	36.80
Carpenters	20.80	Nurses, Licensed Practical	21.40
Cashiers	11.10	Nurses, Registered	35.30
Computer Programmers	n/a	Nursing Assistants	14.40
Computer Systems Analysts	47.30	Office Clerks, General	15.90
Computer User Support Specialists	26.70	Physical Therapists	43.60
Construction Laborers	16.60	Physicians	103.50
Cooks, Restaurant	13.20	Plumbers, Pipefitters and Steamfitters	23.90
Customer Service Representatives	15.30	Police and Sheriff's Patrol Officers	27.30
Dentists	88.30	Postal Service Mail Carriers	25.10
Electricians	24.00	Real Estate Sales Agents	31.60
Engineers, Electrical	46.70	Retail Salespersons	12.70
Fast Food and Counter Workers	10.90	Sales Representatives, Technical/Scientific	47.40
Financial Managers	66.80	Secretaries, Exc. Legal/Medical/Executive	19.10
First-Line Supervisors of Office Workers	28.80	Security Guards	16.80
General and Operations Managers	53.60	Surgeons	n/a
Hairdressers/Cosmetologists	12.60	Teacher Assistants, Exc. Postsecondary*	13.90
Home Health and Personal Care Aides	10.50	Teachers, Secondary School, Exc. Sp. Ed.*	33.00
Janitors and Cleaners	12.30	Telemarketers	13.90
Landscaping/Groundskeeping Workers	14.20	Truck Drivers, Heavy/Tractor-Trailer	19.70
Lawyers	62.90	Truck Drivers, Light/Delivery Services	19.40
Maids and Housekeeping Cleaners	12.20	Waiters and Waitresses	11.60

Note: Wage data covers the Virginia Beach-Norfolk-Newport News, VA-NC Metropolitan Statistical Area;
(*) Hourly wages were calculated from annual wage data based on a 40 hour work week; n/a not available.
Source: Bureau of Labor Statistics, Metro Area Occupational Employment & Wage Estimates, May 2020

Employment by Industry

Sector	MSA[1]		U.S.
	Number of Employees	Percent of Total	Percent of Total
Construction, Mining, and Logging	40,100	5.3	5.5
Education and Health Services	108,600	14.2	16.3
Financial Activities	38,800	5.1	6.1
Government	156,600	20.5	15.2
Information	9,200	1.2	1.9
Leisure and Hospitality	77,000	10.1	9.0
Manufacturing	56,600	7.4	8.5
Other Services	31,700	4.2	3.8
Professional and Business Services	113,300	14.8	14.4
Retail Trade	85,500	11.2	10.9
Transportation, Warehousing, and Utilities	27,800	3.6	4.6
Wholesale Trade	18,200	2.4	3.9

Note: Figures are non-farm employment as of December 2020. Figures are not seasonally adjusted and include workers 16 years of age and older; (1) Figures cover the Virginia Beach-Norfolk-Newport News, VA-NC Metropolitan Statistical Area
Source: Bureau of Labor Statistics, Current Employment Statistics, Employment, Hours, and Earnings

Employment by Occupation

Occupation Classification	City (%)	MSA[1] (%)	U.S. (%)
Management, Business, Science, and Arts	41.5	38.9	38.5
Natural Resources, Construction, and Maintenance	9.0	9.7	8.9
Production, Transportation, and Material Moving	9.3	11.7	13.2
Sales and Office	23.2	22.1	21.6
Service	17.0	17.6	17.8

Note: Figures cover employed civilians 16 years of age and older; (1) Figures cover the Virginia Beach-Norfolk-Newport News, VA-NC Metropolitan Statistical Area
Source: U.S. Census Bureau, 2015-2019 American Community Survey 5-Year Estimates

Occupations with Greatest Projected Employment Growth: 2020 – 2022

Occupation[1]	2020 Employment	2022 Projected Employment	Numeric Employment Change	Percent Employment Change
Retail Salespersons	81,130	93,780	12,650	15.6
Combined Food Preparation and Serving Workers, Including Fast Food	66,410	75,450	9,040	13.6
Cashiers	105,090	113,180	8,090	7.7
Waiters and Waitresses	46,090	53,400	7,310	15.9
Fitness Trainers and Aerobics Instructors	8,900	15,470	6,570	73.8
Laborers and Freight, Stock, and Material Movers, Hand	55,200	60,910	5,710	10.3
Childcare Workers	18,440	24,050	5,610	30.4
Customer Service Representatives	67,210	72,440	5,230	7.8
Management Analysts	62,240	67,200	4,960	8.0
Software Developers, Applications	40,250	44,610	4,360	10.8

Note: Projections cover Virginia; (1) Sorted by numeric employment change
Source: www.projectionscentral.com, State Occupational Projections, 2020–2022 Short-Term Projections

Fastest-Growing Occupations: 2020 – 2022

Occupation[1]	2020 Employment	2022 Projected Employment	Numeric Employment Change	Percent Employment Change
Fitness Trainers and Aerobics Instructors	8,900	15,470	6,570	73.8
Education Administrators, Preschool and Childcare Center/Program	830	1,180	350	42.2
Locker Room, Coatroom, and Dressing Room Attendants	130	180	50	38.5
Preschool Teachers, Except Special Education	7,830	10,600	2,770	35.4
Childcare Workers	18,440	24,050	5,610	30.4
Ushers, Lobby Attendants, and Ticket Takers	1,070	1,390	320	29.9
First-Line Supervisors of Personal Service Workers	5,310	6,750	1,440	27.1
Funeral Service Managers	300	380	80	26.7
Jewelers and Precious Stone and Metal Workers	300	380	80	26.7
Shampooers	800	1,010	210	26.3

Note: Projections cover Virginia; (1) Sorted by percent employment change and excludes occupations with numeric employment change less than 50
Source: www.projectionscentral.com, State Occupational Projections, 2020–2022 Short-Term Projections

TAXES

State Corporate Income Tax Rates

State	Tax Rate (%)	Income Brackets ($)	Num. of Brackets	Financial Institution Tax Rate (%)[a]	Federal Income Tax Ded.
Virginia	6.0	Flat rate	1	6.0	No

Note: Tax rates as of January 1, 2021; (a) Rates listed are the corporate income tax rate applied to financial institutions or excise taxes based on income. Some states have other taxes based upon the value of deposits or shares.
Source: Federation of Tax Administrators, State Corporate Income Tax Rates, January 1, 2021

State Individual Income Tax Rates

State	Tax Rate (%)	Income Brackets ($)	Personal Exemptions ($)			Standard Ded. ($)	
			Single	Married	Depend.	Single	Married
Virginia	2.0 - 5.75	3,000 - 17,001	930	1,860	930	4,500	9,000

Note: Tax rates as of January 1, 2021; Local- and county-level taxes are not included; Federal income tax is not deductible on state income tax returns
Source: Federation of Tax Administrators, State Individual Income Tax Rates, January 1, 2021

Various State Sales and Excise Tax Rates

State	State Sales Tax (%)	Gasoline[1] (¢/gal.)	Cigarette[2] ($/pack)	Spirits[3] ($/gal.)	Wine[4] ($/gal.)	Beer[5] ($/gal.)	Recreational Marijuana (%)
Virginia	5.3	29.4	0.6	19.89	1.51	0.26	(s)

Note: All tax rates as of January 1, 2021; (1) The American Petroleum Institute has developed a methodology for determining the average tax rate on a gallon of fuel. Rates may include any of the following: excise taxes, environmental fees, storage tank fees, other fees or taxes, general sales tax, and local taxes; (2) The federal excise tax of $1.0066 per pack and local taxes are not included; (3) Rates are those applicable to off-premise sales of 40% alcohol by volume (a.b.v.) distilled spirits in 750ml containers. Local excise taxes are excluded; (4) Rates are those applicable to off-premise sales of 11% a.b.v. non-carbonated wine in 750ml containers; (5) Rates are those applicable to off-premise sales of 4.7% a.b.v. beer in 12 ounce containers; (s) The Virginia legislature passed a bill in 2021 that would legalize recreational marijuana sales starting in 2024
Source: Tax Foundation, 2021 Facts & Figures: How Does Your State Compare?

State Business Tax Climate Index Rankings

State	Overall Rank	Corporate Tax Rank	Individual Income Tax Rank	Sales Tax Rank	Property Tax Rank	Unemployment Insurance Tax Rank
Virginia	26	16	35	11	27	46

Note: The index is a measure of how each state's tax laws affect economic performance. The lower the rank, the more favorable a state's tax system is for business. States without a given tax are given a ranking of 1. The scores/rankings for the District of Columbia do not affect other states. The 2021 index represents the tax climate as of July 1, 2020.
Source: Tax Foundation, State Business Tax Climate Index 2021

TRANSPORTATION

Means of Transportation to Work

Area	Car/Truck/Van Drove Alone	Car/Truck/Van Car-pooled	Public Transportation Bus	Public Transportation Subway	Public Transportation Railroad	Bicycle	Walked	Other Means	Worked at Home
City	82.1	8.6	0.7	0.0	0.0	0.5	2.4	1.6	3.9
MSA[1]	81.3	8.3	1.4	0.0	0.0	0.4	3.3	1.4	3.8
U.S.	76.3	9.0	2.4	1.9	0.6	0.5	2.7	1.4	5.2

Note: Figures are percentages and cover workers 16 years of age and older; (1) Figures cover the Virginia Beach-Norfolk-Newport News, VA-NC Metropolitan Statistical Area
Source: U.S. Census Bureau, 2015-2019 American Community Survey 5-Year Estimates

Travel Time to Work

Area	Less Than 10 Minutes	10 to 19 Minutes	20 to 29 Minutes	30 to 44 Minutes	45 to 59 Minutes	60 to 89 Minutes	90 Minutes or More
City	10.7	29.8	28.1	22.3	5.1	2.7	1.4
MSA[1]	11.3	30.6	23.9	21.4	7.1	4.0	1.7
U.S.	12.2	28.4	20.8	20.8	8.3	6.4	2.9

Note: Note: Figures are percentages and include workers 16 years old and over; (1) Figures cover the Virginia Beach-Norfolk-Newport News, VA-NC Metropolitan Statistical Area
Source: U.S. Census Bureau, 2015-2019 American Community Survey 5-Year Estimates

Key Congestion Measures

Measure	1982	1992	2002	2012	2017
Annual Hours of Delay, Total (000)	7,377	17,075	30,430	36,852	40,510
Annual Hours of Delay, Per Auto Commuter	15	26	39	39	46
Annual Congestion Cost, Total (million $)	55	179	408	654	741
Annual Congestion Cost, Per Auto Commuter ($)	309	493	685	650	692

Note: Covers the Virginia Beach VA urban area
Source: Texas A&M Transportation Institute, 2019 Urban Mobility Report

Freeway Travel Time Index

Measure	1982	1987	1992	1997	2002	2007	2012	2017
Urban Area Index[1]	1.06	1.08	1.11	1.15	1.17	1.18	1.18	1.17
Urban Area Rank[1,2]	43	44	49	41	41	44	40	49

Note: Freeway Travel Time Index—the ratio of travel time in the peak period to the travel time at free-flow conditions. For example, a value of 1.30 indicates a 20-minute free-flow trip takes 26 minutes in the peak (20 minutes x 1.30 = 26 minutes); (1) Covers the Virginia Beach VA urban area; (2) Rank is based on 101 larger urban areas (#1 = highest travel time index)
Source: Texas A&M Transportation Institute, 2019 Urban Mobility Report

Public Transportation

Agency Name / Mode of Transportation	Vehicles Operated in Maximum Service[1]	Annual Unlinked Passenger Trips[2] (in thous.)	Annual Passenger Miles[3] (in thous.)
Hampton Roads Transit (HRT)			
Bus (directly operated)	243	11,102.4	59,926.2
Demand Response (purchased transportation)	88	326.4	3,228.1
Demand Response Taxi (purchased transportation)	20	46.9	479.1
Ferryboat (purchased transportation)	2	301.3	214.2
Light Rail (directly operated)	6	1,429.0	4,798.1
Vanpool (purchased transportation)	48	126.8	4,140.7

Note: (1) Number of revenue vehicles operated by the given mode and type of service to meet the annual maximum service requirement. This is the revenue vehicle count during the peak season of the year; on the week and day that maximum service is provided. Vehicles operated in maximum service (VOMS) exclude atypical days and one-time special events; (2) Number of passengers who boarded public transportation vehicles. Passengers are counted each time they board a vehicle no matter how many vehicles they use to travel from their origin to their destination. (3) Sum of the distances ridden by all passengers during the entire fiscal year.
Source: Federal Transit Administration, National Transit Database, 2019

Air Transportation

Airport Name and Code / Type of Service	Passenger Airlines[1]	Passenger Enplanements	Freight Carriers[2]	Freight (lbs)
Norfolk International (ORF)				
Domestic service (U.S. carriers - 2020)	24	884,502	11	24,497,098
International service (U.S. carriers - 2019)	3	292	1	20,738

Note: (1) Includes all U.S.-based major, minor and commuter airlines that carried at least one passenger during the year; (2) Includes all U.S.-based airlines and freight carriers that transported at least one pound of freight during the year.
Source: Bureau of Transportation Statistics, The Intermodal Transportation Database, Air Carriers: T-100 Domestic Market (U.S. Carriers), 2020; Bureau of Transportation Statistics, The Intermodal Transportation Database, Air Carriers: T-100 International Market (U.S. Carriers), 2019

BUSINESSES

Major Business Headquarters

Company Name	Industry	Rankings	
		Fortune[1]	Forbes[2]
No companies listed	-	-	-

Note: (1) Companies that produce a 10-K are ranked 1 to 500 based on 2019 revenue; (2) All private companies with at least $2 billion in annual revenue through the end of their most current fiscal year are ranked 1 to 219; companies listed are headquartered in the city; dashes indicate no ranking
Source: Fortune, "Fortune 500," June/July 2020; Forbes, "America's Largest Private Companies," 2020

Fastest-Growing Businesses

According to *Inc.*, Virginia Beach is home to one of America's 500 fastest-growing private companies: **Kern Technology Group** (#407). Criteria: must be an independent, privately-held, for-profit, U.S. corporation, proprietorship or partnership as of December 31, 2019; revenues must be at least $100,000 in 2016 and $2 million in 2019; must have four-year operating/sales history. *Inc., "America's 500 Fastest-Growing Private Companies," 2020*

Living Environment

COST OF LIVING

Cost of Living Index

Composite Index	Groceries	Housing	Utilities	Trans-portation	Health Care	Misc. Goods/ Services
96.2	97.3	91.4	102.9	92.4	94.0	99.0

Note: The Cost of Living Index measures regional differences in the cost of consumer goods and services, excluding taxes and non-consumer expenditures, for professional and managerial households in the top income quintile. It is based on more than 50,000 prices covering almost 60 different items for which prices are collected three times a year by chambers of commerce, economic development organizations or university applied economic centers in each participating urban area. The numbers shown should be read as a percentage above or below the national average of 100. For example, a value of 115.4 in the groceries column indicates that grocery prices are 15.4% higher than the national average. Small differences in the index numbers should not be interpreted as significant; Figures cover the Hampton Roads-SE Virginia urban area.
Source: The Council for Community and Economic Research, Cost of Living Index, 2020

Grocery Prices

Area[1]	T-Bone Steak ($/pound)	Frying Chicken ($/pound)	Whole Milk ($/half gal.)	Eggs ($/dozen)	Orange Juice ($/64 oz.)	Coffee ($/11.5 oz.)
City[2]	11.03	1.20	1.75	1.35	3.88	3.85
Avg.	11.78	1.39	2.05	1.47	3.57	4.34
Min.	8.03	0.94	1.03	0.74	2.94	3.02
Max.	15.86	2.65	4.31	3.77	5.44	8.69

*Note: (1) Values for the local area are compared with the average, minimum and maximum values for all 284 areas in the Cost of Living Index; (2) Figures cover the Hampton Roads-SE Virginia urban area; **T-Bone Steak** (price per pound); **Frying Chicken** (price per pound, whole fryer); **Whole Milk** (half gallon carton); **Eggs** (price per dozen, Grade A, large); **Orange Juice** (64 oz. Tropicana or Florida Natural); **Coffee** (11.5 oz. can, vacuum-packed, Maxwell House, Hills Bros, or Folgers).*
Source: The Council for Community and Economic Research, Cost of Living Index, 2020

Housing and Utility Costs

Area[1]	New Home Price ($)	Apartment Rent ($/month)	All Electric ($/month)	Part Electric ($/month)	Other Energy ($/month)	Telephone ($/month)
City[2]	317,054	1,200	-	97.52	76.48	185.90
Avg.	368,594	1,168	170.86	100.47	65.28	184.30
Min.	190,567	502	91.58	31.42	26.08	169.60
Max.	2,227,806	4,738	470.38	280.31	280.06	206.50

*Note: (1) Values for the local area are compared with the average, minimum and maximum values for all 284 areas in the Cost of Living Index; (2) Figures cover the Hampton Roads-SE Virginia urban area; **New Home Price** (2,400 sf living area, 8,000 sf lot, in urban area with full utilities); **Apartment Rent** (950 sf 2 bedroom/1.5 or 2 bath, unfurnished, excluding all utilities except water); **All Electric** (average monthly cost for an all-electric home); **Part Electric** (average monthly cost for a part-electric home); **Other Energy** (average monthly cost for natural gas, fuel oil, coal, wood, and any other forms of energy except electricity); **Telephone** (price includes the base monthly rate plus taxes and fees for three lines of mobile phone service).*
Source: The Council for Community and Economic Research, Cost of Living Index, 2020

Health Care, Transportation, and Other Costs

Area[1]	Doctor ($/visit)	Dentist ($/visit)	Optometrist ($/visit)	Gasoline ($/gallon)	Beauty Salon ($/visit)	Men's Shirt ($)
City[2]	83.17	103.67	98.57	2.00	38.97	36.02
Avg.	115.44	99.32	108.10	2.21	39.27	31.37
Min.	36.68	59.00	51.36	1.71	19.00	11.00
Max.	219.00	153.10	250.97	3.46	82.05	58.33

*Note: (1) Values for the local area are compared with the average, minimum and maximum values for all 284 areas in the Cost of Living Index; (2) Figures cover the Hampton Roads-SE Virginia urban area; **Doctor** (general practitioners routine exam of an established patient); **Dentist** (adult teeth cleaning and periodic oral examination); **Optometrist** (full vision eye exam for established adult patient); **Gasoline** (one gallon regular unleaded, national brand, including all taxes, cash price at self-service pump if available); **Beauty Salon** (woman's shampoo, trim, and blow-dry); **Men's Shirt** (cotton/polyester dress shirt, pinpoint weave, long sleeves).*
Source: The Council for Community and Economic Research, Cost of Living Index, 2020

HOUSING

Homeownership Rate

Area	2012 (%)	2013 (%)	2014 (%)	2015 (%)	2016 (%)	2017 (%)	2018 (%)	2019 (%)	2020 (%)
MSA[1]	62.0	63.3	64.1	59.4	59.6	65.3	62.8	63.0	65.8
U.S.	65.4	65.1	64.5	63.7	63.4	63.9	64.4	64.6	66.6

Note: (1) Figures cover the Virginia Beach-Norfolk-Newport News, VA-NC Metropolitan Statistical Area
Source: U.S. Census Bureau, Housing Vacancies and Homeownership Annual Statistics: 2012-2020

House Price Index (HPI)

Area	National Ranking[2]	Quarterly Change (%)	One-Year Change (%)	Five-Year Change (%)	Since 1991Q1 (%)
MSA[1]	144	1.54	5.90	17.40	170.16
U.S.[3]	–	3.81	10.77	38.99	205.12

Note: The HPI is a weighted repeat sales index. It measures average price changes in repeat sales or refinancings on the same properties. This information is obtained by reviewing repeat mortgage transactions on single-family properties whose mortgages have been purchased or securitized by Fannie Mae or Freddie Mac since January 1975; (1) Figures cover the Virginia Beach-Norfolk-Newport News, VA-NC Metropolitan Statistical Area; (2) Rankings are based on annual percentage change for all metro areas containing at least 15,000 transactions over the last 10 years and ranges from 1 to 253; (3) figures based on a weighted average of Census Division estimates using a seasonally adjusted, purchase-only index; all figures are for the period ending December 31, 2020
Source: Federal Housing Finance Agency, Change in Metropolitan Area House Price Indexes, April 7, 2021

Median Single-Family Home Prices

Area	2018	2019	2020p	Percent Change 2019 to 2020
MSA[1]	219.0	235.0	275.0	17.0
U.S. Average	261.6	274.6	299.9	9.2

Note: Figures are median sales prices of existing single-family homes in thousands of dollars; (p) preliminary; (1) Figures cover the Virginia Beach-Norfolk-Newport News, VA-NC Metropolitan Statistical Area
Source: National Association of Realtors, Median Sales Price of Existing Single-Family Homes for Metropolitan Areas, 4th Quarter 2020

Qualifying Income Based on Median Sales Price of Existing Single-Family Homes

Area	With 5% Down ($)	With 10% Down ($)	With 20% Down ($)
MSA[1]	52,014	49,276	43,801
U.S. Average	59,266	56,147	49,908

Note: Figures are preliminary; Qualifying income is based on a mortgage rate of 2.81%. Monthly principal and interest payment is limited to 25% of income; (1) Figures cover the Virginia Beach-Norfolk-Newport News, VA-NC Metropolitan Statistical Area
Source: National Association of Realtors, Qualifying Income Based on Median Sales Price of Existing Single-Family Homes for Metropolitan Areas, 4th Quarter 2020

Home Value Distribution

Area	Under $50,000	$50,000 -$99,999	$100,000 -$149,999	$150,000 -$199,999	$200,000 -$299,999	$300,000 -$499,999	$500,000 -$999,999	$1,000,000 or more
City	2.2	1.5	6.1	12.6	33.7	30.5	11.1	2.3
MSA[1]	3.3	3.8	10.2	17.0	31.5	25.1	7.7	1.2
U.S.	6.9	12.0	13.3	14.0	19.6	19.3	11.4	3.4

Note: Figures are percentages and cover owner-occupied housing units; (1) Figures cover the Virginia Beach-Norfolk-Newport News, VA-NC Metropolitan Statistical Area
Source: U.S. Census Bureau, 2015-2019 American Community Survey 5-Year Estimates

Year Housing Structure Built

Area	2010 or Later	2000 -2009	1990 -1999	1980 -1989	1970 -1979	1960 -1969	1950 -1959	1940 -1949	Before 1940	Median Year
City	4.9	10.8	13.7	27.9	21.4	12.8	6.1	1.3	1.1	1983
MSA[1]	6.0	12.7	15.2	18.9	15.8	11.8	9.7	4.2	5.7	1981
U.S.	5.2	14.0	13.9	13.4	15.2	10.6	10.3	4.9	12.6	1978

Note: Figures are percentages except for Median Year; Note: (1) Figures cover the Virginia Beach-Norfolk-Newport News, VA-NC Metropolitan Statistical Area
Source: U.S. Census Bureau, 2015-2019 American Community Survey 5-Year Estimates

Gross Monthly Rent

Area	Under $500	$500 -$999	$1,000 -$1,499	$1,500 -$1,999	$2,000 -$2,499	$2,500 -$2,999	$3,000 and up	Median ($)
City	3.2	12.0	47.9	26.8	6.9	1.7	1.6	1,367
MSA[1]	7.0	26.2	41.2	18.4	4.9	1.3	1.0	1,180
U.S.	9.4	36.2	30.0	14.0	5.6	2.4	2.4	1,062

Note: Figures are percentages except for Median; Gross rent is the contract rent plus the estimated average monthly cost of utilities (electricity, gas, and water and sewer) and fuels (oil, coal, kerosene, wood, etc.) if these are paid by the renter (or paid for the renter by someone else); (1) Figures cover the Virginia Beach-Norfolk-Newport News, VA-NC Metropolitan Statistical Area
Source: U.S. Census Bureau, 2015-2019 American Community Survey 5-Year Estimates

HEALTH

Health Risk Factors

Category	MSA[1] (%)	U.S. (%)
Adults aged 18–64 who have any kind of health care coverage	85.6	87.3
Adults who reported being in good or better health	84.1	82.4
Adults who have been told they have high blood cholesterol	31.5	33.0
Adults who have been told they have high blood pressure	33.3	32.3
Adults who are current smokers	16.2	17.1
Adults who currently use E-cigarettes	5.6	4.6
Adults who currently use chewing tobacco, snuff, or snus	2.3	4.0
Adults who are heavy drinkers[2]	6.2	6.3
Adults who are binge drinkers[3]	19.0	17.4
Adults who are overweight (BMI 25.0 - 29.9)	37.2	35.3
Adults who are obese (BMI 30.0 - 99.8)	32.4	31.3
Adults who participated in any physical activities in the past month	74.5	74.4
Adults who always or nearly always wears a seat belt	95.0	94.3

Note: (1) Figures cover the Virginia Beach-Norfolk-Newport News, VA-NC Metropolitan Statistical Area;
(2) Heavy drinkers are classified as adult men having more than 14 drinks per week and adult women having
more than 7 drinks per week; (3) Binge drinkers are classified as males having five or more drinks on one
occasion or females having four or more drinks on one occasion
Source: Centers for Disease Control and Prevention, Behaviorial Risk Factor Surveillance System, SMART:
Selected Metropolitan Area Risk Trends, 2017

Acute and Chronic Health Conditions

Category	MSA[1] (%)	U.S. (%)
Adults who have ever been told they had a heart attack	4.3	4.2
Adults who have ever been told they have angina or coronary heart disease	3.8	3.9
Adults who have ever been told they had a stroke	3.9	3.0
Adults who have ever been told they have asthma	16.2	14.2
Adults who have ever been told they have arthritis	26.8	24.9
Adults who have ever been told they have diabetes[2]	12.1	10.5
Adults who have ever been told they had skin cancer	5.3	6.2
Adults who have ever been told they had any other types of cancer	6.9	7.1
Adults who have ever been told they have COPD	6.1	6.5
Adults who have ever been told they have kidney disease	3.1	3.0
Adults who have ever been told they have a form of depression	19.6	20.5

Note: (1) Figures cover the Virginia Beach-Norfolk-Newport News, VA-NC Metropolitan Statistical Area; (2)
Figures do not include pregnancy-related, borderline, or pre-diabetes
Source: Centers for Disease Control and Prevention, Behaviorial Risk Factor Surveillance System, SMART:
Selected Metropolitan Area Risk Trends, 2017

Health Screening and Vaccination Rates

Category	MSA[1] (%)	U.S. (%)
Adults aged 65+ who have had flu shot within the past year	69.3	60.7
Adults aged 65+ who have ever had a pneumonia vaccination	78.4	75.4
Adults who have ever been tested for HIV	50.5	36.1
Adults who have ever had the shingles or zoster vaccine?	30.3	28.9
Adults who have had their blood cholesterol checked within the last five years	86.9	85.9

Note: n/a not available; (1) Figures cover the Virginia Beach-Norfolk-Newport News, VA-NC Metropolitan
Statistical Area.
Source: Centers for Disease Control and Prevention, Behaviorial Risk Factor Surveillance System, SMART:
Selected Metropolitan Area Risk Trends, 2017

Disability Status

Category	MSA[1] (%)	U.S. (%)
Adults who reported being deaf	7.0	6.7
Are you blind or have serious difficulty seeing, even when wearing glasses?	4.6	4.5
Are you limited in any way in any of your usual activities due of arthritis?	13.9	12.9
Do you have difficulty doing errands alone?	5.8	6.8
Do you have difficulty dressing or bathing?	3.1	3.6
Do you have serious difficulty concentrating/remembering/making decisions?	10.5	10.7
Do you have serious difficulty walking or climbing stairs?	13.1	13.6

Note: (1) Figures cover the Virginia Beach-Norfolk-Newport News, VA-NC Metropolitan Statistical Area.
Source: Centers for Disease Control and Prevention, Behaviorial Risk Factor Surveillance System, SMART:
Selected Metropolitan Area Risk Trends, 2017

Mortality Rates for the Top 10 Causes of Death in the U.S.

ICD-10[a] Sub-Chapter	ICD-10[a] Code	Age-Adjusted Mortality Rate[1] per 100,000 population	
		County[2]	U.S.
Malignant neoplasms	C00-C97	147.3	149.2
Ischaemic heart diseases	I20-I25	67.5	90.5
Other forms of heart disease	I30-I51	65.3	52.2
Chronic lower respiratory diseases	J40-J47	30.6	39.6
Other degenerative diseases of the nervous system	G30-G31	35.6	37.6
Cerebrovascular diseases	I60-I69	42.2	37.2
Other external causes of accidental injury	W00-X59	27.9	36.1
Organic, including symptomatic, mental disorders	F01-F09	33.6	29.4
Hypertensive diseases	I10-I15	10.9	24.1
Diabetes mellitus	E10-E14	17.5	21.5

Note: (a) ICD-10 = International Classification of Diseases 10th Revision; (1) Mortality rates are a three-year average covering 2017-2019; (2) Figures cover Virginia Beach city.
Source: Centers for Disease Control and Prevention, National Center for Health Statistics. Underlying Cause of Death 1999-2019 on CDC WONDER Online Database

Mortality Rates for Selected Causes of Death

ICD-10[a] Sub-Chapter	ICD-10[a] Code	Age-Adjusted Mortality Rate[1] per 100,000 population	
		County[2]	U.S.
Assault	X85-Y09	5.3	6.0
Diseases of the liver	K70-K76	12.5	14.4
Human immunodeficiency virus (HIV) disease	B20-B24	Unreliable	1.5
Influenza and pneumonia	J09-J18	6.8	13.8
Intentional self-harm	X60-X84	13.1	14.1
Malnutrition	E40-E46	2.5	2.3
Obesity and other hyperalimentation	E65-E68	1.6	2.1
Renal failure	N17-N19	16.2	12.6
Transport accidents	V01-V99	6.8	12.3
Viral hepatitis	B15-B19	Suppressed	1.2

Note: (a) ICD-10 = International Classification of Diseases 10th Revision; (1) Mortality rates are a three-year average covering 2017-2019; (2) Figures cover Virginia Beach city; Data are suppressed when the data meet the criteria for confidentiality constraints; Mortality rates are flagged as unreliable when the rate would be calculated with a numerator of 20 or less.
Source: Centers for Disease Control and Prevention, National Center for Health Statistics. Underlying Cause of Death 1999-2019 on CDC WONDER Online Database

Health Insurance Coverage

Area	With Health Insurance	With Private Health Insurance	With Public Health Insurance	Without Health Insurance	Population Under Age 19 Without Health Insurance
City	92.4	80.7	25.8	7.6	3.8
MSA[1]	91.6	75.2	30.5	8.4	4.6
U.S.	91.2	67.9	35.1	8.8	5.1

Note: Figures are percentages that cover the civilian noninstitutionalized population; (1) Figures cover the Virginia Beach-Norfolk-Newport News, VA-NC Metropolitan Statistical Area
Source: U.S. Census Bureau, 2015-2019 American Community Survey 5-Year Estimates

Number of Medical Professionals

Area	MDs[3]	DOs[3,4]	Dentists	Podiatrists	Chiropractors	Optometrists
Ind. City[1] (number)	1,135	60	348	34	123	76
Ind. City[1] (rate[2])	252.3	13.3	77.3	7.6	27.3	16.9
U.S. (rate[2])	282.9	22.7	71.2	6.2	28.1	16.9

51810
Note: Data as of 2019 unless noted; (1) Data covers Virginia Beach independent city; (2) Rate per 100,000 population; (3) Data as of 2018 and includes all active, non-federal physicians; (4) Doctor of Osteopathic Medicine
Source: U.S. Department of Health and Human Services, Health Resources and Services Administration, Bureau of Health Professions, Area Resource File (ARF) 2019-2020

Best Hospitals

According to *U.S. News,* the Virginia Beach-Norfolk-Newport News, VA-NC metro area is home to one of the best hospitals in the U.S.: **Sentara Norfolk General Hospital** (1 adult specialty). The hospital listed was nationally ranked in at least one of 16 adult or 10 pediatric specialties. Only 134 hospitals nationwide were nationally ranked in one or more adult or pediatric specialty; this number increases to 178 counting specialized centers within hospitals. Twenty hospitals in the U.S. made the Honor Roll. The Best Hospitals Honor Roll takes both the national rankings and the procedure and condition ratings into account. Hospitals received points if they were nationally ranked in one of the 16 adult specialties—the higher they ranked, the more points they got—and how many ratings of "high performing" they earned in the 10 procedures and conditions. *U.S. News Online, "America's Best Hospitals 2020-21"*

EDUCATION

Public School District Statistics

District Name	Schls	Pupils	Pupil/ Teacher Ratio	Minority Pupils[1] (%)	Free Lunch Eligible[2] (%)	IEP[3] (%)
Virginia Beach City Pblc Schs	87	68,624	15.9	51.8	31.6	11.8

Note: Table includes school districts with 2,000 or more students; (1) Percentage of students that are not non-Hispanic white; (2) Percentage of students that are eligible for the free lunch program; (3) Percentage of students that have an Individualized Education Program.
Source: U.S. Department of Education, National Center for Education Statistics, Common Core of Data, Local Education Agency (School District) Universe Survey: School Year 2018-2019; U.S. Department of Education, National Center for Education Statistics, Common Core of Data, Public Elementary/Secondary School Universe Survey: School Year 2018-2019

Highest Level of Education

Area	Less than H.S.	H.S. Diploma	Some College, No Deg.	Associate Degree	Bachelor's Degree	Master's Degree	Prof. School Degree	Doctorate Degree
City	6.5	21.0	25.7	10.9	22.6	10.2	2.1	1.1
MSA[1]	8.6	24.9	24.7	9.9	19.5	9.3	1.8	1.2
U.S.	12.0	27.0	20.4	8.5	19.8	8.8	2.1	1.4

Note: Figures cover persons age 25 and over; (1) Figures cover the Virginia Beach-Norfolk-Newport News, VA-NC Metropolitan Statistical Area
Source: U.S. Census Bureau, 2015-2019 American Community Survey 5-Year Estimates

Educational Attainment by Race

Area	High School Graduate or Higher (%)					Bachelor's Degree or Higher (%)				
	Total	White	Black	Asian	Hisp.[2]	Total	White	Black	Asian	Hisp.[2]
City	93.5	95.3	91.1	88.2	84.5	36.0	38.8	26.4	40.6	25.5
MSA[1]	91.4	93.9	87.2	87.3	84.0	31.9	36.2	22.1	43.3	24.8
U.S.	88.0	89.9	86.0	87.1	68.7	32.1	33.5	21.6	54.3	16.4

Note: Figures shown cover persons 25 years old and over; (1) Figures cover the Virginia Beach-Norfolk-Newport News, VA-NC Metropolitan Statistical Area; (2) People of Hispanic origin can be of any race
Source: U.S. Census Bureau, 2015-2019 American Community Survey 5-Year Estimates

School Enrollment by Grade and Control

Area	Preschool (%)		Kindergarten (%)		Grades 1 - 4 (%)		Grades 5 - 8 (%)		Grades 9 - 12 (%)	
	Public	Private	Public	Private	Public	Private	Public	Private	Public	Private
City	37.7	62.3	77.3	22.7	90.2	9.8	88.7	11.3	92.7	7.3
MSA[1]	53.4	46.6	83.0	17.0	89.4	10.6	89.3	10.7	91.4	8.6
U.S.	59.1	40.9	87.6	12.4	89.5	10.5	89.4	10.6	90.1	9.9

Note: Figures shown cover persons 3 years old and over; (1) Figures cover the Virginia Beach-Norfolk-Newport News, VA-NC Metropolitan Statistical Area
Source: U.S. Census Bureau, 2015-2019 American Community Survey 5-Year Estimates

Higher Education

Four-Year Colleges			Two-Year Colleges			Medical Schools[1]	Law Schools[2]	Voc/ Tech[3]
Public	Private Non-profit	Private For-profit	Public	Private Non-profit	Private For-profit			
0	3	6	0	1	1	0	1	5

Note: Figures cover institutions located within the city limits and include main campuses only; (1) includes schools accredited by the Liaison Committee on Medical Education and the American Osteopathic Association's Commission on Osteopathic College Accreditation; (2) includes ABA-accredited schools, schools with provisional ABA accreditation, and state accredited schools; (3) includes all schools with programs that are less than 2 years.
Source: National Center for Education Statistics, Integrated Postsecondary Education System (IPEDS), 2019-20; Wikipedia, List of Medical Schools in the United States, accessed April 2, 2021; Wikipedia, List of Law Schools in the United States, accessed April 2, 2021

According to *U.S. News & World Report,* the Virginia Beach-Norfolk-Newport News, VA-NC metro area is home to one of the top 200 national universities in the U.S.: **William & Mary** (#39 tie). The indicators used to capture academic quality fall into a number of categories: assessment by administrators at peer institutions; retention of students; faculty resources; student selectivity; financial resources; alumni giving; high school counselor ratings of colleges; and graduation rate. *U.S. News & World Report, "America's Best Colleges 2021"*

According to *U.S. News & World Report,* the Virginia Beach-Norfolk-Newport News, VA-NC metro area is home to one of the top 100 law schools in the U.S.: **William & Mary Law School** (#35 tie). The rankings are based on a weighted average of 12 measures of quality: peer assessment score; assessment score by lawyers/judges; median LSAT scores; median undergrad GPA; acceptance rate; employment rates for graduates; placement success; bar passage rate; faculty resources; expenditures per student; student/faculty ratio; and library resources. *U.S. News & World Report, "America's Best Graduate Schools, Law, 2022"*

According to *U.S. News & World Report,* the Virginia Beach-Norfolk-Newport News, VA-NC metro area is home to one of the top 75 business schools in the U.S.: **William & Mary** (#71). The rankings are based on a weighted average of the following nine measures: quality assessment; peer assessment; recruiter assessment; placement success; mean starting salary and bonus; student selectivity; mean GMAT and GRE scores; mean undergraduate GPA; and acceptance rate. *U.S. News & World Report, "America's Best Graduate Schools, Business, 2022"*

EMPLOYERS

Major Employers

Company Name	Industry
Bank of America, National Association	National commerical banks
Chesapeake Hospital Authority	General medical & surgical hospitals
Children's Health System	Specialty hospitals, except psychiatric
City Line Apts.	Apartment building operators
City of Newport News	Municipal government
City of Virginia Beach	Municipal government
Cox Communications Hampton Roads	Cable & other pay television services
Ford Motor Company	Truck & tractor truck assembly
Gwaltney of Smithfield	Meat packing plants
Hampton Training School for Nurses	General medical & surgical hospitals
Northrop Grumman Systems Corporation	Systems integration services
Old Dominion University	University
Riverside Hospital	General medical & surgical hospitals
STIHL Incorporated	Power-driven handtools
The College of William & Mary	Colleges & universities
The Colonial Williamsburg Foundation	Management consulting services
The Smithfield Packing Company	Hams & picnics, from meat slaughtered on site
U.S. Navy	Offices & clinics of medical doctors
Williamsburg James City Co. Pub Schls	Schools & educational services, nec

Note: Companies shown are located within the Virginia Beach-Norfolk-Newport News, VA-NC Metropolitan Statistical Area.
Source: Hoovers.com; Wikipedia

PUBLIC SAFETY

Crime Rate

Area	All Crimes	Violent Crimes				Property Crimes		
		Murder	Rape[3]	Robbery	Aggrav. Assault	Burglary	Larceny -Theft	Motor Vehicle Theft
City	1,890.0	6.7	17.6	43.6	61.5	118.0	1,513.7	128.9
Suburbs[1]	3,057.1	8.5	39.5	83.1	293.8	282.1	2,149.5	200.6
Metro[2]	2,759.6	8.0	33.9	73.0	234.6	240.3	1,987.4	182.3
U.S.	2,489.3	5.0	42.6	81.6	250.2	340.5	1,549.5	219.9

Note: Figures are crimes per 100,000 population; (1) All areas within the metro area that are located outside the city limits; (2) Figures cover the Virginia Beach-Norfolk-Newport News, VA-NC Metropolitan Statistical Area; (3) All figures shown were reported using the revised Uniform Crime Reporting (UCR) definition of rape.
Source: FBI Uniform Crime Reports, 2019

Hate Crimes

Area	Number of Quarters Reported	Number of Incidents per Bias Motivation					
		Race/Ethnicity/ Ancestry	Religion	Sexual Orientation	Disability	Gender	Gender Identity
City	4	1	1	0	0	0	0
U.S.	4	3,963	1,521	1,195	157	69	198

Source: Federal Bureau of Investigation, Hate Crime Statistics 2019

Identity Theft Consumer Reports

Area	Reports	Reports per 100,000 Population	Rank[2]
MSA[1]	4,272	242	169
U.S.	1,387,615	423	-

Note: (1) Figures cover the Virginia Beach-Norfolk-Newport News, VA-NC Metropolitan Statistical Area; (2) Rank ranges from 1 to 391 where 1 indicates greatest number of identity theft reports per 100,000 population
Source: Federal Trade Commission, Consumer Sentinel Network Data Book 2020

Fraud and Other Consumer Reports

Area	Reports	Reports per 100,000 Population	Rank[2]
MSA[1]	17,494	989	22
U.S.	3,385,133	1,031	-

Note: (1) Figures cover the Virginia Beach-Norfolk-Newport News, VA-NC Metropolitan Statistical Area; (2) Rank ranges from 1 to 391 where 1 indicates greatest number of fraud and other consumer reports per 100,000 population
Source: Federal Trade Commission, Consumer Sentinel Network Data Book 2020

POLITICS

2020 Presidential Election Results

Area	Biden	Trump	Jorgensen	Hawkins	Other
Virginia Beach City	51.6	46.2	1.8	0.0	0.4
U.S.	51.3	46.8	1.2	0.3	0.5

Note: Results are percentages and may not add to 100% due to rounding
Source: Dave Leip's Atlas of U.S. Presidential Elections

SPORTS

Professional Sports Teams

Team Name	League	Year Established
No teams are located in the metro area		

Source: Wikipedia, Major Professional Sports Teams of the United States and Canada, April 6, 2021

CLIMATE

Average and Extreme Temperatures

Temperature	Jan	Feb	Mar	Apr	May	Jun	Jul	Aug	Sep	Oct	Nov	Dec	Yr.
Extreme High (°F)	78	81	88	97	100	101	103	104	99	95	86	80	104
Average High (°F)	48	51	58	68	76	84	88	86	80	70	61	52	69
Average Temp. (°F)	41	42	49	58	67	75	79	78	72	62	53	44	60
Average Low (°F)	32	33	40	48	57	66	71	70	64	53	44	35	51
Extreme Low (°F)	-3	8	18	28	36	45	54	49	45	27	20	7	-3

Note: Figures cover the years 1948-1995
Source: National Climatic Data Center, International Station Meteorological Climate Summary, 9/96

Average Precipitation/Snowfall/Humidity

Precip./Humidity	Jan	Feb	Mar	Apr	May	Jun	Jul	Aug	Sep	Oct	Nov	Dec	Yr.
Avg. Precip. (in.)	3.6	3.3	3.8	3.0	3.7	3.5	5.2	5.3	3.9	3.3	3.0	3.1	44.8
Avg. Snowfall (in.)	3	3	1	Tr	0	0	0	0	0	0	Tr	1	8
Avg. Rel. Hum. 7am (%)	74	74	74	73	77	79	81	84	83	82	79	75	78
Avg. Rel. Hum. 4pm (%)	59	56	53	50	56	57	60	63	62	60	58	59	58

Note: Figures cover the years 1948-1995; Tr = Trace amounts (<0.05 in. of rain; <0.5 in. of snow)
Source: National Climatic Data Center, International Station Meteorological Climate Summary, 9/96

Weather Conditions

Temperature			Daytime Sky			Precipitation		
10°F & below	32°F & below	90°F & above	Clear	Partly cloudy	Cloudy	0.01 inch or more precip.	0.1 inch or more snow/ice	Thunder-storms
< 1	53	33	89	149	127	115	5	38

Note: Figures are average number of days per year and cover the years 1948-1995
Source: National Climatic Data Center, International Station Meteorological Climate Summary, 9/96

HAZARDOUS WASTE

Superfund Sites

The Virginia Beach-Norfolk-Newport News, VA-NC metro area is home to 14 sites on the EPA's Superfund National Priorities List: **Abex Corp.** (final); **Atlantic Wood Industries, Inc.** (final); **Chisman Creek** (final); **Former Nansemond Ordnance Depot** (final); **Fort Eustis (USARMY)** (final); **Langley Air Force Base/Nasa Langley Research Center** (final); **Naval Amphibious Base Little Creek** (final); **Naval Weapons Station - Yorktown** (final); **Norfolk Naval Base (Sewells Point Naval Complex)** (final); **Norfolk Naval Shipyard** (final); **NWS Yorktown - Cheatham Annex** (final); **Peck Iron and Metal** (final); **Saunders Supply Co.** (final); **Saint Juliens Creek Annex (U.S. Navy)** (final). There are a total of 1,375 Superfund sites with a status of proposed or final on the list in the U.S. *U.S. Environmental Protection Agency, National Priorities List, April 7, 2021*

AIR QUALITY

Air Quality Trends: Ozone

	1990	1995	2000	2005	2010	2015	2016	2017	2018	2019
MSA[1]	0.085	0.084	0.083	0.078	0.074	0.061	0.062	0.059	0.061	0.059
U.S.	0.088	0.089	0.082	0.080	0.073	0.068	0.069	0.068	0.069	0.065

Note: (1) Data covers the Virginia Beach-Norfolk-Newport News, VA-NC Metropolitan Statistical Area. The values shown are the composite ozone concentration averages among trend sites based on the highest fourth daily maximum 8-hour concentration in parts per million. These trends are based on sites having an adequate record of monitoring data during the trend period. Data from exceptional events are included.
Source: U.S. Environmental Protection Agency, Air Quality Monitoring Information, "Air Quality Trends by City, 1990-2019"

Air Quality Index

Area	Percent of Days when Air Quality was...[2]					AQI Statistics[2]	
	Good	Moderate	Unhealthy for Sensitive Groups	Unhealthy	Very Unhealthy	Maximum	Median
MSA[1]	86.8	13.2	0.0	0.0	0.0	97	40

Note: (1) Data covers the Virginia Beach-Norfolk-Newport News, VA-NC Metropolitan Statistical Area; (2) Based on 365 days with AQI data in 2019. Air Quality Index (AQI) is an index for reporting daily air quality. EPA calculates the AQI for five major air pollutants regulated by the Clean Air Act: ground-level ozone, particle pollution (aka particulate matter), carbon monoxide, sulfur dioxide, and nitrogen dioxide. The AQI runs from 0 to 500. The higher the AQI value, the greater the level of air pollution and the greater the health concern. There are six AQI categories: "Good" AQI is between 0 and 50. Air quality is considered satisfactory; "Moderate" AQI is between 51 and 100. Air quality is acceptable; "Unhealthy for Sensitive Groups" When AQI values are between 101 and 150, members of sensitive groups may experience health effects; "Unhealthy" When AQI values are between 151 and 200 everyone may begin to experience health effects; "Very Unhealthy" AQI values between 201 and 300 trigger a health alert; "Hazardous" AQI values over 300 trigger warnings of emergency conditions (not shown).
Source: U.S. Environmental Protection Agency, Air Quality Index Report, 2019

Air Quality Index Pollutants

Area	Percent of Days when AQI Pollutant was...[2]					
	Carbon Monoxide	Nitrogen Dioxide	Ozone	Sulfur Dioxide	Particulate Matter 2.5	Particulate Matter 10
MSA[1]	0.0	12.1	61.9	0.0	26.0	0.0

Note: (1) Data covers the Virginia Beach-Norfolk-Newport News, VA-NC Metropolitan Statistical Area; (2) Based on 365 days with AQI data in 2019. The Air Quality Index (AQI) is an index for reporting daily air quality. EPA calculates the AQI for five major air pollutants regulated by the Clean Air Act: ground-level ozone, particle pollution (also known as particulate matter), carbon monoxide, sulfur dioxide, and nitrogen dioxide. The AQI runs from 0 to 500. The higher the AQI value, the greater the level of air pollution and the greater the health concern.
Source: U.S. Environmental Protection Agency, Air Quality Index Report, 2019

Maximum Air Pollutant Concentrations: Particulate Matter, Ozone, CO and Lead

	Particulate Matter 10 (ug/m^3)	Particulate Matter 2.5 Wtd AM (ug/m^3)	Particulate Matter 2.5 24-Hr (ug/m^3)	Ozone (ppm)	Carbon Monoxide (ppm)	Lead (ug/m^3)
MSA[1] Level	20	7.1	18	0.061	1	n/a
NAAQS[2]	150	15	35	0.075	9	0.15
Met NAAQS[2]	Yes	Yes	Yes	Yes	Yes	n/a

Note: (1) Data covers the Virginia Beach-Norfolk-Newport News, VA-NC Metropolitan Statistical Area; Data from exceptional events are included; (2) National Ambient Air Quality Standards; ppm = parts per million; ug/m^3 = micrograms per cubic meter; n/a not available.
Concentrations: Particulate Matter 10 (coarse particulate)—highest second maximum 24-hour concentration; Particulate Matter 2.5 Wtd AM (fine particulate)—highest weighted annual mean concentration; Particulate Matter 2.5 24-Hour (fine particulate)—highest 98th percentile 24-hour concentration; Ozone—highest fourth daily maximum 8-hour concentration; Carbon Monoxide—highest second maximum non-overlapping 8-hour concentration; Lead—maximum running 3-month average
Source: U.S. Environmental Protection Agency, Air Quality Monitoring Information, "Air Quality Statistics by City, 2019"

Maximum Air Pollutant Concentrations: Nitrogen Dioxide and Sulfur Dioxide

	Nitrogen Dioxide AM (ppb)	Nitrogen Dioxide 1-Hr (ppb)	Sulfur Dioxide AM (ppb)	Sulfur Dioxide 1-Hr (ppb)	Sulfur Dioxide 24-Hr (ppb)
MSA[1] Level	8	40	n/a	3	n/a
NAAQS[2]	53	100	30	75	140
Met NAAQS[2]	Yes	Yes	n/a	Yes	n/a

Note: (1) Data covers the Virginia Beach-Norfolk-Newport News, VA-NC Metropolitan Statistical Area; Data from exceptional events are included; (2) National Ambient Air Quality Standards; ppm = parts per million; ug/m³ = micrograms per cubic meter; n/a not available.
Concentrations: Nitrogen Dioxide AM—highest arithmetic mean concentration; Nitrogen Dioxide 1-Hr—highest 98th percentile 1-hour daily maximum concentration; Sulfur Dioxide AM—highest annual mean concentration; Sulfur Dioxide 1-Hr—highest 99th percentile 1-hour daily maximum concentration; Sulfur Dioxide 24-Hr—highest second maximum 24-hour concentration
Source: U.S. Environmental Protection Agency, Air Quality Monitoring Information, "Air Quality Statistics by City, 2019"

Washington, D.C.

Background

The city and federal district of Washington, D.C., with its more than 150 foreign embassies, consulates and ambassadors' residences, is definitely cosmopolitan.

In 1793, the first cornerstone of the White House was laid. In 1800, the north wing was completed, a drifting Congress found its home, and President John Adams was the first president to reside at the White House. The building was burned down by the British in 1814 (during the War of 1812), and its final reconstruction was completed in 1891.

The young capital, which grows more confident and worldly every year, is renowned for its brilliant annual springtime display of cherry blossoms, as well as a breathtaking collection of architectural styles, including Greek Revival, Federal, Victorian, and Baroque; in fact, six of the top ten buildings in the American Institute of Architects' 2007 ranking of America's Favorite Architecture are in the District of Columbia. Some of the city's monuments and well-known sites include the Washington Monument, Lincoln Memorial, the White House, Jefferson Memorial, Vietnam Veterans Memorial, and Arlington National Cemetery. In 2004, the National World War II Memorial was dedicated, as part of a four-day World War II Reunion, and the United States Air Force Memorial was completed in 2006.

As the political machine of the country, the main industry is government. A second major employer for the city proper is the tourism industry; it is one of the most visited cities in the world, with more than 20 million annual tourists. Other industries in D.C. include education, finance, public policy and scientific research. In a recent survey, Washington was ranked as one of the most competitive financial centers in both the country and also the world. Washington is also home to five major universities—American, Georgetown, George Washington, Howard, and the Catholic University of America.

On September 11, 2001, the city suffered an attack orchestrated by Saudi terrorist Osama bin Laden as part of a wider assault on the U.S. that included the World Trade Center in New York on the same day. An airplane crashed through the Pentagon, after, it is believed, terrorists on board were unable to locate their original target—either the White House or the Capitol, killing several hundred people. On January 6, 2021, hundreds stormed the Capitol building, believing that Joe Biden, winner of the 2020 presidential election, stole the election. Several were killed, many were injured in a harrowing attempt at overthrowing the government. Both these major incidents has led to tightening of security in the district itself.

Despite such destruction, D.C. continues to be in an urban renaissance. Recent construction projects include the DC Streetcar system, a new Metro line, and Capital Bikeshare, one of the largest bicycle sharing systems in the country.

The Walter E. Washington Convention Center, open since 2004, hosts hundreds of events and welcomes over a million visitors annually. The convention center has sparked a new phase in the economic development of the city's northeast downtown area, which was devastated by the riots of 1968. In addition to the convention center, City Museum opened up across the street at the old Carnegie Library. Just a few blocks south, restaurants fill the vicinity of the International Spy Museum and the Verizon Center, home to the NBA Wizards, WNBA Mystics, and the NHL Capitals. In 2005 the Montreal Expos baseball team became the Washington Nationals and the team moved to Washington D.C. Today they play at Nationals Park, a state-of-the-art, 41,000-seat facility, and the underdog team won the 2019 World Series.

As part of D.C.'s vibrant cultural scene, the John F. Kennedy Center for the Performing Arts was renovated in 2005, with improved access and visual improvements to its façade. More recently completed was the renovation of the Eisenhower Theater in the JFK Center.

In addition, the Smithsonian Institution's National Air and Space Museum has expanded into a second museum near the Washington Dulles International Airport in Virginia, which is called the Steven F. Udvar-Hazy Center. Other museums in the city include the National Gallery of Art, U.S. Holocaust Memorial Museum, the Corcoran Gallery, the Phillips Collection, the Hirshhorn Museum and Sculpture Garden, and the many other Smithsonian museums. One of the city's newest museums, the National Museum of the American Indian, is housed in a dramatic building on the National Mall, with a mission to explore and celebrate the histories and cultures of Native Americans from North, Central, and South America.

Washington, a global media center, has bureaus of all worldwide major news outlets and the country's largest concentrations of journalists. It is also home to Black Entertainment Television, C-SPAN, National Public Radio, the Washington Post Company and XM Satellite Radio.

Summertime in Washington is warm and humid; winters are cold, but usually not severe.

Rankings

General Rankings

- In its eighth annual survey, *Travel + Leisure* readers nominated their favorite small cities and towns in America—those with 100,000 or fewer residents—voting on numerous attractive features in categories including culture, food and drink, quality of life, style, and people. After 50,000 votes, Washington was ranked #16 among the proposed favorites. *www.travelandleisure.com, "America's Favorite Cities," October 20, 2017*

- The human resources consulting firm Mercer ranked 231 major cities worldwide in terms of overall quality of life. Washington ranked #53. Criteria: political, social, economic, and socio-cultural factors; medical and health considerations; schools and education; public services and transportation; recreation; consumer goods; housing; and natural environment. *Mercer, "Mercer 2019 Quality of Living Survey," March 13, 2019*

- Washington appeared on *Travel + Leisure's* list of the 15 best cities in the United States. The city was ranked #13. Criteria: sights/landmarks; culture; food; friendliness; shopping; and overall value. *Travel + Leisure, "The World's Best Awards 2020" July 8, 2020*

- For its 33rd annual "Readers' Choice Awards" survey, *Condé Nast Traveler* ranked its readers' favorite cities in the U.S. These places brought feelings of comfort in a time of limited travel. The list was broken into large cities and cities under 250,000. Washington ranked #2 in the big city category. *Condé Nast Traveler, Readers' Choice Awards 2020, "Best Big Cities in the U.S." October 6, 2020*

Business/Finance Rankings

- According to *Business Insider*, the Washington metro area is a prime place to run a startup or move an existing business to. The area ranked #15. Nearly 190 metro areas were analyzed on overall economic health and investments. Data was based on the 2019 U.S. Census Bureau American Community Survey, the marketing company PitchBook, Bureau of Labor Statistics employment report, and Zillow. Criteria: percentage of change in typical home values and employment rates; quarterly venture capital investment activity; and median household income. *www.businessinsider.com, "The 25 Best Cities to Start a Business-Or Move Your Current One," January 12, 2021*

- Based on metro area social media reviews, the employment opinion group Glassdoor surveyed 50 of the most populous U.S. metro areas and equally weighed cost of living, hiring opportunity, and job satisfaction to compose a list of "25 Best Cities for Jobs." Median pay and home value, and number of active job openings were also factored in. The Washington metro area was ranked #17 in overall job satisfaction. *www.glassdoor.com, "Best Cities for Jobs," February 25, 2020*

- The Brookings Institution ranked the nation's largest cities based on income inequality. Washington was ranked #2 (#1 = greatest inequality). Criteria: the "95/20 ratio," a figure representing the income at which a household earns more than 95 percent of all other households, divided by the income at which a household earns more than only 20 percent of all other households. *Brookings Institution, "Household Income Inequality, Largest Cities of 97 Large U.S. Metro Areas, 2014-2016," February 5, 2018*

- The Brookings Institution ranked the 100 largest metro areas in the U.S. based on income inequality. Washington was ranked #70 (#1 = greatest inequality). Criteria: the "95/20 ratio," a figure representing the income at which a household earns more than 95 percent of all other households, divided by the income at which a household earns more than only 20 percent of all other households. *Brookings Institution, "Household Income Inequality, 100 Largest U.S. Metro Areas, 2014-2016," February 5, 2018*

- *Forbes* ranked the 100 largest metro areas in the U.S. in terms of the "Best Cities for Young Professionals." The Washington metro area ranked #7 out of 25. Criteria: median rent of a two-bedroom apartment; job growth and unemployment rate; median salary of college graduates with 5 or less years of work experience; networking opportunities; social outlook; percentage of population 25 years of age and older with college degrees. *Forbes.com, "America's 25 Best Cities for Young Professionals in 2017," May 22, 2017*

- Payscale.com ranked the 32 largest metro areas in terms of wage growth. The Washington metro area ranked #21. Criteria: private-sector and education professional wage growth between the 4th quarter of 2019 and the 4th quarter of 2020. *PayScale, "Wage Trends by Metro Area-4th Quarter," January 11, 2021*

- The Washington metro area was identified as one of the most debt-ridden places in America by the finance site Credit.com. The metro area was ranked #1. Criteria: residents' average credit card debt as well as median income. *Credit.com, "25 Cities With the Most Credit Card Debt," February 28, 2018*

- For its annual survey of the "Most Expensive U.S. Cities to Live In," Kiplinger applied Cost of Living Index statistics developed by the Council for Community and Economic Research to U.S. Census Bureau population and median household income data for 256 urban areas. Washington was among the 20 most expensive in the country. *Kiplinger.com, "The 20 Most Expensive Cities in the U.S.," July 29, 2020*

- Washington was identified as one of America's most frugal metro areas by *Coupons.com*. The city ranked #1 out of 25. Criteria: digital coupon usage. *Coupons.com, "America's Most Frugal Cities of 2017," March 22, 2018*

- Washington was cited as one of America's top metros for new and expanded facility projects in 2020. The area ranked #10 in the large metro area category (population over 1 million). *Site Selection, "Top Metros of 2020," March 2021*

- The Washington metro area appeared on the Milken Institute "2021 Best Performing Cities" list. Rank: #79 out of 200 large metro areas (population over 250,000). Criteria: job growth; wage and salary growth; high-tech output growth; housing affordability; household broadband access. *Milken Institute, "Best-Performing Cities 2021," February 16, 2021*

- *Forbes* ranked the 200 most populous metro areas to determine the nation's "Best Places for Business and Careers." The Washington metro area was ranked #59. Criteria: costs (business and living); job growth (past and projected); income growth; quality of life; educational attainment (college and high school); projected economic growth; cultural and leisure opportunities; workplace tolerance laws; net migration patterns. *Forbes, "The Best Places for Business and Careers 2019: Seattle Still On Top," October 30, 2019*

- Mercer Human Resources Consulting ranked 209 cities worldwide in terms of cost-of-living. Washington ranked #32 (the lower the ranking, the higher the cost-of-living). The survey measured the comparative cost of over 200 items (such as housing, food, clothing, household goods, transportation, and entertainment) in each location. *Mercer, "2020 Cost of Living Survey," June 9, 2020*

Culture/Performing Arts Rankings

- Washington was selected as one of the 25 best cities for moviemakers in North America. COVID-19 has spurred a quest for great film cities that offer more creative space, lower costs, and more great outdoors. NYC & LA were intentionally excluded. Criteria: longstanding reputations as film-friendly communities; efforts to deal with pandemic-specific challenges; and establish appropriate COVID-19 guidelines. The city was ranked #20. *MovieMaker Magazine, "Best Places to Live and Work as a Moviemaker, 2021," January 26, 2021*

Dating/Romance Rankings

- Washington was selected as one of the best cities for post grads by *Rent.com*. The city ranked among the top 10. Criteria: jobs per capita; unemployment rate; mean annual income; cost of living; rental inventory. *Rent.com, "Best Cities for College Grads," December 11, 2018*

Education Rankings

- Personal finance website *WalletHub* analyzed the 150 largest U.S. metropolitan statistical areas to determine where the most educated Americans are putting their degrees to work. Criteria: education levels; percentage of workers with degrees; education quality and attainment gap; public school quality rankings; quality and enrollment of each metro area's universities. Washington was ranked #3 (#1 = most educated city). *www.WalletHub.com, "Most and Least Educated Cities in America," July 20, 2020*

- Washington was selected as one of America's most literate cities. The city ranked #2 out of the 84 largest U.S. cities. Criteria: number of booksellers; library resources; Internet resources; educational attainment; periodical publishing resources; newspaper circulation. *Central Connecticut State University, "America's Most Literate Cities, 2018," February 2019*

Environmental Rankings

- The U.S. Environmental Protection Agency (EPA) released a list of U.S. metropolitan areas with the most ENERGY STAR certified buildings in 2019. The Washington metro area was ranked #2 out of 25. *U.S. Environmental Protection Agency, "2020 Energy Star Top Cities," March 2020*

- Washington was highlighted as one of the 25 most ozone-polluted metro areas in the U.S. during 2016 through 2018. The area ranked #20. *American Lung Association, "State of the Air 2020," April 21, 2020*

Food/Drink Rankings

- The U.S. Chamber of Commerce Foundation conducted an in-depth study on local food truck regulations, surveyed 288 food truck owners, and ranked 20 major American cities based on how friendly they are for operating a food truck. The compiled index assessed the following: procedures for obtaining permits and licenses; complying with restrictions; and financial obligations associated with operating a food truck. Washington ranked #19 overall (1 being the best). *www.foodtrucknation.us, "Food Truck Nation," March 20, 2018*

Health/Fitness Rankings

- The Sharecare Community Well-Being Index evaluates 10 individual and social health factors in order to measure what matters to Americans in the co mmunities in which they live. The Washington metro area was one of the five communities where social determinants of health were the highest. Criteria: access to food, healthcare, and community resources; housing and transportation; economic security. The area ranked #0. *www.sharecare.com, "Community Well-Being Index: 2019 Metro Area & County Rankings Report," August 31, 2020*

- For each of the 100 largest cities in the United States, the American Fitness Index®, published by the American College of Sports Medicine and the Anthem Foundation, evaluated community infrastructure and 33 health behaviors including preventive health, levels of chronic disease conditions, pedestrian safety, air quality, and community resources that support physical activity. Washington ranked #6 for "community fitness." *americanfitnessindex.org, "2020 ACSM American Fitness Index Summary Report," July 14, 2020*

- Washington was identified as one of the 10 most walkable cities in the U.S. by Walk Score. The city ranked #7. Walk Score measures walkability by analyzing hundreds of walking routes to nearby amenities, and also measures pedestrian friendliness by analyzing population density and road metrics such as block length and intersection density. *WalkScore.com, April 13, 2021*

- The Washington metro area was identified as one of the worst cities for bed bugs in America by pest control company Orkin. The area ranked #3 out of 50 based on the number of bed bug treatments Orkin performed from December 2019 to November 2020. *Orkin, "New Year, New Top City on Orkin's 2021 Bed Bug Cities List: Chicago," February 1, 2021*

- Washington was identified as a "2021 Spring Allergy Capital." The area ranked #61 out of 100. Three groups of factors were used to identify the most challenging cities for people with allergies during the spring season: annual spring pollen levels; over the counter medicine use; number of board-certified allergy specialists. *Asthma and Allergy Foundation of America, "Spring Allergy Capitals 2021," February 23, 2021*

- Washington was identified as a "2021 Fall Allergy Capital." The area ranked #82 out of 100. Three groups of factors were used to identify the most challenging cities for people with allergies during the fall season: annual fall pollen levels; over the counter medicine use; number of board-certified allergy specialists. *Asthma and Allergy Foundation of America, "Fall Allergy Capitals 2021," February 23, 2021*

- Washington was identified as a "2019 Asthma Capital." The area ranked #28 out of the nation's 100 largest metropolitan areas. Criteria: estimated asthma prevalence; crude death rate from asthma; and ER visits due to asthma. Risk factors analyzed but not factored in the rankings: annual pollen score; annual air quality; public smoking laws; number of board-certified asthma specialists; rescue medication use; controller medication use; uninsured rate; poverty rate. *Asthma and Allergy Foundation of America, "Asthma Capitals 2019: The Most Challenging Places to Live With Asthma," May 7, 2019*

Pet Rankings

- Washington appeared on *The Dogington Post* site as one of the top cities for dog lovers, ranking #5 out of 20. The real estate brokerage, Redfin and Rover, the largest pet sitter and dog walker network, compiled a list from over 14,000 U.S. cities to come up with a "Rover Rank." Criteria: highest count of dog walks, the city's Walk Score®, for-sale home listings that mention "dog," number of dog walkers and pet sitters and the hours spent and distance logged. *www.dogingtonpost.com, "The 20 Most Dog-Friendly Cities of 2019," April 4, 2019*

Real Estate Rankings

- FitSmallBusiness looked at 50 of the largest metropolitan areas in the U.S. to determine which metro was the best to start a real estate business. Data was compiled from such sources as: Zillow, Trulia, U.S. Census Bureau, and the Bureau of Labor Statistics. Criteria: location; inventory; annual wages; median sales price of homes; days on the market; median price cut percentage; and other factors that would influence real estate professional growth. The Washington metro area ranked #5. *fitsmallbusiness.com, "The Best Cities to Become a Real Estate Agent in 2018," January 30, 2018*

- *WalletHub* compared the most populated U.S. cities to determine which had the best markets for real estate agents. Washington ranked #9 where demand was high and pay was the best. Criteria: sales per agent; annual median wage for real-estate agents; monthly average starting salary for real estate agents; real estate job density and competition; unemployment rate; home turnover rate; housing-market health index; and other relevant metrics. *www.WalletHub.com, "2019's Best Places to Be a Real Estate Agent," April 24, 2019*

- The Washington metro area was identified as one of the 20 least affordable housing markets in the U.S. in 2020. The area ranked #168 out of 183 markets. Criteria: qualification for a mortgage loan with a 10 percent down payment on a typical home. *National Association of Realtors®, Qualifying Income Based on Sales Price of Existing Single-Family Homes for Metropolitan Areas, 2020*

- Washington was ranked #153 out of 268 metro areas in terms of housing affordability in 2020 by the National Association of Home Builders (#1 = most affordable). Criteria: the share of homes sold in that area affordable to a family earning the local median income, based on standard mortgage underwriting criteria. *National Association of Home Builders®, NAHB-Wells Fargo Housing Opportunity Index, 4th Quarter 2020*

Safety Rankings

- To identify the most dangerous cities in America, 24/7 Wall Street focused on violent crime categories—murder, non-negligent manslaughter, rape, robbery, and aggravated assault—and property crime as reported in the FBI's 2019 annual Uniform Crime Report. Criteria also included median income from American Community Survey and unemployment figures from Bureau of Labor Statistics. For cities with populations over 100,000, Washington was ranked #29. *247wallst.com, "America's 50 Most Dangerous Cities" November 16, 2020*

- Allstate ranked the 200 largest cities in America in terms of driver safety. Washington ranked #199. Criteria: internal property damage claims over a two-year period from January 2016 to December 2017. The report helps increase the importance of safety and awareness behind the wheel. *Allstate, "Allstate America's Best Drivers Report, 2019" June 24, 2019*

- Washington was identified as one of the most dangerous cities in America by NeighborhoodScout. The city ranked #52 out of 100 (#1 = most dangerous). Criteria: number of violent crimes per 1,000 residents. The editors evaluated cities with 25,000 or more residents. *NeighborhoodScout.com, "2021 Top 100 Most Dangerous Cities in the U.S.," January 2, 2021*

- The National Insurance Crime Bureau ranked 384 metro areas in the U.S. in terms of per capita rates of vehicle theft. The Washington metro area ranked #230 (#1 = highest rate). Criteria: number of vehicle theft offenses per 100,000 inhabitants in 2019. *National Insurance Crime Bureau, "Hot Spots 2019," July 21, 2020*

Seniors/Retirement Rankings

- From its Best Cities for Successful Aging indexes, the Milken Institute generated rankings for metropolitan areas, weighing data in nine categories—health care, wellness, living arrangements, transportation and convenience, financial characteristics, education, employment, community engagement, and overall livability. The Washington metro area was ranked #48 overall in the large metro area category. *Milken Institute, "Best Cities for Successful Aging, 2017" March 14, 2017*

Sports/Recreation Rankings

- Washington was chosen as one of America's best cities for bicycling. The city ranked #11 out of 50. Criteria: cycling infrastructure that is safe and friendly for all ages; energy and bike culture. The editors evaluated cities with populations of 100,000 or more. *Bicycling, "The 50 Best Bike Cities in America," October 10, 2018*

Transportation Rankings

- Business Insider presented an AllTransit Performance Score ranking of public transportation in major U.S. cities and towns, with populations over 250,000, in which Washington earned the #4-ranked "Transit Score," awarded for frequency of service, access to jobs, quality and number of stops, and affordability. *www.businessinsider.com, "The 17 Major U.S. Cities with the Best Public Transportation," April 17, 2018*

- The business website 24/7 Wall Street reviewed U.S. Census data to identify the 25 cities where the largest share of households do not own a vehicle. Washington held the #3 position. *247wallst.com, "Cities Where No One Wants to Drive," February 15, 2017*

- Washington was identified as one of the most congested metro areas in the U.S. The area ranked #3 out of 10. Criteria: yearly delay per auto commuter in hours. *Texas A&M Transportation Institute, "2019 Urban Mobility Report," December 2019*

- According to the INRIX "2019 Global Traffic Scorecard," Washington was identified as one of the most congested metro areas in the U.S. The area ranked #5 out of 10. Criteria: average annual time spent in traffic and average cost of congestion per motorist. *Inrix.com, "Congestion Costs Each American Nearly 100 hours, $1,400 A Year," March 9, 2020*

Women/Minorities Rankings

- Personal finance website *WalletHub* compared more than 180 U.S. cities across two key dimensions, "Hispanic Business-Friendliness" and "Hispanic Purchasing Power," to arrive at the most favorable conditions for Hispanic entrepreneurs. Washington was ranked #90 out of 182. Criteria includes: share of Hispanic-Owned Businesses; Hispanic entrepreneurship rate to median annual income of Hispanics; Small Business-Friendliness score; cost of living; and number of Hispanics with at least a bachelor's degree. *WalletHub.com, "2019's Best Cities for Hispanic Entrepreneurs," May 1, 2019*

Miscellaneous Rankings

- While the majority of travel ground to a halt in 2020, plugged-in travel influencers and experts were able to rediscover their local regions. Washington appeared on a *Forbes* list of 15 U.S. cities that provided solace as well as local inspiration. Whether it be quirky things to see and do, delicious take out, outdoor exploring and daytrips, these places are must-see destinations. *Forbes, "Bucket List Travel: The 15 Best U.S. Destinations For 2021," January 1, 2021*

- The watchdog site, Charity Navigator, conducted a study of charities in major markets both to analyze statistical differences in their financial, accountability, and transparency practices and to track year-to-year variations in individual philanthropic communities. The Washington metro area was ranked #24 among the 30 metro markets in the rating category of Overall Score. *www.charitynavigator.org, "2017 Metro Market Study," May 1, 2017*

- *WalletHub* compared the 150 most populated U.S. cities to determine their operating efficiency. A "Quality of City Services" score was constructed for each city and then divided by the total budget per capita to reveal which were managed the best. Washington ranked #150. Criteria: financial stability; economy; education; safety; health; infrastructure and pollution. *www.WalletHub.com, "2020's Best- & Worst-Run Cities in America," June 29, 2020*

- The National Alliance to End Homelessness listed the 25 most populous metro areas with the highest rate of homelessness. The Washington metro area had a high rate of homelessness. Criteria: number of homeless people per 10,000 population in 2016. *National Alliance to End Homelessness, "Homelessness in the 25 Most Populous U.S. Metro Areas," September 1, 2017*

Business Environment

DEMOGRAPHICS

Population Growth

Area	1990 Census	2000 Census	2010 Census	2019* Estimate	Population Growth (%) 1990-2019	Population Growth (%) 2010-2019
City	606,900	572,059	601,723	692,683	14.1	15.1
MSA[1]	4,122,914	4,796,183	5,582,170	6,196,585	50.3	11.0
U.S.	248,709,873	281,421,906	308,745,538	324,697,795	30.6	5.2

Note: (1) Figures cover the Washington-Arlington-Alexandria, DC-VA-MD-WV Metropolitan Statistical Area; (*) 2015-2019 5-year estimated population
Source: U.S. Census Bureau, 1990 Census, Census 2000, Census 2010, 2015-2019 American Community Survey 5-Year Estimates

Household Size

Area	Persons in Household (%) One	Two	Three	Four	Five	Six	Seven or More	Average Household Size
City	44.1	31.1	11.7	7.9	3.2	1.3	0.8	2.30
MSA[1]	27.2	30.8	16.5	14.7	6.5	2.6	1.6	2.80
U.S.	27.9	33.9	15.6	12.9	6.0	2.3	1.4	2.60

Note: (1) Figures cover the Washington-Arlington-Alexandria, DC-VA-MD-WV Metropolitan Statistical Area
Source: U.S. Census Bureau, 2015-2019 American Community Survey 5-Year Estimates

Race

Area	White Alone[2] (%)	Black Alone[2] (%)	Asian Alone[2] (%)	AIAN[3] Alone[2] (%)	NHOPI[4] Alone[2] (%)	Other Race Alone[2] (%)	Two or More Races (%)
City	41.3	46.3	4.0	0.3	0.1	5.0	3.1
MSA[1]	53.5	25.3	10.1	0.3	0.1	6.5	4.2
U.S.	72.5	12.7	5.5	0.8	0.2	4.9	3.3

Note: (1) Figures cover the Washington-Arlington-Alexandria, DC-VA-MD-WV Metropolitan Statistical Area; (2) Alone is defined as not being in combination with one or more other races; (3) American Indian and Alaska Native; (4) Native Hawaiian and Other Pacific Islander
Source: U.S. Census Bureau, 2015-2019 American Community Survey 5-Year Estimates

Hispanic or Latino Origin

Area	Total (%)	Mexican (%)	Puerto Rican (%)	Cuban (%)	Other (%)
City	11.0	2.0	0.9	0.4	7.6
MSA[1]	15.8	2.3	1.1	0.3	12.1
U.S.	18.0	11.2	1.7	0.7	4.3

Note: Persons of Hispanic or Latino origin can be of any race; (1) Figures cover the Washington-Arlington-Alexandria, DC-VA-MD-WV Metropolitan Statistical Area
Source: U.S. Census Bureau, 2015-2019 American Community Survey 5-Year Estimates

Ancestry

Area	German	Irish	English	American	Italian	Polish	French[2]	Scottish	Dutch
City	6.9	6.7	5.2	2.3	3.9	2.2	1.5	1.4	0.7
MSA[1]	9.3	8.3	6.9	4.1	4.3	2.3	1.6	1.6	0.7
U.S.	13.3	9.7	7.2	6.2	5.1	2.8	2.3	1.7	1.2

Note: Figures are the percentage of the total population reporting a particular ancestry. The nine most commonly reported ancestries in the U.S. are shown. Figures include multiple ancestries (e.g. if a person reported being Irish and Italian, they were included in both columns); (1) Figures cover the Washington-Arlington-Alexandria, DC-VA-MD-WV Metropolitan Statistical Area; (2) Excludes Basque
Source: U.S. Census Bureau, 2015-2019 American Community Survey 5-Year Estimates

Foreign-born Population

Area	Percent of Population Born in Any Foreign Country	Asia	Mexico	Europe	Caribbean	Central America[2]	South America	Africa	Canada
City	13.7	3.0	0.6	2.5	1.2	2.6	1.3	2.1	0.3
MSA[1]	22.8	8.2	0.8	1.8	1.1	4.9	2.2	3.5	0.2
U.S.	13.6	4.2	3.5	1.5	1.3	1.1	1.0	0.7	0.2

Note: (1) Figures cover the Washington-Arlington-Alexandria, DC-VA-MD-WV Metropolitan Statistical Area; (2) Excludes Mexico.
Source: U.S. Census Bureau, 2015-2019 American Community Survey 5-Year Estimates

Marital Status

Area	Never Married	Now Married[2]	Separated	Widowed	Divorced
City	56.4	28.9	2.1	4.1	8.5
MSA[1]	36.1	48.9	1.9	4.4	8.8
U.S.	33.4	48.1	1.9	5.8	10.9

Note: Figures are percentages and cover the population 15 years of age and older; (1) Figures cover the Washington-Arlington-Alexandria, DC-VA-MD-WV Metropolitan Statistical Area; (2) Excludes separated
Source: U.S. Census Bureau, 2015-2019 American Community Survey 5-Year Estimates

Disability by Age

Area	All Ages	Under 18 Years Old	18 to 64 Years Old	65 Years and Over
City	11.7	4.1	9.6	35.3
MSA[1]	8.7	3.0	6.7	29.1
U.S.	12.6	4.2	10.3	34.5

Note: Figures show percent of the civilian noninstitutionalized population that reported having a disability. Disability status is determined from six types of difficulty: vision, hearing, cognitive, ambulatory, self-care, and independent living. For children under 5 years old, hearing and vision difficulty are used to determine disability status. For children between the ages of 5 and 14, disability status is determined from hearing, vision, cognitive, ambulatory, and self-care difficulties. For people aged 15 years and older, they are considered to have a disability if they have difficulty with any one of the six difficulty types; Note: (1) Figures cover the Washington-Arlington-Alexandria, DC-VA-MD-WV Metropolitan Statistical Area
Source: U.S. Census Bureau, 2015-2019 American Community Survey 5-Year Estimates

Age

Area	Percent of Population									Median Age
	Under Age 5	Age 5–19	Age 20–34	Age 35–44	Age 45–54	Age 55–64	Age 65–74	Age 75–84	Age 85+	
City	6.5	14.5	31.0	14.8	11.0	10.1	7.0	3.5	1.6	34.0
MSA[1]	6.5	19.0	21.3	14.3	14.0	12.1	7.7	3.6	1.4	37.0
U.S.	6.1	19.1	20.7	12.6	13.0	12.9	9.1	4.6	1.9	38.1

Note: (1) Figures cover the Washington-Arlington-Alexandria, DC-VA-MD-WV Metropolitan Statistical Area
Source: U.S. Census Bureau, 2015-2019 American Community Survey 5-Year Estimates

Gender

Area	Males	Females	Males per 100 Females
City	328,644	364,039	90.3
MSA[1]	3,028,975	3,167,610	95.6
U.S.	159,886,919	164,810,876	97.0

Note: (1) Figures cover the Washington-Arlington-Alexandria, DC-VA-MD-WV Metropolitan Statistical Area
Source: U.S. Census Bureau, 2015-2019 American Community Survey 5-Year Estimates

Religious Groups by Family

Area	Catholic	Baptist	Non-Den.	Methodist[2]	Lutheran	LDS[3]	Pente-costal	Presby-terian[4]	Muslim[5]	Judaism
MSA[1]	14.5	7.3	4.9	4.5	1.3	1.2	1.1	1.4	2.4	1.2
U.S.	19.1	9.3	4.0	4.0	2.3	2.0	1.9	1.6	0.8	0.7

Note: Figures are the number of adherents as a percentage of the total population; (1) Figures cover the Washington-Arlington-Alexandria, DC-VA-MD-WV Metropolitan Statistical Area; (2) Methodist/Pietist; (3) Latter Day Saints; (4) Reformed; (5) Figures are estimates
Source: Association of Statisticians of American Religious Bodies, 2010 U.S. Religion Census: Religious Congregations & Membership Study

Religious Groups by Tradition

Area	Catholic	Evangelical Protestant	Mainline Protestant	Other Tradition	Black Protestant	Orthodox
MSA[1]	14.5	12.4	8.8	5.9	2.3	0.6
U.S.	19.1	16.2	7.3	4.3	1.6	0.3

Note: Figures are the number of adherents as a percentage of the total population; (1) Figures cover the Washington-Arlington-Alexandria, DC-VA-MD-WV Metropolitan Statistical Area
Source: Association of Statisticians of American Religious Bodies, 2010 U.S. Religion Census: Religious Congregations & Membership Study

ECONOMY

Gross Metropolitan Product

Area	2017	2018	2019	2020	Rank[2]
MSA[1]	539.6	562.6	585.8	612.1	4

Note: Figures are in billions of dollars; (1) Figures cover the Washington-Arlington-Alexandria, DC-VA-MD-WV Metropolitan Statistical Area; (2) Rank is based on 2018 data and ranges from 1 to 381
Source: U.S. Conference of Mayors, U.S. Metro Economies: GMP & Employment 2018-2020, September 2019

Economic Growth

Area	2015-17 (%)	2018 (%)	2019 (%)	2020 (%)	Rank[2]
MSA[1]	2.0	2.3	2.4	2.1	131
U.S.	1.9	2.9	2.3	2.1	–

Note: Figures are real gross metropolitan product (GMP) growth rates and represent average annual percent change; (1) Figures cover the Washington-Arlington-Alexandria, DC-VA-MD-WV Metropolitan Statistical Area; (2) Rank is based on 2017 2-year average annual percent change and ranges from 1 to 381
Source: U.S. Conference of Mayors, U.S. Metro Economies: GMP & Employment 2018-2020, September 2019

Metropolitan Area Exports

Area	2014	2015	2016	2017	2018	2019	Rank[2]
MSA[1]	13,053.6	13,900.4	13,582.4	12,736.1	13,602.7	14,563.8	25

Note: Figures are in millions of dollars; (1) Figures cover the Washington-Arlington-Alexandria, DC-VA-MD-WV Metropolitan Statistical Area; (2) Rank is based on 2019 data and ranges from 1 to 386
Source: U.S. Department of Commerce, International Trade Administration, Office of Trade and Economic Analysis, Industry and Analysis, Exports by Metropolitan Area, data extracted March 24, 2021

Building Permits

Area	Single-Family			Multi-Family			Total		
	2018	2019	Pct. Chg.	2018	2019	Pct. Chg.	2018	2019	Pct. Chg.
City	112	168	50.0	4,503	5,777	28.3	4,615	5,945	28.8
MSA[1]	13,588	12,977	-4.5	12,169	13,827	13.6	25,757	26,804	4.1
U.S.	855,300	862,100	0.7	473,500	523,900	10.6	1,328,800	1,386,000	4.3

Note: (1) Figures cover the Washington-Arlington-Alexandria, DC-VA-MD-WV Metropolitan Statistical Area; Figures represent new, privately-owned housing units authorized (unadjusted data); All permit data are based on estimates with imputation
Source: U.S. Census Bureau, Manufacturing, Mining, and Construction Statistics, Building Permits, 2018, 2019

Bankruptcy Filings

Area	Business Filings			Nonbusiness Filings		
	2019	2020	% Chg.	2019	2020	% Chg.
District of Columbia	50	50	0.0	789	449	-43.1
U.S.	22,780	21,655	-4.9	752,160	522,808	-30.5

Note: Business filings include Chapter 7, Chapter 9, Chapter 11, Chapter 12, Chapter 13, Chapter 15, and Section 304; Nonbusiness filings include Chapter 7, Chapter 11, and Chapter 13
Source: Administrative Office of the U.S. Courts, Business and Nonbusiness Bankruptcy, County Cases Commenced by Chapter of the Bankruptcy Code, During the 12-Month Period Ending December 31, 2019 and Business and Nonbusiness Bankruptcy, County Cases Commenced by Chapter of the Bankruptcy Code, During the 12-Month Period Ending December 31, 2020

Housing Vacancy Rates

Area	Gross Vacancy Rate[2] (%)			Year-Round Vacancy Rate[3] (%)			Rental Vacancy Rate[4] (%)			Homeowner Vacancy Rate[5] (%)		
	2018	2019	2020	2018	2019	2020	2018	2019	2020	2018	2019	2020
MSA[1]	7.0	7.1	6.5	6.7	6.7	6.2	6.2	5.6	5.5	1.1	1.1	0.7
U.S.	12.3	12.0	10.6	9.7	9.5	8.2	6.9	6.7	6.3	1.5	1.4	1.0

Note: (1) Figures cover the Washington-Arlington-Alexandria, DC-VA-MD-WV Metropolitan Statistical Area; (2) The percentage of the total housing inventory that is vacant; (3) The percentage of the housing inventory (excluding seasonal units) that is year-round vacant; (4) The percentage of rental inventory that is vacant for rent; (5) The percentage of homeowner inventory that is vacant for sale
Source: U.S. Census Bureau, Housing Vacancies and Homeownership Annual Statistics: 2018, 2019, 2020

INCOME

Income

Area	Per Capita ($)	Median Household ($)	Average Household ($)
City	56,147	86,420	127,890
MSA[1]	49,881	103,751	134,513
U.S.	34,103	62,843	88,607

Note: (1) Figures cover the Washington-Arlington-Alexandria, DC-VA-MD-WV Metropolitan Statistical Area
Source: U.S. Census Bureau, 2015-2019 American Community Survey 5-Year Estimates

Household Income Distribution

Area	Percent of Households Earning							
	Under $15,000	$15,000 -$24,999	$25,000 -$34,999	$35,000 -$49,999	$50,000 -$74,999	$75,000 -$99,999	$100,000 -$149,999	$150,000 and up
City	12.9	6.0	5.9	7.7	12.2	10.6	16.4	28.2
MSA[1]	5.8	4.1	4.8	7.5	13.3	12.6	19.9	31.9
U.S.	10.3	8.9	8.9	12.3	17.2	12.7	15.1	14.5

Note: (1) Figures cover the Washington-Arlington-Alexandria, DC-VA-MD-WV Metropolitan Statistical Area
Source: U.S. Census Bureau, 2015-2019 American Community Survey 5-Year Estimates

Poverty Rate

Area	All Ages	Under 18 Years Old	18 to 64 Years Old	65 Years and Over
City	16.2	24.0	14.5	14.5
MSA[1]	7.8	9.9	7.2	7.2
U.S.	13.4	18.5	12.6	9.3

Note: Figures are percentage of people whose income during the past 12 months was below the poverty level;
(1) Figures cover the Washington-Arlington-Alexandria, DC-VA-MD-WV Metropolitan Statistical Area
Source: U.S. Census Bureau, 2015-2019 American Community Survey 5-Year Estimates

CITY FINANCES

City Government Finances

Component	2017 ($000)	2017 ($ per capita)
Total Revenues	14,034,422	20,877
Total Expenditures	14,562,674	21,663
Debt Outstanding	14,417,441	21,447
Cash and Securities[1]	12,792,967	19,031

Note: (1) Cash and security holdings of a government at the close of its fiscal year,
including those of its dependent agencies, utilities, and liquor stores.
Source: U.S. Census Bureau, State & Local Government Finances 2017

City Government Revenue by Source

Source	2017 ($000)	2017 ($ per capita)	2017 (%)
General Revenue			
From Federal Government	3,824,420	5,689	27.3
From State Government	223,295	332	1.6
From Local Governments	8,077	12	0.1
Taxes			
Property	2,431,971	3,618	17.3
Sales and Gross Receipts	1,814,410	2,699	12.9
Personal Income	1,958,277	2,913	14.0
Corporate Income	554,245	824	3.9
Motor Vehicle License	45,915	68	0.3
Other Taxes	651,050	968	4.6
Current Charges	838,144	1,247	6.0
Liquor Store	0	0	0.0
Utility	180,561	269	1.3
Employee Retirement	619,695	922	4.4

Source: U.S. Census Bureau, State & Local Government Finances 2017

City Government Expenditures by Function

Function	2017 ($000)	2017 ($ per capita)	2017 (%)
General Direct Expenditures			
Air Transportation	0	0	0.0
Corrections	157,189	233	1.1
Education	2,906,833	4,324	20.0
Employment Security Administration	41,679	62	0.3
Financial Administration	276,338	411	1.9
Fire Protection	281,620	418	1.9
General Public Buildings	217,212	323	1.5
Governmental Administration, Other	87,341	129	0.6
Health	396,883	590	2.7
Highways	455,133	677	3.1
Hospitals	263,983	392	1.8
Housing and Community Development	766,629	1,140	5.3
Interest on General Debt	587,928	874	4.0
Judicial and Legal	148,175	220	1.0
Libraries	93,064	138	0.6
Parking	29,560	44	0.2
Parks and Recreation	258,569	384	1.8
Police Protection	633,302	942	4.3
Public Welfare	3,929,827	5,846	27.0
Sewerage	554,324	824	3.8
Solid Waste Management	127,136	189	0.9
Veterans' Services	0	0	0.0
Liquor Store	0	0	0.0
Utility	324,777	483	2.2
Employee Retirement	155,935	232	1.1

Source: U.S. Census Bureau, State & Local Government Finances 2017

EMPLOYMENT

Labor Force and Employment

Area	Civilian Labor Force			Workers Employed		
	Dec. 2019	Dec. 2020	% Chg.	Dec. 2019	Dec. 2020	% Chg.
City	416,329	413,158	-0.8	397,389	376,699	-5.2
MD[1]	2,779,621	2,686,651	-3.3	2,705,388	2,537,166	-6.2
U.S.	164,007,000	160,017,000	-2.4	158,504,000	149,613,000	-5.6

Note: Data is not seasonally adjusted and covers workers 16 years of age and older; (1) Figures cover the Washington-Arlington-Alexandria, DC-VA-MD-WV Metropolitan Division
Source: Bureau of Labor Statistics, Local Area Unemployment Statistics

Unemployment Rate

Area	2020											
	Jan.	Feb.	Mar.	Apr.	May	Jun.	Jul.	Aug.	Sep.	Oct.	Nov.	Dec.
City	5.0	4.9	5.5	10.6	9.0	9.2	9.5	8.9	8.8	8.2	8.4	8.8
MD[1]	3.1	3.0	3.4	10.0	8.9	8.4	8.1	6.9	6.9	6.4	5.7	5.6
U.S.	4.0	3.8	4.5	14.4	13.0	11.2	10.5	8.5	7.7	6.6	6.4	6.5

Note: Data is not seasonally adjusted and covers workers 16 years of age and older; (1) Figures cover the Washington-Arlington-Alexandria, DC-VA-MD-WV Metropolitan Division
Source: Bureau of Labor Statistics, Local Area Unemployment Statistics

Average Wages

Occupation	$/Hr.	Occupation	$/Hr.
Accountants and Auditors	47.10	Maintenance and Repair Workers	24.30
Automotive Mechanics	27.30	Marketing Managers	84.60
Bookkeepers	24.80	Network and Computer Systems Admin.	49.30
Carpenters	25.00	Nurses, Licensed Practical	26.80
Cashiers	13.20	Nurses, Registered	40.10
Computer Programmers	50.50	Nursing Assistants	16.20
Computer Systems Analysts	56.10	Office Clerks, General	20.90
Computer User Support Specialists	32.00	Physical Therapists	46.00
Construction Laborers	18.40	Physicians	98.70
Cooks, Restaurant	15.40	Plumbers, Pipefitters and Steamfitters	27.90
Customer Service Representatives	21.20	Police and Sheriff's Patrol Officers	37.00
Dentists	105.60	Postal Service Mail Carriers	25.70
Electricians	31.70	Real Estate Sales Agents	32.60
Engineers, Electrical	62.60	Retail Salespersons	15.10
Fast Food and Counter Workers	13.60	Sales Representatives, Technical/Scientific	60.70
Financial Managers	85.20	Secretaries, Exc. Legal/Medical/Executive	23.80
First-Line Supervisors of Office Workers	34.60	Security Guards	22.30
General and Operations Managers	74.90	Surgeons	128.60
Hairdressers/Cosmetologists	19.20	Teacher Assistants, Exc. Postsecondary*	17.50
Home Health and Personal Care Aides	14.10	Teachers, Secondary School, Exc. Sp. Ed.*	41.60
Janitors and Cleaners	16.30	Telemarketers	14.50
Landscaping/Groundskeeping Workers	17.20	Truck Drivers, Heavy/Tractor-Trailer	24.40
Lawyers	89.50	Truck Drivers, Light/Delivery Services	22.50
Maids and Housekeeping Cleaners	15.40	Waiters and Waitresses	16.00

Note: Wage data covers the Washington-Arlington-Alexandria, DC-VA-MD-WV Metropolitan Statistical Area; (*) Hourly wages were calculated from annual wage data based on a 40 hour work week; n/a not available.
Source: Bureau of Labor Statistics, Metro Area Occupational Employment & Wage Estimates, May 2020

Employment by Industry

Sector	MD[1]		U.S.
	Number of Employees	Percent of Total	Percent of Total
Construction, Mining, and Logging	130,400	5.0	5.5
Education and Health Services	335,100	12.9	16.3
Financial Activities	117,700	4.5	6.1
Government	594,100	22.8	15.2
Information	61,900	2.4	1.9
Leisure and Hospitality	191,200	7.3	9.0
Manufacturing	36,800	1.4	8.5
Other Services	167,900	6.5	3.8
Professional and Business Services	639,100	24.6	14.4
Retail Trade	210,000	8.1	10.9
Transportation, Warehousing, and Utilities	68,800	2.6	4.6
Wholesale Trade	48,500	1.9	3.9

Note: Figures are non-farm employment as of December 2020. Figures are not seasonally adjusted and include workers 16 years of age and older; (1) Figures cover the Washington-Arlington-Alexandria, DC-VA-MD-WV Metropolitan Division
Source: Bureau of Labor Statistics, Current Employment Statistics, Employment, Hours, and Earnings

Employment by Occupation

Occupation Classification	City (%)	MSA[1] (%)	U.S. (%)
Management, Business, Science, and Arts	63.6	52.7	38.5
Natural Resources, Construction, and Maintenance	2.7	6.8	8.9
Production, Transportation, and Material Moving	4.1	6.6	13.2
Sales and Office	15.1	17.8	21.6
Service	14.5	16.1	17.8

Note: Figures cover employed civilians 16 years of age and older; (1) Figures cover the Washington-Arlington-Alexandria, DC-VA-MD-WV Metropolitan Statistical Area
Source: U.S. Census Bureau, 2015-2019 American Community Survey 5-Year Estimates

Occupations with Greatest Projected Employment Growth: 2019 – 2021

Occupation[1]	2019 Employment	2021 Projected Employment	Numeric Employment Change	Percent Employment Change
Total,, All Occupations	818,160	846,830	28,670	3.5
Management Analysts	24,690	25,900	1,210	4.9
Public Relations Specialists	18,040	19,200	1,160	6.4
General and Operations Managers	31,260	32,360	1,100	3.5
Lawyers	39,840	40,890	1,050	2.6
Janitors and Cleaners,, Except Maids and Housekeeping Cleaners	16,340	17,050	710	4.3
Computer Occupations,, All Other	22,030	22,730	700	3.2
Combined Food Preparation and Serving Workers,, Including Fast Food	9,520	10,200	680	7.1
Business Operations Specialists,, All Other	39,740	40,380	640	1.6
Market Research Analysts and Marketing Specialists	6,660	7,210	550	8.3

Note: Projections cover District of Columbia; Projections for 2020-2022 were not available at time of publication; (1) Sorted by numeric employment change
Source: www.projectionscentral.com, State Occupational Projections, 2019–2021 Short-Term Projections

Fastest-Growing Occupations: 2019 – 2021

Occupation[1]	2019 Employment	2021 Projected Employment	Numeric Employment Change	Percent Employment Change
Information Security Analysts	1,590	1,780	190	11.9
Helpers—Pipelayers,, Plumbers,, Pipefitters,, and Steamfitters	600	660	60	10.0
Market Research Analysts and Marketing Specialists	6,660	7,210	550	8.3
Software Developers,, Applications	2,780	3,010	230	8.3
Cooks,, Restaurant	6,550	7,090	540	8.2
Counter and Rental Clerks	860	930	70	8.1
Social Science Research Assistants	3,250	3,510	260	8.0
Physician Assistants	630	680	50	7.9
Baggage Porters and Bellhops	650	700	50	7.7
First-Line Supervisors of Construction Trades and Extraction Workers	1,050	1,130	80	7.6

Note: Projections cover District of Columbia; Projections for 2020-2022 were not available at time of publication; (1) Sorted by percent employment change and excludes occupations with numeric employment change less than 50
Source: www.projectionscentral.com, State Occupational Projections, 2019–2021 Short-Term Projections

TAXES

State Corporate Income Tax Rates

State	Tax Rate (%)	Income Brackets ($)	Num. of Brackets	Financial Institution Tax Rate (%)[a]	Federal Income Tax Ded.
D.C.	8.25 (b)	Flat rate	1	8.25 (b)	No

Note: Tax rates as of January 1, 2021; (a) Rates listed are the corporate income tax rate applied to financial institutions or excise taxes based on income. Some states have other taxes based upon the value of deposits or shares; (b) Minimum tax is $800 in California, $250 in District of Columbia, $50 in Arizona and North Dakota (banks), $400 ($100 banks) in Rhode Island, $200 per location in South Dakota (banks), $100 in Utah, $300 in Vermont.
Source: Federation of Tax Administrators, State Corporate Income Tax Rates, January 1, 2021

State Individual Income Tax Rates

State	Tax Rate (%)	Income Brackets ($)	Personal Exemptions ($) Single	Married	Depend.	Standard Ded. ($) Single	Married
D.C.	4.0 - 8.95	10,000 - 1 million	(d)	(d)	(d)	12,550	25,100 (d)

Note: Tax rates as of January 1, 2021; Local- and county-level taxes are not included; Federal income tax is not deductible on state income tax returns; (d) These states use the personal exemption/standard deduction amounts provided in the federal Internal Revenue Code.
Source: Federation of Tax Administrators, State Individual Income Tax Rates, January 1, 2021

Various State Sales and Excise Tax Rates

State	State Sales Tax (%)	Gasoline[1] (¢/gal.)	Cigarette[2] ($/pack)	Spirits[3] ($/gal.)	Wine[4] ($/gal.)	Beer[5] ($/gal.)	Recreational Marijuana (%)
D.C.	6	28.8	5	6.2	1.89	0.72	(p)

Note: All tax rates as of January 1, 2021; (1) The American Petroleum Institute has developed a methodology for determining the average tax rate on a gallon of fuel. Rates may include any of the following: excise taxes, environmental fees, storage tank fees, other fees or taxes, general sales tax, and local taxes; (2) The federal excise tax of $1.0066 per pack and local taxes are not included; (3) Rates are those applicable to off-premise sales of 40% alcohol by volume (a.b.v.) distilled spirits in 750ml containers. Local excise taxes are excluded; (4) Rates are those applicable to off-premise sales of 11% a.b.v. non-carbonated wine in 750ml containers; (5) Rates are those applicable to off-premise sales of 4.7% a.b.v. beer in 12 ounce containers; (p) District of Columbia voters approved legalization and purchase of marijuana in 2014 but federal law prohibits any action to implement it.
Source: Tax Foundation, 2021 Facts & Figures: How Does Your State Compare?

State Business Tax Climate Index Rankings

State	Overall Rank	Corporate Tax Rank	Individual Income Tax Rank	Sales Tax Rank	Property Tax Rank	Unemployment Insurance Tax Rank
District of Columbia	46	17	45	34	49	37

Note: The index is a measure of how each state's tax laws affect economic performance. The lower the rank, the more favorable a state's tax system is for business. States without a given tax are given a ranking of 1. The scores/rankings for the District of Columbia do not affect other states. The 2021 index represents the tax climate as of July 1, 2020.
Source: Tax Foundation, State Business Tax Climate Index 2021

TRANSPORTATION

Means of Transportation to Work

Area	Car/Truck/Van Drove Alone	Car-pooled	Public Transportation Bus	Subway	Railroad	Bicycle	Walked	Other Means	Worked at Home
City	33.5	5.2	13.2	21.1	0.3	4.5	13.4	2.3	6.6
MSA[1]	65.8	9.3	4.8	7.8	0.8	0.9	3.3	1.5	5.9
U.S.	76.3	9.0	2.4	1.9	0.6	0.5	2.7	1.4	5.2

Note: Figures are percentages and cover workers 16 years of age and older; (1) Figures cover the Washington-Arlington-Alexandria, DC-VA-MD-WV Metropolitan Statistical Area
Source: U.S. Census Bureau, 2015-2019 American Community Survey 5-Year Estimates

Travel Time to Work

Area	Less Than 10 Minutes	10 to 19 Minutes	20 to 29 Minutes	30 to 44 Minutes	45 to 59 Minutes	60 to 89 Minutes	90 Minutes or More
City	4.9	18.5	22.5	32.4	12.6	7.1	2.0
MSA[1]	5.9	18.9	17.7	25.7	14.2	13.1	4.6
U.S.	12.2	28.4	20.8	20.8	8.3	6.4	2.9

Note: Note: Figures are percentages and include workers 16 years old and over; (1) Figures cover the Washington-Arlington-Alexandria, DC-VA-MD-WV Metropolitan Statistical Area
Source: U.S. Census Bureau, 2015-2019 American Community Survey 5-Year Estimates

Key Congestion Measures

Measure	1982	1992	2002	2012	2017
Annual Hours of Delay, Total (000)	46,620	100,013	157,422	219,081	247,811
Annual Hours of Delay, Per Auto Commuter	36	59	75	90	102
Annual Congestion Cost, Total (million $)	350	1,055	2,130	3,926	4,575
Annual Congestion Cost, Per Auto Commuter ($)	849	1,253	1,538	1,677	1,840

Note: Covers the Washington DC-VA-MD urban area
Source: Texas A&M Transportation Institute, 2019 Urban Mobility Report

Freeway Travel Time Index

Measure	1982	1987	1992	1997	2002	2007	2012	2017
Urban Area Index[1]	1.15	1.20	1.25	1.28	1.31	1.35	1.34	1.35
Urban Area Rank[1,2]	8	5	4	6	6	6	8	7

Note: Freeway Travel Time Index—the ratio of travel time in the peak period to the travel time at free-flow conditions. For example, a value of 1.30 indicates a 20-minute free-flow trip takes 26 minutes in the peak (20 minutes x 1.30 = 26 minutes); (1) Covers the Washington DC-VA-MD urban area; (2) Rank is based on 101 larger urban areas (#1 = highest travel time index)
Source: Texas A&M Transportation Institute, 2019 Urban Mobility Report

Public Transportation

Agency Name / Mode of Transportation	Vehicles Operated in Maximum Service[1]	Annual Unlinked Passenger Trips[2] (in thous.)	Annual Passenger Miles[3] (in thous.)
Washington Metropolitan Area Transit Authority (WMATA)			
Bus (directly operated)	1,286	122,127.1	358,532.9
Bus (purchased transportation)	93	1,206.1	9,025.8
Demand Response (purchased transportation)	754	2,212.7	21,875.3
Demand Response Taxi (purchased transportation)	338	135.6	2,502.4
Heavy Rail (directly operated)	920	228,974.8	1,313,511.2

Note: (1) Number of revenue vehicles operated by the given mode and type of service to meet the annual maximum service requirement. This is the revenue vehicle count during the peak season of the year; on the week and day that maximum service is provided. Vehicles operated in maximum service (VOMS) exclude atypical days and one-time special events; (2) Number of passengers who boarded public transportation vehicles. Passengers are counted each time they board a vehicle no matter how many vehicles they use to travel from their origin to their destination. (3) Sum of the distances ridden by all passengers during the entire fiscal year.
Source: Federal Transit Administration, National Transit Database, 2019

Air Transportation

Airport Name and Code / Type of Service	Passenger Airlines[1]	Passenger Enplanements	Freight Carriers[2]	Freight (lbs)
Ronald Reagan Washington National (DCA)				
Domestic service (U.S. carriers - 2020)	22	3,540,437	9	928,115
International service (U.S. carriers - 2019)	5	49,029	2	13,617
Dulles International (IAD)				
Domestic service (U.S. carriers - 2020)	26	2,904,308	11	92,412,405
International service (U.S. carriers - 2019)	9	1,602,485	3	38,087,697

Note: (1) Includes all U.S.-based major, minor and commuter airlines that carried at least one passenger during the year; (2) Includes all U.S.-based airlines and freight carriers that transported at least one pound of freight during the year.
Source: Bureau of Transportation Statistics, The Intermodal Transportation Database, Air Carriers: T-100 Domestic Market (U.S. Carriers), 2020; Bureau of Transportation Statistics, The Intermodal Transportation Database, Air Carriers: T-100 International Market (U.S. Carriers), 2019

BUSINESSES

Major Business Headquarters

Company Name	Industry	Rankings Fortune[1]	Rankings Forbes[2]
Danaher	Scientific, Photographic and Control Equipment	161	-
Fannie Mae	Diversified Financials	24	-

Note: (1) Companies that produce a 10-K are ranked 1 to 500 based on 2019 revenue; (2) All private companies with at least $2 billion in annual revenue through the end of their most current fiscal year are ranked 1 to 219; companies listed are headquartered in the city; dashes indicate no ranking
Source: Fortune, "Fortune 500," June/July 2020; Forbes, "America's Largest Private Companies," 2020

Fastest-Growing Businesses

According to *Fortune*, Washington is home to one of the 100 fastest-growing companies in the world: **CoStar Group** (#29). Companies were ranked by their revenue growth rate; their EPS growth rate; and their three-year annualized total return to investors for the period ending June 30, 2020. Criteria for inclusion: a company, foreign or domestic, must trade on a major U.S. stock exchange; must file quarterly reports with the SEC; must have a minimum market capitalization of $250 million; must have a stock price of at least $5 on June 30, 2020; must have been trading continuously since June 30, 2017; must have revenue and net income for the four quarters ended on or before April 30, 2020, of at least $50 million and $10 million, respectively; and must have posted a compound annual growth in revenue and earnings per share of at least 15% annually over the three years ending on or before April 30, 2020. Real estate investment trusts, limited-liability companies, limited parterships, business development companies, closed-end investment firms, companies about to be acquired, and companies that lost money in the quarter ending April 30, 2020 were excluded. *Fortune, "100 Fastest-Growing Companies," 2020*

According to *Initiative for a Competitive Inner City (ICIC)*, Washington is home to two of America's 100 fastest-growing "inner city" companies: **Grubb's Southeast Pharmacy and Mini Mart** (#65); **TCG** (#74). Criteria for inclusion: company must be headquartered in or have 51 percent or more of its physical operations in an economically distressed urban area; must be an independent, for-profit corporation, partnership or proprietorship; must have 10 or more employees and have a five-year sales history that includes sales of at least $200,000 in the base year and at least $1 million in the current year with no decrease in sales over the two most recent years. Companies were ranked overall by revenue growth over the five-year period between 2015 and 2019. *Initiative for a Competitive Inner City (ICIC), "Inner City 100 Companies," 2020*

According to Deloitte, Washington is home to four of North America's 500 fastest-growing high-technology companies: **Fundrise** (#252); **Clutch** (#358); **Mapbox, Inc.** (#387); **Thycotic** (#479). Companies are ranked by percentage growth in revenue over a four-year period. Criteria for inclusion: company must be headquartered within North America; must own proprietary intellectual property or technology that is sold to customers in products that contributes to a significant portion of the company's operating revenue; must have been in business for a minumum of four years with 2016 operating revenues of at least $50,000 USD/CD and 2019 operating revenues of at least $5 million USD/CD. *Deloitte, 2020 Technology Fast 500*™

Minority Business Opportunity

Washington is home to four companies which are on the *Black Enterprise* Industrial/Service list (100 largest companies based on gross sales): **Frontier Development & Hospitality Group** (#63); **Howard Stirk Holdings** (#74); **JMA Solutions** (#79); **Logistics Systems** (#84). Criteria: operational in previous calendar year; at least 51% black-owned and manufactures/owns the product it sells or provides industrial or consumer services. Brokerages, real estate firms and firms that provide professional services are not eligible. *Black Enterprise, B.E. 100s, 2019*

Washington is home to one company which is on the *Black Enterprise* Bank list (15 largest banks based on total assets, capital, deposits and loans, including mortgage-backed securities for the calendar year): **Industrial Bank** (#4). Only commercial banks or savings and loans that are classified by the Federal Reserve as black institutions and have been fully operational for the previous calendar year were considered. *Black Enterprise, B.E. 100s, 2019*

Washington is home to one company which is on the *Black Enterprise* Private Equity list (10 largest private equity firms based on capital under management): **Grain Management** (#4). Criteria: company must be operational in previous calendar year and be at least 51% black-owned. *Black Enterprise, B.E. 100s, 2019*

Living Environment

COST OF LIVING

Cost of Living Index

Composite Index	Groceries	Housing	Utilities	Trans-portation	Health Care	Misc. Goods/Services
159.3	115.6	272.7	113.0	105.6	92.9	121.7

Note: The Cost of Living Index measures regional differences in the cost of consumer goods and services, excluding taxes and non-consumer expenditures, for professional and managerial households in the top income quintile. It is based on more than 50,000 prices covering almost 60 different items for which prices are collected three times a year by chambers of commerce, economic development organizations or university applied economic centers in each participating urban area. The numbers shown should be read as a percentage above or below the national average of 100. For example, a value of 115.4 in the groceries column indicates that grocery prices are 15.4% higher than the national average. Small differences in the index numbers should not be interpreted as significant; Figures cover the Washington DC urban area.
Source: The Council for Community and Economic Research, Cost of Living Index, 2020

Grocery Prices

Area[1]	T-Bone Steak ($/pound)	Frying Chicken ($/pound)	Whole Milk ($/half gal.)	Eggs ($/dozen)	Orange Juice ($/64 oz.)	Coffee ($/11.5 oz.)
City[2]	13.57	1.80	2.46	1.80	3.91	4.77
Avg.	11.78	1.39	2.05	1.47	3.57	4.34
Min.	8.03	0.94	1.03	0.74	2.94	3.02
Max.	15.86	2.65	4.31	3.77	5.44	8.69

Note: (1) Values for the local area are compared with the average, minimum and maximum values for all 284 areas in the Cost of Living Index; (2) Figures cover the Washington DC urban area; **T-Bone Steak** (price per pound); **Frying Chicken** (price per pound, whole fryer); **Whole Milk** (half gallon carton); **Eggs** (price per dozen, Grade A, large); **Orange Juice** (64 oz. Tropicana or Florida Natural); **Coffee** (11.5 oz. can, vacuum-packed, Maxwell House, Hills Bros, or Folgers).
Source: The Council for Community and Economic Research, Cost of Living Index, 2020

Housing and Utility Costs

Area[1]	New Home Price ($)	Apartment Rent ($/month)	All Electric ($/month)	Part Electric ($/month)	Other Energy ($/month)	Telephone ($/month)
City[2]	1,020,885	3,033	-	135.39	69.36	184.50
Avg.	368,594	1,168	170.86	100.47	65.28	184.30
Min.	190,567	502	91.58	31.42	26.08	169.60
Max.	2,227,806	4,738	470.38	280.31	280.06	206.50

Note: (1) Values for the local area are compared with the average, minimum and maximum values for all 284 areas in the Cost of Living Index; (2) Figures cover the Washington DC urban area; **New Home Price** (2,400 sf living area, 8,000 sf lot, in urban area with full utilities); **Apartment Rent** (950 sf 2 bedroom/1.5 or 2 bath, unfurnished, excluding all utilities except water); **All Electric** (average monthly cost for an all-electric home); **Part Electric** (average monthly cost for a part-electric home); **Other Energy** (average monthly cost for natural gas, fuel oil, coal, wood, and any other forms of energy except electricity); **Telephone** (price includes the base monthly rate plus taxes and fees for three lines of mobile phone service).
Source: The Council for Community and Economic Research, Cost of Living Index, 2020

Health Care, Transportation, and Other Costs

Area[1]	Doctor ($/visit)	Dentist ($/visit)	Optometrist ($/visit)	Gasoline ($/gallon)	Beauty Salon ($/visit)	Men's Shirt ($)
City[2]	109.41	94.31	79.25	2.31	66.76	37.74
Avg.	115.44	99.32	108.10	2.21	39.27	31.37
Min.	36.68	59.00	51.36	1.71	19.00	11.00
Max.	219.00	153.10	250.97	3.46	82.05	58.33

Note: (1) Values for the local area are compared with the average, minimum and maximum values for all 284 areas in the Cost of Living Index; (2) Figures cover the Washington DC urban area; **Doctor** (general practitioners routine exam of an established patient); **Dentist** (adult teeth cleaning and periodic oral examination); **Optometrist** (full vision eye exam for established adult patient); **Gasoline** (one gallon regular unleaded, national brand, including all taxes, cash price at self-service pump if available); **Beauty Salon** (woman's shampoo, trim, and blow-dry); **Men's Shirt** (cotton/polyester dress shirt, pinpoint weave, long sleeves).
Source: The Council for Community and Economic Research, Cost of Living Index, 2020

HOUSING

Homeownership Rate

Area	2012 (%)	2013 (%)	2014 (%)	2015 (%)	2016 (%)	2017 (%)	2018 (%)	2019 (%)	2020 (%)
MSA[1]	66.9	66.0	65.0	64.6	63.1	63.3	62.9	64.7	67.9
U.S.	65.4	65.1	64.5	63.7	63.4	63.9	64.4	64.6	66.6

Note: (1) Figures cover the Washington-Arlington-Alexandria, DC-VA-MD-WV Metropolitan Statistical Area
Source: U.S. Census Bureau, Housing Vacancies and Homeownership Annual Statistics: 2012-2020

House Price Index (HPI)

Area	National Ranking[2]	Quarterly Change (%)	One-Year Change (%)	Five-Year Change (%)	Since 1991Q1 (%)
MD[1]	189	1.67	5.16	21.40	197.71
U.S.[3]	–	3.81	10.77	38.99	205.12

Note: The HPI is a weighted repeat sales index. It measures average price changes in repeat sales or refinancings on the same properties. This information is obtained by reviewing repeat mortgage transactions on single-family properties whose mortgages have been purchased or securitized by Fannie Mae or Freddie Mac since January 1975; (1) Figures cover the Washington-Arlington-Alexandria, DC-VA-MD-WV Metropolitan Division; (2) Rankings are based on annual percentage change for all metro areas containing at least 15,000 transactions over the last 10 years and ranges from 1 to 253; (3) figures based on a weighted average of Census Division estimates using a seasonally adjusted, purchase-only index; all figures are for the period ending December 31, 2020
Source: Federal Housing Finance Agency, Change in Metropolitan Area House Price Indexes, April 7, 2021

Median Single-Family Home Prices

Area	2018	2019	2020[p]	Percent Change 2019 to 2020
MSA[1]	424.0	440.9	475.4	7.8
U.S. Average	261.6	274.6	299.9	9.2

Note: Figures are median sales prices of existing single-family homes in thousands of dollars; (p) preliminary; (1) Figures cover the Washington-Arlington-Alexandria, DC-VA-MD-WV Metropolitan Statistical Area
Source: National Association of Realtors, Median Sales Price of Existing Single-Family Homes for Metropolitan Areas, 4th Quarter 2020

Qualifying Income Based on Median Sales Price of Existing Single-Family Homes

Area	With 5% Down ($)	With 10% Down ($)	With 20% Down ($)
MSA[1]	91,507	86,691	77,058
U.S. Average	59,266	56,147	49,908

Note: Figures are preliminary; Qualifying income is based on a mortgage rate of 2.81%. Monthly principal and interest payment is limited to 25% of income; (1) Figures cover the Washington-Arlington-Alexandria, DC-VA-MD-WV Metropolitan Statistical Area
Source: National Association of Realtors, Qualifying Income Based on Median Sales Price of Existing Single-Family Homes for Metropolitan Areas, 4th Quarter 2020

Home Value Distribution

Area	Under $50,000	$50,000 -$99,999	$100,000 -$149,999	$150,000 -$199,999	$200,000 -$299,999	$300,000 -$499,999	$500,000 -$999,999	$1,000,000 or more
City	1.2	0.8	1.1	1.9	9.5	25.7	41.0	18.8
MSA[1]	1.5	1.0	2.1	4.7	17.1	35.8	31.2	6.7
U.S.	6.9	12.0	13.3	14.0	19.6	19.3	11.4	3.4

Note: Figures are percentages and cover owner-occupied housing units; (1) Figures cover the Washington-Arlington-Alexandria, DC-VA-MD-WV Metropolitan Statistical Area
Source: U.S. Census Bureau, 2015-2019 American Community Survey 5-Year Estimates

Year Housing Structure Built

Area	2010 or Later	2000 -2009	1990 -1999	1980 -1989	1970 -1979	1960 -1969	1950 -1959	1940 -1949	Before 1940	Median Year
City	7.3	8.1	3.3	4.4	7.1	11.4	12.6	11.7	34.1	1953
MSA[1]	6.7	14.5	14.4	15.8	14.0	12.0	9.4	4.9	8.3	1981
U.S.	5.2	14.0	13.9	13.4	15.2	10.6	10.3	4.9	12.6	1978

Note: Figures are percentages except for Median Year; Note: (1) Figures cover the Washington-Arlington-Alexandria, DC-VA-MD-WV Metropolitan Statistical Area
Source: U.S. Census Bureau, 2015-2019 American Community Survey 5-Year Estimates

Gross Monthly Rent

Area	Under $500	$500 -$999	$1,000 -$1,499	$1,500 -$1,999	$2,000 -$2,499	$2,500 -$2,999	$3,000 and up	Median ($)
City	10.4	13.2	24.7	21.1	13.6	8.2	8.9	1,541
MSA[1]	4.6	7.8	25.4	32.2	16.6	7.3	6.1	1,690
U.S.	9.4	36.2	30.0	14.0	5.6	2.4	2.4	1,062

Note: Figures are percentages except for Median; Gross rent is the contract rent plus the estimated average monthly cost of utilities (electricity, gas, and water and sewer) and fuels (oil, coal, kerosene, wood, etc.) if these are paid by the renter (or paid for the renter by someone else); (1) Figures cover the Washington-Arlington-Alexandria, DC-VA-MD-WV Metropolitan Statistical Area
Source: U.S. Census Bureau, 2015-2019 American Community Survey 5-Year Estimates

HEALTH

Health Risk Factors

Category	MD[1] (%)	U.S. (%)
Adults aged 18–64 who have any kind of health care coverage	89.0	87.3
Adults who reported being in good or better health	87.1	82.4
Adults who have been told they have high blood cholesterol	32.0	33.0
Adults who have been told they have high blood pressure	27.0	32.3
Adults who are current smokers	11.2	17.1
Adults who currently use E-cigarettes	2.7	4.6
Adults who currently use chewing tobacco, snuff, or snus	2.1	4.0
Adults who are heavy drinkers[2]	6.0	6.3
Adults who are binge drinkers[3]	16.3	17.4
Adults who are overweight (BMI 25.0 - 29.9)	35.6	35.3
Adults who are obese (BMI 30.0 - 99.8)	27.6	31.3
Adults who participated in any physical activities in the past month	77.4	74.4
Adults who always or nearly always wears a seat belt	96.3	94.3

Note: (1) Figures cover the Washington-Arlington-Alexandria, DC-VA-MD-WV Metropolitan Division; (2) Heavy drinkers are classified as adult men having more than 14 drinks per week and adult women having more than 7 drinks per week; (3) Binge drinkers are classified as males having five or more drinks on one occasion or females having four or more drinks on one occasion
Source: Centers for Disease Control and Prevention, Behaviorial Risk Factor Surveillance System, SMART: Selected Metropolitan Area Risk Trends, 2017

Acute and Chronic Health Conditions

Category	MD[1] (%)	U.S. (%)
Adults who have ever been told they had a heart attack	2.9	4.2
Adults who have ever been told they have angina or coronary heart disease	2.6	3.9
Adults who have ever been told they had a stroke	2.6	3.0
Adults who have ever been told they have asthma	12.7	14.2
Adults who have ever been told they have arthritis	20.4	24.9
Adults who have ever been told they have diabetes[2]	7.7	10.5
Adults who have ever been told they had skin cancer	4.8	6.2
Adults who have ever been told they had any other types of cancer	5.6	7.1
Adults who have ever been told they have COPD	4.7	6.5
Adults who have ever been told they have kidney disease	2.2	3.0
Adults who have ever been told they have a form of depression	14.2	20.5

Note: (1) Figures cover the Washington-Arlington-Alexandria, DC-VA-MD-WV Metropolitan Division; (2) Figures do not include pregnancy-related, borderline, or pre-diabetes
Source: Centers for Disease Control and Prevention, Behaviorial Risk Factor Surveillance System, SMART: Selected Metropolitan Area Risk Trends, 2017

Health Screening and Vaccination Rates

Category	MD[1] (%)	U.S. (%)
Adults aged 65+ who have had flu shot within the past year	64.7	60.7
Adults aged 65+ who have ever had a pneumonia vaccination	74.3	75.4
Adults who have ever been tested for HIV	52.3	36.1
Adults who have ever had the shingles or zoster vaccine?	29.8	28.9
Adults who have had their blood cholesterol checked within the last five years	89.2	85.9

Note: n/a not available; (1) Figures cover the Washington-Arlington-Alexandria, DC-VA-MD-WV Metropolitan Division.
Source: Centers for Disease Control and Prevention, Behaviorial Risk Factor Surveillance System, SMART: Selected Metropolitan Area Risk Trends, 2017

Disability Status

Category	MD[1] (%)	U.S. (%)
Adults who reported being deaf	4.9	6.7
Are you blind or have serious difficulty seeing, even when wearing glasses?	3.8	4.5
Are you limited in any way in any of your usual activities due of arthritis?	10.0	12.9
Do you have difficulty doing errands alone?	4.6	6.8
Do you have difficulty dressing or bathing?	3.0	3.6
Do you have serious difficulty concentrating/remembering/making decisions?	7.5	10.7
Do you have serious difficulty walking or climbing stairs?	9.7	13.6

Note: (1) Figures cover the Washington-Arlington-Alexandria, DC-VA-MD-WV Metropolitan Division.
Source: Centers for Disease Control and Prevention, Behaviorial Risk Factor Surveillance System, SMART: Selected Metropolitan Area Risk Trends, 2017

Mortality Rates for the Top 10 Causes of Death in the U.S.

ICD-10[a] Sub-Chapter	ICD-10[a] Code	Age-Adjusted Mortality Rate[1] per 100,000 population	
		County[2]	U.S.
Malignant neoplasms	C00-C97	152.1	149.2
Ischaemic heart diseases	I20-I25	101.2	90.5
Other forms of heart disease	I30-I51	37.3	52.2
Chronic lower respiratory diseases	J40-J47	20.4	39.6
Other degenerative diseases of the nervous system	G30-G31	25.1	37.6
Cerebrovascular diseases	I60-I69	36.8	37.2
Other external causes of accidental injury	W00-X59	53.2	36.1
Organic, including symptomatic, mental disorders	F01-F09	22.8	29.4
Hypertensive diseases	I10-I15	49.6	24.1
Diabetes mellitus	E10-E14	20.2	21.5

Note: (a) ICD-10 = International Classification of Diseases 10th Revision; (1) Mortality rates are a three-year average covering 2017-2019; (2) Figures cover District of Columbia.
Source: Centers for Disease Control and Prevention, National Center for Health Statistics. Underlying Cause of Death 1999-2019 on CDC WONDER Online Database

Mortality Rates for Selected Causes of Death

ICD-10[a] Sub-Chapter	ICD-10[a] Code	Age-Adjusted Mortality Rate[1] per 100,000 population	
		County[2]	U.S.
Assault	X85-Y09	18.5	6.0
Diseases of the liver	K70-K76	10.2	14.4
Human immunodeficiency virus (HIV) disease	B20-B24	9.5	1.5
Influenza and pneumonia	J09-J18	11.1	13.8
Intentional self-harm	X60-X84	6.8	14.1
Malnutrition	E40-E46	1.0	2.3
Obesity and other hyperalimentation	E65-E68	2.2	2.1
Renal failure	N17-N19	7.8	12.6
Transport accidents	V01-V99	5.9	12.3
Viral hepatitis	B15-B19	3.3	1.2

Note: (a) ICD-10 = International Classification of Diseases 10th Revision; (1) Mortality rates are a three-year average covering 2017-2019; (2) Figures cover District of Columbia; Data are suppressed when the data meet the criteria for confidentiality constraints; Mortality rates are flagged as unreliable when the rate would be calculated with a numerator of 20 or less.
Source: Centers for Disease Control and Prevention, National Center for Health Statistics. Underlying Cause of Death 1999-2019 on CDC WONDER Online Database

Health Insurance Coverage

Area	With Health Insurance	With Private Health Insurance	With Public Health Insurance	Without Health Insurance	Population Under Age 19 Without Health Insurance
City	96.3	70.4	35.6	3.7	2.0
MSA[1]	92.4	78.2	25.2	7.6	4.5
U.S.	91.2	67.9	35.1	8.8	5.1

Note: Figures are percentages that cover the civilian noninstitutionalized population; (1) Figures cover the Washington-Arlington-Alexandria, DC-VA-MD-WV Metropolitan Statistical Area
Source: U.S. Census Bureau, 2015-2019 American Community Survey 5-Year Estimates

Number of Medical Professionals

Area	MDs[3]	DOs[3,4]	Dentists	Podiatrists	Chiropractors	Optometrists
DC[1] (number)	5,469	117	868	63	66	102
DC[1] (rate[2])	779.6	16.7	123.0	8.9	9.4	14.5
U.S. (rate[2])	282.9	22.7	71.2	6.2	28.1	16.9

11001
Note: Data as of 2019 unless noted; (1) Data covers the District of Columbia; (2) Rate per 100,000 population; (3) Data as of 2018 and includes all active, non-federal physicians; (4) Doctor of Osteopathic Medicine
Source: U.S. Department of Health and Human Services, Health Resources and Services Administration, Bureau of Health Professions, Area Resource File (ARF) 2019-2020

Best Hospitals

According to *U.S. News,* the Washington-Arlington-Alexandria, DC-VA-MD-WV metro area is home to two of the best hospitals in the U.S.: **Inova Fairfax Hospital** (1 adult specialty); **MedStar Heart & Vascular Institute at MedStar Washington Hospital** (1 adult specialty). The hospitals listed were nationally ranked in at least one of 16 adult or 10 pediatric specialties. Only 134 hospitals nationwide were nationally ranked in one or more adult or pediatric specialty; this number increases to 178 counting specialized centers within hospitals. Twenty hospitals in the U.S. made the Honor Roll. The Best Hospitals Honor Roll takes both the national rankings and the procedure and condition ratings into account. Hospitals received points if they were nationally ranked in one of the 16 adult special-ties—the higher they ranked, the more points they got—and how many ratings of "high performing"

they earned in the 10 procedures and conditions. *U.S. News Online, "America's Best Hospitals 2020-21"*

According to *U.S. News,* the Washington-Arlington-Alexandria, DC-VA-MD-WV metro area is home to one of the best children's hospitals in the U.S.: **Children's National Hospital** (Honor Roll/10 pediatric specialties). The hospital listed was highly ranked in at least one of 10 pediatric specialties. Eighty-eight children's hospitals in the U.S. were nationally ranked in at least one specialty. Hospitals received points for being ranked in a specialty, and the 10 hospitals with the most points across the 10 specialties make up the Honor Roll. *U.S. News Online, "America's Best Children's Hospitals 2020-21"*

EDUCATION

Public School District Statistics

District Name	Schls	Pupils	Pupil/ Teacher Ratio	Minority Pupils[1] (%)	Free Lunch Eligible[2] (%)	IEP[3] (%)
District of Columbia Public Schls	113	49,065	12.1	84.2	n/a	15.8
Friendship PCS	13	4,011	13.2	99.6	n/a	14.5
Kipp DC PCS	16	6,283	13.7	99.8	n/a	14.5

Note: Table includes school districts with 2,000 or more students; (1) Percentage of students that are not non-Hispanic white; (2) Percentage of students that are eligible for the free lunch program; (3) Percentage of students that have an Individualized Education Program.
Source: U.S. Department of Education, National Center for Education Statistics, Common Core of Data, Local Education Agency (School District) Universe Survey: School Year 2018-2019; U.S. Department of Education, National Center for Education Statistics, Common Core of Data, Public Elementary/Secondary School Universe Survey: School Year 2018-2019

Best High Schools

According to *U.S. News,* Washington is home to three of the top 500 high schools in the U.S.: **School Without Walls High School** (#73); **Benjamin Banneker Academy High School** (#99); **BASIS DC** (#227). Nearly 18,000 public, magnet and charter schools were ranked based on their performance on state assessments and how well they prepare students for college. *U.S. News & World Report, "Best High Schools 2020"*

Highest Level of Education

Area	Less than H.S.	H.S. Diploma	Some College, No Deg.	Associate Degree	Bachelor's Degree	Master's Degree	Prof. School Degree	Doctorate Degree
City	9.1	16.8	12.6	3.0	24.8	21.2	8.4	4.2
MSA[1]	9.1	18.2	16.0	5.9	25.8	17.6	4.3	3.2
U.S.	12.0	27.0	20.4	8.5	19.8	8.8	2.1	1.4

Note: Figures cover persons age 25 and over; (1) Figures cover the Washington-Arlington-Alexandria, DC-VA-MD-WV Metropolitan Statistical Area
Source: U.S. Census Bureau, 2015-2019 American Community Survey 5-Year Estimates

Educational Attainment by Race

Area	High School Graduate or Higher (%)					Bachelor's Degree or Higher (%)				
	Total	White	Black	Asian	Hisp.[2]	Total	White	Black	Asian	Hisp.[2]
City	90.9	98.1	86.3	94.9	73.1	58.5	89.5	27.3	81.9	47.3
MSA[1]	90.9	94.1	91.5	91.1	68.0	50.9	59.2	34.8	65.1	25.7
U.S.	88.0	89.9	86.0	87.1	68.7	32.1	33.5	21.6	54.3	16.4

Note: Figures shown cover persons 25 years old and over; (1) Figures cover the Washington-Arlington-Alexandria, DC-VA-MD-WV Metropolitan Statistical Area; (2) People of Hispanic origin can be of any race
Source: U.S. Census Bureau, 2015-2019 American Community Survey 5-Year Estimates

School Enrollment by Grade and Control

Area	Preschool (%)		Kindergarten (%)		Grades 1 - 4 (%)		Grades 5 - 8 (%)		Grades 9 - 12 (%)	
	Public	Private	Public	Private	Public	Private	Public	Private	Public	Private
City	77.1	22.9	92.3	7.7	87.6	12.4	82.7	17.3	82.6	17.4
MSA[1]	44.9	55.1	86.1	13.9	88.7	11.3	87.9	12.1	88.3	11.7
U.S.	59.1	40.9	87.6	12.4	89.5	10.5	89.4	10.6	90.1	9.9

Note: Figures shown cover persons 3 years old and over; (1) Figures cover the Washington-Arlington-Alexandria, DC-VA-MD-WV Metropolitan Statistical Area
Source: U.S. Census Bureau, 2015-2019 American Community Survey 5-Year Estimates

Higher Education

Four-Year Colleges			Two-Year Colleges			Medical Schools[1]	Law Schools[2]	Voc/ Tech[3]
Public	Private Non-profit	Private For-profit	Public	Private Non-profit	Private For-profit			
2	13	3	0	1	1	3	6	3

Note: Figures cover institutions located within the city limits and include main campuses only; (1) includes schools accredited by the Liaison Committee on Medical Education and the American Osteopathic Association's Commission on Osteopathic College Accreditation; (2) includes ABA-accredited schools, schools with provisional ABA accreditation, and state accredited schools; (3) includes all schools with programs that are less than 2 years.
Source: National Center for Education Statistics, Integrated Postsecondary Education System (IPEDS), 2019-20; Wikipedia, List of Medical Schools in the United States, accessed April 2, 2021; Wikipedia, List of Law Schools in the United States, accessed April 2, 2021

According to *U.S. News & World Report,* the Washington-Arlington-Alexandria, DC-VA-MD-WV metro division is home to eight of the top 200 national universities in the U.S.: **Georgetown University** (#23); **University of Maryland—College Park** (#58 tie); **George Washington University** (#66 tie); **American University** (#76 tie); **Howard University** (#80 tie); **Gallaudet University** (#124 tie); **The Catholic University of America** (#143 tie); **George Mason University** (#143 tie). The indicators used to capture academic quality fall into a number of categories: assessment by administrators at peer institutions; retention of students; faculty resources; student selectivity; financial resources; alumni giving; high school counselor ratings of colleges; and graduation rate. *U.S. News & World Report, "America's Best Colleges 2021"*

According to *U.S. News & World Report,* the Washington-Arlington-Alexandria, DC-VA-MD-WV metro division is home to five of the top 100 law schools in the U.S.: **Georgetown University** (#15); **George Washington University** (#27 tie); **George Mason University** (#41 tie); **American University (Washington)** (#81 tie); **Howard University** (#91 tie). The rankings are based on a weighted average of 12 measures of quality: peer assessment score; assessment score by lawyers/judges; median LSAT scores; median undergrad GPA; acceptance rate; employment rates for graduates; placement success; bar passage rate; faculty resources; expenditures per student; student/faculty ratio; and library resources. *U.S. News & World Report, "America's Best Graduate Schools, Law, 2022"*

According to *U.S. News & World Report,* the Washington-Arlington-Alexandria, DC-VA-MD-WV metro division is home to two of the top 75 medical schools for research in the U.S.: **Georgetown University** (#55 tie); **George Washington University** (#60). The rankings are based on a weighted average of 11 measures of quality: quality assessment; peer assessment score; assessment score by residency directors; research activity; total research activity; average research activity per faculty member; student selectivity; median MCAT total score; median undergraduate GPA; acceptance rate; and faculty resources. *U.S. News & World Report, "America's Best Graduate Schools, Medical, 2022"*

According to *U.S. News & World Report,* the Washington-Arlington-Alexandria, DC-VA-MD-WV metro division is home to four of the top 75 business schools in the U.S.: **Georgetown University (McDonough)** (#21); **University of Maryland—College Park (Smith)** (#42 tie); **George Washington University** (#53 tie); **Howard University** (#64 tie). The rankings are based on a weighted average of the following nine measures: quality assessment; peer assessment; recruiter assessment; placement success; mean starting salary and bonus; student selectivity; mean GMAT and GRE scores; mean undergraduate GPA; and acceptance rate. *U.S. News & World Report, "America's Best Graduate Schools, Business, 2022"*

EMPLOYERS

Major Employers

Company Name	Industry
Adventist HealthCare	General medical & surgical hospitals
Bechtel National	Engineering services
Computer Sciences Corporation	Computer related consulting services
Federal Aviation Administration	Air traffic control operations, government
Federal Bureau of Investigation	Police protection
Howard University	Colleges & universities
HR Solutions	Human resource consulting services
Internal Revenue Service	Finance, taxation, and monetary policy
Intl Bank for Recons. & Dev.	Foreign trade & international banks
Natl Inst of Standards & Technology	Administration of general economic programs
Office of the Secretary of Defense	National security
U.S. Department of Agriculture	Regulation of agricultural marketing
U.S. Department of Commerce	Regulation, miscellaneous commercial sectors
U.S. Department of Labor	Administration of social & manpower programs
U.S. Department of the Army	National security
U.S. Department of the Navy	National security
U.S. Department of Transportation	Regulation, administration of transportation
U.S. Environmental Protection Agency	Land, mineral, & wildlife conservation
U.S. Fish and Wildlife Service	Fish & wildlife conservation agency, government
Washington Hospital Center Corporation	General medical & surgical hospitals

Note: Companies shown are located within the Washington-Arlington-Alexandria, DC-VA-MD-WV Metropolitan Statistical Area.
Source: Hoovers.com; Wikipedia

Best Companies to Work For

Arnold & Porter; EAB; Finnegan; FINRA (Financial Industry Regulatory Authority), headquartered in Washington, are among the "100 Best Companies for Working Mothers." Criteria: paid time off and leaves; workforce profile; benefits; women's issues and advancement; flexible work; company culture and work life programs. *Working Mother, "100 Best Companies for Working Mothers," 2020*

Fannie Mae; FINRA (Financial Industry Regulatory Authority), headquartered in Washington, are among the "100 Best Places to Work in IT." To qualify, companies had to be U.S.-based organizations or be non-U.S.-based employers that met the following criteria: have a minimum of 300 total employees at a U.S. headquarters and a minimum of 30 IT employees in the U.S., with at least 50% of their IT employees based in the U.S. The best places to work were selected based on compensation, benefits, work/life balance, employee morale, and satisfaction with training and development programs. In addition, *InsiderPro* and *Computerworld* looked at retention efforts, programs for recognizing and rewarding outstanding performances, and benefits such as flextime, elder care and child care, and reimbursement for college tuition and the cost of pursuing technology certifications. *InsiderPro and Computerworld, "100 Best Places to Work in IT," 2020*

Arnold & Porter; FINRA (Financial Industry Regulatory Authority), headquartered in Washington, are among the "Best Companies for Dads." *Working Mother's* newest list recognizes the growing importance companies place on giving dads time off and support for their families. Rankings are determined by measuring gender-neutral or paternity leave offered, as well as actual time taken, phase-back policies, child- and dependent-care benefits, and corporate support groups for men and dads. *Working Mother, "Best Companies for Dads," 2020*

PUBLIC SAFETY

Crime Rate

Area	All Crimes	Violent Crimes				Property Crimes		
		Murder	Rape[3]	Robbery	Aggrav. Assault	Burglary	Larceny -Theft	Motor Vehicle Theft
City	5,223.0	23.5	48.5	334.3	570.9	260.7	3,659.5	325.6
Suburbs[1]	n/a	n/a	26.7	61.2	96.5	98.4	1,055.9	126.4
Metro[2]	n/a	n/a	29.8	99.9	163.6	121.4	1,424.4	154.6
U.S.	2,489.3	5.0	42.6	81.6	250.2	340.5	1,549.5	219.9

Note: Figures are crimes per 100,000 population; (1) All areas within the metro area that are located outside the city limits; (2) Figures cover the Washington-Arlington-Alexandria, DC-VA-MD-WV Metropolitan Division; (3) All figures shown were reported using the revised Uniform Crime Reporting (UCR) definition of rape.
Source: FBI Uniform Crime Reports, 2019

Hate Crimes

Area	Number of Quarters Reported	Number of Incidents per Bias Motivation					
		Race/Ethnicity/ Ancestry	Religion	Sexual Orientation	Disability	Gender	Gender Identity
City	4	107	5	60	1	2	27
U.S.	4	3,963	1,521	1,195	157	69	198

Source: Federal Bureau of Investigation, Hate Crime Statistics 2019

Identity Theft Consumer Reports

Area	Reports	Reports per 100,000 Population	Rank[2]
MSA[1]	17,447	278	137
U.S.	1,387,615	423	-

Note: (1) Figures cover the Washington-Arlington-Alexandria, DC-VA-MD-WV Metropolitan Statistical Area;
(2) Rank ranges from 1 to 391 where 1 indicates greatest number of identity theft reports per 100,000 population
Source: Federal Trade Commission, Consumer Sentinel Network Data Book 2020

Fraud and Other Consumer Reports

Area	Reports	Reports per 100,000 Population	Rank[2]
MSA[1]	67,314	1,072	14
U.S.	3,385,133	1,031	-

Note: (1) Figures cover the Washington-Arlington-Alexandria, DC-VA-MD-WV Metropolitan Statistical Area;
(2) Rank ranges from 1 to 391 where 1 indicates greatest number of fraud and other consumer reports per 100,000 population
Source: Federal Trade Commission, Consumer Sentinel Network Data Book 2020

POLITICS

2020 Presidential Election Results

Area	Biden	Trump	Jorgensen	Hawkins	Other
District of Columbia	92.1	5.4	0.6	0.5	1.4
U.S.	51.3	46.8	1.2	0.3	0.5

Note: Results are percentages and may not add to 100% due to rounding
Source: Dave Leip's Atlas of U.S. Presidential Elections

SPORTS

Professional Sports Teams

Team Name	League	Year Established
D.C. United	Major League Soccer (MLS)	1996
Washington Capitals	National Hockey League (NHL)	1974
Washington Nationals	Major League Baseball (MLB)	2005
Washington Redskins	National Football League (NFL)	1937
Washington Wizards	National Basketball Association (NBA)	1973

Note: Includes teams located in the Washington-Arlington-Alexandria, DC-VA-MD-WV Metropolitan Statistical Area.
Source: Wikipedia, Major Professional Sports Teams of the United States and Canada, April 6, 2021

CLIMATE

Average and Extreme Temperatures

Temperature	Jan	Feb	Mar	Apr	May	Jun	Jul	Aug	Sep	Oct	Nov	Dec	Yr.
Extreme High (°F)	79	82	89	95	97	101	104	103	101	94	86	75	104
Average High (°F)	43	46	55	67	76	84	88	86	80	69	58	47	67
Average Temp. (°F)	36	38	46	57	66	75	79	78	71	60	49	39	58
Average Low (°F)	28	30	37	46	56	65	70	69	62	50	40	31	49
Extreme Low (°F)	-5	4	14	24	34	47	54	49	39	29	16	3	-5

Note: Figures cover the years 1945-1990
Source: National Climatic Data Center, International Station Meteorological Climate Summary, 9/96

Average Precipitation/Snowfall/Humidity

Precip./Humidity	Jan	Feb	Mar	Apr	May	Jun	Jul	Aug	Sep	Oct	Nov	Dec	Yr.
Avg. Precip. (in.)	2.8	2.6	3.3	2.9	4.0	3.4	4.1	4.2	3.3	2.9	3.0	3.1	39.5
Avg. Snowfall (in.)	6	6	2	Tr	0	0	0	0	0	Tr	1	3	18
Avg. Rel. Hum. 7am (%)	71	70	70	70	74	75	77	80	82	80	76	72	75
Avg. Rel. Hum. 4pm (%)	54	50	46	45	51	52	53	54	54	53	53	55	52

Note: Figures cover the years 1945-1990; Tr = Trace amounts (<0.05 in. of rain; <0.5 in. of snow)
Source: National Climatic Data Center, International Station Meteorological Climate Summary, 9/96

Weather Conditions

Temperature			Daytime Sky			Precipitation		
10°F & below	32°F & below	90°F & above	Clear	Partly cloudy	Cloudy	0.01 inch or more precip.	0.1 inch or more snow/ice	Thunder-storms
2	71	34	84	143	138	112	9	30

Note: Figures are average number of days per year and cover the years 1945-1990
Source: National Climatic Data Center, International Station Meteorological Climate Summary, 9/96

HAZARDOUS WASTE

Superfund Sites

The Washington-Arlington-Alexandria, DC-VA-MD-WV metro division is home to 10 sites on the EPA's Superfund National Priorities List: **Andrews Air Force Base** (final); **Avtex Fibers, Inc.** (final); **Beltsville Agricultural Research Center (USDA)** (final); **Brandywine Drmo** (final); **Culpeper Wood Preservers, Inc.** (final); **Hidden Lane Landfill** (final); **Indian Head Naval Surface Warfare Center** (final); **L.A. Clarke & Son** (final); **Marine Corps Combat Development Command** (final); **Washington Navy Yard** (final). There are a total of 1,375 Superfund sites with a status of proposed or final on the list in the U.S. *U.S. Environmental Protection Agency, National Priorities List, April 7, 2021*

AIR QUALITY

Air Quality Trends: Ozone

	1990	1995	2000	2005	2010	2015	2016	2017	2018	2019
MSA[1]	0.088	0.093	0.082	0.081	0.077	0.067	0.069	0.065	0.066	0.061
U.S.	0.088	0.089	0.082	0.080	0.073	0.068	0.069	0.068	0.069	0.065

Note: (1) Data covers the Washington-Arlington-Alexandria, DC-VA-MD-WV Metropolitan Statistical Area. The values shown are the composite ozone concentration averages among trend sites based on the highest fourth daily maximum 8-hour concentration in parts per million. These trends are based on sites having an adequate record of monitoring data during the trend period. Data from exceptional events are included.
Source: U.S. Environmental Protection Agency, Air Quality Monitoring Information, "Air Quality Trends by City, 1990-2019"

Air Quality Index

Area	Percent of Days when Air Quality was...[2]					AQI Statistics[2]	
	Good	Moderate	Unhealthy for Sensitive Groups	Unhealthy	Very Unhealthy	Maximum	Median
MSA[1]	57.3	39.7	2.7	0.3	0.0	157	47

Note: (1) Data covers the Washington-Arlington-Alexandria, DC-VA-MD-WV Metropolitan Statistical Area; (2) Based on 365 days with AQI data in 2019. Air Quality Index (AQI) is an index for reporting daily air quality. EPA calculates the AQI for five major air pollutants regulated by the Clean Air Act: ground-level ozone, particle pollution (aka particulate matter), carbon monoxide, sulfur dioxide, and nitrogen dioxide. The AQI runs from 0 to 500. The higher the AQI value, the greater the level of air pollution and the greater the health concern. There are six AQI categories: "Good" AQI is between 0 and 50. Air quality is considered satisfactory; "Moderate" AQI is between 51 and 100. Air quality is acceptable; "Unhealthy for Sensitive Groups" When AQI values are between 101 and 150, members of sensitive groups may experience health effects; "Unhealthy" When AQI values are between 151 and 200 everyone may begin to experience health effects; "Very Unhealthy" AQI values between 201 and 300 trigger a health alert; "Hazardous" AQI values over 300 trigger warnings of emergency conditions (not shown).
Source: U.S. Environmental Protection Agency, Air Quality Index Report, 2019

Air Quality Index Pollutants

Area	Percent of Days when AQI Pollutant was...[2]					
	Carbon Monoxide	Nitrogen Dioxide	Ozone	Sulfur Dioxide	Particulate Matter 2.5	Particulate Matter 10
MSA[1]	0.0	6.8	61.9	0.0	31.2	0.0

Note: (1) Data covers the Washington-Arlington-Alexandria, DC-VA-MD-WV Metropolitan Statistical Area; (2) Based on 365 days with AQI data in 2019. The Air Quality Index (AQI) is an index for reporting daily air quality. EPA calculates the AQI for five major air pollutants regulated by the Clean Air Act: ground-level ozone, particle pollution (also known as particulate matter), carbon monoxide, sulfur dioxide, and nitrogen dioxide. The AQI runs from 0 to 500. The higher the AQI value, the greater the level of air pollution and the greater the health concern.
Source: U.S. Environmental Protection Agency, Air Quality Index Report, 2019

Maximum Air Pollutant Concentrations: Particulate Matter, Ozone, CO and Lead

	Particulate Matter 10 (ug/m³)	Particulate Matter 2.5 Wtd AM (ug/m³)	Particulate Matter 2.5 24-Hr (ug/m³)	Ozone (ppm)	Carbon Monoxide (ppm)	Lead (ug/m³)
MSA[1] Level	46	9.1	25	0.075	2	n/a
NAAQS[2]	150	15	35	0.075	9	0.15
Met NAAQS[2]	Yes	Yes	Yes	Yes	Yes	n/a

Note: (1) Data covers the Washington-Arlington-Alexandria, DC-VA-MD-WV Metropolitan Statistical Area; Data from exceptional events are included; (2) National Ambient Air Quality Standards; ppm = parts per million; ug/m³ = micrograms per cubic meter; n/a not available.
Concentrations: Particulate Matter 10 (coarse particulate)—highest second maximum 24-hour concentration; Particulate Matter 2.5 Wtd AM (fine particulate)—highest weighted annual mean concentration; Particulate Matter 2.5 24-Hour (fine particulate)—highest 98th percentile 24-hour concentration; Ozone—highest fourth daily maximum 8-hour concentration; Carbon Monoxide—highest second maximum non-overlapping 8-hour concentration; Lead—maximum running 3-month average
Source: U.S. Environmental Protection Agency, Air Quality Monitoring Information, "Air Quality Statistics by City, 2019"

Maximum Air Pollutant Concentrations: Nitrogen Dioxide and Sulfur Dioxide

	Nitrogen Dioxide AM (ppb)	Nitrogen Dioxide 1-Hr (ppb)	Sulfur Dioxide AM (ppb)	Sulfur Dioxide 1-Hr (ppb)	Sulfur Dioxide 24-Hr (ppb)
MSA[1] Level	16	49	n/a	5	n/a
NAAQS[2]	53	100	30	75	140
Met NAAQS[2]	Yes	Yes	n/a	Yes	n/a

Note: (1) Data covers the Washington-Arlington-Alexandria, DC-VA-MD-WV Metropolitan Statistical Area; Data from exceptional events are included; (2) National Ambient Air Quality Standards; ppm = parts per million; ug/m³ = micrograms per cubic meter; n/a not available.
Concentrations: Nitrogen Dioxide AM—highest arithmetic mean concentration; Nitrogen Dioxide 1-Hr—highest 98th percentile 1-hour daily maximum concentration; Sulfur Dioxide AM—highest annual mean concentration; Sulfur Dioxide 1-Hr—highest 99th percentile 1-hour daily maximum concentration; Sulfur Dioxide 24-Hr—highest second maximum 24-hour concentration
Source: U.S. Environmental Protection Agency, Air Quality Monitoring Information, "Air Quality Statistics by City, 2019"

Winston-Salem, North Carolina

Background

The "Twin City" of Winston-Salem was formed by joining the towns of Winston and Salem, North Carolina. The combined name was created in 1899, due to a mistake by a postal office employee, and Winston-Salem became the official name in 1913. The newly named city became known as the "Twin City."

The town of Salem, North Carolina dates back to January of 1753 when the Moravain Church purchased approximately 100,000 acres to form their first community in North Carolina. The eastern European based church settled in the Wachovia Tract. The settlement, originally known as Bethabara, was renamed Salem, from the Hebrew word for peace, in 1766. The community was established around a town square with all of the property owned by the church. The Moravain congregation specified that all of the town's residents needed to be members of the church and enforced control by only leasing land to church members. The Moravains, known for their craftsmanship and artistry, as well arts and culture, soon established the town as an economic trade center. In 1856 the town of Salem was officially incorporated in what is now Forsyth County.

Winston, North Carolina was established in 1849 when Forsyth County purchased the land from the Moravain congregation of Salem. Situated to the north of Salem, Winston was officially named in 1851 after local politician and revolutionary war hero Mayor John Winston. At the end of the Civil War in 1865, Winston became a major industrial center. Soon Winston and Salem both began work to connect to the North Carolina Railroad to further strengthen their economies. In 1868, Winston's first tobacco factories were built by Thomas Jethro Brown and followed by Pleasant Henderson Hanes. Richard Joshua Reynolds started his tobacco factory in 1875. Winston had nearly 40 tobacco factories by mid 1880. After over two decades of competition, Reynolds bought out Hanes, the last of the smaller companies, and thus began the reign of the tobacco giant R.J. Reynolds Tobacco Company. Pleasant Henderson Hanes reinvested his proceeds and founded the P.H. Hanes Knitting Company manufacturing men's underwear.

The tobacco and textile industries fueled the economy of Winston-Salem. In 1917, 180 houses were built by the Reynold's Company, known as "Reynoldstown." The employees of R.J. Reynolds were able to purchase these houses at cost. The tobacco company built the Reynold's Building in 1929. This 21-story skyscraper, one of the tallest buildings in the United States at the time, became the prototype to the Empire State Building.

The surging economy brought about the merger of the Wachovia National Bank (established in 1879) and Wachovia Loan and Trust (established in 1879) to form the Wachovia Bank and Trust in 1911. In 2001 the bank became Wachovia and, in 2009, Wells Fargo. Today, Winston-Salem is headquarters to many thriving companies including Branch Banking and Trust Company (BB&T), HanesBrands, Krispy Kreme Doughnuts, Lowe's Foods, and Reynolds American (parent of R.J. Reynolds Tobacco Company).

> Krispy Kreme Doughnuts launches COVID-19 vaccination campaign by offering free original glazed doughnut daily through end of year to vaccinated customers.

The city's downtown's Wake-Forest Innovation Quarter features business, education in biomedical research and engineering, information technology and digital media, as well as public gathering spaces, apartment living and community events. Popular attractions include Reynolds Gardens, Wake Forest University Museum of Anthropology, children's museums Kaleideum North and Kaleideum Downtown, and the New Winston Museum.

Salem's Moravain Easter Sunrise Service has been an annual tradition since 1772 and the city is known as "Easter City." Like many small towns, Salem Tavern boasts that, on May 31st and June 1st, George Washington slept there while passing through North Carolina

Winston-Salem's climate has a humid, sub-tropical climate, characterized by cool winters and hot, humid summers.

Rankings

General Rankings

■ In their seventh annual survey, Livability.com looked at data for more than 1,000 small to mid-sized U.S. cities to determine the rankings for Livability's "Top 100 Best Places to Live" in 2020. Winston-Salem ranked #92. Criteria: housing and affordable living; vibrant economy; social and civic engagement; education; demographics; health care options; transportation & infrastructure; and abundant lifestyle amenities. *Livability.com, "Top 100 Best Places to Live 2020" October 2020*

Business/Finance Rankings

■ The Brookings Institution ranked the nation's largest cities based on income inequality. Winston-Salem was ranked #28 (#1 = greatest inequality). Criteria: the "95/20 ratio," a figure representing the income at which a household earns more than 95 percent of all other households, divided by the income at which a household earns more than only 20 percent of all other households. *Brookings Institution, "Household Income Inequality, Largest Cities of 97 Large U.S. Metro Areas, 2014-2016," February 5, 2018*

■ The Brookings Institution ranked the 100 largest metro areas in the U.S. based on income inequality. Winston-Salem was ranked #52 (#1 = greatest inequality). Criteria: the "95/20 ratio," a figure representing the income at which a household earns more than 95 percent of all other households, divided by the income at which a household earns more than only 20 percent of all other households. *Brookings Institution, "Household Income Inequality, 100 Largest U.S. Metro Areas, 2014-2016," February 5, 2018*

■ The Winston-Salem metro area appeared on the Milken Institute "2021 Best Performing Cities" list. Rank: #122 out of 200 large metro areas (population over 250,000). Criteria: job growth; wage and salary growth; high-tech output growth; housing affordability; household broadband access. *Milken Institute, "Best-Performing Cities 2021," February 16, 2021*

■ *Forbes* ranked the 200 most populous metro areas to determine the nation's "Best Places for Business and Careers." The Winston-Salem metro area was ranked #69. Criteria: costs (business and living); job growth (past and projected); income growth; quality of life; educational attainment (college and high school); projected economic growth; cultural and leisure opportunities; workplace tolerance laws; net migration patterns. *Forbes, "The Best Places for Business and Careers 2019: Seattle Still On Top," October 30, 2019*

■ Mercer Human Resources Consulting ranked 209 cities worldwide in terms of cost-of-living. Winston-Salem ranked #132 (the lower the ranking, the higher the cost-of-living). The survey measured the comparative cost of over 200 items (such as housing, food, clothing, household goods, transportation, and entertainment) in each location. *Mercer, "2020 Cost of Living Survey," June 9, 2020*

Education Rankings

■ Personal finance website *WalletHub* analyzed the 150 largest U.S. metropolitan statistical areas to determine where the most educated Americans are putting their degrees to work. Criteria: education levels; percentage of workers with degrees; education quality and attainment gap; public school quality rankings; quality and enrollment of each metro area's universities. Winston-Salem was ranked #113 (#1 = most educated city). *www.WalletHub.com, "Most and Least Educated Cities in America, " July 20, 2020*

Health/Fitness Rankings

■ For each of the 100 largest cities in the United States, the American Fitness Index®, published by the American College of Sports Medicine and the Anthem Foundation, evaluated community infrastructure and 33 health behaviors including preventive health, levels of chronic disease conditions, pedestrian safety, air quality, and community resources that support physical activity. Winston-Salem ranked #70 for "community fitness." *americanfitnessindex.org, "2020 ACSM American Fitness Index Summary Report," July 14, 2020*

■ Winston-Salem was identified as a "2021 Spring Allergy Capital." The area ranked #40 out of 100. Three groups of factors were used to identify the most challenging cities for people with allergies during the spring season: annual spring pollen levels; over the counter medicine use; number of board-certified allergy specialists. *Asthma and Allergy Foundation of America, "Spring Allergy Capitals 2021," February 23, 2021*

- Winston-Salem was identified as a "2021 Fall Allergy Capital." The area ranked #64 out of 100. Three groups of factors were used to identify the most challenging cities for people with allergies during the fall season: annual fall pollen levels; over the counter medicine use; number of board-certified allergy specialists. *Asthma and Allergy Foundation of America, "Fall Allergy Capitals 2021," February 23, 2021*

Real Estate Rankings

- The Winston-Salem metro area was identified as one of the 20 best housing markets in the U.S. in 2020. The area ranked #13 out of 180 markets. Criteria: year-over-year change of median sales price of existing single-family homes between the 4th quarter of 2019 and the 4th quarter of 2020. *National Association of Realtors®, Median Sales Price of Existing Single-Family Homes for Metropolitan Areas, 4th Quarter 2020*

- Winston-Salem was ranked #61 out of 268 metro areas in terms of housing affordability in 2020 by the National Association of Home Builders (#1 = most affordable). Criteria: the share of homes sold in that area affordable to a family earning the local median income, based on standard mortgage underwriting criteria. *National Association of Home Builders®, NAHB-Wells Fargo Housing Opportunity Index, 4th Quarter 2020*

Safety Rankings

- Allstate ranked the 200 largest cities in America in terms of driver safety. Winston-Salem ranked #28. Criteria: internal property damage claims over a two-year period from January 2016 to December 2017. The report helps increase the importance of safety and awareness behind the wheel. *Allstate, "Allstate America's Best Drivers Report, 2019" June 24, 2019*

- The National Insurance Crime Bureau ranked 384 metro areas in the U.S. in terms of per capita rates of vehicle theft. The Winston-Salem metro area ranked #145 (#1 = highest rate). Criteria: number of vehicle theft offenses per 100,000 inhabitants in 2019. *National Insurance Crime Bureau, "Hot Spots 2019," July 21, 2020*

Seniors/Retirement Rankings

- From its Best Cities for Successful Aging indexes, the Milken Institute generated rankings for metropolitan areas, weighing data in nine categories—health care, wellness, living arrangements, transportation and convenience, financial characteristics, education, employment, community engagement, and overall livability. The Winston-Salem metro area was ranked #95 overall in the large metro area category. *Milken Institute, "Best Cities for Successful Aging, 2017" March 14, 2017*

- Winston-Salem made the 2020 *Forbes* list of "25 Best Places to Retire." Criteria, focused on high-quality retirement living at an affordable price, include: housing/living costs compared to the national average and state taxes; air quality; crime rates; good economic outlook; home price appreciation; risk associated with climate-change; availability of medical care; bikeability; walkability; healthy living. *Forbes.com, "The Best Places to Retire in 2020," August 14, 2020*

Business Environment

DEMOGRAPHICS

Population Growth

Area	1990 Census	2000 Census	2010 Census	2019* Estimate	Population Growth (%) 1990-2019	Population Growth (%) 2010-2019
City	168,139	185,776	229,617	244,115	45.2	6.3
MSA[1]	361,091	421,961	666,216	477,717	84.5	39.5
U.S.	248,709,873	281,421,906	308,745,538	324,697,795	30.6	5.2

Note: (1) Figures cover the Winston-Salem, NC Metropolitan Statistical Area; (*) 2015-2019 5-year estimated population
Source: U.S. Census Bureau, 1990 Census, Census 2000, Census 2010, 2015-2019 American Community Survey 5-Year Estimates

Household Size

Area	Persons in Household (%) One	Two	Three	Four	Five	Six	Seven or More	Average Household Size
City	35.7	31.5	15.1	9.4	5.3	1.8	1.1	2.50
MSA[1]	29.5	36.0	15.5	11.3	5.0	1.7	1.0	2.50
U.S.	27.9	33.9	15.6	12.9	6.0	2.3	1.4	2.60

Note: (1) Figures cover the Winston-Salem, NC Metropolitan Statistical Area
Source: U.S. Census Bureau, 2015-2019 American Community Survey 5-Year Estimates

Race

Area	White Alone[2] (%)	Black Alone[2] (%)	Asian Alone[2] (%)	AIAN[3] Alone[2] (%)	NHOPI[4] Alone[2] (%)	Other Race Alone[2] (%)	Two or More Races (%)
City	56.6	34.9	2.5	0.3	0.1	2.8	2.8
MSA[1]	75.8	17.8	1.8	0.4	0.1	2.0	2.2
U.S.	72.5	12.7	5.5	0.8	0.2	4.9	3.3

Note: (1) Figures cover the Winston-Salem, NC Metropolitan Statistical Area; (2) Alone is defined as not being in combination with one or more other races; (3) American Indian and Alaska Native; (4) Native Hawaiian and Other Pacific Islander
Source: U.S. Census Bureau, 2015-2019 American Community Survey 5-Year Estimates

Hispanic or Latino Origin

Area	Total (%)	Mexican (%)	Puerto Rican (%)	Cuban (%)	Other (%)
City	15.0	9.9	1.4	0.2	3.5
MSA[1]	10.2	6.7	0.9	0.2	2.5
U.S.	18.0	11.2	1.7	0.7	4.3

Note: Persons of Hispanic or Latino origin can be of any race; (1) Figures cover the Winston-Salem, NC Metropolitan Statistical Area
Source: U.S. Census Bureau, 2015-2019 American Community Survey 5-Year Estimates

Ancestry

Area	German	Irish	English	American	Italian	Polish	French[2]	Scottish	Dutch
City	9.6	6.8	7.8	5.2	2.8	1.1	1.3	2.3	1.0
MSA[1]	11.7	7.8	9.0	9.8	2.5	1.0	1.3	2.4	1.1
U.S.	13.3	9.7	7.2	6.2	5.1	2.8	2.3	1.7	1.2

Note: Figures are the percentage of the total population reporting a particular ancestry. The nine most commonly reported ancestries in the U.S. are shown. Figures include multiple ancestries (e.g. if a person reported being Irish and Italian, they were included in both columns); (1) Figures cover the Winston-Salem, NC Metropolitan Statistical Area; (2) Excludes Basque
Source: U.S. Census Bureau, 2015-2019 American Community Survey 5-Year Estimates

Foreign-born Population

Area	Percent of Population Born in Any Foreign Country	Asia	Mexico	Europe	Caribbean	Central America[2]	South America	Africa	Canada
City	9.9	2.1	4.3	0.7	0.4	1.1	0.5	0.6	0.1
MSA[1]	6.8	1.4	3.0	0.6	0.2	0.9	0.4	0.3	0.1
U.S.	13.6	4.2	3.5	1.5	1.3	1.1	1.0	0.7	0.2

Note: (1) Figures cover the Winston-Salem, NC Metropolitan Statistical Area; (2) Excludes Mexico.
Source: U.S. Census Bureau, 2015-2019 American Community Survey 5-Year Estimates

Marital Status

Area	Never Married	Now Married[2]	Separated	Widowed	Divorced
City	40.4	39.9	2.8	5.9	11.1
MSA[1]	29.8	49.6	2.5	6.8	11.3
U.S.	33.4	48.1	1.9	5.8	10.9

Note: Figures are percentages and cover the population 15 years of age and older; (1) Figures cover the Winston-Salem, NC Metropolitan Statistical Area; (2) Excludes separated
Source: U.S. Census Bureau, 2015-2019 American Community Survey 5-Year Estimates

Disability by Age

Area	All Ages	Under 18 Years Old	18 to 64 Years Old	65 Years and Over
City	9.8	2.8	8.3	28.6
MSA[1]	12.7	3.8	10.2	33.8
U.S.	12.6	4.2	10.3	34.5

Note: Figures show percent of the civilian noninstitutionalized population that reported having a disability. Disability status is determined from six types of difficulty: vision, hearing, cognitive, ambulatory, self-care, and independent living. For children under 5 years old, hearing and vision difficulty are used to determine disability status. For children between the ages of 5 and 14, disability status is determined from hearing, vision, cognitive, ambulatory, and self-care difficulties. For people aged 15 years and older, they are considered to have a disability if they have difficulty with any one of the six difficulty types; Note: (1) Figures cover the Winston-Salem, NC Metropolitan Statistical Area
Source: U.S. Census Bureau, 2015-2019 American Community Survey 5-Year Estimates

Age

Area	Percent of Population									Median Age
	Under Age 5	Age 5–19	Age 20–34	Age 35–44	Age 45–54	Age 55–64	Age 65–74	Age 75–84	Age 85+	
City	6.5	20.9	21.8	12.4	12.1	12.0	8.1	4.3	1.7	35.5
MSA[1]	5.7	19.4	18.3	11.9	14.1	13.7	9.9	5.3	1.8	40.6
U.S.	6.1	19.1	20.7	12.6	13.0	12.9	9.1	4.6	1.9	38.1

Note: (1) Figures cover the Winston-Salem, NC Metropolitan Statistical Area
Source: U.S. Census Bureau, 2015-2019 American Community Survey 5-Year Estimates

Gender

Area	Males	Females	Males per 100 Females
City	114,592	129,523	88.5
MSA[1]	320,092	346,124	92.5
U.S.	159,886,919	164,810,876	97.0

Note: (1) Figures cover the Winston-Salem, NC Metropolitan Statistical Area
Source: U.S. Census Bureau, 2015-2019 American Community Survey 5-Year Estimates

Religious Groups by Family

Area	Catholic	Baptist	Non-Den.	Methodist[2]	Lutheran	LDS[3]	Pentecostal	Presbyterian[4]	Muslim[5]	Judaism
MSA[1]	3.6	17.5	9.4	12.4	0.7	0.7	2.6	2.2	0.3	0.1
U.S.	19.1	9.3	4.0	4.0	2.3	2.0	1.9	1.6	0.8	0.7

Note: Figures are the number of adherents as a percentage of the total population; (1) Figures cover the Winston-Salem, NC Metropolitan Statistical Area; (2) Methodist/Pietist; (3) Latter Day Saints; (4) Reformed; (5) Figures are estimates
Source: Association of Statisticians of American Religious Bodies, 2010 U.S. Religion Census: Religious Congregations & Membership Study

Religious Groups by Tradition

Area	Catholic	Evangelical Protestant	Mainline Protestant	Other Tradition	Black Protestant	Orthodox
MSA[1]	3.6	29.2	15.7	1.3	2.3	0.3
U.S.	19.1	16.2	7.3	4.3	1.6	0.3

Note: Figures are the number of adherents as a percentage of the total population; (1) Figures cover the Winston-Salem, NC Metropolitan Statistical Area
Source: Association of Statisticians of American Religious Bodies, 2010 U.S. Religion Census: Religious Congregations & Membership Study

ECONOMY

Gross Metropolitan Product

Area	2017	2018	2019	2020	Rank[2]
MSA[1]	29.7	31.2	32.5	33.8	88

Note: Figures are in billions of dollars; (1) Figures cover the Winston-Salem, NC Metropolitan Statistical Area; (2) Rank is based on 2018 data and ranges from 1 to 381
Source: U.S. Conference of Mayors, U.S. Metro Economies: GMP & Employment 2018-2020, September 2019

Economic Growth

Area	2015-17 (%)	2018 (%)	2019 (%)	2020 (%)	Rank[2]
MSA[1]	-0.2	2.6	2.6	1.6	314
U.S.	1.9	2.9	2.3	2.1	–

Note: Figures are real gross metropolitan product (GMP) growth rates and represent average annual percent change; (1) Figures cover the Winston-Salem, NC Metropolitan Statistical Area; (2) Rank is based on 2017 2-year average annual percent change and ranges from 1 to 381
Source: U.S. Conference of Mayors, U.S. Metro Economies: GMP & Employment 2018-2020, September 2019

Metropolitan Area Exports

Area	2014	2015	2016	2017	2018	2019	Rank[2]
MSA[1]	1,441.9	1,267.4	1,234.6	1,131.7	1,107.5	1,209.1	137

Note: Figures are in millions of dollars; (1) Figures cover the Winston-Salem, NC Metropolitan Statistical Area; (2) Rank is based on 2019 data and ranges from 1 to 386
Source: U.S. Department of Commerce, International Trade Administration, Office of Trade and Economic Analysis, Industry and Analysis, Exports by Metropolitan Area, data extracted March 24, 2021

Building Permits

Area	Single-Family			Multi-Family			Total		
	2018	2019	Pct. Chg.	2018	2019	Pct. Chg.	2018	2019	Pct. Chg.
City	1,251	1,185	-5.3	84	0	-100.0	1,335	1,185	-11.2
MSA[1]	3,123	3,160	1.2	376	174	-53.7	3,499	3,334	-4.7
U.S.	855,300	862,100	0.7	473,500	523,900	10.6	1,328,800	1,386,000	4.3

Note: (1) Figures cover the Winston-Salem, NC Metropolitan Statistical Area; Figures represent new, privately-owned housing units authorized (unadjusted data); All permit data are based on estimates with imputation
Source: U.S. Census Bureau, Manufacturing, Mining, and Construction Statistics, Building Permits, 2018, 2019

Bankruptcy Filings

Area	Business Filings			Nonbusiness Filings		
	2019	2020	% Chg.	2019	2020	% Chg.
Forsyth County	17	15	-11.8	537	363	-32.4
U.S.	22,780	21,655	-4.9	752,160	522,808	-30.5

Note: Business filings include Chapter 7, Chapter 9, Chapter 11, Chapter 12, Chapter 13, Chapter 15, and Section 304; Nonbusiness filings include Chapter 7, Chapter 11, and Chapter 13
Source: Administrative Office of the U.S. Courts, Business and Nonbusiness Bankruptcy, County Cases Commenced by Chapter of the Bankruptcy Code, During the 12-Month Period Ending December 31, 2019 and Business and Nonbusiness Bankruptcy, County Cases Commenced by Chapter of the Bankruptcy Code, During the 12-Month Period Ending December 31, 2020

Housing Vacancy Rates

Area	Gross Vacancy Rate[2] (%)			Year-Round Vacancy Rate[3] (%)			Rental Vacancy Rate[4] (%)			Homeowner Vacancy Rate[5] (%)		
	2018	2019	2020	2018	2019	2020	2018	2019	2020	2018	2019	2020
MSA[1]	n/a	n/a	n/a	n/a	n/a	n/a	n/a	n/a	n/a	n/a	n/a	n/a
U.S.	12.3	12.0	10.6	9.7	9.5	8.2	6.9	6.7	6.3	1.5	1.4	1.0

Note: (1) Figures cover the Winston-Salem, NC Metropolitan Statistical Area; (2) The percentage of the total housing inventory that is vacant; (3) The percentage of the housing inventory (excluding seasonal units) that is year-round vacant; (4) The percentage of rental inventory that is vacant for rent; (5) The percentage of homeowner inventory that is vacant for sale; n/a not available
Source: U.S. Census Bureau, Housing Vacancies and Homeownership Annual Statistics: 2018, 2019, 2020

INCOME

Income

Area	Per Capita ($)	Median Household ($)	Average Household ($)
City	28,821	45,750	71,423
MSA[1]	28,986	50,774	71,206
U.S.	34,103	62,843	88,607

Note: (1) Figures cover the Winston-Salem, NC Metropolitan Statistical Area
Source: U.S. Census Bureau, 2015-2019 American Community Survey 5-Year Estimates

Household Income Distribution

Area	Percent of Households Earning							
	Under $15,000	$15,000 -$24,999	$25,000 -$34,999	$35,000 -$49,999	$50,000 -$74,999	$75,000 -$99,999	$100,000 -$149,999	$150,000 and up
City	15.4	11.8	11.9	14.3	16.9	11.2	9.8	8.7
MSA[1]	12.1	11.3	11.0	14.8	18.0	12.8	11.6	8.3
U.S.	10.3	8.9	8.9	12.3	17.2	12.7	15.1	14.5

Note: (1) Figures cover the Winston-Salem, NC Metropolitan Statistical Area
Source: U.S. Census Bureau, 2015-2019 American Community Survey 5-Year Estimates

Poverty Rate

Area	All Ages	Under 18 Years Old	18 to 64 Years Old	65 Years and Over
City	20.7	32.0	18.6	10.4
MSA[1]	16.0	24.8	14.6	9.0
U.S.	13.4	18.5	12.6	9.3

Note: Figures are percentage of people whose income during the past 12 months was below the poverty level;
(1) Figures cover the Winston-Salem, NC Metropolitan Statistical Area
Source: U.S. Census Bureau, 2015-2019 American Community Survey 5-Year Estimates

CITY FINANCES

City Government Finances

Component	2017 ($000)	2017 ($ per capita)
Total Revenues	431,534	1,789
Total Expenditures	539,004	2,235
Debt Outstanding	778,899	3,229
Cash and Securities[1]	149,252	619

Note: (1) Cash and security holdings of a government at the close of its fiscal year,
including those of its dependent agencies, utilities, and liquor stores.
Source: U.S. Census Bureau, State & Local Government Finances 2017

City Government Revenue by Source

Source	2017 ($000)	2017 ($ per capita)	2017 (%)
General Revenue			
From Federal Government	20,275	84	4.7
From State Government	29,794	124	6.9
From Local Governments	1,349	6	0.3
Taxes			
Property	122,178	507	28.3
Sales and Gross Receipts	45,163	187	10.5
Personal Income	0	0	0.0
Corporate Income	0	0	0.0
Motor Vehicle License	2,458	10	0.6
Other Taxes	1,675	7	0.4
Current Charges	86,934	360	20.1
Liquor Store	34,873	145	8.1
Utility	57,523	238	13.3
Employee Retirement	15,042	62	3.5

Source: U.S. Census Bureau, State & Local Government Finances 2017

City Government Expenditures by Function

Function	2017 ($000)	2017 ($ per capita)	2017 (%)
General Direct Expenditures			
Air Transportation	0	0	0.0
Corrections	0	0	0.0
Education	0	0	0.0
Employment Security Administration	0	0	0.0
Financial Administration	3,819	15	0.7
Fire Protection	34,162	141	6.3
General Public Buildings	15,029	62	2.8
Governmental Administration, Other	12,803	53	2.4
Health	0	0	0.0
Highways	34,606	143	6.4
Hospitals	0	0	0.0
Housing and Community Development	31,481	130	5.8
Interest on General Debt	40,725	168	7.6
Judicial and Legal	1,366	5	0.3
Libraries	0	0	0.0
Parking	1,832	7	0.3
Parks and Recreation	47,517	197	8.8
Police Protection	79,207	328	14.7
Public Welfare	0	0	0.0
Sewerage	66,610	276	12.4
Solid Waste Management	31,789	131	5.9
Veterans' Services	0	0	0.0
Liquor Store	29,272	121	5.4
Utility	86,361	358	16.0
Employee Retirement	10,503	43	1.9

Source: U.S. Census Bureau, State & Local Government Finances 2017

EMPLOYMENT

Labor Force and Employment

Area	Civilian Labor Force			Workers Employed		
	Dec. 2019	Dec. 2020	% Chg.	Dec. 2019	Dec. 2020	% Chg.
City	118,986	117,479	-1.3	114,945	109,601	-4.6
MSA[1]	329,944	323,658	-1.9	319,404	304,539	-4.7
U.S.	164,007,000	160,017,000	-2.4	158,504,000	149,613,000	-5.6

Note: Data is not seasonally adjusted and covers workers 16 years of age and older; (1) Figures cover the Winston-Salem, NC Metropolitan Statistical Area
Source: Bureau of Labor Statistics, Local Area Unemployment Statistics

Unemployment Rate

Area	2020											
	Jan.	Feb.	Mar.	Apr.	May	Jun.	Jul.	Aug.	Sep.	Oct.	Nov.	Dec.
City	4.2	3.7	4.3	12.9	13.9	8.8	10.3	8.0	8.2	6.9	6.8	6.7
MSA[1]	3.9	3.5	4.1	12.7	12.7	7.7	8.8	6.6	6.8	5.9	6.0	5.9
U.S.	4.0	3.8	4.5	14.4	13.0	11.2	10.5	8.5	7.7	6.6	6.4	6.5

Note: Data is not seasonally adjusted and covers workers 16 years of age and older; (1) Figures cover the Winston-Salem, NC Metropolitan Statistical Area
Source: Bureau of Labor Statistics, Local Area Unemployment Statistics

Average Wages

Occupation	$/Hr.	Occupation	$/Hr.
Accountants and Auditors	35.90	Maintenance and Repair Workers	19.90
Automotive Mechanics	20.20	Marketing Managers	64.50
Bookkeepers	19.60	Network and Computer Systems Admin.	39.50
Carpenters	19.80	Nurses, Licensed Practical	22.10
Cashiers	10.20	Nurses, Registered	34.00
Computer Programmers	42.80	Nursing Assistants	13.80
Computer Systems Analysts	44.70	Office Clerks, General	16.40
Computer User Support Specialists	24.70	Physical Therapists	47.60
Construction Laborers	15.80	Physicians	59.30
Cooks, Restaurant	10.90	Plumbers, Pipefitters and Steamfitters	21.40
Customer Service Representatives	17.30	Police and Sheriff's Patrol Officers	21.50
Dentists	72.90	Postal Service Mail Carriers	26.10
Electricians	22.40	Real Estate Sales Agents	29.80
Engineers, Electrical	43.40	Retail Salespersons	12.80
Fast Food and Counter Workers	10.40	Sales Representatives, Technical/Scientific	46.10
Financial Managers	73.60	Secretaries, Exc. Legal/Medical/Executive	18.60
First-Line Supervisors of Office Workers	26.30	Security Guards	19.10
General and Operations Managers	59.20	Surgeons	n/a
Hairdressers/Cosmetologists	12.90	Teacher Assistants, Exc. Postsecondary*	11.40
Home Health and Personal Care Aides	11.40	Teachers, Secondary School, Exc. Sp. Ed.*	24.50
Janitors and Cleaners	11.70	Telemarketers	n/a
Landscaping/Groundskeeping Workers	14.40	Truck Drivers, Heavy/Tractor-Trailer	23.70
Lawyers	60.40	Truck Drivers, Light/Delivery Services	17.90
Maids and Housekeeping Cleaners	11.30	Waiters and Waitresses	10.40

Note: Wage data covers the Winston-Salem, NC Metropolitan Statistical Area; (*) Hourly wages were calculated from annual wage data based on a 40 hour work week; n/a not available.
Source: Bureau of Labor Statistics, Metro Area Occupational Employment & Wage Estimates, May 2020

Employment by Industry

Sector	MSA[1]		U.S.
	Number of Employees	Percent of Total	Percent of Total
Construction, Mining, and Logging	11,900	4.5	5.5
Education and Health Services	54,900	20.9	16.3
Financial Activities	13,000	4.9	6.1
Government	30,000	11.4	15.2
Information	1,600	0.6	1.9
Leisure and Hospitality	24,300	9.2	9.0
Manufacturing	33,100	12.6	8.5
Other Services	8,100	3.1	3.8
Professional and Business Services	35,400	13.5	14.4
Retail Trade	31,000	11.8	10.9
Transportation, Warehousing, and Utilities	11,800	4.5	4.6
Wholesale Trade	7,700	2.9	3.9

Note: Figures are non-farm employment as of December 2020. Figures are not seasonally adjusted and include workers 16 years of age and older; (1) Figures cover the Winston-Salem, NC Metropolitan Statistical Area
Source: Bureau of Labor Statistics, Current Employment Statistics, Employment, Hours, and Earnings

Employment by Occupation

Occupation Classification	City (%)	MSA[1] (%)	U.S. (%)
Management, Business, Science, and Arts	39.5	35.9	38.5
Natural Resources, Construction, and Maintenance	6.7	9.2	8.9
Production, Transportation, and Material Moving	14.1	17.4	13.2
Sales and Office	21.3	21.2	21.6
Service	18.5	16.4	17.8

Note: Figures cover employed civilians 16 years of age and older; (1) Figures cover the Winston-Salem, NC Metropolitan Statistical Area
Source: U.S. Census Bureau, 2015-2019 American Community Survey 5-Year Estimates

Occupations with Greatest Projected Employment Growth: 2020 – 2022

Occupation[1]	2020 Employment	2022 Projected Employment	Numeric Employment Change	Percent Employment Change
Laborers and Freight, Stock, and Material Movers, Hand	90,950	94,250	3,300	3.6
Stockers and Order Fillers	99,690	102,690	3,000	3.0
Software Developers and Software Quality Assurance Analysts and Testers	74,740	76,850	2,110	2.8
Registered Nurses	87,970	89,970	2,000	2.3
Project Management Specialists and Business Operations Specialists, All Other	62,540	63,660	1,120	1.8
Computer Systems Analysts (SOC 2018)	40,350	41,450	1,100	2.7
Insurance Sales Agents	13,950	14,920	970	7.0
Industrial Truck and Tractor Operators	22,480	23,360	880	3.9
Loan Officers	12,610	13,430	820	6.5
Customer Service Representatives	80,790	81,600	810	1.0

Note: Projections cover North Carolina; (1) Sorted by numeric employment change
Source: www.projectionscentral.com, State Occupational Projections, 2020–2022 Short-Term Projections

Fastest-Growing Occupations: 2020 – 2022

Occupation[1]	2020 Employment	2022 Projected Employment	Numeric Employment Change	Percent Employment Change
Statisticians	1,420	1,540	120	8.5
Operations Research Analysts	2,490	2,700	210	8.4
Butchers and Meat Cutters	2,650	2,860	210	7.9
Insurance Sales Agents	13,950	14,920	970	7.0
Loan Interviewers and Clerks	6,000	6,420	420	7.0
Brokerage Clerks	1,590	1,700	110	6.9
Veterinary Assistants and Laboratory Animal Caretakers	3,590	3,830	240	6.7
Personal Financial Advisors	8,760	9,330	570	6.5
Loan Officers	12,610	13,430	820	6.5
Veterinary Technologists and Technicians	3,040	3,230	190	6.3

Note: Projections cover North Carolina; (1) Sorted by percent employment change and excludes occupations with numeric employment change less than 50
Source: www.projectionscentral.com, State Occupational Projections, 2020–2022 Short-Term Projections

TAXES

State Corporate Income Tax Rates

State	Tax Rate (%)	Income Brackets ($)	Num. of Brackets	Financial Institution Tax Rate (%)[a]	Federal Income Tax Ded.
North Carolina	2.5	Flat rate	1	2.5	No

Note: Tax rates as of January 1, 2021; (a) Rates listed are the corporate income tax rate applied to financial institutions or excise taxes based on income. Some states have other taxes based upon the value of deposits or shares.
Source: Federation of Tax Administrators, State Corporate Income Tax Rates, January 1, 2021

State Individual Income Tax Rates

State	Tax Rate (%)	Income Brackets ($)	Personal Exemptions ($)			Standard Ded. ($)	
			Single	Married	Depend.	Single	Married
North Carolina	5.25	Flat rate	None	None	None	10,750	21,500

Note: Tax rates as of January 1, 2021; Local- and county-level taxes are not included; Federal income tax is not deductible on state income tax returns
Source: Federation of Tax Administrators, State Individual Income Tax Rates, January 1, 2021

Various State Sales and Excise Tax Rates

State	State Sales Tax (%)	Gasoline[1] (¢/gal.)	Cigarette[2] ($/pack)	Spirits[3] ($/gal.)	Wine[4] ($/gal.)	Beer[5] ($/gal.)	Recreational Marijuana (%)
North Carolina	4.75	36.35	0.45	14.58	1	0.62	Not legal

Note: All tax rates as of January 1, 2021; (1) The American Petroleum Institute has developed a methodology for determining the average tax rate on a gallon of fuel. Rates may include any of the following: excise taxes, environmental fees, storage tank fees, other fees or taxes, general sales tax, and local taxes; (2) The federal excise tax of $1.0066 per pack and local taxes are not included; (3) Rates are those applicable to off-premise sales of 40% alcohol by volume (a.b.v.) distilled spirits in 750ml containers. Local excise taxes are excluded; (4) Rates are those applicable to off-premise sales of 11% a.b.v. non-carbonated wine in 750ml containers; (5) Rates are those applicable to off-premise sales of 4.7% a.b.v. beer in 12 ounce containers.
Source: Tax Foundation, 2021 Facts & Figures: How Does Your State Compare?

State Business Tax Climate Index Rankings

State	Overall Rank	Corporate Tax Rank	Individual Income Tax Rank	Sales Tax Rank	Property Tax Rank	Unemployment Insurance Tax Rank
North Carolina	10	4	16	22	26	10

Note: The index is a measure of how each state's tax laws affect economic performance. The lower the rank, the more favorable a state's tax system is for business. States without a given tax are given a ranking of 1. The scores/rankings for the District of Columbia do not affect other states. The 2021 index represents the tax climate as of July 1, 2020.
Source: Tax Foundation, State Business Tax Climate Index 2021

TRANSPORTATION

Means of Transportation to Work

Area	Car/Truck/Van		Public Transportation			Bicycle	Walked	Other Means	Worked at Home
	Drove Alone	Car-pooled	Bus	Subway	Railroad				
City	81.9	8.3	1.7	0.0	0.0	0.2	2.1	1.1	4.7
MSA[1]	83.6	8.9	0.7	0.0	0.0	0.1	1.3	0.9	4.5
U.S.	76.3	9.0	2.4	1.9	0.6	0.5	2.7	1.4	5.2

Note: Figures are percentages and cover workers 16 years of age and older; (1) Figures cover the Winston-Salem, NC Metropolitan Statistical Area
Source: U.S. Census Bureau, 2015-2019 American Community Survey 5-Year Estimates

Travel Time to Work

Area	Less Than 10 Minutes	10 to 19 Minutes	20 to 29 Minutes	30 to 44 Minutes	45 to 59 Minutes	60 to 89 Minutes	90 Minutes or More
City	13.6	40.8	23.8	13.7	4.2	2.1	1.8
MSA[1]	12.0	33.3	24.5	19.1	6.1	2.8	2.1
U.S.	12.2	28.4	20.8	20.8	8.3	6.4	2.9

Note: Note: Figures are percentages and include workers 16 years old and over; (1) Figures cover the Winston-Salem, NC Metropolitan Statistical Area
Source: U.S. Census Bureau, 2015-2019 American Community Survey 5-Year Estimates

Key Congestion Measures

Measure	1982	1992	2002	2012	2017
Annual Hours of Delay, Total (000)	684	1,496	4,426	6,513	7,930
Annual Hours of Delay, Per Auto Commuter	6	9	18	21	27
Annual Congestion Cost, Total (million $)	5	16	59	115	145
Annual Congestion Cost, Per Auto Commuter ($)	94	141	327	377	445

Note: Covers the Winston-Salem NC urban area
Source: Texas A&M Transportation Institute, 2019 Urban Mobility Report

Freeway Travel Time Index

Measure	1982	1987	1992	1997	2002	2007	2012	2017
Urban Area Index[1]	1.03	1.05	1.05	1.08	1.10	1.11	1.11	1.11
Urban Area Rank[1,2]	76	79	92	88	91	95	94	96

Note: Freeway Travel Time Index—the ratio of travel time in the peak period to the travel time at free-flow conditions. For example, a value of 1.30 indicates a 20-minute free-flow trip takes 26 minutes in the peak (20 minutes x 1.30 = 26 minutes); (1) Covers the Winston-Salem NC urban area; (2) Rank is based on 101 larger urban areas (#1 = highest travel time index)
Source: Texas A&M Transportation Institute, 2019 Urban Mobility Report

Public Transportation

Agency Name / Mode of Transportation	Vehicles Operated in Maximum Service[1]	Annual Unlinked Passenger Trips[2] (in thous.)	Annual Passenger Miles[3] (in thous.)
Winston-Salem Transit Authority (WSTA)			
Bus (directly operated)	38	2,471.6	7,199.9
Demand Response (directly operated)	33	225.1	1,975.9

Note: (1) Number of revenue vehicles operated by the given mode and type of service to meet the annual maximum service requirement. This is the revenue vehicle count during the peak season of the year; on the week and day that maximum service is provided. Vehicles operated in maximum service (VOMS) exclude atypical days and one-time special events; (2) Number of passengers who boarded public transportation vehicles. Passengers are counted each time they board a vehicle no matter how many vehicles they use to travel from their origin to their destination. (3) Sum of the distances ridden by all passengers during the entire fiscal year.
Source: Federal Transit Administration, National Transit Database, 2019

Air Transportation

Airport Name and Code / Type of Service	Passenger Airlines[1]	Passenger Enplanements	Freight Carriers[2]	Freight (lbs)
Piedmont Triad International Airport (23 miles) (GSO)				
Domestic service (U.S. carriers - 2020)	23	379,379	18	107,216,252
International service (U.S. carriers - 2019)	1	12	1	60,916

Note: (1) Includes all U.S.-based major, minor and commuter airlines that carried at least one passenger during the year; (2) Includes all U.S.-based airlines and freight carriers that transported at least one pound of freight during the year.
Source: Bureau of Transportation Statistics, The Intermodal Transportation Database, Air Carriers: T-100 Domestic Market (U.S. Carriers), 2020; Bureau of Transportation Statistics, The Intermodal Transportation Database, Air Carriers: T-100 International Market (U.S. Carriers), 2019

BUSINESSES

Major Business Headquarters

Company Name	Industry	Rankings	
		Fortune[1]	Forbes[2]
Hanesbrands	Apparel	436	-

Note: (1) Companies that produce a 10-K are ranked 1 to 500 based on 2019 revenue; (2) All private companies with at least $2 billion in annual revenue through the end of their most current fiscal year are ranked 1 to 219; companies listed are headquartered in the city; dashes indicate no ranking
Source: Fortune, "Fortune 500," June/July 2020; Forbes, "America's Largest Private Companies," 2020

Living Environment

COST OF LIVING

Cost of Living Index

Composite Index	Groceries	Housing	Utilities	Trans-portation	Health Care	Misc. Goods/ Services
94.3	101.1	79.9	93.7	99.7	116.7	98.8

Note: The Cost of Living Index measures regional differences in the cost of consumer goods and services, excluding taxes and non-consumer expenditures, for professional and managerial households in the top income quintile. It is based on more than 50,000 prices covering almost 60 different items for which prices are collected three times a year by chambers of commerce, economic development organizations or university applied economic centers in each participating urban area. The numbers shown should be read as a percentage above or below the national average of 100. For example, a value of 115.4 in the groceries column indicates that grocery prices are 15.4% higher than the national average. Small differences in the index numbers should not be interpreted as significant; Figures cover the Winston-Salem NC urban area.
Source: The Council for Community and Economic Research, Cost of Living Index, 2020

Grocery Prices

Area[1]	T-Bone Steak ($/pound)	Frying Chicken ($/pound)	Whole Milk ($/half gal.)	Eggs ($/dozen)	Orange Juice ($/64 oz.)	Coffee ($/11.5 oz.)
City[2]	11.86	1.27	1.55	1.45	3.94	4.03
Avg.	11.78	1.39	2.05	1.47	3.57	4.34
Min.	8.03	0.94	1.03	0.74	2.94	3.02
Max.	15.86	2.65	4.31	3.77	5.44	8.69

*Note: (1) Values for the local area are compared with the average, minimum and maximum values for all 284 areas in the Cost of Living Index; (2) Figures cover the Winston-Salem NC urban area; **T-Bone Steak** (price per pound); **Frying Chicken** (price per pound, whole fryer); **Whole Milk** (half gallon carton); **Eggs** (price per dozen, Grade A, large); **Orange Juice** (64 oz. Tropicana or Florida Natural); **Coffee** (11.5 oz. can, vacuum-packed, Maxwell House, Hills Bros, or Folgers).*
Source: The Council for Community and Economic Research, Cost of Living Index, 2020

Housing and Utility Costs

Area[1]	New Home Price ($)	Apartment Rent ($/month)	All Electric ($/month)	Part Electric ($/month)	Other Energy ($/month)	Telephone ($/month)
City[2]	248,204	1,242	158.18	-	-	169.60
Avg.	368,594	1,168	170.86	100.47	65.28	184.30
Min.	190,567	502	91.58	31.42	26.08	169.60
Max.	2,227,806	4,738	470.38	280.31	280.06	206.50

*Note: (1) Values for the local area are compared with the average, minimum and maximum values for all 284 areas in the Cost of Living Index; (2) Figures cover the Winston-Salem NC urban area; **New Home Price** (2,400 sf living area, 8,000 sf lot, in urban area with full utilities); **Apartment Rent** (950 sf 2 bedroom/1.5 or 2 bath, unfurnished, excluding all utilities except water); **All Electric** (average monthly cost for an all-electric home); **Part Electric** (average monthly cost for a part-electric home); **Other Energy** (average monthly cost for natural gas, fuel oil, coal, wood, and any other forms of energy except electricity); **Telephone** (price includes the base monthly rate plus taxes and fees for three lines of mobile phone service).*
Source: The Council for Community and Economic Research, Cost of Living Index, 2020

Health Care, Transportation, and Other Costs

Area[1]	Doctor ($/visit)	Dentist ($/visit)	Optometrist ($/visit)	Gasoline ($/gallon)	Beauty Salon ($/visit)	Men's Shirt ($)
City[2]	124.74	139.81	109.70	2.12	35.48	39.18
Avg.	115.44	99.32	108.10	2.21	39.27	31.37
Min.	36.68	59.00	51.36	1.71	19.00	11.00
Max.	219.00	153.10	250.97	3.46	82.05	58.33

*Note: (1) Values for the local area are compared with the average, minimum and maximum values for all 284 areas in the Cost of Living Index; (2) Figures cover the Winston-Salem NC urban area; **Doctor** (general practitioners routine exam of an established patient); **Dentist** (adult teeth cleaning and periodic oral examination); **Optometrist** (full vision eye exam for established adult patient); **Gasoline** (one gallon regular unleaded, national brand, including all taxes, cash price at self-service pump if available); **Beauty Salon** (woman's shampoo, trim, and blow-dry); **Men's Shirt** (cotton/polyester dress shirt, pinpoint weave, long sleeves).*
Source: The Council for Community and Economic Research, Cost of Living Index, 2020

HOUSING

Homeownership Rate

Area	2012 (%)	2013 (%)	2014 (%)	2015 (%)	2016 (%)	2017 (%)	2018 (%)	2019 (%)	2020 (%)
MSA[1]	n/a	n/a	n/a	n/a	n/a	n/a	n/a	n/a	n/a
U.S.	65.4	65.1	64.5	63.7	63.4	63.9	64.4	64.6	66.6

Note: (1) Figures cover the Winston-Salem, NC Metropolitan Statistical Area; n/a not available
Source: U.S. Census Bureau, Housing Vacancies and Homeownership Annual Statistics: 2012-2020

House Price Index (HPI)

Area	National Ranking[2]	Quarterly Change (%)	One-Year Change (%)	Five-Year Change (%)	Since 1991Q1 (%)
MSA[1]	94	2.58	6.92	28.40	118.04
U.S.[3]	–	3.81	10.77	38.99	205.12

Note: The HPI is a weighted repeat sales index. It measures average price changes in repeat sales or refinancings on the same properties. This information is obtained by reviewing repeat mortgage transactions on single-family properties whose mortgages have been purchased or securitized by Fannie Mae or Freddie Mac since January 1975; (1) Figures cover the Winston-Salem, NC Metropolitan Statistical Area; (2) Rankings are based on annual percentage change for all metro areas containing at least 15,000 transactions over the last 10 years and ranges from 1 to 253; (3) figures based on a weighted average of Census Division estimates using a seasonally adjusted, purchase-only index; all figures are for the period ending December 31, 2020
Source: Federal Housing Finance Agency, Change in Metropolitan Area House Price Indexes, April 7, 2021

Median Single-Family Home Prices

Area	2018	2019	2020[p]	Percent Change 2019 to 2020
MSA[1]	165.4	177.3	202.4	14.2
U.S. Average	261.6	274.6	299.9	9.2

Note: Figures are median sales prices of existing single-family homes in thousands of dollars; (p) preliminary; (1) Figures cover the Winston-Salem, NC Metropolitan Statistical Area
Source: National Association of Realtors, Median Sales Price of Existing Single-Family Homes for Metropolitan Areas, 4th Quarter 2020

Qualifying Income Based on Median Sales Price of Existing Single-Family Homes

Area	With 5% Down ($)	With 10% Down ($)	With 20% Down ($)
MSA[1]	40,949	38,794	34,484
U.S. Average	59,266	56,147	49,908

Note: Figures are preliminary; Qualifying income is based on a mortgage rate of 2.81%. Monthly principal and interest payment is limited to 25% of income; (1) Figures cover the Winston-Salem, NC Metropolitan Statistical Area
Source: National Association of Realtors, Qualifying Income Based on Median Sales Price of Existing Single-Family Homes for Metropolitan Areas, 4th Quarter 2020

Home Value Distribution

Area	Under $50,000	$50,000 -$99,999	$100,000 -$149,999	$150,000 -$199,999	$200,000 -$299,999	$300,000 -$499,999	$500,000 -$999,999	$1,000,000 or more
City	6.6	19.7	24.8	20.8	13.4	8.8	5.2	0.8
MSA[1]	7.4	16.9	24.5	20.0	17.2	9.9	3.5	0.6
U.S.	6.9	12.0	13.3	14.0	19.6	19.3	11.4	3.4

Note: Figures are percentages and cover owner-occupied housing units; (1) Figures cover the Winston-Salem, NC Metropolitan Statistical Area
Source: U.S. Census Bureau, 2015-2019 American Community Survey 5-Year Estimates

Year Housing Structure Built

Area	2010 or Later	2000 -2009	1990 -1999	1980 -1989	1970 -1979	1960 -1969	1950 -1959	1940 -1949	Before 1940	Median Year
City	4.7	14.0	12.1	14.3	16.7	13.6	11.8	5.4	7.4	1977
MSA[1]	4.5	15.6	17.2	15.7	16.7	10.9	8.9	4.3	6.3	1982
U.S.	5.2	14.0	13.9	13.4	15.2	10.6	10.3	4.9	12.6	1978

Note: Figures are percentages except for Median Year; Note: (1) Figures cover the Winston-Salem, NC Metropolitan Statistical Area
Source: U.S. Census Bureau, 2015-2019 American Community Survey 5-Year Estimates

Gross Monthly Rent

Area	Under $500	$500 -$999	$1,000 -$1,499	$1,500 -$1,999	$2,000 -$2,499	$2,500 -$2,999	$3,000 and up	Median ($)
City	10.9	62.6	21.5	3.5	0.9	0.2	0.4	806
MSA[1]	12.9	63.9	18.9	3.1	0.7	0.2	0.2	773
U.S.	9.4	36.2	30.0	14.0	5.6	2.4	2.4	1,062

Note: Figures are percentages except for Median; Gross rent is the contract rent plus the estimated average monthly cost of utilities (electricity, gas, and water and sewer) and fuels (oil, coal, kerosene, wood, etc.) if these are paid by the renter (or paid for the renter by someone else); (1) Figures cover the Winston-Salem, NC Metropolitan Statistical Area
Source: U.S. Census Bureau, 2015-2019 American Community Survey 5-Year Estimates

HEALTH

Health Risk Factors

Category	MSA[1] (%)	U.S. (%)
Adults aged 18–64 who have any kind of health care coverage	n/a	87.3
Adults who reported being in good or better health	n/a	82.4
Adults who have been told they have high blood cholesterol	n/a	33.0
Adults who have been told they have high blood pressure	n/a	32.3
Adults who are current smokers	n/a	17.1
Adults who currently use E-cigarettes	n/a	4.6
Adults who currently use chewing tobacco, snuff, or snus	n/a	4.0
Adults who are heavy drinkers[2]	n/a	6.3
Adults who are binge drinkers[3]	n/a	17.4
Adults who are overweight (BMI 25.0 - 29.9)	n/a	35.3
Adults who are obese (BMI 30.0 - 99.8)	n/a	31.3
Adults who participated in any physical activities in the past month	n/a	74.4
Adults who always or nearly always wears a seat belt	n/a	94.3

Note: n/a not available; (1) Figures cover the Winston-Salem, NC Metropolitan Statistical Area; (2) Heavy drinkers are classified as adult men having more than 14 drinks per week and adult women having more than 7 drinks per week; (3) Binge drinkers are classified as males having five or more drinks on one occasion or females having four or more drinks on one occasion
Source: Centers for Disease Control and Prevention, Behaviorial Risk Factor Surveillance System, SMART: Selected Metropolitan Area Risk Trends, 2017

Acute and Chronic Health Conditions

Category	MSA[1] (%)	U.S. (%)
Adults who have ever been told they had a heart attack	n/a	4.2
Adults who have ever been told they have angina or coronary heart disease	n/a	3.9
Adults who have ever been told they had a stroke	n/a	3.0
Adults who have ever been told they have asthma	n/a	14.2
Adults who have ever been told they have arthritis	n/a	24.9
Adults who have ever been told they have diabetes[2]	n/a	10.5
Adults who have ever been told they had skin cancer	n/a	6.2
Adults who have ever been told they had any other types of cancer	n/a	7.1
Adults who have ever been told they have COPD	n/a	6.5
Adults who have ever been told they have kidney disease	n/a	3.0
Adults who have ever been told they have a form of depression	n/a	20.5

Note: n/a not available; (1) Figures cover the Winston-Salem, NC Metropolitan Statistical Area; (2) Figures do not include pregnancy-related, borderline, or pre-diabetes
Source: Centers for Disease Control and Prevention, Behaviorial Risk Factor Surveillance System, SMART: Selected Metropolitan Area Risk Trends, 2017

Health Screening and Vaccination Rates

Category	MSA[1] (%)	U.S. (%)
Adults aged 65+ who have had flu shot within the past year	n/a	60.7
Adults aged 65+ who have ever had a pneumonia vaccination	n/a	75.4
Adults who have ever been tested for HIV	n/a	36.1
Adults who have ever had the shingles or zoster vaccine?	n/a	28.9
Adults who have had their blood cholesterol checked within the last five years	n/a	85.9

Note: n/a not available; (1) Figures cover the Winston-Salem, NC Metropolitan Statistical Area.
Source: Centers for Disease Control and Prevention, Behaviorial Risk Factor Surveillance System, SMART: Selected Metropolitan Area Risk Trends, 2017

Disability Status

Category	MSA[1] (%)	U.S. (%)
Adults who reported being deaf	n/a	6.7
Are you blind or have serious difficulty seeing, even when wearing glasses?	n/a	4.5
Are you limited in any way in any of your usual activities due of arthritis?	n/a	12.9
Do you have difficulty doing errands alone?	n/a	6.8
Do you have difficulty dressing or bathing?	n/a	3.6
Do you have serious difficulty concentrating/remembering/making decisions?	n/a	10.7
Do you have serious difficulty walking or climbing stairs?	n/a	13.6

Note: n/a not available; (1) Figures cover the Winston-Salem, NC Metropolitan Statistical Area.
Source: Centers for Disease Control and Prevention, Behaviorial Risk Factor Surveillance System, SMART: Selected Metropolitan Area Risk Trends, 2017

Mortality Rates for the Top 10 Causes of Death in the U.S.

ICD-10[a] Sub-Chapter	ICD-10[a] Code	Age-Adjusted Mortality Rate[1] per 100,000 population	
		County[2]	U.S.
Malignant neoplasms	C00-C97	155.7	149.2
Ischaemic heart diseases	I20-I25	78.3	90.5
Other forms of heart disease	I30-I51	55.4	52.2
Chronic lower respiratory diseases	J40-J47	44.4	39.6
Other degenerative diseases of the nervous system	G30-G31	42.8	37.6
Cerebrovascular diseases	I60-I69	44.4	37.2
Other external causes of accidental injury	W00-X59	48.9	36.1
Organic, including symptomatic, mental disorders	F01-F09	41.4	29.4
Hypertensive diseases	I10-I15	17.8	24.1
Diabetes mellitus	E10-E14	24.2	21.5

Note: (a) ICD-10 = International Classification of Diseases 10th Revision; (1) Mortality rates are a three-year average covering 2017-2019; (2) Figures cover Forsyth County.
Source: Centers for Disease Control and Prevention, National Center for Health Statistics. Underlying Cause of Death 1999-2019 on CDC WONDER Online Database

Mortality Rates for Selected Causes of Death

ICD-10[a] Sub-Chapter	ICD-10[a] Code	Age-Adjusted Mortality Rate[1] per 100,000 population	
		County[2]	U.S.
Assault	X85-Y09	8.4	6.0
Diseases of the liver	K70-K76	12.6	14.4
Human immunodeficiency virus (HIV) disease	B20-B24	2.4	1.5
Influenza and pneumonia	J09-J18	15.3	13.8
Intentional self-harm	X60-X84	10.9	14.1
Malnutrition	E40-E46	2.4	2.3
Obesity and other hyperalimentation	E65-E68	3.1	2.1
Renal failure	N17-N19	16.6	12.6
Transport accidents	V01-V99	12.1	12.3
Viral hepatitis	B15-B19	Unreliable	1.2

Note: (a) ICD-10 = International Classification of Diseases 10th Revision; (1) Mortality rates are a three-year average covering 2017-2019; (2) Figures cover Forsyth County; Data are suppressed when the data meet the criteria for confidentiality constraints; Mortality rates are flagged as unreliable when the rate would be calculated with a numerator of 20 or less.
Source: Centers for Disease Control and Prevention, National Center for Health Statistics. Underlying Cause of Death 1999-2019 on CDC WONDER Online Database

Health Insurance Coverage

Area	With Health Insurance	With Private Health Insurance	With Public Health Insurance	Without Health Insurance	Population Under Age 19 Without Health Insurance
City	87.6	62.4	36.3	12.4	4.9
MSA[1]	89.1	66.0	35.7	10.9	4.9
U.S.	91.2	67.9	35.1	8.8	5.1

Note: Figures are percentages that cover the civilian noninstitutionalized population; (1) Figures cover the Winston-Salem, NC Metropolitan Statistical Area
Source: U.S. Census Bureau, 2015-2019 American Community Survey 5-Year Estimates

Number of Medical Professionals

Area	MDs[3]	DOs[3,4]	Dentists	Podiatrists	Chiropractors	Optometrists
County[1] (number)	2,504	111	238	22	63	68
County[1] (rate[2])	660.3	29.3	62.3	5.8	16.5	17.8
U.S. (rate[2])	282.9	22.7	71.2	6.2	28.1	16.9

37067

Note: Data as of 2019 unless noted; (1) Data covers Forsyth County; (2) Rate per 100,000 population; (3) Data as of 2018 and includes all active, non-federal physicians; (4) Doctor of Osteopathic Medicine
Source: U.S. Department of Health and Human Services, Health Resources and Services Administration, Bureau of Health Professions, Area Resource File (ARF) 2019-2020

EDUCATION

Public School District Statistics

District Name	Schls	Pupils	Pupil/ Teacher Ratio	Minority Pupils[1] (%)	Free Lunch Eligible[2] (%)	IEP[3] (%)
Winston Salem/Forsyth Co. Schls	79	54,707	14.5	62.8	58.5	13.6

Note: Table includes school districts with 2,000 or more students; (1) Percentage of students that are not non-Hispanic white; (2) Percentage of students that are eligible for the free lunch program; (3) Percentage of students that have an Individualized Education Program.
Source: U.S. Department of Education, National Center for Education Statistics, Common Core of Data, Local Education Agency (School District) Universe Survey: School Year 2018-2019; U.S. Department of Education, National Center for Education Statistics, Common Core of Data, Public Elementary/Secondary School Universe Survey: School Year 2018-2019

Highest Level of Education

Area	Less than H.S.	H.S. Diploma	Some College, No Deg.	Associate Degree	Bachelor's Degree	Master's Degree	Prof. School Degree	Doctorate Degree
City	11.8	24.9	21.5	7.4	20.8	8.9	3.0	1.9
MSA[1]	13.0	29.4	21.6	9.3	17.4	6.5	1.6	1.2
U.S.	12.0	27.0	20.4	8.5	19.8	8.8	2.1	1.4

Note: Figures cover persons age 25 and over; (1) Figures cover the Winston-Salem, NC Metropolitan Statistical Area
Source: U.S. Census Bureau, 2015-2019 American Community Survey 5-Year Estimates

Educational Attainment by Race

Area	High School Graduate or Higher (%)					Bachelor's Degree or Higher (%)				
	Total	White	Black	Asian	Hisp.[2]	Total	White	Black	Asian	Hisp.[2]
City	88.2	89.9	87.8	87.7	58.1	34.5	41.8	21.0	65.7	13.5
MSA[1]	87.0	87.9	86.9	87.2	56.7	26.6	27.7	20.6	54.6	12.2
U.S.	88.0	89.9	86.0	87.1	68.7	32.1	33.5	21.6	54.3	16.4

Note: Figures shown cover persons 25 years old and over; (1) Figures cover the Winston-Salem, NC Metropolitan Statistical Area; (2) People of Hispanic origin can be of any race
Source: U.S. Census Bureau, 2015-2019 American Community Survey 5-Year Estimates

School Enrollment by Grade and Control

Area	Preschool (%)		Kindergarten (%)		Grades 1 - 4 (%)		Grades 5 - 8 (%)		Grades 9 - 12 (%)	
	Public	Private	Public	Private	Public	Private	Public	Private	Public	Private
City	55.3	44.7	94.1	5.9	93.3	6.7	90.8	9.2	93.2	6.8
MSA[1]	56.2	43.8	91.8	8.2	93.0	7.0	90.3	9.7	90.8	9.2
U.S.	59.1	40.9	87.6	12.4	89.5	10.5	89.4	10.6	90.1	9.9

Note: Figures shown cover persons 3 years old and over; (1) Figures cover the Winston-Salem, NC Metropolitan Statistical Area
Source: U.S. Census Bureau, 2015-2019 American Community Survey 5-Year Estimates

Higher Education

Four-Year Colleges			Two-Year Colleges			Medical Schools[1]	Law Schools[2]	Voc/ Tech[3]
Public	Private Non-profit	Private For-profit	Public	Private Non-profit	Private For-profit			
1	3	0	1	0	0	1	1	2

Note: Figures cover institutions located within the city limits and include main campuses only; (1) includes schools accredited by the Liaison Committee on Medical Education and the American Osteopathic Association's Commission on Osteopathic College Accreditation; (2) includes ABA-accredited schools, schools with provisional ABA accreditation, and state accredited schools; (3) includes all schools with programs that are less than 2 years.
Source: National Center for Education Statistics, Integrated Postsecondary Education System (IPEDS), 2019-20; Wikipedia, List of Medical Schools in the United States, accessed April 2, 2021; Wikipedia, List of Law Schools in the United States, accessed April 2, 2021

According to *U.S. News & World Report*, the Winston-Salem, NC metro area is home to one of the top 200 national universities in the U.S.: **Wake Forest University** (#28 tie). The indicators used to capture academic quality fall into a number of categories: assessment by administrators at peer institutions; retention of students; faculty resources; student selectivity; financial resources; alumni giving; high school counselor ratings of colleges; and graduation rate. *U.S. News & World Report, "America's Best Colleges 2021"*

According to *U.S. News & World Report*, the Winston-Salem, NC metro area is home to one of the top 100 law schools in the U.S.: **Wake Forest University** (#41 tie). The rankings are based on a weighted average of 12 measures of quality: peer assessment score; assessment score by lawyers/judges; median LSAT scores; median undergrad GPA; acceptance rate; employment rates for graduates; placement success; bar passage rate; faculty resources; expenditures per student; student/faculty ratio; and library resources. *U.S. News & World Report, "America's Best Graduate Schools, Law, 2022"*

According to *U.S. News & World Report,* the Winston-Salem, NC metro area is home to one of the top 75 medical schools for research in the U.S.: **Wake Forest University** (#48 tie). The rankings are based on a weighted average of 11 measures of quality: quality assessment; peer assessment score; assessment score by residency directors; research activity; total research activity; average research activity per faculty member; student selectivity; median MCAT total score; median undergraduate GPA; acceptance rate; and faculty resources. *U.S. News & World Report, "America's Best Graduate Schools, Medical, 2022"*

EMPLOYERS

Major Employers

Company Name	Industry
B/E Aerospace	Aerospace manufacturing
BB&T	Financial services headquarters
City of Winston-Salem	Municipal government
Deere-Hitachi	Machinery manufacturing
Forsyth Medical Center and Affiliates	Medical center & health services
Forsyth Technical Community College	Education
Hanesbrands	Apparel manufacturing
Lowes Food Stores	Retail grocery
Pepsi	Consumer goods operations
Reynolds American	Tobacco manufacturing
Wake Forest Baptist Medical Center	Academic medical center
Wake Forest University	Education
Wells Fargo	Financial services
Winston-Salem State University	Education
Winston-Salem/Forsyth County Schools	Educational system

Note: Companies shown are located within the Winston-Salem, NC Metropolitan Statistical Area.
Source: Hoovers.com; Wikipedia

PUBLIC SAFETY

Crime Rate

Area	All Crimes	Violent Crimes				Property Crimes		
		Murder	Rape[3]	Robbery	Aggrav. Assault	Burglary	Larceny -Theft	Motor Vehicle Theft
City	n/a	n/a	n/a	n/a	n/a	n/a	n/a	n/a
Suburbs[1]	n/a	n/a	n/a	n/a	n/a	n/a	n/a	n/a
Metro[2]	n/a	n/a	n/a	n/a	n/a	n/a	n/a	n/a
U.S.	2,593.1	5.0	44.0	86.1	248.2	378.0	1,601.6	230.2

Note: Figures are crimes per 100,000 population; (1) All areas within the metro area that are located outside the city limits; (2) Figures cover the Winston-Salem, NC Metropolitan Statistical Area; n/a not available; (3) All figures shown were reported using the revised Uniform Crime Reporting (UCR) definition of rape.
Source: FBI Uniform Crime Reports, 2018 (data for 2019 was not available)

Hate Crimes

Area	Number of Quarters Reported	Number of Incidents per Bias Motivation					
		Race/Ethnicity/ Ancestry	Religion	Sexual Orientation	Disability	Gender	Gender Identity
City	n/a	n/a	n/a	n/a	n/a	n/a	n/a
U.S.	4	3,963	1,521	1,195	157	69	198

Note: n/a not available.
Source: Federal Bureau of Investigation, Hate Crime Statistics 2019

Identity Theft Consumer Reports

Area	Reports	Reports per 100,000 Population	Rank[2]
MSA[1]	1,390	206	202
U.S.	1,387,615	423	-

Note: (1) Figures cover the Winston-Salem, NC Metropolitan Statistical Area; (2) Rank ranges from 1 to 391 where 1 indicates greatest number of identity theft reports per 100,000 population
Source: Federal Trade Commission, Consumer Sentinel Network Data Book 2020

Fraud and Other Consumer Reports

Area	Reports	Reports per 100,000 Population	Rank[2]
MSA[1]	4,696	695	192
U.S.	3,385,133	1,031	-

Note: (1) Figures cover the Winston-Salem, NC Metropolitan Statistical Area; (2) Rank ranges from 1 to 391 where 1 indicates greatest number of fraud and other consumer reports per 100,000 population
Source: Federal Trade Commission, Consumer Sentinel Network Data Book 2020

POLITICS

2020 Presidential Election Results

Area	Biden	Trump	Jorgensen	Hawkins	Other
Forsyth County	56.2	42.3	0.9	0.2	0.4
U.S.	51.3	46.8	1.2	0.3	0.5

Note: Results are percentages and may not add to 100% due to rounding
Source: Dave Leip's Atlas of U.S. Presidential Elections

SPORTS

Professional Sports Teams

Team Name	League	Year Established
No teams are located in the metro area		

Source: Wikipedia, Major Professional Sports Teams of the United States and Canada, April 6, 2021

CLIMATE

Average and Extreme Temperatures

Temperature	Jan	Feb	Mar	Apr	May	Jun	Jul	Aug	Sep	Oct	Nov	Dec	Yr.
Extreme High (°F)	78	81	89	91	96	102	102	103	100	95	85	78	103
Average High (°F)	48	51	60	70	78	84	87	86	80	70	60	50	69
Average Temp. (°F)	38	41	49	58	67	74	78	76	70	59	49	40	58
Average Low (°F)	28	30	37	46	55	63	67	66	59	47	37	30	47
Extreme Low (°F)	-8	-1	5	23	32	42	49	45	37	20	10	0	-8

Note: Figures cover the years 1948-1990
Source: National Climatic Data Center, International Station Meteorological Climate Summary, 9/96

Average Precipitation/Snowfall/Humidity

Precip./Humidity	Jan	Feb	Mar	Apr	May	Jun	Jul	Aug	Sep	Oct	Nov	Dec	Yr.
Avg. Precip. (in.)	3.2	3.4	3.7	3.1	3.7	3.8	4.5	4.2	3.4	3.4	2.9	3.3	42.5
Avg. Snowfall (in.)	4	3	2	Tr	0	0	0	0	0	0	Tr	1	10
Avg. Rel. Hum. 7am (%)	80	78	78	77	82	84	87	90	90	88	83	80	83
Avg. Rel. Hum. 4pm (%)	53	50	47	44	51	54	57	58	56	51	51	54	52

Note: Figures cover the years 1948-1990; Tr = Trace amounts (<0.05 in. of rain; <0.5 in. of snow)
Source: National Climatic Data Center, International Station Meteorological Climate Summary, 9/96

Weather Conditions

Temperature			Daytime Sky			Precipitation		
10°F & below	32°F & below	90°F & above	Clear	Partly cloudy	Cloudy	0.01 inch or more precip.	0.1 inch or more snow/ice	Thunderstorms
3	85	32	94	143	128	113	5	43

Note: Figures are average number of days per year and cover the years 1948-1990
Source: National Climatic Data Center, International Station Meteorological Climate Summary, 9/96

HAZARDOUS WASTE

Superfund Sites

The Winston-Salem, NC metro area is home to one site on the EPA's Superfund National Priorities List: **Holcomb Creosote Co** (final). There are a total of 1,375 Superfund sites with a status of proposed or final on the list in the U.S. *U.S. Environmental Protection Agency, National Priorities List, April 7, 2021*

AIR QUALITY

Air Quality Trends: Ozone

	1990	1995	2000	2005	2010	2015	2016	2017	2018	2019
MSA[1]	0.084	0.086	0.089	0.080	0.078	0.065	0.069	0.066	0.064	0.062
U.S.	0.088	0.089	0.082	0.080	0.073	0.068	0.069	0.068	0.069	0.065

Note: (1) Data covers the Winston-Salem, NC Metropolitan Statistical Area. The values shown are the composite ozone concentration averages among trend sites based on the highest fourth daily maximum 8-hour concentration in parts per million. These trends are based on sites having an adequate record of monitoring data during the trend period. Data from exceptional events are included.
Source: U.S. Environmental Protection Agency, Air Quality Monitoring Information, "Air Quality Trends by City, 1990-2019"

Air Quality Index

Area	Percent of Days when Air Quality was...[2]					AQI Statistics[2]	
	Good	Moderate	Unhealthy for Sensitive Groups	Unhealthy	Very Unhealthy	Maximum	Median
MSA[1]	61.6	38.4	0.0	0.0	0.0	97	45

Note: (1) Data covers the Winston-Salem, NC Metropolitan Statistical Area; (2) Based on 365 days with AQI data in 2019. Air Quality Index (AQI) is an index for reporting daily air quality. EPA calculates the AQI for five major air pollutants regulated by the Clean Air Act: ground-level ozone, particle pollution (aka particulate matter), carbon monoxide, sulfur dioxide, and nitrogen dioxide. The AQI runs from 0 to 500. The higher the AQI value, the greater the level of air pollution and the greater the health concern. There are six AQI categories: "Good" AQI is between 0 and 50. Air quality is considered satisfactory; "Moderate" AQI is between 51 and 100. Air quality is acceptable; "Unhealthy for Sensitive Groups" When AQI values are between 101 and 150, members of sensitive groups may experience health effects; "Unhealthy" When AQI values are between 151 and 200 everyone may begin to experience health effects; "Very Unhealthy" AQI values between 201 and 300 trigger a health alert; "Hazardous" AQI values over 300 trigger warnings of emergency conditions (not shown).
Source: U.S. Environmental Protection Agency, Air Quality Index Report, 2019

Air Quality Index Pollutants

Area	Percent of Days when AQI Pollutant was...[2]					
	Carbon Monoxide	Nitrogen Dioxide	Ozone	Sulfur Dioxide	Particulate Matter 2.5	Particulate Matter 10
MSA[1]	0.0	2.7	47.1	0.0	50.1	0.0

Note: (1) Data covers the Winston-Salem, NC Metropolitan Statistical Area; (2) Based on 365 days with AQI data in 2019. The Air Quality Index (AQI) is an index for reporting daily air quality. EPA calculates the AQI for five major air pollutants regulated by the Clean Air Act: ground-level ozone, particle pollution (also known as particulate matter), carbon monoxide, sulfur dioxide, and nitrogen dioxide. The AQI runs from 0 to 500. The higher the AQI value, the greater the level of air pollution and the greater the health concern.
Source: U.S. Environmental Protection Agency, Air Quality Index Report, 2019

Maximum Air Pollutant Concentrations: Particulate Matter, Ozone, CO and Lead

	Particulate Matter 10 (ug/m^3)	Particulate Matter 2.5 Wtd AM (ug/m^3)	Particulate Matter 2.5 24-Hr (ug/m^3)	Ozone (ppm)	Carbon Monoxide (ppm)	Lead (ug/m^3)
MSA[1] Level	33	9.5	24	0.065	n/a	n/a
NAAQS[2]	150	15	35	0.075	9	0.15
Met NAAQS[2]	Yes	Yes	Yes	Yes	n/a	n/a

Note: (1) Data covers the Winston-Salem, NC Metropolitan Statistical Area; Data from exceptional events are included; (2) National Ambient Air Quality Standards; ppm = parts per million; ug/m³ = micrograms per cubic meter; n/a not available.
Concentrations: Particulate Matter 10 (coarse particulate)—highest second maximum 24-hour concentration; Particulate Matter 2.5 Wtd AM (fine particulate)—highest weighted annual mean concentration; Particulate Matter 2.5 24-Hour (fine particulate)—highest 98th percentile 24-hour concentration; Ozone—highest fourth daily maximum 8-hour concentration; Carbon Monoxide—highest second maximum non-overlapping 8-hour concentration; Lead—maximum running 3-month average
Source: U.S. Environmental Protection Agency, Air Quality Monitoring Information, "Air Quality Statistics by City, 2019"

Maximum Air Pollutant Concentrations: Nitrogen Dioxide and Sulfur Dioxide

	Nitrogen Dioxide AM (ppb)	Nitrogen Dioxide 1-Hr (ppb)	Sulfur Dioxide AM (ppb)	Sulfur Dioxide 1-Hr (ppb)	Sulfur Dioxide 24-Hr (ppb)
MSA[1] Level	7	34	n/a	5	n/a
NAAQS[2]	53	100	30	75	140
Met NAAQS[2]	Yes	Yes	n/a	Yes	n/a

Note: (1) Data covers the Winston-Salem, NC Metropolitan Statistical Area; Data from exceptional events are included; (2) National Ambient Air Quality Standards; ppm = parts per million; ug/m³ = micrograms per cubic meter; n/a not available.
Concentrations: Nitrogen Dioxide AM—highest arithmetic mean concentration; Nitrogen Dioxide 1-Hr—highest 98th percentile 1-hour daily maximum concentration; Sulfur Dioxide AM—highest annual mean concentration; Sulfur Dioxide 1-Hr—highest 99th percentile 1-hour daily maximum concentration; Sulfur Dioxide 24-Hr—highest second maximum 24-hour concentration
Source: U.S. Environmental Protection Agency, Air Quality Monitoring Information, "Air Quality Statistics by City, 2019"

Appendixes

Appendix A: Comparative Statistics

Table of Contents

Population Growth: City

Area	1990 Census	2000 Census	2010 Census	2019* Estimate	Population Growth (%)	
					1990-2019	2010-2019
Albuquerque, NM	388,375	448,607	545,852	559,374	44.0	2.5
Allentown, PA	105,066	106,632	118,032	120,915	15.1	2.4
Anchorage, AK	226,338	260,283	291,826	293,531	29.7	0.6
Ann Arbor, MI	111,018	114,024	113,934	120,735	8.8	6.0
Athens, GA	86,561	100,266	115,452	124,719	44.1	8.0
Atlanta, GA	394,092	416,474	420,003	488,800	24.0	16.4
Austin, TX	499,053	656,562	790,390	950,807	90.5	20.3
Baton Rouge, LA	223,299	227,818	229,493	224,149	0.4	-2.3
Boise City, ID	144,317	185,787	205,671	226,115	56.7	9.9
Boston, MA	574,283	589,141	617,594	684,379	19.2	10.8
Boulder, CO	87,737	94,673	97,385	106,392	21.3	9.2
Cape Coral, FL	75,507	102,286	154,305	183,942	143.6	19.2
Cedar Rapids, IA	110,829	120,758	126,326	132,301	19.4	4.7
Charleston, SC	96,102	96,650	120,083	135,257	40.7	12.6
Charlotte, NC	428,283	540,828	731,424	857,425	100.2	17.2
Chicago, IL	2,783,726	2,896,016	2,695,598	2,709,534	-2.7	0.5
Cincinnati, OH	363,974	331,285	296,943	301,394	-17.2	1.5
Clarksville, TN	78,569	103,455	132,929	152,934	94.6	15.0
Cleveland, OH	505,333	478,403	396,815	385,282	-23.8	-2.9
College Station, TX	53,318	67,890	93,857	113,686	113.2	21.1
Colorado Springs, CO	283,798	360,890	416,427	464,871	63.8	11.6
Columbia, MO	71,069	84,531	108,500	121,230	70.6	11.7
Columbia, SC	115,475	116,278	129,272	133,273	15.4	3.1
Columbus, OH	648,656	711,470	787,033	878,553	35.4	11.6
Dallas, TX	1,006,971	1,188,580	1,197,816	1,330,612	32.1	11.1
Davenport, IA	95,705	98,359	99,685	102,169	6.8	2.5
Denver, CO	467,153	554,636	600,158	705,576	51.0	17.6
Des Moines, IA	193,569	198,682	203,433	215,636	11.4	6.0
Durham, NC	151,737	187,035	228,330	269,702	77.7	18.1
Edison, NJ	88,680	97,687	99,967	100,447	13.3	0.5
El Paso, TX	515,541	563,662	649,121	679,813	31.9	4.7
Fargo, ND	74,372	90,599	105,549	121,889	63.9	15.5
Fayetteville, NC	118,247	121,015	200,564	210,432	78.0	4.9
Fort Collins, CO	89,555	118,652	143,986	165,609	84.9	15.0
Fort Wayne, IN	205,671	205,727	253,691	265,752	29.2	4.8
Fort Worth, TX	448,311	534,694	741,206	874,401	95.0	18.0
Grand Rapids, MI	189,145	197,800	188,040	198,401	4.9	5.5
Greeley, CO	60,887	76,930	92,889	105,888	73.9	14.0
Green Bay, WI	96,466	102,313	104,057	104,777	8.6	0.7
Greensboro, NC	193,389	223,891	269,666	291,303	50.6	8.0
Honolulu, HI	376,465	371,657	337,256	348,985	-7.3	3.5
Houston, TX	1,697,610	1,953,631	2,099,451	2,310,432	36.1	10.0
Huntsville, AL	161,842	158,216	180,105	196,219	21.2	8.9
Indianapolis, IN	730,993	781,870	820,445	864,447	18.3	5.4
Jacksonville, FL	635,221	735,617	821,784	890,467	40.2	8.4
Kansas City, MO	434,967	441,545	459,787	486,404	11.8	5.8
Lafayette, LA	104,735	110,257	120,623	126,666	20.9	5.0
Lakeland, FL	73,375	78,452	97,422	107,922	47.1	10.8
Las Vegas, NV	261,374	478,434	583,756	634,773	142.9	8.7
Lexington, KY	225,366	260,512	295,803	320,601	42.3	8.4
Lincoln, NE	193,629	225,581	258,379	283,839	46.6	9.9
Little Rock, AR	177,519	183,133	193,524	197,958	11.5	2.3
Los Angeles, CA	3,487,671	3,694,820	3,792,621	3,966,936	13.7	4.6
Louisville, KY	269,160	256,231	597,337	617,790	129.5	3.4
Madison, WI	193,451	208,054	233,209	254,977	31.8	9.3

Table continued on following page.

Area	1990 Census	2000 Census	2010 Census	2019* Estimate	Population Growth (%)	
					1990-2019	2010-2019
Manchester, NH	99,567	107,006	109,565	112,109	12.6	2.3
Memphis, TN	660,536	650,100	646,889	651,932	-1.3	0.8
Miami, FL	358,843	362,470	399,457	454,279	26.6	13.7
Midland, TX	89,358	94,996	111,147	138,549	55.0	24.7
Milwaukee, WI	628,095	596,974	594,833	594,548	-5.3	0.0
Minneapolis, MN	368,383	382,618	382,578	420,324	14.1	9.9
Nashville, TN	488,364	545,524	601,222	663,750	35.9	10.4
New Haven, CT	130,474	123,626	129,779	130,331	-0.1	0.4
New Orleans, LA	496,938	484,674	343,829	390,845	-21.3	13.7
New York, NY	7,322,552	8,008,278	8,175,133	8,419,316	15.0	3.0
Oklahoma City, OK	445,065	506,132	579,999	643,692	44.6	11.0
Omaha, NE	371,972	390,007	408,958	475,862	27.9	16.4
Orlando, FL	161,172	185,951	238,300	280,832	74.2	17.8
Peoria, IL	114,341	112,936	115,007	113,532	-0.7	-1.3
Philadelphia, PA	1,585,577	1,517,550	1,526,006	1,579,075	-0.4	3.5
Phoenix, AZ	989,873	1,321,045	1,445,632	1,633,017	65.0	13.0
Pittsburgh, PA	369,785	334,563	305,704	302,205	-18.3	-1.1
Portland, OR	485,833	529,121	583,776	645,291	32.8	10.5
Providence, RI	160,734	173,618	178,042	179,494	11.7	0.8
Provo, UT	87,148	105,166	112,488	116,403	33.6	3.5
Raleigh, NC	226,841	276,093	403,892	464,485	104.8	15.0
Reno, NV	139,950	180,480	225,221	246,500	76.1	9.4
Richmond, VA	202,783	197,790	204,214	226,622	11.8	11.0
Riverside, CA	226,232	255,166	303,871	326,414	44.3	7.4
Rochester, MN	74,151	85,806	106,769	115,557	55.8	8.2
Sacramento, CA	368,923	407,018	466,488	500,930	35.8	7.4
Salt Lake City, UT	159,796	181,743	186,440	197,756	23.8	6.1
San Antonio, TX	997,258	1,144,646	1,327,407	1,508,083	51.2	13.6
San Diego, CA	1,111,048	1,223,400	1,307,402	1,409,573	26.9	7.8
San Francisco, CA	723,959	776,733	805,235	874,961	20.9	8.7
San Jose, CA	784,324	894,943	945,942	1,027,690	31.0	8.6
Santa Rosa, CA	123,297	147,595	167,815	179,701	45.7	7.1
Savannah, GA	138,038	131,510	136,286	145,403	5.3	6.7
Seattle, WA	516,262	563,374	608,660	724,305	40.3	19.0
Sioux Falls, SD	102,262	123,975	153,888	177,117	73.2	15.1
Springfield, IL	108,997	111,454	116,250	115,888	6.3	-0.3
Tallahassee, FL	128,014	150,624	181,376	191,279	49.4	5.5
Tampa, FL	279,960	303,447	335,709	387,916	38.6	15.6
Tucson, AZ	417,942	486,699	520,116	541,482	29.6	4.1
Tulsa, OK	367,241	393,049	391,906	402,324	9.6	2.7
Tuscaloosa, AL	81,075	77,906	90,468	99,390	22.6	9.9
Virginia Beach, VA	393,069	425,257	437,994	450,201	14.5	2.8
Washington, DC	606,900	572,059	601,723	692,683	14.1	15.1
Wichita, KS	313,693	344,284	382,368	389,877	24.3	2.0
Winston-Salem, NC	168,139	185,776	229,617	244,115	45.2	6.3
U.S.	248,709,873	281,421,906	308,745,538	324,697,795	30.6	5.2

Note: (*) 2014-2019 5-year estimated population
Source: U.S. Census Bureau, 1990 Census, Census 2000, Census 2010, 2015-2019 American Community Survey 5-Year Estimates

Population Growth: Metro Area

Area	1990 Census	2000 Census	2010 Census	2019* Estimate	Population Growth (%)	
					1990-2019	2010-2019
Albuquerque, NM	599,416	729,649	887,077	912,108	52.2	2.8
Allentown, PA	686,666	740,395	821,173	837,610	22.0	2.0
Anchorage, AK	266,021	319,605	380,821	398,900	50.0	4.7
Ann Arbor, MI	282,937	322,895	344,791	367,000	29.7	6.4
Athens, GA	136,025	166,079	192,541	208,457	53.2	8.3
Atlanta, GA	3,069,411	4,247,981	5,268,860	5,862,424	91.0	11.3
Austin, TX	846,217	1,249,763	1,716,289	2,114,441	149.9	23.2
Baton Rouge, LA	623,853	705,973	802,484	854,318	36.9	6.5
Boise City, ID	319,596	464,840	616,561	710,743	122.4	15.3
Boston, MA	4,133,895	4,391,344	4,552,402	4,832,346	16.9	6.1
Boulder, CO	208,898	269,758	294,567	322,510	54.4	9.5
Cape Coral, FL	335,113	440,888	618,754	737,468	120.1	19.2
Cedar Rapids, IA	210,640	237,230	257,940	270,056	28.2	4.7
Charleston, SC	506,875	549,033	664,607	774,508	52.8	16.5
Charlotte, NC	1,024,331	1,330,448	1,758,038	2,545,560	148.5	44.8
Chicago, IL	8,182,076	9,098,316	9,461,105	9,508,605	16.2	0.5
Cincinnati, OH	1,844,917	2,009,632	2,130,151	2,201,741	19.3	3.4
Clarksville, TN	189,277	232,000	273,949	299,470	58.2	9.3
Cleveland, OH	2,102,219	2,148,143	2,077,240	2,056,898	-2.2	-1.0
College Station, TX	150,998	184,885	228,660	258,029	70.9	12.8
Colorado Springs, CO	409,482	537,484	645,613	723,498	76.7	12.1
Columbia, MO	122,010	145,666	172,786	205,369	68.3	18.9
Columbia, SC	548,325	647,158	767,598	824,278	50.3	7.4
Columbus, OH	1,405,176	1,612,694	1,836,536	2,077,761	47.9	13.1
Dallas, TX	3,989,294	5,161,544	6,371,773	7,320,663	83.5	14.9
Davenport, IA	368,151	376,019	379,690	381,175	3.5	0.4
Denver, CO	1,666,935	2,179,296	2,543,482	2,892,066	73.5	13.7
Des Moines, IA	416,346	481,394	569,633	680,439	63.4	19.5
Durham, NC	344,646	426,493	504,357	626,695	81.8	24.3
Edison, NJ	16,845,992	18,323,002	18,897,109	19,294,236	14.5	2.1
El Paso, TX	591,610	679,622	800,647	840,477	42.1	5.0
Fargo, ND	153,296	174,367	208,777	240,421	56.8	15.2
Fayetteville, NC	297,422	336,609	366,383	519,101	74.5	41.7
Fort Collins, CO	186,136	251,494	299,630	344,786	85.2	15.1
Fort Wayne, IN	354,435	390,156	416,257	406,305	14.6	-2.4
Fort Worth, TX	3,989,294	5,161,544	6,371,773	7,320,663	83.5	14.9
Grand Rapids, MI	645,914	740,482	774,160	1,062,392	64.5	37.2
Greeley, CO	131,816	180,926	252,825	305,345	131.6	20.8
Green Bay, WI	243,698	282,599	306,241	319,401	31.1	4.3
Greensboro, NC	540,257	643,430	723,801	762,063	41.1	5.3
Honolulu, HI	836,231	876,156	953,207	984,821	17.8	3.3
Houston, TX	3,767,335	4,715,407	5,946,800	6,884,138	82.7	15.8
Huntsville, AL	293,047	342,376	417,593	457,003	55.9	9.4
Indianapolis, IN	1,294,217	1,525,104	1,756,241	2,029,472	56.8	15.6
Jacksonville, FL	925,213	1,122,750	1,345,596	1,503,574	62.5	11.7
Kansas City, MO	1,636,528	1,836,038	2,035,334	2,124,518	29.8	4.4
Lafayette, LA	208,740	239,086	273,738	489,914	134.7	79.0
Lakeland, FL	405,382	483,924	602,095	686,218	69.3	14.0
Las Vegas, NV	741,459	1,375,765	1,951,269	2,182,004	194.3	11.8
Lexington, KY	348,428	408,326	472,099	510,647	46.6	8.2
Lincoln, NE	229,091	266,787	302,157	330,329	44.2	9.3
Little Rock, AR	535,034	610,518	699,757	737,015	37.8	5.3
Los Angeles, CA	11,273,720	12,365,627	12,828,837	13,249,614	17.5	3.3
Louisville, KY	1,055,973	1,161,975	1,283,566	1,257,088	19.0	-2.1
Madison, WI	432,323	501,774	568,593	653,725	51.2	15.0

Table continued on following page.

Area	1990 Census	2000 Census	2010 Census	2019* Estimate	Population Growth (%)	
					1990-2019	2010-2019
Manchester, NH	336,073	380,841	400,721	413,035	22.9	3.1
Memphis, TN	1,067,263	1,205,204	1,316,100	1,339,623	25.5	1.8
Miami, FL	4,056,100	5,007,564	5,564,635	6,090,660	50.2	9.5
Midland, TX	106,611	116,009	136,872	173,816	63.0	27.0
Milwaukee, WI	1,432,149	1,500,741	1,555,908	1,575,223	10.0	1.2
Minneapolis, MN	2,538,834	2,968,806	3,279,833	3,573,609	40.8	9.0
Nashville, TN	1,048,218	1,311,789	1,589,934	1,871,903	78.6	17.7
New Haven, CT	804,219	824,008	862,477	857,513	6.6	-0.6
New Orleans, LA	1,264,391	1,316,510	1,167,764	1,267,777	0.3	8.6
New York, NY	16,845,992	18,323,002	18,897,109	19,294,236	14.5	2.1
Oklahoma City, OK	971,042	1,095,421	1,252,987	1,382,841	42.4	10.4
Omaha, NE	685,797	767,041	865,350	931,779	35.9	7.7
Orlando, FL	1,224,852	1,644,561	2,134,411	2,508,970	104.8	17.5
Peoria, IL	358,552	366,899	379,186	406,883	13.5	7.3
Philadelphia, PA	5,435,470	5,687,147	5,965,343	6,079,130	11.8	1.9
Phoenix, AZ	2,238,480	3,251,876	4,192,887	4,761,603	112.7	13.6
Pittsburgh, PA	2,468,289	2,431,087	2,356,285	2,331,447	-5.5	-1.1
Portland, OR	1,523,741	1,927,881	2,226,009	2,445,761	60.5	9.9
Providence, RI	1,509,789	1,582,997	1,600,852	1,618,268	7.2	1.1
Provo, UT	269,407	376,774	526,810	616,791	128.9	17.1
Raleigh, NC	541,081	797,071	1,130,490	1,332,311	146.2	17.9
Reno, NV	257,193	342,885	425,417	460,924	79.2	8.3
Richmond, VA	949,244	1,096,957	1,258,251	1,269,530	33.7	0.9
Riverside, CA	2,588,793	3,254,821	4,224,851	4,560,470	76.2	7.9
Rochester, MN	141,945	163,618	186,011	217,964	53.6	17.2
Sacramento, CA	1,481,126	1,796,857	2,149,127	2,315,980	56.4	7.8
Salt Lake City, UT	768,075	968,858	1,124,197	1,201,043	56.4	6.8
San Antonio, TX	1,407,745	1,711,703	2,142,508	2,468,193	75.3	15.2
San Diego, CA	2,498,016	2,813,833	3,095,313	3,316,073	32.7	7.1
San Francisco, CA	3,686,592	4,123,740	4,335,391	4,701,332	27.5	8.4
San Jose, CA	1,534,280	1,735,819	1,836,911	1,987,846	29.6	8.2
Santa Rosa, CA	388,222	458,614	483,878	499,772	28.7	3.3
Savannah, GA	258,060	293,000	347,611	386,036	49.6	11.1
Seattle, WA	2,559,164	3,043,878	3,439,809	3,871,323	51.3	12.5
Sioux Falls, SD	153,500	187,093	228,261	259,348	69.0	13.6
Springfield, IL	189,550	201,437	210,170	209,167	10.3	-0.5
Tallahassee, FL	259,096	320,304	367,413	382,197	47.5	4.0
Tampa, FL	2,067,959	2,395,997	2,783,243	3,097,859	49.8	11.3
Tucson, AZ	666,880	843,746	980,263	1,027,207	54.0	4.8
Tulsa, OK	761,019	859,532	937,478	990,544	30.2	5.7
Tuscaloosa, AL	176,123	192,034	219,461	250,681	42.3	14.2
Virginia Beach, VA	1,449,389	1,576,370	1,671,683	1,761,729	21.5	5.4
Washington, DC	4,122,914	4,796,183	5,582,170	6,196,585	50.3	11.0
Wichita, KS	511,111	571,166	623,061	637,690	24.8	2.3
Winston-Salem, NC	361,091	421,961	477,717	666,216	84.5	39.5
U.S.	248,709,873	281,421,906	308,745,538	324,697,795	30.6	5.2

Note: (*) 2014-2019 5-year estimated population; Figures cover the Metropolitan Statistical Area (MSA)—see Appendix B for areas included

Source: U.S. Census Bureau, 1990 Census, Census 2000, Census 2010, 2015-2019 American Community Survey 5-Year Estimates

Household Size: City

City	Persons in Household (%)							Average Household Size
	One	Two	Three	Four	Five	Six	Seven or More	
Albuquerque, NM	34.6	33.7	13.8	10.7	4.5	1.5	0.8	2.47
Allentown, PA	27.6	28.9	15.4	13.8	8.0	3.6	2.3	2.73
Anchorage, AK	26.3	33.0	16.9	12.5	6.6	2.4	2.0	2.69
Ann Arbor, MI	34.6	37.8	11.7	10.4	3.0	1.5	0.8	2.26
Athens, GA	33.4	35.2	14.5	11.2	3.6	1.4	0.4	2.35
Atlanta, GA	46.7	30.7	10.6	7.2	2.9	1.0	0.6	2.19
Austin, TX	34.5	32.7	14.3	11.3	4.4	1.5	0.9	2.44
Baton Rouge, LA	36.1	32.4	15.6	9.0	4.1	1.7	0.9	2.58
Boise City, ID	34.1	34.1	14.3	10.3	4.6	1.4	0.8	2.43
Boston, MA	36.2	32.4	15.4	9.4	3.9	1.6	0.8	2.36
Boulder, CO	33.8	36.8	14.5	10.9	2.7	0.7	0.3	2.27
Cape Coral, FL	23.7	43.0	14.2	12.3	4.4	1.6	0.5	2.81
Cedar Rapids, IA	34.1	33.9	14.0	10.5	4.4	2.2	0.6	2.33
Charleston, SC	35.4	37.8	14.2	9.0	2.4	0.6	0.1	2.31
Charlotte, NC	32.9	32.2	15.5	11.9	4.8	1.5	0.8	2.56
Chicago, IL	37.1	29.7	13.8	10.2	5.1	2.2	1.5	2.48
Cincinnati, OH	44.3	30.1	12.0	7.5	3.5	1.3	0.8	2.10
Clarksville, TN	24.7	30.7	19.6	15.1	5.8	2.3	1.3	2.66
Cleveland, OH	44.4	27.5	13.1	8.0	4.2	1.6	0.9	2.18
College Station, TX	29.7	33.8	16.5	14.1	3.5	1.8	0.4	2.53
Colorado Springs, CO	28.6	35.1	14.6	12.2	5.8	2.2	1.0	2.52
Columbia, MO	32.7	32.8	15.0	12.9	4.7	1.1	0.4	2.33
Columbia, SC	40.6	33.0	12.3	8.9	3.6	0.8	0.5	2.21
Columbus, OH	35.5	32.4	13.9	10.1	4.8	1.8	1.2	2.39
Dallas, TX	35.3	29.1	13.7	11.2	6.2	2.5	1.7	2.56
Davenport, IA	35.3	33.5	13.1	9.7	5.2	1.8	1.0	2.46
Denver, CO	38.2	32.9	12.0	9.5	4.3	1.6	1.2	2.29
Des Moines, IA	34.1	30.5	14.7	11.4	5.3	2.2	1.5	2.45
Durham, NC	33.9	33.5	15.4	10.1	4.4	1.6	0.8	2.36
Edison, NJ	18.9	29.0	21.1	20.3	6.4	2.5	1.5	2.86
El Paso, TX	25.5	28.5	17.7	15.9	7.5	3.2	1.3	2.97
Fargo, ND	36.4	34.0	14.4	8.9	4.2	1.3	0.5	2.14
Fayetteville, NC	35.6	31.3	15.3	10.7	4.2	1.8	0.8	2.42
Fort Collins, CO	24.7	37.9	17.8	13.8	4.3	0.9	0.4	2.44
Fort Wayne, IN	32.1	33.0	14.3	11.2	5.9	2.2	1.0	2.45
Fort Worth, TX	26.1	28.8	16.5	15.1	7.8	3.3	2.1	2.89
Grand Rapids, MI	33.1	31.4	13.8	11.1	5.9	2.5	1.9	2.53
Greeley, CO	26.0	31.4	16.1	13.3	8.2	3.2	1.3	2.72
Green Bay, WI	34.1	32.1	12.7	11.3	6.5	1.5	1.5	2.39
Greensboro, NC	34.2	33.1	15.4	10.2	4.6	1.4	0.7	2.37
Honolulu, HI	33.4	31.3	14.3	10.6	5.1	2.3	2.6	2.60
Houston, TX	32.3	28.9	15.2	12.3	6.6	2.8	1.7	2.65
Huntsville, AL	35.7	34.3	14.5	9.4	4.1	1.2	0.4	2.21
Indianapolis, IN	37.8	31.3	13.2	9.6	4.9	1.9	1.0	2.51
Jacksonville, FL	30.4	33.7	16.6	11.4	5.0	1.7	0.9	2.57
Kansas City, MO	37.0	31.9	12.9	10.0	4.9	1.8	1.1	2.35
Lafayette, LA	35.1	34.5	13.9	9.5	3.9	1.7	1.0	2.40
Lakeland, FL	33.1	37.5	14.3	8.9	3.6	1.6	0.7	2.50
Las Vegas, NV	30.6	31.6	15.3	11.5	6.2	2.7	1.7	2.70
Lexington, KY	31.5	35.0	15.1	11.2	4.6	1.6	0.6	2.37
Lincoln, NE	31.5	34.8	13.9	11.5	5.2	2.0	0.9	2.38
Little Rock, AR	36.6	32.0	14.0	10.1	4.6	1.8	0.7	2.37
Los Angeles, CA	30.2	28.8	15.3	13.0	6.8	2.9	2.5	2.80
Louisville, KY	33.3	32.9	15.3	10.5	4.8	1.8	1.0	2.43

Table continued on following page.

City	Persons in Household (%)							Average Household Size
	One	Two	Three	Four	Five	Six	Seven or More	
Madison, WI	35.3	36.2	13.2	9.8	3.7	1.1	0.4	2.21
Manchester, NH	31.4	34.1	16.5	10.7	4.4	1.6	1.0	2.37
Memphis, TN	37.1	30.3	14.8	9.8	4.2	2.2	1.3	2.53
Miami, FL	37.3	31.0	16.1	8.8	3.9	1.5	0.9	2.51
Midland, TX	26.1	31.2	16.4	14.4	7.3	3.0	1.3	2.90
Milwaukee, WI	36.3	29.3	14.0	10.4	5.7	2.4	1.6	2.51
Minneapolis, MN	40.4	31.2	11.9	9.5	3.5	1.7	1.5	2.28
Nashville, TN	33.9	33.9	15.2	9.6	4.5	1.6	1.0	2.36
New Haven, CT	38.4	27.3	15.4	9.9	5.3	2.3	1.0	2.46
New Orleans, LA	45.9	29.2	12.6	7.8	2.6	1.0	0.6	2.45
New York, NY	32.2	28.4	16.2	12.5	5.9	2.5	2.0	2.60
Oklahoma City, OK	31.1	32.1	14.5	12.2	6.2	2.5	1.1	2.60
Omaha, NE	32.6	32.0	13.5	11.2	6.0	2.7	1.6	2.48
Orlando, FL	33.6	33.1	16.7	9.8	4.0	1.8	0.6	2.48
Peoria, IL	38.2	31.4	13.3	9.1	5.2	1.7	0.9	2.37
Philadelphia, PA	37.5	29.2	14.7	10.4	4.8	1.9	1.3	2.55
Phoenix, AZ	27.9	30.0	15.2	12.9	7.3	3.7	2.7	2.85
Pittsburgh, PA	43.6	32.4	12.8	6.7	2.5	1.1	0.6	2.02
Portland, OR	34.0	34.8	14.1	10.8	3.8	1.4	0.8	2.34
Providence, RI	33.2	29.0	15.6	11.7	7.0	1.7	1.5	2.67
Provo, UT	13.2	33.1	18.8	16.1	7.9	7.1	3.4	3.17
Raleigh, NC	33.0	32.4	15.2	12.4	4.7	1.3	0.6	2.42
Reno, NV	33.0	33.4	14.6	10.5	5.1	1.8	1.4	2.36
Richmond, VA	43.4	32.8	12.0	6.8	2.9	1.2	0.6	2.39
Riverside, CA	20.4	27.5	17.7	15.5	10.1	4.7	3.8	3.43
Rochester, MN	31.0	33.2	14.4	13.0	4.7	1.8	1.5	2.40
Sacramento, CA	30.9	30.7	14.7	12.1	6.0	2.9	2.3	2.66
Salt Lake City, UT	36.1	32.2	13.5	9.9	4.2	2.0	1.7	2.42
San Antonio, TX	29.9	29.5	16.2	12.9	6.7	2.8	1.7	2.96
San Diego, CA	27.5	33.4	16.1	13.1	5.7	2.3	1.5	2.70
San Francisco, CA	35.6	33.6	14.3	9.7	3.7	1.4	1.3	2.36
San Jose, CA	19.4	28.8	18.6	17.9	8.1	3.5	3.4	3.12
Santa Rosa, CA	28.2	32.6	15.3	13.2	6.2	2.3	2.0	2.66
Savannah, GA	33.5	34.0	15.6	9.8	4.3	1.4	1.0	2.55
Seattle, WA	38.5	35.6	12.5	8.8	2.9	0.8	0.6	2.11
Sioux Falls, SD	32.0	34.0	13.0	12.2	5.3	2.0	1.1	2.37
Springfield, IL	38.0	34.0	13.3	8.7	3.1	1.4	1.0	2.20
Tallahassee, FL	35.0	33.0	16.8	10.2	3.6	0.9	0.1	2.33
Tampa, FL	35.7	31.5	15.3	10.8	4.2	1.5	0.6	2.47
Tucson, AZ	34.6	31.2	14.7	10.8	5.1	2.0	1.3	2.42
Tulsa, OK	35.1	32.5	13.6	10.2	5.1	2.1	1.1	2.41
Tuscaloosa, AL	35.4	33.7	15.9	9.9	3.4	1.0	0.4	2.55
Virginia Beach, VA	24.4	34.4	17.5	14.8	5.8	1.9	0.8	2.58
Washington, DC	44.0	31.0	11.7	7.8	3.1	1.2	0.8	2.30
Wichita, KS	33.3	31.3	13.4	11.3	6.5	2.7	1.2	2.51
Winston-Salem, NC	35.7	31.5	15.0	9.4	5.2	1.8	1.1	2.46
U.S.	27.8	33.9	15.5	12.9	5.9	2.2	1.4	2.62

U.S. Census Bureau, 2015-2019 American Community Survey 5-Year Estimates

Household Size: Metro Area

Metro Area	Persons in Household (%)							Average Household Size
	One	Two	Three	Four	Five	Six	Seven or More	
Albuquerque, NM	31.4	35.2	14.4	10.8	5.0	1.9	1.1	2.56
Allentown, PA	26.1	35.4	15.7	13.4	6.0	2.1	1.0	2.54
Anchorage, AK	25.5	33.6	16.4	12.7	6.8	2.6	2.1	2.83
Ann Arbor, MI	29.6	36.9	13.7	12.3	4.5	1.8	1.0	2.45
Athens, GA	28.9	35.3	15.2	13.1	4.8	1.6	0.8	2.50
Atlanta, GA	26.7	31.6	16.9	14.3	6.3	2.4	1.4	2.74
Austin, TX	27.9	33.1	15.5	13.9	6.0	2.1	1.2	2.71
Baton Rouge, LA	28.6	33.8	16.7	12.3	5.6	1.8	0.9	2.69
Boise City, ID	27.8	34.4	14.3	12.0	7.0	2.7	1.6	2.68
Boston, MA	27.7	33.0	16.6	14.3	5.4	1.7	0.9	2.55
Boulder, CO	28.7	36.3	15.5	12.9	4.6	1.2	0.4	2.44
Cape Coral, FL	28.0	44.7	11.5	9.0	4.1	1.6	0.8	2.64
Cedar Rapids, IA	29.6	36.5	13.8	11.9	5.0	2.0	0.8	2.41
Charleston, SC	29.1	35.6	16.5	11.7	4.6	1.5	0.6	2.60
Charlotte, NC	27.1	34.0	16.3	14.0	5.5	1.8	0.9	2.63
Chicago, IL	28.9	31.1	15.6	13.7	6.6	2.4	1.4	2.66
Cincinnati, OH	28.8	34.3	15.1	12.7	5.7	1.9	1.0	2.50
Clarksville, TN	24.9	32.2	18.3	14.2	6.2	2.5	1.2	2.64
Cleveland, OH	34.0	33.8	14.2	10.7	4.5	1.5	0.8	2.34
College Station, TX	28.1	33.9	15.7	13.2	5.1	2.6	1.2	2.61
Colorado Springs, CO	25.0	35.4	15.6	13.4	6.5	2.4	1.3	2.64
Columbia, MO	30.1	34.4	15.1	13.2	4.8	1.3	0.7	2.41
Columbia, SC	29.8	34.3	15.6	12.1	5.2	1.7	0.9	2.53
Columbus, OH	28.5	33.9	15.6	12.9	5.9	1.9	1.0	2.55
Dallas, TX	25.0	30.6	16.8	15.2	7.5	2.9	1.7	2.83
Davenport, IA	31.1	35.7	13.2	11.9	5.3	1.7	0.8	2.42
Denver, CO	28.2	34.3	14.9	13.2	5.7	2.1	1.3	2.57
Des Moines, IA	27.9	34.2	14.6	13.8	6.2	2.1	0.8	2.50
Durham, NC	30.5	35.7	15.4	11.2	4.8	1.3	0.7	2.42
Edison, NJ	28.0	29.4	16.9	14.5	6.5	2.4	1.9	2.70
El Paso, TX	23.8	28.1	17.8	16.5	8.3	3.5	1.6	3.06
Fargo, ND	31.1	35.0	14.5	11.6	5.0	1.5	0.8	2.31
Fayetteville, NC	30.7	31.5	16.0	12.4	5.8	2.2	1.0	2.64
Fort Collins, CO	24.2	40.2	15.7	12.3	5.1	1.5	0.5	2.45
Fort Wayne, IN	28.9	34.3	14.4	12.2	6.3	2.4	1.2	2.52
Fort Worth, TX	25.0	30.6	16.8	15.2	7.5	2.9	1.7	2.83
Grand Rapids, MI	24.8	34.6	14.9	14.3	6.9	2.7	1.4	2.65
Greeley, CO	20.5	33.4	16.7	15.7	8.3	3.2	1.8	2.85
Green Bay, WI	28.3	36.9	14.1	12.2	5.8	1.5	0.9	2.40
Greensboro, NC	29.4	35.0	16.1	11.4	5.0	1.8	1.0	2.48
Honolulu, HI	24.0	30.5	16.7	13.5	7.3	3.5	4.1	3.03
Houston, TX	24.1	29.7	17.1	15.6	8.1	3.1	1.9	2.89
Huntsville, AL	29.4	35.1	15.5	12.2	5.1	1.7	0.6	2.47
Indianapolis, IN	30.1	33.5	14.8	12.8	5.7	1.9	0.9	2.56
Jacksonville, FL	27.1	35.6	16.6	12.4	5.3	1.8	0.8	2.62
Kansas City, MO	29.0	34.1	14.8	12.9	5.8	2.0	1.1	2.52
Lafayette, LA	26.9	34.0	16.7	12.9	6.1	2.1	1.0	2.65
Lakeland, FL	25.2	37.9	15.1	11.6	5.9	2.5	1.4	2.86
Las Vegas, NV	28.5	32.8	15.3	12.3	6.5	2.6	1.7	2.76
Lexington, KY	28.4	35.6	15.9	12.3	5.0	1.7	0.7	2.44
Lincoln, NE	30.1	35.7	13.7	11.9	5.3	2.0	1.0	2.41
Little Rock, AR	29.8	34.2	15.9	11.8	5.2	1.8	0.8	2.55
Los Angeles, CA	24.5	28.6	17.0	15.4	7.9	3.4	2.8	2.99
Louisville, KY	30.3	34.1	15.7	11.7	5.1	1.8	0.9	2.51

Table continued on following page.

Metro Area	Persons in Household (%)							Average Household Size
	One	Two	Three	Four	Five	Six	Seven or More	
Madison, WI	30.1	36.8	14.0	12.1	4.6	1.4	0.7	2.35
Manchester, NH	25.5	36.2	16.4	13.5	5.2	1.9	1.0	2.51
Memphis, TN	29.8	32.5	16.2	12.3	5.3	2.2	1.3	2.64
Miami, FL	28.2	32.6	16.8	13.2	5.8	2.1	1.1	2.82
Midland, TX	26.3	30.8	15.9	14.4	7.8	2.9	1.6	2.93
Milwaukee, WI	31.5	34.3	14.0	11.9	5.2	1.8	0.9	2.45
Minneapolis, MN	27.9	34.1	14.8	13.6	5.8	2.1	1.3	2.56
Nashville, TN	26.0	34.8	16.7	13.3	5.8	2.0	1.0	2.59
New Haven, CT	31.2	33.0	16.1	12.3	4.8	1.7	0.7	2.51
New Orleans, LA	33.4	32.2	15.4	11.5	4.6	1.6	0.9	2.58
New York, NY	28.0	29.4	16.9	14.5	6.5	2.4	1.9	2.70
Oklahoma City, OK	28.2	34.1	15.4	12.6	6.0	2.3	1.1	2.62
Omaha, NE	28.4	33.9	14.3	12.6	6.4	2.7	1.5	2.54
Orlando, FL	24.8	34.2	17.4	13.9	5.9	2.3	1.1	2.83
Peoria, IL	31.3	35.3	14.0	11.0	5.2	2.0	0.8	2.42
Philadelphia, PA	29.1	32.3	16.2	13.5	5.7	1.9	1.0	2.60
Phoenix, AZ	26.4	34.4	14.4	12.6	6.7	3.0	2.2	2.76
Pittsburgh, PA	33.2	35.5	14.3	10.8	4.0	1.3	0.5	2.25
Portland, OR	26.8	35.4	15.3	13.4	5.3	2.2	1.2	2.56
Providence, RI	29.8	33.3	16.6	12.8	5.0	1.5	0.7	2.48
Provo, UT	11.9	28.6	15.6	15.6	12.4	9.0	6.5	3.55
Raleigh, NC	25.0	33.1	17.6	15.3	6.1	1.8	0.8	2.64
Reno, NV	28.2	35.0	15.5	11.4	5.7	2.3	1.5	2.47
Richmond, VA	29.4	34.2	16.0	12.3	5.3	1.8	0.7	2.57
Riverside, CA	20.4	28.3	16.3	16.0	10.1	4.9	3.7	3.28
Rochester, MN	27.2	36.2	14.1	13.5	5.3	2.2	1.2	2.45
Sacramento, CA	25.3	33.2	15.9	14.4	6.6	2.7	1.7	2.74
Salt Lake City, UT	22.4	30.5	15.8	14.3	8.6	4.9	3.2	3.00
San Antonio, TX	26.3	31.2	16.5	13.8	7.1	3.0	1.7	3.00
San Diego, CA	23.8	32.6	16.9	14.7	7.0	2.8	1.9	2.87
San Francisco, CA	26.2	31.9	16.9	14.8	6.1	2.2	1.6	2.71
San Jose, CA	20.1	30.6	18.8	17.7	7.2	2.9	2.4	2.96
Santa Rosa, CA	27.4	34.8	15.4	12.9	5.9	2.0	1.3	2.59
Savannah, GA	28.0	35.9	16.1	12.2	5.0	1.5	0.9	2.62
Seattle, WA	27.1	34.5	16.0	13.5	5.2	2.0	1.3	2.54
Sioux Falls, SD	28.6	35.0	13.6	13.1	6.2	2.1	1.1	2.46
Springfield, IL	32.9	35.7	14.0	10.6	4.2	1.6	0.7	2.30
Tallahassee, FL	30.5	35.2	17.0	11.0	4.2	1.2	0.5	2.43
Tampa, FL	30.8	36.7	14.7	10.8	4.4	1.5	0.8	2.51
Tucson, AZ	30.5	35.8	13.7	11.2	5.1	2.0	1.3	2.46
Tulsa, OK	28.2	34.5	15.2	12.1	5.9	2.4	1.2	2.56
Tuscaloosa, AL	29.4	35.0	16.4	11.5	5.3	1.3	0.8	2.69
Virginia Beach, VA	27.2	34.1	17.3	13.1	5.3	1.8	0.9	2.55
Washington, DC	27.2	30.8	16.5	14.6	6.5	2.6	1.6	2.75
Wichita, KS	29.9	32.8	14.0	11.6	7.0	2.8	1.4	2.56
Winston-Salem, NC	29.5	35.9	15.4	11.3	5.0	1.6	0.9	2.46
U.S.	27.8	33.9	15.5	12.9	5.9	2.2	1.4	2.62

Note: Figures cover the Metropolitan Statistical Area (MSA)—see Appendix B for areas included
Source: U.S. Census Bureau, 2015-2019 American Community Survey 5-Year Estimates

Race: City

City	White Alone[1] (%)	Black Alone[1] (%)	Asian Alone[1] (%)	AIAN[2] Alone[2] (%)	NHOPI[3] Alone[1] (%)	Other Race Alone[1] (%)	Two or More Races (%)
Albuquerque, NM	73.9	3.3	2.9	4.7	0.1	10.6	4.4
Allentown, PA	62.3	14.7	2.9	0.7	0.1	14.7	4.6
Anchorage, AK	62.6	5.6	9.6	7.9	2.4	2.4	9.5
Ann Arbor, MI	71.1	6.8	16.9	0.4	0.1	0.7	4.1
Athens, GA	63.2	28.0	3.9	0.1	0.1	2.1	2.6
Atlanta, GA	40.9	51.0	4.4	0.3	0.0	1.0	2.4
Austin, TX	72.6	7.8	7.6	0.7	0.1	7.8	3.5
Baton Rouge, LA	38.7	54.7	3.5	0.3	0.1	1.5	1.3
Boise City, ID	89.3	1.9	2.8	0.5	0.2	1.9	3.4
Boston, MA	52.8	25.2	9.7	0.3	0.1	6.7	5.3
Boulder, CO	87.4	1.2	5.8	0.2	0.1	1.5	3.8
Cape Coral, FL	89.5	5.2	1.8	0.2	0.0	1.8	1.6
Cedar Rapids, IA	83.9	7.8	2.9	0.3	0.2	1.1	3.8
Charleston, SC	74.1	21.7	1.9	0.1	0.1	0.6	1.5
Charlotte, NC	48.8	35.2	6.5	0.4	0.1	6.1	2.8
Chicago, IL	50.0	29.6	6.6	0.3	0.0	10.6	2.8
Cincinnati, OH	50.7	42.3	2.2	0.1	0.1	0.9	3.7
Clarksville, TN	65.1	24.3	2.5	0.7	0.5	1.8	5.2
Cleveland, OH	40.0	48.8	2.6	0.5	0.1	3.6	4.4
College Station, TX	77.8	7.6	10.1	0.3	0.0	1.5	2.7
Colorado Springs, CO	78.5	6.5	2.9	0.8	0.3	5.1	5.9
Columbia, MO	77.1	10.9	6.2	0.4	0.1	0.9	4.4
Columbia, SC	53.4	39.8	2.7	0.1	0.2	1.0	2.8
Columbus, OH	58.6	29.0	5.8	0.3	0.0	2.1	4.2
Dallas, TX	62.7	24.3	3.4	0.3	0.0	6.9	2.4
Davenport, IA	81.4	11.3	2.3	0.5	0.0	1.0	3.5
Denver, CO	76.1	9.2	3.7	0.9	0.2	6.1	3.8
Des Moines, IA	75.8	11.4	6.2	0.4	0.1	2.3	3.9
Durham, NC	49.2	38.7	5.4	0.3	0.0	3.4	3.2
Edison, NJ	35.3	8.2	48.7	0.3	0.1	4.0	3.5
El Paso, TX	80.1	3.6	1.4	0.6	0.2	11.4	2.7
Fargo, ND	84.6	7.0	3.5	1.2	0.0	0.5	3.1
Fayetteville, NC	44.6	42.1	2.9	1.1	0.4	2.9	6.1
Fort Collins, CO	88.3	1.6	3.5	1.0	0.1	1.5	4.0
Fort Wayne, IN	73.4	15.1	4.7	0.2	0.1	2.1	4.5
Fort Worth, TX	63.8	18.9	4.6	0.5	0.1	9.0	3.2
Grand Rapids, MI	67.2	18.6	2.4	0.4	0.0	5.7	5.6
Greeley, CO	88.3	2.4	1.4	1.2	0.2	3.7	2.8
Green Bay, WI	76.7	4.2	4.2	3.5	0.0	6.0	5.4
Greensboro, NC	47.3	41.4	5.0	0.5	0.1	2.7	3.0
Honolulu, HI	17.2	2.0	53.2	0.1	8.0	0.9	18.4
Houston, TX	57.0	22.6	6.8	0.3	0.1	11.1	2.2
Huntsville, AL	61.3	30.7	2.6	0.4	0.1	2.0	2.8
Indianapolis, IN	60.9	28.6	3.4	0.3	0.0	3.5	3.3
Jacksonville, FL	58.2	31.0	4.8	0.2	0.1	2.1	3.6
Kansas City, MO	60.9	28.2	2.7	0.4	0.2	4.0	3.6
Lafayette, LA	64.0	30.9	2.2	0.3	0.0	0.6	2.1
Lakeland, FL	72.3	20.5	2.2	0.4	0.1	2.8	1.8
Las Vegas, NV	61.9	12.2	6.9	0.9	0.8	12.1	5.2
Lexington, KY	74.9	14.6	3.8	0.2	0.0	2.8	3.8
Lincoln, NE	84.9	4.4	4.6	0.7	0.1	1.5	3.9
Little Rock, AR	50.3	42.0	3.3	0.3	0.1	1.8	2.3
Los Angeles, CA	52.1	8.9	11.6	0.7	0.2	22.8	3.8
Louisville, KY	69.9	23.6	2.7	0.2	0.1	1.0	2.6

Table continued on following page.

City	White Alone[1] (%)	Black Alone[1] (%)	Asian Alone[1] (%)	AIAN[2] Alone[1] (%)	NHOPI[3] Alone[1] (%)	Other Race Alone[1] (%)	Two or More Races (%)
Madison, WI	78.6	7.0	9.0	0.5	0.1	1.4	3.5
Manchester, NH	84.8	6.1	5.1	0.1	0.0	0.9	3.0
Memphis, TN	29.2	64.1	1.7	0.2	0.0	3.3	1.5
Miami, FL	76.1	16.8	1.1	0.2	0.0	4.0	1.7
Midland, TX	80.6	7.8	2.2	0.6	0.1	6.4	2.3
Milwaukee, WI	44.4	38.7	4.3	0.6	0.0	8.0	4.0
Minneapolis, MN	63.6	19.2	5.9	1.4	0.0	5.0	4.8
Nashville, TN	63.5	27.6	3.7	0.2	0.1	2.4	2.6
New Haven, CT	44.4	32.6	5.0	0.4	0.0	13.1	4.4
New Orleans, LA	33.9	59.5	2.9	0.2	0.0	1.5	1.9
New York, NY	42.7	24.3	14.1	0.4	0.1	14.7	3.6
Oklahoma City, OK	67.7	14.3	4.5	2.9	0.1	4.1	6.3
Omaha, NE	77.5	12.3	3.8	0.6	0.0	2.3	3.4
Orlando, FL	61.3	24.5	4.2	0.2	0.0	6.2	3.5
Peoria, IL	60.1	27.1	6.1	0.3	0.0	2.1	4.3
Philadelphia, PA	40.7	42.1	7.2	0.4	0.0	6.5	3.1
Phoenix, AZ	72.9	7.1	3.8	2.1	0.2	10.0	3.9
Pittsburgh, PA	66.8	23.0	5.8	0.2	0.0	0.6	3.5
Portland, OR	77.4	5.8	8.2	0.8	0.6	1.9	5.3
Providence, RI	55.1	16.8	6.0	1.0	0.1	16.3	4.7
Provo, UT	87.9	0.9	2.7	0.8	1.3	2.2	4.2
Raleigh, NC	58.3	29.0	4.6	0.4	0.0	4.8	2.9
Reno, NV	75.4	2.8	6.7	1.0	0.8	8.5	4.8
Richmond, VA	45.5	46.9	2.1	0.4	0.0	1.7	3.4
Riverside, CA	58.3	6.2	7.6	0.8	0.3	22.0	4.9
Rochester, MN	79.4	8.2	7.3	0.5	0.1	1.1	3.4
Sacramento, CA	46.3	13.2	18.9	0.7	1.7	11.7	7.4
Salt Lake City, UT	72.8	2.6	5.4	1.5	1.6	12.7	3.3
San Antonio, TX	80.3	7.0	2.8	0.8	0.1	6.0	3.0
San Diego, CA	65.1	6.4	16.7	0.5	0.4	5.6	5.3
San Francisco, CA	46.4	5.2	34.4	0.4	0.4	7.7	5.6
San Jose, CA	39.9	3.0	35.9	0.6	0.5	14.8	5.3
Santa Rosa, CA	66.8	2.6	5.5	1.3	0.6	17.1	6.0
Savannah, GA	38.9	53.9	2.6	0.3	0.1	1.4	2.8
Seattle, WA	67.3	7.3	15.4	0.5	0.3	2.3	6.9
Sioux Falls, SD	84.5	6.2	2.5	2.1	0.0	1.6	3.2
Springfield, IL	72.9	19.9	3.1	0.1	0.0	0.5	3.5
Tallahassee, FL	56.2	35.0	4.6	0.2	0.0	1.1	2.9
Tampa, FL	65.4	23.6	4.3	0.3	0.1	2.5	3.9
Tucson, AZ	72.1	5.2	3.2	3.7	0.2	10.2	5.4
Tulsa, OK	64.3	15.2	3.4	4.5	0.1	4.9	7.5
Tuscaloosa, AL	51.2	44.0	2.5	0.3	0.1	0.9	1.0
Virginia Beach, VA	66.3	19.0	6.7	0.3	0.1	2.1	5.6
Washington, DC	41.3	46.3	4.0	0.3	0.1	5.0	3.1
Wichita, KS	74.3	10.9	5.1	1.0	0.1	4.2	4.4
Winston-Salem, NC	56.6	34.9	2.5	0.3	0.1	2.8	2.8
U.S.	72.5	12.7	5.5	0.8	0.2	4.9	3.3

Note: (1) Alone is defined as not being in combination with one or more other races; (2) American Indian and Alaska Native; (3) Native Hawaiian and Other Pacific Islander
Source: U.S. Census Bureau, 2015-2019 American Community Survey 5-Year Estimates

Race: Metro Area

Metro Area	White Alone[1] (%)	Black Alone[1] (%)	Asian Alone[1] (%)	AIAN[2] Alone[1] (%)	NHOPI[3] Alone[1] (%)	Other Race Alone[1] (%)	Two or More Races (%)
Albuquerque, NM	74.9	2.7	2.3	6.0	0.1	10.0	4.0
Allentown, PA	84.0	6.0	2.9	0.2	0.0	3.7	3.1
Anchorage, AK	68.0	4.4	7.5	7.5	1.9	1.8	9.0
Ann Arbor, MI	73.6	11.9	9.1	0.4	0.0	0.8	4.2
Athens, GA	72.0	20.6	3.1	0.1	0.1	1.8	2.3
Atlanta, GA	53.4	34.2	5.9	0.4	0.0	3.4	2.7
Austin, TX	76.0	7.3	5.9	0.5	0.1	6.7	3.6
Baton Rouge, LA	59.2	35.3	1.9	0.2	0.0	1.4	1.9
Boise City, ID	88.0	1.0	1.9	0.7	0.2	4.6	3.5
Boston, MA	76.0	8.3	7.9	0.2	0.0	4.2	3.3
Boulder, CO	89.0	0.9	4.7	0.4	0.1	1.8	3.0
Cape Coral, FL	84.4	8.6	1.6	0.2	0.1	3.4	1.8
Cedar Rapids, IA	89.4	4.8	2.0	0.2	0.1	0.7	2.8
Charleston, SC	67.6	25.6	1.8	0.3	0.1	1.9	2.7
Charlotte, NC	66.9	22.8	3.7	0.4	0.1	3.6	2.5
Chicago, IL	65.7	16.6	6.6	0.3	0.0	8.0	2.7
Cincinnati, OH	81.8	12.0	2.6	0.1	0.0	0.9	2.6
Clarksville, TN	72.7	19.1	1.9	0.6	0.4	1.3	4.1
Cleveland, OH	73.4	19.9	2.3	0.2	0.0	1.3	2.9
College Station, TX	77.0	11.5	5.3	0.4	0.1	3.0	2.8
Colorado Springs, CO	80.1	6.2	2.7	0.8	0.4	4.0	5.9
Columbia, MO	82.3	8.6	3.9	0.4	0.1	0.9	3.8
Columbia, SC	59.6	33.4	2.1	0.2	0.1	1.8	2.7
Columbus, OH	75.3	15.5	4.2	0.2	0.0	1.3	3.4
Dallas, TX	68.3	15.8	6.9	0.5	0.1	5.4	3.0
Davenport, IA	85.1	7.6	2.3	0.3	0.0	1.7	3.0
Denver, CO	81.0	5.7	4.2	0.8	0.1	4.4	3.7
Des Moines, IA	86.9	5.2	3.9	0.3	0.1	1.1	2.5
Durham, NC	62.5	26.6	4.5	0.4	0.0	3.0	3.1
Edison, NJ	57.5	17.3	11.2	0.3	0.0	10.5	3.1
El Paso, TX	79.6	3.3	1.2	0.6	0.1	12.4	2.7
Fargo, ND	88.0	5.1	2.5	1.2	0.1	0.6	2.7
Fayetteville, NC	53.8	32.6	2.0	2.0	0.3	4.1	5.3
Fort Collins, CO	91.3	1.0	2.2	0.8	0.1	1.5	3.2
Fort Wayne, IN	80.4	10.6	3.5	0.2	0.0	1.7	3.6
Fort Worth, TX	68.3	15.8	6.9	0.5	0.1	5.4	3.0
Grand Rapids, MI	83.9	6.7	2.6	0.3	0.0	2.9	3.5
Greeley, CO	90.3	1.2	1.6	0.8	0.1	3.0	3.0
Green Bay, WI	87.1	2.1	2.7	2.2	0.0	2.9	3.0
Greensboro, NC	63.0	26.8	3.7	0.5	0.1	3.3	2.6
Honolulu, HI	20.9	2.4	42.7	0.2	9.5	1.0	23.2
Houston, TX	65.0	17.3	7.7	0.4	0.1	7.0	2.5
Huntsville, AL	70.5	22.1	2.4	0.6	0.1	1.5	2.8
Indianapolis, IN	76.6	15.2	3.2	0.2	0.0	2.0	2.7
Jacksonville, FL	69.3	21.5	3.8	0.3	0.1	1.8	3.4
Kansas City, MO	78.3	12.3	2.9	0.4	0.2	2.7	3.3
Lafayette, LA	70.6	24.6	1.7	0.3	0.0	0.8	2.0
Lakeland, FL	77.1	15.3	1.8	0.3	0.0	3.0	2.5
Las Vegas, NV	60.2	11.7	9.7	0.9	0.8	11.5	5.4
Lexington, KY	80.7	11.0	2.7	0.2	0.0	2.3	3.1
Lincoln, NE	86.6	3.8	4.0	0.7	0.1	1.3	3.5
Little Rock, AR	70.3	23.3	1.7	0.4	0.1	1.6	2.5
Los Angeles, CA	53.6	6.6	16.0	0.7	0.3	18.8	4.0
Louisville, KY	79.4	14.8	2.1	0.2	0.0	0.9	2.5

Table continued on following page.

Metro Area	White Alone[1] (%)	Black Alone[1] (%)	Asian Alone[1] (%)	AIAN[2] Alone[1] (%)	NHOPI[3] Alone[1] (%)	Other Race Alone[1] (%)	Two or More Races (%)
Madison, WI	86.0	4.4	5.0	0.3	0.0	1.4	2.8
Manchester, NH	89.4	2.9	4.0	0.1	0.1	0.9	2.5
Memphis, TN	46.3	47.1	2.1	0.2	0.0	2.3	1.9
Miami, FL	70.2	21.2	2.5	0.2	0.0	3.5	2.3
Midland, TX	82.1	6.5	1.9	0.6	0.1	6.4	2.4
Milwaukee, WI	72.5	16.5	3.7	0.4	0.0	3.8	2.9
Minneapolis, MN	78.7	8.5	6.6	0.6	0.0	2.2	3.4
Nashville, TN	77.6	15.3	2.8	0.2	0.0	1.6	2.5
New Haven, CT	73.3	13.5	4.0	0.2	0.0	5.7	3.3
New Orleans, LA	57.3	35.1	2.9	0.4	0.0	2.2	2.0
New York, NY	57.5	17.3	11.2	0.3	0.0	10.5	3.1
Oklahoma City, OK	73.7	10.2	3.2	3.6	0.1	2.8	6.5
Omaha, NE	84.0	7.7	2.9	0.5	0.1	1.9	2.9
Orlando, FL	69.7	16.6	4.3	0.3	0.1	5.7	3.3
Peoria, IL	85.4	8.8	2.3	0.2	0.0	0.8	2.4
Philadelphia, PA	66.6	21.0	5.9	0.2	0.0	3.4	2.8
Phoenix, AZ	77.8	5.5	4.0	2.3	0.2	6.5	3.7
Pittsburgh, PA	86.6	8.1	2.3	0.1	0.0	0.4	2.5
Portland, OR	81.1	2.8	6.7	0.8	0.5	3.0	5.0
Providence, RI	81.7	5.9	3.0	0.4	0.1	5.7	3.2
Provo, UT	91.7	0.6	1.5	0.5	0.9	1.8	3.1
Raleigh, NC	67.2	20.0	5.7	0.4	0.0	3.7	2.9
Reno, NV	77.6	2.3	5.3	1.6	0.6	8.1	4.4
Richmond, VA	61.1	29.7	3.8	0.3	0.1	1.8	3.1
Riverside, CA	60.5	7.4	6.8	0.8	0.3	19.5	4.7
Rochester, MN	87.4	4.5	4.3	0.3	0.1	1.1	2.4
Sacramento, CA	65.0	7.1	13.3	0.6	0.9	6.5	6.6
Salt Lake City, UT	79.7	1.8	3.9	0.8	1.4	9.0	3.4
San Antonio, TX	80.7	6.8	2.5	0.6	0.1	5.9	3.4
San Diego, CA	70.7	5.0	11.9	0.7	0.4	6.0	5.2
San Francisco, CA	49.0	7.3	26.1	0.5	0.7	10.2	6.2
San Jose, CA	45.6	2.4	35.4	0.5	0.4	10.4	5.2
Santa Rosa, CA	74.8	1.7	4.1	0.9	0.3	12.9	5.4
Savannah, GA	59.6	33.3	2.2	0.3	0.1	1.5	3.0
Seattle, WA	68.3	5.8	13.6	0.8	0.9	3.7	6.8
Sioux Falls, SD	88.3	4.5	1.8	1.6	0.0	1.1	2.7
Springfield, IL	82.8	12.1	1.9	0.1	0.1	0.4	2.6
Tallahassee, FL	60.6	32.7	2.7	0.2	0.0	1.3	2.4
Tampa, FL	77.8	12.2	3.4	0.3	0.1	2.9	3.3
Tucson, AZ	76.0	3.6	2.9	3.9	0.2	8.6	4.9
Tulsa, OK	71.2	8.0	2.5	7.3	0.1	2.7	8.2
Tuscaloosa, AL	60.6	35.8	1.4	0.2	0.0	0.8	1.1
Virginia Beach, VA	59.0	30.6	3.8	0.3	0.1	1.8	4.5
Washington, DC	53.5	25.3	10.1	0.3	0.1	6.5	4.2
Wichita, KS	80.9	7.5	3.7	0.9	0.1	2.9	4.0
Winston-Salem, NC	75.8	17.8	1.8	0.4	0.1	2.0	2.2
U.S.	72.5	12.7	5.5	0.8	0.2	4.9	3.3

Note: (1) Figures cover the Metropolitan Statistical Area (MSA)—see Appendix B for areas included; (1) Alone is defined as not being in combination with one or more other races; (2) American Indian and Alaska Native; (3) Native Hawaiian & Other Pacific Islander
Source: U.S. Census Bureau, 2015-2019 American Community Survey 5-Year Estimates

Hispanic Origin: City

City	Hispanic or Latino (%)	Mexican (%)	Puerto Rican (%)	Cuban (%)	Other Hispanic or Latino (%)
Albuquerque, NM	49.2	28.0	0.6	0.5	20.2
Allentown, PA	52.5	1.9	28.8	0.9	20.9
Anchorage, AK	9.2	4.8	1.4	0.1	2.8
Ann Arbor, MI	4.8	2.2	0.4	0.3	1.9
Athens, GA	10.9	6.7	0.7	0.4	3.1
Atlanta, GA	4.3	2.0	0.6	0.3	1.4
Austin, TX	33.9	27.2	0.9	0.7	5.2
Baton Rouge, LA	3.7	1.1	0.3	0.2	2.1
Boise City, ID	9.0	7.2	0.3	0.0	1.5
Boston, MA	19.8	1.2	5.3	0.5	12.9
Boulder, CO	9.7	6.0	0.4	0.4	2.9
Cape Coral, FL	20.9	2.0	5.0	7.8	6.1
Cedar Rapids, IA	4.0	2.8	0.2	0.0	1.0
Charleston, SC	3.2	1.3	0.5	0.2	1.2
Charlotte, NC	14.3	5.3	1.2	0.5	7.3
Chicago, IL	28.8	21.3	3.6	0.3	3.5
Cincinnati, OH	3.8	1.2	0.6	0.1	2.0
Clarksville, TN	11.5	5.2	3.7	0.3	2.3
Cleveland, OH	11.9	1.3	8.5	0.2	1.9
College Station, TX	15.8	11.2	0.3	0.4	3.9
Colorado Springs, CO	17.6	11.3	1.4	0.5	4.5
Columbia, MO	3.6	2.2	0.3	0.1	1.1
Columbia, SC	5.5	2.1	1.3	0.3	1.7
Columbus, OH	6.2	3.2	0.9	0.1	1.9
Dallas, TX	41.8	35.4	0.5	0.3	5.5
Davenport, IA	8.7	7.8	0.3	0.0	0.5
Denver, CO	29.9	23.7	0.6	0.2	5.4
Des Moines, IA	13.6	10.6	0.4	0.1	2.4
Durham, NC	13.8	6.1	1.1	0.2	6.4
Edison, NJ	9.9	1.8	2.5	0.8	4.8
El Paso, TX	81.4	76.9	1.1	0.1	3.2
Fargo, ND	3.0	1.9	0.4	0.0	0.6
Fayetteville, NC	12.4	4.2	4.1	0.4	3.7
Fort Collins, CO	11.6	8.2	0.4	0.1	3.0
Fort Wayne, IN	9.2	6.8	0.5	0.1	1.7
Fort Worth, TX	35.1	30.6	1.1	0.3	3.1
Grand Rapids, MI	16.1	9.5	1.5	0.2	4.8
Greeley, CO	38.6	31.0	0.6	0.3	6.7
Green Bay, WI	15.8	12.5	1.4	0.1	1.8
Greensboro, NC	7.9	4.7	0.7	0.2	2.2
Honolulu, HI	7.3	2.0	1.8	0.2	3.4
Houston, TX	45.0	31.8	0.6	0.8	11.7
Huntsville, AL	6.2	3.8	0.9	0.2	1.4
Indianapolis, IN	10.5	7.1	0.6	0.2	2.6
Jacksonville, FL	10.0	2.0	3.0	1.2	3.7
Kansas City, MO	10.6	8.0	0.4	0.3	1.9
Lafayette, LA	3.6	1.4	0.2	0.2	1.7
Lakeland, FL	16.4	3.5	6.3	2.5	4.0
Las Vegas, NV	33.1	24.7	1.2	1.3	5.9
Lexington, KY	7.2	4.8	0.7	0.2	1.5
Lincoln, NE	7.6	5.5	0.3	0.2	1.6
Little Rock, AR	7.4	4.8	0.3	0.3	2.1
Los Angeles, CA	48.5	32.2	0.4	0.4	15.4
Louisville, KY	5.6	2.0	0.5	1.9	1.2
Madison, WI	7.0	4.1	0.7	0.2	2.0

Table continued on following page.

City	Hispanic or Latino (%)	Mexican (%)	Puerto Rican (%)	Cuban (%)	Other Hispanic or Latino (%)
Manchester, NH	10.4	1.5	4.4	0.1	4.4
Memphis, TN	7.2	5.1	0.3	0.2	1.6
Miami, FL	72.7	1.9	3.4	35.0	32.4
Midland, TX	44.2	40.6	0.5	0.9	2.2
Milwaukee, WI	19.0	13.4	4.4	0.2	1.1
Minneapolis, MN	9.6	5.8	0.5	0.2	3.1
Nashville, TN	10.5	6.2	0.6	0.4	3.4
New Haven, CT	31.2	5.6	17.6	0.3	7.7
New Orleans, LA	5.5	1.3	0.3	0.4	3.5
New York, NY	29.1	4.0	8.1	0.5	16.5
Oklahoma City, OK	19.7	16.6	0.3	0.1	2.8
Omaha, NE	13.9	10.7	0.4	0.1	2.7
Orlando, FL	32.6	1.9	15.6	3.0	12.0
Peoria, IL	6.3	4.6	0.4	0.1	1.1
Philadelphia, PA	14.7	1.3	8.8	0.3	4.3
Phoenix, AZ	42.6	38.3	0.7	0.3	3.3
Pittsburgh, PA	3.2	1.0	0.7	0.2	1.3
Portland, OR	9.7	6.8	0.4	0.4	2.1
Providence, RI	43.3	1.8	9.3	0.3	31.9
Provo, UT	16.7	11.3	0.5	0.1	4.7
Raleigh, NC	11.2	5.1	1.2	0.4	4.5
Reno, NV	24.7	19.2	0.5	0.3	4.7
Richmond, VA	6.9	1.7	0.7	0.2	4.3
Riverside, CA	53.7	47.1	0.8	0.2	5.6
Rochester, MN	5.9	3.7	0.4	0.2	1.6
Sacramento, CA	28.9	24.6	0.7	0.2	3.3
Salt Lake City, UT	21.8	16.9	0.3	0.4	4.2
San Antonio, TX	64.2	56.9	1.3	0.3	5.7
San Diego, CA	30.3	26.6	0.7	0.2	2.8
San Francisco, CA	15.2	7.8	0.6	0.3	6.6
San Jose, CA	31.6	27.1	0.6	0.1	3.7
Santa Rosa, CA	32.8	28.8	0.4	0.1	3.5
Savannah, GA	5.8	2.3	1.5	0.2	1.8
Seattle, WA	6.7	3.9	0.4	0.2	2.1
Sioux Falls, SD	5.5	3.1	0.4	0.1	1.9
Springfield, IL	2.8	1.5	0.5	0.1	0.7
Tallahassee, FL	6.7	1.2	1.4	1.3	2.8
Tampa, FL	26.4	3.1	7.6	8.0	7.7
Tucson, AZ	43.6	39.5	0.8	0.2	3.1
Tulsa, OK	16.5	13.2	0.6	0.2	2.6
Tuscaloosa, AL	3.2	1.6	0.1	0.2	1.4
Virginia Beach, VA	8.2	2.5	2.4	0.3	3.0
Washington, DC	11.0	2.0	0.9	0.4	7.6
Wichita, KS	17.2	14.7	0.4	0.2	1.9
Winston-Salem, NC	15.0	9.9	1.4	0.2	3.5
U.S.	18.0	11.2	1.7	0.7	4.3

Note: Persons of Hispanic or Latino origin can be of any race
Source: U.S. Census Bureau, 2015-2019 American Community Survey 5-Year Estimates

Hispanic Origin: Metro Area

Metro Area	Hispanic or Latino (%)	Mexican (%)	Puerto Rican (%)	Cuban (%)	Other Hispanic or Latino (%)
Albuquerque, NM	49.0	27.7	0.5	0.4	20.4
Allentown, PA	17.0	1.2	9.2	0.3	6.2
Anchorage, AK	8.1	4.2	1.2	0.2	2.4
Ann Arbor, MI	4.7	2.6	0.3	0.2	1.6
Athens, GA	8.6	5.0	0.7	0.3	2.6
Atlanta, GA	10.7	5.6	1.0	0.4	3.6
Austin, TX	32.4	26.8	0.9	0.5	4.3
Baton Rouge, LA	4.0	1.5	0.3	0.2	2.0
Boise City, ID	13.7	11.6	0.3	0.1	1.6
Boston, MA	11.1	0.7	2.9	0.2	7.3
Boulder, CO	13.9	10.4	0.4	0.3	2.8
Cape Coral, FL	21.4	6.0	4.3	4.9	6.2
Cedar Rapids, IA	3.0	2.1	0.1	0.0	0.8
Charleston, SC	5.6	2.7	0.8	0.1	2.0
Charlotte, NC	10.1	4.7	1.0	0.4	4.1
Chicago, IL	22.1	17.3	2.2	0.2	2.4
Cincinnati, OH	3.2	1.5	0.4	0.1	1.2
Clarksville, TN	8.8	4.2	2.7	0.2	1.7
Cleveland, OH	5.8	1.3	3.4	0.1	1.0
College Station, TX	24.9	21.4	0.2	0.2	3.0
Colorado Springs, CO	16.7	10.3	1.7	0.4	4.4
Columbia, MO	3.2	2.1	0.2	0.1	0.8
Columbia, SC	5.5	2.8	1.1	0.2	1.4
Columbus, OH	4.2	2.1	0.7	0.1	1.3
Dallas, TX	28.9	23.9	0.7	0.3	4.0
Davenport, IA	8.7	7.7	0.4	0.1	0.6
Denver, CO	23.1	17.6	0.6	0.2	4.7
Des Moines, IA	7.1	5.4	0.2	0.1	1.4
Durham, NC	11.1	5.7	0.9	0.2	4.3
Edison, NJ	24.6	3.0	6.2	0.8	14.7
El Paso, TX	82.5	78.2	1.0	0.1	3.2
Fargo, ND	3.2	2.2	0.3	0.0	0.7
Fayetteville, NC	12.1	5.3	3.5	0.3	2.9
Fort Collins, CO	11.5	8.4	0.3	0.1	2.6
Fort Wayne, IN	7.0	5.2	0.4	0.1	1.3
Fort Worth, TX	28.9	23.9	0.7	0.3	4.0
Grand Rapids, MI	9.6	6.7	0.8	0.3	1.8
Greeley, CO	29.4	24.2	0.4	0.3	4.6
Green Bay, WI	7.4	5.8	0.7	0.0	0.9
Greensboro, NC	8.4	5.5	0.7	0.2	1.9
Honolulu, HI	9.8	2.9	3.1	0.1	3.7
Houston, TX	37.3	27.8	0.7	0.6	8.3
Huntsville, AL	5.2	3.2	0.7	0.2	1.0
Indianapolis, IN	6.7	4.4	0.5	0.1	1.7
Jacksonville, FL	8.9	1.8	2.8	1.2	3.1
Kansas City, MO	9.0	6.9	0.4	0.2	1.6
Lafayette, LA	4.0	2.1	0.2	0.2	1.5
Lakeland, FL	22.5	7.5	9.3	1.6	4.0
Las Vegas, NV	31.1	23.1	1.1	1.4	5.6
Lexington, KY	6.2	4.2	0.5	0.1	1.3
Lincoln, NE	6.8	4.9	0.3	0.2	1.5
Little Rock, AR	5.3	3.7	0.2	0.1	1.3
Los Angeles, CA	45.0	35.0	0.4	0.4	9.3
Louisville, KY	4.9	2.4	0.4	1.1	1.1
Madison, WI	5.7	3.6	0.5	0.1	1.5

Table continued on following page.

Metro Area	Hispanic or Latino (%)	Mexican (%)	Puerto Rican (%)	Cuban (%)	Other Hispanic or Latino (%)
Manchester, NH	6.8	1.0	2.5	0.2	3.0
Memphis, TN	5.6	4.0	0.2	0.1	1.2
Miami, FL	45.2	2.5	3.9	19.0	19.8
Midland, TX	44.7	41.6	0.5	0.7	1.9
Milwaukee, WI	10.7	7.4	2.3	0.1	0.9
Minneapolis, MN	5.9	3.8	0.3	0.1	1.6
Nashville, TN	7.3	4.4	0.5	0.2	2.2
New Haven, CT	18.1	1.9	10.6	0.4	5.3
New Orleans, LA	8.8	1.9	0.5	0.6	5.9
New York, NY	24.6	3.0	6.2	0.8	14.7
Oklahoma City, OK	13.3	10.9	0.3	0.1	2.0
Omaha, NE	10.4	7.9	0.4	0.1	2.0
Orlando, FL	30.7	2.9	15.2	2.4	10.1
Peoria, IL	3.5	2.5	0.3	0.0	0.6
Philadelphia, PA	9.4	1.9	4.6	0.3	2.7
Phoenix, AZ	30.9	27.1	0.7	0.3	2.8
Pittsburgh, PA	1.8	0.5	0.5	0.1	0.7
Portland, OR	12.0	9.2	0.4	0.2	2.2
Providence, RI	12.9	0.9	4.3	0.2	7.4
Provo, UT	11.7	7.7	0.3	0.1	3.7
Raleigh, NC	10.6	5.5	1.3	0.4	3.4
Reno, NV	24.3	18.9	0.6	0.3	4.4
Richmond, VA	6.3	1.6	1.0	0.2	3.5
Riverside, CA	51.0	44.4	0.8	0.3	5.5
Rochester, MN	4.4	2.9	0.2	0.1	1.2
Sacramento, CA	21.6	17.7	0.7	0.2	3.1
Salt Lake City, UT	18.0	13.3	0.5	0.1	4.1
San Antonio, TX	55.4	48.8	1.3	0.2	5.0
San Diego, CA	33.7	30.0	0.7	0.2	2.8
San Francisco, CA	21.8	14.2	0.7	0.2	6.7
San Jose, CA	26.5	22.1	0.5	0.1	3.7
Santa Rosa, CA	26.7	22.6	0.4	0.1	3.6
Savannah, GA	6.2	2.9	1.2	0.4	1.6
Seattle, WA	10.0	7.1	0.6	0.2	2.2
Sioux Falls, SD	4.3	2.5	0.3	0.1	1.5
Springfield, IL	2.3	1.3	0.4	0.1	0.5
Tallahassee, FL	6.6	1.9	1.3	1.0	2.4
Tampa, FL	19.6	3.8	6.2	4.0	5.6
Tucson, AZ	37.2	33.5	0.8	0.2	2.7
Tulsa, OK	9.9	7.8	0.4	0.1	1.6
Tuscaloosa, AL	3.5	2.2	0.2	0.1	1.0
Virginia Beach, VA	6.7	2.2	2.0	0.3	2.3
Washington, DC	15.8	2.3	1.1	0.3	12.1
Wichita, KS	13.1	11.0	0.4	0.1	1.5
Winston-Salem, NC	10.2	6.7	0.9	0.2	2.5
U.S.	18.0	11.2	1.7	0.7	4.3

Note: Persons of Hispanic or Latino origin can be of any race; Figures cover the Metropolitan Statistical Area (MSA)—see Appendix B for areas included
Source: U.S. Census Bureau, 2015-2019 American Community Survey 5-Year Estimates

Age: City

City	Under Age 5	Age 5–19	Age 20–34	Age 35–44	Age 45–54	Age 55–64	Age 65–74	Age 75–84	Age 85+	Median Age
Albuquerque, NM	5.9	19.0	22.6	13.0	12.0	12.2	8.8	4.4	1.8	36.6
Allentown, PA	7.6	22.8	24.6	11.9	11.3	10.0	6.5	3.3	2.0	31.6
Anchorage, AK	7.2	19.6	25.4	12.9	12.3	12.2	7.0	2.6	0.9	33.6
Ann Arbor, MI	3.7	18.5	40.1	9.5	8.3	8.2	6.8	3.4	1.5	27.5
Athens, GA	5.3	20.8	34.5	11.2	8.8	8.8	6.3	3.2	1.0	28.0
Atlanta, GA	5.4	16.9	30.7	13.8	11.8	9.8	6.8	3.4	1.4	33.3
Austin, TX	6.4	16.7	30.2	16.0	11.9	9.8	5.6	2.3	1.0	33.3
Baton Rouge, LA	6.7	19.6	28.3	10.5	10.1	11.1	8.0	3.9	1.9	31.5
Boise City, ID	5.7	18.9	23.1	14.0	12.3	12.0	8.4	3.7	1.8	36.6
Boston, MA	5.0	15.4	34.8	12.4	10.9	10.1	6.6	3.3	1.6	32.2
Boulder, CO	2.9	18.7	37.6	10.2	10.4	8.9	6.6	3.0	1.6	28.6
Cape Coral, FL	4.4	15.9	15.7	11.4	14.2	15.7	13.2	6.7	2.8	46.7
Cedar Rapids, IA	6.5	18.9	22.8	13.0	11.6	11.9	8.4	4.4	2.4	36.3
Charleston, SC	6.0	14.5	29.8	12.4	10.7	11.9	9.0	3.7	1.9	34.8
Charlotte, NC	6.8	19.4	25.1	14.8	13.1	10.7	6.4	2.8	1.1	34.2
Chicago, IL	6.3	17.0	27.3	14.0	11.9	10.9	7.2	3.7	1.5	34.6
Cincinnati, OH	7.1	19.0	28.3	11.3	10.5	11.6	7.0	3.3	1.9	32.2
Clarksville, TN	9.0	20.6	30.7	13.0	10.0	8.5	5.2	2.1	0.9	29.6
Cleveland, OH	6.3	18.3	23.7	11.5	12.4	13.8	8.0	4.2	1.8	36.3
College Station, TX	5.1	22.9	42.6	9.9	6.8	6.0	4.3	1.9	0.6	23.0
Colorado Springs, CO	6.5	19.3	24.6	12.6	11.9	11.6	8.1	3.8	1.5	34.7
Columbia, MO	5.9	19.0	34.6	11.0	9.5	9.4	6.0	3.2	1.3	28.5
Columbia, SC	5.1	23.2	31.9	10.1	10.1	9.4	6.2	2.8	1.2	28.5
Columbus, OH	7.3	18.2	29.4	12.9	11.3	10.6	6.2	2.7	1.3	32.2
Dallas, TX	7.5	19.9	26.4	13.7	11.8	10.4	6.1	2.9	1.2	32.7
Davenport, IA	6.4	19.2	21.8	12.3	12.3	12.7	8.6	4.1	2.5	36.7
Denver, CO	6.1	15.7	29.2	15.9	11.6	10.0	7.0	3.1	1.5	34.5
Des Moines, IA	6.9	19.7	24.5	13.0	12.0	11.8	7.1	3.3	1.6	34.2
Durham, NC	6.8	18.4	26.7	14.0	11.9	10.7	7.1	3.0	1.4	33.9
Edison, NJ	6.1	18.4	17.9	15.7	14.0	13.1	8.4	4.1	2.3	39.6
El Paso, TX	7.4	22.2	23.2	12.4	11.7	10.6	7.1	3.9	1.7	32.9
Fargo, ND	6.7	17.4	32.0	12.3	9.5	10.1	6.6	3.3	2.0	31.0
Fayetteville, NC	7.7	18.9	30.9	11.0	9.8	10.1	6.7	3.5	1.4	30.0
Fort Collins, CO	5.0	19.5	33.9	11.6	9.7	9.5	6.3	3.0	1.3	29.3
Fort Wayne, IN	7.1	20.6	22.2	12.1	11.7	12.1	8.3	3.8	1.8	35.0
Fort Worth, TX	8.0	22.5	23.3	14.0	12.4	10.1	5.9	2.6	1.2	32.6
Grand Rapids, MI	6.9	18.6	30.3	11.2	10.1	10.8	6.6	3.4	2.1	31.4
Greeley, CO	6.5	23.6	24.8	12.0	10.9	10.5	6.8	3.4	1.7	31.5
Green Bay, WI	7.6	20.3	22.8	12.4	12.3	11.8	7.2	3.7	1.9	34.5
Greensboro, NC	6.0	19.9	24.0	12.5	12.4	11.5	8.0	3.9	1.8	35.1
Honolulu, HI	5.2	14.1	22.0	13.0	12.8	12.9	10.5	5.5	3.9	41.5
Houston, TX	7.6	19.9	25.9	14.0	11.7	10.4	6.3	3.0	1.2	33.0
Huntsville, AL	6.1	17.6	23.8	11.6	12.1	12.7	8.9	5.2	2.1	36.9
Indianapolis, IN	7.3	19.8	24.1	12.8	11.9	11.9	7.2	3.4	1.5	34.2
Jacksonville, FL	6.9	18.3	23.3	12.7	12.8	12.5	8.2	3.8	1.5	35.9
Kansas City, MO	6.8	18.4	24.6	13.2	12.0	12.2	7.5	3.6	1.7	35.1
Lafayette, LA	5.7	18.5	24.4	11.5	11.5	13.5	8.9	4.2	1.7	35.8
Lakeland, FL	4.9	17.8	19.9	11.9	11.4	11.9	11.8	7.2	3.2	41.1
Las Vegas, NV	6.4	19.5	20.2	13.3	13.4	12.1	9.1	4.3	1.5	37.8
Lexington, KY	6.1	18.4	26.0	13.1	11.8	11.5	7.8	3.7	1.5	34.6
Lincoln, NE	6.5	19.9	26.7	12.4	10.5	10.9	7.7	3.6	1.7	32.7
Little Rock, AR	6.7	18.8	22.1	13.5	11.9	12.8	8.4	3.6	2.2	36.7
Los Angeles, CA	5.9	17.5	25.7	14.3	13.2	11.0	7.0	3.6	1.7	35.6
Louisville, KY	6.5	18.5	21.5	12.4	12.8	13.4	8.7	4.3	1.9	37.6

Table continued on following page.

City	Percent of Population									Median Age
	Under Age 5	Age 5–19	Age 20–34	Age 35–44	Age 45–54	Age 55–64	Age 65–74	Age 75–84	Age 85+	
Madison, WI	4.9	16.4	35.5	12.2	9.7	9.7	6.9	3.2	1.5	31.0
Manchester, NH	6.0	15.7	26.6	12.8	13.2	12.4	7.2	3.7	2.3	36.0
Memphis, TN	7.6	19.9	23.7	12.0	11.8	12.0	7.7	3.6	1.5	34.0
Miami, FL	5.9	13.4	23.0	14.6	14.5	11.8	8.5	5.8	2.6	40.1
Midland, TX	8.8	21.0	25.5	13.0	10.8	10.5	5.7	3.1	1.6	31.7
Milwaukee, WI	7.4	21.9	25.6	12.6	11.2	10.7	6.3	2.8	1.4	31.5
Minneapolis, MN	6.5	16.9	32.0	13.8	10.8	10.1	6.3	2.6	1.1	32.3
Nashville, TN	6.8	17.0	27.6	13.8	11.8	11.4	7.1	3.3	1.3	34.2
New Haven, CT	6.3	21.2	29.6	12.6	11.1	8.9	6.4	2.7	1.2	30.8
New Orleans, LA	5.9	16.6	24.6	13.4	12.1	13.3	8.7	3.7	1.7	36.8
New York, NY	6.5	16.5	24.3	13.7	12.7	11.8	8.1	4.4	2.0	36.7
Oklahoma City, OK	7.6	20.6	23.1	13.4	11.5	11.5	7.4	3.5	1.5	34.1
Omaha, NE	7.3	20.4	22.9	12.7	11.9	11.9	7.6	3.6	1.7	34.5
Orlando, FL	6.7	15.9	29.7	15.1	12.1	10.1	6.3	2.7	1.2	33.8
Peoria, IL	7.6	19.5	22.5	12.1	11.3	11.8	8.4	4.4	2.4	35.2
Philadelphia, PA	6.7	18.0	26.2	12.4	11.7	11.6	7.7	4.0	1.8	34.4
Phoenix, AZ	7.2	21.6	23.2	13.8	12.8	10.9	6.5	2.9	1.2	33.8
Pittsburgh, PA	4.7	15.4	33.3	10.6	9.5	11.8	8.1	4.3	2.3	32.9
Portland, OR	5.3	14.6	25.9	17.1	13.1	11.3	8.0	3.3	1.5	37.1
Providence, RI	6.3	21.9	28.3	12.3	10.9	9.4	5.9	3.2	1.7	30.6
Provo, UT	7.1	20.7	47.4	8.3	5.4	5.0	3.1	2.0	0.9	23.6
Raleigh, NC	5.9	18.9	27.5	14.5	12.7	9.9	6.4	2.9	1.3	33.6
Reno, NV	6.2	17.8	24.7	12.6	11.7	12.2	9.3	4.1	1.4	35.8
Richmond, VA	5.9	15.6	30.2	11.8	11.2	12.4	7.7	3.3	1.8	34.0
Riverside, CA	6.2	22.3	26.5	12.4	12.0	10.0	6.3	3.1	1.3	31.6
Rochester, MN	7.2	18.8	22.6	13.1	11.6	11.8	8.0	4.6	2.4	35.7
Sacramento, CA	6.6	18.8	25.4	13.5	11.6	11.1	7.8	3.5	1.8	34.5
Salt Lake City, UT	6.2	17.1	31.6	13.8	10.1	10.2	6.6	3.2	1.3	32.3
San Antonio, TX	6.9	21.0	24.2	13.2	12.0	10.7	7.1	3.5	1.5	33.6
San Diego, CA	5.9	16.8	27.4	13.9	12.3	11.0	7.3	3.7	1.6	34.9
San Francisco, CA	4.5	10.5	29.0	15.8	13.2	11.6	8.5	4.5	2.5	38.2
San Jose, CA	6.1	18.4	22.7	14.4	13.9	11.8	7.3	3.7	1.5	36.7
Santa Rosa, CA	5.9	17.8	21.2	12.8	12.6	12.9	9.6	4.8	2.3	38.8
Savannah, GA	6.4	18.2	29.1	11.6	10.4	11.2	7.7	3.7	1.7	32.6
Seattle, WA	4.8	12.8	31.8	15.3	12.3	10.7	7.4	3.3	1.8	35.3
Sioux Falls, SD	7.5	19.9	23.5	13.3	11.4	11.7	7.6	3.4	1.7	34.4
Springfield, IL	6.1	18.2	20.2	11.6	12.2	14.0	10.0	5.3	2.3	39.4
Tallahassee, FL	4.9	19.2	38.0	10.0	8.8	8.7	6.3	2.8	1.2	26.9
Tampa, FL	6.4	18.5	24.2	13.5	13.4	11.8	7.3	3.5	1.5	35.7
Tucson, AZ	6.0	19.1	26.5	11.9	10.9	11.2	8.3	4.2	1.9	33.7
Tulsa, OK	7.1	20.0	22.8	12.4	11.4	12.3	8.1	4.0	1.9	35.1
Tuscaloosa, AL	5.2	22.9	29.5	10.0	9.9	10.3	6.9	3.9	1.4	29.3
Virginia Beach, VA	6.3	18.2	23.7	13.0	12.7	12.1	8.1	4.0	1.6	36.2
Washington, DC	6.5	14.5	31.0	14.8	11.0	10.1	7.0	3.5	1.6	34.0
Wichita, KS	7.0	20.7	22.4	11.9	11.6	12.5	8.2	3.9	1.8	35.0
Winston-Salem, NC	6.5	20.9	21.8	12.4	12.1	12.0	8.1	4.3	1.7	35.5
U.S.	6.1	19.1	20.7	12.6	13.0	12.9	9.1	4.6	1.9	38.1

Source: U.S. Census Bureau, 2015-2019 American Community Survey 5-Year Estimates

Age: Metro Area

Metro Area	Percent of Population									Median Age
	Under Age 5	Age 5–19	Age 20–34	Age 35–44	Age 45–54	Age 55–64	Age 65–74	Age 75–84	Age 85+	
Albuquerque, NM	5.7	19.2	20.7	12.6	12.4	13.2	9.8	4.7	1.8	38.2
Allentown, PA	5.3	18.7	18.6	11.9	13.8	14.1	9.9	5.2	2.6	41.4
Anchorage, AK	7.2	20.2	24.0	13.0	12.4	12.4	7.2	2.6	0.9	34.0
Ann Arbor, MI	4.9	19.5	27.4	11.5	11.8	11.5	8.2	3.7	1.6	33.6
Athens, GA	5.4	21.1	27.1	12.0	11.0	10.7	7.8	3.8	1.2	32.2
Atlanta, GA	6.4	21.0	20.6	14.0	14.3	11.8	7.5	3.2	1.1	36.4
Austin, TX	6.4	19.7	24.3	15.5	12.9	10.6	6.7	2.7	1.1	34.7
Baton Rouge, LA	6.5	20.1	22.7	12.7	12.2	12.2	8.4	3.9	1.4	35.6
Boise City, ID	6.3	21.7	20.0	13.4	12.5	11.8	8.7	4.0	1.4	36.3
Boston, MA	5.3	17.7	22.2	12.5	13.7	13.2	8.8	4.4	2.1	38.7
Boulder, CO	4.6	19.0	24.3	12.6	13.1	12.7	8.4	3.7	1.6	36.6
Cape Coral, FL	4.7	15.2	15.8	10.3	11.9	14.1	15.5	9.3	3.3	48.5
Cedar Rapids, IA	6.2	19.5	19.6	12.7	12.9	12.9	9.0	4.8	2.3	38.4
Charleston, SC	6.1	18.5	22.1	13.2	12.7	12.8	9.3	3.9	1.5	37.2
Charlotte, NC	6.2	20.2	20.1	13.9	14.2	12.1	8.2	3.8	1.4	37.5
Chicago, IL	6.1	19.4	21.0	13.3	13.3	12.7	8.2	4.1	1.8	37.5
Cincinnati, OH	6.3	20.1	19.9	12.4	13.2	13.4	8.7	4.2	1.9	37.9
Clarksville, TN	8.4	20.8	27.0	12.4	10.8	9.8	6.6	3.2	1.2	31.1
Cleveland, OH	5.6	18.1	18.9	11.6	13.3	14.5	10.1	5.4	2.5	41.3
College Station, TX	6.1	20.9	32.9	11.0	9.5	9.2	6.1	3.0	1.2	27.8
Colorado Springs, CO	6.6	20.2	23.6	12.5	12.1	12.1	7.9	3.5	1.3	34.6
Columbia, MO	5.8	19.4	28.5	11.6	10.7	11.3	7.5	3.7	1.4	32.1
Columbia, SC	5.8	20.2	21.6	12.5	12.7	12.7	8.9	4.1	1.5	36.6
Columbus, OH	6.7	19.8	22.2	13.4	13.0	12.1	7.8	3.6	1.5	36.0
Dallas, TX	7.0	21.8	21.5	14.2	13.4	11.2	6.8	3.1	1.1	34.8
Davenport, IA	6.2	19.3	18.3	12.3	12.5	13.8	10.0	5.3	2.4	39.7
Denver, CO	6.1	18.9	22.6	14.6	13.2	12.1	7.8	3.3	1.4	36.5
Des Moines, IA	7.0	20.5	20.7	13.7	12.8	11.9	7.9	3.9	1.6	36.2
Durham, NC	5.7	18.6	22.3	13.0	13.0	12.6	9.1	4.0	1.7	37.6
Edison, NJ	6.1	17.8	21.2	13.1	13.6	12.8	8.6	4.6	2.2	38.6
El Paso, TX	7.6	22.8	23.3	12.5	11.5	10.4	6.7	3.7	1.5	32.2
Fargo, ND	7.1	19.5	27.4	12.8	10.5	10.7	6.6	3.4	1.9	32.5
Fayetteville, NC	7.7	20.7	25.7	12.5	11.4	10.6	7.0	3.4	1.1	32.3
Fort Collins, CO	5.1	18.4	25.2	12.3	11.2	12.6	9.4	4.1	1.7	36.0
Fort Wayne, IN	7.0	21.1	20.1	12.3	12.4	12.6	8.6	4.1	1.8	36.4
Fort Worth, TX	7.0	21.8	21.5	14.2	13.4	11.2	6.8	3.1	1.1	34.8
Grand Rapids, MI	6.5	20.6	21.8	12.3	12.4	12.5	8.1	4.0	1.9	35.8
Greeley, CO	7.2	22.1	21.5	13.6	12.2	11.5	7.4	3.2	1.2	34.4
Green Bay, WI	6.2	19.7	19.2	12.4	13.4	13.7	9.0	4.6	1.8	38.8
Greensboro, NC	5.8	19.7	19.8	12.1	13.7	13.0	9.3	4.7	1.9	38.8
Honolulu, HI	6.4	17.0	22.6	12.7	12.1	11.9	9.4	5.0	2.9	37.9
Houston, TX	7.3	21.9	21.7	14.2	12.8	11.2	6.8	3.0	1.0	34.3
Huntsville, AL	5.8	19.0	20.3	12.4	14.1	13.5	8.6	4.5	1.6	38.7
Indianapolis, IN	6.7	20.5	20.7	13.2	13.1	12.3	8.0	3.8	1.6	36.5
Jacksonville, FL	6.2	18.5	20.7	12.7	13.3	13.2	9.5	4.3	1.6	38.3
Kansas City, MO	6.5	20.0	20.0	13.2	12.9	12.8	8.5	4.2	1.8	37.4
Lafayette, LA	6.9	20.2	21.3	12.6	12.4	12.9	8.1	4.0	1.6	36.0
Lakeland, FL	5.8	18.8	19.0	11.8	12.1	12.3	11.4	6.7	2.1	40.2
Las Vegas, NV	6.3	19.3	21.1	13.8	13.3	11.7	8.9	4.2	1.3	37.3
Lexington, KY	6.2	19.0	23.2	13.0	12.6	12.1	8.3	4.0	1.5	36.1
Lincoln, NE	6.4	20.4	25.0	12.3	10.9	11.4	8.1	3.8	1.8	33.7
Little Rock, AR	6.4	19.6	21.3	12.9	12.4	12.5	8.9	4.2	1.8	36.9
Los Angeles, CA	6.0	18.6	22.7	13.5	13.6	12.0	7.7	4.0	1.9	36.8
Louisville, KY	6.1	18.7	19.9	12.8	13.3	13.6	9.3	4.4	1.8	39.0

Table continued on following page.

Metro Area	Percent of Population									Median Age
	Under Age 5	Age 5–19	Age 20–34	Age 35–44	Age 45–54	Age 55–64	Age 65–74	Age 75–84	Age 85+	
Madison, WI	5.6	18.2	24.4	13.0	12.3	12.5	8.5	3.8	1.7	36.2
Manchester, NH	5.2	17.8	19.8	12.3	14.9	14.7	9.0	4.3	1.9	40.7
Memphis, TN	6.8	20.7	20.8	12.7	12.9	12.5	8.3	3.8	1.4	36.3
Miami, FL	5.7	17.0	19.4	13.1	14.2	12.8	9.4	5.8	2.7	41.0
Midland, TX	8.8	22.1	24.4	13.1	10.6	10.8	5.8	3.1	1.5	31.7
Milwaukee, WI	6.2	19.6	20.4	12.5	12.8	13.3	8.7	4.3	2.2	37.8
Minneapolis, MN	6.5	19.7	20.7	13.3	13.3	13.0	8.0	3.8	1.7	37.1
Nashville, TN	6.4	19.4	22.1	13.7	13.3	12.3	8.0	3.6	1.3	36.4
New Haven, CT	5.2	18.2	20.2	11.8	13.7	13.8	9.5	4.9	2.6	40.3
New Orleans, LA	6.2	18.3	21.0	12.8	12.8	13.7	9.3	4.3	1.7	38.3
New York, NY	6.1	17.8	21.2	13.1	13.6	12.8	8.6	4.6	2.2	38.6
Oklahoma City, OK	6.8	20.6	22.2	13.0	11.8	12.0	8.1	3.9	1.6	35.2
Omaha, NE	7.2	21.0	20.8	13.2	12.3	12.2	8.0	3.8	1.6	35.7
Orlando, FL	5.9	18.7	22.2	13.7	13.3	11.7	8.5	4.3	1.7	37.2
Peoria, IL	6.3	19.1	18.5	12.3	12.6	13.5	9.9	5.3	2.6	39.9
Philadelphia, PA	5.9	18.6	20.7	12.3	13.4	13.5	8.9	4.6	2.1	38.8
Phoenix, AZ	6.4	20.3	21.0	13.1	12.5	11.4	8.9	4.6	1.7	36.7
Pittsburgh, PA	5.1	16.5	19.2	11.5	13.1	15.2	10.8	5.8	3.0	43.1
Portland, OR	5.7	18.1	21.3	14.7	13.3	12.5	9.0	3.8	1.7	38.1
Providence, RI	5.2	17.9	20.5	11.9	13.9	13.9	9.5	4.8	2.5	40.3
Provo, UT	9.6	28.3	26.8	12.6	8.4	6.7	4.5	2.3	0.8	24.8
Raleigh, NC	6.2	20.8	20.4	14.8	14.5	11.6	7.4	3.2	1.2	36.7
Reno, NV	6.0	18.1	21.5	12.2	12.8	13.2	10.2	4.4	1.4	38.5
Richmond, VA	5.8	18.7	20.7	12.8	13.6	13.5	9.2	4.1	1.8	38.8
Riverside, CA	6.8	22.1	21.8	12.8	12.5	11.2	7.5	3.8	1.4	34.5
Rochester, MN	6.7	19.8	18.9	12.6	12.4	13.4	8.8	5.0	2.3	38.4
Sacramento, CA	6.1	19.6	21.0	12.8	12.8	12.6	8.8	4.3	1.9	37.4
Salt Lake City, UT	7.6	22.6	23.3	14.6	11.2	10.1	6.4	3.0	1.1	32.7
San Antonio, TX	6.9	21.4	22.2	13.3	12.4	11.2	7.6	3.7	1.5	34.7
San Diego, CA	6.3	18.2	24.2	13.3	12.5	11.7	7.9	4.0	1.8	35.8
San Francisco, CA	5.5	16.5	22.0	14.5	13.8	12.6	8.7	4.4	2.1	39.0
San Jose, CA	6.1	18.6	22.3	14.5	13.8	11.7	7.4	4.0	1.8	37.1
Santa Rosa, CA	5.0	17.2	18.7	12.4	13.0	14.5	11.6	5.1	2.2	42.1
Savannah, GA	6.6	19.4	23.2	12.9	12.1	11.9	8.5	4.0	1.5	35.6
Seattle, WA	6.1	17.6	23.0	14.3	13.4	12.4	7.9	3.5	1.6	37.0
Sioux Falls, SD	7.6	20.7	21.4	13.5	11.8	12.0	7.8	3.4	1.8	35.2
Springfield, IL	5.8	19.0	18.4	12.2	13.1	14.2	10.1	5.1	2.1	40.4
Tallahassee, FL	5.2	18.9	27.4	11.5	11.2	11.8	8.7	3.8	1.5	33.8
Tampa, FL	5.4	16.8	18.9	12.4	13.5	13.6	10.9	6.0	2.5	42.1
Tucson, AZ	5.7	18.6	21.5	11.4	11.2	12.6	10.9	6.0	2.2	38.5
Tulsa, OK	6.7	20.5	20.1	12.6	12.4	12.7	8.9	4.5	1.7	37.0
Tuscaloosa, AL	6.0	20.5	24.3	11.8	11.5	12.0	8.4	4.1	1.5	34.4
Virginia Beach, VA	6.3	18.6	23.4	12.3	12.4	12.7	8.5	4.2	1.7	36.3
Washington, DC	6.5	19.0	21.3	14.3	14.0	12.1	7.7	3.6	1.4	37.0
Wichita, KS	6.9	21.3	20.4	12.1	11.8	12.7	8.3	4.3	1.9	36.0
Winston-Salem, NC	5.7	19.4	18.3	11.9	14.1	13.7	9.9	5.3	1.8	40.6
U.S.	6.1	19.1	20.7	12.6	13.0	12.9	9.1	4.6	1.9	38.1

Note: Figures cover the Metropolitan Statistical Area (MSA)—see Appendix B for areas included
Source: U.S. Census Bureau, 2015-2019 American Community Survey 5-Year Estimates

Religious Groups by Family

Area[1]	Catholic	Baptist	Non-Den.	Methodist[2]	Lutheran	LDS[3]	Pentecostal	Presbyterian[4]	Muslim[5]	Judaism
Albuquerque, NM	27.1	3.7	4.2	1.4	0.9	2.3	1.4	1.0	0.2	0.2
Allentown, PA	23.1	0.4	1.9	3.9	7.9	0.3	0.4	6.2	0.6	0.6
Anchorage, AK	6.9	5.0	6.4	1.3	1.9	5.1	1.8	0.6	0.2	0.1
Ann Arbor, MI	12.3	2.2	1.5	3.0	2.8	0.8	1.9	2.9	1.2	0.9
Athens, GA	4.4	16.2	2.2	8.3	0.3	0.8	2.8	2.0	0.3	0.2
Atlanta, GA	7.4	17.4	6.8	7.8	0.5	0.7	2.6	1.8	0.7	0.5
Austin, TX	16.0	10.3	4.5	3.6	1.9	1.1	0.8	1.0	1.2	0.2
Baton Rouge, LA	22.5	18.2	9.6	4.6	0.2	0.7	1.1	0.6	0.2	0.1
Boise City, ID	8.0	2.9	4.1	2.1	1.1	15.8	2.3	0.6	0.1	0.1
Boston, MA	44.3	1.1	1.0	0.9	0.3	0.4	0.6	1.6	0.4	1.4
Boulder, CO	20.1	2.3	4.7	1.7	3.0	2.9	0.4	2.0	0.1	0.7
Cape Coral, FL	16.2	4.9	3.0	2.5	1.1	0.5	4.3	1.4	0.9	0.2
Cedar Rapids, IA	18.8	2.3	3.0	7.3	11.3	0.8	1.8	3.2	0.5	0.1
Charleston, SC	6.1	12.4	7.0	10.0	1.1	0.9	2.0	2.3	0.1	0.3
Charlotte, NC	5.9	17.2	6.7	8.6	1.3	0.7	3.2	4.5	0.2	0.3
Chicago, IL	34.2	3.2	4.4	1.9	3.0	0.3	1.2	1.9	3.2	0.8
Cincinnati, OH	19.0	9.5	3.6	3.8	1.1	0.5	2.2	1.5	0.2	0.5
Clarksville, TN	4.0	30.9	2.2	6.1	0.5	1.5	1.8	1.0	0.1	<0.1
Cleveland, OH	28.8	4.3	3.3	2.8	2.5	0.3	1.1	2.0	0.1	1.4
College Station, TX	11.7	15.6	3.9	4.7	1.5	1.2	0.6	0.9	1.1	<0.1
Colorado Springs, CO	8.3	4.3	7.4	2.4	1.9	3.0	1.0	2.0	<0.1	0.1
Columbia, MO	6.6	14.6	5.4	4.3	1.7	1.3	1.0	2.3	0.3	0.2
Columbia, SC	3.1	18.0	5.2	9.3	3.4	1.0	2.6	3.3	0.1	0.2
Columbus, OH	11.7	5.3	3.5	4.7	2.4	0.7	1.9	2.0	0.8	0.5
Dallas, TX	13.3	18.7	7.7	5.2	0.7	1.1	2.1	0.9	2.4	0.3
Davenport, IA	14.9	4.9	2.7	5.3	8.6	0.8	1.4	2.9	0.9	0.1
Denver, CO	16.0	2.9	4.6	1.7	2.1	2.4	1.2	1.5	0.5	0.6
Des Moines, IA	13.6	4.7	3.3	6.9	8.2	0.9	2.3	2.9	0.3	0.3
Durham, NC	5.0	13.8	5.6	8.1	0.4	0.7	1.3	2.5	0.4	0.5
Edison, NJ	36.9	1.8	1.7	1.3	0.7	0.3	0.8	1.0	2.3	4.7
El Paso, TX	43.2	3.7	4.9	0.8	0.3	1.5	1.4	0.2	<0.1	0.2
Fargo, ND	17.4	0.4	0.4	3.3	32.5	0.6	1.5	1.8	0.1	<0.1
Fayetteville, NC	2.6	14.1	10.4	6.2	0.1	1.4	4.8	2.1	0.1	<0.1
Fort Collins, CO	11.8	2.2	6.3	4.3	3.4	2.9	4.7	1.9	0.1	<0.1
Fort Wayne, IN	14.2	6.0	6.8	5.1	8.5	0.4	1.4	1.6	0.2	0.1
Fort Worth, TX	13.3	18.7	7.7	5.2	0.7	1.1	2.1	0.9	2.4	0.3
Grand Rapids, MI	17.1	1.7	8.3	3.0	2.1	0.5	1.1	9.9	1.0	0.1
Greeley, CO	13.5	1.8	1.5	2.6	2.0	1.9	1.8	1.4	0.1	<0.1
Green Bay, WI	42.0	0.7	3.4	2.2	12.7	0.3	0.6	1.0	0.1	<0.1
Greensboro, NC	2.6	12.8	7.4	9.8	0.6	0.8	2.4	3.1	0.6	0.4
Honolulu, HI	18.2	1.9	2.2	0.8	0.3	5.1	4.1	1.4	<0.1	<0.1
Houston, TX	17.0	16.0	7.2	4.8	1.0	1.1	1.5	0.8	2.6	0.3
Huntsville, AL	3.9	27.6	3.1	7.5	0.7	1.1	1.2	1.7	0.2	0.1
Indianapolis, IN	10.5	10.2	7.1	4.9	1.6	0.7	1.6	1.6	0.2	0.3
Jacksonville, FL	9.8	18.5	7.7	4.5	0.6	1.1	1.9	1.6	0.6	0.4
Kansas City, MO	12.6	13.1	5.2	5.8	2.2	2.4	2.6	1.6	0.3	0.4
Lafayette, LA	47.0	14.7	3.9	2.5	0.2	0.4	2.9	0.1	0.1	<0.1
Lakeland, FL	7.5	13.6	5.0	3.9	0.9	0.7	4.0	1.6	0.4	<0.1
Las Vegas, NV	18.1	2.9	3.0	0.4	0.7	6.3	1.5	0.2	<0.1	0.3
Lexington, KY	6.7	24.9	2.3	5.9	0.4	1.0	2.1	1.3	0.1	0.3
Lincoln, NE	14.7	2.4	1.9	7.1	11.2	1.1	1.4	3.9	0.2	0.1
Little Rock, AR	4.5	25.9	6.0	7.3	0.5	0.9	2.8	0.8	0.1	0.1
Los Angeles, CA	33.8	2.7	3.6	1.0	0.6	1.7	1.7	0.9	0.7	0.9
Louisville, KY	13.6	25.0	1.7	3.7	0.6	0.8	0.9	1.1	0.5	0.4
Madison, WI	21.8	1.1	1.5	3.6	12.7	0.5	0.3	2.1	0.4	0.4

Table continued on following page.

Area[1]	Catholic	Baptist	Non-Den.	Methodist[2]	Lutheran	LDS[3]	Pentecostal	Presbyterian[4]	Muslim[5]	Judaism
Manchester, NH	31.1	1.3	2.3	1.1	0.5	0.6	0.4	2.0	0.3	0.5
Memphis, TN	5.2	30.8	5.4	6.2	0.3	0.6	4.7	2.4	0.3	0.6
Miami, FL	18.5	5.3	4.1	1.2	0.4	0.5	1.7	0.6	0.9	1.5
Midland, TX	22.4	25.2	8.8	4.2	0.6	1.2	1.6	1.8	3.7	<0.1
Milwaukee, WI	24.6	3.1	3.8	1.5	10.7	0.4	1.9	1.5	0.5	0.5
Minneapolis, MN	21.7	2.4	2.9	2.7	14.4	0.6	1.7	1.8	0.4	0.7
Nashville, TN	4.1	25.2	5.8	6.1	0.3	0.7	2.1	2.1	0.3	0.1
New Haven, CT	35.3	1.4	1.9	1.5	0.6	0.3	1.0	2.2	0.5	1.2
New Orleans, LA	31.5	8.4	3.7	2.6	0.8	0.5	2.1	0.5	0.4	0.5
New York, NY	36.9	1.8	1.7	1.3	0.7	0.3	0.8	1.0	2.3	4.7
Oklahoma City, OK	6.3	25.3	7.0	10.6	0.7	1.2	3.1	0.9	0.2	0.1
Omaha, NE	21.6	4.5	1.8	3.9	7.8	1.7	1.2	2.2	0.5	0.4
Orlando, FL	13.2	6.9	5.6	2.9	0.9	0.9	3.2	1.3	1.3	0.2
Peoria, IL	11.4	5.5	5.2	4.9	6.1	0.5	1.5	2.8	5.2	0.1
Philadelphia, PA	33.4	3.9	2.8	2.9	1.8	0.3	0.8	2.1	1.2	1.3
Phoenix, AZ	13.3	3.4	5.1	1.0	1.6	6.1	2.9	0.6	0.1	0.3
Pittsburgh, PA	32.8	2.3	2.8	5.6	3.3	0.3	1.1	4.6	0.3	0.7
Portland, OR	10.5	2.3	4.5	1.0	1.6	3.7	2.0	0.9	0.1	0.3
Providence, RI	47.0	1.4	1.2	0.8	0.5	0.3	0.5	1.0	0.1	0.7
Provo, UT	1.3	<0.1	<0.1	0.1	<0.1	88.5	0.1	<0.1	<0.1	<0.1
Raleigh, NC	9.1	12.1	5.9	6.7	0.9	0.8	2.2	2.2	0.9	0.3
Reno, NV	14.3	1.5	3.1	0.9	0.7	4.6	1.9	0.4	<0.1	0.1
Richmond, VA	5.9	19.9	5.4	6.1	0.6	0.9	1.8	2.1	2.7	0.3
Riverside, CA	24.8	2.6	5.5	0.6	0.5	2.4	1.5	0.6	0.5	<0.1
Rochester, MN	23.3	1.6	4.6	4.8	21.0	1.1	1.2	2.9	0.2	0.2
Sacramento, CA	16.1	3.1	4.0	1.7	0.7	3.3	2.0	0.8	0.8	0.2
Salt Lake City, UT	8.9	0.8	0.5	0.5	0.5	58.9	0.6	0.3	0.4	0.1
San Antonio, TX	28.4	8.5	6.0	3.0	1.6	1.4	1.3	0.7	0.9	0.2
San Diego, CA	25.9	2.0	4.8	1.1	0.9	2.3	1.0	0.9	0.7	0.5
San Francisco, CA	20.7	2.5	2.4	1.9	0.5	1.5	1.2	1.1	1.2	0.8
San Jose, CA	26.0	1.3	4.2	1.0	0.5	1.4	1.1	0.7	1.0	0.6
Santa Rosa, CA	22.2	1.3	1.5	0.9	0.9	1.9	0.6	0.9	0.4	0.4
Savannah, GA	7.0	19.6	6.9	8.9	1.6	0.9	2.3	1.0	0.1	0.8
Seattle, WA	12.3	2.1	5.0	1.2	2.0	3.3	2.8	1.4	0.4	0.4
Sioux Falls, SD	14.9	3.0	1.5	3.8	21.4	0.7	1.0	6.2	0.3	<0.1
Springfield, IL	15.5	11.7	2.7	6.8	5.6	0.7	4.9	2.0	1.5	0.2
Tallahassee, FL	4.8	16.0	6.7	9.1	0.4	1.0	2.1	1.5	0.8	0.3
Tampa, FL	10.8	7.0	3.7	3.4	0.9	0.6	2.1	0.9	1.2	0.4
Tucson, AZ	20.7	3.3	3.7	1.3	1.5	2.9	1.5	1.0	<0.1	0.5
Tulsa, OK	5.8	22.9	7.6	9.2	0.7	1.1	3.3	1.2	0.3	0.2
Tuscaloosa, AL	1.7	32.2	4.5	8.3	<0.1	0.6	1.5	1.3	0.1	<0.1
Virginia Beach, VA	6.4	11.5	6.1	5.2	0.7	0.9	1.9	2.0	2.0	0.3
Washington, DC	14.5	7.3	4.8	4.5	1.2	1.1	1.0	1.3	2.3	1.1
Wichita, KS	14.5	13.4	3.1	7.1	1.7	1.4	1.9	1.6	0.1	<0.1
Winston-Salem, NC	3.5	17.4	9.3	12.4	0.7	0.6	2.5	2.2	0.3	0.1
U.S.	19.1	9.3	4.0	4.0	2.3	2.0	1.9	1.6	0.8	0.7

Note: Figures are the number of adherents as a percentage of the total population; (1) Figures cover the Metropolitan Statistical Area—see Appendix B for areas included; (2) Methodist/Pietist; (3) Latter Day Saints; (4) Reformed; (5) Figures are estimates
Source: Association of Statisticians of American Religious Bodies, 2010 U.S. Religion Census: Religious Congregations & Membership Study

Religious Groups by Tradition

Area	Catholic	Evangelical Protestant	Mainline Protestant	Other Tradition	Black Protestant	Orthodox
Albuquerque, NM	27.1	11.2	3.2	3.9	0.2	0.1
Allentown, PA	23.1	5.3	17.7	3.0	0.1	0.6
Anchorage, AK	6.9	15.6	3.5	6.8	0.3	0.6
Ann Arbor, MI	12.3	7.3	7.5	3.7	1.5	0.2
Athens, GA	4.4	21.1	9.7	1.7	2.4	0.1
Atlanta, GA	7.4	26.0	9.8	2.9	3.1	0.2
Austin, TX	16.0	16.1	6.3	3.9	1.3	0.1
Baton Rouge, LA	22.5	24.8	5.6	1.5	5.1	<0.1
Boise City, ID	8.0	12.9	4.3	16.7	<0.1	<0.1
Boston, MA	44.3	3.2	4.5	3.4	0.1	1.0
Boulder, CO	20.1	9.7	6.4	4.8	<0.1	0.2
Cape Coral, FL	16.2	14.3	4.6	2.0	0.3	0.1
Cedar Rapids, IA	18.8	13.7	17.5	1.9	0.1	0.2
Charleston, SC	6.1	19.6	11.1	1.8	7.3	0.1
Charlotte, NC	5.9	27.5	13.3	1.6	2.7	0.4
Chicago, IL	34.2	9.7	5.1	5.0	2.0	0.9
Cincinnati, OH	19.0	15.5	7.1	1.5	1.1	0.1
Clarksville, TN	4.0	35.3	7.2	1.6	2.4	<0.1
Cleveland, OH	28.8	9.0	7.5	2.6	2.1	0.8
College Station, TX	11.7	20.6	6.6	2.5	0.9	<0.1
Colorado Springs, CO	8.3	15.2	5.3	3.7	0.4	0.1
Columbia, MO	6.6	19.9	10.4	2.3	0.4	0.1
Columbia, SC	3.1	25.5	13.4	2.1	5.4	0.1
Columbus, OH	11.7	11.8	9.5	3.1	1.1	0.2
Dallas, TX	13.3	28.3	6.9	4.7	1.7	0.1
Davenport, IA	14.9	11.3	15.1	2.3	1.5	0.1
Denver, CO	16.0	11.0	4.5	4.6	0.3	0.3
Des Moines, IA	13.6	12.3	16.8	1.8	0.9	0.1
Durham, NC	5.0	19.3	11.7	2.9	3.1	<0.1
Edison, NJ	36.9	3.9	4.1	8.3	1.2	0.9
El Paso, TX	43.2	10.8	1.2	2.0	0.2	<0.1
Fargo, ND	17.4	10.7	30.8	0.8	<0.1	<0.1
Fayetteville, NC	2.6	26.7	7.8	1.7	4.3	0.1
Fort Collins, CO	11.8	18.8	5.9	3.9	<0.1	0.1
Fort Wayne, IN	14.2	24.6	9.1	0.9	2.4	0.2
Fort Worth, TX	13.3	28.3	6.9	4.7	1.7	0.1
Grand Rapids, MI	17.1	20.7	7.5	2.1	1.0	0.2
Greeley, CO	13.5	9.2	3.8	2.1	<0.1	<0.1
Green Bay, WI	42.0	14.1	8.1	0.6	<0.1	<0.1
Greensboro, NC	2.6	23.2	14.0	2.1	2.6	<0.1
Honolulu, HI	18.2	9.6	2.9	8.4	<0.1	<0.1
Houston, TX	17.0	24.9	6.6	4.9	1.3	0.2
Huntsville, AL	3.9	33.3	9.6	1.8	1.8	<0.1
Indianapolis, IN	10.5	18.2	9.6	1.6	1.8	0.2
Jacksonville, FL	9.8	27.1	5.6	2.9	4.2	0.2
Kansas City, MO	12.6	20.5	9.9	3.6	2.6	0.1
Lafayette, LA	47.0	12.7	3.2	0.7	9.2	<0.1
Lakeland, FL	7.5	24.6	5.2	1.4	1.7	<0.1
Las Vegas, NV	18.1	7.7	1.3	7.6	0.4	0.4
Lexington, KY	6.7	28.3	10.2	1.7	2.0	0.1
Lincoln, NE	14.7	14.8	16.2	2.0	0.1	<0.1
Little Rock, AR	4.5	33.9	8.1	1.7	3.4	<0.1
Los Angeles, CA	33.8	9.0	2.3	4.6	0.8	0.6
Louisville, KY	13.6	24.5	7.1	2.0	2.9	<0.1
Madison, WI	21.8	7.2	15.3	2.2	0.1	<0.1

Table continued on following page.

Area	Catholic	Evangelical Protestant	Mainline Protestant	Other Tradition	Black Protestant	Orthodox
Manchester, NH	31.1	5.1	4.4	1.8	<0.1	0.7
Memphis, TN	5.2	29.4	8.3	2.1	13.4	<0.1
Miami, FL	18.5	11.4	2.4	3.5	1.7	0.2
Midland, TX	22.4	35.4	7.2	5.3	1.0	<0.1
Milwaukee, WI	24.6	14.6	7.1	2.3	2.4	0.6
Minneapolis, MN	21.7	12.8	14.5	2.2	0.4	0.2
Nashville, TN	4.1	32.9	8.0	1.7	3.3	0.4
New Haven, CT	35.3	3.8	6.1	2.3	0.7	0.4
New Orleans, LA	31.5	12.7	4.0	2.1	2.9	0.1
New York, NY	36.9	3.9	4.1	8.3	1.2	0.9
Oklahoma City, OK	6.3	39.0	9.8	2.7	1.9	0.1
Omaha, NE	21.6	12.1	10.7	3.2	1.4	0.1
Orlando, FL	13.2	17.8	4.7	3.2	1.2	0.3
Peoria, IL	11.4	18.9	11.1	6.1	0.9	0.1
Philadelphia, PA	33.4	6.3	8.9	3.7	1.7	0.4
Phoenix, AZ	13.3	13.2	2.6	7.8	0.1	0.3
Pittsburgh, PA	32.8	7.3	13.8	2.0	0.8	0.6
Portland, OR	10.5	11.6	3.6	5.2	0.1	0.3
Providence, RI	47.0	2.8	4.7	1.6	<0.1	0.5
Provo, UT	1.3	0.4	<0.1	88.8	<0.1	<0.1
Raleigh, NC	9.1	19.9	10.1	3.2	1.7	0.2
Reno, NV	14.3	7.6	1.9	5.1	0.2	0.1
Richmond, VA	5.9	23.6	13.3	4.5	2.4	0.1
Riverside, CA	24.8	11.4	1.3	3.7	0.8	0.1
Rochester, MN	23.3	18.9	21.0	2.0	<0.1	0.1
Sacramento, CA	16.1	11.3	2.2	5.8	0.5	0.3
Salt Lake City, UT	8.9	2.6	1.2	60.0	0.1	0.4
San Antonio, TX	28.4	16.9	5.0	3.1	0.4	<0.1
San Diego, CA	25.9	9.7	2.4	5.2	0.3	0.2
San Francisco, CA	20.7	6.1	3.8	5.2	1.0	0.6
San Jose, CA	26.0	8.2	2.4	6.8	0.1	0.4
Santa Rosa, CA	22.2	5.3	2.3	4.8	<0.1	0.2
Savannah, GA	7.0	25.0	9.4	2.6	8.5	0.1
Seattle, WA	12.3	11.9	4.6	5.9	0.3	0.4
Sioux Falls, SD	14.9	12.9	28.0	1.2	0.1	0.1
Springfield, IL	15.5	21.4	11.6	3.1	2.1	0.1
Tallahassee, FL	4.8	21.9	6.3	2.9	9.1	0.1
Tampa, FL	10.8	13.6	5.1	3.1	1.1	0.8
Tucson, AZ	20.7	10.0	3.7	4.5	0.4	0.2
Tulsa, OK	5.8	34.6	11.2	2.1	1.5	<0.1
Tuscaloosa, AL	1.7	35.2	6.4	0.9	8.5	<0.1
Virginia Beach, VA	6.4	18.0	9.4	3.9	2.2	0.3
Washington, DC	14.5	12.4	8.7	5.9	2.3	0.6
Wichita, KS	14.5	20.7	11.0	2.4	1.8	0.2
Winston-Salem, NC	3.5	29.1	15.6	1.2	2.2	0.2
U.S.	19.1	16.2	7.3	4.3	1.6	0.3

Note: Figures are the number of adherents as a percentage of the total population; (1) Figures cover the Metropolitan Statistical Area—see Appendix B for areas included
Source: Association of Statisticians of American Religious Bodies, 2010 U.S. Religion Census: Religious Congregations & Membership Study

Ancestry: City

City	German	Irish	English	American	Italian	Polish	French[1]	Scottish	Dutch
Albuquerque, NM	9.0	7.0	6.4	3.8	2.9	1.4	1.7	1.6	0.7
Allentown, PA	10.3	4.9	1.7	2.1	4.4	1.7	0.9	0.5	1.1
Anchorage, AK	14.4	9.7	7.8	3.6	3.0	2.1	2.4	2.6	1.4
Ann Arbor, MI	17.1	9.9	9.5	3.8	4.9	6.0	3.0	2.7	2.3
Athens, GA	8.4	8.2	8.0	4.3	3.0	1.6	1.7	2.7	1.0
Atlanta, GA	6.1	5.6	7.2	5.4	2.6	1.4	1.7	1.8	0.6
Austin, TX	10.4	7.4	7.4	3.1	3.0	1.7	2.3	2.0	0.8
Baton Rouge, LA	5.2	5.0	4.5	5.5	3.3	0.4	6.9	1.3	0.3
Boise City, ID	16.7	11.8	18.5	4.5	3.7	1.7	2.4	3.9	1.7
Boston, MA	4.6	13.4	4.3	2.5	7.7	2.2	1.9	1.2	0.5
Boulder, CO	17.4	12.1	10.5	2.5	6.0	3.5	2.6	3.2	1.3
Cape Coral, FL	14.1	11.5	7.3	15.3	10.4	3.5	2.2	1.6	1.2
Cedar Rapids, IA	30.6	13.8	7.8	4.5	1.9	1.6	2.3	1.6	1.9
Charleston, SC	10.4	9.9	9.9	23.1	4.4	1.9	2.2	2.7	0.7
Charlotte, NC	8.7	7.0	6.6	4.7	3.4	1.6	1.4	1.9	0.7
Chicago, IL	7.3	7.5	2.4	2.0	4.0	5.6	1.0	0.6	0.5
Cincinnati, OH	17.7	10.0	5.3	3.9	3.5	1.7	1.6	1.2	0.8
Clarksville, TN	10.7	8.3	5.6	7.8	3.5	1.5	1.8	1.3	1.1
Cleveland, OH	9.0	8.3	2.6	2.1	4.8	3.8	0.9	0.6	0.5
College Station, TX	16.9	8.9	7.7	3.5	3.5	2.3	3.5	2.3	0.7
Colorado Springs, CO	18.6	11.0	9.7	4.3	4.8	2.3	2.9	2.6	1.5
Columbia, MO	23.9	12.3	8.8	5.6	3.7	2.4	2.5	1.9	1.5
Columbia, SC	9.9	6.9	8.3	5.3	2.9	1.3	2.0	2.2	0.8
Columbus, OH	16.4	10.1	6.1	4.3	4.9	2.2	1.7	1.7	0.9
Dallas, TX	5.1	4.0	4.5	3.8	1.5	0.8	1.2	1.1	0.4
Davenport, IA	28.8	15.3	6.3	4.0	2.3	2.1	1.5	1.5	1.8
Denver, CO	13.8	9.7	7.8	2.9	4.6	2.7	2.3	2.1	1.4
Des Moines, IA	20.3	11.6	6.6	3.6	3.9	1.0	1.8	1.3	2.6
Durham, NC	7.4	5.8	7.0	4.3	2.8	1.7	1.6	1.5	0.6
Edison, NJ	4.9	6.8	1.6	1.7	7.8	4.6	0.8	0.6	0.3
El Paso, TX	3.6	2.3	1.7	2.4	1.2	0.5	0.8	0.4	0.2
Fargo, ND	37.1	8.8	3.9	2.2	1.1	3.1	3.6	1.2	1.1
Fayetteville, NC	8.8	6.9	6.6	3.9	2.8	1.4	1.5	1.8	0.6
Fort Collins, CO	22.5	12.7	11.4	3.7	5.3	3.0	3.3	2.9	1.8
Fort Wayne, IN	24.3	9.5	6.9	5.7	2.4	2.1	3.0	1.5	1.3
Fort Worth, TX	7.4	6.0	5.6	5.0	1.9	0.9	1.5	1.4	0.7
Grand Rapids, MI	15.0	8.7	7.0	2.3	3.0	6.8	2.2	1.6	13.9
Greeley, CO	18.4	8.5	6.8	4.2	2.5	1.4	1.6	2.1	1.0
Green Bay, WI	29.5	9.3	3.8	3.4	2.3	7.9	4.2	0.6	3.0
Greensboro, NC	7.0	5.5	7.3	4.8	2.4	1.1	1.1	1.7	0.7
Honolulu, HI	4.1	3.3	2.8	1.2	1.8	0.7	0.8	0.6	0.3
Houston, TX	4.8	3.6	3.7	4.0	1.5	0.8	1.6	0.9	0.4
Huntsville, AL	8.6	8.8	8.7	11.4	2.4	0.9	1.8	2.0	0.9
Indianapolis, IN	13.5	8.6	5.9	5.9	2.2	1.6	1.5	1.5	1.0
Jacksonville, FL	7.9	7.8	6.0	5.4	3.8	1.5	1.4	1.5	0.8
Kansas City, MO	15.4	10.5	7.0	3.9	3.5	1.4	2.0	1.6	1.1
Lafayette, LA	7.4	5.5	5.7	6.4	3.8	0.4	17.8	1.1	0.5
Lakeland, FL	10.1	8.1	8.7	8.1	4.5	1.8	2.6	1.7	1.4
Las Vegas, NV	8.9	7.7	5.6	3.4	5.3	2.1	1.8	1.3	0.8
Lexington, KY	13.7	11.8	10.8	9.2	2.9	1.7	1.9	2.9	1.1
Lincoln, NE	33.2	11.3	8.0	3.6	2.3	2.5	2.1	1.5	2.0
Little Rock, AR	7.1	6.8	7.5	5.5	1.6	0.9	1.8	1.6	0.5
Los Angeles, CA	3.9	3.5	2.8	3.6	2.6	1.4	1.1	0.7	0.4
Louisville, KY	15.1	11.5	7.8	8.7	2.5	1.0	1.9	1.6	0.9
Madison, WI	31.4	12.4	8.1	2.0	4.1	5.7	2.9	1.5	1.8
Manchester, NH	6.6	19.3	9.0	2.9	8.2	3.9	13.5	3.2	0.5

Table continued on following page.

City	German	Irish	English	American	Italian	Polish	French[1]	Scottish	Dutch
Memphis, TN	3.4	4.2	3.9	3.9	1.6	0.7	1.0	1.0	0.3
Miami, FL	1.5	1.2	0.8	3.3	2.3	0.7	0.9	0.2	0.2
Midland, TX	6.8	6.0	6.7	4.4	1.4	0.6	1.6	1.6	0.7
Milwaukee, WI	16.3	5.6	2.1	1.2	2.7	6.6	1.3	0.5	0.7
Minneapolis, MN	20.9	10.1	5.6	1.8	2.7	4.0	2.5	1.4	1.4
Nashville, TN	8.4	7.9	7.3	8.2	2.4	1.3	1.7	1.9	0.8
New Haven, CT	4.1	6.5	3.2	1.1	7.7	2.1	1.3	0.6	0.5
New Orleans, LA	6.1	5.4	4.1	2.5	3.9	0.9	5.4	1.1	0.4
New York, NY	2.9	4.4	1.6	4.2	6.2	2.4	0.8	0.5	0.3
Oklahoma City, OK	10.6	8.1	6.2	5.9	1.9	0.8	1.5	1.5	0.9
Omaha, NE	25.2	13.1	6.9	3.0	4.1	3.6	2.0	1.3	1.4
Orlando, FL	6.3	5.3	4.5	5.6	4.3	1.6	1.7	1.3	0.5
Peoria, IL	18.3	11.3	6.7	4.7	3.1	1.9	2.1	1.2	1.0
Philadelphia, PA	6.4	10.4	2.6	2.3	7.4	3.3	0.7	0.5	0.3
Phoenix, AZ	9.9	7.1	5.5	3.0	3.8	2.0	1.7	1.3	0.9
Pittsburgh, PA	18.7	14.6	5.1	3.6	12.3	6.9	1.6	1.4	0.6
Portland, OR	15.9	11.1	10.5	4.6	4.3	2.3	3.0	2.9	1.9
Providence, RI	3.2	7.6	3.9	2.9	7.2	1.9	2.9	0.8	0.3
Provo, UT	10.1	4.1	23.0	3.0	2.0	0.8	1.6	4.8	1.4
Raleigh, NC	8.9	7.5	9.0	12.2	4.0	2.2	1.7	2.3	0.6
Reno, NV	12.8	10.8	9.1	3.9	6.1	1.7	2.6	2.2	1.1
Richmond, VA	6.9	6.3	7.4	4.2	3.5	1.3	1.4	2.1	0.5
Riverside, CA	5.9	4.6	4.1	3.1	2.9	0.9	1.6	1.0	0.8
Rochester, MN	29.1	11.3	6.1	3.0	2.0	3.6	2.1	1.3	1.7
Sacramento, CA	6.7	6.1	4.5	1.7	3.5	0.9	1.5	1.2	0.8
Salt Lake City, UT	10.4	6.7	14.9	3.3	3.3	1.5	2.0	3.3	1.9
San Antonio, TX	6.8	4.3	3.6	3.1	1.6	1.0	1.3	0.9	0.4
San Diego, CA	8.3	7.0	5.5	2.4	4.1	1.7	1.8	1.4	0.8
San Francisco, CA	7.1	7.7	5.1	2.8	4.5	1.8	2.3	1.4	0.8
San Jose, CA	5.0	4.0	3.5	1.8	3.3	0.9	1.2	0.8	0.5
Santa Rosa, CA	11.4	10.1	8.9	2.8	7.4	1.4	3.0	2.2	1.2
Savannah, GA	5.5	6.7	4.6	3.6	2.8	1.2	1.6	1.6	0.7
Seattle, WA	14.8	11.4	10.1	2.3	4.4	2.7	3.0	2.9	1.6
Sioux Falls, SD	35.1	11.2	5.3	3.2	1.5	1.7	2.2	1.2	5.6
Springfield, IL	20.1	12.8	9.0	4.8	4.7	2.1	2.3	1.7	1.2
Tallahassee, FL	8.5	8.1	7.8	3.8	3.7	1.8	1.9	2.1	0.7
Tampa, FL	8.7	8.0	6.0	6.2	6.0	2.0	2.0	1.5	0.8
Tucson, AZ	11.0	8.2	6.4	3.0	3.6	1.9	2.0	1.5	0.9
Tulsa, OK	11.0	9.1	7.5	6.2	2.0	0.9	1.9	2.0	1.0
Tuscaloosa, AL	5.8	6.6	5.6	7.3	2.3	0.9	1.2	2.2	0.6
Virginia Beach, VA	11.7	11.0	9.1	9.4	5.6	2.4	2.3	2.3	0.9
Washington, DC	6.9	6.7	5.2	2.3	3.9	2.2	1.5	1.4	0.7
Wichita, KS	19.3	9.5	7.8	5.0	1.7	1.0	2.2	1.6	1.5
Winston-Salem, NC	9.6	6.8	7.8	5.2	2.8	1.1	1.3	2.3	1.0
U.S.	13.3	9.7	7.2	6.2	5.1	2.8	2.3	1.7	1.2

Note: Figures are the percentage of the total population reporting a particular ancestry. The nine most commonly reported ancestries in the U.S. are shown. Figures include multiple ancestries (e.g. if a person reported being Irish and Italian, they were included in both columns); (1) Excludes Basque
Source: U.S. Census Bureau, 2015-2019 American Community Survey 5-Year Estimates

Ancestry: Metro Area

Metro Area	German	Irish	English	American	Italian	Polish	French[1]	Scottish	Dutch
Albuquerque, NM	8.7	6.8	6.4	4.3	2.8	1.3	1.7	1.6	0.7
Allentown, PA	24.3	13.5	5.8	4.5	12.8	5.2	1.6	1.1	2.3
Anchorage, AK	15.3	10.0	7.9	4.1	3.1	2.1	2.7	2.6	1.5
Ann Arbor, MI	19.0	10.7	9.9	6.6	4.7	6.4	3.1	2.6	2.1
Athens, GA	8.6	9.4	9.1	7.9	2.8	1.2	1.6	2.8	0.9
Atlanta, GA	6.6	6.6	7.2	9.2	2.5	1.2	1.4	1.7	0.6
Austin, TX	12.3	7.7	7.9	3.8	2.7	1.6	2.4	2.0	0.8
Baton Rouge, LA	6.8	6.6	5.0	7.8	4.7	0.5	12.3	1.1	0.3
Boise City, ID	16.1	9.6	17.1	5.1	3.4	1.2	2.4	3.2	2.1
Boston, MA	5.9	20.8	9.4	3.5	13.1	3.4	4.5	2.3	0.6
Boulder, CO	18.9	11.5	11.6	3.5	5.4	3.3	2.7	3.3	1.5
Cape Coral, FL	13.5	11.0	8.1	14.3	7.7	3.3	2.3	1.8	1.3
Cedar Rapids, IA	34.2	14.5	8.0	4.7	1.9	1.2	2.4	1.5	2.0
Charleston, SC	9.9	9.7	8.2	13.3	3.7	1.9	2.0	2.5	0.8
Charlotte, NC	11.0	8.4	7.8	9.1	3.9	1.7	1.6	2.3	0.9
Chicago, IL	14.3	10.8	4.2	2.6	6.6	8.8	1.4	0.9	1.2
Cincinnati, OH	27.2	13.8	8.3	7.1	4.2	1.6	1.9	1.8	1.2
Clarksville, TN	11.1	9.0	6.4	9.3	2.8	1.4	1.8	1.6	0.9
Cleveland, OH	18.8	13.4	7.0	3.8	9.8	7.7	1.5	1.5	0.9
College Station, TX	14.0	8.0	6.6	3.9	2.9	2.0	2.5	2.0	0.6
Colorado Springs, CO	18.8	10.9	9.4	4.4	4.9	2.4	2.8	2.7	1.5
Columbia, MO	25.0	11.9	9.0	6.8	3.0	1.7	2.4	2.0	1.5
Columbia, SC	10.0	7.4	7.3	8.5	2.3	1.1	1.7	2.0	0.7
Columbus, OH	21.8	12.6	8.5	6.3	5.4	2.4	1.9	2.1	1.3
Dallas, TX	8.6	6.5	6.7	6.3	2.1	1.1	1.7	1.6	0.7
Davenport, IA	27.7	14.7	7.6	4.2	2.4	2.1	1.8	1.5	2.0
Denver, CO	17.5	10.7	9.3	3.9	5.0	2.5	2.5	2.4	1.5
Des Moines, IA	27.1	13.0	8.4	4.3	3.2	1.3	1.9	1.7	3.8
Durham, NC	8.9	7.4	9.3	6.0	3.1	1.8	1.8	2.3	0.8
Edison, NJ	6.2	9.2	2.7	4.4	12.2	3.8	0.9	0.7	0.6
El Paso, TX	3.4	2.2	1.6	2.3	1.1	0.5	0.8	0.4	0.2
Fargo, ND	37.4	8.2	4.3	2.0	1.1	2.8	3.1	1.2	1.2
Fayetteville, NC	8.7	7.0	6.6	5.6	3.0	1.4	1.5	2.2	0.6
Fort Collins, CO	24.3	12.8	12.2	4.4	4.9	2.7	3.4	3.2	2.2
Fort Wayne, IN	27.0	9.3	7.2	6.9	2.6	2.1	3.3	1.6	1.4
Fort Worth, TX	8.6	6.5	6.7	6.3	2.1	1.1	1.7	1.6	0.7
Grand Rapids, MI	20.0	10.1	8.8	3.7	3.1	6.6	2.9	1.8	18.9
Greeley, CO	22.0	9.9	8.7	4.9	3.6	2.1	2.1	1.9	1.4
Green Bay, WI	36.3	9.7	4.1	3.6	2.2	9.8	4.3	0.7	4.4
Greensboro, NC	8.0	6.6	8.2	8.3	2.3	1.1	1.2	1.9	0.8
Honolulu, HI	5.1	3.8	3.3	1.3	2.0	0.9	1.1	0.9	0.4
Houston, TX	7.8	5.3	5.2	4.3	2.0	1.2	2.1	1.2	0.6
Huntsville, AL	8.9	9.5	9.3	12.2	2.2	1.1	1.8	2.1	1.0
Indianapolis, IN	17.3	10.0	8.0	9.3	2.7	1.9	1.8	1.8	1.4
Jacksonville, FL	10.0	9.6	7.9	7.9	4.6	1.9	1.9	2.0	0.9
Kansas City, MO	20.7	12.3	9.7	5.4	3.3	1.5	2.3	1.9	1.4
Lafayette, LA	6.3	4.2	3.8	9.0	2.4	0.4	18.4	0.7	0.3
Lakeland, FL	8.9	7.4	7.3	13.2	3.6	1.7	2.0	1.5	1.0
Las Vegas, NV	8.7	7.2	5.6	3.4	5.0	1.9	1.7	1.2	0.7
Lexington, KY	13.0	11.8	10.9	13.6	2.6	1.5	1.8	2.7	1.1
Lincoln, NE	34.6	11.1	8.0	3.7	2.2	2.5	2.1	1.4	2.2
Little Rock, AR	9.3	8.8	7.9	7.9	1.5	1.0	1.7	1.9	1.0
Los Angeles, CA	5.2	4.2	3.8	3.6	2.9	1.2	1.2	0.9	0.6
Louisville, KY	17.2	12.4	9.1	10.1	2.4	1.1	2.1	1.9	1.0
Madison, WI	37.1	13.1	8.5	2.8	3.8	5.4	2.8	1.5	1.9
Manchester, NH	8.4	20.8	13.0	3.5	10.0	4.4	12.4	3.4	0.8

Table continued on following page.

Metro Area	German	Irish	English	American	Italian	Polish	French[1]	Scottish	Dutch
Memphis, TN	5.2	6.3	6.0	7.1	2.1	0.7	1.2	1.4	0.5
Miami, FL	4.4	4.3	2.7	6.0	5.0	1.9	1.2	0.6	0.4
Midland, TX	6.9	6.1	6.4	4.5	1.4	0.6	1.6	1.5	0.6
Milwaukee, WI	33.0	9.8	4.3	2.0	4.3	10.8	2.5	0.9	1.3
Minneapolis, MN	29.1	10.9	5.6	3.1	2.6	4.4	3.3	1.3	1.5
Nashville, TN	10.0	9.6	9.2	10.8	2.7	1.4	1.8	2.2	1.0
New Haven, CT	7.9	14.9	6.8	2.7	20.6	6.2	3.5	1.2	0.6
New Orleans, LA	9.7	7.4	4.5	5.0	7.9	0.7	11.7	1.0	0.4
New York, NY	6.2	9.2	2.7	4.4	12.2	3.8	0.9	0.7	0.6
Oklahoma City, OK	12.0	9.1	7.2	7.6	2.0	0.9	1.7	1.7	1.2
Omaha, NE	29.2	13.6	7.9	3.6	3.9	3.7	2.1	1.4	1.7
Orlando, FL	8.2	7.3	6.1	7.6	5.1	1.9	1.9	1.4	0.7
Peoria, IL	27.2	12.4	9.1	6.7	3.9	2.0	2.4	1.8	1.6
Philadelphia, PA	14.6	18.0	7.0	3.2	13.0	5.0	1.4	1.3	0.8
Phoenix, AZ	12.5	8.3	7.7	3.9	4.4	2.4	2.1	1.6	1.1
Pittsburgh, PA	26.1	17.3	8.0	3.7	15.6	8.4	1.8	1.9	1.1
Portland, OR	17.2	10.4	10.4	4.7	3.9	1.8	2.9	2.9	1.9
Providence, RI	4.5	17.6	10.6	3.4	13.6	3.7	9.4	1.6	0.4
Provo, UT	10.5	4.8	26.7	4.7	2.4	0.6	1.9	4.9	1.6
Raleigh, NC	10.3	9.0	10.1	10.3	4.8	2.2	1.9	2.5	0.9
Reno, NV	13.6	10.9	9.4	3.9	6.5	1.8	2.8	2.2	1.2
Richmond, VA	9.2	7.9	10.7	6.7	3.7	1.6	1.6	2.1	0.7
Riverside, CA	7.1	5.6	4.5	2.9	3.0	0.9	1.6	1.0	0.9
Rochester, MN	35.4	11.7	6.2	3.2	1.7	3.3	2.2	1.3	2.0
Sacramento, CA	10.6	8.1	7.5	2.8	4.8	1.3	2.1	1.7	1.1
Salt Lake City, UT	10.0	5.6	20.0	4.3	2.9	0.9	1.8	3.9	2.0
San Antonio, TX	10.1	5.5	5.1	3.5	1.9	1.5	1.7	1.2	0.5
San Diego, CA	9.3	7.6	6.2	2.7	4.1	1.7	2.0	1.5	1.0
San Francisco, CA	7.6	7.2	5.7	2.4	4.7	1.5	1.9	1.5	0.8
San Jose, CA	6.1	4.8	4.5	1.9	3.7	1.2	1.5	1.1	0.7
Santa Rosa, CA	12.9	12.2	9.8	2.7	8.6	1.8	3.3	2.6	1.4
Savannah, GA	9.1	9.7	7.4	7.9	3.3	1.3	1.8	1.8	0.7
Seattle, WA	14.6	9.7	9.3	3.2	3.7	1.9	2.8	2.6	1.5
Sioux Falls, SD	37.2	10.8	5.2	3.8	1.4	1.6	2.1	1.0	6.4
Springfield, IL	23.5	13.6	10.0	5.6	5.0	2.0	2.4	1.9	1.4
Tallahassee, FL	8.4	8.2	8.0	5.2	3.3	1.6	1.9	2.3	0.9
Tampa, FL	12.3	10.8	7.8	8.6	7.5	3.0	2.6	1.8	1.1
Tucson, AZ	13.4	9.1	8.2	3.3	4.0	2.3	2.3	1.9	1.1
Tulsa, OK	12.9	10.5	8.0	6.7	1.9	1.0	2.1	2.0	1.2
Tuscaloosa, AL	5.1	6.5	5.3	11.4	1.6	0.6	1.0	1.8	0.5
Virginia Beach, VA	9.8	8.8	8.7	9.3	4.1	1.8	1.9	1.9	0.8
Washington, DC	9.3	8.3	6.9	4.1	4.3	2.3	1.6	1.6	0.7
Wichita, KS	21.8	9.9	8.1	6.7	1.7	1.0	2.3	1.9	1.6
Winston-Salem, NC	11.7	7.8	9.0	9.8	2.5	1.0	1.3	2.4	1.1
U.S.	13.3	9.7	7.2	6.2	5.1	2.8	2.3	1.7	1.2

Note: Figures are the percentage of the total population reporting a particular ancestry. The nine most commonly reported ancestries in the U.S. are shown. Figures include multiple ancestries (e.g. if a person reported being Irish and Italian, they were included in both columns); Figures cover the Metropolitan Statistical Area—see Appendix B for areas included; (1) Excludes Basque
Source: U.S. Census Bureau, 2015-2019 American Community Survey 5-Year Estimates

Foreign-Born Population: City

City	Any Foreign Country	Asia	Mexico	Europe	Caribbean	Central America[1]	South America	Africa	Canada
					Percent of Population Born in				
Albuquerque, NM	9.9	2.4	5.3	0.8	0.3	0.2	0.4	0.4	0.1
Allentown, PA	19.2	3.6	1.0	0.8	9.0	1.3	2.5	0.8	0.1
Anchorage, AK	10.9	6.2	0.9	1.1	0.5	0.1	0.5	0.6	0.4
Ann Arbor, MI	19.1	12.7	0.4	3.0	0.2	0.1	0.8	0.9	0.9
Athens, GA	10.1	2.9	3.0	0.9	0.4	1.0	1.0	0.7	0.2
Atlanta, GA	7.6	3.2	0.7	1.3	0.6	0.1	0.6	0.7	0.3
Austin, TX	18.8	6.0	7.4	1.3	0.6	1.7	0.6	0.8	0.3
Baton Rouge, LA	5.5	2.8	0.4	0.5	0.2	1.0	0.2	0.3	0.0
Boise City, ID	6.4	2.7	1.0	1.4	0.1	0.1	0.3	0.6	0.2
Boston, MA	28.3	7.6	0.4	3.4	8.2	2.6	2.4	3.1	0.4
Boulder, CO	11.0	4.4	1.2	2.8	0.2	0.3	1.0	0.3	0.4
Cape Coral, FL	15.2	1.4	0.7	2.1	6.8	0.7	2.8	0.1	0.6
Cedar Rapids, IA	6.1	2.7	0.7	0.5	0.1	0.1	0.2	1.5	0.1
Charleston, SC	4.8	1.7	0.6	1.3	0.4	0.1	0.3	0.2	0.2
Charlotte, NC	16.7	5.4	2.6	1.2	1.1	2.8	1.4	1.9	0.2
Chicago, IL	20.6	5.2	8.4	3.5	0.4	0.9	1.1	1.0	0.2
Cincinnati, OH	6.0	1.8	0.3	0.8	0.2	0.9	0.3	1.6	0.2
Clarksville, TN	5.3	1.7	1.1	0.9	0.4	0.4	0.4	0.3	0.1
Cleveland, OH	5.9	2.5	0.3	1.0	0.5	0.4	0.3	0.7	0.1
College Station, TX	13.4	7.9	1.6	1.0	0.1	0.5	1.2	0.9	0.2
Colorado Springs, CO	7.5	2.1	2.1	1.5	0.3	0.3	0.3	0.4	0.4
Columbia, MO	9.1	5.3	0.5	1.3	0.1	0.3	0.3	1.0	0.2
Columbia, SC	5.0	2.1	0.5	0.8	0.3	0.3	0.5	0.4	0.1
Columbus, OH	12.7	5.1	1.2	0.8	0.5	0.5	0.3	4.2	0.1
Dallas, TX	24.8	2.8	15.4	0.7	0.4	2.6	0.6	1.9	0.2
Davenport, IA	4.5	1.6	1.9	0.4	0.3	0.0	0.0	0.2	0.1
Denver, CO	15.0	3.0	7.3	1.4	0.3	0.8	0.5	1.4	0.3
Des Moines, IA	12.5	4.5	3.3	0.9	0.1	1.1	0.2	2.3	0.1
Durham, NC	15.0	4.6	2.8	1.1	0.6	3.2	0.7	1.5	0.4
Edison, NJ	46.9	37.6	1.0	2.8	1.5	0.3	1.7	1.8	0.2
El Paso, TX	23.1	1.1	20.7	0.5	0.1	0.3	0.2	0.2	0.0
Fargo, ND	9.0	3.5	0.1	1.0	0.2	0.1	0.2	3.7	0.2
Fayetteville, NC	7.1	2.3	0.6	1.0	0.9	0.8	0.6	0.6	0.1
Fort Collins, CO	6.8	3.0	1.2	1.4	0.1	0.2	0.4	0.3	0.2
Fort Wayne, IN	8.2	3.9	1.9	0.8	0.1	0.7	0.3	0.4	0.1
Fort Worth, TX	16.8	3.4	9.8	0.6	0.3	0.9	0.5	1.2	0.2
Grand Rapids, MI	10.9	2.3	3.3	1.2	0.6	1.8	0.2	1.3	0.3
Greeley, CO	11.5	1.0	7.4	0.4	0.2	1.2	0.2	1.1	0.1
Green Bay, WI	9.9	2.0	5.9	0.5	0.1	0.6	0.2	0.5	0.0
Greensboro, NC	11.0	3.9	2.0	1.2	0.6	0.6	0.5	2.0	0.2
Honolulu, HI	27.4	23.2	0.1	0.8	0.1	0.1	0.2	0.1	0.2
Houston, TX	29.3	6.0	11.4	1.1	1.1	6.3	1.3	1.9	0.2
Huntsville, AL	6.6	2.3	1.7	0.7	0.4	0.5	0.2	0.6	0.1
Indianapolis, IN	9.7	2.8	3.0	0.5	0.4	0.9	0.3	1.6	0.1
Jacksonville, FL	11.3	4.0	0.6	1.8	2.0	0.8	1.3	0.6	0.2
Kansas City, MO	8.2	2.5	2.3	0.6	0.5	0.6	0.3	1.2	0.1
Lafayette, LA	4.3	1.8	0.5	0.7	0.2	0.4	0.2	0.2	0.1
Lakeland, FL	10.9	1.8	1.3	0.8	4.0	0.5	1.4	0.2	0.9
Las Vegas, NV	21.0	5.3	9.2	1.6	1.1	2.3	0.8	0.4	0.4
Lexington, KY	9.7	3.7	2.4	1.0	0.2	0.5	0.3	1.2	0.2
Lincoln, NE	8.5	4.5	1.3	0.9	0.2	0.4	0.3	0.8	0.1
Little Rock, AR	7.7	2.7	2.3	0.7	0.1	1.0	0.3	0.5	0.1
Los Angeles, CA	36.9	11.0	12.5	2.4	0.3	8.4	1.1	0.7	0.4
Louisville, KY	7.7	2.5	0.7	0.9	1.6	0.4	0.3	1.2	0.1

Table continued on following page.

City	Percent of Population Born in								
	Any Foreign Country	Asia	Mexico	Europe	Caribbean	Central America[1]	South America	Africa	Canada
Madison, WI	12.1	6.7	1.5	1.4	0.2	0.3	0.8	1.0	0.3
Manchester, NH	14.5	5.1	0.5	2.5	1.6	1.2	0.8	1.9	0.8
Memphis, TN	6.2	1.5	2.2	0.3	0.2	0.9	0.2	0.8	0.1
Miami, FL	58.3	1.1	0.9	2.0	32.5	11.9	9.6	0.3	0.2
Midland, TX	14.1	1.8	8.6	0.3	1.2	0.6	0.4	0.8	0.4
Milwaukee, WI	10.0	2.9	4.8	0.8	0.4	0.2	0.2	0.7	0.1
Minneapolis, MN	15.6	4.0	2.4	1.3	0.3	0.4	1.3	5.6	0.3
Nashville, TN	13.3	4.0	3.1	0.9	0.4	1.9	0.3	2.5	0.2
New Haven, CT	17.8	4.6	3.1	1.9	2.5	1.0	2.9	1.2	0.5
New Orleans, LA	5.5	2.0	0.3	0.8	0.3	1.5	0.3	0.2	0.1
New York, NY	36.8	10.9	2.0	5.3	10.2	1.4	4.8	1.7	0.3
Oklahoma City, OK	11.8	3.3	6.0	0.4	0.2	1.0	0.3	0.6	0.1
Omaha, NE	10.7	3.4	3.8	0.6	0.1	1.0	0.3	1.3	0.1
Orlando, FL	22.0	2.9	0.5	1.5	6.9	1.2	8.0	0.6	0.3
Peoria, IL	7.6	4.7	1.2	0.5	0.1	0.2	0.3	0.3	0.1
Philadelphia, PA	14.1	5.5	0.5	2.2	2.7	0.6	0.9	1.6	0.1
Phoenix, AZ	19.4	3.4	11.9	1.3	0.3	0.9	0.4	0.8	0.4
Pittsburgh, PA	9.0	4.8	0.3	1.9	0.3	0.1	0.5	0.8	0.2
Portland, OR	13.5	5.9	2.0	2.7	0.3	0.5	0.3	1.0	0.5
Providence, RI	28.7	4.2	0.6	2.2	12.3	5.0	1.4	2.7	0.2
Provo, UT	11.0	2.0	4.4	0.5	0.1	0.6	2.3	0.3	0.4
Raleigh, NC	13.4	3.9	2.7	1.4	0.9	1.4	0.7	2.1	0.3
Reno, NV	15.9	5.3	6.2	1.3	0.2	1.6	0.4	0.3	0.3
Richmond, VA	7.0	1.5	0.8	0.7	0.4	2.5	0.4	0.6	0.2
Riverside, CA	22.6	5.1	13.2	0.9	0.2	2.0	0.6	0.3	0.2
Rochester, MN	14.1	5.8	1.5	1.6	0.2	0.2	0.5	3.9	0.2
Sacramento, CA	22.2	10.7	6.9	1.5	0.1	0.8	0.2	0.6	0.2
Salt Lake City, UT	17.1	4.6	6.4	2.0	0.3	0.6	1.3	1.0	0.4
San Antonio, TX	14.3	2.6	9.1	0.6	0.2	0.8	0.4	0.3	0.1
San Diego, CA	26.1	11.9	9.1	2.3	0.2	0.5	0.8	0.9	0.4
San Francisco, CA	34.3	22.2	2.4	4.5	0.2	2.5	1.0	0.5	0.6
San Jose, CA	39.7	25.6	9.0	2.2	0.1	1.0	0.6	0.8	0.4
Santa Rosa, CA	20.1	4.0	11.6	1.7	0.0	0.9	0.3	0.8	0.3
Savannah, GA	6.2	2.7	0.7	0.9	0.4	0.4	0.5	0.3	0.1
Seattle, WA	18.8	10.6	1.2	2.5	0.1	0.5	0.5	2.1	1.0
Sioux Falls, SD	8.5	2.3	0.5	0.9	0.1	0.9	0.1	3.5	0.1
Springfield, IL	4.5	2.5	0.4	0.5	0.2	0.1	0.2	0.5	0.1
Tallahassee, FL	8.1	3.6	0.2	0.9	1.0	0.4	0.7	0.9	0.3
Tampa, FL	17.2	3.8	1.1	1.4	6.9	1.1	2.0	0.4	0.4
Tucson, AZ	15.3	2.7	9.5	1.0	0.1	0.4	0.3	0.9	0.3
Tulsa, OK	11.2	2.7	5.6	0.5	0.2	1.0	0.4	0.5	0.1
Tuscaloosa, AL	4.6	2.2	0.5	0.4	0.1	0.9	0.1	0.3	0.1
Virginia Beach, VA	9.4	4.9	0.5	1.6	0.7	0.6	0.5	0.4	0.1
Washington, DC	13.7	3.0	0.6	2.5	1.2	2.6	1.3	2.1	0.3
Wichita, KS	10.2	3.8	4.3	0.5	0.1	0.6	0.2	0.6	0.1
Winston-Salem, NC	9.9	2.1	4.3	0.7	0.4	1.1	0.5	0.6	0.1
U.S.	13.6	4.2	3.5	1.5	1.3	1.1	1.0	0.7	0.2

Note: (1) Excludes Mexico
Source: U.S. Census Bureau, 2015-2019 American Community Survey 5-Year Estimates

Foreign-Born Population: Metro Area

Metro Area	Any Foreign Country	Asia	Mexico	Europe	Caribbean	Central America[1]	South America	Africa	Canada
					Percent of Population Born in				
Albuquerque, NM	8.9	1.8	5.2	0.7	0.3	0.2	0.3	0.3	0.1
Allentown, PA	9.3	2.8	0.4	1.6	2.2	0.6	1.2	0.5	0.1
Anchorage, AK	8.9	4.9	0.7	1.1	0.4	0.1	0.4	0.5	0.3
Ann Arbor, MI	12.5	7.4	0.4	2.1	0.2	0.3	0.5	0.9	0.6
Athens, GA	7.8	2.3	2.1	0.8	0.3	0.9	0.7	0.5	0.1
Atlanta, GA	13.8	4.6	2.6	1.2	1.4	1.1	1.1	1.6	0.2
Austin, TX	15.2	4.5	6.4	1.1	0.4	1.2	0.6	0.7	0.3
Baton Rouge, LA	4.0	1.5	0.7	0.3	0.2	0.9	0.2	0.2	0.1
Boise City, ID	6.5	1.6	2.7	1.0	0.0	0.2	0.3	0.3	0.3
Boston, MA	18.9	6.1	0.2	3.3	3.4	1.6	2.1	1.6	0.5
Boulder, CO	10.7	3.5	2.8	2.3	0.1	0.3	0.7	0.3	0.5
Cape Coral, FL	16.7	1.3	2.5	2.0	5.9	1.8	2.0	0.1	1.1
Cedar Rapids, IA	3.8	1.8	0.5	0.4	0.1	0.1	0.1	0.8	0.1
Charleston, SC	5.4	1.5	1.1	1.0	0.3	0.5	0.5	0.2	0.2
Charlotte, NC	10.1	3.0	2.1	1.1	0.6	1.4	0.9	0.9	0.2
Chicago, IL	17.7	5.2	6.5	3.7	0.3	0.6	0.6	0.6	0.2
Cincinnati, OH	4.8	2.1	0.5	0.7	0.1	0.4	0.2	0.7	0.1
Clarksville, TN	4.1	1.3	0.7	0.7	0.3	0.3	0.3	0.3	0.1
Cleveland, OH	6.0	2.2	0.3	2.2	0.2	0.2	0.2	0.4	0.2
College Station, TX	12.5	4.2	5.5	0.7	0.1	0.5	0.7	0.7	0.1
Colorado Springs, CO	6.9	1.9	1.8	1.6	0.3	0.3	0.3	0.4	0.3
Columbia, MO	6.1	3.3	0.4	1.0	0.1	0.2	0.2	0.6	0.2
Columbia, SC	5.0	1.6	1.1	0.7	0.3	0.5	0.3	0.4	0.1
Columbus, OH	8.2	3.6	0.7	0.8	0.3	0.3	0.2	2.2	0.1
Dallas, TX	18.7	5.3	8.4	0.8	0.3	1.5	0.6	1.5	0.2
Davenport, IA	5.2	1.7	1.9	0.5	0.1	0.1	0.1	0.8	0.1
Denver, CO	12.1	3.3	4.9	1.4	0.2	0.5	0.5	1.0	0.3
Des Moines, IA	7.7	3.0	1.5	1.1	0.1	0.5	0.2	1.2	0.1
Durham, NC	11.7	3.6	2.6	1.4	0.4	2.0	0.5	0.9	0.4
Edison, NJ	29.5	8.7	1.5	4.4	6.9	2.0	4.4	1.4	0.2
El Paso, TX	24.2	1.0	22.0	0.4	0.1	0.3	0.2	0.2	0.0
Fargo, ND	6.7	2.7	0.2	0.8	0.1	0.1	0.2	2.4	0.3
Fayetteville, NC	6.2	1.6	1.4	0.9	0.7	0.8	0.4	0.3	0.1
Fort Collins, CO	5.6	1.9	1.3	1.3	0.1	0.2	0.4	0.2	0.2
Fort Wayne, IN	6.3	3.0	1.4	0.7	0.1	0.5	0.2	0.3	0.1
Fort Worth, TX	18.7	5.3	8.4	0.8	0.3	1.5	0.6	1.5	0.2
Grand Rapids, MI	6.8	2.1	1.8	1.0	0.4	0.6	0.1	0.5	0.2
Greeley, CO	8.7	0.9	5.9	0.4	0.2	0.6	0.2	0.5	0.1
Green Bay, WI	5.1	1.5	2.4	0.5	0.0	0.4	0.1	0.2	0.1
Greensboro, NC	8.8	2.9	2.5	0.8	0.4	0.6	0.4	1.0	0.2
Honolulu, HI	19.7	16.1	0.2	0.7	0.1	0.1	0.3	0.1	0.2
Houston, TX	23.4	6.0	8.9	1.0	0.8	3.6	1.3	1.4	0.3
Huntsville, AL	5.1	1.9	1.2	0.7	0.3	0.4	0.2	0.4	0.2
Indianapolis, IN	7.0	2.6	1.7	0.6	0.2	0.5	0.3	0.9	0.1
Jacksonville, FL	9.3	3.1	0.5	1.7	1.5	0.6	1.1	0.4	0.3
Kansas City, MO	6.9	2.3	2.0	0.6	0.2	0.6	0.3	0.7	0.1
Lafayette, LA	3.3	1.2	0.7	0.3	0.2	0.5	0.1	0.2	0.1
Lakeland, FL	10.0	1.3	2.3	0.9	2.8	0.6	1.4	0.2	0.5
Las Vegas, NV	22.2	7.2	8.2	1.6	1.1	2.0	0.9	0.8	0.4
Lexington, KY	7.5	2.6	2.1	0.9	0.2	0.5	0.2	0.8	0.1
Lincoln, NE	7.5	4.0	1.1	0.8	0.2	0.3	0.3	0.7	0.1
Little Rock, AR	4.3	1.4	1.3	0.5	0.1	0.6	0.2	0.2	0.1
Los Angeles, CA	33.1	12.8	12.1	1.7	0.3	4.3	0.9	0.6	0.3
Louisville, KY	5.9	1.9	0.9	0.7	0.9	0.3	0.2	0.7	0.1

Table continued on following page.

Metro Area	Percent of Population Born in								
	Any Foreign Country	Asia	Mexico	Europe	Caribbean	Central America[1]	South America	Africa	Canada
Madison, WI	7.6	3.6	1.2	1.0	0.1	0.2	0.6	0.6	0.2
Manchester, NH	9.7	3.6	0.4	1.8	1.0	0.5	0.8	0.9	0.8
Memphis, TN	5.3	1.7	1.6	0.4	0.2	0.5	0.2	0.6	0.1
Miami, FL	40.7	2.1	1.1	2.3	21.2	4.2	8.8	0.4	0.5
Midland, TX	13.4	1.6	8.8	0.3	1.0	0.5	0.3	0.6	0.3
Milwaukee, WI	7.4	2.8	2.3	1.3	0.2	0.2	0.2	0.4	0.1
Minneapolis, MN	10.7	4.2	1.3	1.1	0.2	0.4	0.5	2.8	0.2
Nashville, TN	8.3	2.6	2.0	0.7	0.2	1.0	0.3	1.1	0.2
New Haven, CT	12.7	3.3	1.0	2.8	1.9	0.5	1.9	0.9	0.3
New Orleans, LA	7.6	2.1	0.6	0.6	0.7	2.7	0.5	0.3	0.1
New York, NY	29.5	8.7	1.5	4.4	6.9	2.0	4.4	1.4	0.2
Oklahoma City, OK	7.9	2.4	3.5	0.4	0.1	0.6	0.3	0.4	0.1
Omaha, NE	7.4	2.4	2.5	0.6	0.1	0.7	0.2	0.9	0.1
Orlando, FL	18.5	3.0	1.1	1.5	5.7	1.1	5.2	0.6	0.3
Peoria, IL	3.3	1.7	0.6	0.4	0.0	0.1	0.1	0.1	0.1
Philadelphia, PA	11.0	4.5	0.9	1.9	1.3	0.4	0.6	1.1	0.2
Phoenix, AZ	14.3	3.4	7.2	1.3	0.3	0.6	0.3	0.5	0.6
Pittsburgh, PA	3.9	2.0	0.1	1.0	0.1	0.1	0.2	0.3	0.1
Portland, OR	12.6	5.0	3.1	2.3	0.1	0.5	0.3	0.6	0.4
Providence, RI	13.3	2.3	0.2	4.2	2.3	1.4	1.0	1.6	0.2
Provo, UT	7.3	1.1	2.8	0.5	0.1	0.5	1.6	0.2	0.3
Raleigh, NC	12.3	4.4	2.6	1.4	0.6	1.1	0.6	1.2	0.4
Reno, NV	14.0	3.9	6.1	1.1	0.2	1.5	0.4	0.3	0.3
Richmond, VA	7.9	3.2	0.6	1.0	0.4	1.4	0.5	0.6	0.1
Riverside, CA	21.3	4.9	12.3	0.8	0.2	1.7	0.6	0.4	0.3
Rochester, MN	8.5	3.4	1.0	1.1	0.1	0.3	0.3	2.1	0.2
Sacramento, CA	18.6	8.8	4.7	2.7	0.1	0.6	0.3	0.5	0.3
Salt Lake City, UT	12.4	3.1	4.6	1.2	0.1	0.6	1.4	0.6	0.3
San Antonio, TX	11.8	2.2	7.3	0.6	0.2	0.7	0.4	0.3	0.1
San Diego, CA	23.4	9.0	10.1	1.8	0.2	0.5	0.6	0.6	0.4
San Francisco, CA	30.7	17.5	4.9	2.9	0.2	2.5	1.0	0.7	0.5
San Jose, CA	38.6	25.4	7.0	3.1	0.1	0.9	0.7	0.7	0.5
Santa Rosa, CA	16.4	2.9	9.0	1.9	0.1	0.9	0.5	0.4	0.4
Savannah, GA	5.7	2.0	1.1	0.8	0.5	0.4	0.4	0.3	0.2
Seattle, WA	18.7	9.9	2.4	2.6	0.2	0.5	0.5	1.5	0.7
Sioux Falls, SD	6.2	1.6	0.4	0.7	0.1	0.7	0.1	2.4	0.1
Springfield, IL	3.1	1.6	0.3	0.4	0.1	0.1	0.1	0.3	0.1
Tallahassee, FL	6.1	2.2	0.5	0.8	0.9	0.5	0.5	0.6	0.2
Tampa, FL	13.9	2.8	1.3	2.2	3.7	0.8	1.9	0.5	0.6
Tucson, AZ	13.0	2.3	7.6	1.2	0.1	0.3	0.3	0.6	0.4
Tulsa, OK	6.6	1.9	2.9	0.5	0.1	0.5	0.3	0.3	0.1
Tuscaloosa, AL	3.4	1.1	0.9	0.4	0.1	0.6	0.1	0.2	0.1
Virginia Beach, VA	6.5	2.8	0.4	1.1	0.6	0.7	0.4	0.4	0.1
Washington, DC	22.8	8.2	0.8	1.8	1.1	4.9	2.2	3.5	0.2
Wichita, KS	7.4	2.7	3.0	0.4	0.1	0.4	0.2	0.4	0.1
Winston-Salem, NC	6.8	1.4	3.0	0.6	0.2	0.9	0.4	0.3	0.1
U.S.	13.6	4.2	3.5	1.5	1.3	1.1	1.0	0.7	0.2

Note: Figures cover the Metropolitan Statistical Area—see Appendix B for areas included; (1) Excludes Mexico
Source: U.S. Census Bureau, 2015-2019 American Community Survey 5-Year Estimates

Marital Status: City

City	Never Married	Now Married[1]	Separated	Widowed	Divorced
Albuquerque, NM	37.7	40.8	1.5	5.6	14.4
Allentown, PA	47.4	33.2	3.6	5.4	10.4
Anchorage, AK	34.5	48.4	1.8	3.6	11.7
Ann Arbor, MI	56.5	33.8	0.4	2.6	6.6
Athens, GA	54.4	32.2	1.6	3.5	8.2
Atlanta, GA	55.2	27.3	1.9	5.1	10.5
Austin, TX	43.2	40.9	1.7	3.1	11.0
Baton Rouge, LA	50.2	30.4	2.0	6.4	11.0
Boise City, ID	34.1	46.7	0.9	4.5	13.9
Boston, MA	56.0	30.3	2.6	3.9	7.2
Boulder, CO	55.6	32.4	0.8	2.6	8.6
Cape Coral, FL	25.5	52.0	1.5	7.3	13.7
Cedar Rapids, IA	35.2	45.7	1.0	6.0	12.1
Charleston, SC	41.9	41.6	1.5	5.2	9.7
Charlotte, NC	40.7	42.5	2.6	4.0	10.2
Chicago, IL	48.7	35.5	2.3	5.2	8.3
Cincinnati, OH	52.0	28.3	2.4	5.1	12.1
Clarksville, TN	30.2	50.9	2.2	4.0	12.6
Cleveland, OH	51.4	25.1	3.2	6.2	14.1
College Station, TX	59.7	32.4	0.8	2.1	5.0
Colorado Springs, CO	31.2	49.5	1.6	4.6	13.1
Columbia, MO	48.0	39.0	1.2	3.4	8.4
Columbia, SC	55.8	27.8	2.6	4.4	9.4
Columbus, OH	45.0	36.3	2.1	4.3	12.4
Dallas, TX	41.6	40.4	3.2	4.5	10.4
Davenport, IA	36.7	42.6	1.5	6.3	12.9
Denver, CO	42.5	39.5	1.8	4.0	12.2
Des Moines, IA	39.0	40.0	2.0	5.3	13.7
Durham, NC	43.1	39.9	2.5	4.3	10.2
Edison, NJ	25.7	61.0	1.0	6.1	6.2
El Paso, TX	35.3	44.5	3.5	5.8	10.8
Fargo, ND	42.8	42.9	1.1	4.5	8.7
Fayetteville, NC	38.4	40.7	3.6	5.5	11.8
Fort Collins, CO	46.6	40.6	0.8	3.3	8.7
Fort Wayne, IN	35.3	44.4	1.5	5.8	13.0
Fort Worth, TX	35.4	46.3	2.3	4.5	11.4
Grand Rapids, MI	46.2	36.9	1.3	5.1	10.4
Greeley, CO	35.8	46.0	1.7	5.1	11.3
Green Bay, WI	37.9	43.2	1.5	5.1	12.3
Greensboro, NC	42.2	38.4	2.6	5.7	11.0
Honolulu, HI	36.2	45.8	1.2	6.9	9.9
Houston, TX	41.0	41.3	3.2	4.6	9.9
Huntsville, AL	34.9	44.8	2.0	6.0	12.3
Indianapolis, IN	42.9	37.7	1.8	5.1	12.5
Jacksonville, FL	35.5	42.6	2.2	5.6	14.0
Kansas City, MO	39.7	39.9	2.1	5.4	12.9
Lafayette, LA	42.2	38.8	1.7	6.0	11.2
Lakeland, FL	34.9	41.7	2.1	8.2	13.1
Las Vegas, NV	34.9	43.3	2.3	5.5	14.1
Lexington, KY	38.8	43.1	1.7	4.6	11.8
Lincoln, NE	39.0	45.6	1.0	4.4	10.0
Little Rock, AR	37.7	39.9	2.5	6.2	13.7
Los Angeles, CA	45.8	38.8	2.6	4.6	8.2
Louisville, KY	36.3	42.1	2.1	6.1	13.4
Madison, WI	50.2	37.3	0.8	3.3	8.4
Manchester, NH	38.8	39.9	2.0	5.8	13.4

Table continued on following page.

City	Never Married	Now Married[1]	Separated	Widowed	Divorced
Memphis, TN	47.8	31.3	3.7	5.8	11.4
Miami, FL	40.2	36.0	3.7	6.6	13.5
Midland, TX	30.1	51.1	2.1	5.1	11.6
Milwaukee, WI	53.3	30.0	1.9	4.6	10.2
Minneapolis, MN	50.5	34.4	1.6	2.9	10.5
Nashville, TN	40.7	40.8	1.8	4.7	11.9
New Haven, CT	57.8	26.1	1.9	4.3	9.9
New Orleans, LA	49.2	29.4	2.7	5.9	12.8
New York, NY	43.4	40.4	3.0	5.4	7.8
Oklahoma City, OK	33.3	45.8	2.3	5.4	13.2
Omaha, NE	36.4	45.9	1.6	4.8	11.2
Orlando, FL	43.0	36.5	3.1	4.1	13.3
Peoria, IL	40.5	39.9	1.3	6.2	12.1
Philadelphia, PA	50.7	30.6	3.3	6.2	9.3
Phoenix, AZ	39.2	42.1	2.0	4.3	12.4
Pittsburgh, PA	52.4	30.7	1.9	5.8	9.3
Portland, OR	41.3	40.9	1.5	3.8	12.5
Providence, RI	54.4	30.6	2.3	4.2	8.5
Provo, UT	47.7	44.6	1.1	2.0	4.5
Raleigh, NC	42.7	40.3	2.5	3.7	10.8
Reno, NV	35.5	42.5	2.2	4.8	14.9
Richmond, VA	52.7	27.3	3.0	5.4	11.6
Riverside, CA	43.1	40.8	2.4	4.7	9.0
Rochester, MN	32.1	52.3	1.0	5.2	9.4
Sacramento, CA	40.2	41.0	2.4	5.1	11.4
Salt Lake City, UT	42.4	41.4	1.5	3.9	10.8
San Antonio, TX	39.0	40.6	3.1	5.2	12.1
San Diego, CA	40.0	44.3	1.7	4.1	9.8
San Francisco, CA	45.8	40.3	1.3	4.6	7.9
San Jose, CA	35.4	51.0	1.6	4.2	7.8
Santa Rosa, CA	34.6	44.5	1.9	5.5	13.5
Savannah, GA	47.5	31.2	3.0	5.9	12.4
Seattle, WA	44.5	41.1	1.2	3.4	9.9
Sioux Falls, SD	33.6	48.8	1.4	5.0	11.1
Springfield, IL	37.5	40.8	1.5	6.4	13.7
Tallahassee, FL	56.3	29.3	1.3	3.3	9.8
Tampa, FL	40.4	38.4	2.7	5.0	13.6
Tucson, AZ	42.5	36.0	2.2	5.4	14.0
Tulsa, OK	34.5	42.5	2.4	5.9	14.8
Tuscaloosa, AL	53.2	30.8	1.9	4.3	9.9
Virginia Beach, VA	30.4	51.1	2.4	5.0	11.1
Washington, DC	56.4	28.9	2.1	4.1	8.5
Wichita, KS	33.5	45.6	2.0	5.6	13.3
Winston-Salem, NC	40.4	39.9	2.8	5.9	11.1
U.S.	33.4	48.1	1.9	5.8	10.9

Note: Figures are percentages and cover the population 15 years of age and older; (1) Excludes separated
Source: U.S. Census Bureau, 2015-2019 American Community Survey 5-Year Estimates

Marital Status: Metro Area

Metro Area	Never Married	Now Married[1]	Separated	Widowed	Divorced
Albuquerque, NM	34.9	43.9	1.5	5.8	13.9
Allentown, PA	32.3	49.3	2.1	6.4	9.9
Anchorage, AK	33.9	48.7	1.8	3.7	11.9
Ann Arbor, MI	43.0	44.1	0.8	3.7	8.4
Athens, GA	42.7	41.9	1.6	4.7	9.1
Atlanta, GA	35.3	47.4	1.9	4.6	10.8
Austin, TX	36.4	47.4	1.7	3.7	10.8
Baton Rouge, LA	37.2	43.2	2.1	6.1	11.4
Boise City, ID	29.6	52.2	1.1	4.5	12.6
Boston, MA	37.1	47.5	1.5	5.1	8.7
Boulder, CO	38.1	46.2	1.0	3.7	11.0
Cape Coral, FL	26.2	50.8	1.6	8.2	13.2
Cedar Rapids, IA	30.0	52.0	0.9	5.8	11.2
Charleston, SC	34.5	46.9	2.4	5.5	10.7
Charlotte, NC	32.6	49.4	2.4	5.2	10.3
Chicago, IL	37.0	46.9	1.6	5.5	8.9
Cincinnati, OH	32.3	49.0	1.6	5.7	11.3
Clarksville, TN	28.3	52.5	2.0	5.1	12.0
Cleveland, OH	34.9	45.0	1.6	6.6	11.8
College Station, TX	46.3	40.1	1.9	3.8	7.9
Colorado Springs, CO	29.5	53.1	1.5	4.2	11.8
Columbia, MO	40.0	44.6	1.2	4.4	9.7
Columbia, SC	36.6	44.2	2.8	5.7	10.7
Columbus, OH	34.7	47.0	1.7	4.9	11.6
Dallas, TX	32.8	50.3	2.1	4.4	10.5
Davenport, IA	29.9	50.2	1.3	6.6	12.0
Denver, CO	33.1	49.6	1.4	4.1	11.8
Des Moines, IA	29.9	52.1	1.3	5.0	11.8
Durham, NC	36.9	45.4	2.3	5.1	10.2
Edison, NJ	37.8	46.3	2.3	5.7	7.9
El Paso, TX	35.4	45.2	3.5	5.5	10.3
Fargo, ND	36.8	49.6	0.9	4.3	8.3
Fayetteville, NC	33.8	46.1	3.2	5.8	11.2
Fort Collins, CO	34.8	50.1	0.9	4.0	10.2
Fort Wayne, IN	31.5	49.6	1.3	5.7	11.9
Fort Worth, TX	32.8	50.3	2.1	4.4	10.5
Grand Rapids, MI	32.7	51.3	1.0	4.9	10.2
Greeley, CO	28.2	55.2	1.4	4.5	10.8
Green Bay, WI	30.2	53.2	0.9	5.2	10.5
Greensboro, NC	33.6	46.1	2.7	6.3	11.3
Honolulu, HI	33.9	50.1	1.2	6.3	8.6
Houston, TX	33.7	49.8	2.5	4.5	9.6
Huntsville, AL	30.1	50.8	1.7	5.6	11.8
Indianapolis, IN	33.5	47.9	1.4	5.3	11.9
Jacksonville, FL	31.4	47.8	1.9	5.8	13.2
Kansas City, MO	30.5	50.4	1.6	5.4	12.0
Lafayette, LA	34.7	46.2	1.9	6.0	11.3
Lakeland, FL	31.8	46.9	2.1	7.2	12.1
Las Vegas, NV	34.7	43.9	2.3	5.2	13.9
Lexington, KY	34.3	46.5	1.7	5.1	12.3
Lincoln, NE	36.7	48.2	0.9	4.4	9.7
Little Rock, AR	30.7	47.4	2.1	6.3	13.6
Los Angeles, CA	39.9	44.7	2.1	4.9	8.4
Louisville, KY	31.6	47.4	1.9	6.1	13.0
Madison, WI	36.5	48.8	0.8	4.2	9.6
Manchester, NH	30.4	51.3	1.4	5.3	11.6

Table continued on following page.

Metro Area	Never Married	Now Married[1]	Separated	Widowed	Divorced
Memphis, TN	38.4	42.0	2.9	5.7	11.0
Miami, FL	34.6	43.3	2.8	6.4	12.8
Midland, TX	29.2	51.8	2.0	5.0	11.9
Milwaukee, WI	37.0	46.4	1.1	5.5	10.1
Minneapolis, MN	33.2	51.4	1.0	4.3	10.1
Nashville, TN	32.0	50.3	1.6	5.0	11.2
New Haven, CT	37.9	43.6	1.3	6.2	10.9
New Orleans, LA	37.8	41.3	2.3	6.3	12.2
New York, NY	37.8	46.3	2.3	5.7	7.9
Oklahoma City, OK	31.4	48.3	2.0	5.6	12.7
Omaha, NE	31.4	51.6	1.3	4.9	10.7
Orlando, FL	34.8	46.0	2.2	5.2	11.8
Peoria, IL	29.9	50.3	1.1	7.0	11.8
Philadelphia, PA	37.2	45.5	2.1	6.0	9.2
Phoenix, AZ	34.0	47.2	1.6	5.1	12.1
Pittsburgh, PA	31.7	49.4	1.7	7.3	9.9
Portland, OR	32.1	50.0	1.4	4.5	12.0
Providence, RI	36.0	45.2	1.6	6.1	11.0
Provo, UT	32.3	58.4	1.0	2.7	5.6
Raleigh, NC	32.0	51.7	2.3	4.2	9.9
Reno, NV	30.9	48.6	1.9	4.9	13.7
Richmond, VA	34.9	46.0	2.5	5.8	10.9
Riverside, CA	36.0	47.0	2.3	5.1	9.6
Rochester, MN	27.8	56.9	0.8	5.1	9.4
Sacramento, CA	33.5	48.2	2.1	5.2	10.9
Salt Lake City, UT	32.1	52.1	1.7	3.8	10.3
San Antonio, TX	35.1	45.6	2.6	5.2	11.5
San Diego, CA	35.9	47.6	1.7	4.7	10.1
San Francisco, CA	36.3	48.7	1.5	4.7	8.8
San Jose, CA	33.6	53.2	1.4	4.2	7.5
Santa Rosa, CA	32.1	47.8	1.7	5.3	13.1
Savannah, GA	34.9	44.9	2.2	5.8	12.1
Seattle, WA	32.6	50.8	1.4	4.2	11.0
Sioux Falls, SD	30.2	53.1	1.2	5.0	10.5
Springfield, IL	32.1	47.5	1.3	6.1	13.0
Tallahassee, FL	43.9	39.0	1.6	4.6	10.9
Tampa, FL	31.2	45.9	2.1	7.0	13.9
Tucson, AZ	34.4	45.0	1.8	5.9	12.9
Tulsa, OK	28.4	50.3	1.9	6.2	13.2
Tuscaloosa, AL	40.8	41.1	2.1	5.6	10.3
Virginia Beach, VA	33.5	47.3	2.7	5.6	11.0
Washington, DC	36.1	48.9	1.9	4.4	8.8
Wichita, KS	30.0	50.3	1.6	5.9	12.2
Winston-Salem, NC	29.8	49.6	2.5	6.8	11.3
U.S.	33.4	48.1	1.9	5.8	10.9

Note: Figures are percentages and cover the population 15 years of age and older; Figures cover the Metropolitan Statistical Area—see Appendix B for areas included; (1) Excludes separated
Source: U.S. Census Bureau, 2015-2019 American Community Survey 5-Year Estimates

Disability by Age: City

City	All Ages	Under 18 Years Old	18 to 64 Years Old	65 Years and Over
Albuquerque, NM	13.4	4.1	11.7	34.9
Allentown, PA	17.1	9.2	16.9	37.5
Anchorage, AK	11.4	3.6	10.3	36.3
Ann Arbor, MI	7.1	3.0	4.9	25.7
Athens, GA	11.5	6.6	9.4	35.1
Atlanta, GA	11.9	4.7	9.7	36.8
Austin, TX	8.4	3.9	6.9	30.7
Baton Rouge, LA	16.8	8.5	14.6	40.3
Boise City, ID	10.9	3.3	9.0	31.7
Boston, MA	11.9	5.3	8.9	41.0
Boulder, CO	6.3	2.8	4.5	23.5
Cape Coral, FL	12.9	3.4	9.3	29.9
Cedar Rapids, IA	10.6	3.5	8.5	29.7
Charleston, SC	9.9	2.8	7.2	30.6
Charlotte, NC	7.9	2.5	6.5	29.7
Chicago, IL	10.5	2.9	8.3	35.5
Cincinnati, OH	13.3	5.5	11.9	35.8
Clarksville, TN	14.9	4.7	16.1	41.1
Cleveland, OH	20.0	8.6	18.8	44.3
College Station, TX	6.3	3.8	4.9	28.7
Colorado Springs, CO	13.0	4.6	11.7	33.8
Columbia, MO	10.1	2.9	8.0	38.2
Columbia, SC	12.6	5.4	10.8	35.7
Columbus, OH	11.7	5.0	10.5	35.3
Dallas, TX	9.6	3.3	8.1	35.0
Davenport, IA	12.4	4.8	10.3	33.5
Denver, CO	9.6	3.5	7.4	33.5
Des Moines, IA	14.0	5.8	12.7	38.2
Durham, NC	9.1	2.9	7.3	31.9
Edison, NJ	8.2	3.3	5.3	29.0
El Paso, TX	13.7	5.0	11.3	43.4
Fargo, ND	10.0	2.8	7.7	36.5
Fayetteville, NC	17.5	6.7	16.6	44.5
Fort Collins, CO	7.9	2.8	6.0	30.0
Fort Wayne, IN	13.6	5.2	12.6	34.0
Fort Worth, TX	10.2	3.8	9.1	35.9
Grand Rapids, MI	13.2	5.4	12.0	35.8
Greeley, CO	11.2	2.3	10.2	36.2
Green Bay, WI	13.0	6.6	11.6	32.5
Greensboro, NC	10.7	4.3	8.7	30.9
Honolulu, HI	11.2	2.6	7.1	31.4
Houston, TX	9.5	3.2	7.7	35.6
Huntsville, AL	13.7	4.8	11.2	34.7
Indianapolis, IN	13.3	5.1	12.0	37.5
Jacksonville, FL	13.5	5.0	11.5	37.6
Kansas City, MO	12.7	3.9	11.2	36.2
Lafayette, LA	12.4	3.7	10.7	32.7
Lakeland, FL	15.8	4.3	11.8	37.1
Las Vegas, NV	12.9	3.7	10.8	36.3
Lexington, KY	12.4	4.5	10.7	34.3
Lincoln, NE	10.8	4.4	8.6	32.7
Little Rock, AR	13.4	5.8	11.5	35.4
Los Angeles, CA	10.1	3.1	7.3	37.3
Louisville, KY	14.8	4.6	13.4	36.4
Madison, WI	8.0	3.2	6.2	26.3

Table continued on following page.

City	All Ages	Under 18 Years Old	18 to 64 Years Old	65 Years and Over
Manchester, NH	14.1	6.0	11.7	39.8
Memphis, TN	13.5	5.1	12.0	37.8
Miami, FL	11.8	3.9	7.7	36.3
Midland, TX	9.7	2.4	8.2	38.5
Milwaukee, WI	13.0	5.7	11.8	38.8
Minneapolis, MN	11.2	4.7	10.1	32.9
Nashville, TN	11.5	4.0	9.8	35.4
New Haven, CT	10.2	5.2	8.6	31.9
New Orleans, LA	14.2	5.0	12.3	36.4
New York, NY	10.8	3.4	7.9	35.1
Oklahoma City, OK	13.2	4.2	12.0	38.6
Omaha, NE	10.9	3.3	9.7	32.3
Orlando, FL	10.1	5.4	8.2	32.5
Peoria, IL	12.4	3.2	11.0	33.2
Philadelphia, PA	16.7	6.0	15.0	43.2
Phoenix, AZ	10.7	3.9	9.5	34.7
Pittsburgh, PA	13.9	6.9	10.7	36.8
Portland, OR	12.1	4.1	10.0	35.4
Providence, RI	13.3	5.5	12.2	38.5
Provo, UT	8.2	4.2	6.8	38.3
Raleigh, NC	9.0	4.7	6.8	31.6
Reno, NV	12.2	5.2	10.3	30.7
Richmond, VA	15.2	6.7	13.2	38.0
Riverside, CA	11.2	3.9	9.1	40.7
Rochester, MN	10.5	4.7	8.2	30.1
Sacramento, CA	11.6	3.2	9.3	38.0
Salt Lake City, UT	10.8	3.2	9.1	35.7
San Antonio, TX	14.6	5.8	13.2	41.1
San Diego, CA	9.2	3.3	6.5	32.4
San Francisco, CA	10.2	2.3	6.3	35.2
San Jose, CA	8.6	2.6	6.1	33.1
Santa Rosa, CA	12.0	4.0	9.9	30.5
Savannah, GA	15.2	6.1	12.5	43.4
Seattle, WA	9.2	2.5	6.9	30.9
Sioux Falls, SD	10.2	3.3	9.0	30.1
Springfield, IL	14.9	5.8	12.9	33.6
Tallahassee, FL	9.9	4.7	8.2	30.5
Tampa, FL	12.2	3.7	9.9	39.4
Tucson, AZ	15.3	5.5	13.2	39.5
Tulsa, OK	14.5	4.7	13.5	36.2
Tuscaloosa, AL	11.1	2.8	9.5	32.4
Virginia Beach, VA	11.2	3.5	9.4	31.6
Washington, DC	11.7	4.1	9.6	35.3
Wichita, KS	13.7	4.6	12.4	36.3
Winston-Salem, NC	9.8	2.8	8.3	28.6
U.S.	12.6	4.2	10.3	34.5

Note: Figures show percent of the civilian noninstitutionalized population that reported having a disability. Disability status is determined from from six types of difficulty: vision, hearing, cognitive, ambulatory, self-care, and independent living. For children under 5 years old, hearing and vision difficulty are used to determine disability status. For children between the ages of 5 and 14, disability status is determined from hearing, vision, cognitive, ambulatory, and self-care difficulties. For people aged 15 years and older, they are considered to have a disability if they have difficulty with any one of the six difficulty types.
Source: U.S. Census Bureau, 2015-2019 American Community Survey 5-Year Estimates

Disability by Age: Metro Area

Metro Area	All Ages	Under 18 Years Old	18 to 64 Years Old	65 Years and Over
Albuquerque, NM	14.3	4.1	12.2	36.6
Allentown, PA	13.3	5.7	10.8	31.8
Anchorage, AK	11.9	3.7	11.0	36.5
Ann Arbor, MI	9.4	3.7	7.3	27.9
Athens, GA	12.5	6.0	10.1	35.8
Atlanta, GA	10.0	3.5	8.4	32.5
Austin, TX	9.2	3.7	7.6	31.4
Baton Rouge, LA	14.8	6.2	13.0	38.1
Boise City, ID	12.0	4.0	10.5	33.0
Boston, MA	10.6	4.0	7.8	31.3
Boulder, CO	8.1	3.0	6.1	25.6
Cape Coral, FL	13.9	3.8	9.9	28.2
Cedar Rapids, IA	10.4	3.6	8.1	29.8
Charleston, SC	12.2	4.0	10.0	33.9
Charlotte, NC	10.5	3.4	8.7	32.4
Chicago, IL	9.9	3.0	7.7	31.8
Cincinnati, OH	12.4	4.7	10.6	32.7
Clarksville, TN	16.5	5.7	16.6	43.2
Cleveland, OH	14.2	5.2	11.7	33.8
College Station, TX	9.5	4.1	7.3	35.2
Colorado Springs, CO	12.4	4.4	11.4	32.7
Columbia, MO	12.1	4.0	10.0	37.2
Columbia, SC	14.1	4.6	12.2	36.8
Columbus, OH	12.0	4.7	10.3	33.7
Dallas, TX	9.5	3.4	7.9	33.7
Davenport, IA	12.3	4.4	9.6	31.8
Denver, CO	9.3	3.2	7.4	30.8
Des Moines, IA	10.6	4.0	8.9	31.4
Durham, NC	11.4	3.9	9.1	32.3
Edison, NJ	10.0	3.2	7.2	31.6
El Paso, TX	13.8	5.5	11.5	44.6
Fargo, ND	9.5	3.1	7.4	33.9
Fayetteville, NC	16.4	6.0	15.7	43.7
Fort Collins, CO	9.7	3.1	7.4	28.1
Fort Wayne, IN	12.6	4.5	11.3	32.8
Fort Worth, TX	9.5	3.4	7.9	33.7
Grand Rapids, MI	11.4	4.0	9.8	31.7
Greeley, CO	10.3	3.0	8.9	34.6
Green Bay, WI	11.2	4.7	9.1	29.4
Greensboro, NC	12.7	4.5	10.7	32.5
Honolulu, HI	10.9	2.9	7.4	32.8
Houston, TX	9.4	3.3	7.8	34.0
Huntsville, AL	13.7	4.9	11.3	37.7
Indianapolis, IN	12.2	4.5	10.5	35.0
Jacksonville, FL	13.2	4.7	11.0	34.7
Kansas City, MO	12.1	3.9	10.2	34.2
Lafayette, LA	14.5	5.0	12.9	39.1
Lakeland, FL	15.4	5.7	12.4	34.7
Las Vegas, NV	12.1	3.8	9.9	34.8
Lexington, KY	13.5	5.1	11.8	35.5
Lincoln, NE	10.7	4.1	8.4	32.5
Little Rock, AR	15.7	5.9	13.8	39.5
Los Angeles, CA	9.6	3.0	6.8	33.9
Louisville, KY	14.1	4.2	12.4	35.5
Madison, WI	8.9	3.4	6.9	26.9

Table continued on following page.

Metro Area	All Ages	Under 18 Years Old	18 to 64 Years Old	65 Years and Over
Manchester, NH	11.8	4.7	9.5	31.8
Memphis, TN	12.9	4.5	11.2	36.4
Miami, FL	10.9	3.4	7.2	32.1
Midland, TX	9.8	2.3	8.3	39.5
Milwaukee, WI	11.4	4.2	9.1	31.6
Minneapolis, MN	9.9	3.7	8.0	30.0
Nashville, TN	12.0	4.0	10.2	35.2
New Haven, CT	11.6	4.0	8.8	31.5
New Orleans, LA	14.4	5.0	12.3	36.6
New York, NY	10.0	3.2	7.2	31.6
Oklahoma City, OK	13.9	4.3	12.2	39.4
Omaha, NE	11.0	3.5	9.6	32.2
Orlando, FL	12.2	5.1	9.6	34.5
Peoria, IL	12.0	3.4	9.5	32.2
Philadelphia, PA	12.7	4.6	10.5	33.4
Phoenix, AZ	11.5	3.7	9.3	32.6
Pittsburgh, PA	14.5	5.4	11.4	33.8
Portland, OR	11.9	3.9	9.7	34.1
Providence, RI	13.6	5.2	11.2	33.3
Provo, UT	7.8	3.3	7.1	32.8
Raleigh, NC	9.6	3.8	7.7	32.1
Reno, NV	12.1	4.7	9.9	30.7
Richmond, VA	12.6	5.0	10.4	32.6
Riverside, CA	11.3	3.6	9.1	37.5
Rochester, MN	10.2	4.0	7.7	29.4
Sacramento, CA	11.5	3.4	9.0	34.8
Salt Lake City, UT	9.4	3.5	8.3	32.4
San Antonio, TX	14.0	5.3	12.5	39.2
San Diego, CA	9.9	3.2	7.2	32.8
San Francisco, CA	9.7	2.9	6.8	31.5
San Jose, CA	8.1	2.4	5.4	31.2
Santa Rosa, CA	11.9	3.8	9.4	28.5
Savannah, GA	13.7	5.5	11.6	37.0
Seattle, WA	10.8	3.5	8.7	33.4
Sioux Falls, SD	9.9	3.1	8.8	29.7
Springfield, IL	13.7	5.4	11.4	32.9
Tallahassee, FL	12.7	5.9	10.2	33.9
Tampa, FL	14.0	4.4	10.8	34.3
Tucson, AZ	15.3	5.1	12.5	35.1
Tulsa, OK	14.5	4.6	12.9	37.9
Tuscaloosa, AL	14.4	4.0	12.4	40.2
Virginia Beach, VA	13.1	4.7	11.1	34.4
Washington, DC	8.7	3.0	6.7	29.1
Wichita, KS	13.4	4.9	11.7	36.1
Winston-Salem, NC	12.7	3.8	10.2	33.8
U.S.	12.6	4.2	10.3	34.5

Note: Figures show percent of the civilian noninstitutionalized population that reported having a disability. Disability status is determined from from six types of difficulty: vision, hearing, cognitive, ambulatory, self-care, and independent living. For children under 5 years old, hearing and vision difficulty are used to determine disability status. For children between the ages of 5 and 14, disability status is determined from hearing, vision, cognitive, ambulatory, and self-care difficulties. For people aged 15 years and older, they are considered to have a disability if they have difficulty with any one of the six difficulty types; Figures cover the Metropolitan Statistical Area—see Appendix B for areas included
Source: U.S. Census Bureau, 2015-2019 American Community Survey 5-Year Estimates

Male/Female Ratio: City

City	Males	Females	Males per 100 Females
Albuquerque, NM	272,468	286,906	95.0
Allentown, PA	59,101	61,814	95.6
Anchorage, AK	149,670	143,861	104.0
Ann Arbor, MI	60,089	60,646	99.1
Athens, GA	59,357	65,362	90.8
Atlanta, GA	237,192	251,608	94.3
Austin, TX	482,605	468,202	103.1
Baton Rouge, LA	107,345	116,804	91.9
Boise City, ID	112,637	113,478	99.3
Boston, MA	328,503	355,876	92.3
Boulder, CO	55,160	51,232	107.7
Cape Coral, FL	91,158	92,784	98.2
Cedar Rapids, IA	64,863	67,438	96.2
Charleston, SC	63,863	71,394	89.5
Charlotte, NC	412,035	445,390	92.5
Chicago, IL	1,317,791	1,391,743	94.7
Cincinnati, OH	145,900	155,494	93.8
Clarksville, TN	76,399	76,535	99.8
Cleveland, OH	185,274	200,008	92.6
College Station, TX	58,117	55,569	104.6
Colorado Springs, CO	232,440	232,431	100.0
Columbia, MO	58,250	62,980	92.5
Columbia, SC	67,638	65,635	103.1
Columbus, OH	429,868	448,685	95.8
Dallas, TX	657,714	672,898	97.7
Davenport, IA	50,216	51,953	96.7
Denver, CO	353,311	352,265	100.3
Des Moines, IA	106,316	109,320	97.3
Durham, NC	126,897	142,805	88.9
Edison, NJ	50,210	50,237	99.9
El Paso, TX	332,917	346,896	96.0
Fargo, ND	61,988	59,901	103.5
Fayetteville, NC	105,869	104,563	101.2
Fort Collins, CO	83,175	82,434	100.9
Fort Wayne, IN	128,483	137,269	93.6
Fort Worth, TX	428,238	446,163	96.0
Grand Rapids, MI	97,940	100,461	97.5
Greeley, CO	52,657	53,231	98.9
Green Bay, WI	51,929	52,848	98.3
Greensboro, NC	135,572	155,731	87.1
Honolulu, HI	173,837	175,148	99.3
Houston, TX	1,153,417	1,157,015	99.7
Huntsville, AL	94,803	101,416	93.5
Indianapolis, IN	416,893	447,554	93.1
Jacksonville, FL	431,133	459,334	93.9
Kansas City, MO	235,974	250,430	94.2
Lafayette, LA	61,742	64,924	95.1
Lakeland, FL	51,105	56,817	89.9
Las Vegas, NV	316,556	318,217	99.5
Lexington, KY	157,231	163,370	96.2
Lincoln, NE	142,589	141,250	100.9
Little Rock, AR	94,939	103,019	92.2
Los Angeles, CA	1,964,984	2,001,952	98.2
Louisville, KY	299,406	318,384	94.0
Madison, WI	126,190	128,787	98.0

Table continued on following page.

City	Males	Females	Males per 100 Females
Manchester, NH	56,510	55,599	101.6
Memphis, TN	308,460	343,472	89.8
Miami, FL	224,810	229,469	98.0
Midland, TX	70,558	67,991	103.8
Milwaukee, WI	286,081	308,467	92.7
Minneapolis, MN	212,823	207,501	102.6
Nashville, TN	319,844	343,906	93.0
New Haven, CT	61,926	68,405	90.5
New Orleans, LA	185,513	205,332	90.3
New York, NY	4,015,982	4,403,334	91.2
Oklahoma City, OK	316,500	327,192	96.7
Omaha, NE	234,719	241,143	97.3
Orlando, FL	134,785	146,047	92.3
Peoria, IL	54,542	58,990	92.5
Philadelphia, PA	747,479	831,596	89.9
Phoenix, AZ	813,775	819,242	99.3
Pittsburgh, PA	147,776	154,429	95.7
Portland, OR	319,869	325,422	98.3
Providence, RI	86,874	92,620	93.8
Provo, UT	57,489	58,914	97.6
Raleigh, NC	223,942	240,543	93.1
Reno, NV	124,568	121,932	102.2
Richmond, VA	107,430	119,192	90.1
Riverside, CA	162,664	163,750	99.3
Rochester, MN	56,262	59,295	94.9
Sacramento, CA	245,188	255,742	95.9
Salt Lake City, UT	100,748	97,008	103.9
San Antonio, TX	744,596	763,487	97.5
San Diego, CA	711,134	698,439	101.8
San Francisco, CA	446,286	428,675	104.1
San Jose, CA	518,708	508,982	101.9
Santa Rosa, CA	86,927	92,774	93.7
Savannah, GA	69,220	76,183	90.9
Seattle, WA	366,442	357,863	102.4
Sioux Falls, SD	88,410	88,707	99.7
Springfield, IL	54,935	60,953	90.1
Tallahassee, FL	90,053	101,226	89.0
Tampa, FL	188,134	199,782	94.2
Tucson, AZ	269,403	272,079	99.0
Tulsa, OK	195,534	206,790	94.6
Tuscaloosa, AL	47,718	51,672	92.3
Virginia Beach, VA	221,324	228,877	96.7
Washington, DC	328,644	364,039	90.3
Wichita, KS	191,730	198,147	96.8
Winston-Salem, NC	114,592	129,523	88.5
U.S.	159,886,919	164,810,876	97.0

Source: U.S. Census Bureau, 2015-2019 American Community Survey 5-Year Estimates

Male/Female Ratio: Metro Area

Metro Area	Males	Females	Males per 100 Females
Albuquerque, NM	448,642	463,466	96.8
Allentown, PA	411,125	426,485	96.4
Anchorage, AK	204,508	194,392	105.2
Ann Arbor, MI	181,923	185,077	98.3
Athens, GA	100,687	107,770	93.4
Atlanta, GA	2,834,134	3,028,290	93.6
Austin, TX	1,059,553	1,054,888	100.4
Baton Rouge, LA	417,717	436,601	95.7
Boise City, ID	354,905	355,838	99.7
Boston, MA	2,347,899	2,484,447	94.5
Boulder, CO	162,211	160,299	101.2
Cape Coral, FL	361,232	376,236	96.0
Cedar Rapids, IA	133,800	136,256	98.2
Charleston, SC	378,374	396,134	95.5
Charlotte, NC	1,235,495	1,310,065	94.3
Chicago, IL	4,654,160	4,854,445	95.9
Cincinnati, OH	1,079,705	1,122,036	96.2
Clarksville, TN	151,723	147,747	102.7
Cleveland, OH	993,227	1,063,671	93.4
College Station, TX	129,895	128,134	101.4
Colorado Springs, CO	365,383	358,115	102.0
Columbia, MO	100,711	104,658	96.2
Columbia, SC	399,998	424,280	94.3
Columbus, OH	1,022,627	1,055,134	96.9
Dallas, TX	3,601,569	3,719,094	96.8
Davenport, IA	187,831	193,344	97.1
Denver, CO	1,445,090	1,446,976	99.9
Des Moines, IA	336,082	344,357	97.6
Durham, NC	301,581	325,114	92.8
Edison, NJ	9,327,459	9,966,777	93.6
El Paso, TX	413,883	426,594	97.0
Fargo, ND	120,992	119,429	101.3
Fayetteville, NC	257,939	261,162	98.8
Fort Collins, CO	172,000	172,786	99.5
Fort Wayne, IN	198,843	207,462	95.8
Fort Worth, TX	3,601,569	3,719,094	96.8
Grand Rapids, MI	527,777	534,615	98.7
Greeley, CO	154,294	151,051	102.1
Green Bay, WI	159,123	160,278	99.3
Greensboro, NC	364,321	397,742	91.6
Honolulu, HI	496,066	488,755	101.5
Houston, TX	3,417,036	3,467,102	98.6
Huntsville, AL	224,226	232,777	96.3
Indianapolis, IN	991,392	1,038,080	95.5
Jacksonville, FL	733,355	770,219	95.2
Kansas City, MO	1,042,927	1,081,591	96.4
Lafayette, LA	238,957	250,957	95.2
Lakeland, FL	336,279	349,939	96.1
Las Vegas, NV	1,089,228	1,092,776	99.7
Lexington, KY	249,429	261,218	95.5
Lincoln, NE	165,977	164,352	101.0
Little Rock, AR	356,611	380,404	93.7
Los Angeles, CA	6,533,214	6,716,400	97.3
Louisville, KY	613,822	643,266	95.4
Madison, WI	325,952	327,773	99.4

Table continued on following page.

Metro Area	Males	Females	Males per 100 Females
Manchester, NH	205,394	207,641	98.9
Memphis, TN	640,257	699,366	91.5
Miami, FL	2,959,743	3,130,917	94.5
Midland, TX	87,984	85,832	102.5
Milwaukee, WI	767,950	807,273	95.1
Minneapolis, MN	1,771,443	1,802,166	98.3
Nashville, TN	913,820	958,083	95.4
New Haven, CT	413,519	443,994	93.1
New Orleans, LA	612,116	655,661	93.4
New York, NY	9,327,459	9,966,777	93.6
Oklahoma City, OK	682,133	700,708	97.3
Omaha, NE	461,556	470,223	98.2
Orlando, FL	1,226,241	1,282,729	95.6
Peoria, IL	200,311	206,572	97.0
Philadelphia, PA	2,939,397	3,139,733	93.6
Phoenix, AZ	2,366,181	2,395,422	98.8
Pittsburgh, PA	1,135,076	1,196,371	94.9
Portland, OR	1,210,509	1,235,252	98.0
Providence, RI	785,383	832,885	94.3
Provo, UT	311,659	305,132	102.1
Raleigh, NC	649,577	682,734	95.1
Reno, NV	232,199	228,725	101.5
Richmond, VA	613,475	656,055	93.5
Riverside, CA	2,270,726	2,289,744	99.2
Rochester, MN	107,432	110,532	97.2
Sacramento, CA	1,132,519	1,183,461	95.7
Salt Lake City, UT	603,034	598,009	100.8
San Antonio, TX	1,220,720	1,247,473	97.9
San Diego, CA	1,669,515	1,646,558	101.4
San Francisco, CA	2,325,587	2,375,745	97.9
San Jose, CA	1,004,573	983,273	102.2
Santa Rosa, CA	244,045	255,727	95.4
Savannah, GA	187,309	198,727	94.3
Seattle, WA	1,938,723	1,932,600	100.3
Sioux Falls, SD	130,188	129,160	100.8
Springfield, IL	100,527	108,640	92.5
Tallahassee, FL	184,249	197,948	93.1
Tampa, FL	1,502,972	1,594,887	94.2
Tucson, AZ	505,666	521,541	97.0
Tulsa, OK	486,355	504,189	96.5
Tuscaloosa, AL	120,524	130,157	92.6
Virginia Beach, VA	867,843	893,886	97.1
Washington, DC	3,028,975	3,167,610	95.6
Wichita, KS	316,050	321,640	98.3
Winston-Salem, NC	320,092	346,124	92.5
U.S.	159,886,919	164,810,876	97.0

Note: Figures cover the Metropolitan Statistical Area (MSA)—see Appendix B for areas included
Source: U.S. Census Bureau, 2015-2019 American Community Survey 5-Year Estimates

Gross Metropolitan Product

MSA[1]	2017	2018	2019	2020	Rank[2]
Albuquerque, NM	42.8	44.4	46.3	48.6	68
Allentown, PA	43.9	46.2	48.1	49.9	64
Anchorage, AK	27.4	28.3	29.3	30.6	102
Ann Arbor, MI	23.5	24.6	25.5	26.4	112
Athens, GA	10.1	10.5	10.8	11.2	205
Atlanta, GA	391.0	409.9	431.6	452.0	10
Austin, TX	145.1	156.6	164.6	174.0	25
Baton Rouge, LA	53.2	56.3	58.3	61.0	59
Boise City, ID	33.9	36.5	38.7	40.8	79
Boston, MA	449.5	472.7	493.6	515.0	8
Boulder, CO	25.6	27.2	28.7	29.9	107
Cape Coral, FL	28.3	30.0	31.8	33.4	93
Cedar Rapids, IA	17.8	18.4	18.8	19.4	141
Charleston, SC	42.5	44.6	46.7	49.0	67
Charlotte, NC	174.1	185.6	195.5	205.3	20
Chicago, IL	683.3	716.3	743.3	770.7	3
Cincinnati, OH	137.2	143.5	150.7	156.1	29
Clarksville, TN	11.0	11.6	12.2	12.6	194
Cleveland, OH	138.3	145.9	152.3	157.1	28
College Station, TX	9.9	10.6	11.2	11.7	204
Colorado Springs, CO	33.1	34.9	36.6	38.5	84
Columbia, MO	9.2	9.6	9.9	10.3	220
Columbia, SC	41.4	42.3	43.9	45.8	73
Columbus, OH	135.6	142.2	148.6	154.7	32
Dallas, TX	522.3	556.9	586.7	620.6	5
Davenport, IA	19.8	20.7	21.6	22.3	124
Denver, CO	211.6	225.3	235.8	246.9	18
Des Moines, IA	55.0	57.7	60.3	62.8	58
Durham, NC	43.4	45.5	48.0	50.7	65
Edison, NJ	1,765.5	1,851.9	1,932.1	2,007.4	1
El Paso, TX	28.3	29.4	30.5	31.5	97
Fargo, ND	15.3	16.1	16.8	17.5	156
Fayetteville, NC	17.2	17.6	18.1	18.8	149
Fort Collins, CO	17.4	18.4	19.7	20.7	139
Fort Wayne, IN	21.9	22.9	23.9	24.8	117
Fort Worth, TX	522.3	556.9	586.7	620.6	5
Grand Rapids, MI	60.6	63.6	66.2	68.3	54
Greeley, CO	12.8	13.8	14.7	15.6	178
Green Bay, WI	19.4	20.4	21.3	22.1	128
Greensboro, NC	41.5	43.0	44.3	45.7	71
Honolulu, HI	68.2	70.5	73.2	75.5	50
Houston, TX	478.1	513.9	546.1	583.7	7
Huntsville, AL	25.9	27.2	28.4	29.8	106
Indianapolis, IN	140.6	147.0	152.8	159.1	27
Jacksonville, FL	77.6	82.8	86.5	90.6	45
Kansas City, MO	131.8	138.2	144.1	149.7	33
Lafayette, LA	21.4	23.0	24.0	25.4	116
Lakeland, FL	21.4	22.6	23.6	24.6	119
Las Vegas, NV	112.8	119.1	124.1	130.3	36
Lexington, KY	29.7	30.8	31.9	33.0	90
Lincoln, NE	19.7	20.6	21.2	22.0	125
Little Rock, AR	38.5	39.8	41.1	42.7	76
Los Angeles, CA	1,067.7	1,125.5	1,164.2	1,207.3	2
Louisville, KY	75.3	78.1	81.3	83.9	48
Madison, WI	49.5	52.1	54.5	56.5	61
Manchester, NH	28.7	30.0	31.2	32.5	94

Table continued on following page.

MSA[1]	2017	2018	2019	2020	Rank[2]
Memphis, TN	72.9	76.2	79.4	82.2	49
Miami, FL	349.2	369.5	386.7	403.4	12
Midland, TX	27.1	35.0	38.1	44.4	83
Milwaukee, WI	104.6	109.2	112.8	116.2	37
Minneapolis, MN	260.9	273.1	284.6	296.0	14
Nashville, TN	134.3	142.5	149.8	156.5	30
New Haven, CT	46.1	47.8	49.7	51.2	62
New Orleans, LA	76.7	81.0	83.8	87.5	46
New York, NY	1,765.5	1,851.9	1,932.1	2,007.4	1
Oklahoma City, OK	74.2	79.6	83.2	88.3	47
Omaha, NE	63.3	65.9	68.5	71.0	52
Orlando, FL	134.1	142.4	150.7	158.6	31
Peoria, IL	19.2	20.1	20.9	21.6	133
Philadelphia, PA	445.1	465.5	485.8	504.6	9
Phoenix, AZ	248.0	264.9	280.3	294.0	16
Pittsburgh, PA	147.4	156.4	162.8	168.5	26
Portland, OR	165.9	175.7	183.8	191.1	21
Providence, RI	84.0	86.8	89.5	93.0	44
Provo, UT	25.7	27.9	29.5	31.2	104
Raleigh, NC	83.2	88.3	92.8	97.8	42
Reno, NV	26.8	28.8	30.8	32.3	99
Richmond, VA	83.0	87.2	91.0	94.7	43
Riverside, CA	161.6	171.0	178.3	186.9	22
Rochester, MN	12.6	13.2	13.9	14.4	182
Sacramento, CA	129.3	137.0	144.3	151.5	34
Salt Lake City, UT	87.9	93.6	97.8	102.5	41
San Antonio, TX	126.1	134.5	140.1	148.6	35
San Diego, CA	237.2	249.4	260.3	272.1	17
San Francisco, CA	512.2	547.3	578.7	605.5	6
San Jose, CA	281.6	303.1	321.2	334.7	13
Santa Rosa, CA	29.3	30.4	31.4	32.5	91
Savannah, GA	18.8	19.7	20.6	21.2	134
Seattle, WA	367.9	397.5	416.9	435.0	11
Sioux Falls, SD	19.6	20.5	21.5	22.4	127
Springfield, IL	10.3	10.7	11.0	11.4	202
Tallahassee, FL	16.4	17.1	17.9	18.7	152
Tampa, FL	148.2	156.6	164.0	172.0	24
Tucson, AZ	39.9	41.7	43.6	45.5	74
Tulsa, OK	57.2	60.9	63.7	67.4	55
Tuscaloosa, AL	11.8	12.4	13.0	13.4	190
Virginia Beach, VA	95.2	99.3	103.6	107.4	39
Washington, DC	539.6	562.6	585.8	612.1	4
Wichita, KS	34.3	35.7	37.0	38.0	81
Winston-Salem, NC	29.7	31.2	32.5	33.8	88

Note: Figures are in billions of dollars; (1) Metropolitan Statistical Area—see Appendix B for areas included; (2) Rank is based on 2018 data and ranges from 1 to 381.
Source: The U.S. Conference of Mayors, U.S. Metro Economies: GMP & Employment 2018-2020, September 2019

Economic Growth

MSA[1]	2015-17 (%)	2018 (%)	2019 (%)	2020 (%)	Rank[2]
Albuquerque, NM	0.7	1.4	2.6	2.5	252
Allentown, PA	1.2	2.6	2.3	1.6	210
Anchorage, AK	-1.5	-0.9	2.4	0.6	353
Ann Arbor, MI	2.1	2.5	1.9	1.3	123
Athens, GA	6.8	1.5	1.3	1.4	6
Atlanta, GA	3.7	2.8	3.6	2.6	47
Austin, TX	6.3	4.4	3.5	2.6	9
Baton Rouge, LA	1.6	0.8	1.2	2.4	170
Boise City, ID	3.7	5.5	4.1	3.2	45
Boston, MA	2.0	3.0	2.8	2.1	134
Boulder, CO	2.5	4.1	3.9	2.1	98
Cape Coral, FL	2.7	3.7	3.7	3.0	83
Cedar Rapids, IA	-1.6	0.9	0.8	1.0	354
Charleston, SC	5.0	2.4	2.9	2.6	16
Charlotte, NC	3.4	4.2	3.7	2.8	51
Chicago, IL	0.8	2.3	2.0	1.6	247
Cincinnati, OH	2.0	1.7	3.3	1.4	132
Clarksville, TN	-0.6	3.0	3.0	1.6	331
Cleveland, OH	1.7	1.9	2.8	0.9	160
College Station, TX	1.0	3.4	3.3	1.4	224
Colorado Springs, CO	2.9	3.1	3.0	2.8	73
Columbia, MO	0.9	1.6	1.5	1.8	242
Columbia, SC	0.8	-0.1	1.9	2.3	245
Columbus, OH	2.0	2.1	2.6	1.9	130
Dallas, TX	2.7	2.8	3.7	2.7	87
Davenport, IA	-0.2	2.4	2.4	1.2	311
Denver, CO	2.6	3.7	3.0	1.9	89
Des Moines, IA	2.8	1.8	2.7	1.9	78
Durham, NC	-2.0	2.9	3.7	3.5	363
Edison, NJ	1.3	2.6	2.6	1.6	196
El Paso, TX	0.9	1.5	1.6	1.4	244
Fargo, ND	0.4	2.1	2.6	2.0	283
Fayetteville, NC	-1.0	0.0	1.2	1.5	343
Fort Collins, CO	5.3	3.7	4.7	3.1	14
Fort Wayne, IN	1.9	2.5	2.5	1.3	149
Fort Worth, TX	2.7	2.8	3.7	2.7	87
Grand Rapids, MI	1.9	3.4	2.3	1.2	139
Greeley, CO	4.1	5.3	4.5	3.9	33
Green Bay, WI	1.2	3.2	2.6	1.2	203
Greensboro, NC	-0.2	1.5	1.2	1.2	312
Honolulu, HI	1.6	1.0	1.9	0.9	165
Houston, TX	-1.7	2.9	4.6	3.1	360
Huntsville, AL	1.8	3.0	2.5	2.7	155
Indianapolis, IN	2.5	1.9	2.1	2.0	101
Jacksonville, FL	4.1	4.3	2.6	2.5	34
Kansas City, MO	0.6	2.6	2.4	1.7	263
Lafayette, LA	-4.9	2.6	3.0	2.0	380
Lakeland, FL	2.7	3.2	2.5	2.4	82
Las Vegas, NV	1.5	3.1	2.3	2.7	182
Lexington, KY	1.6	1.3	2.0	1.1	167
Lincoln, NE	0.3	2.1	1.3	1.5	287
Little Rock, AR	0.4	0.9	1.6	1.5	286
Los Angeles, CA	2.3	3.5	1.8	1.6	110
Louisville, KY	0.7	1.4	2.3	1.2	254
Madison, WI	2.4	3.2	2.8	1.7	107
Manchester, NH	2.7	2.6	2.3	1.8	84

Table continued on following page.

MSA[1]	2015-17 (%)	2018 (%)	2019 (%)	2020 (%)	Rank[2]
Memphis, TN	0.1	2.3	2.3	1.4	299
Miami, FL	3.2	3.5	2.9	2.1	56
Midland, TX	1.0	13.0	9.2	3.6	231
Milwaukee, WI	0.9	2.1	1.5	0.9	243
Minneapolis, MN	1.9	2.3	2.5	1.9	144
Nashville, TN	4.0	3.9	3.3	2.3	39
New Haven, CT	1.2	1.7	2.1	0.9	204
New Orleans, LA	-0.6	1.2	1.3	2.0	329
New York, NY	1.3	2.6	2.6	1.6	196
Oklahoma City, OK	0.7	2.8	2.9	2.2	259
Omaha, NE	0.6	1.7	2.2	1.5	272
Orlando, FL	2.4	3.8	4.0	3.0	109
Peoria, IL	-4.0	2.5	2.0	1.3	376
Philadelphia, PA	1.4	1.9	2.7	1.7	188
Phoenix, AZ	3.3	4.5	4.0	2.7	54
Pittsburgh, PA	2.0	2.6	2.5	1.3	137
Portland, OR	3.9	3.5	2.6	1.6	42
Providence, RI	0.7	1.0	1.3	1.7	262
Provo, UT	6.6	6.5	4.0	3.7	7
Raleigh, NC	3.1	3.9	3.4	3.3	62
Reno, NV	4.3	5.3	4.9	2.5	27
Richmond, VA	1.5	3.0	2.6	1.8	179
Riverside, CA	3.0	3.4	2.3	2.6	65
Rochester, MN	3.6	2.9	3.1	1.1	48
Sacramento, CA	2.6	3.6	3.4	2.7	90
Salt Lake City, UT	2.3	3.7	2.6	2.7	114
San Antonio, TX	4.2	2.0	2.7	1.7	30
San Diego, CA	3.1	3.0	2.6	2.3	64
San Francisco, CA	4.8	5.1	4.3	2.5	18
San Jose, CA	7.0	6.0	4.6	2.2	5
Santa Rosa, CA	2.5	1.2	1.7	1.1	100
Savannah, GA	2.3	2.7	2.4	1.2	115
Seattle, WA	4.3	6.3	3.4	2.4	29
Sioux Falls, SD	1.2	1.6	3.2	2.2	206
Springfield, IL	-0.8	0.8	1.4	0.9	337
Tallahassee, FL	3.1	2.6	2.8	1.9	61
Tampa, FL	2.7	3.5	2.9	2.6	85
Tucson, AZ	2.0	2.7	2.8	2.0	133
Tulsa, OK	-3.3	1.3	3.1	1.7	373
Tuscaloosa, AL	1.0	2.8	3.4	1.5	227
Virginia Beach, VA	-0.4	2.2	2.5	1.4	323
Washington, DC	2.0	2.3	2.4	2.1	131
Wichita, KS	1.9	1.5	1.8	0.5	141
Winston-Salem, NC	-0.2	2.6	2.6	1.6	314
U.S.	1.9	2.9	2.3	2.1	–

Note: Figures are real gross metropolitan product (GMP) growth rates and represent annual average percent change; (1) Metropolitan Statistical Area—see Appendix B for areas included; (2) Rank is based on 2017 2-year average annual percent change and ranges from 1 to 381
Source: The U.S. Conference of Mayors, U.S. Metro Economies: GMP & Employment 2018-2020, September 2019

Metropolitan Area Exports

Area	2014	2015	2016	2017	2018	2019	Rank[2]
Albuquerque, NM	1,564.0	1,761.2	999.7	624.2	771.5	1,629.7	114
Allentown, PA	3,152.5	3,439.9	3,657.2	3,639.4	3,423.2	3,796.3	66
Anchorage, AK	571.8	421.9	1,215.4	1,675.9	1,510.8	1,348.0	132
Ann Arbor, MI	1,213.6	1,053.0	1,207.9	1,447.4	1,538.7	1,432.7	128
Athens, GA	320.8	327.4	332.1	297.7	378.2	442.1	219
Atlanta, GA	19,870.3	19,163.9	20,480.1	21,748.0	24,091.6	25,800.8	14
Austin, TX	9,400.0	10,094.5	10,682.7	12,451.5	12,929.9	12,509.0	30
Baton Rouge, LA	7,528.3	6,505.4	6,580.5	8,830.3	10,506.1	8,981.2	40
Boise City, ID	3,143.4	2,668.0	3,021.7	2,483.3	2,771.7	2,062.8	101
Boston, MA	23,378.5	21,329.5	21,168.0	23,116.2	24,450.1	23,505.8	17
Boulder, CO	1,016.1	1,039.1	956.3	1,012.0	1,044.1	1,014.9	158
Cape Coral, FL	496.6	487.3	540.3	592.3	668.0	694.9	190
Cedar Rapids, IA	879.0	873.5	945.0	1,071.6	1,025.0	1,028.4	157
Charleston, SC	5,866.7	6,457.5	9,508.1	8,845.2	10,943.2	16,337.9	23
Charlotte, NC	12,885.3	13,985.8	11,944.1	13,122.5	14,083.2	13,892.4	27
Chicago, IL	47,340.1	44,820.9	43,932.7	46,140.2	47,287.8	42,438.8	4
Cincinnati, OH	22,280.7	24,127.0	26,326.2	28,581.8	27,396.3	28,778.3	11
Clarksville, TN	323.7	296.5	376.1	360.2	435.5	341.8	241
Cleveland, OH	10,706.5	9,629.7	8,752.9	8,944.9	9,382.9	8,829.9	41
College Station, TX	129.7	122.5	113.2	145.4	153.0	160.5	313
Colorado Springs, CO	856.6	832.4	786.9	819.7	850.6	864.2	172
Columbia, MO	237.7	214.0	213.7	224.0	238.6	291.4	260
Columbia, SC	2,007.9	2,011.8	2,007.7	2,123.9	2,083.8	2,184.6	97
Columbus, OH	6,245.6	6,201.6	5,675.4	5,962.2	7,529.5	7,296.6	47
Dallas, TX	28,669.4	27,372.9	27,187.8	30,269.1	36,260.9	39,474.0	7
Davenport, IA	6,563.2	5,711.8	4,497.6	5,442.7	6,761.9	6,066.3	51
Denver, CO	4,958.6	3,909.5	3,649.3	3,954.7	4,544.3	4,555.6	61
Des Moines, IA	1,361.8	1,047.8	1,052.2	1,141.2	1,293.7	1,437.8	126
Durham, NC	2,934.0	2,807.2	2,937.4	3,128.4	3,945.8	4,452.9	62
Edison, NJ	105,266.6	95,645.4	89,649.5	93,693.7	97,692.4	87,365.7	2
El Paso, TX	20,079.3	24,560.9	26,452.8	25,814.1	30,052.0	32,749.6	10
Fargo, ND	782.8	543.2	474.5	519.5	553.5	515.0	207
Fayetteville, NC	375.8	256.3	179.8	231.6	260.5	287.8	263
Fort Collins, CO	1,037.4	990.7	993.8	1,034.1	1,021.8	1,060.0	152
Fort Wayne, IN	1,581.1	1,529.0	1,322.2	1,422.8	1,593.3	1,438.5	125
Fort Worth, TX	28,669.4	27,372.9	27,187.8	30,269.1	36,260.9	39,474.0	7
Grand Rapids, MI	5,244.5	5,143.0	5,168.5	5,385.8	5,420.9	5,214.1	55
Greeley, CO	1,343.6	1,240.1	1,539.6	1,492.8	1,366.5	1,439.2	124
Green Bay, WI	988.7	968.1	1,044.0	1,054.8	1,044.3	928.2	167
Greensboro, NC	3,505.5	3,286.1	3,730.4	3,537.9	3,053.5	2,561.8	87
Honolulu, HI	765.5	446.4	330.3	393.6	438.9	308.6	250
Houston, TX	118,966.0	97,054.3	84,105.5	95,760.3	120,714.3	129,656.0	1
Huntsville, AL	1,440.4	1,344.7	1,827.3	1,889.2	1,608.7	1,534.2	122
Indianapolis, IN	9,539.4	9,809.4	9,655.4	10,544.2	11,069.9	11,148.7	33
Jacksonville, FL	2,473.7	2,564.4	2,159.0	2,141.7	2,406.7	2,975.5	79
Kansas City, MO	8,262.9	6,723.2	6,709.8	7,015.0	7,316.9	7,652.6	45
Lafayette, LA	1,532.7	1,165.2	1,335.2	954.8	1,001.7	1,086.2	148
Lakeland, FL	2,151.9	1,318.6	995.5	1,147.2	1,299.8	1,141.5	143
Las Vegas, NV	2,509.7	2,916.2	2,312.3	2,710.6	2,240.6	2,430.8	90
Lexington, KY	2,191.4	2,065.7	2,069.6	2,119.8	2,148.0	2,093.8	100
Lincoln, NE	1,173.9	1,189.3	796.9	860.9	885.6	807.0	177
Little Rock, AR	2,463.5	1,777.5	1,871.0	2,146.1	1,607.4	1,642.5	113
Los Angeles, CA	75,471.2	61,758.7	61,245.7	63,752.9	64,814.6	61,041.1	3
Louisville, KY	8,877.3	8,037.9	7,793.3	8,925.9	8,987.0	9,105.5	39
Madison, WI	2,369.5	2,280.4	2,204.8	2,187.7	2,460.2	2,337.6	93
Manchester, NH	1,575.4	1,556.6	1,465.2	1,714.7	1,651.4	1,587.1	118

Table continued on following page.

Area	2014	2015	2016	2017	2018	2019	Rank[2]
Memphis, TN	11,002.0	11,819.5	11,628.7	11,233.9	12,695.4	13,751.7	28
Miami, FL	37,969.5	33,258.5	32,734.5	34,780.5	35,650.2	35,498.9	8
Midland, TX	122.7	110.1	69.6	69.4	63.6	63.7	357
Milwaukee, WI	8,696.0	7,953.6	7,256.2	7,279.1	7,337.6	6,896.3	49
Minneapolis, MN	21,198.2	19,608.6	18,329.2	19,070.9	20,016.2	18,633.0	22
Nashville, TN	9,620.9	9,353.0	9,460.1	10,164.3	8,723.7	7,940.7	44
New Haven, CT	1,834.5	1,756.3	1,819.8	1,876.3	2,082.3	2,133.8	98
New Orleans, LA	34,881.5	27,023.3	29,518.8	31,648.5	36,570.4	34,109.6	9
New York, NY	105,266.6	95,645.4	89,649.5	93,693.7	97,692.4	87,365.7	2
Oklahoma City, OK	1,622.0	1,353.1	1,260.0	1,278.8	1,489.4	1,434.5	127
Omaha, NE	4,528.5	3,753.4	3,509.7	3,756.2	4,371.6	3,725.7	68
Orlando, FL	3,134.8	3,082.7	3,363.9	3,196.7	3,131.7	3,363.9	73
Peoria, IL	11,234.8	9,826.9	7,260.1	9,403.6	9,683.6	8,151.9	42
Philadelphia, PA	26,321.3	24,236.1	21,359.9	21,689.7	23,663.2	24,721.3	15
Phoenix, AZ	12,764.4	13,821.5	12,838.2	13,223.1	13,614.9	15,136.6	24
Pittsburgh, PA	10,015.8	9,137.1	7,971.0	9,322.7	9,824.2	9,672.9	38
Portland, OR	18,667.2	18,847.8	20,256.8	20,788.8	21,442.9	23,761.9	16
Providence, RI	6,595.1	5,048.8	6,595.7	7,125.4	6,236.6	7,424.8	46
Provo, UT	2,533.4	2,216.4	1,894.8	2,065.3	1,788.1	1,783.7	107
Raleigh, NC	2,713.1	2,553.4	2,620.4	2,865.8	3,193.2	3,546.8	70
Reno, NV	2,138.9	1,943.3	2,382.1	2,517.3	2,631.7	2,598.3	86
Richmond, VA	3,307.0	3,325.9	3,525.7	3,663.7	3,535.0	3,203.2	76
Riverside, CA	9,134.8	8,970.0	10,211.6	8,782.3	9,745.7	9,737.6	37
Rochester, MN	720.5	530.2	398.0	495.3	537.6	390.1	235
Sacramento, CA	7,143.9	8,101.2	7,032.1	6,552.6	6,222.8	5,449.2	53
Salt Lake City, UT	8,361.5	10,380.5	8,653.7	7,916.9	9,748.6	13,273.9	29
San Antonio, TX	25,781.8	15,919.2	5,621.2	9,184.1	11,678.1	11,668.0	32
San Diego, CA	18,585.7	17,439.7	18,086.6	18,637.1	20,156.8	19,774.1	20
San Francisco, CA	26,863.7	25,061.1	24,506.3	29,103.8	27,417.0	28,003.8	12
San Jose, CA	21,128.8	19,827.2	21,716.8	21,464.7	22,224.2	20,909.4	19
Santa Rosa, CA	1,103.7	1,119.8	1,194.3	1,168.2	1,231.7	1,234.5	135
Savannah, GA	5,093.4	5,447.5	4,263.4	4,472.0	5,407.8	4,925.5	58
Seattle, WA	61,938.4	67,226.4	61,881.0	59,007.0	59,742.9	41,249.0	5
Sioux Falls, SD	455.3	375.0	334.3	386.8	400.0	431.5	224
Springfield, IL	94.4	111.7	88.3	107.5	91.2	99.8	338
Tallahassee, FL	174.0	191.2	223.1	241.1	270.8	219.7	291
Tampa, FL	5,817.3	5,660.4	5,702.9	6,256.0	4,966.7	6,219.7	50
Tucson, AZ	2,277.4	2,485.9	2,563.9	2,683.9	2,824.8	2,943.7	81
Tulsa, OK	3,798.5	2,699.7	2,363.0	2,564.7	3,351.7	3,399.2	72
Tuscaloosa, AL	n/a	n/a	n/a	n/a	n/a	n/a	400
Virginia Beach, VA	3,573.2	3,556.4	3,291.1	3,307.2	3,950.6	3,642.4	69
Washington, DC	13,053.6	13,900.4	13,582.4	12,736.1	13,602.7	14,563.8	25
Wichita, KS	4,011.7	3,717.6	3,054.9	3,299.2	3,817.0	3,494.7	71
Winston-Salem, NC	1,441.9	1,267.4	1,234.6	1,131.7	1,107.5	1,209.1	137

Note: Figures are in millions of dollars; (1) Metropolitan Statistical Area—see Appendix B for areas included; (2) Rank is based on 2019 data and ranges from 1 to 386
Source: U.S. Department of Commerce, International Trade Administration, Office of Trade and Economic Analysis, Industry and Analysis, Exports by Metropolitan Area, extracted March 24, 2021

Building Permits: City

City	Single-Family			Multi-Family			Total		
	2018	2019	Pct. Chg.	2018	2019	Pct. Chg.	2018	2019	Pct. Chg.
Albuquerque, NM	1,115	906	-18.7	0	188	–	1,115	1,094	-1.9
Allentown, PA	0	0	0.0	0	0	0.0	0	0	0.0
Anchorage, AK	869	838	-3.6	214	221	3.3	1,083	1,059	-2.2
Ann Arbor, MI	126	96	-23.8	0	0	0.0	126	96	-23.8
Athens, GA	345	517	49.9	261	766	193.5	606	1,283	111.7
Atlanta, GA	1,184	728	-38.5	5,312	2,555	-51.9	6,496	3,283	-49.5
Austin, TX	4,433	4,568	3.0	8,850	10,141	14.6	13,283	14,709	10.7
Baton Rouge, LA	282	354	25.5	58	0	-100.0	340	354	4.1
Boise City, ID	844	698	-17.3	296	883	198.3	1,140	1,581	38.7
Boston, MA	49	37	-24.5	3,553	2,956	-16.8	3,602	2,993	-16.9
Boulder, CO	80	41	-48.8	667	286	-57.1	747	327	-56.2
Cape Coral, FL	2,245	1,878	-16.3	356	810	127.5	2,601	2,688	3.3
Cedar Rapids, IA	147	173	17.7	325	197	-39.4	472	370	-21.6
Charleston, SC	810	828	2.2	354	360	1.7	1,164	1,188	2.1
Charlotte, NC	n/a	n/a	n/a	n/a	n/a	n/a	n/a	n/a	n/a
Chicago, IL	439	410	-6.6	6,010	7,504	24.9	6,449	7,914	22.7
Cincinnati, OH	98	135	37.8	632	992	57.0	730	1,127	54.4
Clarksville, TN	669	1,428	113.5	269	160	-40.5	938	1,588	69.3
Cleveland, OH	114	78	-31.6	34	19	-44.1	148	97	-34.5
College Station, TX	459	398	-13.3	572	219	-61.7	1,031	617	-40.2
Colorado Springs, CO	n/a	n/a	n/a	n/a	n/a	n/a	n/a	n/a	n/a
Columbia, MO	261	338	29.5	2	166	8,200.0	263	504	91.6
Columbia, SC	449	464	3.3	28	10	-64.3	477	474	-0.6
Columbus, OH	555	512	-7.7	3,742	2,258	-39.7	4,297	2,770	-35.5
Dallas, TX	2,009	2,093	4.2	6,038	6,000	-0.6	8,047	8,093	0.6
Davenport, IA	68	122	79.4	0	196	–	68	318	367.6
Denver, CO	2,428	2,257	-7.0	5,450	5,073	-6.9	7,878	7,330	-7.0
Des Moines, IA	180	391	117.2	391	279	-28.6	571	670	17.3
Durham, NC	1,894	1,945	2.7	1,336	1,884	41.0	3,230	3,829	18.5
Edison, NJ	71	55	-22.5	100	175	75.0	171	230	34.5
El Paso, TX	1,588	1,873	17.9	621	413	-33.5	2,209	2,286	3.5
Fargo, ND	313	311	-0.6	897	172	-80.8	1,210	483	-60.1
Fayetteville, NC	241	240	-0.4	0	282	–	241	522	116.6
Fort Collins, CO	398	316	-20.6	673	632	-6.1	1,071	948	-11.5
Fort Wayne, IN	n/a	n/a	n/a	n/a	n/a	n/a	n/a	n/a	n/a
Fort Worth, TX	5,477	5,063	-7.6	3,833	6,276	63.7	9,310	11,339	21.8
Grand Rapids, MI	124	153	23.4	690	183	-73.5	814	336	-58.7
Greeley, CO	348	170	-51.1	190	697	266.8	538	867	61.2
Green Bay, WI	101	63	-37.6	0	0	0.0	101	63	-37.6
Greensboro, NC	597	548	-8.2	249	385	54.6	846	933	10.3
Honolulu, HI	n/a	n/a	n/a	n/a	n/a	n/a	n/a	n/a	n/a
Houston, TX	5,417	5,120	-5.5	7,820	10,343	32.3	13,237	15,463	16.8
Huntsville, AL	1,241	1,436	15.7	71	167	135.2	1,312	1,603	22.2
Indianapolis, IN	1,090	1,153	5.8	1,196	1,229	2.8	2,286	2,382	4.2
Jacksonville, FL	3,780	4,155	9.9	3,223	2,650	-17.8	7,003	6,805	-2.8
Kansas City, MO	813	619	-23.9	1,341	879	-34.5	2,154	1,498	-30.5
Lafayette, LA	n/a	n/a	n/a	n/a	n/a	n/a	n/a	n/a	n/a
Lakeland, FL	435	606	39.3	0	953	–	435	1,559	258.4
Las Vegas, NV	1,794	1,885	5.1	179	780	335.8	1,973	2,665	35.1
Lexington, KY	733	579	-21.0	1,056	804	-23.9	1,789	1,383	-22.7
Lincoln, NE	859	863	0.5	673	864	28.4	1,532	1,727	12.7
Little Rock, AR	325	480	47.7	145	539	271.7	470	1,019	116.8
Los Angeles, CA	2,636	2,647	0.4	13,663	11,740	-14.1	16,299	14,387	-11.7
Louisville, KY	1,183	1,207	2.0	2,080	2,204	6.0	3,263	3,411	4.5

Table continued on following page.

City	Single-Family			Multi-Family			Total		
	2018	2019	Pct. Chg.	2018	2019	Pct. Chg.	2018	2019	Pct. Chg.
Madison, WI	334	426	27.5	1,109	1,232	11.1	1,443	1,658	14.9
Manchester, NH	151	106	-29.8	59	26	-55.9	210	132	-37.1
Memphis, TN	n/a	n/a	n/a	n/a	n/a	n/a	n/a	n/a	n/a
Miami, FL	80	107	33.8	4,545	4,361	-4.0	4,625	4,468	-3.4
Midland, TX	1,222	1,290	5.6	0	0	0.0	1,222	1,290	5.6
Milwaukee, WI	39	15	-61.5	717	178	-75.2	756	193	-74.5
Minneapolis, MN	162	122	-24.7	3,463	4,691	35.5	3,625	4,813	32.8
Nashville, TN	3,560	3,830	7.6	3,268	5,935	81.6	6,828	9,765	43.0
New Haven, CT	4	4	0.0	456	695	52.4	460	699	52.0
New Orleans, LA	524	558	6.5	779	748	-4.0	1,303	1,306	0.2
New York, NY	417	332	-20.4	20,493	26,215	27.9	20,910	26,547	27.0
Oklahoma City, OK	2,955	3,243	9.7	142	128	-9.9	3,097	3,371	8.8
Omaha, NE	1,237	1,179	-4.7	1,650	965	-41.5	2,887	2,144	-25.7
Orlando, FL	790	747	-5.4	2,289	1,887	-17.6	3,079	2,634	-14.5
Peoria, IL	32	33	3.1	0	0	0.0	32	33	3.1
Philadelphia, PA	683	894	30.9	2,556	3,672	43.7	3,239	4,566	41.0
Phoenix, AZ	3,732	4,175	11.9	3,530	5,723	62.1	7,262	9,898	36.3
Pittsburgh, PA	90	78	-13.3	553	582	5.2	643	660	2.6
Portland, OR	775	703	-9.3	4,873	4,391	-9.9	5,648	5,094	-9.8
Providence, RI	1	14	1,300.0	0	183	–	1	197	19,600.0
Provo, UT	171	174	1.8	286	140	-51.0	457	314	-31.3
Raleigh, NC	1,304	380	-70.9	2,907	827	-71.6	4,211	1,207	-71.3
Reno, NV	1,351	1,176	-13.0	1,883	2,144	13.9	3,234	3,320	2.7
Richmond, VA	273	353	29.3	290	887	205.9	563	1,240	120.2
Riverside, CA	171	170	-0.6	503	509	1.2	674	679	0.7
Rochester, MN	347	296	-14.7	1,068	478	-55.2	1,415	774	-45.3
Sacramento, CA	1,610	1,538	-4.5	714	1,463	104.9	2,324	3,001	29.1
Salt Lake City, UT	109	127	16.5	793	3,359	323.6	902	3,486	286.5
San Antonio, TX	3,266	3,890	19.1	2,663	5,306	99.2	5,929	9,196	55.1
San Diego, CA	774	580	-25.1	3,678	3,361	-8.6	4,452	3,941	-11.5
San Francisco, CA	28	22	-21.4	5,150	3,178	-38.3	5,178	3,200	-38.2
San Jose, CA	238	514	116.0	2,598	1,831	-29.5	2,836	2,345	-17.3
Santa Rosa, CA	1,632	939	-42.5	69	251	263.8	1,701	1,190	-30.0
Savannah, GA	399	339	-15.0	0	0	0.0	399	339	-15.0
Seattle, WA	523	507	-3.1	7,395	10,277	39.0	7,918	10,784	36.2
Sioux Falls, SD	1,083	1,013	-6.5	898	643	-28.4	1,981	1,656	-16.4
Springfield, IL	74	57	-23.0	219	112	-48.9	293	169	-42.3
Tallahassee, FL	396	407	2.8	1,128	1,275	13.0	1,524	1,682	10.4
Tampa, FL	1,109	1,159	4.5	679	3,618	432.8	1,788	4,777	167.2
Tucson, AZ	680	999	46.9	860	817	-5.0	1,540	1,816	17.9
Tulsa, OK	471	629	33.5	343	580	69.1	814	1,209	48.5
Tuscaloosa, AL	353	321	-9.1	469	844	80.0	822	1,165	41.7
Virginia Beach, VA	534	667	24.9	245	683	178.8	779	1,350	73.3
Washington, DC	112	168	50.0	4,503	5,777	28.3	4,615	5,945	28.8
Wichita, KS	532	618	16.2	326	364	11.7	858	982	14.5
Winston-Salem, NC	1,251	1,185	-5.3	84	0	-100.0	1,335	1,185	-11.2
U.S.	855,300	862,100	0.7	473,500	523,900	10.6	1,328,800	1,386,000	4.3

Note: Figures represent new, privately-owned housing units authorized (unadjusted data); All permit data are based on estimates with imputation

Source: U.S. Census Bureau, Manufacturing, Mining, and Construction Statistics, Building Permits, 2018, 2019

Building Permits: Metro Area

Metro Area	Single-Family			Multi-Family			Total		
	2018	2019	Pct. Chg.	2018	2019	Pct. Chg.	2018	2019	Pct. Chg.
Albuquerque, NM	2,086	1,872	-10.3	100	276	176.0	2,186	2,148	-1.7
Allentown, PA	1,082	1,078	-0.4	164	267	62.8	1,246	1,345	7.9
Anchorage, AK	938	878	-6.4	321	285	-11.2	1,259	1,163	-7.6
Ann Arbor, MI	652	608	-6.7	153	207	35.3	805	815	1.2
Athens, GA	729	821	12.6	340	770	126.5	1,069	1,591	48.8
Atlanta, GA	26,506	26,261	-0.9	12,935	6,575	-49.2	39,441	32,836	-16.7
Austin, TX	17,030	18,426	8.2	13,005	13,611	4.7	30,035	32,037	6.7
Baton Rouge, LA	3,509	3,612	2.9	413	10	-97.6	3,922	3,622	-7.6
Boise City, ID	6,923	7,570	9.3	1,994	3,062	53.6	8,917	10,632	19.2
Boston, MA	4,930	4,299	-12.8	9,253	10,789	16.6	14,183	15,088	6.4
Boulder, CO	899	742	-17.5	2,055	908	-55.8	2,954	1,650	-44.1
Cape Coral, FL	5,803	5,633	-2.9	3,918	3,472	-11.4	9,721	9,105	-6.3
Cedar Rapids, IA	490	509	3.9	469	305	-35.0	959	814	-15.1
Charleston, SC	4,787	4,758	-0.6	2,215	1,937	-12.6	7,002	6,695	-4.4
Charlotte, NC	16,407	16,253	-0.9	9,802	8,384	-14.5	26,209	24,637	-6.0
Chicago, IL	8,546	7,598	-11.1	9,135	10,487	14.8	17,681	18,085	2.3
Cincinnati, OH	4,282	4,488	4.8	1,794	1,535	-14.4	6,076	6,023	-0.9
Clarksville, TN	1,516	2,332	53.8	287	325	13.2	1,803	2,657	47.4
Cleveland, OH	2,733	2,584	-5.5	248	448	80.6	2,981	3,032	1.7
College Station, TX	1,023	1,091	6.6	833	389	-53.3	1,856	1,480	-20.3
Colorado Springs, CO	4,229	4,051	-4.2	1,505	1,457	-3.2	5,734	5,508	-3.9
Columbia, MO	555	633	14.1	2	166	8,200.0	557	799	43.4
Columbia, SC	4,478	4,209	-6.0	474	215	-54.6	4,952	4,424	-10.7
Columbus, OH	4,493	4,389	-2.3	4,947	3,701	-25.2	9,440	8,090	-14.3
Dallas, TX	36,832	34,939	-5.1	27,061	27,769	2.6	63,893	62,708	-1.9
Davenport, IA	490	533	8.8	69	268	288.4	559	801	43.3
Denver, CO	11,808	11,081	-6.2	9,921	8,227	-17.1	21,729	19,308	-11.1
Des Moines, IA	3,233	3,915	21.1	1,690	1,354	-19.9	4,923	5,269	7.0
Durham, NC	3,289	3,561	8.3	2,127	2,234	5.0	5,416	5,795	7.0
Edison, NJ	11,077	11,072	0.0	38,615	50,096	29.7	49,692	61,168	23.1
El Paso, TX	1,751	2,433	38.9	665	633	-4.8	2,416	3,066	26.9
Fargo, ND	1,080	939	-13.1	1,233	486	-60.6	2,313	1,425	-38.4
Fayetteville, NC	803	1,547	92.7	16	292	1,725.0	819	1,839	124.5
Fort Collins, CO	1,679	1,580	-5.9	1,265	910	-28.1	2,944	2,490	-15.4
Fort Wayne, IN	1,343	1,330	-1.0	541	626	15.7	1,884	1,956	3.8
Fort Worth, TX	36,832	34,939	-5.1	27,061	27,769	2.6	63,893	62,708	-1.9
Grand Rapids, MI	2,749	2,531	-7.9	1,105	1,624	47.0	3,854	4,155	7.8
Greeley, CO	3,194	3,335	4.4	913	1,052	15.2	4,107	4,387	6.8
Green Bay, WI	766	723	-5.6	435	407	-6.4	1,201	1,130	-5.9
Greensboro, NC	1,949	2,002	2.7	275	421	53.1	2,224	2,423	8.9
Honolulu, HI	983	912	-7.2	1,427	1,367	-4.2	2,410	2,279	-5.4
Houston, TX	40,321	39,507	-2.0	16,967	24,165	42.4	57,288	63,672	11.1
Huntsville, AL	2,870	3,399	18.4	71	167	135.2	2,941	3,566	21.3
Indianapolis, IN	7,291	7,120	-2.3	1,603	2,601	62.3	8,894	9,721	9.3
Jacksonville, FL	10,755	11,583	7.7	4,695	3,104	-33.9	15,450	14,687	-4.9
Kansas City, MO	5,608	4,811	-14.2	4,660	4,536	-2.7	10,268	9,347	-9.0
Lafayette, LA	1,657	1,632	-1.5	30	34	13.3	1,687	1,666	-1.2
Lakeland, FL	5,331	6,435	20.7	0	2,291	–	5,331	8,726	63.7
Las Vegas, NV	9,721	10,042	3.3	2,323	3,861	66.2	12,044	13,903	15.4
Lexington, KY	1,404	1,308	-6.8	1,368	938	-31.4	2,772	2,246	-19.0
Lincoln, NE	1,117	1,088	-2.6	687	1,010	47.0	1,804	2,098	16.3
Little Rock, AR	1,819	1,921	5.6	355	1,084	205.4	2,174	3,005	38.2
Los Angeles, CA	10,042	9,306	-7.3	19,482	21,248	9.1	29,524	30,554	3.5
Louisville, KY	3,104	3,122	0.6	2,409	2,644	9.8	5,513	5,766	4.6

Table continued on following page.

Metro Area	Single-Family			Multi-Family			Total		
	2018	2019	Pct. Chg.	2018	2019	Pct. Chg.	2018	2019	Pct. Chg.
Madison, WI	1,623	1,536	-5.4	2,029	1,807	-10.9	3,652	3,343	-8.5
Manchester, NH	709	691	-2.5	697	561	-19.5	1,406	1,252	-11.0
Memphis, TN	3,185	3,319	4.2	1,307	355	-72.8	4,492	3,674	-18.2
Miami, FL	7,022	7,241	3.1	12,531	13,447	7.3	19,553	20,688	5.8
Midland, TX	1,227	1,306	6.4	0	0	0.0	1,227	1,306	6.4
Milwaukee, WI	1,712	1,494	-12.7	2,057	925	-55.0	3,769	2,419	-35.8
Minneapolis, MN	8,985	9,610	7.0	9,221	12,804	38.9	18,206	22,414	23.1
Nashville, TN	13,470	14,460	7.3	5,689	8,242	44.9	19,159	22,702	18.5
New Haven, CT	406	399	-1.7	760	1,054	38.7	1,166	1,453	24.6
New Orleans, LA	3,046	3,241	6.4	818	785	-4.0	3,864	4,026	4.2
New York, NY	11,077	11,072	0.0	38,615	50,096	29.7	49,692	61,168	23.1
Oklahoma City, OK	5,430	5,924	9.1	300	633	111.0	5,730	6,557	14.4
Omaha, NE	2,791	2,633	-5.7	1,997	1,467	-26.5	4,788	4,100	-14.4
Orlando, FL	16,455	14,995	-8.9	12,427	9,475	-23.8	28,882	24,470	-15.3
Peoria, IL	228	218	-4.4	106	90	-15.1	334	308	-7.8
Philadelphia, PA	6,875	6,963	1.3	6,281	8,644	37.6	13,156	15,607	18.6
Phoenix, AZ	23,526	25,026	6.4	7,817	10,847	38.8	31,343	35,873	14.5
Pittsburgh, PA	2,977	2,830	-4.9	1,060	1,154	8.9	4,037	3,984	-1.3
Portland, OR	6,869	7,688	11.9	7,311	9,127	24.8	14,180	16,815	18.6
Providence, RI	1,553	1,592	2.5	410	456	11.2	1,963	2,048	4.3
Provo, UT	5,516	5,423	-1.7	1,325	1,524	15.0	6,841	6,947	1.5
Raleigh, NC	11,160	11,142	-0.2	4,790	2,178	-54.5	15,950	13,320	-16.5
Reno, NV	2,255	2,157	-4.3	2,195	3,106	41.5	4,450	5,263	18.3
Richmond, VA	4,498	4,481	-0.4	1,563	3,859	146.9	6,061	8,340	37.6
Riverside, CA	11,591	11,147	-3.8	3,218	3,452	7.3	14,809	14,599	-1.4
Rochester, MN	690	614	-11.0	1,126	497	-55.9	1,816	1,111	-38.8
Sacramento, CA	6,393	7,184	12.4	1,480	2,247	51.8	7,873	9,431	19.8
Salt Lake City, UT	5,391	4,760	-11.7	3,359	5,920	76.2	8,750	10,680	22.1
San Antonio, TX	8,013	9,103	13.6	3,484	6,792	94.9	11,497	15,895	38.3
San Diego, CA	3,489	3,019	-13.5	6,345	5,197	-18.1	9,834	8,216	-16.5
San Francisco, CA	4,048	4,076	0.7	13,373	9,805	-26.7	17,421	13,881	-20.3
San Jose, CA	2,466	2,603	5.6	6,278	3,627	-42.2	8,744	6,230	-28.8
Santa Rosa, CA	3,169	2,079	-34.4	110	350	218.2	3,279	2,429	-25.9
Savannah, GA	2,080	2,151	3.4	1,078	440	-59.2	3,158	2,591	-18.0
Seattle, WA	9,134	8,737	-4.3	19,052	17,862	-6.2	28,186	26,599	-5.6
Sioux Falls, SD	1,380	1,376	-0.3	1,008	743	-26.3	2,388	2,119	-11.3
Springfield, IL	193	149	-22.8	313	180	-42.5	506	329	-35.0
Tallahassee, FL	2,073	1,070	-48.4	1,128	1,275	13.0	3,201	2,345	-26.7
Tampa, FL	14,228	14,670	3.1	3,224	8,870	175.1	17,452	23,540	34.9
Tucson, AZ	3,240	3,490	7.7	1,164	823	-29.3	4,404	4,313	-2.1
Tulsa, OK	2,845	3,377	18.7	567	929	63.8	3,412	4,306	26.2
Tuscaloosa, AL	578	630	9.0	469	844	80.0	1,047	1,474	40.8
Virginia Beach, VA	4,168	4,345	4.2	1,436	1,563	8.8	5,604	5,908	5.4
Washington, DC	13,588	12,977	-4.5	12,169	13,827	13.6	25,757	26,804	4.1
Wichita, KS	1,223	1,389	13.6	735	737	0.3	1,958	2,126	8.6
Winston-Salem, NC	3,123	3,160	1.2	376	174	-53.7	3,499	3,334	-4.7
U.S.	855,300	862,100	0.7	473,500	523,900	10.6	1,328,800	1,386,000	4.3

Note: Figures cover the Metropolitan Statistical Area—see Appendix B for areas included; Figures represent new, privately-owned housing units authorized (unadjusted data); All permit data are based on estimates with imputation
Source: U.S. Census Bureau, Manufacturing, Mining, and Construction Statistics, Building Permits, 2018, 2019

Housing Vacancy Rates

Metro Area[1]	Gross Vacancy Rate[2] (%)			Year-Round Vacancy Rate[3] (%)			Rental Vacancy Rate[4] (%)			Homeowner Vacancy Rate[5] (%)		
	2018	2019	2020	2018	2019	2020	2018	2019	2020	2018	2019	2020
Albuquerque, NM	8.3	7.9	5.1	7.9	7.4	4.9	7.8	6.5	5.4	1.8	1.9	1.4
Allentown, PA	9.3	7.7	4.9	7.1	5.8	4.8	5.7	4.0	3.9	0.9	1.4	0.7
Anchorage, AK	n/a	n/a	n/a	n/a	n/a	n/a	n/a	n/a	n/a	n/a	n/a	n/a
Ann Arbor, MI	n/a	n/a	n/a	n/a	n/a	n/a	n/a	n/a	n/a	n/a	n/a	n/a
Athens, GA	n/a	n/a	n/a	n/a	n/a	n/a	n/a	n/a	n/a	n/a	n/a	n/a
Atlanta, GA	7.8	7.6	5.8	7.4	7.3	5.4	6.6	7.0	6.4	1.1	1.3	0.8
Austin, TX	9.7	10.7	7.0	8.7	10.3	6.8	7.0	8.2	6.6	1.2	1.8	2.0
Baton Rouge, LA	13.0	13.9	12.6	11.8	13.0	11.8	7.6	10.2	7.4	1.4	1.9	1.7
Boise City, ID	n/a	n/a	n/a	n/a	n/a	n/a	n/a	n/a	n/a	n/a	n/a	n/a
Boston, MA	7.5	7.1	6.8	6.5	6.2	5.6	3.8	3.6	4.7	1.0	0.8	0.4
Boulder, CO	n/a	n/a	n/a	n/a	n/a	n/a	n/a	n/a	n/a	n/a	n/a	n/a
Cape Coral, FL	41.5	40.0	35.1	16.6	17.9	15.8	5.8	8.5	15.5	3.0	2.3	1.9
Cedar Rapids, IA	n/a	n/a	n/a	n/a	n/a	n/a	n/a	n/a	n/a	n/a	n/a	n/a
Charleston, SC	16.0	18.4	18.1	14.5	16.6	16.5	17.0	16.7	27.7	3.4	2.2	2.3
Charlotte, NC	8.5	9.3	6.6	8.1	9.0	6.3	5.6	7.6	5.6	1.7	1.8	1.0
Chicago, IL	7.5	7.6	7.4	7.4	7.6	7.2	7.0	5.7	7.4	1.6	1.5	1.2
Cincinnati, OH	6.8	8.6	6.6	6.7	8.4	6.2	4.4	10.7	7.9	1.5	1.1	0.7
Clarksville, TN	n/a	n/a	n/a	n/a	n/a	n/a	n/a	n/a	n/a	n/a	n/a	n/a
Cleveland, OH	10.4	10.1	9.3	10.3	9.9	8.8	6.9	3.8	5.5	0.9	1.1	0.7
College Station, TX	n/a	n/a	n/a	n/a	n/a	n/a	n/a	n/a	n/a	n/a	n/a	n/a
Colorado Springs, CO	n/a	n/a	n/a	n/a	n/a	n/a	n/a	n/a	n/a	n/a	n/a	n/a
Columbia, MO	n/a	n/a	n/a	n/a	n/a	n/a	n/a	n/a	n/a	n/a	n/a	n/a
Columbia, SC	8.9	10.6	7.2	8.8	10.4	7.1	9.4	9.3	4.5	1.9	1.5	0.7
Columbus, OH	7.4	4.5	4.7	7.4	4.2	4.5	8.6	4.3	5.9	1.5	0.8	0.3
Dallas, TX	7.8	7.6	6.4	7.6	7.3	6.4	7.4	6.9	7.2	1.4	1.5	0.7
Davenport, IA	n/a	n/a	n/a	n/a	n/a	n/a	n/a	n/a	n/a	n/a	n/a	n/a
Denver, CO	8.0	7.5	5.8	7.4	7.0	5.1	3.8	4.7	4.8	0.9	1.0	0.5
Des Moines, IA	n/a	n/a	n/a	n/a	n/a	n/a	n/a	n/a	n/a	n/a	n/a	n/a
Durham, NC	n/a	n/a	n/a	n/a	n/a	n/a	n/a	n/a	n/a	n/a	n/a	n/a
Edison, NJ	10.3	9.2	9.1	9.1	7.8	7.8	4.5	4.3	4.5	1.6	1.4	1.3
El Paso, TX	n/a	n/a	n/a	n/a	n/a	n/a	n/a	n/a	n/a	n/a	n/a	n/a
Fargo, ND	n/a	n/a	n/a	n/a	n/a	n/a	n/a	n/a	n/a	n/a	n/a	n/a
Fayetteville, NC	n/a	n/a	n/a	n/a	n/a	n/a	n/a	n/a	n/a	n/a	n/a	n/a
Fort Collins, CO	n/a	n/a	n/a	n/a	n/a	n/a	n/a	n/a	n/a	n/a	n/a	n/a
Fort Wayne, IN	n/a	n/a	n/a	n/a	n/a	n/a	n/a	n/a	n/a	n/a	n/a	n/a
Fort Worth, TX	7.8	7.6	6.4	7.6	7.3	6.4	7.4	6.9	7.2	1.4	1.5	0.7
Grand Rapids, MI	8.9	7.4	7.1	6.8	5.1	4.7	6.8	4.5	4.6	0.3	0.5	1.1
Greeley, CO	n/a	n/a	n/a	n/a	n/a	n/a	n/a	n/a	n/a	n/a	n/a	n/a
Green Bay, WI	n/a	n/a	n/a	n/a	n/a	n/a	n/a	n/a	n/a	n/a	n/a	n/a
Greensboro, NC	11.6	9.9	8.3	11.5	9.5	8.2	11.4	8.1	7.2	1.0	0.7	0.7
Honolulu, HI	14.0	11.7	10.0	12.9	10.9	9.6	6.5	5.7	5.5	1.4	1.8	1.0
Houston, TX	8.8	9.8	6.8	8.2	9.1	6.3	8.8	11.4	9.7	2.0	1.9	1.1
Huntsville, AL	n/a	n/a	n/a	n/a	n/a	n/a	n/a	n/a	n/a	n/a	n/a	n/a
Indianapolis, IN	8.7	7.2	7.3	8.6	6.7	7.0	9.9	7.0	10.4	1.5	1.5	0.8
Jacksonville, FL	10.1	10.1	9.5	9.3	9.8	9.3	5.6	5.2	7.5	1.3	1.0	1.5
Kansas City, MO	7.8	8.9	9.1	7.7	8.7	9.1	7.9	10.0	9.4	1.2	1.4	0.7
Lafayette, LA	n/a	n/a	n/a	n/a	n/a	n/a	n/a	n/a	n/a	n/a	n/a	n/a
Lakeland, FL	n/a	n/a	n/a	n/a	n/a	n/a	n/a	n/a	n/a	n/a	n/a	n/a
Las Vegas, NV	11.4	10.2	7.8	10.4	9.5	7.1	6.8	5.5	5.0	0.9	2.0	1.1
Lexington, KY	n/a	n/a	n/a	n/a	n/a	n/a	n/a	n/a	n/a	n/a	n/a	n/a
Lincoln, NE	n/a	n/a	n/a	n/a	n/a	n/a	n/a	n/a	n/a	n/a	n/a	n/a
Little Rock, AR	10.5	9.9	9.4	10.2	9.6	9.1	10.9	11.4	9.1	1.8	1.7	1.3
Los Angeles, CA	6.6	6.3	5.5	6.2	5.8	4.8	4.0	4.0	3.6	1.2	1.1	0.6
Louisville, KY	7.6	7.9	6.9	7.4	7.8	6.9	7.7	10.6	6.4	1.4	0.7	1.4

Table continued on following page.

Metro Area[1]	Gross Vacancy Rate[2] (%)			Year-Round Vacancy Rate[3] (%)			Rental Vacancy Rate[4] (%)			Homeowner Vacancy Rate[5] (%)		
	2018	2019	2020	2018	2019	2020	2018	2019	2020	2018	2019	2020
Madison, WI	n/a	n/a	n/a	n/a	n/a	n/a	n/a	n/a	n/a	n/a	n/a	n/a
Manchester, NH	n/a	n/a	n/a	n/a	n/a	n/a	n/a	n/a	n/a	n/a	n/a	n/a
Memphis, TN	12.6	9.9	7.3	12.5	9.9	7.0	11.7	10.6	6.6	1.6	1.4	1.0
Miami, FL	14.9	14.1	12.6	7.9	7.4	6.8	7.4	7.0	5.4	1.9	1.8	1.4
Midland, TX	n/a	n/a	n/a	n/a	n/a	n/a	n/a	n/a	n/a	n/a	n/a	n/a
Milwaukee, WI	8.1	8.0	6.6	7.8	7.8	6.3	5.9	6.6	4.6	1.4	0.6	0.6
Minneapolis, MN	3.9	4.4	4.7	3.3	3.8	3.7	4.1	4.1	4.0	0.4	0.5	0.5
Nashville, TN	5.9	7.8	6.5	5.8	7.5	6.1	7.5	8.6	7.3	0.8	1.2	0.7
New Haven, CT	10.9	11.9	9.4	10.0	11.1	8.4	5.6	8.3	7.8	1.4	1.5	0.2
New Orleans, LA	11.9	12.9	10.7	11.8	12.8	9.8	9.7	9.4	6.1	1.7	1.8	1.3
New York, NY	10.3	9.2	9.1	9.1	7.8	7.8	4.5	4.3	4.5	1.6	1.4	1.3
Oklahoma City, OK	11.5	10.8	7.5	11.2	10.4	7.3	11.8	8.6	6.4	2.7	2.7	0.9
Omaha, NE	7.1	5.6	5.6	6.1	4.8	5.3	7.1	6.3	6.5	0.7	0.6	0.5
Orlando, FL	19.4	16.0	12.9	16.2	12.7	9.8	5.8	8.3	8.6	2.6	2.5	1.2
Peoria, IL	n/a	n/a	n/a	n/a	n/a	n/a	n/a	n/a	n/a	n/a	n/a	n/a
Philadelphia, PA	9.0	8.3	6.0	8.9	8.1	5.8	6.4	7.1	5.4	1.2	1.3	0.7
Phoenix, AZ	12.6	10.3	8.9	7.8	6.2	5.3	6.2	5.0	4.9	1.4	1.0	0.7
Pittsburgh, PA	10.2	10.6	11.5	9.9	10.3	11.3	6.3	7.3	9.3	2.2	1.2	1.0
Portland, OR	6.8	6.6	5.5	6.0	5.6	4.9	3.8	4.4	4.3	1.4	0.9	0.8
Providence, RI	10.3	9.8	8.7	8.5	8.2	6.6	5.0	4.2	3.5	1.1	0.9	0.8
Provo, UT	n/a	n/a	n/a	n/a	n/a	n/a	n/a	n/a	n/a	n/a	n/a	n/a
Raleigh, NC	6.7	6.6	4.6	6.6	6.5	4.5	6.4	7.0	2.3	0.9	0.8	0.4
Reno, NV	n/a	n/a	n/a	n/a	n/a	n/a	n/a	n/a	n/a	n/a	n/a	n/a
Richmond, VA	8.0	8.5	6.0	8.0	8.5	6.0	5.4	9.5	2.7	2.1	1.3	0.9
Riverside, CA	15.1	14.9	11.8	9.1	9.6	7.5	5.1	4.5	4.4	1.6	1.7	0.8
Rochester, MN	n/a	n/a	n/a	n/a	n/a	n/a	n/a	n/a	n/a	n/a	n/a	n/a
Sacramento, CA	8.6	7.8	6.1	7.9	7.1	5.8	5.1	4.2	4.2	1.5	0.8	1.0
Salt Lake City, UT	5.0	4.8	5.7	4.7	4.8	5.6	6.1	5.0	6.2	0.5	0.8	0.3
San Antonio, TX	6.7	9.0	7.4	5.8	8.2	6.7	7.4	10.1	7.2	0.6	2.0	1.0
San Diego, CA	7.6	7.5	6.0	7.4	7.3	5.6	4.5	5.8	3.9	0.7	0.8	0.8
San Francisco, CA	7.5	7.1	6.4	7.4	6.9	6.2	5.4	3.8	5.3	0.9	0.9	0.5
San Jose, CA	5.8	5.6	4.7	5.8	5.6	4.7	4.6	3.7	4.4	0.5	0.5	n/a
Santa Rosa, CA	n/a	n/a	n/a	n/a	n/a	n/a	n/a	n/a	n/a	n/a	n/a	n/a
Savannah, GA	n/a	n/a	n/a	n/a	n/a	n/a	n/a	n/a	n/a	n/a	n/a	n/a
Seattle, WA	5.9	5.5	4.7	5.4	5.2	4.5	4.8	4.4	3.6	0.8	1.0	0.6
Sioux Falls, SD	n/a	n/a	n/a	n/a	n/a	n/a	n/a	n/a	n/a	n/a	n/a	n/a
Springfield, IL	n/a	n/a	n/a	n/a	n/a	n/a	n/a	n/a	n/a	n/a	n/a	n/a
Tallahassee, FL	n/a	n/a	n/a	n/a	n/a	n/a	n/a	n/a	n/a	n/a	n/a	n/a
Tampa, FL	16.1	16.2	13.0	11.9	12.7	10.1	9.9	10.7	8.9	2.1	1.6	1.5
Tucson, AZ	12.5	14.8	12.1	8.1	9.2	7.7	4.4	7.3	8.6	1.8	1.5	0.5
Tulsa, OK	11.7	8.4	9.4	11.6	8.0	8.8	10.1	8.5	8.6	2.6	1.6	0.8
Tuscaloosa, AL	n/a	n/a	n/a	n/a	n/a	n/a	n/a	n/a	n/a	n/a	n/a	n/a
Virginia Beach, VA	8.9	10.4	7.9	7.6	9.3	7.0	7.1	7.1	5.5	1.2	2.2	0.6
Washington, DC	7.0	7.1	6.5	6.7	6.7	6.2	6.2	5.6	5.5	1.1	1.1	0.7
Wichita, KS	n/a	n/a	n/a	n/a	n/a	n/a	n/a	n/a	n/a	n/a	n/a	n/a
Winston-Salem, NC	n/a	n/a	n/a	n/a	n/a	n/a	n/a	n/a	n/a	n/a	n/a	n/a
U.S.	12.3	12.0	10.6	9.7	9.5	8.2	6.9	6.7	6.3	1.5	1.4	1.0

Note: (1) Metropolitan Statistical Area—see Appendix B for areas included; (2) The percentage of the total housing inventory that is vacant; (3) The percentage of the housing inventory (excluding seasonal units) that is year-round vacant; (4) The percentage of rental inventory that is vacant for rent; (5) The percentage of homeowner inventory that is vacant for sale; n/a not available
Source: U.S. Census Bureau, Housing Vacancies and Homeownership Annual Statistics: 2018, 2019, 2020

Bankruptcy Filings

City	Area Covered	Business Filings			Nonbusiness Filings		
		2019	2020	% Chg.	2019	2020	% Chg.
Albuquerque, NM	Bernalillo County	30	33	10.0	1,071	872	-18.6
Allentown, PA	Lehigh County	16	10	-37.5	599	433	-27.7
Anchorage, AK	Anchorage Borough	17	20	17.6	176	137	-22.2
Ann Arbor, MI	Washtenaw County	10	13	30.0	654	454	-30.6
Athens, GA	Clarke County	0	5	n/a	338	228	-32.5
Atlanta, GA	Fulton County	173	152	-12.1	4,013	2,591	-35.4
Austin, TX	Travis County	118	175	48.3	737	529	-28.2
Baton Rouge, LA	East Baton Rouge Parish	37	49	32.4	771	435	-43.6
Boise City, ID	Ada County	26	19	-26.9	878	589	-32.9
Boston, MA	Suffolk County	47	37	-21.3	530	279	-47.4
Boulder, CO	Boulder County	30	42	40.0	372	286	-23.1
Cape Coral, FL	Lee County	57	79	38.6	1,254	1,112	-11.3
Cedar Rapids, IA	Linn County	11	9	-18.2	365	285	-21.9
Charleston, SC	Charleston County	19	21	10.5	356	261	-26.7
Charlotte, NC	Mecklenburg County	64	45	-29.7	1,020	639	-37.4
Chicago, IL	Cook County	413	335	-18.9	27,789	16,384	-41.0
Cincinnati, OH	Hamilton County	48	25	-47.9	2,519	1,845	-26.8
Clarksville, TN	Montgomery County	11	6	-45.5	829	579	-30.2
Cleveland, OH	Cuyahoga County	69	96	39.1	6,013	4,189	-30.3
College Station, TX	Brazos County	7	6	-14.3	105	87	-17.1
Colorado Springs, CO	El Paso County	39	30	-23.1	1,525	1,154	-24.3
Columbia, MO	Boone County	6	8	33.3	375	263	-29.9
Columbia, SC	Richland County	11	12	9.1	837	520	-37.9
Columbus, OH	Franklin County	72	86	19.4	4,342	2,960	-31.8
Dallas, TX	Dallas County	355	568	60.0	3,572	2,452	-31.4
Davenport, IA	Scott County	10	7	-30.0	329	246	-25.2
Denver, CO	Denver County	68	91	33.8	1,338	1,029	-23.1
Des Moines, IA	Polk County	28	12	-57.1	962	782	-18.7
Durham, NC	Durham County	16	18	12.5	395	223	-43.5
Edison, NJ	Middlesex County	46	31	-32.6	1,718	1,097	-36.1
El Paso, TX	El Paso County	63	42	-33.3	2,079	1,290	-38.0
Fargo, ND	Cass County	4	5	25.0	198	183	-7.6
Fayetteville, NC	Cumberland County	8	8	0.0	795	506	-36.4
Fort Collins, CO	Larimer County	29	28	-3.4	558	404	-27.6
Fort Wayne, IN	Allen County	15	15	0.0	1,294	1,057	-18.3
Fort Worth, TX	Tarrant County	242	271	12.0	4,040	2,937	-27.3
Grand Rapids, MI	Kent County	35	47	34.3	935	613	-34.4
Greeley, CO	Weld County	20	21	5.0	691	509	-26.3
Green Bay, WI	Brown County	25	9	-64.0	599	418	-30.2
Greensboro, NC	Guilford County	25	21	-16.0	758	471	-37.9
Honolulu, HI	Honolulu County	35	46	31.4	1,225	1,106	-9.7
Houston, TX	Harris County	411	608	47.9	4,527	2,967	-34.5
Huntsville, AL	Madison County	20	42	110.0	1,463	1,024	-30.0
Indianapolis, IN	Marion County	100	39	-61.0	4,465	3,319	-25.7
Jacksonville, FL	Duval County	75	57	-24.0	2,349	1,604	-31.7
Kansas City, MO	Jackson County	36	26	-27.8	2,080	1,394	-33.0
Lafayette, LA	Lafayette Parish	44	22	-50.0	560	306	-45.4
Lakeland, FL	Polk County	31	53	71.0	1,466	1,168	-20.3
Las Vegas, NV	Clark County	228	204	-10.5	8,184	6,529	-20.2
Lexington, KY	Fayette County	56	54	-3.6	749	520	-30.6
Lincoln, NE	Lancaster County	16	11	-31.3	653	485	-25.7
Little Rock, AR	Pulaski County	233	30	-87.1	2,318	1,519	-34.5
Los Angeles, CA	Los Angeles County	882	857	-2.8	18,304	13,323	-27.2
Louisville, KY	Jefferson County	50	39	-22.0	2,893	2,174	-24.9
Madison, WI	Dane County	34	28	-17.6	773	527	-31.8

Table continued on following page.

City	Area Covered	Business Filings			Nonbusiness Filings		
		2019	2020	% Chg.	2019	2020	% Chg.
Manchester, NH	Hillsborough County	25	27	8.0	519	339	-34.7
Memphis, TN	Shelby County	72	41	-43.1	9,622	5,523	-42.6
Miami, FL	Miami-Dade County	215	322	49.8	8,490	7,108	-16.3
Midland, TX	Midland County	32	11	-65.6	72	48	-33.3
Milwaukee, WI	Milwaukee County	43	48	11.6	6,315	4,019	-36.4
Minneapolis, MN	Hennepin County	62	92	48.4	2,032	1,552	-23.6
Nashville, TN	Davidson County	53	60	13.2	2,051	1,330	-35.2
New Haven, CT	New Haven County	47	33	-29.8	1,884	1,258	-33.2
New Orleans, LA	Orleans Parish	36	21	-41.7	683	391	-42.8
New York, NY	Bronx County	44	24	-45.5	2,486	1,498	-39.7
New York, NY	Kings County	327	182	-44.3	2,743	1,710	-37.7
New York, NY	New York County	244	480	96.7	1,210	854	-29.4
New York, NY	Queens County	206	127	-38.3	3,708	1,990	-46.3
New York, NY	Richmond County	22	19	-13.6	835	459	-45.0
Oklahoma City, OK	Oklahoma County	89	139	56.2	2,147	1,679	-21.8
Omaha, NE	Douglas County	39	16	-59.0	1,283	1,064	-17.1
Orlando, FL	Orange County	154	167	8.4	2,956	2,477	-16.2
Peoria, IL	Peoria County	16	6	-62.5	548	391	-28.6
Philadelphia, PA	Philadelphia County	88	116	31.8	2,222	1,162	-47.7
Phoenix, AZ	Maricopa County	344	261	-24.1	11,095	8,954	-19.3
Pittsburgh, PA	Allegheny County	140	116	-17.1	2,280	1,700	-25.4
Portland, OR	Multnomah County	62	59	-4.8	1,394	1,147	-17.7
Providence, RI	Providence County	38	29	-23.7	1,246	887	-28.8
Provo, UT	Utah County	37	31	-16.2	1,408	1,151	-18.3
Raleigh, NC	Wake County	91	75	-17.6	1,314	882	-32.9
Reno, NV	Washoe County	34	44	29.4	960	765	-20.3
Richmond, VA	Richmond city	18	21	16.7	897	695	-22.5
Riverside, CA	Riverside County	165	145	-12.1	6,195	4,455	-28.1
Rochester, MN	Olmsted County	9	4	-55.6	151	138	-8.6
Sacramento, CA	Sacramento County	95	124	30.5	3,208	2,300	-28.3
Salt Lake City, UT	Salt Lake County	56	60	7.1	4,109	3,232	-21.3
San Antonio, TX	Bexar County	191	128	-33.0	2,173	1,445	-33.5
San Diego, CA	San Diego County	308	269	-12.7	7,366	5,848	-20.6
San Francisco, CA	San Francisco County	58	67	15.5	564	384	-31.9
San Jose, CA	Santa Clara County	94	86	-8.5	1,446	1,018	-29.6
Santa Rosa, CA	Sonoma County	32	29	-9.4	531	388	-26.9
Savannah, GA	Chatham County	18	13	-27.8	1,220	729	-40.2
Seattle, WA	King County	115	96	-16.5	2,174	1,516	-30.3
Sioux Falls, SD	Minnehaha County	18	11	-38.9	349	268	-23.2
Springfield, IL	Sangamon County	8	8	0.0	436	311	-28.7
Tallahassee, FL	Leon County	35	17	-51.4	446	288	-35.4
Tampa, FL	Hillsborough County	155	110	-29.0	3,356	2,538	-24.4
Tucson, AZ	Pima County	50	32	-36.0	2,438	1,727	-29.2
Tulsa, OK	Tulsa County	44	45	2.3	1,555	1,163	-25.2
Tuscaloosa, AL	Tuscaloosa County	9	10	11.1	1,246	799	-35.9
Virginia Beach, VA	Virginia Beach city	18	14	-22.2	1,606	1,206	-24.9
Washington, DC	District of Columbia	50	50	0.0	789	449	-43.1
Wichita, KS	Sedgwick County	30	15	-50.0	1,381	941	-31.9
Winston-Salem, NC	Forsyth County	17	15	-11.8	537	363	-32.4
U.S.	U.S.	22,780	21,655	-4.9	752,160	522,808	-30.5

Note: Business filings include Chapter 7, Chapter 9, Chapter 11, Chapter 12, Chapter 13, Chapter 15, and Section 304; Nonbusiness filings include Chapter 7, Chapter 11, and Chapter 13
Source: Administrative Office of the U.S. Courts, Business and Nonbusiness Bankruptcy, County Cases Commenced by Chapter of the Bankruptcy Code, During the 12-Month Period Ending December 31, 2019 and Business and Nonbusiness Bankruptcy, County Cases Commenced by Chapter of the Bankruptcy Code, During the 12-Month Period Ending December 31, 2020

Income: City

City	Per Capita ($)	Median Household ($)	Average Household ($)
Albuquerque, NM	30,403	52,911	72,265
Allentown, PA	20,792	41,167	56,842
Anchorage, AK	41,415	84,928	109,988
Ann Arbor, MI	42,674	65,745	96,906
Athens, GA	23,726	38,311	59,118
Atlanta, GA	47,424	59,948	106,300
Austin, TX	43,043	71,576	102,876
Baton Rouge, LA	28,491	44,470	70,902
Boise City, ID	34,636	60,035	82,424
Boston, MA	44,690	71,115	107,608
Boulder, CO	44,942	69,520	109,410
Cape Coral, FL	29,970	61,599	76,925
Cedar Rapids, IA	32,290	58,511	75,289
Charleston, SC	42,872	68,438	98,288
Charlotte, NC	38,000	62,817	94,516
Chicago, IL	37,103	58,247	90,713
Cincinnati, OH	30,531	40,640	65,213
Clarksville, TN	25,239	53,604	65,458
Cleveland, OH	21,223	30,907	46,137
College Station, TX	27,541	45,820	73,853
Colorado Springs, CO	34,076	64,712	84,708
Columbia, MO	30,244	51,276	74,727
Columbia, SC	30,461	47,286	76,118
Columbus, OH	29,322	53,745	69,315
Dallas, TX	34,479	52,580	86,393
Davenport, IA	28,645	51,029	68,559
Denver, CO	43,770	68,592	99,151
Des Moines, IA	28,554	53,525	69,074
Durham, NC	34,329	58,905	82,573
Edison, NJ	44,667	103,076	127,171
El Paso, TX	22,734	47,568	64,025
Fargo, ND	35,205	55,551	78,237
Fayetteville, NC	24,823	45,024	58,752
Fort Collins, CO	34,482	65,866	87,406
Fort Wayne, IN	26,970	49,411	65,377
Fort Worth, TX	29,531	62,187	82,977
Grand Rapids, MI	26,120	50,103	65,615
Greeley, CO	26,222	57,586	72,302
Green Bay, WI	26,618	49,251	64,595
Greensboro, NC	29,628	48,964	71,453
Honolulu, HI	37,834	71,465	97,456
Houston, TX	32,521	52,338	84,179
Huntsville, AL	35,634	55,305	80,877
Indianapolis, IN	28,363	47,873	68,367
Jacksonville, FL	30,064	54,701	74,873
Kansas City, MO	32,348	54,194	75,137
Lafayette, LA	32,998	51,264	78,055
Lakeland, FL	28,042	47,511	67,899
Las Vegas, NV	30,761	56,354	79,657
Lexington, KY	34,442	57,291	83,111
Lincoln, NE	31,301	57,746	76,763
Little Rock, AR	35,966	51,485	83,730
Los Angeles, CA	35,261	62,142	96,416
Louisville, KY	30,943	53,436	74,580
Madison, WI	38,285	65,332	87,055
Manchester, NH	31,951	60,711	75,665

Table continued on following page.

City	Per Capita ($)	Median Household ($)	Average Household ($)
Memphis, TN	25,605	41,228	62,588
Miami, FL	28,804	39,049	68,105
Midland, TX	40,252	79,329	112,701
Milwaukee, WI	23,462	41,838	57,332
Minneapolis, MN	38,808	62,583	89,282
Nashville, TN	35,243	59,828	83,348
New Haven, CT	26,429	42,222	65,362
New Orleans, LA	31,385	41,604	71,938
New York, NY	39,828	63,998	102,946
Oklahoma City, OK	30,567	55,557	77,896
Omaha, NE	33,401	60,092	82,945
Orlando, FL	32,085	51,757	75,669
Peoria, IL	31,497	51,771	74,900
Philadelphia, PA	27,924	45,927	68,379
Phoenix, AZ	29,343	57,459	80,631
Pittsburgh, PA	34,083	48,711	72,981
Portland, OR	41,310	71,005	95,998
Providence, RI	26,560	45,610	71,136
Provo, UT	20,792	48,888	69,265
Raleigh, NC	38,494	67,266	94,359
Reno, NV	34,475	58,790	81,700
Richmond, VA	33,549	47,250	76,182
Riverside, CA	26,028	69,045	85,486
Rochester, MN	39,518	73,106	96,015
Sacramento, CA	31,956	62,335	83,189
Salt Lake City, UT	36,779	60,676	88,127
San Antonio, TX	25,894	52,455	70,778
San Diego, CA	41,112	79,673	108,864
San Francisco, CA	68,883	112,449	160,396
San Jose, CA	46,599	109,593	142,635
Santa Rosa, CA	36,935	75,630	96,786
Savannah, GA	25,664	43,307	63,984
Seattle, WA	59,835	92,263	128,184
Sioux Falls, SD	33,065	59,912	79,847
Springfield, IL	34,607	54,648	77,473
Tallahassee, FL	27,677	45,734	66,889
Tampa, FL	36,169	53,833	87,818
Tucson, AZ	23,655	43,425	58,057
Tulsa, OK	30,970	47,650	73,816
Tuscaloosa, AL	26,437	45,268	68,837
Virginia Beach, VA	37,776	76,610	96,936
Washington, DC	56,147	86,420	127,890
Wichita, KS	28,806	52,620	71,335
Winston-Salem, NC	28,821	45,750	71,423
U.S.	34,103	62,843	88,607

Source: U.S. Census Bureau, 2015-2019 American Community Survey 5-Year Estimates

Income: Metro Area

Metro Area	Per Capita ($)	Median Household ($)	Average Household ($)
Albuquerque, NM	29,747	54,072	73,512
Allentown, PA	34,637	67,652	88,415
Anchorage, AK	38,725	83,048	105,968
Ann Arbor, MI	41,399	72,586	101,787
Athens, GA	27,653	47,214	70,940
Atlanta, GA	35,296	68,316	94,723
Austin, TX	39,827	76,844	104,847
Baton Rouge, LA	31,082	58,912	81,614
Boise City, ID	30,508	60,568	80,438
Boston, MA	47,604	90,333	122,399
Boulder, CO	46,826	83,019	115,966
Cape Coral, FL	33,543	57,832	82,544
Cedar Rapids, IA	34,039	64,687	82,498
Charleston, SC	35,011	63,649	88,023
Charlotte, NC	34,558	63,217	89,212
Chicago, IL	38,157	71,770	100,233
Cincinnati, OH	34,575	63,987	86,633
Clarksville, TN	25,931	53,027	67,368
Cleveland, OH	33,785	56,008	79,168
College Station, TX	27,698	50,240	73,129
Colorado Springs, CO	33,795	68,687	88,185
Columbia, MO	29,534	54,808	74,042
Columbia, SC	29,894	55,971	75,154
Columbus, OH	34,441	65,150	87,472
Dallas, TX	35,278	70,281	97,589
Davenport, IA	31,571	58,531	76,075
Denver, CO	41,988	79,664	106,322
Des Moines, IA	36,310	70,126	90,791
Durham, NC	36,322	62,289	90,054
Edison, NJ	43,409	78,773	116,604
El Paso, TX	21,644	46,795	62,663
Fargo, ND	35,812	64,666	85,794
Fayetteville, NC	24,228	48,459	61,989
Fort Collins, CO	37,363	71,881	93,301
Fort Wayne, IN	29,383	55,341	73,578
Fort Worth, TX	35,278	70,281	97,589
Grand Rapids, MI	31,388	63,302	83,235
Greeley, CO	31,793	74,150	89,427
Green Bay, WI	32,520	62,405	79,316
Greensboro, NC	28,787	50,891	71,256
Honolulu, HI	36,816	85,857	109,304
Houston, TX	34,400	67,516	97,410
Huntsville, AL	34,918	64,483	86,328
Indianapolis, IN	33,699	61,552	85,193
Jacksonville, FL	33,304	61,723	84,690
Kansas City, MO	35,761	66,632	89,308
Lafayette, LA	27,955	51,955	72,041
Lakeland, FL	24,864	50,584	66,810
Las Vegas, NV	30,704	59,340	80,762
Lexington, KY	33,153	58,685	82,094
Lincoln, NE	32,360	61,031	80,274
Little Rock, AR	30,599	54,746	76,145
Los Angeles, CA	35,916	72,998	104,698
Louisville, KY	32,630	59,158	80,682
Madison, WI	39,484	72,374	93,923
Manchester, NH	40,955	81,460	103,090

Table continued on following page.

Metro Area	Per Capita ($)	Median Household ($)	Average Household ($)
Memphis, TN	29,453	53,209	76,187
Miami, FL	32,522	56,775	86,518
Midland, TX	38,966	79,140	109,861
Milwaukee, WI	35,491	62,389	86,290
Minneapolis, MN	41,204	80,421	104,946
Nashville, TN	35,479	66,347	91,202
New Haven, CT	38,009	69,905	94,740
New Orleans, LA	31,072	53,084	76,818
New York, NY	43,409	78,773	116,604
Oklahoma City, OK	31,301	59,084	80,805
Omaha, NE	34,825	67,885	88,578
Orlando, FL	29,875	58,368	80,864
Peoria, IL	32,575	59,397	79,057
Philadelphia, PA	39,091	72,343	100,889
Phoenix, AZ	32,522	63,883	87,543
Pittsburgh, PA	36,208	60,535	82,754
Portland, OR	38,544	74,792	97,930
Providence, RI	35,991	67,818	89,281
Provo, UT	26,153	74,387	93,213
Raleigh, NC	38,370	75,851	100,551
Reno, NV	36,087	64,801	89,057
Richmond, VA	36,413	68,529	92,171
Riverside, CA	27,003	65,121	85,373
Rochester, MN	38,754	73,697	95,925
Sacramento, CA	35,563	72,280	96,023
Salt Lake City, UT	32,829	74,842	96,196
San Antonio, TX	29,071	60,327	81,852
San Diego, CA	38,073	78,980	106,600
San Francisco, CA	55,252	106,025	147,703
San Jose, CA	55,547	122,478	163,355
Santa Rosa, CA	42,178	81,018	108,169
Savannah, GA	32,088	59,459	82,125
Seattle, WA	45,750	86,856	115,653
Sioux Falls, SD	33,453	65,621	83,463
Springfield, IL	35,603	62,533	82,720
Tallahassee, FL	28,766	51,874	72,487
Tampa, FL	32,276	55,285	78,248
Tucson, AZ	29,707	53,379	73,554
Tulsa, OK	30,633	55,739	77,341
Tuscaloosa, AL	25,759	50,408	67,811
Virginia Beach, VA	33,907	66,759	86,062
Washington, DC	49,881	103,751	134,513
Wichita, KS	29,414	57,379	74,900
Winston-Salem, NC	28,986	50,774	71,206
U.S.	34,103	62,843	88,607

Note: Figures cover the Metropolitan Statistical Area (MSA)—see Appendix B for areas included
Source: U.S. Census Bureau, 2015-2019 American Community Survey 5-Year Estimates

Household Income Distribution: City

City	Percent of Households Earning							
	Under $15,000	$15,000 -$24,999	$25,000 -$34,999	$35,000 -$49,999	$50,000 -$74,999	$75,000 -$99,999	$100,000 -$149,999	$150,000 and up
Albuquerque, NM	13.1	10.8	10.4	13.1	17.7	12.0	13.3	9.4
Allentown, PA	15.9	13.8	13.0	15.2	19.3	10.2	8.0	4.5
Anchorage, AK	5.3	5.1	6.3	9.9	17.4	13.8	20.5	21.6
Ann Arbor, MI	14.5	7.3	7.6	9.3	15.8	11.4	14.5	19.7
Athens, GA	21.0	14.6	11.3	13.3	14.1	8.7	9.9	7.2
Atlanta, GA	15.4	9.6	8.0	10.6	14.8	10.3	12.8	18.5
Austin, TX	8.6	6.5	7.9	11.6	17.5	12.3	16.6	19.0
Baton Rouge, LA	18.2	13.1	11.0	12.0	15.5	9.1	11.4	9.7
Boise City, ID	10.2	9.7	9.3	13.2	18.2	12.3	14.8	12.3
Boston, MA	16.1	8.1	6.3	8.4	13.0	10.3	15.7	22.2
Boulder, CO	13.6	7.5	7.3	10.0	14.3	10.1	13.9	23.4
Cape Coral, FL	8.7	7.8	9.1	13.7	20.5	15.8	15.3	9.1
Cedar Rapids, IA	9.0	8.8	10.0	13.9	20.9	13.4	15.1	8.9
Charleston, SC	11.2	7.7	7.0	10.7	17.0	12.8	17.4	16.1
Charlotte, NC	8.6	7.9	9.7	13.3	17.9	12.5	14.6	15.5
Chicago, IL	14.0	10.3	8.9	11.0	15.1	11.2	13.8	15.7
Cincinnati, OH	21.1	12.6	11.2	12.3	15.6	9.1	9.4	8.7
Clarksville, TN	10.4	8.7	11.3	16.2	20.8	14.2	12.7	5.6
Cleveland, OH	27.1	15.1	12.9	13.7	14.2	7.9	5.7	3.4
College Station, TX	21.3	11.1	9.2	11.2	12.4	10.9	12.5	11.4
Colorado Springs, CO	8.8	8.3	8.5	12.5	19.0	13.8	16.2	12.8
Columbia, MO	14.8	10.6	9.8	13.8	15.2	11.2	13.6	11.0
Columbia, SC	17.9	11.5	10.8	11.7	15.6	10.9	10.4	11.2
Columbus, OH	12.1	9.7	10.2	14.4	19.5	13.3	13.4	7.3
Dallas, TX	11.8	10.4	10.7	14.7	17.9	10.6	10.8	13.1
Davenport, IA	12.5	11.4	10.6	14.6	19.1	12.3	12.1	7.4
Denver, CO	10.0	7.3	7.9	11.3	17.3	12.5	15.7	18.1
Des Moines, IA	12.0	10.6	10.2	14.2	19.9	13.7	12.4	7.1
Durham, NC	10.3	8.4	10.0	13.5	17.4	12.7	14.5	13.2
Edison, NJ	4.9	4.3	4.1	8.9	12.6	13.7	21.3	30.1
El Paso, TX	14.3	12.2	11.1	14.3	19.1	10.8	11.5	6.7
Fargo, ND	11.1	10.1	9.7	13.8	18.2	14.0	12.6	10.4
Fayetteville, NC	14.5	12.0	12.4	16.4	19.2	11.1	9.3	5.2
Fort Collins, CO	9.7	8.7	8.0	12.2	17.1	12.9	15.8	15.5
Fort Wayne, IN	11.5	11.3	11.9	15.8	19.4	12.6	10.8	6.6
Fort Worth, TX	10.2	8.3	9.5	12.0	18.8	13.4	15.5	12.3
Grand Rapids, MI	13.0	11.8	10.0	15.2	19.4	12.7	11.7	6.4
Greeley, CO	11.9	9.8	8.3	13.5	18.9	13.7	15.7	8.1
Green Bay, WI	11.9	10.9	11.8	16.2	19.6	12.6	11.4	5.5
Greensboro, NC	13.5	10.9	11.5	15.1	18.0	11.2	11.3	8.4
Honolulu, HI	10.1	6.9	6.8	11.8	16.8	12.8	17.0	17.6
Houston, TX	12.6	11.1	10.8	13.5	16.7	10.6	11.3	13.5
Huntsville, AL	13.7	10.7	10.0	11.8	15.2	10.9	13.9	13.8
Indianapolis, IN	13.5	11.1	11.8	15.3	17.9	11.3	11.0	8.0
Jacksonville, FL	11.3	9.4	10.1	14.6	19.4	13.2	12.9	9.2
Kansas City, MO	12.1	10.1	10.4	14.0	17.6	12.2	13.5	10.1
Lafayette, LA	15.8	11.1	10.1	12.0	17.1	10.2	11.1	12.7
Lakeland, FL	12.5	11.9	12.5	15.3	19.2	11.7	9.9	7.1
Las Vegas, NV	11.8	9.5	9.7	13.8	17.5	13.0	14.0	10.7
Lexington, KY	11.5	9.6	9.9	13.0	17.6	12.2	14.2	12.1
Lincoln, NE	9.6	9.2	10.5	13.9	19.3	13.0	14.7	9.9
Little Rock, AR	12.7	11.0	10.4	14.7	16.5	10.4	11.2	13.0
Los Angeles, CA	12.4	9.3	8.7	11.5	15.4	11.4	14.4	16.9
Louisville, KY	12.4	10.3	10.2	13.9	17.8	12.5	12.7	10.1

Table continued on following page.

City	Percent of Households Earning							
	Under $15,000	$15,000 -$24,999	$25,000 -$34,999	$35,000 -$49,999	$50,000 -$74,999	$75,000 -$99,999	$100,000 -$149,999	$150,000 and up
Madison, WI	10.3	7.6	8.8	12.1	17.7	13.3	16.4	13.6
Manchester, NH	10.1	8.6	9.9	12.5	19.8	13.3	16.3	9.3
Memphis, TN	18.3	13.5	11.8	14.6	16.5	9.4	8.8	7.0
Miami, FL	20.8	14.1	11.6	12.3	14.5	8.8	8.6	9.4
Midland, TX	6.7	6.7	6.9	9.8	17.3	13.7	18.0	20.8
Milwaukee, WI	17.8	13.1	11.7	15.1	17.2	10.6	9.6	4.8
Minneapolis, MN	13.0	8.7	8.2	11.6	16.0	12.3	14.6	15.5
Nashville, TN	9.8	8.5	9.3	14.1	18.9	13.6	14.3	11.8
New Haven, CT	20.2	11.9	11.1	12.5	15.8	9.6	9.7	9.4
New Orleans, LA	22.1	12.2	10.3	11.5	14.2	8.8	9.9	10.9
New York, NY	14.3	9.0	7.9	10.2	14.3	11.1	14.3	18.9
Oklahoma City, OK	11.3	9.5	10.0	14.0	18.6	12.6	13.3	10.7
Omaha, NE	10.5	8.8	8.8	13.5	18.5	13.4	14.4	12.1
Orlando, FL	12.5	10.4	11.1	14.2	19.8	10.9	10.8	10.3
Peoria, IL	16.8	11.0	8.8	12.0	17.3	11.6	11.8	10.7
Philadelphia, PA	19.1	11.2	10.2	12.7	15.8	10.5	11.0	9.4
Phoenix, AZ	10.4	9.3	9.5	14.3	18.5	12.6	13.6	11.9
Pittsburgh, PA	17.5	11.6	10.0	11.8	15.9	11.3	11.2	10.6
Portland, OR	10.6	7.2	7.8	10.4	16.4	13.0	16.9	17.7
Providence, RI	20.2	12.0	9.0	11.4	16.7	11.1	10.0	9.7
Provo, UT	12.2	12.9	12.3	13.5	18.9	11.8	10.6	7.8
Raleigh, NC	7.3	7.3	8.9	13.2	18.4	13.5	15.8	15.6
Reno, NV	9.2	9.5	9.5	14.5	18.6	12.7	14.5	11.5
Richmond, VA	17.6	11.0	10.1	13.3	16.2	10.2	10.5	11.0
Riverside, CA	9.0	7.6	8.3	11.4	17.8	14.8	17.6	13.6
Rochester, MN	8.2	7.0	7.1	11.6	17.6	14.1	17.8	16.6
Sacramento, CA	11.3	9.0	8.7	11.7	17.3	13.1	15.6	13.3
Salt Lake City, UT	12.0	8.5	9.1	12.4	17.6	12.5	14.3	13.7
San Antonio, TX	12.7	10.4	10.6	14.0	19.0	12.1	12.5	8.7
San Diego, CA	8.1	6.6	6.8	10.0	15.9	12.9	17.8	21.8
San Francisco, CA	9.7	5.8	4.9	6.2	9.8	9.0	15.6	38.9
San Jose, CA	6.2	4.8	4.9	7.2	12.0	10.7	18.0	36.2
Santa Rosa, CA	7.0	5.9	7.1	11.0	18.4	14.8	18.5	17.3
Savannah, GA	17.5	13.1	10.9	14.8	16.5	10.9	9.7	6.7
Seattle, WA	8.8	5.3	5.6	8.7	13.5	11.4	18.3	28.4
Sioux Falls, SD	8.8	8.3	10.7	13.2	19.0	14.4	15.2	10.5
Springfield, IL	13.7	10.7	9.6	12.1	17.2	13.0	12.9	10.9
Tallahassee, FL	16.8	10.9	11.7	13.8	17.3	10.2	10.4	8.8
Tampa, FL	14.6	10.3	9.9	12.2	15.8	10.7	12.0	14.6
Tucson, AZ	15.8	13.2	11.7	15.6	17.9	10.8	9.7	5.3
Tulsa, OK	14.2	11.6	11.2	15.2	17.4	10.3	10.1	10.0
Tuscaloosa, AL	19.4	11.0	11.0	12.3	16.5	9.4	10.2	10.2
Virginia Beach, VA	5.3	5.4	7.4	11.7	19.1	15.8	19.9	15.4
Washington, DC	12.9	6.0	5.9	7.7	12.2	10.6	16.4	28.2
Wichita, KS	12.3	10.5	10.5	14.6	18.7	12.0	12.8	8.7
Winston-Salem, NC	15.4	11.8	11.9	14.3	16.9	11.2	9.8	8.7
U.S.	10.3	8.9	8.9	12.3	17.2	12.7	15.1	14.5

Source: U.S. Census Bureau, 2015-2019 American Community Survey 5-Year Estimates

Household Income Distribution: Metro Area

Metro Area	Percent of Households Earning							
	Under $15,000	$15,000 -$24,999	$25,000 -$34,999	$35,000 -$49,999	$50,000 -$74,999	$75,000 -$99,999	$100,000 -$149,999	$150,000 and up
Albuquerque, NM	12.4	10.7	10.0	13.3	18.0	12.5	13.1	9.8
Allentown, PA	7.9	8.4	8.7	12.2	17.9	13.9	16.9	14.2
Anchorage, AK	6.1	5.6	6.5	9.9	17.2	13.7	20.5	20.5
Ann Arbor, MI	10.6	7.1	7.1	10.5	16.0	12.5	16.7	19.6
Athens, GA	16.4	12.1	10.3	13.5	15.2	10.2	12.6	9.6
Atlanta, GA	8.4	7.6	8.3	12.1	17.8	13.3	16.2	16.1
Austin, TX	7.3	6.0	7.3	11.1	17.3	13.3	18.1	19.8
Baton Rouge, LA	12.6	9.8	9.4	11.5	16.4	11.9	15.5	12.9
Boise City, ID	9.5	8.6	9.4	13.5	19.8	13.6	15.2	10.5
Boston, MA	8.8	6.2	5.8	8.3	13.5	11.8	18.5	27.1
Boulder, CO	8.5	6.0	6.6	10.2	14.5	12.4	17.2	24.5
Cape Coral, FL	9.4	9.1	10.3	13.9	19.6	13.2	13.3	11.3
Cedar Rapids, IA	7.7	7.9	9.1	13.3	19.3	14.4	16.9	11.4
Charleston, SC	10.0	8.4	8.5	12.1	18.4	13.5	15.6	13.6
Charlotte, NC	8.9	8.6	9.2	12.7	18.1	13.0	15.1	14.4
Chicago, IL	9.3	7.9	7.8	10.8	16.0	12.8	17.0	18.4
Cincinnati, OH	10.2	8.7	8.6	11.8	17.6	13.2	16.0	13.8
Clarksville, TN	11.4	9.1	10.8	16.0	19.7	13.7	12.4	6.8
Cleveland, OH	12.6	9.7	9.8	13.0	17.4	12.4	13.9	11.2
College Station, TX	16.3	11.0	9.8	12.7	15.8	11.5	12.8	10.2
Colorado Springs, CO	7.8	7.4	8.1	12.0	19.0	14.3	17.4	13.9
Columbia, MO	12.0	10.0	10.1	13.9	17.4	12.8	14.2	9.5
Columbia, SC	12.2	9.1	10.1	13.4	18.4	13.4	13.6	9.8
Columbus, OH	9.2	8.1	8.6	12.4	18.2	13.5	16.5	13.5
Dallas, TX	7.7	7.1	8.3	12.0	17.8	13.2	16.7	17.2
Davenport, IA	10.2	9.4	9.5	13.4	19.0	13.8	15.4	9.3
Denver, CO	6.7	5.8	6.7	10.8	17.1	13.7	18.9	20.2
Des Moines, IA	7.2	7.5	8.1	12.0	18.8	14.4	17.6	14.3
Durham, NC	10.0	8.6	9.3	12.7	16.8	12.6	14.7	15.3
Edison, NJ	10.5	7.5	7.0	9.3	13.9	11.4	16.4	24.1
El Paso, TX	14.6	12.2	11.4	14.5	19.0	10.8	11.2	6.3
Fargo, ND	9.4	8.6	8.2	12.1	18.3	15.3	15.7	12.4
Fayetteville, NC	13.8	11.1	11.2	15.5	18.9	12.5	11.5	5.6
Fort Collins, CO	7.9	7.9	7.3	11.6	17.2	14.1	17.9	16.1
Fort Wayne, IN	9.4	9.8	10.9	14.8	19.8	13.7	13.3	8.3
Fort Worth, TX	7.7	7.1	8.3	12.0	17.8	13.2	16.7	17.2
Grand Rapids, MI	7.6	9.0	8.8	13.5	19.8	14.4	15.9	11.0
Greeley, CO	7.7	6.9	7.2	11.0	17.7	16.3	19.3	13.9
Green Bay, WI	8.2	8.5	9.5	13.5	19.2	14.6	16.4	10.0
Greensboro, NC	12.4	10.8	11.3	14.7	18.2	12.2	11.9	8.6
Honolulu, HI	7.1	5.1	5.9	9.6	15.8	13.9	20.2	22.5
Houston, TX	8.8	8.3	8.7	11.7	16.8	12.3	15.8	17.7
Huntsville, AL	10.4	9.2	8.8	11.5	16.1	12.5	16.4	15.0
Indianapolis, IN	9.6	8.7	9.4	13.2	17.9	13.3	15.1	12.8
Jacksonville, FL	9.5	8.3	9.2	13.4	18.8	13.6	14.7	12.4
Kansas City, MO	8.4	7.8	8.7	12.6	17.8	13.9	16.8	14.1
Lafayette, LA	14.4	11.5	10.3	12.4	16.1	12.4	13.4	9.6
Lakeland, FL	11.1	11.2	11.2	16.0	19.9	12.6	11.3	6.8
Las Vegas, NV	10.2	8.8	9.7	13.9	18.6	13.5	14.5	11.0
Lexington, KY	10.9	9.4	9.7	13.1	17.5	13.1	14.7	11.5
Lincoln, NE	8.9	8.8	9.9	13.4	19.0	13.3	15.9	10.8
Little Rock, AR	12.0	10.0	10.4	13.7	18.1	11.9	14.1	9.8
Los Angeles, CA	9.6	7.7	7.6	10.6	15.6	12.4	16.5	20.1
Louisville, KY	10.2	9.3	9.4	13.6	18.4	13.4	14.4	11.4

Table continued on following page.

Metro Area	Percent of Households Earning							
	Under $15,000	$15,000 -$24,999	$25,000 -$34,999	$35,000 -$49,999	$50,000 -$74,999	$75,000 -$99,999	$100,000 -$149,999	$150,000 and up
Madison, WI	7.3	6.8	7.9	11.9	17.8	14.4	18.5	15.5
Manchester, NH	6.3	6.3	7.3	9.8	16.1	13.8	19.9	20.5
Memphis, TN	13.2	10.6	10.2	13.4	17.4	11.8	13.0	10.4
Miami, FL	11.8	9.9	9.8	13.0	17.2	11.7	13.3	13.4
Midland, TX	6.9	6.9	7.1	9.9	17.1	13.5	18.1	20.6
Milwaukee, WI	10.4	9.1	8.7	12.7	17.1	12.9	15.8	13.2
Minneapolis, MN	6.7	6.1	6.7	10.6	16.4	14.2	19.4	19.7
Nashville, TN	8.0	7.5	8.6	13.0	18.6	14.1	16.2	14.0
New Haven, CT	10.0	8.2	7.6	11.1	16.2	12.5	16.5	17.9
New Orleans, LA	14.8	10.9	9.6	12.2	16.4	11.6	13.0	11.5
New York, NY	10.5	7.5	7.0	9.3	13.9	11.4	16.4	24.1
Oklahoma City, OK	10.1	9.2	9.6	13.6	18.8	13.3	14.1	11.2
Omaha, NE	8.4	7.7	8.0	12.3	18.1	14.4	17.5	13.5
Orlando, FL	9.5	9.2	10.1	14.0	18.9	13.1	13.7	11.5
Peoria, IL	10.4	9.1	9.0	13.2	19.5	13.5	14.8	10.5
Philadelphia, PA	10.0	7.8	7.7	10.4	15.6	12.6	16.6	19.3
Phoenix, AZ	8.9	8.0	8.8	13.0	18.5	13.4	15.7	13.7
Pittsburgh, PA	10.6	9.7	9.3	12.3	17.4	12.9	15.5	12.3
Portland, OR	7.7	6.7	7.4	11.1	17.3	14.0	18.3	17.6
Providence, RI	11.0	8.8	7.9	10.8	15.9	13.2	17.0	15.4
Provo, UT	6.1	6.2	7.5	11.8	18.9	16.1	19.5	14.0
Raleigh, NC	6.5	6.6	7.6	11.7	17.1	13.7	18.2	18.6
Reno, NV	7.9	8.4	8.5	13.2	18.9	13.8	16.3	13.1
Richmond, VA	9.0	7.4	8.0	12.4	17.2	13.4	17.3	15.3
Riverside, CA	9.4	8.5	8.8	11.9	17.6	13.5	16.5	13.8
Rochester, MN	7.1	7.0	7.4	11.6	18.0	14.2	18.8	16.0
Sacramento, CA	9.1	7.6	7.7	10.6	16.6	13.1	17.4	17.9
Salt Lake City, UT	6.5	5.9	7.2	11.4	19.1	15.2	19.2	15.5
San Antonio, TX	10.3	8.9	9.4	12.8	18.7	13.2	14.8	11.9
San Diego, CA	7.6	6.7	7.1	10.3	16.1	13.0	18.0	21.1
San Francisco, CA	7.2	5.2	5.2	7.2	11.7	11.0	17.5	35.0
San Jose, CA	5.5	4.3	4.5	6.6	10.8	10.0	17.5	40.9
Santa Rosa, CA	6.7	6.0	6.8	10.0	16.6	14.2	18.5	21.1
Savannah, GA	10.6	9.5	9.2	13.0	17.8	13.8	14.6	11.4
Seattle, WA	6.7	5.4	5.9	9.5	15.7	13.3	19.5	23.9
Sioux Falls, SD	7.6	7.5	9.7	12.5	19.2	15.6	16.9	11.0
Springfield, IL	10.5	9.0	8.9	11.9	17.4	14.1	16.1	12.0
Tallahassee, FL	13.5	10.2	10.8	13.9	17.5	12.1	12.2	9.7
Tampa, FL	10.9	10.0	10.3	14.0	18.0	12.4	13.2	11.1
Tucson, AZ	12.0	10.6	10.2	14.3	18.2	12.3	12.7	9.6
Tulsa, OK	10.9	10.0	10.1	14.0	18.4	12.6	13.4	10.4
Tuscaloosa, AL	16.4	10.6	10.2	12.4	17.8	11.5	12.7	8.4
Virginia Beach, VA	8.7	7.7	8.2	12.3	18.8	14.4	17.1	12.7
Washington, DC	5.8	4.1	4.8	7.5	13.3	12.6	19.9	31.9
Wichita, KS	10.5	9.5	9.7	14.2	19.2	13.1	14.5	9.4
Winston-Salem, NC	12.1	11.3	11.0	14.8	18.0	12.8	11.6	8.3
U.S.	10.3	8.9	8.9	12.3	17.2	12.7	15.1	14.5

Note: Figures cover the Metropolitan Statistical Area (MSA)—see Appendix B for areas included
Source: Source: U.S. Census Bureau, 2015-2019 American Community Survey 5-Year Estimates

Poverty Rate: City

City	All Ages	Under 18 Years Old	18 to 64 Years Old	65 Years and Over
Albuquerque, NM	16.9	24.0	16.1	9.5
Allentown, PA	25.7	37.4	22.4	15.8
Anchorage, AK	9.0	13.1	8.1	5.5
Ann Arbor, MI	22.3	9.8	27.3	7.7
Athens, GA	29.9	33.7	32.2	9.4
Atlanta, GA	20.8	33.5	18.1	16.1
Austin, TX	13.2	18.0	12.3	9.4
Baton Rouge, LA	24.8	35.7	23.9	11.5
Boise City, ID	13.7	16.2	13.6	10.7
Boston, MA	18.9	27.7	16.5	20.9
Boulder, CO	20.4	6.3	25.2	6.9
Cape Coral, FL	10.4	13.1	10.3	8.6
Cedar Rapids, IA	12.5	17.0	12.2	7.0
Charleston, SC	13.2	14.7	13.8	8.8
Charlotte, NC	12.8	18.6	11.4	8.6
Chicago, IL	18.4	26.8	16.2	15.5
Cincinnati, OH	26.3	39.0	24.2	13.9
Clarksville, TN	14.5	18.5	13.5	9.0
Cleveland, OH	32.7	48.2	29.8	20.5
College Station, TX	29.6	12.3	35.9	7.9
Colorado Springs, CO	11.7	15.8	11.1	7.0
Columbia, MO	21.8	15.1	26.2	5.0
Columbia, SC	21.8	26.8	21.9	13.2
Columbus, OH	19.5	29.3	17.4	11.6
Dallas, TX	18.9	29.3	15.6	14.4
Davenport, IA	16.6	24.3	15.5	9.0
Denver, CO	12.9	18.2	11.6	10.9
Des Moines, IA	16.1	23.2	14.7	9.3
Durham, NC	15.9	24.5	14.3	8.4
Edison, NJ	5.7	6.8	5.1	6.8
El Paso, TX	19.1	27.1	15.9	17.6
Fargo, ND	13.2	12.8	14.3	7.6
Fayetteville, NC	19.3	28.0	17.4	11.6
Fort Collins, CO	16.3	10.3	19.3	7.7
Fort Wayne, IN	16.0	24.1	14.5	7.5
Fort Worth, TX	14.5	20.0	12.5	11.4
Grand Rapids, MI	20.4	28.9	19.4	10.1
Greeley, CO	16.2	19.6	16.1	9.3
Green Bay, WI	14.9	19.7	13.9	9.7
Greensboro, NC	18.5	26.7	17.1	11.5
Honolulu, HI	10.6	12.2	10.1	10.9
Houston, TX	20.1	31.2	16.6	14.2
Huntsville, AL	16.8	25.5	16.2	7.9
Indianapolis, IN	18.0	26.8	16.1	10.2
Jacksonville, FL	14.9	21.9	13.0	11.3
Kansas City, MO	16.1	24.3	14.5	9.6
Lafayette, LA	19.7	27.7	18.9	11.4
Lakeland, FL	16.4	23.5	15.5	12.3
Las Vegas, NV	15.3	21.3	14.1	10.6
Lexington, KY	16.8	20.4	17.5	7.4
Lincoln, NE	13.5	14.2	14.8	6.4
Little Rock, AR	16.6	23.8	15.2	10.9
Los Angeles, CA	18.0	25.7	16.0	15.6
Louisville, KY	15.9	24.0	14.6	9.4
Madison, WI	16.9	11.8	19.9	5.9

Table continued on following page.

City	All Ages	Under 18 Years Old	18 to 64 Years Old	65 Years and Over
Manchester, NH	14.1	19.8	13.2	10.1
Memphis, TN	25.1	40.8	21.1	13.6
Miami, FL	23.4	31.8	19.0	31.6
Midland, TX	9.2	11.5	7.7	11.8
Milwaukee, WI	25.4	36.7	22.7	13.6
Minneapolis, MN	19.1	25.5	18.2	13.2
Nashville, TN	15.1	24.2	13.2	9.2
New Haven, CT	26.5	36.2	24.7	16.3
New Orleans, LA	23.7	34.2	21.6	18.1
New York, NY	17.9	25.1	15.6	18.2
Oklahoma City, OK	16.1	23.7	14.2	9.0
Omaha, NE	13.4	18.7	12.3	8.5
Orlando, FL	17.2	24.4	15.4	14.8
Peoria, IL	19.7	24.6	20.1	10.1
Philadelphia, PA	24.3	34.8	22.2	17.6
Phoenix, AZ	18.0	26.6	15.6	10.8
Pittsburgh, PA	20.5	27.2	20.7	12.8
Portland, OR	13.7	15.5	13.9	10.4
Providence, RI	25.5	34.7	23.0	20.6
Provo, UT	26.3	19.6	30.2	7.9
Raleigh, NC	12.6	17.8	11.9	6.7
Reno, NV	13.5	15.8	14.0	8.2
Richmond, VA	23.2	37.0	21.5	13.2
Riverside, CA	13.9	17.9	13.0	10.5
Rochester, MN	10.1	12.8	10.0	5.7
Sacramento, CA	16.6	21.9	15.5	12.3
Salt Lake City, UT	16.6	20.4	16.4	10.9
San Antonio, TX	17.8	26.1	15.4	12.8
San Diego, CA	12.8	15.7	12.6	9.4
San Francisco, CA	10.3	10.0	9.7	13.6
San Jose, CA	8.7	9.3	8.4	9.5
Santa Rosa, CA	10.3	13.7	9.8	7.7
Savannah, GA	21.9	30.9	20.8	12.4
Seattle, WA	11.0	10.9	10.9	11.2
Sioux Falls, SD	10.4	12.9	9.9	8.0
Springfield, IL	18.6	29.8	17.5	8.4
Tallahassee, FL	26.4	24.3	29.3	9.9
Tampa, FL	18.6	26.5	16.2	17.6
Tucson, AZ	22.5	30.5	21.9	13.0
Tulsa, OK	19.4	29.7	17.7	8.8
Tuscaloosa, AL	24.0	24.2	26.6	10.3
Virginia Beach, VA	7.3	10.2	6.9	4.5
Washington, DC	16.2	24.0	14.5	14.5
Wichita, KS	15.9	22.0	15.0	8.8
Winston-Salem, NC	20.7	32.0	18.6	10.4
U.S.	13.4	18.5	12.6	9.3

Note: Figures are percentage of people whose income during the past 12 months was below the poverty level;
Source: U.S. Census Bureau, 2015-2019 American Community Survey 5-Year Estimates

Poverty Rate: Metro Area

Metro Area	All Ages	Under 18 Years Old	18 to 64 Years Old	65 Years and Over
Albuquerque, NM	16.2	22.6	15.5	10.1
Allentown, PA	10.4	16.3	9.3	6.8
Anchorage, AK	9.4	12.8	8.6	6.0
Ann Arbor, MI	14.0	12.0	16.1	6.7
Athens, GA	22.0	25.1	23.8	8.1
Atlanta, GA	12.1	17.4	10.7	8.6
Austin, TX	10.8	13.3	10.5	7.2
Baton Rouge, LA	15.9	21.8	14.9	10.0
Boise City, ID	11.9	13.5	11.8	9.1
Boston, MA	9.3	11.3	8.8	9.1
Boulder, CO	11.7	8.5	13.8	6.3
Cape Coral, FL	13.1	22.1	12.8	7.9
Cedar Rapids, IA	10.0	12.8	9.8	6.6
Charleston, SC	12.9	18.9	11.7	8.7
Charlotte, NC	11.7	16.5	10.7	8.2
Chicago, IL	11.8	16.5	10.7	9.1
Cincinnati, OH	12.2	16.8	11.5	7.8
Clarksville, TN	14.7	19.0	13.7	9.7
Cleveland, OH	14.3	20.7	13.6	9.0
College Station, TX	22.7	20.1	25.8	9.1
Colorado Springs, CO	10.0	13.1	9.6	6.3
Columbia, MO	17.2	15.0	20.1	6.5
Columbia, SC	15.0	20.2	14.3	9.5
Columbus, OH	13.2	18.5	12.2	7.9
Dallas, TX	11.7	16.6	10.1	8.5
Davenport, IA	12.5	18.8	11.5	7.5
Denver, CO	8.8	11.4	8.3	6.9
Des Moines, IA	9.3	11.6	9.0	6.3
Durham, NC	14.2	20.6	13.6	7.8
Edison, NJ	12.8	17.7	11.4	12.0
El Paso, TX	20.2	28.6	16.7	18.6
Fargo, ND	11.1	11.1	11.9	6.3
Fayetteville, NC	17.9	24.8	16.3	11.4
Fort Collins, CO	11.6	9.4	13.5	6.4
Fort Wayne, IN	13.0	19.4	11.7	6.5
Fort Worth, TX	11.7	16.6	10.1	8.5
Grand Rapids, MI	11.0	13.7	10.9	6.9
Greeley, CO	10.0	12.0	9.5	8.4
Green Bay, WI	9.6	12.5	9.0	7.3
Greensboro, NC	16.0	23.2	14.9	10.0
Honolulu, HI	8.3	10.1	7.8	7.8
Houston, TX	13.7	19.8	11.7	10.0
Huntsville, AL	12.7	18.5	11.8	7.7
Indianapolis, IN	12.4	17.5	11.4	7.4
Jacksonville, FL	12.6	17.7	11.6	8.9
Kansas City, MO	10.5	15.0	9.6	6.8
Lafayette, LA	19.1	26.4	17.4	13.7
Lakeland, FL	15.8	24.7	14.5	9.9
Las Vegas, NV	13.7	19.3	12.6	9.2
Lexington, KY	15.8	20.9	15.9	7.6
Lincoln, NE	12.2	12.5	13.5	5.8
Little Rock, AR	15.1	20.5	14.2	9.7
Los Angeles, CA	13.9	19.2	12.5	12.2
Louisville, KY	12.5	18.2	11.6	7.9
Madison, WI	10.3	8.7	11.8	5.6

Table continued on following page.

Metro Area	All Ages	Under 18 Years Old	18 to 64 Years Old	65 Years and Over
Manchester, NH	7.8	9.4	7.6	6.1
Memphis, TN	17.6	27.8	15.0	10.1
Miami, FL	14.6	20.2	12.6	15.1
Midland, TX	9.5	13.2	7.5	11.1
Milwaukee, WI	13.3	19.3	12.3	8.4
Minneapolis, MN	8.6	11.0	8.1	6.6
Nashville, TN	11.4	15.7	10.6	7.6
New Haven, CT	11.7	17.3	11.0	7.6
New Orleans, LA	17.3	25.2	15.7	12.5
New York, NY	12.8	17.7	11.4	12.0
Oklahoma City, OK	13.9	19.0	13.2	7.5
Omaha, NE	10.3	13.5	9.6	7.2
Orlando, FL	13.7	19.6	12.5	9.9
Peoria, IL	12.2	15.5	12.4	6.9
Philadelphia, PA	12.4	16.9	11.7	8.6
Phoenix, AZ	13.7	19.6	12.8	8.2
Pittsburgh, PA	11.2	14.9	11.0	8.0
Portland, OR	10.6	13.1	10.5	7.7
Providence, RI	12.0	16.9	11.1	9.6
Provo, UT	10.7	9.5	12.0	5.5
Raleigh, NC	9.8	13.4	9.1	6.3
Reno, NV	11.2	14.0	11.2	7.7
Richmond, VA	11.2	15.8	10.5	7.6
Riverside, CA	14.8	20.5	13.2	10.7
Rochester, MN	8.3	10.4	8.1	5.6
Sacramento, CA	13.4	16.8	13.2	8.9
Salt Lake City, UT	9.0	10.7	8.6	6.7
San Antonio, TX	14.4	20.6	12.7	10.4
San Diego, CA	11.6	14.7	11.1	8.9
San Francisco, CA	9.0	10.2	8.7	8.7
San Jose, CA	7.5	7.9	7.3	8.0
Santa Rosa, CA	9.2	10.7	9.4	7.0
Savannah, GA	13.7	18.4	13.1	8.7
Seattle, WA	9.0	10.8	8.6	7.8
Sioux Falls, SD	8.7	10.4	8.3	7.2
Springfield, IL	14.2	22.8	13.2	6.9
Tallahassee, FL	20.0	22.1	21.9	8.4
Tampa, FL	13.5	18.6	12.8	10.3
Tucson, AZ	16.8	23.9	16.9	8.8
Tulsa, OK	14.3	20.9	13.3	7.7
Tuscaloosa, AL	19.2	24.7	19.2	10.6
Virginia Beach, VA	11.3	17.1	10.2	6.9
Washington, DC	7.8	9.9	7.2	7.2
Wichita, KS	13.0	17.4	12.3	8.2
Winston-Salem, NC	16.0	24.8	14.6	9.0
U.S.	13.4	18.5	12.6	9.3

Note: Figures are percentage of people whose income during the past 12 months was below the poverty level;
Figures cover the Metropolitan Statistical Area—see Appendix B for areas included
Source: U.S. Census Bureau, 2015-2019 American Community Survey 5-Year Estimates

Employment by Industry

Metro Area[1]	(A)	(B)	(C)	(D)	(E)	(F)	(G)	(H)	(I)	(J)	(K)	(L)	(M)	(N)
Albuquerque, NM	6.8	n/a	17.3	4.9	20.9	1.3	8.7	3.8	n/a	2.8	16.5	10.9	2.8	2.9
Allentown, PA	3.5	n/a	20.8	3.6	10.5	1.2	7.7	10.5	n/a	3.4	12.8	10.8	10.9	3.8
Anchorage, AK	7.4	6.0	19.2	4.6	20.8	2.1	8.0	1.1	1.3	3.4	10.9	12.1	6.9	2.9
Ann Arbor, MI	2.2	n/a	13.3	3.0	38.3	2.8	4.6	6.3	n/a	2.5	14.0	7.3	2.2	3.0
Athens, GA	n/a	n/a	n/a	n/a	29.7	n/a	10.2	n/a	n/a	n/a	9.1	11.3	n/a	n/a
Atlanta, GA	4.7	4.6	13.1	6.6	12.0	3.5	8.8	6.0	<0.1	3.3	19.5	10.5	6.1	5.3
Austin, TX	6.4	n/a	11.2	6.2	16.9	3.6	9.5	5.8	n/a	3.8	18.6	10.0	2.6	4.9
Baton Rouge, LA	10.7	10.5	13.5	4.2	20.0	1.1	8.8	7.5	0.1	3.8	12.3	10.5	3.9	3.3
Boise City, ID	8.2	n/a	14.3	6.0	13.6	1.0	9.2	8.1	n/a	3.4	15.2	11.9	3.8	4.7
Boston, MA[4]	4.1	n/a	22.8	8.6	11.0	3.4	6.3	4.2	n/a	3.1	22.3	8.0	2.4	3.2
Boulder, CO	3.0	n/a	13.3	3.8	18.9	4.5	6.5	11.3	n/a	3.1	21.2	9.5	1.1	3.5
Cape Coral, FL	12.6	n/a	11.4	4.9	15.8	0.9	13.5	2.4	n/a	4.0	14.0	14.9	2.4	2.8
Cedar Rapids, IA	6.0	n/a	14.8	8.2	11.3	2.1	6.8	14.0	n/a	3.4	10.2	11.0	7.7	4.1
Charleston, SC	5.7	n/a	11.9	4.4	18.2	1.5	11.5	7.6	n/a	3.8	15.5	12.3	4.2	2.9
Charlotte, NC	5.6	n/a	10.1	9.1	12.8	1.9	9.4	8.5	n/a	3.5	17.4	10.6	6.1	4.6
Chicago, IL[2]	3.5	3.4	16.5	7.8	11.4	1.8	6.5	7.6	<0.1	4.1	19.1	9.6	6.4	5.1
Cincinnati, OH	4.2	n/a	15.8	6.9	11.8	1.2	8.9	10.5	n/a	3.4	15.7	10.1	5.7	5.2
Clarksville, TN	3.8	n/a	12.9	3.3	20.6	1.0	12.1	11.7	n/a	3.4	10.6	13.9	2.9	n/a
Cleveland, OH	3.7	n/a	19.4	6.5	12.8	1.2	8.3	11.2	n/a	3.3	15.0	9.7	3.6	4.8
College Station, TX	5.7	n/a	10.1	3.1	37.9	1.1	11.3	4.4	n/a	2.5	9.0	10.4	1.7	2.2
Colorado Springs, CO	6.3	n/a	14.7	6.5	18.4	1.8	9.5	4.0	n/a	5.9	16.6	11.6	2.2	2.0
Columbia, MO	n/a	n/a	n/a	n/a	29.2	n/a	n/a	n/a	n/a	n/a	n/a	10.9	n/a	n/a
Columbia, SC	4.4	n/a	12.2	8.1	21.7	1.2	8.9	7.9	n/a	3.8	12.4	10.8	4.4	3.6
Columbus, OH	4.1	n/a	14.5	8.0	16.4	1.3	7.6	6.7	n/a	3.6	16.4	9.3	7.9	3.7
Dallas, TX[2]	5.4	n/a	11.7	9.7	11.9	2.5	8.5	6.7	n/a	2.8	19.5	9.5	5.6	5.6
Davenport, IA	n/a	n/a	n/a	n/a	n/a	n/a	n/a	n/a	n/a	n/a	n/a	n/a	n/a	n/a
Denver, CO	7.5	n/a	12.8	7.7	13.5	3.4	7.3	4.7	n/a	3.7	18.8	9.7	5.5	5.0
Des Moines, IA	5.8	n/a	13.9	15.8	12.6	1.6	7.8	5.6	n/a	3.5	13.7	10.9	3.4	4.9
Durham, NC	2.9	n/a	22.1	5.1	19.9	1.7	6.2	10.4	n/a	3.3	15.3	7.4	2.5	2.6
Edison, NJ[2]	3.8	n/a	22.7	9.4	14.1	3.8	6.0	2.7	n/a	3.8	16.4	8.9	4.2	3.7
El Paso, TX	5.5	n/a	14.8	4.1	22.2	1.4	10.5	5.1	n/a	2.5	11.8	12.3	5.5	3.7
Fargo, ND	6.4	n/a	19.3	8.3	13.3	2.1	8.1	7.1	n/a	3.4	9.5	10.9	4.6	6.4
Fayetteville, NC	3.7	n/a	11.5	2.9	31.8	0.7	11.5	6.2	n/a	3.3	8.6	13.6	3.9	1.5
Fort Collins, CO	7.0	n/a	11.2	4.1	25.0	1.8	8.8	8.4	n/a	3.8	12.2	11.7	2.3	3.1
Fort Wayne, IN	5.3	n/a	19.1	5.5	8.8	0.9	8.4	16.5	n/a	4.7	9.9	11.3	4.6	4.6
Fort Worth, TX[2]	6.8	n/a	12.8	6.3	12.8	0.8	10.1	9.2	n/a	3.5	11.5	11.8	9.0	4.9
Grand Rapids, MI	4.7	n/a	17.6	5.0	9.0	1.0	5.8	20.4	n/a	3.7	13.6	9.2	3.5	5.9
Greeley, CO	14.9	n/a	9.8	4.2	15.9	0.4	8.1	13.1	n/a	3.4	10.7	10.5	4.6	4.0
Green Bay, WI	4.8	n/a	15.5	6.8	11.1	0.8	7.5	17.9	n/a	4.7	11.1	9.6	5.1	4.7
Greensboro, NC	4.5	n/a	14.3	5.2	12.1	1.2	8.5	14.5	n/a	3.3	13.0	11.1	6.4	5.3
Honolulu, HI	6.5	n/a	15.2	5.3	22.5	1.3	12.0	2.1	n/a	4.1	12.8	9.7	4.8	3.2
Houston, TX	8.9	6.7	13.2	5.4	14.0	0.9	9.5	6.9	2.2	3.5	16.1	10.1	5.7	5.2
Huntsville, AL	4.0	n/a	8.7	2.9	21.2	0.8	8.0	10.6	n/a	3.2	25.5	10.4	1.6	2.5
Indianapolis, IN	5.5	5.4	15.1	6.7	12.7	1.0	8.5	8.4	<0.1	3.5	15.9	9.8	7.9	4.4
Jacksonville, FL	6.6	6.5	15.4	9.6	10.8	1.2	10.4	4.4	<0.1	3.4	15.6	11.3	7.1	3.6
Kansas City, MO	4.9	n/a	14.6	7.4	13.7	1.3	8.1	7.4	n/a	3.8	17.7	10.3	5.7	4.6
Lafayette, LA	10.1	4.9	16.8	5.2	13.4	1.0	10.1	7.0	5.2	3.4	11.1	14.0	3.2	4.2
Lakeland, FL	6.3	n/a	14.6	5.8	11.7	0.7	8.7	7.2	n/a	2.5	13.9	13.5	10.0	4.5
Las Vegas, NV	7.0	6.9	11.4	5.8	11.2	1.0	21.4	2.6	<0.1	2.9	14.3	12.4	7.0	2.5
Lexington, KY	5.0	n/a	13.0	3.7	19.4	0.9	8.8	10.5	n/a	3.6	14.8	11.2	4.7	3.9
Lincoln, NE	5.1	n/a	16.6	6.8	21.9	1.7	7.6	7.0	n/a	3.6	11.4	9.8	5.9	2.3
Little Rock, AR	4.9	n/a	16.7	6.3	19.3	1.4	8.0	5.3	n/a	5.0	12.5	11.2	4.6	4.2
Los Angeles, CA[2]	3.5	3.5	20.1	5.1	13.4	4.3	8.5	7.4	<0.1	2.8	14.4	9.7	5.4	4.8
Louisville, KY	4.3	n/a	14.3	7.3	10.8	1.2	7.8	12.6	n/a	3.5	13.1	10.0	10.2	4.4
Madison, WI	4.6	n/a	12.6	5.9	21.5	4.5	6.4	9.1	n/a	5.2	13.5	10.3	2.4	3.6
Manchester, NH[3]	5.0	n/a	22.6	7.2	10.6	2.8	6.7	7.0	n/a	3.7	15.2	11.5	3.2	4.0

Table continued on following page.

Metro Area[1]	(A)	(B)	(C)	(D)	(E)	(F)	(G)	(H)	(I)	(J)	(K)	(L)	(M)	(N)
Memphis, TN	3.6	n/a	14.6	4.5	12.9	0.7	8.9	6.8	n/a	4.2	15.4	10.0	12.6	5.3
Miami, FL[2]	4.5	4.4	16.5	7.2	12.1	1.6	9.2	3.7	<0.1	3.9	15.9	12.0	7.1	6.0
Midland, TX	28.0	n/a	7.3	4.8	11.2	0.7	10.1	3.3	n/a	3.7	9.4	10.5	5.2	5.2
Milwaukee, WI	3.6	3.6	20.5	6.0	9.6	1.5	7.1	13.9	<0.1	5.4	14.3	9.4	3.6	4.5
Minneapolis, MN	4.3	n/a	17.7	8.7	12.9	1.6	5.3	10.2	n/a	3.6	16.6	9.8	4.0	4.7
Nashville, TN	4.8	n/a	14.8	6.9	11.8	2.4	9.2	7.9	n/a	3.8	17.3	10.0	6.5	4.0
New Haven, CT[3]	3.5	n/a	28.4	4.0	12.7	1.3	6.5	8.2	n/a	3.5	10.9	9.6	7.1	3.8
New Orleans, LA	5.6	4.9	19.1	5.2	13.5	1.0	11.9	5.6	0.7	4.0	13.2	11.5	5.2	3.8
New York, NY[2]	3.8	n/a	22.7	9.4	14.1	3.8	6.0	2.7	n/a	3.8	16.4	8.9	4.2	3.7
Oklahoma City, OK	6.0	4.8	15.4	5.4	20.2	0.9	10.4	5.2	1.2	4.3	12.8	10.7	4.8	3.4
Omaha, NE	6.2	n/a	16.0	9.2	13.2	1.9	8.5	6.8	n/a	3.5	14.3	10.9	5.5	3.4
Orlando, FL	7.0	7.0	13.1	6.5	10.6	2.0	15.1	4.0	<0.1	3.3	18.2	12.2	3.7	3.8
Peoria, IL	4.7	n/a	19.8	4.4	11.9	0.9	7.3	13.0	n/a	4.7	13.0	11.5	4.4	3.8
Philadelphia, PA[2]	2.6	n/a	32.1	6.3	14.4	1.9	6.0	3.5	n/a	3.7	14.7	7.7	4.1	2.4
Phoenix, AZ	6.2	6.1	15.9	9.4	11.1	1.6	8.9	6.1	0.1	3.0	16.8	11.3	5.3	3.7
Pittsburgh, PA	5.8	5.1	22.8	6.8	10.2	1.6	7.5	7.2	0.6	3.7	15.5	10.6	4.4	3.4
Portland, OR	6.4	6.3	15.8	6.2	12.4	2.1	6.3	10.6	0.1	3.2	16.4	10.4	4.8	4.8
Providence, RI[3]	4.5	4.5	21.4	6.6	13.2	1.0	8.6	8.7	<0.1	4.0	13.1	11.6	3.4	3.2
Provo, UT	9.5	n/a	18.7	4.3	11.9	4.7	8.2	7.3	n/a	2.1	15.2	13.2	1.7	2.6
Raleigh, NC	6.5	n/a	12.4	5.1	14.9	3.4	9.0	4.6	n/a	3.9	20.5	11.6	3.4	4.0
Reno, NV	7.4	7.2	11.5	4.5	12.4	1.2	12.3	10.3	0.2	2.3	14.4	9.9	9.3	3.9
Richmond, VA	6.1	n/a	14.7	8.0	16.4	0.9	7.9	4.6	n/a	4.2	17.2	10.3	5.3	3.8
Riverside, CA	7.3	7.2	16.6	2.8	16.2	0.5	8.3	6.0	<0.1	2.4	10.4	11.8	12.9	4.2
Rochester, MN	4.0	n/a	44.7	2.3	10.5	1.1	5.8	8.3	n/a	2.9	4.7	10.6	2.2	2.3
Sacramento, CA	7.5	7.5	16.4	5.3	24.0	1.0	8.0	3.6	<0.1	2.8	13.8	10.5	4.0	2.7
Salt Lake City, UT	6.6	n/a	11.6	8.3	14.1	2.7	7.5	7.8	n/a	2.7	17.5	10.4	5.9	4.4
San Antonio, TX	5.8	5.2	15.1	8.9	16.6	1.7	10.8	4.8	0.5	3.2	14.7	10.6	3.8	3.4
San Diego, CA	6.3	6.3	15.2	5.3	16.9	1.5	9.3	8.1	<0.1	2.9	18.2	10.4	2.6	2.8
San Francisco, CA[2]	3.9	3.9	13.5	7.9	11.9	10.3	6.5	3.4	<0.1	2.9	26.8	6.6	3.9	1.9
San Jose, CA	4.8	4.7	15.9	3.5	8.7	10.0	5.4	15.7	<0.1	1.9	22.3	7.2	1.6	2.6
Santa Rosa, CA	8.7	8.6	17.4	3.9	14.2	1.1	8.2	11.8	0.1	3.0	11.9	12.9	2.3	4.0
Savannah, GA	4.6	n/a	14.0	3.2	13.0	0.8	12.2	9.3	n/a	3.7	14.3	11.8	9.1	3.4
Seattle, WA[2]	6.3	6.2	13.1	5.2	12.2	8.1	6.2	8.6	<0.1	3.4	16.4	12.8	3.4	3.9
Sioux Falls, SD	5.5	n/a	22.2	9.9	9.4	1.5	7.8	9.0	n/a	3.7	9.4	12.0	3.6	5.4
Springfield, IL	3.3	n/a	20.4	6.0	25.9	1.7	6.6	2.8	n/a	5.7	10.5	11.7	2.0	2.7
Tallahassee, FL	4.5	n/a	13.7	4.2	32.8	1.7	9.4	1.9	n/a	5.0	12.8	10.0	1.3	2.0
Tampa, FL	6.2	6.1	15.5	9.2	11.2	1.7	9.9	4.9	<0.1	3.3	18.7	11.7	3.2	3.9
Tucson, AZ	5.3	4.8	18.1	4.6	19.8	1.3	9.3	7.1	0.5	3.3	12.2	11.3	5.4	1.8
Tulsa, OK	6.7	5.6	16.1	5.1	12.7	1.3	9.5	11.1	1.0	4.4	13.0	11.1	4.9	3.6
Tuscaloosa, AL	6.4	n/a	8.3	3.8	26.4	0.8	9.2	16.5	n/a	3.8	9.2	10.3	2.8	1.9
Virginia Beach, VA	5.2	n/a	14.2	5.0	20.5	1.2	10.0	7.4	n/a	4.1	14.8	11.2	3.6	2.3
Washington, DC[2]	5.0	n/a	12.8	4.5	22.8	2.3	7.3	1.4	n/a	6.4	24.5	8.0	2.6	1.8
Wichita, KS	5.8	n/a	16.3	4.1	14.3	1.2	10.3	15.5	n/a	3.5	11.8	10.6	3.3	2.8
Winston-Salem, NC	4.5	n/a	20.8	4.9	11.4	0.6	9.2	12.6	n/a	3.0	13.4	11.8	4.4	2.9
U.S.	5.5	5.1	16.3	6.1	15.2	1.9	9.0	8.5	0.4	3.8	14.4	10.9	4.6	3.9

Note: All figures are percentages covering non-farm employment as of December 2020 and are not seasonally adjusted;
(1) Figures cover the Metropolitan Statistical Area (MSA) except where noted. See Appendix B for areas included; (2) Metropolitan Division; (3) New England City and Town Area; (4) New England City and Town Area Division; (A) Construction, Mining, and Logging (some areas report Construction separate from Mining and Logging); (B) Construction; (C) Education and Health Services; (D) Financial Activities; (E) Government; (F) Information; (G) Leisure and Hospitality; (H) Manufacturing; (I) Mining and Logging; (J) Other Services; (K) Professional and Business Services; (L) Retail Trade; (M) Transportation and Utilities; (N) Wholesale Trade; n/a not available
Source: Bureau of Labor Statistics, Current Employment Statistics, Employment, Hours, and Earnings, December 2020

Labor Force, Employment and Job Growth: City

City	Civilian Labor Force			Workers Employed		
	Dec. 2019	Dec. 2020	% Chg.	Dec. 2019	Dec. 2020	% Chg.
Albuquerque, NM	284,609	280,764	-1.3	273,259	260,057	-4.8
Allentown, PA	56,275	55,559	-1.2	52,716	50,085	-4.9
Anchorage, AK	147,801	150,509	1.8	140,718	142,180	1.0
Ann Arbor, MI	66,802	63,917	-4.3	65,636	62,017	-5.5
Athens, GA	59,225	58,747	-0.8	57,596	55,706	-3.2
Atlanta, GA	264,779	266,767	0.7	256,964	248,040	-3.4
Austin, TX	601,055	606,519	0.9	587,607	576,501	-1.8
Baton Rouge, LA	111,969	112,989	0.9	106,514	104,304	-2.0
Boise City, ID	134,753	133,502	-0.9	131,600	127,739	-2.9
Boston, MA	399,841	382,754	-4.2	391,993	354,899	-9.4
Boulder, CO	66,229	64,864	-2.0	65,025	60,677	-6.6
Cape Coral, FL	93,172	90,468	-2.9	90,578	86,083	-4.9
Cedar Rapids, IA	73,629	67,681	-8.0	71,125	64,790	-8.9
Charleston, SC	75,308	72,571	-3.6	73,919	69,583	-5.8
Charlotte, NC	499,499	492,206	-1.4	483,932	461,278	-4.6
Chicago, IL	1,322,199	1,308,831	-1.0	1,281,869	1,177,846	-8.1
Cincinnati, OH	147,410	148,764	0.9	142,030	139,857	-1.5
Clarksville, TN	63,787	65,851	3.2	61,432	60,949	-0.7
Cleveland, OH	156,471	151,177	-3.3	149,465	137,384	-8.0
College Station, TX	62,425	62,445	0.0	60,916	59,698	-2.0
Colorado Springs, CO	238,705	245,635	2.9	232,124	223,547	-3.7
Columbia, MO	68,108	67,049	-1.5	66,459	64,199	-3.4
Columbia, SC	58,665	58,030	-1.0	57,222	55,091	-3.7
Columbus, OH	478,751	473,342	-1.1	463,416	448,688	-3.1
Dallas, TX	703,081	714,931	1.6	681,628	663,820	-2.6
Davenport, IA	51,918	47,841	-7.8	49,753	45,379	-8.7
Denver, CO	423,917	436,113	2.8	414,090	395,349	-4.5
Des Moines, IA	115,631	106,451	-7.9	111,652	101,736	-8.8
Durham, NC	150,280	147,613	-1.7	145,981	139,307	-4.5
Edison, NJ	55,345	54,084	-2.2	54,066	51,214	-5.2
El Paso, TX	305,478	303,471	-0.6	295,039	280,221	-5.0
Fargo, ND	69,702	73,397	5.3	68,423	71,067	3.8
Fayetteville, NC	76,883	75,832	-1.3	73,263	69,057	-5.7
Fort Collins, CO	103,931	102,364	-1.5	101,963	94,647	-7.1
Fort Wayne, IN	128,470	131,139	2.0	124,594	125,226	0.5
Fort Worth, TX	444,954	448,335	0.7	431,424	417,064	-3.3
Grand Rapids, MI	103,987	101,472	-2.4	100,701	95,669	-5.0
Greeley, CO	55,458	56,828	2.4	54,063	51,159	-5.3
Green Bay, WI	53,859	54,419	1.0	52,110	51,623	-0.9
Greensboro, NC	147,165	143,483	-2.5	141,957	132,895	-6.3
Honolulu, HI	452,859	447,861	-1.1	443,191	411,864	-7.0
Houston, TX	1,168,794	1,162,957	-0.5	1,128,145	1,071,532	-5.0
Huntsville, AL	99,396	97,639	-1.7	97,185	94,305	-2.9
Indianapolis, IN	446,151	467,925	4.8	433,373	443,878	2.4
Jacksonville, FL	469,934	463,646	-1.3	457,089	438,293	-4.1
Kansas City, MO	262,205	262,873	0.2	252,990	245,170	-3.0
Lafayette, LA	59,376	59,649	0.4	56,669	56,144	-0.9
Lakeland, FL	47,582	47,525	-0.1	46,092	44,428	-3.6
Las Vegas, NV	316,225	301,287	-4.7	305,003	270,332	-11.3
Lexington, KY	175,216	173,151	-1.1	170,118	164,394	-3.3
Lincoln, NE	160,552	162,129	0.9	156,783	157,418	0.4
Little Rock, AR	96,600	95,461	-1.1	93,594	90,677	-3.1
Los Angeles, CA	2,095,690	1,987,043	-5.1	2,011,531	1,777,290	-11.6
Louisville, KY	402,027	394,489	-1.8	388,284	371,824	-4.2
Madison, WI	157,534	157,457	0.0	154,347	151,326	-1.9

Table continued on following page.

City	Civilian Labor Force			Workers Employed		
	Dec. 2019	Dec. 2020	% Chg.	Dec. 2019	Dec. 2020	% Chg.
Manchester, NH	66,041	64,338	-2.5	64,553	61,492	-4.7
Memphis, TN	299,167	316,351	5.7	287,040	285,384	-0.5
Miami, FL	234,913	222,511	-5.2	231,476	205,346	-11.2
Midland, TX	88,858	84,069	-5.3	87,068	77,687	-10.7
Milwaukee, WI	271,222	276,192	1.8	260,380	253,283	-2.7
Minneapolis, MN	245,206	236,236	-3.6	238,869	224,977	-5.8
Nashville, TN	413,927	420,401	1.5	404,589	396,582	-1.9
New Haven, CT	65,459	65,774	0.4	63,121	59,553	-5.6
New Orleans, LA	179,138	182,736	2.0	170,426	162,218	-4.8
New York, NY	4,055,234	3,856,031	-4.9	3,932,458	3,408,146	-13.3
Oklahoma City, OK	322,420	325,821	1.0	313,116	308,959	-1.3
Omaha, NE	243,405	245,582	0.8	236,406	237,000	0.2
Orlando, FL	170,544	162,722	-4.5	166,541	149,954	-9.9
Peoria, IL	50,615	47,156	-6.8	47,924	43,020	-10.2
Philadelphia, PA	729,738	699,455	-4.1	690,247	634,633	-8.0
Phoenix, AZ	885,177	887,360	0.2	853,111	820,050	-3.8
Pittsburgh, PA	157,702	150,397	-4.6	151,169	140,388	-7.1
Portland, OR	376,061	380,047	1.0	366,666	355,132	-3.1
Providence, RI	86,891	84,686	-2.5	83,544	77,341	-7.4
Provo, UT	68,223	69,278	1.5	66,963	67,577	0.9
Raleigh, NC	260,153	256,088	-1.5	252,404	241,439	-4.3
Reno, NV	139,960	134,597	-3.8	136,175	127,830	-6.1
Richmond, VA	119,856	116,571	-2.7	116,483	108,936	-6.4
Riverside, CA	156,209	155,456	-0.4	151,257	142,354	-5.8
Rochester, MN	65,938	64,249	-2.5	64,352	61,741	-4.0
Sacramento, CA	237,846	239,336	0.6	230,186	217,425	-5.5
Salt Lake City, UT	117,922	119,415	1.2	115,531	115,159	-0.3
San Antonio, TX	740,486	738,883	-0.2	720,097	690,895	-4.0
San Diego, CA	724,077	722,739	-0.1	704,952	665,731	-5.5
San Francisco, CA	589,286	566,193	-3.9	578,146	529,919	-8.3
San Jose, CA	558,215	552,450	-1.0	545,337	515,386	-5.4
Santa Rosa, CA	90,456	87,703	-3.0	88,298	81,635	-7.5
Savannah, GA	66,855	68,668	2.7	64,804	63,654	-1.7
Seattle, WA	475,147	468,970	-1.3	464,721	440,258	-5.2
Sioux Falls, SD	106,508	105,414	-1.0	103,166	102,274	-0.8
Springfield, IL	56,539	55,105	-2.5	54,362	51,115	-5.9
Tallahassee, FL	102,369	97,422	-4.8	99,536	91,619	-7.9
Tampa, FL	205,639	203,778	-0.9	200,162	191,493	-4.3
Tucson, AZ	271,283	268,958	-0.8	259,611	246,980	-4.8
Tulsa, OK	196,335	194,348	-1.0	190,196	182,480	-4.0
Tuscaloosa, AL	48,708	47,374	-2.7	47,449	45,126	-4.9
Virginia Beach, VA	234,164	226,000	-3.4	228,643	216,261	-5.4
Washington, DC	416,329	413,158	-0.7	397,389	376,699	-5.2
Wichita, KS	189,743	189,451	-0.1	183,423	180,980	-1.3
Winston-Salem, NC	118,986	117,479	-1.2	114,945	109,601	-4.6
U.S.	164,007,000	160,017,000	-2.4	158,504,000	149,613,000	-5.6

Note: Data is not seasonally adjusted and covers workers 16 years of age and older
Source: Bureau of Labor Statistics, Local Area Unemployment Statistics

Labor Force, Employment and Job Growth: Metro Area

Metro Area[1]	Civilian Labor Force			Workers Employed		
	Dec. 2019	Dec. 2020	% Chg.	Dec. 2019	Dec. 2020	% Chg.
Albuquerque, NM	442,230	434,669	-1.7	423,884	402,897	-4.9
Allentown, PA	448,501	434,989	-3.0	428,188	408,208	-4.6
Anchorage, AK	195,036	197,957	1.5	184,796	186,758	1.0
Ann Arbor, MI	200,349	192,221	-4.0	196,082	185,271	-5.5
Athens, GA	99,032	97,723	-1.3	96,483	93,287	-3.3
Atlanta, GA	3,128,881	3,107,968	-0.6	3,045,413	2,939,513	-3.4
Austin, TX	1,255,200	1,267,150	0.9	1,224,993	1,202,103	-1.8
Baton Rouge, LA	417,880	416,461	-0.3	399,191	391,186	-2.0
Boise City, ID	381,230	377,479	-0.9	371,231	360,351	-2.9
Boston, MA[4]	1,694,809	1,609,639	-5.0	1,662,542	1,505,214	-9.4
Boulder, CO	197,746	194,238	-1.7	193,839	180,878	-6.6
Cape Coral, FL	353,248	344,421	-2.5	344,074	327,001	-4.9
Cedar Rapids, IA	148,694	136,358	-8.3	143,975	131,243	-8.8
Charleston, SC	395,683	381,666	-3.5	387,938	365,144	-5.8
Charlotte, NC	1,373,470	1,344,434	-2.1	1,331,441	1,267,112	-4.8
Chicago, IL[2]	3,687,479	3,541,085	-3.9	3,574,836	3,232,803	-9.5
Cincinnati, OH	1,128,063	1,122,791	-0.4	1,090,733	1,069,559	-1.9
Clarksville, TN	118,102	120,516	2.0	113,647	112,488	-1.0
Cleveland, OH	1,049,216	997,566	-4.9	1,009,725	921,287	-8.7
College Station, TX	137,059	137,930	0.6	133,696	130,968	-2.0
Colorado Springs, CO	356,603	365,426	2.4	346,681	333,941	-3.6
Columbia, MO	99,481	97,891	-1.6	97,069	93,768	-3.4
Columbia, SC	403,325	396,126	-1.7	394,519	379,089	-3.9
Columbus, OH	1,105,853	1,087,829	-1.6	1,070,103	1,037,232	-3.0
Dallas, TX[2]	2,719,675	2,742,810	0.8	2,640,356	2,571,653	-2.6
Davenport, IA	194,473	181,630	-6.6	185,909	172,320	-7.3
Denver, CO	1,688,220	1,720,681	1.9	1,650,053	1,575,283	-4.5
Des Moines, IA	366,728	336,296	-8.3	356,630	324,997	-8.8
Durham, NC	305,270	298,535	-2.2	296,522	283,058	-4.5
Edison, NJ[2]	7,008,087	6,694,644	-4.4	6,780,009	6,077,482	-10.3
El Paso, TX	367,648	366,204	-0.3	354,536	336,718	-5.0
Fargo, ND	138,402	143,685	3.8	135,435	139,201	2.7
Fayetteville, NC	148,437	145,648	-1.8	141,883	133,739	-5.7
Fort Collins, CO	209,156	205,612	-1.6	205,003	190,294	-7.1
Fort Wayne, IN	216,998	220,641	1.6	210,942	212,055	0.5
Fort Worth, TX[2]	1,311,941	1,316,316	0.3	1,273,454	1,230,725	-3.3
Grand Rapids, MI	575,885	557,316	-3.2	561,939	534,032	-4.9
Greeley, CO	172,545	174,099	0.9	168,655	159,598	-5.3
Green Bay, WI	172,794	173,847	0.6	167,575	165,813	-1.0
Greensboro, NC	371,920	360,292	-3.1	359,136	336,201	-6.3
Honolulu, HI	452,859	447,861	-1.1	443,191	411,864	-7.0
Houston, TX	3,462,635	3,445,575	-0.4	3,336,616	3,169,170	-5.0
Huntsville, AL	229,898	224,806	-2.2	225,028	218,441	-2.9
Indianapolis, IN	1,060,176	1,101,669	3.9	1,032,445	1,057,751	2.4
Jacksonville, FL	794,684	779,448	-1.9	774,172	742,219	-4.1
Kansas City, MO	1,145,405	1,145,812	0.0	1,109,920	1,089,310	-1.8
Lafayette, LA	210,923	212,283	0.6	200,667	199,150	-0.7
Lakeland, FL	308,057	308,560	0.1	298,597	287,817	-3.6
Las Vegas, NV	1,136,500	1,084,944	-4.5	1,096,609	971,954	-11.3
Lexington, KY	273,326	269,822	-1.2	265,044	256,418	-3.2
Lincoln, NE	186,998	188,745	0.9	182,613	183,294	0.3
Little Rock, AR	354,854	348,009	-1.9	343,794	333,024	-3.1
Los Angeles, CA[2]	5,171,306	4,867,991	-5.8	4,946,895	4,270,635	-13.6
Louisville, KY	674,729	662,325	-1.8	652,752	628,916	-3.6
Madison, WI	390,192	389,396	-0.2	381,370	373,552	-2.0

Table continued on following page.

Metro Area[1]	Civilian Labor Force			Workers Employed		
	Dec. 2019	Dec. 2020	% Chg.	Dec. 2019	Dec. 2020	% Chg.
Manchester, NH[3]	123,691	119,789	-3.1	121,082	115,342	-4.7
Memphis, TN	647,507	668,382	3.2	622,648	618,793	-0.6
Miami, FL[2]	1,377,214	1,301,119	-5.5	1,353,568	1,197,859	-11.5
Midland, TX	110,792	105,257	-5.0	108,522	96,833	-10.7
Milwaukee, WI	811,069	812,442	0.1	785,335	763,907	-2.7
Minneapolis, MN	2,037,880	1,953,111	-4.1	1,976,964	1,864,309	-5.7
Nashville, TN	1,102,127	1,112,635	0.9	1,076,372	1,054,820	-2.0
New Haven, CT[3]	331,537	326,637	-1.4	321,457	303,291	-5.6
New Orleans, LA	596,687	591,186	-0.9	570,042	542,565	-4.8
New York, NY[2]	7,008,087	6,694,644	-4.4	6,780,009	6,077,482	-10.3
Oklahoma City, OK	687,962	693,472	0.8	668,536	660,099	-1.2
Omaha, NE	496,578	495,217	-0.2	483,022	480,259	-0.5
Orlando, FL	1,372,173	1,294,626	-5.6	1,337,648	1,204,999	-9.9
Peoria, IL	173,154	158,961	-8.2	165,096	148,160	-10.2
Philadelphia, PA[2]	1,031,591	989,425	-4.0	980,295	906,853	-7.4
Phoenix, AZ	2,548,680	2,536,430	-0.4	2,456,125	2,361,237	-3.8
Pittsburgh, PA	1,217,975	1,157,008	-5.0	1,162,800	1,080,640	-7.0
Portland, OR	1,332,520	1,316,280	-1.2	1,294,803	1,235,940	-4.5
Providence, RI[3]	695,900	674,373	-3.0	673,941	622,895	-7.5
Provo, UT	319,576	325,243	1.7	313,261	316,139	0.9
Raleigh, NC	731,065	715,982	-2.0	709,901	678,982	-4.3
Reno, NV	261,692	251,522	-3.8	254,486	238,896	-6.1
Richmond, VA	692,884	665,116	-4.0	675,329	631,884	-6.4
Riverside, CA	2,087,383	2,086,402	0.0	2,014,602	1,896,009	-5.8
Rochester, MN	125,263	121,785	-2.7	121,567	117,057	-3.7
Sacramento, CA	1,104,616	1,096,884	-0.7	1,069,620	1,010,465	-5.5
Salt Lake City, UT	679,607	687,168	1.1	665,544	663,455	-0.3
San Antonio, TX	1,218,568	1,213,928	-0.3	1,184,374	1,136,070	-4.0
San Diego, CA	1,597,099	1,593,875	-0.2	1,552,857	1,466,461	-5.5
San Francisco, CA[2]	1,054,065	1,010,523	-4.1	1,034,791	948,543	-8.3
San Jose, CA	1,090,183	1,071,686	-1.7	1,065,627	1,007,069	-5.5
Santa Rosa, CA	259,689	250,632	-3.4	253,575	234,440	-7.5
Savannah, GA	187,692	190,082	1.2	182,609	179,365	-1.7
Seattle, WA[2]	1,724,567	1,722,800	-0.1	1,683,121	1,619,303	-3.7
Sioux Falls, SD	155,466	153,813	-1.0	150,743	149,521	-0.8
Springfield, IL	106,114	102,509	-3.4	102,129	96,019	-5.9
Tallahassee, FL	195,372	185,262	-5.1	190,212	175,456	-7.7
Tampa, FL	1,566,692	1,540,183	-1.6	1,525,133	1,459,839	-4.2
Tucson, AZ	504,172	497,081	-1.4	483,909	460,365	-4.8
Tulsa, OK	481,673	474,408	-1.5	466,612	447,916	-4.0
Tuscaloosa, AL	120,183	116,579	-3.0	117,420	111,848	-4.7
Virginia Beach, VA	858,173	834,317	-2.7	834,872	790,145	-5.3
Washington, DC[2]	2,779,621	2,686,651	-3.3	2,705,388	2,537,166	-6.2
Wichita, KS	315,547	315,051	-0.1	305,590	301,566	-1.3
Winston-Salem, NC	329,944	323,658	-1.9	319,404	304,539	-4.6
U.S.	164,007,000	160,017,000	-2.4	158,504,000	149,613,000	-5.6

Note: Data is not seasonally adjusted and covers workers 16 years of age and older; (1) Figures cover the Metropolitan Statistical Area (MSA) except where noted. See Appendix B for areas included; (2) Metropolitan Division; (3) New England City and Town Area; (4) New England City and Town Area Division
Source: Bureau of Labor Statistics, Local Area Unemployment Statistics

Unemployment Rate: City

City	2020											
	Jan.	Feb.	Mar.	Apr.	May	Jun.	Jul.	Aug.	Sep.	Oct.	Nov.	Dec.
Albuquerque, NM	4.4	4.4	5.5	12.8	9.4	9.1	13.2	11.2	9.5	7.5	6.3	7.4
Allentown, PA	6.6	6.6	8.2	20.1	18.3	19.8	19.0	16.9	12.9	12.1	10.7	9.9
Anchorage, AK	5.1	4.5	4.7	13.9	12.3	12.0	10.8	6.5	6.4	5.3	6.0	5.5
Ann Arbor, MI	2.0	1.8	1.9	12.4	11.6	8.9	6.6	5.7	5.0	3.3	2.8	3.0
Athens, GA	3.5	3.5	4.7	12.2	9.0	7.7	7.9	5.8	5.9	4.3	5.1	5.2
Atlanta, GA	3.6	3.7	5.4	13.4	11.9	11.0	10.6	8.6	8.4	6.1	7.4	7.0
Austin, TX	2.6	2.5	3.6	12.5	11.6	7.4	6.9	5.6	6.4	4.9	5.7	4.9
Baton Rouge, LA	5.7	4.1	6.2	14.7	15.0	11.6	11.3	9.1	8.8	10.1	9.2	7.7
Boise City, ID	2.8	2.4	2.3	12.6	9.6	5.9	5.2	4.0	5.8	5.3	4.8	4.3
Boston, MA	2.7	2.6	2.4	14.6	16.6	19.3	18.2	12.9	11.1	7.7	6.6	7.3
Boulder, CO	2.1	2.4	4.2	9.4	8.1	9.6	6.5	5.4	4.9	4.9	4.7	6.5
Cape Coral, FL	3.2	3.0	4.4	16.2	14.0	10.0	11.0	7.2	6.0	5.2	5.2	4.8
Cedar Rapids, IA	4.0	3.5	4.1	14.2	12.9	11.3	9.3	10.1	6.8	4.7	4.9	4.3
Charleston, SC	2.2	2.3	2.5	14.6	14.0	9.9	9.7	7.1	5.0	3.9	3.9	4.1
Charlotte, NC	3.8	3.5	4.0	13.0	13.9	8.8	10.2	8.0	8.1	6.8	6.7	6.3
Chicago, IL	3.7	3.5	5.0	18.7	17.2	18.6	15.2	15.5	14.4	10.5	8.6	10.0
Cincinnati, OH	4.7	4.3	4.7	15.1	13.7	12.7	11.1	11.2	10.0	7.5	6.4	6.0
Clarksville, TN	4.4	4.3	3.8	17.2	11.3	11.2	11.4	9.9	7.3	8.4	5.8	7.4
Cleveland, OH	5.9	6.4	9.0	26.1	21.9	19.4	17.3	15.9	15.3	10.3	9.0	9.1
College Station, TX	2.8	2.6	3.7	8.2	8.1	5.9	5.3	4.2	4.7	3.9	4.9	4.4
Colorado Springs, CO	3.3	3.4	6.1	13.0	10.0	10.7	7.1	6.4	6.1	6.1	6.2	9.0
Columbia, MO	3.1	2.4	2.5	6.6	6.7	5.8	5.2	5.2	3.0	2.7	2.9	4.3
Columbia, SC	3.1	3.1	3.1	8.9	10.2	9.1	9.1	6.9	5.1	4.4	4.6	5.1
Columbus, OH	4.1	3.7	4.1	14.6	12.4	11.3	9.8	9.8	8.8	6.5	5.7	5.2
Dallas, TX	3.4	3.3	4.8	13.0	12.8	8.9	8.4	7.1	8.4	6.9	8.0	7.1
Davenport, IA	4.9	4.2	4.7	15.4	15.0	12.1	10.3	9.6	7.0	5.2	5.3	5.1
Denver, CO	2.8	2.8	5.3	13.4	11.5	12.0	8.8	7.9	7.3	7.3	7.2	9.3
Des Moines, IA	4.6	4.0	4.4	14.6	14.0	12.2	9.5	9.1	6.6	4.6	4.5	4.4
Durham, NC	3.4	3.1	3.7	10.1	11.4	7.6	8.8	6.7	6.8	5.7	5.7	5.6
Edison, NJ	2.8	2.7	2.4	11.7	11.3	12.7	11.0	8.4	4.9	5.8	7.4	5.3
El Paso, TX	3.8	3.6	5.1	14.5	14.0	9.1	8.4	6.9	8.1	6.7	8.9	7.7
Fargo, ND	2.5	2.3	2.3	9.6	8.5	7.0	5.5	4.0	3.0	3.1	3.1	3.2
Fayetteville, NC	5.8	5.2	6.0	15.7	16.8	10.8	12.9	10.1	10.4	9.0	9.0	8.9
Fort Collins, CO	2.4	2.5	4.4	11.5	8.7	9.3	6.2	5.5	5.1	5.0	5.0	7.5
Fort Wayne, IN	3.6	3.5	3.2	20.6	14.9	12.9	9.6	7.7	6.8	6.0	5.6	4.5
Fort Worth, TX	3.5	3.3	5.0	13.5	13.1	8.9	8.3	7.1	8.1	6.7	7.9	7.0
Grand Rapids, MI	3.8	3.2	3.3	26.7	22.0	16.0	11.5	10.0	8.7	5.9	5.2	5.7
Greeley, CO	3.1	3.2	5.6	10.3	9.3	11.2	8.4	7.9	7.5	7.3	7.7	10.0
Green Bay, WI	4.2	3.8	3.2	14.6	14.4	10.2	8.1	7.0	5.1	5.7	4.9	5.1
Greensboro, NC	4.4	4.0	4.6	15.3	15.8	10.0	11.6	9.1	9.0	7.7	7.7	7.4
Honolulu, HI	2.8	2.5	2.1	20.5	20.8	12.2	11.5	11.0	13.6	12.4	9.1	8.0
Houston, TX	3.9	3.7	5.4	14.4	14.1	10.0	9.8	8.4	9.8	7.7	8.8	7.9
Huntsville, AL	2.8	2.4	2.6	11.8	8.6	7.5	7.8	5.6	6.4	5.3	3.8	3.4
Indianapolis, IN	3.4	3.2	3.1	14.0	11.3	12.6	9.9	8.4	7.7	7.0	6.4	5.1
Jacksonville, FL	3.3	3.1	4.6	11.5	11.0	8.4	9.7	6.4	5.5	5.6	5.7	5.5
Kansas City, MO	4.1	3.7	4.1	11.7	12.3	9.2	9.0	9.0	5.7	4.9	5.0	6.7
Lafayette, LA	5.4	4.0	6.1	13.5	12.8	9.3	9.1	7.2	7.0	7.9	7.0	5.9
Lakeland, FL	3.8	3.5	4.9	11.4	12.0	9.4	10.7	7.3	6.4	6.5	6.9	6.5
Las Vegas, NV	4.0	3.9	7.3	32.1	27.1	16.7	15.8	14.9	13.9	13.5	11.7	10.3
Lexington, KY	3.5	3.1	4.1	14.1	9.0	4.5	4.6	6.7	4.8	6.2	4.5	5.1
Lincoln, NE	2.8	2.7	3.7	9.6	5.3	5.9	5.2	3.9	3.3	2.7	2.7	2.9
Little Rock, AR	3.7	3.6	4.6	12.0	11.7	10.4	10.1	10.4	9.8	7.9	7.7	5.0
Los Angeles, CA	4.5	4.6	6.6	20.7	21.0	20.0	18.8	17.1	15.5	11.8	10.6	10.6
Louisville, KY	4.1	3.7	4.7	16.5	11.7	5.3	5.3	7.7	5.6	7.4	5.4	5.7
Madison, WI	2.7	2.3	1.9	10.4	9.7	7.8	6.2	5.4	3.9	4.3	3.7	3.9

Table continued on following page.

| City | 2020 | | | | | | | | | | | |
---	Jan.	Feb.	Mar.	Apr.	May	Jun.	Jul.	Aug.	Sep.	Oct.	Nov.	Dec.
Manchester, NH	3.0	3.0	2.7	20.0	18.4	10.5	9.2	7.8	6.7	4.5	4.3	4.4
Memphis, TN	4.9	4.9	4.2	14.5	12.9	15.3	17.4	16.3	12.5	13.1	8.7	9.8
Miami, FL	1.4	1.4	3.7	12.4	12.8	12.5	15.4	8.6	13.6	9.3	8.4	7.7
Midland, TX	2.3	2.3	3.3	9.9	12.3	9.2	9.1	7.8	9.2	7.7	8.8	7.6
Milwaukee, WI	4.9	4.7	4.1	15.8	15.7	13.1	11.4	10.1	8.2	9.2	7.9	8.3
Minneapolis, MN	2.5	2.6	2.8	10.0	11.6	11.4	10.5	10.3	7.8	5.2	4.6	4.8
Nashville, TN	2.7	2.7	2.4	16.1	12.3	12.0	12.3	10.6	7.7	6.9	4.7	5.7
New Haven, CT	4.9	4.8	4.0	7.0	8.8	10.6	11.8	9.7	9.1	7.5	10.0	9.5
New Orleans, LA	5.5	4.2	6.3	22.2	20.7	15.9	15.1	12.6	12.4	15.1	13.6	11.2
New York, NY	3.8	3.8	4.2	15.5	20.2	18.7	18.8	14.9	14.7	11.7	11.7	11.6
Oklahoma City, OK	2.9	2.7	2.7	15.8	13.7	7.2	7.6	5.9	5.5	6.3	6.0	5.2
Omaha, NE	3.5	3.3	4.8	10.8	6.6	7.5	6.8	5.2	4.5	3.5	3.3	3.5
Orlando, FL	2.8	2.7	4.0	18.2	21.7	16.9	17.0	12.0	10.4	9.0	8.6	7.8
Peoria, IL	5.2	4.3	4.0	19.2	18.0	16.5	13.8	13.2	11.8	8.5	8.6	8.8
Philadelphia, PA	6.0	5.9	7.0	17.0	16.4	18.2	18.1	15.8	12.0	10.8	9.7	9.3
Phoenix, AZ	4.0	3.9	5.5	12.9	8.8	10.5	11.3	6.5	6.9	8.4	8.2	7.6
Pittsburgh, PA	4.7	4.6	5.6	15.2	13.6	13.8	14.6	12.2	8.9	7.7	6.9	6.7
Portland, OR	3.2	3.2	3.4	16.2	15.9	14.3	13.1	10.7	9.0	7.5	6.4	6.6
Providence, RI	4.7	4.7	5.9	19.5	18.7	15.2	14.9	16.7	13.3	8.5	8.5	8.7
Provo, UT	2.3	2.3	3.2	6.4	5.3	4.0	3.2	3.0	3.3	2.6	2.8	2.5
Raleigh, NC	3.6	3.3	3.9	12.4	13.2	8.2	9.1	6.9	6.9	5.9	5.9	5.7
Reno, NV	3.4	3.2	5.5	20.9	16.9	9.1	8.5	7.6	7.0	6.5	5.7	5.0
Richmond, VA	3.5	3.2	3.8	14.1	12.1	11.8	12.1	9.5	9.3	7.6	6.5	6.5
Riverside, CA	3.9	3.8	4.8	13.5	13.6	13.4	12.6	9.7	9.4	8.2	7.4	8.4
Rochester, MN	2.3	2.5	2.5	7.2	10.4	9.1	7.5	6.7	4.9	4.0	3.6	3.9
Sacramento, CA	4.0	3.8	4.9	14.5	14.5	14.0	13.1	10.4	10.2	8.7	8.0	9.2
Salt Lake City, UT	2.6	2.6	4.1	12.8	10.9	7.4	6.1	5.3	5.4	4.2	4.2	3.6
San Antonio, TX	3.2	3.1	4.5	13.8	13.0	8.5	8.3	6.9	7.9	6.3	7.4	6.5
San Diego, CA	3.2	3.1	4.0	14.7	14.9	13.7	12.2	9.3	8.7	7.1	6.3	7.9
San Francisco, CA	2.3	2.3	3.1	12.6	12.7	12.5	11.1	8.5	8.3	6.7	5.7	6.4
San Jose, CA	2.8	2.7	3.6	13.8	13.1	12.4	10.9	8.4	8.1	6.5	5.7	6.7
Santa Rosa, CA	3.0	2.9	3.8	14.9	13.6	12.2	10.4	8.0	7.7	6.7	6.1	6.9
Savannah, GA	3.7	3.7	5.1	18.5	13.7	11.3	11.0	8.8	8.8	6.3	7.5	7.3
Seattle, WA	2.4	2.2	5.3	13.7	13.2	9.0	7.9	6.8	6.5	4.2	3.9	6.1
Sioux Falls, SD	3.5	3.3	3.1	11.6	10.4	7.3	6.0	4.6	3.7	3.2	3.2	3.0
Springfield, IL	3.8	3.2	2.9	14.9	14.2	13.2	10.5	10.0	9.2	6.5	6.9	7.2
Tallahassee, FL	3.4	3.0	4.4	9.2	9.1	7.8	9.5	6.2	5.3	5.7	6.0	6.0
Tampa, FL	3.1	3.0	4.3	12.6	12.2	9.7	11.6	7.8	6.6	6.4	6.4	6.0
Tucson, AZ	4.7	4.4	6.3	13.8	9.2	10.9	11.7	6.6	7.1	8.7	8.6	8.2
Tulsa, OK	3.2	3.1	3.0	16.2	14.2	7.9	8.6	6.8	6.4	7.4	7.1	6.1
Tuscaloosa, AL	3.2	2.7	3.0	17.9	11.9	10.4	10.6	7.6	8.6	7.0	5.0	4.7
Virginia Beach, VA	2.9	2.6	3.1	12.2	9.4	8.2	7.7	6.0	5.9	4.6	4.2	4.3
Washington, DC	5.0	4.9	5.5	10.6	9.0	9.2	9.5	8.9	8.8	8.2	8.4	8.8
Wichita, KS	4.0	4.1	3.5	19.2	15.6	12.1	12.3	11.6	9.1	7.4	7.0	4.5
Winston-Salem, NC	4.2	3.7	4.3	12.9	13.9	8.8	10.3	8.0	8.2	6.9	6.8	6.7
U.S.	4.0	3.8	4.5	14.4	13.0	11.2	10.5	8.5	7.7	6.6	6.4	6.5

Note: Data is not seasonally adjusted and covers workers 16 years of age and older; All figures are percentages
Source: Bureau of Labor Statistics, Local Area Unemployment Statistics

Unemployment Rate: Metro Area

Metro Area[1]	2020											
	Jan.	Feb.	Mar.	Apr.	May	Jun.	Jul.	Aug.	Sep.	Oct.	Nov.	Dec.
Albuquerque, NM	4.6	4.6	5.7	12.3	9.1	9.0	13.1	11.1	9.5	7.5	6.4	7.3
Allentown, PA	5.0	5.0	5.7	16.2	13.8	14.1	12.8	10.6	7.5	6.9	6.5	6.2
Anchorage, AK	5.7	5.0	5.2	14.3	12.5	12.2	11.0	6.6	6.5	5.3	6.1	5.7
Ann Arbor, MI	2.5	2.2	2.3	14.8	13.9	10.7	8.0	6.9	6.1	4.0	3.4	3.6
Athens, GA	3.2	3.3	4.3	11.1	8.0	6.7	6.7	4.9	4.9	3.7	4.4	4.5
Atlanta, GA	3.2	3.3	4.4	12.7	9.9	8.6	8.6	6.4	6.6	4.6	5.6	5.4
Austin, TX	2.8	2.6	3.8	12.2	11.4	7.3	6.8	5.5	6.3	5.0	5.9	5.1
Baton Rouge, LA	5.1	3.8	5.6	13.0	12.6	9.6	9.2	7.2	7.0	8.0	7.2	6.1
Boise City, ID	3.2	2.7	2.6	12.3	9.2	5.8	5.2	4.1	6.0	5.4	4.9	4.5
Boston, MA[4]	2.7	2.6	2.4	14.2	15.3	16.9	15.5	10.7	9.3	6.7	5.9	6.5
Boulder, CO	2.4	2.4	4.4	9.7	8.3	9.6	6.7	5.8	5.3	5.2	5.1	6.9
Cape Coral, FL	3.1	3.0	4.3	14.6	13.0	9.6	10.7	7.1	5.9	5.4	5.4	5.1
Cedar Rapids, IA	3.8	3.4	3.9	12.5	11.1	9.6	7.9	8.3	5.6	3.8	4.1	3.8
Charleston, SC	2.4	2.5	2.6	12.1	12.2	9.0	9.2	6.9	5.0	4.0	4.0	4.3
Charlotte, NC	3.7	3.4	3.9	12.7	13.2	8.3	9.3	7.1	7.0	5.9	5.9	5.8
Chicago, IL[2]	3.8	3.7	3.9	16.4	15.8	15.7	13.3	13.0	12.2	8.8	8.9	8.7
Cincinnati, OH	4.3	4.0	4.4	14.1	11.2	9.0	7.6	7.9	6.8	5.6	4.8	4.7
Clarksville, TN	4.6	4.4	4.3	16.1	10.5	8.8	9.0	8.5	6.2	7.5	5.4	6.7
Cleveland, OH	5.0	5.4	6.2	21.8	17.3	12.7	9.2	8.1	8.8	7.2	7.1	7.6
College Station, TX	2.9	2.7	3.9	8.7	8.7	6.3	5.8	4.7	5.5	4.5	5.5	5.0
Colorado Springs, CO	3.3	3.4	6.2	12.6	9.7	10.5	6.9	6.2	5.9	6.0	6.0	8.6
Columbia, MO	3.2	2.5	2.6	6.5	6.5	5.7	5.1	5.1	2.9	2.6	2.8	4.2
Columbia, SC	2.7	2.8	2.8	8.5	9.3	7.8	7.8	6.0	4.4	3.7	3.8	4.3
Columbus, OH	4.2	3.8	4.2	13.7	11.0	9.9	8.3	8.3	7.4	5.5	4.9	4.7
Dallas, TX[2]	3.3	3.2	4.6	12.6	12.1	8.1	7.5	6.2	7.3	5.9	7.1	6.2
Davenport, IA	4.7	4.0	4.0	15.3	14.4	11.5	9.4	8.5	7.1	5.0	5.0	5.1
Denver, CO	2.7	2.8	5.2	12.3	10.5	11.1	7.9	7.0	6.5	6.5	6.4	8.5
Des Moines, IA	3.5	3.0	3.4	11.8	10.9	9.2	7.2	6.7	4.8	3.3	3.5	3.4
Durham, NC	3.5	3.1	3.7	9.6	10.6	6.9	7.9	5.9	6.0	5.2	5.2	5.2
Edison, NJ[2]	3.8	3.6	3.8	15.1	16.3	18.3	17.6	14.0	10.7	10.5	10.4	9.2
El Paso, TX	4.0	3.8	5.4	14.9	14.6	9.5	8.8	7.3	8.6	7.1	9.4	8.1
Fargo, ND	2.8	2.6	2.5	7.7	7.2	6.4	5.1	3.9	3.0	2.9	3.0	3.1
Fayetteville, NC	5.4	4.9	5.6	14.6	15.4	9.8	11.6	9.1	9.3	8.2	8.3	8.2
Fort Collins, CO	2.5	2.6	4.7	11.1	8.6	9.2	6.2	5.6	5.2	5.1	5.2	7.4
Fort Wayne, IN	3.4	3.3	3.0	19.4	13.5	11.2	8.2	6.5	5.7	5.1	4.8	3.9
Fort Worth, TX[2]	3.3	3.2	4.7	13.1	12.6	8.3	7.7	6.5	7.5	6.1	7.3	6.5
Grand Rapids, MI	2.9	2.5	2.6	21.5	17.1	12.0	8.4	7.2	6.3	4.2	3.7	4.2
Greeley, CO	2.7	2.9	5.1	9.9	8.6	10.1	7.3	6.6	6.3	6.2	6.4	8.3
Green Bay, WI	4.0	3.7	3.1	12.9	12.1	8.6	6.7	5.6	4.1	4.8	4.2	4.6
Greensboro, NC	4.3	3.9	4.5	14.8	14.5	9.0	10.2	7.8	7.9	6.9	6.9	6.7
Honolulu, HI	2.8	2.5	2.1	20.5	20.8	12.2	11.5	11.0	13.6	12.4	9.1	8.0
Houston, TX	4.1	3.9	5.5	14.3	13.9	9.7	9.5	8.1	9.6	7.7	8.9	8.0
Huntsville, AL	2.7	2.3	2.5	10.7	7.4	6.4	6.4	4.5	5.1	4.2	3.1	2.8
Indianapolis, IN	3.2	2.9	2.8	13.3	10.2	10.6	7.8	6.6	6.0	5.4	5.0	4.0
Jacksonville, FL	3.1	3.0	4.3	11.2	10.4	7.8	8.8	5.7	4.8	4.8	5.0	4.8
Kansas City, MO	3.7	3.4	3.5	11.3	10.8	7.8	7.6	7.3	5.0	4.4	4.4	4.9
Lafayette, LA	5.7	4.3	6.4	13.0	12.4	9.2	9.1	7.4	7.3	8.2	7.3	6.2
Lakeland, FL	3.7	3.5	4.9	14.0	17.6	13.6	13.2	9.2	7.9	7.1	7.0	6.7
Las Vegas, NV	3.9	3.9	7.2	34.0	28.8	17.8	16.6	15.6	14.6	13.7	11.8	10.4
Lexington, KY	3.7	3.3	4.2	15.2	9.1	4.4	4.5	6.5	4.7	6.1	4.4	5.0
Lincoln, NE	2.7	2.6	3.7	9.3	5.2	5.7	5.0	3.8	3.2	2.7	2.7	2.9
Little Rock, AR	3.7	3.6	4.6	10.9	10.2	9.0	8.3	8.4	7.8	6.4	6.4	4.3
Los Angeles, CA[2]	4.9	4.7	5.6	18.2	18.8	17.9	18.2	17.5	13.2	12.0	11.9	12.3
Louisville, KY	3.9	3.5	4.3	16.8	11.8	6.5	5.6	7.0	5.3	6.5	4.9	5.0
Madison, WI	3.1	2.8	2.3	11.1	9.7	7.5	6.0	5.1	3.7	4.2	3.7	4.1

Table continued on following page.

Metro Area[1]	2020											
	Jan.	Feb.	Mar.	Apr.	May	Jun.	Jul.	Aug.	Sep.	Oct.	Nov.	Dec.
Manchester, NH[3]	2.8	2.8	2.5	17.4	15.8	9.0	7.9	6.5	5.6	3.8	3.7	3.7
Memphis, TN	4.4	4.4	3.8	12.8	10.7	11.9	13.1	11.9	9.2	9.6	6.7	7.4
Miami, FL[2]	1.8	1.6	2.2	10.3	10.3	10.1	15.2	9.1	12.6	8.5	8.2	7.9
Midland, TX	2.4	2.3	3.4	10.1	12.6	9.5	9.5	8.1	9.5	8.0	9.3	8.0
Milwaukee, WI	4.0	3.8	3.2	13.6	12.9	10.2	8.6	7.5	5.9	6.6	5.7	6.0
Minneapolis, MN	3.1	3.1	3.1	9.2	10.1	9.2	8.2	7.8	5.9	4.2	4.0	4.5
Nashville, TN	2.8	2.8	2.5	15.2	11.1	10.2	10.0	8.4	6.1	6.1	4.2	5.2
New Haven, CT[3]	4.2	4.1	3.4	7.2	8.5	9.3	9.7	7.7	7.1	5.5	7.4	7.1
New Orleans, LA	5.2	3.9	5.9	19.0	17.4	12.8	11.9	9.7	9.4	11.2	10.0	8.2
New York, NY[2]	3.8	3.6	3.8	15.1	16.3	18.3	17.6	14.0	10.7	10.5	10.4	9.2
Oklahoma City, OK	2.9	2.7	2.7	14.8	12.9	6.9	7.1	5.6	5.1	5.9	5.6	4.8
Omaha, NE	3.2	3.1	4.3	10.0	6.4	6.9	6.0	4.6	3.9	3.0	2.9	3.0
Orlando, FL	3.0	2.9	4.2	16.8	21.1	16.1	15.4	10.8	9.2	7.8	7.4	6.9
Peoria, IL	5.0	4.2	3.8	17.7	15.4	13.5	10.8	9.8	8.6	6.1	6.3	6.8
Philadelphia, PA[2]	5.5	5.4	6.4	16.3	15.5	17.0	16.7	14.5	10.9	9.8	8.8	8.3
Phoenix, AZ	4.0	3.8	5.4	12.5	8.3	9.8	10.4	5.9	6.2	7.4	7.4	6.9
Pittsburgh, PA	5.2	5.2	6.1	16.4	13.6	12.9	13.1	10.9	7.9	6.9	6.3	6.6
Portland, OR	3.4	3.5	3.6	14.2	14.0	11.8	11.2	9.1	7.9	6.6	5.8	6.1
Providence, RI[3]	4.1	4.1	4.7	18.2	16.7	13.7	12.7	12.7	10.1	6.5	6.8	7.6
Provo, UT	2.5	2.5	3.6	7.9	6.2	4.4	3.6	3.4	3.8	3.1	3.3	2.8
Raleigh, NC	3.5	3.2	3.7	11.0	11.5	7.0	7.9	6.0	6.1	5.2	5.2	5.2
Reno, NV	3.4	3.2	5.6	20.4	16.0	8.7	8.2	7.3	6.7	6.3	5.6	5.0
Richmond, VA	3.1	2.8	3.4	11.2	9.4	8.9	8.8	6.9	6.8	5.5	4.9	5.0
Riverside, CA	4.1	4.0	5.2	14.7	15.1	14.3	13.4	10.5	10.2	8.7	7.9	9.1
Rochester, MN	3.1	3.1	3.1	6.9	9.3	8.1	6.6	5.8	4.2	3.5	3.4	3.9
Sacramento, CA	3.9	3.8	4.8	14.0	13.7	12.8	11.6	9.0	8.7	7.3	6.7	7.9
Salt Lake City, UT	2.6	2.7	4.0	11.2	9.4	6.4	5.3	4.7	5.2	4.1	4.2	3.5
San Antonio, TX	3.2	3.1	4.5	13.3	12.7	8.3	8.0	6.6	7.7	6.2	7.3	6.4
San Diego, CA	3.3	3.2	4.2	15.0	15.2	13.8	12.4	9.5	8.9	7.5	6.6	8.0
San Francisco, CA[2]	2.2	2.2	3.0	12.1	12.0	11.8	10.3	7.9	7.7	6.3	5.4	6.1
San Jose, CA	2.7	2.7	3.5	12.0	11.3	10.8	9.5	7.3	7.0	5.8	5.2	6.0
Santa Rosa, CA	2.9	2.8	3.7	14.5	13.0	11.6	10.0	7.5	7.2	6.0	5.5	6.5
Savannah, GA	3.3	3.3	4.4	15.3	10.8	8.6	8.5	6.5	6.7	4.7	5.6	5.6
Seattle, WA[2]	2.7	2.6	5.3	16.2	12.6	10.7	9.5	7.9	7.4	6.5	6.1	6.0
Sioux Falls, SD	3.4	3.2	3.0	10.5	9.4	6.7	5.6	4.3	3.4	3.0	3.0	2.8
Springfield, IL	3.9	3.2	2.9	14.2	13.1	11.7	9.2	8.7	7.8	5.5	5.9	6.3
Tallahassee, FL	3.2	2.9	4.2	8.3	8.1	7.0	8.4	5.5	4.7	5.0	5.4	5.3
Tampa, FL	3.1	3.0	4.3	13.2	12.2	9.0	10.2	6.7	5.7	5.4	5.5	5.2
Tucson, AZ	4.5	4.2	6.0	12.8	8.4	9.9	10.6	5.9	6.3	7.8	7.7	7.4
Tulsa, OK	3.2	3.0	3.0	15.1	12.9	7.1	7.6	6.1	5.7	6.6	6.4	5.6
Tuscaloosa, AL	2.9	2.5	2.8	16.6	10.8	9.0	9.1	6.3	7.1	6.0	4.4	4.1
Virginia Beach, VA	3.3	3.0	3.6	12.1	10.0	9.2	9.2	7.4	7.2	5.8	5.1	5.3
Washington, DC[2]	3.1	3.0	3.4	10.0	8.9	8.4	8.1	6.9	6.9	6.4	5.7	5.6
Wichita, KS	3.8	3.8	3.3	17.7	14.1	10.8	11.0	10.3	8.0	6.6	6.5	4.3
Winston-Salem, NC	3.9	3.5	4.1	12.7	12.7	7.7	8.8	6.6	6.8	5.9	6.0	5.9
U.S.	4.0	3.8	4.5	14.4	13.0	11.2	10.5	8.5	7.7	6.6	6.4	6.5

Note: Data is not seasonally adjusted and covers workers 16 years of age and older; All figures are percentages; (1) Figures cover the Metropolitan Statistical Area (MSA) except where noted. See Appendix B for areas included; (2) Metropolitan Division; (3) New England City and Town Area; (4) New England City and Town Area Division
Source: Bureau of Labor Statistics, Local Area Unemployment Statistics

Average Hourly Wages: Occupations A – C

Metro Area[1]	Accountants/ Auditors	Automotive Mechanics	Book-keepers	Carpenters	Cashiers	Computer Program-mers	Computer Systems Analysts
Albuquerque, NM	33.46	21.98	20.06	20.67	11.88	38.33	39.87
Allentown, PA	36.61	21.48	20.16	23.11	11.53	40.11	42.51
Anchorage, AK	39.02	22.66	23.63	33.12	14.55	44.08	41.47
Ann Arbor, MI	36.68	30.73	21.60	27.75	12.05	38.47	40.58
Athens, GA	31.72	20.47	17.40	19.07	10.70	32.83	43.69
Atlanta, GA	42.18	23.13	21.75	20.56	11.10	44.52	45.29
Austin, TX	37.28	26.39	20.95	19.33	12.25	42.42	41.18
Baton Rouge, LA	31.10	22.33	19.99	24.74	10.14	40.35	39.72
Boise City, ID	36.48	21.60	20.17	18.39	12.59	32.61	45.73
Boston, MA[2]	43.60	24.14	25.10	31.31	14.22	49.27	50.79
Boulder, CO	40.09	24.42	22.25	25.30	14.13	39.10	48.44
Cape Coral, FL	31.26	21.32	20.50	19.97	11.99	42.99	37.54
Cedar Rapids, IA	35.32	22.27	19.62	24.33	11.59	39.02	40.35
Charleston, SC	32.87	23.69	18.26	28.28	11.63	39.15	41.06
Charlotte, NC	42.38	23.40	20.71	19.73	10.98	48.79	48.01
Chicago, IL	37.81	24.87	22.39	34.74	12.61	49.84	45.00
Cincinnati, OH	36.81	22.26	20.71	24.06	11.71	44.99	47.80
Clarksville, TN	30.21	18.81	18.23	18.80	11.06	n/a	36.97
Cleveland, OH	36.64	22.16	20.46	25.76	12.11	39.60	40.53
College Station, TX	29.37	25.23	17.40	20.32	11.70	48.32	38.11
Colorado Springs, CO	36.33	25.52	19.93	24.48	13.94	34.84	49.76
Columbia, MO	29.02	20.93	17.87	24.13	11.10	30.68	38.55
Columbia, SC	29.39	21.06	17.97	23.15	10.58	43.48	37.52
Columbus, OH	36.98	21.18	21.79	24.76	11.99	44.57	44.18
Dallas, TX	40.31	23.53	21.33	19.85	11.39	53.87	49.58
Davenport, IA	32.27	20.88	19.51	25.19	11.12	42.62	44.10
Denver, CO	42.62	24.69	22.73	25.92	14.48	43.53	51.32
Des Moines, IA	37.04	24.11	21.99	22.21	11.87	35.53	42.70
Durham, NC	39.14	22.27	21.86	19.68	10.92	47.50	45.42
Edison, NJ	50.83	24.31	24.50	34.16	14.25	46.28	55.05
El Paso, TX	31.64	16.30	16.08	16.69	10.53	40.15	37.37
Fargo, ND	32.72	24.61	20.00	23.07	12.34	36.01	42.32
Fayetteville, NC	35.70	17.98	17.77	19.91	10.55	30.98	38.38
Fort Collins, CO	35.94	24.03	21.32	23.09	14.29	35.42	42.76
Fort Wayne, IN	34.36	18.77	19.67	20.21	11.30	25.61	37.13
Fort Worth, TX	40.31	23.53	21.33	19.85	11.39	53.87	49.58
Grand Rapids, MI	33.78	21.17	19.56	23.43	11.96	34.14	37.61
Greeley, CO	39.19	25.37	20.19	22.97	13.76	n/a	58.55
Green Bay, WI	33.64	20.09	20.68	26.03	11.26	37.56	39.08
Greensboro, NC	38.57	22.14	19.86	17.69	10.55	40.70	45.51
Honolulu, HI	31.74	25.73	21.44	39.88	13.68	39.65	38.51
Houston, TX	40.30	22.98	21.66	21.53	11.62	49.83	59.65
Huntsville, AL	35.97	23.40	20.47	20.55	10.97	41.94	49.70
Indianapolis, IN	37.22	21.50	20.88	24.11	11.33	45.99	40.06
Jacksonville, FL	32.52	20.49	20.33	19.12	11.34	38.38	37.87
Kansas City, MO	35.61	23.49	20.58	28.51	12.02	42.04	36.99
Lafayette, LA	31.83	18.68	18.14	19.37	9.98	35.29	39.77
Lakeland, FL	36.15	22.44	18.64	18.81	11.96	31.46	37.47
Las Vegas, NV	33.27	21.01	20.44	29.29	12.02	41.98	43.58
Lexington, KY	34.06	20.09	19.10	22.60	11.15	37.18	39.27
Lincoln, NE	33.35	22.34	19.37	19.78	11.87	36.02	36.79
Little Rock, AR	32.28	20.29	18.68	20.70	11.78	37.05	35.10
Los Angeles, CA	40.22	25.83	24.20	32.37	14.82	47.38	53.54
Louisville, KY	36.49	20.16	19.65	25.97	11.25	36.56	41.09
Madison, WI	35.56	23.85	21.38	27.06	12.20	51.95	44.21

Table continued on following page.

Metro Area[1]	Accountants/ Auditors	Automotive Mechanics	Book-keepers	Carpenters	Cashiers	Computer Program-mers	Computer Systems Analysts
Manchester, NH[2]	36.21	23.60	20.53	22.51	11.60	33.07	45.34
Memphis, TN	34.52	25.99	21.21	21.37	10.80	41.07	39.88
Miami, FL	38.52	21.77	21.28	20.93	11.76	41.74	44.55
Midland, TX	49.58	30.42	23.19	20.45	13.31	57.40	n/a
Milwaukee, WI	36.97	21.67	21.43	27.70	11.60	40.27	40.47
Minneapolis, MN	37.42	23.75	22.79	27.95	13.27	43.22	49.04
Nashville, TN	34.65	21.80	21.53	22.23	11.54	45.25	40.00
New Haven, CT[2]	40.03	23.80	23.77	29.32	12.79	47.26	46.09
New Orleans, LA	33.52	19.89	18.98	22.06	10.47	49.80	46.68
New York, NY	50.83	24.31	24.50	34.16	14.25	46.28	55.05
Oklahoma City, OK	38.02	23.73	19.72	20.80	11.03	38.30	38.44
Omaha, NE	35.78	22.47	20.56	19.96	12.22	38.65	41.38
Orlando, FL	35.16	19.62	20.04	21.12	11.70	41.55	44.36
Peoria, IL	38.38	20.73	18.98	31.69	11.40	39.55	45.55
Philadelphia, PA	41.21	22.53	22.28	30.86	11.77	48.82	50.50
Phoenix, AZ	36.29	22.21	21.58	23.50	13.39	44.18	44.56
Pittsburgh, PA	35.65	20.59	19.36	28.43	11.02	41.89	41.16
Portland, OR	38.49	24.48	22.58	29.13	14.68	45.18	48.24
Providence, RI[2]	41.50	21.85	22.70	25.77	13.17	51.83	47.51
Provo, UT	30.23	23.85	19.47	21.85	12.14	42.53	40.09
Raleigh, NC	36.22	23.93	20.23	20.64	11.17	47.69	47.56
Reno, NV	31.29	25.37	21.43	25.23	12.11	44.10	43.87
Richmond, VA	39.89	24.49	21.27	22.33	11.07	45.10	47.11
Riverside, CA	36.22	24.02	22.43	26.58	14.92	43.59	43.34
Rochester, MN	33.90	21.22	20.99	26.07	12.84	29.59	41.46
Sacramento, CA	40.32	26.48	22.61	28.08	15.49	39.13	50.27
Salt Lake City, UT	33.91	21.58	20.00	22.62	12.06	41.48	37.30
San Antonio, TX	35.76	20.68	20.96	20.42	11.81	46.43	47.72
San Diego, CA	43.00	25.61	23.56	28.60	14.50	48.42	45.56
San Francisco, CA	48.60	31.07	26.61	36.44	16.58	60.30	60.27
San Jose, CA	49.48	30.53	27.26	31.80	17.29	54.58	64.41
Santa Rosa, CA	44.34	28.46	26.79	35.33	15.89	44.87	43.31
Savannah, GA	33.08	25.13	20.20	22.91	10.51	38.06	49.67
Seattle, WA	42.21	26.17	24.43	33.25	16.50	n/a	54.00
Sioux Falls, SD	34.97	20.87	17.77	18.73	12.24	28.31	37.94
Springfield, IL	34.50	21.31	20.55	29.86	11.24	47.45	45.09
Tallahassee, FL	27.29	21.76	19.47	20.05	11.07	31.03	29.13
Tampa, FL	37.28	21.62	20.88	19.31	11.46	38.78	42.77
Tucson, AZ	34.29	21.59	18.88	20.44	13.57	42.88	41.83
Tulsa, OK	36.62	19.11	21.11	24.67	11.12	40.37	45.55
Tuscaloosa, AL	34.36	20.19	17.36	19.72	10.43	30.43	43.48
Virginia Beach, VA	36.21	25.63	20.21	20.84	11.14	n/a	47.27
Washington, DC	47.13	27.27	24.81	24.98	13.22	50.51	56.09
Wichita, KS	33.82	18.41	17.96	18.76	11.17	39.71	36.62
Winston-Salem, NC	35.91	20.17	19.63	19.79	10.16	42.82	44.65

Notes: (1) Figures cover the Metropolitan Statistical Area (MSA) except where noted. See Appendix B for areas included;
(2) New England City and Town Area; n/a not available
Source: Bureau of Labor Statistics, May 2020 Metro Area Occupational Employment and Wage Estimates

Average Hourly Wages: Occupations C – E

Metro Area	Comp. User Support Specialists	Construction Laborers	Cooks, Restaurant	Customer Service Reps.	Dentists	Electricians	Engineers, Electrical
Albuquerque, NM	21.74	16.94	12.77	16.16	77.97	23.25	58.20
Allentown, PA	27.07	21.92	13.74	17.59	66.64	27.36	50.31
Anchorage, AK	29.69	26.02	14.62	19.54	101.03	33.57	54.83
Ann Arbor, MI	23.79	22.53	15.59	18.78	71.19	33.74	42.05
Athens, GA	21.34	14.82	12.71	15.83	n/a	26.34	51.49
Atlanta, GA	28.15	16.51	13.35	17.73	77.08	27.77	47.62
Austin, TX	25.88	15.85	13.15	17.26	77.48	25.85	52.09
Baton Rouge, LA	24.19	17.93	12.04	16.40	91.40	26.16	53.11
Boise City, ID	24.03	16.83	12.67	16.30	105.24	24.69	48.27
Boston, MA[2]	33.22	28.35	16.99	22.68	100.75	34.07	55.65
Boulder, CO	30.99	18.47	15.58	20.26	107.71	26.35	52.75
Cape Coral, FL	23.30	16.84	15.40	16.51	83.47	21.88	53.83
Cedar Rapids, IA	20.83	19.76	11.87	19.74	55.16	29.19	51.76
Charleston, SC	26.66	16.83	13.15	18.77	70.75	22.35	47.79
Charlotte, NC	25.75	15.96	13.03	18.80	83.93	22.29	48.47
Chicago, IL	26.71	32.05	14.66	20.08	92.31	40.50	46.52
Cincinnati, OH	24.74	22.97	12.99	17.97	103.00	23.55	43.84
Clarksville, TN	20.86	15.26	10.88	16.79	n/a	23.71	42.56
Cleveland, OH	24.39	23.80	13.11	19.37	101.12	29.21	41.38
College Station, TX	21.68	15.89	11.24	14.68	n/a	24.78	19.71
Colorado Springs, CO	26.65	17.48	14.36	17.16	59.66	24.26	52.77
Columbia, MO	21.99	19.97	12.27	15.32	95.89	22.23	n/a
Columbia, SC	24.58	16.93	11.80	16.92	63.01	25.77	44.63
Columbus, OH	26.89	24.18	13.34	18.35	92.26	22.93	42.67
Dallas, TX	24.78	17.39	13.00	18.59	110.94	23.96	51.08
Davenport, IA	23.82	20.58	11.98	17.03	77.64	28.51	47.09
Denver, CO	30.27	19.27	15.39	19.75	99.20	26.85	47.84
Des Moines, IA	26.48	18.81	14.39	21.09	90.74	24.79	40.35
Durham, NC	30.19	15.67	14.28	19.11	109.88	24.99	48.84
Edison, NJ	31.34	29.45	17.33	21.93	81.29	40.48	54.54
El Paso, TX	20.29	13.74	11.29	12.83	92.58	18.18	41.46
Fargo, ND	22.59	21.54	15.48	18.69	83.78	28.94	47.67
Fayetteville, NC	23.78	15.30	11.83	16.47	92.25	21.06	41.81
Fort Collins, CO	28.31	18.20	14.74	17.04	84.69	30.01	52.44
Fort Wayne, IN	23.05	19.96	13.24	18.84	80.13	26.13	48.46
Fort Worth, TX	24.78	17.39	13.00	18.59	110.94	23.96	51.08
Grand Rapids, MI	25.00	17.99	13.49	18.78	115.44	23.51	39.99
Greeley, CO	28.57	18.27	15.14	16.42	80.53	27.27	51.35
Green Bay, WI	25.96	20.76	13.61	18.77	105.02	27.59	40.42
Greensboro, NC	24.49	15.45	12.56	18.30	72.13	23.33	49.13
Honolulu, HI	25.51	30.70	16.72	19.16	103.97	38.38	43.60
Houston, TX	24.90	17.92	12.03	17.51	69.53	25.57	54.61
Huntsville, AL	24.21	15.88	12.69	17.48	78.91	23.75	51.86
Indianapolis, IN	24.33	19.53	13.36	18.96	69.38	28.17	44.98
Jacksonville, FL	24.83	16.85	12.99	17.90	72.89	21.37	45.99
Kansas City, MO	26.35	22.20	13.89	18.68	82.22	29.28	43.98
Lafayette, LA	26.20	17.63	13.15	16.07	n/a	23.40	43.43
Lakeland, FL	26.15	16.45	12.88	15.53	97.38	19.94	43.16
Las Vegas, NV	24.94	17.98	15.83	17.00	98.54	33.90	40.75
Lexington, KY	25.92	18.55	13.47	16.56	n/a	23.98	41.54
Lincoln, NE	22.54	17.18	14.40	16.32	60.36	24.62	47.42
Little Rock, AR	23.55	14.24	11.97	17.45	95.92	19.85	44.73
Los Angeles, CA	29.62	23.18	15.95	20.32	65.87	37.25	58.88
Louisville, KY	24.98	18.87	13.45	17.72	61.30	28.14	42.60
Madison, WI	28.38	20.82	13.02	20.69	117.88	28.07	46.09

Table continued on following page.

Metro Area	Comp. User Support Specialists	Construction Laborers	Cooks, Restaurant	Customer Service Reps.	Dentists	Electricians	Engineers, Electrical
Manchester, NH[2]	27.45	19.30	15.58	20.34	111.95	26.41	52.51
Memphis, TN	23.06	15.86	12.46	18.07	71.03	24.89	46.46
Miami, FL	26.17	16.41	14.96	17.41	100.72	22.68	46.88
Midland, TX	24.74	17.43	13.11	17.41	n/a	28.94	52.80
Milwaukee, WI	25.85	23.25	13.14	20.22	98.32	33.98	44.41
Minneapolis, MN	28.26	28.53	16.38	21.32	105.18	35.78	50.53
Nashville, TN	24.09	17.16	13.19	18.01	75.33	25.45	45.40
New Haven, CT[2]	28.52	22.06	15.54	20.29	120.40	34.67	50.33
New Orleans, LA	24.41	16.66	12.31	16.48	74.68	27.52	54.15
New York, NY	31.34	29.45	17.33	21.93	81.29	40.48	54.54
Oklahoma City, OK	24.90	16.58	13.18	16.47	80.68	24.21	47.52
Omaha, NE	25.85	18.60	13.66	18.15	113.83	27.78	44.63
Orlando, FL	24.93	16.61	14.06	17.02	81.37	22.29	50.42
Peoria, IL	27.32	20.86	13.39	15.80	118.44	33.87	n/a
Philadelphia, PA	29.11	24.78	14.84	20.23	81.37	36.95	53.04
Phoenix, AZ	25.78	19.60	14.46	18.18	97.79	23.86	48.56
Pittsburgh, PA	24.98	21.30	13.04	18.03	71.78	31.54	47.12
Portland, OR	29.15	23.09	16.02	20.20	107.31	37.04	46.08
Providence, RI[2]	29.98	26.78	15.08	19.39	120.18	28.88	52.32
Provo, UT	26.06	16.78	13.93	16.82	n/a	22.38	35.78
Raleigh, NC	27.29	16.83	15.74	18.53	95.72	21.78	48.22
Reno, NV	24.94	20.58	14.82	17.38	99.87	26.92	43.83
Richmond, VA	26.74	15.20	12.97	17.99	79.04	26.98	47.93
Riverside, CA	29.70	24.28	15.12	19.74	84.77	26.51	48.20
Rochester, MN	27.37	23.17	14.87	17.51	93.21	30.42	48.07
Sacramento, CA	41.51	24.49	15.22	21.08	93.37	30.07	52.08
Salt Lake City, UT	26.07	18.26	13.09	18.57	60.05	26.94	47.95
San Antonio, TX	23.60	16.05	12.33	16.77	72.46	25.37	45.10
San Diego, CA	29.34	23.87	15.90	20.38	53.63	30.22	50.09
San Francisco, CA	37.82	28.43	19.21	24.01	85.30	51.29	58.99
San Jose, CA	34.93	27.64	17.22	22.94	94.63	41.61	72.35
Santa Rosa, CA	28.84	25.31	17.33	20.34	98.37	35.19	50.52
Savannah, GA	24.02	16.07	12.17	14.71	84.25	25.83	59.47
Seattle, WA	30.88	27.11	17.85	22.61	81.64	39.81	57.72
Sioux Falls, SD	20.11	16.27	13.58	17.26	78.71	24.23	46.65
Springfield, IL	29.20	26.62	11.66	17.52	86.11	34.16	45.48
Tallahassee, FL	21.83	14.26	13.54	16.05	78.74	21.70	44.42
Tampa, FL	24.82	15.90	13.00	17.32	71.77	22.08	46.52
Tucson, AZ	24.98	17.41	13.83	16.79	102.12	25.23	44.68
Tulsa, OK	24.46	16.60	12.51	16.05	n/a	23.73	49.81
Tuscaloosa, AL	29.04	15.01	10.38	16.06	73.08	25.65	43.67
Virginia Beach, VA	26.72	16.64	13.23	15.33	88.32	23.97	46.70
Washington, DC	32.03	18.44	15.40	21.22	105.63	31.72	62.57
Wichita, KS	22.03	16.12	12.82	16.56	77.90	25.06	43.33
Winston-Salem, NC	24.73	15.83	10.93	17.29	72.88	22.44	43.40

Notes: (1) Figures cover the Metropolitan Statistical Area (MSA) except where noted. See Appendix B for areas included; (2) New England City and Town Area; n/a not available
Source: Bureau of Labor Statistics, May 2020 Metro Area Occupational Employment and Wage Estimates

Average Hourly Wages: Occupations F – H

Metro Area	Fast Food and Counter Workers	Financial Managers	First-Line Supervisors/ of Office Workers	General and Operations Managers	Hair-dressers/ Cosme-tologists	Home Health and Personal Care Aides	Janitors/ Cleaners
Albuquerque, NM	10.64	55.09	27.54	56.14	10.84	11.86	12.36
Allentown, PA	11.10	75.32	28.94	57.29	15.22	12.94	15.88
Anchorage, AK	12.54	54.93	32.38	58.03	14.27	16.10	16.48
Ann Arbor, MI	11.86	65.04	29.64	68.81	13.02	12.34	16.01
Athens, GA	9.77	52.35	24.64	45.41	10.25	12.00	12.46
Atlanta, GA	9.99	72.80	28.87	59.99	18.33	12.85	12.66
Austin, TX	11.34	72.96	31.36	57.34	15.92	11.06	14.50
Baton Rouge, LA	9.49	53.55	24.60	56.42	14.04	9.70	10.97
Boise City, ID	9.99	52.76	27.07	43.73	14.95	14.05	13.26
Boston, MA[2]	14.13	79.09	34.34	73.18	21.89	16.31	18.88
Boulder, CO	13.56	90.36	31.98	76.38	20.61	16.10	17.25
Cape Coral, FL	10.94	54.85	27.05	47.49	15.61	12.65	14.35
Cedar Rapids, IA	11.05	59.04	28.10	53.31	14.88	14.05	15.15
Charleston, SC	10.81	69.92	27.74	59.94	15.78	12.19	11.86
Charlotte, NC	10.65	83.71	28.74	64.43	15.60	11.20	12.26
Chicago, IL	11.94	75.24	32.97	66.06	15.60	13.73	15.85
Cincinnati, OH	11.06	67.69	29.76	59.57	14.55	12.32	15.23
Clarksville, TN	9.43	50.27	22.51	45.76	11.69	11.14	13.50
Cleveland, OH	11.12	73.35	29.66	63.12	15.00	11.54	14.61
College Station, TX	10.09	63.69	26.16	45.76	13.83	10.56	13.33
Colorado Springs, CO	12.80	71.91	28.53	62.51	19.89	14.62	14.95
Columbia, MO	12.41	57.39	26.61	41.33	15.87	12.15	14.70
Columbia, SC	9.32	58.42	27.64	54.33	17.75	11.20	12.24
Columbus, OH	10.98	68.77	29.82	58.25	17.11	12.26	14.37
Dallas, TX	10.98	77.10	30.67	62.23	12.81	10.68	14.25
Davenport, IA	10.58	53.76	26.30	48.05	13.57	13.27	14.93
Denver, CO	13.34	85.61	32.53	74.73	20.09	14.62	14.92
Des Moines, IA	11.04	66.80	31.26	53.18	15.31	14.13	13.43
Durham, NC	11.19	79.52	30.27	68.80	15.35	11.60	14.70
Edison, NJ	14.03	103.21	36.45	82.87	18.53	15.37	18.58
El Paso, TX	9.41	51.61	24.23	45.01	11.55	9.04	10.97
Fargo, ND	12.69	70.22	27.09	55.50	16.88	15.07	14.65
Fayetteville, NC	10.16	61.97	24.74	57.51	12.44	10.47	12.75
Fort Collins, CO	13.48	72.34	28.34	58.87	16.06	15.01	15.54
Fort Wayne, IN	10.87	57.58	28.51	55.31	13.03	12.24	11.86
Fort Worth, TX	10.98	77.10	30.67	62.23	12.81	10.68	14.25
Grand Rapids, MI	11.69	58.03	27.84	58.14	16.59	12.98	14.15
Greeley, CO	13.23	81.29	30.36	63.01	16.59	15.20	15.03
Green Bay, WI	10.40	60.24	30.04	66.79	14.46	12.75	14.61
Greensboro, NC	9.88	69.84	27.42	63.64	12.88	11.02	12.65
Honolulu, HI	13.15	60.38	29.59	58.24	18.80	14.07	16.41
Houston, TX	10.42	74.03	29.80	61.00	11.85	10.15	12.52
Huntsville, AL	9.32	65.66	26.99	71.84	11.25	9.93	12.52
Indianapolis, IN	10.96	68.18	30.65	59.89	15.32	12.21	13.87
Jacksonville, FL	10.31	63.49	28.46	52.07	16.47	12.37	12.06
Kansas City, MO	11.82	72.08	30.56	53.57	15.00	12.06	14.78
Lafayette, LA	9.61	49.98	24.38	59.04	11.41	9.98	11.01
Lakeland, FL	10.43	52.81	26.80	46.19	12.89	11.86	12.29
Las Vegas, NV	10.95	57.63	25.95	62.09	10.29	12.47	15.19
Lexington, KY	9.92	57.27	28.00	48.43	11.98	12.60	13.88
Lincoln, NE	11.43	58.67	26.69	50.22	13.35	13.55	13.37
Little Rock, AR	10.81	54.43	25.88	49.18	12.59	11.53	12.24
Los Angeles, CA	14.39	76.00	30.99	67.85	18.20	14.88	17.45
Louisville, KY	10.27	58.62	27.96	50.02	15.10	14.08	13.55

Table continued on following page.

Metro Area	Fast Food and Counter Workers	Financial Managers	First-Line Supervisors/ of Office Workers	General and Operations Managers	Hair-dressers/ Cosme-tologists	Home Health and Personal Care Aides	Janitors/ Cleaners
Madison, WI	11.02	71.61	31.88	65.89	13.94	13.95	15.37
Manchester, NH[2]	11.88	67.78	32.11	65.40	13.19	14.37	14.07
Memphis, TN	9.95	56.29	27.64	55.82	14.51	10.93	12.43
Miami, FL	10.90	72.93	30.04	55.19	13.80	12.10	12.75
Midland, TX	11.26	68.87	32.21	66.38	12.71	11.08	12.72
Milwaukee, WI	10.56	72.24	32.60	73.76	15.73	12.15	14.55
Minneapolis, MN	12.90	71.92	31.32	62.40	16.45	14.26	16.97
Nashville, TN	10.76	59.60	28.46	59.95	15.12	11.82	14.02
New Haven, CT[2]	13.15	67.42	33.60	71.07	15.79	14.00	17.93
New Orleans, LA	10.17	61.27	24.86	60.79	9.97	9.90	11.80
New York, NY	14.03	103.21	36.45	82.87	18.53	15.37	18.58
Oklahoma City, OK	10.46	56.40	26.50	53.95	13.21	11.30	12.31
Omaha, NE	11.57	60.81	27.79	51.20	17.22	12.78	14.62
Orlando, FL	10.44	67.64	27.02	50.37	14.70	12.02	12.97
Peoria, IL	10.98	60.22	28.72	50.68	14.84	12.88	12.80
Philadelphia, PA	11.82	82.22	33.44	74.57	16.17	12.96	15.31
Phoenix, AZ	13.06	64.55	29.32	58.07	16.74	13.34	14.73
Pittsburgh, PA	10.89	70.81	29.25	62.42	13.16	12.79	14.91
Portland, OR	13.97	65.29	30.19	61.17	16.58	15.31	16.47
Providence, RI[2]	13.21	78.87	33.57	71.70	16.31	15.37	15.75
Provo, UT	10.47	59.60	25.62	41.04	16.12	13.22	12.21
Raleigh, NC	10.01	68.49	28.13	70.88	14.20	11.45	12.29
Reno, NV	10.29	63.61	28.05	58.60	14.28	11.98	14.42
Richmond, VA	10.56	75.79	29.92	63.13	17.54	10.69	11.90
Riverside, CA	14.71	62.41	29.71	57.31	15.64	14.69	18.37
Rochester, MN	12.92	53.96	27.84	50.55	14.11	14.58	15.51
Sacramento, CA	14.18	65.80	31.37	59.57	16.75	14.17	17.86
Salt Lake City, UT	10.14	56.64	27.69	44.41	16.35	14.68	12.49
San Antonio, TX	11.01	67.11	26.77	61.53	12.89	10.91	12.76
San Diego, CA	14.44	74.59	31.30	69.74	18.23	14.88	17.57
San Francisco, CA	16.35	92.01	36.43	78.04	18.55	16.57	20.31
San Jose, CA	16.36	92.45	34.48	84.61	18.18	15.80	19.37
Santa Rosa, CA	14.43	69.07	31.18	61.63	17.02	16.21	17.54
Savannah, GA	10.40	49.27	26.00	50.31	11.68	11.70	12.39
Seattle, WA	16.04	76.28	37.04	73.17	22.82	16.24	21.21
Sioux Falls, SD	11.13	74.37	26.26	71.01	14.81	13.74	13.97
Springfield, IL	10.42	56.43	28.36	47.01	22.21	12.19	14.82
Tallahassee, FL	10.45	47.46	29.66	45.46	13.94	12.80	12.76
Tampa, FL	10.81	67.64	29.24	54.46	14.14	11.61	16.79
Tucson, AZ	12.90	53.26	25.41	46.52	16.70	13.18	14.72
Tulsa, OK	9.55	71.06	28.40	51.58	13.46	10.71	12.05
Tuscaloosa, AL	9.61	66.99	25.70	56.16	13.19	9.91	13.78
Virginia Beach, VA	10.94	66.75	28.75	53.58	12.55	10.52	12.31
Washington, DC	13.58	85.16	34.55	74.88	19.24	14.06	16.30
Wichita, KS	9.74	62.41	27.44	50.93	12.99	11.16	13.86
Winston-Salem, NC	10.40	73.56	26.29	59.21	12.93	11.42	11.67

Notes: (1) Figures cover the Metropolitan Statistical Area (MSA) except where noted. See Appendix B for areas included;
(2) New England City and Town Area; n/a not available
Source: Bureau of Labor Statistics, May 2020 Metro Area Occupational Employment and Wage Estimates

Average Hourly Wages: Occupations L – N

Metro Area	Landscapers	Lawyers	Maids/House-keepers	Main-tenance/Repairers	Marketing Managers	Network Admin.	Nurses, Licensed Practical
Albuquerque, NM	14.47	55.30	10.78	19.40	47.06	39.32	24.25
Allentown, PA	16.36	68.66	12.98	22.76	63.74	37.86	24.54
Anchorage, AK	17.23	55.18	15.11	24.45	49.02	39.64	33.65
Ann Arbor, MI	16.81	55.39	13.25	22.11	61.92	39.05	25.79
Athens, GA	16.07	37.80	10.10	17.26	61.63	32.23	21.52
Atlanta, GA	15.33	71.75	10.69	20.23	70.03	43.84	23.16
Austin, TX	15.64	69.36	11.26	18.11	74.00	41.06	23.83
Baton Rouge, LA	15.13	54.49	10.56	21.06	50.44	37.90.	20.42
Boise City, ID	15.86	54.48	11.86	19.32	63.98	39.11	23.88
Boston, MA[2]	20.13	84.41	16.40	25.61	74.50	48.82	29.40
Boulder, CO	19.74	n/a	14.29	23.36	85.29	44.95	26.24
Cape Coral, FL	14.77	n/a	11.54	19.02	54.42	35.40	21.43
Cedar Rapids, IA	16.24	55.33	12.33	22.65	68.01	40.48	21.30
Charleston, SC	15.16	52.10	11.57	19.55	60.30	41.69	23.22
Charlotte, NC	15.09	69.55	11.69	21.36	72.17	40.33	22.77
Chicago, IL	16.89	76.45	14.09	23.38	68.69	43.67	28.45
Cincinnati, OH	14.62	67.43	12.24	21.32	66.12	38.88	23.84
Clarksville, TN	14.10	38.91	11.38	21.41	n/a	33.32	20.91
Cleveland, OH	17.07	71.56	12.07	21.06	66.16	42.80	23.78
College Station, TX	14.63	61.53	11.96	17.32	77.65	33.45	23.37
Colorado Springs, CO	15.28	57.73	13.68	20.63	80.71	39.94	27.45
Columbia, MO	14.70	43.61	11.43	15.89	54.36	34.22	21.46
Columbia, SC	13.75	57.84	11.26	19.16	57.61	38.25	21.20
Columbus, OH	15.69	54.42	12.55	21.51	73.13	41.93	22.50
Dallas, TX	16.49	72.23	12.05	21.14	74.99	43.23	25.11
Davenport, IA	16.09	70.60	11.68	20.79	61.19	37.00	21.77
Denver, CO	18.07	73.11	13.60	21.58	83.15	46.05	27.16
Des Moines, IA	17.08	63.08	12.53	21.27	64.28	41.04	23.35
Durham, NC	15.20	59.34	13.46	22.26	74.28	46.08	24.21
Edison, NJ	18.58	86.62	18.17	24.50	93.77	50.99	27.54
El Paso, TX	11.21	60.78	9.75	15.17	54.66	32.96	23.69
Fargo, ND	18.32	54.07	13.61	21.03	61.56	36.75	22.24
Fayetteville, NC	12.88	59.59	10.39	19.76	54.51	41.86	22.65
Fort Collins, CO	16.84	69.74	14.18	21.34	88.50	36.89	25.42
Fort Wayne, IN	14.26	59.12	11.29	21.47	60.08	32.57	22.79
Fort Worth, TX	16.49	72.23	12.05	21.14	74.99	43.23	25.11
Grand Rapids, MI	16.69	57.05	13.11	19.48	60.07	34.56	23.52
Greeley, CO	18.15	51.46	13.31	22.36	72.61	35.49	28.99
Green Bay, WI	16.03	51.55	12.13	22.68	60.63	33.41	20.81
Greensboro, NC	13.66	59.43	10.64	20.20	69.84	41.07	22.20
Honolulu, HI	19.34	56.12	19.89	24.13	52.09	40.41	26.08
Houston, TX	14.69	70.00	11.44	20.96	78.48	46.20	23.54
Huntsville, AL	15.69	56.43	10.54	17.99	72.22	40.01	19.99
Indianapolis, IN	16.30	60.41	12.05	20.39	61.76	40.98	23.39
Jacksonville, FL	14.63	61.24	12.55	19.96	68.66	37.71	22.65
Kansas City, MO	19.56	62.18	12.00	21.06	69.34	41.35	23.04
Lafayette, LA	15.41	45.40	9.86	17.55	43.77	34.54	19.08
Lakeland, FL	14.43	44.81	11.52	20.58	62.00	36.25	20.98
Las Vegas, NV	15.39	63.43	15.89	22.82	65.55	42.05	28.50
Lexington, KY	15.36	51.94	11.20	20.46	50.14	30.83	21.39
Lincoln, NE	14.29	56.03	13.51	21.24	43.46	35.90	22.16
Little Rock, AR	13.87	42.89	11.04	16.67	55.06	35.22	21.72
Los Angeles, CA	19.04	86.64	16.19	22.77	77.25	46.74	29.91
Louisville, KY	15.83	57.01	12.16	22.04	68.47	37.55	21.89
Madison, WI	17.69	57.68	14.08	21.18	64.29	37.64	23.27

Table continued on following page.

Metro Area	Landscapers	Lawyers	Maids/House-keepers	Main-tenance/Repairers	Marketing Managers	Network Admin.	Nurses, Licensed Practical
Manchester, NH[2]	16.72	66.91	12.82	23.16	75.31	41.64	27.45
Memphis, TN	13.86	51.22	11.39	19.63	47.56	36.25	21.46
Miami, FL	14.82	81.48	11.96	18.62	65.38	41.99	23.34
Midland, TX	16.68	79.48	12.97	19.94	81.11	44.09	25.03
Milwaukee, WI	17.16	67.17	13.05	22.36	65.22	36.67	25.10
Minneapolis, MN	18.17	65.42	15.37	24.86	74.13	42.76	25.10
Nashville, TN	14.16	62.16	12.20	20.31	59.03	37.49	21.95
New Haven, CT[2]	21.07	72.97	14.36	24.76	62.79	46.03	27.76
New Orleans, LA	13.11	59.17	11.03	19.02	48.62	34.09	21.91
New York, NY	18.58	86.62	18.17	24.50	93.77	50.99	27.54
Oklahoma City, OK	14.58	60.36	11.38	18.60	66.70	37.72	21.30
Omaha, NE	16.84	60.84	12.85	21.39	53.21	40.66	22.70
Orlando, FL	14.06	58.70	11.93	18.05	58.36	40.84	22.30
Peoria, IL	14.85	63.40	12.71	20.89	71.93	35.66	22.80
Philadelphia, PA	16.87	73.14	14.54	22.62	75.68	41.45	27.69
Phoenix, AZ	14.91	68.90	13.30	20.64	64.49	42.05	27.24
Pittsburgh, PA	15.16	60.20	12.74	21.02	67.26	38.22	21.99
Portland, OR	18.52	68.32	15.17	22.37	65.90	43.03	27.81
Providence, RI[2]	17.76	61.76	15.61	24.03	78.17	44.50	28.42
Provo, UT	16.13	73.52	12.41	20.26	54.83	39.72	22.86
Raleigh, NC	15.42	66.00	12.05	21.71	71.46	43.77	23.23
Reno, NV	15.83	59.64	13.96	23.28	55.19	41.53	30.36
Richmond, VA	15.83	67.92	12.10	21.90	74.21	43.79	23.80
Riverside, CA	16.79	79.37	15.65	22.90	62.78	43.26	29.90
Rochester, MN	17.47	56.23	13.55	20.95	55.51	38.82	24.74
Sacramento, CA	19.87	73.57	18.56	22.64	73.63	45.57	31.24
Salt Lake City, UT	16.86	72.69	12.37	20.90	62.53	39.60	25.62
San Antonio, TX	14.36	61.79	11.83	18.51	71.37	38.99	22.64
San Diego, CA	16.37	70.82	15.49	22.57	71.15	47.47	31.68
San Francisco, CA	21.71	97.08	21.46	27.95	94.36	51.30	35.83
San Jose, CA	22.59	111.35	19.47	26.36	101.54	64.55	36.51
Santa Rosa, CA	19.15	84.04	16.93	25.05	77.45	43.90	35.97
Savannah, GA	14.12	60.11	10.61	17.68	53.92	36.94	21.45
Seattle, WA	20.08	66.70	16.36	24.21	81.40	48.50	29.46
Sioux Falls, SD	16.01	62.19	11.67	19.64	66.03	32.40	19.44
Springfield, IL	16.70	50.23	12.27	21.57	51.93	37.76	21.99
Tallahassee, FL	13.54	48.96	10.81	17.35	47.03	31.12	20.87
Tampa, FL	14.01	57.69	11.21	18.38	70.07	40.32	22.60
Tucson, AZ	14.30	70.81	14.77	18.16	54.39	37.56	26.53
Tulsa, OK	14.93	68.67	11.08	18.93	66.79	35.66	21.60
Tuscaloosa, AL	14.92	54.99	10.48	16.55	46.18	36.95	19.30
Virginia Beach, VA	14.23	62.89	12.23	19.55	70.12	36.79	21.44
Washington, DC	17.19	89.46	15.44	24.33	84.55	49.25	26.79
Wichita, KS	13.64	47.07	11.59	18.91	59.34	35.01	21.14
Winston-Salem, NC	14.43	60.44	11.31	19.93	64.53	39.48	22.11

Notes: (1) Figures cover the Metropolitan Statistical Area (MSA) except where noted. See Appendix B for areas included;
(2) New England City and Town Area; n/a not available
Source: Bureau of Labor Statistics, May 2020 Metro Area Occupational Employment and Wage Estimates

Average Hourly Wages: Occupations N – P

Metro Area	Nurses, Registered	Nursing Assistants	Office Clerks	Physical Therapists	Physicians	Plumbers	Police Officers
Albuquerque, NM	36.89	14.68	13.26	42.37	93.46	22.34	27.77
Allentown, PA	34.19	16.29	18.15	42.47	n/a	33.01	34.49
Anchorage, AK	45.34	19.45	21.95	50.03	131.18	42.17	46.36
Ann Arbor, MI	39.09	17.55	16.78	42.90	92.84	35.65	33.41
Athens, GA	34.14	13.24	15.96	38.70	95.71	n/a	21.06
Atlanta, GA	36.53	16.57	17.83	42.77	127.01	26.53	24.70
Austin, TX	35.23	14.69	19.62	41.53	107.02	25.23	36.91
Baton Rouge, LA	31.33	12.25	13.85	43.09	104.38	29.38	21.21
Boise City, ID	35.63	14.84	17.45	39.54	115.74	24.22	30.14
Boston, MA[2]	47.79	18.34	21.18	41.62	86.54	40.46	37.76
Boulder, CO	39.80	17.23	22.67	44.97	132.80	25.79	40.27
Cape Coral, FL	34.06	15.25	17.14	41.34	125.98	21.62	26.01
Cedar Rapids, IA	29.59	14.88	18.09	37.39	120.60	29.06	31.16
Charleston, SC	33.46	14.93	15.18	37.56	134.84	26.03	24.33
Charlotte, NC	33.86	14.08	17.52	41.50	100.25	21.86	25.91
Chicago, IL	37.48	15.55	19.15	47.77	108.91	44.20	39.61
Cincinnati, OH	34.60	15.17	18.74	43.02	116.48	26.11	33.14
Clarksville, TN	31.25	13.32	15.39	43.19	113.83	24.00	22.17
Cleveland, OH	35.16	14.82	19.54	42.93	n/a	32.16	31.03
College Station, TX	33.67	12.92	15.42	40.64	n/a	20.44	31.50
Colorado Springs, CO	36.85	15.90	20.41	41.34	106.98	24.78	35.01
Columbia, MO	31.38	14.29	16.36	37.16	123.11	31.70	24.57
Columbia, SC	31.88	13.61	13.78	42.64	92.46	20.01	21.56
Columbus, OH	33.37	13.95	19.08	42.28	108.46	28.16	39.05
Dallas, TX	37.50	14.89	18.25	46.10	98.81	24.37	35.24
Davenport, IA	28.77	14.33	15.96	38.74	125.45	28.20	29.69
Denver, CO	38.12	17.19	22.26	42.29	119.46	29.30	41.15
Des Moines, IA	30.83	15.70	19.88	41.96	118.88	25.94	33.62
Durham, NC	34.04	14.98	18.39	37.70	60.22	23.42	25.52
Edison, NJ	45.63	19.48	19.03	47.81	99.88	35.78	41.48
El Paso, TX	35.14	13.03	15.07	46.19	113.76	18.19	30.62
Fargo, ND	35.67	16.56	20.46	39.52	n/a	26.34	32.53
Fayetteville, NC	36.31	12.73	15.84	41.85	125.79	21.51	22.19
Fort Collins, CO	37.00	16.20	20.49	38.37	114.80	26.03	40.60
Fort Wayne, IN	30.07	14.32	16.90	42.52	122.85	27.79	29.01
Fort Worth, TX	37.50	14.89	18.25	46.10	98.81	24.37	35.24
Grand Rapids, MI	33.54	14.54	18.46	40.21	103.72	25.17	30.97
Greeley, CO	34.49	15.51	21.15	43.71	117.71	25.41	36.09
Green Bay, WI	33.10	15.41	17.63	43.41	134.65	32.94	34.68
Greensboro, NC	33.75	13.32	16.51	43.44	133.51	24.87	24.42
Honolulu, HI	51.33	18.53	18.01	46.01	129.46	32.64	39.30
Houston, TX	40.85	14.11	20.18	40.55	97.14	26.71	32.55
Huntsville, AL	28.17	13.37	12.64	41.60	126.02	26.09	25.95
Indianapolis, IN	33.96	14.71	18.04	42.89	125.04	25.96	31.19
Jacksonville, FL	32.50	13.39	16.95	39.98	120.42	22.43	28.73
Kansas City, MO	33.77	14.40	17.65	42.64	77.69	32.53	27.86
Lafayette, LA	n/a	10.90	13.13	41.06	97.24	26.72	20.08
Lakeland, FL	31.77	13.41	16.98	45.93	111.82	21.29	28.08
Las Vegas, NV	44.58	16.81	18.26	54.41	112.43	29.48	38.04
Lexington, KY	30.92	14.26	16.76	41.60	117.61	30.48	23.72
Lincoln, NE	32.83	14.76	15.31	41.91	114.19	26.77	31.80
Little Rock, AR	33.20	13.43	17.00	37.99	90.23	22.80	24.32
Los Angeles, CA	54.38	18.28	19.87	50.77	111.66	29.04	53.23
Louisville, KY	31.94	14.54	17.26	41.20	119.15	28.33	25.33
Madison, WI	39.58	17.70	19.30	41.01	123.11	32.30	31.59

Table continued on following page.

Metro Area	Nurses, Registered	Nursing Assistants	Office Clerks	Physical Therapists	Physicians	Plumbers	Police Officers
Manchester, NH[2]	36.90	16.63	19.87	40.56	145.31	27.62	30.42
Memphis, TN	32.84	13.99	16.64	44.13	60.99	25.56	24.96
Miami, FL	34.76	13.66	17.51	39.20	103.07	22.66	35.19
Midland, TX	32.87	15.50	19.18	51.29	n/a	22.43	32.02
Milwaukee, WI	36.90	15.65	18.75	43.06	118.39	34.14	36.14
Minneapolis, MN	41.41	18.64	20.45	41.29	113.38	39.45	38.98
Nashville, TN	32.75	13.98	17.06	37.77	98.61	27.20	25.18
New Haven, CT[2]	41.58	17.50	19.49	48.99	109.62	37.97	36.22
New Orleans, LA	34.10	12.28	13.40	43.01	105.80	27.86	24.02
New York, NY	45.63	19.48	19.03	47.81	99.88	35.78	41.48
Oklahoma City, OK	32.94	13.44	15.49	43.27	98.08	27.58	27.64
Omaha, NE	33.90	15.61	17.67	40.54	113.21	33.69	32.51
Orlando, FL	32.37	13.57	17.28	41.78	87.69	21.20	28.75
Peoria, IL	32.97	14.10	18.03	42.48	108.82	38.03	26.30
Philadelphia, PA	38.45	15.82	19.59	45.60	110.75	33.19	36.66
Phoenix, AZ	39.13	16.56	20.25	44.20	117.44	25.87	34.93
Pittsburgh, PA	33.74	15.25	17.82	41.00	61.88	31.40	32.43
Portland, OR	47.45	18.03	19.73	44.08	84.07	37.75	39.52
Providence, RI[2]	39.75	16.41	19.47	41.73	101.63	29.94	31.88
Provo, UT	32.54	14.31	17.04	43.98	101.67	26.23	26.67
Raleigh, NC	33.71	14.25	17.60	40.47	131.23	21.78	25.39
Reno, NV	38.61	15.69	19.47	43.31	n/a	32.93	n/a
Richmond, VA	38.19	14.34	17.47	48.16	100.13	24.50	28.11
Riverside, CA	52.80	17.66	18.80	49.86	101.93	28.90	50.52
Rochester, MN	34.67	17.06	18.54	41.15	120.62	35.99	33.04
Sacramento, CA	64.59	20.17	19.88	53.64	125.17	30.79	48.23
Salt Lake City, UT	34.93	15.33	17.52	39.40	120.03	26.94	30.14
San Antonio, TX	36.11	13.97	17.09	41.28	104.54	21.49	29.60
San Diego, CA	53.66	19.08	19.89	47.32	115.36	30.73	44.39
San Francisco, CA	71.73	23.28	23.83	49.69	90.09	51.01	58.93
San Jose, CA	70.61	20.18	21.97	51.92	106.37	40.79	63.02
Santa Rosa, CA	60.02	18.91	21.01	52.11	110.94	36.11	55.62
Savannah, GA	31.19	12.86	17.14	42.25	79.65	25.97	22.03
Seattle, WA	45.73	18.20	21.98	44.19	121.55	39.45	41.70
Sioux Falls, SD	29.70	13.76	13.70	35.64	136.24	21.69	30.58
Springfield, IL	34.64	14.66	18.74	44.92	131.59	36.97	33.66
Tallahassee, FL	31.79	12.60	14.97	40.99	100.02	21.64	27.13
Tampa, FL	34.28	14.08	17.66	39.93	104.01	22.02	30.94
Tucson, AZ	36.86	15.70	19.72	42.86	96.12	24.44	31.18
Tulsa, OK	32.44	13.14	16.37	41.95	101.73	26.45	27.25
Tuscaloosa, AL	28.76	12.79	12.79	47.83	104.43	22.88	26.12
Virginia Beach, VA	35.27	14.43	15.93	43.59	103.50	23.91	27.28
Washington, DC	40.14	16.19	20.88	46.02	98.67	27.93	37.03
Wichita, KS	28.59	13.31	14.06	43.59	72.44	23.76	23.57
Winston-Salem, NC	33.96	13.84	16.40	47.63	59.26	21.42	21.49

Notes: (1) Figures cover the Metropolitan Statistical Area (MSA) except where noted. See Appendix B for areas included;
(2) New England City and Town Area; n/a not available
Source: Bureau of Labor Statistics, May 2020 Metro Area Occupational Employment and Wage Estimates

Average Hourly Wages: Occupations P – S

Metro Area	Postal Mail Carriers	R.E. Sales Agents	Retail Sales-persons	Sales Reps., Technical/ Scientific	Secretaries, Exc. Leg./ Med./Exec.	Security Guards	Surgeons
Albuquerque, NM	25.35	27.94	13.71	53.85	17.98	14.03	117.34
Allentown, PA	25.45	20.93	13.51	35.66	18.99	14.13	n/a
Anchorage, AK	25.19	35.74	16.71	41.68	21.33	21.46	n/a
Ann Arbor, MI	25.59	23.92	15.17	50.25	21.85	18.21	n/a
Athens, GA	24.88	27.22	12.23	22.13	15.66	15.56	121.05
Atlanta, GA	25.44	35.07	13.86	41.84	17.67	13.91	120.75
Austin, TX	25.90	32.45	13.91	51.09	18.80	16.12	123.62
Baton Rouge, LA	25.30	20.08	12.82	38.42	17.00	15.22	140.15
Boise City, ID	25.46	19.41	14.97	29.05	17.35	13.31	97.30
Boston, MA[2]	26.35	43.81	16.09	51.61	23.99	18.44	130.15
Boulder, CO	25.69	29.36	16.67	52.42	20.24	16.82	138.32
Cape Coral, FL	25.50	25.90	13.39	35.11	18.26	13.12	117.59
Cedar Rapids, IA	25.60	20.45	13.27	55.20	19.13	17.64	n/a
Charleston, SC	25.11	24.16	14.34	31.33	17.96	15.38	n/a
Charlotte, NC	25.80	26.82	14.40	45.84	19.39	15.19	n/a
Chicago, IL	25.88	21.35	14.74	43.30	20.83	16.67	126.47
Cincinnati, OH	26.01	22.97	14.27	54.66	18.99	17.36	136.71
Clarksville, TN	25.31	13.84	13.05	28.37	16.54	17.01	n/a
Cleveland, OH	25.57	25.39	13.80	44.45	18.72	15.88	n/a
College Station, TX	25.72	26.12	12.40	38.39	16.65	12.99	n/a
Colorado Springs, CO	25.33	36.06	15.75	51.66	17.72	16.33	138.49
Columbia, MO	24.78	15.74	16.35	37.54	17.90	15.12	n/a
Columbia, SC	25.03	21.37	13.33	35.54	19.69	15.89	n/a
Columbus, OH	25.57	24.24	14.13	43.53	19.06	17.50	130.76
Dallas, TX	25.84	32.44	14.22	42.11	19.17	15.96	96.15
Davenport, IA	25.05	35.10	16.04	41.15	17.40	16.63	n/a
Denver, CO	25.33	43.38	16.33	53.97	20.86	17.65	122.99
Des Moines, IA	25.38	24.89	13.93	48.46	21.68	16.81	n/a
Durham, NC	26.10	23.48	12.83	64.20	20.51	24.93	n/a
Edison, NJ	25.82	47.39	17.06	53.94	21.58	18.33	103.27
El Paso, TX	25.52	28.82	11.77	n/a	15.48	12.85	n/a
Fargo, ND	25.35	30.08	15.57	41.70	19.41	14.99	n/a
Fayetteville, NC	25.38	31.75	12.89	n/a	17.36	19.85	n/a
Fort Collins, CO	25.02	28.43	15.06	44.49	18.64	14.53	n/a
Fort Wayne, IN	25.01	23.92	13.59	39.15	18.02	17.34	102.77
Fort Worth, TX	25.84	32.44	14.22	42.11	19.17	15.96	96.15
Grand Rapids, MI	25.56	26.79	14.74	36.78	18.94	14.23	n/a
Greeley, CO	24.67	n/a	17.48	42.69	18.73	16.81	n/a
Green Bay, WI	25.05	27.21	15.84	45.73	18.17	14.03	n/a
Greensboro, NC	26.02	21.07	13.99	47.50	18.17	14.07	n/a
Honolulu, HI	26.27	34.78	16.86	41.95	22.13	16.81	125.38
Houston, TX	25.54	30.11	13.06	45.56	19.08	14.70	109.57
Huntsville, AL	25.08	n/a	14.19	40.45	17.89	15.08	n/a
Indianapolis, IN	25.51	24.10	15.14	58.59	18.14	15.06	83.72
Jacksonville, FL	26.36	32.81	12.90	55.76	18.29	12.98	n/a
Kansas City, MO	25.56	25.16	14.32	42.28	18.80	19.75	134.82
Lafayette, LA	25.61	20.02	13.19	41.34	15.02	11.63	n/a
Lakeland, FL	25.73	24.66	13.99	50.71	16.80	13.69	125.71
Las Vegas, NV	25.67	33.49	14.32	55.81	19.28	15.70	n/a
Lexington, KY	25.61	21.40	13.53	40.76	18.81	13.31	n/a
Lincoln, NE	25.26	26.16	13.66	39.84	18.52	17.86	142.38
Little Rock, AR	25.59	n/a	13.77	31.84	16.05	14.70	n/a
Los Angeles, CA	26.77	29.45	17.09	49.22	22.28	16.50	89.22
Louisville, KY	25.74	31.08	13.26	42.65	18.47	13.24	134.53
Madison, WI	24.45	22.36	15.01	38.52	20.01	18.11	n/a

Table continued on following page.

Metro Area	Postal Mail Carriers	R.E. Sales Agents	Retail Sales-persons	Sales Reps., Technical/ Scientific	Secretaries, Exc. Leg./ Med./Exec.	Security Guards	Surgeons
Manchester, NH[2]	25.30	23.78	14.27	48.55	18.80	17.13	n/a
Memphis, TN	25.90	28.54	14.05	42.81	18.28	13.18	n/a
Miami, FL	25.74	33.05	14.10	43.52	17.95	14.33	102.70
Midland, TX	24.14	43.87	15.66	47.47	18.67	17.54	n/a
Milwaukee, WI	25.52	24.22	15.05	42.81	19.69	15.28	n/a
Minneapolis, MN	25.48	22.43	15.67	43.88	21.10	18.83	n/a
Nashville, TN	25.66	22.88	14.62	38.86	20.08	14.59	87.98
New Haven, CT[2]	25.57	n/a	15.78	51.87	23.42	16.82	n/a
New Orleans, LA	25.18	n/a	12.85	32.30	17.67	14.16	n/a
New York, NY	25.82	47.39	17.06	53.94	21.58	18.33	103.27
Oklahoma City, OK	25.83	27.06	14.42	47.84	16.56	17.63	n/a
Omaha, NE	25.62	26.55	14.47	27.54	18.29	18.67	97.62
Orlando, FL	25.63	21.86	13.90	45.86	17.38	13.36	107.64
Peoria, IL	25.20	22.91	13.31	41.09	16.53	18.73	n/a
Philadelphia, PA	25.80	23.80	15.36	39.35	20.84	15.80	127.73
Phoenix, AZ	26.14	25.87	15.31	45.74	18.93	15.32	n/a
Pittsburgh, PA	25.28	35.64	14.07	41.12	18.26	14.45	n/a
Portland, OR	25.16	27.75	16.66	51.50	22.16	16.55	137.03
Providence, RI[2]	25.36	34.42	16.55	43.31	22.02	15.82	135.97
Provo, UT	25.17	19.82	14.08	35.28	17.09	18.95	n/a
Raleigh, NC	25.99	25.85	13.72	53.76	18.82	16.13	n/a
Reno, NV	25.58	18.91	16.30	50.40	20.94	18.12	n/a
Richmond, VA	25.32	31.14	14.11	52.19	19.17	13.71	129.69
Riverside, CA	26.10	n/a	16.16	47.48	21.05	16.42	116.37
Rochester, MN	24.97	25.68	15.36	44.55	18.15	15.79	n/a
Sacramento, CA	26.14	40.54	16.20	49.21	21.10	17.05	n/a
Salt Lake City, UT	25.55	n/a	15.78	45.08	19.50	17.37	120.78
San Antonio, TX	25.93	30.87	13.97	43.36	17.05	16.35	n/a
San Diego, CA	26.30	n/a	16.36	49.07	21.27	16.24	n/a
San Francisco, CA	26.61	35.07	18.15	57.04	25.23	20.24	120.47
San Jose, CA	26.28	48.70	20.75	69.16	24.97	21.24	124.63
Santa Rosa, CA	25.08	n/a	18.83	58.81	22.47	17.86	n/a
Savannah, GA	25.33	26.46	13.07	42.67	16.91	15.61	135.03
Seattle, WA	25.94	34.15	18.51	53.25	23.36	19.56	110.96
Sioux Falls, SD	25.69	n/a	16.24	59.28	14.98	14.66	135.63
Springfield, IL	25.77	19.54	14.55	41.97	17.85	23.01	137.30
Tallahassee, FL	25.24	26.87	14.02	38.03	17.26	13.85	n/a
Tampa, FL	25.84	27.84	14.16	38.88	17.85	16.60	99.80
Tucson, AZ	26.13	28.26	14.92	41.86	17.67	14.50	n/a
Tulsa, OK	25.76	43.74	13.54	39.78	16.99	15.16	n/a
Tuscaloosa, AL	24.94	29.55	14.23	n/a	17.36	13.60	n/a
Virginia Beach, VA	25.12	31.60	12.74	47.42	19.12	16.77	n/a
Washington, DC	25.68	32.62	15.08	60.70	23.83	22.34	128.61
Wichita, KS	25.19	34.94	16.50	48.42	17.11	15.40	n/a
Winston-Salem, NC	26.12	29.77	12.78	46.13	18.63	19.14	n/a

Notes: (1) Figures cover the Metropolitan Statistical Area (MSA) except where noted. See Appendix B for areas included; (2) New England City and Town Area; n/a not available
Source: Bureau of Labor Statistics, May 2020 Metro Area Occupational Employment and Wage Estimates

Average Hourly Wages: Occupations T – W

Metro Area	Teacher Assistants[3]	Teachers, Secondary School[3]	Telemarketers	Truck Drivers, Heavy	Truck Drivers, Light	Waiters/ Waitresses
Albuquerque, NM	10.86	25.68	n/a	20.15	18.42	10.00
Allentown, PA	14.41	34.29	13.77	23.61	17.65	13.50
Anchorage, AK	19.53	40.19	n/a	28.67	24.80	12.41
Ann Arbor, MI	14.25	30.94	n/a	23.07	20.97	12.42
Athens, GA	9.86	28.26	n/a	24.12	22.33	11.05
Atlanta, GA	11.99	30.58	13.88	24.03	19.17	11.09
Austin, TX	12.63	28.51	16.75	21.42	23.43	11.41
Baton Rouge, LA	10.61	25.88	13.65	20.24	16.72	9.75
Boise City, ID	13.33	24.81	13.26	22.95	18.28	12.34
Boston, MA[2]	18.17	39.93	18.30	25.04	22.25	16.02
Boulder, CO	16.60	33.44	n/a	21.44	21.14	15.29
Cape Coral, FL	14.99	31.83	13.57	21.06	18.21	12.55
Cedar Rapids, IA	12.78	25.85	12.92	18.16	16.81	10.61
Charleston, SC	12.41	28.34	9.27	20.05	17.41	9.82
Charlotte, NC	12.78	25.96	16.80	23.25	17.99	11.80
Chicago, IL	14.87	39.72	15.22	26.10	23.89	11.30
Cincinnati, OH	14.28	30.87	15.21	24.06	19.05	11.05
Clarksville, TN	13.56	33.45	n/a	19.83	19.57	10.91
Cleveland, OH	14.60	34.51	11.42	23.90	19.82	10.71
College Station, TX	9.90	23.45	n/a	18.16	17.70	9.94
Colorado Springs, CO	14.25	25.06	16.71	23.30	19.39	15.23
Columbia, MO	13.47	25.88	n/a	21.47	19.86	11.41
Columbia, SC	12.27	28.01	16.21	21.90	17.53	9.40
Columbus, OH	14.60	33.80	14.44	22.67	19.28	11.77
Dallas, TX	11.50	28.25	17.10	24.27	20.71	9.50
Davenport, IA	13.57	27.87	14.32	23.94	17.03	11.62
Denver, CO	15.53	29.76	18.67	26.50	20.37	15.26
Des Moines, IA	13.66	29.67	14.89	24.12	16.86	10.63
Durham, NC	12.80	26.34	12.24	19.82	20.75	12.65
Edison, NJ	17.07	43.94	18.00	27.38	21.27	18.12
El Paso, TX	13.05	30.31	10.36	23.37	17.27	9.93
Fargo, ND	16.34	31.20	n/a	24.48	20.00	12.90
Fayetteville, NC	11.91	22.89	n/a	17.95	17.42	9.29
Fort Collins, CO	14.31	n/a	n/a	22.10	18.76	16.23
Fort Wayne, IN	12.40	26.62	n/a	21.76	19.38	13.50
Fort Worth, TX	11.50	28.25	17.10	24.27	20.71	9.50
Grand Rapids, MI	14.25	29.14	12.06	22.41	20.39	14.47
Greeley, CO	14.61	25.80	n/a	25.81	20.06	12.56
Green Bay, WI	16.03	28.94	n/a	22.82	19.81	9.89
Greensboro, NC	12.38	24.19	n/a	24.63	17.87	10.40
Honolulu, HI	15.68	n/a	12.79	25.82	18.43	30.11
Houston, TX	10.92	29.18	14.80	23.21	20.42	11.44
Huntsville, AL	10.13	26.12	n/a	19.59	17.60	9.19
Indianapolis, IN	13.05	27.37	16.60	23.26	20.81	12.55
Jacksonville, FL	12.80	30.73	12.86	21.69	18.78	12.21
Kansas City, MO	13.33	26.10	15.91	24.16	18.51	11.20
Lafayette, LA	11.30	25.17	n/a	20.88	14.72	9.79
Lakeland, FL	11.20	24.22	12.40	22.02	22.47	11.43
Las Vegas, NV	15.75	28.05	12.82	23.35	17.59	13.15
Lexington, KY	15.32	28.71	n/a	25.24	22.54	10.77
Lincoln, NE	14.87	30.70	11.05	26.01	19.74	10.59
Little Rock, AR	11.35	26.77	12.43	24.40	14.91	10.92
Los Angeles, CA	18.25	41.94	15.89	24.13	21.40	16.07
Louisville, KY	15.06	27.29	n/a	25.60	20.42	11.01
Madison, WI	15.69	27.83	12.02	25.51	18.09	12.03

Table continued on following page.

Metro Area	Teacher Assistants[3]	Teachers, Secondary School[3]	Telemarketers	Truck Drivers, Heavy	Truck Drivers, Light	Waiters/ Waitresses
Manchester, NH[2]	15.12	28.80	n/a	24.56	18.27	13.46
Memphis, TN	12.21	26.97	15.50	22.93	19.09	9.84
Miami, FL	13.47	31.76	14.05	19.63	17.20	12.57
Midland, TX	10.43	28.63	n/a	24.50	21.89	9.28
Milwaukee, WI	16.15	29.89	16.04	24.97	17.36	11.33
Minneapolis, MN	16.69	31.99	18.31	25.51	21.47	15.04
Nashville, TN	13.09	25.02	18.69	25.40	17.83	9.89
New Haven, CT[2]	15.38	37.68	17.96	24.73	19.11	13.86
New Orleans, LA	12.38	26.55	17.07	22.70	18.90	9.90
New York, NY	17.07	43.94	18.00	27.38	21.27	18.12
Oklahoma City, OK	10.86	23.79	14.03	24.44	18.01	11.61
Omaha, NE	14.35	30.82	12.49	21.91	18.84	10.79
Orlando, FL	13.12	27.96	12.95	22.29	19.05	12.53
Peoria, IL	12.78	28.02	16.30	23.04	19.39	10.60
Philadelphia, PA	14.25	34.95	17.40	25.10	20.12	13.00
Phoenix, AZ	13.68	27.18	16.21	23.93	19.25	19.03
Pittsburgh, PA	14.11	34.46	12.75	26.03	17.58	13.55
Portland, OR	17.44	39.42	18.26	25.23	20.13	15.65
Providence, RI[2]	17.30	37.01	16.66	24.14	20.19	14.06
Provo, UT	13.67	38.46	14.13	20.44	18.31	12.13
Raleigh, NC	11.87	27.24	n/a	22.00	16.96	11.79
Reno, NV	10.42	25.59	14.61	25.19	21.37	11.35
Richmond, VA	12.74	n/a	14.96	23.73	21.33	12.03
Riverside, CA	17.96	41.62	15.27	25.57	22.32	14.16
Rochester, MN	15.75	30.87	n/a	23.53	16.41	15.44
Sacramento, CA	17.41	39.16	15.61	25.88	19.96	16.21
Salt Lake City, UT	13.35	29.93	12.47	24.57	20.04	10.55
San Antonio, TX	11.97	28.34	19.63	20.54	21.17	10.02
San Diego, CA	16.96	41.03	15.07	24.67	23.99	15.63
San Francisco, CA	19.29	44.41	n/a	27.78	25.20	19.64
San Jose, CA	19.75	44.47	16.69	27.47	24.95	17.28
Santa Rosa, CA	17.76	42.66	n/a	26.90	23.21	17.56
Savannah, GA	12.45	26.54	n/a	22.16	17.24	9.30
Seattle, WA	19.79	38.01	21.37	26.88	22.88	20.75
Sioux Falls, SD	12.32	23.01	n/a	22.48	18.48	10.59
Springfield, IL	12.03	27.07	n/a	24.22	18.96	10.05
Tallahassee, FL	13.00	24.52	14.79	20.09	17.87	12.10
Tampa, FL	14.49	30.07	13.79	20.31	17.75	14.24
Tucson, AZ	13.63	21.17	14.70	23.53	18.79	17.12
Tulsa, OK	11.41	26.46	12.45	27.46	18.88	9.11
Tuscaloosa, AL	9.49	24.81	n/a	20.28	18.27	9.02
Virginia Beach, VA	13.86	32.96	13.91	19.71	19.40	11.59
Washington, DC	17.52	41.57	14.54	24.43	22.49	15.99
Wichita, KS	13.20	27.00	12.02	22.85	17.72	9.40
Winston-Salem, NC	11.38	24.47	n/a	23.68	17.90	10.37

Notes: (1) Figures cover the Metropolitan Statistical Area (MSA) except where noted. See Appendix B for areas included;
(2) New England City and Town Area; (3) Hourly wages were calculated from annual wage data assuming a 40 hour work week;
n/a not available
Source: Bureau of Labor Statistics, May 2020 Metro Area Occupational Employment and Wage Estimates

Means of Transportation to Work: City

City	Car/Truck/Van		Public Transportation			Bicycle	Walked	Other Means	Worked at Home
	Drove Alone	Car-pooled	Bus	Subway	Railroad				
Albuquerque, NM	80.6	9.0	1.8	0.0	0.1	1.1	1.9	1.0	4.4
Allentown, PA	67.4	17.2	4.9	0.0	0.0	0.1	5.4	1.2	3.9
Anchorage, AK	76.3	11.8	1.5	0.0	0.0	1.3	2.9	2.3	4.0
Ann Arbor, MI	54.0	6.4	10.3	0.2	0.0	3.9	16.5	0.7	8.0
Athens, GA	72.5	10.0	4.6	0.0	0.0	1.4	4.4	1.5	5.6
Atlanta, GA	67.1	6.3	6.6	3.4	0.2	1.1	5.0	2.2	8.1
Austin, TX	73.7	9.1	3.2	0.1	0.1	1.3	2.4	1.3	8.7
Baton Rouge, LA	80.3	9.8	2.4	0.0	0.0	0.6	3.4	0.6	2.9
Boise City, ID	79.6	7.3	0.6	0.0	0.0	2.8	2.5	1.1	6.0
Boston, MA	38.3	5.9	13.5	17.8	1.1	2.3	15.1	2.6	3.4
Boulder, CO	50.8	5.5	7.3	0.0	0.0	9.9	11.1	1.1	14.5
Cape Coral, FL	81.7	9.0	0.1	0.0	0.0	0.2	0.8	1.2	7.0
Cedar Rapids, IA	84.0	8.2	0.8	0.0	0.0	0.5	1.7	1.1	3.6
Charleston, SC	76.4	7.0	0.8	0.0	0.0	2.4	5.0	1.7	6.8
Charlotte, NC	76.3	9.3	2.4	0.4	0.2	0.1	2.1	1.5	7.7
Chicago, IL	48.8	7.7	13.3	13.0	1.8	1.7	6.5	2.0	5.2
Cincinnati, OH	72.3	8.8	7.0	0.0	0.0	0.4	5.7	1.1	4.7
Clarksville, TN	85.9	7.8	0.9	0.0	0.0	0.0	1.3	1.3	2.7
Cleveland, OH	69.3	10.8	8.9	0.5	0.1	0.6	5.1	1.5	3.2
College Station, TX	78.2	9.3	2.8	0.0	0.0	2.1	2.7	1.0	3.8
Colorado Springs, CO	77.8	10.9	0.9	0.0	0.0	0.6	1.9	0.9	6.9
Columbia, MO	77.1	10.5	1.3	0.0	0.0	1.3	4.8	0.9	4.2
Columbia, SC	64.1	6.1	1.8	0.0	0.0	0.5	21.9	2.2	3.4
Columbus, OH	79.4	8.3	3.1	0.0	0.0	0.6	3.1	1.1	4.4
Dallas, TX	76.7	11.0	2.9	0.4	0.3	0.2	2.1	1.5	4.9
Davenport, IA	85.6	6.6	0.9	0.0	0.0	0.4	2.3	0.5	3.7
Denver, CO	69.1	7.7	4.4	0.9	0.5	2.2	4.7	1.9	8.5
Des Moines, IA	80.1	9.7	2.2	0.1	0.0	0.4	2.9	1.2	3.5
Durham, NC	76.9	9.3	3.6	0.0	0.0	0.6	2.4	1.3	5.8
Edison, NJ	69.4	9.0	0.5	0.5	12.6	0.3	1.7	1.2	4.8
El Paso, TX	81.1	10.6	1.6	0.0	0.0	0.2	1.4	1.9	3.2
Fargo, ND	82.8	8.3	0.9	0.0	0.0	0.6	3.7	0.8	2.9
Fayetteville, NC	77.2	9.4	0.6	0.0	0.0	0.2	7.8	1.7	3.1
Fort Collins, CO	71.9	7.2	2.2	0.0	0.0	5.4	4.2	1.0	8.0
Fort Wayne, IN	83.4	9.6	0.8	0.0	0.0	0.3	1.6	0.7	3.7
Fort Worth, TX	81.5	11.4	0.6	0.0	0.2	0.2	1.2	0.8	4.1
Grand Rapids, MI	75.3	11.1	3.6	0.1	0.0	1.1	4.1	1.0	3.8
Greeley, CO	79.5	11.3	0.6	0.0	0.0	0.7	2.8	1.2	3.9
Green Bay, WI	79.7	10.2	1.4	0.0	0.0	0.5	2.3	1.9	3.9
Greensboro, NC	81.9	7.6	1.9	0.0	0.0	0.2	1.9	0.9	5.6
Honolulu, HI	57.2	13.0	11.6	0.0	0.0	1.6	8.5	4.0	3.9
Houston, TX	77.7	10.4	3.5	0.1	0.0	0.4	2.0	2.0	4.0
Huntsville, AL	86.1	7.0	0.4	0.0	0.0	0.2	1.3	1.1	4.0
Indianapolis, IN	82.0	9.2	1.8	0.0	0.0	0.5	1.9	1.1	3.5
Jacksonville, FL	80.3	9.2	1.8	0.0	0.0	0.5	1.7	1.6	4.8
Kansas City, MO	81.5	7.8	2.5	0.0	0.0	0.2	2.0	1.2	4.9
Lafayette, LA	84.3	6.7	1.2	0.0	0.0	1.2	2.3	0.9	3.5
Lakeland, FL	80.5	10.5	0.8	0.0	0.0	0.3	1.6	1.8	4.6
Las Vegas, NV	78.0	9.8	3.4	0.0	0.0	0.2	1.5	2.8	4.2
Lexington, KY	78.5	9.3	1.9	0.0	0.0	0.6	3.7	1.5	4.4
Lincoln, NE	81.0	9.0	1.3	0.0	0.0	1.2	3.4	0.6	3.4
Little Rock, AR	81.6	9.8	0.9	0.0	0.0	0.1	1.8	1.5	4.2
Los Angeles, CA	69.6	8.8	7.8	0.9	0.2	1.0	3.4	2.0	6.3
Louisville, KY	79.6	8.9	3.1	0.0	0.0	0.4	2.0	1.8	4.3

Table continued on following page.

City	Car/Truck/Van		Public Transportation			Bicycle	Walked	Other Means	Worked at Home
	Drove Alone	Car-pooled	Bus	Subway	Railroad				
Madison, WI	64.3	7.0	9.1	0.0	0.1	4.5	9.1	1.3	4.7
Manchester, NH	79.1	11.0	0.7	0.0	0.1	0.3	3.2	1.3	4.2
Memphis, TN	82.0	10.5	1.4	0.0	0.0	0.2	1.6	1.3	2.9
Miami, FL	69.4	8.3	7.9	1.0	0.2	0.9	4.0	3.2	5.2
Midland, TX	85.1	10.1	0.2	0.0	0.0	0.1	0.6	1.0	2.8
Milwaukee, WI	72.8	10.2	7.2	0.0	0.1	0.8	4.6	0.8	3.5
Minneapolis, MN	60.5	7.4	11.2	1.1	0.2	4.0	7.4	2.3	5.8
Nashville, TN	77.7	10.0	2.0	0.0	0.1	0.2	2.4	1.2	6.4
New Haven, CT	58.7	9.1	10.5	0.1	1.1	3.1	11.4	1.2	4.7
New Orleans, LA	68.0	9.1	5.9	0.0	0.0	3.1	5.4	2.7	5.7
New York, NY	22.3	4.5	10.1	43.9	1.5	1.3	10.0	2.2	4.3
Oklahoma City, OK	82.6	10.5	0.5	0.0	0.0	0.1	1.5	1.1	3.6
Omaha, NE	81.7	9.1	1.4	0.0	0.0	0.3	2.3	1.3	4.0
Orlando, FL	79.0	8.0	3.4	0.1	0.0	0.6	1.8	1.9	5.3
Peoria, IL	80.1	9.5	2.4	0.0	0.0	0.3	2.7	1.1	3.7
Philadelphia, PA	50.3	8.2	16.0	5.6	2.8	2.1	8.5	2.3	4.2
Phoenix, AZ	74.6	12.6	2.7	0.1	0.1	0.6	1.6	1.9	5.9
Pittsburgh, PA	55.3	8.1	16.9	0.4	0.0	1.8	10.7	1.2	5.6
Portland, OR	57.3	8.3	9.9	0.9	0.3	6.0	5.8	3.0	8.5
Providence, RI	64.5	12.0	5.2	0.1	1.2	0.7	9.5	1.3	5.5
Provo, UT	62.0	11.8	2.6	0.2	1.1	2.4	13.0	1.6	5.3
Raleigh, NC	78.2	8.0	1.9	0.1	0.0	0.4	1.6	1.3	8.5
Reno, NV	75.2	12.6	2.3	0.0	0.0	0.8	3.6	1.1	4.4
Richmond, VA	71.1	9.5	5.5	0.1	0.1	2.1	5.2	1.8	4.6
Riverside, CA	76.4	12.6	1.7	0.0	0.7	0.7	2.6	1.1	4.2
Rochester, MN	70.6	12.5	6.2	0.0	0.0	1.0	4.3	0.9	4.4
Sacramento, CA	74.4	10.4	2.0	0.2	0.4	1.9	2.8	2.2	5.6
Salt Lake City, UT	67.8	10.5	4.8	0.4	0.8	2.5	5.1	2.7	5.5
San Antonio, TX	78.7	11.3	2.9	0.0	0.0	0.2	1.7	1.5	3.8
San Diego, CA	74.7	8.6	3.6	0.0	0.1	0.8	3.1	1.8	7.2
San Francisco, CA	32.1	6.9	22.0	8.8	1.7	4.0	11.8	6.1	6.6
San Jose, CA	75.8	11.7	2.6	0.3	1.2	0.8	1.8	1.6	4.2
Santa Rosa, CA	77.9	11.5	1.6	0.0	0.1	1.2	1.7	1.1	4.8
Savannah, GA	72.0	11.0	4.4	0.1	0.0	1.7	4.7	1.9	4.2
Seattle, WA	46.5	7.2	20.1	1.3	0.1	3.5	11.3	2.5	7.4
Sioux Falls, SD	84.3	8.5	0.8	0.0	0.0	0.5	2.0	0.6	3.4
Springfield, IL	81.8	7.9	2.2	0.1	0.0	0.7	2.1	1.3	3.9
Tallahassee, FL	78.5	8.7	2.4	0.0	0.0	0.8	3.3	1.5	4.8
Tampa, FL	77.1	8.8	2.1	0.0	0.0	1.0	2.4	1.5	6.9
Tucson, AZ	74.5	10.6	3.3	0.0	0.0	2.4	3.1	1.7	4.5
Tulsa, OK	80.2	10.7	0.9	0.0	0.0	0.3	1.8	2.1	4.0
Tuscaloosa, AL	84.2	8.1	0.8	0.1	0.0	0.5	1.8	0.6	3.9
Virginia Beach, VA	82.1	8.6	0.7	0.0	0.0	0.5	2.4	1.6	3.9
Washington, DC	33.5	5.2	13.2	21.1	0.3	4.5	13.4	2.3	6.6
Wichita, KS	83.5	9.5	0.7	0.0	0.0	0.3	1.5	1.3	3.2
Winston-Salem, NC	81.9	8.3	1.7	0.0	0.0	0.2	2.1	1.1	4.7
U.S.	76.3	9.0	2.4	1.9	0.6	0.5	2.7	1.4	5.2

Note: Figures are percentages and cover workers 16 years of age and older
Source: U.S. Census Bureau, 2015-2019 American Community Survey 5-Year Estimates

Means of Transportation to Work: Metro Area

Metro Area	Car/Truck/Van		Public Transportation			Bicycle	Walked	Other Means	Worked at Home
	Drove Alone	Car-pooled	Bus	Subway	Railroad				
Albuquerque, NM	80.6	9.6	1.3	0.0	0.2	0.8	1.7	1.1	4.8
Allentown, PA	81.7	8.4	1.5	0.1	0.1	0.2	2.4	1.1	4.6
Anchorage, AK	75.7	11.5	1.3	0.0	0.0	1.0	2.7	3.2	4.5
Ann Arbor, MI	71.8	7.9	5.1	0.1	0.0	1.6	7.0	0.6	5.9
Athens, GA	76.3	10.3	2.8	0.0	0.0	0.9	2.9	1.2	5.6
Atlanta, GA	77.3	9.2	2.0	0.8	0.1	0.2	1.3	1.6	7.4
Austin, TX	76.3	9.2	1.8	0.1	0.1	0.8	1.8	1.2	8.8
Baton Rouge, LA	84.8	8.7	0.8	0.0	0.0	0.3	1.5	0.9	3.1
Boise City, ID	79.9	8.9	0.3	0.0	0.0	1.2	1.7	1.1	6.8
Boston, MA	66.4	7.2	4.1	6.7	2.2	1.1	5.4	1.7	5.3
Boulder, CO	65.0	7.2	4.7	0.0	0.0	4.2	5.0	1.0	12.8
Cape Coral, FL	79.0	10.2	0.6	0.0	0.0	0.6	1.2	2.0	6.3
Cedar Rapids, IA	84.7	7.5	0.5	0.0	0.0	0.3	2.0	0.7	4.2
Charleston, SC	81.1	8.2	0.7	0.0	0.0	0.7	2.3	1.2	5.8
Charlotte, NC	80.4	8.9	1.1	0.2	0.1	0.1	1.4	1.2	6.6
Chicago, IL	70.0	7.7	4.4	4.4	3.3	0.7	3.0	1.4	5.2
Cincinnati, OH	82.3	8.0	1.7	0.0	0.0	0.2	2.0	0.8	5.0
Clarksville, TN	84.0	8.1	0.7	0.0	0.0	0.1	3.1	1.3	2.7
Cleveland, OH	81.4	7.7	2.7	0.2	0.1	0.3	2.2	1.1	4.4
College Station, TX	79.8	10.7	1.7	0.0	0.0	1.3	1.9	1.1	3.5
Colorado Springs, CO	77.0	10.4	0.6	0.0	0.0	0.4	3.4	1.0	7.0
Columbia, MO	78.9	10.7	0.8	0.0	0.0	0.8	3.3	0.9	4.5
Columbia, SC	80.7	8.6	0.6	0.0	0.0	0.1	4.4	1.9	3.6
Columbus, OH	82.2	7.6	1.6	0.0	0.0	0.4	2.2	1.0	5.0
Dallas, TX	80.6	9.7	0.9	0.2	0.2	0.1	1.2	1.2	5.8
Davenport, IA	85.6	6.8	0.9	0.0	0.0	0.2	2.0	0.9	3.6
Denver, CO	75.3	8.1	2.8	0.6	0.3	0.8	2.2	1.5	8.4
Des Moines, IA	83.6	7.8	1.1	0.0	0.0	0.2	1.8	0.8	4.6
Durham, NC	76.5	8.7	3.4	0.0	0.0	0.7	2.8	1.3	6.7
Edison, NJ	49.2	6.3	7.5	20.0	3.9	0.7	5.9	2.0	4.5
El Paso, TX	80.7	10.6	1.3	0.0	0.0	0.1	1.6	2.1	3.5
Fargo, ND	82.2	8.6	0.7	0.0	0.0	0.5	2.8	0.8	4.4
Fayetteville, NC	81.3	9.2	0.3	0.0	0.0	0.1	4.2	1.4	3.4
Fort Collins, CO	74.9	8.0	1.5	0.0	0.0	3.1	2.7	1.2	8.6
Fort Wayne, IN	83.9	9.0	0.6	0.0	0.0	0.3	1.4	0.7	4.2
Fort Worth, TX	80.6	9.7	0.9	0.2	0.2	0.1	1.2	1.2	5.8
Grand Rapids, MI	81.9	9.1	1.4	0.0	0.0	0.5	2.2	0.8	4.2
Greeley, CO	80.4	9.6	0.5	0.0	0.0	0.3	1.9	1.0	6.2
Green Bay, WI	83.8	7.9	0.7	0.0	0.0	0.2	1.8	0.9	4.7
Greensboro, NC	82.7	9.0	0.9	0.0	0.0	0.1	1.4	0.9	4.9
Honolulu, HI	64.7	14.2	8.0	0.0	0.0	0.9	5.5	2.7	4.0
Houston, TX	80.8	9.8	1.9	0.0	0.0	0.2	1.3	1.4	4.5
Huntsville, AL	88.0	6.2	0.2	0.0	0.0	0.1	0.8	1.0	3.7
Indianapolis, IN	83.2	8.3	0.8	0.0	0.0	0.3	1.5	0.9	4.9
Jacksonville, FL	80.9	8.2	1.2	0.0	0.0	0.5	1.5	1.7	6.0
Kansas City, MO	83.7	7.8	0.8	0.0	0.0	0.1	1.2	0.9	5.4
Lafayette, LA	84.8	8.2	0.5	0.0	0.0	0.4	1.9	1.1	3.0
Lakeland, FL	83.4	9.4	0.5	0.0	0.0	0.4	1.0	1.4	4.0
Las Vegas, NV	78.8	9.8	3.3	0.0	0.0	0.3	1.5	2.2	4.2
Lexington, KY	79.9	9.3	1.3	0.0	0.0	0.4	3.1	1.3	4.6
Lincoln, NE	81.3	8.9	1.1	0.0	0.0	1.1	3.3	0.6	3.7
Little Rock, AR	83.9	9.5	0.5	0.0	0.0	0.2	1.3	1.1	3.5
Los Angeles, CA	75.1	9.5	4.1	0.4	0.3	0.7	2.5	1.6	5.8
Louisville, KY	82.0	8.5	1.8	0.0	0.0	0.2	1.6	1.3	4.6

Table continued on following page.

Metro Area	Car/Truck/Van		Public Transportation			Bicycle	Walked	Other Means	Worked at Home
	Drove Alone	Car-pooled	Bus	Subway	Railroad				
Madison, WI	75.0	7.5	4.2	0.0	0.0	2.2	5.0	0.9	5.1
Manchester, NH	81.4	8.1	0.8	0.0	0.1	0.1	2.1	0.9	6.4
Memphis, TN	84.6	9.2	0.7	0.0	0.0	0.1	1.0	1.1	3.3
Miami, FL	77.9	9.1	2.8	0.3	0.2	0.6	1.6	1.8	5.7
Midland, TX	84.8	9.7	0.2	0.0	0.0	0.1	1.1	0.8	3.3
Milwaukee, WI	80.9	7.8	3.1	0.0	0.1	0.5	2.6	0.7	4.3
Minneapolis, MN	77.5	8.1	4.1	0.2	0.2	0.8	2.3	1.1	5.8
Nashville, TN	80.8	9.4	0.9	0.0	0.1	0.1	1.3	1.1	6.3
New Haven, CT	78.3	8.4	2.8	0.1	0.9	0.5	3.3	1.0	4.7
New Orleans, LA	78.1	9.8	2.3	0.0	0.0	1.1	2.5	1.7	4.5
New York, NY	49.2	6.3	7.5	20.0	3.9	0.7	5.9	2.0	4.5
Oklahoma City, OK	83.2	9.4	0.4	0.0	0.0	0.3	1.6	1.0	4.1
Omaha, NE	83.8	8.2	0.8	0.0	0.0	0.2	1.7	1.0	4.2
Orlando, FL	79.7	9.8	1.5	0.0	0.1	0.4	1.1	1.6	5.9
Peoria, IL	84.9	7.3	1.1	0.0	0.0	0.3	2.1	0.9	3.6
Philadelphia, PA	72.5	7.6	5.0	1.9	2.3	0.6	3.6	1.3	5.2
Phoenix, AZ	76.1	11.1	1.7	0.1	0.0	0.8	1.5	1.8	7.0
Pittsburgh, PA	76.6	8.3	5.1	0.2	0.0	0.3	3.4	1.1	5.0
Portland, OR	70.3	9.1	4.8	0.7	0.2	2.2	3.4	2.0	7.4
Providence, RI	80.7	8.6	1.5	0.2	1.0	0.2	3.1	0.8	3.9
Provo, UT	73.1	11.4	1.1	0.2	0.9	0.9	4.1	1.2	7.2
Raleigh, NC	79.7	8.3	0.8	0.0	0.0	0.2	1.1	0.9	8.9
Reno, NV	77.2	12.0	1.8	0.0	0.0	0.6	2.6	1.1	4.7
Richmond, VA	81.1	8.6	1.4	0.0	0.1	0.5	1.7	1.3	5.3
Riverside, CA	78.9	11.5	0.9	0.1	0.4	0.3	1.5	1.3	5.3
Rochester, MN	74.1	11.5	4.0	0.0	0.0	0.6	3.6	0.8	5.3
Sacramento, CA	76.8	9.4	1.6	0.2	0.2	1.4	1.8	1.5	7.1
Salt Lake City, UT	75.4	11.1	2.1	0.3	0.5	0.8	2.1	1.5	6.2
San Antonio, TX	79.5	10.7	1.9	0.0	0.0	0.2	1.7	1.3	4.7
San Diego, CA	76.2	8.6	2.5	0.0	0.2	0.6	2.9	1.9	7.0
San Francisco, CA	57.6	9.5	7.6	7.6	1.5	1.9	4.7	3.0	6.6
San Jose, CA	74.9	10.6	2.4	0.3	1.5	1.7	2.1	1.6	5.0
Santa Rosa, CA	74.6	11.3	1.6	0.0	0.2	1.0	2.7	1.3	7.4
Savannah, GA	79.5	9.7	1.8	0.1	0.0	0.8	2.4	1.6	4.2
Seattle, WA	67.5	10.0	8.7	0.4	0.5	1.1	4.0	1.5	6.2
Sioux Falls, SD	84.3	8.1	0.5	0.0	0.0	0.4	2.1	0.6	4.1
Springfield, IL	83.3	8.0	1.3	0.1	0.0	0.5	1.7	1.0	4.3
Tallahassee, FL	81.1	9.2	1.4	0.0	0.0	0.6	2.0	1.3	4.3
Tampa, FL	78.9	8.8	1.3	0.0	0.0	0.6	1.4	1.6	7.4
Tucson, AZ	76.8	10.0	2.2	0.0	0.0	1.5	2.3	1.8	5.4
Tulsa, OK	82.8	9.6	0.4	0.0	0.0	0.2	1.2	1.5	4.2
Tuscaloosa, AL	85.3	9.0	0.5	0.0	0.0	0.2	1.1	0.5	3.4
Virginia Beach, VA	81.3	8.3	1.4	0.0	0.0	0.4	3.3	1.4	3.8
Washington, DC	65.8	9.3	4.8	7.8	0.8	0.9	3.3	1.5	5.9
Wichita, KS	84.0	8.7	0.4	0.0	0.0	0.4	1.7	1.2	3.5
Winston-Salem, NC	83.6	8.9	0.7	0.0	0.0	0.1	1.3	0.9	4.5
U.S.	76.3	9.0	2.4	1.9	0.6	0.5	2.7	1.4	5.2

Note: Figures are percentages and cover workers 16 years of age and older; (1) Figures cover the Metropolitan Statistical Area—see Appendix B for areas included
Source: U.S. Census Bureau, 2015-2019 American Community Survey 5-Year Estimates

Travel Time to Work: City

City	Less Than 10 Minutes	10 to 19 Minutes	20 to 29 Minutes	30 to 44 Minutes	45 to 59 Minutes	60 to 89 Minutes	90 Minutes or More
Albuquerque, NM	11.1	35.8	28.1	17.7	3.1	2.8	1.4
Allentown, PA	11.5	34.8	28.6	14.6	4.2	4.1	2.2
Anchorage, AK	16.3	44.7	23.7	10.4	2.3	1.1	1.5
Ann Arbor, MI	12.9	45.5	19.9	13.3	5.3	2.4	0.7
Athens, GA	17.4	48.3	16.9	8.8	3.6	3.0	2.0
Atlanta, GA	6.8	28.7	26.4	22.2	7.6	5.2	3.1
Austin, TX	9.5	31.8	24.3	22.1	7.1	3.8	1.4
Baton Rouge, LA	11.9	39.3	25.5	15.1	3.6	2.8	1.9
Boise City, ID	13.7	46.2	25.8	10.4	1.5	1.3	1.1
Boston, MA	7.1	19.1	19.6	30.3	12.1	9.6	2.2
Boulder, CO	17.6	45.9	16.3	10.3	5.6	3.3	1.0
Cape Coral, FL	7.9	23.9	23.5	26.5	10.4	5.8	2.0
Cedar Rapids, IA	18.0	49.5	18.0	9.7	2.2	1.5	1.1
Charleston, SC	11.4	31.9	26.3	21.1	6.5	1.5	1.3
Charlotte, NC	8.2	28.3	26.6	24.4	7.1	3.5	2.0
Chicago, IL	4.5	16.0	17.4	30.6	15.3	12.8	3.5
Cincinnati, OH	11.0	33.2	27.0	19.2	4.5	3.2	1.9
Clarksville, TN	10.8	34.3	24.5	15.6	5.7	7.4	1.7
Cleveland, OH	9.4	33.3	27.0	19.5	5.0	3.7	2.0
College Station, TX	16.5	56.7	17.6	5.9	0.5	1.8	1.2
Colorado Springs, CO	11.6	35.9	28.5	15.2	3.5	3.0	2.3
Columbia, MO	20.2	55.0	11.8	8.2	2.8	0.8	1.2
Columbia, SC	31.3	36.6	17.6	9.7	1.8	1.8	1.2
Columbus, OH	10.0	34.5	29.8	18.8	3.7	2.1	1.1
Dallas, TX	7.9	26.6	23.0	26.5	8.0	5.9	2.0
Davenport, IA	17.0	47.8	20.8	9.0	3.1	1.2	1.0
Denver, CO	7.5	28.5	24.6	26.0	8.0	3.9	1.5
Des Moines, IA	13.0	43.8	27.2	11.9	1.9	1.1	1.0
Durham, NC	9.4	37.4	26.3	18.0	4.5	3.0	1.6
Edison, NJ	6.4	23.1	17.4	18.1	11.2	14.0	9.7
El Paso, TX	9.8	34.4	27.7	19.6	4.4	2.2	1.9
Fargo, ND	20.9	54.9	17.6	3.3	1.0	1.4	0.8
Fayetteville, NC	20.6	37.5	22.3	12.5	3.3	2.1	1.6
Fort Collins, CO	16.5	42.6	19.9	11.0	5.1	3.5	1.4
Fort Wayne, IN	12.2	40.5	27.4	12.5	3.1	2.4	1.9
Fort Worth, TX	8.4	28.3	22.5	23.9	8.7	6.2	2.0
Grand Rapids, MI	15.0	42.9	24.4	11.6	3.3	2.0	0.9
Greeley, CO	16.1	37.4	16.2	14.7	5.9	7.4	2.3
Green Bay, WI	18.1	48.8	19.4	7.7	3.1	1.8	1.1
Greensboro, NC	12.1	41.4	24.1	14.7	3.5	2.6	1.6
Honolulu, HI	7.9	35.3	23.7	22.0	5.5	4.3	1.4
Houston, TX	7.3	25.5	22.2	27.8	8.9	6.4	1.9
Huntsville, AL	12.8	41.7	26.3	15.2	2.3	0.7	0.9
Indianapolis, IN	9.7	30.0	29.9	22.1	4.3	2.5	1.5
Jacksonville, FL	8.3	27.7	27.5	25.6	6.5	2.9	1.6
Kansas City, MO	11.4	33.4	28.1	20.0	4.5	1.6	1.1
Lafayette, LA	16.4	42.1	20.4	12.5	2.5	2.8	3.3
Lakeland, FL	10.8	43.4	20.1	14.4	5.8	3.5	2.0
Las Vegas, NV	6.9	23.9	29.3	28.7	6.4	2.7	2.0
Lexington, KY	12.4	38.0	27.6	14.9	3.2	2.5	1.4
Lincoln, NE	17.2	44.8	23.1	9.3	2.5	2.1	1.1
Little Rock, AR	14.0	44.4	26.5	10.8	2.0	1.3	1.1
Los Angeles, CA	5.9	21.8	19.0	28.3	10.8	10.5	3.8
Louisville, KY	9.3	32.4	30.1	20.3	4.4	2.2	1.4
Madison, WI	14.4	40.7	24.1	15.3	2.9	1.9	0.8

Table continued on following page.

City	Less Than 10 Minutes	10 to 19 Minutes	20 to 29 Minutes	30 to 44 Minutes	45 to 59 Minutes	60 to 89 Minutes	90 Minutes or More
Manchester, NH	14.1	38.3	19.2	14.5	5.9	4.8	3.2
Memphis, TN	10.2	32.9	30.2	20.5	3.6	1.6	1.0
Miami, FL	4.9	21.3	22.7	31.7	10.2	7.4	1.8
Midland, TX	16.1	49.1	17.2	11.1	2.6	2.0	1.9
Milwaukee, WI	10.1	36.6	25.8	19.3	4.0	2.7	1.5
Minneapolis, MN	8.1	32.0	30.9	20.9	4.2	2.8	1.2
Nashville, TN	8.7	29.1	26.2	23.8	7.2	3.5	1.5
New Haven, CT	13.6	40.4	20.1	13.1	4.7	4.7	3.4
New Orleans, LA	9.9	33.9	25.4	19.7	4.5	4.2	2.3
New York, NY	3.8	12.1	13.4	27.1	16.4	19.5	7.7
Oklahoma City, OK	11.2	35.5	29.5	17.7	3.3	1.5	1.3
Omaha, NE	14.0	41.0	27.8	12.4	2.3	1.5	0.9
Orlando, FL	7.8	27.2	25.9	26.7	6.8	3.4	2.2
Peoria, IL	18.6	49.5	19.8	7.6	1.9	1.8	0.8
Philadelphia, PA	6.1	18.7	19.7	28.0	12.6	10.6	4.4
Phoenix, AZ	8.8	26.7	25.5	24.9	7.5	4.7	1.9
Pittsburgh, PA	9.4	31.5	25.8	22.9	5.1	3.7	1.6
Portland, OR	7.8	26.3	27.0	24.5	7.7	4.9	1.8
Providence, RI	12.2	39.9	20.8	14.3	5.6	4.1	3.1
Provo, UT	21.3	45.3	17.3	9.0	2.7	2.9	1.4
Raleigh, NC	9.8	33.0	25.8	21.0	5.7	3.1	1.7
Reno, NV	14.4	43.5	22.1	12.1	3.7	2.7	1.5
Richmond, VA	9.8	37.9	28.5	16.4	3.2	2.6	1.5
Riverside, CA	8.9	26.2	19.9	21.7	7.6	9.4	6.4
Rochester, MN	19.3	55.7	13.6	6.3	2.2	1.7	1.2
Sacramento, CA	8.0	31.2	25.1	22.5	5.9	4.0	3.3
Salt Lake City, UT	12.3	45.3	22.8	13.0	3.6	1.9	1.0
San Antonio, TX	8.5	30.8	27.2	22.1	6.1	3.3	2.0
San Diego, CA	7.6	32.1	27.6	21.7	5.7	3.4	1.8
San Francisco, CA	3.8	18.0	20.5	30.3	12.3	11.2	3.9
San Jose, CA	5.1	22.4	22.1	27.7	10.8	8.7	3.1
Santa Rosa, CA	13.8	39.2	21.7	13.6	3.9	4.6	3.2
Savannah, GA	16.0	40.0	22.3	12.8	4.4	3.2	1.4
Seattle, WA	6.7	23.4	24.4	28.6	10.5	5.0	1.5
Sioux Falls, SD	16.1	52.3	22.4	5.4	1.4	1.3	1.1
Springfield, IL	18.2	51.5	18.5	6.1	1.8	2.3	1.6
Tallahassee, FL	14.6	44.7	23.9	12.3	2.1	1.3	1.0
Tampa, FL	11.1	30.5	23.6	21.8	6.7	4.3	1.9
Tucson, AZ	11.9	34.4	25.0	19.7	4.8	2.5	1.6
Tulsa, OK	14.6	44.5	25.7	10.5	2.0	1.5	1.2
Tuscaloosa, AL	14.6	44.8	25.9	7.4	3.5	2.8	1.0
Virginia Beach, VA	10.7	29.8	28.1	22.3	5.1	2.7	1.4
Washington, DC	4.9	18.5	22.5	32.4	12.6	7.1	2.0
Wichita, KS	14.2	44.9	27.2	9.7	1.7	1.2	1.2
Winston-Salem, NC	13.6	40.8	23.8	13.7	4.2	2.1	1.8
U.S.	12.2	28.4	20.8	20.8	8.3	6.4	2.9

Note: Figures are percentages and include workers 16 years old and over
Source: U.S. Census Bureau, 2015-2019 American Community Survey 5-Year Estimates

Travel Time to Work: Metro Area

Metro Area	Less Than 10 Minutes	10 to 19 Minutes	20 to 29 Minutes	30 to 44 Minutes	45 to 59 Minutes	60 to 89 Minutes	90 Minutes or More
Albuquerque, NM	10.8	31.6	26.2	20.5	5.7	3.6	1.6
Allentown, PA	12.4	27.6	23.1	18.1	7.4	7.3	4.1
Anchorage, AK	15.7	41.0	21.8	10.8	4.3	4.0	2.5
Ann Arbor, MI	10.6	32.7	24.5	19.3	7.6	4.1	1.3
Athens, GA	14.1	41.1	21.4	12.9	4.7	3.5	2.2
Atlanta, GA	7.0	22.1	19.6	24.9	12.3	10.4	3.8
Austin, TX	9.6	27.1	22.3	23.1	10.0	6.1	1.8
Baton Rouge, LA	9.8	27.7	22.0	22.5	9.2	6.5	2.3
Boise City, ID	12.7	34.6	25.6	18.4	5.1	2.2	1.3
Boston, MA	9.0	22.0	17.9	24.4	12.1	11.0	3.7
Boulder, CO	13.7	34.4	21.4	17.6	7.0	4.6	1.3
Cape Coral, FL	8.7	25.3	23.1	25.6	10.2	5.1	2.0
Cedar Rapids, IA	17.4	40.6	21.6	13.1	3.9	2.0	1.3
Charleston, SC	8.7	25.6	24.3	26.0	9.3	4.4	1.7
Charlotte, NC	9.3	27.1	22.7	24.0	9.6	5.2	2.1
Chicago, IL	8.2	21.5	18.4	25.2	12.4	10.8	3.5
Cincinnati, OH	10.9	27.5	25.3	23.4	7.8	3.6	1.5
Clarksville, TN	15.2	32.1	21.1	17.4	6.1	6.0	2.1
Cleveland, OH	11.2	28.3	25.5	23.1	7.3	3.3	1.4
College Station, TX	15.6	49.4	19.1	10.1	2.3	2.1	1.5
Colorado Springs, CO	11.6	32.8	27.2	17.4	5.0	3.7	2.3
Columbia, MO	17.5	45.5	17.3	12.4	4.3	1.5	1.4
Columbia, SC	12.5	29.6	23.5	22.3	6.8	3.4	1.9
Columbus, OH	11.0	29.7	26.3	21.8	6.6	3.2	1.4
Dallas, TX	8.6	25.0	21.3	25.6	10.5	7.0	2.1
Davenport, IA	17.9	37.4	24.3	13.6	3.7	1.9	1.3
Denver, CO	8.0	24.9	23.0	26.3	10.2	5.8	1.8
Des Moines, IA	15.2	35.2	27.3	16.3	3.4	1.5	1.1
Durham, NC	9.8	31.6	24.8	21.2	6.8	4.2	1.5
Edison, NJ	6.7	18.2	16.1	23.9	12.7	15.3	7.1
El Paso, TX	10.7	32.6	26.8	20.6	4.9	2.4	2.0
Fargo, ND	18.5	50.6	19.3	7.0	2.0	1.6	1.1
Fayetteville, NC	14.4	29.4	23.3	20.1	6.6	4.1	2.1
Fort Collins, CO	14.5	34.6	22.0	15.6	6.4	5.1	1.9
Fort Wayne, IN	12.7	36.5	28.2	15.0	3.5	2.3	1.8
Fort Worth, TX	8.6	25.0	21.3	25.6	10.5	7.0	2.1
Grand Rapids, MI	14.8	35.3	24.9	16.1	5.0	2.5	1.5
Greeley, CO	11.9	27.1	19.2	22.3	9.5	7.5	2.5
Green Bay, WI	18.1	40.0	21.7	12.9	3.8	2.0	1.5
Greensboro, NC	12.2	34.8	25.3	18.4	5.0	2.6	1.7
Honolulu, HI	9.0	24.9	19.6	25.3	9.8	8.5	3.0
Houston, TX	7.7	23.3	19.4	26.5	11.8	8.9	2.5
Huntsville, AL	10.3	32.1	27.8	21.7	5.6	1.6	1.0
Indianapolis, IN	11.4	27.5	24.4	24.1	7.6	3.5	1.5
Jacksonville, FL	8.8	25.4	24.4	26.0	9.0	4.5	1.8
Kansas City, MO	12.2	30.7	25.2	21.7	6.6	2.6	1.1
Lafayette, LA	15.1	32.4	21.0	18.4	5.2	3.7	4.3
Lakeland, FL	8.4	30.0	21.7	21.0	9.9	6.3	2.7
Las Vegas, NV	7.4	27.5	29.0	26.1	5.4	2.7	1.9
Lexington, KY	14.3	34.6	25.1	17.7	4.5	2.5	1.3
Lincoln, NE	17.1	41.8	23.8	11.2	2.9	2.0	1.2
Little Rock, AR	12.6	33.0	23.4	19.9	7.0	2.8	1.3
Los Angeles, CA	6.9	24.4	19.5	25.4	10.2	9.8	3.7
Louisville, KY	9.7	29.9	27.3	22.6	6.4	2.6	1.5
Madison, WI	15.6	32.6	24.3	18.6	5.2	2.5	1.1

Table continued on following page.

Metro Area	Less Than 10 Minutes	10 to 19 Minutes	20 to 29 Minutes	30 to 44 Minutes	45 to 59 Minutes	60 to 89 Minutes	90 Minutes or More
Manchester, NH	11.1	29.7	19.7	19.8	8.6	7.2	3.9
Memphis, TN	10.2	28.3	26.7	24.1	6.8	2.7	1.2
Miami, FL	6.4	22.6	22.0	27.9	10.3	8.1	2.7
Midland, TX	15.8	46.2	17.9	12.5	3.1	2.6	1.8
Milwaukee, WI	11.9	31.6	25.8	21.3	5.5	2.5	1.4
Minneapolis, MN	10.2	27.3	25.1	23.7	8.1	4.3	1.4
Nashville, TN	9.2	26.5	21.7	23.4	10.6	6.6	2.0
New Haven, CT	11.5	31.8	22.9	19.5	6.6	4.8	2.9
New Orleans, LA	10.5	30.6	22.2	20.9	7.6	5.6	2.5
New York, NY	6.7	18.2	16.1	23.9	12.7	15.3	7.1
Oklahoma City, OK	12.3	32.0	25.7	20.3	5.7	2.4	1.5
Omaha, NE	13.9	36.4	27.5	15.8	3.7	1.7	1.0
Orlando, FL	7.1	22.9	22.9	28.1	11.1	5.6	2.3
Peoria, IL	18.6	34.8	23.6	15.1	4.4	2.1	1.4
Philadelphia, PA	9.2	23.6	20.3	24.0	11.1	8.5	3.3
Phoenix, AZ	9.9	26.2	23.7	23.7	9.0	5.7	1.9
Pittsburgh, PA	11.8	26.6	21.0	22.8	9.5	6.2	2.1
Portland, OR	10.2	26.9	22.6	23.1	9.3	5.8	2.1
Providence, RI	11.9	29.9	21.9	19.6	7.6	5.9	3.2
Provo, UT	18.0	35.3	20.1	15.5	5.6	3.9	1.6
Raleigh, NC	8.9	27.5	24.4	23.9	8.7	4.8	1.9
Reno, NV	12.1	37.7	25.0	16.6	4.2	2.7	1.7
Richmond, VA	8.7	29.1	27.4	23.2	6.3	3.1	2.0
Riverside, CA	9.4	26.2	18.6	19.7	8.5	10.4	7.2
Rochester, MN	18.9	41.6	18.4	12.8	3.9	2.7	1.7
Sacramento, CA	9.9	28.2	22.3	23.0	8.1	4.9	3.5
Salt Lake City, UT	10.5	33.4	27.0	19.6	5.6	2.8	1.1
San Antonio, TX	9.0	28.1	24.3	23.2	8.5	4.7	2.2
San Diego, CA	8.2	28.9	24.3	23.5	7.7	5.1	2.2
San Francisco, CA	6.4	22.0	17.4	23.7	12.5	12.9	5.1
San Jose, CA	6.6	25.0	22.6	25.1	9.6	7.8	3.2
Santa Rosa, CA	15.1	32.2	20.4	16.8	5.8	5.9	3.9
Savannah, GA	11.0	30.6	24.1	21.2	7.7	4.1	1.3
Seattle, WA	7.7	22.2	20.8	25.5	11.4	9.0	3.4
Sioux Falls, SD	16.5	44.0	24.6	10.0	2.4	1.4	1.2
Springfield, IL	15.6	42.6	23.6	11.5	2.7	2.3	1.7
Tallahassee, FL	11.0	34.3	24.8	20.4	5.6	2.4	1.5
Tampa, FL	9.6	26.9	21.6	23.0	10.1	6.5	2.3
Tucson, AZ	10.7	28.9	24.6	23.6	7.4	3.0	1.9
Tulsa, OK	13.3	33.9	26.5	18.1	4.5	2.2	1.4
Tuscaloosa, AL	11.3	32.4	26.5	16.5	6.6	5.0	1.7
Virginia Beach, VA	11.3	30.6	23.9	21.4	7.1	4.0	1.7
Washington, DC	5.9	18.9	17.7	25.7	14.2	13.1	4.6
Wichita, KS	16.3	37.5	26.5	14.3	2.8	1.4	1.3
Winston-Salem, NC	12.0	33.3	24.5	19.1	6.1	2.8	2.1
U.S.	12.2	28.4	20.8	20.8	8.3	6.4	2.9

Note: Figures are percentages and include workers 16 years old and over; Figures cover the Metropolitan Statistical Area—see Appendix B for areas included
Source: U.S. Census Bureau, 2015-2019 American Community Survey 5-Year Estimates

2020 Presidential Election Results

City	Area Covered	Biden	Trump	Jorgensen	Hawkins	Other
Albuquerque, NM	Bernalillo County	61.0	36.6	1.5	0.5	0.4
Allentown, PA	Lehigh County	53.1	45.5	1.2	0.1	0.2
Anchorage, AK	State of Alaska	42.8	52.8	2.5	0.0	1.9
Ann Arbor, MI	Washtenaw County	72.4	25.9	0.9	0.3	0.4
Athens, GA	Clarke County	70.1	28.1	1.6	0.1	0.1
Atlanta, GA	Fulton County	72.6	26.2	1.2	0.0	0.0
Austin, TX	Travis County	71.4	26.4	1.5	0.3	0.4
Baton Rouge, LA	East Baton Rouge Parish	55.5	42.5	1.2	0.0	0.8
Boise City, ID	Ada County	46.1	50.0	2.0	0.1	1.8
Boston, MA	Suffolk County	80.6	17.5	0.9	0.5	0.5
Boulder, CO	Boulder County	77.2	20.6	1.2	0.3	0.6
Cape Coral, FL	Lee County	39.9	59.1	0.5	0.1	0.3
Cedar Rapids, IA	Linn County	55.6	41.9	1.6	0.3	0.7
Charleston, SC	Charleston County	55.5	42.6	1.5	0.3	0.1
Charlotte, NC	Mecklenburg County	66.7	31.6	1.0	0.3	0.5
Chicago, IL	Cook County	74.2	24.0	0.8	0.5	0.5
Cincinnati, OH	Hamilton County	57.1	41.3	1.2	0.3	0.0
Clarksville, TN	Montgomery County	42.3	55.0	1.9	0.2	0.7
Cleveland, OH	Cuyahoga County	66.4	32.3	0.7	0.3	0.3
College Station, TX	Brazos County	41.6	55.9	2.1	0.3	0.1
Colorado Springs, CO	El Paso County	42.7	53.5	2.4	0.3	1.0
Columbia, MO	Boone County	54.8	42.3	2.2	0.3	0.4
Columbia, SC	Richland County	68.4	30.1	1.0	0.4	0.1
Columbus, OH	Franklin County	64.7	33.4	1.2	0.3	0.4
Dallas, TX	Dallas County	64.9	33.3	1.0	0.4	0.4
Davenport, IA	Scott County	50.7	47.2	1.2	0.2	0.7
Denver, CO	Denver County	79.6	18.2	1.2	0.3	0.7
Des Moines, IA	Polk County	56.5	41.3	1.3	0.2	0.7
Durham, NC	Durham County	80.4	18.0	0.8	0.3	0.4
Edison, NJ	Middlesex County	60.2	38.2	0.7	0.3	0.6
El Paso, TX	El Paso County	66.7	31.6	1.0	0.5	0.2
Fargo, ND	Cass County	46.8	49.5	2.9	0.0	0.7
Fayetteville, NC	Cumberland County	57.4	40.8	1.1	0.3	0.4
Fort Collins, CO	Larimer County	56.2	40.8	1.8	0.3	0.9
Fort Wayne, IN	Allen County	43.2	54.3	2.2	0.0	0.3
Fort Worth, TX	Tarrant County	49.3	49.1	1.2	0.3	0.0
Grand Rapids, MI	Kent County	51.9	45.8	1.5	0.3	0.5
Greeley, CO	Weld County	39.6	57.6	1.7	0.2	0.9
Green Bay, WI	Brown County	45.5	52.7	1.3	0.0	0.5
Greensboro, NC	Guilford County	60.8	37.7	0.8	0.2	0.4
Honolulu, HI	Honolulu County	62.5	35.7	0.9	0.6	0.4
Houston, TX	Harris County	56.0	42.7	1.0	0.3	0.0
Huntsville, AL	Madison County	44.8	52.8	1.9	0.0	0.5
Indianapolis, IN	Marion County	63.3	34.3	1.8	0.1	0.4
Jacksonville, FL	Duval County	51.1	47.3	1.0	0.2	0.5
Kansas City, MO	Jackson County	59.8	37.9	1.4	0.4	0.5
Lafayette, LA	Lafayette Parish	34.7	63.3	1.3	0.0	0.7
Lakeland, FL	Polk County	42.2	56.6	0.8	0.1	0.4
Las Vegas, NV	Clark County	53.7	44.3	0.9	0.0	1.1
Lexington, KY	Fayette County	59.2	38.5	1.6	0.1	0.6
Lincoln, NE	Lancaster County	52.3	44.6	2.4	0.0	0.7
Little Rock, AR	Pulaski County	60.0	37.5	1.0	0.3	1.3
Los Angeles, CA	Los Angeles County	71.0	26.9	0.8	0.5	0.8
Louisville, KY	Jefferson County	59.1	39.0	1.2	0.1	0.7
Madison, WI	Dane County	75.5	22.9	1.1	0.1	0.6
Manchester, NH	Hillsborough County	52.8	45.2	1.7	0.0	0.3

Table continued on following page.

City	Area Covered	Biden	Trump	Jorgensen	Hawkins	Other
Memphis, TN	Shelby County	64.4	34.0	0.6	0.2	0.8
Miami, FL	Miami-Dade County	53.3	46.0	0.3	0.1	0.3
Midland, TX	Midland County	20.9	77.3	1.3	0.2	0.2
Milwaukee, WI	Milwaukee County	69.1	29.3	0.9	0.0	0.7
Minneapolis, MN	Hennepin County	70.5	27.2	1.0	0.3	1.0
Nashville, TN	Davidson County	64.5	32.4	1.1	0.2	1.8
New Haven, CT	New Haven County	58.0	40.6	0.9	0.4	0.0
New Orleans, LA	Orleans Parish	83.1	15.0	0.9	0.0	1.0
New York, NY	Bronx County	83.3	15.9	0.2	0.3	0.3
New York, NY	Kings County	76.8	22.1	0.3	0.4	0.4
New York, NY	New York County	86.4	12.2	0.5	0.4	0.5
New York, NY	Queens County	72.0	26.9	0.3	0.4	0.4
New York, NY	Richmond County	42.0	56.9	0.4	0.3	0.4
Oklahoma City, OK	Oklahoma County	48.1	49.2	1.8	0.0	0.9
Omaha, NE	Douglas County	54.4	43.1	2.0	0.0	0.6
Orlando, FL	Orange County	60.9	37.8	0.7	0.2	0.4
Peoria, IL	Peoria County	51.9	45.6	1.6	0.6	0.4
Philadelphia, PA	Philadelphia County	81.2	17.9	0.7	0.1	0.2
Phoenix, AZ	Maricopa County	50.1	48.0	1.5	0.0	0.3
Pittsburgh, PA	Allegheny County	59.4	39.0	1.2	0.0	0.4
Portland, OR	Multnomah County	79.2	17.9	1.2	0.6	1.0
Providence, RI	Providence County	60.5	37.6	0.8	0.0	1.0
Provo, UT	Utah County	26.3	66.7	3.6	0.3	3.1
Raleigh, NC	Wake County	62.3	35.8	1.2	0.3	0.5
Reno, NV	Washoe County	50.8	46.3	1.4	0.0	1.5
Richmond, VA	Richmond City	82.9	14.9	1.5	0.0	0.6
Riverside, CA	Riverside County	53.0	45.0	1.0	0.3	0.6
Rochester, MN	Olmsted County	54.2	43.4	1.2	0.3	0.9
Sacramento, CA	Sacramento County	61.4	36.1	1.4	0.5	0.7
Salt Lake City, UT	Salt Lake County	53.0	42.1	2.2	0.4	2.2
San Antonio, TX	Bexar County	58.2	40.1	1.1	0.4	0.2
San Diego, CA	San Diego County	60.2	37.5	1.3	0.5	0.5
San Francisco, CA	San Francisco County	85.3	12.7	0.7	0.6	0.7
San Jose, CA	Santa Clara County	72.6	25.2	1.1	0.5	0.6
Santa Rosa, CA	Sonoma County	74.5	23.0	1.3	0.6	0.6
Savannah, GA	Chatham County	58.6	39.9	1.4	0.0	0.0
Seattle, WA	King County	75.0	22.2	1.5	0.5	0.8
Sioux Falls, SD	Minnehaha County	43.8	53.3	2.8	0.0	0.0
Springfield, IL	Sangamon County	46.7	51.1	1.4	0.6	0.3
Tallahassee, FL	Leon County	63.3	35.1	0.8	0.2	0.5
Tampa, FL	Hillsborough County	52.7	45.8	0.8	0.2	0.5
Tucson, AZ	Pima County	58.4	39.8	1.5	0.0	0.3
Tulsa, OK	Tulsa County	40.9	56.5	1.8	0.0	0.8
Tuscaloosa, AL	Tuscaloosa County	41.9	56.7	1.0	0.0	0.4
Virginia Beach, VA	Virginia Beach City	51.6	46.2	1.8	0.0	0.4
Washington, DC	District of Columbia	92.1	5.4	0.6	0.5	1.4
Wichita, KS	Sedgwick County	42.6	54.4	2.4	0.0	0.5
Winston-Salem, NC	Forsyth County	56.2	42.3	0.9	0.2	0.4
U.S.	U.S.	51.3	46.8	1.2	0.3	0.5

Note: Results are percentages and may not add to 100% due to rounding
Source: Dave Leip's Atlas of U.S. Presidential Elections

House Price Index (HPI)

Metro Area[1]	National Ranking[3]	Quarterly Change (%)	One-Year Change (%)	Five-Year Change (%)	Since 1991Q1 (%)
Albuquerque, NM	42	2.20	7.86	27.05	163.46
Allentown, PA	59	2.10	7.47	23.78	102.86
Anchorage, AK	205	1.39	4.88	9.73	184.56
Ann Arbor, MI	224	0.98	3.78	29.65	164.45
Athens, GA	66	1.41	7.40	43.79	181.78
Atlanta, GA	110	1.95	6.57	40.75	164.55
Austin, TX	30	3.27	8.26	41.08	401.86
Baton Rouge, LA	230	1.37	3.54	17.61	188.52
Boise City, ID	1	4.90	13.83	78.91	350.41
Boston, MA[2]	167	1.93	5.51	29.37	228.40
Boulder, CO	227	1.79	3.59	36.23	436.16
Cape Coral, FL	84	3.11	7.07	33.53	188.18
Cedar Rapids, IA	218	1.99	4.00	17.00	130.16
Charleston, SC	130	1.32	6.11	36.39	284.93
Charlotte, NC	60	2.55	7.46	41.48	183.15
Chicago, IL[2]	239	1.11	2.98	16.74	122.65
Cincinnati, OH	98	1.97	6.79	31.23	131.06
Clarksville, TN	n/a	n/a	n/a	n/a	n/a
Cleveland, OH	50	2.24	7.63	30.38	104.70
College Station, TX	n/a	n/a	n/a	n/a	n/a
Colorado Springs, CO	19	3.08	8.89	51.30	301.84
Columbia, MO	212	1.63	4.42	20.40	150.92
Columbia, SC	181	1.37	5.23	24.67	125.47
Columbus, OH	65	2.05	7.40	37.73	163.06
Dallas, TX[2]	206	2.07	4.81	38.75	203.48
Davenport, IA	225	0.97	3.73	15.46	153.27
Denver, CO	164	1.71	5.57	42.32	404.42
Des Moines, IA	237	1.39	3.15	20.11	154.39
Durham, NC	161	1.51	5.61	34.97	182.89
Edison, NJ[2]	220	1.50	3.91	23.15	199.59
El Paso, TX	158	1.05	5.68	18.03	118.41
Fargo, ND	240	0.70	2.82	16.07	201.82
Fayetteville, NC	n/a	n/a	n/a	n/a	n/a
Fort Collins, CO	217	1.38	4.19	38.15	365.72
Fort Wayne, IN	53	1.29	7.55	35.84	111.44
Fort Worth, TX[2]	191	2.39	5.13	42.54	191.04
Grand Rapids, MI	71	2.11	7.32	44.57	175.35
Greeley, CO	177	1.80	5.33	46.65	333.63
Green Bay, WI	169	2.46	5.48	28.92	157.42
Greensboro, NC	128	1.99	6.14	27.91	106.32
Honolulu, HI	250	1.23	0.53	16.08	154.83
Houston, TX	211	1.45	4.53	23.50	211.24
Huntsville, AL	9	3.60	9.98	30.56	124.28
Indianapolis, IN	46	2.17	7.74	36.43	135.15
Jacksonville, FL	136	2.34	6.06	43.85	224.14
Kansas City, MO	75	2.00	7.29	37.81	175.77
Lafayette, LA	221	0.62	3.89	8.70	180.99
Lakeland, FL	8	4.29	10.11	53.44	194.73
Las Vegas, NV	171	1.70	5.46	50.47	163.25
Lexington, KY	200	1.46	5.04	28.47	155.18
Lincoln, NE	198	2.22	5.09	30.00	177.71
Little Rock, AR	196	1.79	5.10	16.24	131.58
Los Angeles, CA[2]	193	1.98	5.13	31.04	214.04
Louisville, KY	111	2.46	6.56	29.08	178.89
Madison, WI	202	1.80	4.96	27.32	218.96

Table continued on following page.

Metro Area[1]	National Ranking[3]	Quarterly Change (%)	One-Year Change (%)	Five-Year Change (%)	Since 1991Q1 (%)
Manchester, NH	17	3.48	9.02	33.95	167.53
Memphis, TN	90	1.82	6.94	33.17	120.34
Miami, FL[2]	124	1.83	6.32	38.91	334.89
Midland, TX	n/a	n/a	n/a	n/a	n/a
Milwaukee, WI	172	1.59	5.45	26.53	171.34
Minneapolis, MN	157	1.56	5.70	30.96	210.96
Nashville, TN	88	1.88	6.96	45.40	266.19
New Haven, CT	99	2.80	6.78	15.33	80.58
New Orleans, LA	174	2.09	5.37	22.52	226.15
New York, NY[2]	220	1.50	3.91	23.15	199.59
Oklahoma City, OK	182	1.07	5.23	21.46	179.09
Omaha, NE	154	1.72	5.74	31.76	176.42
Orlando, FL	119	1.83	6.36	44.80	198.33
Peoria, IL	238	0.87	3.00	6.40	120.92
Philadelphia, PA[2]	145	1.50	5.90	33.20	191.57
Phoenix, AZ	7	3.44	10.26	47.39	283.82
Pittsburgh, PA	123	1.67	6.33	26.47	167.39
Portland, OR	127	2.22	6.27	37.96	381.42
Providence, RI	89	2.66	6.95	31.83	154.93
Provo, UT	23	3.08	8.61	46.91	339.23
Raleigh, NC	159	1.84	5.67	34.46	180.65
Reno, NV	96	2.61	6.81	48.07	229.64
Richmond, VA	134	2.05	6.10	28.56	172.25
Riverside, CA	86	2.74	7.03	34.65	169.25
Rochester, MN	116	1.70	6.45	32.58	175.69
Sacramento, CA	93	2.73	6.92	37.42	166.72
Salt Lake City, UT	15	3.24	9.07	50.25	408.84
San Antonio, TX	149	2.10	5.83	34.99	224.63
San Diego, CA	141	1.97	6.01	30.38	235.91
San Francisco, CA[2]	253	-3.20	-6.72	10.12	283.50
San Jose, CA	251	0.55	0.10	18.04	296.60
Santa Rosa, CA	246	1.59	2.15	26.52	225.13
Savannah, GA	214	0.50	4.40	33.56	221.18
Seattle, WA[2]	97	2.16	6.81	48.46	324.48
Sioux Falls, SD	139	2.09	6.03	29.70	212.39
Springfield, IL	248	0.83	1.79	8.16	85.25
Tallahassee, FL	186	1.55	5.20	30.45	154.52
Tampa, FL	33	2.36	8.17	52.43	254.29
Tucson, AZ	29	2.33	8.30	39.73	202.45
Tulsa, OK	179	1.98	5.26	22.61	153.16
Tuscaloosa, AL	n/a	n/a	n/a	n/a	n/a
Virginia Beach, VA	144	1.54	5.90	17.40	170.16
Washington, DC[2]	189	1.67	5.16	21.40	197.71
Wichita, KS	49	1.50	7.67	27.26	136.03
Winston-Salem, NC	94	2.58	6.92	28.40	118.04
U.S.[4]	—	3.81	10.77	38.99	205.12

Note: The HPI is a weighted repeat sales index. It measures average price changes in repeat sales or refinancings on the same properties. This information is obtained by reviewing repeat mortgage transactions on single-family properties whose mortgages have been purchased or securitized by Fannie Mae or Freddie Mac since January 1975; (1) figures cover the Metropolitan Statistical Area (MSA) unless noted otherwise—see Appendix B for areas included; (2) Metropolitan Division—see Appendix B for areas included; (3) Rankings are based on annual percentage change, for all MSAs containing at least 15,000 transactions over the last 10 years and ranges from 1 to 253; (4) figures based on a weighted division average; all figures are for the period ended December 31, 2020; n/a not available
Source: Federal Housing Finance Agency, Change in Metropolitan Area House Price Indexes, April 7, 2021

Home Value Distribution: City

Area	Under $50,000	$50,000 -$99,999	$100,000 -$149,999	$150,000 -$199,999	$200,000 -$299,999	$300,000 -$499,999	$500,000 -$999,999	$1,000,000 or more
Albuquerque, NM	4.5	4.4	16.9	25.1	29.5	15.9	3.3	0.5
Allentown, PA	4.5	22.0	35.2	24.0	8.7	4.1	1.1	0.4
Anchorage, AK	5.3	1.9	4.8	7.0	26.9	40.9	12.2	1.0
Ann Arbor, MI	1.3	3.6	6.0	8.2	25.2	37.6	15.7	2.4
Athens, GA	6.3	12.9	19.9	21.9	20.3	12.7	5.4	0.7
Atlanta, GA	4.5	10.1	9.6	10.6	16.6	19.7	20.2	8.8
Austin, TX	2.2	2.2	4.8	9.1	24.3	33.0	20.1	4.3
Baton Rouge, LA	5.6	17.7	15.6	19.4	21.4	12.9	5.8	1.6
Boise City, ID	3.9	1.9	8.6	17.4	31.6	26.6	9.0	1.0
Boston, MA	1.6	0.3	0.4	1.4	8.2	34.1	40.4	13.5
Boulder, CO	3.8	1.7	1.8	3.3	4.1	13.3	48.9	23.1
Cape Coral, FL	1.6	3.1	11.1	22.6	34.1	20.2	6.5	0.9
Cedar Rapids, IA	5.5	16.3	34.2	20.9	16.3	5.1	1.4	0.2
Charleston, SC	1.5	2.6	4.6	8.2	26.4	31.1	19.0	6.6
Charlotte, NC	2.1	8.2	17.3	17.6	21.0	19.5	10.9	3.4
Chicago, IL	2.7	7.0	11.1	15.0	23.8	24.1	12.5	3.9
Cincinnati, OH	6.9	25.4	22.2	11.9	14.7	11.5	6.2	1.3
Clarksville, TN	4.3	14.1	28.9	26.6	19.0	5.6	0.9	0.5
Cleveland, OH	28.8	44.0	14.0	5.9	3.6	2.1	1.2	0.4
College Station, TX	2.1	1.3	7.4	21.9	35.6	24.9	6.1	0.9
Colorado Springs, CO	3.0	2.1	6.5	14.5	33.6	30.4	8.6	1.2
Columbia, MO	3.4	7.4	19.0	22.8	25.7	17.2	4.2	0.3
Columbia, SC	4.5	15.3	19.7	16.0	15.6	16.5	10.9	1.6
Columbus, OH	5.9	19.5	23.8	20.7	19.8	7.9	2.0	0.3
Dallas, TX	6.7	19.2	15.4	10.7	12.6	17.6	13.2	4.6
Davenport, IA	6.3	24.6	28.4	16.1	15.6	7.4	1.1	0.4
Denver, CO	1.3	1.6	3.3	6.8	19.5	34.6	27.3	5.6
Des Moines, IA	5.9	21.6	33.1	20.5	12.1	4.8	1.8	0.2
Durham, NC	1.8	5.3	14.5	20.5	30.8	20.3	5.9	1.0
Edison, NJ	2.1	1.8	1.9	2.7	17.0	47.4	25.4	1.6
El Paso, TX	5.1	25.0	32.7	18.5	12.5	4.8	1.2	0.3
Fargo, ND	4.0	4.3	12.6	25.0	30.8	18.6	4.0	0.6
Fayetteville, NC	5.0	26.2	28.2	19.3	13.7	5.5	1.7	0.3
Fort Collins, CO	3.2	1.1	1.5	3.6	19.8	52.8	16.7	1.3
Fort Wayne, IN	10.6	30.1	28.9	16.1	9.6	3.7	0.9	0.1
Fort Worth, TX	6.2	17.3	17.6	19.3	22.9	11.9	4.0	0.8
Grand Rapids, MI	4.7	19.6	30.0	24.3	15.0	5.0	1.3	0.2
Greeley, CO	7.1	2.5	7.2	15.2	36.3	27.2	4.3	0.2
Green Bay, WI	3.3	20.8	35.3	20.4	12.8	5.7	1.5	0.3
Greensboro, NC	3.5	19.2	24.5	18.3	18.2	11.4	3.7	1.2
Honolulu, HI	0.8	0.8	0.8	1.4	7.2	22.6	42.5	24.0
Houston, TX	5.4	19.6	18.1	13.0	14.5	15.8	10.0	3.6
Huntsville, AL	5.3	17.9	15.0	16.6	22.8	16.6	4.6	1.1
Indianapolis, IN	7.1	22.9	27.0	18.8	12.5	8.0	3.1	0.7
Jacksonville, FL	7.4	15.2	17.4	19.0	24.0	11.9	3.9	1.2
Kansas City, MO	11.2	17.4	19.4	18.4	18.5	10.8	3.6	0.7
Lafayette, LA	5.5	8.2	14.9	23.2	23.8	16.0	6.5	1.9
Lakeland, FL	18.2	15.4	16.7	19.4	18.7	8.6	2.6	0.5
Las Vegas, NV	2.4	4.3	8.7	15.4	31.4	27.3	8.6	1.9
Lexington, KY	2.6	8.8	21.0	21.1	22.4	16.6	6.0	1.4
Lincoln, NE	3.5	9.8	25.5	23.9	23.3	11.2	2.4	0.5
Little Rock, AR	6.5	19.3	16.8	17.5	15.9	15.4	7.0	1.6
Los Angeles, CA	1.2	0.8	0.7	0.8	4.8	25.2	44.5	22.1
Louisville, KY	5.5	15.7	24.8	18.2	17.6	13.0	4.4	0.8
Madison, WI	1.6	2.6	8.5	18.5	35.6	25.7	6.7	0.8

Table continued on following page.

Area	Under $50,000	$50,000 -$99,999	$100,000 -$149,999	$150,000 -$199,999	$200,000 -$299,999	$300,000 -$499,999	$500,000 -$999,999	$1,000,000 or more
Manchester, NH	1.9	3.0	8.3	21.6	47.9	15.7	1.4	0.2
Memphis, TN	14.5	34.7	17.4	12.4	9.9	6.8	3.3	1.0
Miami, FL	2.2	4.6	6.0	9.8	24.1	29.6	16.1	7.5
Midland, TX	4.9	9.0	12.7	17.4	28.4	18.3	7.8	1.4
Milwaukee, WI	9.1	27.3	29.6	17.9	10.6	3.6	1.5	0.4
Minneapolis, MN	1.4	4.0	10.7	16.1	31.3	24.7	10.0	1.9
Nashville, TN	2.1	5.0	13.5	17.4	27.0	23.1	10.0	1.9
New Haven, CT	2.7	7.9	14.1	25.8	28.0	14.9	6.0	0.7
New Orleans, LA	2.8	7.9	13.8	18.6	19.9	20.5	13.0	3.7
New York, NY	2.9	1.3	1.9	2.4	6.6	23.7	41.4	19.9
Oklahoma City, OK	7.9	18.0	19.9	20.8	18.9	10.2	3.4	0.8
Omaha, NE	4.2	14.8	25.8	21.8	19.0	10.5	3.2	0.7
Orlando, FL	2.9	10.7	13.4	13.0	24.6	24.6	8.8	2.1
Peoria, IL	12.6	25.4	21.8	15.6	13.8	8.1	2.4	0.4
Philadelphia, PA	6.7	19.4	18.6	18.0	19.6	11.3	5.1	1.3
Phoenix, AZ	4.3	6.3	11.0	17.7	26.4	23.0	9.6	1.7
Pittsburgh, PA	11.8	27.6	18.0	12.8	12.4	10.6	5.7	1.0
Portland, OR	1.9	0.8	1.5	3.8	16.7	41.6	30.5	3.2
Providence, RI	2.1	5.3	16.9	25.7	23.9	15.6	8.6	1.9
Provo, UT	3.5	1.2	6.4	13.5	34.5	29.0	9.8	2.2
Raleigh, NC	2.0	2.7	11.4	19.4	27.1	24.8	10.8	1.8
Reno, NV	4.1	2.9	3.7	7.5	22.3	43.2	13.7	2.5
Richmond, VA	2.0	11.4	13.9	15.4	20.8	21.7	11.5	3.3
Riverside, CA	2.9	1.6	1.7	3.4	17.5	55.6	15.4	1.9
Rochester, MN	2.9	4.5	16.5	26.0	27.6	17.9	4.2	0.4
Sacramento, CA	2.5	2.0	3.5	7.2	26.0	39.6	17.2	2.0
Salt Lake City, UT	2.9	1.4	6.7	13.0	23.6	29.7	19.5	3.3
San Antonio, TX	6.8	24.5	20.0	18.4	17.9	9.4	2.5	0.6
San Diego, CA	1.6	1.0	0.8	1.1	5.3	27.4	47.6	15.3
San Francisco, CA	1.1	0.5	0.4	0.3	1.2	3.9	34.9	57.8
San Jose, CA	1.5	1.4	1.4	0.9	1.9	7.2	50.0	35.6
Santa Rosa, CA	2.7	2.0	1.7	1.5	5.2	30.6	50.0	6.2
Savannah, GA	6.1	20.2	20.4	19.5	18.7	9.4	4.6	1.1
Seattle, WA	0.6	0.4	0.4	1.0	5.0	22.3	52.5	17.8
Sioux Falls, SD	5.5	6.6	17.7	24.4	27.0	14.4	3.8	0.7
Springfield, IL	10.0	24.9	23.4	15.7	15.7	7.9	2.3	0.2
Tallahassee, FL	2.9	9.9	16.8	19.3	26.8	19.3	4.0	1.0
Tampa, FL	3.8	10.8	11.7	14.7	20.7	20.1	13.6	4.5
Tucson, AZ	10.6	13.5	22.6	24.6	19.6	6.8	1.9	0.3
Tulsa, OK	9.0	22.8	22.3	15.7	13.8	10.4	4.9	1.2
Tuscaloosa, AL	4.4	11.2	21.2	19.0	19.4	15.1	8.2	1.4
Virginia Beach, VA	2.2	1.5	6.1	12.6	33.7	30.5	11.1	2.3
Washington, DC	1.2	0.8	1.1	1.9	9.5	25.7	41.0	18.8
Wichita, KS	8.4	26.6	22.6	18.2	14.6	7.0	2.3	0.3
Winston-Salem, NC	6.6	19.7	24.8	20.8	13.4	8.8	5.2	0.8
U.S.	6.9	12.0	13.3	14.0	19.6	19.3	11.4	3.4

Note: Figures are percentages and cover owner-occupied housing units.
Source: U.S. Census Bureau, 2015-2019 American Community Survey 5-Year Estimates

Home Value Distribution: Metro Area

MSA[1]	Under $50,000	$50,000 -$99,999	$100,000 -$149,999	$150,000 -$199,999	$200,000 -$299,999	$300,000 -$499,999	$500,000 -$999,999	$1,000,000 or more
Albuquerque, NM	5.8	7.6	16.8	22.7	25.8	15.5	4.8	1.0
Allentown, PA	3.8	7.3	14.4	20.0	28.2	21.4	4.3	0.6
Anchorage, AK	4.9	2.6	5.2	9.3	29.6	37.3	10.3	0.9
Ann Arbor, MI	5.5	6.1	8.0	13.7	24.9	28.8	11.3	1.7
Athens, GA	8.8	12.2	17.4	17.3	21.0	16.1	6.2	1.0
Atlanta, GA	3.7	9.2	14.8	18.0	22.5	20.7	9.3	1.8
Austin, TX	3.3	3.9	6.9	12.7	27.8	28.3	13.9	3.2
Baton Rouge, LA	8.7	12.3	15.0	20.4	24.0	14.3	4.3	1.0
Boise City, ID	4.4	4.2	11.1	17.9	28.9	25.3	7.3	1.0
Boston, MA	1.6	1.0	1.6	3.6	14.5	38.5	31.8	7.4
Boulder, CO	2.9	1.1	1.3	2.9	10.6	31.6	38.3	11.3
Cape Coral, FL	6.2	8.9	11.8	16.4	24.5	20.2	9.2	2.8
Cedar Rapids, IA	6.5	13.7	27.1	19.7	20.8	9.2	2.4	0.6
Charleston, SC	6.0	7.5	11.6	15.3	23.1	21.1	11.7	3.7
Charlotte, NC	4.8	11.4	16.7	17.1	21.5	18.7	7.8	1.9
Chicago, IL	3.2	7.2	12.4	16.4	25.5	23.1	9.9	2.4
Cincinnati, OH	4.8	15.3	21.4	18.8	21.0	13.6	4.3	0.7
Clarksville, TN	6.6	17.3	23.7	21.4	19.5	9.0	1.8	0.7
Cleveland, OH	7.6	20.0	21.6	17.9	18.4	10.7	3.0	0.7
College Station, TX	10.0	13.0	13.2	18.1	23.3	16.1	5.3	1.0
Colorado Springs, CO	3.1	2.0	6.1	14.3	31.7	31.1	10.4	1.2
Columbia, MO	5.4	11.2	19.9	20.9	22.9	14.8	4.3	0.7
Columbia, SC	8.6	16.9	22.6	18.7	17.1	11.2	4.2	0.8
Columbus, OH	4.8	13.1	18.2	18.8	23.1	16.5	4.9	0.7
Dallas, TX	4.5	11.1	14.5	15.9	23.1	20.9	7.9	1.9
Davenport, IA	7.3	23.5	24.9	17.5	15.3	9.1	2.0	0.4
Denver, CO	2.2	1.3	2.3	5.3	19.2	42.7	23.3	3.5
Des Moines, IA	4.5	11.9	19.7	19.9	24.4	14.9	4.2	0.5
Durham, NC	5.0	7.8	14.2	16.4	23.6	22.0	9.7	1.4
Edison, NJ	2.0	1.4	2.4	3.9	13.2	35.1	32.1	9.9
El Paso, TX	7.7	26.8	31.4	17.2	11.2	4.3	1.1	0.2
Fargo, ND	3.7	5.3	13.1	23.0	30.1	19.4	4.8	0.7
Fayetteville, NC	8.8	21.8	23.2	20.1	18.1	6.2	1.5	0.4
Fort Collins, CO	3.9	1.4	1.6	4.7	20.7	46.4	19.1	2.2
Fort Wayne, IN	8.4	24.8	26.3	17.2	13.7	7.2	2.0	0.4
Fort Worth, TX	4.5	11.1	14.5	15.9	23.1	20.9	7.9	1.9
Grand Rapids, MI	6.7	11.6	20.2	21.8	22.4	13.0	3.6	0.7
Greeley, CO	4.6	2.7	4.6	9.7	28.6	36.6	12.0	1.1
Green Bay, WI	4.0	11.9	22.8	22.2	24.5	11.3	2.6	0.6
Greensboro, NC	7.0	19.7	23.7	17.7	17.2	10.7	3.4	0.7
Honolulu, HI	0.7	0.6	0.8	1.0	5.0	19.6	54.6	17.7
Houston, TX	5.3	12.1	16.7	17.8	22.0	16.9	6.9	2.3
Huntsville, AL	6.4	13.8	17.3	19.0	23.7	15.1	3.9	0.8
Indianapolis, IN	5.6	16.1	22.3	19.0	18.5	13.4	4.4	0.8
Jacksonville, FL	5.8	12.0	14.1	16.8	24.6	18.1	6.7	1.8
Kansas City, MO	6.2	12.8	17.6	18.7	22.7	16.1	5.0	0.9
Lafayette, LA	14.7	16.0	16.1	19.5	19.3	10.1	3.5	0.8
Lakeland, FL	14.7	18.2	16.8	18.6	20.6	8.3	2.2	0.6
Las Vegas, NV	3.5	4.3	8.0	14.1	31.6	28.6	8.2	1.7
Lexington, KY	3.5	9.9	22.0	20.7	21.4	15.4	5.9	1.3
Lincoln, NE	3.2	9.4	23.4	22.6	23.4	13.8	3.7	0.5
Little Rock, AR	7.9	17.6	22.4	19.5	18.4	10.1	3.2	0.9
Los Angeles, CA	1.9	1.4	0.9	1.2	4.9	25.2	47.5	17.0
Louisville, KY	4.8	13.7	22.6	18.9	20.8	13.6	4.5	0.9
Madison, WI	2.1	3.9	9.7	16.6	32.4	26.6	7.5	1.2

Table continued on following page.

MSA[1]	Under $50,000	$50,000 -$99,999	$100,000 -$149,999	$150,000 -$199,999	$200,000 -$299,999	$300,000 -$499,999	$500,000 -$999,999	$1,000,000 or more
Manchester, NH	1.9	2.5	5.9	12.0	37.5	32.8	6.7	0.7
Memphis, TN	9.1	21.8	18.2	16.5	18.6	11.2	3.6	0.9
Miami, FL	4.0	7.1	8.7	11.9	22.9	28.5	12.5	4.5
Midland, TX	8.7	10.4	11.9	15.9	26.2	17.9	7.5	1.3
Milwaukee, WI	3.7	8.8	15.1	18.2	27.1	20.0	6.0	1.1
Minneapolis, MN	2.7	2.7	7.9	16.7	32.8	27.1	8.8	1.4
Nashville, TN	2.9	6.1	13.1	16.5	25.6	23.0	10.5	2.3
New Haven, CT	2.0	4.9	10.6	17.0	29.8	26.8	7.6	1.2
New Orleans, LA	4.2	9.0	16.8	20.8	24.8	16.4	6.4	1.6
New York, NY	2.0	1.4	2.4	3.9	13.2	35.1	32.1	9.9
Oklahoma City, OK	7.5	17.7	21.3	19.6	18.4	10.9	3.7	1.0
Omaha, NE	3.9	12.1	23.4	21.0	22.0	13.5	3.4	0.7
Orlando, FL	6.1	8.5	11.7	17.0	28.6	20.3	6.2	1.7
Peoria, IL	8.6	25.9	23.0	17.4	15.3	7.6	1.9	0.4
Philadelphia, PA	3.4	7.3	10.2	14.8	26.3	26.2	10.1	1.7
Phoenix, AZ	5.5	5.2	8.7	15.2	28.2	25.2	9.8	2.2
Pittsburgh, PA	8.8	20.3	19.2	17.8	17.5	12.0	3.6	0.7
Portland, OR	3.2	1.3	2.1	4.9	21.0	42.8	22.1	2.6
Providence, RI	2.1	2.0	5.7	14.1	33.3	31.2	10.0	1.7
Provo, UT	2.4	0.9	3.6	10.1	32.2	37.0	12.1	1.7
Raleigh, NC	3.5	5.0	11.9	15.5	25.7	27.6	9.6	1.3
Reno, NV	4.0	2.8	4.2	7.5	23.6	38.4	15.4	4.1
Richmond, VA	2.4	5.3	11.7	18.2	29.4	23.7	8.2	1.2
Riverside, CA	4.9	3.4	4.1	6.8	21.0	40.8	17.0	2.0
Rochester, MN	4.6	6.8	16.1	22.2	24.5	19.3	5.5	1.0
Sacramento, CA	2.8	1.7	2.2	4.5	17.7	42.3	25.8	3.0
Salt Lake City, UT	2.9	1.2	5.2	11.5	29.6	34.2	13.7	1.7
San Antonio, TX	6.8	18.2	16.6	17.7	20.5	14.2	4.9	1.2
San Diego, CA	2.5	1.9	1.4	1.4	5.2	29.3	46.1	12.2
San Francisco, CA	1.2	0.9	0.8	0.8	2.8	13.2	43.9	36.2
San Jose, CA	1.3	1.0	1.2	0.9	1.8	6.4	40.1	47.3
Santa Rosa, CA	2.6	2.6	1.6	1.2	4.2	22.2	51.9	13.7
Savannah, GA	5.7	11.2	17.1	19.2	23.1	14.9	7.1	1.6
Seattle, WA	2.5	1.2	2.0	4.2	15.3	34.2	32.0	8.5
Sioux Falls, SD	5.6	7.7	16.6	22.7	26.5	15.7	4.4	0.8
Springfield, IL	8.2	23.3	22.4	17.8	18.2	8.0	1.9	0.2
Tallahassee, FL	8.3	15.3	16.5	16.9	22.4	15.2	4.6	0.8
Tampa, FL	8.8	13.0	13.5	16.7	23.7	16.4	6.4	1.6
Tucson, AZ	8.4	10.7	16.2	19.9	22.5	15.4	5.8	1.0
Tulsa, OK	9.4	18.7	21.7	19.4	17.3	9.4	3.4	0.8
Tuscaloosa, AL	13.0	14.9	17.5	20.5	19.7	9.8	3.9	0.7
Virginia Beach, VA	3.3	3.8	10.2	17.0	31.5	25.1	7.7	1.2
Washington, DC	1.5	1.0	2.1	4.7	17.1	35.8	31.2	6.7
Wichita, KS	8.3	24.2	22.6	19.1	15.6	7.8	2.0	0.4
Winston-Salem, NC	7.4	16.9	24.5	20.0	17.2	9.9	3.5	0.6
U.S.	6.9	12.0	13.3	14.0	19.6	19.3	11.4	3.4

Note: (1) Figures cover the Metropolitan Statistical Area (MSA)—see Appendix B for areas included; Figures are percentages and cover owner-occupied housing units.
Source: U.S. Census Bureau, 2015-2019 American Community Survey 5-Year Estimates

Homeownership Rate

Metro Area	2012	2013	2014	2015	2016	2017	2018	2019	2020
Albuquerque, NM	62.8	65.9	64.4	64.3	66.9	67.0	67.9	70.0	69.5
Allentown, PA	75.5	71.5	68.2	69.2	68.9	73.1	72.1	67.8	68.8
Anchorage, AK	n/a	n/a	n/a	n/a	n/a	n/a	n/a	n/a	n/a
Ann Arbor, MI	n/a	n/a	n/a	n/a	n/a	n/a	n/a	n/a	n/a
Athens, GA	n/a	n/a	n/a	n/a	n/a	n/a	n/a	n/a	n/a
Atlanta, GA	62.1	61.6	61.6	61.7	61.5	62.4	64.0	64.2	66.4
Austin, TX	60.1	59.6	61.1	57.5	56.5	55.6	56.1	59.0	65.4
Baton Rouge, LA	71.4	66.6	64.8	64.2	64.8	66.9	66.6	66.2	72.1
Boise City, ID	n/a	n/a	n/a	n/a	n/a	n/a	n/a	n/a	n/a
Boston, MA	66.0	66.3	62.8	59.3	58.9	58.8	61.0	60.9	61.2
Boulder, CO	n/a	n/a	n/a	n/a	n/a	n/a	n/a	n/a	n/a
Cape Coral, FL	n/a	n/a	n/a	62.9	66.5	65.5	75.1	72.0	77.4
Cedar Rapids, IA	n/a	n/a	n/a	n/a	n/a	n/a	n/a	n/a	n/a
Charleston, SC	n/a	n/a	n/a	65.8	62.1	67.7	68.8	70.7	75.5
Charlotte, NC	58.3	58.9	58.1	62.3	66.2	64.6	67.9	72.3	73.3
Chicago, IL	67.1	68.2	66.3	64.3	64.5	64.1	64.6	63.4	66.0
Cincinnati, OH	63.4	63.3	65.5	65.9	64.9	65.7	67.3	67.4	71.1
Clarksville, TN	n/a	n/a	n/a	n/a	n/a	n/a	n/a	n/a	n/a
Cleveland, OH	64.2	65.8	69.2	68.4	64.8	66.6	66.7	64.4	66.3
College Station, TX	n/a	n/a	n/a	n/a	n/a	n/a	n/a	n/a	n/a
Colorado Springs, CO	n/a	n/a	n/a	n/a	n/a	n/a	n/a	n/a	n/a
Columbia, MO	n/a	n/a	n/a	n/a	n/a	n/a	n/a	n/a	n/a
Columbia, SC	65.6	68.9	69.5	66.1	63.9	70.7	69.3	65.9	69.7
Columbus, OH	60.7	60.5	60.0	59.0	57.5	57.9	64.8	65.7	65.6
Dallas, TX	61.8	59.9	57.7	57.8	59.7	61.8	62.0	60.6	64.7
Davenport, IA	n/a	n/a	n/a	n/a	n/a	n/a	n/a	n/a	n/a
Denver, CO	61.8	61.0	61.9	61.6	61.6	59.3	60.1	63.5	62.9
Des Moines, IA	n/a	n/a	n/a	n/a	n/a	n/a	n/a	n/a	n/a
Durham, NC	n/a	n/a	n/a	n/a	n/a	n/a	n/a	n/a	n/a
Edison, NJ	51.5	50.6	50.7	49.9	50.4	49.9	49.7	50.4	50.9
El Paso, TX	n/a	n/a	n/a	n/a	n/a	n/a	n/a	n/a	n/a
Fargo, ND	n/a	n/a	n/a	n/a	n/a	n/a	n/a	n/a	n/a
Fayetteville, NC	n/a	n/a	n/a	n/a	n/a	n/a	n/a	n/a	n/a
Fort Collins, CO	n/a	n/a	n/a	n/a	n/a	n/a	n/a	n/a	n/a
Fort Wayne, IN	n/a	n/a	n/a	n/a	n/a	n/a	n/a	n/a	n/a
Fort Worth, TX	61.8	59.9	57.7	57.8	59.7	61.8	62.0	60.6	64.7
Grand Rapids, MI	76.9	73.7	71.6	75.8	76.2	71.7	73.0	75.2	71.8
Greeley, CO	n/a	n/a	n/a	n/a	n/a	n/a	n/a	n/a	n/a
Green Bay, WI	n/a	n/a	n/a	n/a	n/a	n/a	n/a	n/a	n/a
Greensboro, NC	64.9	67.9	68.1	65.4	62.9	61.9	63.2	61.7	65.8
Honolulu, HI	56.1	57.9	58.2	59.6	57.9	53.8	57.7	59.0	56.9
Houston, TX	62.1	60.5	60.4	60.3	59.0	58.9	60.1	61.3	65.3
Huntsville, AL	n/a	n/a	n/a	n/a	n/a	n/a	n/a	n/a	n/a
Indianapolis, IN	67.1	67.5	66.9	64.6	63.9	63.9	64.3	66.2	70.0
Jacksonville, FL	66.6	69.9	65.3	62.5	61.8	65.2	61.4	63.1	64.8
Kansas City, MO	65.1	65.6	66.1	65.0	62.4	62.4	64.3	65.0	66.7
Lafayette, LA	n/a	n/a	n/a	n/a	n/a	n/a	n/a	n/a	n/a
Lakeland, FL	n/a	n/a	n/a	n/a	n/a	n/a	n/a	n/a	n/a
Las Vegas, NV	52.6	52.8	53.2	52.1	51.3	54.4	58.1	56.0	57.3
Lexington, KY	n/a	n/a	n/a	n/a	n/a	n/a	n/a	n/a	n/a
Lincoln, NE	n/a	n/a	n/a	n/a	n/a	n/a	n/a	n/a	n/a
Little Rock, AR	n/a	n/a	n/a	65.8	64.9	61.0	62.2	65.0	67.7
Los Angeles, CA	49.9	48.7	49.0	49.1	47.1	49.1	49.5	48.2	48.5
Louisville, KY	63.3	64.5	68.9	67.7	67.6	71.7	67.9	64.9	69.3
Madison, WI	n/a	n/a	n/a	n/a	n/a	n/a	n/a	n/a	n/a
Manchester, NH	n/a	n/a	n/a	n/a	n/a	n/a	n/a	n/a	n/a

Table continued on following page.

Metro Area	2012	2013	2014	2015	2016	2017	2018	2019	2020
Memphis, TN	60.5	56.2	57.2	59.6	61.8	62.4	63.5	63.7	62.5
Miami, FL	61.8	60.1	58.8	58.6	58.4	57.9	59.9	60.4	60.6
Midland, TX	n/a	n/a	n/a	n/a	n/a	n/a	n/a	n/a	n/a
Milwaukee, WI	61.9	60.0	55.9	57.0	60.4	63.9	62.3	56.9	58.5
Minneapolis, MN	70.8	71.7	69.7	67.9	69.1	70.1	67.8	70.2	73.0
Nashville, TN	64.9	63.9	67.1	67.4	65.0	69.4	68.3	69.8	69.8
New Haven, CT	62.2	62.0	62.4	64.6	59.4	58.7	65.0	65.1	63.4
New Orleans, LA	62.4	61.4	60.6	62.8	59.3	61.7	62.6	61.1	66.3
New York, NY	51.5	50.6	50.7	49.9	50.4	49.9	49.7	50.4	50.9
Oklahoma City, OK	67.3	67.6	65.7	61.4	63.1	64.7	64.6	64.3	68.3
Omaha, NE	72.4	70.6	68.7	69.6	69.2	65.5	67.8	66.9	68.6
Orlando, FL	68.0	65.5	62.3	58.4	58.5	59.5	58.5	56.1	64.2
Peoria, IL	n/a	n/a	n/a	n/a	n/a	n/a	n/a	n/a	n/a
Philadelphia, PA	69.5	69.1	67.0	67.0	64.7	65.6	67.4	67.4	69.2
Phoenix, AZ	63.1	62.2	61.9	61.0	62.6	64.0	65.3	65.9	67.9
Pittsburgh, PA	67.9	68.3	69.1	71.0	72.2	72.7	71.7	71.5	69.8
Portland, OR	63.9	60.9	59.8	58.9	61.8	61.1	59.2	60.0	62.5
Providence, RI	61.7	60.1	61.6	60.0	57.5	58.6	61.3	63.5	64.8
Provo, UT	n/a	n/a	n/a	n/a	n/a	n/a	n/a	n/a	n/a
Raleigh, NC	67.7	65.5	65.5	67.4	65.9	68.2	64.9	63.0	68.2
Reno, NV	n/a	n/a	n/a	n/a	n/a	n/a	n/a	n/a	n/a
Richmond, VA	67.0	65.4	72.6	67.4	61.7	63.1	62.9	66.4	66.5
Riverside, CA	58.2	56.3	56.8	61.1	62.9	59.9	62.3	64.4	65.8
Rochester, MN	n/a	n/a	n/a	n/a	n/a	n/a	n/a	n/a	n/a
Sacramento, CA	58.6	60.4	60.1	60.8	60.5	60.1	64.1	61.6	63.4
Salt Lake City, UT	66.9	66.8	68.2	69.1	69.2	68.1	69.5	69.2	68.0
San Antonio, TX	67.5	70.1	70.2	66.0	61.6	62.5	64.4	62.6	64.2
San Diego, CA	55.4	55.0	57.4	51.8	53.3	56.0	56.1	56.7	57.8
San Francisco, CA	53.2	55.2	54.6	56.3	55.8	55.7	55.6	52.8	53.0
San Jose, CA	58.6	56.4	56.4	50.7	49.9	50.4	50.4	52.4	52.6
Santa Rosa, CA	n/a	n/a	n/a	n/a	n/a	n/a	n/a	n/a	n/a
Savannah, GA	n/a	n/a	n/a	n/a	n/a	n/a	n/a	n/a	n/a
Seattle, WA	60.4	61.0	61.3	59.5	57.7	59.5	62.5	61.5	59.4
Sioux Falls, SD	n/a	n/a	n/a	n/a	n/a	n/a	n/a	n/a	n/a
Springfield, IL	n/a	n/a	n/a	n/a	n/a	n/a	n/a	n/a	n/a
Tallahassee, FL	n/a	n/a	n/a	n/a	n/a	n/a	n/a	n/a	n/a
Tampa, FL	67.0	65.3	64.9	64.9	62.9	60.4	64.9	68.0	72.2
Tucson, AZ	64.9	66.1	66.7	61.4	56.0	60.1	63.8	60.1	67.1
Tulsa, OK	66.5	64.1	65.3	65.2	65.4	66.8	68.3	70.5	70.1
Tuscaloosa, AL	n/a	n/a	n/a	n/a	n/a	n/a	n/a	n/a	n/a
Virginia Beach, VA	62.0	63.3	64.1	59.4	59.6	65.3	62.8	63.0	65.8
Washington, DC	66.9	66.0	65.0	64.6	63.1	63.3	62.9	64.7	67.9
Wichita, KS	n/a	n/a	n/a	n/a	n/a	n/a	n/a	n/a	n/a
Winston-Salem, NC	n/a	n/a	n/a	n/a	n/a	n/a	n/a	n/a	n/a
U.S.	65.4	65.1	64.5	63.7	63.4	63.9	64.4	64.6	66.6

Note: Figures are percentages and cover the Metropolitan Statistical Area—see Appendix B for areas included; n/a not available
Source: U.S. Census Bureau, Housing Vacancies and Homeownership Annual Statistics: 2012-2020

Year Housing Structure Built: City

City	2010 or Later	2000 -2009	1990 -1999	1980 -1989	1970 -1979	1960 -1969	1950 -1959	1940 -1949	Before 1940	Median Year
Albuquerque, NM	4.3	16.3	15.3	15.5	19.6	10.3	11.5	4.4	2.8	1981
Allentown, PA	2.1	5.0	3.8	5.5	10.6	12.1	16.1	7.2	37.6	1953
Anchorage, AK	3.5	12.2	11.6	26.4	28.2	10.8	6.0	1.0	0.3	1981
Ann Arbor, MI	3.7	6.3	10.8	10.8	17.2	18.2	12.6	5.0	15.6	1969
Athens, GA	3.8	17.7	20.3	15.6	16.5	12.2	6.6	2.4	4.8	1985
Atlanta, GA	8.1	22.3	10.6	7.9	8.4	12.6	11.7	6.1	12.3	1979
Austin, TX	12.8	18.1	15.7	19.6	15.9	7.6	4.9	2.6	2.8	1988
Baton Rouge, LA	5.9	9.9	8.7	12.9	22.4	17.3	11.7	5.9	5.3	1974
Boise City, ID	6.5	11.9	22.5	15.0	19.2	7.1	7.1	4.4	6.2	1984
Boston, MA	5.0	6.5	4.2	5.9	7.9	7.8	7.3	5.8	49.6	1941
Boulder, CO	6.2	7.7	11.2	17.3	21.5	18.3	8.1	2.0	7.6	1976
Cape Coral, FL	3.8	37.8	17.8	22.9	11.9	4.7	0.8	0.2	0.1	1995
Cedar Rapids, IA	6.9	11.1	13.0	8.2	14.4	13.9	12.3	4.2	16.0	1972
Charleston, SC	12.3	20.3	12.8	13.8	10.2	8.3	6.1	4.1	12.2	1987
Charlotte, NC	8.9	23.1	19.4	15.1	12.0	9.5	6.6	2.6	2.8	1991
Chicago, IL	2.6	8.0	4.9	4.3	7.5	9.7	11.9	9.3	41.8	1949
Cincinnati, OH	2.3	3.7	4.2	5.3	9.9	13.0	12.2	8.1	41.2	1951
Clarksville, TN	13.0	22.8	20.9	13.2	12.4	8.6	4.7	2.5	2.0	1993
Cleveland, OH	1.7	3.8	3.2	2.4	5.4	7.1	12.5	11.3	52.6	<1940
College Station, TX	16.2	24.0	19.8	16.0	16.5	4.0	2.2	0.7	0.6	1995
Colorado Springs, CO	6.5	15.7	15.9	18.6	18.3	10.2	7.1	1.9	5.8	1984
Columbia, MO	12.6	21.5	17.9	12.0	12.5	10.7	5.1	2.2	5.5	1991
Columbia, SC	6.1	15.8	11.6	8.9	10.1	11.9	13.6	11.2	10.8	1972
Columbus, OH	5.9	11.4	15.4	13.0	15.0	12.0	10.8	5.0	11.6	1977
Dallas, TX	7.1	10.6	10.3	17.2	17.3	13.4	13.7	5.2	5.2	1977
Davenport, IA	3.4	8.6	7.9	5.9	15.7	13.3	11.2	5.6	28.5	1964
Denver, CO	9.0	11.3	6.6	7.4	14.2	10.9	15.0	6.6	18.9	1969
Des Moines, IA	3.2	7.3	6.5	6.4	13.4	10.5	15.2	8.2	29.3	1958
Durham, NC	11.6	21.0	16.3	15.4	10.5	8.8	6.6	3.8	6.1	1989
Edison, NJ	1.7	4.7	9.3	23.3	13.6	20.3	17.4	4.5	5.1	1972
El Paso, TX	9.8	15.2	13.4	14.0	16.5	10.8	11.5	4.1	4.6	1982
Fargo, ND	16.1	15.8	16.5	13.8	14.0	6.0	6.9	2.6	8.2	1989
Fayetteville, NC	6.9	11.9	18.1	16.9	21.6	13.2	6.6	2.9	1.8	1982
Fort Collins, CO	10.2	17.5	21.3	15.2	18.8	7.1	3.2	1.6	5.2	1989
Fort Wayne, IN	1.5	6.6	14.3	11.7	16.7	15.0	12.2	6.6	15.3	1970
Fort Worth, TX	9.9	24.5	11.5	13.2	9.8	8.2	11.3	5.3	6.3	1987
Grand Rapids, MI	2.5	4.2	6.1	7.0	8.5	10.3	15.7	8.9	36.8	1953
Greeley, CO	6.3	19.3	15.7	10.1	21.2	10.3	6.7	2.6	7.8	1982
Green Bay, WI	1.6	7.6	10.3	12.9	17.8	13.1	15.0	5.7	16.0	1970
Greensboro, NC	5.2	15.0	17.9	16.6	14.4	11.2	10.2	3.8	5.5	1983
Honolulu, HI	4.2	6.9	7.9	9.5	25.3	22.8	12.8	5.5	5.1	1971
Houston, TX	8.6	13.4	9.9	14.6	21.1	13.4	10.3	4.5	4.3	1978
Huntsville, AL	11.8	12.9	10.8	15.6	13.2	21.0	9.5	2.4	2.8	1981
Indianapolis, IN	3.4	9.2	13.2	12.1	13.5	13.1	12.7	6.1	16.8	1971
Jacksonville, FL	6.2	19.3	15.3	15.5	12.7	10.0	11.1	4.8	5.1	1984
Kansas City, MO	4.6	9.9	9.3	8.6	12.0	12.7	14.3	6.3	22.1	1966
Lafayette, LA	7.2	13.3	10.4	18.0	21.7	13.4	9.0	3.9	3.1	1979
Lakeland, FL	3.4	15.1	13.2	19.6	20.2	10.4	8.8	3.3	6.0	1981
Las Vegas, NV	5.2	23.0	32.0	16.6	9.9	7.4	4.2	1.3	0.5	1993
Lexington, KY	6.1	15.5	15.8	14.0	15.0	13.5	9.7	3.1	7.3	1981
Lincoln, NE	7.3	13.7	15.0	10.4	15.3	10.0	11.2	3.0	14.0	1978
Little Rock, AR	6.2	11.2	11.2	14.3	19.6	15.2	9.9	5.2	7.1	1976
Los Angeles, CA	3.2	5.6	5.7	10.2	13.7	14.1	17.4	9.8	20.3	1962
Louisville, KY	4.3	11.0	11.7	6.9	12.7	13.8	14.8	7.4	17.4	1968
Madison, WI	7.1	14.4	13.1	10.9	13.9	11.5	10.4	4.8	14.0	1977

Table continued on following page.

City	2010 or Later	2000 -2009	1990 -1999	1980 -1989	1970 -1979	1960 -1969	1950 -1959	1940 -1949	Before 1940	Median Year
Manchester, NH	1.9	6.7	8.1	15.9	10.4	7.9	10.3	6.1	32.6	1961
Memphis, TN	2.0	7.0	10.0	12.4	18.2	14.9	19.1	8.7	7.7	1970
Miami, FL	7.6	19.0	6.4	8.3	13.3	9.8	14.7	11.7	9.2	1973
Midland, TX	12.9	8.5	13.8	18.4	11.7	11.6	18.5	3.0	1.5	1982
Milwaukee, WI	1.5	3.3	2.9	3.9	8.7	11.1	20.2	9.8	38.6	1951
Minneapolis, MN	5.8	6.7	3.6	6.8	9.0	7.5	9.5	6.8	44.3	1948
Nashville, TN	9.3	14.6	12.4	15.3	14.8	12.2	10.6	4.5	6.2	1981
New Haven, CT	3.1	4.8	2.6	7.1	8.0	9.7	9.4	7.5	47.7	1943
New Orleans, LA	3.4	7.1	3.5	7.3	13.7	11.1	12.1	7.7	34.0	1957
New York, NY	2.8	5.6	3.7	4.8	7.1	12.5	13.0	9.9	40.6	1949
Oklahoma City, OK	9.4	13.1	9.5	14.9	16.1	12.6	10.6	5.5	8.4	1978
Omaha, NE	3.4	7.4	13.0	11.0	15.6	14.6	11.1	4.2	19.7	1970
Orlando, FL	9.6	21.6	16.3	16.9	13.9	7.2	8.6	2.9	3.0	1989
Peoria, IL	3.3	8.7	7.4	6.8	15.2	12.5	14.0	7.9	24.3	1963
Philadelphia, PA	2.7	3.0	3.2	3.7	7.1	10.7	16.3	11.6	41.7	1947
Phoenix, AZ	4.3	16.7	16.3	17.1	19.6	11.7	10.1	2.5	1.8	1983
Pittsburgh, PA	2.3	3.0	3.5	4.4	6.7	8.7	12.6	8.9	49.8	1940
Portland, OR	5.8	10.5	8.8	6.4	10.7	9.2	12.0	8.2	28.3	1962
Providence, RI	0.6	4.5	3.7	5.5	9.2	5.9	7.6	6.8	56.2	<1940
Provo, UT	4.6	11.8	21.1	14.3	17.7	10.4	7.6	5.1	7.3	1981
Raleigh, NC	10.7	25.0	19.0	17.3	10.6	7.7	4.5	2.1	3.1	1992
Reno, NV	6.2	19.7	19.2	13.9	18.3	9.5	7.2	3.0	3.0	1987
Richmond, VA	4.0	5.4	4.9	6.3	11.3	12.4	15.0	9.1	31.7	1956
Riverside, CA	2.8	11.5	10.6	16.4	18.4	12.1	16.0	5.0	7.2	1975
Rochester, MN	8.9	18.3	14.3	14.6	13.0	10.1	9.6	3.3	7.9	1984
Sacramento, CA	2.3	15.7	8.9	15.7	14.6	11.7	12.4	7.9	10.9	1975
Salt Lake City, UT	5.3	6.6	7.4	7.7	12.1	10.0	13.2	8.7	29.1	1959
San Antonio, TX	7.3	15.9	13.7	16.6	15.0	10.2	10.1	5.7	5.6	1982
San Diego, CA	3.9	10.3	11.4	17.7	21.2	12.5	12.1	4.3	6.7	1977
San Francisco, CA	3.7	6.6	4.3	5.3	7.6	8.2	8.4	9.1	46.8	1944
San Jose, CA	5.2	9.3	10.6	12.9	24.2	18.6	11.0	3.0	5.2	1975
Santa Rosa, CA	2.9	12.4	13.0	19.4	21.8	11.8	8.2	4.9	5.6	1979
Savannah, GA	6.3	11.3	7.4	9.8	12.7	12.6	15.0	8.1	16.7	1968
Seattle, WA	10.4	13.2	8.3	7.9	8.2	8.7	9.8	8.3	25.2	1968
Sioux Falls, SD	13.3	18.3	15.1	10.5	13.8	7.3	9.1	3.8	8.6	1987
Springfield, IL	2.3	8.8	12.6	9.6	16.5	12.7	11.3	7.0	19.2	1970
Tallahassee, FL	3.9	18.2	20.8	17.7	18.0	9.2	7.5	3.2	1.5	1986
Tampa, FL	7.8	17.9	12.4	11.8	11.9	10.0	14.4	5.2	8.7	1980
Tucson, AZ	2.6	12.6	13.4	16.2	21.4	11.5	14.8	3.9	3.7	1978
Tulsa, OK	3.6	6.1	9.5	13.3	21.0	14.4	16.8	6.4	9.0	1972
Tuscaloosa, AL	12.9	17.6	15.5	11.5	13.7	10.4	8.8	5.2	4.3	1987
Virginia Beach, VA	4.9	10.8	13.7	27.9	21.4	12.8	6.1	1.3	1.1	1983
Washington, DC	7.3	8.1	3.3	4.4	7.1	11.4	12.6	11.7	34.1	1953
Wichita, KS	4.2	10.2	12.9	12.5	12.8	9.3	20.0	7.4	10.7	1972
Winston-Salem, NC	4.7	14.0	12.1	14.3	16.7	13.6	11.8	5.4	7.4	1977
U.S.	5.2	14.0	13.9	13.4	15.2	10.6	10.3	4.9	12.6	1978

Note: Figures are percentages except for Median Year
Source: U.S. Census Bureau, 2015-2019 American Community Survey 5-Year Estimates

Year Housing Structure Built: Metro Area

Metro Area	2010 or Later	2000 -2009	1990 -1999	1980 -1989	1970 -1979	1960 -1969	1950 -1959	1940 -1949	Before 1940	Median Year
Albuquerque, NM	4.2	17.6	18.2	17.0	18.0	9.2	9.1	3.7	3.0	1984
Allentown, PA	3.0	11.5	10.6	11.1	12.0	9.7	11.2	5.3	25.5	1968
Anchorage, AK	4.5	17.2	13.0	25.7	24.4	9.0	5.0	0.9	0.4	1984
Ann Arbor, MI	3.7	13.2	17.0	11.5	16.1	12.6	10.1	4.2	11.8	1977
Athens, GA	5.0	18.1	21.7	17.4	15.3	10.1	5.5	2.0	5.0	1987
Atlanta, GA	6.2	24.3	21.5	17.7	13.0	7.6	4.8	1.9	2.9	1991
Austin, TX	16.4	25.1	18.1	16.4	11.6	4.9	3.3	1.8	2.3	1995
Baton Rouge, LA	9.4	19.8	14.6	15.0	17.4	10.2	6.9	2.9	3.9	1986
Boise City, ID	10.5	24.6	21.4	10.3	16.2	4.7	4.4	3.0	4.9	1993
Boston, MA	4.0	7.6	7.4	10.4	11.2	10.2	10.8	5.3	33.2	1961
Boulder, CO	6.5	12.1	19.3	17.2	20.8	11.6	4.6	1.5	6.4	1983
Cape Coral, FL	5.6	31.3	17.7	21.4	14.8	5.5	2.5	0.5	0.7	1993
Cedar Rapids, IA	6.8	14.2	14.6	7.5	13.4	12.3	9.9	3.6	17.7	1975
Charleston, SC	11.9	21.4	16.6	16.4	14.2	8.2	5.2	2.4	3.6	1990
Charlotte, NC	9.2	24.1	19.5	13.5	11.5	8.4	6.5	3.1	4.2	1991
Chicago, IL	2.4	11.5	11.1	9.0	14.2	11.6	13.0	6.1	21.0	1968
Cincinnati, OH	3.7	12.4	14.4	10.7	13.8	10.7	11.9	4.9	17.6	1974
Clarksville, TN	10.7	20.0	20.9	12.1	15.2	9.2	6.2	2.5	3.1	1991
Cleveland, OH	2.3	7.1	8.7	6.8	12.4	13.4	18.1	7.6	23.7	1960
College Station, TX	12.7	21.0	17.7	17.0	15.8	6.1	5.2	2.0	2.4	1991
Colorado Springs, CO	7.6	18.8	16.9	17.5	17.0	8.9	6.5	1.6	5.2	1986
Columbia, MO	9.5	19.4	18.0	12.8	15.4	10.1	5.3	2.5	7.2	1988
Columbia, SC	8.0	19.5	18.5	14.3	15.9	9.7	7.0	3.3	3.8	1987
Columbus, OH	5.8	14.2	16.5	11.7	14.4	11.1	10.2	4.1	12.2	1979
Dallas, TX	10.0	20.0	16.1	18.1	14.2	8.7	7.5	2.7	2.7	1988
Davenport, IA	3.6	7.5	8.3	6.4	16.6	13.4	11.9	7.1	25.2	1964
Denver, CO	7.4	16.4	15.2	14.2	18.6	9.3	9.2	2.8	6.8	1982
Des Moines, IA	10.4	16.7	12.6	8.7	13.6	8.6	9.1	4.2	16.1	1979
Durham, NC	9.3	19.7	18.7	15.8	12.4	9.2	6.4	3.0	5.6	1989
Edison, NJ	2.8	6.7	6.1	7.7	9.8	13.7	15.9	8.8	28.6	1958
El Paso, TX	11.0	16.5	14.6	14.5	15.7	9.7	10.1	3.6	4.2	1985
Fargo, ND	15.1	18.4	14.2	11.2	14.9	6.9	7.4	2.7	9.1	1988
Fayetteville, NC	9.3	17.9	21.7	14.5	16.4	9.6	5.6	2.4	2.5	1989
Fort Collins, CO	10.3	18.8	20.1	13.5	19.1	7.1	3.6	1.7	5.8	1989
Fort Wayne, IN	3.8	11.0	15.2	10.9	15.2	13.0	10.8	5.4	14.7	1974
Fort Worth, TX	10.0	20.0	16.1	18.1	14.2	8.7	7.5	2.7	2.7	1988
Grand Rapids, MI	4.7	12.4	16.3	12.1	14.0	9.5	10.4	5.0	15.7	1977
Greeley, CO	10.9	28.6	16.3	7.4	15.2	6.2	4.4	2.4	8.6	1994
Green Bay, WI	5.2	15.0	16.4	12.4	15.4	9.6	9.3	4.2	12.4	1979
Greensboro, NC	5.0	15.9	18.9	14.5	14.7	10.9	9.5	4.5	6.1	1983
Honolulu, HI	5.1	10.2	11.5	12.2	24.1	18.9	10.7	4.0	3.3	1975
Houston, TX	11.9	21.5	14.4	15.5	16.9	8.4	6.2	2.6	2.4	1989
Huntsville, AL	10.8	19.7	17.8	16.1	11.3	13.7	6.4	1.9	2.2	1989
Indianapolis, IN	6.5	15.5	16.7	10.6	12.5	10.6	10.3	4.4	12.8	1979
Jacksonville, FL	8.6	22.7	16.6	16.6	12.4	8.0	8.0	3.4	3.9	1989
Kansas City, MO	4.8	13.7	14.5	12.3	15.4	11.6	11.4	4.4	11.8	1977
Lafayette, LA	9.5	16.6	12.9	15.5	16.4	10.4	9.3	4.1	5.2	1983
Lakeland, FL	5.8	23.8	17.7	18.2	15.1	7.7	6.5	2.1	3.2	1989
Las Vegas, NV	7.2	30.1	29.1	14.6	10.6	5.1	2.2	0.7	0.4	1996
Lexington, KY	6.4	17.2	17.0	13.9	14.8	11.5	8.0	3.3	7.9	1983
Lincoln, NE	7.3	14.1	15.1	10.1	15.6	10.0	10.3	2.8	14.7	1978
Little Rock, AR	9.3	18.2	16.7	13.7	17.0	10.8	7.1	3.4	3.7	1986
Los Angeles, CA	2.9	6.1	7.6	12.3	16.1	15.9	18.7	8.4	11.9	1967
Louisville, KY	4.4	13.1	14.2	9.2	15.2	12.4	12.6	6.2	12.8	1974
Madison, WI	6.5	16.2	15.6	11.1	15.0	9.6	7.8	3.5	14.6	1980

Table continued on following page.

Metro Area	2010 or Later	2000 -2009	1990 -1999	1980 -1989	1970 -1979	1960 -1969	1950 -1959	1940 -1949	Before 1940	Median Year
Manchester, NH	3.0	10.1	10.3	20.9	15.3	9.6	7.1	3.7	19.9	1976
Memphis, TN	4.2	15.7	17.1	13.7	16.2	10.8	11.9	5.3	5.1	1980
Miami, FL	4.1	13.0	15.1	19.4	21.4	12.3	9.8	2.8	2.1	1981
Midland, TX	14.0	11.4	14.5	18.0	11.2	10.5	15.9	2.8	1.7	1984
Milwaukee, WI	2.7	8.2	10.8	8.0	13.0	11.5	16.3	6.8	22.9	1964
Minneapolis, MN	5.1	14.3	14.4	14.5	14.7	9.8	9.7	3.7	13.9	1979
Nashville, TN	10.7	19.7	17.8	14.3	13.6	9.2	6.9	3.1	4.7	1989
New Haven, CT	1.8	5.6	7.1	12.3	13.3	12.3	15.2	7.1	25.2	1962
New Orleans, LA	3.8	11.9	9.8	13.3	19.3	13.6	10.1	4.8	13.5	1974
New York, NY	2.8	6.7	6.1	7.7	9.8	13.7	15.9	8.8	28.6	1958
Oklahoma City, OK	9.3	15.0	11.1	14.8	17.2	12.0	9.6	4.8	6.2	1980
Omaha, NE	6.8	14.3	13.0	9.9	14.6	12.0	8.7	3.4	17.2	1976
Orlando, FL	8.8	23.8	20.6	20.2	12.8	5.9	5.2	1.2	1.5	1992
Peoria, IL	3.1	9.0	8.6	6.0	17.3	12.3	14.3	8.0	21.4	1965
Philadelphia, PA	3.1	7.8	9.6	10.0	12.1	11.9	15.7	7.5	22.2	1964
Phoenix, AZ	6.6	25.4	20.3	17.2	16.1	7.3	5.1	1.2	0.9	1991
Pittsburgh, PA	2.8	6.5	7.7	7.5	11.9	11.5	16.7	8.9	26.4	1959
Portland, OR	6.3	14.5	18.6	11.3	17.2	8.4	7.1	4.6	11.9	1981
Providence, RI	1.9	6.3	8.1	11.1	12.2	11.0	11.6	6.6	31.4	1960
Provo, UT	14.0	25.9	19.2	9.3	13.6	5.0	5.4	3.1	4.6	1995
Raleigh, NC	12.7	25.9	23.0	15.2	9.3	5.9	3.7	1.6	2.8	1995
Reno, NV	5.5	21.1	20.6	15.2	18.9	8.9	5.3	2.2	2.3	1988
Richmond, VA	5.9	14.9	15.3	16.1	15.1	9.7	9.4	4.3	9.2	1981
Riverside, CA	4.2	20.5	14.6	21.9	15.7	8.9	8.5	2.8	2.8	1985
Rochester, MN	7.0	18.0	14.3	12.1	13.5	9.0	8.0	3.4	14.6	1981
Sacramento, CA	3.5	17.6	15.1	16.6	18.3	10.9	10.0	3.7	4.2	1982
Salt Lake City, UT	8.9	15.5	15.5	12.6	18.4	8.8	8.7	3.6	8.0	1982
San Antonio, TX	11.4	20.2	14.5	15.4	13.5	8.4	7.7	4.2	4.6	1988
San Diego, CA	3.7	12.0	12.5	18.6	22.6	12.2	10.7	3.5	4.2	1979
San Francisco, CA	3.2	7.7	8.2	11.1	14.9	13.4	13.7	7.8	19.9	1966
San Jose, CA	5.6	9.0	10.6	12.6	21.6	18.0	13.9	3.6	5.1	1974
Santa Rosa, CA	2.5	10.6	13.6	18.6	21.0	11.6	8.5	5.0	8.4	1978
Savannah, GA	9.0	20.7	16.3	13.8	12.0	7.8	8.1	4.3	8.0	1987
Seattle, WA	7.7	15.2	15.5	14.4	14.2	11.0	7.4	4.4	10.1	1982
Sioux Falls, SD	11.9	18.7	15.3	9.5	14.0	6.8	8.1	3.7	12.1	1986
Springfield, IL	3.1	9.9	13.2	9.1	16.9	11.9	11.6	6.7	17.5	1971
Tallahassee, FL	4.0	18.7	22.6	19.2	16.2	8.3	6.6	2.6	1.7	1988
Tampa, FL	5.6	16.4	14.1	20.1	21.0	9.5	8.5	2.0	2.7	1983
Tucson, AZ	4.5	18.6	17.5	17.8	19.6	8.5	8.9	2.5	2.2	1985
Tulsa, OK	6.7	14.4	12.7	14.3	19.3	10.5	10.6	4.5	7.0	1979
Tuscaloosa, AL	9.2	18.7	18.7	14.2	14.6	9.7	7.1	4.0	3.9	1988
Virginia Beach, VA	6.0	12.7	15.2	18.9	15.8	11.8	9.7	4.2	5.7	1981
Washington, DC	6.7	14.5	14.4	15.8	14.0	12.0	9.4	4.9	8.3	1981
Wichita, KS	4.7	11.9	14.1	12.2	13.3	8.5	17.9	6.0	11.3	1975
Winston-Salem, NC	4.5	15.6	17.2	15.7	16.7	10.9	8.9	4.3	6.3	1982
U.S.	5.2	14.0	13.9	13.4	15.2	10.6	10.3	4.9	12.6	1978

Note: Figures are percentages except for Median Year; Figures cover the Metropolitan Statistical Area—see Appendix B for areas included
Source: U.S. Census Bureau, 2015-2019 American Community Survey 5-Year Estimates

Gross Monthly Rent: City

City	Under $500	$500 -$999	$1,000 -$1,499	$1,500 -$1,999	$2,000 -$2,499	$2,500 -$2,999	$3,000 and up	Median ($)
Albuquerque, NM	8.1	54.4	29.1	6.5	1.1	0.3	0.4	873
Allentown, PA	10.0	39.6	38.7	10.0	1.4	0.3	0.0	1,004
Anchorage, AK	4.0	21.8	36.9	19.9	11.7	4.1	1.4	1,320
Ann Arbor, MI	4.6	23.6	39.5	19.8	7.3	2.4	2.8	1,237
Athens, GA	7.9	59.5	24.2	6.6	1.4	0.2	0.1	856
Atlanta, GA	11.3	27.5	33.6	18.8	5.6	1.7	1.5	1,153
Austin, TX	3.1	18.1	45.2	22.4	7.1	2.3	1.8	1,280
Baton Rouge, LA	10.1	54.4	25.7	5.9	3.2	0.5	0.3	879
Boise City, ID	5.6	50.5	34.7	6.9	1.4	0.3	0.7	957
Boston, MA	16.5	11.4	16.6	22.7	15.3	8.2	9.3	1,620
Boulder, CO	2.8	9.4	35.1	25.4	14.8	5.5	6.9	1,554
Cape Coral, FL	0.9	22.4	46.8	22.5	5.0	1.0	1.4	1,244
Cedar Rapids, IA	15.8	61.0	20.2	1.5	0.6	0.3	0.7	767
Charleston, SC	6.4	20.8	40.8	22.1	5.9	1.8	2.2	1,257
Charlotte, NC	3.8	30.9	46.3	14.5	2.9	0.8	0.7	1,135
Chicago, IL	9.6	31.9	31.5	15.2	6.7	3.0	2.1	1,112
Cincinnati, OH	19.1	56.0	18.0	4.5	1.3	0.4	0.7	738
Clarksville, TN	5.8	48.7	35.6	7.8	1.8	0.1	0.1	961
Cleveland, OH	21.9	58.1	15.8	2.7	0.9	0.3	0.2	719
College Station, TX	3.2	48.7	27.6	14.1	5.0	1.0	0.5	983
Colorado Springs, CO	3.9	34.3	38.3	17.5	3.5	1.8	0.7	1,131
Columbia, MO	6.1	58.0	26.4	5.7	3.3	0.3	0.2	887
Columbia, SC	10.1	48.2	31.9	7.6	1.6	0.1	0.5	933
Columbus, OH	6.4	48.7	35.7	7.1	1.5	0.4	0.3	961
Dallas, TX	4.3	41.0	36.7	11.7	3.6	1.4	1.1	1,052
Davenport, IA	9.2	68.6	16.4	3.2	0.8	0.7	1.1	771
Denver, CO	8.2	18.4	35.8	23.2	9.6	3.2	1.6	1,311
Des Moines, IA	8.6	61.1	25.1	4.1	0.9	0.2	0.1	855
Durham, NC	7.4	36.4	42.6	10.3	2.0	0.5	0.8	1,058
Edison, NJ	2.8	5.8	39.4	35.3	13.2	2.6	0.9	1,528
El Paso, TX	15.2	53.4	25.4	4.9	0.5	0.3	0.2	837
Fargo, ND	7.0	65.6	20.7	5.3	1.1	0.2	0.1	823
Fayetteville, NC	5.6	51.7	36.6	5.2	0.7	0.2	0.1	947
Fort Collins, CO	2.9	20.0	39.7	26.3	9.1	1.4	0.7	1,346
Fort Wayne, IN	11.5	71.0	15.0	1.5	0.7	0.2	0.1	764
Fort Worth, TX	4.9	39.7	35.0	15.5	3.1	0.9	0.9	1,060
Grand Rapids, MI	10.2	48.9	31.0	6.5	2.8	0.5	0.1	925
Greeley, CO	9.2	40.3	32.2	14.0	3.2	0.6	0.5	1,007
Green Bay, WI	12.0	71.3	15.4	1.0	0.1	0.1	0.2	730
Greensboro, NC	6.8	61.7	26.0	3.4	1.2	0.4	0.5	877
Honolulu, HI	6.9	13.3	30.4	22.3	11.3	6.7	9.2	1,491
Houston, TX	3.8	42.7	34.6	12.8	3.3	1.4	1.4	1,041
Huntsville, AL	11.3	59.9	24.2	3.2	0.5	0.6	0.4	827
Indianapolis, IN	6.2	58.7	28.2	5.3	1.0	0.2	0.3	892
Jacksonville, FL	6.6	36.6	42.2	11.8	2.2	0.3	0.4	1,065
Kansas City, MO	8.7	48.0	33.8	7.2	1.5	0.5	0.4	941
Lafayette, LA	9.9	54.6	27.8	6.1	1.3	0.3	0.1	890
Lakeland, FL	5.6	44.6	39.6	7.9	1.4	0.6	0.3	999
Las Vegas, NV	4.7	35.4	41.8	13.8	2.9	0.8	0.6	1,102
Lexington, KY	8.1	52.5	30.6	5.8	2.2	0.4	0.3	896
Lincoln, NE	9.5	58.4	25.0	4.9	0.8	0.3	1.0	852
Little Rock, AR	9.9	54.3	29.0	4.8	0.8	0.6	0.6	872
Los Angeles, CA	5.3	15.7	32.0	22.6	12.4	6.1	5.9	1,450
Louisville, KY	13.7	54.1	25.9	4.9	0.7	0.4	0.3	846
Madison, WI	3.4	34.3	42.0	13.9	4.1	1.3	1.0	1,118

Table continued on following page.

City	Under $500	$500 -$999	$1,000 -$1,499	$1,500 -$1,999	$2,000 -$2,499	$2,500 -$2,999	$3,000 and up	Median ($)
Manchester, NH	7.4	28.2	45.1	15.4	2.5	0.7	0.6	1,135
Memphis, TN	8.1	54.6	31.2	4.7	0.9	0.2	0.2	901
Miami, FL	10.7	26.3	30.0	17.0	9.3	3.8	2.9	1,183
Midland, TX	1.7	26.0	41.3	19.5	7.5	2.9	1.2	1,262
Milwaukee, WI	9.1	60.2	24.2	4.7	1.2	0.4	0.2	858
Minneapolis, MN	12.8	35.3	30.2	14.4	4.7	1.4	1.1	1,027
Nashville, TN	8.7	31.5	39.8	14.1	4.0	1.1	0.8	1,100
New Haven, CT	13.3	18.7	41.2	19.5	5.1	1.5	0.8	1,196
New Orleans, LA	12.8	37.4	33.7	11.5	3.0	0.9	0.6	998
New York, NY	10.6	14.6	28.1	22.1	11.0	5.6	8.0	1,443
Oklahoma City, OK	8.1	57.1	27.0	6.0	1.2	0.4	0.4	871
Omaha, NE	7.7	51.6	31.4	7.0	1.3	0.3	0.7	923
Orlando, FL	3.7	24.7	48.8	17.6	4.0	0.8	0.4	1,196
Peoria, IL	15.6	58.0	20.6	3.7	1.0	0.3	0.9	806
Philadelphia, PA	11.0	35.4	34.7	11.6	4.4	1.5	1.3	1,042
Phoenix, AZ	4.5	40.2	40.2	11.5	2.4	0.6	0.5	1,053
Pittsburgh, PA	13.6	40.7	28.8	11.2	4.0	1.0	0.7	958
Portland, OR	6.5	22.1	38.1	20.9	8.1	2.7	1.6	1,248
Providence, RI	19.5	31.1	35.2	9.8	2.6	0.7	1.1	994
Provo, UT	12.8	49.7	24.3	10.2	2.3	0.5	0.2	877
Raleigh, NC	3.9	31.6	47.0	13.2	3.0	0.5	0.8	1,121
Reno, NV	5.6	42.2	33.7	14.3	3.2	0.5	0.6	1,029
Richmond, VA	12.6	35.0	37.0	11.7	2.7	0.3	0.6	1,025
Riverside, CA	3.4	16.0	39.3	28.9	9.9	1.8	0.7	1,378
Rochester, MN	9.1	43.7	30.2	13.0	1.7	0.9	1.3	974
Sacramento, CA	5.9	24.1	38.5	23.4	6.1	1.4	0.6	1,263
Salt Lake City, UT	8.9	42.8	31.8	12.5	3.1	0.6	0.4	985
San Antonio, TX	7.6	43.3	36.4	10.0	1.7	0.4	0.6	992
San Diego, CA	3.4	10.2	25.9	26.9	18.7	8.9	6.0	1,695
San Francisco, CA	9.3	13.0	15.6	15.3	13.6	11.7	21.4	1,895
San Jose, CA	4.5	6.9	13.6	20.9	19.2	16.2	18.7	2,107
Santa Rosa, CA	5.4	8.4	30.1	27.8	18.2	6.9	3.2	1,609
Savannah, GA	10.0	38.1	39.8	8.9	1.8	0.5	1.0	1,019
Seattle, WA	6.5	10.0	27.1	28.0	14.9	7.0	6.4	1,614
Sioux Falls, SD	8.5	65.9	19.8	4.0	0.6	0.5	0.8	827
Springfield, IL	12.4	62.3	19.5	3.4	1.1	1.1	0.2	805
Tallahassee, FL	5.3	42.2	39.8	8.5	3.2	0.6	0.3	1,023
Tampa, FL	8.1	30.2	37.6	16.0	4.8	1.9	1.5	1,131
Tucson, AZ	7.9	57.2	27.6	5.4	1.1	0.4	0.5	846
Tulsa, OK	10.9	59.4	24.1	3.6	1.0	0.5	0.6	829
Tuscaloosa, AL	13.1	57.0	22.2	4.6	1.9	0.3	1.0	844
Virginia Beach, VA	3.2	12.0	47.9	26.8	6.9	1.7	1.6	1,367
Washington, DC	10.4	13.2	24.7	21.1	13.6	8.2	8.9	1,541
Wichita, KS	11.6	61.3	22.4	3.3	0.6	0.2	0.7	809
Winston-Salem, NC	10.9	62.6	21.5	3.5	0.9	0.2	0.4	806
U.S.	9.4	36.2	30.0	14.0	5.6	2.4	2.4	1,062

Note: Figures are percentages except for Median; Gross rent is the contract rent plus the estimated average monthly cost of utilities (electricity, gas, and water and sewer) and fuels (oil, coal, kerosene, wood, etc.) if these are paid by the renter (or paid for the renter by someone else).
Source: U.S. Census Bureau, 2015-2019 American Community Survey 5-Year Estimates

Gross Monthly Rent: Metro Area

MSA[1]	Under $500	$500 -$999	$1,000 -$1,499	$1,500 -$1,999	$2,000 -$2,499	$2,500 -2,999	$3,000 and up	Median ($)
Albuquerque, NM	8.0	52.5	30.1	7.5	1.1	0.3	0.4	892
Allentown, PA	9.5	34.3	38.5	13.6	2.6	0.7	0.8	1,066
Anchorage, AK	4.2	23.2	37.1	19.7	10.8	3.7	1.3	1,288
Ann Arbor, MI	5.5	33.9	37.6	14.7	4.5	1.6	2.2	1,114
Athens, GA	8.4	59.5	23.6	6.2	1.5	0.5	0.2	853
Atlanta, GA	4.8	28.9	45.0	16.1	3.4	0.9	0.8	1,156
Austin, TX	3.1	19.4	44.5	22.7	6.7	2.1	1.6	1,273
Baton Rouge, LA	8.9	50.9	29.0	7.6	2.9	0.4	0.3	922
Boise City, ID	8.2	47.3	34.8	7.4	1.6	0.4	0.5	958
Boston, MA	12.4	13.4	25.6	23.5	13.2	6.1	5.8	1,475
Boulder, CO	4.0	11.7	34.6	27.2	13.3	5.0	4.2	1,495
Cape Coral, FL	4.2	29.8	43.3	14.3	4.8	1.6	2.0	1,154
Cedar Rapids, IA	16.9	60.9	18.9	1.9	0.5	0.3	0.7	753
Charleston, SC	6.1	29.6	40.2	17.0	4.2	1.5	1.4	1,156
Charlotte, NC	6.1	41.0	37.9	11.2	2.4	0.8	0.6	1,030
Chicago, IL	7.7	32.0	34.9	15.8	5.8	2.2	1.7	1,122
Cincinnati, OH	12.3	54.7	24.8	5.7	1.5	0.4	0.7	842
Clarksville, TN	8.7	49.9	32.7	7.3	1.3	0.2	0.0	919
Cleveland, OH	13.0	57.6	23.2	4.3	1.1	0.3	0.5	817
College Station, TX	6.3	51.7	26.5	10.6	3.6	0.8	0.5	935
Colorado Springs, CO	3.8	31.8	36.9	21.1	4.0	1.8	0.6	1,173
Columbia, MO	7.9	59.1	25.3	4.5	2.8	0.3	0.2	862
Columbia, SC	7.6	50.4	32.4	7.2	1.5	0.5	0.4	933
Columbus, OH	7.6	48.3	34.3	7.3	1.6	0.5	0.4	953
Dallas, TX	3.4	33.2	40.0	16.3	4.7	1.4	1.0	1,139
Davenport, IA	15.1	61.8	17.1	3.9	0.9	0.4	0.8	765
Denver, CO	5.1	16.7	37.2	26.2	10.2	2.9	1.7	1,380
Des Moines, IA	7.3	54.0	30.1	6.2	1.3	0.2	0.7	904
Durham, NC	7.9	38.7	39.1	10.0	2.5	0.6	1.1	1,033
Edison, NJ	9.4	13.9	30.7	23.1	11.0	5.3	6.7	1,439
El Paso, TX	15.0	53.4	25.4	5.2	0.5	0.3	0.2	837
Fargo, ND	8.0	62.0	21.3	6.7	1.4	0.4	0.3	837
Fayetteville, NC	7.3	50.9	33.4	7.2	1.1	0.1	0.1	932
Fort Collins, CO	4.1	23.2	37.4	25.2	7.7	1.7	0.7	1,297
Fort Wayne, IN	11.5	69.3	16.1	2.0	0.8	0.2	0.1	771
Fort Worth, TX	3.4	33.2	40.0	16.3	4.7	1.4	1.0	1,139
Grand Rapids, MI	8.8	56.1	26.7	5.7	1.9	0.3	0.3	884
Greeley, CO	7.7	36.4	33.4	16.3	4.0	1.0	1.2	1,085
Green Bay, WI	9.9	69.3	18.6	1.4	0.3	0.2	0.3	784
Greensboro, NC	9.6	63.4	22.4	2.9	1.0	0.3	0.5	834
Honolulu, HI	5.6	10.4	24.1	20.3	14.1	10.0	15.5	1,745
Houston, TX	3.8	37.0	37.0	15.6	4.0	1.4	1.2	1,101
Huntsville, AL	10.9	59.8	24.0	3.9	0.6	0.5	0.3	836
Indianapolis, IN	6.3	54.7	30.5	6.4	1.4	0.3	0.5	916
Jacksonville, FL	5.9	34.8	41.3	13.6	3.2	0.7	0.6	1,093
Kansas City, MO	8.2	46.4	34.4	8.0	2.0	0.5	0.6	961
Lafayette, LA	15.3	57.0	21.5	4.8	1.2	0.1	0.1	811
Lakeland, FL	6.7	45.8	33.6	11.3	1.8	0.5	0.3	978
Las Vegas, NV	2.8	34.4	42.1	15.9	3.5	0.8	0.6	1,132
Lexington, KY	9.6	55.1	28.1	4.9	1.7	0.3	0.3	867
Lincoln, NE	9.9	58.2	24.9	4.8	0.8	0.4	1.0	848
Little Rock, AR	10.1	58.9	25.0	4.7	0.6	0.4	0.3	845
Los Angeles, CA	4.2	12.7	30.8	25.7	14.0	6.7	5.9	1,545
Louisville, KY	13.1	54.3	26.6	4.6	0.8	0.4	0.3	854
Madison, WI	5.0	40.5	38.5	11.6	2.9	0.9	0.6	1,046

Table continued on following page.

MSA[1]	Under $500	$500 -$999	$1,000 -$1,499	$1,500 -$1,999	$2,000 -$2,499	$2,500 -2,999	$3,000 and up	Median ($)
Manchester, NH	6.9	24.7	42.8	19.9	4.2	0.9	0.5	1,191
Memphis, TN	7.8	50.9	32.8	6.4	1.5	0.3	0.3	930
Miami, FL	5.2	17.0	37.9	24.5	9.5	3.4	2.4	1,363
Midland, TX	2.0	25.1	41.0	20.1	7.5	3.2	1.1	1,269
Milwaukee, WI	7.7	54.1	28.9	6.7	1.6	0.5	0.3	903
Minneapolis, MN	9.2	32.4	35.9	16.1	4.2	1.2	1.1	1,102
Nashville, TN	8.0	35.2	38.0	13.3	3.6	1.1	0.8	1,073
New Haven, CT	10.4	24.6	41.3	17.0	4.6	1.2	1.0	1,153
New Orleans, LA	9.3	41.9	35.6	10.0	2.2	0.6	0.5	991
New York, NY	9.4	13.9	30.7	23.1	11.0	5.3	6.7	1,439
Oklahoma City, OK	8.2	56.4	27.3	6.2	1.3	0.3	0.4	876
Omaha, NE	8.2	50.7	31.0	7.5	1.4	0.4	0.7	927
Orlando, FL	2.9	25.1	46.3	19.7	4.2	1.1	0.7	1,210
Peoria, IL	16.6	60.9	17.6	2.6	1.0	0.4	1.0	764
Philadelphia, PA	8.1	29.1	38.4	15.9	5.4	1.7	1.4	1,143
Phoenix, AZ	3.6	34.4	40.9	15.4	3.6	1.1	1.1	1,124
Pittsburgh, PA	15.6	51.9	23.2	6.0	1.9	0.6	0.8	831
Portland, OR	4.8	20.9	42.1	21.8	7.1	1.8	1.4	1,271
Providence, RI	16.0	37.6	31.8	10.3	2.8	0.6	0.7	968
Provo, UT	6.6	39.1	33.3	15.8	3.7	0.9	0.6	1,054
Raleigh, NC	4.9	32.8	43.7	13.4	3.4	0.8	1.0	1,113
Reno, NV	4.9	39.3	34.7	15.9	3.7	0.8	0.8	1,074
Richmond, VA	7.3	30.2	44.1	13.9	2.9	0.8	0.8	1,117
Riverside, CA	4.2	22.6	34.7	23.5	9.9	3.7	1.5	1,326
Rochester, MN	11.5	47.5	27.7	10.0	1.5	0.7	0.9	908
Sacramento, CA	4.6	22.7	37.5	23.2	8.1	2.4	1.4	1,290
Salt Lake City, UT	5.4	33.3	41.2	15.4	3.3	0.8	0.7	1,114
San Antonio, TX	7.0	40.8	36.6	11.8	2.3	0.7	0.8	1,024
San Diego, CA	3.5	9.9	28.1	27.2	17.0	8.2	6.2	1,658
San Francisco, CA	6.0	9.4	17.2	21.4	18.2	11.9	15.8	1,905
San Jose, CA	3.5	5.8	11.6	18.8	20.7	17.2	22.4	2,249
Santa Rosa, CA	5.2	10.6	27.7	27.0	17.3	7.6	4.5	1,621
Savannah, GA	7.3	33.4	43.3	12.0	2.8	0.4	0.8	1,086
Seattle, WA	5.1	14.0	31.4	27.7	12.8	5.0	4.0	1,492
Sioux Falls, SD	9.4	64.4	20.0	4.4	0.7	0.4	0.8	829
Springfield, IL	11.4	63.1	19.9	3.6	0.9	0.9	0.2	818
Tallahassee, FL	6.9	44.2	36.9	8.4	2.9	0.5	0.2	991
Tampa, FL	4.9	33.9	40.4	14.9	3.6	1.4	1.0	1,115
Tucson, AZ	7.2	51.4	30.9	7.5	1.6	0.7	0.8	907
Tulsa, OK	10.7	56.8	26.1	4.4	1.0	0.5	0.5	852
Tuscaloosa, AL	17.1	54.6	21.8	4.2	1.5	0.2	0.6	819
Virginia Beach, VA	7.0	26.2	41.2	18.4	4.9	1.3	1.0	1,180
Washington, DC	4.6	7.8	25.4	32.2	16.6	7.3	6.1	1,690
Wichita, KS	11.4	60.3	22.5	4.0	0.9	0.3	0.7	818
Winston-Salem, NC	12.9	63.9	18.9	3.1	0.7	0.2	0.2	773
U.S.	9.4	36.2	30.0	14.0	5.6	2.4	2.4	1,062

Note: (1) Figures cover the Metropolitan Statistical Area (MSA)—see Appendix B for areas included; Figures are percentages except for Median; Gross rent is the contract rent plus the estimated average monthly cost of utilities (electricity, gas, and water and sewer) and fuels (oil, coal, kerosene, wood, etc.) if these are paid by the renter (or paid for the renter by someone else).
Source: U.S. Census Bureau, 2015-2019 American Community Survey 5-Year Estimates

Highest Level of Education: City

City	Less than H.S.	H.S. Diploma	Some College, No Deg.	Associate Degree	Bachelors Degree	Masters Degree	Profess. School Degree	Doctorate Degree
Albuquerque, NM	10.3	22.5	23.4	8.5	19.4	10.6	2.7	2.5
Allentown, PA	21.0	38.0	18.3	7.4	9.6	3.9	1.0	0.8
Anchorage, AK	6.1	23.4	25.4	9.0	22.2	9.5	3.1	1.3
Ann Arbor, MI	2.7	7.1	10.0	4.2	30.2	26.9	7.1	11.7
Athens, GA	12.1	19.8	17.1	6.9	22.1	13.4	3.0	5.6
Atlanta, GA	9.1	18.9	15.3	4.9	28.9	15.1	5.3	2.5
Austin, TX	10.6	15.6	16.7	5.4	32.3	13.6	3.3	2.5
Baton Rouge, LA	12.0	27.8	22.5	4.5	19.3	8.8	2.6	2.5
Boise City, ID	4.9	21.4	23.1	9.1	26.8	10.1	2.7	1.9
Boston, MA	12.8	19.7	13.1	4.6	27.0	14.5	4.8	3.4
Boulder, CO	3.1	6.2	11.1	3.6	36.2	24.7	6.4	8.7
Cape Coral, FL	8.2	37.3	21.0	10.1	15.8	5.3	1.3	0.9
Cedar Rapids, IA	6.7	26.6	22.2	12.4	22.9	6.6	1.5	1.0
Charleston, SC	5.1	17.6	16.3	7.9	33.8	12.6	4.5	2.2
Charlotte, NC	10.9	17.1	20.0	7.7	28.9	11.7	2.6	1.1
Chicago, IL	14.9	22.5	17.3	5.8	23.3	11.3	3.3	1.6
Cincinnati, OH	11.9	24.4	19.1	7.4	21.4	10.4	3.1	2.1
Clarksville, TN	7.1	27.9	26.9	10.5	18.7	6.9	0.8	1.2
Cleveland, OH	19.2	32.7	23.2	7.4	10.9	4.5	1.4	0.7
College Station, TX	5.6	11.4	17.0	7.4	29.3	15.7	3.3	10.3
Colorado Springs, CO	6.1	20.0	23.4	10.6	24.3	12.0	2.0	1.5
Columbia, MO	4.8	18.1	18.7	6.2	27.4	14.9	4.6	5.3
Columbia, SC	10.6	20.1	18.6	6.9	24.4	12.8	3.9	2.7
Columbus, OH	10.2	25.5	20.6	7.2	23.8	9.4	1.9	1.5
Dallas, TX	22.5	21.7	17.8	4.6	21.0	8.3	2.9	1.1
Davenport, IA	9.5	32.5	21.8	10.7	17.0	6.3	1.5	0.8
Denver, CO	12.0	16.8	16.5	5.3	30.2	13.1	4.2	2.0
Des Moines, IA	13.7	29.5	21.2	8.9	18.6	5.5	1.7	0.9
Durham, NC	11.9	16.4	15.5	6.5	25.8	14.7	4.2	4.8
Edison, NJ	7.9	19.5	11.7	5.4	30.0	20.3	2.8	2.5
El Paso, TX	19.7	23.0	24.0	8.2	16.7	6.4	1.2	0.8
Fargo, ND	5.7	20.9	19.6	13.8	28.0	8.0	2.1	1.8
Fayetteville, NC	8.3	24.4	29.4	10.6	18.0	6.7	1.5	1.0
Fort Collins, CO	3.5	15.1	17.7	8.3	32.3	16.8	2.4	4.0
Fort Wayne, IN	11.5	28.2	22.1	10.3	18.3	7.1	1.4	1.0
Fort Worth, TX	17.8	24.9	20.8	6.9	20.0	7.1	1.5	1.1
Grand Rapids, MI	13.3	21.9	20.5	7.9	24.4	8.7	2.0	1.4
Greeley, CO	15.5	27.2	23.4	9.1	15.4	7.2	1.2	1.0
Green Bay, WI	12.5	31.4	20.1	11.2	17.9	5.1	1.1	0.7
Greensboro, NC	10.2	21.5	21.7	8.4	24.1	10.0	2.3	1.8
Honolulu, HI	11.0	23.5	18.3	10.1	23.7	8.3	3.2	2.0
Houston, TX	21.1	22.8	17.8	5.5	20.0	8.6	2.6	1.6
Huntsville, AL	9.0	18.7	20.3	7.9	26.4	13.8	1.8	2.2
Indianapolis, IN	14.2	27.9	19.4	7.6	20.0	7.6	2.1	1.1
Jacksonville, FL	10.5	28.4	22.3	10.1	19.1	7.0	1.7	0.8
Kansas City, MO	10.0	25.3	22.0	7.4	22.2	9.3	2.5	1.2
Lafayette, LA	10.5	27.0	20.0	4.3	25.6	8.5	2.7	1.4
Lakeland, FL	12.0	33.0	19.5	9.6	16.8	6.7	1.6	0.9
Las Vegas, NV	15.2	27.6	24.6	8.0	16.0	5.9	1.9	0.8
Lexington, KY	8.8	19.6	20.5	7.5	24.4	12.0	4.1	3.2
Lincoln, NE	6.7	21.3	21.2	11.2	24.8	9.8	2.2	2.8
Little Rock, AR	8.7	22.2	21.1	6.2	23.7	11.0	4.3	2.8
Los Angeles, CA	22.5	19.2	17.6	6.2	22.6	7.6	2.8	1.4
Louisville, KY	10.4	28.6	22.9	8.1	17.9	8.5	2.3	1.2
Madison, WI	4.5	14.2	15.3	8.0	32.1	16.2	4.2	5.3

Table continued on following page.

City	Less than H.S.	H.S. Diploma	Some College, No Deg.	Associate Degree	Bachelors Degree	Masters Degree	Profess. School Degree	Doctorate Degree
Manchester, NH	12.7	29.1	18.9	9.3	20.3	7.3	1.7	0.9
Memphis, TN	14.3	30.6	23.3	5.6	15.7	7.1	2.0	1.3
Miami, FL	22.0	28.4	12.5	7.4	17.9	7.1	3.6	1.1
Midland, TX	14.9	25.2	23.2	7.7	20.7	5.9	1.7	0.7
Milwaukee, WI	16.0	30.2	21.9	7.2	15.9	6.5	1.3	0.9
Minneapolis, MN	10.0	15.1	17.1	7.3	30.4	13.6	4.0	2.5
Nashville, TN	11.2	22.3	18.9	6.4	25.8	10.3	2.9	2.1
New Haven, CT	14.4	32.2	14.0	4.5	15.7	10.7	4.2	4.3
New Orleans, LA	13.5	22.8	21.5	4.7	21.2	9.9	4.4	2.0
New York, NY	17.8	24.0	13.7	6.3	22.2	11.2	3.2	1.5
Oklahoma City, OK	13.6	25.4	22.9	7.3	19.7	7.5	2.4	1.1
Omaha, NE	10.5	22.3	21.9	7.7	24.3	8.9	2.9	1.5
Orlando, FL	9.6	23.2	18.4	10.8	25.4	8.3	3.0	1.3
Peoria, IL	10.6	24.3	21.5	8.6	20.7	10.2	2.7	1.3
Philadelphia, PA	15.3	32.6	16.7	5.7	17.3	8.1	2.6	1.6
Phoenix, AZ	18.1	23.6	22.0	7.7	18.3	7.3	2.0	1.0
Pittsburgh, PA	7.1	25.5	15.1	7.9	23.2	13.1	4.3	3.9
Portland, OR	7.6	15.1	20.3	6.6	30.1	13.8	4.1	2.4
Providence, RI	18.4	31.4	15.2	5.0	16.1	8.6	2.9	2.5
Provo, UT	7.1	14.3	26.5	8.9	29.7	8.9	1.6	2.8
Raleigh, NC	8.2	15.6	17.8	7.5	32.4	13.1	3.1	2.3
Reno, NV	11.0	22.2	25.0	8.2	20.6	8.4	2.3	2.3
Richmond, VA	14.6	21.8	18.4	5.6	23.5	11.0	3.1	2.0
Riverside, CA	19.4	26.3	23.7	7.7	13.5	6.4	1.4	1.7
Rochester, MN	6.0	18.7	17.2	11.4	25.7	12.1	5.2	3.7
Sacramento, CA	14.7	21.3	22.4	8.5	21.2	7.7	2.9	1.3
Salt Lake City, UT	11.2	17.5	17.7	7.0	25.7	12.5	4.6	3.7
San Antonio, TX	17.6	26.3	22.4	7.7	16.6	6.7	1.7	1.0
San Diego, CA	11.9	15.1	19.7	7.4	27.0	12.2	3.7	3.0
San Francisco, CA	11.5	12.1	13.3	5.0	34.8	15.4	5.0	2.8
San Jose, CA	15.4	16.6	16.8	7.5	25.7	13.6	2.0	2.5
Santa Rosa, CA	13.8	19.3	24.5	9.8	20.1	8.0	2.9	1.5
Savannah, GA	12.4	26.8	25.9	6.7	17.8	7.6	1.6	1.2
Seattle, WA	5.2	9.6	15.0	6.2	36.7	18.1	5.3	3.9
Sioux Falls, SD	7.7	24.8	20.8	11.5	23.8	8.1	2.2	1.1
Springfield, IL	8.7	25.9	22.1	7.6	21.5	9.8	3.3	1.2
Tallahassee, FL	6.5	17.0	19.0	9.3	26.2	13.8	3.9	4.3
Tampa, FL	12.1	25.6	16.0	7.7	23.3	9.6	3.9	1.7
Tucson, AZ	15.0	23.6	25.6	8.4	16.5	7.8	1.4	1.6
Tulsa, OK	12.7	25.3	22.6	7.9	20.7	7.2	2.5	1.1
Tuscaloosa, AL	10.9	27.3	19.9	5.0	21.0	10.3	2.5	3.1
Virginia Beach, VA	6.5	21.0	25.7	10.9	22.6	10.2	2.1	1.1
Washington, DC	9.1	16.8	12.6	3.0	24.8	21.2	8.4	4.2
Wichita, KS	11.7	26.4	24.0	7.9	19.1	8.1	1.8	1.1
Winston-Salem, NC	11.8	24.9	21.5	7.4	20.8	8.9	3.0	1.9
U.S.	12.0	27.0	20.4	8.5	19.8	8.8	2.1	1.4

Note: Figures cover persons age 25 and over
Source: U.S. Census Bureau, 2015-2019 American Community Survey 5-Year Estimates

Highest Level of Education: Metro Area

Metro Area	Less than H.S.	H.S. Diploma	Some College, No Deg.	Associate Degree	Bachelors Degree	Masters Degree	Profess. School Degree	Doctorate Degree
Albuquerque, NM	11.4	24.6	23.3	8.5	17.9	9.8	2.3	2.2
Allentown, PA	10.0	34.2	17.1	9.3	18.3	8.4	1.6	1.2
Anchorage, AK	6.3	26.0	26.2	9.1	20.1	8.5	2.6	1.2
Ann Arbor, MI	4.7	14.6	17.6	7.1	26.3	18.8	4.7	6.0
Athens, GA	12.2	24.5	16.8	7.1	19.9	11.8	3.1	4.5
Atlanta, GA	10.4	23.9	19.5	7.6	24.0	10.6	2.5	1.5
Austin, TX	10.1	19.1	19.6	6.5	28.8	11.6	2.5	1.9
Baton Rouge, LA	12.6	32.2	21.4	6.2	18.0	6.6	1.7	1.3
Boise City, ID	8.2	25.8	24.8	9.4	21.3	7.4	1.7	1.3
Boston, MA	8.3	22.1	14.5	7.0	26.0	15.2	3.5	3.3
Boulder, CO	5.0	11.7	15.1	6.1	34.0	18.8	4.1	5.2
Cape Coral, FL	11.6	31.0	20.3	8.9	17.6	7.2	2.2	1.2
Cedar Rapids, IA	5.7	29.0	21.5	12.8	21.9	6.9	1.4	0.8
Charleston, SC	9.3	25.4	20.1	9.5	23.0	8.9	2.4	1.2
Charlotte, NC	11.0	23.5	21.1	9.2	23.5	9.0	1.8	0.9
Chicago, IL	11.3	23.9	19.5	7.2	23.0	10.9	2.6	1.4
Cincinnati, OH	9.0	29.7	19.2	8.4	21.0	9.3	2.0	1.4
Clarksville, TN	9.3	30.2	25.4	10.3	16.1	6.8	1.1	0.9
Cleveland, OH	9.4	28.9	21.8	8.7	18.9	8.7	2.4	1.2
College Station, TX	13.4	22.2	20.4	6.5	20.6	9.6	2.2	5.1
Colorado Springs, CO	5.6	20.5	24.0	11.3	23.5	11.8	1.8	1.4
Columbia, MO	6.4	23.7	19.8	7.4	24.5	11.3	3.2	3.7
Columbia, SC	10.1	26.9	21.2	9.0	20.1	9.2	1.8	1.5
Columbus, OH	8.5	27.7	19.6	7.5	23.4	9.7	2.2	1.4
Dallas, TX	14.4	22.3	21.1	7.0	23.0	9.2	1.9	1.1
Davenport, IA	9.0	30.5	23.0	10.5	17.2	7.3	1.5	0.8
Denver, CO	8.8	19.9	19.8	7.7	27.7	11.8	2.7	1.6
Des Moines, IA	7.5	25.6	20.2	10.3	25.4	7.7	2.2	1.1
Durham, NC	11.2	19.8	16.1	7.6	23.2	13.2	4.0	4.9
Edison, NJ	13.5	24.7	14.8	6.7	23.4	12.1	3.3	1.6
El Paso, TX	21.7	23.7	23.1	8.2	15.7	5.7	1.1	0.7
Fargo, ND	5.2	21.0	21.0	14.2	27.4	7.9	1.8	1.5
Fayetteville, NC	10.4	27.3	27.5	11.1	15.7	6.2	1.0	0.8
Fort Collins, CO	4.1	19.0	20.4	9.2	28.0	13.9	2.1	3.2
Fort Wayne, IN	10.4	29.2	21.7	10.9	18.4	6.9	1.5	0.9
Fort Worth, TX	14.4	22.3	21.1	7.0	23.0	9.2	1.9	1.1
Grand Rapids, MI	8.8	27.2	22.0	9.3	21.8	8.1	1.7	1.1
Greeley, CO	11.9	27.3	24.1	9.1	18.6	7.0	1.1	0.9
Green Bay, WI	8.0	32.1	19.7	12.4	19.6	6.0	1.5	0.7
Greensboro, NC	13.2	26.7	21.7	8.9	19.2	7.5	1.5	1.3
Honolulu, HI	8.1	25.9	20.3	10.7	22.9	8.1	2.5	1.5
Houston, TX	16.3	23.2	20.6	7.1	21.0	8.4	2.0	1.5
Huntsville, AL	9.8	22.7	20.2	8.1	24.2	11.9	1.4	1.7
Indianapolis, IN	10.3	27.9	19.3	7.9	22.4	8.8	2.2	1.3
Jacksonville, FL	9.1	27.7	21.8	10.0	20.6	7.9	1.9	1.1
Kansas City, MO	8.0	25.5	21.6	7.7	23.5	10.2	2.3	1.2
Lafayette, LA	15.9	36.4	18.6	5.7	16.4	5.0	1.3	0.7
Lakeland, FL	15.0	34.7	20.9	9.2	13.2	5.2	1.1	0.7
Las Vegas, NV	13.9	28.5	25.1	8.1	16.2	5.8	1.6	0.8
Lexington, KY	9.9	24.2	20.8	7.9	21.3	10.3	3.2	2.4
Lincoln, NE	6.3	21.9	21.2	11.7	24.5	9.7	2.2	2.6
Little Rock, AR	9.6	29.3	23.0	7.8	18.9	8.0	2.1	1.5
Los Angeles, CA	19.3	19.8	19.2	7.2	22.4	8.2	2.5	1.4
Louisville, KY	9.9	29.6	22.3	8.6	17.9	8.4	2.2	1.1
Madison, WI	4.7	21.0	17.9	10.3	27.7	12.1	3.0	3.2

Table continued on following page.

Metro Area	Less than H.S.	H.S. Diploma	Some College, No Deg.	Associate Degree	Bachelors Degree	Masters Degree	Profess. School Degree	Doctorate Degree
Manchester, NH	7.9	25.8	18.2	10.0	24.3	10.9	1.6	1.3
Memphis, TN	12.0	29.2	23.5	7.1	17.4	7.9	1.9	1.2
Miami, FL	14.5	26.5	17.4	9.3	20.2	7.9	2.9	1.2
Midland, TX	15.7	25.9	23.5	7.8	19.3	5.8	1.4	0.6
Milwaukee, WI	8.5	26.5	20.6	8.7	23.0	9.0	2.3	1.3
Minneapolis, MN	6.4	21.2	20.0	10.4	27.4	10.4	2.6	1.6
Nashville, TN	10.0	26.4	20.2	7.3	23.5	9.0	2.2	1.6
New Haven, CT	9.9	30.7	17.1	7.3	18.6	11.2	3.1	2.1
New Orleans, LA	13.1	28.2	22.5	5.8	19.0	7.3	2.8	1.2
New York, NY	13.5	24.7	14.8	6.7	23.4	12.1	3.3	1.6
Oklahoma City, OK	11.0	27.3	23.6	7.5	19.6	7.6	2.0	1.3
Omaha, NE	8.3	23.8	22.5	9.1	23.8	9.0	2.3	1.3
Orlando, FL	10.5	25.8	19.9	11.5	21.3	7.8	2.0	1.0
Peoria, IL	8.3	30.5	23.2	10.4	18.1	7.2	1.5	0.9
Philadelphia, PA	9.3	29.0	16.7	7.1	22.4	10.8	2.7	1.9
Phoenix, AZ	12.5	23.0	24.4	8.6	20.0	8.3	1.9	1.2
Pittsburgh, PA	6.1	32.4	16.4	10.2	21.3	9.8	2.3	1.7
Portland, OR	7.9	19.9	23.6	8.8	24.7	10.5	2.6	1.9
Providence, RI	12.3	28.8	18.0	8.6	19.6	9.2	1.9	1.5
Provo, UT	5.5	16.8	26.7	10.7	27.7	9.2	1.6	1.7
Raleigh, NC	8.3	17.7	18.2	9.0	29.6	12.6	2.4	2.2
Reno, NV	11.3	23.6	25.7	8.6	19.2	7.8	2.1	1.8
Richmond, VA	10.1	25.1	20.0	7.4	23.1	10.5	2.3	1.6
Riverside, CA	18.9	26.6	24.6	8.2	13.9	5.6	1.3	0.9
Rochester, MN	5.9	23.9	19.1	12.4	22.7	9.7	3.8	2.5
Sacramento, CA	10.7	21.2	24.7	9.9	21.8	7.8	2.6	1.4
Salt Lake City, UT	9.2	23.0	23.9	9.0	22.5	8.7	2.3	1.5
San Antonio, TX	14.9	26.3	22.6	8.0	18.0	7.5	1.7	1.0
San Diego, CA	12.6	18.2	22.3	8.1	23.8	10.0	2.9	2.1
San Francisco, CA	10.9	15.5	17.3	6.6	29.3	13.7	3.8	2.9
San Jose, CA	11.9	14.4	15.4	6.9	27.3	17.5	2.7	3.9
Santa Rosa, CA	11.2	18.7	25.0	9.6	22.2	8.6	3.1	1.6
Savannah, GA	10.2	26.3	24.2	7.9	19.5	8.4	2.2	1.3
Seattle, WA	7.4	19.4	21.0	9.3	26.6	11.7	2.7	2.0
Sioux Falls, SD	7.1	26.1	20.6	12.7	23.2	7.3	2.0	1.0
Springfield, IL	7.4	27.7	22.7	8.3	21.2	9.0	2.6	1.0
Tallahassee, FL	9.4	23.7	19.8	8.7	22.0	10.4	2.9	3.1
Tampa, FL	10.4	28.9	20.5	9.8	19.6	7.6	2.0	1.2
Tucson, AZ	11.6	22.2	25.1	8.7	18.7	9.4	2.3	2.0
Tulsa, OK	10.6	29.1	23.7	8.9	18.9	6.3	1.7	0.9
Tuscaloosa, AL	12.9	31.7	21.1	6.9	16.6	7.5	1.4	1.9
Virginia Beach, VA	8.6	24.9	24.7	9.9	19.5	9.3	1.8	1.2
Washington, DC	9.1	18.2	16.0	5.9	25.8	17.6	4.3	3.2
Wichita, KS	9.9	26.5	24.4	8.6	19.6	8.3	1.7	1.0
Winston-Salem, NC	13.0	29.4	21.6	9.3	17.4	6.5	1.6	1.2
U.S.	12.0	27.0	20.4	8.5	19.8	8.8	2.1	1.4

Note: Figures cover persons age 25 and over; Figures cover the Metropolitan Statistical Area—see Appendix B for areas included
Source: U.S. Census Bureau, 2015-2019 American Community Survey 5-Year Estimates

School Enrollment by Grade and Control: City

City	Preschool (%)		Kindergarten (%)		Grades 1 - 4 (%)		Grades 5 - 8 (%)		Grades 9 - 12 (%)	
	Public	Private	Public	Private	Public	Private	Public	Private	Public	Private
Albuquerque, NM	59.3	40.7	87.2	12.8	91.8	8.2	90.0	10.0	92.0	8.0
Allentown, PA	73.8	26.2	82.8	17.2	87.8	12.2	88.3	11.7	89.0	11.0
Anchorage, AK	56.6	43.4	94.0	6.0	92.3	7.7	92.5	7.5	95.1	4.9
Ann Arbor, MI	25.7	74.3	94.1	5.9	91.8	8.2	87.6	12.4	94.2	5.8
Athens, GA	67.9	32.1	92.6	7.4	91.9	8.1	88.8	11.2	88.5	11.5
Atlanta, GA	54.3	45.7	84.5	15.5	87.8	12.2	79.5	20.5	80.1	19.9
Austin, TX	51.0	49.0	86.9	13.1	89.3	10.7	88.9	11.1	91.0	9.0
Baton Rouge, LA	66.8	33.2	75.3	24.7	80.3	19.7	79.5	20.5	80.8	19.2
Boise City, ID	30.6	69.4	84.8	15.2	90.0	10.0	91.7	8.3	89.1	10.9
Boston, MA	50.7	49.3	84.9	15.1	85.7	14.3	86.8	13.2	87.8	12.2
Boulder, CO	44.0	56.0	84.5	15.5	92.5	7.5	93.4	6.6	92.2	7.8
Cape Coral, FL	84.8	15.2	94.8	5.2	92.0	8.0	93.0	7.0	91.8	8.2
Cedar Rapids, IA	67.5	32.5	86.4	13.6	88.9	11.1	93.0	7.0	90.0	10.0
Charleston, SC	41.2	58.9	78.8	21.2	83.4	16.6	78.9	21.1	78.9	21.1
Charlotte, NC	47.5	52.5	90.5	9.5	90.7	9.3	87.6	12.4	89.8	10.2
Chicago, IL	58.4	41.6	79.9	20.1	85.9	14.1	85.4	14.6	87.4	12.6
Cincinnati, OH	64.7	35.3	73.1	26.9	77.6	22.4	80.1	19.9	80.8	19.2
Clarksville, TN	57.3	42.7	90.6	9.4	93.7	6.3	92.5	7.5	92.4	7.6
Cleveland, OH	74.3	25.7	79.3	20.7	79.6	20.4	77.9	22.1	79.8	20.2
College Station, TX	46.9	53.1	85.1	14.9	86.5	13.5	93.5	6.5	92.7	7.3
Colorado Springs, CO	57.1	42.9	89.3	10.7	92.5	7.5	92.5	7.5	92.0	8.0
Columbia, MO	36.1	63.9	76.7	23.3	87.5	12.5	88.1	11.9	88.8	11.2
Columbia, SC	57.2	42.8	74.3	25.7	88.1	11.9	87.7	12.3	86.7	13.3
Columbus, OH	60.3	39.7	85.3	14.7	87.7	12.3	87.2	12.8	87.3	12.7
Dallas, TX	69.2	30.8	91.0	9.0	92.0	8.0	91.7	8.3	91.6	8.4
Davenport, IA	57.0	43.0	86.1	13.9	89.3	10.7	84.3	15.7	92.8	7.2
Denver, CO	64.4	35.6	86.3	13.7	91.4	8.6	91.0	9.0	91.4	8.6
Des Moines, IA	73.0	27.0	90.0	10.0	89.0	11.0	91.7	8.3	92.3	7.7
Durham, NC	52.1	47.9	91.9	8.1	88.8	11.2	87.3	12.7	89.7	10.3
Edison, NJ	30.2	69.8	67.7	32.3	90.1	9.9	90.0	10.0	91.6	8.4
El Paso, TX	78.5	21.5	93.3	6.7	95.0	5.0	94.6	5.4	96.2	3.8
Fargo, ND	53.4	46.6	94.7	5.3	90.4	9.6	89.3	10.7	93.7	6.3
Fayetteville, NC	63.5	36.5	88.7	11.3	87.2	12.8	87.4	12.6	89.7	10.3
Fort Collins, CO	41.9	58.1	91.7	8.3	94.5	5.5	95.1	4.9	94.6	5.4
Fort Wayne, IN	45.5	54.5	83.5	16.5	79.5	20.5	82.2	17.8	81.3	18.7
Fort Worth, TX	62.0	38.0	87.1	12.9	92.6	7.4	90.7	9.3	92.8	7.2
Grand Rapids, MI	60.4	39.6	74.5	25.5	83.4	16.6	83.4	16.6	84.9	15.1
Greeley, CO	69.6	30.4	83.6	16.4	91.5	8.5	92.6	7.4	95.3	4.7
Green Bay, WI	71.8	28.2	85.7	14.3	90.6	9.4	84.6	15.4	91.1	8.9
Greensboro, NC	53.2	46.8	89.5	10.5	93.4	6.6	90.2	9.8	91.6	8.4
Honolulu, HI	34.7	65.3	79.6	20.4	83.3	16.7	73.0	27.0	74.8	25.2
Houston, TX	66.9	33.1	90.8	9.2	94.2	5.8	92.7	7.3	93.5	6.5
Huntsville, AL	59.4	40.6	87.2	12.8	80.1	19.9	82.9	17.1	84.8	15.2
Indianapolis, IN	61.8	38.2	85.6	14.4	88.5	11.5	87.1	12.9	89.2	10.8
Jacksonville, FL	57.5	42.5	84.3	15.7	84.3	15.7	81.7	18.3	83.5	16.5
Kansas City, MO	57.7	42.3	85.3	14.7	90.1	9.9	88.3	11.7	85.4	14.6
Lafayette, LA	60.7	39.3	64.2	35.8	74.4	25.6	73.3	26.7	80.6	19.4
Lakeland, FL	61.7	38.3	85.0	15.0	83.6	16.4	83.7	16.3	88.0	12.0
Las Vegas, NV	65.7	34.3	88.6	11.4	91.3	8.7	91.7	8.3	93.0	7.0
Lexington, KY	44.2	55.8	86.4	13.6	87.2	12.8	86.6	13.4	86.1	13.9
Lincoln, NE	44.8	55.2	73.8	26.2	84.9	15.1	86.5	13.5	86.4	13.6
Little Rock, AR	60.3	39.7	82.3	17.7	82.7	17.3	82.0	18.0	79.8	20.2
Los Angeles, CA	60.2	39.8	88.1	11.9	89.0	11.0	88.6	11.4	88.8	11.2
Louisville, KY	51.1	48.9	80.2	19.8	83.4	16.6	79.9	20.1	79.3	20.7
Madison, WI	53.6	46.4	85.3	14.7	88.4	11.6	87.0	13.0	91.0	9.0

Table continued on following page.

City	Preschool (%)		Kindergarten (%)		Grades 1 - 4 (%)		Grades 5 - 8 (%)		Grades 9 - 12 (%)	
	Public	Private	Public	Private	Public	Private	Public	Private	Public	Private
Manchester, NH	52.6	47.4	86.1	13.9	89.9	10.1	93.1	6.9	89.5	10.5
Memphis, TN	67.2	32.8	87.3	12.7	87.9	12.1	87.2	12.8	85.5	14.5
Miami, FL	56.0	44.0	86.7	13.3	88.1	11.9	85.6	14.4	90.8	9.2
Midland, TX	64.4	35.6	89.1	10.9	86.0	14.0	88.3	11.7	89.9	10.1
Milwaukee, WI	73.5	26.5	79.4	20.6	77.1	22.9	75.8	24.2	81.4	18.6
Minneapolis, MN	53.4	46.6	85.1	14.9	88.2	11.8	88.9	11.1	87.7	12.3
Nashville, TN	50.7	49.3	87.4	12.6	85.6	14.4	83.4	16.6	82.0	18.0
New Haven, CT	83.6	16.4	94.0	6.0	94.8	5.2	93.8	6.2	92.2	7.8
New Orleans, LA	50.3	49.7	77.0	23.0	80.1	19.9	80.0	20.0	78.9	21.1
New York, NY	60.9	39.1	79.2	20.8	82.7	17.3	82.2	17.8	82.3	17.7
Oklahoma City, OK	73.4	26.6	91.7	8.3	91.8	8.2	91.0	9.0	90.2	9.8
Omaha, NE	53.5	46.5	82.0	18.0	83.5	16.5	85.3	14.7	83.2	16.8
Orlando, FL	62.2	37.8	86.4	13.6	91.2	8.8	85.0	15.0	93.3	6.7
Peoria, IL	60.1	39.9	70.0	30.0	83.9	16.1	83.4	16.6	88.7	11.3
Philadelphia, PA	56.8	43.2	79.1	20.9	79.1	20.9	80.6	19.4	80.1	19.9
Phoenix, AZ	62.7	37.3	90.0	10.0	92.9	7.1	92.4	7.6	93.1	6.9
Pittsburgh, PA	48.0	52.0	77.1	22.9	73.1	26.9	75.8	24.2	81.5	18.5
Portland, OR	39.4	60.6	84.8	15.2	88.0	12.0	87.1	12.9	85.1	14.9
Providence, RI	51.6	48.4	87.8	12.2	86.0	14.0	85.4	14.6	88.6	11.4
Provo, UT	53.8	46.2	95.7	4.3	93.9	6.1	95.8	4.2	88.5	11.5
Raleigh, NC	43.5	56.5	89.3	10.7	90.6	9.4	89.2	10.8	90.6	9.4
Reno, NV	60.7	39.3	86.1	13.9	94.1	5.9	93.2	6.8	94.0	6.0
Richmond, VA	58.6	41.4	91.1	8.9	87.8	12.2	80.8	19.2	87.1	12.9
Riverside, CA	66.0	34.0	90.5	9.5	94.0	6.0	93.6	6.4	95.0	5.0
Rochester, MN	50.9	49.1	80.4	19.6	86.9	13.1	87.1	12.9	91.4	8.6
Sacramento, CA	68.9	31.1	92.8	7.2	93.2	6.8	92.9	7.1	92.6	7.4
Salt Lake City, UT	47.7	52.3	88.2	11.8	91.2	8.8	91.0	9.0	92.8	7.2
San Antonio, TX	70.1	29.9	90.3	9.7	93.1	6.9	92.9	7.1	92.6	7.4
San Diego, CA	52.5	47.5	92.9	7.1	90.9	9.1	91.2	8.8	91.5	8.5
San Francisco, CA	37.5	62.5	73.1	26.9	72.2	27.8	68.1	31.9	75.0	25.0
San Jose, CA	41.9	58.1	81.2	18.8	87.0	13.0	87.0	13.0	86.8	13.2
Santa Rosa, CA	53.6	46.4	94.6	5.4	95.9	4.1	92.5	7.5	92.0	8.0
Savannah, GA	67.6	32.4	93.0	7.0	90.1	9.9	91.0	9.0	89.6	10.4
Seattle, WA	32.6	67.4	79.7	20.3	81.6	18.4	75.9	24.1	79.8	20.2
Sioux Falls, SD	51.1	48.9	87.3	12.7	88.2	11.8	87.5	12.5	84.2	15.8
Springfield, IL	65.7	34.3	80.4	19.6	81.9	18.1	83.9	16.1	85.6	14.4
Tallahassee, FL	48.6	51.4	86.3	13.7	85.9	14.1	83.3	16.7	87.4	12.6
Tampa, FL	49.9	50.1	83.4	16.6	89.5	10.5	85.7	14.3	84.5	15.5
Tucson, AZ	74.0	26.0	85.8	14.2	89.6	10.4	91.3	8.7	92.8	7.2
Tulsa, OK	67.6	32.4	87.1	12.9	88.3	11.7	85.8	14.2	85.2	14.8
Tuscaloosa, AL	62.5	37.5	91.8	8.2	86.2	13.8	92.2	7.8	85.1	14.9
Virginia Beach, VA	37.7	62.3	77.3	22.7	90.2	9.8	88.7	11.3	92.7	7.3
Washington, DC	77.1	22.9	92.3	7.7	87.6	12.4	82.7	17.3	82.6	17.4
Wichita, KS	62.5	37.5	83.7	16.3	85.4	14.6	84.7	15.3	84.2	15.8
Winston-Salem, NC	55.3	44.7	94.1	5.9	93.3	6.7	90.8	9.2	93.2	6.8
U.S.	59.1	40.9	87.6	12.4	89.5	10.5	89.4	10.6	90.1	9.9

Note: Figures shown cover persons 3 years old and over
Source: U.S. Census Bureau, 2015-2019 American Community Survey 5-Year Estimates

School Enrollment by Grade and Control: Metro Area

Metro Area	Preschool (%)		Kindergarten (%)		Grades 1 - 4 (%)		Grades 5 - 8 (%)		Grades 9 - 12 (%)	
	Public	Private	Public	Private	Public	Private	Public	Private	Public	Private
Albuquerque, NM	64.5	35.5	85.6	14.4	90.1	9.9	89.4	10.6	91.7	8.3
Allentown, PA	49.0	51.0	85.5	14.5	89.4	10.6	90.5	9.5	91.0	9.0
Anchorage, AK	58.3	41.7	92.4	7.6	90.7	9.3	90.5	9.5	92.8	7.2
Ann Arbor, MI	49.6	50.4	89.6	10.4	87.3	12.7	87.7	12.3	91.8	8.2
Athens, GA	67.9	32.1	90.9	9.1	90.1	9.9	86.0	14.0	86.7	13.3
Atlanta, GA	56.0	44.0	86.9	13.1	91.0	9.0	89.2	10.8	89.9	10.1
Austin, TX	51.5	48.5	88.1	11.9	90.7	9.3	90.7	9.3	92.4	7.6
Baton Rouge, LA	57.1	42.9	76.9	23.1	81.4	18.6	81.7	18.3	81.4	18.6
Boise City, ID	37.7	62.3	86.1	13.9	91.1	8.9	92.8	7.2	90.5	9.5
Boston, MA	45.7	54.3	87.7	12.3	91.2	8.8	89.8	10.2	86.9	13.1
Boulder, CO	50.7	49.3	84.7	15.3	90.8	9.2	90.8	9.2	93.9	6.1
Cape Coral, FL	65.5	34.5	89.7	10.3	92.6	7.4	91.5	8.5	90.8	9.2
Cedar Rapids, IA	69.1	30.9	87.8	12.2	89.0	11.0	92.3	7.7	92.3	7.7
Charleston, SC	51.2	48.8	86.2	13.8	89.8	10.2	89.3	10.7	90.4	9.6
Charlotte, NC	50.2	49.8	90.0	10.0	90.5	9.5	88.9	11.1	90.4	9.6
Chicago, IL	58.0	42.0	84.8	15.2	89.3	10.7	89.0	11.0	90.6	9.4
Cincinnati, OH	53.4	46.6	78.8	21.2	83.1	16.9	83.9	16.1	82.5	17.5
Clarksville, TN	62.9	37.1	92.1	7.9	88.8	11.2	89.5	10.5	89.0	11.0
Cleveland, OH	54.9	45.1	81.2	18.8	81.4	18.6	82.0	18.0	84.1	15.9
College Station, TX	60.1	39.9	86.1	13.9	88.9	11.1	92.4	7.6	93.3	6.7
Colorado Springs, CO	62.1	37.9	89.5	10.5	92.5	7.5	92.6	7.4	92.2	7.8
Columbia, MO	47.1	52.9	84.2	15.8	88.0	12.0	89.0	11.0	90.3	9.7
Columbia, SC	57.9	42.1	88.4	11.6	91.0	9.0	92.1	7.9	92.9	7.1
Columbus, OH	55.0	45.0	85.2	14.8	88.8	11.2	88.9	11.1	89.3	10.7
Dallas, TX	58.9	41.1	90.2	9.8	92.6	7.4	92.3	7.7	92.4	7.6
Davenport, IA	69.0	31.0	89.9	10.1	91.6	8.4	91.6	8.4	93.2	6.8
Denver, CO	59.6	40.4	90.1	9.9	92.5	7.5	92.0	8.0	91.9	8.1
Des Moines, IA	65.6	34.4	87.6	12.4	91.6	8.4	91.3	8.7	92.1	7.9
Durham, NC	49.5	50.5	88.6	11.4	89.6	10.4	88.8	11.2	90.8	9.2
Edison, NJ	54.8	45.2	82.3	17.7	85.6	14.4	85.7	14.3	85.1	14.9
El Paso, TX	81.0	19.0	93.9	6.1	95.1	4.9	94.8	5.2	96.4	3.6
Fargo, ND	58.8	41.2	93.6	6.4	89.5	10.5	89.3	10.7	93.8	6.2
Fayetteville, NC	63.5	36.5	88.7	11.3	87.7	12.3	88.9	11.1	89.4	10.6
Fort Collins, CO	52.2	47.8	91.0	9.0	92.3	7.7	91.9	8.1	91.4	8.6
Fort Wayne, IN	42.6	57.4	78.5	21.5	77.9	22.1	79.3	20.7	81.7	18.3
Fort Worth, TX	58.9	41.1	90.2	9.8	92.6	7.4	92.3	7.7	92.4	7.6
Grand Rapids, MI	62.5	37.5	82.2	17.8	84.8	15.2	86.2	13.8	86.1	13.9
Greeley, CO	69.7	30.3	89.1	10.9	91.9	8.1	94.0	6.0	93.9	6.1
Green Bay, WI	69.2	30.8	85.4	14.6	88.9	11.1	88.4	11.6	93.2	6.8
Greensboro, NC	50.5	49.5	89.4	10.6	90.3	9.7	89.1	10.9	90.3	9.7
Honolulu, HI	36.3	63.7	80.0	20.0	85.3	14.7	78.3	21.7	76.8	23.2
Houston, TX	58.1	41.9	90.2	9.8	93.1	6.9	93.0	7.0	93.3	6.7
Huntsville, AL	54.3	45.7	85.8	14.2	82.9	17.1	82.7	17.3	86.0	14.0
Indianapolis, IN	53.8	46.2	87.2	12.8	89.5	10.5	89.2	10.8	89.2	10.8
Jacksonville, FL	55.1	44.9	86.2	13.8	86.3	13.7	84.3	15.7	86.7	13.3
Kansas City, MO	58.1	41.9	88.5	11.5	89.6	10.4	89.2	10.8	89.4	10.6
Lafayette, LA	66.9	33.1	79.2	20.8	81.0	19.0	79.8	20.2	81.3	18.7
Lakeland, FL	69.5	30.5	85.9	14.1	89.0	11.0	86.1	13.9	90.5	9.5
Las Vegas, NV	61.7	38.3	89.8	10.2	92.5	7.5	92.9	7.1	93.4	6.6
Lexington, KY	47.1	52.9	83.9	16.1	88.1	11.9	86.9	13.1	86.8	13.2
Lincoln, NE	44.3	55.7	75.3	24.7	84.3	15.7	86.7	13.3	86.9	13.1
Little Rock, AR	63.2	36.8	87.1	12.9	88.9	11.1	88.9	11.1	87.4	12.6
Los Angeles, CA	58.5	41.5	88.4	11.6	90.8	9.2	91.0	9.0	91.4	8.6
Louisville, KY	49.2	50.8	82.9	17.1	84.2	15.8	81.4	18.6	81.3	18.7
Madison, WI	66.3	33.7	88.6	11.4	90.0	10.0	90.0	10.0	94.2	5.8

Table continued on following page.

Metro Area	Preschool (%)		Kindergarten (%)		Grades 1 - 4 (%)		Grades 5 - 8 (%)		Grades 9 - 12 (%)	
	Public	Private	Public	Private	Public	Private	Public	Private	Public	Private
Manchester, NH	42.4	57.6	83.7	16.3	87.1	12.9	89.9	10.1	88.9	11.1
Memphis, TN	61.4	38.6	86.2	13.8	86.6	13.4	86.3	13.7	84.7	15.3
Miami, FL	50.3	49.7	83.3	16.7	86.2	13.8	86.7	13.3	87.2	12.8
Midland, TX	64.3	35.7	89.1	10.9	86.9	13.1	90.0	10.0	90.3	9.7
Milwaukee, WI	56.6	43.4	80.0	20.0	80.5	19.5	79.7	20.3	85.2	14.8
Minneapolis, MN	59.4	40.6	88.5	11.5	89.4	10.6	90.1	9.9	91.6	8.4
Nashville, TN	47.3	52.7	86.2	13.8	87.1	12.9	86.3	13.7	84.4	15.6
New Haven, CT	65.1	34.9	90.7	9.3	92.2	7.8	90.5	9.5	89.3	10.7
New Orleans, LA	53.6	46.4	77.3	22.7	78.1	21.9	77.7	22.3	76.0	24.0
New York, NY	54.8	45.2	82.3	17.7	85.6	14.4	85.7	14.3	85.1	14.9
Oklahoma City, OK	72.1	27.9	90.7	9.3	91.2	8.8	90.8	9.2	90.7	9.3
Omaha, NE	57.3	42.7	85.4	14.6	85.7	14.3	87.2	12.8	85.9	14.1
Orlando, FL	55.2	44.8	81.0	19.0	86.3	13.7	85.6	14.4	89.6	10.4
Peoria, IL	61.4	38.6	82.9	17.1	89.1	10.9	89.1	10.9	91.0	9.0
Philadelphia, PA	46.0	54.0	81.8	18.2	84.9	15.1	84.9	15.1	83.3	16.7
Phoenix, AZ	60.3	39.7	89.4	10.6	92.0	8.0	92.5	7.5	92.9	7.1
Pittsburgh, PA	49.3	50.7	85.0	15.0	88.0	12.0	88.3	11.7	89.8	10.2
Portland, OR	42.8	57.2	86.2	13.8	89.0	11.0	89.5	10.5	90.3	9.7
Providence, RI	53.8	46.2	89.9	10.1	90.4	9.6	89.6	10.4	88.5	11.5
Provo, UT	53.3	46.7	91.6	8.4	92.9	7.1	94.4	5.6	94.4	5.6
Raleigh, NC	38.9	61.1	88.2	11.8	89.0	11.0	87.8	12.2	89.9	10.1
Reno, NV	58.2	41.8	85.6	14.4	92.7	7.3	92.9	7.1	93.2	6.8
Richmond, VA	41.9	58.1	89.0	11.0	89.8	10.2	88.6	11.4	90.3	9.7
Riverside, CA	68.6	31.4	91.8	8.2	94.4	5.6	94.2	5.8	94.9	5.1
Rochester, MN	62.6	37.4	85.5	14.5	87.3	12.7	89.1	10.9	92.1	7.9
Sacramento, CA	62.3	37.7	90.7	9.3	92.4	7.6	92.5	7.5	93.1	6.9
Salt Lake City, UT	54.5	45.5	88.8	11.2	92.6	7.4	93.4	6.6	93.7	6.3
San Antonio, TX	65.9	34.1	90.4	9.6	92.9	7.1	92.1	7.9	92.5	7.5
San Diego, CA	54.0	46.0	90.5	9.5	92.1	7.9	92.1	7.9	92.4	7.6
San Francisco, CA	41.3	58.7	84.2	15.8	86.3	13.7	85.8	14.2	87.2	12.8
San Jose, CA	36.2	63.8	81.2	18.8	85.7	14.3	85.4	14.6	86.2	13.8
Santa Rosa, CA	48.6	51.4	93.0	7.0	92.8	7.2	90.3	9.7	90.9	9.1
Savannah, GA	58.3	41.7	92.2	7.8	86.1	13.9	87.8	12.2	85.9	14.1
Seattle, WA	41.4	58.6	83.9	16.1	88.3	11.7	88.3	11.7	90.5	9.5
Sioux Falls, SD	53.6	46.4	88.3	11.7	88.4	11.6	89.2	10.8	86.8	13.2
Springfield, IL	66.2	33.8	86.4	13.6	87.2	12.8	88.6	11.4	90.1	9.9
Tallahassee, FL	49.6	50.4	86.3	13.7	86.0	14.0	81.7	18.3	86.2	13.8
Tampa, FL	57.1	42.9	84.8	15.2	86.9	13.1	87.1	12.9	88.3	11.7
Tucson, AZ	65.7	34.3	87.8	12.2	90.4	9.6	90.1	9.9	92.1	7.9
Tulsa, OK	69.4	30.6	88.7	11.3	88.9	11.1	88.2	11.8	87.7	12.3
Tuscaloosa, AL	66.5	33.5	89.8	10.2	87.4	12.6	90.3	9.7	86.1	13.9
Virginia Beach, VA	53.4	46.6	83.0	17.0	89.4	10.6	89.3	10.7	91.4	8.6
Washington, DC	44.9	55.1	86.1	13.9	88.7	11.3	87.9	12.1	88.3	11.7
Wichita, KS	63.1	36.9	83.3	16.7	86.3	13.7	87.3	12.7	86.6	13.4
Winston-Salem, NC	56.2	43.8	91.8	8.2	93.0	7.0	90.3	9.7	90.8	9.2
U.S.	59.1	40.9	87.6	12.4	89.5	10.5	89.4	10.6	90.1	9.9

Note: Figures shown cover persons 3 years old and over; Figures cover the Metropolitan Statistical Area—see Appendix B for areas included

Source: U.S. Census Bureau, 2015-2019 American Community Survey 5-Year Estimates

Educational Attainment by Race: City

City	High School Graduate or Higher (%)					Bachelor's Degree or Higher (%)				
	Total	White	Black	Asian	Hisp.[1]	Total	White	Black	Asian	Hisp.[1]
Albuquerque, NM	89.7	91.1	92.0	85.5	82.5	35.2	38.1	31.2	48.3	21.5
Allentown, PA	79.0	81.5	83.0	81.3	68.2	15.3	17.9	7.3	37.1	6.0
Anchorage, AK	93.9	96.5	93.6	84.0	85.3	36.1	43.2	19.6	25.2	22.3
Ann Arbor, MI	97.3	98.1	90.6	97.8	92.0	76.0	78.4	38.2	86.4	68.6
Athens, GA	87.9	90.9	81.5	94.5	57.0	44.0	54.8	18.6	73.2	19.8
Atlanta, GA	90.9	97.7	84.4	96.1	82.5	51.8	78.0	25.7	84.6	46.0
Austin, TX	89.4	91.2	89.6	93.9	72.3	51.7	55.1	28.8	77.0	25.8
Baton Rouge, LA	88.0	96.2	82.2	84.1	73.9	33.2	53.4	15.9	54.7	21.7
Boise City, ID	95.1	95.7	86.2	89.1	84.2	41.6	41.8	29.9	51.2	22.0
Boston, MA	87.2	93.0	83.8	78.9	70.0	49.7	65.7	21.8	53.2	23.7
Boulder, CO	96.9	97.5	92.2	96.1	76.4	76.0	76.9	39.9	80.4	42.1
Cape Coral, FL	91.8	92.3	89.3	88.5	86.9	23.3	23.7	19.8	24.7	18.7
Cedar Rapids, IA	93.3	94.7	83.4	83.8	75.8	32.1	32.7	15.0	51.2	21.0
Charleston, SC	94.9	97.4	86.9	93.5	91.4	53.1	61.0	22.3	67.3	45.6
Charlotte, NC	89.1	92.7	90.4	81.4	60.0	44.3	55.4	29.4	58.3	17.0
Chicago, IL	85.1	88.7	85.2	87.1	68.4	39.5	50.9	21.4	60.5	16.5
Cincinnati, OH	88.1	92.1	83.0	93.1	73.2	37.1	52.6	14.5	80.7	31.0
Clarksville, TN	92.9	93.5	92.6	85.2	87.2	27.6	28.1	24.7	41.9	18.2
Cleveland, OH	80.8	83.3	80.0	71.5	67.4	17.5	24.9	9.7	39.5	9.0
College Station, TX	94.4	95.1	87.8	95.2	85.6	58.6	58.8	29.4	80.9	45.8
Colorado Springs, CO	93.9	95.3	94.2	86.3	80.6	39.9	42.7	25.7	48.4	20.9
Columbia, MO	95.2	96.3	90.0	94.6	91.4	52.2	54.8	21.2	73.9	36.0
Columbia, SC	89.4	95.4	81.8	96.8	86.4	43.8	62.6	19.6	78.1	35.2
Columbus, OH	89.8	92.0	86.8	85.3	75.6	36.6	42.3	19.7	57.7	23.2
Dallas, TX	77.5	75.2	86.8	85.5	51.1	33.4	38.9	19.4	65.8	11.0
Davenport, IA	90.5	92.2	83.6	69.2	72.8	25.6	27.4	10.5	28.0	15.5
Denver, CO	88.0	90.3	86.9	83.4	64.7	49.4	54.5	24.7	53.9	15.9
Des Moines, IA	86.3	89.7	81.3	60.8	57.2	26.7	29.2	13.6	20.3	9.0
Durham, NC	88.1	90.1	87.6	90.5	49.4	49.6	60.1	34.2	73.9	13.6
Edison, NJ	92.1	92.8	94.7	93.0	82.0	55.5	37.2	35.0	77.0	24.1
El Paso, TX	80.3	81.1	95.7	90.1	76.4	25.1	25.7	30.5	54.0	20.7
Fargo, ND	94.3	96.1	81.9	71.8	92.0	40.0	41.7	20.2	46.6	21.2
Fayetteville, NC	91.7	93.7	90.6	86.3	88.5	27.2	31.3	22.9	43.0	21.7
Fort Collins, CO	96.5	96.9	97.0	93.4	84.3	55.5	55.8	40.2	72.3	34.2
Fort Wayne, IN	88.5	91.9	84.4	52.6	61.8	27.8	30.7	15.6	28.3	9.8
Fort Worth, TX	82.2	84.4	88.6	80.8	59.2	29.7	33.8	21.5	42.8	12.2
Grand Rapids, MI	86.7	90.8	83.2	72.3	50.3	36.4	43.1	17.4	43.9	11.9
Greeley, CO	84.5	86.2	79.2	80.0	65.6	24.8	25.9	16.6	43.4	8.4
Green Bay, WI	87.5	90.4	83.1	74.3	53.5	24.8	27.0	15.3	20.0	6.5
Greensboro, NC	89.8	93.4	88.5	75.2	64.2	38.2	49.1	24.5	41.9	18.2
Honolulu, HI	89.0	97.6	97.5	85.5	91.9	37.2	53.0	24.5	36.6	27.9
Houston, TX	78.9	78.0	88.8	86.9	58.5	32.9	37.4	22.6	58.9	13.6
Huntsville, AL	91.0	94.0	85.4	91.1	63.8	44.1	50.3	28.4	59.3	22.8
Indianapolis, IN	85.8	88.0	84.6	76.2	57.3	30.9	36.0	18.2	47.1	12.5
Jacksonville, FL	89.5	91.0	86.7	88.7	82.3	28.6	31.5	19.1	49.5	24.6
Kansas City, MO	90.0	93.2	86.5	80.3	70.2	35.2	43.5	16.6	47.2	18.6
Lafayette, LA	89.5	93.6	79.4	94.8	57.4	38.2	47.0	15.1	56.8	21.2
Lakeland, FL	88.0	89.3	83.3	81.6	78.8	25.9	27.5	15.7	51.0	19.5
Las Vegas, NV	84.8	87.5	89.2	91.1	63.5	24.6	26.9	18.2	40.7	9.9
Lexington, KY	91.2	93.4	85.4	91.1	61.0	43.6	47.7	19.5	68.5	19.2
Lincoln, NE	93.3	95.0	86.1	79.2	70.1	39.6	40.7	23.8	46.7	19.3
Little Rock, AR	91.3	93.8	88.2	95.3	61.3	41.8	54.6	22.6	70.2	10.2
Los Angeles, CA	77.5	80.9	88.7	90.3	56.3	34.4	39.8	26.5	54.9	12.3
Louisville, KY	89.6	90.7	86.9	81.4	80.2	29.9	32.9	17.8	49.0	25.8
Madison, WI	95.5	96.8	87.6	92.5	77.3	57.9	59.7	22.7	71.7	34.2

Table continued on following page.

City	High School Graduate or Higher (%)					Bachelor's Degree or Higher (%)				
	Total	White	Black	Asian	Hisp.[1]	Total	White	Black	Asian	Hisp.[1]
Manchester, NH	87.3	88.4	79.2	76.4	67.0	30.1	29.7	22.1	44.6	14.9
Memphis, TN	85.7	91.7	84.1	87.0	49.5	26.2	44.5	15.9	57.0	11.2
Miami, FL	78.0	78.7	74.2	90.4	75.3	29.6	32.2	14.8	63.5	25.9
Midland, TX	85.1	85.8	85.6	81.7	71.3	28.9	30.3	18.1	51.7	11.9
Milwaukee, WI	84.0	89.1	83.0	68.8	62.2	24.6	35.3	12.6	27.1	9.3
Minneapolis, MN	90.0	96.2	74.6	82.6	59.9	50.4	61.2	14.3	54.8	21.0
Nashville, TN	88.8	90.4	88.2	77.9	57.0	41.1	46.5	27.6	49.2	15.4
New Haven, CT	85.6	87.5	87.2	96.8	70.9	34.9	46.6	19.9	78.7	13.6
New Orleans, LA	86.5	95.7	81.0	75.8	80.9	37.6	63.9	19.7	40.4	35.9
New York, NY	82.2	88.7	83.5	76.1	68.9	38.1	51.0	24.4	42.4	18.6
Oklahoma City, OK	86.4	87.5	89.0	81.2	54.5	30.7	33.2	20.3	41.4	10.4
Omaha, NE	89.5	91.5	86.9	70.4	54.3	37.7	40.7	18.9	49.4	12.0
Orlando, FL	90.4	92.8	84.6	92.6	86.8	38.1	43.3	21.8	60.3	28.8
Peoria, IL	89.4	92.4	81.4	94.7	71.6	34.9	39.6	13.4	75.4	21.9
Philadelphia, PA	84.7	89.2	84.6	73.0	67.2	29.7	41.6	17.3	40.3	14.6
Phoenix, AZ	81.9	84.0	87.5	84.9	62.1	28.6	30.2	21.8	57.4	10.3
Pittsburgh, PA	92.9	94.5	88.6	90.9	87.1	44.6	50.2	18.4	78.3	48.4
Portland, OR	92.4	94.8	85.9	76.9	76.1	50.4	54.3	23.9	41.2	31.0
Providence, RI	81.6	86.4	84.4	79.3	71.9	30.1	38.0	19.1	48.1	10.4
Provo, UT	92.9	93.1	98.0	93.2	75.2	43.1	43.4	27.2	52.9	18.6
Raleigh, NC	91.8	95.9	89.7	86.8	61.2	50.9	61.8	31.0	60.0	21.9
Reno, NV	89.0	91.4	91.3	91.6	64.6	33.5	35.3	21.2	48.1	12.5
Richmond, VA	85.4	92.3	78.8	81.7	50.8	39.6	61.8	15.5	62.5	14.3
Riverside, CA	80.6	83.5	92.0	87.2	68.5	23.0	23.8	26.5	47.8	11.8
Rochester, MN	94.0	96.3	77.2	83.8	74.1	46.7	47.8	18.0	59.9	26.2
Sacramento, CA	85.3	89.2	90.1	79.7	73.0	33.1	39.6	21.0	37.4	17.7
Salt Lake City, UT	88.8	94.2	82.2	83.8	62.2	46.5	51.8	26.7	61.5	16.5
San Antonio, TX	82.4	82.4	91.1	87.2	74.8	26.0	26.0	23.9	53.1	16.4
San Diego, CA	88.1	89.2	91.3	88.7	69.1	45.9	48.1	25.8	53.8	20.4
San Francisco, CA	88.5	96.7	88.4	79.3	78.9	58.1	73.8	30.5	46.7	34.2
San Jose, CA	84.6	88.6	91.8	87.0	67.5	43.7	44.2	35.5	55.9	15.9
Santa Rosa, CA	86.2	91.3	87.6	87.1	62.8	32.6	37.4	30.2	40.2	12.1
Savannah, GA	87.6	93.0	83.3	85.8	79.4	28.2	42.9	15.5	46.7	27.1
Seattle, WA	94.8	97.8	86.8	88.4	83.5	64.0	69.8	29.5	61.5	43.0
Sioux Falls, SD	92.3	94.7	74.7	70.8	65.3	35.2	37.6	14.3	36.4	14.3
Springfield, IL	91.3	93.4	81.2	91.7	87.8	35.8	38.6	17.8	64.9	33.6
Tallahassee, FL	93.5	96.4	88.2	96.0	88.5	48.2	56.9	28.1	80.7	39.6
Tampa, FL	87.9	90.1	82.9	86.7	78.3	38.6	44.4	16.8	63.0	23.5
Tucson, AZ	85.0	88.0	84.3	86.7	72.7	27.4	30.1	21.3	48.0	14.0
Tulsa, OK	87.3	89.9	88.8	74.8	57.6	31.5	36.5	17.6	37.8	10.7
Tuscaloosa, AL	89.1	94.4	84.1	84.5	73.8	36.9	54.1	17.6	53.0	11.5
Virginia Beach, VA	93.5	95.3	91.1	88.2	84.5	36.0	38.8	26.4	40.6	25.5
Washington, DC	90.9	98.1	86.3	94.9	73.1	58.5	89.5	27.3	81.9	47.3
Wichita, KS	88.3	90.4	87.4	81.3	62.8	30.1	32.9	15.2	36.3	13.0
Winston-Salem, NC	88.2	89.9	87.8	87.7	58.1	34.5	41.8	21.0	65.7	13.5
U.S.	88.0	89.9	86.0	87.1	68.7	32.1	33.5	21.6	54.3	16.4

Note: Figures shown cover persons 25 years old and over; (1) People of Hispanic origin can be of any race
Source: U.S. Census Bureau, 2015-2019 American Community Survey 5-Year Estimates

Educational Attainment by Race: Metro Area

Metro Area	High School Graduate or Higher (%)					Bachelor's Degree or Higher (%)				
	Total	White	Black	Asian	Hisp.[1]	Total	White	Black	Asian	Hisp.[1]
Albuquerque, NM	88.6	90.4	91.0	87.3	81.1	32.2	35.0	30.4	47.8	19.1
Allentown, PA	90.0	91.1	88.0	87.5	74.9	29.5	30.1	19.5	54.6	13.2
Anchorage, AK	93.7	95.6	93.5	83.9	86.3	32.3	37.0	19.5	25.0	21.3
Ann Arbor, MI	95.3	96.3	89.2	96.6	85.5	55.9	57.7	27.4	83.0	42.9
Athens, GA	87.8	90.1	80.3	91.0	60.0	39.4	44.5	17.6	69.9	22.2
Atlanta, GA	89.6	91.0	90.5	87.5	64.9	38.6	42.6	30.2	58.1	20.6
Austin, TX	89.9	91.4	91.0	92.5	74.0	44.8	46.7	29.1	71.8	23.0
Baton Rouge, LA	87.4	90.5	82.8	86.1	67.5	27.6	31.9	18.5	53.2	16.4
Boise City, ID	91.8	93.4	88.7	86.6	67.8	31.7	32.5	27.9	46.7	11.4
Boston, MA	91.7	94.3	85.2	86.0	72.0	48.1	50.6	26.3	62.3	22.8
Boulder, CO	95.0	95.8	87.8	93.8	71.6	62.1	62.8	30.5	72.5	26.5
Cape Coral, FL	88.4	90.0	79.5	88.6	71.0	28.2	29.4	15.9	45.3	14.8
Cedar Rapids, IA	94.3	95.2	84.0	81.4	77.6	31.0	31.3	15.4	51.7	22.0
Charleston, SC	90.7	93.7	84.4	86.3	71.1	35.6	42.6	16.5	49.0	20.5
Charlotte, NC	89.0	90.8	88.4	84.9	63.1	35.1	37.7	25.9	58.1	17.7
Chicago, IL	88.7	91.4	87.8	90.7	68.0	38.0	41.6	22.7	64.7	14.8
Cincinnati, OH	91.0	91.9	86.6	88.9	74.1	33.6	34.8	19.2	65.9	24.6
Clarksville, TN	90.7	91.2	89.6	85.6	86.2	24.8	24.9	22.2	43.3	19.1
Cleveland, OH	90.6	92.3	85.2	86.8	74.6	31.2	34.5	15.1	61.5	15.8
College Station, TX	86.6	87.3	85.3	94.0	63.3	37.5	39.3	16.5	78.4	15.9
Colorado Springs, CO	94.4	95.5	94.5	87.4	82.7	38.5	40.5	27.2	44.8	20.9
Columbia, MO	93.6	94.3	89.3	93.9	86.8	42.7	43.8	18.8	71.2	34.4
Columbia, SC	89.9	91.7	87.9	90.5	65.1	32.7	37.3	23.2	58.9	20.0
Columbus, OH	91.5	92.7	87.4	88.5	76.6	36.7	38.3	21.5	63.7	25.6
Dallas, TX	85.6	85.9	91.0	88.8	60.3	35.2	35.8	27.4	62.0	14.0
Davenport, IA	91.0	92.6	79.5	80.4	72.9	26.9	27.6	13.8	46.8	15.6
Denver, CO	91.2	92.8	89.8	86.0	71.0	43.8	46.2	27.0	52.1	16.7
Des Moines, IA	92.5	94.2	84.6	74.1	62.8	36.5	37.6	19.8	38.7	13.6
Durham, NC	88.8	91.0	86.3	91.3	52.7	45.3	51.4	28.8	72.3	16.9
Edison, NJ	86.5	90.8	85.4	83.5	71.4	40.4	46.0	25.6	54.5	19.6
El Paso, TX	78.3	79.5	95.3	90.1	74.4	23.2	24.0	29.9	52.6	19.2
Fargo, ND	94.8	96.1	81.7	78.4	83.4	38.6	39.8	22.2	46.8	19.5
Fayetteville, NC	89.6	91.5	89.7	84.8	80.2	23.7	25.6	21.5	39.3	19.3
Fort Collins, CO	95.9	96.2	95.7	92.2	83.8	47.3	47.5	37.8	62.7	25.1
Fort Wayne, IN	89.6	91.9	85.2	57.5	63.5	27.8	29.4	15.8	33.7	10.4
Fort Worth, TX	85.6	85.9	91.0	88.8	60.3	35.2	35.8	27.4	62.0	14.0
Grand Rapids, MI	91.2	93.1	85.7	75.2	63.7	32.7	34.3	18.3	37.3	14.2
Greeley, CO	88.1	89.1	84.2	87.9	66.6	27.5	28.0	27.2	42.4	9.1
Green Bay, WI	92.0	93.5	83.2	83.1	57.0	27.8	28.5	17.3	44.2	9.2
Greensboro, NC	86.8	88.9	86.1	76.4	57.6	29.5	32.0	23.0	42.6	13.7
Honolulu, HI	91.9	97.3	97.0	88.8	93.4	35.0	48.3	29.9	36.1	25.2
Houston, TX	83.7	83.6	91.0	87.8	64.1	32.8	33.3	27.5	56.6	15.0
Huntsville, AL	90.2	91.6	86.8	92.7	66.6	39.2	40.9	31.4	61.9	24.3
Indianapolis, IN	89.7	91.3	85.9	82.6	63.7	34.7	36.7	20.7	56.2	17.6
Jacksonville, FL	90.9	92.2	87.2	89.4	84.3	31.4	33.8	19.7	49.7	27.0
Kansas City, MO	92.0	93.6	88.5	85.5	69.0	37.1	39.7	20.7	54.8	17.8
Lafayette, LA	84.1	87.0	76.3	73.1	63.9	23.4	26.4	13.0	34.9	12.3
Lakeland, FL	85.0	86.1	82.2	80.4	73.1	20.2	20.6	15.0	41.5	14.6
Las Vegas, NV	86.1	88.3	89.7	90.4	66.8	24.5	25.9	17.8	38.8	10.5
Lexington, KY	90.1	91.6	85.1	91.1	60.8	37.3	39.2	19.0	64.5	16.9
Lincoln, NE	93.7	95.2	86.1	78.9	70.4	39.0	39.8	23.9	46.3	19.7
Little Rock, AR	90.4	91.8	87.4	90.5	67.5	30.4	32.7	21.8	54.3	13.8
Los Angeles, CA	80.7	83.2	89.9	88.2	62.2	34.5	36.6	27.3	53.4	13.3
Louisville, KY	90.1	90.9	87.2	86.3	74.0	29.6	31.0	18.3	54.2	22.7
Madison, WI	95.3	96.2	88.8	90.9	76.4	46.1	46.2	23.9	68.0	26.7

Table continued on following page.

Metro Area	High School Graduate or Higher (%)					Bachelor's Degree or Higher (%)				
	Total	White	Black	Asian	Hisp.[1]	Total	White	Black	Asian	Hisp.[1]
Manchester, NH	92.1	92.6	83.7	88.3	71.7	38.1	37.4	24.0	64.8	19.4
Memphis, TN	88.0	91.9	85.2	87.9	57.7	28.3	35.7	19.1	58.2	14.8
Miami, FL	85.5	86.9	81.4	87.5	80.0	32.3	35.4	19.8	51.6	27.7
Midland, TX	84.3	84.9	85.7	83.4	69.6	27.1	28.3	18.3	54.5	10.6
Milwaukee, WI	91.5	94.4	83.8	83.5	68.7	35.6	39.9	14.3	51.0	14.5
Minneapolis, MN	93.6	96.3	82.6	81.2	68.5	42.0	44.3	22.0	45.3	20.1
Nashville, TN	90.0	90.9	88.5	84.0	62.9	36.2	37.5	28.2	51.5	17.3
New Haven, CT	90.1	91.8	87.6	90.1	74.4	35.0	37.4	20.2	65.3	15.6
New Orleans, LA	86.9	90.6	82.0	77.4	75.1	30.3	36.8	18.7	38.7	19.2
New York, NY	86.5	90.8	85.4	83.5	71.4	40.4	46.0	25.6	54.5	19.6
Oklahoma City, OK	89.0	89.9	90.0	84.3	60.6	30.5	32.0	21.3	46.0	13.2
Omaha, NE	91.7	93.1	88.0	76.7	61.2	36.3	37.7	21.5	49.7	14.8
Orlando, FL	89.5	91.1	85.8	88.8	83.6	32.2	33.9	22.8	52.3	23.2
Peoria, IL	91.7	92.9	80.3	92.4	75.4	27.7	28.1	12.8	69.8	20.9
Philadelphia, PA	90.7	93.2	87.5	84.6	70.1	37.9	42.1	21.4	57.1	17.8
Phoenix, AZ	87.5	89.1	90.1	88.6	68.5	31.5	32.3	25.7	58.9	13.1
Pittsburgh, PA	93.9	94.4	89.7	88.2	88.0	34.9	35.3	20.2	70.7	36.8
Portland, OR	92.1	93.5	88.2	86.7	68.7	39.8	40.3	28.0	52.1	19.5
Providence, RI	87.7	89.2	85.5	85.5	73.3	32.3	33.7	22.3	51.6	14.0
Provo, UT	94.5	94.9	97.4	94.6	75.3	40.3	40.6	35.4	58.9	20.2
Raleigh, NC	91.7	94.1	89.0	92.4	62.5	46.8	50.5	30.8	73.2	20.1
Reno, NV	88.7	91.0	90.3	91.8	63.3	30.8	32.5	21.7	45.4	11.0
Richmond, VA	89.9	92.8	85.0	88.8	67.3	37.4	43.4	21.8	64.0	21.3
Riverside, CA	81.1	83.7	89.6	90.4	67.4	21.7	22.0	23.8	48.6	10.7
Rochester, MN	94.1	95.5	78.3	84.4	71.3	38.7	38.7	18.1	58.0	23.1
Sacramento, CA	89.3	92.0	90.4	84.3	74.1	33.5	34.8	23.0	44.1	17.9
Salt Lake City, UT	90.8	94.0	85.4	86.8	69.0	35.0	37.2	25.1	51.4	14.3
San Antonio, TX	85.1	85.3	92.2	87.5	76.1	28.2	28.4	28.8	51.7	17.2
San Diego, CA	87.4	88.2	91.8	89.2	69.8	38.8	39.5	25.9	51.3	17.8
San Francisco, CA	89.1	93.6	90.7	87.3	71.5	49.7	56.1	28.8	55.4	21.7
San Jose, CA	88.1	90.4	92.0	90.8	69.3	51.5	49.4	38.2	65.5	17.6
Santa Rosa, CA	88.8	92.9	89.3	88.9	64.6	35.5	39.3	29.8	44.4	14.1
Savannah, GA	89.8	92.0	86.2	84.2	81.2	31.5	36.7	19.8	45.2	26.2
Seattle, WA	92.6	95.0	89.6	88.8	73.3	43.0	43.8	25.8	56.1	22.4
Sioux Falls, SD	92.9	94.5	75.5	72.1	66.9	33.5	35.0	14.4	37.1	15.6
Springfield, IL	92.6	93.9	81.6	92.7	87.0	33.9	35.2	17.4	64.0	31.5
Tallahassee, FL	90.6	93.9	83.5	96.3	82.1	38.4	44.1	23.0	79.3	30.2
Tampa, FL	89.6	90.8	87.0	85.4	80.2	30.4	30.9	22.4	51.7	22.6
Tucson, AZ	88.4	90.9	87.6	88.0	75.8	32.4	35.1	25.6	53.1	16.3
Tulsa, OK	89.4	90.9	89.5	77.7	63.4	27.7	29.8	19.2	37.0	12.4
Tuscaloosa, AL	87.1	89.9	82.8	81.1	70.1	27.4	33.4	16.2	51.8	11.5
Virginia Beach, VA	91.4	93.9	87.2	87.3	84.0	31.9	36.2	22.1	43.3	24.8
Washington, DC	90.9	94.1	91.5	91.1	68.0	50.9	59.2	34.8	65.1	25.7
Wichita, KS	90.1	91.7	87.1	81.9	65.8	30.6	32.3	17.2	36.9	15.3
Winston-Salem, NC	87.0	87.9	86.9	87.2	56.7	26.6	27.7	20.6	54.6	12.2
U.S.	88.0	89.9	86.0	87.1	68.7	32.1	33.5	21.6	54.3	16.4

Note: Figures shown cover persons 25 years old and over; Figures cover the Metropolitan Statistical Area—see Appendix B for areas included; (1) People of Hispanic origin can be of any race
Source: U.S. Census Bureau, 2015-2019 American Community Survey 5-Year Estimates

Cost of Living Index

Urban Area	Composite	Groceries	Housing	Utilities	Transp.	Health	Misc.
Albuquerque, NM	93.8	104.8	84.5	87.7	97.2	99.8	96.6
Allentown, PA	104.4	98.4	114.0	103.4	104.8	94.6	100.6
Anchorage, AK	124.5	132.6	140.0	124.0	114.8	144.2	109.7
Ann Arbor, MI	n/a	n/a	n/a	n/a	n/a	n/a	n/a
Athens, GA	n/a	n/a	n/a	n/a	n/a	n/a	n/a
Atlanta, GA	102.8	103.4	103.5	85.1	103.6	107.1	106.0
Austin, TX	99.7	91.2	105.5	95.2	90.7	105.8	101.4
Baton Rouge	99.4	102.6	92.3	85.4	100.5	104.5	106.5
Boise City, ID	98.7	94.5	97.5	81.9	108.5	103.0	102.8
Boston, MA	151.0	109.3	228.6	120.5	112.0	118.3	129.3
Boulder, CO	n/a	n/a	n/a	n/a	n/a	n/a	n/a
Cape Coral, FL	100.6	107.8	89.6	98.8	98.7	108.5	106.3
Cedar Rapids, IA	96.2	94.8	83.0	102.1	96.6	107.0	103.9
Charleston, SC	97.2	99.7	93.2	120.4	86.6	97.5	95.9
Charlotte, NC	98.2	101.7	88.8	95.6	90.7	105.1	106.0
Chicago, IL	120.6	101.9	155.7	92.4	125.9	100.0	109.4
Cincinnati, OH	99.7	91.2	105.5	95.2	90.7	105.8	101.4
Clarksville, TN	n/a	n/a	n/a	n/a	n/a	n/a	n/a
Cleveland, OH	96.9	106.0	83.3	96.1	99.4	104.4	102.6
College Station, TX	n/a	n/a	n/a	n/a	n/a	n/a	n/a
Colorado Springs, CO	101.1	95.9	101.3	97.2	97.7	108.6	104.1
Columbia, MO	91.8	95.5	75.0	100.0	92.0	102.6	99.8
Columbia, SC	93.5	103.1	72.7	126.2	87.1	79.9	100.5
Columbus, OH	92.6	98.6	81.2	89.1	95.5	88.5	99.7
Dallas, TX	108.2	100.2	118.8	106.8	96.7	105.4	106.7
Davenport, IA	92.0	99.7	76.9	98.9	105.8	105.3	93.7
Denver, CO	111.3	98.3	139.3	80.5	100.9	103.6	106.6
Des Moines, IA	89.9	95.2	80.2	90.1	99.1	95.4	92.3
Durham, NC	n/a	n/a	n/a	n/a	n/a	n/a	n/a
Edison, NJ[1]	120.6	108.7	149.3	105.8	107.8	102.5	112.4
El Paso, TX	87.7	102.3	73.7	85.7	99.0	99.3	89.0
Fargo, ND	98.6	111.5	77.6	90.5	100.4	120.1	108.9
Fayetteville, NC	n/a	n/a	n/a	n/a	n/a	n/a	n/a
Fort Collins, CO	n/a	n/a	n/a	n/a	n/a	n/a	n/a
Fort Wayne, IN	86.9	86.7	62.3	95.7	99.5	101.5	98.6
Fort Worth, TX	94.9	92.4	88.4	107.2	96.9	101.5	96.2
Grand Rapids, MI	94.1	92.8	87.4	98.5	104.1	92.3	96.3
Greeley, CO	n/a	n/a	n/a	n/a	n/a	n/a	n/a
Green Bay, WI	91.1	91.0	77.9	97.4	97.7	101.8	96.6
Greensboro, NC[2]	90.8	101.4	66.7	94.6	92.0	119.5	100.5
Honolulu, HI	192.9	165.0	332.6	172.3	138.2	118.8	124.2
Houston, TX	95.8	88.4	91.2	105.8	95.2	92.0	100.3
Huntsville, AL	91.3	95.1	66.6	99.0	97.3	96.4	104.7
Indianapolis, IN	92.4	94.1	78.4	105.4	97.9	90.6	98.0
Jacksonville, FL	91.7	98.4	88.0	97.7	86.0	83.7	92.7
Kansas City, MO	95.8	102.4	82.6	100.6	92.6	105.9	101.7
Lafayette, LA	88.9	101.8	72.0	88.0	104.7	88.0	93.3
Lakeland, FL	n/a	n/a	n/a	n/a	n/a	n/a	n/a
Las Vegas, NV	103.6	95.8	118.3	98.6	114.0	100.2	94.2
Lexington, KY	92.7	89.9	83.7	95.6	96.7	78.9	100.7
Lincoln, NE	93.0	95.6	78.7	90.2	93.4	105.8	102.2
Little Rock, AR	96.0	95.1	88.1	97.4	94.7	89.6	103.2
Los Angeles, CA	146.7	116.3	230.6	106.2	134.8	110.8	112.0
Louisville, KY	94.1	91.8	79.8	94.6	98.1	105.2	103.7
Madison, WI	107.0	107.6	108.6	99.8	104.4	124.0	106.0
Manchester, NH	108.9	102.2	109.6	117.9	104.1	116.0	108.9

Table continued on following page.

Urban Area	Composite	Groceries	Housing	Utilities	Transp.	Health	Misc.
Memphis, TN	99.7	91.2	105.5	95.2	90.7	105.8	101.4
Miami, FL	115.0	110.5	144.3	102.0	101.5	100.6	102.7
Midland, TX	102.1	93.6	91.5	106.6	104.1	96.5	112.6
Milwaukee, WI	96.7	93.4	100.5	94.8	99.8	115.9	92.4
Minneapolis, MN	106.6	103.6	102.9	97.5	104.4	105.6	113.9
Nashville, TN	98.9	99.5	98.5	97.0	97.9	92.4	100.4
New Haven, CT	122.3	111.0	128.5	136.7	110.6	115.8	121.9
New Orleans, LA	105.0	102.6	125.5	81.5	101.3	115.1	96.1
New York, NY[3]	181.6	128.4	339.0	121.4	113.7	107.1	123.1
Oklahoma City, OK	86.0	93.3	69.6	95.3	86.2	95.0	92.1
Omaha, NE	92.3	96.8	83.6	99.4	98.3	96.4	93.3
Orlando, FL	92.1	100.7	85.1	97.2	89.3	88.3	94.1
Peoria, IL	92.9	89.7	76.5	93.7	106.3	96.8	102.7
Philadelphia, PA	110.9	118.7	116.5	105.6	116.1	101.8	104.8
Phoenix, AZ	99.3	99.7	103.8	109.5	107.2	90.1	91.9
Pittsburgh, PA	103.1	111.9	105.7	116.1	114.0	93.1	92.6
Portland, OR	134.7	112.4	186.4	87.1	131.0	115.6	119.4
Providence, RI	119.2	106.7	132.8	126.4	112.1	109.3	114.6
Provo, UT	98.2	93.0	96.1	84.7	100.7	94.5	105.4
Raleigh, NC	95.4	92.7	89.0	98.3	90.9	103.8	100.9
Reno, NV	114.1	118.7	125.8	85.9	126.3	113.9	107.6
Richmond, VA	94.2	89.0	86.0	97.6	86.9	106.7	102.1
Riverside, CA	99.7	91.2	105.5	95.2	90.7	105.8	101.4
Rochester, MN	n/a	n/a	n/a	n/a	n/a	n/a	n/a
Sacramento, CA	118.4	120.2	134.2	102.9	139.0	113.6	104.8
Salt Lake City, UT	103.6	108.0	106.7	87.8	103.6	105.7	103.6
San Antonio, TX	89.5	88.0	82.2	87.6	89.1	87.2	96.5
San Diego, CA	142.1	116.1	216.3	123.2	129.2	107.3	107.3
San Francisco, CA	197.9	131.3	368.9	123.0	145.3	129.6	133.4
San Jose, CA	n/a	n/a	n/a	n/a	n/a	n/a	n/a
Santa Rosa, CA	n/a	n/a	n/a	n/a	n/a	n/a	n/a
Savannah, GA	89.5	95.7	66.2	96.0	94.9	106.1	100.0
Seattle, WA	157.5	129.1	227.6	108.0	137.8	128.6	136.2
Sioux Falls, SD	92.5	96.3	86.3	84.7	91.9	107.7	96.3
Springfield, IL	n/a	n/a	n/a	n/a	n/a	n/a	n/a
Tallahassee, FL	97.5	107.4	93.3	86.5	96.2	99.6	99.9
Tampa, FL	91.2	104.8	79.2	85.9	99.4	98.3	93.7
Tucson, AZ	97.5	100.5	87.9	99.9	101.1	98.7	102.0
Tulsa, OK	86.0	96.2	62.7	99.5	84.4	91.6	96.1
Tuscaloosa, AL	n/a	n/a	n/a	n/a	n/a	n/a	n/a
Virginia Beach, VA[4]	94.1	92.7	89.1	97.4	92.2	90.4	98.7
Washington, DC	159.9	116.0	277.1	117.9	110.6	95.8	118.1
Wichita, KS	91.1	94.3	69.6	99.3	95.3	96.1	102.5
Winston-Salem, NC	90.8	101.4	66.7	94.6	92.0	119.5	100.5
U.S.	100.0	100.0	100.0	100.0	100.0	100.0	100.0

Note: The Cost of Living Index measures regional differences in the cost of consumer goods and services, excluding taxes and non-consumer expenditures, for professional and managerial households in the top income quintile. It is based on more than 50,000 prices covering almost 60 different items for which prices are collected three times a year by chambers of commerce, economic development organizations or university applied economic centers in each participating urban area. The numbers shown should be read as a percentage above or below the national average of 100. For example, a value of 115.4 in the groceries column indicates that grocery prices are 15.4% higher than the national average. Small differences in the index numbers should not be interpreted as significant. In cases where data is not available for the city, data for the metro area or for a neighboring city has been provided and noted as follows: (1) Middlesex-Monmouth NJ; (2) Winston-Salem, NC; (3) Brooklyn, NY; (4) Hampton Roads-SE Virginia
Source: The Council for Community and Economic Research (formerly ACCRA), Cost of Living Index, 2020

Grocery Prices

Urban Area	T-Bone Steak ($/pound)	Frying Chicken ($/pound)	Whole Milk ($/half gal.)	Eggs ($/dozen)	Orange Juice ($/64 oz.)	Coffee ($/11.5 oz.)
Albuquerque, NM	11.18	1.16	2.10	1.41	3.96	4.63
Allentown, PA	13.52	1.36	2.09	1.36	3.47	3.73
Anchorage, AK	13.95	1.71	2.73	2.19	4.39	5.84
Ann Arbor, MI	n/a	n/a	n/a	n/a	n/a	n/a
Athens, GA	n/a	n/a	n/a	n/a	n/a	n/a
Atlanta, GA	14.32	1.30	1.99	1.25	3.76	4.92
Austin, TX	9.67	1.02	1.84	1.39	3.22	4.23
Baton Rouge	11.70	1.42	2.65	1.53	3.69	4.26
Boise City, ID	11.77	1.13	1.37	1.18	3.69	4.46
Boston, MA	13.53	1.64	2.27	2.00	3.73	4.41
Boulder, CO	n/a	n/a	n/a	n/a	n/a	n/a
Cape Coral, FL	11.21	1.92	2.40	1.51	3.36	3.34
Cedar Rapids, IA	10.99	1.68	2.49	1.24	3.31	4.86
Charleston, SC	12.80	1.27	2.25	1.26	3.53	4.42
Charlotte, NC	12.19	1.46	1.69	1.34	3.54	4.02
Chicago, IL	12.67	1.99	2.42	1.47	3.96	4.48
Cincinnati, OH	13.16	1.25	1.42	1.09	3.61	4.28
Clarksville, TN	n/a	n/a	n/a	n/a	n/a	n/a
Cleveland, OH	14.49	1.83	1.55	1.32	3.72	4.57
College Station, TX	n/a	n/a	n/a	n/a	n/a	n/a
Colorado Springs, CO	13.95	1.39	1.76	1.27	3.39	4.55
Columbia, MO	11.89	1.53	2.18	1.08	3.56	4.44
Columbia, SC	12.24	1.40	2.19	1.31	3.54	4.28
Columbus, OH	12.68	1.16	1.58	1.17	3.53	7.19
Dallas, TX	10.44	1.48	1.97	1.15	3.45	4.51
Davenport, IA	11.56	1.53	2.60	1.32	3.44	4.60
Denver, CO	12.57	1.48	1.76	1.46	3.36	4.17
Des Moines, IA	12.05	1.51	2.18	1.34	3.05	4.24
Durham, NC	n/a	n/a	n/a	n/a	n/a	n/a
Edison, NJ[1]	13.96	1.67	2.41	1.60	3.51	4.06
El Paso, TX	10.83	2.02	2.67	1.85	3.93	5.38
Fargo, ND	n/a	n/a	n/a	n/a	n/a	n/a
Fayetteville, NC	n/a	n/a	n/a	n/a	n/a	n/a
Fort Collins, CO	n/a	n/a	n/a	n/a	n/a	n/a
Fort Wayne, IN	11.87	1.07	1.31	0.74	3.13	3.47
Fort Worth, TX	9.35	1.87	1.92	1.26	3.55	4.49
Grand Rapids, MI	12.68	1.12	1.59	1.25	3.34	3.25
Greeley, CO	n/a	n/a	n/a	n/a	n/a	n/a
Green Bay, WI	11.37	1.10	1.93	1.51	3.64	4.47
Greensboro, NC[2]	11.86	1.27	1.55	1.45	3.94	4.03
Honolulu, HI	13.84	2.45	4.31	3.77	5.44	8.69
Houston, TX	11.29	1.13	1.58	1.42	3.50	3.84
Huntsville, AL	13.10	1.45	1.62	0.95	3.75	4.36
Indianapolis, IN	11.98	1.37	1.68	1.13	3.34	4.17
Jacksonville, FL	12.36	1.49	2.21	1.46	3.30	3.86
Kansas City, MO	11.83	1.92	1.87	1.17	3.22	3.44
Lafayette, LA	11.14	1.16	2.19	1.69	3.82	4.26
Lakeland, FL	n/a	n/a	n/a	n/a	n/a	n/a
Las Vegas, NV	10.89	1.35	2.46	2.07	3.99	4.69
Lexington, KY	10.82	1.11	1.64	1.16	3.18	3.69
Lincoln, NE	11.88	1.46	2.21	1.42	3.03	4.13
Little Rock, AR	10.99	1.16	1.78	1.43	3.23	3.89
Los Angeles, CA	12.32	1.72	2.19	2.88	4.09	4.90
Louisville, KY	12.70	1.09	1.15	1.02	3.13	4.01
Madison, WI	14.10	1.61	2.26	1.17	3.46	4.65

Table continued on following page.

Urban Area	T-Bone Steak ($/pound)	Frying Chicken ($/pound)	Whole Milk ($/half gal.)	Eggs ($/dozen)	Orange Juice ($/64 oz.)	Coffee ($/11.5 oz.)
Manchester, NH	13.66	1.19	2.79	1.52	3.41	3.66
Memphis, TN	9.64	0.98	1.79	1.27	3.09	4.05
Miami, FL	12.55	1.73	3.16	1.71	3.67	4.00
Midland, TX	10.05	1.16	1.51	1.47	3.37	4.14
Milwaukee, WI	12.91	1.22	1.98	1.11	3.38	4.14
Minneapolis, MN	13.63	2.10	2.60	1.81	3.71	4.67
Nashville, TN	13.20	1.42	1.96	1.05	3.65	4.37
New Haven, CT	10.42	1.51	2.52	1.73	3.32	4.03
New Orleans, LA	10.51	1.21	2.30	1.63	3.63	3.83
New York, NY[3]	15.20	2.36	2.82	2.78	4.36	4.74
Oklahoma City, OK	11.70	1.34	1.87	1.23	3.23	4.07
Omaha, NE	11.27	1.24	2.00	1.87	3.47	4.87
Orlando, FL	11.14	1.27	2.39	1.31	3.60	3.91
Peoria, IL	10.98	1.03	1.32	0.93	3.45	5.99
Philadelphia, PA	13.82	1.60	2.18	1.99	4.08	4.54
Phoenix, AZ	13.58	1.68	1.63	1.80	3.71	4.84
Pittsburgh, PA	13.64	1.61	2.03	1.35	3.36	4.62
Portland, OR	11.98	1.58	2.12	2.36	4.10	5.30
Providence, RI	12.73	1.75	2.52	2.17	3.57	4.42
Provo, UT	11.04	1.66	1.50	1.46	3.65	4.66
Raleigh, NC	10.15	0.97	1.61	1.19	3.79	3.83
Reno, NV	12.84	1.58	2.93	2.07	3.36	5.86
Richmond, VA	11.36	1.05	1.58	0.86	3.20	3.78
Riverside, CA	n/a	n/a	n/a	n/a	n/a	n/a
Rochester, MN	n/a	n/a	n/a	n/a	n/a	n/a
Sacramento, CA	10.84	1.31	2.66	2.50	4.16	5.46
Salt Lake City, UT	11.44	1.81	1.73	1.32	3.44	4.51
San Antonio, TX	9.89	1.01	1.63	1.66	3.14	3.93
San Diego, CA	12.27	1.72	2.19	2.88	4.09	5.21
San Francisco, CA	14.94	1.80	2.83	3.16	4.26	6.63
San Jose, CA	n/a	n/a	n/a	n/a	n/a	n/a
Santa Rosa, CA	n/a	n/a	n/a	n/a	n/a	n/a
Savannah, GA	11.65	1.51	1.76	1.50	3.22	3.92
Seattle, WA	12.88	2.15	2.50	2.13	4.05	6.00
Sioux Falls, SD	n/a	n/a	n/a	n/a	n/a	n/a
Springfield, IL	n/a	n/a	n/a	n/a	n/a	n/a
Tallahassee, FL	11.54	1.56	2.71	1.70	3.95	3.85
Tampa, FL	11.11	1.74	2.66	1.68	3.43	4.28
Tucson, AZ	13.61	1.65	1.59	1.89	3.70	5.03
Tulsa, OK	11.20	1.30	2.00	1.38	3.44	3.89
Tuscaloosa, AL	n/a	n/a	n/a	n/a	n/a	n/a
Virginia Beach, VA[4]	11.03	1.20	1.75	1.35	3.88	3.85
Washington, DC	13.57	1.80	2.46	1.80	3.91	4.77
Wichita, KS	11.94	1.23	1.75	0.94	3.70	4.17
Winston-Salem, NC	11.86	1.27	1.55	1.45	3.94	4.03
Average*	11.78	1.39	2.05	1.47	3.57	4.34
Minimum*	8.03	0.94	1.03	0.74	2.94	3.02
Maximum*	15.86	2.65	4.31	3.77	5.44	8.69

*Note: **T-Bone Steak** (price per pound); **Frying Chicken** (price per pound, whole fryer); **Whole Milk** (half gallon carton); **Eggs** (price per dozen, Grade A, large); **Orange Juice** (64 oz. Tropicana or Florida Natural); **Coffee** (11.5 oz. can, vacuum-packed, Maxwell House, Hills Bros, or Folgers); (*) Average, minimum, and maximum values for all 284 areas in the Cost of Living Index report; n/a not available; In cases where data is not available for the city, data for the metro area or for a neighboring city has been provided and noted as follows: (1) Middlesex-Monmouth NJ; (2) Winston-Salem, NC; (3) Brooklyn, NY; (4) Hampton Roads-SE Virginia Source: The Council for Community and Economic Research (formerly ACCRA), Cost of Living Index, 2020*

Housing and Utility Costs

Urban Area	New Home Price ($)	Apartment Rent ($/month)	All Electric ($/month)	Part Electric ($/month)	Other Energy ($/month)	Telephone ($/month)
Albuquerque, NM	329,645	874	-	114.55	40.75	183.90
Allentown, PA	397,306	1,488	-	100.14	86.52	189.10
Anchorage, AK	535,483	1,257	-	111.07	136.23	184.30
Ann Arbor, MI	n/a	n/a	n/a	n/a	n/a	n/a
Athens, GA	n/a	n/a	n/a	n/a	n/a	n/a
Atlanta, GA	380,418	1,245	-	87.42	33.41	185.10
Austin, TX	370,234	1,530	-	105.65	45.12	185.50
Baton Rouge	333,881	1,144	101.95	-	-	179.00
Boise City, ID	366,858	1,252	-	63.83	62.43	170.20
Boston, MA	744,522	3,157	-	72.47	161.39	181.10
Boulder, CO	n/a	n/a	n/a	n/a	n/a	n/a
Cape Coral, FL	328,513	1,061	158.56	-	-	187.80
Cedar Rapids, IA	322,911	831	-	139.90	48.93	180.80
Charleston, SC	325,960	1,372	228.13	-	-	187.30
Charlotte, NC	269,325	1,257	158.05	-	-	179.90
Chicago, IL	537,912	2,334	-	80.80	51.09	203.20
Cincinnati, OH	293,448	944	-	76.98	57.83	179.10
Clarksville, TN	n/a	n/a	n/a	n/a	n/a	n/a
Cleveland, OH	291,327	1,120	-	84.52	69.85	180.60
College Station, TX	n/a	n/a	n/a	n/a	n/a	n/a
Colorado Springs, CO	377,643	1,386	-	89.03	76.10	182.20
Columbia, MO	313,945	808	-	96.59	60.50	190.50
Columbia, SC	258,420	885	-	116.56	131.89	185.80
Columbus, OH	281,476	1,136	-	68.54	59.10	179.90
Dallas, TX	371,745	1,705	-	133.58	55.19	185.50
Davenport, IA	248,085	880	-	85.19	52.80	191.30
Denver, CO	530,852	1,545	-	59.31	46.19	186.50
Des Moines, IA	300,464	712	-	79.70	55.44	180.80
Durham, NC	n/a	n/a	n/a	n/a	n/a	n/a
Edison, NJ[1]	532,983	1,597	-	102.88	71.38	179.90
El Paso, TX	242,558	908	-	93.81	45.21	185.50
Fargo, ND	n/a	n/a	n/a	n/a	n/a	n/a
Fayetteville, NC	n/a	n/a	n/a	n/a	n/a	n/a
Fort Collins, CO	n/a	n/a	n/a	n/a	n/a	n/a
Fort Wayne, IN	204,729	859	-	93.81	50.38	184.30
Fort Worth, TX	258,331	1,164	-	133.52	54.42	184.70
Grand Rapids, MI	299,711	1,144	-	102.23	68.00	181.00
Greeley, CO	n/a	n/a	n/a	n/a	n/a	n/a
Green Bay, WI	304,129	813	-	82.41	78.05	179.40
Greensboro, NC[2]	248,204	1,242	158.18	-	-	169.60
Honolulu, HI	1,386,483	3,315	470.38	-	-	178.30
Houston, TX	297,296	1,119	-	161.68	38.31	184.00
Huntsville, AL	256,311	792	156.41	-	-	181.80
Indianapolis, IN	278,798	1,039	-	104.81	67.00	184.30
Jacksonville, FL	275,940	1,277	158.65	-	-	188.30
Kansas City, MO	299,164	1,207	-	96.98	60.15	189.70
Lafayette, LA	244,456	952	-	88.34	52.94	180.20
Lakeland, FL	n/a	n/a	n/a	n/a	n/a	n/a
Las Vegas, NV	412,949	1,205	-	120.44	50.07	175.30
Lexington, KY	309,955	976	-	79.97	77.60	206.50
Lincoln, NE	296,778	867	-	70.14	53.85	194.40
Little Rock, AR	371,333	740	-	85.47	57.54	197.30
Los Angeles, CA	841,834	2,775	-	122.73	62.94	189.50
Louisville, KY	273,187	1,038	-	80.02	77.60	180.80
Madison, WI	433,233	1,119	-	103.73	65.58	179.40

Table continued on following page.

Urban Area	New Home Price ($)	Apartment Rent ($/month)	All Electric ($/month)	Part Electric ($/month)	Other Energy ($/month)	Telephone ($/month)
Manchester, NH	362,551	1,625	-	117.62	88.11	180.00
Memphis, TN	273,404	903	-	90.75	43.22	185.00
Miami, FL	447,771	2,208	162.18	-	-	188.20
Midland, TX	301,432	1,078	-	125.29	39.71	184.40
Milwaukee, WI	358,549	1,315	-	102.30	56.96	178.70
Minneapolis, MN	386,294	1,204	-	95.03	65.60	181.00
Nashville, TN	339,380	1,130	-	88.87	55.47	185.00
New Haven, CT	393,588	1,995	-	170.80	131.69	178.60
New Orleans, LA	520,536	1,618	-	58.74	38.53	180.20
New York, NY[3]	1,278,996	3,486	-	95.03	78.96	189.50
Oklahoma City, OK	258,612	873	-	92.78	58.17	188.40
Omaha, NE	305,521	1,100	-	89.62	56.82	194.40
Orlando, FL	294,196	1,148	164.06	-	-	187.90
Peoria, IL	306,592	771	-	80.23	81.73	191.30
Philadelphia, PA	426,075	1,517	-	100.69	93.28	192.10
Phoenix, AZ	362,970	1,639	189.67	-	-	178.50
Pittsburgh, PA	378,703	1,232	-	108.94	101.72	190.60
Portland, OR	623,494	2,459	-	81.22	62.64	170.50
Providence, RI	430,197	1,800	-	125.74	114.83	189.00
Provo, UT	382,813	1,129	-	68.02	58.46	187.20
Raleigh, NC	308,897	1,309	-	103.82	58.98	179.90
Reno, NV	489,573	1,330	-	82.05	42.67	177.90
Richmond, VA	318,880	1,135	-	94.98	81.43	178.00
Riverside, CA	n/a	n/a	n/a	n/a	n/a	n/a
Rochester, MN	n/a	n/a	n/a	n/a	n/a	n/a
Sacramento, CA	484,470	1,948	-	145.58	46.79	186.50
Salt Lake City, UT	401,866	1,164	-	74.91	60.06	187.80
San Antonio, TX	271,143	1,396	-	96.33	37.17	184.30
San Diego, CA	797,634	2,351	-	183.35	64.21	176.00
San Francisco, CA	1,362,163	4,098	-	183.22	84.62	198.20
San Jose, CA	n/a	n/a	n/a	n/a	n/a	n/a
Santa Rosa, CA	n/a	n/a	n/a	n/a	n/a	n/a
Savannah, GA	218,111	905	155.12	-	-	182.20
Seattle, WA	854,748	2,680	186.95	-	-	194.20
Sioux Falls, SD	n/a	n/a	n/a	n/a	n/a	n/a
Springfield, IL	n/a	n/a	n/a	n/a	n/a	n/a
Tallahassee, FL	344,867	1,132	124.57	-	-	189.90
Tampa, FL	278,508	1,296	165.98	-	-	189.50
Tucson, AZ	372,120	955	-	121.08	48.38	185.50
Tulsa, OK	239,022	680	-	87.50	59.74	188.20
Tuscaloosa, AL	n/a	n/a	n/a	n/a	n/a	n/a
Virginia Beach, VA[4]	317,054	1,200	-	97.52	76.48	185.90
Washington, DC	1,020,885	3,033	-	135.39	69.36	184.50
Wichita, KS	254,831	771	-	100.11	56.39	188.70
Winston-Salem, NC	248,204	1,242	158.18	-	-	169.60
Average*	368,594	1,168	170.86	100.47	65.28	184.30
Minimum*	190,567	502	91.58	31.42	26.08	169.60
Maximum*	2,227,806	4,738	470.38	280.31	280.06	206.50

Note: **New Home Price** (2,400 sf living area, 8,000 sf lot, in urban area with full utilities); **Apartment Rent** (950 sf 2 bedroom/1.5 or 2 bath, unfurnished, excluding all utilities except water); **All Electric** (average monthly cost for an all-electric home); **Part Electric** (average monthly cost for a part-electric home); **Other Energy** (average monthly cost for natural gas, fuel oil, coal, wood, and any other forms of energy except electricity); **Telephone** (price includes the base monthly rate plus taxes and fees for three lines of mobile phone service); (*) Average, minimum, and maximum values for all 284 areas in the Cost of Living Index report; n/a not available; In cases where data is not available for the city, data for the metro area or for a neighboring city has been provided and noted as follows: (1) Middlesex-Monmouth NJ; (2) Winston-Salem, NC; (3) Brooklyn, NY; (4) Hampton Roads-SE Virginia
Source: The Council for Community and Economic Research (formerly ACCRA), Cost of Living Index, 2020

Health Care, Transportation, and Other Costs

Urban Area	Doctor ($/visit)	Dentist ($/visit)	Optometrist ($/visit)	Gasoline ($/gallon)	Beauty Salon ($/visit)	Men's Shirt ($)
Albuquerque, NM	106.93	98.97	108.12	1.85	39.81	30.50
Allentown, PA	75.54	110.86	106.13	2.54	43.55	25.80
Anchorage, AK	206.08	147.12	219.89	2.59	54.87	16.85
Ann Arbor, MI	n/a	n/a	n/a	n/a	n/a	n/a
Athens, GA	n/a	n/a	n/a	n/a	n/a	n/a
Atlanta, GA	119.80	105.78	110.27	2.23	47.13	27.27
Austin, TX	117.55	121.27	114.00	2.00	50.41	32.54
Baton Rouge	114.78	104.33	127.76	1.89	50.62	40.67
Boise City, ID	124.87	83.97	133.84	2.37	36.81	42.44
Boston, MA	194.00	108.27	102.75	2.19	64.17	44.46
Boulder, CO	n/a	n/a	n/a	n/a	n/a	n/a
Cape Coral, FL	123.46	110.14	85.53	2.45	33.41	25.30
Cedar Rapids, IA	122.25	115.00	102.58	2.15	37.59	28.78
Charleston, SC	131.23	102.76	81.87	2.06	57.83	27.44
Charlotte, NC	121.12	112.88	119.06	2.35	39.10	31.86
Chicago, IL	104.96	101.82	96.76	2.51	65.57	32.92
Cincinnati, OH	109.23	105.08	96.61	2.29	34.80	33.72
Clarksville, TN	n/a	n/a	n/a	n/a	n/a	n/a
Cleveland, OH	121.47	119.67	86.00	2.25	31.40	37.72
College Station, TX	n/a	n/a	n/a	n/a	n/a	n/a
Colorado Springs, CO	126.71	105.77	114.08	2.41	42.90	28.17
Columbia, MO	126.58	89.08	104.24	1.99	39.17	33.37
Columbia, SC	102.00	59.00	51.67	2.00	41.63	20.62
Columbus, OH	130.99	84.54	59.28	2.38	39.83	34.09
Dallas, TX	121.08	133.84	97.86	1.92	44.45	38.73
Davenport, IA	142.33	96.83	93.08	2.16	34.50	43.03
Denver, CO	111.77	105.51	104.86	2.49	44.29	30.30
Des Moines, IA	110.85	82.19	108.45	2.17	32.13	15.16
Durham, NC	n/a	n/a	n/a	n/a	n/a	n/a
Edison, NJ[1]	94.50	113.15	101.33	2.26	36.40	41.77
El Paso, TX	133.61	82.94	87.16	2.15	30.42	28.66
Fargo, ND	n/a	n/a	n/a	n/a	n/a	n/a
Fayetteville, NC	n/a	n/a	n/a	n/a	n/a	n/a
Fort Collins, CO	n/a	n/a	n/a	n/a	n/a	n/a
Fort Wayne, IN	129.50	94.17	89.56	2.30	33.00	33.48
Fort Worth, TX	91.05	108.33	92.25	1.83	53.57	39.58
Grand Rapids, MI	98.00	94.78	105.11	2.23	32.55	17.24
Greeley, CO	n/a	n/a	n/a	n/a	n/a	n/a
Green Bay, WI	176.50	81.33	74.00	1.71	22.70	30.51
Greensboro, NC[2]	124.74	139.81	109.70	2.12	35.48	39.18
Honolulu, HI	145.88	86.68	195.37	3.30	70.00	58.06
Houston, TX	88.11	111.03	119.84	1.92	61.37	33.46
Huntsville, AL	112.22	100.06	109.44	2.06	33.33	31.87
Indianapolis, IN	88.25	92.92	65.90	2.12	37.63	42.14
Jacksonville, FL	77.42	94.87	70.67	2.20	56.67	23.45
Kansas City, MO	108.18	107.03	106.75	2.02	38.27	33.28
Lafayette, LA	113.42	79.60	103.22	1.92	40.73	32.66
Lakeland, FL	n/a	n/a	n/a	n/a	n/a	n/a
Las Vegas, NV	106.13	96.98	105.92	2.36	46.67	29.07
Lexington, KY	82.39	76.80	74.07	2.08	37.90	38.67
Lincoln, NE	148.06	94.73	104.48	2.20	40.62	43.69
Little Rock, AR	125.22	69.23	101.50	1.89	42.83	35.86
Los Angeles, CA	125.00	110.78	125.58	3.31	76.50	32.87
Louisville, KY	133.98	82.89	71.56	2.28	49.58	32.27
Madison, WI	201.33	113.22	57.00	2.18	48.44	33.55

Table continued on following page.

Urban Area	Doctor ($/visit)	Dentist ($/visit)	Optometrist ($/visit)	Gasoline ($/gallon)	Beauty Salon ($/visit)	Men's Shirt ($)
Manchester, NH	152.49	121.64	101.89	2.00	41.18	34.23
Memphis, TN	84.25	77.68	74.47	1.94	36.63	25.89
Miami, FL	111.06	107.78	105.63	2.24	70.00	23.08
Midland, TX	98.67	109.17	103.22	2.03	33.61	25.58
Milwaukee, WI	175.40	101.10	60.00	2.01	41.93	22.41
Minneapolis, MN	147.85	86.94	89.59	2.06	34.39	34.39
Nashville, TN	94.18	107.94	91.08	2.05	35.67	32.97
New Haven, CT	130.27	107.76	112.13	2.30	47.72	35.60
New Orleans, LA	156.11	111.89	94.77	2.02	48.89	27.54
New York, NY[3]	116.89	116.47	100.16	2.32	70.14	49.22
Oklahoma City, OK	112.21	93.98	102.53	1.90	40.17	18.12
Omaha, NE	119.00	78.66	114.83	2.07	34.01	23.77
Orlando, FL	83.46	97.71	100.39	2.10	54.17	17.78
Peoria, IL	114.08	79.00	141.52	2.36	30.00	29.99
Philadelphia, PA	133.89	96.86	108.61	2.43	60.55	31.89
Phoenix, AZ	96.33	89.83	96.17	2.49	41.67	27.57
Pittsburgh, PA	93.55	102.37	90.39	2.55	34.18	22.73
Portland, OR	168.67	101.75	146.25	2.78	56.44	41.23
Providence, RI	157.87	92.75	131.39	2.15	48.53	38.26
Provo, UT	99.81	84.76	97.49	2.39	36.53	24.62
Raleigh, NC	145.22	99.00	98.89	2.27	48.42	30.33
Reno, NV	155.00	114.56	117.17	2.98	40.13	21.17
Richmond, VA	139.74	99.40	116.20	2.01	44.43	29.26
Riverside, CA	n/a	n/a	n/a	n/a	n/a	n/a
Rochester, MN	n/a	n/a	n/a	n/a	n/a	n/a
Sacramento, CA	194.75	94.80	148.50	3.24	62.28	24.56
Salt Lake City, UT	107.49	101.65	89.78	2.44	34.97	23.53
San Antonio, TX	86.07	87.61	97.83	1.90	45.96	31.37
San Diego, CA	125.00	107.18	117.65	3.24	64.57	32.48
San Francisco, CA	149.63	132.68	144.57	3.46	82.05	42.08
San Jose, CA	n/a	n/a	n/a	n/a	n/a	n/a
Santa Rosa, CA	n/a	n/a	n/a	n/a	n/a	n/a
Savannah, GA	109.21	127.37	93.79	2.10	35.80	25.61
Seattle, WA	136.39	143.77	158.73	3.19	50.33	36.89
Sioux Falls, SD	n/a	n/a	n/a	n/a	n/a	n/a
Springfield, IL	n/a	n/a	n/a	n/a	n/a	n/a
Tallahassee, FL	126.07	111.09	69.75	2.25	36.64	33.99
Tampa, FL	99.22	105.57	99.12	2.11	37.26	23.11
Tucson, AZ	138.05	91.20	96.00	2.14	51.51	49.50
Tulsa, OK	109.61	90.61	99.06	1.77	35.56	23.57
Tuscaloosa, AL	n/a	n/a	n/a	n/a	n/a	n/a
Virginia Beach, VA[4]	83.17	103.67	98.57	2.00	38.97	36.02
Washington, DC	109.41	94.31	79.25	2.31	66.76	37.74
Wichita, KS	100.20	86.82	148.22	2.03	39.58	43.51
Winston-Salem, NC	124.74	139.81	109.70	2.12	35.48	39.18
Average*	115.44	99.32	108.10	2.21	39.27	31.37
Minimum*	36.68	59.00	51.36	1.71	19.00	11.00
Maximum*	219.00	153.10	250.97	3.46	82.05	58.33

Note: **Doctor** (general practitioners routine exam of an established patient); **Dentist** (adult teeth cleaning and periodic oral examination); **Optometrist** (full vision eye exam for established adult patient); **Gasoline** (one gallon regular unleaded, national brand, including all taxes, cash price at self-service pump if available); **Beauty Salon** (woman's shampoo, trim, and blow-dry); **Men's Shirt** (cotton/polyester dress shirt, pinpoint weave, long sleeves); (*) Average, minimum, and maximum values for all 284 areas in the Cost of Living Index report; n/a not available; In cases where data is not available for the city, data for the metro area or for a neighboring city has been provided and noted as follows: (1) Middlesex-Monmouth NJ; (2) Winston-Salem, NC; (3) Brooklyn, NY; (4) Hampton Roads-SE Virginia
Source: The Council for Community and Economic Research (formerly ACCRA), Cost of Living Index, 2020

Number of Medical Professionals

City	Area Covered	MDs[1]	DOs[1,2]	Dentists	Podiatrists	Chiropractors	Optometrists
Albuquerque, NM	Bernalillo County	457.1	20.1	87.2	9.9	24.4	16.9
Allentown, PA	Lehigh County	347.8	83.3	88.3	12.2	29.5	20.0
Anchorage, AK	Anchorage Borough	360.0	46.1	128.5	4.9	63.2	31.3
Ann Arbor, MI	Washtenaw County	1,272.3	41.4	183.4	7.3	26.7	17.1
Athens, GA	Clarke County	313.5	14.9	53.8	4.7	21.0	16.4
Atlanta, GA	Fulton County	510.9	12.8	71.1	5.3	55.1	17.2
Austin, TX	Travis County	320.3	19.2	72.2	4.2	34.0	16.3
Baton Rouge, LA	East Baton Rouge Parish	388.4	7.2	75.9	4.5	12.5	13.9
Boise City, ID	Ada County	290.3	33.1	81.0	3.5	55.4	19.5
Boston, MA	Suffolk County	1,479.8	15.2	222.3	10.0	14.1	34.1
Boulder, CO	Boulder County	351.8	32.7	106.1	6.1	80.9	26.4
Cape Coral, FL	Lee County	190.7	29.8	49.8	8.3	27.4	12.6
Cedar Rapids, IA	Linn County	185.1	22.1	73.7	8.4	59.5	18.1
Charleston, SC	Charleston County	796.9	31.0	109.6	4.9	50.8	21.9
Charlotte, NC	Mecklenburg County	329.6	14.2	69.9	3.4	32.8	14.0
Chicago, IL	Cook County	432.8	23.4	94.5	12.4	28.7	20.8
Cincinnati, OH	Hamilton County	612.8	25.1	75.7	10.0	20.3	21.8
Clarksville, TN	Montgomery County	95.5	14.6	46.9	2.4	13.4	12.9
Cleveland, OH	Cuyahoga County	714.3	51.5	109.6	18.1	18.4	17.2
College Station, TX	Brazos County	258.7	19.0	52.4	3.1	17.5	15.7
Colorado Springs, CO	El Paso County	196.9	31.0	104.5	4.4	43.6	24.6
Columbia, MO	Boone County	815.9	59.8	69.8	5.5	35.5	27.2
Columbia, SC	Richland County	356.3	15.9	91.6	7.2	23.8	19.7
Columbus, OH	Franklin County	424.6	61.9	93.1	7.1	24.8	27.1
Dallas, TX	Dallas County	335.5	20.5	86.8	4.0	36.5	13.5
Davenport, IA	Scott County	233.2	52.1	79.2	4.6	182.7	16.8
Denver, CO	Denver County	595.6	32.7	76.3	6.6	36.2	16.9
Des Moines, IA	Polk County	213.2	96.7	73.9	10.8	55.3	21.0
Durham, NC	Durham County	1,131.3	15.8	75.0	4.0	19.3	14.6
Edison, NJ	Middlesex County	375.0	19.5	90.9	9.9	25.5	20.0
El Paso, TX	El Paso County	195.0	12.9	46.5	3.9	8.7	10.1
Fargo, ND	Cass County	392.7	19.4	79.7	4.4	73.1	31.3
Fayetteville, NC	Cumberland County	200.3	23.1	104.9	6.0	9.8	18.2
Fort Collins, CO	Larimer County	239.5	29.9	79.6	5.9	55.5	21.0
Fort Wayne, IN	Allen County	264.5	27.5	66.4	5.5	21.9	25.8
Fort Worth, TX	Tarrant County	183.1	34.4	60.4	4.4	27.0	15.9
Grand Rapids, MI	Kent County	343.8	69.5	74.6	4.7	37.0	25.1
Greeley, CO	Weld County	129.9	16.5	45.9	2.8	22.8	12.3
Green Bay, WI	Brown County	244.7	24.3	80.5	3.4	46.9	18.1
Greensboro, NC	Guilford County	252.9	14.1	57.0	5.0	14.1	10.2
Honolulu, HI	Honolulu County	351.0	17.3	101.1	3.4	19.6	24.3
Houston, TX	Harris County	333.5	11.5	70.7	4.7	22.3	20.4
Huntsville, AL	Madison County	275.5	12.0	56.6	3.8	23.3	19.0
Indianapolis, IN	Marion County	438.4	21.4	90.3	6.1	15.8	19.8
Jacksonville, FL	Duval County	351.1	22.9	83.3	8.4	25.0	16.2
Kansas City, MO	Jackson County	307.2	59.9	90.2	6.4	45.2	20.2
Lafayette, LA	Lafayette Parish	367.7	9.9	68.7	3.7	32.7	13.1
Lakeland, FL	Polk County	124.5	10.0	34.1	4.3	18.1	9.7
Las Vegas, NV	Clark County	177.4	34.8	63.7	4.3	19.6	13.1
Lexington, KY	Fayette County	728.8	36.6	148.5	7.4	22.6	23.2
Lincoln, NE	Lancaster County	218.3	12.6	101.5	5.3	45.1	21.6
Little Rock, AR	Pulaski County	737.4	14.3	77.6	4.6	22.5	21.4
Los Angeles, CA	Los Angeles County	302.4	13.5	89.6	6.4	30.1	18.7
Louisville, KY	Jefferson County	476.6	13.3	109.6	7.8	28.8	15.5
Madison, WI	Dane County	610.2	21.2	73.9	4.6	44.1	22.3
Manchester, NH	Hillsborough County	237.8	25.3	82.7	5.5	25.9	20.1

Table continued on following page.

City	Area Covered	MDs[1]	DOs[1,2]	Dentists	Podiatrists	Chiropractors	Optometrists
Memphis, TN	Shelby County	403.7	10.3	73.6	3.6	13.2	31.6
Miami, FL	Miami-Dade County	344.1	16.5	69.8	10.3	18.3	14.4
Midland, TX	Midland County	150.1	9.3	54.9	2.3	13.6	11.9
Milwaukee, WI	Milwaukee County	374.6	21.6	83.9	7.7	20.4	10.9
Minneapolis, MN	Hennepin County	524.3	22.3	99.8	5.2	73.2	21.5
Nashville, TN	Davidson County	647.2	12.2	81.1	4.3	25.6	16.9
New Haven, CT	New Haven County	556.7	10.7	79.9	10.1	26.9	17.3
New Orleans, LA	Orleans Parish	808.2	18.2	74.3	3.8	9.5	6.2
New York, NY	New York City	483.9	16.6	91.0	13.6	16.5	17.6
Oklahoma City, OK	Oklahoma County	410.1	41.7	105.6	5.3	27.3	18.3
Omaha, NE	Douglas County	540.6	27.5	97.0	5.3	41.1	20.5
Orlando, FL	Orange County	311.3	22.1	50.7	3.7	26.6	12.8
Peoria, IL	Peoria County	558.6	41.5	86.5	8.4	50.8	20.6
Philadelphia, PA	Philadelphia County	571.9	44.8	81.1	17.2	15.6	17.7
Phoenix, AZ	Maricopa County	245.6	31.3	68.2	6.6	33.2	15.5
Pittsburgh, PA	Allegheny County	642.7	43.9	98.1	10.9	44.7	20.9
Portland, OR	Multnomah County	634.2	31.0	99.8	5.3	74.7	22.4
Providence, RI	Providence County	496.3	18.1	60.6	9.9	20.3	20.7
Provo, UT	Utah County	116.3	19.0	61.0	4.6	25.5	11.0
Raleigh, NC	Wake County	276.9	11.4	71.6	3.5	26.5	16.6
Reno, NV	Washoe County	294.4	20.9	70.0	4.0	28.0	24.0
Richmond, VA	Richmond City	740.3	28.4	143.2	10.8	7.4	16.5
Riverside, CA	Riverside County	127.8	15.3	52.4	2.6	16.3	12.8
Rochester, MN	Olmsted County	2,492.4	48.6	126.3	6.3	41.1	24.0
Sacramento, CA	Sacramento County	315.5	15.7	78.3	4.6	22.0	18.1
Salt Lake City, UT	Salt Lake County	376.7	17.1	78.4	6.5	27.1	13.5
San Antonio, TX	Bexar County	324.7	18.6	89.2	5.3	16.3	18.1
San Diego, CA	San Diego County	325.9	18.3	90.9	4.3	34.4	19.1
San Francisco, CA	San Francisco County	814.1	13.6	156.7	10.4	39.6	29.4
San Jose, CA	Santa Clara County	421.9	10.9	118.4	6.8	42.7	27.5
Santa Rosa, CA	Sonoma County	279.6	18.2	93.7	6.7	40.9	18.2
Savannah, GA	Chatham County	352.0	18.0	69.8	6.9	19.0	13.5
Seattle, WA	King County	489.5	15.6	109.7	6.4	46.7	21.8
Sioux Falls, SD	Minnehaha County	362.3	25.7	55.4	6.2	58.0	19.2
Springfield, IL	Sangamon County	631.8	26.1	85.3	5.7	40.1	21.1
Tallahassee, FL	Leon County	304.5	14.1	49.0	3.4	23.8	18.7
Tampa, FL	Hillsborough County	344.9	26.1	58.9	5.6	26.4	14.2
Tucson, AZ	Pima County	361.9	24.6	65.1	5.4	19.1	15.9
Tulsa, OK	Tulsa County	269.3	122.0	69.7	4.0	38.8	23.5
Tuscaloosa, AL	Tuscaloosa County	228.0	9.1	49.7	5.3	20.5	15.8
Virginia Beach, VA	Virginia Beach City	252.3	13.3	77.3	7.6	27.3	16.9
Washington, DC	District of Columbia	779.6	16.7	123.0	8.9	9.4	14.5
Wichita, KS	Sedgwick County	258.0	35.2	65.9	2.5	42.6	28.1
Winston-Salem, NC	Forsyth County	660.3	29.3	62.3	5.8	16.5	17.8
U.S.	U.S.	282.9	22.7	71.2	6.2	28.1	16.9

Note: All figures are rates per 100,000 population; Data as of 2019 unless noted; (1) Data as of 2018 and includes all active, non-federal physicians; (2) Doctor of Osteopathic Medicine
Source: U.S. Department of Health and Human Services, Health Resources and Services Administration, Bureau of Health Professions, Area Resource File (ARF) 2019-2020

Health Insurance Coverage: City

City	With Health Insurance	With Private Health Insurance	With Public Health Insurance	Without Health Insurance	Population Under Age 19 Without Health Insurance
Albuquerque, NM	92.1	60.9	43.0	7.9	3.4
Allentown, PA	88.8	47.3	49.7	11.2	5.0
Anchorage, AK	88.8	70.3	30.4	11.2	8.2
Ann Arbor, MI	97.3	87.7	19.7	2.7	1.1
Athens, GA	86.5	68.5	26.9	13.5	7.3
Atlanta, GA	89.7	69.2	28.3	10.3	4.9
Austin, TX	86.4	73.3	20.2	13.6	8.9
Baton Rouge, LA	90.3	59.2	41.1	9.7	3.5
Boise City, ID	91.1	75.8	26.8	8.9	4.4
Boston, MA	96.5	67.2	36.7	3.5	1.3
Boulder, CO	95.9	84.0	20.1	4.1	1.2
Cape Coral, FL	87.4	65.9	36.8	12.6	8.6
Cedar Rapids, IA	95.5	74.3	34.3	4.5	2.7
Charleston, SC	91.9	78.0	25.5	8.1	3.3
Charlotte, NC	87.5	68.5	26.3	12.5	6.4
Chicago, IL	90.4	60.3	36.9	9.6	3.4
Cincinnati, OH	92.7	59.1	41.6	7.3	4.5
Clarksville, TN	91.6	71.5	33.7	8.4	3.4
Cleveland, OH	92.3	44.0	57.3	7.7	3.1
College Station, TX	92.0	85.0	13.7	8.0	4.9
Colorado Springs, CO	92.2	68.7	36.6	7.8	4.2
Columbia, MO	93.2	81.9	20.6	6.8	3.6
Columbia, SC	91.2	72.0	29.7	8.8	2.7
Columbus, OH	91.0	64.0	34.8	9.0	5.4
Dallas, TX	76.4	51.8	30.3	23.6	14.8
Davenport, IA	94.4	66.2	40.2	5.6	3.3
Denver, CO	90.7	65.5	33.0	9.3	4.2
Des Moines, IA	93.1	64.7	41.0	6.9	3.5
Durham, NC	87.5	68.8	28.3	12.5	7.3
Edison, NJ	94.6	81.1	22.8	5.4	1.3
El Paso, TX	80.9	54.7	33.8	19.1	9.1
Fargo, ND	93.5	80.6	24.3	6.5	4.1
Fayetteville, NC	90.0	65.3	40.4	10.0	3.3
Fort Collins, CO	94.0	78.7	24.3	6.0	5.0
Fort Wayne, IN	91.0	65.0	36.5	9.0	5.6
Fort Worth, TX	81.7	60.6	27.5	18.3	11.7
Grand Rapids, MI	91.4	62.1	39.6	8.6	3.9
Greeley, CO	91.5	63.7	38.4	8.5	4.3
Green Bay, WI	92.1	66.1	35.9	7.9	3.7
Greensboro, NC	89.7	65.9	34.1	10.3	4.5
Honolulu, HI	96.1	77.7	34.5	3.9	2.4
Houston, TX	76.9	51.9	30.8	23.1	13.1
Huntsville, AL	90.2	72.8	32.9	9.8	4.2
Indianapolis, IN	89.5	62.3	36.7	10.5	6.0
Jacksonville, FL	88.0	64.7	33.9	12.0	6.8
Kansas City, MO	88.2	68.6	29.1	11.8	6.6
Lafayette, LA	91.3	67.0	35.3	8.7	3.1
Lakeland, FL	90.0	62.2	41.4	10.0	5.2
Las Vegas, NV	87.7	61.6	36.0	12.3	7.2
Lexington, KY	93.2	71.6	32.5	6.8	4.3
Lincoln, NE	92.3	78.5	25.2	7.7	5.2
Little Rock, AR	91.6	65.6	37.6	8.4	4.8
Los Angeles, CA	88.6	54.4	40.5	11.4	4.2
Louisville, KY	94.6	67.1	40.3	5.4	2.7
Madison, WI	96.0	83.8	22.2	4.0	2.2

Table continued on following page.

City	With Health Insurance	With Private Health Insurance	With Public Health Insurance	Without Health Insurance	Population Under Age 19 Without Health Insurance
Manchester, NH	90.1	64.0	36.3	9.9	3.7
Memphis, TN	86.3	55.7	41.0	13.7	6.3
Miami, FL	80.2	46.7	36.7	19.8	8.6
Midland, TX	83.3	71.1	19.7	16.7	14.7
Milwaukee, WI	90.7	54.1	44.9	9.3	3.3
Minneapolis, MN	93.4	66.8	34.5	6.6	3.4
Nashville, TN	87.9	67.1	29.8	12.1	6.9
New Haven, CT	91.1	50.8	46.7	8.9	2.8
New Orleans, LA	90.8	56.3	42.9	9.2	3.4
New York, NY	92.5	58.3	43.0	7.5	2.4
Oklahoma City, OK	85.4	64.0	32.1	14.6	7.1
Omaha, NE	89.8	71.3	27.7	10.2	5.8
Orlando, FL	84.8	62.3	29.4	15.2	7.5
Peoria, IL	94.2	65.7	41.1	5.8	3.0
Philadelphia, PA	91.9	56.9	45.2	8.1	3.5
Phoenix, AZ	85.9	57.2	36.0	14.1	9.5
Pittsburgh, PA	94.7	73.5	33.4	5.3	3.3
Portland, OR	93.6	71.5	32.0	6.4	2.8
Providence, RI	92.5	53.2	46.4	7.5	3.1
Provo, UT	88.8	77.8	17.3	11.2	10.7
Raleigh, NC	89.8	74.2	24.5	10.2	5.4
Reno, NV	90.2	68.4	32.1	9.8	8.1
Richmond, VA	88.0	62.6	34.9	12.0	6.5
Riverside, CA	90.6	58.9	38.2	9.4	3.6
Rochester, MN	95.7	79.4	30.4	4.3	2.4
Sacramento, CA	94.2	62.2	42.1	5.8	2.2
Salt Lake City, UT	87.4	72.5	22.1	12.6	11.7
San Antonio, TX	83.3	60.1	32.7	16.7	8.6
San Diego, CA	92.2	69.7	31.6	7.8	3.6
San Francisco, CA	96.3	75.7	29.4	3.7	1.5
San Jose, CA	94.8	72.3	30.4	5.2	2.1
Santa Rosa, CA	92.4	67.6	37.9	7.6	4.9
Savannah, GA	83.0	57.3	34.5	17.0	7.7
Seattle, WA	95.8	80.6	24.0	4.2	1.4
Sioux Falls, SD	92.2	77.2	26.5	7.8	4.9
Springfield, IL	95.7	69.1	42.2	4.3	1.7
Tallahassee, FL	91.6	76.3	25.1	8.4	4.2
Tampa, FL	88.3	62.5	32.9	11.7	5.4
Tucson, AZ	88.5	56.5	42.8	11.5	8.1
Tulsa, OK	83.4	58.9	35.1	16.6	8.2
Tuscaloosa, AL	92.6	72.0	31.2	7.4	2.5
Virginia Beach, VA	92.4	80.7	25.8	7.6	3.8
Washington, DC	96.3	70.4	35.6	3.7	2.0
Wichita, KS	87.9	67.3	32.3	12.1	6.6
Winston-Salem, NC	87.6	62.4	36.3	12.4	4.9
U.S.	91.2	67.9	35.1	8.8	5.1

Note: Figures are percentages that cover the civilian noninstitutionalized population
Source: U.S. Census Bureau, 2015-2019 American Community Survey 5-Year Estimates

Health Insurance Coverage: Metro Area

Metro Area	With Health Insurance	With Private Health Insurance	With Public Health Insurance	Without Health Insurance	Population Under Age 19 Without Health Insurance
Albuquerque, NM	91.7	60.2	44.2	8.3	4.1
Allentown, PA	94.5	73.3	35.4	5.5	3.0
Anchorage, AK	87.8	68.3	31.3	12.2	9.4
Ann Arbor, MI	96.5	83.3	25.9	3.5	1.8
Athens, GA	87.6	69.5	28.5	12.4	6.7
Atlanta, GA	87.2	69.3	26.8	12.8	7.5
Austin, TX	87.5	74.5	21.7	12.5	8.1
Baton Rouge, LA	91.7	66.4	35.5	8.3	3.3
Boise City, ID	89.6	71.7	30.2	10.4	4.8
Boston, MA	97.1	76.7	32.7	2.9	1.3
Boulder, CO	95.4	79.5	25.6	4.6	2.1
Cape Coral, FL	86.7	62.4	43.6	13.3	9.3
Cedar Rapids, IA	96.5	77.1	33.1	3.5	2.0
Charleston, SC	89.5	71.1	31.4	10.5	5.7
Charlotte, NC	89.8	70.7	29.3	10.2	4.8
Chicago, IL	92.4	70.2	31.7	7.6	3.2
Cincinnati, OH	94.8	73.1	32.8	5.2	3.1
Clarksville, TN	91.8	69.1	37.2	8.2	5.3
Cleveland, OH	94.7	69.2	38.4	5.3	3.4
College Station, TX	87.4	73.5	23.1	12.6	8.4
Colorado Springs, CO	92.8	71.1	35.3	7.2	4.1
Columbia, MO	92.8	79.5	24.1	7.2	4.6
Columbia, SC	90.5	70.4	33.6	9.5	3.7
Columbus, OH	93.3	71.2	32.1	6.7	4.2
Dallas, TX	83.6	66.0	24.9	16.4	11.0
Davenport, IA	95.3	72.9	37.3	4.7	2.7
Denver, CO	92.6	72.6	29.2	7.4	4.0
Des Moines, IA	95.6	77.4	31.2	4.4	2.2
Durham, NC	89.7	71.7	29.7	10.3	6.1
Edison, NJ	92.8	67.2	36.0	7.2	2.9
El Paso, TX	79.7	52.6	33.9	20.3	9.8
Fargo, ND	94.6	82.1	24.4	5.4	4.2
Fayetteville, NC	89.3	64.6	38.7	10.7	3.6
Fort Collins, CO	94.1	76.0	29.1	5.9	4.7
Fort Wayne, IN	91.5	69.2	33.1	8.5	6.4
Fort Worth, TX	83.6	66.0	24.9	16.4	11.0
Grand Rapids, MI	94.6	75.5	31.5	5.4	3.1
Greeley, CO	92.1	70.1	32.2	7.9	4.6
Green Bay, WI	94.8	75.7	30.4	5.2	3.6
Greensboro, NC	89.6	65.5	35.2	10.4	4.7
Honolulu, HI	96.7	80.4	32.2	3.3	2.0
Houston, TX	81.9	62.1	26.6	18.1	11.1
Huntsville, AL	91.4	76.2	29.9	8.6	3.3
Indianapolis, IN	91.9	71.6	31.0	8.1	5.3
Jacksonville, FL	89.1	68.7	32.7	10.9	6.6
Kansas City, MO	91.1	75.3	27.2	8.9	5.2
Lafayette, LA	90.1	62.1	38.5	9.9	3.6
Lakeland, FL	87.3	59.0	41.4	12.7	7.2
Las Vegas, NV	88.3	64.2	33.7	11.7	7.4
Lexington, KY	93.7	70.8	34.5	6.3	4.0
Lincoln, NE	92.9	79.5	24.9	7.1	4.8
Little Rock, AR	92.4	67.0	38.9	7.6	4.4
Los Angeles, CA	90.9	60.6	37.4	9.1	3.8
Louisville, KY	94.6	71.4	36.4	5.4	3.3
Madison, WI	96.1	83.5	24.7	3.9	2.1

Table continued on following page.

Metro Area	With Health Insurance	With Private Health Insurance	With Public Health Insurance	Without Health Insurance	Population Under Age 19 Without Health Insurance
Manchester, NH	93.8	76.9	28.9	6.2	2.6
Memphis, TN	89.2	64.7	35.4	10.8	5.0
Miami, FL	84.9	58.9	33.6	15.1	7.8
Midland, TX	83.6	71.1	20.2	16.4	14.0
Milwaukee, WI	94.4	71.8	34.1	5.6	2.4
Minneapolis, MN	95.7	78.0	29.6	4.3	3.0
Nashville, TN	90.7	72.1	28.7	9.3	5.1
New Haven, CT	95.0	68.2	38.7	5.0	2.2
New Orleans, LA	90.3	60.4	40.1	9.7	3.7
New York, NY	92.8	67.2	36.0	7.2	2.9
Oklahoma City, OK	87.5	68.6	30.8	12.5	6.2
Omaha, NE	92.3	75.9	27.0	7.7	4.3
Orlando, FL	87.6	65.5	31.5	12.4	6.9
Peoria, IL	95.2	73.5	37.2	4.8	2.9
Philadelphia, PA	94.4	73.2	34.0	5.6	2.9
Phoenix, AZ	89.5	65.4	34.9	10.5	8.2
Pittsburgh, PA	96.2	77.0	35.8	3.8	1.7
Portland, OR	94.0	73.3	32.6	6.0	2.8
Providence, RI	96.1	70.9	38.8	3.9	2.1
Provo, UT	91.9	81.7	17.4	8.1	6.0
Raleigh, NC	91.0	75.9	24.8	9.0	4.6
Reno, NV	90.6	69.8	32.2	9.4	7.7
Richmond, VA	91.8	75.2	29.4	8.2	4.6
Riverside, CA	91.4	57.5	42.0	8.6	3.9
Rochester, MN	95.5	79.9	30.3	4.5	3.7
Sacramento, CA	94.9	69.3	38.2	5.1	2.5
Salt Lake City, UT	89.7	77.5	20.1	10.3	8.2
San Antonio, TX	85.3	65.1	31.0	14.7	8.1
San Diego, CA	92.2	68.4	33.8	7.8	3.8
San Francisco, CA	95.7	75.5	30.5	4.3	2.1
San Jose, CA	95.6	76.7	27.4	4.4	1.9
Santa Rosa, CA	93.9	71.6	36.7	6.1	3.2
Savannah, GA	87.0	67.6	30.1	13.0	6.2
Seattle, WA	94.4	75.9	29.2	5.6	2.5
Sioux Falls, SD	92.8	78.9	25.1	7.2	4.5
Springfield, IL	96.2	74.3	37.4	3.8	1.6
Tallahassee, FL	91.2	73.4	30.0	8.8	4.6
Tampa, FL	88.1	63.3	36.8	11.9	6.3
Tucson, AZ	90.8	62.2	42.6	9.2	7.1
Tulsa, OK	86.6	65.8	32.6	13.4	7.6
Tuscaloosa, AL	92.3	70.5	33.7	7.7	2.5
Virginia Beach, VA	91.6	75.2	30.5	8.4	4.6
Washington, DC	92.4	78.2	25.2	7.6	4.5
Wichita, KS	89.8	71.6	30.3	10.2	5.8
Winston-Salem, NC	89.1	66.0	35.7	10.9	4.9
U.S.	91.2	67.9	35.1	8.8	5.1

Note: Figures are percentages that cover the civilian noninstitutionalized population; Figures cover the Metropolitan Statistical Area (MSA)—see Appendix B for areas included
Source: U.S. Census Bureau, 2015-2019 American Community Survey 5-Year Estimates

Crime Rate: City

City	All Crimes	Violent Crimes				Property Crimes		
		Murder	Rape	Robbery	Aggrav. Assault	Burglary	Larceny -Theft	Motor Vehicle Theft
Albuquerque, NM	n/a	14.9	86.5	302.4	948.0	n/a	3,672.1	965.4
Allentown, PA	2,669.6	5.7	52.5	139.5	188.7	427.6	1,656.1	199.4
Anchorage, AK	5,505.8	11.1	187.7	215.8	829.9	588.0	3,141.1	532.1
Ann Arbor, MI	1,979.8	1.6	62.7	37.4	149.7	160.3	1,455.7	112.3
Athens, GA[2]	3,562.0	4.8	45.6	98.5	266.6	546.8	2,415.5	184.1
Atlanta, GA[1]	5,423.2	17.7	49.4	221.5	480.1	621.2	3,366.4	666.8
Austin, TX	4,111.4	3.2	54.2	98.5	245.0	440.5	2,962.9	307.1
Baton Rouge, LA	6,226.7	31.7	23.6	292.3	588.7	1,023.3	3,904.9	362.1
Boise City, ID	1,859.8	1.7	70.9	19.0	188.9	203.2	1,276.2	99.9
Boston, MA	n/a	6.0	33.1	148.7	419.5	243.7	1,515.1	n/a
Boulder, CO	3,282.4	0.9	37.8	34.1	183.4	373.2	2,421.7	231.3
Cape Coral, FL	1,237.0	2.6	8.2	18.5	87.0	141.1	895.5	83.9
Cedar Rapids, IA	3,593.1	1.5	20.1	61.9	173.9	624.6	2,438.7	272.4
Charleston, SC	2,632.8	5.8	36.9	68.7	261.8	211.2	1,688.9	359.5
Charlotte, NC	4,665.2	10.9	33.6	209.2	485.8	574.6	2,997.5	353.7
Chicago, IL	3,925.8	18.2	65.1	294.9	565.0	353.8	2,293.4	335.5
Cincinnati, OH	5,147.1	21.1	92.3	287.5	443.7	911.5	2,945.6	445.4
Clarksville, TN	3,370.7	8.8	64.4	72.5	433.1	339.4	2,160.7	291.9
Cleveland, OH	5,983.8	24.1	125.4	496.3	870.8	1,129.0	2,610.6	727.6
College Station, TX	1,948.1	0.8	40.3	36.1	111.5	327.9	1,282.2	149.3
Colorado Springs, CO	4,251.7	4.8	89.9	101.1	389.2	500.4	2,521.6	644.6
Columbia, MO	2,914.8	8.8	55.2	59.2	197.6	399.1	1,944.5	250.4
Columbia, SC	6,027.4	21.7	65.8	164.4	523.2	684.7	3,898.6	669.0
Columbus, OH	3,811.3	8.9	97.3	199.8	197.3	641.1	2,274.1	392.8
Dallas, TX	4,184.2	14.5	58.5	322.7	467.2	675.6	1,893.4	752.4
Davenport, IA	4,421.2	2.0	82.0	121.1	389.7	727.6	2,763.9	335.0
Denver, CO	4,492.4	9.2	97.8	165.3	476.6	544.2	2,473.0	726.3
Des Moines, IA	4,802.5	6.4	53.6	129.6	522.5	1,045.9	2,443.4	601.2
Durham, NC	4,537.6	13.2	43.2	223.3	450.3	703.6	2,833.6	270.4
Edison, NJ	1,450.9	1.0	9.0	18.9	54.8	137.6	1,139.8	89.7
El Paso, TX	1,863.7	5.8	45.1	49.2	252.5	152.6	1,234.6	123.9
Fargo, ND	3,572.4	3.9	87.1	61.2	298.2	651.4	2,163.7	306.9
Fayetteville, NC	4,401.4	11.4	55.8	134.1	674.1	651.2	2,691.1	183.7
Fort Collins, CO	2,389.9	0.6	24.0	21.1	171.5	204.8	1,834.5	133.4
Fort Wayne, IN	3,122.5	9.7	53.8	132.5	165.6	367.5	2,182.5	210.9
Fort Worth, TX	3,132.8	7.5	51.4	106.2	279.4	433.7	1,890.3	364.4
Grand Rapids, MI	2,545.1	4.0	71.4	135.8	426.2	294.8	1,364.7	248.3
Greeley, CO	2,680.0	1.8	65.0	61.3	225.2	309.4	1,737.2	280.1
Green Bay, WI	2,145.9	2.9	74.3	46.7	380.0	233.4	1,290.6	118.1
Greensboro, NC	4,507.7	14.4	37.9	208.4	558.0	743.2	2,614.5	331.2
Honolulu, HI	n/a	n/a	n/a	n/a	n/a	n/a	n/a	n/a
Houston, TX	5,391.7	11.7	53.0	388.3	619.2	723.3	3,040.2	556.0
Huntsville, AL[2]	5,635.0	11.3	88.1	184.5	621.0	731.7	3,462.6	535.9
Indianapolis, IN[1]	5,402.0	18.5	77.1	351.1	826.1	893.6	2,671.9	563.7
Jacksonville, FL	3,956.9	14.2	60.9	142.3	430.0	539.6	2,460.9	309.0
Kansas City, MO	5,287.3	30.2	70.0	290.9	1,040.2	619.0	2,470.5	766.4
Lafayette, LA	4,829.0	11.1	12.6	116.8	383.6	814.6	3,236.9	253.4
Lakeland, FL	3,189.7	6.2	56.1	86.4	163.0	390.2	2,306.7	180.9
Las Vegas, NV	3,302.8	5.0	86.3	127.1	312.8	638.7	1,694.3	438.6
Lexington, KY	3,294.7	8.0	53.7	111.0	123.9	471.4	2,248.9	277.9
Lincoln, NE	3,133.7	1.7	110.9	57.0	213.3	339.4	2,255.4	155.9
Little Rock, AR	7,638.8	19.2	105.4	197.1	1,195.2	887.2	4,696.0	538.9
Los Angeles, CA	3,115.5	6.4	56.6	240.4	428.7	343.9	1,649.9	389.5
Louisville, KY	4,578.4	13.9	29.8	149.2	494.0	638.9	2,670.2	582.4

Table continued on following page.

City	All Crimes	Violent Crimes				Property Crimes		
		Murder	Rape	Robbery	Aggrav. Assault	Burglary	Larceny -Theft	Motor Vehicle Theft
Madison, WI	2,833.9	1.5	41.0	83.1	234.2	400.4	1,865.1	208.6
Manchester, NH	2,972.7	5.3	54.9	117.8	422.5	264.8	1,970.9	136.4
Memphis, TN	8,029.9	29.2	72.0	373.9	1,426.3	1,204.3	4,302.1	622.1
Miami, FL	4,260.9	8.9	31.6	160.0	392.5	368.6	2,959.2	340.1
Midland, TX[1]	2,261.0	3.6	42.8	42.1	199.2	269.9	1,504.9	198.5
Milwaukee, WI	3,887.3	16.4	72.3	323.4	920.4	608.2	1,362.8	583.8
Minneapolis, MN	5,442.7	10.7	106.5	299.1	509.5	788.1	3,056.0	672.8
Nashville, TN	5,114.2	12.1	63.7	287.8	709.5	490.9	3,150.5	399.8
New Haven, CT	4,694.5	10.0	34.5	246.0	604.6	505.0	2,743.4	551.0
New Orleans, LA	6,437.3	30.7	196.2	256.8	661.1	543.2	4,001.3	748.0
New York, NY	2,030.3	3.8	33.1	159.9	374.0	117.5	1,276.2	65.9
Oklahoma City, OK	4,813.7	11.4	81.9	135.0	493.9	943.3	2,572.2	576.1
Omaha, NE	4,256.7	4.9	80.6	110.3	417.0	357.9	2,615.8	670.2
Orlando, FL	5,565.2	8.6	69.8	183.5	476.5	501.2	3,889.5	436.1
Peoria, IL	4,792.9	22.5	58.6	241.5	721.0	683.2	2,666.8	399.3
Philadelphia, PA[1]	4,005.6	22.1	69.0	331.6	486.0	409.4	2,329.5	357.9
Phoenix, AZ	4,013.5	7.8	67.4	189.3	434.4	560.8	2,334.7	419.0
Pittsburgh, PA[1]	3,594.8	18.8	40.0	230.0	289.9	443.2	2,331.9	241.0
Portland, OR	5,748.0	4.4	55.6	147.9	336.8	634.3	3,597.6	971.4
Providence, RI	3,507.4	7.2	59.0	134.1	295.9	397.7	2,349.8	263.7
Provo, UT	1,623.0	0.9	37.5	11.1	65.7	139.1	1,259.5	109.2
Raleigh, NC	2,038.8	1.0	34.3	67.4	153.0	251.1	1,375.4	156.5
Reno, NV	2,658.9	4.7	70.0	121.1	362.1	323.2	1,314.3	463.5
Richmond, VA	3,962.4	23.8	19.5	166.9	252.7	427.4	2,702.0	370.1
Riverside, CA	3,443.6	5.1	41.7	142.8	316.3	390.7	2,099.6	447.4
Rochester, MN	2,096.1	0.8	52.4	28.7	132.8	238.4	1,535.5	107.4
Sacramento, CA	3,809.2	6.6	24.7	202.2	393.6	582.4	2,071.1	528.7
Salt Lake City, UT	6,369.7	6.4	115.6	199.1	391.3	637.3	4,397.7	622.4
San Antonio, TX	5,032.7	6.7	104.5	126.0	471.1	524.1	3,301.1	499.0
San Diego, CA	2,244.2	3.5	38.9	93.4	226.0	245.7	1,278.0	358.7
San Francisco, CA	6,175.2	4.5	36.6	344.8	283.7	524.1	4,501.9	479.6
San Jose, CA	2,858.0	3.1	64.5	128.7	242.0	395.6	1,435.0	589.0
Santa Rosa, CA	2,097.4	1.7	82.1	70.8	327.2	273.2	1,167.6	174.8
Savannah, GA[1]	2,865.5	11.6	35.1	110.2	248.5	364.9	1,824.4	270.8
Seattle, WA	5,081.0	3.7	46.9	175.3	359.6	944.1	3,074.2	477.3
Sioux Falls, SD	3,528.6	2.2	62.5	36.6	381.9	374.4	2,316.5	354.5
Springfield, IL	5,218.0	7.9	94.4	181.8	493.0	908.3	3,300.9	231.7
Tallahassee, FL	4,675.5	10.3	101.0	129.2	456.2	608.4	3,022.5	348.0
Tampa, FL	2,033.7	7.7	30.0	71.2	296.1	255.2	1,242.9	130.6
Tucson, AZ	3,960.4	7.3	96.1	201.5	383.5	455.3	2,406.4	410.3
Tulsa, OK	6,298.2	13.7	84.9	178.7	709.5	1,206.4	3,350.0	755.0
Tuscaloosa, AL[1]	4,843.6	4.9	46.2	137.6	316.4	739.9	3,289.0	309.5
Virginia Beach, VA	1,890.0	6.7	17.6	43.6	61.5	118.0	1,513.7	128.9
Washington, DC	5,223.0	23.5	48.5	334.3	570.9	260.7	3,659.5	325.6
Wichita, KS	6,462.8	9.0	94.1	118.2	919.8	686.3	4,044.6	590.9
Winston-Salem, NC	n/a	n/a	n/a	n/a	n/a	n/a	n/a	n/a
U.S.	2,489.3	5.0	42.6	81.6	250.2	340.5	1,549.5	219.9

Note: Figures are crimes per 100,000 population in 2019 except where noted; n/a not available; (1) 2018 data; (2) 2017 data
Source: FBI Uniform Crime Reports, 2017, 2018, 2019

Crime Rate: Suburbs

Suburbs[1]	All Crimes	Violent Crimes				Property Crimes		
		Murder	Rape	Robbery	Aggrav. Assault	Burglary	Larceny -Theft	Motor Vehicle Theft
Albuquerque, NM	n/a	2.5	28.6	23.0	502.8	n/a	995.5	214.2
Allentown, PA	n/a	n/a	n/a	n/a	n/a	n/a	n/a	n/a
Anchorage, AK	5,634.3	10.9	32.6	92.4	277.1	787.8	3,955.4	478.1
Ann Arbor, MI	2,017.9	2.4	69.1	38.7	296.3	218.0	1,258.3	135.0
Athens, GA[3]	1,855.9	1.2	18.1	14.5	111.2	289.0	1,349.3	72.5
Atlanta, GA[2]	2,666.3	4.6	24.0	82.5	168.8	373.2	1,770.4	242.7
Austin, TX	1,564.4	1.9	43.6	23.6	126.5	212.3	1,059.4	97.1
Baton Rouge, LA	3,048.0	7.9	29.9	42.8	339.8	380.5	2,107.7	139.3
Boise City, ID	1,329.9	1.2	52.7	7.5	176.3	201.4	798.8	92.1
Boston, MA	n/a	1.4	30.1	41.9	212.4	126.0	804.5	n/a
Boulder, CO	2,439.7	0.9	83.1	20.9	175.3	269.8	1,686.5	203.0
Cape Coral, FL	1,476.1	3.1	40.1	61.0	201.4	186.4	880.9	103.2
Cedar Rapids, IA	911.9	0.0	21.6	5.0	95.2	183.1	523.4	83.6
Charleston, SC	3,168.8	9.6	42.3	61.1	290.1	419.0	2,025.9	320.8
Charlotte, NC	n/a	n/a	n/a	n/a	n/a	n/a	n/a	n/a
Chicago, IL	n/a	n/a	n/a	n/a	n/a	n/a	n/a	n/a
Cincinnati, OH	1,749.6	1.5	34.0	32.1	73.6	224.7	1,269.6	114.0
Clarksville, TN	1,876.6	4.7	31.4	23.3	124.1	401.6	1,146.8	144.8
Cleveland, OH	1,401.7	1.8	21.7	34.6	90.5	189.4	985.7	77.9
College Station, TX	2,466.8	2.7	79.5	46.6	193.9	419.9	1,565.3	158.9
Colorado Springs, CO	1,634.0	3.7	56.3	25.7	166.4	213.4	951.5	216.8
Columbia, MO	1,774.1	3.5	37.8	13.0	145.2	253.8	1,150.8	170.0
Columbia, SC	3,564.0	5.9	45.8	67.3	428.2	503.6	2,152.4	360.8
Columbus, OH	1,836.3	2.6	36.4	25.9	60.9	251.9	1,366.9	91.7
Dallas, TX	n/a	n/a	n/a	n/a	n/a	n/a	n/a	n/a
Davenport, IA	1,880.3	2.2	46.1	31.4	202.5	306.7	1,169.0	122.5
Denver, CO	n/a	n/a	n/a	n/a	n/a	n/a	n/a	n/a
Des Moines, IA	n/a	n/a	n/a	n/a	n/a	n/a	n/a	n/a
Durham, NC	1,853.6	2.7	22.5	32.4	157.6	332.5	1,221.8	84.0
Edison, NJ	n/a	n/a	n/a	n/a	n/a	n/a	n/a	n/a
El Paso, TX	1,251.9	0.6	37.2	15.8	195.1	156.6	746.2	100.4
Fargo, ND	1,642.9	0.0	34.9	22.4	76.5	277.5	1,087.8	143.8
Fayetteville, NC	n/a	n/a	n/a	n/a	n/a	n/a	n/a	n/a
Fort Collins, CO	1,855.9	1.1	44.9	14.6	189.3	184.4	1,296.7	124.9
Fort Wayne, IN	1,097.2	2.8	35.5	32.1	128.3	146.4	649.7	102.5
Fort Worth, TX	n/a	n/a	n/a	n/a	n/a	n/a	n/a	n/a
Grand Rapids, MI	n/a	1.8	81.2	19.6	146.3	n/a	933.5	85.2
Greeley, CO	1,419.9	1.4	41.0	12.3	90.5	171.1	940.9	162.6
Green Bay, WI	928.9	0.9	26.1	3.2	61.9	81.6	725.8	29.3
Greensboro, NC	2,421.7	6.7	29.9	53.7	258.8	475.5	1,421.1	175.9
Honolulu, HI	n/a	n/a	n/a	n/a	n/a	n/a	n/a	n/a
Houston, TX	n/a	n/a	n/a	n/a	n/a	n/a	n/a	n/a
Huntsville, AL[3]	2,220.1	4.2	32.4	31.2	227.3	432.2	1,337.1	155.6
Indianapolis, IN[2]	1,699.1	2.5	23.1	28.7	114.1	199.2	1,200.7	130.7
Jacksonville, FL	1,592.3	2.2	35.2	25.3	166.6	235.0	1,031.9	96.1
Kansas City, MO	n/a	n/a	n/a	n/a	n/a	n/a	n/a	n/a
Lafayette, LA	2,832.6	6.6	29.8	51.6	358.4	551.2	1,694.4	140.6
Lakeland, FL	1,687.2	2.6	17.0	33.6	217.9	249.4	1,045.5	121.2
Las Vegas, NV	2,501.4	4.6	36.8	114.4	354.9	390.7	1,310.3	289.7
Lexington, KY	2,369.2	0.5	30.9	28.3	60.2	318.5	1,748.7	182.1
Lincoln, NE	1,017.1	0.0	77.9	0.0	41.1	119.0	705.4	73.6
Little Rock, AR	n/a	6.8	60.7	54.6	393.0	n/a	n/a	278.3
Los Angeles, CA	2,574.0	4.1	31.4	148.3	263.3	400.2	1,366.0	360.7
Louisville, KY	1,847.8	1.9	21.7	30.8	98.0	230.7	1,263.0	201.7

Table continued on following page.

Suburbs[1]	All Crimes	Violent Crimes				Property Crimes		
		Murder	Rape	Robbery	Aggrav. Assault	Burglary	Larceny -Theft	Motor Vehicle Theft
Madison, WI	1,351.6	1.0	24.7	18.3	82.4	169.4	971.3	84.6
Manchester, NH	1,000.0	1.6	42.2	12.2	35.9	81.4	789.2	37.5
Memphis, TN	2,498.8	6.8	34.3	50.8	297.1	361.2	1,515.0	233.6
Miami, FL	3,417.0	6.9	35.0	125.5	289.7	268.7	2,428.8	262.4
Midland, TX[2]	2,400.0	11.5	25.9	31.7	368.8	299.6	1,293.6	368.8
Milwaukee, WI	1,671.2	1.4	20.7	24.3	79.0	124.4	1,348.6	72.7
Minneapolis, MN	2,224.5	1.6	36.4	48.6	98.2	238.6	1,611.4	189.7
Nashville, TN	1,872.5	2.8	29.2	26.7	236.4	201.0	1,238.9	137.5
New Haven, CT	1,934.6	2.2	24.3	47.9	77.5	206.4	1,361.4	214.9
New Orleans, LA	2,472.9	9.3	22.9	43.8	209.1	290.9	1,767.8	129.1
New York, NY	n/a	n/a	n/a	n/a	n/a	n/a	n/a	n/a
Oklahoma City, OK	2,410.6	4.4	46.1	32.5	150.0	447.5	1,495.7	234.3
Omaha, NE	1,880.3	2.3	43.8	23.0	147.2	232.1	1,212.2	219.7
Orlando, FL	2,485.9	4.1	42.0	75.9	269.2	341.2	1,573.1	180.5
Peoria, IL	1,462.2	1.7	46.0	15.2	161.7	265.2	890.0	82.4
Philadelphia, PA[2]	1,935.5	7.6	16.3	96.8	235.8	202.8	1,235.3	140.9
Phoenix, AZ	n/a	2.9	40.6	49.3	192.6	n/a	1,530.6	165.3
Pittsburgh, PA[2]	1,402.7	3.5	23.7	33.2	168.7	159.1	958.5	55.9
Portland, OR	2,077.6	1.6	48.3	37.5	128.0	233.0	1,381.8	247.4
Providence, RI	1,466.1	1.7	43.0	37.4	173.7	203.4	912.5	94.2
Provo, UT	1,312.0	1.1	30.2	7.2	46.1	131.5	1,018.1	77.8
Raleigh, NC	1,325.7	2.1	14.8	21.7	90.6	209.5	912.4	74.6
Reno, NV	1,965.3	1.4	55.1	47.4	262.9	331.5	1,041.2	225.8
Richmond, VA	2,045.4	4.9	28.3	37.0	106.2	170.5	1,580.8	117.6
Riverside, CA	2,643.4	5.8	29.0	111.1	273.8	441.1	1,367.7	414.9
Rochester, MN	653.1	1.0	9.7	2.9	67.2	122.6	407.8	41.9
Sacramento, CA	2,195.0	3.4	28.3	73.9	172.0	335.6	1,366.4	215.3
Salt Lake City, UT	3,178.0	2.3	62.6	48.1	186.0	349.3	2,211.9	317.8
San Antonio, TX	1,855.5	2.5	37.7	25.0	148.4	294.5	1,199.2	148.3
San Diego, CA	1,801.2	1.9	28.6	81.2	214.0	218.1	1,020.7	236.8
San Francisco, CA	2,534.2	1.3	42.6	87.1	128.4	294.1	1,778.4	202.3
San Jose, CA	2,582.6	1.5	27.9	54.6	118.4	291.8	1,875.3	213.0
Santa Rosa, CA	1,577.8	1.9	41.0	36.6	283.0	232.0	903.5	79.7
Savannah, GA[2]	3,497.3	5.3	37.2	67.1	245.2	497.1	2,366.1	279.1
Seattle, WA	n/a	n/a	n/a	n/a	n/a	n/a	n/a	n/a
Sioux Falls, SD	1,221.6	1.2	42.1	3.6	128.8	358.7	568.1	119.2
Springfield, IL	1,395.2	1.1	40.2	32.6	269.7	340.4	605.7	105.5
Tallahassee, FL	2,203.5	2.6	40.1	31.7	278.9	510.7	1,198.9	140.5
Tampa, FL	1,969.7	3.4	37.9	46.7	187.8	210.4	1,356.1	127.3
Tucson, AZ	2,634.2	3.2	25.3	38.5	115.5	349.9	1,905.9	195.9
Tulsa, OK	2,046.1	4.5	38.9	18.4	159.8	420.8	1,190.3	213.3
Tuscaloosa, AL[2]	2,503.0	3.3	28.5	41.7	249.6	518.3	1,449.1	212.5
Virginia Beach, VA	3,057.1	8.5	39.5	83.1	293.8	282.1	2,149.5	200.6
Washington, DC	n/a	n/a	26.7	61.2	96.5	98.4	1,055.9	126.4
Wichita, KS	n/a	1.6	42.3	14.5	156.8	271.8	n/a	129.8
Winston-Salem, NC	n/a	n/a	n/a	n/a	n/a	n/a	n/a	n/a
U.S.	2,489.3	5.0	42.6	81.6	250.2	340.5	1,549.5	219.9

Note: Figures are crimes per 100,000 population in 2019 except where noted; n/a not available; (1) All areas within the metro area that are located outside the city limits; (2) 2018 data; (3) 2017 data
Source: FBI Uniform Crime Reports, 2017, 2018, 2019

Crime Rate: Metro Area

Metro Area[1]	All Crimes	Violent Crimes				Property Crimes		
		Murder	Rape	Robbery	Aggrav. Assault	Burglary	Larceny -Theft	Motor Vehicle Theft
Albuquerque, NM	n/a	10.1	64.0	194.0	775.3	n/a	2,633.7	674.0
Allentown, PA	n/a	n/a	n/a	n/a	n/a	n/a	n/a	n/a
Anchorage, AK	5,513.6	11.1	178.4	208.4	796.7	600.1	3,190.1	528.8
Ann Arbor, MI	2,005.3	2.1	67.0	38.3	248.1	199.0	1,323.3	127.5
Athens, GA[4]	2,882.3	3.4	34.7	65.0	204.7	444.1	1,990.8	139.7
Atlanta, GA[3]	2,895.7	5.7	26.1	94.1	194.7	393.9	1,903.2	278.0
Austin, TX	2,697.1	2.5	48.3	56.9	179.2	313.8	1,905.9	190.5
Baton Rouge, LA	3,871.0	14.1	28.3	107.4	404.3	547.0	2,573.0	197.0
Boise City, ID	1,493.5	1.3	58.3	11.1	180.2	201.9	946.2	94.5
Boston, MA[2]	n/a	3.0	31.1	78.6	283.6	166.5	1,048.9	n/a
Boulder, CO	2,717.9	0.9	68.2	25.3	178.0	303.9	1,929.3	212.4
Cape Coral, FL	1,415.7	3.0	32.0	50.3	172.4	174.9	884.6	98.3
Cedar Rapids, IA	2,229.3	0.7	20.9	33.0	133.8	400.0	1,464.5	176.4
Charleston, SC	3,076.7	8.9	41.4	62.4	285.2	383.3	1,968.0	327.5
Charlotte, NC	n/a	n/a	n/a	n/a	n/a	n/a	n/a	n/a
Chicago, IL[2]	n/a	n/a	n/a	n/a	n/a	n/a	n/a	n/a
Cincinnati, OH	2,214.3	4.1	42.0	67.0	124.2	318.7	1,498.9	159.4
Clarksville, TN	2,648.0	6.8	48.4	48.7	283.6	369.5	1,670.2	220.7
Cleveland, OH	2,254.7	5.9	41.0	120.5	235.8	364.4	1,288.2	198.9
College Station, TX	2,233.6	1.9	61.8	41.9	156.8	378.5	1,438.0	154.6
Colorado Springs, CO	3,313.4	4.4	77.8	74.1	309.4	397.5	1,958.8	491.3
Columbia, MO	2,454.0	6.7	48.2	40.5	176.4	340.4	1,623.9	217.9
Columbia, SC	3,955.7	8.4	49.0	82.7	443.3	532.4	2,430.1	409.8
Columbus, OH	2,676.7	5.3	62.3	99.9	119.0	417.5	1,752.9	219.8
Dallas, TX[2]	n/a	n/a	n/a	n/a	n/a	n/a	n/a	n/a
Davenport, IA	2,565.2	2.1	55.8	55.5	253.0	420.1	1,598.8	179.8
Denver, CO	n/a	n/a	n/a	n/a	n/a	n/a	n/a	n/a
Des Moines, IA	n/a	n/a	n/a	n/a	n/a	n/a	n/a	n/a
Durham, NC	3,020.8	7.3	31.5	115.4	284.9	493.9	1,922.7	165.1
Edison, NJ[2]	n/a	n/a	n/a	n/a	n/a	n/a	n/a	n/a
El Paso, TX	1,749.1	4.9	43.7	42.9	241.7	153.3	1,143.1	119.5
Fargo, ND	2,635.2	2.0	61.8	42.4	190.5	469.8	1,641.1	227.6
Fayetteville, NC	n/a	n/a	n/a	n/a	n/a	n/a	n/a	n/a
Fort Collins, CO	2,112.3	0.8	34.8	17.7	180.7	194.2	1,555.0	129.0
Fort Wayne, IN	2,418.7	7.3	47.5	97.6	152.6	290.7	1,649.8	173.2
Fort Worth, TX[2]	n/a	n/a	n/a	n/a	n/a	n/a	n/a	n/a
Grand Rapids, MI	n/a	2.2	79.4	41.3	198.6	n/a	1,014.1	115.7
Greeley, CO	1,848.3	1.6	49.2	28.9	136.3	218.1	1,211.6	202.6
Green Bay, WI	1,324.3	1.5	41.8	17.3	165.3	130.9	909.3	58.2
Greensboro, NC	3,226.1	9.7	33.0	113.3	374.2	578.8	1,881.3	235.7
Honolulu, HI	n/a	n/a	n/a	n/a	n/a	n/a	n/a	n/a
Houston, TX	n/a	n/a	n/a	n/a	n/a	n/a	n/a	n/a
Huntsville, AL[4]	3,685.7	7.3	56.3	97.0	396.3	560.7	2,249.3	318.9
Indianapolis, IN[3]	3,285.3	9.3	46.3	166.8	419.1	496.7	1,830.9	316.2
Jacksonville, FL	2,980.1	9.2	50.3	94.0	321.2	413.8	1,870.6	221.0
Kansas City, MO	n/a	n/a	n/a	n/a	n/a	n/a	n/a	n/a
Lafayette, LA	3,349.4	7.8	25.3	68.5	365.0	619.4	2,093.7	169.8
Lakeland, FL	1,922.4	3.2	23.1	41.8	209.3	271.5	1,242.9	130.5
Las Vegas, NV	3,089.8	4.9	73.2	123.7	324.0	572.8	1,592.2	399.1
Lexington, KY	2,949.0	5.2	45.2	80.1	100.1	414.3	2,062.1	242.1
Lincoln, NE	2,843.7	1.5	106.4	49.2	189.7	309.2	2,043.0	144.7
Little Rock, AR	n/a	10.1	72.6	92.6	607.0	n/a	n/a	347.8
Los Angeles, CA[2]	2,790.2	5.1	41.5	185.0	329.4	377.7	1,479.4	372.2
Louisville, KY	3,300.8	8.3	26.0	93.8	308.7	447.9	2,011.8	404.3

Table continued on following page.

Metro Area[1]	All Crimes	Violent Crimes				Property Crimes		
		Murder	Rape	Robbery	Aggrav. Assault	Burglary	Larceny -Theft	Motor Vehicle Theft
Madison, WI	1,932.4	1.2	31.0	43.6	141.9	259.9	1,321.5	133.2
Manchester, NH	1,534.7	2.6	45.6	40.8	140.7	131.1	1,109.5	64.3
Memphis, TN	5,173.9	17.6	52.5	207.1	843.3	769.0	2,863.0	421.5
Miami, FL[2]	3,563.1	7.3	34.4	131.5	307.5	286.0	2,520.6	275.9
Midland, TX[3]	2,288.6	5.1	39.5	40.1	232.9	275.8	1,463.0	232.3
Milwaukee, WI	2,501.8	7.0	40.0	136.4	394.4	305.7	1,353.9	264.3
Minneapolis, MN	2,605.3	2.7	44.7	78.3	146.9	303.6	1,782.3	246.9
Nashville, TN	3,020.0	6.1	41.4	119.1	403.9	303.6	1,915.5	230.4
New Haven, CT	2,383.4	3.5	25.9	80.1	163.2	255.0	1,586.2	269.5
New Orleans, LA	3,701.4	15.9	76.6	109.8	349.1	369.1	2,459.9	320.9
New York, NY[2]	n/a	n/a	n/a	n/a	n/a	n/a	n/a	n/a
Oklahoma City, OK	3,530.9	7.7	62.8	80.3	310.3	678.7	1,997.6	393.6
Omaha, NE	3,059.7	3.6	62.0	66.4	281.1	294.5	1,908.8	443.3
Orlando, FL	2,829.9	4.6	45.1	87.9	292.4	359.1	1,831.9	209.0
Peoria, IL	2,386.5	7.5	49.5	78.0	316.9	381.2	1,383.1	170.3
Philadelphia, PA[2,3]	3,462.1	18.3	55.2	270.0	420.3	355.2	2,042.3	300.9
Phoenix, AZ	n/a	4.6	49.8	97.1	275.1	n/a	1,804.9	251.9
Pittsburgh, PA[3]	1,687.7	5.5	25.8	58.8	184.5	196.1	1,137.0	80.0
Portland, OR	3,049.5	2.4	50.2	66.7	183.3	339.3	1,968.5	439.1
Providence, RI	1,692.5	2.3	44.8	48.1	187.3	225.0	1,071.9	113.0
Provo, UT	1,368.4	1.1	31.6	7.9	49.6	132.9	1,061.8	83.5
Raleigh, NC	1,570.3	1.7	21.5	37.4	112.0	223.8	1,071.2	102.7
Reno, NV	2,336.2	3.2	63.1	86.8	315.9	327.1	1,187.2	352.9
Richmond, VA	2,388.9	8.3	26.7	60.3	132.4	216.6	1,781.7	162.9
Riverside, CA	2,700.9	5.7	29.9	113.4	276.9	437.5	1,420.4	417.2
Rochester, MN	1,425.3	0.9	32.6	16.7	102.3	184.6	1,011.3	76.9
Sacramento, CA	2,548.0	4.1	27.5	102.0	220.5	389.6	1,520.5	283.8
Salt Lake City, UT	3,700.3	3.0	71.3	72.8	219.5	396.4	2,569.6	367.6
San Antonio, TX	3,796.6	5.1	78.5	86.7	345.6	434.8	2,483.3	362.6
San Diego, CA	1,992.1	2.6	33.1	86.4	219.1	230.0	1,131.6	289.3
San Francisco, CA[2]	4,482.9	3.0	39.4	225.0	211.5	417.2	3,236.0	350.7
San Jose, CA	2,725.6	2.3	46.9	93.1	182.6	345.7	1,646.7	408.3
Santa Rosa, CA	1,763.5	1.8	55.7	48.8	298.8	246.8	997.9	113.7
Savannah, GA[3]	3,107.5	9.2	35.9	93.7	247.2	415.6	2,032.0	274.0
Seattle, WA[2]	n/a	n/a	n/a	n/a	n/a	n/a	n/a	n/a
Sioux Falls, SD	2,815.3	1.9	56.2	26.4	303.7	369.5	1,775.9	281.7
Springfield, IL	3,514.4	4.8	70.3	115.3	393.5	655.2	2,099.8	175.4
Tallahassee, FL	3,458.0	6.5	71.0	81.2	368.9	560.3	2,124.4	245.8
Tampa, FL	1,977.8	4.0	36.9	49.8	201.5	216.1	1,341.8	127.7
Tucson, AZ	3,328.8	5.3	62.4	123.9	255.9	405.1	2,168.0	308.2
Tulsa, OK	3,757.4	8.2	57.4	83.0	381.0	737.0	2,059.5	431.3
Tuscaloosa, AL[3]	3,445.1	4.0	35.6	80.3	276.5	607.5	2,189.7	251.6
Virginia Beach, VA	2,759.6	8.0	33.9	73.0	234.6	240.3	1,987.4	182.3
Washington, DC[2]	n/a	n/a	29.8	99.9	163.6	121.4	1,424.4	154.6
Wichita, KS	n/a	6.1	74.0	77.9	623.3	525.2	n/a	411.7
Winston-Salem, NC[3]	n/a	n/a	n/a	n/a	n/a	n/a	n/a	n/a
U.S.	2,489.3	5.0	42.6	81.6	250.2	340.5	1,549.5	219.9

Note: Figures are crimes per 100,000 population in 2019 except where noted; n/a not available; (1) Figures cover the Metropolitan Statistical Area except where noted; (2) Metropolitan Division (MD); (3) 2018 data; (4) 2017 data
Source: FBI Uniform Crime Reports, 2017, 2018, 2019

Temperature & Precipitation: Yearly Averages and Extremes

City	Extreme Low (°F)	Average Low (°F)	Average Temp. (°F)	Average High (°F)	Extreme High (°F)	Average Precip. (in.)	Average Snow (in.)
Albuquerque, NM	-17	43	57	70	105	8.5	11
Allentown, PA	-12	42	52	61	105	44.2	32
Anchorage, AK	-34	29	36	43	85	15.7	71
Ann Arbor, MI	-21	39	49	58	104	32.4	41
Athens, GA	-8	52	62	72	105	49.8	2
Atlanta, GA	-8	52	62	72	105	49.8	2
Austin, TX	-2	58	69	79	109	31.1	1
Baton Rouge, LA	8	57	68	78	103	58.5	Trace
Boise City, ID	-25	39	51	63	111	11.8	22
Boston, MA	-12	44	52	59	102	42.9	41
Boulder, CO	-25	37	51	64	103	15.5	63
Cape Coral, FL	26	65	75	84	103	53.9	0
Cedar Rapids, IA	-34	36	47	57	105	34.4	33
Charleston, SC	6	55	66	76	104	52.1	1
Charlotte, NC	-5	50	61	71	104	42.8	6
Chicago, IL	-27	40	49	59	104	35.4	39
Cincinnati, OH	-25	44	54	64	103	40.9	23
Clarksville, TN	-17	49	60	70	107	47.4	11
Cleveland, OH	-19	41	50	59	104	37.1	55
College Station, TX	-2	58	69	79	109	31.1	1
Colorado Springs, CO	-24	36	49	62	99	17.0	48
Columbia, MO	-20	44	54	64	111	40.6	25
Columbia, SC	-1	51	64	75	107	48.3	2
Columbus, OH	-19	42	52	62	104	37.9	28
Dallas, TX	-2	56	67	77	112	33.9	3
Davenport, IA	-24	40	50	60	108	31.8	33
Denver, CO	-25	37	51	64	103	15.5	63
Des Moines, IA	-24	40	50	60	108	31.8	33
Durham, NC	-9	48	60	71	105	42.0	8
Edison, NJ	-8	46	55	63	105	43.5	27
El Paso, TX	-8	50	64	78	114	8.6	6
Fargo, ND	-36	31	41	52	106	19.6	40
Fayetteville, NC	-9	48	60	71	105	42.0	8
Fort Collins, CO	-25	37	51	64	103	15.5	63
Fort Wayne, IN	-22	40	50	60	106	35.9	33
Fort Worth, TX	-1	55	66	76	113	32.3	3
Grand Rapids, MI	-22	38	48	57	102	34.7	73
Greeley, CO	-25	37	51	64	103	15.5	63
Green Bay, WI	-31	34	44	54	99	28.3	46
Greensboro, NC	-8	47	58	69	103	42.5	10
Honolulu, HI	52	70	77	84	94	22.4	0
Houston, TX	7	58	69	79	107	46.9	Trace
Huntsville, AL	-11	50	61	71	104	56.8	4
Indianapolis, IN	-23	42	53	62	104	40.2	25
Jacksonville, FL	7	58	69	79	103	52.0	0
Kansas City, MO	-23	44	54	64	109	38.1	21
Lafayette, LA	8	57	68	78	103	58.5	Trace
Lakeland, FL	18	63	73	82	99	46.7	Trace
Las Vegas, NV	8	53	67	80	116	4.0	1
Lexington, KY	-21	45	55	65	103	45.1	17
Lincoln, NE	-33	39	51	62	108	29.1	27
Little Rock, AR	-5	51	62	73	112	50.7	5
Los Angeles, CA	27	55	63	70	110	11.3	Trace
Louisville, KY	-20	46	57	67	105	43.9	17
Madison, WI	-37	35	46	57	104	31.1	42

Table continued on following page.

City	Extreme Low (°F)	Average Low (°F)	Average Temp. (°F)	Average High (°F)	Extreme High (°F)	Average Precip. (in.)	Average Snow (in.)
Manchester, NH	-33	34	46	57	102	36.9	63
Memphis, TN	0	52	65	77	107	54.8	1
Miami, FL	30	69	76	83	98	57.1	0
Midland, TX	-11	50	64	77	116	14.6	4
Milwaukee, WI	-26	38	47	55	103	32.0	49
Minneapolis, MN	-34	35	45	54	105	27.1	52
Nashville, TN	-17	49	60	70	107	47.4	11
New Haven, CT	-7	44	52	60	103	41.4	25
New Orleans, LA	11	59	69	78	102	60.6	Trace
New York, NY	-2	47	55	62	104	47.0	23
Oklahoma City, OK	-8	49	60	71	110	32.8	10
Omaha, NE	-23	40	51	62	110	30.1	29
Orlando, FL	19	62	72	82	100	47.7	Trace
Peoria, IL	-26	41	51	61	113	35.4	23
Philadelphia, PA	-7	45	55	64	104	41.4	22
Phoenix, AZ	17	59	72	86	122	7.3	Trace
Pittsburgh, PA	-18	41	51	60	103	37.1	43
Portland, OR	-3	45	54	62	107	37.5	7
Providence, RI	-13	42	51	60	104	45.3	35
Provo, UT	-22	40	52	64	107	15.6	63
Raleigh, NC	-9	48	60	71	105	42.0	8
Reno, NV	-16	33	50	67	105	7.2	24
Richmond, VA	-8	48	58	69	105	43.0	13
Riverside, CA	24	53	66	78	114	n/a	n/a
Rochester, MN	-40	34	44	54	102	29.4	47
Sacramento, CA	18	48	61	73	115	17.3	Trace
Salt Lake City, UT	-22	40	52	64	107	15.6	63
San Antonio, TX	0	58	69	80	108	29.6	1
San Diego, CA	29	57	64	71	111	9.5	Trace
San Francisco, CA	24	49	57	65	106	19.3	Trace
San Jose, CA	21	50	59	68	105	13.5	Trace
Santa Rosa, CA	23	42	57	71	109	29.0	n/a
Savannah, GA	3	56	67	77	105	50.3	Trace
Seattle, WA	0	44	52	59	99	38.4	13
Sioux Falls, SD	-36	35	46	57	110	24.6	38
Springfield, IL	-24	44	54	63	112	34.9	21
Tallahassee, FL	6	56	68	79	103	63.3	Trace
Tampa, FL	18	63	73	82	99	46.7	Trace
Tucson, AZ	16	55	69	82	117	11.6	2
Tulsa, OK	-8	50	61	71	112	38.9	10
Tuscaloosa, AL	-6	51	63	74	106	53.5	2
Virginia Beach, VA	-3	51	60	69	104	44.8	8
Washington, DC	-5	49	58	67	104	39.5	18
Wichita, KS	-21	45	57	68	113	29.3	17
Winston-Salem, NC	-8	47	58	69	103	42.5	10

Source: National Climatic Data Center, International Station Meteorological Climate Summary, 9/96

Weather Conditions

City	Temperature			Daytime Sky			Precipitation		
	10°F & below	32°F & below	90°F & above	Clear	Partly cloudy	Cloudy	0.01 inch or more precip.	1.0 inch or more snow/ice	Thunder-storms
Albuquerque, NM	4	114	65	140	161	64	60	9	38
Allentown, PA	n/a	123	15	77	148	140	123	20	31
Anchorage, AK	n/a	194	n/a	50	115	200	113	49	2
Ann Arbor, MI	n/a	136	12	74	134	157	135	38	32
Athens, GA	1	49	38	98	147	120	116	3	48
Atlanta, GA	1	49	38	98	147	120	116	3	48
Austin, TX	< 1	20	111	105	148	112	83	1	41
Baton Rouge, LA	< 1	21	86	99	150	116	113	< 1	73
Boise City, ID	n/a	124	45	106	133	126	91	22	14
Boston, MA	n/a	97	12	88	127	150	253	48	18
Boulder, CO	24	155	33	99	177	89	90	38	39
Cape Coral, FL	n/a	n/a	115	93	220	52	110	0	92
Cedar Rapids, IA	n/a	156	16	89	132	144	109	28	42
Charleston, SC	< 1	33	53	89	162	114	114	1	59
Charlotte, NC	1	65	44	98	142	125	113	3	41
Chicago, IL	n/a	132	17	83	136	146	125	31	38
Cincinnati, OH	14	107	23	80	126	159	127	25	39
Clarksville, TN	5	76	51	98	135	132	119	8	54
Cleveland, OH	n/a	123	12	63	127	175	157	48	34
College Station, TX	< 1	20	111	105	148	112	83	1	41
Colorado Springs, CO	21	161	18	108	157	100	98	33	49
Columbia, MO	17	108	36	99	127	139	110	17	52
Columbia, SC	< 1	58	77	97	149	119	110	1	53
Columbus, OH	n/a	118	19	72	137	156	136	29	40
Dallas, TX	1	34	102	108	160	97	78	2	49
Davenport, IA	n/a	137	26	99	129	137	106	25	46
Denver, CO	24	155	33	99	177	89	90	38	39
Des Moines, IA	n/a	137	26	99	129	137	106	25	46
Durham, NC	n/a	n/a	39	98	143	124	110	3	42
Edison, NJ	n/a	90	24	80	146	139	122	16	46
El Paso, TX	1	59	106	147	164	54	49	3	35
Fargo, ND	n/a	180	15	81	145	139	100	38	31
Fayetteville, NC	n/a	n/a	39	98	143	124	110	3	42
Fort Collins, CO	24	155	33	99	177	89	90	38	39
Fort Wayne, IN	n/a	131	16	75	140	150	131	31	39
Fort Worth, TX	1	40	100	123	136	106	79	3	47
Grand Rapids, MI	n/a	146	11	67	119	179	142	57	34
Greeley, CO	24	155	33	99	177	89	90	38	39
Green Bay, WI	n/a	163	7	86	125	154	120	40	33
Greensboro, NC	3	85	32	94	143	128	113	5	43
Honolulu, HI	n/a	n/a	23	25	286	54	98	0	7
Houston, TX	n/a	n/a	96	83	168	114	101	1	62
Huntsville, AL	2	66	49	70	118	177	116	2	54
Indianapolis, IN	19	119	19	83	128	154	127	24	43
Jacksonville, FL	< 1	16	83	86	181	98	114	1	65
Kansas City, MO	22	110	39	112	134	119	103	17	51
Lafayette, LA	< 1	21	86	99	150	116	113	< 1	73
Lakeland, FL	n/a	n/a	85	81	204	80	107	< 1	87
Las Vegas, NV	< 1	37	134	185	132	48	27	2	13
Lexington, KY	11	96	22	86	136	143	129	17	44
Lincoln, NE	n/a	145	40	108	135	122	94	19	46
Little Rock, AR	1	57	73	110	142	113	104	4	57
Los Angeles, CA	0	< 1	5	131	125	109	34	0	1
Louisville, KY	8	90	35	82	143	140	125	15	45

Table continued on following page.

City	Temperature			Daytime Sky			Precipitation		
	10°F & below	32°F & below	90°F & above	Clear	Partly cloudy	Cloudy	0.01 inch or more precip.	1.0 inch or more snow/ice	Thunder-storms
Madison, WI	n/a	161	14	88	119	158	118	38	40
Manchester, NH	n/a	171	12	87	131	147	125	32	19
Memphis, TN	1	53	86	101	152	112	104	2	59
Miami, FL	n/a	n/a	55	48	263	54	128	0	74
Midland, TX	1	62	102	144	138	83	52	3	38
Milwaukee, WI	n/a	141	10	90	118	157	126	38	35
Minneapolis, MN	n/a	156	16	93	125	147	113	41	37
Nashville, TN	5	76	51	98	135	132	119	8	54
New Haven, CT	n/a	n/a	7	80	146	139	118	17	22
New Orleans, LA	0	13	70	90	169	106	114	1	69
New York, NY	n/a	n/a	18	85	166	114	120	11	20
Oklahoma City, OK	5	79	70	124	131	110	80	8	50
Omaha, NE	n/a	139	35	100	142	123	97	20	46
Orlando, FL	n/a	n/a	90	76	208	81	115	0	80
Peoria, IL	n/a	127	27	89	127	149	115	22	49
Philadelphia, PA	5	94	23	81	146	138	117	14	27
Phoenix, AZ	0	10	167	186	125	54	37	< 1	23
Pittsburgh, PA	n/a	121	8	62	137	166	154	42	35
Portland, OR	n/a	37	11	67	116	182	152	4	7
Providence, RI	n/a	117	9	85	134	146	123	21	21
Provo, UT	n/a	128	56	94	152	119	92	38	38
Raleigh, NC	n/a	n/a	39	98	143	124	110	3	42
Reno, NV	14	178	50	143	139	83	50	17	14
Richmond, VA	3	79	41	90	147	128	115	7	43
Riverside, CA	0	4	82	124	178	63	n/a	n/a	5
Rochester, MN	n/a	165	9	87	126	152	114	40	41
Sacramento, CA	0	21	73	175	111	79	58	< 1	2
Salt Lake City, UT	n/a	128	56	94	152	119	92	38	38
San Antonio, TX	n/a	n/a	112	97	153	115	81	1	36
San Diego, CA	0	< 1	4	115	126	124	40	0	5
San Francisco, CA	0	6	4	136	130	99	63	< 1	5
San Jose, CA	0	5	5	106	180	79	57	< 1	6
Santa Rosa, CA	n/a	43	30	n/a	365	n/a	n/a	n/a	2
Savannah, GA	< 1	29	70	97	155	113	111	< 1	63
Seattle, WA	n/a	38	3	57	121	187	157	8	8
Sioux Falls, SD	n/a	n/a	n/a	95	136	134	n/a	n/a	n/a
Springfield, IL	19	111	34	96	126	143	111	18	49
Tallahassee, FL	< 1	31	86	93	175	97	114	1	83
Tampa, FL	n/a	n/a	85	81	204	80	107	< 1	87
Tucson, AZ	0	18	140	177	119	69	54	2	42
Tulsa, OK	6	78	74	117	141	107	88	8	50
Tuscaloosa, AL	1	57	59	91	161	113	119	1	57
Virginia Beach, VA	< 1	53	33	89	149	127	115	5	38
Washington, DC	2	71	34	84	144	137	112	9	30
Wichita, KS	13	110	63	117	132	116	87	13	54
Winston-Salem, NC	3	85	32	94	143	128	113	5	43

Note: Figures are average number of days per year
Source: National Climatic Data Center, International Station Meteorological Climate Summary, 9/96

Air Quality Index

MSA[1] (Days[2])	Percent of Days when Air Quality was...					AQI Statistics	
	Good	Moderate	Unhealthy for Sensitive Groups	Unhealthy	Very Unhealthy	Maximum	Median
Albuquerque, NM (365)	44.1	54.8	1.1	0.0	0.0	108	53
Allentown, PA (365)	75.3	23.6	1.1	0.0	0.0	119	42
Anchorage, AK (365)	71.8	24.9	2.2	1.1	0.0	160	31
Ann Arbor, MI (365)	80.5	19.5	0.0	0.0	0.0	88	39
Athens, GA (365)	67.1	32.9	0.0	0.0	0.0	87	44
Atlanta, GA (365)	44.4	50.4	4.9	0.3	0.0	172	52
Austin, TX (365)	68.2	31.2	0.5	0.0	0.0	115	44
Baton Rouge, LA (365)	61.4	36.2	2.5	0.0	0.0	119	45
Boise City, ID (365)	67.9	31.2	0.5	0.3	0.0	165	44
Boston, MA (365)	79.7	20.0	0.3	0.0	0.0	122	43
Boulder, CO (365)	62.2	36.4	1.4	0.0	0.0	119	47
Cape Coral, FL (365)	89.9	9.9	0.3	0.0	0.0	108	36
Cedar Rapids, IA (365)	78.6	21.4	0.0	0.0	0.0	84	39
Charleston, SC (357)	84.3	15.4	0.3	0.0	0.0	140	38
Charlotte, NC (365)	54.8	40.3	4.9	0.0	0.0	136	49
Chicago, IL (365)	33.2	62.2	4.4	0.3	0.0	174	55
Cincinnati, OH (365)	38.1	56.4	5.5	0.0	0.0	147	54
Clarksville, TN (365)	84.1	15.9	0.0	0.0	0.0	87	40
Cleveland, OH (365)	50.7	47.4	1.9	0.0	0.0	119	50
College Station, TX (352)	100.0	0.0	0.0	0.0	0.0	17	0
Colorado Springs, CO (365)	71.0	29.0	0.0	0.0	0.0	100	45
Columbia, MO (245)	97.6	2.4	0.0	0.0	0.0	71	38
Columbia, SC (365)	72.3	27.1	0.5	0.0	0.0	136	43
Columbus, OH (365)	64.9	34.8	0.3	0.0	0.0	101	46
Dallas, TX (365)	49.6	42.5	7.7	0.3	0.0	156	51
Davenport, IA (365)	59.5	39.7	0.8	0.0	0.0	115	46
Denver, CO (365)	24.9	69.0	5.5	0.5	0.0	154	58
Des Moines, IA (365)	83.8	16.2	0.0	0.0	0.0	100	39
Durham, NC (365)	75.3	24.7	0.0	0.0	0.0	92	44
Edison, NJ (365)	46.3	49.3	4.4	0.0	0.0	150	51
El Paso, TX (365)	40.3	56.2	3.0	0.5	0.0	157	53
Fargo, ND (363)	90.1	9.4	0.3	0.3	0.0	156	33
Fayetteville, NC (363)	77.7	22.3	0.0	0.0	0.0	84	41
Fort Collins, CO (365)	57.0	41.4	1.6	0.0	0.0	129	48
Fort Wayne, IN (365)	64.7	35.1	0.3	0.0	0.0	101	45
Fort Worth, TX (365)	49.6	42.5	7.7	0.3	0.0	156	51
Grand Rapids, MI (365)	81.6	18.4	0.0	0.0	0.0	100	38
Greeley, CO (365)	69.0	30.1	0.8	0.0	0.0	125	45
Green Bay, WI (365)	85.2	14.8	0.0	0.0	0.0	97	36
Greensboro, NC (365)	79.7	20.3	0.0	0.0	0.0	90	43
Honolulu, HI (365)	92.9	7.1	0.0	0.0	0.0	94	29
Houston, TX (365)	46.8	44.7	7.1	1.1	0.3	202	52
Huntsville, AL (361)	70.6	29.4	0.0	0.0	0.0	93	44
Indianapolis, IN (365)	40.5	58.1	1.4	0.0	0.0	119	54
Jacksonville, FL (365)	67.1	32.6	0.3	0.0	0.0	114	43
Kansas City, MO (365)	57.5	42.2	0.3	0.0	0.0	137	47
Lafayette, LA (365)	76.7	23.3	0.0	0.0	0.0	84	41
Lakeland, FL (365)	86.0	14.0	0.0	0.0	0.0	100	36
Las Vegas, NV (365)	42.2	56.4	1.4	0.0	0.0	122	54
Lexington, KY (365)	83.0	17.0	0.0	0.0	0.0	80	42
Lincoln, NE (360)	93.9	6.1	0.0	0.0	0.0	66	31
Little Rock, AR (365)	64.4	35.6	0.0	0.0	0.0	79	45
Los Angeles, CA (365)	18.1	57.0	17.0	7.7	0.3	201	72
Louisville, KY (365)	53.4	45.5	1.1	0.0	0.0	136	49

Table continued on following page.

MSA[1] (Days[2])	Percent of Days when Air Quality was...					AQI Statistics	
	Good	Moderate	Unhealthy for Sensitive Groups	Unhealthy	Very Unhealthy	Maximum	Median
Madison, WI (365)	78.1	21.9	0.0	0.0	0.0	93	39
Manchester, NH (365)	96.7	3.3	0.0	0.0	0.0	80	37
Memphis, TN (365)	60.5	38.1	1.4	0.0	0.0	148	45
Miami, FL (364)	78.3	21.2	0.5	0.0	0.0	146	41
Midland, TX (n/a)	n/a	n/a	n/a	n/a	n/a	n/a	n/a
Milwaukee, WI (365)	69.6	29.6	0.8	0.0	0.0	115	44
Minneapolis, MN (365)	58.6	40.5	0.5	0.3	0.0	200	46
Nashville, TN (365)	62.7	37.0	0.3	0.0	0.0	101	45
New Haven, CT (365)	76.7	19.5	3.3	0.5	0.0	159	41
New Orleans, LA (365)	62.7	36.7	0.5	0.0	0.0	112	45
New York, NY (365)	46.3	49.3	4.4	0.0	0.0	150	51
Oklahoma City, OK (365)	55.9	43.6	0.5	0.0	0.0	119	48
Omaha, NE (365)	77.5	22.5	0.0	0.0	0.0	97	40
Orlando, FL (365)	81.1	17.3	1.6	0.0	0.0	122	39
Peoria, IL (365)	78.1	21.4	0.5	0.0	0.0	101	41
Philadelphia, PA (365)	49.3	46.3	4.4	0.0	0.0	150	51
Phoenix, AZ (365)	13.7	71.5	11.5	0.5	0.8	886	74
Pittsburgh, PA (365)	35.3	60.3	3.3	1.1	0.0	161	56
Portland, OR (365)	78.1	21.1	0.8	0.0	0.0	128	38
Providence, RI (365)	79.2	20.3	0.5	0.0	0.0	126	44
Provo, UT (365)	69.3	30.4	0.3	0.0	0.0	107	46
Raleigh, NC (365)	65.5	34.5	0.0	0.0	0.0	93	46
Reno, NV (365)	66.8	33.2	0.0	0.0	0.0	97	46
Richmond, VA (365)	74.5	25.5	0.0	0.0	0.0	100	44
Riverside, CA (365)	11.5	48.8	21.6	15.9	2.2	213	89
Rochester, MN (364)	86.0	14.0	0.0	0.0	0.0	84	36
Sacramento, CA (365)	47.1	47.1	5.8	0.0	0.0	140	52
Salt Lake City, UT (365)	46.3	49.0	4.7	0.0	0.0	136	51
San Antonio, TX (365)	53.7	44.7	1.4	0.3	0.0	169	49
San Diego, CA (365)	23.8	69.3	6.3	0.5	0.0	169	64
San Francisco, CA (365)	69.6	27.9	2.5	0.0	0.0	150	43
San Jose, CA (365)	72.1	26.8	1.1	0.0	0.0	136	43
Santa Rosa, CA (365)	95.3	4.7	0.0	0.0	0.0	87	33
Savannah, GA (365)	80.8	19.2	0.0	0.0	0.0	87	39
Seattle, WA (365)	64.7	34.8	0.5	0.0	0.0	142	45
Sioux Falls, SD (365)	87.9	11.8	0.3	0.0	0.0	105	36
Springfield, IL (360)	79.7	20.3	0.0	0.0	0.0	87	40
Tallahassee, FL (365)	74.5	25.2	0.3	0.0	0.0	119	40
Tampa, FL (365)	73.2	25.2	1.6	0.0	0.0	132	43
Tucson, AZ (365)	61.6	37.8	0.5	0.0	0.0	103	47
Tulsa, OK (365)	68.2	31.2	0.5	0.0	0.0	105	45
Tuscaloosa, AL (264)	90.9	9.1	0.0	0.0	0.0	87	35
Virginia Beach, VA (365)	86.8	13.2	0.0	0.0	0.0	97	40
Washington, DC (365)	57.3	39.7	2.7	0.3	0.0	157	47
Wichita, KS (365)	82.5	17.5	0.0	0.0	0.0	97	40
Winston-Salem, NC (365)	61.6	38.4	0.0	0.0	0.0	97	45

Note: The Air Quality Index (AQI) is an index for reporting daily air quality. EPA calculates the AQI for five major air pollutants regulated by the Clean Air Act: ground-level ozone, particle pollution (also known as particulate matter), carbon monoxide, sulfur dioxide, and nitrogen dioxide. The AQI runs from 0 to 500. The higher the AQI value, the greater the level of air pollution and the greater the health concern. There are six AQI categories: "Good" The AQI is between 0 and 50. Air quality is considered satisfactory; "Moderate" The AQI is between 51 and 100. Air quality is acceptable; "Unhealthy for Sensitive Groups" When AQI values are between 101 and 150, members of sensitive groups may experience health effects; "Unhealthy" When AQI values are between 151 and 200 everyone may begin to experience health effects; "Very Unhealthy" AQI values between 201 and 300 trigger a health alert; "Hazardous" AQI values over 300 trigger health warnings of emergency conditions; Data covers the entire county unless noted otherwise; (1) Data covers the Metropolitan Statistical Area—see Appendix B for areas included; (2) Number of days with AQI data in 2019
Source: U.S. Environmental Protection Agency, Air Quality Index Report, 2019

Air Quality Index Pollutants

MSA[1] (Days[2])	Percent of Days when AQI Pollutant was...					
	Carbon Monoxide	Nitrogen Dioxide	Ozone	Sulfur Dioxide	Particulate Matter 2.5	Particulate Matter 10
Albuquerque, NM (365)	0.0	0.0	69.0	0.0	18.1	12.9
Allentown, PA (365)	0.0	3.6	61.4	0.0	35.1	0.0
Anchorage, AK (365)	1.4	0.0	0.0	0.0	69.9	28.8
Ann Arbor, MI (365)	0.0	0.0	66.6	0.0	33.4	0.0
Athens, GA (365)	0.0	0.0	37.3	0.0	62.7	0.0
Atlanta, GA (365)	0.0	2.5	46.8	0.0	50.7	0.0
Austin, TX (365)	0.0	1.9	48.8	0.0	49.3	0.0
Baton Rouge, LA (365)	0.0	1.6	47.9	0.3	50.1	0.0
Boise City, ID (365)	0.0	1.1	44.4	0.0	51.0	3.6
Boston, MA (365)	0.0	4.1	57.5	0.0	38.4	0.0
Boulder, CO (365)	0.0	0.0	73.7	0.0	26.3	0.0
Cape Coral, FL (365)	0.0	0.0	68.8	0.0	30.1	1.1
Cedar Rapids, IA (365)	0.0	0.0	47.9	1.1	51.0	0.0
Charleston, SC (357)	0.0	0.0	67.2	0.0	32.5	0.3
Charlotte, NC (365)	0.0	0.0	66.6	0.0	33.4	0.0
Chicago, IL (365)	0.0	5.5	24.1	4.9	62.5	3.0
Cincinnati, OH (365)	0.0	1.6	41.4	6.0	50.1	0.8
Clarksville, TN (365)	0.0	0.0	72.9	0.0	27.1	0.0
Cleveland, OH (365)	0.0	0.3	40.5	0.5	55.1	3.6
College Station, TX (352)	0.0	0.0	0.0	100.0	0.0	0.0
Colorado Springs, CO (365)	0.0	0.0	94.5	0.0	4.9	0.5
Columbia, MO (245)	0.0	0.0	100.0	0.0	0.0	0.0
Columbia, SC (365)	0.0	0.0	71.8	0.0	28.2	0.0
Columbus, OH (365)	0.0	1.4	49.0	0.0	49.3	0.3
Dallas, TX (365)	0.0	3.0	56.2	0.0	40.8	0.0
Davenport, IA (365)	0.0	0.0	37.8	0.0	41.9	20.3
Denver, CO (365)	0.0	16.4	57.8	0.3	17.3	8.2
Des Moines, IA (365)	0.0	0.8	67.4	0.0	31.8	0.0
Durham, NC (365)	0.0	0.0	56.7	1.6	41.6	0.0
Edison, NJ (365)	0.0	17.5	39.2	0.0	43.3	0.0
El Paso, TX (365)	0.0	5.8	55.9	0.0	37.5	0.8
Fargo, ND (363)	0.0	2.5	72.7	0.0	24.2	0.6
Fayetteville, NC (363)	0.0	0.0	56.7	0.0	42.1	1.1
Fort Collins, CO (365)	0.0	0.0	92.3	0.0	7.7	0.0
Fort Wayne, IN (365)	0.0	0.0	48.5	0.0	51.5	0.0
Fort Worth, TX (365)	0.0	3.0	56.2	0.0	40.8	0.0
Grand Rapids, MI (365)	0.0	2.5	69.9	0.0	26.3	1.4
Greeley, CO (365)	0.0	0.0	64.7	0.0	35.3	0.0
Green Bay, WI (365)	0.0	0.0	51.0	1.1	47.9	0.0
Greensboro, NC (365)	0.0	0.0	63.6	0.0	29.3	7.1
Honolulu, HI (365)	0.3	0.8	71.8	17.8	9.0	0.3
Houston, TX (365)	0.0	4.4	47.1	0.5	47.1	0.8
Huntsville, AL (361)	0.0	0.0	42.9	0.0	55.1	1.9
Indianapolis, IN (365)	0.0	0.0	34.2	1.1	64.7	0.0
Jacksonville, FL (365)	0.0	0.0	48.2	2.7	49.0	0.0
Kansas City, MO (365)	0.0	2.5	48.2	0.0	45.5	3.8
Lafayette, LA (365)	0.0	0.0	58.4	0.0	41.6	0.0
Lakeland, FL (365)	0.0	0.0	67.9	0.5	31.5	0.0
Las Vegas, NV (365)	0.3	5.5	69.0	0.0	23.0	2.2
Lexington, KY (365)	0.0	2.7	52.9	0.0	44.4	0.0
Lincoln, NE (360)	0.0	0.0	63.6	21.1	15.3	0.0
Little Rock, AR (365)	0.0	0.5	40.0	0.0	59.5	0.0
Los Angeles, CA (365)	0.0	9.0	56.2	0.0	32.3	2.5
Louisville, KY (365)	0.0	2.7	45.8	0.0	51.5	0.0

Table continued on following page.

MSA[1] (Days[2])	Percent of Days when AQI Pollutant was...					
	Carbon Monoxide	Nitrogen Dioxide	Ozone	Sulfur Dioxide	Particulate Matter 2.5	Particulate Matter 10
Madison, WI (365)	0.0	0.0	45.5	0.0	54.5	0.0
Manchester, NH (365)	0.0	0.0	97.5	0.0	2.5	0.0
Memphis, TN (365)	0.0	2.5	51.0	0.0	46.6	0.0
Miami, FL (364)	0.3	3.6	37.4	0.0	58.5	0.3
Midland, TX (n/a)	n/a	n/a	n/a	n/a	n/a	n/a
Milwaukee, WI (365)	0.0	2.7	51.8	0.0	43.3	2.2
Minneapolis, MN (365)	0.0	1.4	31.2	1.1	43.0	23.3
Nashville, TN (365)	0.0	6.8	40.5	0.0	52.6	0.0
New Haven, CT (365)	0.0	4.1	67.7	0.0	27.1	1.1
New Orleans, LA (365)	0.0	0.8	45.8	8.8	44.4	0.3
New York, NY (365)	0.0	17.5	39.2	0.0	43.3	0.0
Oklahoma City, OK (365)	0.0	1.1	52.9	0.0	45.8	0.3
Omaha, NE (365)	0.0	0.0	52.3	3.3	40.8	3.6
Orlando, FL (365)	0.0	0.0	80.5	0.0	19.5	0.0
Peoria, IL (365)	0.0	0.0	55.6	0.5	43.8	0.0
Philadelphia, PA (365)	0.0	3.6	50.1	0.0	46.3	0.0
Phoenix, AZ (365)	0.0	0.8	46.3	0.0	19.7	33.2
Pittsburgh, PA (365)	0.0	0.0	29.3	6.3	64.4	0.0
Portland, OR (365)	0.0	2.2	56.4	0.0	41.4	0.0
Providence, RI (365)	0.0	2.2	70.7	0.0	26.8	0.3
Provo, UT (365)	0.0	1.9	81.4	0.0	16.2	0.5
Raleigh, NC (365)	0.3	0.3	46.8	0.0	52.6	0.0
Reno, NV (365)	0.0	1.1	80.5	0.0	17.0	1.4
Richmond, VA (365)	0.0	4.4	67.4	0.0	28.2	0.0
Riverside, CA (365)	0.0	3.0	62.5	0.0	24.4	10.1
Rochester, MN (364)	0.0	0.0	53.6	0.0	46.4	0.0
Sacramento, CA (365)	0.0	0.3	71.0	0.0	27.1	1.6
Salt Lake City, UT (365)	0.0	8.8	67.1	0.0	22.7	1.4
San Antonio, TX (365)	0.0	0.8	44.1	0.0	54.8	0.3
San Diego, CA (365)	0.0	0.5	48.2	0.0	50.4	0.8
San Francisco, CA (365)	0.0	6.3	52.1	0.0	41.6	0.0
San Jose, CA (365)	0.0	0.5	64.7	0.0	33.7	1.1
Santa Rosa, CA (365)	0.0	0.8	70.7	0.0	25.8	2.7
Savannah, GA (365)	0.0	0.0	40.0	15.9	44.1	0.0
Seattle, WA (365)	0.0	8.5	43.3	0.0	48.2	0.0
Sioux Falls, SD (365)	0.0	2.5	84.1	0.0	12.9	0.5
Springfield, IL (360)	0.0	0.0	50.8	0.0	49.2	0.0
Tallahassee, FL (365)	0.0	0.0	47.7	0.0	52.3	0.0
Tampa, FL (365)	0.0	0.0	58.4	1.1	39.5	1.1
Tucson, AZ (365)	0.0	0.3	71.5	0.0	5.5	22.7
Tulsa, OK (365)	0.0	0.0	65.2	0.0	34.8	0.0
Tuscaloosa, AL (264)	0.0	0.0	71.2	0.0	28.8	0.0
Virginia Beach, VA (365)	0.0	12.1	61.9	0.0	26.0	0.0
Washington, DC (365)	0.0	6.8	61.9	0.0	31.2	0.0
Wichita, KS (365)	0.0	1.4	72.6	0.0	23.6	2.5
Winston-Salem, NC (365)	0.0	2.7	47.1	0.0	50.1	0.0

Note: The Air Quality Index (AQI) is an index for reporting daily air quality. EPA calculates the AQI for five major air pollutants regulated by the Clean Air Act: ground-level ozone, particle pollution (also known as particulate matter), carbon monoxide, sulfur dioxide, and nitrogen dioxide. The AQI runs from 0 to 500. The higher the AQI value, the greater the level of air pollution and the greater the health concern; (1) Data covers the Metropolitan Statistical Area—see Appendix B for areas included; (2) Number of days with AQI data in 2019
Source: U.S. Environmental Protection Agency, Air Quality Index Report, 2019

Air Quality Trends: Ozone

MSA[1]	1990	1995	2000	2005	2010	2015	2016	2017	2018	2019
Albuquerque, NM	0.072	0.070	0.072	0.073	0.066	0.066	0.065	0.069	0.074	0.067
Allentown, PA	0.093	0.091	0.091	0.086	0.080	0.070	0.073	0.067	0.067	0.064
Anchorage, AK	n/a	n/a	n/a	n/a	n/a	n/a	n/a	n/a	n/a	n/a
Ann Arbor, MI	n/a	n/a	n/a	n/a	n/a	n/a	n/a	n/a	n/a	n/a
Athens, GA	n/a	n/a	n/a	n/a	n/a	n/a	n/a	n/a	n/a	n/a
Atlanta, GA	0.104	0.103	0.101	0.087	0.076	0.070	0.073	0.068	0.068	0.071
Austin, TX	0.088	0.089	0.088	0.082	0.074	0.073	0.064	0.070	0.072	0.065
Baton Rouge, LA	0.105	0.091	0.090	0.090	0.075	0.069	0.066	0.069	0.069	0.066
Boise City, ID	n/a	n/a	n/a	n/a	n/a	n/a	n/a	n/a	n/a	n/a
Boston, MA	n/a	n/a	n/a	n/a	n/a	n/a	n/a	n/a	n/a	n/a
Boulder, CO	n/a	n/a	n/a	n/a	n/a	n/a	n/a	n/a	n/a	n/a
Cape Coral, FL	n/a	n/a	n/a	n/a	n/a	n/a	n/a	n/a	n/a	n/a
Cedar Rapids, IA	n/a	n/a	n/a	n/a	n/a	n/a	n/a	n/a	n/a	n/a
Charleston, SC	0.068	0.071	0.078	0.073	0.067	0.054	0.059	0.062	0.058	0.064
Charlotte, NC	n/a	n/a	n/a	n/a	n/a	n/a	n/a	n/a	n/a	n/a
Chicago, IL	0.074	0.094	0.073	0.084	0.070	0.066	0.074	0.071	0.073	0.069
Cincinnati, OH	0.091	0.091	0.081	0.085	0.075	0.068	0.071	0.067	0.074	0.067
Clarksville, TN	n/a	n/a	n/a	n/a	n/a	n/a	n/a	n/a	n/a	n/a
Cleveland, OH	0.085	0.092	0.076	0.083	0.077	0.071	0.072	0.070	0.074	0.070
College Station, TX	n/a	n/a	n/a	n/a	n/a	n/a	n/a	n/a	n/a	n/a
Colorado Springs, CO	n/a	n/a	n/a	n/a	n/a	n/a	n/a	n/a	n/a	n/a
Columbia, MO	n/a	n/a	n/a	n/a	n/a	n/a	n/a	n/a	n/a	n/a
Columbia, SC	0.093	0.079	0.096	0.082	0.070	0.056	0.065	0.059	0.060	0.066
Columbus, OH	0.090	0.091	0.085	0.084	0.073	0.066	0.069	0.065	0.062	0.060
Dallas, TX	0.095	0.105	0.096	0.097	0.080	0.077	0.070	0.073	0.078	0.071
Davenport, IA	n/a	n/a	n/a	n/a	n/a	n/a	n/a	n/a	n/a	n/a
Denver, CO	0.077	0.070	0.069	0.072	0.070	0.073	0.071	0.072	0.071	0.068
Des Moines, IA	n/a	n/a	n/a	n/a	n/a	n/a	n/a	n/a	n/a	n/a
Durham, NC	n/a	n/a	n/a	n/a	n/a	n/a	n/a	n/a	n/a	n/a
Edison, NJ	0.101	0.106	0.090	0.091	0.081	0.075	0.073	0.070	0.073	0.067
El Paso, TX	0.080	0.078	0.082	0.074	0.072	0.071	0.068	0.073	0.077	0.074
Fargo, ND	n/a	n/a	n/a	n/a	n/a	n/a	n/a	n/a	n/a	n/a
Fayetteville, NC	0.087	0.081	0.086	0.084	0.071	0.060	0.064	0.063	0.064	0.061
Fort Collins, CO	0.066	0.072	0.074	0.076	0.072	0.069	0.070	0.067	0.073	0.065
Fort Wayne, IN	0.086	0.094	0.086	0.081	0.067	0.061	0.068	0.063	0.071	0.063
Fort Worth, TX	0.095	0.105	0.096	0.097	0.080	0.077	0.070	0.073	0.078	0.071
Grand Rapids, MI	0.102	0.089	0.073	0.085	0.071	0.066	0.075	0.065	0.072	0.065
Greeley, CO	n/a	n/a	n/a	n/a	n/a	n/a	n/a	n/a	n/a	n/a
Green Bay, WI	n/a	n/a	n/a	n/a	n/a	n/a	n/a	n/a	n/a	n/a
Greensboro, NC	n/a	n/a	n/a	n/a	n/a	n/a	n/a	n/a	n/a	n/a
Honolulu, HI	0.034	0.049	0.044	0.042	0.046	0.048	0.047	0.046	0.046	0.053
Houston, TX	0.119	0.114	0.102	0.087	0.079	0.083	0.066	0.070	0.073	0.074
Huntsville, AL	0.079	0.080	0.088	0.075	0.071	0.063	0.066	0.063	0.065	0.063
Indianapolis, IN	0.084	0.094	0.081	0.080	0.069	0.064	0.070	0.067	0.073	0.067
Jacksonville, FL	0.080	0.068	0.072	0.076	0.068	0.060	0.057	0.059	0.060	0.062
Kansas City, MO	0.075	0.098	0.088	0.084	0.072	0.063	0.066	0.069	0.073	0.063
Lafayette, LA	n/a	n/a	n/a	n/a	n/a	n/a	n/a	n/a	n/a	n/a
Lakeland, FL	0.066	0.071	0.079	0.074	0.064	0.062	0.064	0.072	0.065	0.066
Las Vegas, NV	n/a	n/a	n/a	n/a	n/a	n/a	n/a	n/a	n/a	n/a
Lexington, KY	0.078	0.088	0.077	0.078	0.070	0.069	0.066	0.063	0.063	0.059
Lincoln, NE	0.057	0.060	0.057	0.056	0.050	0.061	0.058	0.062	0.062	0.056
Little Rock, AR	0.080	0.086	0.090	0.083	0.072	0.063	0.064	0.060	0.066	0.059
Los Angeles, CA	0.134	0.114	0.091	0.085	0.076	0.083	0.083	0.093	0.084	0.080
Louisville, KY	0.075	0.087	0.088	0.083	0.076	0.070	0.070	0.064	0.067	0.064
Madison, WI	0.077	0.084	0.072	0.079	0.062	0.064	0.068	0.064	0.066	0.059
Manchester, NH	n/a	n/a	n/a	n/a	n/a	n/a	n/a	n/a	n/a	n/a

Table continued on following page.

MSA[1]	1990	1995	2000	2005	2010	2015	2016	2017	2018	2019
Memphis, TN	0.088	0.095	0.092	0.086	0.076	0.065	0.069	0.063	0.069	0.065
Miami, FL	0.068	0.072	0.075	0.065	0.064	0.061	0.061	0.064	0.064	0.058
Midland, TX	n/a	n/a	n/a	n/a	n/a	n/a	n/a	n/a	n/a	n/a
Milwaukee, WI	0.095	0.106	0.082	0.092	0.079	0.069	0.074	0.072	0.073	0.066
Minneapolis, MN	0.068	0.084	0.065	0.074	0.066	0.061	0.061	0.062	0.065	0.059
Nashville, TN	0.089	0.092	0.084	0.078	0.073	0.065	0.067	0.063	0.068	0.064
New Haven, CT	n/a	n/a	n/a	n/a	n/a	n/a	n/a	n/a	n/a	n/a
New Orleans, LA	0.082	0.088	0.091	0.079	0.074	0.067	0.065	0.063	0.065	0.062
New York, NY	0.101	0.106	0.090	0.091	0.081	0.075	0.073	0.070	0.073	0.067
Oklahoma City, OK	0.078	0.086	0.082	0.077	0.071	0.067	0.066	0.070	0.072	0.067
Omaha, NE	0.054	0.075	0.063	0.069	0.058	0.055	0.063	0.061	0.063	0.050
Orlando, FL	0.081	0.075	0.080	0.083	0.069	0.060	0.064	0.067	0.062	0.062
Peoria, IL	0.071	0.082	0.072	0.075	0.064	0.062	0.067	0.066	0.070	0.063
Philadelphia, PA	0.102	0.109	0.099	0.091	0.083	0.074	0.075	0.073	0.075	0.067
Phoenix, AZ	0.080	0.087	0.082	0.077	0.076	0.072	0.071	0.075	0.074	0.071
Pittsburgh, PA	0.080	0.095	0.082	0.082	0.075	0.069	0.068	0.066	0.068	0.062
Portland, OR	0.081	0.065	0.059	0.059	0.056	0.064	0.057	0.073	0.062	0.058
Providence, RI	0.106	0.107	0.087	0.090	0.072	0.070	0.075	0.076	0.074	0.064
Provo, UT	0.070	0.068	0.083	0.078	0.070	0.073	0.072	0.073	0.073	0.073
Raleigh, NC	0.093	0.081	0.087	0.082	0.071	0.065	0.069	0.066	0.063	0.064
Reno, NV	0.074	0.069	0.067	0.069	0.068	0.071	0.070	0.068	0.077	0.063
Richmond, VA	0.083	0.089	0.080	0.082	0.079	0.062	0.065	0.063	0.062	0.061
Riverside, CA	0.146	0.129	0.104	0.102	0.093	0.094	0.096	0.099	0.097	0.091
Rochester, MN	n/a	n/a	n/a	n/a	n/a	n/a	n/a	n/a	n/a	n/a
Sacramento, CA	0.088	0.093	0.087	0.087	0.074	0.074	0.077	0.073	0.079	0.068
Salt Lake City, UT	n/a	n/a	n/a	n/a	n/a	n/a	n/a	n/a	n/a	n/a
San Antonio, TX	0.090	0.095	0.078	0.084	0.072	0.079	0.071	0.073	0.072	0.075
San Diego, CA	0.112	0.093	0.084	0.079	0.075	0.070	0.073	0.077	0.069	0.071
San Francisco, CA	0.058	0.074	0.057	0.057	0.061	0.062	0.059	0.060	0.053	0.060
San Jose, CA	0.079	0.085	0.070	0.065	0.073	0.067	0.063	0.065	0.061	0.062
Santa Rosa, CA	0.063	0.071	0.061	0.050	0.053	0.059	0.055	0.062	0.055	0.056
Savannah, GA	n/a	n/a	n/a	n/a	n/a	n/a	n/a	n/a	n/a	n/a
Seattle, WA	0.082	0.062	0.056	0.053	0.053	0.059	0.054	0.076	0.067	0.052
Sioux Falls, SD	n/a	n/a	n/a	n/a	n/a	n/a	n/a	n/a	n/a	n/a
Springfield, IL	n/a	n/a	n/a	n/a	n/a	n/a	n/a	n/a	n/a	n/a
Tallahassee, FL	n/a	n/a	n/a	n/a	n/a	n/a	n/a	n/a	n/a	n/a
Tampa, FL	0.080	0.075	0.081	0.075	0.067	0.062	0.064	0.064	0.065	0.065
Tucson, AZ	0.073	0.078	0.074	0.075	0.068	0.065	0.065	0.070	0.069	0.065
Tulsa, OK	0.086	0.091	0.081	0.072	0.069	0.061	0.064	0.065	0.067	0.062
Tuscaloosa, AL	n/a	n/a	n/a	n/a	n/a	n/a	n/a	n/a	n/a	n/a
Virginia Beach, VA	0.085	0.084	0.083	0.078	0.074	0.061	0.062	0.059	0.061	0.059
Washington, DC	0.088	0.093	0.082	0.081	0.077	0.067	0.069	0.065	0.066	0.061
Wichita, KS	0.077	0.069	0.080	0.074	0.075	0.064	0.062	0.063	0.064	0.062
Winston-Salem, NC	0.084	0.086	0.089	0.080	0.078	0.065	0.069	0.066	0.064	0.062
U.S.	0.088	0.089	0.082	0.080	0.073	0.068	0.069	0.068	0.069	0.065

Note: (1) Data covers the Metropolitan Statistical Area—see Appendix B for areas included; n/a not available. The values shown are the composite ozone concentration averages among trend sites based on the highest fourth daily maximum 8-hour concentration in parts per million. These trends are based on sites having an adequate record of monitoring data during the trend period. Data from exceptional events are included.
Source: U.S. Environmental Protection Agency, Air Quality Monitoring Information, "Air Quality Trends by City, 1990-2019"

Maximum Air Pollutant Concentrations: Particulate Matter, Ozone, CO and Lead

Metro Aea	PM 10 (ug/m³)	PM 2.5 Wtd AM (ug/m³)	PM 2.5 24-Hr (ug/m³)	Ozone (ppm)	Carbon Monoxide (ppm)	Lead (ug/m³)
Albuquerque, NM	141	7.7	20	0.069	1	n/a
Allentown, PA	31	8.5	26	0.065	n/a	0.04
Anchorage, AK	148	8.2	42	n/a	2	n/a
Ann Arbor, MI	n/a	8.5	22	0.060	n/a	n/a
Athens, GA	n/a	9.8	21	0.063	n/a	n/a
Atlanta, GA	40	10.8	24	0.075	2	n/a
Austin, TX	38	9.5	21	0.065	2	n/a
Baton Rouge, LA	51	9.2	23	0.070	1	0
Boise City, ID	83	6.9	25	0.057	1	n/a
Boston, MA	34	7.5	17	0.065	1	n/a
Boulder, CO	52	7.4	36	0.069	n/a	n/a
Cape Coral, FL	51	7.4	14	0.062	n/a	n/a
Cedar Rapids, IA	38	7.9	20	0.060	n/a	n/a
Charleston, SC	54	6.9	14	0.064	n/a	n/a
Charlotte, NC	36	9.5	18	0.074	1	n/a
Chicago, IL	73	10.8	26	0.071	2	0.19
Cincinnati, OH	108	11.9	26	0.072	2	n/a
Clarksville, TN	n/a	n/a	n/a	0.061	n/a	n/a
Cleveland, OH	79	10.8	26	0.071	2	0.01
College Station, TX	n/a	n/a	n/a	n/a	n/a	n/a
Colorado Springs, CO	32	5.0	13	0.065	2	n/a
Columbia, MO	n/a	n/a	n/a	0.058	n/a	n/a
Columbia, SC	35	7.2	15	0.067	1	n/a
Columbus, OH	39	9.7	22	0.068	1	n/a
Dallas, TX	40	9.0	19	0.076	1	0.23
Davenport, IA	129	8.6	22	0.066	1	n/a
Denver, CO	111	10.0	29	0.078	2	n/a
Des Moines, IA	39	7.0	19	0.064	1	n/a
Durham, NC	27	7.7	15	0.063	n/a	n/a
Edison, NJ	34	11.0	24	0.073	2	n/a
El Paso, TX	79	8.5	25	0.075	2	0.01
Fargo, ND	78	6.5	18	0.062	n/a	n/a
Fayetteville, NC	30	7.4	16	0.061	n/a	n/a
Fort Collins, CO	n/a	6.0	20	0.071	1	n/a
Fort Wayne, IN	n/a	9.0	22	0.063	n/a	n/a
Fort Worth, TX	40	9.0	19	0.076	1	0.23
Grand Rapids, MI	104	8.3	24	0.065	1	0.01
Greeley, CO	n/a	9.0	26	0.065	1	n/a
Green Bay, WI	n/a	7.3	19	0.061	n/a	n/a
Greensboro, NC	33	6.8	15	0.064	n/a	n/a
Honolulu, HI	32	3.9	8	0.053	1	n/a
Houston, TX	63	10.7	27	0.081	2	n/a
Huntsville, AL	34	7.4	14	0.063	n/a	n/a
Indianapolis, IN	57	12.6	27	0.067	2	n/a
Jacksonville, FL	57	8.6	20	0.065	1	n/a
Kansas City, MO	71	7.6	17	0.064	1	n/a
Lafayette, LA	52	7.9	17	0.063	n/a	n/a
Lakeland, FL	57	7.7	19	0.067	n/a	n/a
Las Vegas, NV	104	8.0	26	0.070	2	n/a
Lexington, KY	28	8.0	17	0.059	n/a	n/a
Lincoln, NE	n/a	6.5	17	0.056	n/a	n/a
Little Rock, AR	38	10.3	23	0.060	1	n/a
Los Angeles, CA	159	11.0	28	0.101	3	0.02
Louisville, KY	40	10.5	23	0.068	2	n/a
Madison, WI	35	8.0	21	0.059	n/a	n/a

Table continued on following page.

Metro Aea	PM 10 (ug/m³)	PM 2.5 Wtd AM (ug/m³)	PM 2.5 24-Hr (ug/m³)	Ozone (ppm)	Carbon Monoxide (ppm)	Lead (ug/m³)
Manchester, NH	n/a	3.0	10	0.057	0	n/a
Memphis, TN	54	8.8	19	0.070	1	n/a
Miami, FL	54	8.9	19	0.060	2	n/a
Midland, TX	n/a	n/a	n/a	n/a	n/a	n/a
Milwaukee, WI	58	9.3	24	0.068	1	n/a
Minneapolis, MN	98	8.0	23	0.062	1	0.07
Nashville, TN	32	9.2	18	0.066	1	n/a
New Haven, CT	67	7.7	18	0.084	1	n/a
New Orleans, LA	79	7.8	17	0.063	2	0.09
New York, NY	34	11.0	24	0.073	2	n/a
Oklahoma City, OK	63	10.0	21	0.066	1	n/a
Omaha, NE	50	7.8	22	0.062	2	0.06
Orlando, FL	49	6.9	16	0.072	1	n/a
Peoria, IL	n/a	8.0	19	0.064	n/a	n/a
Philadelphia, PA	49	9.8	26	0.072	2	0
Phoenix, AZ	990	10.9	30	0.076	2	0.05
Pittsburgh, PA	86	12.2	39	0.064	3	0
Portland, OR	32	7.0	25	0.065	1	n/a
Providence, RI	37	8.3	18	0.066	2	n/a
Provo, UT	53	6.1	21	0.066	1	n/a
Raleigh, NC	30	8.9	17	0.064	1	n/a
Reno, NV	78	6.0	16	0.066	2	n/a
Richmond, VA	27	8.4	20	0.064	1	n/a
Riverside, CA	243	12.8	36	0.106	1	0.01
Rochester, MN	n/a	n/a	n/a	0.054	n/a	n/a
Sacramento, CA	90	8.4	30	0.079	1	n/a
Salt Lake City, UT	67	9.0	31	0.073	1	n/a
San Antonio, TX	42	8.9	21	0.075	1	n/a
San Diego, CA	153	13.7	27	0.076	2	0.02
San Francisco, CA	34	9.4	19	0.072	2	n/a
San Jose, CA	75	9.1	21	0.064	2	0.07
Santa Rosa, CA	73	5.7	14	0.056	1	n/a
Savannah, GA	n/a	n/a	n/a	0.060	n/a	n/a
Seattle, WA	22	8.5	28	0.056	1	n/a
Sioux Falls, SD	37	3.9	16	0.065	1	n/a
Springfield, IL	n/a	8.2	18	0.062	n/a	n/a
Tallahassee, FL	n/a	7.7	20	0.063	1	n/a
Tampa, FL	64	7.7	17	0.070	1	0.09
Tucson, AZ	139	3.8	9	0.065	1	n/a
Tulsa, OK	36	8.7	22	0.066	1	0.01
Tuscaloosa, AL	n/a	7.9	15	0.060	n/a	n/a
Virginia Beach, VA	20	7.1	18	0.061	1	n/a
Washington, DC	46	9.1	25	0.075	2	n/a
Wichita, KS	64	7.5	18	0.062	n/a	n/a
Winston-Salem, NC	33	9.5	24	0.065	n/a	n/a
NAAQS[1]	150	15.0	35	0.075	9	0.15

Note: Data from exceptional events are included; Data covers the Metropolitan Statistical Area—see Appendix B for areas included;
(1) National Ambient Air Quality Standards; ppm = parts per million; ug/m³ = micrograms per cubic meter; n/a not available
Concentrations: Particulate Matter 10 (coarse particulate)—highest second maximum 24-hour concentration; Particulate Matter 2.5 Wtd AM (fine particulate)—highest weighted annual mean concentration; Particulate Matter 2.5 24-Hour (fine particulate)—highest 98th percentile 24-hour concentration; Ozone—highest fourth daily maximum 8-hour concentration; Carbon Monoxide—highest second maximum non-overlapping 8-hour concentration; Lead—maximum running 3-month average
Source: U.S. Environmental Protection Agency, Air Quality Monitoring Information, "Air Quality Statistics by City, 2019"

Maximum Air Pollutant Concentrations: Nitrogen Dioxide and Sulfur Dioxide

Metro Area	Nitrogen Dioxide AM (ppb)	Nitrogen Dioxide 1-Hr (ppb)	Sulfur Dioxide AM (ppb)	Sulfur Dioxide 1-Hr (ppb)	Sulfur Dioxide 24-Hr (ppb)
Albuquerque, NM	9	44	n/a	4	n/a
Allentown, PA	11	43	n/a	6	n/a
Anchorage, AK	n/a	n/a	n/a	n/a	n/a
Ann Arbor, MI	n/a	n/a	n/a	n/a	n/a
Athens, GA	n/a	n/a	n/a	n/a	n/a
Atlanta, GA	16	50	n/a	5	n/a
Austin, TX	12	32	n/a	2	n/a
Baton Rouge, LA	10	45	n/a	16	n/a
Boise City, ID	n/a	n/a	n/a	3	n/a
Boston, MA	14	49	n/a	10	n/a
Boulder, CO	n/a	n/a	n/a	n/a	n/a
Cape Coral, FL	n/a	n/a	n/a	n/a	n/a
Cedar Rapids, IA	n/a	n/a	n/a	25	n/a
Charleston, SC	n/a	n/a	n/a	14	n/a
Charlotte, NC	11	37	n/a	3	n/a
Chicago, IL	17	56	n/a	79	n/a
Cincinnati, OH	18	49	n/a	134	n/a
Clarksville, TN	n/a	n/a	n/a	n/a	n/a
Cleveland, OH	10	45	n/a	23	n/a
College Station, TX	n/a	n/a	n/a	8	n/a
Colorado Springs, CO	n/a	n/a	n/a	10	n/a
Columbia, MO	n/a	n/a	n/a	n/a	n/a
Columbia, SC	3	31	n/a	3	n/a
Columbus, OH	10	42	n/a	n/a	n/a
Dallas, TX	12	46	n/a	7	n/a
Davenport, IA	n/a	n/a	n/a	5	n/a
Denver, CO	27	69	n/a	7	n/a
Des Moines, IA	6	37	n/a	n/a	n/a
Durham, NC	n/a	n/a	n/a	41	n/a
Edison, NJ	21	66	n/a	11	n/a
El Paso, TX	14	n/a	n/a	n/a	n/a
Fargo, ND	4	39	n/a	3	n/a
Fayetteville, NC	n/a	n/a	n/a	n/a	n/a
Fort Collins, CO	n/a	n/a	n/a	n/a	n/a
Fort Wayne, IN	n/a	n/a	n/a	n/a	n/a
Fort Worth, TX	12	46	Sulfur	7	Sulfur
Grand Rapids, MI	6	36	n/a	14	n/a
Greeley, CO	n/a	n/a	n/a	n/a	n/a
Green Bay, WI	n/a	n/a	n/a	5	n/a
Greensboro, NC	n/a	n/a	n/a	n/a	n/a
Honolulu, HI	4	28	n/a	62	n/a
Houston, TX	17	56	n/a	14	n/a
Huntsville, AL	n/a	n/a	n/a	n/a	n/a
Indianapolis, IN	9	37	n/a	n/a	n/a
Jacksonville, FL	11	39	n/a	41	n/a
Kansas City, MO	11	47	n/a	7	n/a
Lafayette, LA	n/a	n/a	n/a	n/a	n/a
Lakeland, FL	n/a	n/a	n/a	26	n/a
Las Vegas, NV	24	58	n/a	5	n/a
Lexington, KY	6	42	n/a	4	n/a
Lincoln, NE	n/a	n/a	n/a	33	n/a
Little Rock, AR	8	38	n/a	13	n/a
Los Angeles, CA	23	78	n/a	8	n/a
Louisville, KY	15	49	n/a	15	n/a
Madison, WI	n/a	n/a	n/a	2	n/a

Table continued on following page.

Metro Area	Nitrogen Dioxide AM (ppb)	Nitrogen Dioxide 1-Hr (ppb)	Sulfur Dioxide AM (ppb)	Sulfur Dioxide 1-Hr (ppb)	Sulfur Dioxide 24-Hr (ppb)
Manchester, NH	n/a	n/a	n/a	1	n/a
Memphis, TN	10	40	n/a	2	n/a
Miami, FL	15	48	n/a	1	n/a
Midland, TX	n/a	n/a	n/a	n/a	n/a
Milwaukee, WI	13	47	n/a	4	n/a
Minneapolis, MN	8	41	n/a	10	n/a
Nashville, TN	14	51	n/a	n/a	n/a
New Haven, CT	12	46	n/a	2	n/a
New Orleans, LA	10	43	n/a	53	n/a
New York, NY	21	66	n/a	11	n/a
Oklahoma City, OK	12	n/a	n/a	1	n/a
Omaha, NE	n/a	n/a	n/a	38	n/a
Orlando, FL	4	30	n/a	3	n/a
Peoria, IL	n/a	n/a	n/a	17	n/a
Philadelphia, PA	13	52	n/a	17	n/a
Phoenix, AZ	25	52	n/a	5	n/a
Pittsburgh, PA	10	37	n/a	80	n/a
Portland, OR	11	33	n/a	3	n/a
Providence, RI	17	52	n/a	2	n/a
Provo, UT	9	42	n/a	n/a	n/a
Raleigh, NC	9	34	n/a	2	n/a
Reno, NV	11	46	n/a	3	n/a
Richmond, VA	12	43	n/a	14	n/a
Riverside, CA	29	74	n/a	7	n/a
Rochester, MN	n/a	n/a	n/a	n/a	n/a
Sacramento, CA	12	55	n/a	3	n/a
Salt Lake City, UT	18	55	n/a	13	n/a
San Antonio, TX	7	40	n/a	4	n/a
San Diego, CA	14	47	n/a	1	n/a
San Francisco, CA	15	48	n/a	15	n/a
San Jose, CA	14	52	n/a	2	n/a
Santa Rosa, CA	4	28	n/a	n/a	n/a
Savannah, GA	n/a	n/a	n/a	50	n/a
Seattle, WA	18	57	n/a	6	n/a
Sioux Falls, SD	5	31	n/a	2	n/a
Springfield, IL	n/a	n/a	n/a	n/a	n/a
Tallahassee, FL	n/a	n/a	n/a	n/a	n/a
Tampa, FL	10	37	n/a	11	n/a
Tucson, AZ	7	30	n/a	1	n/a
Tulsa, OK	7	n/a	n/a	6	n/a
Tuscaloosa, AL	n/a	n/a	n/a	n/a	n/a
Virginia Beach, VA	8	40	n/a	3	n/a
Washington, DC	16	49	n/a	5	n/a
Wichita, KS	6	21	n/a	3	n/a
Winston-Salem, NC	7	34	n/a	5	n/a
NAAQS[1]	53	100	30	75	140

Note: Data from exceptional events are included; Data covers the Metropolitan Statistical Area—see Appendix B for areas included;
(1) National Ambient Air Quality Standards; ppb = parts per billion; n/a not available
Concentrations: Nitrogen Dioxide AM—highest arithmetic mean concentration; Nitrogen Dioxide 1-Hr—highest 98th percentile 1-hour
daily maximum concentration; Sulfur Dioxide AM—highest annual mean concentration; Sulfur Dioxide 1-Hr—highest 99th percentile
1-hour daily maximum concentration; Sulfur Dioxide 24-Hr—highest second maximum 24-hour concentration
Source: U.S. Environmental Protection Agency, Air Quality Monitoring Information, "Air Quality Statistics by City, 2019"

Appendix B: Metropolitan Area Definitions

Metropolitan Statistical Areas (MSA), Metropolitan Divisions (MD), New England City and Town Areas (NECTA), and New England City and Town Area Divisions (NECTAD)

Note: In March 2020, the Office of Management and Budget (OMB) announced changes to metropolitan and micropolitan statistical area definitions. Both current and historical definitions (December 2009) are shown below. If the change only affected the name of the metro area, the counties included were not repeated.

Albuquerque, NM MSA
Bernalillo, Sandoval, Torrance, and Valencia Counties

Allentown-Bethlehem-Easton, PA-NJ MSA
Carbon, Lehigh, and Northampton Counties, PA; Warren County, NJ

Anchorage, AK MSA
Anchorage Municipality and Matanuska-Susitna Borough

Ann Arbor, MI MSA
Washtenaw County

Athens-Clarke County, GA MSA
Clarke, Madison, Oconee, and Oglethorpe Counties

Atlanta-Sandy Springs-Roswell, GA MSA
Barrow, Bartow, Butts, Carroll, Cherokee, Clayton, Cobb, Coweta, Dawson, DeKalb, Douglas, Fayette, Forsyth, Fulton, Gwinnett, Haralson, Heard, Henry, Jasper, Lamar, Meriwether, Morgan, Newton, Paulding, Pickens, Pike, Rockdale, Spalding, and Walton Counties
Previously Atlanta-Sandy Springs-Marietta, GA MSA
Barrow, Bartow, Butts, Carroll, Cherokee, Clayton, Cobb, Coweta, Dawson, DeKalb, Douglas, Fayette, Forsyth, Fulton, Gwinnett, Haralson, Heard, Henry, Jasper, Lamar, Meriwether, Newton, Paulding, Pickens, Pike, Rockdale, Spalding, and Walton Counties

Austin-Round Rock, TX MSA
Previously Austin-Round Rock-San Marcos, TX MSA
Bastrop, Caldwell, Hays, Travis, and Williamson Counties

Baton Rouge, LA MSA
Ascension, East Baton Rouge, East Feliciana, Iberville, Livingston, Pointe Coupee, St. Helena, West Baton Rouge, and West Feliciana Parishes
Previously Baton Rouge, LA MSA
Ascension, East Baton Rouge, Livingston, and West Baton Rouge Parishes

Boise City, ID MSA
Previously Boise City-Nampa, ID MSA
Ada, Boise, Canyon, Gem, and Owyhee Counties

Boston, MA

Boston-Cambridge-Newton, MA-NH MSA
Previously Boston-Cambridge-Quincy, MA-NH MSA
Essex, Middlesex, Norfolk, Plymouth, and Suffolk Counties, MA; Rockingham and Strafford Counties, NH

Boston, MA MD
Previously Boston-Quincy, MA MD
Norfolk, Plymouth, and Suffolk Counties

Boston-Cambridge-Nashua, MA-NH NECTA
Includes 157 cities and towns in Massachusetts and 34 cities and towns in New Hampshire
Previously Boston-Cambridge-Quincy, MA-NH NECTA
Includes 155 cities and towns in Massachusetts and 38 cities and towns in New Hampshire

Boston-Cambridge-Newton, MA NECTA Division
Includes 92 cities and towns in Massachusetts
Previously Boston-Cambridge-Quincy, MA NECTA Division
Includes 97 cities and towns in Massachusetts

Boulder, CO MSA
Boulder County

Cape Coral-Fort Myers, FL MSA
Lee County

Cedar Rapids, IA, MSA
Benton, Jones, and Linn Counties

Charleston-North Charleston, SC MSA
Previously Charleston-North Charleston- Summerville, SC MSA
Berkeley, Charleston, and Dorchester Counties

Charlotte-Concord-Gastonia, NC-SC MSA
Cabarrus, Gaston, Iredell, Lincoln, Mecklenburg, Rowan, and Union Counties, NC; Chester, Lancaster, and York Counties, SC
Previously Charlotte-Gastonia-Rock Hill, NC-SC MSA
Anson, Cabarrus, Gaston, Mecklenburg, and Union Counties, NC; York County, SC

Chicago, IL

Chicago-Naperville-Elgin, IL-IN-WI MSA
Previous name: Chicago-Joliet-Naperville, IL-IN-WI MSA
Cook, DeKalb, DuPage, Grundy, Kane, Kendall, Lake, McHenry, and Will Counties, IL; Jasper, Lake, Newton, and Porter Counties, IN; Kenosha County, WI

Chicago-Naperville-Arlington Heights, IL MD
Cook, DuPage, Grundy, Kendall, McHenry, and Will Counties
Previous name: Chicago-Joliet-Naperville, IL MD
Cook, DeKalb, DuPage, Grundy, Kane, Kendall, McHenry, and Will Counties

Elgin, IL MD
DeKalb and Kane Counties
Previously part of the Chicago-Joliet-Naperville, IL MD

Gary, IN MD
Jasper, Lake, Newton, and Porter Counties

Lake County-Kenosha County, IL-WI MD
Lake County, IL; Kenosha County, WI

Cincinnati, OH-KY-IN MSA
Brown, Butler, Clermont, Hamilton, and Warren Counties, OH; Boone, Bracken, Campbell, Gallatin, Grant, Kenton, and Pendleton County, KY; Dearborn, Franklin, Ohio, and Union Counties, IN
Previously Cincinnati-Middletown, OH-KY-IN MSA
Brown, Butler, Clermont, Hamilton, and Warren Counties, OH; Boone, Bracken, Campbell, Gallatin, Grant, Kenton, and Pendleton County, KY; Dearborn, Franklin, and Ohio Counties, IN

Clarksville, TN-KY MSA
Montgomery and Stewart Counties, TN; Christian and Trigg Counties, KY

Cleveland-Elyria-Mentor, OH MSA
Cuyahoga, Geauga, Lake, Lorain, and Medina Counties

College Station-Bryan, TX MSA
Brazos, Burleson and Robertson Counties

Colorado Springs, CO MSA
El Paso and Teller Counties

Columbia, MO MSA
Boone and Howard Counties

Columbia, SC MSA
Calhoun, Fairfield, Kershaw, Lexington, Richland and Saluda Counties

Columbus, OH MSA
Delaware, Fairfield, Franklin, Licking, Madison, Morrow, Pickaway, and Union Counties

Dallas, TX

Dallas-Fort Worth-Arlington, TX MSA
Collin, Dallas, Denton, Ellis, Hunt, Johnson, Kaufman, Parker, Rockwall, Tarrant, and Wise Counties

Dallas-Plano-Irving, TX MD
Collin, Dallas, Denton, Ellis, Hunt, Kaufman, and Rockwall Counties

Davenport-Moline-Rock Island, IA-IL MSA
Henry, Mercer, and Rock Island Counties, IA; Scott County

Denver-Aurora-Lakewood, CO MSA
Previously Denver-Aurora-Broomfield, CO MSA
Adams, Arapahoe, Broomfield, Clear Creek, Denver, Douglas, Elbert, Gilpin, Jefferson, and Park Counties

Des Moines-West Des Moines, IA MSA
Dallas, Guthrie, Madison, Polk, and Warren Counties

Durham-Chapel Hill, NC MSA
Chatham, Durham, Orange, and Person Counties

Edison, NJ
See New York, NY (New York-Jersey City-White Plains, NY-NJ MD)

El Paso, TX MSA
El Paso County

Fargo, ND-MN MSA
Cass County, ND; Clay County, MN

Fayetteville, NC MSA
Cumberland, and Hoke Counties

Fort Collins, CO MSA
Previously Fort Collins-Loveland, CO MSA
Larimer County

Fort Wayne, IN MSA
Allen, Wells, and Whitley Counties

Fort Worth, TX

Dallas-Fort Worth-Arlington, TX MSA
Collin, Dallas, Denton, Ellis, Hunt, Johnson, Kaufman, Parker, Rockwall, Tarrant, and Wise Counties

Fort Worth-Arlington, TX MD
Hood, Johnson, Parker, Somervell, Tarrant, and Wise Counties

Grand Rapids-Wyoming, MI MSA
Barry, Kent, Montcalm, and Ottawa Counties
Previously Grand Rapids-Wyoming, MI MSA
Barry, Ionia, Kent, and Newaygo Counties

Greeley, CO MSA
Weld County

Green Bay, WI MSA
Brown, Kewaunee, and Oconto Counties

Greensboro-High Point, NC MSA
Guilford, Randolph, and Rockingham Counties

Honolulu, HI MSA
Honolulu County

Houston-The Woodlands-Sugar Land-Baytown, TX MSA
Austin, Brazoria, Chambers, Fort Bend, Galveston, Harris, Liberty, Montgomery, and Waller Counties
Previously Houston-Sugar Land-Baytown, TX MSA
Austin, Brazoria, Chambers, Fort Bend, Galveston, Harris, Liberty, Montgomery, San Jacinto, and Waller Counties

Huntsville, AL MSA
Limestone and Madison Counties

Indianapolis-Carmel, IN MSA
Boone, Brown, Hamilton, Hancock, Hendricks, Johnson, Marion, Morgan, Putnam, and Shelby Counties

Jacksonville, FL MSA
Baker, Clay, Duval, Nassau, and St. Johns Counties

Kansas City, MO-KS MSA
Franklin, Johnson, Leavenworth, Linn, Miami, and Wyandotte Counties, KS; Bates, Caldwell, Cass, Clay, Clinton, Jackson, Lafayette, Platte, and Ray Counties, MO

Lafayette, LA MSA
Acadia, Iberia, Lafayette, St. Martin, and Vermilion Parishes

Lakeland-Winter Haven, FL MSA
Polk County

Las Vegas-Henderson-Paradise, NV MSA
Previously Las Vegas-Paradise, NV MSA
Clark County

Lexington-Fayette, KY MSA
Bourbon, Clark, Fayette, Jessamine, Scott, and Woodford Counties

Lincoln, NE MSA
Lancaster and Seward Counties

Little Rock-North Little Rock-Conway, AR MSA
Faulkner, Grant, Lonoke, Perry, Pulaski, and Saline Counties

Los Angeles, CA

Los Angeles-Long Beach-Anaheim, CA MSA
Previously Los Angeles-Long Beach-Santa Ana, CA MSA
Los Angeles and Orange Counties

Los Angeles-Long Beach-Glendale, CA MD
Los Angeles County

Anaheim-Santa Ana-Irvine, CA MD
Previously Santa Ana-Anaheim-Irvine, CA MD
Orange County

Louisville/Jefferson, KY-IN MSA
Clark, Floyd, Harrison, Scott, and Washington Counties, IN; Bullitt, Henry, Jefferson, Oldham, Shelby, Spencer, and Trimble Counties, KY

Madison, WI MSA
Columbia, Dane, and Iowa Counties

Manchester, NH

Manchester-Nashua, NH MSA
Hillsborough County

Manchester, NH NECTA
Includes 11 cities and towns in New Hampshire
Previously Manchester, NH NECTA
Includes 9 cities and towns in New Hampshire

Memphis, TN-AR-MS MSA
Fayette, Shelby and Tipton Counties, TN; Crittenden County, AR; DeSoto, Marshall, Tate and Tunica Counties, MS

Miami, FL

Miami-Fort Lauderdale-West Palm Beach, FL MSA
Previously Miami-Fort Lauderdale-Pompano Beach, FL MSA
Broward, Miami-Dade, and Palm Beach Counties

Miami-Miami Beach-Kendall, FL MD
Miami-Dade County

Midland, TX MSA
Martin, and Midland Counties

Milwaukee-Waukesha-West Allis, WI MSA
Milwaukee, Ozaukee, Washington, and Waukesha Counties

Minneapolis-St. Paul-Bloomington, MN-WI MSA
Anoka, Carver, Chisago, Dakota, Hennepin, Isanti, Le Sueur, Mille Lacs, Ramsey, Scott, Sherburne, Sibley, Washington, and Wright Counties, MN; Pierce and St. Croix Counties, WI

Nashville-Davidson-Murfreesboro-Franklin, TN MSA
Cannon, Cheatham, Davidson, Dickson, Hickman, Macon, Robertson, Rutherford, Smith, Sumner, Trousdale, Williamson, and Wilson Counties

New Haven-Milford, CT MSA
New Haven County

New Orleans-Metarie-Kenner, LA MSA
Jefferson, Orleans, Plaquemines, St. Bernard, St. Charles, St. James, St. John the Baptist, and St. Tammany Parish
Previously New Orleans-Metarie-Kenner, LA MSA
Jefferson, Orleans, Plaquemines, St. Bernard, St. Charles, St. John the Baptist, and St. Tammany Parish

New York, NY

New York-Newark-Jersey City, NY-NJ-PA MSA
Bergen, Essex, Hudson, Hunterdon, Middlesex, Monmouth, Morris, Ocean, Passaic, Somerset, Sussex, and Union Counties, NJ; Bronx, Dutchess, Kings, Nassau, New York, Orange, Putnam, Queens, Richmond, Rockland, Suffolk, and Westchester Counties, NY; Pike County, PA
Previous name: New York-Northern New Jersey-Long Island, NY-NJ-PA MSA
Bergen, Essex, Hudson, Hunterdon, Middlesex, Monmouth, Morris, Ocean, Passaic, Somerset, Sussex, and Union Counties, NJ; Bronx, Kings, Nassau, New York, Putnam, Queens, Richmond, Rockland, Suffolk, and Westchester Counties, NY; Pike County, PA

Dutchess County-Putnam County, NY MD
Dutchess and Putnam Counties
Dutchess County was previously part of the Poughkeepsie-Newburgh-Middletown, NY MSA. Putnam County was previously part of the New York-Wayne-White Plains, NY-NJ MD

Nassau-Suffolk, NY MD
Nassau and Suffolk Counties

New York-Jersey City-White Plains, NY-NJ MD
Bergen, Hudson, Middlesex, Monmouth, Ocean, and Passaic Counties, NJ; Bronx, Kings, New York, Orange, Queens, Richmond, Rockland, and Westchester Counties, NY
Previous name: New York-Wayne-White Plains, NY-NJ MD
Bergen, Hudson, and Passaic Counties, NJ; Bronx, Kings, New York, Putnam, Queens, Richmond, Rockland, and Westchester Counties, NY

Newark, NJ-PA MD
Essex, Hunterdon, Morris, Somerset, Sussex, and Union Counties, NJ; Pike County, PA
Previous name: Newark-Union, NJ-PA MD
Essex, Hunterdon, Morris, Sussex, and Union Counties, NJ; Pike County, PA

Oklahoma City, OK MSA
Canadian, Cleveland, Grady, Lincoln, Logan, McClain, and Oklahoma Counties

Omaha-Council Bluffs, NE-IA MSA
Harrison, Mills, and Pottawattamie Counties, IA; Cass, Douglas, Sarpy, Saunders, and Washington Counties, NE

Orlando-Kissimmee-Sanford, FL MSA
Lake, Orange, Osceola, and Seminole Counties

Peoria, IL MSA
Marshall, Peoria, Stark, Tazewell, and Woodford Counties

Philadelphia, PA

Philadelphia-Camden-Wilmington, PA-NJ-DE-MD MSA
New Castle County, DE; Cecil County, MD; Burlington, Camden, Gloucester, and Salem Counties, NJ; Bucks, Chester, Delaware, Montgomery, and Philadelphia Counties, PA

Camden, NJ MD
Burlington, Camden, and Gloucester Counties

Montgomery County-Bucks County-Chester County, PA MD
Bucks, Chester, and Montgomery Counties
Previously part of the Philadelphia, PA MD

Philadelphia, PA MD
Delaware and Philadelphia Counties
Previous name: Philadelphia, PA MD
Bucks, Chester, Delaware, Montgomery, and Philadelphia Counties

Wilmington, DE-MD-NJ MD
New Castle County, DE; Cecil County, MD; Salem County, NJ

Phoenix-Mesa-Scottsdale, AZ MSA
Previously Phoenix-Mesa-Glendale, AZ MSA
Maricopa and Pinal Counties

Pittsburgh, PA MSA
Allegheny, Armstrong, Beaver, Butler, Fayette, Washington, and Westmoreland Counties

Portland-Vancouver-Hillsboro, OR-WA MSA
Clackamas, Columbia, Multnomah, Washington, and Yamhill Counties, OR; Clark and Skamania Counties, WA

Providence, RI

Providence-New Bedford-Fall River, RI-MA MSA
Previously Providence-New Bedford-Fall River, RI-MA MSA
Bristol County, MA; Bristol, Kent, Newport, Providence, and
Washington Counties, RI

Providence-Warwick, RI-MA NECTA
Includes 12 cities and towns in Massachusetts and 36 cities and towns
in Rhode Island
Previously Providence-Fall River-Warwick, RI-MA NECTA
Includes 12 cities and towns in Massachusetts and 37 cities and towns
in Rhode Island

Provo-Orem, UT MSA
Juab and Utah Counties

Raleigh, NC MSA
Previously Raleigh-Cary, NC MSA
Franklin, Johnston, and Wake Counties

Reno, NV MSA
Previously Reno-Sparks, NV MSA
Storey and Washoe Counties

Richmond, VA MSA
Amelia, Caroline, Charles City, Chesterfield, Dinwiddie, Goochland,
Hanover, Henrico, King William, New Kent, Powhatan, Prince
George, and Sussex Counties; Colonial Heights, Hopewell,
Petersburg, and Richmond Cities

Riverside-San Bernardino-Ontario, CA MSA
Riverside and San Bernardino Counties

Rochester, MN MSA
Dodge, Fillmore, Olmsted, and Wabasha Counties

Sacramento—Roseville—Arden-Arcade, CA MSA
El Dorado, Placer, Sacramento, and Yolo Counties

Salt Lake City, UT MSA
Salt Lake and Tooele Counties

San Antonio-New Braunfels, TX MSA
Atascosa, Bandera, Bexar, Comal, Guadalupe, Kendall, Medina, and
Wilson Counties

San Diego-Carlsbad, CA MSA
Previously San Diego-Carlsbad-San Marcos, CA MSA
San Diego County

San Francisco, CA

San Francisco-Oakland-Hayward, CA MSA
Previously San Francisco-Oakland- Fremont, CA MSA
Alameda, Contra Costa, Marin, San Francisco, and San Mateo Counties

San Francisco-Redwood City-South San Francisco, CA MD
San Francisco and San Mateo Counties

Previously San Francisco-San Mateo-Redwood City, CA MD
Marin, San Francisco, and San Mateo Counties

San Jose-Sunnyvale-Santa Clara, CA MSA
San Benito and Santa Clara Counties

Santa Rosa, CA MSA
Previously Santa Rosa-Petaluma, CA MSA
Sonoma County

Savannah, GA MSA
Bryan, Chatham, and Effingham Counties

Seattle, WA

Seattle-Tacoma-Bellevue, WA MSA
King, Pierce, and Snohomish Counties

Seattle-Bellevue-Everett, WA MD
King and Snohomish Counties

Sioux Falls, SD MSA
Lincoln, McCook, Minnehaha, and Turner Counties

Springfield, IL MSA
Menard and Sangamon Counties

Tallahassee, FL MSA
Gadsden, Jefferson, Leon, and Wakulla Counties

Tampa-St. Petersburg-Clearwater, FL MSA
Hernando, Hillsborough, Pasco, and Pinellas Counties

Tucson, AZ MSA
Pima County

Tulsa, OK MSA
Creek, Okmulgee, Osage, Pawnee, Rogers, Tulsa, and Wagoner
Counties

Tuscaloosa, AL MSA
Hale, Pickens, and Tuscaloosa Counties

Virginia Beach-Norfolk-Newport News, VA-NC MSA
Currituck County, NC; Chesapeake, Hampton, Newport News,
Norfolk, Poquoson, Portsmouth, Suffolk, Virginia Beach and
Williamsburg cities, VA; Gloucester, Isle of Wight, James City,
Mathews, Surry, and York Counties, VA

Washington, DC

Washington-Arlington-Alexandria, DC-VA-MD-WV MSA
District of Columbia; Calvert, Charles, Frederick, Montgomery, and
Prince George's Counties, MD; Alexandria, Fairfax, Falls Church,
Fredericksburg, Manassas Park, and Manassas cities, VA; Arlington,
Clarke, Culpepper, Fairfax, Fauquier, Loudoun, Prince William,
Rappahannock, Spotsylvania, Stafford, and Warren Counties, VA;
Jefferson County, WV
Previously Washington-Arlington-Alexandria, DC-VA-MD-WV MSA
District of Columbia; Calvert, Charles, Frederick, Montgomery, and
Prince George's Counties, MD; Alexandria, Fairfax, Falls Church,
Fredericksburg, Manassas Park, and Manassas cities, VA; Arlington,
Clarke, Fairfax, Fauquier, Loudoun, Prince William, Spotsylvania,
Stafford, and Warren Counties, VA; Jefferson County, WV

Washington-Arlington-Alexandria, DC-VA-MD-WV MD
District of Columbia; Calvert, Charles, and Prince George's Counties,
MD; Alexandria, Fairfax, Falls Church, Fredericksburg, Manassas
Park, and Manassas cities, VA; Arlington, Clarke, Culpepper, Fairfax,
Fauquier, Loudoun, Prince William, Rappahannock, Spotsylvania,
Stafford, and Warren Counties, VA; Jefferson County, WV
Previously Washington-Arlington-Alexandria, DC-VA-MD-WV MD
District of Columbia; Calvert, Charles, and Prince George's Counties,
MD; Alexandria, Fairfax, Falls Church, Fredericksburg, Manassas
Park, and Manassas cities, VA; Arlington, Clarke, Fairfax, Fauquier,
Loudoun, Prince William, Spotsylvania, Stafford, and Warren
Counties, VA; Jefferson County, WV

Wichita, KS MSA
Butler, Harvey, Kingman, Sedgwick, and Sumner Counties

Winston-Salem, NC MSA
Davidson, Davie, Forsyth, Stokes, and Yadkin Counties

Appendix C: Government Type and Primary County

This appendix includes the government structure of each place included in this book. It also includes the county or county equivalent in which each place is located. If a place spans more than one county, the county in which the majority of the population resides is shown.

Albuquerque, NM
Government Type: City
County: Bernalillo

Allentown, PA
Government Type: City
County: Lehigh

Anchorage, AK
Government Type: Municipality
Borough: Anchorage

Ann Arbor, MI
Government Type: City
County: Washtenaw

Athens, GA
Government Type: Consolidated
  city-county
County: Clarke

Atlanta, GA
Government Type: City
County: Fulton

Austin, TX
Government Type: City
County: Travis

Baton Rouge, LA
Government Type: Consolidated city-parish
Parish: East Baton Rouge

Boise City, ID
Government Type: City
County: Ada

Boston, MA
Government Type: City
County: Suffolk

Boulder, CO
Government Type: City
County: Boulder

Cape Coral, FL
Government Type: City
County: Lee

Cedar Rapids, IA
Government Type: City
County: Linn

Charleston, SC
Government Type: City
County: Charleston

Charlotte, NC
Government Type: City
County: Mecklenburg

Chicago, IL
Government Type: City
County: Cook

Cincinnati, OH
Government Type: City
County: Hamilton

Clarksville, TN
Government Type: City
County: Montgomery

Cleveland, OH
Government Type: City
County: Cuyahoga

College Station, TX
Government Type: City
County: Brazos

Colorado Springs, CO
Government Type: City
County: El Paso

Columbia, MO
Government Type: City
County: Boone

Columbia, SC
Government Type: City
County: Richland

Columbus, OH
Government Type: City
County: Franklin

Dallas, TX
Government Type: City
County: Dallas

Davenport, IA
Government Type: City
County: Scott

Denver, CO
Government Type: City
County: Denver

Des Moines, IA
Government Type: City
County: Polk

Durham, NC
Government Type: City
County: Durham

Edison, NJ
Government Type: Township
County: Middlesex

El Paso, TX
Government Type: City
County: El Paso

Fargo, ND
Government Type: City
County: Cass

Fayetteville, NC
Government Type: City
County: Cumberland

Fort Collins, CO
Government Type: City
County: Larimer

Fort Wayne, IN
Government Type: City
County: Allen

Fort Worth, TX
Government Type: City
County: Tarrant

Grand Rapids, MI
Government Type: City
County: Kent

Greeley, CO
Government Type: City
County: Weld

Green Bay, WI
Government Type: City
County: Brown

Greensboro, NC
Government Type: City
County: Guilford

Honolulu, HI
Government Type: Census Designated Place
  (CDP)
County: Honolulu

Houston, TX
Government Type: City
County: Harris

Huntsville, AL
Government Type: City
County: Madison

Indianapolis, IN
Government Type: City
County: Marion

Jacksonville, FL
Government Type: City
County: Duval

Kansas City, MO
Government Type: City
County: Jackson

Lafayette, LA
Government Type: City
Parish: Lafayette

Lakeland, FL
Government Type: City
County: Polk

Las Vegas, NV
Government Type: City
County: Clark

Lexington, KY
Government Type: Consolidated city-county
County: Fayette

Lincoln, NE
Government Type: City
County: Lancaster

Little Rock, AR
Government Type: City
County: Pulaski

Los Angeles, CA
Government Type: City
County: Los Angeles

Louisville, KY
Government Type: Consolidated city-county
County: Jefferson

Madison, WI
Government Type: City
County: Dane

Manchester, NH
Government Type: City
County: Hillsborough

Memphis, TN
Government Type: City
County: Shelby

Miami, FL
Government Type: City
County: Miami-Dade

Midland, TX
Government Type: City
County: Midland

Milwaukee, WI
Government Type: City
County: Milwaukee

Minneapolis, MN
Government Type: City
County: Hennepin

Nashville, TN
Government Type: Consolidated city-county
County: Davidson

New Haven, CT
Government Type: City
County: New Haven

New Orleans, LA
Government Type: City
Parish: Orleans

New York, NY
Government Type: City
Counties: Bronx; Kings; New York; Queens; Staten Island

Oklahoma City, OK
Government Type: City
County: Oklahoma

Omaha, NE
Government Type: City
County: Douglas

Orlando, FL
Government Type: City
County: Orange

Peoria, IL
Government Type: City
County: Peoria

Philadelphia, PA
Government Type: City
County: Philadelphia

Phoenix, AZ
Government Type: City
County: Maricopa

Pittsburgh, PA
Government Type: City
County: Allegheny

Portland, OR
Government Type: City
County: Multnomah

Providence, RI
Government Type: City
County: Providence

Provo, UT
Government Type: City
County: Utah

Raleigh, NC
Government Type: City
County: Wake

Reno, NV
Government Type: City
County: Washoe

Richmond, VA
Government Type: Independent city
County: Richmond city

Riverside, CA
Government Type: City
County: Riverside

Rochester, MN
Government Type: City
County: Olmsted

Sacramento, CA
Government Type: City
County: Sacramento

Salt Lake City, UT
Government Type: City
County: Salt Lake

San Antonio, TX
Government Type: City
County: Bexar

San Diego, CA
Government Type: City
County: San Diego

San Francisco, CA
Government Type: City
County: San Francisco

San Jose, CA
Government Type: City
County: Santa Clara

Santa Rosa, CA
Government Type: City
County: Sonoma

Savannah, GA
Government Type: City
County: Chatham

Seattle, WA
Government Type: City
County: King

Sioux Falls, SD
Government Type: City
County: Minnehaha

Springfield, IL
Government Type: City
County: Sangamon

Tallahassee, FL
Government Type: City
County: Leon

Tampa, FL
Government Type: City
County: Hillsborough

Tucson, AZ
Government Type: City
County: Pima

Tulsa, OK
Government Type: City
County: Tulsa

Tuscaloosa, AL
Government Type: City
County: Tuscaloosa

Virginia Beach, VA
Government Type: Independent city
County: Virginia Beach city

Washington, DC
Government Type: City
County: District of Columbia

Wichita, KS
Government Type: City
County: Sedgwick

Winston-Salem, NC
Government Type: City
County: Forsyth

Appendix D: Chambers of Commerce

Albuquerque, NM
Albuquerque Chamber of Commerce
P.O. Box 25100
Albuquerque, NM 87125
Phone: (505) 764-3700
Fax: (505) 764-3714
http://www.abqchamber.com

Albuquerque Economic Development Dept
851 University Blvd SE, Suite 203
Albuquerque, NM 87106
Phone: (505) 246-6200
Fax: (505) 246-6219
http://www.cabq.gov/econdev

Allentown, PA
Greater Lehigh Valley Chamber of
Commerce
Allentown Office
840 Hamilton Street, Suite 205
Allentown, PA 18101
Phone: (610) 751-4929
Fax: (610) 437-4907
http://www.lehighvalleychamber.org

Anchorage, AK
Anchorage Chamber of Commerce
1016 W Sixth Avenue
Suite 303
Anchorage, AK 99501
Phone: (907) 272-2401
Fax: (907) 272-4117
http://www.anchoragechamber.org

Anchorage Economic Development
Department
900 W 5th Avenue
Suite 300
Anchorage, AK 99501
Phone: (907) 258-3700
Fax: (907) 258-6646
http://aedcweb.com

Ann Arbor, MI
Ann Arbor Area Chamber of Commerce
115 West Huron
3rd Floor
Ann Arbor, MI 48104
Phone: (734) 665-4433
Fax: (734) 665-4191
http://www.annarborchamber.org

Ann Arbor Economic Development
Department
201 S Division
Suite 430
Ann Arbor, MI 48104
Phone: (734) 761-9317
http://www.annarborspark.org

Athens, GA
Athens Area Chamber of Commerce
246 W Hancock Avenue
Athens, GA 30601
Phone: (706) 549-6800
Fax: (706) 549-5636
http://www.aacoc.org

Athens-Clarke County Economic
Development Department
246 W. Hancock Avenue
Athens, GA 30601
Phone: (706) 613-3233
Fax: (706) 613-3812
http://www.athensbusiness.org

Atlanta, GA
Metro Atlanta Chamber of Commerce
235 Andrew Young International Blvd NW
Atlanta, GA 30303
Phone: (404) 880-9000
Fax: (404) 586-8464
http://www.metroatlantachamber.com

Austin, TX
Greater Austin Chamber of Commerce
210 Barton Springs Road
Suite 400
Austin, TX 78704
Phone: (512) 478-9383
Fax: (512) 478-6389
http://www.austin-chamber.org

Baton Rouge, LA
Baton Rouge Area Chamber
451 Florida Street
Suite 1050
Baton Rouge, LA 70801
Phone (225) 381-7125
http://www.brac.org

Boise City, ID
Boise Metro Chamber of Commerce
250 S 5th Street
Suite 800
Boise City, ID 83701
Phone: (208) 472-5200
Fax: (208) 472-5201
http://www.boisechamber.org

Boston, MA
Greater Boston Chamber of Commerce
265 Franklin Street
12th Floor
Boston, MA 02110
Phone: (617) 227-4500
Fax: (617) 227-7505
http://www.bostonchamber.com

Boulder, CO
Boulder Chamber of Commerce
2440 Pearl Street
Boulder, CO 80302
Phone: (303) 442-1044
Fax: (303) 938-8837
http://www.boulderchamber.com

City of Boulder Economic Vitality Program
P.O. Box 791
Boulder, CO 80306
Phone: (303) 441-3090
http://www.bouldercolorado.gov

Cape Coral, FL
Chamber of Commerce of Cape Coral
2051 Cape Coral Parkway East
Cape Coral, FL 33904
Phone: (239) 549-6900
Fax: (239) 549-9609
http://www.capecoralchamber.com

Cedar Rapids, IA
Cedar Rapids Chamber of Commerce
424 First Avenue NE
Cedar Rapids, IA 52401
Phone: (319) 398-5317
Fax: (319) 398-5228
http://www.cedarrapids.org

Cedar Rapids Economic Development
50 Second Avenue Bridge
Sixth Floor
Cedar Rapids, IA 52401-1256
Phone: (319) 286-5041
Fax: (319) 286-5141
http://www.cedar-rapids.org

Charleston, SC
Charleston Metro Chamber of Commerce
P.O. Box 975
Charleston, SC 29402
Phone: (843) 577-2510
http://www.charlestonchamber.net

Charlotte, NC
Charlotte Chamber of Commerce
330 S Tryon Street
P.O. Box 32785
Charlotte, NC 28232
Phone: (704) 378-1300
Fax: (704) 374-1903
http://www.charlottechamber.com

Charlotte Regional Partnership
1001 Morehead Square Drive
Suite 200
Charlotte, NC 28203
Phone: (704) 347-8942
Fax: (704) 347-8981
http://www.charlotteusa.com

Chicago, IL
Chicagoland Chamber of Commerce
200 E Randolph Street
Suite 2200
Chicago, IL 60601-6436
Phone: (312) 494-6700
Fax: (312) 861-0660
http://www.chicagolandchamber.org

City of Chicago Department of Planning
and Development
City Hall, Room 1000
121 North La Salle Street
Chicago, IL 60602
Phone: (312) 744-4190
Fax: (312) 744-2271
https://www.cityofchicago.org/city/en/
depts/dcd.html

Cincinnati, OH
Cincinnati USA Regional Chamber
3 East 4th Street
Suite 200
Cincinnati, Ohio 45202
Phone: (513) 579-3111
https://www.cincinnatichamber.com

Clarksville, TN
Clarksville Area Chamber of Commerce
25 Jefferson Street
Suite 300
Clarksville, TN 37040
Phone: (931) 647-2331
http://www.clarksvillechamber.com

Cleveland, OH
Greater Cleveland Partnership
1240 Huron Rd. E
Suite 300
Cleveland, OH 44115
Phone: (216) 621-3300
https://www.gcpartnership.com

College Station, TX
Bryan-College Station Chamber of
Commerce
4001 East 29th St, Suite 175
Bryan, TX 77802
Phone: (979) 260-5200
http://www.bcschamber.org

Colorado Springs, CO
Colorado Springs Chamber and EDC
102 South Tejon Street
Suite 430
Colorado Springs, CO 80903
Phone: (719) 471-8183
https://coloradospringschamberedc.com

Columbia, MO
Columbia Chamber of Commerce
300 South Providence Rd.
P.O. Box 1016
Columbia, MO 65205-1016
Phone: (573) 874-1132
Fax: (573) 443-3986
http://www.columbiamochamber.com

Columbia, SC
The Columbia Chamber
930 Richland Street
Columbia, SC 29201
Phone: (803) 733-1110
Fax: (803) 733-1113
http://www.columbiachamber.com

Columbus, OH
Greater Columbus Chamber
37 North High Street
Columbus, OH 43215
Phone: (614) 221-1321
Fax: (614) 221-1408
http://www.columbus.org

Dallas, TX
City of Dallas Economic Development
Department
1500 Marilla Street
5C South
Dallas, TX 75201
Phone: (214) 670-1685
Fax: (214) 670-0158
http://www.dallas-edd.org

Greater Dallas Chamber of Commerce
700 North Pearl Street
Suite1200
Dallas, TX 75201
Phone: (214) 746-6600
Fax: (214) 746-6799
http://www.dallaschamber.org

Davenport, IA
Quad Cities Chamber
331 W. 3rd Street
Suite 100
Davenport, IA 52801
Phone: (563) 322-1706
https://quadcitieschamber.com

Denver, CO
Denver Metro Chamber of Commerce
1445 Market Street
Denver, CO 80202
Phone: (303) 534-8500
Fax: (303) 534-3200
http://www.denverchamber.org

Downtown Denver Partnership
511 16th Street
Suite 200
Denver, CO 80202
Phone: (303) 534-6161
Fax: (303) 534-2803
http://www.downtowndenver.com

Des Moines, IA
Des Moines Downtown Chamber
301 Grand Ave
Des Moines, IA 50309
Phone: (515) 309-3229
http://desmoinesdowntownchamber.com

Greater Des Moines Partnership
700 Locust Street
Suite 100
Des Moines, IA 50309
Phone: (515) 286-4950
Fax: (515) 286-4974
http://www.desmoinesmetro.com

Durham, NC
Durham Chamber of Commerce
P.O. Box 3829
Durham, NC 27702
Phone: (919) 682-2133
Fax: (919) 688-8351
http://www.durhamchamber.org

North Carolina Institute of Minority
Economic Development
114 W Parish Street
Durham, NC 27701
Phone: (919) 956-8889
Fax: (919) 688-7668
http://www.ncimed.com

Edison, NJ
Edison Chamber of Commerce
939 Amboy Avenue
Edison, NJ 08837
Phone: (732) 738-9482
http://www.edisonchamber.com

El Paso, TX
City of El Paso Department of Economic
Development
2 Civic Center Plaza
El Paso, TX 79901
Phone: (915) 541-4000
Fax: (915) 541-1316
http://www.elpasotexas.gov

Greater El Paso Chamber of Commerce
10 Civic Center Plaza
El Paso, TX 79901
Phone: (915) 534-0500
Fax: (915) 534-0510
http://www.elpaso.org

Southwest Indiana Chamber
318 Main Street
Suite 401
Evansville, IN 47708
Phone: (812) 425-8147
Fax: (812) 421-5883
https://swinchamber.com

Fargo, ND
Chamber of Commerce of Fargo Moorhead
202 First Avenue North
Fargo, ND 56560
Phone: (218) 233-1100
Fax: (218) 233-1200
http://www.fmchamber.com

Greater Fargo-Moorhead Economic
Development Corporation
51 Broadway, Suite 500
Fargo, ND 58102
Phone: (701) 364-1900
Fax: (701) 293-7819
http://www.gfmedc.com

Fayetteville, NC
Fayetteville Regional Chamber
1019 Hay Street
Fayetteville, NC 28305
Phone: (910) 483-8133
Fax: (910) 483-0263
http://www.fayettevillencchamber.org

Fort Collins, CO
Fort Collins Chamber of Commerce
225 South Meldrum
Fort Collins, CO 80521
Phone: (970) 482-3746
Fax: (970) 482-3774
https://fortcollinschamber.com

Fort Wayne, IN
City of Fort Wayne Economic Development
1 Main St
1 Main Street
Fort Wayne, IN 46802
Phone: (260) 427-1111
Fax: (260) 427-1375
http://www.cityoffortwayne.org

Greater Fort Wayne Chamber of Commerce
826 Ewing Street
Fort Wayne, IN 46802
Phone: (260) 424-1435
Fax: (260) 426-7232
http://www.fwchamber.org

Fort Worth, TX
City of Fort Worth Economic Development
City Hall
900 Monroe Street
Suite 301
Fort Worth, TX 76102
Phone: (817) 392-6103
Fax: (817) 392-2431
http://www.fortworthgov.org

Fort Worth Chamber of Commerce
777 Taylor Street
Suite 900
Fort Worth, TX 76102-4997
Phone: (817) 336-2491
Fax: (817) 877-4034
http://www.fortworthchamber.com

Grand Rapids, MI
Grands Rapids Area Chamber of Commerce
111 Pearl Street N.W.
Grand Rapids, MI 49503
Phone: (616) 771-0300
Fax: (616) 771-0318
http://www.grandrapids.org

Greeley, CO
Greeley Chamber of Commerce
902 7th Avenue
Greeley, CO 80631
Phone: (970) 352-3566
https://greeleychamber.com

Green Bay, WI
Economic Development
100 N Jefferson St
Room 202
Green Bay, WI 54301
Phone: (920) 448-3397
Fax: (920) 448-3063
http://www.ci.green-bay.wi.us

Green Bay Area Chamber of Commerce
300 N. Broadway
Suite 3A
Green Bay, WI 54305-1660
Phone: (920) 437-8704
Fax: (920) 593-3468
http://www.titletown.org

Greensboro, NC
Greensboro Area Chamber of Commerce
342 N. Elm Street
Greensboro, NC 27401
Phone: (336) 387-8301
Fax: (336) 275-9299
http://www.greensboro.org

Honolulu, HI
The Chamber of Commerce of Hawaii
1132 Bishop Street
Suite 402
Honolulu, HI 96813
Phone: (808) 545-4300
Fax: (808) 545-4369
http://www.cochawaii.com

Houston, TX
Greater Houston Partnership
1200 Smith Street
Suite 700
Houston, TX 77002-4400
Phone: (713) 844-3600
Fax: (713) 844-0200
http://www.houston.org

Huntsville, AL
Chamber of Commerce of
Huntsville/Madison County
225 Church Street
Huntsville, AL 35801
Phone: (256) 535-2000
Fax: (256) 535-2015
http://www.huntsvillealabamausa.com

Indianapolis, IN
Greater Indianapolis Chamber of Commerce
111 Monument Circle
Suite 1950
Indianapolis, IN 46204
Phone: (317) 464-2222
Fax: (317) 464-2217
http://www.indychamber.com

The Indy Partnership
111 Monument Circle
Suite 1800
Indianapolis, IN 46204
Phone: (317) 236-6262
Fax: (317) 236-6275
http://indypartnership.com

Jacksonville, FL
Jacksonville Chamber of Commerce
3 Independent Drive
Jacksonville, FL 32202
Phone: (904) 366-6600
Fax: (904) 632-0617
http://www.myjaxchamber.com

Kansas City, MO
Greater Kansas City Chamber of Commerce
2600 Commerce Tower
911 Main Street
Kansas City, MO 64105
Phone: (816) 221-2424
Fax: (816) 221-7440
http://www.kcchamber.com

Kansas City Area Development Council
2600 Commerce Tower
911 Main Street
Kansas City, MO 64105
Phone: (816) 221-2121
Fax: (816) 842-2865
http://www.thinkkc.com

Lafayette, LA
Greater Lafayette Chamber of Commerce
804 East Saint Mary Blvd.
Lafayette, LA 70503
Phone: (337) 233-2705
Fax: (337) 234-8671
http://www.lafchamber.org

Lakeland, FL
Lakeland Chamber of Commerce
35 Lake Morton Dr.
Lakeland, FL 33801
Phone: (863) 688-8551
https://www.lakelandchamber.com

Las Vegas, NV
Las Vegas Chamber of Commerce
6671 Las Vegas Blvd South
Suite 300
Las Vegas, NV 89119
Phone: (702) 735-1616
Fax: (702) 735-0406
http://www.lvchamber.org

Las Vegas Office of Business Development
400 Stewart Avenue
City Hall
Las Vegas, NV 89101
Phone: (702) 229-6011
Fax: (702) 385-3128
http://www.lasvegasnevada.gov

Lexington, KY
Greater Lexington Chamber of Commerce
330 East Main Street
Suite 100
Lexington, KY 40507
Phone: (859) 254-4447
Fax: (859) 233-3304
http://www.commercelexington.com

Lexington Downtown Development
Authority
101 East Vine Street
Suite 500
Lexington, KY 40507
Phone: (859) 425-2296
Fax: (859) 425-2292
http://www.lexingtondda.com

Lincoln, NE
Lincoln Chamber of Commerce
1135 M Street
Suite 200
Lincoln, NE 68508
Phone: (402) 436-2350
Fax: (402) 436-2360
http://www.lcoc.com

Little Rock, AR
Little Rock Regional Chamber
One Chamber Plaza
Little Rock, AR 72201
Phone: (501) 374-2001
Fax: (501) 374-6018
http://www.littlerockchamber.com

Los Angeles, CA
Los Angeles Area Chamber of Commerce
350 South Bixel Street
Los Angeles, CA 90017
Phone: (213) 580-7500
Fax: (213) 580-7511
http://www.lachamber.org

Los Angeles County Economic
Development Corporation
444 South Flower Street
34th Floor
Los Angeles, CA 90071
Phone: (213) 622-4300
Fax: (213) 622-7100
http://www.laedc.org

Louisville, KY
The Greater Louisville Chamber of
Commerce
614 West Main Street
Suite 6000
Louisville, KY 40202
Phone: (502) 625-0000
Fax: (502) 625-0010
http://www.greaterlouisville.com

Madison, WI
Greater Madison Chamber of Commerce
615 East Washington Avenue
P.O. Box 71
Madison, WI 53701-0071
Phone: (608) 256-8348
Fax: (608) 256-0333
http://www.greatermadisonchamber.com

Manchester, NH
Greater Manchester Chamber of Commerce
889 Elm Street
Manchester, NH 03101
Phone: (603) 666-6600
Fax: (603) 626-0910
http://www.manchester-chamber.org

Manchester Economic Development Office
One City Hall Plaza
Manchester, NH 03101
Phone: (603) 624-6505
Fax: (603) 624-6308
http://www.yourmanchesternh.com

Memphis, TN
Greater Memphis Chamber
22 North Front Street, Suite 200
Memphis, TN 38103-2100
Phone: (901) 543-3500
https://memphischamber.com

Miami, FL
Greater Miami Chamber of Commerce
1601 Biscayne Boulevard
Ballroom Level
Miami, FL 33132-1260
Phone: (305) 350-7700
Fax: (305) 374-6902
http://www.miamichamber.com

The Beacon Council
80 Southwest 8th Street
Suite 2400
Miami, FL 33130
Phone: (305) 579-1300
Fax: (305) 375-0271
http://www.beaconcouncil.com

Midland, TX
Midland Chamber of Commerce
109 N. Main
Midland, TX 79701
Phone: (432) 683-3381
Fax: (432) 686-3556
http://www.midlandtxchamber.com

Milwaukee, WI
Greater Milwaukee Chamber of Commerce
6815 W. Capitol Drive
Suite 300
Milwaukee, WI 53216
Phone: (414) 465-2422
http://www.gmcofc.org

Metropolitan Milwaukee Association of
Commerce
756 N. Milwaukee Street
Suite 400
Milwaukee, WI 53202
Phone: (414) 287-4100
Fax: (414) 271-7753
https://www.mmac.org

Minneapolis, MN
Minneapolis Community Development
Agency
Crown Roller Mill
105 5th Avenue South
Suite 200
Minneapolis, MN 55401
Phone: (612) 673-5095
Fax: (612) 673-5100
http://www.ci.minneapolis.mn.us

Minneapolis Regional Chamber
81 South Ninth Street
Suite 200
Minneapolis, MN 55402
Phone: (612) 370-9100
Fax: (612) 370-9195
http://www.minneapolischamber.org

Nashville, TN
Nashville Area Chamber of Commerce
211 Commerce Street
Suite 100
Nashville, TN 37201
Phone: (615) 743-3000
Fax: (615) 256-3074
http://www.nashvillechamber.com

Tennessee Valley Authority Economic
Development
400 West Summit Hill Drive
Knoxville TN 37902
Phone: (865) 632-2101
http://www.tvaed.com

New Haven, CT
Greater New Haven Chamber of Commerce
900 Chapel Street
10th Floor
New Haven, CT 06510
Phone: (203) 787-6735
https://www.gnhcc.com

New Orleans, LA
New Orleans Chamber of Commerce
1515 Poydras Street
Suite 1010
New Orleans, LA 70112
Phone: (504) 799-4260
Fax: (504) 799-4259
http://www.neworleanschamber.org

New York, NY
New York City Economic Development
Corporation
110 William Street
New York, NY 10038
Phone: (212) 619-5000
http://www.nycedc.com

The Partnership for New York City
One Battery Park Plaza
5th Floor
New York, NY 10004
Phone: (212) 493-7400
Fax: (212) 344-3344
http://www.pfnyc.org

Oklahoma City, OK
Greater Oklahoma City Chamber of
Commerce
123 Park Avenue
Oklahoma City, OK 73102
Phone: (405) 297-8900
Fax: (405) 297-8916
http://www.okcchamber.com

Omaha, NE
Omaha Chamber of Commerce
1301 Harney Street
Omaha, NE 68102
Phone: (402) 346-5000
Fax: (402) 346-7050
http://www.omahachamber.org

Orlando, FL
Metro Orlando Economic Development
Commission of Mid-Florida
301 East Pine Street
Suite 900
Orlando, FL 32801
Phone: (407) 422-7159
Fax: (407) 425.6428
http://www.orlandoedc.com

Orlando Regional Chamber of Commerce
75 South Ivanhoe Boulevard
P.O. Box 1234
Orlando, FL 32802
Phone: (407) 425-1234
Fax: (407) 839-5020
http://www.orlando.org

Peoria, IL
Peoria Area Chamber
100 SW Water Street
Peoria, IL 61602
Phone: (309) 495-5900
http://www.peoriachamber.org

Philadelphia, PA
Greater Philadelphia Chamber of
Commerce
200 South Broad Street
Suite 700
Philadelphia, PA 19102
Phone: (215) 545-1234
Fax: (215) 790-3600
http://www.greaterphilachamber.com

Phoenix, AZ
Greater Phoenix Chamber of Commerce
201 North Central Avenue
27th Floor
Phoenix, AZ 85073
Phone: (602) 495-2195
Fax: (602) 495-8913
http://www.phoenixchamber.com

Greater Phoenix Economic Council
2 North Central Avenue
Suite 2500
Phoenix, AZ 85004
Phone: (602) 256-7700
Fax: (602) 256-7744
http://www.gpec.org

Pittsburgh, PA
Allegheny County Industrial Development
Authority
425 6th Avenue
Suite 800
Pittsburgh, PA 15219
Phone: (412) 350-1067
Fax: (412) 642-2217
http://www.alleghenycounty.us

Greater Pittsburgh Chamber of Commerce
425 6th Avenue
12th Floor
Pittsburgh, PA 15219
Phone: (412) 392-4500
Fax: (412) 392-4520
http://www.alleghenyconference.org

Portland, OR
Portland Business Alliance
200 SW Market Street
Suite 1770
Portland, OR 97201
Phone: (503) 224-8684
Fax: (503) 323-9186
http://www.portlandalliance.com

Providence, RI
Greater Providence Chamber of Commerce
30 Exchange Terrace
Fourth Floor
Providence, RI 02903
Phone: (401) 521-5000
Fax: (401) 351-2090
http://www.provchamber.com

Rhode Island Economic Development
Corporation
Providence City Hall
25 Dorrance Street
Providence, RI 02903
Phone: (401) 421-7740
Fax: (401) 751-0203
http://www.providenceri.com

Provo, UT
Provo-Orem Chamber of Commerce
51 South University Avenue
Suite 215
Provo, UT 84601
Phone: (801) 851-2555
Fax: (801) 851-2557
http://www.thechamber.org

Raleigh, NC
Greater Raleigh Chamber of Commerce
800 South Salisbury Street
Raleigh, NC 27601-2978
Phone: (919) 664-7000
Fax: (919) 664-7099
http://www.raleighchamber.org

Reno, NV
Greater Reno-Sparks Chamber of
Commerce
1 East First Street
16th Floor
Reno, NV 89505
Phone: (775) 337-3030
Fax: (775) 337-3038
http://www.reno-sparkschamber.org

The Chamber Reno-Sparks-Northern
Nevada
449 S. Virginia St.
2nd Floor
Reno, NV 89501
Phone: (775) 636-9550
http://www.thechambernv.org

Richmond, VA
Greater Richmond Chamber
600 East Main Street
Suite 700
Richmond, VA 23219
Phone: (804) 648-1234
http://www.grcc.com

Greater Richmond Partnership
901 East Byrd Street
Suite 801
Richmond, VA 23219-4070
Phone: (804) 643-3227
Fax: (804) 343-7167
http://www.grpva.com

Riverside, CA
Greater Riverside Chambers of Commerce
3985 University Avenue
Riverside, CA 92501
Phone: (951) 683-7100
https://www.riverside-chamber.com

Rochester, MN
Rochester Area Chamber of Commerce
220 South Broadway
Suite 100
Rochester, MN 55904
Phone: (507) 288-1122
Fax: (507) 282-8960
http://www.rochestermnchamber.com

Sacramento, CA
Sacramento Metro Chamber
One Capitol Mall
Suite 700
Sacramento, CA 95814
Phone: (916) 552-6800
https://metrochamber.org

Salt Lake City, UT
Department of Economic Development
451 South State Street
Room 425
Salt Lake City, UT 84111
Phone: (801) 535-7240
Fax: (801) 535-6331
http://www.slcgov.com/economic-developm
ent

Salt Lake Chamber
175 E. University Blvd. (400 S)
Suite 600
Salt Lake City, UT 84111
Phone: (801) 364-3631
http://www.slchamber.com

San Antonio, TX
The Greater San Antonio Chamber of
Commerce
602 E. Commerce Street
San Antonio, TX 78205
Phone: (210) 229-2100
Fax: (210) 229-1600
http://www.sachamber.org

San Antonio Economic Development
Department
P.O. Box 839966
San Antonio, TX 78283-3966
Phone: (210) 207-8080
Fax: (210) 207-8151
http://www.sanantonio.gov/edd

San Diego, CA
San Diego Economic Development Corp.
401 B Street
Suite 1100
San Diego, CA 92101
Phone: (619) 234-8484
Fax: (619) 234-1935
http://www.sandiegobusiness.org

San Diego Regional Chamber of Commerce
402 West Broadway
Suite 1000
San Diego, CA 92101-3585
Phone: (619) 544-1300
Fax: (619) 744-7481
http://www.sdchamber.org

San Francisco, CA
San Francisco Chamber of Commerce
235 Montgomery Street
12th Floor
San Francisco, CA 94104
Phone: (415) 392-4520
Fax: (415) 392-0485
http://www.sfchamber.com

San Jose, CA
Office of Economic Development
60 South Market Street
Suite 470
San Jose, CA 95113
Phone: (408) 277-5880
Fax: (408) 277-3615
http://www.sba.gov

The Silicon Valley Organization
101 W Santa Clara Street
San Jose, CA 95113
Phone: (408) 291-5250
https://www.thesvo.com

Santa Rosa, CA
Santa Rosa Chamber of Commerce
1260 North Dutton Avenue
Suite 272
Santa Rosa, CA 95401
Phone: (707) 545-1414
http://www.santarosachamber.com

Savannah, GA
Economic Development Authority
131 Hutchinson Island Road
4th Floor
Savannah, GA 31421
Phone: (912) 447-8450
Fax: (912) 447-8455
http://www.seda.org

Savannah Chamber of Commerce
101 E. Bay Street
Savannah, GA 31402
Phone: (912) 644-6400
Fax: (912) 644-6499
http://www.savannahchamber.com

Seattle, WA
Greater Seattle Chamber of Commerce
1301 Fifth Avenue
Suite 2500
Seattle, WA 98101
Phone: (206) 389-7200
Fax: (206) 389-7288
http://www.seattlechamber.com

Sioux Falls, SD
Sioux Falls Area Chamber of Commerce
200 N. Phillips Avenue
Suite 102
Sioux Falls, SD 57104
Phone: (605) 336-1620
Fax: (605) 336-6499
http://www.siouxfallschamber.com

Springfield, IL
The Greater Springfield Chamber of
Commerce
1011 S. Second Street
Springfield, IL 62704
Phone: (217) 525-1173
Fax: (217) 525-8768
http://www.gscc.org

Tallahassee, FL
Greater Tallahassee Chamber of Commerce
300 E. Park Avenue
P.O. Box 1638
Tallahassee, FL 32301
Phone: (850) 224-8116
Fax: (850) 561-3860
http://www.talchamber.com

Tampa, FL
Greater Tampa Chamber of Commerce
P.O. Box 420
Tampa, FL 33601-0420
Phone: (813) 276-9401
Fax: (813) 229-7855
http://www.tampachamber.com

Tucson, AZ
Tucson Metro Chamber
212 E. Broadway Blvd
Tucson, AZ 85701
Phone: (520) 792-1212
https://tucsonchamber.org

Tulsa, OK
Tulsa Regional Chamber
One West Third Street
Suite 100
Tulsa, OK 74103
Phone: (918) 585-1201
https://www.tulsachamber.com

Tuscaloosa, AL
The Chamber of Commerce of West
Alabama
2201 Jack Warner Parkway
Building C
Tuscaloosa, AL 35401
Phone: (205) 758-7588
https://tuscaloosachamber.com

Virginia Beach, VA
Hampton Roads Chamber of Commerce
500 East Main Street
Suite 700
Virginia Beach, VA 23510
Phone: (757) 664-2531
http://www.hamptonroadschamber.com

Washington, DC
District of Columbia Chamber of
Commerce
1213 K Street NW
Washington, DC 20005
Phone: (202) 347-7201
Fax: (202) 638-6762
http://www.dcchamber.org

District of Columbia Office of Planning and
Economic Development
J.A. Wilson Building
1350 Pennsylvania Ave NW
Suite 317
Washington, DC 20004
Phone: (202) 727-6365
Fax: (202) 727-6703
http://www.dcbiz.dc.gov

Wichita, KS
Wichita Regional Chamber of Commerce
350 W Douglas Avennue
Wichita, KS 67202
Phone: (316) 265-7771
https://www.wichitachamber.org

Winston-Salem, NC
Winston-Salem Chamber of Commerce
411 West Fourth Street
Suite 211
Winston-Salem, NC 27101
Phone: (336) 728-9200
http://www.winstonsalem.com

Appendix E: State Departments of Labor

Alabama
Alabama Department of Labor
P.O. Box 303500
Montgomery, AL 36130-3500
Phone: (334) 242-3072
https://www.labor.alabama.gov

Alaska
Dept of Labor and Workforce Devel.
P.O. Box 11149
Juneau, AK 99822-2249
Phone: (907) 465-2700
http://www.labor.state.ak.us

Arizona
Industrial Commission or Arizona
800 West Washington Street
Phoenix, AZ 85007
Phone: (602) 542-4411
https://www.azica.gov

Arkansas
Department of Labor
10421 West Markham
Little Rock, AR 72205
Phone: (501) 682-4500
http://www.labor.ar.gov

California
Labor and Workforce Development
445 Golden Gate Ave., 10th Floor
San Francisco, CA 94102
Phone: (916) 263-1811
http://www.labor.ca.gov

Colorado
Dept of Labor and Employment
633 17th St., 2nd Floor
Denver, CO 80202-3660
Phone: (888) 390-7936
https://www.colorado.gov/CDLE

Connecticut
Department of Labor
200 Folly Brook Blvd.
Wethersfield, CT 06109-1114
Phone: (860) 263-6000
http://www.ctdol.state.ct.us

Delaware
Department of Labor
4425 N. Market St., 4th Floor
Wilmington, DE 19802
Phone: (302) 451-3423
http://dol.delaware.gov

District of Columbia
Department of Employment Services
614 New York Ave., NE, Suite 300
Washington, DC 20002
Phone: (202) 671-1900
http://does.dc.gov

Florida
Florida Department of Economic
Opportunity
The Caldwell Building
107 East Madison St. Suite 100
Tallahassee, FL 32399-4120
Phone: (800) 342-3450
http://www.floridajobs.org

Georgia
Department of Labor
Sussex Place, Room 600
148 Andrew Young Intl Blvd., NE
Atlanta, GA 30303
Phone: (404) 656-3011
http://dol.georgia.gov

Hawaii
Dept of Labor & Industrial Relations
830 Punchbowl Street
Honolulu, HI 96813
Phone: (808) 586-8842
http://labor.hawaii.gov

Idaho
Department of Labor
317 W. Main St.
Boise, ID 83735-0001
Phone: (208) 332-3579
http://www.labor.idaho.gov

Illinois
Department of Labor
160 N. LaSalle Street, 13th Floor
Suite C-1300
Chicago, IL 60601
Phone: (312) 793-2800
https://www.illinois.gov/idol

Indiana
Indiana Department of Labor
402 West Washington Street, Room W195
Indianapolis, IN 46204
Phone: (317) 232-2655
http://www.in.gov/dol

Iowa
Iowa Workforce Development
1000 East Grand Avenue
Des Moines, IA 50319-0209
Phone: (515) 242-5870
http://www.iowadivisionoflabor.gov

Kansas
Department of Labor
401 S.W. Topeka Blvd.
Topeka, KS 66603-3182
Phone: (785) 296-5000
http://www.dol.ks.gov

Kentucky
Department of Labor
1047 U.S. Hwy 127 South, Suite 4
Frankfort, KY 40601-4381
Phone: (502) 564-3070
http://www.labor.ky.gov

Louisiana
Louisiana Workforce Commission
1001 N. 23rd Street
Baton Rouge, LA 70804-9094
Phone: (225) 342-3111
http://www.laworks.net

Maine
Department of Labor
45 Commerce Street
Augusta, ME 04330
Phone: (207) 623-7900
http://www.state.me.us/labor

Maryland
Department of Labor, Licensing &
Regulation
500 N. Calvert Street
Suite 401
Baltimore, MD 21202
Phone: (410) 767-2357
http://www.dllr.state.md.us

Massachusetts
Dept of Labor & Workforce Development
One Ashburton Place
Room 2112
Boston, MA 02108
Phone: (617) 626-7100
http://www.mass.gov/lwd

Michigan
Department of Licensing and Regulatory
Affairs
611 W. Ottawa
P.O. Box 30004
Lansing, MI 48909
Phone: (517) 373-1820
http://www.michigan.gov/lara

Minnesota
Dept of Labor and Industry
443 Lafayette Road North
Saint Paul, MN 55155
Phone: (651) 284-5070
http://www.doli.state.mn.us

Mississippi
Dept of Employment Security
P.O. Box 1699
Jackson, MS 39215-1699
Phone: (601) 321-6000
http://www.mdes.ms.gov

Missouri
Labor and Industrial Relations
P.O. Box 599
3315 W. Truman Boulevard
Jefferson City, MO 65102-0599
Phone: (573) 751-7500
https://labor.mo.gov

Montana
Dept of Labor and Industry
P.O. Box 1728
Helena, MT 59624-1728
Phone: (406) 444-9091
http://www.dli.mt.gov

Nebraska
Department of Labor
550 S 16th Street
Lincoln, NE 68508
Phone: (402) 471-9000
https://dol.nebraska.gov

Nevada
Dept of Business and Industry
3300 W. Sahara Ave
Suite 425
Las Vegas, NV 89102
Phone: (702) 486-2750
http://business.nv.gov

New Hampshire
Department of Labor
State Office Park South
95 Pleasant Street
Concord, NH 03301
Phone: (603) 271-3176
https://www.nh.gov/labor

New Jersey
Department of Labor & Workforce
Development
John Fitch Plaza, 13th Floor
Suite D
Trenton, NJ 08625-0110
Phone: (609) 777-3200
http://lwd.dol.state.nj.us/labor

New Mexico
Department of Workforce Solutions
401 Broadway, NE
Albuquerque, NM 87103-1928
Phone: (505) 841-8450
https://www.dws.state.nm.us

New York
Department of Labor
State Office Bldg. # 12
W.A. Harriman Campus
Albany, NY 12240
Phone: (518) 457-9000
https://www.labor.ny.gov

North Carolina
Department of Labor
4 West Edenton Street
Raleigh, NC 27601-1092
Phone: (919) 733-7166
https://www.labor.nc.gov

North Dakota
North Dakota Department of Labor and
Human Rights
State Capitol Building
600 East Boulevard, Dept 406
Bismark, ND 58505-0340
Phone: (701) 328-2660
http://www.nd.gov/labor

Ohio
Department of Commerce
77 South High Street, 22nd Floor
Columbus, OH 43215
Phone: (614) 644-2239
http://www.com.state.oh.us

Oklahoma
Department of Labor
4001 N. Lincoln Blvd.
Oklahoma City, OK 73105-5212
Phone: (405) 528-1500
https://www.ok.gov/odol

Oregon
Bureau of Labor and Industries
800 NE Oregon St., #32
Portland, OR 97232
Phone: (971) 673-0761
http://www.oregon.gov/boli

Pennsylvania
Dept of Labor and Industry
1700 Labor and Industry Bldg
7th and Forster Streets
Harrisburg, PA 17120
Phone: (717) 787-5279
http://www.dli.pa.gov

Rhode Island
Department of Labor and Training
1511 Pontiac Avenue
Cranston, RI 02920
Phone: (401) 462-8000
http://www.dlt.state.ri.us

South Carolina
Dept of Labor, Licensing & Regulations
P.O. Box 11329
Columbia, SC 29211-1329
Phone: (803) 896-4300
http://www.llr.state.sc.us

South Dakota
Department of Labor & Regulation
700 Governors Drive
Pierre, SD 57501-2291
Phone: (605) 773-3682
http://dlr.sd.gov

Tennessee
Dept of Labor & Workforce Development
Andrew Johnson Tower
710 James Robertson Pkwy
Nashville, TN 37243-0655
Phone: (615) 741-6642
http://www.tn.gov/workforce

Texas
Texas Workforce Commission
101 East 15th St.
Austin, TX 78778
Phone: (512) 475-2670
http://www.twc.state.tx.us

Utah
Utah Labor Commission
160 East 300 South, 3rd Floor
Salt Lake City, UT 84114-6600
Phone: (801) 530-6800
https://laborcommission.utah.gov

Vermont
Department of Labor
5 Green Mountain Drive
P.O. Box 488
Montpelier, VT 05601-0488
Phone: (802) 828-4000
http://labor.vermont.gov

Virginia
Dept of Labor and Industry
Powers-Taylor Building
13 S. 13th Street
Richmond, VA 23219
Phone: (804) 371-2327
http://www.doli.virginia.gov

Washington
Dept of Labor and Industries
P.O. Box 44001
Olympia, WA 98504-4001
Phone: (360) 902-4200
http://www.lni.wa.gov

West Virginia
Division of Labor
749 B Building 6
Capitol Complex
Charleston, WV 25305
Phone: (304) 558-7890
https://labor.wv.gov

Wisconsin
Dept of Workforce Development
201 E. Washington Ave., #A400
P.O. Box 7946
Madison, WI 53707-7946
Phone: (608) 266-6861
http://dwd.wisconsin.gov

Wyoming
Department of Workforce Services
1510 East Pershing Blvd.
Cheyenne, WY 82002
Phone: (307) 777-7261
http://www.wyomingworkforce.org

2021 Title List

Visit www.GreyHouse.com for Product Information, Table of Contents, and Sample Pages.

Opinions Throughout History

Opinions Throughout History: The Death Penalty
Opinions Throughout History: Diseases & Epidemics
Opinions Throughout History: Drug Use & Abuse
Opinions Throughout History: The Environment
Opinions Throughout History: Gender: Roles & Rights
Opinions Throughout History: Globalization
Opinions Throughout History: Guns in America
Opinions Throughout History: Immigration
Opinions Throughout History: Law Enforcement in America
Opinions Throughout History: National Security vs. Civil &
    Privacy Rights
Opinions Throughout History: Presidential Authority
Opinions Throughout History: Robotics & Artificial Intelligence
Opinions Throughout History: Social Media Issues
Opinions Throughout History: Sports & Games
Opinions Throughout History: Voters' Rights

This is Who We Were

This is Who We Were: Colonial America (1492-1775)
This is Who We Were: 1880-1899
This is Who We Were: In the 1900s
This is Who We Were: In the 1910s
This is Who We Were: In the 1920s
This is Who We Were: A Companion to the 1940 Census
This is Who We Were: In the 1940s (1940-1949)
This is Who We Were: In the 1950s
This is Who We Were: In the 1960s
This is Who We Were: In the 1970s
This is Who We Were: In the 1980s
This is Who We Were: In the 1990s
This is Who We Were: In the 2000s
This is Who We Were: In the 2010s

Working Americans

Working Americans—Vol. 1: The Working Class
Working Americans—Vol. 2: The Middle Class
Working Americans—Vol. 3: The Upper Class
Working Americans—Vol. 4: Children
Working Americans—Vol. 5: At War
Working Americans—Vol. 6: Working Women
Working Americans—Vol. 7: Social Movements
Working Americans—Vol. 8: Immigrants
Working Americans—Vol. 9: Revolutionary War to the Civil War
Working Americans—Vol. 10: Sports & Recreation
Working Americans—Vol. 11: Inventors & Entrepreneurs
Working Americans—Vol. 12: Our History through Music
Working Americans—Vol. 13: Education & Educators
Working Americans—Vol. 14: African Americans
Working Americans—Vol. 15: Politics & Politicians
Working Americans—Vol. 16: Farming & Ranching
Working Americans—Vol. 17: Teens in America

Education

Complete Learning Disabilities Resource Guide
Educators Resource Guide
The Comparative Guide to Elem. & Secondary Schools
Charter School Movement
Special Education: A Reference Book for Policy & Curriculum
    Development

Grey House Health & Wellness Guides

Autoimmune Disorders Handbook & Resource Guide
Cancer Handbook & Resource Guide
Cardiovascular Disease Handbook & Resource Guide
Dementia Handbook & Resource Guide

Consumer Health

Autoimmune Disorders Handbook & Resource Guide
Cancer Handbook & Resource Guide
Cardiovascular Disease Handbook & Resource Guide
Comparative Guide to American Hospitals
Complete Mental Health Resource Guide
Complete Resource Guide for Pediatric Disorders
Complete Resource Guide for People with Chronic Illness
Complete Resource Guide for People with Disabilities
Older Americans Information Resource

General Reference

African Biographical Dictionary
American Environmental Leaders
America's College Museums
Constitutional Amendments
Encyclopedia of African-American Writing
Encyclopedia of Invasions & Conquests
Encyclopedia of Prisoners of War & Internment
Encyclopedia of Rural America
Encyclopedia of the Continental Congresses
Encyclopedia of the United States Cabinet
Encyclopedia of War Journalism
The Environmental Debate
The Evolution Wars: A Guide to the Debates
Financial Literacy Starter Kit
From Suffrage to the Senate
The Gun Debate: Gun Rights & Gun Control in the U.S.
History of Canada
Historical Warrior Peoples & Modern Fighting Groups
Human Rights and the United States
Political Corruption in America
Privacy Rights in the Digital Age
The Religious Right and American Politics
Speakers of the House of Representatives, 1789-2021
US Land & Natural Resources Policy
The Value of a Dollar 1600-1865 Colonial to Civil War
The Value of a Dollar 1860-2019
World Cultural Leaders of the 20th Century

Business Information

Business Information Resources
The Complete Broadcasting Industry Guide: Television, Radio,
    Cable & Streaming
Directory of Mail Order Catalogs
Environmental Resource Handbook
Food & Beverage Market Place
The Grey House Guide to Homeland Security Resources
The Grey House Performing Arts Industry Guide
Guide to Healthcare Group Purchasing Organizations
Guide to U.S. HMOs and PPOs
Guide to Venture Capital & Private Equity Firms
Hudson's Washington News Media Contacts Guide
New York State Directory
Sports Market Place

2021 Title List

Visit www.GreyHouse.com for Product Information, Table of Contents, and Sample Pages.

Statistics & Demographics

America's Top-Rated Cities
America's Top-Rated Smaller Cities
The Comparative Guide to American Suburbs
Profiles of America
Profiles of California
Profiles of Florida
Profiles of Illinois
Profiles of Indiana
Profiles of Massachusetts
Profiles of Michigan
Profiles of New Jersey
Profiles of New York
Profiles of North Carolina & South Carolina
Profiles of Ohio
Profiles of Pennsylvania
Profiles of Texas
Profiles of Virginia
Profiles of Wisconsin

Canadian Resources

Associations Canada
Canadian Almanac & Directory
Canadian Environmental Resource Guide
Canadian Parliamentary Guide
Canadian Venture Capital & Private Equity Firms
Canadian Who's Who
Cannabis Canada
Careers & Employment Canada
Financial Post: Directory of Directors
Financial Services Canada
FP Bonds: Corporate
FP Bonds: Government
FP Equities: Preferreds & Derivatives
FP Survey: Industrials
FP Survey: Mines & Energy
FP Survey: Predecessor & Defunct
Health Guide Canada
Libraries Canada
Major Canadian Cities: Compared & Ranked, First Edition

Weiss Financial Ratings

Financial Literacy Basics
Financial Literacy: How to Become an Investor
Financial Literacy: Planning for the Future
Weiss Ratings Consumer Guides
Weiss Ratings Guide to Banks
Weiss Ratings Guide to Credit Unions
Weiss Ratings Guide to Health Insurers
Weiss Ratings Guide to Life & Annuity Insurers
Weiss Ratings Guide to Property & Casualty Insurers
Weiss Ratings Investment Research Guide to Bond & Money
    Market Mutual Funds
Weiss Ratings Investment Research Guide to Exchange-Traded
    Funds
Weiss Ratings Investment Research Guide to Stock Mutual Funds
Weiss Ratings Investment Research Guide to Stocks

Books in Print Series

American Book Publishing Record® Annual
American Book Publishing Record® Monthly
Books In Print®
Books In Print® Supplement
Books Out Loud™
Bowker's Complete Video Directory™
Children's Books In Print®
El-Hi Textbooks & Serials In Print®
Forthcoming Books®
Law Books & Serials In Print™
Medical & Health Care Books In Print™
Publishers, Distributors & Wholesalers of the US™
Subject Guide to Books In Print®
Subject Guide to Children's Books In Print®

Grey House Publishing | Salem Press | H.W. Wilson | 4919 Route, 22 PO Box 56, Amenia NY 12501-0056

2021 Title List

Visit www.SalemPress.com for Product Information, Table of Contents, and Sample Pages.

LITERATURE
Critical Insights: Authors

Louisa May Alcott
Sherman Alexie
Isabel Allende
Maya Angelou
Isaac Asimov
Margaret Atwood
Jane Austen
James Baldwin
Saul Bellow
Roberto Bolano
Ray Bradbury
Gwendolyn Brooks
Albert Camus
Raymond Carver
Willa Cather
Geoffrey Chaucer
John Cheever
Joseph Conrad
Charles Dickens
Emily Dickinson
Frederick Douglass
T. S. Eliot
George Eliot
Harlan Ellison
Louise Erdrich
William Faulkner
F. Scott Fitzgerald
Gustave Flaubert
Horton Foote
Benjamin Franklin
Robert Frost
Neil Gaiman
Gabriel Garcia Marquez
Thomas Hardy
Nathaniel Hawthorne
Robert A. Heinlein
Lillian Hellman
Ernest Hemingway
Langston Hughes
Zora Neale Hurston
Henry James
Thomas Jefferson
James Joyce
Jamaica Kincaid
Stephen King
Martin Luther King, Jr.
Barbara Kingsolver
Abraham Lincoln
Mario Vargas Llosa
Jack London
James McBride
Cormac McCarthy
Herman Melville
Arthur Miller
Toni Morrison
Alice Munro
Tim O'Brien
Flannery O'Connor
Eugene O'Neill

George Orwell
Sylvia Plath
Philip Roth
Salman Rushdie
Mary Shelley
John Steinbeck
Amy Tan
Leo Tolstoy
Mark Twain
John Updike
Kurt Vonnegut
Alice Walker
David Foster Wallace
Edith Wharton
Walt Whitman
Oscar Wilde
Tennessee Williams
Richard Wright
Malcolm X

Critical Insights: Works

Absalom, Absalom!
Adventures of Huckleberry Finn
Aeneid
All Quiet on the Western Front
Animal Farm
Anna Karenina
The Awakening
The Bell Jar
Beloved
Billy Budd, Sailor
The Book Thief
Brave New World
The Canterbury Tales
Catch-22
The Catcher in the Rye
The Crucible
Death of a Salesman
The Diary of a Young Girl
Dracula
Fahrenheit 451
The Grapes of Wrath
Great Expectations
The Great Gatsby
Hamlet
The Handmaid's Tale
Harry Potter Series
Heart of Darkness
The Hobbit
The House on Mango Street
How the Garcia Girls Lost Their Accents
The Hunger Games Trilogy
I Know Why the Caged Bird Sings
In Cold Blood
The Inferno
Invisible Man
Jane Eyre
The Joy Luck Club
King Lear
The Kite Runner
Life of Pi
Little Women

Lolita
Lord of the Flies
Macbeth
The Metamorphosis
Midnight's Children
A Midsummer Night's Dream
Moby-Dick
Mrs. Dalloway
Nineteen Eighty-Four
The Odyssey
Of Mice and Men
One Flew Over the Cuckoo's Nest
One Hundred Years of Solitude
Othello
The Outsiders
Paradise Lost
The Pearl
The Poetry of Baudelaire
The Poetry of Edgar Allan Poe
A Portrait of the Artist as a Young Man
Pride and Prejudice
The Red Badge of Courage
Romeo and Juliet
The Scarlet Letter
Short Fiction of Flannery O'Connor
Slaughterhouse-Five
The Sound and the Fury
A Streetcar Named Desire
The Sun Also Rises
A Tale of Two Cities
The Tales of Edgar Allan Poe
Their Eyes Were Watching God
Things Fall Apart
To Kill a Mockingbird
War and Peace
The Woman Warrior

Critical Insights: Themes

The American Comic Book
American Creative Non-Fiction
The American Dream
American Multicultural Identity
American Road Literature
American Short Story
American Sports Fiction
The American Thriller
American Writers in Exile
Censored & Banned Literature
Civil Rights Literature, Past & Present
Coming of Age
Conspiracies
Contemporary Canadian Fiction
Contemporary Immigrant Short Fiction
Contemporary Latin American Fiction
Contemporary Speculative Fiction
Crime and Detective Fiction
Crisis of Faith
Cultural Encounters
Dystopia
Family
The Fantastic
Feminism

2021 Title List

Visit www.SalemPress.com for Product Information, Table of Contents, and Sample Pages.

Flash Fiction
Gender, Sex and Sexuality
Good & Evil
The Graphic Novel
Greed
Harlem Renaissance
The Hero's Quest
Historical Fiction
Holocaust Literature
The Immigrant Experience
Inequality
LGBTQ Literature
Literature in Times of Crisis
Literature of Protest
Magical Realism
Midwestern Literature
Modern Japanese Literature
Nature & the Environment
Paranoia, Fear & Alienation
Patriotism
Political Fiction
Postcolonial Literature
Pulp Fiction of the '20s and '30s
Rebellion
Russia's Golden Age
Satire
The Slave Narrative
Social Justice and American Literature
Southern Gothic Literature
Southwestern Literature
Survival
Technology & Humanity
Violence in Literature
Virginia Woolf & 20th Century Women Writers
War

Critical Insights: Film
Bonnie & Clyde
Casablanca
Alfred Hitchcock
Stanley Kubrick

Critical Approaches to Literature
Critical Approaches to Literature: Feminist
Critical Approaches to Literature: Moral
Critical Approaches to Literature: Multicultural
Critical Approaches to Literature: Psychological

Critical Surveys of Literature
Critical Survey of American Literature
Critical Survey of Drama
Critical Survey of Graphic Novels: Heroes & Superheroes
Critical Survey of Graphic Novels: History, Theme, and
    Technique
Critical Survey of Graphic Novels: Independents and
    Underground Classics
Critical Survey of Graphic Novels: Manga
Critical Survey of Long Fiction
Critical Survey of Mystery and Detective Fiction
Critical Survey of Mythology & Folklore: Gods & Goddesses
Critical Survey of Mythology & Folklore: Heroes and Heroines
Critical Survey of Mythology & Folklore: Love, Sexuality, and
    Desire
Critical Survey of Mythology & Folklore: World Mythology
Critical Survey of Poetry
Critical Survey of Poetry: Contemporary Poets
Critical Survey of Science Fiction & Fantasy Literature
Critical Survey of Shakespeare's Plays
Critical Survey of Shakespeare's Sonnets
Critical Survey of Short Fiction
Critical Survey of World Literature
Critical Survey of Young Adult Literature

Cyclopedia of Literary Characters & Places
Cyclopedia of Literary Characters
Cyclopedia of Literary Places

Introduction to Literary Context
American Poetry of the 20th Century
American Post-Modernist Novels
American Short Fiction
English Literature
Plays
World Literature

Magill's Literary Annual
Magill's Literary Annual, 2021
Magill's Literary Annual, 2020
Magill's Literary Annual, 2019

Masterplots
Masterplots, Fourth Edition
Masterplots, 2010-2018 Supplement

Notable Writers
Notable African American Writers
Notable American Women Writers
Notable Mystery & Detective Fiction Writers
Notable Native American Writers & Writers of the American West
Novels into Film: Adaptations & Interpretation
Recommended Reading: 600 Classics Reviewed

Grey House Publishing | Salem Press | H.W. Wilson | 4919 Route, 22 PO Box 56, Amenia NY 12501-0056

2021 Title List

HISTORY

The Decades

The 1910s in America
The Twenties in America
The Thirties in America
The Forties in America
The Fifties in America
The Sixties in America
The Seventies in America
The Eighties in America
The Nineties in America
The 2000s in America
The 2010s in America

Defining Documents in American History

Defining Documents: The 1900s
Defining Documents: The 1910s
Defining Documents: The 1920s
Defining Documents: The 1930s
Defining Documents: The 1950s
Defining Documents: The 1960s
Defining Documents: The 1970s
Defining Documents: American Citizenship
Defining Documents: The American Economy
Defining Documents: The American Revolution
Defining Documents: The American West
Defining Documents: Business Ethics
Defining Documents: Capital Punishment
Defining Documents: Civil Rights
Defining Documents: Civil War
Defining Documents: The Cold War
Defining Documents: Dissent & Protest
Defining Documents: Drug Policy
Defining Documents: The Emergence of Modern America
Defining Documents: Environment & Conservation
Defining Documents: Espionage & Intrigue
Defining Documents: Exploration and Colonial America
Defining Documents: The Formation of the States
Defining Documents: The Free Press
Defining Documents: The Gun Debate
Defining Documents: Immigration & Immigrant Communities
Defining Documents: The Legacy of 9/11
Defining Documents: LGBTQ+
Defining Documents: Manifest Destiny and the New Nation
Defining Documents: Native Americans
Defining Documents: Political Campaigns, Candidates & Discourse
Defining Documents: Postwar 1940s
Defining Documents: Prison Reform
Defining Documents: Secrets, Leaks & Scandals
Defining Documents: Slavery
Defining Documents: Supreme Court Decisions
Defining Documents: Reconstruction Era
Defining Documents: The Vietnam War
Defining Documents: U.S. Involvement in the Middle East
Defining Documents: World War I
Defining Documents: World War II

Defining Documents in World History

Defining Documents: The 17th Century
Defining Documents: The 18th Century
Defining Documents: The 19th Century
Defining Documents: The 20th Century (1900-1950)
Defining Documents: The Ancient World
Defining Documents: Asia
Defining Documents: Genocide & the Holocaust
Defining Documents: Nationalism & Populism
Defining Documents: Pandemics, Plagues & Public Health
Defining Documents: Renaissance & Early Modern Era
Defining Documents: The Middle Ages
Defining Documents: The Middle East
Defining Documents: Women's Rights

Great Events from History

Great Events from History: The Ancient World
Great Events from History: The Middle Ages
Great Events from History: The Renaissance & Early Modern Era
Great Events from History: The 17th Century
Great Events from History: The 18th Century
Great Events from History: The 19th Century
Great Events from History: The 20th Century, 1901-1940
Great Events from History: The 20th Century, 1941-1970
Great Events from History: The 20th Century, 1971-2000
Great Events from History: Modern Scandals
Great Events from History: African American History
Great Events from History: The 21st Century, 2000-2016
Great Events from History: LGBTQ Events
Great Events from History: Human Rights

Great Lives from History

Computer Technology Innovators
Fashion Innovators
Great Athletes
Great Athletes of the Twenty-First Century
Great Lives from History: African Americans
Great Lives from History: American Heroes
Great Lives from History: American Women
Great Lives from History: Asian and Pacific Islander Americans
Great Lives from History: Inventors & Inventions
Great Lives from History: Jewish Americans
Great Lives from History: Latinos
Great Lives from History: Scientists and Science
Great Lives from History: The 17th Century
Great Lives from History: The 18th Century
Great Lives from History: The 19th Century
Great Lives from History: The 20th Century
Great Lives from History: The 21st Century, 2000-2017
Great Lives from History: The Ancient World
Great Lives from History: The Incredibly Wealthy
Great Lives from History: The Middle Ages
Great Lives from History: The Renaissance & Early Modern Era
Human Rights Innovators
Internet Innovators
Music Innovators
Musicians and Composers of the 20th Century
World Political Innovators

2021 Title List

Visit www.SalemPress.com for Product Information, Table of Contents, and Sample Pages.

History & Government

American First Ladies
American Presidents
The 50 States
The Ancient World: Extraordinary People in Extraordinary
    Societies
The Bill of Rights
The Criminal Justice System
The U.S. Supreme Court

SOCIAL SCIENCES

Civil Rights Movements: Past & Present
Countries, Peoples and Cultures
Countries: Their Wars & Conflicts: A World Survey
Education Today: Issues, Policies & Practices
Encyclopedia of American Immigration
Ethics: Questions & Morality of Human Actions
Issues in U.S. Immigration
Principles of Sociology: Group Relationships & Behavior
Principles of Sociology: Personal Relationships & Behavior
Principles of Sociology: Societal Issues & Behavior
Racial & Ethnic Relations in America
World Geography

SCIENCE

Ancient Creatures
Applied Science
Applied Science: Engineering & Mathematics
Applied Science: Science & Medicine
Applied Science: Technology
Biomes and Ecosystems
Earth Science: Earth Materials and Resources
Earth Science: Earth's Surface and History
Earth Science: Earth's Weather, Water and Atmosphere
Earth Science: Physics and Chemistry of the Earth
Encyclopedia of Climate Change
Encyclopedia of Energy
Encyclopedia of Environmental Issues
Encyclopedia of Global Resources
Encyclopedia of Mathematics and Society
Forensic Science
Notable Natural Disasters
The Solar System
USA in Space

Principles of Science

Principles of Anatomy
Principles of Astronomy
Principles of Behavioral Science
Principles of Biology
Principles of Biotechnology
Principles of Botany
Principles of Chemistry
Principles of Climatology
Principles of Information Technology
Principles of Computer Science
Principles of Ecology
Principles of Energy
Principles of Geology

Principles of Marine Science
Principles of Mathematics
Principles of Modern Agriculture
Principles of Pharmacology
Principles of Physical Science
Principles of Physics
Principles of Programming & Coding
Principles of Robotics & Artificial Intelligence
Principles of Scientific Research
Principles of Sustainability
Principles of Zoology

HEALTH

Addictions, Substance Abuse & Alcoholism
Adolescent Health & Wellness
Aging
Cancer
Community & Family Health Issues
Integrative, Alternative & Complementary Medicine
Genetics and Inherited Conditions
Infectious Diseases and Conditions
Magill's Medical Guide
Nutrition
Psychology & Behavioral Health
Women's Health

Principles of Health

Principles of Health: Allergies & Immune Disorders
Principles of Health: Anxiety & Stress
Principles of Health: Depression
Principles of Health: Diabetes
Principles of Health: Nursing
Principles of Health: Obesity
Principles of Health: Pain Management
Principles of Health: Prescription Drug Abuse

Grey House Publishing | Salem Press | H.W. Wilson | 4919 Route, 22 PO Box 56, Amenia NY 12501-0056

2021 Title List

Visit www.SalemPress.com for Product Information, Table of Contents, and Sample Pages.

CAREERS

Careers: Paths to Entrepreneurship
Careers in the Arts: Fine, Performing & Visual
Careers in Building Construction
Careers in Business
Careers in Chemistry
Careers in Communications & Media
Careers in Education & Training
Careers in Environment & Conservation
Careers in Financial Services
Careers in Forensic Science
Careers in Gaming
Careers in Green Energy
Careers in Healthcare
Careers in Hospitality & Tourism
Careers in Human Services
Careers in Information Technology
Careers in Law, Criminal Justice & Emergency Services
Careers in the Music Industry
Careers in Manufacturing & Production
Careers in Nursing
Careers in Physics
Careers in Protective Services
Careers in Psychology & Behavioral Health
Careers in Public Administration
Careers in Sales, Insurance & Real Estate
Careers in Science & Engineering
Careers in Social Media
Careers in Sports & Fitness
Careers in Sports Medicine & Training
Careers in Technical Services & Equipment Repair
Careers in Transportation
Careers in Writing & Editing
Careers Outdoors
Careers Overseas
Careers Working with Infants & Children
Careers Working with Animals

BUSINESS

Principles of Business: Accounting
Principles of Business: Economics
Principles of Business: Entrepreneurship
Principles of Business: Finance
Principles of Business: Globalization
Principles of Business: Leadership
Principles of Business: Management
Principles of Business: Marketing

Grey House Publishing | Salem Press | H.W. Wilson | 4919 Route, 22 PO Box 56, Amenia NY 12501-0056

2021 Title List

Visit www.HWWilsonInPrint.com for Product Information, Table of Contents, and Sample Pages.

The Reference Shelf

Affordable Housing
Aging in America
Alternative Facts, Post-Truth and the Information War
The American Dream
American Military Presence Overseas
Arab Spring
Artificial Intelligence
The Business of Food
Campaign Trends & Election Law
College Sports
Conspiracy Theories
Democracy Evolving
The Digital Age
Dinosaurs
Embracing New Paradigms in Education
Faith & Science
Families - Traditional & New Structures
Food Insecurity & Hunger in the United States
Future of U.S. Economic Relations: Mexico, Cuba, &
    Venezuela
Global Climate Change
Graphic Novels and Comic Books
Guns in America
Hate Crimes
Immigration
Internet Abuses & Privacy Rights
Internet Law
LGBTQ in the 21st Century
Marijuana Reform
National Debate Topic 2014/2015: The Ocean
National Debate Topic 2015/2016: Surveillance
National Debate Topic 2016/2017: US/China Relations
National Debate Topic 2017/2018: Education Reform
National Debate Topic 2018/2019: Immigration
National Debate Topic 2019/2021: Arms Sales
National Debate Topic 2020/2021: Criminal Justice Reform
National Debate Topic 2021/2022
New Frontiers in Space
The News and its Future
Policing in 2020
Politics of the Oceans
Pollution
Prescription Drug Abuse
Propaganda and Misinformation
Racial Tension in a Postracial Age
Reality Television
Representative American Speeches, Annual Edition
Rethinking Work
Revisiting Gender
Robotics
Russia
Social Networking
The South China Sea Conflict
Space Exploration and Development
Sports in America
The Supreme Court
The Transformation of American Cities
The Two Koreas
U.S. Infrastructure
Vaccinations
Whistleblowers

Core Collections

Children's Core Collection
Fiction Core Collection
Graphic Novels Core Collection
Middle & Junior High School Core
Public Library Core Collection: Nonfiction
Senior High Core Collection
Young Adult Fiction Core Collection

Current Biography

Current Biography Cumulative Index 1946-2021
Current Biography Monthly Magazine
Current Biography Yearbook

Readers' Guide to Periodical Literature

Abridged Readers' Guide to Periodical Literature
Readers' Guide to Periodical Literature

Indexes

Index to Legal Periodicals & Books
Short Story Index
Book Review Digest

Sears List

Sears List of Subject Headings
Sears: Lista de Encabezamientos de Materia

History

American Game Changers: Invention, Innovation &
    Transformation
American Reformers
Speeches of the American Presidents

Facts About Series

Facts About the 20th Century
Facts About American Immigration
Facts About China
Facts About the Presidents
Facts About the World's Languages

Nobel Prize Winners

Nobel Prize Winners: 1901-1986
Nobel Prize Winners: 1987-1991
Nobel Prize Winners: 1992-1996
Nobel Prize Winners: 1997-2001
Nobel Prize Winners: 2002-2018

Famous First Facts

Famous First Facts
Famous First Facts About American Politics
Famous First Facts About Sports
Famous First Facts About the Environment
Famous First Facts: International Edition

American Book of Days

The American Book of Days
The International Book of Days

Grey House Publishing | Salem Press | H.W. Wilson | 4919 Route, 22 PO Box 56, Amenia NY 12501-0056